Fodor's 2022

ESSENTIAL SPAIN

Date: 2/16/22

914.6 FOD 2022
Fodor's 2022 essential Spain

O9-BTL-646

Welcome to Spain

Spain conjures images of flamenco dancers, café-lined plazas, white hillside villages, and soaring cathedrals. Beyond these traditional associations, this modern country offers top-notch art museums, inventive cuisine, and exciting nightlife. From the Pyrenees to the coast, its landscapes and varied cultures are worth exploring. Especially enticing is the national insistence on enjoying everyday pleasures. This book was produced in the middle of the COVID-19 pandemic. As you plan your upcoming travels to Spain, please confirm that places are still open and let us know when we need to make updates by writing to us: editors@fodors.com.

TOP REASONS TO GO

★ **Cool Cities:** Barcelona, Madrid, Seville, Granada, Valencia, Bilbao, San Sebastián, and Salamanca.

★ **Amazing Architecture:** From the Moorish Alhambra to Gaudí's eclectic Sagrada Família.

★ **History:** From Segovia's Roman aqueduct to Córdoba's Mezquita, history comes alive.

★ **Superlative Art:** Masterpieces by Goya, El Greco, Picasso, Dalí, and Miró thrill.

★ **Tapas and Wine:** Spain's justly famed small bites pair perfectly with its Riojas.

★ **Beautiful Beaches:** From Barcelona's city beaches to Ibiza's celebrated strands.

Contents

Fodor's Features

Contents

MAPS

Chapter 1
EXPERIENCE SPAIN

25 ULTIMATE EXPERIENCES

Spain offers terrific experiences that should be on every traveler's list. Here are Fodor's top picks for a memorable trip.

1 Park Güell

A sweeping view of Barcelona awaits you at this architectural park, Gaudí's pièce de résistance in urban planning. Peer out from the mosaic benches over gingerbread-like houses and fountains guarded by giant tiled lizards. (Ch. 8)

2 Picos de Europa

A national park where you can hike between lakes, meadows, and snowy peaks, this mountain range on Spain's northern coast is a top outdoor adventure. (Ch. 5)

3 Gorgeous Cathedrals

Towering temples in cities including León and Burgos have been presided over by bishops for centuries and are some of the greatest marvels in Spain. (Ch. 4)

4 Food tours

Take a delicious dive into Spanish culture by trying dishes like tortilla española (Spanish potato omelet) and paella with a local guide who knows the best haunts.

5 Guggenheim Bilbao

Thought-provoking works by world-renowned international artists will entrance you at Bilbao's riverfront museum, a titanium work of art itself. (Ch. 6)

6 Beaches

You can't go wrong on the Iberian Peninsula, where you can choose between the sun-drenched beaches of the Mediterranean and the wild, brisk shores of the Atlantic.

7 Flamenco

A foot-stomping whirlwind of click-clacking castanets, guitar solos, and gut-wrenching vocals will have you shouting "¡Olé!" at the tablaos (flamenco venues) of Sevilla. (Ch. 11)

8 El Escorial

A leisurely day trip from the hustle and bustle of Madrid, this medieval town's main attraction is a gargantuan royal residence set high on a hill. (Ch. 4)

9 Córdoba Mosque

The ancient Mezquita's engraved columns and candy cane–striped double arches are an enchanting reminder of Andalusia's 10th-century Islamic grandeur. (Ch. 11)

10 Barri Gòtic

Barcelona's most ancient quarter is a maze of cobblestone streets and stone arcades that empty into medieval plaças. It also boasts some of the city's chicest boutiques. (Ch. 8)

11 Rioja wine caves

Don't miss the bodegas in Haro, in the heart of Rioja Alta, for their centuries of history and mysterious cellars, draped with penicillin mold and cobwebs. (Ch. 6)

12 Mérida

Tour the remnants of an ancient Roman city, home to one of the best-preserved stone amphitheaters in Europe. The UNESCO site is the largest of its kind in Spain. (Ch. 4)

13 Canary Islands volcanoes

The tallest mountain in Spain is also an active volcano—and you can climb it. Make it to the peak of 12,000-foot El Teide, and you'll be rewarded with bird's-eye views. (Ch. 14)

14 Alhambra

Nothing epitomizes the Moors' power and ingenuity like this centuries-old fortress. Set aside a few hours to take in arched courtyards and intricate arabesques. (Ch. 12)

15 Sagrada Família

Gaudí's iconic church is a soaring fantasy world of vivid stained glass and zoomorphic motifs. It is slated for completion in 2026 after 150 years of construction. (Ch. 8)

16 Toledo

When Toledo was the ancient capital of Spain, Muslims, Jews, and Christians cohabitated in harmony—hence the city's nickname, "City of Three Cultures." (Ch. 4)

17 Skiing

Some of the best slopes in western Europe (and with reasonable ticket prices) can be found in the Pyrenees, the mountain range Spain shares with France and Andorra. (Ch. 7)

18 Retiro Park

The tree-shaded trails, artwork, and gardens here are an oasis right in Madrid's city center. Look for the Palacio de Cristal, an impressive iron-and-glass greenhouse. (Ch. 3)

19 ¡Feria!

Vibrant ferias, or fairs, are some of the country's wildest parties, with traditional dance performances, carnival rides, street food, and makeshift discotecas. (Ch. 11)

20 Paradores

Want to hole up in a property with personality and a true sense of place? Look to the paradores, a state-run network of accommodations in historic buildings.

21 Cuenca's hanging houses

It doesn't get much more picturesque than these buildings perched on a cliffside overlooking the Huécar River. They seem to defy gravity as they jut over the ravine. (Ch. 4)

22 Museums in Madrid

Madrid's Golden Triangle is home to three world-class museums within blocks of each other. Don't miss Picasso's Guernica at Museo Reina Sofia. (Ch. 3)

23 Segovia aqueduct

This work of Roman engineering has stood for more than 2,000 years—mind-boggling, considering that mortar is entirely absent from construction. (Ch. 4)

24 Pueblos blancos

Road trip through these stark white villages on Andalusian hilltops, one of southern Spain's most postcard-perfect attractions. (Ch. 11)

25 Santiago de Compostela

The best way to reach the Galician capital is hiking the Camino de Santiago, an old Christian pilgrimage route; you don't have to be religious to appreciate the hike. (Ch. 5)

WHAT'S WHERE

1 Madrid. Its boundless energy creates sights and sounds larger than life. The Prado, Reina Sofía, and Thyssen-Bornemisza museums make this one of the greatest repositories of Western art in the world.

2 Central Spain. From Madrid there are several important excursions, notably Toledo, as well as Segovia and Salamanca. Other cities in Castile–La Mancha and Castile-León worth visiting include León, Burgos, Soria, Sigüenza, Ávila, and Cuenca. Extremadura, Spain's remote borderland with Portugal, is often overlooked, but has some intriguing places to discover.

3 Galicia and Asturias. On the way to Galicia to pay homage to St. James, pilgrims once crossed Europe to this corner of Spain so remote it was called *finis terrae* ("world's end"). Galicia's capital, Santiago de Compostela, still resonates with mystic importance. In nearby Asturias, villages nestle in green highlands, backed by the snowcapped Picos de Europa mountains, while sandy beaches

stretch along the Atlantic. East, in Cantabria, is the Belle Époque beach resort of Santander.

4 The Basque Country, Navarra, and La Rioja. The Basque region is a country within a country, proud of its own language and culture and home to the wild, dramatic coast of the Bay of Biscay. Nearby Navarra and La Rioja are famous for the running of the bulls in Pamplona and for excellent wines, respectively.

5 The Pyrenees. Cut by some 23 steep north–south valleys on the Spanish side alone, with four independent geographical entities—the valleys of Camprodón, Cerdanya, Aran, and Baztán—the Pyrenees have a wealth of areas to explore, with different cultures and languages, as well as world-class ski resorts.

6 Barcelona. La Rambla, in the heart of the Ciutat Vella, is packed day and night with artists, street entertainers, vendors, and vamps, all preparing you for Barcelona's startling architectural landmarks. But treasures lie beyond the tourist path, including Antoni Gaudí's sinuous Casa Milà and his unique Sagrada Família church, masterpieces of Modernisme.

WHAT'S WHERE

7 Catalonia, Valencia, and the Costa Blanca. The mountain-backed plain of the Levante is dotted with Christian and Moorish landmarks and Roman ruins. Valencia's signature paella fortifies visitors touring the city's medieval masterpieces and modern architecture, while the Costa Blanca has party-till-dawn resort towns. The rice paddies and orange groves of the Costa Blanca lead to the palm-fringed port city of Alicante.

8 Ibiza and the Balearic Islands. Ibiza still generates buzz as a summer playground for club-goers from all over, but even this isle has its quiet coves. Mallorca has some heavily touristed pockets, along with pristine mountain vistas in the island's interior. On serene Menorca, the two cities of Ciutadella and Mahón have different histories, cultures, and points of view.

9 Seville. One of Andalusia's landlocked provinces, seductive Seville is a vibrant city known for its food, Moorish architecture, and flamenco. Don't miss the Mezquita in nearby Córdoba.

10 Granada. Christian and Moorish cultures are dramatically counterposed here. Especially notable is the romantic Alhambra.

11 Costa del Sol and Costa de Almería. A popular "sun-holiday" destination, the Costas have vast holiday resorts occupying much of the Mediterranean coast. Respites include Málaga, a vibrant city with world-class art museums; Marbella, a pristine Andalusian old quarter; and villages such as Casares that seem immune to the goings-on along the water.

12 Canary Islands. Fuerteventura, the least visited and developed of the four largest volcanic islands, boasts endless white beaches, while Gran Canaria is an isle of contrasts from the desert dunes in the south to the verdant central peaks. Lanzarote's ocher-and-gold landscape is dotted with long beaches and white villages. Tenerife has the most attractions plus Spain's highest peak, the Pico de Teide.

Spain Today

POLITICS

Since the advent of democracy in 1978 and until 2014, Spanish politics was dominated by the two largest parties: the socialist Partido Socialista Obrero Español (PSOE) and the right-wing Partido Popular (PP). In 2014, however, as Spain continued to battle an economic crisis and as some high-profile corruption scandals came to light, the political scenario changed. "Renovation" became the watchword, and Spaniards clamored for more ethical behavior from public figures. On the back of this, two new parties entered the political arena: Unidas Podemos (Together We Can), a left-wing grassroots party; and Ciudadanos (Citizens), a pro-business, center-right party that strongly opposes Catalan nationalism. General elections in June 2016 resulted in a deadlock, with no party reaching the required 176-seat majority. The PP under Prime Minister Mariano Rajoy, however, formed a minority government with support from Ciudadanos.

In October 2017, a push for Catalan independence, led by separatist parties, created a major constitutional crisis. Separatist politicians presided over an independence referendum that had been outlawed by Spanish courts. The ruling PP government in Madrid took a hard-line stance against the independence movement, sending national police and civil guards into Catalonia to halt voting. To punish the renegade region, Madrid imposed emergency rule on Catalonia, suspending its autonomy and jailing top regional politicians—who remained in prison until 2021, when they were pardoned. This should ease tensions but it remains to be seen what will follow.

In 2018, Spain's national court found that the ruling PP had been profiting from illegal kickbacks in return for contracts since 1989 and confirmed that the party had been running an illegal, off-the-books accounting structure. The Socialist party under Pedro Sanchez won a parliamentary no-confidence motion and brought down Rajoy's government. Sanchez—who seeks a negotiated solution to the Catalan issue—became prime minister, supported in a coalition by Podemos and regional separatist parties.

Despite the coalition the parties continued to clash over a number of policies. In May 2021, the leader of Podemos, Pablo Iglesias, stepped down as deputy prime minister and Spain faced an uncertain future as the PP and Vox, Spain's populist radical right-wing party, gained ground.

THE ECONOMY

After Spain went into recession in 2008, stringent financial measures were imposed by the European Union and the IMF. Unemployment soared to 26% and youth unemployment reached double that. Since 2014, the economy has bounced back: GDP growth for 2017 was 3.1%, one of the highest rates in Europe, and Spain surpassed the United States to become the world's second-most-visited country after France. When COVID-19 hit in March 2020, it had an unprecedented effect on the economy and GDP shrank by 10.8% (the worst since 1970), the repercussions of which are yet to be fully seen. Despite this, as vaccinations gain ground and restrictions are being lifted, the economy is forecast to bounce back strongly.

RELIGION

The state-funded Catholic Church, closely tied to the right-wing PP and with the national Cadena Cope radio station as its voice, continues to have considerable social and political influence in Spain, with members of secretive groups such as Opus Dei and the Legionarios de Cristo holding key government and industry positions.

Despite the church's influence, at street level Spain has become a secular country, as demonstrated by the fact that 70% of Spaniards supported the decidedly un-Catholic law allowing gay marriage—which has been legal since 2005. And although more than 75% of the population claims to be Catholic, less than 20% go to church on a regular basis.

More than 1 million Muslims reside in Spain, making Islam the country's second-largest religion.

THE ARTS

Spain's devotion to the arts is clearly shown by the attention, both national and international, paid to its annual Princesa de Asturias prize, where Princess Leonor hands out accolades to international high achievers such as Frank Gehry, Francis Ford Coppola, Martin Scorsese, and Marina Abramovic, and to homegrown talent such as the writer Antonio Muñoz Molina and actress and director Núria Espert.

Film is at the forefront of the Spanish arts scene. Spain's most acclaimed director, Pedro Almodóvar, is still at it, releasing a short in 2020 starring Tilda Swinton (filmed during lockdown) and upcoming *Parallel Mothers* starring long-time muse Penelope Cruz. *The Bookshop*, an English-language film directed and produced by Spaniards, won Best Film and Best Director awards at the 2018 Goya Awards, Spain's version of the Oscars.

While authors such as Miguel Delibes, Rosa Montero, and Maruja Torres flourish in Spain, few break onto the international scene, with the exception of Arturo Pérez Reverte, whose books include *Captain Alatriste* and *The Fencing Master*, and Carlos Ruiz Zafón, author of the acclaimed *Shadow of the Wind*, *The Angel's Game*, and *Prisoner of Heaven*.

Spain's contribution to the fine arts is still dominated by three names: the Mallorca-born artist Miquel Barceló; the Basque sculptor Eduardo Chillida (who died in 2002); and the Catalan abstract painter Antoni Tàpies (who passed away in 2012).

SPORTS

With Real Madrid and FC Barcelona firmly established as international brands, and with La Liga recognized as one of the world's most exciting leagues, soccer remains the nation's favorite sport. The national soccer team, known as La Roja (The Red One), won the World Cup in 2010 and has won the European Cup three times—a record tied only by Germany. In other sports, national heroes include Rafael Nadal, the first tennis player to hold Grand Slam titles on clay, grass, and hard court; Garbiñe Muguruza, the 2017 Wimbledon champion; six-time NBA All-Star Pau Gasol and his two-time All-Star brother Marc; and WNBA star Anna Cruz, who plays for the Minnesota Lynx. Motorsports are hugely popular in Spain; Formula 1 champion Fernando Alonso has recently retired but all-time-great Marc Marquez continues to dominate in Grand Prix motorcycle road racing.

IMPACT OF COVID-19 ON SPAIN

Spain was hit hard by COVID-19. The government imposed a state of alarm, closed its borders, and enforced heavy restrictions. All of this had a huge effect on an economy that relies heavily on tourism and which was only just starting to recover from its long economic recession. The state of alarm was lifted in May 2021 and Spain looked optimistically toward a summer tourism revival.

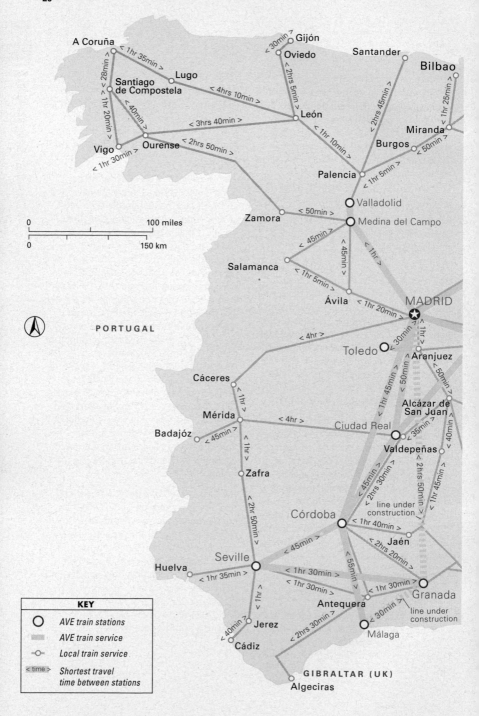

KEY

○	AVE train stations
▬	AVE train service
○─○	Local train service
< time >	Shortest travel time between stations

Travel Times by Train

San Sebastián

FRANCE

< 1hr 55min >

< 25min >
Irún

< 55min >
Pamplona

ANDORRA

Vitoria-
Gasteiz

PYRENEES

< 50min >
Logroño

< 1hr 45min >

Castejón

Huesca

Girona

< 1hr 50min >

< 45min >

Soria

< 1hr 15min >

< 1hr 15min >

COSTA
BRAVA

< 45min >
Zaragoza

Lleida

< 30min >

< 35min >

Barcelona

< 2hrs 40min >

< 1hr 20min >

< 2hrs 20min >

Tarragona

Tortosa

< 1hr 55min >

< 1hr 15min >

Teruel

< 2hrs 50min >

< 3hrs 5min >
Cuenca

Castellón
de la Plana

< 2hrs 5min >

< 3hrs 25min >

< 45min >

< 1hr 40min >

Valencia

< 1hr >

< 1hr 35min >

Albacete

< 1hr 35min >

< 1hr 45min >
Alicante

< 4hrs 45min >

Murcia

< 1hr >

< 2hrs 20min >

Lorca

< 1hr >

< 45min >
Cartagena

Almería

TRAVEL TIMES

Destination	Fastest Times
Madrid to Barcelona	2 hrs 30 min
Madrid to Bilbao	5 hrs 4 min
Madrid to Seville	2 hrs 20 min
Madrid to Granada	3 hrs 17 min
Madrid to Santander	4 hrs 19 min
Madrid to Valencia	1 hr 40 min
Madrid to Santiago de Compostela	5 hrs
Barcelona to Bilbao	6 hrs 34 min
Barcelona to Valencia	3 hrs 8 min
Seville to Granada	3 hr 15 min

Spain's Best Museums

CIUTAT DE LES ARTES I LAS CIÈNCIES (CITY OF ARTS AND SCIENCES), VALENCIA
This incredible collection of buildings in Valencia houses some of the world's most cutting-edge science and art exhibits in an enormous piece of modern architecture.

MUSEU NACIONAL D'ART DE CATALUNYA (MNAC), BARCELONA
Catalonia's national art museum isn't just a literal palace, it's also a shrine to history, culture, and the spirit of the Catalonian people. MNAC has the finest collection of Romanesque frescoes and devotional sculpture in the world, most rescued from abandoned chapels in the Pyrenees in an astonishing feat of restoration.

THEATRE-MUSEU DALÍ, FIGUERES
Dalí himself supervised the renovation work on this former municipal building, recognizable for its red and gold paint job and the iconic white eggs that crown it. The museum pays homage to the artist's creativity and imagination and houses many memorable works. You won't find his greatest paintings here but you will find his crypt!

FUNDACIÓ JOAN MIRÓ, BARCELONA
High on the hill of Montjuïc, overlooking Barcelona, the Fundació Joan Miró houses the largest collection of works by the revolutionary artist, most of which are assembled from his own private collection, as well as temporary exhibitions by new artists. The building was designed by the artist's close friend, the avant-garde architect Josep Lluís Sert.

THE GUGGENHEIM MUSEUM, BILBAO

Frank Gehry's groundbreaking Guggenheim Museum Bilbao is a complex work of art in its own right and one of the great pieces of architecture of the 21st century. It's also one of the world's best contemporary art museums. Highlights include works by Andy Warhol, Anish Kapoor, Jeff Koons, Louise Bourgeois, and Eduardo Chillida.

Centro de Arte Reina Sofía

MUSEU PICASSO, BARCELONA

Five elegant medieval and early Renaissance palaces in Barcelona's La Ribera house a collection of more than 4,000 works by Pablo Picasso, who studied at La Llotja art school. The collection focuses primarily on these formative years and includes pre-adolescent portraits and sketched landscapes.

MUSEO THYSSEN-BORNEMISZA, MADRID

Set in a palace on the Paseo del Prado, the Thyssen offers the opportunity to check a lot of important art off your bucket list as you explore European painting from the Middle Ages through the late 20th century.

CENTRO DE ARTE REINA SOFÍA, MADRID

The Reina Sofía is specifically dedicated to Spanish modern and contemporary art, with works by practically all the major Spanish artists of the 20th century—Picasso, Dalí, Miró, Julio González, Antoni Tàpies, Alfonso Ponce de León, and Antonio Saura. Picasso's *Guernica* is the top attraction.

MUSEO ARQUEOLÓGICO NACIONAL (NATIONAL ARCHEOLOGICAL MUSEUM), MADRID

A modern showcase of ancient treasures, MAN went from hidden gem to one of Madrid's top museums, home to one of the most outstanding archaeological collections in Europe.

MUSEO DEL PRADO, MADRID

The Prado is one of Spain's largest and most visited museums and a highlight of a visit to Madrid. Wander through rooms filled with dazzling works by the great European masters, all housed in a magnificent neoclassical building that first opened more than 200 years ago.

Spain's Best Beaches

CALA MACARELLA AND CALA MACARELLETA, MENORCA
These picture-perfect coves, situated alongside each other on the southwest coast of the island, offer impeccably clear waters, white beaches, and shallow, glimmering rock pools.

PLAYA LOS LANCES, TARIFA
Located where the Mediterranean and the Atlantic meet, Tarifa is ideal for kitesurfing and for spotting dolphins and whales. The main attraction is the 6-mile-long paradise of powdery white sand and the protected nature reserve.

PLAYA DE CORRALEJO, FUERTEVENTURA, CANARY ISLANDS
Incredibly popular with kitesurfers, all the Grandes Playas (or big beaches) of the Corralejo Natural Park offer pristine white powder sand and crystal-clear turquoise water.

BOGATELL, BARCELONA
Barceloneta may be the best known of Barcelona's city beaches, but Bogatell is the beach of choice among locals in the know. Why? Not only is it less crowded than tourist-heavy Barceloneta, it is also cleaner and less popular with local pickpockets. The downside, meanwhile, is that it requires a slightly longer trek from the city center. It's also home to one of Catalonia's best-loved seafood restaurants, Xiringuito Escribà.

PLAYA LAS ARENAS, VALENCIA
Given that Las Arenas literally translates as "the sands," it goes without saying that Valencia's most famous beach has been blessed with some pristine golden powder. The water is calm and shallow, making it suitable for swimmers of all ages and abilities, as well as windsurfing and other water sports. The wide, busy promenade that runs alongside the grand beach is packed with bars and restaurants.

LA CONCHA, SAN SEBASTIÁN
San Sebastián's emblematic seashell-shaped La Concha ranks as one of the most famous urban beaches in the world. Sheltered from the elements by Monte Urgull on one side and Monte Igueldo on the other, and facing Isla de Santa Clara island across a short stretch of water, La Concha's water is nearly always calm, making it an ideal spot for swimming, paddling, and sunbathing.

La Kontxa, San Sebastián

PLAYA DE LA RIBERA, SITGES

The dreamy seaside town of Sitges is located some 40 km (25 miles) down the coast from Barcelona and offers pristine, white powder sand and a lively scene.

EL PLAYAZO, COSTA DE ALMERIA

Few places in Europe remain as wild and unspoiled as Cabo de Gata, the UNESCO Biosphere Reserve in the southeastern corner of the Iberian Peninsula. Its wild, arid landscape is a mix of secluded rocky coves, jagged cliffs, and idyllic white, sandy beaches.

PLAYA DE SES ILLETES, FORMENTERA

While every corner of Formentera screams exclusivity, the chicest spot of all is Platja de Ses Illetes, part of the Ses Salines National Park. The residents are pretty, too.

ISLAS CIES, VIGO

One of the last unspoiled refuges of the Spanish coastline, these islands off the coast of Galicia in northernmost Spain are designated a nature conservation and wildlife site and home to seven beautiful beaches.

ES TRENC, MALLORCA

Popular with nudists and day-trippers, Es Trenc has excellent facilities and a variety of restaurants and beach bars, and is an ideal spot to let it all hang out—if that's what you're into.

PLAYA DE LA VICTORIA, CÁDIZ

The most famous urban beach in the Andalusian city of Cádiz, Playa de la Victoria has a spacious, golden sand beach; a generous boardwalk with a seemingly infinite number of beach bars; and several popular beachfront hotels.

Spain's Most Beautiful Villages

FORNELLS, MENORCA

For a guaranteed quiet escape, head to the northern fishing village of Fornells, whose whitewashed houses wrap around a picturesque marina. Dive by day then make your way to one of the seafood restaurants for the daily catch.

CADAQUÉS, GIRONA

Dalí, Lorca, Duchamp, Buñuel, Picasso—Spain's visionaries flocked to this whitewashed town on the Costa Brava for much the same reasons travelers continue to visit today: its laid-back, bohemian attitude; blindingly white houses; tiny harborside restaurants; and stupefyingly gorgeous sunsets.

CASARES, MÁLAGA

This quintessential Andalusian village—whitewashed houses and terra-cotta roofs—produced one of the region's greatest thinkers and patriots, Blas Infante. Visit the museum in his childhood home, then wander up to the ruins of a Moorish castle.

SAN CRISTÓBAL DE LA LAGUNA

The UNESCO-protected center of San Cristóbal de La Laguna (simply "La Laguna" to locals) takes on a tropical feel with wide plazas, baroque churches, and pastel-painted houses with carved-wood balconies. What La Laguna may lack in beaches (it's 15 minutes from the coast) it makes up for with a student-driven nightlife scene, fascinating history (don't miss the Museo de Historia de Tenerife), and immaculately preserved colonial architecture.

ALQUÉZAR, HUESCA

One of the best-preserved villages of the region of Aragón, sandwiched between Catalonia and Navarra, Alquézar spirals out like a nautilus from its central castillo. Start there and wind your way down to the base of the village through one-car-wide streets and arcaded plazas, pausing at the designated viewpoints to snap pics of the foothills of the Pyrenees.

FORNALUTX, MALLORCA

Overlooking a spectacular backdrop of the Tramuntana mountain range, this is one of Mallorca's highest and most charming villages. The steep cobbled streets are lined with honey-hued stone buildings embellished with bright green shutters and colorful flowers.

CUDILLERO, ASTURIAS
Gravity-defying cliff-top houses? Check. Sleepy port surrounded by cafés and seafood restaurants? Check. Centuries-old churches and palaces? Also yes.

ALMAGRO, CIUDAD REAL
Drama geeks and literature buffs fawn over Almagro, whose Corral de Comedias is the only preserved medieval theater in Europe, founded in 1628. This quaint Manchegan town is known for its *berenjenas de Almagro* (pickled baby eggplant) best sampled at the tapas bars that line the green-and-white Plaza Mayor, a relic of the 1500s; near the plaza are granite mansions bearing the heraldic shields of their former owners and a splendid parador housed in a 17th-century convent.

BEGET, CATALONIA
Beget is nestled against a backdrop of forested mountains, all but hidden amid the lush green valleys of the Pyrenees. Medieval bridges span the river, which flows past the village's historic stone houses and a Romanesque church. There's all manner of hiking trails that start and finish here, best capped off with a *vermut* in the village plaza.

HONDARRIBIA, GIPUZKOA
Hondarribia is one of the Basque Country's most charming towns, thanks to its white, green, and red fishermen's homes and tree-shaded promenades. Wind your way down to the harbor on foot, and ferry over to the town of Hendaye. Then stay at the parador, housed in a medieval bastion.

What to Watch and Read Before You Go to Spain

HOMAGE TO CATALONIA
BY GEORGE ORWELL

Orwell's journals directly document his time at war in Catalonia, and his first-person narrative provides a view of war-torn Barcelona that today may seem wholly foreign.

THE SHADOW OF THE WIND
BY CARLOS RUIZ ZAFÓN

Daniel Sempere is 10 years old when his father, a bookseller in post–civil war Barcelona, takes him to a mysterious labyrinth filled with treasured but forgotten tomes and tells him to pick one that he will then dedicate his life to preserving. What follows is a tale of a young man who discovers a mysterious person—or perhaps creature—is destroying all remaining works of Julián Carax, the author whose book he now protects. *The Shadow of the Wind*'s story of life, death, and history may be fictional, but its setting in a war-torn Spain is forceful, and the fact that it's sold more than 15 million copies hints at its compelling universe.

THE BEST THING THAT CAN HAPPEN TO A CROISSANT
BY PABLO TUSSET

Pablo "Baloo" Miralles is the lazy, debaucherous scion of a well-to-do Spanish family. When his elder (and more accomplished) brother inexplicably disappears, Baloo suddenly finds himself pulled into the dealings of the family's powerful financial firm, a turn of events that inspires him to try to locate his missing sibling. Within this satirical quasi-detective story is a modern-day tale about the city of Barcelona.

FOR WHOM THE BELL TOLLS
BY ERNEST HEMINGWAY

All the typical Hemingway elements are present in this fictional account of the Spanish Civil War: romance, bravado, glory, death, and tragedy. It's an incredibly evocative slice of historical fiction that is almost impossible to put down once started.

MARKS OF IDENTITY BY JUAN GOYTISOLO

A searing masterpiece from one of Spain's greatest novelists and poets describes the return of an exile to Barcelona. Goytisolo comes to the conclusion that every man carries his own exile with him, wherever he lives. The narrator (Goytisolo) rejects Spain itself and searches instead for poetry. This is a shocking and influential work, and an affirmation of the ability of the individual to survive the political tyrannies of the last century and the current one. *Marks of Identity* was banned in Spain until after Franco's death.

MONSIGNOR QUIXOTE
BY GRAHAM GREENE

This novel provides a wonderful journey through Spain in the company of Monsignor Quixote, an aging village priest, and his friend Sancho Panza, the communist ex-mayor. It's a contemporary reimagining of Miguel Cervantes's classic Don Quixote but set in Spain in the 1980s rather than the 1600s.

THE NEW SPANIARDS
BY JOHN HOOPER

How was the transition from dictatorship to democracy accomplished so smoothly? How did a country noted for sexual repression find itself in the European vanguard in legalizing gay marriage? What's the deal with the Spanish royal family? Read Hooper's fascinating study, considered one of the clearest insights into the sociology and culture of modern Spain.

¡AY CARMELA! DIRECTED
BY CARLOS SAURA

This 1990 film portrays the ethical and personal dilemmas a group of nomadic comedians face during the Spanish Civil

War. The film features a scene where Carmela, played by Carmen Maura, tries to teach a Polish prisoner, an International Brigadist, how to pronounce the /ñ/ sound in the word "España."

BIUTIFUL DIRECTED BY ALEJANDRO GONZÁLEZ IÑÁRRITU

Alejandro González Iñárritu's first feature since *Babel,* and his fourth moving film is the story of a single father of two (Javier Bardem) in Barcelona who finds out he has terminal cancer and tries to find someone to care for his children before his death. While melancholy, this is also a story of redemption as a father seeks a better life for his children.

ALL ABOUT MY MOTHER DIRECTED BY PEDRO ALMODÓVAR

After Manuela's 17-year-old son Esteban is killed before her eyes she decides to move to Barcelona in order to find his father, a transvestite named Lola who doesn't know that Esteban exists. It's a brilliantly directed tale which sensitively examines a variety of complex topics such as bereavement, addiction, gender identity, and the impacts of HIV. It also earned director Pedro Almodóvar the Best Director award at the 1999 Cannes Film Festival and the Academy Award for Best Foreign Language Film in 2000.

WOMEN ON THE VERGE OF A NERVOUS BREAKDOWN DIRECTED BY PEDRO ALMODÓVAR

This Academy Award–nominated black comedy was Pedro Almodóvar's international breakthrough and secured his place at the forefront of modern Spanish cinema. Madrid-based Pepa resolves to kill herself with a batch of sleeping-pill-laced gazpacho after her lover leaves her. Fortunately, she is interrupted by a deliciously chaotic series of events.

BELLE EPOQUE DIRECTED BY FERNANDO TRUEBA

It is 1931 in Spain and the country's monarchy is facing its final days. During this time of confusion and conflicting loyalties, Fernando, whose allegiance is to the republic, deserts from the army and goes on the run into the beautiful Spanish countryside. There he meets Manolo, a painter with the same political beliefs and four young, beautiful daughters.

A GUN IN EACH HAND DIRECTED BY CESC GAY

Catalan director Cesc Gay recruited some top-notch Spanish actors and actresses for this comedy. Told through a series of vignettes, *A Gun in Each Hand* explores how changing gender roles in Spain affect modern relationships and speaks to how Spanish ideas about masculinity and relationships are changing, and how the evolution can benefit women in Spain.

PAN'S LABYRINTH DIRECTED BY GUILLERMO DEL TORO

Set in the early years of Franco's dictatorship, this film follows an imaginative kid, Ofelia, who moves with her pregnant mother to her future stepfather's house. In her new home, she meets the faun, Pan, who tells her she might be the lost princess of an underground world. While she faces mythological creatures and terrifying beasts, a rebellion is taking place in her stepfather's military post.

FAMILY UNITED DIRECTED BY DANIEL SANCHEZ AREVALO

Combining two of Spain's greatest passions—football and family—this Spanish comedy takes place at a family wedding in a mountain-village near Madrid during the 2010 World Cup soccer final.

History You Can See

ANCIENT SPAIN

The story of Spain, a romance-tinged tale of counts, caliphs, crusaders, and kings, begins long before written history. The Basques were among the first here, fiercely defending the green mountain valleys of the Pyrenees. Then came the Iberians, believed to have crossed the Mediterranean from North Africa around 3000 BC. The Celts arrived from the north about a thousand years later. The seafaring Phoenicians founded Gadir (now Cádiz) and several coastal cities in the south three millennia ago. The parade continued with the Greeks, who settled parts of the east coast, and then the Carthaginians, who founded Cartagena around 225 BC and dubbed the then-wild, forested, and game-rich country "Ispania," after their word for rabbit: *span*.

What to See: Near Barcelona, on the Costa Brava, rocket yourself back almost 3,000 years at **Ullastret,** a settlement occupied by an Iberian people known as the Indiketas. On a tour, actors guide groups through the homes and fortifications of some of the peninsula's earliest inhabitants, the defensive walls attesting to the constant threat of attack and the bits of pottery evidence of the settlement's early ceramic industry. Not far away in **Empúries** are ruins of the Greek colony established in the 6th century BC. At the **Museo de Cádiz** in Andalusia, you can view sarcophagi dating back to the 1100 BC founding of the city.

In Madrid, the outstanding **National Archaeological Museum** displays more than 1 million years of artifacts unearthed in what is now Spain: from Paleolithic tools found in Madrid's Manzanares River basin to 19th-century textiles and musical instruments.

THE ROMAN EPOCH

Modern civilization in Iberia began with the Romans, who expelled the Carthaginians and turned the peninsula into three imperial provinces. It took the Romans 200 years to subdue the fiercely resisting Iberians, but their influence is seen today in the fortifications, amphitheaters, aqueducts, and other ruins in cities across Spain, as well as in the country's legal system and in the Latin base of Spain's Romance languages and dialects.

What to See: Segovia's nearly 3,000-foot-long **Acueducto Romano** is a marvel of Roman engineering. Mérida's Roman ruins are some of Spain's finest, including its **bridge, theater,** and **outdoor amphitheater.** Tarragona was Rome's most important city in Catalonia, as the **walls, circus,** and **amphitheater** bear witness, while Zaragoza boasts a **Roman amphitheater** and a **Roman fluvial port** that dispatched flat-bottom riverboats loaded with wine and olive oil down the Ebro.

THE VISIGOTHS AND MOORS

In the early 5th century, invading tribes crossed the Pyrenees to attack the weakening Roman Empire. The Visigoths became the dominant force in central and northern Spain by AD 419, establishing their kingdom at Toledo and eventually adopting Christianity. But the Visigoths, too, were to fall before a wave of invaders. The Moors, an Arab-led Berber force, crossed the Strait of Gibraltar in AD 711 and swept through Spain in an astonishingly short time, launching almost eight centuries of Muslim rule. The Moorish architecture and Mudejar Moorish-inspired Gothic decorative details found throughout most of Spain tell much about the splendor of the Islamic culture that flourished here.

What to See: Moorish culture is most spectacularly evident in Andalusia, derived from the Arabic name for the Moorish reign on the Iberian Peninsula, al-Andalus, which meant "western lands." The fairy-tale **Alhambra** palace overlooking Granada captures the refinement of the Moorish aesthetic, while the earlier 9th-century **Mezquita** at Córdoba bears witness to the power of Islam in al-Andalus.

SPAIN'S GOLDEN AGE

By 1085, Alfonso VI of Castile had captured Toledo, giving the Christians a firm grip on the north. In the 13th century, Valencia, Seville, and finally Córdoba—the capital of the Muslim caliphate in Spain—fell to Christian forces, leaving only Granada in Moorish hands. Nearly 200 years later, the so-called Catholic Monarchs—Ferdinand of Aragón and Isabella of Castile—were joined in a marriage that would change the world. Finally, on January 2, 1492—244 years after the fall of Córdoba—Granada surrendered and the Moorish reign was over.

The year 1492 was the beginning of the nation's political golden age: Christian forces conquered Granada and unified all of present-day Spain as a single kingdom; in what was, at the time, viewed as a measure promoting national unity, Jews and Muslims who did not convert to Christianity were expelled from the country. The departure of educated Muslims and Jews was a blow to the nation's agriculture, science, and economy from which it would take nearly 500 years to recover. The Catholic Monarchs and their centralizing successors maintained Spain's unity, but they sacrificed the spirit of international free trade that was bringing prosperity to other parts of Europe. Carlos V weakened Spain with

his penchant for waging war, and his son, Felipe II, followed in the same expensive path, defeating the Turks in 1571 but losing the "Invincible Spanish Armada" in the English Channel in 1588.

What to See: Commemorate Columbus's voyage to America in Seville, Huelva, Granada, Cádiz, and Barcelona, all of which display venues where "the Discoverer" was commissioned, was confirmed, set out from, returned to, or was buried. Wander through the somber **Escorial,** a monastery northwest of Madrid commissioned by Felipe II in 1557 and finished in 1584, the final resting place of most of the Habsburg and Bourbon kings of Spain ever since.

WAR OF THE SPANISH SUCCESSION

The War of the Spanish Succession (1700–14) ended with the fall of Barcelona, which sided with the Habsburg Archduke Carlos against the Bourbon Prince Felipe V. El Born market, completed in 1876, covered the buried remains of the Ribera neighborhood, where the decisive battle took place. Ribera citizens were required to tear down a thousand houses to clear space for the Ciutadella fortress, from which fields of fire were directed, quite naturally, toward the city the Spanish and French forces had taken a year to subdue. The leveled neighborhood, then about a third of Barcelona, was plowed under and forgotten by the victors, though never by barcelonins.

What to See: In Barcelona, the **Fossar de les Moreres cemetery,** next to the Santa María del Mar basilica, remains a powerful symbol for Catalan nationalists who gather there every September 11, Catalonia's National Day, to commemorate the fall of the city in 1714.

SPANISH CIVIL WAR

Spain's early-19th-century War of Independence required five years of bitter guerrilla fighting to rid the peninsula of Napoleonic troops. Later, the Carlist wars set the stage for the Spanish Civil War (1936–39), which claimed more than half a million lives. Intellectuals and leftists sympathized with the elected government; the International Brigades, with many American, British, and Canadian volunteers, took part in some of the worst fighting, including the storied defense of Madrid. But General Francisco Franco, backed by the Catholic Church, got far more help from Nazi Germany, whose Condor legions destroyed the Basque town of Gernika (in a horror made infamous by Picasso's monumental painting *Guernica*), and from Fascist Italy. For three years, European governments stood by as Franco's armies ground their way to victory. After the fall of Barcelona in January 1939, the Republican cause became hopeless. Franco's Nationalist forces entered Madrid on March 27, 1939, and thus began nearly 40 years of dictatorship under Franco. This dark period in recent Spanish history ended on November 20, 1975, when Franco died.

What to See: Snap a shot of **Madrid's Plaza Dos de Mayo,** in the Malasaña neighborhood, where officers Daoiz and Velarde held their ground against the superior French forces at the start of the popular uprising against Napoléon. The archway in the square is all that remains of the armory Daoiz and Velarde defended to the death. Trace the shrapnel marks on the wall of the **Sant Felip Neri church** in Barcelona, evidence of the 1938 bombing of the city by Italian warplanes under Franco's orders. East of Zaragoza, **Belchite** was the scene of bloody fighting during the decisive Battle of the Ebro. The town has been left exactly as it appeared on September 7, 1937, the day the battle ended.

RETURN TO DEMOCRACY

After Franco's death, Spain began the complex process of national reconciliation and a return to democracy. Despite opposition from radical right-wing factions and an attempted coup d'état in February 1981, Spain celebrated the first general elections for 40 years in 1977 and approved a democratic constitution in 1978.

Chapter 2

TRAVEL SMART

Updated by
Joanna Styles

★ **CAPITAL:**
Madrid

♦ **POPULATION:**
46.94 million

☐ **LANGUAGE:**
Spanish

$ **CURRENCY:**
Euro

☏ **COUNTRY CODE:**
34

⚠ **EMERGENCIES:**
112

🚗 **DRIVING:**
On the right

⚡ **ELECTRICITY:**
220v/50 cycles; electrical
plugs have two round prongs

🕔 **TIME:**
Six hours ahead of New York

🌐 **WEB RESOURCES:**
www.spain.info/en
www.parador.es
www.spainisculture.com

Bay of
Biscay

Madrid

SPAIN

Mediterranean Sea

What You Need to Know Before You Go

Should you tip? When can you eat? Do you need to plan ahead for the major attractions or can you just show up? We've got answers and a few tips to help you make the most of your visit to this beautiful country.

CATALAN CULTURE IS STRONG

Before the rise of modern-day Spain there was Aragon, a kingdom on the Iberian Peninsula whose territories included the regions we know as Catalonia and Aragon, as well as Roussillon, a part of southern France. The Catalan people and their culture are tenacious and Barcelona—the capital of Catalonia—remains strongly Catalan. This means that you'll see signage printed in both Spanish and Catalan and will also hear Catalan being spoken. The wealthy Catalan region has about 7.5 million people, with their own language, parliament, flag, and anthem. While you won't be expected to learn the language, it's a sign of respect to learn at least a few Catalan words. (Speaking of regional differences, in the Spanish south, the culture and architecture was strongly influenced by the Moors, the name given to Spain's Muslim population who came across the Straight of Gibraltar from northern Africa.)

AVOID TALKING POLITICS

The Catalan bid for independence is an ongoing and touchy topic in Spain, and it's probably best to avoid asking locals about it. When a majority of the members of the Catalan regional Parliament declared the region's independence from Spain in 2017, a referendum vote was held shortly after and saw most voters indicating that they too wanted to separate from Spain. As a result the central Spanish government cracked down on the separatists, igniting fierce debate and sometimes violent protests. You may notice flags with a single star—known as the Estelada—and oversize yellow ribbons displayed prominently as you explore Barcelona and beyond; these are signs of support for the Catalan secessionist movement.

A SLOWER WAY OF LIFE

Spanish life has a slower rhythm than you may be accustomed to. Meals are later (lunch starts at around 2 and dinner at around 10 or 11) and are languorous experiences that last for hours. Sundays are especially slow, especially in smaller towns (and in the off season) where many stores and some restaurants are closed for the day.

Stores and restaurants keep familiar hours in tourist-centric areas, and while it's unlikely that you'll be refused service if you want to eat lunch at noon, you'll definitely stand out as a tourist. As for the fabled afternoon siesta, while it does still exist in some more rural communities, in cities like Barcelona and Madrid, it really just takes the form of a long, leisurely lunch.

SPAIN IS GAY FRIENDLY

While it's true that Spain is Catholic-majority and generally takes religion quite seriously, this country also legalized gay marriage in 2005, a full decade before the United States. While Spain as a whole is generally tolerant, specific areas have also built international reputations for being welcoming to gay travelers and have gay-friendly beaches, restaurants, and nightclubs, and hold yearly Pride parades. Some particularly welcoming destinations are the capital city Madrid, which is said to be one of the most LGBT-friendly cities in all of Europe, the seaside resort town of Sitges, the island of Maspalomas in the Canary Islands, and parts of the bass-thumping club island Ibiza.

BOOK AHEAD

There are a few major attractions in Spain that rank high on most traveler bucket lists and if you are hoping to check some of the world's top attractions off your list, too, you'll need to plan ahead. For big-ticket sights like the Alhambra, the Sagrada Família, Parc Güell, and the Picasso

Museum, book tickets before you arrive. Otherwise, lines can be long and there is no guarantee that tickets will be available when you visit, especially at peak times. Booking in advance gives you an allocated time (there is zero flexibility with this at most attractions so be sure to arrive on time).

THE RAIN IN SPAIN...

Everyone knows the saying "the rain in Spain stays mainly in the plain," thanks to Eliza Doolittle's elocution exercise in *My Fair Lady*. While you may have sung along as Professor Higgins asked excitedly, "Where does it rain?" It turns out the rain in Spain doesn't really fall or stay upon the plain at all. On the contrary, it favors the country's rocky, steep northwestern corner, Galicia.

PACK FOR A VARIED CLIMATE AND TERRAIN

If you're planning to travel across different regions of Spain, keep in mind that the landscape and climate can change rather dramatically. While Catalonia and Aragon are rolling, arid, and quite dry, Basque Country has generally mild temperatures but significant rainfall, even during the drier months, and southern cities like Seville have a dry Mediterranean climate that can get quite hot during the day. Spain also has placid beaches, coastal plains, tropical islands, and the dramatic Pyrenees mountain range. You'll need to pack accordingly if you will be in more than one climate zone.

SKIP THE PLANE AND TAKE A TRAIN

Flights from one region of Spain to another are cheap and easy, but don't discount the country's high-speed rail network. It's fast, comfortable, and a great way to get from city to city. You can get from Madrid to Seville in 2 hours and 20 minutes without any of the hassles or stresses of air travel. Also, did we mention that you can bring food and alcohol on board with you?

WINE IS INEXPENSIVE

Spain is the third largest producer of wine in the world, after France and Italy, and almost half the wine (in a normal vintage) production is sold at low prices—like 3 to 5 euros a bottle. It's key to a fun and frugal vacation to know that just because this wine is inexpensive, it doesn't mean it's cheap.

DON'T JUST EAT PAELLA

Delicious as it is, there's a lot more to Spanish cuisine than paella. As with any country, Spanish recipes are strongly influenced by culture, tradition, and environment. In northwestern Basque Country the name of the game is pintxos (pronounced pinchos), which is that region's version of tapas—numerous little bites, often on a toothpick, eaten alongside beer or wine. Vegetables are the main attraction in the Navarra region: look for Lodosa piquillo peppers, Tudela artichokes, and white asparagus. On the western border where Spain meets Portugal the greatest treasure is jamón ibérico, thinly sliced cured ham

made from pigs fattened up on foraged acorns. In the Andalusian south—where they were invented—tapas reign supreme. Think about the region you're in before you order. If you're on the coast, fish is the way to go. If you're inland, consider a dish made with meat

GO TO THE BEACH

While most of Europe visits Spain for their beach holidays, the rest of the world is more interested in Spain's vibrant cities, culture, and history. But if you find yourself on one of Spain's gorgeous beaches, you'll wonder why people don't visit for the beaches alone. Spain has a great many seaside towns that offer a range of popular and less-traveled stretches of sand. Even major coastal cities like Barcelona have beaches. If you're looking for something truly special though, head to the Canary Islands, which are famous for their soft sands and clear, azure waters.

TIPPING ISN'T MANDATORY (MOST OF THE TIME)

Thanks to decent worker protections, Spanish servers earn a living wage and don't depend on tips to survive. That said, it is customary in a casual restaurant to round up your bill and leave the change, but it isn't expected or required. If you eat in a formal restaurant there is an expectation that you'll tip, but the maximum is still only 10%.

Getting Here and Around

Air

Flying time from New York to Madrid is about seven hours; from London, it's just over two hours.

Regular nonstop flights serve Spain from many major cities in the eastern United States; flying from other North American cities usually involves a stop. If you're coming from North America and want to land in a city other than Madrid or Barcelona, consider flying a European carrier.

The Visit Europe from oneworld (which includes American Airlines, Iberia, and British Airways among others) is the most useful aviation pass for Spain. It is available only to residents of countries outside Europe and must be booked before departure with a Oneworld member airline. The pass gives you access to 200 destinations in 50 countries in Europe and North Africa. It's available as an add-on to an international flight to Europe booked with any of the airlines in the Oneworld alliance, and is accepted for as long as the international ticket is valid. You must buy a minimum of two coupons for flights within Europe, but there's no maximum.

A number of low-cost carriers operate from the United Kingdom to Spain such as Vueling (⊕ www.vueling.com) and Jet2 (⊕ www.jet2.com). They provide competition to the market's main players, easyJet (⊕ www.easyjet.com) and Ryanair (⊕ www.ryanair.com). All these carriers offer frequent flights, cover small cities as well as large ones, and have very competitive fares.

AIRPORTS

Most flights from North America land in, or pass through, Madrid's Barajas Airport (MAD). The other major gateway is Barcelona's Prat de Llobregat (BCN).

From the United Kingdom and elsewhere in Europe, regular flights also touch down in Málaga (AGP), Alicante (ALC), Palma de Mallorca (PMI), and many other smaller cities.

FLIGHTS

From North America, Air Europa flies to Madrid and Barcelona; American Airlines, part of the Oneworld Alliance, and Iberia fly to Madrid and Barcelona; Delta flies direct to Madrid only. Note that some of these airlines use shared facilities and do not operate their own flights. Within Spain, Iberia is the main domestic airline and also operates low-cost flights through its budget airlines Iberia Express and Vueling. Air Europa and Ryanair both offer inexpensive flights on most domestic routes. The earlier before your travel date you purchase the ticket, the more bargains you're likely to find. Air Europa, Iberia Express, Vueling, and Ryanair also have flights from Spain to other destinations in Europe.

Iberia runs a shuttle, the Puente Áereo, offering flights just over an hour long between Madrid and Barcelona, every 30 minutes (more often during peak travel times) 6:45 am–9:45 pm. You don't need to reserve; you can buy your tickets at the airport ticket counter upon arriving or book online at ⊕ www.iberia.com/es/air-shuttle. Passengers can also use the self-service check-in counters to avoid the line. Puente Áereo departs from Terminal T1 in Barcelona; in Madrid, the shuttle departs from Terminal 4.

Boat

Regular car ferries connect the United Kingdom with northern Spain. Brittany Ferries sails from Plymouth to Santander, and from Portsmouth to Santander and

Bilbao. Trasmediterránea and Baleària connect mainland Spain to the Balearic and Canary islands.

Direct ferries from Spain to Tangier leave daily from Tarifa and Algeciras on FRS, Inter Shipping, and Trasmediterránea. Otherwise, you can take your car either to Ceuta (via Algeciras, on Baleària) or Melilla (via Málaga, on Trasmediterránea)—two Spanish enclaves on the North African coast—and then move on to Morocco.

 # Bus

You can travel to Spain on modern buses (Eurolines/National Express, for example) from major European cities, including London, Paris, Rome, Frankfurt, and Prague. Although it may once have been the case that international bus travel was significantly cheaper than air travel, budget airlines have changed the equation. For perhaps a little more money and a large saving of travel hours, flying is increasingly the better option.

Within Spain, a number of private companies provides bus service, ranging from knee-crunchingly basic to luxurious. Fares are almost always lower than the corresponding train fares, and service covers more towns, though buses are less frequent on weekends. Smaller towns don't usually have a central bus depot, so ask the tourist office where to wait for the bus. Spain's major national long-haul bus line is ALSA.

Most of Spain's larger companies have buses with comfortable seats and adequate legroom; on longer journeys (two hours or longer), a movie is shown on board, and earphones are provided. Except on smaller, regional lines, all buses have bathrooms on board; most

long-haul buses also usually stop at least once every two to three hours for a snack and bathroom break. Smoking is prohibited on board.

ALSA has four luxury classes in addition to its regular seating. Premium, available on limited routes from Madrid, includes a number of services such as à la carte meals and a private waiting room, while Supra+ and Supra Economy include roomy leather seats and onboard meals. You also have the option of *asientos individuales,* individual seats (with no other seat on either side) that line one side of the bus. The last class is Eurobus, with a private waiting room, comfortable seats, and plenty of legroom. The Supra+ and Eurobus usually cost, respectively, up to one-third and one-fourth more than the regular seats.

If you plan to return to your initial destination, you can save by buying a round-trip ticket. Also, some of Spain's smaller, regional bus lines offer multitrip passes, which are worthwhile if you plan to move back and forth between two fixed destinations within the region. Generally, these tickets offer savings of 20% per journey; you can buy them at the station. The general rule for children over 3 is that if they occupy a seat, they pay full fare. Check the bus websites for *ofertas* (special offers).

At bus station ticket counters, most major credit cards (except American Express) are accepted. If you buy your ticket on the bus, it's cash only.

During peak travel times (Easter, August, and Christmas), it's a good idea to make a reservation at least a week in advance.

Getting Here and Around

Car

Your own driver's license is valid in Spain, but U.S. citizens are highly encouraged to obtain an International Driving Permit (IDP). The IDP may facilitate car rental and help you avoid traffic fines—it translates your state-issued driver's license into 10 languages so officials can easily interpret the information on it. Permits are available from the American Automobile Association.

Driving is the best way to see Spain's rural areas. The main cities are connected by a network of excellent four-lane divided highways (*autovías* and *autopistas*), which are designated by the letter *A* and have speed limits—depending on the area—of 80 kph (50 mph)–120 kph (75 mph). If the artery is a toll highway (*peaje*), it is designated *AP.* The letter *N* indicates a *carretera nacional*: a national or intercity route, with local traffic, which may have four or two lanes. Smaller towns and villages are connected by a network of secondary roads maintained by regional, provincial, and local governments, with an alphabet soup of different letter designations.

RENTAL CARS

Alamo, Avis, Budget, Enterprise, Europcar, and Hertz have branches at major Spanish airports and in large cities. Smaller, regional companies and wholesalers offer lower rates. The online outfit Pepe Car has been a big hit with travelers; in general, the earlier you book, the less you pay. Rates run as low as €15 per day, taxes included—but note that pickups at its center-city locations are considerably cheaper than at the airports. All agencies have a range of models, but virtually all cars in Spain have manual transmission. Rates in Madrid begin at the equivalents of $60 per day and $190 per week for an economy car with air-conditioning, manual transmission, and unlimited mileage, including 21% tax. A small car is cheaper and prudent for the tiny roads and parking spaces in many parts of Spain.

Anyone age 18 or older with a valid license can drive in Spain, but most rental agencies will not rent cars to drivers under 23.

GASOLINE

Gas stations are plentiful, and most on major routes and in big cities are open 24 hours. On less-traveled routes, gas stations are usually open 7 am–11 pm. Most stations are self-service, although prices are the same as those at full-service stations. At night, however, you must pay before you fill up. Most pumps offer a choice of gas, including unleaded (*gasolina sin plomo*), high octane, and diesel, so be careful to pick the right one for your car. Prices vary little among stations and were at this writing €1.15 per liter for unleaded. Credit cards are widely accepted.

PARKING

Parking is, almost without exception, a nightmare in Spanish cities. Don't park where the curb is painted yellow or where there is a yellow line painted a few inches from the curb. "No parking" signs are also fairly easy to recognize.

In most cities, there are street-parking spaces marked by blue lines. Look for a nearby machine with a blue-and-white "P" sign to purchase a parking ticket, which you leave inside your car, on the dashboard, before you lock up. Sometimes an attendant will be nearby to answer questions. Parking time limits, fees, and fines vary. Parking lots are available, often underground, but spaces are at a premium. The rule of thumb is to leave your car at your hotel unless absolutely necessary.

ROAD CONDITIONS

Spain's highway system includes some 6,000 km (3,600 miles) of well-maintained superhighways. Still, you'll find some stretches of major national highways that are only two lanes wide, where traffic often backs up behind trucks. Autopista tolls are steep, but as a result these highways are often less crowded than the free ones. If you're driving down through Catalonia, be aware that there are more tolls here than anywhere else in Spain. This can result in a quicker journey but at a sizable cost. If you spring for the autopistas, you'll find that many of the rest stops are nicely landscaped and have cafeterias with decent but overpriced food.

Most Spanish cities have notoriously long morning and evening rush hours. Traffic jams are especially bad in and around Barcelona, Madrid, and Seville. If possible, avoid the morning rush, which can last until noon, and the evening rush, which lasts 7–9. Also be aware that at the beginning, middle, and end of July and August, the country suffers its worst traffic jams (delays of six to eight hours are common) as millions of Spaniards embark on, or return from, their annual vacations.

ROADSIDE EMERGENCIES

Rental agencies Hertz and Avis have (optional) 24-hour breakdown service. If you belong to AAA, you can get emergency assistance from the Spanish counterpart, RACE.

RULES OF THE ROAD

Spaniards drive on the right and pass on the left, so stay in the right-hand lane when not passing. Children under 12 may not ride in the front seat, and seat belts are compulsory for both front- and backseat riders. Speed limits are 30 kph (19 mph) or 50 kph (31 mph) in cities, depending on the type of street, 90 kph (59mph) or 100 kph (62 mph) on national highways, 120 kph (75 mph) on the autopista or autovía. The use of cell phones by drivers, even on the side of the road, is illegal, except with completely hands-free devices.

Severe fines are enforced throughout Spain for driving under the influence of alcohol. Spot Breathalyzer checks are often carried out, and you will be cited if the level of alcohol in your bloodstream is found to be 0.05% or above.

Spanish highway police are increasingly vigilant about speeding and illegal passing. Police are empowered to demand payment on the spot from non-Spanish drivers. Police disproportionately target rental-car drivers for speeding and illegal passing, so play it safe.

 ## Train

The chart here has information about popular train routes. Prices are for one-way fares (depending on seating and where purchased) and subject to change.

International trains run from Madrid to Lisbon (10 hours 30 minutes, overnight) and Barcelona to Paris (6 hours 40 minutes).

Spain's wonderful high-speed train, the 290-kph (180-mph) AVE, travels between Madrid and Seville (with a stop in Córdoba) in 2½ hours; prices start at about €50 each way. It also serves the Madrid–Barcelona route, cutting travel time to just under three hours. From Madrid you can also reach Lleida, Huesca (one AVE train daily), Valencia, Málaga, Toledo, and Valladolid.

From summer 2021, the state-run rail system (RENFE) introduced tariffs based

Getting Here and Around

Train Travel Times

Madrid to Barcelona: €45–€91	High-speed AVE trains make the trip in 2 hours 30 minutes
Madrid to Bilbao: €22–€40	Semi-express Alvia train time is 5 hours 10 minutes
Madrid to Málaga: €35–€70	Fastest AVE trains take 2 hours 25 minutes
Madrid to Seville: €35–€66	Fastest AVE trains take 2 hours 20 minutes
Madrid to Granada: €35–€70	Fastest AVE trains take 3 hours and 20 minutes
Madrid to Santander: €27–€55	Semi-express Alvia is 4 hours 5 minutes
Madrid to Valencia: €23–€80	Fastest AVE trains take 1 hour 42 minutes
Madrid to Santiago de Compostela: €30–€60	Fastest Alvia trains take 4 hours 30 minutes
Barcelona to Bilbao: €30–€50	Running time about 6 hours 36 minutes
Barcelona to Granada: €40–€115	High-speed AVE trains take 6h and 25 min
Barcelona to Valencia: €27–€50	Fastest time 2 hours 40 minutes
Seville to Granada: €24–€50	Running time about 2 hours 20 minutes

on demand on AVE train services. Tickets at less popular times (e.g. mid-day or mid-week) are up to 75% cheaper in all three classes: *Básico, Elige,* and *Premium*. The low-cost AVE service, known as Avlo (*avlorenfe.com*), offers routes between Madrid, Barcelona, and Zarragoza with one-way tickets from as little as €7. The company plans to add other Avlo routes in 2022.

The fast Talgo service is also efficient, but other elements of the rail system are still a bit subpar by European standards, and some long-distance trips with multiple stops can be tediously slow. Although some overnight trains have comfortable sleeper cars, first-class fares that include a sleeping compartment are comparable to, or more expensive than, airfares.

Most Spaniards buy train tickets in advance online or at the train station's *taquilla* (ticket office). The lines can be long, so give yourself plenty of time. For popular train routes, you will need to reserve tickets more than a few days in advance and pick them up at least a day before traveling. The ticket clerks at the stations rarely speak English, so if you need help or advice in planning a more complex train journey, you may be better off going to a travel agency that displays the blue-and-yellow RENFE sign. A small commission (e.g., €2.50) should be expected. For shorter, regional train trips, you can often buy your tickets from machines in the train station. Note that you must provide your full name and identity details (e.g. passport number) for all AVE tickets.

You can use a credit card for train tickets at most city train stations, but in smaller towns and villages it may be cash only. Seat reservations are required on most long-distance and some other trains, particularly high-speed trains, and are wise on any train that might be crowded. You need a reservation if you want a sleeping berth.

The easiest way to make reservations is to go to the English version of the RENFE website (click "Welcome" on the top line) or use the RenfeTicket smartphone app (to buy tickets using the app, you need to register and to have bought a RENFE ticket with your credit card). Book early if you're traveling during Holy Week, on long holiday weekends, or in July and August. (The site allows you to make reservations up to 62 days in advance, which is important in qualifying for online purchase discounts.)

Caveats: You cannot buy tickets online for certain regional lines or for commuter lines (*cercanías*). Station agents cannot alter your reservations; you must do this yourself online. Some ticket types, e.g. Básico for the AVE, allow no changes. The RENFE website may not work with all browsers, but it does accept all major credit cards, including American Express.

DISCOUNTS

If you purchase a ticket on the RENFE website for the AVE or any of the Grandes Líneas (the faster, long-distance trains, including the Talgo) you can get a discount of 20%–60%, depending on how far ahead you book and how you travel: discounts on one-way tickets tend to be higher than on round-trips. Discount availabilities disappear fast: the earliest opportunity is 62 days in advance of travel. If you have a domestic or an international airline ticket and want to take the AVE within 48 hours of your arrival but haven't booked online, you can still get a 10% discount on the AVE one-way ticket and 25% for a round-trip ticket with a dated return. On regional trains, you get a 10% discount on round-trip tickets (15% on AVE medium-distance trains).

If there are more than two of you traveling on the AVE, look for the word "mesa" in the fare column, quoting the price per person for four people traveling together and sitting at the same table. If you select the price, it tells you how much the deal is for one, two, and three people. You have to buy all the tickets at the same time, but they're between 20% and 60% cheaper than regular tickets.

RAIL PASSES

If you're coming from the United States and are planning extensive train travel in Europe, check Rail Europe for Eurail passes. Whichever pass you choose, you must buy it before you leave for Europe.

Spain is one of 33 European countries in which you can use the Eurail Global Pass, which buys you unlimited rail travel in all participating countries for the duration of the pass. Choose from passes that allow a set number of days to travel during a one-, two-, or three-month period, or passes offering continuous travel within the chosen period. There are discounts for children (ages 4–11) and youths (ages 12–27).

If Spain is your only destination, a Eurail Spain Pass allows between three and eight days of unlimited train travel in Spain within a one-month period for $272–$499 (first class) and $204–$337 (second class). There are also combination passes for those visiting Spain and Portugal, Spain and France, and Spain and Italy.

Many travelers assume that rail passes guarantee them seats on the trains they wish to ride: not so. Reserve seats even if you're using a rail pass.

Before You Go

 Immunizations

There are no immunization requirements for visitors traveling to Spain for tourism.

🌐 Passports and Visas

Visitors from the United States, Australia, Canada, New Zealand, and the United Kingdom need a valid passport to enter Spain.

VISAS

Visas are not necessary for those with U.S. passports valid for a minimum of six months and who plan to stay in Spain for tourist or business purposes for up to 90 days. Should you need a visa to stay longer than this, contact the Spanish consulate office nearest to you in the United States to apply for the appropriate documents.

⬛ U.S. Embassy/Consulate

Embassies are located in Madrid while some countries also maintain consulates in Barcelona. The United States also maintains consular agencies in Fuengirola, Las Palmas, Palma de Mallorca, Seville, and Valencia.

📷 What to Pack

Pack light. Although baggage carts are free and plentiful in most Spanish airports, they're rare in smaller train stations and most bus stations. Madrid, north and northeastern Spain, and Granada and the Sierra Nevada can be bitterly cold from late fall through early spring, while the Mediterranean and southern regions are generally much milder, if not warm. It makes sense to wear casual, comfortable clothing and shoes for sightseeing, but you'll want to dress up a bit in large cities, especially for fine restaurants and nightclubs. On the beach, anything goes; it's common to see women of all ages wearing only bikini bottoms, and many of the more remote beaches allow nude sunbathing.

📅 When to Go

High season: June through mid-September is the most expensive and popular time to visit the coast and islands; July and August are especially crowded. Inland cities are quieter but hot, and many businesses close for August. Sunshine is guaranteed almost everywhere, except in the north where weather is changeable.

Low season: Winter offers the least appealing weather, though it's the best time for airfares and hotel deals. The Mediterranean coast can be balmy during the daytime, even in December—and there are no crowds—but nighttime temperatures drop.

Value season: May, June, and September are lovely with warm weather, saner airfares, and good hotel offers. You can hang with the locals without the tourist crowds. October still has great weather, though temperatures start to fall by November. Bring an umbrella in March and April.

Essentials

◎ Communications

PHONES

The country code for Spain is 34. The country code is 1 for the United States and Canada.

If you're going to be traveling in Spain for an extended period, buy a local SIM card (ensure your phone is unlocked), use Skype or FaceTime, or install a free messenger app on your smartphone, such as Viber or WhatsApp

🍴 Dining

Although Spain has always had an extraordinary range of regional cuisines, in the past decade or so its restaurants have won it international recognition at the highest levels. A new generation of Spanish chefs—led by the revolutionary Ferran Adrià—has transformed classic dishes to suit contemporary tastes, drawing on some of the freshest ingredients in Europe and bringing an astonishing range of new technologies into the kitchen.

Smoking is banned in all eating and drinking establishments in Spain.

MEALS AND MEALTIMES

Outside major hotels, which serve morning buffets, breakfast (*desayuno*) is usually limited to coffee and toast or a roll. Lunch (*comida* or *almuerzo*) traditionally consists of an appetizer, a main course, and dessert, followed by coffee and perhaps a liqueur. Between lunch and dinner the best way to snack is to sample some tapas at a bar; normally you can choose from quite a variety. Dinner (*cena*) is somewhat lighter, with perhaps only one course. In addition to à la carte selections, most restaurants offer a *menú del día* (daily fixed-price menu) consisting of a starter, main plate, beverage, and dessert. The menú del día is traditionally offered only at lunch, but increasingly it's also offered at dinner in popular tourist destinations. If your waiter does not suggest it when you're seated, ask for it: "*¿Hay menú del día, por favor?*"

Mealtimes in Spain are later than elsewhere in Europe, and later still in Madrid and the southern region of Andalusia. Lunch starts around 2 or 2:30 (closer to 3 in Madrid) and dinner after 9 (as late as 11 or midnight in Madrid). Weekend eating times, especially dinner, can begin upward of an hour later. In areas with heavy tourist traffic, some restaurants open a bit earlier.

Most prices listed in menus are inclusive of 10% value-added tax (I.V.A.), but not all. If I.V.A. isn't included, it should read, "*10% I.V.A. no incluido en los precios*" at the bottom of the menu. Unless otherwise noted, the restaurants listed in this guide are open daily for lunch and dinner.

Prices in the reviews are the average cost of a main course or equivalent combination of smaller dishes at dinner or, if dinner is not served, at lunch.

PAYING

Credit cards are widely accepted in Spanish restaurants, but some smaller establishments do not take them. If you pay by credit card and you want to leave a small tip above and beyond the service charge, leave the tip in cash. See Tipping for guidelines.

RESERVATIONS AND DRESS

Regardless of where you are, it's a good idea to make a reservation if you can. In some places, it's expected. We only mention them specifically when reservations are essential (there's no other way you'll ever get a table) or when they are not accepted. For popular restaurants,

Essentials

book as far ahead as you can (often 30 days), and reconfirm as soon as you arrive. (Large parties should always call ahead to check the reservations policy.) We mention dress only when men are required to wear a jacket or a jacket and tie.

WINES, BEER, AND SPIRITS

Apart from its famous wines, Spain produces many brands of lager, the most popular of which are San Miguel, Cruzcampo, Aguila, Voll Damm, Mahou, and Estrella. There's also a thriving craft-beer industry and most large towns and cities have bars specializing in local brews. Jerez de la Frontera is Europe's largest producer of brandy and is a major source of sherry. Catalonia is a major producer of cava (sparkling wine). Spanish law prohibits the sale of alcohol to people age 18 or younger.

🛏 Lodging

By law, hotel prices in Spain must be posted at the reception desk and should indicate whether the value-added tax (I.V.A. 10%) is included. Note that high-season rates prevail not only in summer but also during Holy Week and local fiestas. In much of Spain, breakfast is normally *not* included.

HOTELS AND BED-AND-BREAKFASTS

The Spanish government classifies hotels with one to five stars, with an additional rating of five-star GL (Gran Lujo) indicating the highest quality. Although quality is a factor, the rating is technically only an indication of how many facilities the hotel offers. For example, a three-star hotel may be just as comfortable as a four-star hotel but lack a swimming pool.

All hotel entrances are marked with a blue plaque bearing the letter *H* and the number of stars. The letter *R* (for *residencia*) after the letter *H* indicates an establishment with no meal service, with the possible exception of breakfast. The designations *fonda* (*F*), *pensión* (*P*), *casa de huéspedes* (*CH*), and *hostal* (*Hs*) indicate budget accommodations: these are no longer official categories, but you'll still find them across the country. In most cases, especially in smaller villages, rooms in such buildings will be basic but clean; in large cities, these rooms can be downright dreary.

When inquiring in Spanish about whether a hotel has a private bath, ask if it's an *habitación con baño*. Although a single room (*habitación sencilla*) is usually available, singles are often on the small side. Solo travelers might prefer to pay a bit extra for single occupancy of a double room (*habitación doble uso individual*). Make sure you request a double bed (*cama de matrimonio*) if you want one—if you don't ask, you will usually end up with two singles.

The Spanish love small country hotels and agritourism. Rusticae (www.rusticae. es) is an association of more than 120 independently owned hotels in restored palaces, monasteries, mills, and estates, generally in rural Spain. Similar associations serve individual regions, and tourist offices also provide lists of establishments. In Galicia, *pazos* are beautiful, old, often stately homes converted into small luxury hotels; Pazos de Galicia (www. pazosdegalicia.com) is the main organization for them. In Cantabria, *casonas* are small-to-large country houses, but they may not have individual websites, so check the regional tourist office websites for booking and contact information.

A number of *casas rurales* (country houses similar to B&Bs) offer pastoral lodging either in guest rooms or in self-catering cottages. You may also come across the term *finca,* for country estate house. Many *agroturismo* accommodations are fincas converted to upscale B&Bs.

PARADORS

The Spanish government operates nearly 100 paradors—upscale hotels often in historic buildings or near significant sites. Rates are reasonable, considering that most paradores have four- or five-star amenities, and the premises are invariably immaculate and tastefully furnished, often with antiques or reproductions. Each parador has a restaurant serving regional specialties, and you can stop in for a meal without spending the night. Paradors are popular with foreigners and Spaniards alike, so make reservations well in advance.

💲 Taxes

Value-added tax, similar to sales tax, is called I.V.A. in Spain (pronounced "*ee*-vah," for *impuesto sobre el valor añadido*). It's levied on both products and services, such as hotel rooms and restaurant meals. When in doubt about whether tax is included, ask, "*¿Está incluido el I.V.A.?*" The I.V.A. rate for hotels and restaurants is currently 10%, regardless of their number of stars. A special tax law for the Canary Islands allows hotels and restaurants there to charge 7% I.V.A. Menus will generally note at the bottom whether tax is included ("*I.V.A. incluido*") or not ("*más 10% I.V.A.*").

Although food, pharmaceuticals, and household items are taxed at the lowest rate (4%), most consumer goods are now taxed at 21%. A number of shops participate in Global Refund (formerly Europe Tax-Free Shopping), a VAT refund service that makes getting your money back relatively hassle-free. You cannot get a refund on the VAT for such items as meals, or services such as hotel accommodations or taxi fares.

When making a purchase that qualifies for Global Refund, find out whether the merchant gives refunds—not all stores do, nor are they required to—and ask for a V.A.T. refund form. Have the form stamped like any customs form by customs officials when you leave the country or, if you're visiting several European Union countries, when you leave the EU. After you're through passport control, take the form to a refund-service counter for an on-the-spot refund (which is usually the quickest and easiest option), or mail it to the address on the form (or the envelope with it) after you arrive home. You receive the total refund stated on the form, but the processing time can be long, especially if you request a credit-card adjustment.

Global Blue is a Europewide service with 300,000 affiliated stores and more than 700 refund counters at major airports and border crossings. The refund form, called a Tax Free Check or Refund Cheque, is the most common across the European continent. The service issues refunds in the form of cash, check, or credit-card adjustment.

🛎 Tipping

Aside from tipping waiters and taxi drivers, Spaniards tend not to leave extra in addition to the bill. Restaurant checks do not list a service charge on the bill but consider the tip included. If you want to leave a small tip in addition to the bill,

Essentials

tip 5%–10% of the bill (and only if you think the service was worth it), and leave less if you eat tapas or sandwiches at a bar—just enough to round out the bill to the nearest €1.

Tours

SPECIAL-INTEREST TOURS

Madrid and Beyond

An array of customized private luxury tours (no two are the same) are offered by this company, focusing on culinary, cultural, and sports-related themes. ☎ *91/758–0063 in Spain* ⊕ *www.madri-dandbeyond.com* ✉ *Prices available on application.*

Toma Tours

This company provides personalized and small-group tours with the focus on discovering Andalusia's culture, landscape, and gastronomy beyond the guidebook. ☎ *650/733116* ⊕ *tomaandcoe.com* ✉ *From €1690.*

ART

Escorted Spain Tours

Based in the United States, this company offers a range of tours with accents on art, cultural history, and the outdoors. ☎ *800/942–3301* ⊕ *www.escortedspain-tours.com* ✉ *From €1135.*

BIRD-WATCHING

Discovering Doñana

In the Coto Doñana National Park in Andalusia, this company offers some of the best guided bird-watching tours and expeditions in Spain. ☎ *620/964369* ⊕ *www.discoveringdonana.com* ✉ *From €165.*

CULINARY AND WINE

Artisans of Leisure

This company offers personalized food-and-wine and cultural tours to Spain.

☎ *800/214–8144, 212/243–3239* ⊕ *www.artisansofleisure.com* ✉ *From €7685.*

Cellar Tours

Based in Madrid, Cellar Tours offers a wide array of wine and culinary tours to Spain's main wine regions. ☎ *911/436553 in Spain, 310/496–8061 in U.S.* ⊕ *www.cellartours.com* ✉ *From €700.*

HIKING

Spain Adventures

This company offers hiking and biking around Spain, as well as unusual tours such as yoga and cooking. ☎ *772/564–0330* ⊕ *www.spainadventures.com* ✉ *From €3090.*

LANGUAGE PROGRAMS

Go Abroad

This is one of the best resources for language schools and international programs in Spain. ⊕ *www.goabroad.com.*

VOLUNTEER PROGRAMS

Go Abroad

This is the best resource for volunteering and finding paid internships in Spain. ⊕ *www.goabroad.com.*

Spain Savvy

Owned and operated by an American expat in Seville, this company designs custom itineraries including culturally immersive experiences and top-notch properties. ☎ *717/702559* ⊕ *www.spain-savvy.com* ✉ *From €300.*

ONLINE TRAVEL TOOLS

For more information on Spain, visit the Tourist Office of Spain at ⊕ *www.spain.info.* Also check out the sites ⊕ *www.red2000.com/spain* and ⊕ *www.idealspain.com;* the latter focuses more on living, working, or buying property in Spain. For a virtual brochure on Spain's paradores and online booking, go to ⊕ *www.parador.es.*

Contacts

Air

CONTACTS Air Europa. ☎ 911/401501 ⊕ www.aireuropa.com. **Iberia.** ☎ 915/236-568 ⊕ www.iberia.com. **Transportation Security Administration.** ⊕ www.tsa.gov.

AIRLINES Air Europa. ☎ 911/401501 ⊕ www.aireuropa.com. **Iberia Express.** ☎ 919/046342 ⊕ www.iberiaexpress.com. **Vueling.** ☎ 931/225400 ⊕ www.vueling.com.

AIRPORTS Madrid–Barajas (MAD). ✉ Madrid ☎ 902/404704 ⊕ www.aeropuertomadrid-barajas.com. **AENA.** ☎ 913/211000 ⊕ www.aena.es.

Bus

CONTACTS ALSA. ☎ 902/422242 ⊕ www.alsa.es. **Flixbus.** ⊕ www.flixbus.es.

Car

CAR RENTAL COMPANIES Avis. ☎ 800/633-3469, 902/135531 in Spain ⊕ www.avis.com. **Budget.** ☎ 800/404-8033, 902/112585 in Spain ⊕ www.budget.com. **Enterprise.** ☎ 902/100101 in Spain ⊕ www.enterprise.es. **Europcar.** ☎ 911/505000 in Spain ⊕ www.europcar.es. **Hertz.** ☎ 800/654-3131, 917/499069 in Spain ⊕ www.hertz.com. **Pepe Car.** ☎ 916/350317 in Spain ⊕ www.pepecar.com.

EMERGENCY SERVICE RACE. ☎ 900/100992 for info, 900/112222 for assistance ⊕ www.race.es.

Train

TRAIN CONTACTS Eurail. ⊕ www.eurail.com. **Rail Europe.** ⊕ www.raileurope.com. **RENFE.** ☎ 912/320320 for tickets and info ⊕ www.renfe.es.

⚠ Emergencies

FOREIGN EMBASSIES AND CONSULATES U.S. Embassy. ✉ Calle Serrano 75, Madrid ☎ 91/587-2200 U.S.-citizen emergencies ⊕ es.usembassy.gov.

GENERAL EMERGENCY CONTACTS Emergency telephone number. ☎ 112. **Fire department.** ☎ 080. **Local police.** ☎ 092. **Medical service.** ☎ 061. **National police.** ☎ 091.

Lodging

APARTMENT RENTALS HolidayLettings. ⊕ www.holidaylettings.co.uk. **HomeAway.** ⊕ www.homeaway.com. **Interhome.** ☎ 800/268-2615 ⊕ www.interhomeusa.com. **Villas and Apartments Abroad.** ☎ 212/213-6435 ⊕ www.vaanyc.com.

PARADORS Paradores de España. ☎ 913/742500 in Spain ⊕ www.parador.es.

Boat

CONTACTS Balearia. ☎ 912/660215, 084/35087312 From abroad ⊕ www.balearia.com/en. **Brittany Ferries.** ☎ 0330/1597000 in U.K., 902/108147 in Spain ⊕ www.brittany-ferries.com. **FRS.** ☎ 956/681830 ⊕ www.frs.es. **Trasmediterránea.** ☎ 902/454645 ⊕ www.trasmediterranea.es. **Inter Shipping.** ☎ 956/684729.

Great Itineraries

Madrid to the Alhambra, 10-day Itinerary

This trip takes in the best of vibrant Madrid and its world-class art museums and showcases some of Castile's historic gems before whisking you to the Moorish south where Córdoba's majestic mosque, Seville's fragrant orange blossoms, and Granada's "heaven on earth" await.

DAYS 1–3: MADRID

Start the day with a visit to either the **Prado,** the **Museo Thyssen-Bornemisza,** or the **Centro de Arte Reina Sofía.** Then head to the elegant **Plaza Mayor**—a perfect jumping-off point for a tour of the Spanish capital. To the west, see the **Plaza de la Villa, Palacio Real** (the Royal Palace), **Teatro Real** (Royal Theater), and the royal convents; to the south, wander around the maze of streets of **La Latina** and **El Rastro** and try some local tapas.

On Day 2, visit the sprawling **Barrio de las Letras,** centered on the Plaza de Santa Ana. This was the favorite neighborhood of writers during the Spanish golden literary age in the 17th century (Cervantes lies buried under a convent nearby), and it's still crammed with theaters, cafés, and good tapas bars. It borders the Paseo del Prado on the east, allowing you to comfortably walk to any of the art museums in the area. If the weather is pleasant, take an afternoon stroll in the **Parque del Buen Retiro.**

For your third day in the capital, wander in **Chueca** and **Malasaña,** the two funky hipster neighborhoods most favored by young madrileños. Fuencarral, a landmark pedestrianized street that serves as the border between the two, is one of the city's trendiest shopping enclaves. From there you can walk to the **Parque del Oeste** and the **Templo de Debod**—the best spot from which to see the city's sunset. Among the lesser-known museums, consider visiting the captivating **Museo Sorolla,** Goya's frescoes and tomb at the **Ermita de San Antonio de la Florida,** or the **Real Academia de Bellas Artes de San Fernando** for classic painting. People-watch at any of the terrace bars in either Plaza de Chueca or Plaza del Dos de Mayo in Malasaña.

Logistics: If you're traveling light, the subway (Metro Línea 8) or the bus (No. 203 during the day and N27 at night) will take you from the airport to the city for €5. The train costs €2.60 and a taxi is a fixed price of €30. Once in the center consider walking or taking the subway rather than cabbing it in gridlock traffic.

DAYS 4 AND 5: CASTILIAN CITIES

There are several excellent options for half- or full-day side trips from Madrid to occupy Days 4 and 5. **Toledo** and **Segovia** are two of the oldest Castilian cities—both have delightful old quarters dating back to the Romans. There's also **El Escorial,** which houses the massive monastery built by Felipe II. Two other nearby towns also worth visiting are **Aranjuez** and **Alcalá de Henares.**

Logistics: Toledo and Segovia are stops on the high-speed train line (AVE), so you can get to either of them in a half hour from Madrid. To reach the old quarters of both cities, take a bus or cab from the train station or take the bus from Madrid. Buses and trains both go to El Escorial. Reach Aranjuez and Alcalá de Henares via the intercity train system.

DAY 6: CÓRDOBA OR EXTREMADURA

Córdoba, the capital of both Roman and Moorish Spain, was the center of Western art and culture between the 8th and 11th centuries. The city's breathtaking

Mezquita (mosque), which is now a cathedral, and the medieval **Jewish Quarter** bear witness to the city's brilliant past. From Madrid you could also rent a car and visit the lesser-known cities in the north of **Extremadura,** such as **Guadalupe** and **Trujillo,** and overnight in **Cáceres,** a UNESCO World Heritage Site, then return to Madrid the next day.

Logistics: The AVE will take you to Córdoba from Madrid in less than two hours. One alternative is to stay in Toledo, also on the route heading south, and then head to Córdoba the next day, although you need to return to Madrid by train first. Once in Córdoba, take a taxi for a visit out to the summer palace at Medina Azahara.

DAYS 7 AND 8: SEVILLE

Seville's **cathedral,** with its tower La Giralda, **Plaza de Toros Real Maestranza,** and **Barrio de Santa Cruz** are visual feasts. Forty minutes south by train, you can sip the world-famous sherries of **Jerez de la Frontera,** then munch jumbo shrimp on the beach at **Sanlúcar de Barrameda.**

Logistics: From Seville's AVE station, take a taxi to your hotel. After that, walking and hailing the occasional taxi are the best ways to explore the city. A rental car is the best option to reach towns beyond

Tip

Spain's modern freeways and toll highways are as good as any in the world—with the exception of the signs, which are often tiny and hard to decipher as you sweep past them at the routine speed of 120 kph (74 mph).

Seville, except for Jerez de la Frontera, where the train station is an architectural gem in its own right.

DAYS 9 AND 10: GRANADA

The hilltop **Alhambra** palace, Spain's most visited attraction, was conceived by the Moorish caliphs as heaven on earth. Try any of the city's famous tapas bars and tea shops, and make sure to roam the magical, steep streets of the **Albayzín,** the ancient Moorish quarter.

Logistics: The Seville–Granada leg of this trip is best accomplished by renting a car; Antequera makes a good quick stop on the way. However, the Seville–Granada trains (three daily, about 2½ hours, €40) are one alternative. Another idea is to head first from Madrid to Granada, and then from Granada to Seville via Córdoba.

Great Itineraries

Barcelona and the North Coast, 16-day Itinerary

Dive into happening Barcelona, with its unique blend of Gothic and Gaudí architecture, colorful markets, and long city beaches. Then head to the verdant north for culinary sophistication in San Sebastián and to check out the Guggenheim in chic Bilbao. Next, wind your way along the wild, rugged coastline, taking in the mountains, fishing ports, bagpipes, and Europe's best seafood along the way.

DAYS 1–3: BARCELONA

To get a feel for Barcelona, begin with **La Rambla** and the **Boquería** market. Then set off for the **Gothic Quarter** to see the **Catedral de la Seu, Plaça del Rei,** and the Catalan and Barcelona government palaces in **Plaça Sant Jaume.** Next, cross Via Laietana to the **Born-Ribera** (waterfront neighborhood) for the Gothic **Santa Maria del Mar** and nearby **Museu Picasso.**

Make Day 2 a Gaudí day: Visit the **Temple Expiatori de la Sagrada Família,** then **Park Güell.** In the afternoon see the **Casa Milà** and **Casa Batlló,** part of the Manzana de la Discòrdia on Passeig de Gràcia. **Palau Güell,** off the lower Rambla, is probably too much Gaudí for one day, but don't miss it.

On Day 3, climb **Montjuïc** for the **Museu Nacional d'Art de Catalunya,** in the hulking **Palau Nacional.** Investigate the **Fundació Miró, Estadi Olímpic,** the **Mies van der Rohe Pavilion,** and **CaixaForum** exhibition center. At lunchtime, take the cable car across the port for seafood in **Barceloneta** and then stroll along the beach.

Logistics: In Barcelona, walking or taking the subway is better than cabbing it.

DAY 4: SAN SEBASTIÁN

San Sebastián is one of Spain's most beautiful—and delicious—cities. Belle Époque buildings nearly encircle the tiny bay, and tapas bars flourish in the old quarter. Not far from San Sebastián is historic **Pasajes (Pasaia) de San Juan.**

Logistics: Take the train from Barcelona to San Sebastián (5 hours 30 minutes) in the afternoon. You don't need a car in San Sebastián proper, but visits to cider houses in Astigarraga, Chillida Leku on the outskirts of town, and many of the finest restaurants around San Sebastián are possible only with your own transportation or a taxi (the latter with the advantage that you won't get lost). The freeway west to Bilbao is beautiful and fast, but the coastal road is recommended at least as far as Zumaia.

DAYS 5 AND 6: THE BASQUE COAST

The Basque coast between San Sebastián and Bilbao has a succession of fine beaches, rocky cliffs, and picture-perfect fishing ports. The wide beach at **Zarautz,** the fishermen's village of **Getaria,** the **Zuloaga Museum in Zumaia,** and **Bermeo**'s port and fishing museum should all be near the top of your list.

DAYS 7 AND 8: BILBAO

Bilbao's **Guggenheim Museum** is worth a trip for the building itself, and the **Museo de Bellas Artes** has an impressive collection of Basque and Spanish paintings. Restaurants and tapas bars are famously good in Bilbao.

Logistics: In Bilbao, use the subway or the Euskotram, which runs up and down the Nervión estuary.

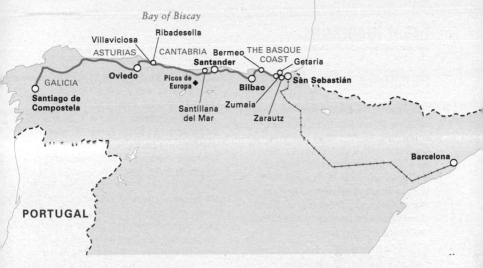

DAYS 9 AND 10: SANTANDER AND CANTABRIA

The elegant beach town of **Santander** has an excellent summer music festival every August. Nearby, **Santillana del Mar** is one of Spain's best Renaissance towns, and the museum of the **Altamira Caves** displays reproductions of the famous underground Neolithic rock paintings discovered here. Exploring the **Picos de Europa** will take you through some of the peninsula's wildest reaches, and the port towns along the coast provide some of Spain's most pristine beaches.

DAYS 11–13: OVIEDO AND ASTURIAS

The coast road through **Ribadesella** and the cider capital **Villaviciosa** to **Oviedo** is scenic and punctuated with tempting beaches. Oviedo, its **cathedral,** and the simplicity of its pre-Romanesque churches are worlds away from the richness of Córdoba's Mezquita and Granada's Alhambra.

Logistics: The A8 coastal freeway gets you quickly and comfortably to Gijón, then hop on the A66 to Oviedo. From there, head back to the A8 and go west

through Avilés and into Galicia via the coastal N634—a slow but scenic route to Santiago.

DAYS 14–16: SANTIAGO DE COMPOSTELA AND GALICIA

Spain's northwest corner, with **Santiago de Compostela** at its spiritual and geographic center, is a green land of bagpipes and apple orchards. The Albariño wine country, along the Río Miño border with Portugal, and the *rías* (estuaries), full of delicious seafood, will keep you steeped in *enxebre*—Gallego for "local specialties and atmosphere."

Logistics: The four-lane freeways AP9 and A6 whisk you from Lugo and Castro to Santiago de Compostela and to the Rías Baixas. By car is the only way to tour Galicia. The AC862 route around the upper northwest corner and the Rías Altas turns into the AP9 coming back into Santiago.

Great Itineraries

Andalusia 7-Day Itinerary

Head south to a land of fiery flamenco passion, unique Moorish treasures, impossibly white villages, and delicious sherry and tapas. As you make your way from Córdoba to Granada via Seville, Jerez de la Frontera, and Málaga, prepare yourself to see some of Europe's finest monuments, prettiest villages, and loveliest—albeit most sweltering—landscapes.

DAY 1: CÓRDOBA

Córdoba's breathtaking **Mezquita** (mosque), now a cathedral, is an Andalusian highlight, and the medieval **Jewish Quarter** is lovely to explore. If you're here during May, visit the **Festival de los Patios** (Patio Festival).

DAYS 2–3: SEVILLE

The city that launched Christopher Columbus to the New World, **Seville** is a treasure trove of sights. Start with the **cathedral** and climb La Giralda for great views of the city. Move on to the richly decorated *alcázar* (fortress), still an official royal residence, with its many beautiful patios, and where, more recently, much of the *Game of Thrones* epic was filmed. The **Jewish Quarter** in Santa Cruz is a charming labyrinth of alleyways and squares. In the afternoon, cross to **Triana** over the Guadalquivir River and lose yourself in the quiet streets, which are the birthplace of many a flamenco artist.

Logistics: Take the high-speed train (AVE) to Seville from Córdoba (45 minutes). Seville is a compact city and easy to navigate so it's best to explore on foot—or pick up a municipal bicycle at one of the hundreds of Sevici bike stations spread out across the city.

DAY 4: JEREZ DE LA FRONTERA AND RONDA VIA ARCOS DE LA FRONTERA

Jerez de la Frontera is the world's sherry headquarters and home to some of the greatest *bodegas* (wineries). Visit Domecq, Harvey, or Sandeman, and, if you have time, watch the world's finest dancing horses at the prestigious Royal Andalusian School of Equestrian Art. The lovely cliff-top village of **Arcos de la Frontera,** one of Andalusia's prettiest *pueblos blancos* (white villages), makes a great stop on the way to **Ronda.** One of the oldest towns in Spain, Ronda is famed for its spectacular position and views; get the best photo from the Juan Peña El Lebrijano Bridge.

Logistics: Rent a car in Seville and take the highway to Jerez de la Frontera before making your way to Ronda via Arcos de la Frontera. If you have time, stop off in the lovely village of Grazalema.

DAY 5: MÁLAGA

Start your exploration of the capital of the **Costa del Sol, Málaga,** with the **Roman theater,** Moorish *alcazaba* (citadel), and Gothic **cathedral.** Stroll down to the Muelle Uno on the port for views of the city skyline and **Gibralfaro** castle before returning to the center to visit the **Museo Picasso** and browse the shops in Larios and surrounding streets.

Logistics: Leave Ronda early and enjoy the scenic drive to Málaga via the A367 and A357. In Málaga, explore on foot, leaving your car in a central lot or at your hotel.

DAYS 6–7: GRANADA

Allow a good half day to visit the hilltop **Alhambra** palace and Generalife gardens. From there, walk down to the city center to the **cathedral** and **Capilla Real,** the shrine of Isabella of Castile and

Ferdinand of Aragón. Finish your day with some tapas at one of the many famous tapas bars. On Day 7, walk up to the Albayzín, the ancient Moorish quarter, for a leisurely wander around the narrow streets. Take your time in the Plaza de San Nicolás and admire the magnificent views of the Alhambra and Sierra Nevada before you leave.

Logistics: The drive to Granada from Málaga takes about 1 hour 30 minutes. Granada is best explored on foot, so leave your car at the hotel.

Madrid and Barcelona, 6-Day Itinerary

Combining Spain's two largest and greatest cities on a six-day itinerary gives you the chance to take in the contrasts of imperial Madrid and Moderniste Barcelona. Both cities are vibrant, energetic cultural centers showcasing some of Europe's greatest art and architecture as well as Spanish gastronomy at its best. You can also get a taste for Spain's late-night fun, sample its colorful markets, and stay at some of the country's best lodgings. However, Madrid and Barcelona

Tip

Rent a car with a GPS navigation system to help you find your way from one Andalusian city to the next. Help with navigating is also useful in the cities themselves.

feel very different, and you'll find huge contrasts in their landscapes, culture, and ambience. By visiting them both you'll get a good idea of the many facets that make up Spain.

For what to do on your days in Madrid, see the "Madrid to the Alhambra" itinerary. For Barcelona, see the "Barcelona, the North Coast, and Galicia" itinerary.

Logistics: Take the high-speed train (AVE) from Madrid to Barcelona (2 hours 30 minutes). For the return journey, fly from Barcelona to Madrid Barajas Airport in time to catch your flight home.

Great Itineraries

5 Days: Madrid Plus Granada or Seville and Side Trips

DAYS 1 AND 2: MADRID

Start the day with a visit to either the Prado, the Museo Thyssen-Bornemisza, or the Centro de Arte Reina Sofía. Then head to the elegant Plaza Mayor—a perfect jumping-off point for a tour of the Spanish capital. To the west, see the Plaza de la Villa, Palacio Real (the Royal Palace), Teatro Real (Royal Theater), and the royal convents; to the south, wander around the maze of streets of La Latina and El Rastro and try some local tapas.

On Day 2, visit the sprawling Barrio de las Letras, centered on the Plaza de Santa Ana. This was the favorite neighborhood of writers during the Spanish golden literary age in the 17th century (Cervantes lies buried under a convent nearby), and it's still crammed with theaters, cafés, and good tapas bars. For here, you can pop to the Paseo del Prado on the east and visit any of the art museums in the area. After lunch, take an afternoon stroll in the Parque del Buen Retiro or wander in Chueca or Malasaña, the two funky hipster neighborhoods favored by young locals. From here, walk to the Parque del Oeste and the Templo de Debod to marvel at the city's sunset.

GRANADA

Getting Here: Four daily flights connect Granada with Madrid and it's easy to get to the city from the airport by taxi, airport bus, or rental car. There are a couple of daily high-speed AVE trains from Madrid to Granada daily.

Day 3: After arriving in Granada, visit the Catholic Monarchs' tomb at the Capilla Real before exploring more Moorish monuments such as the Palacio Madraza (seminary) or El Bañuelo (bathhouse). Stroll around the Moorish Albayzín neighborhood for extraordinary views of Granada's highlight, the Alhambra, and the Sierra Nevada backdrop, extra special at sunset. Dine on the city's excellent tapas or take in a flamenco show.

Day 4: Granada's star of the show is, of course, La Alhambra, the most visited attraction in Spain. Its palace, fortress, patios, gardens, and museums alone merit the trip to Granada and need at least half a day to do them justice. Try to get an early-morning ticket to experience this wonder with less crowds. Note: reserve your ticket as far in advance as possible and show up at your ticketed time (preferably, before) or you will not be allowed entry. Lunch early before you pick up your hire car for a side trip excursion.

EVENING 4, DAY 5: SIDE TRIP OPTIONS

Option 1: Drive north to Priego de Córdoba (1¼ hours) to see one of the region's prettiest towns with a plethora of baroque churches, white facades decked with geraniums and stunning views. From here, drive to Córdoba and your hotel. Spend the next day exploring the Mezquita (mosque) and the Jewish Quarter and dine on the city's famous oxtail stew or *flamenquín* (pork fritter) washed down with local Montilla wine.

Option 2: Drive northeast to Baeza (1½ hours) and then to Úbeda, two jewels in Spain's Renaissance crown. Both are home to stunning architecture, seen in intricate facades on the many monuments; allow more time for Úbeda where you can visit the historic potter's quarter.

Option 3: Head south for the Sierra Nevada (1 hour drive) for a paradise of skiing in winter and trekking and climbing in summer. Or explore the Alpujarras, a unique mountain region dotted with picturesque Moorish villages set in stunning landscapes where time appears to have stopped still.

SEVILLE
Getting Here: Andalusia's second-largest airport, after Málaga, is in Seville and there are flights from Madrid every four hours or so. From Madrid, the best approach to Andalusia is via the high-speed AVE. In just 2½ hours, the spectacular ride winds through olive groves and rolling fields of Castile to Córdoba and on to Seville. From Seville's Santa Justa train station, get a cab (or rental car) to your hotel.

Day 3: Must-sees in the Andalusian capital include the cathedral with its La Giralda tower and the Reales Alcazares Moorish palace. Between visits, explore the nearby Barrio de Santa Cruz neighborhood with its typical architecture, orange blossom trees, and tiny squares. Dine early on delicious tapas at one of the traditional *tavernas* before an evening stroll along the banks of the Guadalquivir River.

Day 4: Start Day 4 with a visit to one of the city's great private houses—Palacio de las Dueñas, Casa de Pilatos, or Palacio de la Condesa de Lebrija—to see how the other half lived in the city. After lunch on tapas, admire the Plaza de Toros Real Maestranza (bullring) and stroll around the Parque de María Luisa before an aperitif in the bar at the Hotel Alfonso XIII. Then take in a flamenco show.

DAY 5: DAY TRIP OPTIONS
Seville is perfectly placed for several excellent side trips: taste the world-famous sherries of Jerez de la Frontera and admire the dancing horses before dining on Spain's freshest seafood at Puerto de Santa María or Sanlúcar de Barrameda; visit Spain's largest and one of its greatest Roman sites at Itálica, just outside Seville; drive to Ronda, one of Andalusia's most beautiful white towns, perched on a river gorge and the cradle of bullfighting; head for Europe's oldest city, the maritime Cádiz and soak up the history in its narrow streets and along the fortress walls; or go to Córdoba where the city's breathtaking Mezquita (mosque) and medieval Jewish Quarter await you. Don't miss the vibrant flower-packed patios while you're there.

Helpful Phrases in Spanish

BASICS

Hello	Hola	oh-lah
Yes/no	Sí/no	see/no
Please	Por favor	pore fah-**vore**
May I?	¿Me permite?	may pair-**mee**-tay
Thank you	Gracias	**Grah**-see-as
You're welcome	De nada	day **nah**-dah
I'm sorry	Lo siento	lo see-**en**-toh
Good morning!	¡Buenos días!	**bway**-nohs **dee**-ahs
Good evening!	¡Buenas tardes! (after 2pm)	**bway**-nahs-**tar**-dess
	¡Buenas noches! (after 8pm)	**bway**-nahs **no**-chess
Good-bye!	¡Adiós!/¡Hasta luego!	ah-dee-**ohss/ah**-stah **lwe**-go
Mr./Mrs.	Señor/Señora	sen-**yor**/ sen-**yohr**-ah
Miss	Señorita	sen-yo-**ree**-tah
Pleased to meet you	Mucho gusto	**moo**-cho **goose**-toh
How are you?	¿Que tal?	keh-tal

NUMBERS

one	un, uno	oon, **oo**-no
two	dos	dos
three	tres	tress
four	cuatro	**kwah**-tro
five	cinco	**sink**-oh
six	seis	saice
seven	siete	see-**et**-eh
eight	ocho	**o**-cho
nine	nueve	new-**eh**-vey
ten	diez	dee-**es**
eleven	once	**ohn**-seh
twelve	doce	**doh**-seh
thirteen	trece	**treh**-seh
fourteen	catorce	ka-**tohr**-seh
fifteen	quince	**keen**-seh
sixteen	dieciséis	dee-es-ee-**saice**
seventeen	diecisiete	dee-**es**-ee-see-**et**-eh
eighteen	dieciocho	dee-**es**-ee-o-cho
nineteen	diecinueve	dee-**es**-ee-new-**ev**-eh
twenty	veinte	**vain**-teh
twenty-one	veintiuno	**vain**-te-**oo**-noh
thirty	treinta	**train**-tah
forty	cuarenta	kwah-**ren**-tah
fifty	cincuenta	seen-**kwen**-tah
sixty	sesenta	sess-**en**-tah
seventy	setenta	set-**en**-tah
eighty	ochenta	oh-**chen**-tah
ninety	noventa	no-**ven**-tah
one hundred	cien	see-**en**
one thousand	mil	meel
one million	un millón	oon meel-**yohn**

COLORS

black	negro	**neh**-groh
blue	azul	ah-**sool**
brown	marrón	mah-**ron**
green	verde	**ver**-deh
orange	naranja	na-**rahn**-hah
red	rojo	**roh**-hoh
white	blanco	**blahn**-koh
yellow	amarillo	ah-mah-**ree**-yoh

DAYS OF THE WEEK

Sunday	domingo	doe-**meen**-goh
Monday	lunes	**loo**-ness
Tuesday	martes	**mahr**-tess
Wednesday	miércoles	me-**air**-koh-less
Thursday	jueves	hoo-**ev**-ess
Friday	viernes	vee-**air**-ness
Saturday	sábado	**sah**-bah-doh

MONTHS

January	enero	eh-**neh**-roh
February	febrero	feh-**breh**-roh
March	marzo	**mahr**-soh
April	abril	ah-**breel**
May	mayo	**my**-oh
June	junio	**hoo**-nee-oh
July	julio	**hoo**-lee-yoh
August	agosto	ah-**ghost**-toh
September	septiembre	sep-tee-**em**-breh
October	octubre	oak-**too**-breh
November	noviembre	no-vee-**em**-breh
December	diciembre	dee-see-**em**-breh

USEFUL WORDS AND PHRASES

Do you speak English?	¿Habla usted inglés?	**ah**-blah oos-**ted** in-**glehs**
I don't speak Spanish.	No hablo español	no **ah**-bloh es-pahn-**yol**
I don't understand.	No entiendo	no en-tee-**en**-doh
I understand.	Entiendo	en-tee-**en**-doh
I don't know.	No sé	no **seh**
I'm American.	Soy americano (americana)	soy ah-meh-**ree**-**kah**-no (ah-meh-ree-**kah**-nah)
What's your name?	¿Cómo se llama?	koh-mo seh **yah**-mah
My name is...	Me llamo...	may **yah**-moh
What time is it?	¿Qué hora es?	keh **o**-rah es
How?	¿Cómo?	**koh**-mo
When?	¿Cuándo?	**kwahn**-doh
Yesterday	Ayer	ah-**yehr**
Today	hoy	oy
Tomorrow	mañana	mahn-**yah**-nah
Tonight	Esta noche	es-tah **no**-cheh
What?	¿Qué?	keh
What is it?	¿Qué es esto?	keh es **es**-toh

Why?	¿Por qué?	pore **keh**
Who?	¿Quién?	kee-**yen**
Where is ...	¿Dónde está ...	dohn-deh es-**tah**
... the train station?	la estación del tren?	la es-tah-see-**on** del trehn
... the subway station?	estación de metro	la es-ta-see-**on** del **meh**-tro
... the bus stop?	la parada del autobus?	la pah-**rah**-dah del ow-toh-**boos**
... the terminal? (airport)	el aeropuerto	el air-oh-**pwar**-toh
... the post office?	la oficina de correos?	la oh-fee-**see**- nah deh koh-**rreh**-os
... the bank?	el banco?	el **bahn**-koh
... the hotel?	el hotel?	el oh-**tel**
... the museum?	el museo?	el moo-**seh**-oh
... the hospital?	el hospital?	el ohss-pee-**tal**
... the elevator?	el ascensor?	el ah-sen-**sohr**
Where are the restrooms?	el baño?	el **bahn**-yoh
Here/there	Aquí/allí	ah-**key**/ah-**yee**
Open/closed	Abierto/cerrado	ah-bee-**er**-toh/ ser-**ah**-doh
Left/right	Izquierda/derecha	iss-key-**eh**-dah/ dare-**eh**-chah
Is it near?	¿Está cerca?	es-**tah** sehr-kah
Is it far?	¿Está lejos?	es-**tah** leh-hoss
I'd like ...	Quisiera ...	kee-see-**ehr**-ah
... a room	un cuarto/una habitación	oon **kwahr**-toh/**oo**-nah ah-bee-tah-see-**on**
... the key	la llave	lah **yah**-veh
... a newspaper	un periódico	oon pehr-ee-**oh**-dee-koh
... a stamp	un sello de correo	oon **seh**-yo deh korr-**eh**-oh
I'd like to buy ...	Quisiera comprar ...	kee-see-**ehr**-ah kohm-**prahr**
... soap	jabón	hah-**bohn**
... suntan lotion	crema solar	**kreh**-mah soh-**lar**
... envelopes	sobres	**so**-brehs
... writing paper	papel	pah-**pel**
... a postcard	una tarjeta postal	oon-ah tar-**het**-ah post-**ahl**
... a ticket	un billete (travel)	oon bee-**yee**-teh
	una entrada (concert etc.)	oona en-**trah**-dah
How much is it?	¿Cuánto cuesta?	**kwahn**-toh **kwes**-tah
It's expensive/ cheap	Es caro/barato	es **kah**-roh/ bah-**rah**-toh
A little/a lot	Un poquito/mucho	oon poh-**kee**-toh/ **moo**-choh
More/less	Más/menos	mahss/**men**-ohss
Enough/too (much)	Suficiente/	soo-fee-see-**en**-teh/
I am ill/sick	Estoy enfermo(a)	es-**toy** en-**fehr**-moh(mah)
Call a doctor	Llame a un medico	ya-meh ah oon **med**-ee-koh

Help!	Socorro	soh-**koh**-roh
Stop!	Pare	**pah**-reh

DINING OUT

I'd like to reserve a table ...	Quisiera reservar una mesa ...	kee-**syeh**-rah rreh-sehr-**bahr** oo-nah **meh**-sah ...
... for two people.	para dos personas.	**pah**-rah dohs pehr-**soh**-nahs
... for this evening.	para esta noche.	**pah**-rah ehs-tah noh-cheh
... for 8 PM	para las ocho de la noche.	**pah**-rah lahs oh-choh deh lah noh-cheh
A bottle of ...	Una botella de ...	oo-nah bo-**teh**-yah deh
A cup of ...	Una taza de ...	oo-nah **tah**-sah deh
A glass of ...	Un vaso (water, soda, etc.) de...	oon **vah**-so deh
	Una copa (wine, spirits, etc.) de...	oona **coh**-pah deh
Bill/check	La cuenta	lah **kwen**-tah
Bread	El pan	el pahn
Breakfast	El desayuno	el deh-sah-**yoon**-oh
Butter	La mantequilla	lah man-teh-**kee**-yah
Coffee	Café	kah-**feh**
Dinner	La cena	lah **seh**-nah
Fork	El tenedor	el ten-eh-**dor**
I don't eat meat	No como carne	noh koh-moh **kahr**-neh
I cannot eat ...	No puedo comer ...	noh **pweh**-doh koh-**mehr**
I'd like to order ...	Quiero pedir ...	**kee**-yehr-oh peh-**deer**
I'd like ...	Me gustaría ...	Meh goo-stah-**ee**-ah
I'm hungry/thirsty	Tengo hambre/sed	**Tehn**-goh **hahm**-breh/seth
Is service/the tip included?	¿Está incluida la propina?	es-**tah** in-cloo-ee-dah lah pro-**pee**-nah
Knife	El cuchillo	el koo-**chee**-yo
Lunch	La comida	lah koh-**mee**-dah
Menu	La carta, el menú	lah **cart**-ah, el meh-**noo**
Napkin	La servilleta	lah sehr-vee-**yet**-ah
Pepper	La pimienta	lah pee-mee-**en**-tah
Plate	plato	**plah**-toh
Please give me ...	Por favor déme ...	pore fah-**vor** **deh**-meh
Salt	La sal	lah sahl
Spoon	Una cuchara	oo-nah koo-**chah**-rah
Sugar	El ázucar	el ah-**su**-kar
Tea	té	teh
Water	agua	ah-**gwah**
Wine	vino	**vee**-noh

On the Calendar

January

La Tamborrada. Every January 19 and 20, more than 100 platoons of donostiarras (San Sebastián natives) dress up as chefs and Napoleonic soldiers and bang drums as they parade through the streets. The tradition was born out of a mockery of Napoleon's troops, who would march around the city in a similar fashion. Today it's San Sebastián's biggest street party. ✉ *San Sebastián.*

Processo dels Tres Tocs *(Procession of the Three Knocks).* This festival, held in Ciutadella on January 17, celebrates the 1287 victory of King Alfonso III of Aragón over the Moors. ✉ *Ciutadella.*

February

Carnival. In February and March, on this first major fiesta of the year after Three Kings' Day (January 6), cities, towns, and villages across the region erupt with festive fun, including parades, parties, and wild costumes.

Festes de Santa Eularia. Ibiza's boisterous winter carnival, held on February 12, includes folk dancing and music. ✉ *Eivissa.*

March

Cherry Blossom Festival *(Fiesta del Cerezo en Flor).* For approximately two weeks between March and early May, depending on the year, Spain's prized cherry-growing region, the Jerte Valley, turns pink and white as more than a million cherry trees bloom in unison. Throughout the area, a series of live concerts, street markets, and gastronomic presentations accompany nature's show. ✉ *Jaraíz de la Vera* ☎ *92/747-2558* ⊕ *www.turismovalledeljerte.com.*

April

Feria de Abril *(April Fair).* Held two weeks after Easter, this secular celebration focuses on horses, pageantry, and bullfights. ✉ *Seville.*

May

Antxua Eguna *(Getaria Anchovy Festival).* Join Getaria locals in early May as they ring in anchovy season with gallons of Txakoli and mountains of grilled fresh fish. ✉ *Getaria.*

Cruces de Mayo *(Festival of Crosses).* Celebrated throughout the Spanish-speaking world, this ancient festival is a highlight of Córdoba's calendar of events, with lots of flower-decked crosses and other floral displays, processions, and music in early May.

Feria Nacional del Queso de Trujillo. Trujillo's cheese festival, in early May, brings together Spain's finest cheese makers with hundreds of varieties to taste and buy (don't pass up Pascualete, named the best cheese in Spain by the World Cheese Awards). The event is understandably popular with foodies. ✉ *Trujillo* ☎ *92/732-1450* ⊕ *www.feriadelquesotrujillo.es.*

Festival de los Patios *(Patio Festival).* This celebration, awarded UNESCO World Heritage status in 2012, is held during the second week of May, a fun time to be in the city, when owners throw open their flower-decked patios to visitors (and to judges, who nominate the best), and the city celebrates with food, drink, and flamenco. ✉ *Córdoba* ⊕ *turismodecordoba.org.*

WOMAD Cáceres. The World of Music, Arts and Dance draws crowds of around 75,000 in early May. Main stages are set up in the magical surroundings of this ancient city's plazas for free concerts, and other events include shows staged in the Gran Teatro, children's events, and a grand procession. ⊠ *Calle San Antón 0, Cáceres* ⊕ *www.womadespana.com.*

June

Festes de Sant Joan. At this event June 23–24, riders in costume parade through the streets of Ciutadella on horseback, urging the horses up to dance on their hind legs while spectators pass dangerously under their hooves. ⊠ *Ciutadella.*

July

Bilbao BBK Live. One of Spain's hottest pop and rock music festivals, BBK Live draws more than 100,000 fans each year with its lineup of big-name artists. In 2021, headliners included The Killers, the Pet Shop Boys, and Bad Bunny. Those with an aversion to mud and noisy campgrounds will appreciate the "glamping" accommodation option. ⊠ *Bilbao* ⊕ *www.bilbaobbklive.com.*

Festival de Teatro Clásico. In Mérida, the highlight of the cultural calendar is this annual festival held in the restored Roman amphitheater from early July through mid-August. It features opera as well as classical drama and celebrated its 65th year in 2019. ⊠ *Pl. Margarita Xirgu, Mérida* ☎ *92/400–9480* ⊕ *www.festivaldemerida.es.*

Jazzaldia. Drawing many of the world's top performers, this late-July festival in San Sebastián attracts an international crowd of jazz devotees. ⊕ *www.jazzaldia.eus.*

Ortigueira Festival. This major Celtic music festival, which takes place in early or mid-July over four days in the coastal city of Ortigueira, attracts folk musicians from around the world. ⊠ *A Coruña* ☎ *981/923093 for tourist office* ⊕ *www.festivaldeortigueira.com.*

San Fermín. Pamplona's main event, immortalized by Ernest Hemingway in his 1926 novel The Sun Also Rises, is best known for its running of the bulls, a tradition that's dangerous for humans and ultimately lethal for the animals involved. Ethics aside, a huge part of the festival is consumed by nontaurine activities such as processions, live music acts, and fireworks. Held each year July 6–14, every day begins at 8 am with a herd of fighting bulls let loose to run through the narrow streets to the bullring alongside daredevils testing their speed and agility in the face of possible injury or death. The atmosphere is electric, and hotel rooms overlooking the course come at a price. Recent years have seen a disturbing increase in sex crimes; it's advisable for travelers, especially women, to take commonsense precautions, including being aware of your surroundings and not walking alone at night. ⊠ *Pamplona* ⊕ *www.sanfermin.com.*

Virgen del Carmen. The patron saint of sailors (Our Lady of Mount Carmel) is honored July 15–16 in Formentera with a blessing of the boats in the harbor. The holiday is also celebrated on Ibiza. ⊠ *Sant Antoni.*

August

Aste Nagusia. The "Big Week," a nine-day event celebrating Basque culture, is held in Bilbao in mid-August with a fine series of street concerts, bullfights, and fireworks displays.

Festa do Viño Albariño (*Albariño Wine Festival*). On the first Sunday of August, the town of Cambados, capital of Albariño

On the Calendar

country, draws thousands to witness its processions, concerts, cultural events, fireworks, and other revelry honoring local vineyards and wineries—including wine tastings from around 40 different Rías Baixas wineries. The festival has been held since the early 1950s. ⊠ *Cambados* ⊕ *www.fiestadelalbariño.com.*

Fiesta de la Virgen Blanca *(Festival of the White Virgin).* This weeklong festival (August 4–9) celebrates Vitoria's patron saint with bullfights and street parties. The festivities begin with the arrival of Celedón, a well-dressed dummy that "flies" over the main square holding an umbrella. ⊠ *Vitoria.*

Sant Ciriac. Capped with a spectacular fireworks display over the walls of Eivissa's old city, this festival (on August 8) celebrates the Reconquest of Ibiza from the Moors. ⊠ *Eivissa.*

Sant Lluís. Celebrations of this saint's day, which are held during the last weekend of August in the town of Sant Lluís, on Menorca, center on an equestrian cavalcade called La Qualcada. ⊠ *Sant Lluís.*

September

Fiestas de la Mare de Déu de Gràcia. Held September 6–9 in Mahón, this celebration is Menorca's final blowout of the season. ⊠ *Mahón.*

Fiesta de Otoño *(Autumn Festival).* In September, this festival in Jerez celebrates the grape harvest and includes a procession, the blessing of the harvest on the steps of the cathedral, and traditional-style grape treading. ⊠ *Jerez de la Frontera.*

San Sebastián Film Festival. Glitterati descend on the city for its international film fest in the second half of September. Exact dates vary, so check the website for details. ⊠ *San Sebastián* ⊕ *www.sansebastianfestival.com.*

October

Festa do Marisco *(Seafood Festival).* Galicia's famous culinary event, held in O Grove in October, draws crowds to feast on a stunning number of seafood delicacies. ⊠ *O Grove* ⊕ *www.turismogrove.es.*

Fiesta de la Rosa del Azafrán *(Consuegra Saffron Festival).* This festival, held in the last weekend of October since 1963, celebrates the annual saffron harvest, one of La Mancha's longest-standing traditions. Watch a saffron-plucking contest, savor locally made manchego cheeses, and marvel at folk dance spectacles—all with a backdrop of Don Quixote–style windmills. ☏ *92/547–5731 Consuegra tourist office* ⊕ *www.consuegra.es.*

December

Encuentros Flamencos. Some of the country's best performers are featured in this early-December event in Granada. ⊠ *Granada.*

Los Escobazos. On December 7, the city is filled with bonfires celebrating the Virgen de la Concepción. Watch out for the locals play-fighting with torches made out of brooms—or if you're feeling daredevilish, join in. ⊠ *Jarandilla de la Vera* ☏ *92/756–0460 tourist office.*

Chapter 3

MADRID

Updated by
Benjamin Kemper

⊙ Sights	🏛 Restaurants	🛏 Hotels	🛍 Shopping	🍸 Nightlife
★★★★☆	★★★★★	★★★★☆	★★★★★	★★★★★

WELCOME TO MADRID

TOP REASONS TO GO

★ **Hit the Centro Histórico:** The Plaza Mayor, on any late night when it's almost empty, evokes the stately, somber glory of Golden Age Spain.

★ **Stroll down museum row:** Feast your eyes on works by your favorite Spanish artists—from Goya to Velázquez to Picasso—in the Prado, Reina Sofía, and Thyssen-Bornemisza.

★ **Nibble tapas into the night:** Indulge in a madrileño style of dining and sample local wines while grazing on small plates (both traditional and modern) on Cava Baja, Calle Ponzano, and beyond.

★ **Relax in the Retiro gardens:** Unwind at a *chiringuito* (refreshment stand) and enjoy some primo people-watching.

★ **Burn the midnight oil:** As other Europeans tuck themselves in, madrileños swarm the bars in lively neighborhoods such as Malasaña, Chueca, Lavapiés, and Barrio de las Letras—and stretch the party until dawn.

Madrid comprises 21 districts, each of which contains several neighborhoods. The most central district is called just that: Centro. There you'll find Madrid's oldest neighborhoods including Sol, Palacio, Chueca, Malasaña, Barrio de las Letras, La Latina, and Lavapiés. Other well-known districts, a term we'll use interchangeably with neighborhoods and barrios for the sake of convenience, are Salamanca, Retiro, Chamberí (north of Centro), Moncloa (east of Chamberí), and Chamartín.

1 Sol. The bustling heart of Madrid with clothes, souvenirs, and tapas bars.

2 Palacio. Madrid's noblest corner home to the Royal Palace, Sabatini Gardens, and Royal Theater.

3 Moncloa. A posh residential quarter with down-home restaurants and a blissfully off-the-radar park.

4 Chueca. The "gayborhood," as famous for its come-one-come-all nightclubs as for its trendy boutiques.

5 Malasaña. Home to bearded-and-bunned expats and Euro-hipsters, third-wave coffee shops, and chic cocktail bars.

6 Barrio de las Letras. Once the stomping grounds of Spain's great writers, now a hub of top-notch tapas bars and hotels.

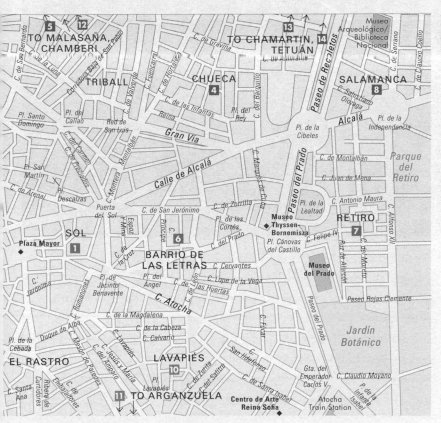

7 Retiro. The surprisingly non-touristy district fringing the city's most iconic park.

8 Salamanca. High-society madrileños flock here for upscale tapas, special-occasion dinners, and exclusive shopping.

9 La Latina. El Rastro flea market lures the crowds to Madrid's most "castizo" (rootsy) neighborhood with a rakish edge.

10 Lavapiés. Ever counter-cultural and rebellious, Lavapiés is a multicultural mecca.

11 Arganzuela. A vibrant modern art center and new riverside park put this blue-collar neighborhood on the map.

12 Chamberí. Welcome to Madrid's newest culinary nerve center lined with restaurants helmed by up-and-coming chefs.

13 Chamartín. Fans cheer till they're hoarse at Real Madrid soccer matches in this northern district.

14 Tetuán. You won't bump into any tour buses in this working-class neighborhood with international restaurants and old-timey tapas bars.

EATING AND DRINKING WELL IN MADRID

A selection of tapas, including smoked ham and roasted peppers.

As Spain's most vibrant melting pot, Madrid is home to countless regional Spanish restaurants serving everything from Valencian paella to Basque *pintxos*, but traditional Madrid fare closely resembles that of Castile.

With a climate sometimes described as *nueve meses de invierno y tres de infierno* (nine months of winter and three of hell), it's no surprise that local grub is often comfort food. Garlic soup, stewed chickpeas, and roast suckling pig and lamb are standard components of Madrid feasts, as are baby goat and deeply flavored beef from Ávila and the Sierra de Guadarrama. *Cocido madrileño* (a meat-packed winter stew) and *callos a la madrileña* (stewed tripe) are favored local specialties, while *jamón ibérico de bellota* (acorn-fed Iberian ham)—a specialty of the *dehesas,* or rolling oak forests of Extremadura and Andalusia—is a staple on special occasions. Seafood is shipped in from the coasts and eaten in shockingly vast quantities for a landlocked capital. Summer recipes hinge on minimally manipulated fruits and vegetables.

TAPAS

Itinerant grazing from tavern to tavern is especially popular in Madrid, beneficiary of tapas traditions from every corner of Spain. The areas around Plaza de Santa Ana, Plaza Mayor, Calle Ponzano, and Cava Baja buzz with excitement as crowds drink beer and wine while devouring platefuls of *boquerones en vinagre* (vinegar-cured anchovies), *calamares a la romana* (fried squid), *albóndigas* (meatballs), and the like.

SOUPS

Sopa de ajo (garlic soup), also known as *sopa castellana,* is a homey soup that starts with an unapologetically garlicky ham-bone stock. Stale bread is then torn in to thicken it up, followed by a cracked egg—a final enriching flourish. *Caldo* (hot chicken or beef broth) served in coffee mugs, a Madrid favorite on wet winter days, is often marketed in restaurant windows (look for "*¡Hay Caldo!*" signs).

STEWS

Cocido madrileño is Madrid's ultimate comfort food and one of its oldest dishes: a boiled dinner of chickpeas, vegetables, potatoes, sausages, pork, and hen simmered for hours and presented in multiple courses. *Estofado de judiones de La Granja* (broad-bean stew) is another soul-satisfying favorite: pork, quail, ham, or whatever meat is available simmers with onions, tomatoes, carrots, and luxuriously creamy broad beans from the Segovian town of La Granja de San Ildefonso.

ROASTS

Asadores (restaurants specializing in roasts) are an institution in and around Madrid, where *cochinillo asado,* or roast suckling pig, is the crown jewel. Wherever you taste it, the preparation is largely the same: milk-fed piglets are

A hearty clam-and-beans stew

Ingredients for a classic cocido madrileño

roasted in oak-burning wood ovens and emerge shatteringly crisp yet tender enough to carve using the edge of a plate. *Lechazo,* or milk-fed lamb, is another asador stalwart that emerges from wood ovens accompanied by the aromas of oak and Castile's wide *meseta*: thistle, rosemary, and thyme.

WINES

The traditional Madrid house wine, a coarse Valdepeñas from La Mancha, south of the capital, has fallen out of favor as better-quality *cuvées* from Rioja and Ribera del Duero (for reds) and Rueda and Rías Baixas (for whites) have become more readily available. Deep-pink *rosados,* the best of which hail from Rioja, Catalonia, and Navarra, are increasingly popular, as is cava, Spanish bubbly from Catalonia. Natural wines—made largely without additives and pesticides in family-run *bodegas* (wineries)—are becoming trendier by the minute and can be enjoyed at a number of specialty bars and restaurants.

Madrid, the Spanish capital since 1561, is Europe's city that never sleeps. A vibrant and increasingly international metropolis, it has an infectious appetite for art, music, and epicurean pleasures yet remains steadfast in its age-old traditions.

Madrid includes plenty of "modern" barrios such as Salamanca, Chamberí, and Chamartín, but the part of the city that draws visitors the world over is its historic center, between the Palacio Real and the city's huge park, the Parque del Buen Retiro. A conglomeration of Belle Époque buildings with intricate facades, terra-cotta-roofed residences, and redbrick Mudejar Revival churches, Madrid is a stately stunner. Madrileños love being outdoors as much as possible: restaurant patios, flea markets, and parks and plazas are always abuzz, particularly if the sun's out.

Then there's the art—the legacy of one of the most important global empires ever assembled. King Carlos I (1500–58), who later became Emperor Carlos V (or Charles V), set out to collect the best specimens from all European schools of art, many of which found their way to Spain's palaces and, later, to the Prado Museum. Between the classical Prado, the contemporary Reina Sofía, the wide-ranging Thyssen-Bornemisza, and Madrid's smaller artistic repositories—the Real Academia de Bellas Artes de San Fernando, the Convento de las Descalzas Reales, the Sorolla Museum, and the Lázaro Galdiano Museum, to name a few—there are more paintings here than you could admire in a lifetime.

Not all of the city's most memorable attractions are centuries old. The CaixaForum arts center is an architectural triumph by Jacques Herzog and Pierre de Meuron. Futuristic towers by Norman Foster and César Pelli have changed the city's northern landscape. Other recent developments include Madrid Río, which added nearly 300 acres of green space and six miles of footpaths along the banks of the Manzanares River.

Planning

When to Go

Madrid is hot and dry in summer—with temperatures reaching 40°C (105°F) in July and August—and chilly and damp in winter, with minimum temperatures around 1°C (low 30s). Snow in the city is rare; in January 2021, Madrid was clobbered by the biggest winter storm in over a half-century. Perhaps the most pleasant time to visit is spring, especially May, when the city honors its patron saint with street fairs and celebrations. June and September to December are also pleasant, generally temperate times to visit.

Avoid Madrid in July and August—especially August, as locals flee the punishing heat for the coasts and mountains, and many restaurants, bars, and shops shutter.

Planning Your Time

Madrid's most valuable art treasures are on display within a few blocks of Paseo del Prado. This area is home to the Museo del Prado, whose collection amasses masterworks by Velázquez, Goya, El Greco, and others; the Centro de Arte Reina Sofía, whose eclectic contemporary art pieces include Picasso's *Guernica*; and the Museo Thyssen-Bornemisza, whose collection stretches from the Renaissance to the 21st century. Each can take hours to explore, so it's best to alternate museum visits with less intellectually rigorous activities. If you're running short on time and want to pack everything in, recharge at tapas bars and cafés in the neighboring Barrio de las Letras.

Any visit to Madrid should include a walk among the historical sights and churches between Puerta del Sol and the Palacio Real. Be sure to stop in the Plaza Mayor, Plaza de la Villa, and Plaza de Oriente.

Getting Here and Around

AIR
Madrid's Adolfo Suárez Madrid–Barajas Airport is Europe's fourth-busiest aviation hub. Terminal 4 (T4) handles flights from 19 carriers, including American Airlines, British Airways, and Iberia. All other U.S. airlines use Terminal 1 (T1).

Airport terminals are connected by bus service and also to Línea 8 of the metro, which reaches the city center in 30–45 minutes for around €5 (€1.50–€2 plus a €3 airport supplement). For €5 there are also convenient buses (Nos. 203 and 203 Exprés) to the Atocha train station (with stops on Calle de O'Donnell and Plaza de Cibeles) and to Avenida de América (note that bus drivers don't take bills greater than €20), where you can catch the metro or a taxi to your hotel. Taxis charge a flat fee of €30 from the airport to anywhere in the city center.

BIKE
BiciMAD (*www.bicimad.com*) is Madrid's bike-share service with docks scattered around the city center. The bikes are electric, meaning you hardly have to pedal, and are an excellent alternative to the metro and buses, provided the weather is good and you're comfortable riding in traffic (separate bike lanes are virtually nonexistent). Avid urban cyclists staying for a month or more may wish to purchase a €25 yearly membership, which drastically lowers the cost of individual rides to €0.60 for up to one hour, but occasional users can pay €2 per 30-minute ride, buying a ticket at each service station. The bikes can be borrowed from, and returned to, any station in the system. In 2021 a "BiciMAD GO" service was added allowing users to retrieve and leave certain bikes directly on the sidewalk; download the BiciMAD app for details.

BUS
Buses are generally less convenient than trains, though they're sometimes faster and cheaper. Madrid has no central bus station: Most destinations south and east of the city center are serviced by Estación del Sur, while Intercambiador de Moncloa and Estación de Avenida de América service northern destinations. All have eponymous metro stops (except for Estación del Sur, serviced by Méndez Álvaro).

Blue city buses (€1.50 one-way) run about 6 am–11:30 pm. Less-frequent night buses run through the night on heavily trafficked routes. Línea Cero (look for buses marked 001 and 002) is a fare-free bus line launched in 2020. As of 2021, contactless credit cards are

Madrid Metro

KEY
- 1 *Metro Terminals*
- O *Metro Stations*
- ▣ *Transfer Stations*
- ┤├ *Railway Lines*
- • *Train Stations*

accepted as payment on all blue buses in addition to cash (exact change is recommended).

BUS STATIONS Estación de Avenida de América. ✉ *Av. de América 9, Salamanca* ☎ *90/242–2242 for ALSA Bus Company* ⊕ *www.crtm.es/tu-transporte-publico/intercambiadores.aspx* Ⓜ *Av. de América.* **Estación del Sur.** ✉ *Calle Méndez Álvaro s/n, Atocha* ☎ *91/468–4200* ⊕ *www.estaciondeautobuses.com* Ⓜ *Méndez Álvaro.* **Intercambiador de Moncloa.** ✉ *Princesa 89, Moncloa* ☎ *012 for Madrid city hotline* ⊕ *www.crtm.es* Ⓜ *Moncloa.*

CAR

It's best to ditch your rental car when in Madrid as traffic and expensive parking cause headaches, though a car is handy for trips to smaller locales with limited public transportation options; many of the nation's highways radiate from Madrid including the A6 (Segovia, Salamanca, Galicia); the A1 (Burgos and the Basque Country); the A2 (Guadalajara, Barcelona, France); the A3 (Cuenca, Valencia, the Mediterranean coast); the A4 (Aranjuez, La Mancha, Granada, Seville); the A42 (Toledo); and the A5 (Talavera de la Reina, Portugal). The city is surrounded by ring roads (M30, M40, and M50), from which most of these highways are easily picked up. There are also toll highways (marked R2, R3, R4, and R5) that bypass major highways, and the A41, a toll highway connecting Madrid and Toledo.

November 2018 marked the beginning of **Madrid Central,** a sweeping, environmentally driven law that prohibits most vehicles—rentals included—from entering the city center. This zone is delineated by double red lines, large roadside signs, and nautilus-like "Madrid Central" logos painted clearly on the asphalt; entering without the proper permissions will result in fines. Be sure to ask your rental car agency about the specific restrictions on your vehicle as they relate to Madrid Central. Zero-emissions vehicles are not affected, so if you plan on driving in the city center, it may be worth spending the extra euros on an eco-friendly car.

SUBWAY

To ride the metro, you must buy a refillable Tarjeta de Transporte Público (Public Transportation Card), which costs an unrefundable €4 and can be obtained at ticketing machines inside any metro station. Each journey costs €1.50–€2, depending on how far you're traveling within the city. There are no free transfers between the metro and bus systems. The **Abono Turístico** (Tourist Pass) allows unlimited use of public buses and the metro for one day (€8.40 for Zone A, €17 for Zone T) to seven days (€35.40 for Zone A, €70.80 for Zone T); buy it at tourist offices, metro stations, and select newsstands. The metro runs 6 am–1:30 am, though a few entrances close earlier.

SUBWAY INFORMATION Metro Madrid. ☎ *90/244–4403* ⊕ *www.metromadrid.es.*

TAXI

Taxis are well-regulated and work under several tariff schemes. Meters start at €2.50 (€3.10 nights, weekends, and holidays). There is a fixed taxi fare of €30 to or from the airport from the city center. Book a taxi by phone or via the Free Now app, which interfaces with official city taxis. Uber and Cabify, back in operation after a brief hiatus due to legal restrictions, are generally more economical than official taxis. In March 2021, it became possible to rent a Lime electric scooter via the Uber app.

The rise of Uber and similar ride-hailing apps has led to a standoff between traditional taxis and vehicles for hire. Taxi strikes are increasingly frequent, so if you plan on using a taxi service, be sure to inquire locally to ensure they're running to cover your bases.

Blablacar is Spain's leading rideshare app in intercity travel. Its free platform allows you to book ahead using a credit card and message your driver to set meeting and drop-off points. Blablacar is the most affordable way to travel to Madrid's outlying cities and beyond as drivers aren't allowed to make a profit (you essentially help the driver offset the price of gas and tolls).

TAXI SERVICES Radio Taxi Gremial. ☎ 91/447–3232, 91/447–5180 ⊕ www. radiotaxigremial.com. **Radioteléfono Taxi.** ☎ 91/547–8200 ⊕ www.radiotelefono-taxi.com. **Tele-Taxi.** ☎ 91/371–2131 ⊕ www.tele-taxi.es.

Tours

Plaza Mayor Tourist Office
Madrid's main tourist office, open 365 days a year, is a treasure trove of maps and resources. Staff happily recommend bus, Segway, cycling, and walking tours to meet your needs. ✉ Casa de la Panadería, Pl. Mayor 27, Sol ☎ 91/578–7810 ⊕ www.esmadrid.com.

BIKE TOURS
Biking in Madrid can be a white-knuckle experience for those unaccustomed to biking in traffic, but for leisurely sightseeing through parks and along the river, bike tours can be a pleasant activity.

BravoBike
BravoBike offers guided bike tours in English (from €15 for two hours). It also offers multiday guided and self-guided bike tours in destinations including Toledo, Segovia, Andalusia, and the Camino de Santiago pilgrimage route. ✉ Calle Juan Álvarez Mendizábal 19, Calle Juan Álvarez Mendizábal 19, Moncloa ☎ 91/758–2945, 60/744–8440 for WhatsApp ⊕ www.bravobike.com ✉ From €15.

BUS TOURS
Madrid City Tours
The ubiquitous red double-decker tourist buses make 1½-hour circuits of the city, allowing you to get on and off at various attractions. Beyond the one- and two-day passes, consider: the "Historic Madrid"

tour, the "Modern Madrid" tour, or the "Night Tour" (June 16–September 15 only), all with recorded English commentary. ☎ 91/369–2732 ⊕ www.madrid.city-tour.com ✉ From €20.

WALKING TOURS
Asociación Nacional de Guías de Turismo (APIT)
This tour operator offers custom history and art walks by government-certified travel guides. ✉ Calle Jacometrezo 4, 9º 13, Sol ☎ 91/542–1214 ⊕ www.apit.es.

Carpetania Madrid
This company offers niche, brainy tours and literary walks on topics like "Women of Malasaña" and "Almodóvar's Madrid." (Spanish only.) ✉ Calle Jesús del Valle 11, Malasaña ☎ 91/531–1418 ⊕ www.carpetaniamadrid.com ✉ From €10.

Devour Madrid
Devour Spain is a dependable food tour company catering to hungry travelers of all interests and ages (kids' tours are available). In Madrid, walks run the gamut from a "Tapas, Taverns & History" neighborhood tapas crawl to a "Prado Museum Tour" that culminates in a lunch at Botín, allegedly the world's oldest restaurant. ✉ Cortes ☎ 94/458–1022, 415/969–9277 U.S. phone number ⊕ www.madridfoodtour.com ✉ From €89.

Walk and Eat
It doesn't get more ear-to-the-ground than these small-group food tours in Malasaña led by a 12-year American expat. On the €89 two-and-a-half-hour mercado tour, one of a handful of itineraries, you'll meet characters ranging from olive vendors to ham slicers to beloved local chefs—and amass a shopping bag of edible souvenirs as you go. ✉ Calle de Santa Lucía, Malasaña ☎ 67/171–7874 ⊕ www.walkandeatspain.com Ⓜ Noviciado.

Where Should I Stay?

	Neighborhood Vibe	Pros	Cons
Palacio, Moncloa, La Latina, and Sol	Anchored by the Plaza Mayor, this historic area is full of narrow streets and taverns.	Has the most traditional feel of Madrid neighborhoods; varied lodging and dining including many inexpensive (though usually undistinguished) *hostales* and old-flavor taverns	Can be tough to navigate; noisy; many tourist traps
Barrio de las Letras (including Carrera de San Jerónimo and Paseo del Prado)	A magnet for style-conscious tourists, this classic literary nest has several pedestrian-only streets.	Picturesque Plaza Santa Ana and Plaza del Ángel; fashionable hotels and restaurants; conveniently located between the oldest part of the city and major art museums	Noisy, especially around Plaza Santa Ana; some bars and restaurants are overpriced
Chueca and Malasaña	Vibrant and bustling, this is where you want to be if you don't plan on being in bed before midnight.	These barrios are alive with busy nightlife, alternative shops, and charming cafés.	Loud, especially on the weekends; 20-minute walk from most major attractions
Salamanca, Retiro, Moncloa, and Chamberí	Swanky, posh, and safe, these are the neighborhoods many high-end hotels and restaurants call home.	Quiet at day's end; plenty of good restaurants and upscale shopping; not touristy	Bland and culturally homogeneous; restaurant staff and locals can be snooty; expensive
Chamartín	Corporate, buttoned-up, and quiet		A taxi or metro ride from sights; mostly unattractive

Restaurants

Spain is an essential foodie pilgrimage, and no Spanish city holds a candle to Madrid when it comes to variety of national and international cuisines. The pandemic hit the restaurant industry hard, but not as hard as it did hotels: Restaurants were largely allowed to remain open in 2020 and 2021, albeit with expanded outdoor dining and strict curfews in place. But lamentably, a number of beloved restaurants were forced to shutter.

Younger madrileños gravitate toward trendy neighborhoods like taberna-lined Malasaña, LGBT-friendly Chueca, rootsy La Latina, and multicultural Lavapiés for their boisterous and affordable restaurants and bars. Dressier travelers and those visiting with family, on the other hand, will feel more at home in the quieter, more sedate restaurants of Salamanca, Chamberí, and Retiro. Of course, these are broad-brush generalizations, and there are plenty of exceptions.

What it Costs in Euros			
$	$$	$$$	$$$$
RESTAURANTS			
under €16	€16–€22	€23–€29	over €29

Hotels

There's a dizzying array of hotels to choose from in Madrid, from grande-dame icons that once hosted Lorca and Hemingway to quirky boutique hotels with art-lined walls and plant-based breakfast buffets.

What it Costs in Euros			
$	$$	$$$	$$$$
HOTELS			
under €125	€125–€174	€175–€225	over €225

Nightlife

Unlike in other European cities, where partying is a pastime geared mostly toward the young, there are plenty of bars and *discotecas* with mixed-age crowds in Madrid, and it's not uncommon for children to play on the sidewalks past midnight while multigenerational families and friends convene over coffee or cocktails at an outdoor café. There's a lot of overlap between dining, bar-hopping, and nightlife in Madrid—some bars serve tapas *and* cocktails *and* blast DJ sets till the wee hours—but this section is geared toward establishments that revolve around drinking, dancing, and entertainment.

Madrid is a sundown-to-sunup party city, but those with earlier bedtimes will feel at home at the sleek cafés, *cervecerías* (pubs), and cocktail bars on Calle Jorge Juan (Barrio Salamanca), Calle Ponzano (Chamberí), and Plaza de Santa Ana (Letras).

More rambunctious party scenes can be found in Malasaña, with its underground *discotecas* and rocker bars around Plaza de Dos de Mayo; Chueca, with its legendary LGBT+ (yet totally hetero-friendly) venues off the eponymous plaza; and Sol, home to a number of popular mega-clubs with flashy visuals and multiple floors.

Shopping

Madrid is a leader in contemporary art and design, but you'll have no trouble finding traditional crafts, such as ceramics, woven baskets, guitars, and leather goods. Note that family-run shops and boutiques generally close during lunch hours, on Saturday afternoon, and on Sunday.

Madrid has three main shopping areas. The most commercial one stretches from Callao to Puerta del Sol (taking in Calle Preciados, Gran Vía, and the streets north of Puerta del Sol) and includes major department stores and international clothing chains such as El Corte Inglés, Zara, Nike, Bershka, and Primark.

The place to shop for timeless, classic fashion is Salamanca, bounded roughly by Serrano, Juan Bravo, Jorge Juan (and its mews), and Velázquez; the shops on Goya extend as far as Alcalá. The streets just off the Plaza de Colón, particularly Calle Serrano and Calle Ortega y Gasset, have the widest selection of designer goods—think Prada, Loewe, Armani, and Louis Vuitton—as well as big-name Spanish designers including Purificación García, Bimbo y Lola, and Roberto Verino. More high-end boutiques can be found on and around Calle Lagasca and Calle Claudio Coello.

For eclectic finds and trendier threads, Chueca, Malasaña, Lavapiés, and the streets around the Conde Duque cultural center are your best bets. Calle

Fuencarral, between Gran Vía and Tribunal metro station, has the most shops in this area with outposts from Diesel, Adidas, and Footlocker—but don't miss out on less-corporate, and often more exciting, boutiques on nearby Calles Hortaleza, Almirante, Piamonte, Velarde, and Corredera Alta de San Pablo. The latter two have several terrific vintage fashion shops.

Sol

This neighborhood, built in the 16th century around the Puerta del Sol, used to mark the city's geographic center, which today sits a tad to its east. Sol encompasses, among other sites, the monumental Plaza Mayor and popular pedestrian shopping area around Callao.

There's never a dull moment in Puerta del Sol, the bustling semicircular plaza where friends gather, buskers perform, and bar crawls begin. The Puerta ("gate") designation is a holdover from when this spot bore entry into the medieval city walls; Sol ("sun"), on the other hand, is a reference to a sun carving that adorned the gate. Let your gaze wander to the clocktower atop the Casa de Correos, the oldest building on the square. It ushers Madrid into the New Year each December as onlookers partake in the Spanish tradition of eating 12 grapes in the last 12 seconds of the year.

 Sights

Mercado de San Miguel

MARKET | Adjacent to the Plaza Mayor, this "gastronomic market" is a feast for the senses. Its bustling interior—a mixture of tapas spots and immaculately arranged grocery stalls—sits beneath a fin-de-siècle glass dome reinforced by elaborate wrought iron. Enjoy a glass of wine and maybe a snack here, but save your appetite: the market, as gorgeous as it may be, has become overpriced and underwhelming in recent years. There are two diamonds in the rough: Amaike-tako, with its Basque-style pintxos, and Daniel Sorlut, a posh oyster bar. ⊠ Pl. de San Miguel, Sol ⊕ www.mercadodesan-miguel.es Ⓜ Ópera.

★ Plaza Mayor

PLAZA/SQUARE | A symbol of imperial Spain's might and grandeur, this public square is often surprisingly quiet, perhaps since most locals wrote it off long ago as too touristy. The plaza was finished in 1619 under Felipe III, whose equestrian statue stands in the center, and is one of the largest in Europe, measuring 360 feet by 300 feet. It's seen it all: *autos-da-fé* (public burnings of heretics), the canonization of saints, criminal executions, royal marriages, bullfights (until 1847), and all manner of other events. The plot was once occupied by a city market, and many of the surrounding streets retain names of the trades and foods once headquartered there (e.g., Cutlers' Street, Lettuce Street). The plaza's oldest building, Casa de la Panadería (Bakery House), has brightly painted murals and gray spires; it is now the tourist office. Opposite sits Casa de la Carnicería (Butcher Shop), now a boutique hotel. The plaza is closed to motorized traffic, making it a pleasant if touristy spot to enjoy a cup of coffee. ⊠ Sol Ⓜ Sol.

Puerta del Sol

PLAZA/SQUARE | Crowded with locals, tourists, hawkers, and street performers, the Puerta del Sol is the nerve center of Madrid. It is in the throes of a massive renovation through at least 2022, so beware of possible closures. A brass plaque in the sidewalk on the south side of the plaza marks Kilometer Zero, the point from which all distances in Spain are measured. The restored 1756 French-Neoclassical building near the marker now houses the offices of the regional government, but during Franco's reign, it was the headquarters of his secret police and is still known colloquially as the Casa de los Gritos (House of Screams). Across the square are a bronze statue of Madrid's official symbol, a bear with a *madroño* (strawberry tree), and a statue of King and Mayor Carlos III on horseback. Puerta del Sol has been the nucleus of countless protests and political movements through the centuries. It was here, in 2011, that the 15-M movement started as sleep-in against government austerity measures and blossomed into an organized anticorporate revolution. The grassroots political party Podemos was created as a result. The 15-M demonstrations would go on to inspire Occupy Wall Street and other future pro-democracy and anti-capitalist protests around the world. ⊠ *Sol* Ⓜ *Sol.*

Real Academia de Bellas Artes de San Fernando (*St. Ferdinand Royal Academy of Fine Arts*)

ART MUSEUM | Designed by José Benito de Churriguera in the waning baroque years of the early 18th century, this museum showcases 500 years of Spanish painting, from José Ribera and Bartolomé Esteban Murillo to Joaquín Sorolla and Ignacio Zuloaga. The tapestries along the stairways are stunning. The gallery displays paintings up to the 18th century, including some by Goya. Guided tours are usually available (check the website for times). The same building houses the Instituto de Calcografía (Prints Institute), which sells limited-edition prints from original plates engraved by Spanish artists. There are often classical concerts and literary events in the small upstairs hall, tickets can be purchased on the website. ⊠ *Calle de Alcalá 13, Sol* 🕿 *91/524–0864* ⊕ *www.realacademiabel-lasartessanfernando.com* ⊘ *Closed Mon.* 🎟 *€8 (free Wed.)* Ⓜ *Sol.*

 Restaurants

La Casa del Abuelo

$$ | **TAPAS** | This rustic tapas hall is the oldest of three branches in a beloved local chain and it's barely changed since it was founded at the beginning of the 20th century. The tapa to try here is *gambas al ajillo*, shrimp sautéed with garlic. **Known for:** killer gambas al ajillo; traditional atmosphere; bold proprietary Toro wines. Ⓢ *Average main: €16* ⊠ *Calle de la Victoria 12, Sol* 🕿 *91/521–2319* ⊕ *www.lacasadelabuelo.es* Ⓜ *Sol.*

La Pulpería de Victoria

$$ | **SPANISH** | **FAMILY** | A modern, urban interpretation of a traditional Galician *pulpería* (octopus restaurant), this casual spot specializes in *polbo á feira*, boiled octopus cut into coins, drizzled with olive oil, and dusted with smoked paprika. Pair it with an icy glass of albariño and a heap of blistered padrón peppers. **Known for:** variety of Galician wines; ocean-fresh shellfish; Galician-style octopus. Ⓢ *Average main: €16* ⊠ *Calle de La Victoria 2, Sol* 🕿 *91/080–4929* ⊕ *www.pulperiade-victoria.com* Ⓜ *Sol.*

Lambuzo

$$ | **SPANISH** | **FAMILY** | This laid-back Andalusian barroom, one of two locations (the other is in Retiro), embodies the soul and joyful spirit of that sunny region. Let cheerful waiters guide you through the extensive menu, which includes fried seafood, unconventional *croquetas* (flecked with garlicky shrimp, for instance), and heftier dishes like cuttlefish meatballs and seared Barbate tuna loin. **Known for:** free marinated carrots with every drink; care-free Andalusian vibe; an ocean's-worth of seafood dishes. Ⓢ *Average main: €16* ⊠ *Calle de las Conchas 9, Sol* 🕿 *91/143–4862* ⊕ *www.barlambuzo.com* ⊘ *Closed Mon. No dinner Sun.* Ⓜ *Ópera.*

Paco Roncero

$$$$ | **ECLECTIC** | Occupying an aerie above one of Madrid's oldest, most exclusive gentlemen's clubs, the dining room and rooftop terrace of this restaurant (formerly known as La Terraza del Casino) are decorated with playful, almost circus-like touches such as bright blue pushcarts,

Sol, Palacio, and MonCloa

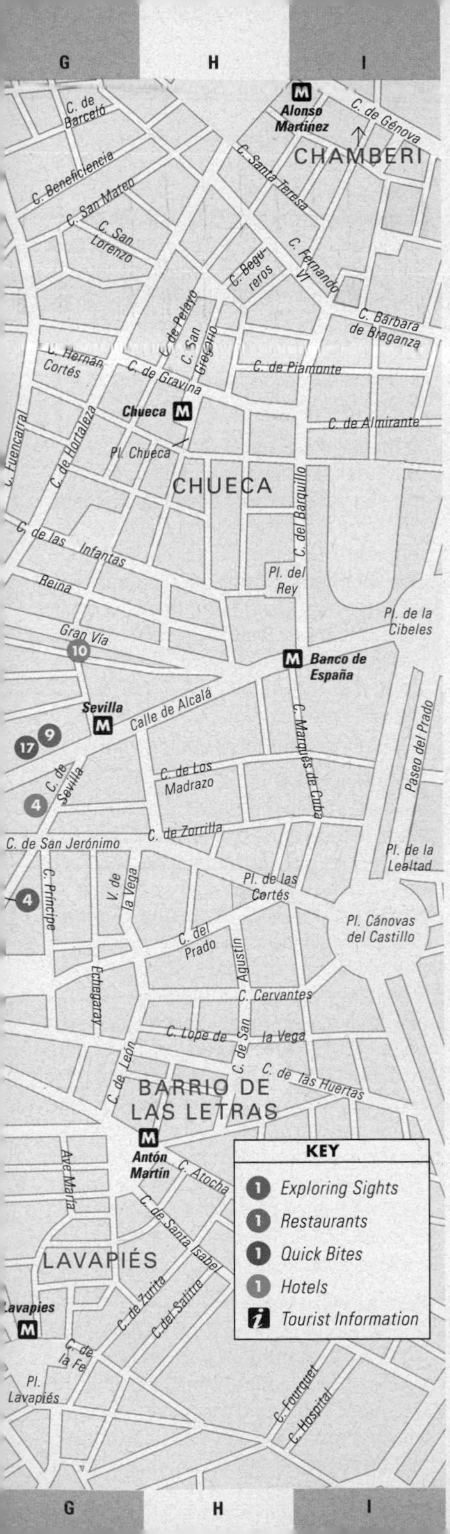

G
H
I
C. de Barceló
Alonso Martínez
C. de Génova
CHAMBERI
C. Santa Teresa
C. Beneficiencia
C. San Mateo
C. San Lorenzo
C. Begu- reros
C. Fernando VI
C. Bárbara de Braganza
C. de Pelayo
C. San Gregorio
C. Hernán Cortés
C. de Gravina
C. de Piamonte
Chueca
C. de Almirante
C. Fuencarral
C. de Hortaleza
Pl. Chueca
CHUECA
C. del Barquillo
C. de las Infantas
Reina
Pl. del Rey
Pl. de la Cibeles
Gran Vía
10
Banco de España
Sevilla
Calle de Alcalá
17
9
C. Marqués de Cuba
Paseo del Prado
C. de Sevilla
4
C. de Los Madrazo
C. de Zorrilla
C. de San Jerónimo
Pl. de la Lealtad
C. Príncipe
V. de la Vega
Pl. de las Cortés
4
Pl. Cánovas del Castillo
C. del Prado
Agustín
Echegaray
C. Cervantes
C. Lope de la Vega
C. San
C. de León
C. de las Huertas
BARRIO DE LAS LETRAS
Antón Martín
Ave María
C. Atocha
C. de Santa Isabel
LAVAPIÉS
Lavapies
C. de Zurita
C. del Salitre
C. de la Fe
Pl. Lavapiés
C. Fourquet
C. Hospital
KEY
Exploring Sights
Restaurants
Quick Bites
Hotels
Tourist Information
G
H
I

Sights

1 Casa de Campo **A4**
2 Catedral de la Almudena................ **B6**
3 Ermita de San Antonio de la Florida **A3**
4 Jardines de Sabatini **B4**
5 Madrid Río............... **A8**
6 Mercado de San Miguel **D6**
7 Monasterio de la Encarnación.............. **C4**
8 Monasterio de las Descalzas Reales....... **D5**
9 Museo Cerralbo......... **B2**
10 Museo del Traje......... **A1**
11 Palacio Real............. **B5**
12 Parque del Oeste **A1**
13 Plaza de la Villa **C6**
14 Plaza de Oriente **C5**
15 Plaza Mayor............. **D6**
16 Puerta del Sol............ **E5**
17 Real Academia de Bellas Artes de San Fernando......... **G5**
18 San Nicolás de los Servitas **C6**
19 Teleférico................ **A4**

Restaurants

1 Casa Lafu **C3**
2 Casa Mingo............. **A4**
3 Cuenllas................. **A1**
4 La Casa del Abuelo..... **G6**
5 La Copita Asturiana **C8**
6 La Pulpería de Victoria.................... **F5**
7 Le Bistroman Atelier **C5**
8 Lambuzo **D5**
9 Paco Roncero........... **G5**
10 Solito Taquería Mexicana................ **D7**

Quick Bites

1 Chocolatería San Ginés................. **E5**
2 Chocolatería Valor...................... **E4**

Hotels

1 Ateneo Hotel **F5**
2 Barceló Torre de Madrid.......... **C2**
3 Dear Hotel **C2**
4 Four Seasons Hotel Madrid **G5**
5 Generator Madrid **D3**
6 Gran Meliá Palacio de Los Duques **C4**
7 Hotel Indigo Madrid – Gran Vía................. **D4**
8 Hotel Indigo Madrid – Princesa **B1**
9 Hotel Intur Palacio San Martín............... **D4**
10 Iberostar Las Letras Gran Vía................. **G4**
11 Mayerling Hotel.......... **E7**
12 Pestana Plaza Mayor............ **D6**
13 Room Mate Laura....... **D5**
14 Room Mate Macarena **E4**
15 Room Mate Mario **D4**

checkered floors, and yellow velvet chairs. The cuisine is just as thrilling and whimsical as the decor with dishes ranging from one-bite *cochinita pibil* tacos to roasted razor clams with green curry. **Known for:** foams, jellies, and sensational flourishes; Instagrammable interiors; two Michelin stars. [$] *Average main: €40* ✉ *Calle Alcalá 15, Sol* ☎ *91/532–1275* 🌐 *www.pacoronceroestaurante.com* 🕒 *Closed Sun. and Mon.* 👔 *Jacket required* [M] *Sol.*

Coffee and Quick Bites

Chocolatería San Ginés

$ | **CAFÉ** | **FAMILY** | San Ginés is to Madrid what Café du Monde is to New Orleans: a historical fried-dough mecca. For generations this 19th-century café has been frying spirals of piping-hot churros and *porras* (the churro's fatter, chewier cousin—try them) day and night. **Known for:** chocolate con churros; a local institution; central location. [$] *Average main: €4* ✉ *Pasadizo de San Ginés, Sol* ✣ *Enter by Arenal 11* ☎ *91/365–6546* 🌐 *www.chocolateriasangines.com* [M] *Sol.*

Hotels

Ateneo Hotel

$ | **HOTEL** | This somewhat old-fashioned but economical property is set in an 18th-century building that was once home to the Ateneo, a club founded in 1835 to promote freedom of thought. **Pros:** some rooms have skylights and balconies; sizable rooms; triples and quadruples available. **Cons:** noisy area; safe yet slightly sketchy street; dated decor. [$] *Rooms from: €100* ✉ *Calle de Montera 22, Sol* ☎ *91/521–2012* 🌐 *www.hotel-ateneo.com* 🛏 *44 rooms* 🍴 *No Meals* [M] *Gran Vía, Sol.*

Four Seasons Hotel Madrid

$$$$ | **HOTEL** | You'll feel like a VIP as you step into the grand lobby—with its gilt-topped columns, enormous central skylight, and sleek spiral staircase—of what was Madrid's most hotly anticipated hotel when it opened in fall 2020. **Pros:** celebrity-chef restaurant; original artwork by emerging Spanish artists; above-and-beyond service touches. **Cons:** conventional interiors; little sense of place; situated above chain restaurants and boutiques. [$] *Rooms from: €695* ✉ *Calle de Sevilla 3, Sol* ☎ *91/088–3333* 🌐 *www.fourseasons.com* 🛏 *200 rooms* 🍴 *No Meals* [M] *Sol.*

★ **Iberostar Las Letras Gran Vía**

$$ | **HOTEL** | A modern, clubby hotel on the stately avenue of Gran Vía, Iberostar Las Letras is a welcoming oasis from the area's constant hubbub of tourists and shoppers. **Pros:** happening rooftop bar; state-of-the-art gym; many rooms have balconies. **Cons:** awkward bathroom design; no spa; finicky a/c. [$] *Rooms from: €150* ✉ *Gran Vía 11, Sol* ☎ *91/523–7980* 🌐 *www.iberostar.com* 🛏 *110 rooms* 🍴 *No Meals* [M] *Banco de España.*

Mayerling Hotel

$$ | **HOTEL** | Minimalism at just the right value is the key at this former textile wholesaler's premises, now a 22-room boutique hotel a few blocks off Plaza Mayor and Plaza de Santa Ana. Serene (if slightly clinical) white rooms come in three sizes—standard, superior, and triple—and are decorated with colorful headboards, charcoal valances, and small open closets. **Pros:** triples available; prime location; 24-hour "help yourself" bar with coffee, snacks, and juices. **Cons:** no restaurant or gym; white walls show smudges; rooms are smallish by U.S. standards. [$] *Rooms from: €140* ✉ *Calle del Conde de Romanones 6, Sol* ☎ *91/420–1580* 🌐 *www.mayerlinghotel.com* 🛏 *22 rooms* 🍴 *No Meals* [M] *Tirso de Molina.*

Pestana Plaza Mayor

$$ | **HOTEL** | Opened in May 2020 Pestana is the newest outpost from the Portuguese boutique hotel chain and Madrid's first hotel situated directly on the Plaza Mayor. **Pros:** cloud-soft beds and linens; sun-drenched breakfast area; upgraded

The Puerta del Sol, Madrid's central transportation hub, is sure to be passed through by every visitor to the city.

rooms have balconies overlooking the plaza. **Cons:** spa has no chairs for lounging by the pool; newfangled interiors clash with the historical building; service foibles. $ *Rooms from: €150* ⊠ *Calle Imperial 8, Sol* ☎ *99/129–3113* ⊕ *www. pestanacollection.com* 🛏 *89 rooms* 🍴 *No Meals* Ⓜ *Sol.*

Nightlife

DANCE CLUBS
★ Cha Chá the Club

DANCE CLUBS | For trendy twentysomethings, there may be no buzzier place to be than this converted multifloor movie theater that erupts into epic DJ-fueled parties. Buy tickets online ahead of time. ⊠ *Calle de Alcalá 20, Sol* ⊕ *www.xceed. me/tickets-club/madrid/cha-cha-the-club* Ⓜ *Sol.*

Cocó Madrid

DANCE CLUBS | This club, with its wild color palette, huge dance floor, and better-than-average cocktails, is best known for its Mondo Disko nights that rage until dawn with house and electronic music often by international DJs. ⊠ *Calle Alcalá 20, Sol* ☎ *91/445–7938* ⊕ *www. mondodisko.es* 🕙 *Closed Mon.–Wed.* Ⓜ *Sevilla.*

Sala El Sol

DANCE CLUBS | Madrid's oldest discoteca continues to win over patrons with all-night dancing to live music (starting around midnight Thursday–Saturday) and DJ sets. ⊠ *Calle Jardines 3, Sol* ☎ *91/532–6490* ⊕ *www.salaelsol.com* 🕙 *Closed Mon.* Ⓜ *Gran Vía.*

MUSIC CLUBS
Costello

LIVE MUSIC | A multiuse space that combines a café and a lounge, this place caters to a relaxed, conversational crowd; the cramped bottom floor is suited to partygoers, with live music. On weekdays, there are theater and stand-up comedy shows. Check the website for events and ticket prices. ⊠ *Calle Caballero de Gracia 10, Sol* ☎ *91/522–1815* ⊕ *www.costelloclub.com* Ⓜ *Gran Vía.*

🎭 Performing Arts

Círculo de Bellas Artes

CONCERTS | Concerts, theater, dance performances, art exhibitions, and other events are all part of the calendar at this performance and entertainment venue. There is also an extremely popular (and overpriced) café and a rooftop restaurant-bar with breathtaking views of the city. ⊠ *Calle del Marqués de Casa Riera 2, Sol* ☎ *90/242-2442* ⊕ *www.circulobellasartes.com* Ⓜ *Banco de España.*

🛍 Shopping

CLOTHING

Capas Seseña

OTHER ACCESSORIES | Seseña is the oldest cape tailor in the world. Since 1901, this family-run business has outfitted the likes of Picasso, Hemingway, and Michael Jackson in traditional merino wool and velvet capes, some lined with red satin. ⊠ *Calle de la Cruz 23, Sol* ☎ *91/531-6840* ⊕ *www.sesena.com* ◔ *Closed Sun.* Ⓜ *Sol.*

CRAFTS AND DESIGN

El Arco Artesanía

CRAFTS | El Arco sells contemporary, whimsical handicrafts from all over Spain, including modern ceramics, handblown glassware, jewelry, and leather items. ⊠ *Pl. Mayor 9, Sol* ☎ *68/904-4374* ⊕ *www.artesaniaelarco.com* Ⓜ *Sol.*

Taller Puntera

CRAFTS | You can watch the artisans at work at this inviting atelier-boutique hybrid situated steps from the Plaza Mayor. Regardless of what catches your eye—a leather card holder, handbag, or perhaps a hand-bound notebook—you'll be pleasantly surprised by the affordable prices. ⊠ *Pl. del Conde de Barajas 4, Sol* ☎ *91/364-2926* ⊕ *www.puntera.com* ◔ *Closed Sun.* Ⓜ *Ópera, Tirso de Molina.*

Gourmet Experience Callao 🍴

On the rooftop of El Corte Inglés, Spain's largest department store, there's a gourmet food court with some of the best views in the city. Grab a couple of tapas and a glass of wine here after perusing the shops around Callao. The space features outposts of well-known Spanish restaurants like La Máquina (seafood) and Asador Imanol (pinchos) as well as international options (hamburgers, Mexican, and Chinese, for example). Take the second entrance to El Corte Inglés as you're walking down Callao on Calle Carmen and across from Fnac.

FANS

★ Casa de Diego

OTHER SPECIALTY STORE | Established in 1800, Casa de Diego manufactures fans, umbrellas, and classic Spanish walking sticks with ornamented silver handles and also sells traditional Spanish ornamental combs, mantillas, and castanets. The British royal family buys autograph fans here for signing on special occasions. ⊠ *Puerta del Sol 12, Sol* ☎ *91/522-6643* ⊕ *www.casadediego.info* ◔ *Closed Sun.* Ⓜ *Sol.*

🏃 Activities

SPAS

Hammam Al Ándalus

SPAS | Walk through a nondescript door off the noisy Plaza de Jacinto Benavente and you're suddenly in a serene Moorish-style bathhouse decorated with carved arches and Andalusian tile. Flickering candles light the way to a steam room, relaxation area, shallow pools of varying temperatures, and, finally, to a massage parlor where professional masseurs offer treatments ranging from 15 minutes to one hour. It's not an authentic hammam by any stretch, but it's the best-priced spa experience in town and a good rainy-day activity for adult travelers. ⊠ *Calle de Atocha 14, Sol* ⊕ *www.madrid.hammamalandalus.com* Ⓢ *€55–120* Ⓜ *Sol.*

Palacio

Madrid's oldest neighborhood, Palacio is the home of the imposing Palacio Real. This is where Muhammad I established the city's first military post in the 9th century, essentially founding the city. The quarter, bounded by the Plaza Mayor to the east, is a maze of cobblestone streets lined with homey restaurants and old-school cafés and shops.

Sights

Catedral de la Almudena

CHURCH | The first stone of the cathedral, which faces the Royal Palace, was laid in 1883 by King Alfonso XII, and the resulting edifice was consecrated by Pope John Paul II in 1993. Built on the site of the old church of Santa María de la Almudena (the city's main mosque during Arab rule), the cathedral has a wooden statue of Madrid's female patron saint, the Virgin of Almudena, reportedly discovered after the Christian Reconquest of Madrid. Legend has it that when the Berbers invaded Spain, the local Christian population hid the statue of the Virgin in a vault carved in the old Roman wall that encircled the city. When the Christians "reconquered" Madrid in 1083, they looked for it, and after nine days of intensive praying—others say it was after a procession honoring the Virgin—the wall opened up to show the statue framed by two lighted candles. The cathedral's name is derived from the place where the relic was found: the wall of the old citadel (in Arabic, *al-mudayna*).

⊠ *Calle Bailén 10, Palacio* ☎ *91/542–2200* ⊕ *www.catedraldelaalmudena.es* Ⓢ *Free; museum and cupola €6* Ⓜ *Ópera.*

Jardines de Sabatini (*Sabatini Gardens*)

GARDEN | The meticulously manicured gardens to the north of the Palacio Real, located where the royal stables once were, are a pleasant place to rest or watch the sun set. ⊠ *Calle Bailén, Palacio* Ⓜ *Ópera.*

Madrid Río

CITY PARK | **FAMILY** | The city's most ambitious urban planning initiative in recent history, Madrid Río, added 32 km (20 miles) of green space and bike-friendly paths along the Manzanares River, beginning at the Puente de los Franceses in the northwest and terminating at the Pasarela Legazpi in the southeast. A popular place to enter is the Puente de Segovia, downhill from the Royal Palace. Outdoor concerts (check out the Veranos de la Villa series; lineups are posted online) and informal riverside dining round out the park's offerings. Note to nature lovers: Madrid Río connects to Casa de Campo, Parque del Oeste, and Madrid's 64-km (40-mile) Anillo Verde ("Green Ring") bike path. ⊠ *Palacio* ⊕ *www.esmadrid.com/en/whats-on/veranos-de-la-villa* Ⓜ *Príncipe Pío, Pirámides, Legazpi.*

Monasterio de la Encarnación (*Monastery of the Incarnation*)

RELIGIOUS BUILDING | Once connected to the Palacio Real by an underground passageway, this cloistered Augustinian convent now houses fewer than a dozen nuns. It was founded in 1611 by Queen Margarita de Austria, the wife of Felipe III, and has several artistic treasures including a reliquary where a vial with the dried blood of St. Pantaleón is said to liquefy every July 27. The ornate church has superb acoustics for medieval and Renaissance choral concerts. ⊠ *Pl. de la Encarnación 1, Palacio* ☎ *91/454–8803 for tourist office* ⊕ *www.patrimonionacional.es/en/real-sitio/*

real-monasterio-de-la-encarnacion ⊠ €6 ⊙ *Closed Mon.* Ⓜ *Ópera.*

★ Monasterio de las Descalzas Reales
(*Monastery of the Royal Discalced/Bare-foot Nuns*)
RELIGIOUS BUILDING | Access to this 16th-century building was restricted for 200 years to noblewomen. Its plain brick-and-stone facade begets an opulent interior strewn with paintings by Francisco de Zurbarán, Titian, and Pieter Brueghel the Elder—all part of the dowry of new monastery inductees—as well as a hall of sumptuous tapestries crafted from drawings by Peter Paul Rubens. The convent was founded in 1559 by Juana of Austria, one of Felipe II's sisters, who ruled Spain while he was in England and the Netherlands. It houses 33 different chapels—the age of Christ when he died and the maximum number of nuns allowed to live at the monastery—and more than 100 sculptures of Jesus as a baby. About 30 nuns (not necessarily of royal blood) still live here and grow vegetables in the convent's garden. You must take a tour in order to visit the convent; tours in English don't follow a set schedule but usually run from 4 pm to close. ⊠ *Pl. de las Descalzas Reales 3, Palacio* ☎ *91/454–8800* ⊕ *www. patrimonionacional.es/en/real-sitio/mon-asterio-de-las-descalzas-reales* ⊠ *From €6* ⊙ *Closed Mon.* Ⓜ *Sol.*

★ Palacio Real (*Royal Palace*)
CASTLE/PALACE | Emblematic of the oldest part of the city, the Royal Palace awes visitors with its sheer size and monumental presence. The palace was commissioned in the early 18th century by the first of Spain's Bourbon rulers, Felipe V. Outside, you can see the classical French architecture on the graceful Patio de Armas; inside, 2,800 rooms compete with each other for over-the-top opulence. A two-hour guided tour in English points out highlights including the Salón de Gasparini, King Carlos III's private apartments; the Salón del Trono, a grand throne room; and the banquet hall, set with gleaming china. Also within are the Museo de Música (Music Museum), with the world's largest collection of five-stringed instruments by Antonio Stradivari; the Painting Gallery, with works by Spanish, Flemish, and Italian artists; the Armería Real (Royal Armory), with suits of armor and medieval torture implements; and the Real Oficina de Farmacia (Royal Pharmacy). The palace also takes in the Biblioteca Real (Royal Library), with a first edition of Miguel de Cervantes's *Don Quixote,* and the Real Cocina (Royal Kitchen; tickets sold separately), which occupies 800 square meters (8,600 square feet) and has remained largely unchanged since the late 18th century. Opened to the public in 2017, its framed hand-written menus, antediluvian wood-burning ovens, enormous copper cauldrons, wooden iceboxes, and nearly 3,000 antique kitchen utensils make it a must-stop for foodies. In 2021 the seven-room Bailén Wing, containing mirrors, tapestries, armaments, and more, reopened after a 25-year hiatus. ⊠ *Calle Bailén, Palacio* ☎ *91/454–8800* ⊕ *www. patrimonionacional.es/visita/palacio-real-de-madrid* ⊠ *From €13* Ⓜ *Ópera.*

Plaza de la Villa
PLAZA/SQUARE | Madrid's town council met in this medieval-looking complex from the Middle Ages until 2009, when it moved to the Palacio de Cibeles. It now houses municipal offices. The oldest building on the plaza is the **Casa de los Lujanes**, the one with the Mudejar tower. Built as a private home in the late 15th century, the house carries the Lujanes crest over the main doorway. Also on the plaza's east end is the brick-and-stone **Casa de la Villa,** built in 1629, a classic example of Dutch-influenced Madrid design, with clean lines and spire-topped corner towers. Connected by an overhead walkway, the **Casa de Cisneros** was commissioned in 1537 by the nephew of Cardinal Cisneros. It's one of Madrid's rare examples of the

flamboyant plateresque style, which has been likened to splashed water. Sadly, none of these landmarks are open to the public. ✉ *Palacio* [M] *Sol, Ópera.*

Plaza de Oriente

PLAZA/SQUARE | This stately plaza, in front of the Palacio Real, is flanked by massive statues of Spanish monarchs. They were meant to be mounted on the railing on top of the palace, but Queen Isabel of Farnesio, one of the first royals to live in the palace, had them removed because she was afraid their enormous weight would bring the roof down. (At least that's the *official* reason; according to local lore, the queen wanted the statues removed because her own likeness wouldn't have been placed front and center.) A Velázquez drawing of King Felipe IV is the inspiration for the statue in the plaza's center. It's the first equestrian bronze ever cast with a rearing horse. The sculptor, Italian artist Pietro de Tacca, enlisted Galileo Galilei's help in configuring the statue's weight so it wouldn't tip over. ✉ *Palacio* [M] *Ópera.*

San Nicolás de los Servitas (*Church of St. Nicholas of the Servites*)

RELIGIOUS BUILDING | There's some debate over whether this church, perhaps the oldest in central Madrid, once formed part of an Arab mosque. It was more likely built after the so-called Reconquest of Madrid in 1083, but the brickwork and horseshoe arches are evidence that it was crafted by either Mudejars (workers of Islamic origin) or Christian Spaniards well versed in the style. Inside, exhibits detail the Islamic history of early Madrid. ✉ *Pl. de San Nicolás, Palacio* ☎ *91/559–4064* 🎟 *Suggested donation* [M] *Ópera.*

🍴 Restaurants

Casa Lafu

$$ | **CHINESE** | **FAMILY** | If you haven't tried Chinese food in Madrid, then you're missing out—the city has some of the best Chinese restaurants in Europe due to a vibrant immigrant community. Casa Lafu, with its serene white-tablecloth dining room, stands out for its expertly prepared repertoire of regional dishes, from Sichuan-style *má là* (spicy) plates to Shanghainese wine-cooked meats and Cantonese dim sum. **Known for:** rare regional specialties; hot pot; white-tablecloth Chinese cuisine at affordable prices. [$] *Average main: €17* ✉ *Calle Flor Baja 1, Palacio* ☎ *91/548–7096* 🌐 *www.casalafu.com* [M] *Santo Domingo.*

★ La Copita Asturiana

$$ | **SPANISH** | In the heart of the tourist fray but blissfully under-the-radar, this teensy, lunch-only restaurant (est. 1959) with an old tin bar serves all the Asturian favorites, from *fabada* (bean stew) to *cachopo* (ham-and-cheese-stuffed cutlets) to ultracreamy rice pudding. Asturian cider is the requisite beverage. **Known for:** kitsch decor; easy-on-the-wallet prices; northern Spanish comfort food. [$] *Average main: €17* ✉ *Calle de Tabernillas 13, Palacio* ☎ *91/365–1063* 🌐 *www.lacopitaasturiana.com* 🕒 *Closed Sat. No dinner* [M] *Tirso de Molina.*

Le Bistroman Atelier

$$$ | **FRENCH** | For a country that borders France, Spain has a surprising dearth of good French restaurants, which makes Le Bistroman all the more remarkable—not only is the food good by Spanish standards, it would be a hit in Paris with its homemade *everything*, from terrines to breads to pastries. Wild game (venison, squab) features prominently on the menu, and other highlights include an old-school cheese cart and throwback desserts like babas au rhum and vanilla bean soufflé. **Known for:** elevated bistro cooking; game meats; varied French wine list. [$] *Average main: €28* ✉ *Calle de la Amnistia 10, Palacio* ☎ *91/447–2713* 🌐 *www.lebistroman.es* 🕒 *Closed Mon. No dinner Sun.* [M] *Ópera.*

Solito Taquería Mexicana

$$ | **MEXICAN** | **FAMILY** | Improbably, some of the best tacos you can gobble down in Madrid are found in tourist central, just off the Plaza Mayor. This inviting taquería, which opened in 2020, is quickly gaining fame for pitch-perfect classics like *cochinita pibil* chalupas, huitlacoche quesadillas, and pozole (choose from three types) as well as real-deal margaritas and *cajeta* crepes. [$] *Average main: €20* ✉ *Calle de la Pasa 4, Palacio* ☎ *91/353–5822* 🌐 *www.solitotaqueria.com* 🕒 *Closed Mon.* [M] *Sol, Tirso de Molina.*

☕ Coffee and Quick Bites

Chocolatería Valor

$ | CAFÉ | FAMILY | Walk along the western side of the Monasterio de las Descalzas Reales until you reach Chocolatería Valor, an ideal spot to indulge in piping-hot churros dipped in thick hot chocolate. **Known for:** outdoor seating; family-friendly atmosphere; one of the best chocolaterías in town. [$] *Average main: €6* ✉ *Calle Postigo de San Martín 7, Palacio* ☎ *91/899–4062* 🌐 *www.valor.es* [M] *Callao.*

🛏 Hotels

Generator Madrid

$ | HOTEL | Generator Madrid might be a budget hotel with shared (up to eight-person) rooms, but it's as much a hotel as any of the major brands. **Pros:** bubbly staff and fellow guests; USB sockets in rooms; PlayStation in the lobby. **Cons:** towels (€5 rental) not included in the rate; storing luggage in lockers is exorbitant at €2 per hour; no laundry facilities or kitchen. [$] *Rooms from: €46* ✉ *Calle de San Bernardo 2, Palacio* ☎ *91/047–9801* 🌐 *www.staygenerator.com/madrid* 🛏 *129 rooms* 🍴 *No Meals* [M] *Callao.*

★ Gran Meliá Palacio de Los Duques

$$$$ | HOTEL | Spanish-art lovers will geek out at the Gran Meliá Palacio de los Duques, a luxury hotel tucked behind Gran Vía where reproductions of famous Diego Velázquez paintings feature in every room. **Pros:** Dos Cielos, one of the city's best hotel restaurants; underfloor heating and deep-soak tubs; rooftop pool and bar. **Cons:** rooftop often off-limits because of private events; no great views from rooms; rooms are less attractive than public areas. [$] *Rooms from: €340* ✉ *Cuesta Santo Domingo 5, Palacio* ☎ *91/276–4747* 🌐 *www.melia.com* 🛏 *180 rooms* 🍴 *No Meals* [M] *Santo Domingo.*

Hotel Indigo Madrid – Gran Vía

$$ | HOTEL | A hip, vibrant hotel off the bustling Gran Vía thoroughfare, Indigo is best known for its stunning rooftop lounge and outdoor infinity pool, rare features in Madrid. **Pros:** restaurant that punches above its weight; surprisingly well-equipped gym; sceney rooftop infinity pool. **Cons:** decor might be gaudy to some; loses much of its vitality in cold-weather months; interior rooms get little natural light. [$] *Rooms from: €142* ✉ *Calle de Silva 6, Palacio* ☎ *91/200–8585* 🌐 *www.indigomadrid.com* 🛏 *85 rooms* 🍴 *No Meals* [M] *Santo Domingo.*

Hotel Intur Palacio San Martín

$$ | HOTEL | In an unbeatable location across from one of Madrid's most celebrated landmarks (Monasterio de las Descalzas Reales), this hotel—once the U.S. embassy and later a luxurious residential building crowded with noblemen—has the architectural bones of a turn-of-the-century mansion with its hand-carved ceilings, marble foyers, and intricate iron balconies. **Pros:** lobby with glass-domed atrium; good variety at breakfast; spacious rooms. **Cons:** loud church bells in the morning; bland interiors; bare-bones gym. [$] *Rooms from: €128* ✉ *Pl. de San Martín 5, Palacio* ☎ *91/701–5000* 🌐 *www.intur.com* 🛏 *103 rooms* 🍴 *No Meals* [M] *Ópera, Callao.*

Room Mate Laura

$$ | HOTEL | A quirky, clubby hotel overlooking Plaza de San Martín near the Royal Theater and Palace, Room Mate Laura feels like a time warp to the early aughts with all-white furniture and bold wall graphics. **Pros:** clean and comfortable;

kitchenettes; free portable Wi-Fi gadgets. **Cons:** no restaurant; only the best rooms have views of the convent; some bathrooms need revamping. $ *Rooms from: €131* ✉ *Travesía de Trujillos 3, Palacio* ☎ *90/081–8320* ⊕ *www.room-mate-hotels.com* ☞ *36 rooms* ⦿ *No Meals* Ⓜ *Ópera.*

Room Mate Macarena

$$ | **HOTEL** | The newest addition to the Room Mate chain, Macarena opened in July 2020 right smack on the Gran Vía thoroughfare. **Pros:** gleaming new property; rooftop open till 2 am on weekends; photogenic and flamboyant design. **Cons:** busy area; pool looks bigger in photos; interiors could be too loud for some. $ *Rooms from: €147* ✉ *Gran Vía 43, Palacio* ☎ *91/116–1191* ⊕ *www.room-mate-hotels.com* ⦿ *No Meals* ☞ *130 rooms* Ⓜ *Santo Domingo, Callao.*

Room Mate Mario

$$ | **HOTEL** | In the city center, steps from the Royal Palace and Teatro Real, Mario is small with limited services but a welcome alternative to Madrid's traditional hotel options at a good price. **Pros:** one of the most affordable Room Mate chain options in Madrid; centrally located; good breakfast served until noon. **Cons:** no restaurant or in-room coffee-making facilities; unremarkable views; cramped entry-level rooms. $ *Rooms from: €131* ✉ *Calle Campomanes 4, Palacio* ☎ *91/548–8548* ⊕ *www.room-mateho-tels.com* ☞ *57 rooms* ⦿ *Free Breakfast* Ⓜ *Ópera.*

 ## Nightlife

DANCE CLUBS
Cool

DANCE CLUBS | This gritty, Berlin-style underground club hosts techno-driven dance parties on weekend nights for a primarily LGBT+ clientele. ✉ *Calle Isabel la Católica 6, Palacio* ☎ *63/459–6212* Ⓜ *Santo Domingo.*

Velvet

DANCE CLUBS | Trippy and chameleonlike, thanks to colorful LED lights and the undulating shapes of the columns and walls, this is the place to go if you want a late-night drink without the thunder of a full-blown DJ. The venue opens at 11 and closes at 5:30 am. ✉ *Calle Jacometrezo 6, Palacio* ☎ *63/341–4887* Ⓜ *Callao.*

MUSIC CLUBS
★ Café Berlín

LIVE MUSIC | For a space so small, Café Berlín packs quite an acoustic punch and draws an international, eclectic crowd. Before midnight, catch nightly live music acts in a panoply of styles (flamenco, swing, soul, and more); from around 1 am on, drop in for the disco-inflected DJ sets that ooze good vibes until 6 am. ✉ *Costanilla de los Ángeles 20, Palacio* ☎ *91/559–7429* ⊕ *www.berlincafe.es* Ⓜ *Santo Domingo.*

El Amante

LIVE MUSIC | With two winding floors filled with nooks hosting the city's best-heeled crowds, this might be the closest thing you'll find in Madrid to a posh private New York club. Music is usually bass-heavy electronic or house. The door is tough, so be sure to dress to impress (no sneakers allowed). Get here before 1:30 am or be ready to wait in line. ✉ *Calle Santiago 3, Palacio* ☎ *91/755–4460* Ⓜ *Ópera.*

Performing Arts

★ Teatro Real

OPERA | This resplendent Neoclassical theater is the city's premier venue for opera and dance performances. Built in 1850, it fell into disuse from 1925 to 1966 because of political upheaval. A major restoration project endowed it with golden balconies, plush seats, and state-of-the-art stage equipment. Opera buffs rave about the choir, said to be one of the best in the world. The theater sometimes hosts flamenco on Friday evenings in the

Did You Know?

In 1997 the Teatro Real returned to its intended use as a dedicated opera house—it was a major European opera venue when it first opened in 1850, but in the interim years it was also used as a parliamentary debate chamber, a dance hall, a temporary war barracks, and even a gunpowder storage facility.

smaller auditorium; check the website for updates. ⊠ *Pl. de Isabel II, Palacio* ☎ *91/516–0660* ⊕ *www.teatroreal.es* Ⓜ *Ópera.*

FLAMENCO
Corral de la Morería
FOLK/TRADITIONAL DANCE | A Michelin-starred dinner followed by a world-class flamenco performance in the same building sounds too good to be true, but at Corral de la Morería, the food (Basque with an Andalusian twist) is as invigorating as the twirling and stomping *bailaoras*. Opt for an elegant, market-driven prix-fixe menu to be enjoyed during the show, or splurge on an exclusive tasting experience at the four-table Gastronómico restaurant that earned the venue its coveted star. Wine pairings, which hinge on rare back-vintage sherries and other *vinos generosos* (fortified wines), are well worth the extra euros. ⊠ *Calle de la Morería 17, Palacio* ☎ *91/365–8446* ⊕ *www.corraldelamoreria.com* Ⓜ *La Latina.*

 Shopping

CERAMICS
★ Antigua Casa Talavera
CRAFTS | Opened in 1904, this is the best of Madrid's many ceramics vendors. Despite the name, the finest wares sold here are from Manises, near Valencia, but the blue-and-yellow Talavera ceramics are also excellent. All pieces are hand-painted and bear traditional Spanish motifs that have been used for centuries. ⊠ *Calle de Isabel la Católica 2, Palacio* ☎ *91/547–3417* ⊕ *www.antiguacasatalavera.com* ☽ *Closed Sun.* Ⓜ *Santo Domingo.*

SPECIALTY STORES
Alambique
OTHER SPECIALTY STORE | Amateur and professional cooks will love this terrific little shop (est. 1978) that sells everything from paella pans to earthenware *cazuelas* to olive-wood cheese boards. Cooking classes (in Spanish) are also available. ⊠ *Pl. de la Encarnación 2, Palacio* ☎ *91/547–4220* ⊕ *www.alambique.com.*

Moncloa

Moncloa is sprawling, diverse, unurbanized in certain pockets, and less touristy than other city-center neighborhoods. It takes in high-society residential communities like Aravaca and Puerta de Hierro, livelier urban areas like Argüelles (where college kids commandeer entire sidewalk cafés), and parks like the manicured Parque del Oeste, sections of the Madrid Río esplanade, and the more rugged Casa de Campo.

 Sights

★ Casa de Campo
CITY PARK | **FAMILY** | Over five times the size of New York's Central Park, Casa de Campo is Madrid's largest park and a nature-lover's paradise, complete with bike trails, picnic tables, pine forests, lakeside restaurants (seek out the newly opened Villa Verbena, run by the folks behind Triciclo, in Barrio de las Letras), and a public outdoor pool (€5 entry). See if you can spot wildlife like hawks, foxes, hares, and red squirrels. The park's name ("country house") is a holdover from when the grounds were the royal family's hunting estate. It became public property in May 1931 with the arrival of the Spanish Second Republic, which dissolved royal landholdings. ⊠ *Moncloa* Ⓜ *Casa de Campo, Lago, Batán.*

Ermita de San Antonio de la Florida (*Goya's Tomb*)
HISTORIC SIGHT | Built between 1792 and 1798 by the Italian architect Francisco Fontana, this Neoclassical chapel was financed by King Carlos IV, who also commissioned Goya to paint the vaults and the main dome. It took him 120 days to fully depict events of the 13th century (St. Anthony of Padua resurrecting a dead

man) as if they had happened five centuries later, with naturalistic images never used before to paint religious scenes. Opposite the image of the frightening dead man on the main dome, Goya painted himself as a man covered with a black cloak. Goya, who died in Bordeaux in 1828, is buried here (without his head, because it was stolen in France) under an unadorned gravestone. ⊠ *Glorieta de San Antonio de la Florida 5, Moncloa* ☎ *91/542–0722* ⊕ *www.sanantoniodelaflorida.es* ✆ *Free* ⊙ *Closed Mon.* Ⓜ *Príncipe Pío.*

Museo Cerralbo

HISTORY MUSEUM | One of Madrid's most captivating museums is also one of its least known. This former palace, built in 1893 by the marquis of the same name, preserves the nobleman's art collection including works by El Greco, Tintoretto, Van Dyck, and Zurbarán. These hang in gilded and frescoed halls appointed with ornate period furniture. ⊠ *Calle de Ventura Rodríguez 17, Moncloa* ☎ *91/547–3646* ⊕ *www.culturaydeporte.gob.es/mcerralbo/en/home.html* ⊙ *Closed Mon. (free Thurs. 5–8 pm, Sat. 2–3 pm, Sun.)* ✆ *€3* Ⓜ *Ventura Rodríguez.*

Museo del Traje (*Costume Museum*)

OTHER MUSEUM | Trace the evolution of dress in Spain here, from rare old royal burial garments to French fashion pieces of Felipe V's reign and the haute couture creations of Balenciaga and Pertegaz. Explanatory notes are in English, and the museum has a superb modern Spanish restaurant, Café de Oriente, overlooking the gardens. ⊠ *Av. Juan de Herrera 2, Moncloa* ☎ *91/550–4700* ⊕ *www.culturaydeporte.gob.es/mtraje/inicio.html* ✆ *€3 (free Sat. after 2:30 and Sun.)* ⊙ *Closed Mon.* Ⓜ *Ciudad Universitaria.*

★ Parque del Oeste

CITY PARK | **FAMILY** | This is many madrileños' favorite park for its pristine yet unmobbed paths and well-pruned lawns and flower beds. From dawn to dusk, expect to see dogs cavorting off leash, couples sprawled out beneath the trees, and groups of friends playing frisbee and *fútbol*. From Paseo del Pintor Rosales, meander downhill toward Avenida de Valladolid, crossing the train tracks, and you'll hit Madrid Río; walk southwest and you'll find Templo de Debod. This park also contains the city's only cable car (see "Teleférico") and, 100 yards beneath it, a rose garden (Rosaleda; free entry) containing some 20,000 specimens of more than 650 rose varieties that reach their peak in May. In the quieter northern section of the park (along Avenida Séneca), you'll happen upon Civil War-era bunkers interspersed among plane tree-lined promenades, a sobering reminder that Parque del Oeste was the western front of Madrid's resistance against Franco's armies. ⊠ *Paseo del Pintor Rosales, Moncloa* Ⓜ *Argüelles, Moncloa, Ventura Rodríguez, Pl. de España.*

Teleférico

VIEWPOINT | **FAMILY** | Kids and adults alike appreciate the sweeping views from this retro cable car, which swoops you 2.5 km (1.6 miles) from the Rosaleda gardens (in the Parque del Oeste) to the center of Casa de Campo in about 10 minutes. If you're feeling active, take a (very) long hike to the top and ride back into the city, or pause in Casa de Campo for primo picnicking. This is not the best way to get to the zoo and theme park, located approximately 2 km (1 mile) from the drop-off point in Casa de Campo. You're better off riding the Teléferico out and back, then taking the bus to the zoo. ⊠ *Estación Terminal Teleférico, Paseo de Pintor Rosales, at Calle Marqués de Urquijo, Moncloa* ☎ *91/541–1118* ⊕ *teleferico.emtmadrid.es* ✆ *From €5* Ⓜ *Argüelles.*

🍴 Restaurants

Casa Mingo

$ | **SPANISH** | **FAMILY** | Madrid's oldest *sidrería* (cider house) is a grand, cathedral-like hall with barrel-lined walls, double-height ceilings, and creaky wooden chairs. The star menu item is roast chicken, hacked up unceremoniously and served swimming in a pool of cider jus—old-school bar food at its finest. **Known for:** a Madrid institution; roast chicken; Asturian cider. $ *Average main: €10* ⊠ *Paseo de la Florida 34, Moncloa* ☎ *91/547–7918* ⊕ *www.casamingo.es* Ⓜ *Príncipe Pío.*

★ Cuenllas

$$$ | SPANISH | Epitomizing Old World luxury, Cuenllas (KWEN-yas) is Moncloa's most iconic dining establishment, in business since 1939. Before or after sitting down at the bar or in the dining room for a meal of Spanish bistro fare (think warm salt cod brandade, Santoña anchovy canapés, and marinated partridge) accompanied by *reserva* wines, peruse the adjoining "Ultramarinos" gourmet shop for edible souvenirs including caviar, cheeses, wines, and homemade charcuterie. **Known for:** standout traditional wine list; charmingly old-fashioned waiters; French-inflected Spanish dining. $ *Average main: €23* ⊠ *Calle Ferraz 5, Moncloa* ☎ *91/559–1705* ⊕ *www.cuenllas.es* ⊘ *Closed Sun.* Ⓜ *Ventura Rodríguez.*

🛏 Hotels

Barceló Torre de Madrid

$$$ | HOTEL | A jewel box of glowing lights, harlequin furniture, and gilded mirrors, the soaring Barceló Torre de Madrid opened in 2017 and remains one of the trendiest hotels in town. **Pros:** sleek pool and spa area; excellent Somos restaurant; cutting-edge design by local artists. **Cons:** short-staffed; Plaza de España under massive renovation; bathing cap required to use the pool. $ *Rooms from: €200* ⊠ *Pl. de España 18, Moncloa* ☎ *91/524–2339* ⊕ *www.barcelo. com* ⊅ *256 rooms* ⑪ *No Meals* Ⓜ *Pl. de España.*

★ Dear Hotel

$$ | HOTEL | Catty-corner to Plaza de España, Dear Hotel is a sleek urban property designed by Tarruella Trenchs Studio, the firm behind such lauded projects as H10 La Mimosa hotel in Barcelona and La Bien Aparecida restaurant in Madrid. **Pros:** swanky rooftop bar with 360-degree views; Scandi chic furnishings; all rooms face out. **Cons:** cramped lobby; no gym or spa; tiny pool. $ *Rooms from: €130* ⊠ *Gran Vía 80, Moncloa* ☎ *91/412–3200* ⊕ *www.dearhotelmadrid.com* ⊅ *162 rooms* ⑪ *No Meals* Ⓜ *Pl. de España.*

Hotel Indigo Madrid – Princesa

$ | HOTEL | This bright, budget option in the heart of residential Argüelles is steps from the bustling shopping street Calle Princesa. **Pros:** rain showers; five-minute walk from Parque del Oeste; cheery decor. **Cons:** so-so breakfast; poor soundproofing; bathrooms are basic. $ *Rooms from: €116* ⊠ *Calle del Marqués de Urquijo 4, Moncloa* ☎ *91/548–1900* ⊕ *www. ihg.com* ⊅ *101 rooms* ⑪ *No Meals* Ⓜ *Argüelles.*

Chueca

Chueca, a subsection of Justicia district, is named after the Plaza de Chueca, which is in turn named after Federico Chueca, author and composer of *zarzuelas* (short musical plays). Today the neighborhood is Spain's most iconic LGBT+ quarter, its unofficial title since the 1980s, when the first gay bars arrived on the scene. Nowadays most young LGBT+ madrileños live and party elsewhere because of the barrio's soaring rents, tourist crowds, and increasingly older clientele, but for a fun, carefree, and rowdy night out, Chueca never disappoints regardless of your sexual orientation. The downside of Chueca's reputation as gay district is that its myriad other attractions—ranging from museums to pretty plazas to fantastic galleries and restaurants—are often overshadowed.

Sights

Museo del Romanticismo (*Museum of Romanticism*)

HISTORY MUSEUM | To catch a glimpse of how the Spanish bourgeoisie lived in the early 19th century, step into this former palace of a marquis. Each room sparkles with ornate period furniture, evocative portraits, and other historical artifacts culled from the height of Spanish Romanticism. It's worth spending a few minutes admiring the flamboyantly decorated fans and backlit lithophanes. The museum can be seen in an hour or two, but don't rush out: the plant-filled interior patio is a lovely, tranquil place to enjoy tea and pastries. ✉ *Calle de San Mateo 13, Chueca* ☎ *91/448–1045* 🌐 *www.culturaydeporte.gob.es/mromanticismo/en/inicio.html* 🎫 *€3* 🕒 *Closed Mon.* [M] *Tribunal.*

Restaurants

Casa Hortensia Restaurante y Sidrería

$$ | **SPANISH** | **FAMILY** | Approximate a vacation to the north of Spain by dining at this true-blue Asturian restaurant (or at the more casual *sidrería,* in the bar area), where that region's unsung comfort-food dishes—such as *fabada* (pork-and-bean stew), Cabrales cheese, and *cachopo* (cheese-stuffed beef cutlets)—take center stage. The obligatory tipple is *sidra,* bone-dry Asturian cider that's aerated using a battery-powered gadget designed for this task. **Known for:** local crowd; authentic fabada; cider bottles with fun DIY aerators. [$] *Average main: €19* ✉ *Calle Farmacia 2, 2nd and 3rd fl., Chueca* ✥ *Situated in what appears to be an apartment building* ☎ *91/539–0090* 🌐 *www.casahortensia.com* 🕒 *Closed Mon. No dinner Sun.* [M] *Chueca.*

★ **Casa Salvador**

$$ | **SPANISH** | Whether you approve of bullfighting or not, the culinary excellence of Casa Salvador—a checkered-tablecloth, taurine-theme restaurant that opened in 1941—isn't up for debate. Sit down to generous servings of feather-light fried hake, hearty oxtail stew, and other stodgy (in the best way) Spanish classics, all served by hale old-school waiters clad in white jackets. **Known for:** cloud-light fried hake and stewed oxtail; walls packed with bullfighting paraphernalia; time-warpy decor. [$] *Average main: €18* ✉ *Calle de Barbieri 12, Chueca* ☎ *91/521–4524* 🌐 *www.casasalvadormadrid.com* 🕒 *Closed Sun.* [M] *Chueca.*

Celso y Manolo

$ | **TAPAS** | Named after the brothers who founded the restaurant (though under new ownership), this place has around a dozen tables and an extensive, eclectic menu geared toward sharing that hinges on natural products—game meats, seafood, cheeses—from the mountainous northerly region of Cantabria. Natural and often organic wines sourced from around the country make for spot-on pairings. **Known for:** varied menu; Cantabrian specialties; market-driven cuisine. [$] *Average main: €14* ✉ *Calle Libertad 1, Chueca* ☎ *91/531–8079* 🌐 *www.celsoymanolo.es* [M] *Chueca.*

NaDo Madrid

$$$$ | **SPANISH** | In a converted brick-walled coal cellar that stretches like a subway tunnel behind an unmarked door is one of Madrid's buzziest restaurants. Galician chef Iván Domínguez coaxes exquisite ingredients from his home region—ocean-fresh cockles, horse mackerel, baby *lágrima* peas, crackly cornbread baked in cabbage leaves—into minimalist fine-dining fare that both surprises and satisfies. **Known for:** open kitchen puts you in the center of the action; ultra-trendy hot spot; creative riffs on traditional Galician cuisine. [$] *Average main: €50* ✉ *Calle de Prim 5, Chueca* ☎ *91/445–1208* 🌐 *www.nado.es* 🕒 *Closed Sun. and Mon.* [M] *Chueca.*

Roostiq

$$ | **EUROPEAN** | Fire is the secret ingredient at Roostiq, where pizzas sizzle and puff in a wood-burning oven and meat, fish, and vegetables char until tender over white-hot embers. Even the cheesecake is of the Basque "burnt" variety, all brown and caramel-ly on the outside and gooey within. **Known for:** trendy industrial digs; open-hearth cooking; Neapolitan-style pizzas. [$] *Average main: €18* ✉ *Calle de Augusto Figueroa 47, Chueca* ☎ *91/853–2434* 🌐 *www.roostiqmadrid.com* ⏲ *No dinner Sun.* [M] *Chueca.*

Coffee and Quick Bites

★ Faraday

$ | **CAFÉ** | Faraday is one of Madrid's trendiest and most pleasant cafés, thanks to meticulously roasted beans, mathematically precise baristas, and gorgeous mid-century modern furniture. **Known for:** great music; excellent coffee; closed 2–4 pm. [$] *Average main: €5* ✉ *Calle de San Lucas 9, Chueca* 🌐 *www.instagram.com/faradaymadrid* [M] *Alonso Martínez, Chueca.*

Hotels

★ Only YOU Boutique Hotel

$$$ | **HOTEL** | The Ibizan owners of this hotel bring that island's mix of glamour, energy, and cutting-edge music and design to one of Madrid's most happening neighborhoods. **Pros:** all-day breakfast; double-paned glass blocks out street noise; excellent tapas restaurant. **Cons:** rooms above Calle Barquillo can be pricey; breakfast quality pales in comparison to dinner; no bathtubs in some upgraded rooms. [$] *Rooms from: €195* ✉ *Calle Barquillo 21, Chueca* ☎ *91/005–2222* 🌐 *www.onlyyouhotels.com* 🛏 *125 rooms* [M] *Chueca.*

The Principal Madrid

$$$$ | **HOTEL** | Dozens of hotels flank Gran Vía, Madrid's main artery, but only The Principal stands above the others—and not just on account of its swanky rooftop cocktail bar. **Pros:** hotel rooftop with 360-degree views; luxury feel with personal touches; Ramón Freixa–helmed restaurant. **Cons:** gym doesn't open until 10 am; rooftop pool is tiny; rooms not properly soundproofed. [$] *Rooms from: €296* ✉ *Calle Marqués de Valdeiglesias 1, Chueca* ☎ *91/521–8743* 🌐 *www.theprincipalmadridhotel.com* 🛏 *76 rooms* 🍴 *No Meals* [M] *Chueca.*

Room Mate Óscar

$$ | **HOTEL** | With one of the busiest rooftop pool bars in the area, Room Mate Oscar is a sceney spot frequented by LGBT+ travelers. **Pros:** rooftop pool and lounge; refreshingly unserious decor; bubbly front-desk staff. **Cons:** lackluster breakfast buffet; noisy street and rooftop; pool only open in summer. [$] *Rooms from: €135* ✉ *Pl. Vázquez de Mella 12, Chueca* ☎ *91/701–1173* 🌐 *www.room-matehotels.com* 🛏 *74 rooms* 🍴 *Free Breakfast* [M] *Chueca.*

URSO Hotel and Spa

$$$ | **HOTEL** | In a regal turn-of-the-20th-century municipal building, this luxury hotel and spa boasts old-world comfort and avant-garde design to satisfy alternative types and jet-setters alike. **Pros:** calm-inducing rooms; stunning facade; Natura Bissé spa with 7-meter hydromassage pool. **Cons:** entry-level rooms are dark and cramped; bar closes at midnight; smallish gym and chilly pool. [$] *Rooms from: €225* ✉ *Calle de Mejía Lequerica 8, Chueca* ☎ *91/444–4458* 🌐 *www.hotelurso.com* 🛏 *78 rooms* 🍴 *No Meals* [M] *Alonso Martínez, Tribunal.*

Nightlife

Most of Chueca's LGBT-oriented venues—including all of those listed below—are welcoming to customers of all genders and sexual orientations.

BARS

Café Belén

CAFÉS | The handful of tables here are rarely empty on weekends, thanks to the candlelit, cozy atmosphere and enormous, open windows. Expect a young, mixed crowd. Weeknights are

Chueca and Malasaña

KEY

- Exploring Sights
- Restaurants
- Quick Bites
- Hotels

Sights	▼
1 Museo del Romanticismo	**D1**
2 Palacio de Liria	**A3**

Restaurants	▼
1 Bar La Gloria	**A1**
2 Bodega de la Ardosa	**C2**
3 Casa Hortensia Restaurante y Sidrería	**D2**
4 Casa Macareno	**B1**
5 Casa Salvador	**D3**
6 Celso y Manolo	**D4**
7 La Colmada	**B1**
8 NaDo Madrid	**E3**
9 Roostiq	**E3**

Quick Bites	▼
1 Faraday	**E2**
2 Misión Café	**C3**
3 Toma Café	**C2**

Hotels	▼
1 Only YOU Boutique Hotel	**E3**
2 The Principal Madrid	**D4**
3 Room Mate Óscar	**D3**
4 URSO Hotel and Spa	**D1**

more mellow. ⊠ *Calle Belén 5, Chueca* ☎ *91/308–2747* ⊕ *www.elcafebelen.com* Ⓜ *Chueca.*

Del Diego

COCKTAIL LOUNGES | There are no fripperies of modern mixology to be found at Del Diego, and that's just how the dyed-in-the-wool regulars like it. This legendary bar has been pouring flawless classic cocktails like dirty martinis and white Russians since the late 1990s, and *amigos*, you better believe they're all that and a bag of chips. ⊠ *Calle de la Reina 12, Chueca* ☎ *91/523–3106* ⊕ *www.deldiego.com* Ⓜ *Gran Vía.*

★ Macera Taller Bar

COCKTAIL LOUNGES | The age-old technique of maceration rules at Macera, where bartenders treat spirits like blank canvases, imbuing them with surprising flavor combinations. Gin is steeped with fresh cilantro, lime, and jalapeño until it achieves a zippy grassy piquancy. Whiskey might be infused with almonds, fresh cherries, mint, or vanilla bean. There's a second outpost on Calle Ventura de la Vega 7 in Barrio de Las Letras. ⊠ *Calle San Mateo 21, Chueca* ☎ *91/011–5810* ⊕ *www.maceradrinks.com* Ⓜ *Alonso Martínez, Tribunal.*

Vinoteca Vides

WINE BARS | This dressed-down wine bar is a great spot to sample classically styled Spanish wines at a terrific price. There's a particularly deep selection of grippy *monastrells*, a dark, high-alcohol grape ubiquitous in southern Spain. ⊠ *Calle Libertad 12, Chueca* ☎ *91/531–8444* ⊕ *www.vinotecavides.es* Ⓜ *Chueca.*

DANCE CLUBS

Fulanita de Tal

DANCE CLUBS | Chueca's favorite lesbian bar hosts popular concerts and dusk-to-3:30 am dance parties in an intimate, unpretentious space. The music varies night to night and mixes pop, oldies, reggaeton, and electro. ⊠ *Calle de Regueros 9, Chueca* ☎ *91/319–5069* ⊕ *www.fulanitadetal.es* ⊘ *Closed Mon.–Thurs.* Ⓜ *Alonso Martínez, Chueca.*

★ Pavoneo

BARS | One of Chueca's buzziest gay bars, Pavoneo caters to well-dressed creatives, selfie-snapping influencers, and models on their nights off. Bartenders may not know what a Negroni is (even if they have all the requisite ingredients), but their sigh-worthy looks make them easy to forgive. ⊠ *Calle de Belén 9, Chueca* ☎ *64/679–6485* ⊘ *Closed Mon.–Wed.* Ⓜ *Chueca.*

MUSIC CLUBS

Café Libertad 8

LIVE MUSIC | Almost every classic madrileño songwriter, musician, and poet has passed through this timeworn hangout (it opens at 3:30 pm and entertainment starts at 9 pm). Acoustic guitar concerts costing €3–6 a head are fantastic—and virtually tourist-free. ⊠ *Calle de la Libertad 8, Chueca* ☎ *91/532–1150* ⊕ *www.libertad8cafe.com* Ⓜ *Chueca.*

Intruso Bar

LIVE MUSIC | Easy to miss (it's tucked inside a building just a block off Fuencarral), this is one of Chueca's best lounge-bars. There are live DJs and funk and jazz bands almost every night from 9 pm playing to a mixed-age crowd. ⊠ *Calle Augusto Figueroa 3, Chueca* ⊕ *www.intrusobar.com* ⊘ *Closed Mon.* Ⓜ *Chueca.*

Museo Chicote

LIVE MUSIC | This landmark cocktail bar–lounge is said to have been one of Hemingway's haunts, and much of the interior can be traced to the 1930s, but modern elements (like the in-house DJ and hordes of international visitors) keep this spot firmly in the present. ⊠ *Gran Vía 12, Chueca* ☎ *91/532–6737* ⊕ *www.museochicote.com* ⊘ *Closed Sun.* Ⓜ *Gran Vía.*

🛍 Shopping

BOUTIQUES AND FASHION

Mans

MEN'S CLOTHING | Owned by Andalusian fashion wunderkind Jaime Álvarez, this is Madrid's most cutting-edge made-to-measure menswear boutique. Ready-made clothes are also available in the shop as well as online. ⊠ *Calle San Bernardino 15, Chueca* ⊕ *www.mansconceptmenswear.com* ⊙ *Closed weekends* Ⓜ *Alonso Martínez, Chueca.*

Oteyza

MIXED CLOTHING | Every garment sold at master tailor Oteyza takes at least two months to make, and the classic craftsmanship shows in the immaculate suits, jackets, and shirts. Get fitted while you're in Madrid and pony up the euros for shipping—you won't regret it. ⊠ *Calle Conde de Xiquena 11, Chueca* ☎ *91/448–8623* ⊕ *www.deoteyza.com* ⊙ *Closed Sun.* Ⓜ *Chueca.*

★ Pez

HOUSEWARES | A favorite among local fashionistas, this store has two branches—one dedicated to high-end women's wear and another to furniture and decor—on the same street. ⊠ *Calle de Regueros 2 and 15, Chueca* ☎ *91/308–6677* ⊕ *www.pez-pez.es* ⊙ *Closed Sun.* Ⓜ *Chueca.*

Próxima Parada

WOMEN'S CLOTHING | The bubbly owner of this womenswear store culls daring, colorful garments from Spanish designers for her devoted (mostly 40-and-above) clientele. ⊠ *Calle Conde de Xiquena 9, Chueca* ☎ *91/523–1929* ⊕ *www.facebook.com/tiendaproximaparada* ⊙ *Closed Sun.* Ⓜ *Chueca.*

CERAMICS

Guille García-Hoz

CERAMICS | This iconic ceramicist is known for painted plates and gleaming white urns decorated with animal motifs. ⊠ *Calle Pelayo 43, Chueca* ☎ *91/308–3149* ⊕ *www.guillegarciahoz.com* ⊙ *Closed Sun.* Ⓜ *Chueca.*

FOOD AND WINE

La Productería

FOOD | You'll find organic local cheeses, gourmet tinned food, charcuterie, and natural wine at this pocket-size shop. ⊠ *Calle de Barbieri 21, Chueca* ☎ *60/835–7175* ⊕ *www.laproducteria.com* ⊙ *Closed Mon. and Tues.* Ⓜ *Chueca.*

Poncelet Punto Selecto Quesos

FOOD | At this gourmet cheese bar and shop, you can find more than 120 different cheeses from all over Spain as well as some 300 others. Marmalades, wines, and other assorted cheese accompaniments are available. ⊠ *Calle de Argensola 27, Chueca* ☎ *91/308–0221* ⊕ *www.poncelet.es* ⊙ *Closed Sun.* Ⓜ *Alonso Martínez.*

Malasaña

Malasaña has a youthful, off-beat pulse rivaled only, perhaps, by Lavapiés, its more multicultural counterpart. Formerly called Barrio de las Maravillas, the neighborhood is centered on Plaza de Dos de Mayo, which commemorates the May 2 uprising against French occupation in 1808. Manuela Malasaña, for whom the barrio is named, was a martyr in the conflict. At the end of the 20th century, Malasaña emerged as an emblem of the Movida Madrileña, its rough-and-ready streets featuring prominently in pop culture thanks to music and film icons like Alaska, Mecano, Hombres G, and Pedro Almodóvar. These days the neighborhood is far cleaner and less rambunctious than it was in its cultural heyday, thanks to massive waves of gentrification in the early 2000s and 2010s, but its rebellious spirit lives on—head to Plaza de Dos de Mayo any weekend night, and you'll see crowds of locals flouting open container laws.

◉ Sights

Palacio de Liria (*Liria Palace*)
HISTORIC HOME | In 2019, this working palace belonging to the House of Alba, one of Spain's most powerful noble families, formally opened to the public. Its sumptuous halls and creaky passages are hung with works selected from what many consider to be Spain's finest private art collection—you'll spot Titians, Rubens, Velázquezes, and other instantly recognizable paintings. In the library, Columbus's diaries from his voyage to the so-called New World are on display as well as the first Spanish-language Bible and other priceless official documents. The Neoclassical palace was built in the 18th century but was bombed to smithereens during the Spanish Civil War (only the facade survived), its works thankfully safeguarded during the conflict. The Duchess of Alba oversaw the reconstruction of the palace to its precise original specifications. Visits are by tour only, but if online tickets are sold out, try your luck as a walk-in. ⊠ *Calle de la Princesa 20, Malasaña* ☎ *91/230–2200* ⊕ *www.palaciodeliria.com* 🎫 *€15 (includes tour)* Ⓜ *Ventura Rodríguez.*

🍴 Restaurants

★ Bar La Gloria
$ | **SPANISH** | **FAMILY** | Your reward for overlooking the soulless Ikea furnishings of this family-run dinette is honest home-cooked food served at exceptionally reasonable prices for the neighborhood. Try Cordoban-style *flamenquines* (ham-and-cheese-stuffed pork), salmon tartare, or (on Sunday) a crave-worthy paella Valenciana. Reservations are a must for Sunday lunch; call ahead to book a table and preorder your paella. **Known for:** local crowd; budget weekday prix fixes; Sunday paella. **$** *Average main: €11* ⊠ *Calle del Noviciado 2, Malasaña* ☎ *91/083–1401* ⊕ *www.barlagloria.es* ⊗ *Closed Mon. No dinner Sun.* Ⓜ *Noviciado.*

Bodega de la Ardosa
$ | **SPANISH** | A 19th-century *bodega* (wine vendor), with barrel tables and dusty gewgaws hanging from the walls, Bodega de la Ardosa is a welcome anachronism in modern Malasaña and a tourist magnet for good reason. The bar's claim to fame—and the dish madrileños make special trips for—is its award-winning *tortilla española*, or Spanish omelet, always warm with a runny center. **Known for:** draft vermú and unfiltered sherry "en rama"; 100-plus years of history; tortilla española. **$** *Average main: €13* ⊠ *Calle Colón 13, Malasaña* ☎ *91/521–4979* ⊕ *www.laardosa.es* Ⓜ *Tribunal.*

★ Casa Macareno
$$ | **TAPAS** | **FAMILY** | Whether you pull up a stool at at the marble bar or sit down for a soup-to-nuts feast in the azulejo-lined dining room, you're in for some of Madrid's finest traditional tapas with a twist here. Madrileños come from far and wide to share heaped plates of *ensaladilla rusa* (tuna-flecked potato salad), a house specialty, as well as textbook-perfect croquetas and hefty steaks served with sherry gravy and house-cut fries. **Known for:** over-and-above service; hidden gem in Malasaña; dependably exceptional old-school tapas. **$** *Average main: €16* ⊠ *Calle de San Vicente Ferrer 44, Malasaña* ☎ *91/166–0921* ⊕ *www.casamacareno.com* Ⓜ *Tribunal, Noviciado.*

La Colmada
$ | **TAPAS** | The first thing you'll notice about this teeny seafood-centric tapas bar is its bright blue walls, a nod to the sea. Sure, you could cobble together a full meal from the menu of delectable cheeses, cured sausages, hams, and *conservas* (canned seafood; seek out La Pureza and Ana María brands), but La Colmada is better suited to casual, booze-fueled snacking. **Known for:** jovial atmosphere; top-quality canned food; affordable Spanish wines. **$** *Average main: €10* ⊠ *Calle del Espíritu Santo*

19, Malasaña ☎ *91/017–6579* ⊕ *www.lacolmada.com* Ⓜ *Tribunal.*

☕ Coffee and Quick Bites

★ Misión Café

$ | CAFÉ | From the owners of Hola Coffee, Madrid's preeminent third-wave coffee shop, is this uber-trendy, roomier outpost two blocks from Gran Vía. Beyond the single-origin espressos and other classics made from roasted-in-house beans, there are warming chai lattes, shrubs, and (seasonal) cold brew. **Known for:** cool-kid hangout; killer pastries; complex brews made with roasted-in-Madrid beans. ⓢ *Average main: €10* ⊠ *Calle de los Reyes 5, Malasaña* ☎ *91/064–0059* ⊕ *www.mision.cafe* Ⓜ *Noviciado, Plaza de España.*

Toma Café

$ | CAFÉ | The originator of Madrid's third-wave coffee revolution, Toma is a Malasaña institution and a favorite among expats and coffee-geek locals. After satisfying your cold brew, flat white, or pour-over cravings, indulge in any of the delicious open-face *tostas*. **Known for:** major expat hangout; always busy; excellent coffee selection. ⓢ *Average main: €8* ⊠ *Calle de la Palma 49, Malasaña* ☎ *91/704–9344* ⊕ *www.tomacafe.es* Ⓜ *Noviciado.*

▼ Nightlife

BARS

V Manneken

BARS | V Manneken is downright deb-onair. Cut-glass decanters filled with Scotch sit on the marble bar top; gold-framed oil paintings accent the walls; and yellowed, out-of-print books sit on tables for you to thumb through while sipping staunchly classic cocktails like Cream Fizzes, Last Words, and Tom Collinses. ⊠ *Calle Marqués de Sta. Ana 30, Malasaña* ☎ *61/564–2480* Ⓜ *Tribunal.*

DANCE CLUBS

Tupper Ware

DANCE CLUBS | Throw on a T-shirt and a pair of ripped jeans and fist-pump the night away at this alternative rock and indie bar that blasts throwback cult classics 'til 3 am. ⊠ *Corredera Alta de San Pablo 26, Malasaña* ☎ *91/446–4204* Ⓜ *Tribunal.*

⬮ Shopping

BOUTIQUES AND FASHION

Sportivo

MEN'S CLOTHING | Time to bust out the big bucks—Sportivo is the best menswear boutique in the city, with two floors of hand-picked garments by the buzziest designers out of Spain, France, Japan, and beyond. ⊠ *Calle Conde Duque 20, Malasaña* ☎ *91/542–5661* ⊕ *www.sportivostore.com.*

Barrio de las Letras

Barrio de las Letras (just "Letras" to locals) is known for its charming balco-nied buildings and electric restaurant and bar scene. It's named for the writers and playwrights of the Spanish Golden Age who lived here. Once a *castizo* (Madrid jargon for "authentic") part of town, Letras is now packed with well-to-do tourists and Madrid's nouveau riche. In short, it's a *scene.*

Letras is a historical (read: unofficial) neighborhood that technically belongs to the district of Cortes, but madrileños use its colloquial, more descriptive name. At the heart of the barrio is Plaza de Santa Ana with its noble buildings, iconic theater, and crowded tapas bars, though you'll see more locals wining and dining on and around the pedestrianized Calle de Huertas. As you explore, remember to look down—sidewalks here bear quotes in bronze from the neighborhood's one-time denizens—Quevedo, Góngora, Lope de Vega, and Cervantes, to name a few.

The vertical outdoor garden is a stunning element of the CaixaForum cultural center. The sculpture in front of the building is changed periodically.

 Sights

CaixaForum

ART MUSEUM | Swiss architects Jacques Herzog and Pierre de Meuron (who designed London's Tate Modern) converted an early-20th-century power station into a stunning arts complex that arguably turns Madrid's "Golden Triangle" of art museums into a quadrilateral. Belonging to one of the country's wealthiest foundations (La Caixa bank), the structure seems to float above the sloped public plaza, with a tall vertical garden designed by French botanist Patrick Blanc on its northern side contrasting with a geometric rust-color roof. Inside, the soaring exhibition halls display ancient as well as contemporary art including pieces from La Caixa's proprietary collection. The Vilaplana restaurant on the fourth floor has good views. Visits are by online ticketing only. ⊠ *Paseo del Prado 36, Barrio de las Letras* ☎ *91/330–7300* ⊕ *www. caixaforum.es* ✉ *€6* Ⓜ *Estación del Arte.*

★ Museo Thyssen-Bornemisza

ART MUSEUM | The far-reaching collection of the Thyssen's almost 1,000 paintings traces the history of Western art with examples from every important movement, from the 13th-century Italian Gothic through 20th-century American pop art. The works were gathered from the 1920s to the 1980s by Swiss industrialist Baron Hans Heinrich Thyssen-Bornemisza and his father and the museum, opened in 1992, occupies the spacious late-18th-century Villahermosa Palace. The baron donated the entire collection to Spain in 1993, and a renovation in 2004 increased the number of paintings on display to include the baroness's personal collection (considered of lesser quality). Critics have described the museum's paintings as the minor works of major artists and the major works of minor artists, but the collection still traces the development of Western humanism as no other in the world. It includes works by Hans Holbein, Gilbert Stuart, many Impressionists

Barrio de las Letras

and Postimpressionists, and a number of German Expressionist paintings. ✉ *Paseo del Prado 8, Barrio de las Letras* ☎ *91/369–0151* 🌐 *www.museothyssen.org* 🎫 *€13* [M] *Banco de España.*

Plaza de Santa Ana

PLAZA/SQUARE | This plaza was the heart of the theater district in the 17th century—the Golden Age of Spanish literature—and is now one of Madrid's many happening nightlife centers. A statue of 17th-century playwright Pedro Calderón de la Barca faces the Teatro Español, where other literary legends such as Lope de Vega, Tirso de Molina, Pedro Calderón de la Barca, and Ramón del Valle-Inclán released some of their plays. Opposite the theater, beside the ME by Meliá hotel, is the diminutive Plaza del Ángel, with one of Madrid's best jazz clubs, Café Central. Cervecería Alemana, a favorite haunt of Hemingway, is on the southeast corner and makes phenomenally tender fried calamari. ✉ *Barrio de las Letras* [M] *Sol, Sevilla.*

🍴 Restaurants

Amano

$$ | TAPAS |"A mano" means "by hand" in Spanish, and lest this experimental white-walled tapas and wine bar (opened in 2019) come across as pretentious, there's an entire section of the menu devoted to finger food. Whet your appetite with one-bite wonders like eggplant salad on Lebanese flatbread, then settle in for heftier plates like salt cod with spinach, pine nuts, olives, and tomatoes. **Known for:** stylish minimalist interiors; varied wine list with French selections; innovative vegetable-driven tapas. [$] *Average main: €18* ✉ *Pl. de Matute 4, Barrio de las Letras* ☎ *91/527–7970* 🌐 *www.amanomadrid.com* [M] *Antón Martín.*

★ Casa González

$ | SPANISH | This gourmet shop (est. 1931) contains a cozy bar where you can sample most of its fare including canned asparagus, charcuterie, anchovies, and a varied, well-priced selection of Spanish cheeses and wines. It also serves good, inexpensive breakfasts. **Known for:** quaint setting; pickled olives; wines and cheeses. [$] *Average main: €6* ✉ *Calle León 12, Barrio de las Letras* ☎ *91/429–5618* 🌐 *www.casagonzalez.es* [M] *Antón Martín.*

El Barril de las Letras

$$$ | SEAFOOD | Seafood lovers shouldn't miss this modern, rustic-chic *marisquería* with original wrought-iron columns, white tablecloths, and ample alfresco seating. The griddled prawns from Dénia are always a treat, as is the cloud-like roasted sole and any number of rice dishes. **Known for:** outdoor dining; impeccable seafood; romantic ambience. [$] *Average main: €25* ✉ *Calle de Cervantes 28, Barrio de las Letras* ☎ *91/186–3632* 🌐 *www.barrildelasletras.com* [M] *Antón Martín.*

Gofio

$$$$ | FUSION | Savor a rare taste of Canary Island cuisine—with quite a few twists—at this envelope-pushing restaurant helmed by Canarian chef Safe Cruz that was awarded a Michelin star in 2019. A recent tasting menu started with olives marinated in green *mojo,* a garlicky cilantro-and-parsley sauce ground in a mortar, and continued with crispy goat tacos or Gomero cheese (smoked tableside) before finishing with *gofio* ice cream, made with the Canarian cornflour from which the restaurant takes its name. **Known for:** gorgeous, uncontrived plating; smoky volcanic wines; Canarian "fusion". [$] *Average main: €50* ✉ *Calle Lope de Vega 9, Barrio de las Letras* ☎ *91/599–4404* 🌐 *www.gofiorestaurant.com* 🕒 *Closed Mon. and Tues.* [M] *Antón Martín.*

La Sanabresa

$ | SPANISH | FAMILY | Most budget prix fixes in Madrid are limited to lunch service, but La Sanabresa offers budget three-course dinner service as well. Choose from a menu of over 20 appetizers and over 40 entrées that reads like a highlight reel of grandmotherly Spanish cuisine: gazpacho, *ensaladilla rusa*, fried anchovies, chicken cutlets, and on and on. **Known for:** satisfying soups and stews; prix fixe menus are a steal; trusty traditional holdout in a gentrified area. $ *Average main: €12* ✉ *Calle del Amor de Dios 12, Barrio de las Letras* ☎ *91/429–0338* ☾ *Closed Sun.* Ⓜ *Antón Martín.*

Taberna de la Dolores

$ | TAPAS | A lively corner bar (established in 1908) with a colorful *trencadís* tiled facade, this is a solid spot for a cold beer and a nosh after visiting the nearby museums. Try the *matrimonio* ("marriage") tapa, which weds a pickled and a cured anchovy on a slice of crusty baguette. **Known for:** mixed crowd of foreigners and locals; refreshing cañas; affordable, no-nonsense tapas. $ *Average main: €12* ✉ *Pl. de Jesús 4, Barrio de las Letras* ☎ *91/429–2243* Ⓜ *Antón Martín.*

★ Taberna La Elisa

$$ | TAPAS | The old-fashioned *azulejo* walls, painted red facade, and squat wooden barstools might fool you into thinking this newcomer is any old tavern, but behind the swinging door, cooks are busy plating novel takes on tapas that you didn't know needed improving. Take the crispy pig ear, doused in the usual spicy *brava*sauce—it gets an unorthodox hit of freshness from tarragon-packed *mojo verde*. **Known for:** trendy crowd; flavor-bomb tapas; Andalusian-style decor. $ *Average main: €16* ✉ *Calle de Santa María 42, Barrio de las Letras* ☎ *91/421–6409* ⊕ *www.eltriciclo.es/la-elisa* Ⓜ *Antón Martín.*

Triciclo

$$$ | TAPAS | Triciclo serves inventive Spanish-style *bistronomie*—think baby Asturian favas with mushrooms and seaweed and spot prawn ravioli with saffron and borage. This may be the only restaurant in town that serves raciones in one-third portions as well as half and full ones—ideal for creating your own

tasting menu whether at the bar or in the dining room. **Known for:** tapas with a modern twist; top-quality ingredients; excellent service. $ *Average main: €23* ✉ *Calle Santa María 28, Barrio de las Letras* ☎ *91/024–4798* ⊕ *www.eltriciclo. es* ☾ *Closed Sun.* Ⓜ *Antón Martín.*

★ Vinoteca Moratín

$$ | SPANISH | You'd be hard-pressed to find a more romantic restaurant than this snug wine bar with a rotating menu of a dozen or so dishes and eclectic Spanish wines. Antique wooden tables are tucked among bookshelves and wine cabinets, and fresh flowers grace the entryway and wait stations. **Known for:** Spanish wine list with quirky small-production bottles; intimate ambience; seasonal bistro fare. $ *Average main: €17* ✉ *Calle de Moratín 36, Barrio de las Letras* ☎ *91/127–6085* ⊕ *www.vinotecamoratin.com* ☾ *Closed Sun. and Mon.* Ⓜ *Antón Martín.*

Coffee and Quick Bites

Chocolat Madrid

$ | CAFÉ | FAMILY | Always crisp and never greasy—that's the mark of a well-made churro, and Madrid Chocolat's piping-hot baskets of fried dough always hit the spot. **Known for:** fast service; city's best churros; bright and comfortable dining area. $ *Average main: €5* ✉ *Calle de Santa María 30, Barrio de las Letras* ⊕ *www.chocolatmadrid.com* Ⓜ *Antón Martín.*

🛏 Hotels

Catalonia Puerta del Sol

$$ | HOTEL | The regal cobblestone corridor leading to the reception desk, the atrium with walls made of granite ashlars, and the magnificent wooden staircase (presided over by a lion statue) reveal this building's 18th-century origins. **Pros:** room service; spacious rooms; grand, quiet building. **Cons:** rooms and common areas lack character; rather uncharming street; smoking permitted in the courtyard. $ *Rooms from: €130* ✉ *Calle de*

Atocha 23, Barrio de las Letras ☎ 91/369–7171 ⊕ www.hoteles-catalonia.es ⇌ 63 rooms ⧉ No Meals Ⓜ Tirso de Molina.

DoubleTree by Hilton Madrid-Prado
$$ | HOTEL | This DoubleTree may appear corporate, but any stuffiness is mitigated by a warm staff eager to help with every need. **Pros:** relaxing earth-tone accents; one of the city's best Japanese restaurants; excellent in-room amenities. **Cons:** no valet parking; dull bar; no sense of place. Ⓢ Rooms from: €174 ⊠ Calle de San Agustín 3, Barrio de las Letras ☎ 91/360–0820 ⊕ www.hilton.com ⇌ 61 rooms ⧉ No Meals Ⓜ Antón Martín.

Gran Hotel Inglés
$$$$ | HOTEL | This legendary hotel, inaugurated in 1853, is the oldest in Madrid—and after a long, painstaking renovation, it reopened in 2018 to great fanfare. **Pros:** one of the city's most iconic hotels; magazine-cover-worthy design; all rooms at least 280 square feet. **Cons:** pricey food and beverages; stairs to get to some rooms; occasional weekend street noise. Ⓢ Rooms from: €343 ⊠ Calle Echegaray 8, Barrio de las Letras ☎ 91/360–0001 ⊕ www.granhotelingles.com ⇌ 48 rooms ⧉ No Meals Ⓜ Sevilla.

Hotel Catalonia Las Cortes
$$ | HOTEL | In a late-18th-century palace formerly owned by the Duke of Noblejas, this hotel, a few yards from Plaza Santa Ana, still bears traces of opulence and grandeur. **Pros:** big walk-in showers; gorgeous architectural details; tastefully decorated rooms. **Cons:** no bar; no gym, pool, or spa; common areas are rather dull. Ⓢ Rooms from: €150 ⊠ Calle del Prado 6, Barrio de las Letras ☎ 91/389–6051 ⊕ www.cataloniahotels.com/en/hotel/catalonia-las-cortes ⇌ 74 rooms ⧉ No Meals Ⓜ Sevilla, Antón Martín.

Hotel Urban
$$$ | HOTEL | A five-minute walk from Puerta del Sol and the Retiro, Hotel Urban blends buttoned-up business-y aesthetics with tropical accents in the form of Papua New Guinean artifacts and other rare museum-grade works. **Pros:** stellar à la carte breakfasts; award-winning restaurants by two celebrity chefs; roof deck that's a destination in itself. **Cons:** interiors stuck in the early 2000s and show wear in spots; tiny gym with no treadmill; smallish rooms with so-so soundproofing. Ⓢ Rooms from: €223 ⊠ Carrera de San Jerónimo 34, Barrio de las Letras ☎ 91/787–7770 ⊕ www.derbyhotels.com ⇌ 103 rooms ⧉ No Meals Ⓜ Sevilla.

★ ME Madrid Reina Victoria
$$$ | HOTEL | In an unbeatable location, this modern hotel bears a few reminders of the era when bullfighters would convene here before setting off to Las Ventas—bulls' heads hang in the lounge and some abstract pictures of bullfighting are scattered around, but the old flair has been superseded by cutting-edge amenities. **Pros:** cool, clubby vibe; rooftop bar boasts great views of city; buzzy restaurant. **Cons:** key cards demagnetize easily; plaza-facing rooms can be noisy; some rooms are cramped. Ⓢ Rooms from: €214 ⊠ Pl. Santa Ana 14, Barrio de las Letras ☎ 91/531–4500 ⊕ www.melia.com ⇌ 192 rooms ⧉ No Meals Ⓜ Sol.

NH Collection Madrid Suecia
$$ | HOTEL | The building housing the NH Collection Madrid Suecia was once home to Ernest Hemingway and Che Guevara; today's guests are decidedly tamer, but the retro aesthetic lives on in the hotel's brown velvet couches, towering tropical plants, and suave concierges. **Pros:** rooftop bar with great views; nine-minute walk from Prado Museum; renovated rooms. **Cons:** overpriced restaurant; robes and slippers not provided in entry-level rooms; windowless gym. Ⓢ Rooms from: €170 ⊠ Calle del Marqués de Casa Riera 4, Barrio de las Letras ☎ 91/200–0570 ⊕ www.nh-hotels.com ⇌ 123 rooms ⧉ No Meals Ⓜ Banco de España.

NH Collection Paseo del Prado

$$ | HOTEL | In a turn-of-the-20th-century palace overlooking Plaza de Neptuno, this hotel preserves the building's erstwhile grandeur with canopy beds, gold-framed mirrors, striped wallpaper, and wing chairs. **Pros:** "lazy Sunday checkout" at 3 pm; within the Golden Triangle of museums; gym with panoramic views. **Cons:** inconsistent food at Estado Puro; need to upgrade to get good views; dated decor. $ *Rooms from: €145* ✉ *Pl. Cánovas del Castillo 4, Barrio de las Letras* ☎ *91/330–2400* ⊕ *www.nh-hoteles.com* ⤵ *115 rooms* ⦿ *No Meals* Ⓜ *Banco de España.*

★ Room Mate Alba

$$ | HOTEL | Opened in 2019, Alba occupies a 17th-century nobleman's home on Letras's most popular pedestrianized street. **Pros:** perks like gym, bar, and free Wi-Fi portal; snazzy property with a youthful feel; breakfast till a cool 12 pm. **Cons:** some street noise in exterior-facing rooms; standard rooms are small; patterns everywhere might be jarring to some. $ *Rooms from: €158* ✉ *Calle Huertas 16, Barrio de las Letras* ☎ *91/080–6471* ⊕ *www.room-mate-hotels.com* ⤵ *80 rooms* ⦿ *No Meals* Ⓜ *Antón Martín.*

Room Mate Alicia

$$ | HOTEL | Room Mate Alicia's all-white lobby, with curving walls, backlit ceiling panels, and gilded columns oozes early 2000s, but its prime location and competitive rates make up for the slightly dated aesthetics. **Pros:** laid-back atmosphere; brightly colored rooms; good value. **Cons:** zero-privacy bathroom spaces; standard rooms are small; no restaurant or gym. $ *Rooms from: €143* ✉ *Calle Prado 2, Barrio de las Letras* ☎ *91/389–6095* ⊕ *www.room-matehoteles.com* ⤵ *34 rooms* ⦿ *No Meals* Ⓜ *Sevilla.*

Urban Sea Atocha 113

$ | HOTEL | A metropolitan outpost of the Blue Sea resort chain, Urban Sea Atocha 113 is a basic 36-room hotel just north of the eponymous railway station. **Pros:** rooftop terrace with gorgeous views; single rooms ideal for solo travelers; equidistant between Barrio de las Letras and Lavapiés. **Cons:** exterior rooms facing Calle Atocha are pricey; bare-bones services; in-room sinks. $ *Rooms from: €100* ✉ *Calle Atocha 113, Barrio de las Letras* ☎ *91/369–2895* ⊕ *www.bluesea-hotels.com* ⤵ *36 rooms* ⦿ *No Meals* Ⓜ *Estación del Arte.*

Westin Palace

$$$$ | HOTEL | An iconic hotel situated inside the "Golden Triangle" (the district connecting the Prado, Reina Sofía, and Thyssen museums), the Westin Palace is known for its unbeatable location, stately facade, and classical decor. **Pros:** rooms have USB ports and antifog mirrors; 24-hour gym with adjoining roof deck; historic grand hotel. **Cons:** last renovation won't meet design lovers' expectations; overpriced; standard rooms face a backstreet. $ *Rooms from: €312* ✉ *Pl. de las Cortés 7, Barrio de las Letras* ☎ *91/360–8000* ⊕ *www.palacemadrid.com* ⤵ *467 rooms* ⦿ *No Meals* Ⓜ *Banco de España, Sevilla.*

🍸 Nightlife

BARS

La Venencia

WINE BARS | This dusty sherry-only bar hasn't changed a lick since the Spanish Civil War, from its no-tipping policy to its salty waiters to its chalked bar tabs. The establishment is named for the tool used to extract sherry through the bunghole of a barrel. No photography allowed. ✉ *Calle de Echegaray 7, Barrio de las Letras* ☎ *91/429–7313* Ⓜ *Sol.*

Radio

COCKTAIL LOUNGES | This sceney bar in the ME Madrid Reina Victoria is split between a bottom-floor lounge and a more exclusive rooftop terrace with 360-degree views—a boon to chic summer revelers both local and international. The doorman planted outside means you shouldn't dress too casual. ✉ *ME Madrid Reina Victoria, Pl. de Santa Ana 14, Barrio de las Letras* ☎ *91/445–6886* ⊕ *www.melia.com* Ⓜ *Antón Martín.*

★ Salmon Guru

COCKTAIL LOUNGES | Regularly featured on best-of lists, Salmon Guru is Madrid's—and perhaps Spain's—most innovative *coctelería*. Come here to impress and to geek out over eye-popping concoctions like the Chipotle Chillón, made with mezcal, absinthe, and chipotle syrup. The *nueva cocina* tapas are almost as impressive as the drinks. ✉ *Calle de Echegaray 21, Barrio de las Letras* ☎ *91/000–6185* ⊕ *www.salmonguru.es* ⊘ *Closed Mon.* Ⓜ *Antón Martín.*

Viva Madrid

COCKTAIL LOUNGES | The Argentine celebrity mixologist behind the bar Salmon Guru has converted one of Madrid's oldest tabernas, built in 1856, into a see-and-be-seen cocktail hot spot. The building's architectural bones remain, from the carved-wood bar to the arched doorways to the tiled walls, but the rest, particularly the flamboyantly garnished drinks and sceney crowd they attract, feels distinctly current. ✉ *Calle Manuel Fernández y González 7, Barrio de las Letras* ☎ *91/605–9774* Ⓜ *Sevilla, Antón Martín.*

DANCE CLUBS

Azúcar

DANCE CLUBS | Salsa dancing is a fixture of Madrid nightlife. Even if you don't have the guts to twirl and shake with the pros on the dance floor, you'll be almost as entertained sipping a mojito on the sidelines. Entry with two cocktail vouchers costs €12. ✉ *Calle de Atocha 107, Barrio de las Letras* ☎ *91/429–6208* ⊘ *Closed Sun.–Wed.* Ⓜ *Estación del Arte.*

★ Teatro Kapital

DANCE CLUBS | Madrid's most famous nightclub, Kapital has seven floors—each of which plays a different type of music (spun by top local and international DJs,

of course)—and room for 2,000 partiers, plus a small movie theater and rooftop terrace. Dress to impress for this one: no sneakers, shorts, or tanks allowed. VIP tables overlooking the dance floor (approximately €170 for four people) are a worthwhile splurge if you can swing it. ✉ *Calle Atocha 125, Barrio de las Letras* ☎ *91/420–2906* ⊕ *www.grupo-kapital.com* Ⓜ *Estación del Arte.*

MUSIC CLUBS

★ Café Central

LIVE MUSIC | Madrid's best-known jazz venue is swanky, and the musicians are often internationally known. Performances are usually 9–11 nightly, and tickets can be bought at the door or online. ✉ *Pl. de Ángel 10, Barrio de las Letras* ☎ *91/369–4143* ⊕ *www.cafecentralmadrid.com* Ⓜ *Antón Martín.*

👜 Shopping

BOUTIQUES AND FASHION

★ Andrés Gallardo

JEWELRY & WATCHES | Madrid's porcelain whisperer, Gallardo fashions second-hand shards and custom-made porcelain elements into runway-ready jewelry and accessories. ✉ *Calle de San Pedro 8, Barrio de las Letras* ☎ *91/053–5352* ⊕ *www.andresgallardo.com* ⊘ *Closed Sun.* Ⓜ *Antón Martín.*

The Concrete Company

MIXED CLOTHING | Fashion designer Fernando García de la Calera is redefining what it means to be a tailor by custom-making garments out of materials usually associated with streetwear, such as denim and canvas. His creations are surprisingly affordable. ✉ *Calle de San Pedro 10, Barrio de las Letras* ☎ *91/242–1803* ⊕ *www.concretemadrid.com* ⊘ *Closed Sun. and Mon.* Ⓜ *Antón Martín.*

Elisa & Eduardo Rivera

MIXED CLOTHING | A block off Plaza de Santa Ana, this is the flagship store of two young Spanish designers with clothes and accessories for both men and women. All garments are made by hand in an atelier 40 minutes north of Madrid. Other stores can be found on Calle Sagasta 4 and Calle Clavel 4. ⊠ *Pl. del Ángel 4, Barrio de las Letras* ☎ *91/843–5852* ⊕ *www.eduardorivera. es* Ⓜ *Sol.*

Santacana

OTHER SPECIALTY STORE | Keep your hands warm—and stylish—during Madrid's chilly winters with a pair of custom hand-made gloves by Santacana, a family-run business that's been open since 1896. ⊠ *Calle Huertas 1, Barrio de las Letras* ☎ *91/704–9670* ⊕ *www.santacana.es* Ⓜ *Antón Martín.*

Retiro

Straighten your tie and zhuzh your hair— you've arrived in the Madrid equivalent of New York's Upper East Side or London's Kensington: a charming, tree-lined play-ground for the rich complete with luxury apartments, Michelin-starred restaurants, and one of Europe's most scenic parks, Parque del Buen Retiro.

But get off the main shopping streets and you'll see that these districts are not all glitz and glam. East and south of the park, in Retiro, you'll find upper-mid-dle-class neighborhoods like Ibiza and Pacífico with their fair share of modest apartments and mom-and-pop bars and restaurants. And in addition to the epon-ymously named park, the Retiro district holds the prestigious Museo del Prado, an essential stop on any Madrid itinerary. The sliver of Retiro real estate called Paseo del Arte, sandwiched between the western side of the park and the Paseo del Prado, is where you'll find some of the city's most exclusive and expensive homes.

◉ Sights

Cuesta de Moyano

PEDESTRIAN MALL | Home to Europe's most expansive permanent book fair since 1925, this pedestrian avenue has around 30 wooden stalls filled with new and second-hand books. In addition to being a pleasant street to stroll—it connects the Paseo del Prado avenue near Atocha station with Madrid's Buen Retiro park—this is also a good place to find collectible and first-edition books. ⊠ *Cuesta de Moyano, Retiro* ⊕ *www. cuestamoyano.es.*

Estación de Atocha

TRAIN/TRAIN STATION | Madrid's main train station is a steel-and-glass hangar built in the late 19th century by Alberto Palacio Elissague, who became famous for his work with Ricardo Velázquez in the cre-ation of the Palacio de Cristal (Glass Pal-ace) in Madrid's Parque del Buen Retiro. Today, following renovations by architect Rafael Moneo, the station's main hall resembles a greenhouse; it's filled with tropical trees and contains a busy turtle pool, a magnet for kids. ⊠ *Paseo de Ato-cha, Retiro* ☎ *91/243–2323* Ⓜ *Estación del Arte, Atocha RENFE.*

Fuente de Cibeles (*Cybele Fountain*)

FOUNTAIN | The Plaza de Cibeles, where three of Madrid's most affluent districts (Centro, Retiro, and Salamanca) inter-sect, is both an epicenter of municipal grandeur and a crash course in Spanish architecture. Two palaces, Buenavista and Linares (baroque and baroque revival, respectively), sit on the northerly corners of the plaza and are dwarfed by the ornate Palacio de Cibeles. In the center of the plaza sits one of Madrid's most defining symbols, the Cybele Fountain, a depiction of the Roman goddess of the Earth driving a lion-drawn chariot. During the civil war, patriotic madrileños risked life and limb to sandbag it as Franco's Nationalist aircraft bombed the city. ⊠ *Retiro* Ⓜ *Banco de España.*

You can rent rowboats at the lake in the Parque del Buen Retiro; it's a great way to cool off in the summer.

★ **Museo del Prado** (*Prado Museum*)
ART MUSEUM | When the Prado was commissioned by King/Mayor Carlos III, in 1785, it was as a natural science museum. By the time the building was completed in 1819, its purpose had changed to exhibiting the art gathered by Spanish royalty since the time of Ferdinand and Isabella. The Prado's jewels are its works by the nation's three great masters: Goya, Velázquez, and El Greco, though the museum also holds masterpieces by Flemish, Dutch, German, French, and Italian artists, collected when their lands were part of the Spanish Empire. The most famous canvas of all, Velázquez's *Las Meninas* (*The Maids of Honor*), combines a self-portrait of the artist with a mirror reflection of the king and queen. Among Goya's early masterpieces are portraits of the family of King Carlos IV; later works include his famous Black Paintings. Other highlights include the *Garden of Earthly Delights* by Hieronymus Bosch and two of El Greco's greatest works, *The Resurrection* and *The Adoration of the Shepherds*.

✉ *Paseo del Prado, Retiro* ☎ *91/330–2800* ⊕ *www.museodelprado.es* ✉ *€15 (permanent collection free Mon.–Sat. 6–8 pm, Sun. 5–7 pm)* Ⓜ *Banco de España, Estación del Arte.*

Museo Nacional de Artes Decorativas
ART MUSEUM | This palatial building showcases 70,000 items including textiles, furniture, jewelry, ceramics, glass, crystal, and metalwork. The collection, displayed in chronological order, starts with medieval and Renaissance items on the first floor and ends with 18th- and 19th-century pieces on the top floor. The ground floor rotates temporary exhibitions and avant-garde works. This museum can be seen as part of the Abono Cinco Palacios, a €12 pass that grants access to five mansion-museums over a 10-day period. ✉ *Montalbán 12, Retiro* ☎ *91/532–6499* ⊕ *mnartesdecorativas. mcu.es* ✉ *€3 (free Thurs. after 5, Sun. all day)* ⊙ *Closed Mon.* Ⓜ *Retiro.*

Palacio de Cibeles (*Cybele Palace*)
VIEWPOINT | This ornate building on the southeast side of Plaza de la Cibeles,

built at the start of the 20th century and formerly called Palacio de Comunicaciones, is a massive stone compound of French, Viennese, and traditional Spanish influences. It first served as the city's main post office and, after renovations, is now an administrative building housing the mayor's office, a cultural center called CentroCentro (a pleasant place to study or work), several exhibition halls, dining options (on the second and sixth floors), and a rooftop lookout. ✉ *Pl. de Cibeles, Retiro* ☎ *91/480–0008* ⊕ *www. centrocentro.org* ⊗ *Closed Mon.* 🎫 *Free, Mirador Madrid €3* Ⓜ *Banco de España.*

★ **Parque del Buen Retiro** (*El Retiro*)
CITY PARK | FAMILY | Once the private playground of royalty, Madrid's crowning park is a vast expanse of green encompassing formal gardens, fountains, lakes, exhibition halls, children's play areas, outdoor cafés, and a puppet theater (shows on Saturday at 1 and on Sunday at 1, 6, and 7). The park, especially lively on weekends, also holds a book fair in May and occasional flamenco concerts in summer. From the entrance at the Puerta de Alcalá, head straight toward the center to find the Estanque (lake), presided over by a grandiose equestrian statue of King Alfonso XII. The 19th-century Palacio de Cristal (Glass Palace) was built to house exotic plants—and, horrifically, actual tribesmen displayed as a "human zoo"—from the Philippines. The Rosaleda (Rose Garden) is bursting with color and heady with floral scents for most of the summer. Madrileños claim that a statue called the *Ángel Caído* (*Fallen Angel*) is the only one in the world depicting the Prince of Darkness before his fall from grace. ✉ *Puerta de Alcalá, Retiro* 🎫 *Free* Ⓜ *Retiro.*

Puerta de Alcalá
NOTABLE BUILDING | This triumphal arch, today a popular backdrop for photos, was built by Carlos III in 1778 to mark the site of one of the ancient city gates. You can still see numerous bullet and cannonball holes on its exterior, left intentionally as a reminder of Madrid's tumultuous past. ✉ *Calle de Alcalá, Retiro* Ⓜ *Retiro.*

Real Fábrica de Tapices
NOTABLE BUILDING | Tired of previous monarchs' dependency on Belgian and Flemish thread mills and craftsmen, King Felipe V decided to establish the Royal Tapestry Factory in Madrid in 1721. It was originally housed near Alonso Martínez and moved to its current location in 1889. Some of Europe's best artists collaborated on the factory's tapestry designs, the most famous of whom was Goya, who produced a number of works on display at the Prado. The factory, the most renowned of its kind in Europe, is still in operation—you can tour the workshop floor and watch weavers at work. They apply traditional weaving techniques from the 18th and 19th centuries to modern and classic designs—including Goya's. Prebooking online is required, and all visitors get a tour (English tours usually at 12:30 pm weekdays; check website for updates). ✉ *Calle de Fuenterrabía 2, Retiro* ☎ *91/434–0550* ⊕ *www. realfabricadetapices.com* ⊗ *Closed weekends and Aug.* ⚲ *Reservation required* 🎫 *€5* Ⓜ *Menéndez Pelayo, Estación del Arte.*

Real Jardín Botánico (*Royal Botanical Garden*)
GARDEN | FAMILY | You don't have to be a horticulturalist to appreciate the breadth of the exotic plant collection here. Opened in 1781 and emblematic of the Age of Enlightenment, this lush Eden of bonsais, orchids, cacti, and more houses more than 5,000 species of living plants and trees in just 20 acres. Its dried specimens number over a million, and many were brought back from exploratory voyages to the New World. ✉ *Pl. de Murillo 2, Retiro* ☎ *91/420–3017* ⊕ *www.rjb.csic. es* 🎫 *€6* Ⓜ *Estación del Arte.*

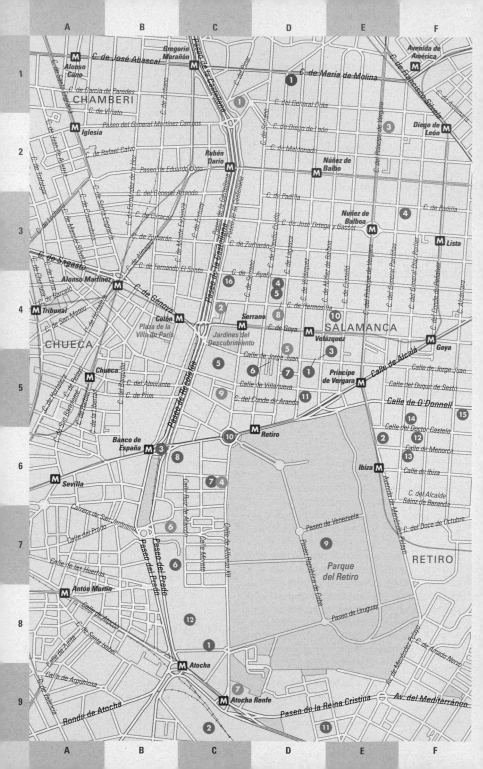

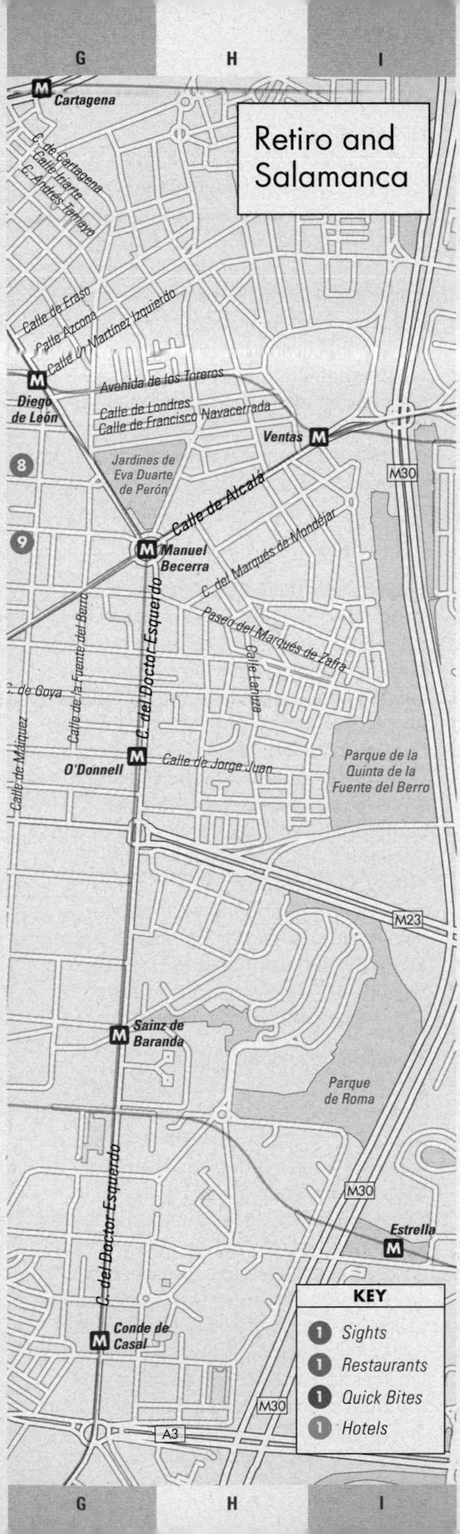

Retiro and Salamanca

KEY
- Sights
- Restaurants
- Quick Bites
- Hotels

🍴 Restaurants

Bar Martín

$ | **SPANISH** | This hole-in-the-wall opened in 1940 serves no-frills Castilian classics like *patatas revolconas* (mashed potatoes with paprika and pork rinds), ham croquettes, and meatballs so good they're often gone before the dinner rush. Don't expect to find a seat unless you go at off hours. **Known for:** affordable Spanish bar food; crowds on weekends; outdoor parkside dining. [$] *Average main: €11* ✉ *Av. de Menéndez Pelayo 17, Retiro* ☎ *91/573–1167* [M] *Ibiza.*

La Castela

$$ | **TAPAS** | **FAMILY** | Traditional taverns with tin-top bars, vermouth on tap, and no-nonsense waiters are a dying breed in Madrid, but this one, just a couple of blocks from the Parque del Buen Retiro, has stood the test of time. It's always busy with locals clamoring over plates of sautéed wild mushrooms, tuna ventresca and roasted pepper salad, and stewed chickpeas with langoustines. **Known for:** neighborhood crowd; friendly staff; colorfully plated tapas. [$] *Average main: €18* ✉ *Calle Doctor Castelo 22, Retiro* ☎ *91/574–0015* 🌐 *www.restaurantelacastela.com* 🕒 *No dinner Sun.* [M] *Ibiza.*

★ La Catapa

$$$ | **SPANISH** | La Catapa's tapas are classic but never old hat, inventive but never pretentious. The burst-in-your-mouth *croquetas* and garlicky razor clams may lure the crowds, but the hidden gems are in the vegetable section: It's hard to decide between the artichoke *menestra* with crisped jamón, ultracreamy *salmorejo* (gazpacho's richer, more garlicky sibling), and umami-packed seared mushrooms. **Known for:** elevated tapas; decadent cream-filled pastry "cigars"; a Retiro institution. [$] *Average main: €23* ✉ *Calle Menorca 14, Retiro* ☎ *68/614–3823* 🕒 *Closed Sun. dinner, Mon.* [M] *Ibiza.*

La Raquetista

$$ | **FUSION** | A relative newcomer on Retiro's traditional tapas scene, La Raquetista has quickly become known for *nueva cocina* dishes like tuna "pastrami," uni with potato cream, and Segovian suckling pig tacos, all served bar-side or in a snug five-table dining room. **Known for:** unusual Spanish wines; to-die-for torreznos (fried pork rinds); eye-popping fusion tapas. [$] *Average main: €21* ✉ *Calle del Dr. Castelo 19, Retiro* ☎ *91/831–1842* 🌐 *www.laraquetista.com* 🕒 *No dinner Sun.* [M] *Ibiza.*

🛏 Hotels

Hotel Palacio Del Retiro, Autograph Collection

$$$ | **HOTEL** | An early-20th-century palace built for a noble family with extravagant habits (the elevator carried their horses up and down from the rooftop exercise ring), this hotel mixes old-world elegance with modern bells and whistles. **Pros:** within walking distance of the Prado; bathrooms stocked with all sorts of complimentary products; spacious, elegant rooms. **Cons:** cumbersome room keys; lower rooms facing the park can get noisy; pricey breakfast. [$] *Rooms from: €195* ✉ *Calle de Alfonso XII 14, Retiro* ☎ *91/523–7460* 🌐 *www.ac-hotels.com* 🛏 *50 rooms* 🍴 *No Meals* [M] *Retiro.*

Mandarin Oriental Ritz, Madrid

$$$$ | **HOTEL** | A €99-million renovation by Mandarin Oriental, completed in April 2021, brought new life to an aging historical hotel overlooking the Prado Museum, replacing heavy Victorian drapes, wingback chairs, and red carpets with muted whites and beiges with gold accents and minimalist contemporary art. **Pros:** Prado- and Retiro-side location; newly renovated in 2021; celebrity chef restaurant. **Cons:** kinks in services and facilities to iron out; some chain hotel blandness; new interiors lack Spanish art and antiques. [$] *Rooms from: €500* ✉ *Pl. de la Lealtad 5, Retiro* ☎ *91/701–6767*

⊕ www.mandarinoriental.com ⇄ 153 rooms ◯❙ No Meals Ⓜ Banco de España.

Only YOU Atocha

$$ | **HOTEL** | One of the trendiest, most youthful hotels in town, Only YOU Atocha has a swanky high-design lobby, rooftop restaurant, spacious gym, and industrial-chic accommodations. **Pros:** gorgeous designer furniture; cloud-soft beds; intriguing pop-ups and events. **Cons:** ugly views of major intersection; food quality falls short across the board; exterior-facing rooms are very noisy. Ⓢ *Rooms from: €160* ⊠ *Paseo de la Infanta Isabel 13, Retiro* ☎ *91/409–7876* ⊕ *www.onlyyouhotels.com* ⇄ *205 rooms* ◯❙ *No Meals* Ⓜ *Estación del Arte.*

Nightlife

Florida Retiro

GATHERING PLACES | Retiro Park became a nightlife destination in 2016 with the opening of Florida Retiro, a see-and-be-seen leisure complex with six separate spaces: El Pabellón, a white-tablecloth restaurant; La Galería, an informal tapas bar; La Terraza, a chic rooftop terrace; Los Kioscos, an indoor-outdoor bar with live music; La Cúpula, a cocktail bar open late; and La Sala, a tony nightclub that heats up on weekends. ⊠ *Parque del Buen Retiro, Paseo de la República Dominicana 1, Retiro* ☎ *91/827–5275* ⊕ *www.floridaretiro.com* Ⓜ *Ibiza.*

🛍 Shopping

Qava

FOOD | Featuring exclusively Spanish cheeses from small producers, Qava, which opened in 2018, doesn't just source and sell killer *quesos* that make great gifts—it also ages each wheel to perfection in on-site "caves." Sample them in an eight-table tasting area alongside carefully selected wines. The 11 pm closing time means you can work Qava into a tapas crawl or—if you're feeling European—make it a final dessert

stop. ⊠ *Calle del Dr. Castelo 34, Retiro* ☎ *91/853–2853* ⊕ *www.qavadequesos.com* Ⓜ *Ibiza, O'Donnell.*

Salamanca

Salamanca was part of the 19th-century city expansion program called the *Ensanche,* which removed the city walls and created new, gridded neighborhoods. The area was originally intended to provide shelter for the working class, but because of its desirable parkside location, it swiftly became a hot spot for the well-to-do, a legacy that remains as the district contains the most expensive homes per square foot in the country.

Sights

★ Mercado de la Paz

MARKET | Salamanca's gleaming high-end market is a hangar-like food emporium selling everything from wild game to softball-size Calanda peaches to sashimi-grade tuna to the finest *jamón* and canned seafood money can buy. Standout restaurants here include Casa Dani (arguably the city's best Spanish omelet; see separate entry), La Despensa (Venezuelan arepas), and Matteo Cucina Italiana (homemade pastas and risotto). ⊠ *Calle Ayala 28, Salamanca* ☎ *91/435–0743* ⊕ *www.mercadodelapaz.com* ◷ *Closed Sun., Sat. after 4 pm* Ⓜ *Serrano.*

Museo Arqueológico Nacional (*Museum of Archaeology*)

HISTORY MUSEUM | FAMILY | This museum boasts three large floors filled with Spanish relics, artifacts, and treasures ranging from ancient history to the 19th century. Among the highlights are *La Dama de Elche* , the bust of a wealthy 5th-century-BC Iberian woman (notice that her headgear vaguely resembles the mantillas and hair combs still associated with traditional Spanish dress); the ancient Visigothic votive crowns discovered in

Continued on page 123

EL PRADO:
MADRID'S BRUSH WITH GREATNESS

One of the world's top museums, the Prado is to Madrid what the Louvre is to Paris, or the Uffizi to Florence: a majestic city landmark and premiere art institution that merits the attention of every traveler who visits the city.

The Prado celebrated its 200th anniversary in 2019, and its unparalleled collection of Spanish paintings (from the Romanesque period to the 19th century—don't expect to find Picassos here) makes it one of the most visited museums in the world. Foreign artists are also well represented—the collection includes masterpieces of European painting such as Hieronymus Bosch's *Garden of Earthly Delights*, *The Annunciation by Fra Angelico*, *Christ Washing the Disciples' Feet* by Tintoretto, and *The Three Graces* by Rubens—but the Prado is best known as home to more paintings by Diego Velázquez and Francisco de Goya than anywhere else.

Originally meant by King Charles III to become a museum of natural history, the Prado nevertheless opened, in 1819, as a sculpture and painting museum under the patronage of his grandchild, King Philip VII. For the first bewildered *madrileños* who crossed the museum's entrance back then, there were only about 300 paintings on display. Today there are more than 3 million visitors a year and 2,000-plus paintings are on display (the whole collection is estimated at about 8,000 canvases, plus 1,000 sculptures).

WHEN TO GO
The best time to visit the Prado is during lunch time, from 1-3, to beat the rush.

HUNGRY?
If your stomach rumbles during your visit, check out the café/restaurant in the foyer of the new building.

CONTACT INFORMATION
✉ Paseo del Prado s/n, 28014 Madrid
☎ (+34) 91 330 2800.
⊕ www.museodelprado.es
Ⓜ Banco de España, Estacíon del Arte

HOURS OF OPERATION
🕙 Mon.–Sat. 10 AM–8 PM, Sun. 10 AM–7 PM, Closed New Year's Day, Fiesta del Trabajo (May 1), and Christmas.

ADMISSION
💳 €15. Free Mon. to Sat. 6 PM–8 PM, Sun. 5 PM-7 PM. To avoid lines, buy tickets in advance online.

The Trinity by El Greco, 1577. Oil on canvas.

THREE GREAT MASTERS

FRANCISCO DE GOYA 1746–1828

Goya's work spans a staggering range of tone, from bucolic to horrific, his idyllic paintings of Spaniards at play and portraits of the family of King Carlos IV contrasting with his dark, disturbing "black paintings." Goya's attraction to the macabre assured him a place in posterity, an ironic statement at the end of a long career in which he served as the official court painter to a succession of Spanish kings, bringing the art of royal portraiture to unknown heights.

Francisco de Goya

Goya found fame in his day as a portraitist, but he is admired by modern audiences for his depictions of the bizarre and the morbid. Beginning as a painter of decorative Rococo figures, he evolved into an artist of great depth in the employ of King Charles IV. The push-pull between Goya's love for his country and his disdain for the enemies of Spain yielded such masterpieces as *Third of May 1808*, painted after the French occupation ended. In the early 19th century, Goya's scandalous *The Naked Maja* brought him before the Spanish Inquisition, whose judgment was to end his tenure as a court painter.

DIEGO VELÁZQUEZ 1599–1660

A native of Seville, Velázquez gained fame at age 24 as court painter to King Philip IV. He developed a lifelike approach to religious art in which both saints and sinners were specific people rather than generic types. The supple brushwork of his ambitious history paintings and portraits was unsurpassed. Several visits to Rome, and his friendship with Rubens, made him the quintessential baroque painter with an international purview.

Diego Velázquez

DOMENIKOS THEOTOKOPOULOS (AKA "EL GRECO") 1541–1614

El Greco's art was one of rapture and devotion, but beyond that his style is almost impossible to categorize. "The Greek" found his way from his native Crete to Spain through Venice; he spent most of his life in Toledo. His twisted, elongated figures imbue both his religious subjects and portraits with a sense of otherworldliness. While his palette and brushstrokes were inspired by Italian Mannerism, his approach to painting was uniquely his own. His inimitable style left few followers.

Domenikos Theotokopoulos

SIX PAINTINGS TO SEE

SATURN DEVOURING ONE OF HIS SONS (1819)
FRANCISCO DE GOYA Y LUCIENTES

In one of fourteen nightmarish "black paintings" executed by Goya to decorate the walls of his home in the later years of his life, the mythological God Kronos, or Saturn, cannibalizes one of his children in order to derail a prophecy that one of them would take over his throne. *Mural transferred to canvas.*

Saturn Devouring One of His Sons

THE GARDEN OF DELIGHTS OR LA PINTURA DEL MADROÑO (1500)
HIËRONYMUS BOSCH

Very little about the small-town environment of the Low Countries where the Roman Catholic Bosch lived in the late Middle Ages can explain his thought-provoking, and downright bizarre, paintings. His depictions of mankind's sins and virtues, and the heavenly rewards or demonic punishments that await us all, have fascinated many generations of viewers. The devout painter has been called a "heretic," and compared to Salvador Dalí for his disturbingly twisted renderings. In this three-panel painting, Adam and Eve are created, mankind celebrates its humanity, and hell awaits the wicked, all within a journey of 152 inches! *Wooden Triptych.*

The Garden of Delights

LAS MENINAS (THE MAIDS OF HONOR) (1656-57)
DIEGO VELÁZQUEZ DE SILVA

Velázquez's masterpiece of spatial perspective occupies pride-of-place in the center of the Spanish baroque galleries. In this complex visual game, *you* are the king and queen of Spain, reflected in a distant hazy mirror as the court painter (Velázquez) pauses in front of his easel to observe your features. The actual subject is the Princess Margarita, heir to the throne in 1656. *Oil on canvas.*

Las Meninas

STILL LIFE (17th Century; no date)
FRANCISCO DE ZURBARÁN

Best known as a painter of contemplative saints, Zurbarán, a native of Extremadura who found success working with Velázquez in Seville, was a peerless observer of beauty in the everyday. His rendering of the surfaces of these homely objects elevates them to the stature of holy relics, urging the viewer to touch them. But the overriding mood is one of serenity and order. *Oil on canvas.*

Still Life

DAVID VICTORIOUS OVER GOLIATH (1599)
MICHELANGELO MERISI (CARAVAGGIO)

Caravaggio used intense contrasts between his dark and light passages (called *chiaroscuro* in Italian) to create drama in his bold baroque paintings. Here, a surprisingly childlike David calmly ties up the severed head of the giant Philistine Goliath, gruesomely featured in the foreground plane of the picture. The astonishing realism of the Italian painter, who was as well known for his tempestuous personal life as for his deftness with a paint brush, had a profound influence on 17th century Spanish art. *Oil on canvas.*

David Victorious over Goliath

THE TRINITY (1577)
DOMENIKOS THEOTOKOPOULOS (EL GRECO)

Soon after arriving in Spain, Domenikos Theotokopoulos created this view of Christ ascending into heaven supported by angels, God the Father, and the Holy Spirit. It was commissioned for the altar of a convent in Toledo. The acid colors recall the Mannerist paintings of Venice, where El Greco was trained, and the distortions of the upward-floating bodies show more gracefulness than the anatomical contortions that characterize his later works. *Oil on canvas.*

The Trinity

PICASSO AND THE PRADO

The Prado contains no modern art, but one of the greatest artists of the 20th century had an important history with the museum. **Pablo Picasso** (1891–1973) served as the director of the Prado during the Spanish civil war, from 1936 to 1939. The Prado was a "phantom museum" in that period, Picasso once noted, since it was closed for most of the war and its collections hidden elsewhere for safety.

Picasso with his wife
Jacqueline Roque

Later that century, the abstract artist's enormous *Guernica* hung briefly on the Prado's walls, returning to Spain from the Museum of Modern Art in 1981. Picasso had stipulated that MoMA give up his anti-war masterpiece after the death of fascist dictator Francisco Franco, and it was displayed at the Prado and the Casón del Buen Retiro until the nearby Reina Sofia was built to house it in 1992.

Picasso in his atelier

1859 near Toledo, believed to date back to the 7th century; and the medieval ivory crucifix of Ferdinand and Sancha. There is also a replica of the early cave paintings in Altamira (access to the real thing, in Cantabria Province, is highly restricted). Consider getting the multimedia guide offering select itineraries to make your visit more manageable. ✉ *Calle de Serrano 13, Salamanca* ☎ *91/577–7912* 🌐 *www.man.es* 🎟 *€3 (free Sat. after 2 and Sun. before 2)* 🕒 *Closed Mon.* [M] *Colón, Serrano.*

🍴 Restaurants

Álbora

$$$ | TAPAS | The owners of this award-winning restaurant also produce cured hams and top-notch canned foods, and these ingredients feature prominently on a menu that manages to be both traditional and creative—unlike the decor, which feels stuck in the early 2000s. There's a tony tapas bar on the street level, ideal for cocktails and quick bites (don't miss the plump Ibérico pork-filled ravioli swimming in *jamón* jus), and a refined tasting-menu restaurant on the second floor. **Known for:** top-quality charcutería; experimental Spanish cuisine; well-heeled clientele. [$] *Average main: €25* ✉ *Calle de Jorge Juan 33, Salamanca* ☎ *91/781–6197* 🌐 *www.restaurantealbora.com* 🕒 *No dinner Sun.* [M] *Velázquez.*

★ Cadaqués

$$$$ | CATALAN | Never has an open kitchen in Madrid been so mesmerizing: At Cadaqués, black-clad cooks tend to rows of paella pans sizzling over pluming orange wood embers and flip Flintstone-worthy steaks and whole fish licked by open flame. It feels like the type of rustic experience you'd encounter at the Mediterranean seaside, but Cadaqués sits squarely on Jorge Juan, one of Madrid's poshest streets. **Known for:** refined Mediterranean décor with well-heeled clientele to match; best rice dishes in town; a slice of the Levant in Madrid. [$] *Average main: €55* ✉ *Calle de Jorge Juan 35, Salamanca* ☎ *91/360–9053* 🌐 *restaurantecadaques.com* [M] *Velázquez.*

Casa Carola

$$$$ | SPANISH | FAMILY | Locals flock to Casa Carola for one dish, *cocido madrileño*, Madrid's famous boiled dinner whose roots can be traced to medieval Spain. Served ritualistically in three courses, or *vuelcos*—broth, then chickpeas and vegetables, then meats—it's an essential Madrid experience, especially in the cold-weather months. **Known for:** warm service; cocido madrileño served in three courses; old-timey interiors. [$] *Average main: €30* ✉ *Calle de Padilla 54, Salamanca* ☎ *91/401–9408* 🌐 *www.casacarola.com* 🕒 *No dinner. Closed mid-June–mid-Sept.* [M] *Lista.*

★ Casa Dani

$ | SPANISH | Casa Dani is a legendary bar in Mercado de la Paz whose tortilla de patata is easily the best in town, and perhaps the country, if first place in the "National Spanish Omelet Championship" of 2019 is any indication. Each hefty wedge is packed with caramelized onions and served hot and slightly runny. **Known for:** possibly world's best tortilla española; long lines that are worth the wait; value prix fixe lunch. [$] *Average main: €12* ✉ *Mercado de la Paz, Calle de Ayala 28, Salamanca* ✥ *Back right corner* ☎ *91/575–5925* 🌐 *www.casadani.es* 🕒 *Closed Sun. No dinner* [M] *Serrano.*

Cinco Jotas Jorge Juan

$$$ | TAPAS | Cinco Jotas Ibérico ham is a sight to behold, translucent and shimmering like shards of red-stained glass, a shade darker than prosciutto and twice as fragrant. That's because this famous producer uses only 100% purebred, acorn-fed Iberian hogs. **Known for:** Ibérico pork dishes; ritzy white-tablecloth patio; the Rolls Royce of jamón. [$] *Average main: €26* ✉ *Calle Puigcerdà, Local 2, Salamanca* ☎ *91/575–4125* 🌐 *www.cincojotas.es* [M] *Serrano.*

The Art Walk (Paseo del Prado)

Any visit to Madrid should include a stroll along Paseo del Prado, lined with world-class museums housed in majestic old buildings. You can tour the area in about two hours (longer if you visit the Prado).

The Paseo del Arte (Art Walk) pass allows you to visit the Prado, the Reina Sofía, and the Thyssen-Bornemisza for approximately €30. You can buy it at any of the three museums and don't have to visit all of them on the same day.

The Paseo del Prado stretches from Plaza de Cibeles to Plaza del Emperador Carlos V (also known as Plaza de Atocha) and is home to Madrid's three main art museums—the Prado, Reina Sofía, and Thyssen-Bornemisza as well as the CaixaForum, an art institution with fabulous temporary exhibitions. In earlier times the Paseo marked the eastern boundary of the city, and in the 17th century it was given a cleaner neoclassical look. A century later, King Carlos III designed a leafy nature walk with glorious fountains and a botanical garden to provide respite to madrileños during the scorching summers.

Start your walk on Plaza Cánovas del Castillo, with its Fuente de Neptuno (Fountain of Neptune); on the northwestern corner is the **Museo Thyssen-Bornemisza**. To your left, across from the plaza, is the elegant, just-renovated Mandarin Oriental Ritz; across from it on the right is the **Museo del Prado**, the best example of neoclassical architecture in the city and one of the world's best-known museums. It was enlarged in 2007 with the addition of what's widely known as "Moneo's cube," architect Rafael Moneo's steel-and-glass building that now encloses the cloister of the old Monasterio de los Jerónimos. The monastery, by far the oldest building in this part of town (built in 1503), is dwarfed by the museum. It once sat at the core of the **Parque del Buen Retiro**, which stretched as far as the Paseo del Prado until the 19th century, when Queen Isabel II sold a third of its terrain to the state. It gets its name from being a retreat where the Habsburg kings would temporarily "retire" from their state affairs. Always bustling, it is a great place to unwind after sightseeing.

To the right of the Prado, across from Murillo Gate, is the **Jardín Botánico**, also a wonderful place to relax with a book or sketch in the shade of an exotic tree. Across the street is a sloping plaza that leads to **CaixaForum**.

The Paseo del Prado ends at the **Estación de Atocha**, a grand old train station resembling the overturned hull of a ship. To its west, across from Calle Atocha, lies **Centro de Arte Reina Sofía**, Madrid's modern art museum and the home of Picasso's *Guernica*.

★ El Paraguas

$$$$ | SPANISH | This low-ceiling dining room filled with plush armchairs, starched white tablecloths, and colorful bouquets is a welcoming spot to feast on refined Asturian dishes like sea urchin gratin, morels stuffed with truffles and foie gras, pheasant with braised green beans, and suckling lamb confit. Weather permitting, you can request a patio table to watch Madrid's one percent parade down Calle Jorge Juan. **Known for:** fantastic seafood; haute Asturian cuisine; romantic dining room and terrace. $ *Average main: €30* ⊠ *Calle Jorge Juan 16, Salamanca* ☎ *91/431–5950* ⊕ *www.elparaguas.com* ⊘ *No dinner Sun.* Ⓜ *Serrano.*

El Pescador

$$$ | SEAFOOD | Owned by the proprietors of one the best fish markets in town, Pescaderías Coruñesas, this seafood restaurant with a warm, modern interior welcomes guests with an impressive window display of fresh seafood—red and white prawns, Kumamoto oysters, goose barnacles, and the renowned Galician Carril clams are just some of what you might see. Fish (including turbot, sole, grouper, and sea bass) is cooked to your liking in the oven, on the grill, in a pan with garlic, or battered and fried. **Known for:** crisp Galician wines; dayboat fish; extravagant seafood displays. $ *Average main: €25* ⊠ *Calle de José Ortega y Gasset 75, Salamanca* ☎ *91/402–1290* ⊕ *www.marisqueriaelpescador.net* ⊘ *Closed Sun.* Ⓜ *Lista, Núñez de Balboa.*

El Rincón de Jaén

$$ | SPANISH | FAMILY | An Andalusian taberna, El Rincón de Jaén evokes the raucous energy and down-home cuisine of that sunny region. Start with *pescaíto frito,* a mix of seafood that's lightly fried and served with lemon halves, before moving on to more substantial dishes like the peeled tomato salad topped with oil-cured tuna belly (easily one of the best salads in town) and whole roasted fish and braised meats. **Known for:** complimentary tapas with drinks; Andalusian joie de vivre; tomato and tuna salad. $ *Average main: €22* ⊠ *Calle Don Ramón de la Cruz 88, Salamanca* ☎ *91/401–6334* ⊕ *elrincondejaen.com* Ⓜ *Lista.*

Estay

$$ | SPANISH | This is a quintessential Salamanca bar-restaurant: spacious, tranquil, and presided over by white-jacketed waitstaff. Try the breakfasts (choose from *pan con tomate,* toast with jam, or a griddled all-butter croissant plus coffee) for €3 and filling prix fixe lunches on weekdays. **Known for:** preppy Salamanca atmosphere; runny tortilla española; weekday prix fixe. $ *Average main: €20* ⊠ *Calle de Hermosilla 46, Salamanca* ☎ *91/578–0470* ⊕ *www.estayrestaurante.com* ⊘ *Closed Sun.* Ⓜ *Velázquez.*

Goizeko Wellington

$$$ | SPANISH | The seasoned Basque chef of this quiet white-tablecloth standby serves dependably delectable fine-dining versions of Spanish classics like steamed hake with seaweed-garlic refrito, cured tuna salad with crab vinaigrette, and a phenomenal roast suckling pig doused in syrupy jus. Save room for house-made desserts, which number over 15 and play nicely with sweet Muscatel wine or sherry. **Known for:** elegant yet comfortable atmosphere; elevated Basque cuisine; excellent acoustics. $ *Average main: €27* ⊠ *Hotel Wellington, Calle de Villanueva 34, Salamanca* ☎ *91/577–6026* ⊕ *www.goizekowellington.es* ⊘ *Closed Sun.* Ⓜ *Retiro, Príncipe de Vergara.*

La Tasquería

$$ | TAPAS | Ever since La Tasquería opened in 2015, its exposed-brick dining room has been drawing restaurant industry pros and food writers with its bold menu revolving around off cuts like liver, kidneys, tripe, and tongue—one-time staples of the Spanish diet that fell out of favor but are now getting a modern makeover. Even the squeamish should consider ordering objectively delectable dishes like lamb necks with corn and huitlacoche and brain-and-potato omelet. **Known for:** craft beers and sherries; offal everything; good-value €55 tasting menu. $ *Average main: €16* ✉ *Calle Duque de Sesto 48, Salamanca* ☎ *91/451–1000* ⊕ *www.latasqueria.com* Ⓜ *Príncipe de Vergara.*

Ten Con Ten
$$$ | SPANISH | This "gin bar" helped start the Spanish *gin-tónic* craze of the late 1980s, and though perhaps not as avant-garde as it once was, the quality of food and drinks at Ten Con Ten is consistently fantastic. Grab a cocktail at one of the wooden high-tops in the bar area, or sit down for a soup-to-nuts dinner in the classy dining room at the back—just remember to book a table weeks, if not months, in advance. **Known for:** hand-cut jamón ibérico; expertly made gin-tónics; memorable gastro-bar fare. $ *Average main: €24* ✉ *Calle de Ayala 6, Salamanca* ☎ *91/575–9254* ⊕ *www.restauranteten-conten.com* Ⓜ *Serrano.*

Coffee and Quick Bites

Religion Specialty Coffee
$ | CAFÉ | After browsing the art collection at Museo Lázaro Galdiano, walk north a block to reach this charming café ideally suited to working and leisurely schmoozing. There are sandwiches, chia bowls, smoothies, and pastries on the menu, in addition to teas and the usual coffee drinks. **Known for:** laptop-friendly; affordable brunch; well-made coffees and teas. $ *Average main: €9* ✉ *Calle de María de Molina 24, Salamanca* ☎ *91/069–8221* ⊕ *www.religioncoffee.es* Ⓜ *Gregorio Marañón.*

Hotels

Barceló Emperatriz
$$ | HOTEL | Worthy of an empress as its name implies, this sumptuous property on a tree-shaded block offers knowledgeable concierge services, healthy breakfast options (tahini toast! spirulina

omelets!), an updated gym, and an extensive pillow menu. **Pros:** private terraces; solid little gym; king-size beds and in-room hot tubs. **Cons:** small pool and gym; 10-minute taxi from center of town; cramped lobby. $ *Rooms from: €155* ✉ *Calle de López de Hoyos 4, Salamanca* ☎ *91/342–2490* ⊕ *www.barcelo.com* ⇆ *146 rooms* ⦶ *No Meals* Ⓜ *Núñez de Balboa.*

Gran Meliá Fénix
$$$ | HOTEL | A Madrid institution that has played host to the likes of the Beatles, Cary Grant, and Rita Hayworth, this hotel has an impressive lobby with marble floors, antique furniture, and a stained-glass dome ceiling. **Pros:** opulent, spacious rooms; celebrity hangout Hortensio restaurant; great breakfast buffet. **Cons:** kitsch Asian decor comes across as insensitive; small bathrooms could use update; elitist VIP policy that excludes standard-room guests from certain areas. $ *Rooms from: €190* ✉ *Calle de Hermosilla 2, Salamanca* ☎ *91/431–6700* ⊕ *www.melia.com* ⇆ *225 rooms* ⦶ *No Meals* Ⓜ *Colón.*

★ Heritage Madrid Hotel
$$$$ | HOTEL | Hotel Orfila's newer stylish sibling, the Relais & Château-approved Heritage lies north of Salamanca's commercial hubbub in a stately residential area. **Pros:** Mario Sandoval-run restaurant; "secret" rooftop bar and terrace; standout old-meets-new furnishings. **Cons:** far from most sights; not the most family-friendly; no gym, pool, or sauna. $ *Rooms from: €300* ✉ *Calle de Diego de León 43, Salamanca* ☎ *91/088–7070* ⊕ *www.heritagemadridhotel.com* ⇆ *46 rooms* ⦶ *No Meals* Ⓜ *Avenida de América.*

ICON Wipton by Petit Palace
$$ | HOTEL | Whites, grays, and dark woods define this boutique hotel on Salamanca's most opulent street, Jorge Juan. **Pros:** calming atmosphere; standout breakfasts; location on main dining and nightlife street. **Cons:** small desks in guest rooms; noise travels from

ground-floor bar; entry-level rooms are a tight fit. $ *Rooms from: €145* ✉ *Calle de Jorge Juan 17, Salamanca* ☎ *91/435–5411* ⊕ *www.iconwipton.com* ⇌ *61 rooms* ❖❘ *No Meals* Ⓜ *Serrano, Velázquez.*

Tótem Madrid
$$$ | HOTEL | Tótem checks all the boxes for a solid boutique hotel: genial service, streamlined design, sought after location, terrific food and cocktails—you name it, they've got it. **Pros:** excellent cocktail bar and restaurant; bubbly service; charming tree-lined block. **Cons:** disappointingly bad breakfast; interior rooms not as pleasant; many attractions not within walking distance. $ *Rooms from: €200* ✉ *Calle Hermosilla 23, Salamanca* ☎ *91/426–0035* ⊕ *www.totem-madrid.com* ⇌ *64 rooms* ❖❘ *No Meals* Ⓜ *Serrano.*

VP Jardín de Recoletos
$$ | HOTEL | FAMILY | This high-end apartment-hotel offers great value on a quiet street just a couple of blocks from Retiro Park, the Prado, and shopping areas. **Pros:** good restaurant; good value with periodic deals via website; spacious rooms with kitchens. **Cons:** breakfast not served in the garden; could use a redesign; the garden closes at midnight and can be noisy. $ *Rooms from: €170* ✉ *Calle Gil de Santivañes 6, Salamanca* ☎ *91/781–1640* ⊕ *www.recoletos-hotel.com* ⇌ *43 rooms* ❖❘ *No Meals* Ⓜ *Colón.*

Nightlife

DANCE CLUBS
Bling Bling
DANCE CLUBS | This glitzy nightclub attracts a well-heeled local crowd with house, reggaeton, and remixed pop tracks. Dress to impress: this isn't an easy door. ✉ *Calle Génova 28, Salamanca* ☎ *91/064–4479* Ⓜ *Colón.*

Performing Arts

Auditorio Nacional de Música
CONCERTS | This is Madrid's main concert hall, with spaces for both symphonic and chamber music. ✉ *Calle del Príncipe de Vergara 146, Salamanca* ☎ *91/337–0140* ⊕ *www.auditorionacional.mcu.es* Ⓜ *Cruz del Rayo.*

★ Cafetín La Quimera
FOLK/TRADITIONAL DANCE | FAMILY | The noncentral location of this old-fashioned flamenco *tablao* keeps the touristy crowds at bay. Choose between a full dinner package (prices vary) or a €20 performance-only ticket and prepare for a soulful, invigorating show. The start time is 10 pm nightly (8 and 10:30 Fri. and Sat.), and there are often after-hours jam sessions on Friday and Saturday night. Informal flamenco classes are held 90 minutes before each performance and cost €18–40 a head depending on party size; reserve online at least 24 hours prior. ✉ *Callede Sancho Dávila 34, Salamanca* ☎ *91/356–9361* ⊕ *www.tablaolaquimera.com* Ⓜ *Ventas, Manuel Becerra.*

🛍 Shopping

BOUTIQUES AND FASHION
Salamanca is Madrid's quintessential shopping district with a high concentration of large and small shops and boutiques on Calles Claudio Coello, Lagasca, and the first few blocks of Serrano.

Adolfo Domínguez
MIXED CLOTHING | This popular Galician designer creates simple, sober, elegant lines for both men and women. Of the numerous locations around the city, the flagship at Calle Serrano 5 is the most varied. There's also a large store at Madrid–Barajas Airport. ✉ *Calle de Serrano 5, Salamanca* ☎ *91/436–2600* ⊕ *www.adolfodominguez.com* Ⓜ *Serrano.*

Loewe
LEATHER GOODS | Luxury Spanish fashion house Loewe (Lo-EH-veh) carries

designer purses, accessories, and clothing made of butter-soft leather in gorgeous jewel tones. The store at Serrano 26 displays the women's collection; men's items are a block away at Serrano 34. The Gran Vía location houses a small fashion museum (free entry) chronicling the history of the iconic brand with pieces dating back to the 19th century. ✉ *Calle de Serrano 26 and 34, Salamanca* ☎ *91/577–6056* ⊕ *www.loewe.com* Ⓜ *Serrano.*

Purificación García

HANDBAGS | For women and men searching for elegant all-day wear, this store offers some standout pieces, particularly handbags. There's another branch at Claudio Coello 95. ✉ *Calle de Serrano 28, Salamanca* ☎ *91/435–8013* ⊕ *www. purificaciongarcia.com* Ⓜ *Serrano.*

FOOD AND WINE
Lavinia

WINE/SPIRITS | Every attendant is a sommelier at this sprawling wine store. Beyond the 4,000-plus bottles from nearly every viticultural region imaginable, there are books, glasses, and bar accessories on sale as well as a Spanish restaurant with some 50 wines by the glass. A small outdoor patio was added recently; call ahead to book. ✉ *Calle de José Ortega y Gasset 16, Salamanca* ☎ *91/426–0604* ⊕ *www.lavinia.es* Ⓜ *Núñez de Balboa.*

Mantequerías Bravo

WINE/SPIRITS | Stock up on Spanish wines, olive oils, cheeses, and hams at this old-timer that's been around since 1931 and is situated in the heart of Salamanca's shopping area. ✉ *Calle de Ayala 24, Salamanca* ☎ *91/576–7641* ⊕ *www. mantequeriasbravo.com* Ⓜ *Serrano.*

JEWELRY
Coolook

JEWELRY & WATCHES | Spanish jeweler Mar Aldeguer sells nature-inspired jewelry made from precious and semiprecious metals and stones at this welcoming boutique. There's another branch at Calle Barquillo 34. ✉ *Calle Serrano 84, Salamanca* ☎ *91/626–3920* ⊕ *www.coolook. es* ⊗ *Closed Tues. and Sun.*

TEXTILES
★ Ábbatte

FABRICS | Every blanket, tablecloth, throw, and rug sold at this deservedly pricey textile shop is woven by hand using the finest natural fibers in the Cistercian abbey of Santa María de la Sierra in Segovia. ✉ *Calle Villanueva 27, Salamanca* ☎ *91/622–5530* ⊕ *www.abbatte.com* ⊗ *Closed Sun.*

La Latina

This is perhaps Madrid's most *castizo* (loosely, "authentic") neighborhood, with its deep-rooted history and hardscrabble spirit. Its layout has changed little since medieval times, with sinuous cobblestone streets emptying onto wide plazas, but its demographic makeup has in the last decade due to soaring rents and the arrival of Airbnb. Though its mom-and-pop businesses preserve the old-world aesthetic of La Latina of yore, the neighborhood has all but lost its original inhabitants and, with them, its pleasingly gritty edge. But that doesn't keep madrileños from flocking here every chance they get, especially around August 15, when the neighborhood's famous Verbena de la Paloma street fair unfolds to the oompah of the *chotis.* When exploring, architecture buffs should keep an eye out for La Latina's *casas a la malicia,* illegally constructed apartments from the 16th to 18th century recognizable for their asymmetrical, randomly placed windows. Their confusing floor plan was intended to dupe the municipal authorities into believing they contained fewer dwellings (allowing landlords to evade property taxes), one of many examples of this neighborhood's unruly character.

Officially part of the Palacio neighborhood, this bustling area bordered by Calle de Segovia to the north; Calle Toledo to the east; Puerta de Toledo to the south; and Calle Bailén, with its imposing Basílica de San Francisco, to the west houses some of the city's oldest buildings, plenty of sloping streets, and an array of unmissable tapas spots—especially on Cava Baja and Cava Alta, and in the area around Plaza de la Paja.

 Sights

Basílica de San Francisco el Grande

CHURCH | In 1760 Carlos III built this basilica on the site of a Franciscan convent, allegedly founded by St. Francis of Assisi in 1217. The dome, 108 feet in diameter, is the largest in Spain, even larger than that of St. Paul's in London. The seven main doors, of American walnut, were carved by Casa Juan Guas. Three chapels adjoin the circular church, the most famous being that of **San Bernardino de Siena** containing a Goya masterpiece depicting a preaching San Bernardino. The figure standing on the right, not looking up, is a self-portrait of Goya. The 16th-century Gothic choir stalls came from La Cartuja del Paular, in rural Segovia Province. ✉ *Pl. de San Francisco, La Latina* ☎ *91/365–3800* 🎫 *€5 guided tour (in Spanish); free Sat.* ⊙ *Closed Mon. and some Sat.* Ⓜ *Puerta de Toledo, La Latina.*

Cava Baja

STREET | Madrid's most popular tapas street is crowded with excellent (if arguably overpriced) tapas bars and traditional *tabernas*. Its lively, and rather touristy, atmosphere spills over onto nearby streets and squares including Almendro, Cava Alta, Plaza del Humilladero, and Plaza de la Paja. Expect full houses and long wait times on weekend nights. ✉ *La Latina* Ⓜ *La Latina.*

Mercado de la Cebada

MARKET | **FAMILY** | An unrenovated building and budget-friendly tapas and groceries make this market a local favorite for both shopping and snacking. The hangar-like space is at its busiest on Saturday from noon to 3 pm, when seafood stalls transform into makeshift fish and shellfish restaurants, frying, steaming, and boiling their freshest wares and serving them on plastic plates alongside jugs of unlabeled table wine—quite the party. Once buzzed and sated, pop into La Pecera, a chic stall dedicated to prints, paintings, and photography by local artists. ✉ *Pl. de la Cebada, La Latina* ☎ *91/366–6966* ⊕ *www. mercadodelacebada.com* ⊙ *Closed Sun.* Ⓜ *La Latina.*

Plaza de la Paja

PLAZA/SQUARE | At the top of a hill, on Costanilla San Andrés, sits the most important square of medieval Madrid. It predates the Plaza Mayor by at least two centuries. The sloped plaza's jewel is the Capilla del Obispo (Bishop's Chapel), built between 1520 and 1530, where peasants deposited their tithes, called *diezmas*—one-tenth of their crop. Architecturally the chapel traces the transition from the blocky Gothic period, which gave the structure its basic shape, to the Renaissance, the source of its decorations. It houses an intricately carved polychrome altarpiece by Francisco Giralta with scenes from the life of Christ. To visit the chapel (*Tuesday 9:30–12:30, Thursday 4–5:30*) reserve in advance (*91/559–2874* or *reservascapilladelobispo@archimadrid. es*). The chapel is part of the complex of the domed church of San Andrés, one of Madrid's oldest. At the northern tip of the plaza there's a pretty little 18th-century park, Jardín del Príncipe de Anglona, that locals call Madrid's secret garden. ✉ *La Latina* Ⓜ *La Latina.*

🍴 **Restaurants**

Casa Botín

$$$ | **SPANISH** | According to *Guinness World Records*, Madrid is home to the world's oldest restaurant, Botín, established in 1725 and a favorite of Ernest

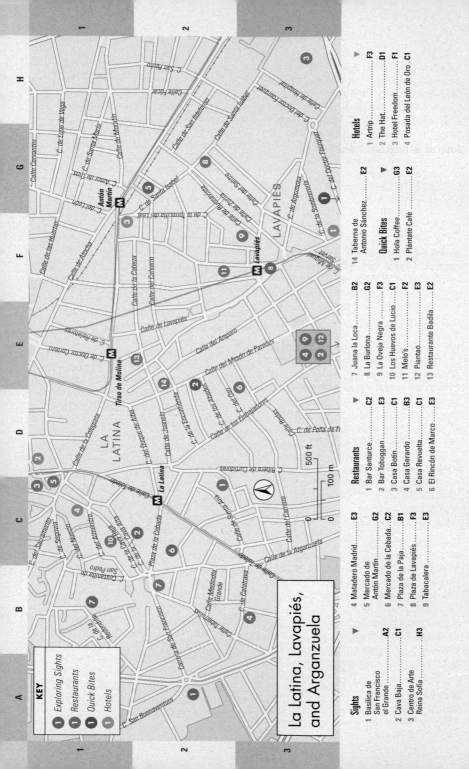

La Latina, Lavapiés, and Arganzuela

KEY

- ● Exploring Sights
- ● Restaurants
- ● Quick Bites
- ● Hotels

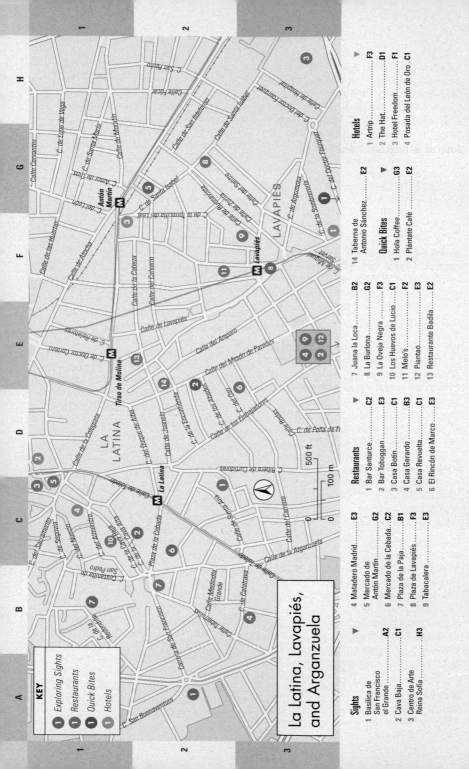

Hemingway. The final scene of *The Sun Also Rises* is set in this very place. **Known for:** world's oldest restaurant; live music ensembles; roast lamb and suckling pig. $ *Average main: €25* ✉ *Calle Cuchilleros 17, La Latina* ☎ *91/366–4217* ⊕ *www. botin.es* Ⓜ *Tirso de Molina.*

★ Casa Gerardo

$ | TAPAS | Huge *tinajas*, clay vessels once filled to the brim with bulk wine (now defunct), sit behind the bar at this raucous no-frills bodega specializing in Spanish cheese and charcuterie. Ask the waiters what they've been drinking and eating lately, and order precisely that. **Known for:** frazzled yet friendly staff; wide selection of wines and charcuterie; unforgettable old-world atmosphere. $ *Average main: €10* ✉ *Calle Calatrava 21, La Latina* ☎ *91/221–9660* Ⓜ *La Latina, Puerta de Toledo.*

★ Casa Revuelta

$ | SPANISH | Many tapas bars serve *pincho de bacalao* (battered cod; an old-school standby) but none hold a candle to Revuelta's rendition, which is crisp, feather-light, and not too salty. Elbow your way to the 1930s-era bar and ask for a "pincho de bacalao" and a glass of Valdepeñas, a Manchegan red that comes chilled in tiny stemless glasses—just like the olden days. **Known for:** time-warp decor; midmorning vermú (vermouth) rush; battered salt cod canapés. $ *Average main: €5* ✉ *Calle Latoneros 3, La Latina* ☎ *91/366–3332* ⊘ *Closed Mon. No dinner Sun.* Ⓜ *La Latina.*

★ Juana la Loca

$$ | TAPAS | This tony gastro-bar serves newfangled tapas that are well worth their higher-than-usual price tag. Spring for the tempura soft-shell crab bao with chive mayonnaise, garlicky artichoke flatbread, or any other tapa *del día*, but whatever you do, order the famous *tortilla de patata* (Spanish omelet), irresistible with its molten core and handfuls of caramelized onions. **Known for:** nueva cocina tapas done right; earth-shatteringly good

tortilla de patata; cheek-by-jowl crowds. $ *Average main: €21* ✉ *Pl. Puerta de Moros 4, La Latina* ☎ *91/366–5500* ⊕ *www.juanalaloca.es* ⊘ *No lunch Mon.* Ⓜ *La Latina.*

Los Huevos de Lucio

$$ | SPANISH | Don't let the crowds dissuade you from entering this Cava Baja stalwart—tables and barstools open up fast. The nonnegotiable dish to try here is *huevos estrellados*, "bashed" fried eggs tucked between olive-oil-fried potatoes and topped with optional add-ons like jamón, *txistorra* sausage, and *pisto* (Spanish ratatouille). **Known for:** uproarious atmosphere; fried egg nirvana; great salads and vegetable dishes. $ *Average main: €16* ✉ *Calle Cava Baja 30, La Latina* ☎ *91/366–2984* ⊕ *www.loshuevosdelucio.com* ⊘ *Closed Tues.* Ⓜ *La Latina.*

🛏 Hotels

★ The Hat

$ | HOTEL | The Hat epitomizes the fast-growing category of "designer hostels," affordable properties geared toward the millennial set with sleek multiperson (and some private) rooms, bumping weekend events, and generous breakfasts. **Pros:** steps from Plaza Mayor; bountiful breakfasts; rooftop bar. **Cons:** some rooms are dark; location means tourists are everywhere; hotel guests not prioritized on rooftop, which fills up fast. $ *Rooms from: €45* ✉ *Calle Imperial 9, La Latina* ☎ *91/772–8572* ⊕ *www. thehatmadrid.com* ⤴ *42 rooms* ⊘| *Free Breakfast* Ⓜ *Tirso de Molina.*

Posada del León de Oro

$$ | HOTEL | More like a luxurious village inn than a metropolitan hotel, this refurbished late-19th-century property was built atop the remains of a stone wall that encircled the city in the 12th century, which you can see through glass floor panels at the hotel entrance and in the casual restaurant. **Pros:** high ceilings with exposed wood beams; unbeatable

A Good Walk: Old Madrid

Wander around Puerta del Sol for a look at Madrid's oldest buildings, bustling taverns, and cobblestone alleys. Allow about two hours, more if you visit the Palacio Real or Monasterio de la Encarnación.

Begin at **Puerta del Sol**, the center of Madrid and a major social and transportation hub, then take Calle Mayor to **Plaza Mayor**. Inaugurated in 1620 on the site of a thriving street market, this is Madrid's historical main square, where you'll find the Casa de la Panadería (Bakery House)—an imposing building with mythological figures painted on its facade, home of the main tourist office.

Exit Plaza Mayor through the "Cutler's Arch" (Arco de Cuchilleros) and go down the stairs: To the right is Calle Cava de San Miguel—an ancient-looking stretch of colorful taverns that inches uphill to the posh Mercado de San Miguel and Calle Mayor; to the left is Calle de Cuchilleros ("Cutlers' Street"), which leads to the Plaza de Puerta Cerrada, or "Closed Gate," named for the city gate that once stood here. The mural up to your right reads *Fui sobre agua edificada; mis muros de fuego son* ("I was built on water; my walls are made of fire"), a reference to the city's origins as a fortress with abundant springs and flint ramparts. Cross the street to **Calle Cava Baja**, packed with taverns and restaurants. At Plaza del Humilladero, walk past Plaza de San Andrés and take Costanilla de San Andrés from Plaza Puerta de Moros, down to **Plaza de la Paja**. The **Capilla del Obispo** (Bishop's Chapel), on the south edge of the plaza, completed in 1535, houses one of Spain's most

magnificent Renaissance altarpieces. Look right on narrow Calle Príncipe Anglona—at its end you'll see a tall redbrick Mudejar tower, the only original element belonging to San Pedro el Real (St. Peter the Royal), one of Madrid's oldest churches.

Cross Calle Segovia to Plaza de la Cruz Verde, take the stairs (Calle del Rollo) to your right, go straight to Calle Cordón, then turn left. Walk up the stairs and cross the Plaza del Cordón and Calle Sacramento to get to **Plaza de la Villa**; noteworthy buildings here are (west) the former city hall main office, finished in 1692; (east) the Casa and Torre de los Lujanes, the oldest civil building in Madrid, dating to the mid-15th century; and (south) the Casa Cisneros, from the 16th century. Turn left on Calle Mayor and walk to Calle San Nicolás; on the corner is the Palacio del Duque de Uceda, a residential building from the 17th century now used as military headquarters. Turn right onto Calle San Nicolás (San Nicolás de los Servitas is Madrid's oldest standing church, with a Mudejar tower dating to the 17th century) and walk to Plaza de Ramales, where you'll find a display of a ruined section of the foundation of the medieval Iglesia de San Juan, demolished in the 19th century. Take Calle San Nicolas until it becomes Calle de Lepanto, which leads to the **Plaza de Oriente.** The equestrian statue of Felipe IV was sculpted from a drawing by Velázquez, who worked and died in what is now a residential building on the east side of the plaza. Take a breather in the plaza, then visit the **Palacio Real**, the adjacent **Jardines de Sabatini**, or nearby **Monasterio de la Encarnación.**

location; restaurant with more than 300 Spanish wines. **Cons:** late-night noise; interior-facing rooms are small; cramped entry-level rooms. ⓈRooms from: €146 ✉ Calle Cava Baja 12, La Latina ☎ 91/119–1494 ⊕ www.posadadelleondeoro.com ⇥ 27 rooms ❑ No Meals Ⓜ La Latina.

ⓎNightlife

BARS
Delic

CAFÉS | This warm, inviting café-bar is an all-hours hangout. Homesick travelers will find comfort in Delic's carrot cake, brownies, and pumpkin pie (seasonal), while low-key revelers will appreciate the bar's coziness and late hours (open until 2:30 am on weekends). ✉ Pl. de la Paja, Costanilla de San Andrés 14, La Latina ☎ 91/364–5450 ⊕ www.delic.es ⊘ Closed Mon. Ⓜ La Latina.

El Viajero

BARS | You can find fine modern raciones here (the ultracreamy burrata stands out), but this place is better known among madrileños for its middle-floor bar, which fills up with a cocktail-drinking after-work crowd, and rooftop terrace decorated with potted plants. Beware of the 10% surcharge that comes with outdoor dining, and expect so-so service. ✉ Pl. de la Cebada 11, La Latina ☎ 91/366–9064 ⊕ www.elviajeromadrid.com ⊘ Closed Sun. night and Mon. Ⓜ La Latina.

★ Sala Equis

CABARET | This uber-trendy cinema-bar hybrid occupies a former adult film theater. The first floor is a high-ceilinged bar with bleacher seating, deckchairs, cushy sofas, and an ivy-covered wall. Head up the stairs, and there's a quieter lounge with velvet walls and warm neon lights; continue to the top floor and you've reached the main attraction, a 55-seat cinema with cocktail service that plays art-house films (buy tickets online in advance). The Spanish movies don't have subtitles, but there are frequent screenings of English films in versión original (undubbed). ✉ Calle del Duque de Alba 4, La Latina ☎ 91/429–6686 ⊕ www.salaequis.es Ⓜ Tirso de Molina.

🛍 Shopping

CRAFTS AND DESIGN
★ Cocol

CRAFTS | There's no better shop in Madrid for top-quality Spanish artisan wares. The shelves in this tiny independently owned boutique off Plaza de la Paja are lined with everything from exquisite Andalusian pottery to hand-sewn blankets, antique esparto baskets, and leather soccer balls. ✉ Costanilla de San Andrés 18, La Latina ☎ 91/919–6770 ⊕ www.cocolmadrid.es Ⓜ La Latina.

FLEA MARKETS
★ El Rastro

MARKET | FAMILY | On Sunday morning, Calle de Ribera de Curtidores is closed to traffic and jammed with outdoor booths selling everything under the sun—this is its weekly transformation into the Rastro flea market. Find everything from antique furniture to rare vinyls of flamenco music and keychains emblazoned with "CNT," Spain's old anarchist trade union. Practice your Spanish by bargaining with vendors over paintings, heraldic iron gates, new and used clothes, and even hashish pipes. Plaza General Vara del Rey has some of El Rastro's best antiques, and the streets beyond—Calles Mira el Río Alta and Mira el Río Baja—boast all sorts of miscellany and bric-a-brac. The market shuts down shortly after 2 pm, in time for a street party to start in the area known as La Latina, centered on the bar El Viajero in Plaza Humilladero. Off the Ribera are two galerías, courtyards with higher-quality, higher-price antiques shops. ✉ Calle de Ribera de Curtidores, La Latina ⊘ Closed Mon.–Sat. Ⓜ La Latina.

The bustling Rastro flea market takes place every Sunday 10–2; you never know what kind of treasures you might find.

FOOD AND WINE

Madrid & Darracott

WINE/SPIRITS | More than just a neighborhood wine shop with a well-curated cellar, Madrid & Darracott, opened in 2019, hosts themed wine tastings Thursday to Sunday evenings in English. Wondering about the difference between Rioja and Ribera del Duero or what makes cava sparkle? Reserve your spot online and show up sober—the pours are generous. ⊠ *Calle del Duque de Rivas 8, La Latina* ☏ *91/219–1975* ⊕ *www.madriddarracott. com* Ⓜ *Tirso de Molina.*

Lavapiés

Lavapiés, which has overtaken Malasaña and La Latina as Madrid's trendiest neighborhood, has the city's highest concentration of immigrants—mostly Chinese, Indian, and North and West African—and as a result the area has plenty of international markets and inexpensive restaurants. The area also has the highest number of extant *corralas*—a type of shared working-class building (now protected by the city after many years of abandonment) that became popular in Madrid in the 17th century. Within, apartments revolve around a central patio, which serves as the community's social hub.

Sights

★ Centro de Arte Reina Sofía

ART MUSEUM | Madrid's premier museum of modern art, housed in a historic hospital building, features more than 1,000 works on four floors (the tip of the iceberg from a collection of over 23,000). Painting is the focus here, but photography and cinema are also represented. The new collection contextualizes the works of the great modern masters— Picasso, Miró, and Salvador Dalí—and of other famed artists, such as Juan Gris, Jorge Oteiza, Pablo Gargallo, Julio Gonzalez, Eduardo Chillida, and Antoni Tàpies, into broader narratives that attempt to better explain the evolution of modern art. This means, for instance, that the Dalís are not all displayed together in a single area, but scattered around the 38 rooms. The museum's showpiece is Picasso's *Guernica,* in Room No. 206 on the second floor. The huge black-and-white canvas depicts the horror of the Nazi Condor Legion's ruthless bombing of innocent civilians in the Basque town of Gernika in 1937 during the Spanish Civil War. Check out the rooftop area for scenic city views. ✉ *Calle de Santa Isabel 52, Lavapiés* ☎ *91/467–5062* 🌐 *www.museoreinasofia.es* 🎫 *From €10 (free Mon. and Wed.–Sat. after 7 pm, Sun. 1:30–7)* 🕓 *Closed Tues.* [M] *Atocha.*

★ Mercado de Antón Martín
MARKET | Go on an international tapas crawl here—nibbling on tacos (at Cutzamala), sushi (at Yokaloka), home-made croissants (at Cafés Tornasol), and more—without so much as stepping outside. Olives from Variantes Juanjo and cheeses from La Quesería make excellent portable picnic snacks. ✉ *Calle de Santa Isabel 5, Lavapiés* ☎ *91/369–0620* 🌐 *www.mercadoantonmartin.com* 🕓 *Closed Sun.* [M] *Antón Martín.*

Plaza de Lavapiés
PLAZA/SQUARE | This oblong plaza is Lavapiés's nerve center. To the east is Calle de la Fe (Street of Faith), named for the church of **San Lorenzo**. ✉ *Lavapiés* [M] *Lavapiés.*

Tabacalera (*Tabacalera Art Promotion*)
ART MUSEUM | This cultural center, which occupies a dilapidated 18th-century cigarette factory, is divided in two parts: on the building's northwest corner, there's the city-funded exhibition and event space (called Espacio Promoción del Arte), a free-entry hub of contemporary art that's always worth peeking into, while at its southwest corner is the city's most famous art squat. The latter (with no official opening schedule) feels like a slice of Copenhagen's Christiania in Madrid with its political, in-your-face graffiti and sculptural art. ✉ *Calle de Embajadores 51, Lavapiés* ☎ *91/701–7045* 🌐 *www.promociondelarte.com/tabacalera* 🎫 *Free* 🕓 *Closed Mon.* [M] *Lavapiés.*

🍴 Restaurants

Bar Santurce
$ | **TAPAS** | This take-no-prisoners *abuelo* bar near the top of the Rastro is famous for griddled sardines, served hot and greasy in an odiferous heap with nothing but a flick of crunchy salt. Beware, supersmellers: *eau de sardine* is potent perfume. **Known for:** inexpensive and unfussy; sardine mecca; busy on Sunday. [$] *Average main: €10* ✉ *Pl. General Vara del Rey 14, Lavapiés* ☎ *64/623–8303* 🌐 *www.sites.google.com/barsanturce.com/barsanturce-en* 🕓 *Closed Mon.* [M] *La Latina.*

El Rincón de Marco
$ | **CUBAN** | **FAMILY** | Step straight into Havana at this hidden Cuban bar and restaurant where *rumbas* and *sones* flow from the speakers and regulars burst into impromptu dance parties. Whatever you end up eating—a €6 *ropa vieja* (cumin-scented beef stew), or perhaps the heftier €10 *picapollo* (fried chicken)—be sure to nab an order or two of fried plantains for the table. **Known for:** music that makes you want to dance; kitschy decor; home-cooked Cuban food. [$] *Average main: €8* ✉ *Calle Cabestreros 8, Lavapiés* ☎ *91/210–7500* 🕓 *Closed Mon.* [M] *Lavapiés.*

La Burlona
$$ | **TAPAS** | Indulge in some self-pampering, or impress a special someone at this sunlight-flooded gastro-tavern with minimalist decor that serves creatively plated dishes that taste as good as they look. Squash blossoms come stuffed with garlicky revolcona potatoes, oysters on the half-shell arrive swimming in house-made Bloody Mary mix, and gazpacho is gussied up with *ají*

amarillo and succulent chunks of seared Almadraba tuna. **Known for:** secret bar below; eye-popping modern tapas; more than 30 small-production wines by the bottle. $ *Average main: €17* ⊠ *Calle de Santa Isabel 40, Lavapiés* ☎ *91/018–0018* ⊘ *Closed Mon.* Ⓜ *Lavapiés.*

La Oveja Negra
$ | VEGETARIAN | Traveling as a vegan in Madrid is becoming easier and easier, thanks to affordable, inviting restaurants with palate-popping food like Oveja Negra. Try vegan takes on Spanish classics: *sidre*-braised soy chorizo, leek-and-squash croquetas, and meatless pâtés, to name a few dishes. **Known for:** punk atmosphere; tasty vegan cuisine; laid-back vibe. $ *Average main: €13* ⊠ *Calle Buenavista 42, Lavapiés* ☎ *65/533–6474* ⊕ *ovejavegana.com* ⊘ *Closed Mon.* Ⓜ *Lavapiés.*

★ Melo's
$ | SPANISH | This beloved old Galician bar changed hands in 2021—it's now run by three twenty-something Madrid natives who couldn't bear to see their favorite neighborhood hangout disappear—but the menu of eight infallible dishes has miraculously stayed the same (save for the addition of battered cod, a secret family recipe of one of the business partners). Come for the ultracreamy croquetas, blistered Padrón peppers, and griddled football-size *zapatilla* sandwiches; stay for the dressed-down conviviality and the *cuncos* (ceramic bowls) overflowing with slatey Albariño. **Known for:** old-school Galician bar food; oversize ham croquetas; battered cod grandfathered in from Casa Revuelta. $ *Average main: €10* ⊠ *Calle del Ave María 44, Lavapiés* ☎ *91/527–5054* ⊘ *Closed Sun. and Mon.* Ⓜ *Lavapiés.*

★ Restaurante Badila
$ | SPANISH | FAMILY | This mom-and-pop neighborhood staple has paper tablecloths, walls hung with ceramic plates, and a chalked menu. The ever-rotating *menú del día* (prix fixe) is the move

here—for €13 (or €15 on Friday and Saturday evening), choose from, say, rustic bean stew, a huge T-bone steak, or a wild-mushroom scramble followed by homemade chocolate cake. **Known for:** great-value prix fixe; bubbly staff; lovingly made modern Spanish food. $ *Average main: €13* ⊠ *Calle de San Pedro Martir 6, Lavapiés* ☎ *91/429–7651* ⊘ *No dinner weekdays* Ⓜ *Tirso de Molina.*

Taberna de Antonio Sánchez
$$ | SPANISH | A Lavapiés landmark opened in 1786, this taberna's regulars have included realist painter Ignacio Zuloaga, countless champion bullfighters, and King Alfonso XIII. Sip on a sudsy *caña*, or half pint, in the creaky bar area, and nibble on house specialties like *cazón en adobo* (fried shark bites with cumin) and *torrijas* (custardy fried bread dusted with cinnamon). **Known for:** cazón (fried shark); centuries-old decor; museum-grade bullfighting paraphernalia. $ *Average main: €16* ⊠ *Calle del Mesón de Paredes, Lavapiés* ☎ *91/539–7826* ⊕ *www.tabernaantoniosanchez.com* ⊘ *No dinner Sun.* Ⓜ *Lavapiés.*

☕ Coffee and Quick Bites

★ Hola Coffee
$ | CAFÉ | Spaniards love their morning cafés con leche and afternoon *cortados* (espresso with steamed milk), but it's not been easy to find a truly great cup of joe in Madrid—until Hola Coffee came along with its multilayered third-wave espressos and cold brews made with beans the company roasts itself. Made-from-scratch baked goods and open-faced sandwiches will make you want to stay awhile. **Known for:** third-wave coffees made with house-roasted beans; alternative music and atmosphere; multilingual expat staff and clientele. $ *Average main: €5* ⊠ *Calle del Dr. Fourquet 33, Lavapiés* ☎ *91/056–8263* ⊕ *www.hola. coffee* Ⓜ *Lavapiés.*

Plántate Café

$ | **CAFÉ** | This coffee shop with exposed-brick walls is an adorable breakfast nook worth seeking out for its single-origin brews and delectable, well-priced brunches. **Known for:** popular with expats; plenty of vegan options; expertly pulled espressos. [$] *Average main: €8* ✉ *Calle del Mesón de Paredes 20, Lavapiés* ☎ *91/023–0291* 🌐 *www.facebook.com/plantatecafe* [M] *Lavapiés.*

Hotels

Artrip

$$ | **HOTEL** | A stone's throw from Madrid's "Golden Triangle" of museums, Artrip is a gem of a budget hotel ideally suited to art-loving travelers. **Pros:** youthful design touches; free portable Wi-Fi; independently owned. **Cons:** small showers; street noise; no parking. [$] *Rooms from: €170* ✉ *Calle de Valencia 11, Lavapiés* ☎ *91/539–3282* 🌐 *www.artriphotel.com* 🛏 *17 rooms* 🍴 *No Meals* [M] *Embajadores.*

Hotel Freedom

$$ | **HOTEL** | **FAMILY** | Rooms in this inexpensive and cheerful hotel overlooking Plaza de Antón Martín have turquoise walls, crimson sofas, and multicolor headboards. **Pros:** immaculately clean; independently owned; trendy location. **Cons:** no breakfast; no restaurant, bar, gym, or room service; lobby-adjacent room is noisy. [$] *Rooms from: €130* ✉ *Calle de Santa Isabel 4, Lavapiés* ☎ *91/073–6271* 🌐 *www.hotel-freedom.hoteles-madrid.net* 🛏 *21 rooms* 🍴 *No Meals* [M] *Antón Martín.*

Nightlife

BARS AND CAFÉS

★ Bendito Vinos y Vinilos

WINE BARS | This unassuming stall inside Mercado de San Fernando is a wine-industry hangout—one of the city's top spots for sampling hard-to-find natural and biodynamic wines from Spain and beyond. Pair whatever wine Ilan, the ever-present barman, is drinking lately with Bendito's hand-selected cheeses and charcuterie sourced from independent producers. Winos looking to spread out should book a table at Bendito's more spacious offshoot, La Cruda, at Calle Divino Vallés 28 in Arganzuela. ✉ *Mercado de San Fernando, Calle de Embajadores 41, Lavapiés* ☎ *66/175–0061* 🌐 *www.benditovino.com* 🕒 *Closed Mon.* [M] *Lavapiés.*

La Caníbal

WINE BARS | At this hot spot for wine geeks, you can pull up a stool and choose from dozens of boutique bottles or some 15 small-production Spanish wines on tap. ✉ *Calle de Argumosa 28, Lavapiés* ☎ *91/539–6057* 🌐 *www.lacanibal.com* [M] *Estación del Arte.*

La Fisna

WINE BARS | This understated yet elegant *vinoteca* pours more than 50 wines by the glass and serves a delectable (if pricey) menu of market-driven tapas. You'd be hard pressed to find a more impressive roster of French wines anywhere in the city. ✉ *Calle Amparo 91, Lavapiés* ☎ *91/539–5615* 🕒 *Closed Sun. and Mon.* [M] *Lavapiés.*

Savas

BARS | Lavapiés upped its cocktail game with Savas, a pocket-size bar that has quickly become a cult hangout for mixology geeks and neighborhood scenesters. The classic cocktails are expertly—think White Russians and Tom Collinses at about €8 apiece—and local craft beers by La Virgen. ✉ *Calle de la Sombrerería 3, Lavapiés* [M] *Lavapiés.*

MUSIC AND DANCE CLUBS

Club 33

DANCE CLUBS | This intimate nightclub caters to a local, alternative crowd and is a favorite stop on the lesbian party circuit, though revelers of all orientations are welcome. ✉ *Calle de la Cabeza 33,*

Lavapiés ☎ *91/369–3302* ⊕ *www.club-33madrid.es* Ⓜ *Lavapiés.*

 Performing Arts

La Casa Encendida

CONCERTS | Film festivals, alternative art shows, dance performances, and weekend events for children are held here. In summer, check the website for outdoor concerts on the rooftop, which is open to the public and a pleasant place to unwind with a book when nothing is on. A coffee and pastry at the Pum Pum Café outpost on the ground floor is always a treat. ✉ *Ronda de Valencia 2, Lavapiés* ☎ *91/506–3875* ⊕ *www.lacasaencendida. es* ✂ *Free* Ⓜ *Embajadores, Lavapiés.*

FLAMENCO
★ **El Juglar**

CONCERTS | Sala Juglar is proof that non-touristy, affordable, and skillful flamenco still exists in Madrid (check the website for weekly performance times). Tropical-inflected dance parties, often held on the weekends, are another draw. ✉ *Calle de Lavapiés 37, Lavapiés* ☎ *91/528–4381* ⊕ *www.salajuglar.com* ☉ *Closed Sun.–Tues.* Ⓜ *Lavapiés.*

Shopping

CRAFTS
★ **Yolanda Andrés**

CRAFTS | These are not your grandma's embroideries: in Yolanda Andrés's thought-provoking pieces, which she describes as "paintings with thread," she interprets the centuries-old technique through a modern-day lens—with stunning results. Beyond the framed artwork (don't miss the technicolor "Artichoke" line), there are embroidered pillowcases, totes, and more. ✉ *Calle Encomienda 15, Lavapiés* ☎ *91/026–0742* ⊕ *www. yolandaandres.com* ☉ *Closed Tues. and Sun.* Ⓜ *Tirso de Molina.*

Arganzuela

Arganzuela is such a huge district that a born-and-bred madrileño would never say, "let's meet in Arganzuela." Locals instead speak in terms of the neighborhood's many subdistricts: Imperial, Legazpi, Las Delicias, Palos de Moguer, La Chopera, Las Acacias, and Atocha. The lack of historical sights—with the notable exception of Matadero Madrid—keeps this blue-collar area largely off tourists' radar.

Sights

★ Matadero Madrid

ARTS CENTER | What was once Madrid's largest slaughterhouse is now one of its most vibrant arts and cultural centers. Built in the early 1900s on a then-undeveloped swath of land on the outskirts of town, the "Matadero Municipal de Legazpi" was in operation from 1925 to 1996. At its peak, it comprised 64 buildings and processed over 500 cattle and 5,000 sheep per day. The complex is a stunning example of Spanish fin-de-siècle civil architecture, all stone-and-redbrick facades punctuated by wide doorways and arched windows. Today its bays are thronged with families, tourists, and plenty of pierced-and-tattooed artists and creative types. Check the website for events ranging from film screenings to poetry slams to art exhibits and design fairs. After moseying from building to building, rest your legs at La Cantina del Matadero, a casual restaurant inside the complex where artists and spectators break bread in the form of tapas and fresh-out-of-the-oven pizzas. ✉ *Plaza de Legazpi 8, Arganzuela* ☎ *91/318–4670* ⊕ *www.mataderomadrid.org* Ⓜ *Legazpi.*

🍴 Restaurants

Bar Toboggan
$ | **INTERNATIONAL** | It's thanks to independently owned gems like Toboggan

A typical evening scene: beer and tapas on the terrace of one of Madrid's many tapas bars

that La Chopera neighborhood is beginning to attract a younger, cooler crowd. This corner bar with outdoor seating serves mouthwatering international tapas ranging from tacos to tortilla to homemade hummus in a sunlit space decorated with plants and metal barstools. **Known for:** local La Virgen beer; excellent tapas and desserts; good-vibes-only atmosphere. [$] *Average main: €8* ✉ *Plaza de Rutilio Gacis 2, Local 1, Arganzuela* ☎ *91/245–6432* 🌐 *www.bartoboggan.com* [M] *Legazpi.*

Piantao

$$$ | **ARGENTINE** | Across the street from Matadero Madrid, this upmarket Argentine *asador* (steak house) hits all the high notes with its daintily crimped empanadas, rustic wooden tables, gutsy South American wines, and—*por supuesto*—flame-licked steaks airlifted in from La Pampa with just the right amount of char. **Known for:** excellent empanadas; industrial yet refined digs; ultrajuicy steaks of Argentine beef. [$] *Average main: €23* ✉ *Paseo de la Chopera 69, Arganzuela* ☎ *91/467–5402* 🌐 *www.piantao.es* 🕓 *Closed Mon.* [M] *Legazpi.*

Nightlife

La Riviera

LIVE MUSIC | One of Madrid's largest nightlife venues, with nine bars and an outdoor terrace, La Riviera hosts big-name DJs, local and international bands, and sundown-to-sunup raves. It's a key party spot on the Madrid Pride week (early July) circuit. Check the website for up-to-date performance schedules. ✉ *Paseo Bajo de la Virgen del Puerto, Arganzuela* ☎ *91/365–2415* 🌐 *www.salariviera.com* [M] *Puerta del Ángel.*

Sala Caracol

LIVE MUSIC | Live techno, jazz, funk, and rock shows with reasonably priced tickets keep music-loving madrileños returning to this underground nightclub just south of Lavapiés. ✉ *Calle de Bernardino Obregón 18, Arganzuela* ☎ *91/527–3594* 🌐 *www.facebook.com/salacaracol* [M] *Embajadores.*

Chamberí

Until recently, Chamberí was largely dismissed as a staid and sleepy residential neighborhood with little to offer tourists, but in the last several years, it has established itself as the city's gastronomic nerve center with innovative tapas bars and fusion fine-dining restaurants springing up left and right.

👁 Sights

Andén Cero (*Platform Zero*)
OTHER MUSEUM | FAMILY | The so-called ghost station of Chamberí is now a locomotive museum managed by Metro Madrid. It occupies the grand old Chamberí station, built in 1919 and defunct since 1966. There are vintage advertisements, old maps, and other memorabilia. Tours (free) and placards are in Spanish only. Don't wait for staff to come fetch you after watching the introductory film—just head down to the platform. ⊠ *Pl. de Chamberí, Chamberí* 🕾 *90/244–4403* ⊕ *www.metromadrid. es/en/who-we-are/anden-cero* 🕙 *Closed Mon.–Wed.* 🎟 *Free* Ⓜ *Iglesia, Bilbao.*

Calle Ponzano
STREET | Locals will tell you that this street boasts more bars per square foot (nearly 100 in total) than anywhere else on earth. Alternative facts aside, there's a bar for every taste here, from tile-walled tabernas to louche cocktail lounges to newfangled fusion spots. Start with a caña (half pint) or glass of *vermú* at a time-worn standby like El Doble (No. 58) or Fide (No. 8) before sampling traditional tapas at Taberna Alipio Ramos (No. 30) or La Máquina (No. 39). More eclectic, refined bites can be found at the tuna-centric DeAtún (No. 59), cheffy Sala de Despiece (No. 11), and modern Basque Arima (No. 51). ⊠ *Calle Ponzano, Chamberí* ⊕ *www. ponzaning.es* Ⓜ *Iglesia, Alonso Cano.*

★ **Mercado de Vallehermoso**
MARKET | Choose from made-to-order *pinsas* (ancient Roman pizzas with a cloudlike crust) at Di Buono, flaky Argentine empanadas at Graciana, refined market cuisine at El 2, and high-octane Thai curries at Kitchen 154, among other flavor-packed options at this city-block-size market in the heart of Chamberí. ⊠ *Calle de Vallehermoso 36, Chamberí* 🕾 *91/138–9995* ⊕ *www.mercadovallehermoso.es* 🕙 *No dinner Sun.* Ⓜ *Quevedo.*

★ **Museo Sorolla**
ART MUSEUM | See the world through the once-in-a-generation eye of Spain's most famous impressionist painter, Joaquín Sorolla (1863–1923), who lived and worked most of his life at this home and garden that he designed and decorated. Every corner is filled with exquisite artwork—including plenty of original Sorollas—and impeccably selected furnishings, which pop against brightly colored walls that evoke the Mediterranean coast, where the painter was born. The museum can be seen as part of the Abono Cinco Palacios, a €12 pass that grants access to five mansion-museums. ⊠ *Paseo del General Martínez Campos 37, Chamberí* 🕾 *91/310–1584* ⊕ *museosorolla.mcu.es* 🎟 *€3 (free Sat. after 2 and all day Sun.)* 🕙 *Closed Mon.* Ⓜ *Rubén Darío, Gregorio Marañón.*

🍴 Restaurants

Las Tortillas de Gabino
$$ | TAPAS | At this lively restaurant you'll find crowds of Spaniards gobbling up one of the city's finest, most upscale renditions of *tortilla española* with unconventional add-ins like octopus, potato chips, and truffles. The menu also includes plenty of equally succulent non-egg choices (the rice dishes in particular stand out). **Known for:** carefully selected wines; date-night ambience; fancy tortillas. 🖹 *Average main: €16* ⊠ *Calle Rafael Calvo 20, Chamberí* 🕾 *91/319–7505* ⊕ *www.*

lastortillasdegabino.com ⊘ *Closed Sun.* Ⓜ *Rubén Darío.*

Perretxico Chamberí

$$ | **BASQUE** | The new Madrid outpost of a legendary Vitoria-Gasteiz (Basque Country) pintxo bar, Perretxico is known for its "cocido donut"—*cocido* being Spain's famous boiled dinner of chickpeas, various meats, and sausages. These are blended into a paste, stuffed inside a doughnut, and served alongside a demitasse of umami-packed bone broth for dunking, a wink to the classic doughnut-coffee combo. **Known for:** Chamberí hot spot; cocido doughnut; inventive Basque pintxos. Ⓢ *Average main: €17* ✉ *Calle Rafael Calvo 29, Chamberí* ☎ *91/192–0069* ⊕ *www.perretxico.es* ⊘ *No dinner Sun.* Ⓜ *Rubén Darío.*

Restaurante Barrera

$$$ | **SPANISH** | Duck into this cozy hole-in-the-wall and be treated like family—Ana, the owner, recites the nightly menu to each table and flits around with a smile until the last guest saunters out. Barrera's famous *patatas revolconas* (paprika-spiced mashed potatoes topped with crispy pork belly), are always on offer; they might be followed by roast suckling lamb, wine-braised meatballs, or seared dayboat fish depending on the night. Inquire about prices when ordering to avoid sticker shock. **Known for:** unhurried all-night dining; homey, romantic atmosphere; terrific patatas revolconas and ensaladilla rusa. Ⓢ *Average main: €25* ✉ *Calle de Alonso Cano 25, Chamberí* ☎ *91/594–1757* ⊘ *Closed Mon. No dinner Sun.* Ⓜ *Alonso Cano.*

Sala de Despiece

$$ | **SPANISH** | The opening of this ultratrendy butcher-shop-theme restaurant spurred the revival of Calle Ponzano as Madrid's most exciting tapas street. Feast on eye-catching, impeccably prepared dishes like carpaccio-truffle roll-ups and grilled octopus slathered in chimichurri. **Known for:** see-and-be-seen crowd; playful industrial decor; local celebrity chef. Ⓢ *Average main: €19* ✉ *Calle de Ponzano 11, Chamberí* ☎ *91/752–6106* ⊕ *www.saladedespiece.com* Ⓜ *Iglesia, Alonso Cano.*

★ Sylkar

$$ | **SPANISH** | **FAMILY** | Budget time for a siesta after dining at this phenomenal down-home restaurant that hasn't changed a lick since opening a half-century ago. Whether you're in the boisterous downstairs bar or cozy upstairs dining room with cloth napkins and popcorn walls, you'll be blown away by Sylkar's lovingly prepared specialties including creamy ham *croquetas*, braised squid in ink sauce, battered hake, and—drum roll, please—the best tortilla española in Madrid for those in the runnier-the-better camp. **Known for:** free tapa with every drink; legendary tortilla española; irreverent banter with the waitstaff. Ⓢ *Average main: €19* ✉ *Calle de Espronceda 17, Chamberí* ☎ *91/554–5703* ⊘ *Closed Sun. No dinner Sat.* Ⓜ *Alonso Cano.*

Taberna San Mamés

$$$ | **SPANISH** | What's that firetruck-red stew on every table in this tiny neighborhood tavern? *Callos a la madrileña*, Madrid-style tripe flavored with industrial quantities of garlic and smoky Extremaduran paprika. Other San Mamés standbys include fried bacalao (salt cod), truffled eggs and potatoes, and steak tartare. Book ahead or show up early (9 pm latest) to snag a table. **Known for:** neighborhood crowd; abuela-approved tripe stew; cozy, traditional digs. Ⓢ *Average main: €27* ✉ *Calle de Bravo Murillo 88, Chamberí* ☎ *91/534–5065* ⊕ *www.tabernasanmames.es* ⊘ *Closed Sun. No dinner Mon.* Ⓜ *Cuatro Caminos.*

Tripea

$$$$ | **FUSION** | Young-gun chef Roberto Martínez Foronda continues to turn food critics' heads with his Spanish-fusion restaurant hidden inside the Mercado de Vallehermoso, Chamberí's traditional market. Martínez's ever-changing tasting menu—a steal at €35—takes cues

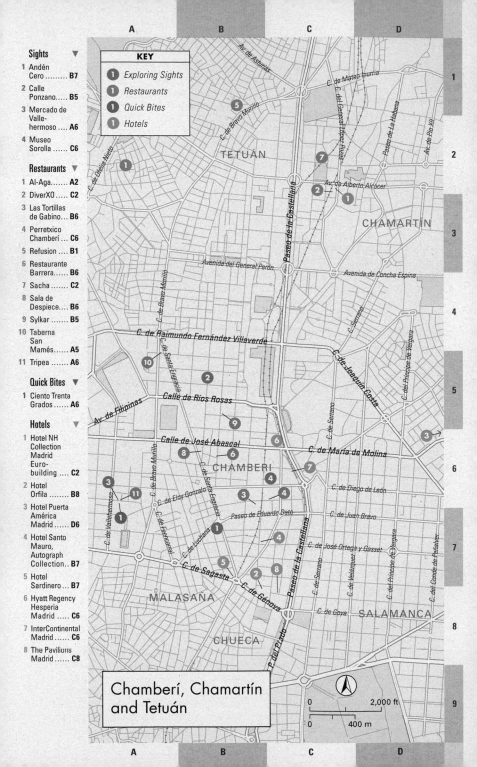

KEY

1 *Exploring Sights*
1 *Restaurants*
1 *Quick Bites*
1 *Hotels*

Chamberí, Chamartín
and Tetuán

0 ___ 2,000 ft
0 ___ 400 m

from *chifa* (Peruvian-Chinese) and *nikkei* (Peruvian-Japanese) culinary canons and incorporates fresh ingredients from the market. **Known for:** foodie buzz; Spanish-fusion cuisine; experimental tasting menus. $ *Average main: €35* ⊠ *Mercado de Vallehermoso, Calle de Vallehermoso 36, Chamberí* ☎ *91/828–6947* ⊕ *www. tripea.es* ⊘ *Closed Sun. and Mon.* Ⓜ *Quevedo.*

☕ Coffee and Quick Bites

Ciento Treinta Grados

$ | CAFÉ | These carb geeks cut no corners—breads here are leavened with sourdough and made with organic stone-ground flours, and the beans for their complex coffees are roasted in house. Drop into the postage-stamp dinette for breakfast or an afternoon pick-me-up, and savor airy all-butter croissants and any range of sweet and savory pastries and breads. Seating is limited and there's no Wi-Fi. **Known for:** house-roasted coffee beans; location across from Mercado de Vallehermoso; sourdough breads and pastries. $ *Average main: €5* ⊠ *Calle de Fernando el Católico 17, Chamberí* ☎ *91/006–7076* ⊕ *cientotreintagrados.com* Ⓜ *Quevedo.*

Hotels

Hotel Orfila

$$$$ | HOTEL | On a leafy residential street not far from Plaza Colón and the gallery-lined Chueca district, this elegant 1886 town house bearing the Relais & Château fleur-de-lis boasts every comfort of larger five-star Madrid hotels—sans the stuffy corporate vibes. **Pros:** attentive service; Mario Sandoval restaurant; year-round dining terrace. **Cons:** no on-site gym; bathrooms could use refurbishing; love-it-or-hate-it Victorian decor. $ *Rooms from: €380* ⊠ *Calle Orfila 6, Chamberí* ☎ *91/702–7770* ⊕ *www.hotelorfila.com* ⇄ *32 rooms* ⦿ *No Meals* Ⓜ *Alonso Martínez.*

Hotel Santo Mauro, Autograph Collection

$$$$ | HOTEL | This fin-de-siècle palace, first a duke's residence and later the Canadian embassy, is now an intimate luxury hotel (managed by Marriott), an oasis of calm removed from the city center. **Pros:** sophisticated restaurant; a world away from the city's hustle and bustle; cushiest beds. **Cons:** a bit of a hike from the main sights; pricey breakfast; some rooms are on the smaller side. $ *Rooms from: €400* ⊠ *Calle Zurbano 36, Chamberí* ☎ *91/319–6900* ⊕ *www. marriott.com* ⇄ *49 rooms* ⦿ *No Meals* Ⓜ *Alonso Martínez, Rubén Darío.*

Hotel Sardinero

$$ | HOTEL | Steps from the trendy Malasaña and gay-friendly Chueca districts, and slightly off the tourist track, Hotel Sardinero occupies a turn-of-the-century palace directly above the Alonso Martínez metro stop. **Pros:** two rooftop terraces; gorgeous neoclassical facade; mellow earth-tone interiors. **Cons:** kettles and coffeemakers only available on request; some guests report plumbing issues; no restaurant. $ *Rooms from: €130* ⊠ *Pl. Alonso Martínez 3, Chamberí* ☎ *91/206–2160* ⊕ *www.hotelsardinero-madrid.com* ⇄ *63 rooms* ⦿ *No Meals* Ⓜ *Alonso Martínez.*

Intercontinental Madrid

$$$$ | HOTEL | Chauffeur-driven town cars snake around the block day and night at the Intercontinental Madrid, a classically decorated hotel frequented by dignitaries, diplomats, and other international bigwigs. **Pros:** dependable if starchy elegance; excellent business facilities; 24-hour gym. **Cons:** cookie-cutter business hotel decor; removed from the center; street-facing rooms can be noisy. $ *Rooms from: €240* ⊠ *Paseo de la Castellana 49, Chamberí* ☎ *91/700–7300* ⊕ *www.ihg.com* ⇄ *302 rooms* ⦿ *No Meals* Ⓜ *Gregorio Marañón.*

★ The Pavilions Madrid

$$ | HOTEL | Hitting the sweet spot between high-end luxury and

3

Madrid CHAMBERÍ

state-of-the-art design, The Pavilions is a boutique hotel that stands out for its original art and sculpture by top Spanish artists, much of it available for purchase. **Pros:** high design on a budget; indoor pool and wellness area; breakfast in solarium. **Cons:** small gym; unexciting block; drab facade. [$] *Rooms from: €150* ✉ *Calle Amador de los Ríos 3, Chamberí* ☎ *91/310–7500* 🌐 *www.pavilionshotels.com/madrid* 🛏 *29 rooms* 🍴 *No Meals* [M] *Colón.*

Nightlife

MUSIC CLUBS

★ Clamores

LIVE MUSIC | Jive to live jazz concerts and world music until 5:30 am on weekdays and 6 am on weekends. Check the website for performance listings and to buy tickets, which rarely creep above €15. ✉ *Calle de Albuquerque 14, Chamberí* ☎ *91/445–5480* 🌐 *www.salaclamores.es* [M] *Bilbao.*

Chamartín

This sprawling neighborhood, which extends to the north of the city from Avenida de América, wasn't annexed to Madrid until 1948. During the following decades, and due to the construction of new sites such as the Chamartín Train Station and the National Auditorium of Music, it has been gaining popularity among madrileños as a good and lively place to live. The area has many office buildings, convention centers, and business hotels.

Restaurants

★ DiverXO

$$$$ | **ECLECTIC** | When you ask a madrileño about a remarkable food experience—something that stirs the senses beyond feeding one's appetite—DiverXO is often the first name you'll hear. There's just one take-no-prisoners tasting menu (called a "canvas") that runs €250. **Known for:** Madrid's only Michelin three-star; courses that use the whole table as a canvas; punk rock fine dining. [$] *Average main: €250* ✉ *NH Hotel Eurobuilding, Calle Padre Damian 23, Chamartín* ☎ *91/570–0766* 🌐 *www.diverxo.com* 🕒 *Closed Sun.–Tues.* [M] *Cuzco.*

Sacha

$$$$ | **SPANISH** | Settle into an unhurried feast at Sacha, a cozy bistro with soul-satisfying food and hand-selected wines, and you might never want to leave—especially if you strike up a conversation with Sacha himself, who's quite the story-teller. The cuisine is regional Spanish—think *butifarra* sausages with sautéed mushrooms or razor clams with black garlic emulsion—with just enough imagination to make you wonder why the restaurant isn't better known. **Known for:** impeccable steak tartare; Spanish bistro fare; hard-to-find wines. [$] *Average main: €30* ✉ *Calle Juan Hurtado de Mendoza 11, Chamartín* ☎ *91/345–5952* 🌐 *www.restaurantesacha.com* 🕒 *Closed Sun.* [M] *Cuzco.*

Hotels

★ Hotel NH Collection Madrid Eurobuilding

$$ | **HOTEL** | The towering NH Collection Madrid Eurobuilding, located blocks from Real Madrid's home stadium, is a state-of-the-art luxury property with large, airy rooms, and an enormous pool and gym complex. **Pros:** bargain rates; 180-degree views from some rooms; excellent gym and spa. **Cons:** hotel can't secure bookings at DiverXO; inconsistent service; very quiet area at night. [$] *Rooms from: €130* ✉ *Calle de Padre Damián 23, Chamartín* ☎ *91/353–7300* 🌐 *www.nh-hotels.com* 🛏 *440 rooms* 🍴 *No Meals* [M] *Cuzco.*

Hotel Puerta América Madrid

$$ | **HOTEL** | Inspired by Paul Eluard's *La Liberté*, whose verses are written across

¡GOOOOOOAALL!

Fútbol (or soccer) is Spain's number-one sport, and Madrid has four teams: Real Madrid, Atlético Madrid, Rayo Vallecano, and Getafe. The two major teams are Real Madrid and Atlético Madrid. For tickets, book online or call a week in advance to reserve and pick them up at the stadium—or, if the match isn't sold out, stand in line at the stadium of your choice. Ticket prices vary according to several factors: the importance of the rival, the seat location, the day of the week the match takes place, whether the match is aired on free TV or not, and the competition (Liga, Copa del Rey, Champions League or Europa League). Final dates and match times are often confirmed only a few days before so it can be hard to reserve in advance. That said, Real Madrid and Atlético Madrid never play at home the same week, so there is a football match every single week in the city.

Stadiums

Campo de Fútbol de Vallecas To enjoy a spirited match without the long lines and inflated price tag, step up to Rayo Vallecano's box office. The team's second-tier status doesn't make the games any less thrilling (think college ball vs. NBA), especially when you catch them on their home turf in Vallecas, which seats 14,708. You can feel good about your ticket purchase, too, since Rayo is known for its community activism. During the COVID-19 crisis, the team's charitable foundation sewed and distributed 12,000 masks for undersupplied hospitals. ✉ *Calle del Payaso Fofó 0, Puente de Villecas* ☎ *91/478–4329* 🌐 *www.rayovallecano.es* [M] *Portazgo.*

Santiago Bernabéu Stadium Home to Real Madrid, this stadium seats 85,400 and offers daytime tours of the facilities. A controversial $590 million renovation is on track to be completed by mid-2022; tour and game schedules may be affected, so check the website for updates. During the COVID-19 outbreak, the stadium was used as a storage facility for medical supplies. ✉ *Paseo de la Castellana 140, Chamartín* ☎ *91/398–4300* 🌐 *www.realmadrid.es* [M] *Santiago Bernabéu.*

Wanda Metrpolitano Since 2017, Atlético Madrid has called this stadium in the San Blas–Canillejas district home. ✉ *Av. de Luis Aragones 4, San Blas–Canilejas* 🌐 *www.atleticodemadrid.com/wandametropolitano* [M] *Estadio Metropolitano.*

the facade, the owners of this hotel granted an unlimited budget to 19 of the world's top architects and designers. **Pros:** candlelit pool and steam room area; 12 hotel designs in one—an architect's dream; top-notch restaurant and bars. **Cons:** frayed at the edges; miles from the center; design impractical in places. [$] *Rooms from: €165* ✉ *Av. de América 41, Chamartín* ☎ *91/744–5400* 🌐 *www.hotelpuertamerica.com* 🛏 *315 rooms* 🍴 *No Meals* [M] *Avenida de América.*

Hyatt Regency Hesperia Madrid
$$$ | **HOTEL** | The legendary Hesperia hotel was bought and renovated by Hyatt Regency is all about business stays. **Pros:** corporate-chic decor; 24-hour room service; dependable service. **Cons:** interior rooms can be dark; stuffy, business feel; miles from the city center. [$] *Rooms from: €215* ✉ *Paseo de la Castellana 57, Chamartín* ☎ *91/210–8800* 🌐 *www.hesperia.com* 🛏 *169 rooms* 🍴 *No Meals* [M] *Gregorio Marañón.*

Tetuán

As Madrid grew dramatically in the second half of the 19th century, rough-and-tumble barrios like Tetuán got a face-lift. Today, its main artery, Bravo Murillo, divides the more developed, business-oriented eastern section from the more residential and multicultural western area of the neighborhood.

 Restaurants

Al-Aga

$ | **MIDDLE EASTERN** | **FAMILY** | Madrileños love kebabs, and the smoky, juicy ones served at Al-Aga may be the city's best. Opened by a family of refugees fleeing Syria's civil war, Al-Aga draws on recipes handed down to the chef and owner, Labib, who cooks with care and attention to detail: Meat is ground by hand for each order, and all the sauces are homemade. **Known for:** Syrian specialties; grab-and-go style; flame-grilled kebabs. $ *Average main: €11* ✉ *Calle Villaamil 52, Tetuán* ☎ *91/070–3115* Ⓜ *Tetuán.*

★ Refusion

$ | **INTERNATIONAL** | **FAMILY** | Refusion's lovingly made international dishes—ranging from Venezuelan tequeños to Sudanese kofta to Syrian fatush—would be worth the quick metro ride to taste even *before* finding out that the restaurant is a cooperative project run by and for young refugees. So you'll not only want to buy the whole menu but also make a few calls to deep-pocketed friends who can help give this new, life-changing business a leg-up. **Known for:** international menu with something for everyone; so affordable; refugee-run restaurant. $ *Average main: €10* ✉ *Calle del Capitán Blanco Argibay 65, Tetuán* ☎ *69/958–1992* ⊕ *www.refusiondelivery.com* ⊗ *No dinner Sun. Closed Mon. and Tues.* Ⓜ *Valdeacederas.*

Nightlife

DANCE CLUBS

Oh My Club

DANCE CLUBS | At this hopping venue, popular among young Latino locals, you'll find plenty of space to dance (under the gaze of go-go girls) to rap, hip-hop, and reggaeton, and also quieter nooks where you can chat and sip a drink. ✉ *Calle Rosario Pino 14, Tetuán* ☎ *91/340–7537* ⊕ *www.ohmyclub.es* Ⓜ *Cuzco.*

Chapter 4

CENTRAL SPAIN

4

Updated by
Benjamin Kemper

⊙ Sights	🍴 Restaurants	🛏 Hotels	🛍 Shopping	🍸 Nightlife
★★★★★	★★★★☆	★★★☆☆	★★★★☆	★★★☆☆

WELCOME TO CENTRAL SPAIN

TOP REASONS TO GO

★ **Discover the Toledo of El Greco:** Tour the Renaissance painter's home and studio on an El Greco–theme tourist trail in the stunning city that the Greek-born painter called home.

★ **Be mesmerized by Cuenca's Hanging Houses:** The Casas Colgadas seem to defy gravity, clinging to a cliffside with views over Castile–La Mancha's parched plains.

★ **Wander Salamanca's old and new cathedrals:** Compare the intricate Late Gothic detail of the new with the Romanesque simplicity of the old.

★ **Visit Segovia's aqueduct:** Miraculously this soaring 2,000-year-old Roman aqueduct, constructed without mortar, still functions today.

★ **Time-travel to the Middle Ages:** The walled city of Cáceres is especially mystical at dusk with its skyline of ancient spires, towers, and cupolas that play host to swooping storks.

1 Toledo. Home to a treasure trove of medieval art and restored synagogues, mosques, and churches

2 Almagro. Relish in small-town charm and evening *tapeos* (tapas crawls) on the plaza.

3 Cuenca. See the Hanging Houses, then explore the Ciudad Encantada ("Enchanted City") with its alien rock formations.

4 Sigüenza. Marvel at one of Spain's most stunning Gothic cathedrals.

5 Segovia. Climb the watchtower of the Alcázar, said to have inspired Walt Disney.

6 Sepúlveda. Explore a medieval dungeon and 11th-century church in a town some call the most beautiful in Spain.

7 San Lorenzo de El Escorial. Bask in the grandeur of Habsburg Spain in the eponymous palace complex.

8 Ávila. Trace some of the best-preserved city walls in Europe and duck into ancient convents.

9 Salamanca. See if you can spot the "lucky frog" on the plateresque facade of Spain's oldest university.

10 Burgos. The famous "morcilla de Burgos" (local blood sausage) is well worth the pilgrimage.

11 León. Snap photos of vivid stained-glass panels in this city's Gothic cathedral.

12 Astorga. Uncover one of Gaudí's least-known masterpieces, the Episcopal Palace.

13 Villafranca del Bierzo. Vineyard-hop through the up-and-coming Bierzo wine region.

14 Jerte and El Valle del Jerte. Attend one of Spain's most breathtaking natural displays.

15 La Vera and Monasterio de Yuste. Come for natural springs, fresh ground *pimentón* (paprika), and the retirement estate of King Carlos V.

16 Cáceres. Time-travel back a few centuries in the UNESCO-protected old town, a filming site for *Game of Thrones*.

17 Trujillo. Learn about Spain's colonial past in the cradle of the conquistadores.

18 Guadalupe. Admire this jewel of a monastery in the foothills of the Sierra de Villuercas.

19 Mérida. Tour the immaculately restored Roman amphitheater.

ASTURIAS

CANTABRIA

NAVARRA

Villafranca
del Bierzo
13

León
11

12

Astorga

GALICIA

10 Burgos

LA RIOJA

Soria

PORTUGAL

Toro

Zamora

Valladolid

6 Sepulveda

Duero R.

ARAGON

CASTILE
AND LEÓN

Medinaceli

Salamanca

9

Segovia

5

Sigüenza

4

Ávila
8

San Lorenzo de
El Escorial
7

MADRID

MADRID

Alcalá de
Henares

SIERRA DE GREDOS

15 La Vera

Cuenca

Plasencia

14

Jerte and
El Valle del Jerte

Aranjuez

Tarancón

3

Toledo
1

CASTILE-
LA MANCHA

Cáceres
16

Trujillo

Guadalupe

17

18

Consuegra

Mota del Cuervo

Alcázar

La Roda

Malagon

Tomelloso

Badajoz

Ciudad
Real

Manzanares

Albacete

19 Mérida

2

EXTREMADURA

Almagro

Valdepenas

Hellín

Zafra

Puertollano

ANDALUSIA

MURCIA

0   30 mi

0   30 km

EATING AND DRINKING WELL IN CENTRAL SPAIN

Roast lamb with potatoes

In Spain's central *meseta*, or arid, high plateau, rustic country cooking provides comfort and energy. Roast lamb, pork, and goat are staples, as are soups; stews; and *migas*, bread crumbs fried with sundry meats and sausages.

Classic Castilian dishes include *cordero* (lamb) and *cochinillo* (suckling pig), roasted in wood-burning ovens, and *perdiz* (partridge), either marinated in escabeche (spiced vinaigrette), or served Toledo-style (braised in white wine). Broad-bean dishes are staples in the areas around Ávila and La Granja (Segovia), while *trucha* (trout) and *cangrejos de río* (crayfish that are virtually always imported these days), are Guadalajara specialties. Some of Castile's most surprising cuisine is found in Cuenca, where Sephardic and Moorish influences appear in dishes like gazpacho *pastor,* a stew made with several meats and a matzo-like flatbread. Across Spain's rural interior, wild mushrooms are a constant, most often cooked with little more than salt and olive oil in earthenware dishes; more elaborate preparations include

WHAT DON QUIXOTE ATE

"Somewhere in La Mancha, in a place whose name I do not care to remember..." begins the epic *Don Quixote*, yet the wines and hearty dishes of this region are some of Spain's most memorable. Cervantine menus based on dishes mentioned in the book are favorites at taverns throughout Quixote country southeast of Madrid. They usually feature *gachas manchegas* (a thick porridge of fried grass-pea flour and pork) and *duelos y quebrantos* (scrambled eggs and bacon).

LAMB

Roast lamb, *cordero asado*, is a favorite throughout Castile, while the subcategory of *lechazo*, or milk-fed lamb, is even more prized for its mild, ultratender meat, one of Spain's great delicacies.

PARTRIDGE

Perdiz a la toledana is one of Castile–La Mancha's most sought-after dishes and a masterpiece of *cocina de caza*, Spanish game-meat cooking. The faintly gamey partridges are slow-braised in wine with vinegar, olive oil, onions, garlic, and bay leaves until the sauce is thick and rich. October to February is hunting season for partridge and the best time to try it—just watch out for steel shot in the meat.

VEGETABLE STEW

La Mancha has moist vegetable-growing pockets along the Tajo River. *Pisto manchego*, a ratatouille-like vegetable stew with peppers, onions, tomatoes, and zucchini, is a classic. Served in earthenware *cazuelas*, often with a fried egg on top, it makes a wonderful light lunch with a bit of crusty bread and a glass of raspy local wine.

MIGAS DEL PASTOR

Translated as "shepherd's breadcrumbs," this ancient dish is made with stale bread that's softened with water

A simple dish of migas is an excellent way to use up leftover bread.

and fried in olive oil with lots of garlic and (optionally) eggs, bacon, chorizo, peppers, or potato. Fresh grapes are a traditional accompaniment.

GAZPACHO PASTOR (SHEPHERD'S STEW)

Andalusian gazpacho is a cold soup, but in La Mancha, especially around Cuenca, gazpacho is a thick, hot braise made with virtually everything in the barnyard. Partridge, hare, rabbit, hen, peppers, paprika, and *tortas de cenceña* (a flatbread with Jewish roots made especially for this dish) all find their way into the pot.

WINES OF CENTRAL SPAIN

Central Spain's finest wines are red, and most are bold, oaky, and high in alcohol. Wines made in the traditional style include Dominio de Valdepusa's Petit Verdot and Syrah blends (Toledo); Ribera del Duero's famed Tempranillos by Pingus, Protos, and Pago de Carraovejas; Extremadura's concentrated reds from Bodegas Habla and Ruiz Torres; and Bierzo's berry-forward Mencías from the likes of Descendientes de J. Palacios. Notable natural and/or biodynamic wineries in this area include Esencia Rural (Toledo), Envínate (Extremadura), Uva de Vida (Toledo), and Vinos Ambiz (Ávila). Winery visits are generally by appointment only.

Pisto manchego incorporates a variety of stewed vegetables.

Madrid, in the center of Spain, is an excellent jumping-off point for exploring, and the high-speed train puts many destinations within easy reach. The "Castiles," which bracket Madrid to the north and south, and Extremadura, bordering Portugal, are steeped in tradition and feel a world away from the ultramodern Spanish capital.

There's something of an underlying unity in Castile, the high, wide steppe of central Spain planted with olive trees and grapevines and punctuated with tiny medieval towns and the occasional scrubby sierra.

Over the centuries, poets and authors have characterized Castile as austere and melancholy. Gaunt mountain ranges frame the horizons; gorges and rocky outcrops break up flat expanses; and the fields around Ávila and Segovia are littered with giant boulders. Castilian villages are built predominantly of granite, and their severe, formidable look contrasts markedly with the whitewashed walls of most of southern Spain.

The very name Extremadura, literally "the far end of the Duero" (as in the Douro River), expresses the wild, isolated, and end-of-the-line character of the region bordering Portugal. With its poor soil and minimal industry, Extremadura hardly experienced the economic booms felt in other parts of Spain, and it's still the country's poorest province—but for the tourist, this otherworldly, lost-in-time feel is unforgettable. No other place in Spain has as many Roman monuments as

Mérida, capital of the vast Roman province of Lusitania, which included most of the western half of the Iberian Peninsula. Mérida guarded the Vía de la Plata, the major Roman highway that crossed Extremadura from north to south, connecting Gijón with Seville. The economy and the arts declined after the Romans left, but the region revived in the 16th century when explorers and conquerors of the so-called New World—from Francisco Pizarro and Hernán Cortés to Francisco de Orellana, first navigator of the Amazon—returned to their birthplace. These men built the magnificent palaces that now glorify towns such as Cáceres and Trujillo, and they turned the remote monastery of Guadalupe into one of the great artistic repositories of Spain.

MAJOR REGIONS

Castile–La Mancha is the land of Don Quixote, Miguel de Cervantes's chivalrous hero. Some of Spain's oldest and noblest cities are found here, steeped in culture and legend, though many have fallen into neglect due to rural flight and lack of investment. Traditional towns here are treeless warrens of whitewashed one-floor houses with indigo-painted plinths—squint and you could be in North

Africa. Toledo, the pre-Madrid capital of Castile, is the main destination, though travelers willing to venture farther afield can explore Cuenca with its Hanging Houses; Almagro with its green-and-white plaza and splendid parador; or Consuegra or Campo de Criptana, both of which sit under the gaze of Don Quixote-esque windmills.

Castile and León is Spain's windswept interior, stretching from the dry plains of Castile–La Mancha to the hilly vineyards of Ribera del Duero, and up to the foot of several mountain ranges: the Sierra de Gredos, Sierra de Francia, and northward toward the towering Picos de Europa. The area combines two of Spain's old kingdoms, Léon and Old Castile, each with their many treasures of palaces, castles, and cathedrals. The region's crown jewel is Segovia with its Roman aqueduct and 12th-century *alcázar*, though medieval Ávila is a close second. Farther north lie Salamanca, dominated by dusky sandstone buildings, and the ancient capitals of Burgos and León. Burgos, an early outpost of Christianity, has what most consider the most beautiful Gothic cathedral in Spain. León is a vibrant college town with a budget-friendly tapas scene and nationally famous modern art museum.

Rugged **Extremadura** is a nature lover's paradise, so bring your mountain bike (or plan on renting one), hiking boots, and binoculars. The lush Jerte Valley and the craggy peaks of the Sierra de Gredos mark upper Extremadura's fertile landscape. South of the Jerte Valley is the 15th-century Yuste Monastery in the village of Cuacos de Yuste. Don't miss medieval Cáceres—boasting one of the best-preserved old towns in Europe—and Mérida, with its immaculately preserved Roman amphitheater. Extremadura's other main towns—Badajoz, Trujillo, Olivenza, and Zafra—are charming (if a tad sleepy) and virtually tourist-free.

Planning

When to Go

July and August can be brutally hot, and November through February can get bitterly cold, especially in the mountains. May and October, when the weather is sunny but relatively cool, are the two best months to visit.

Spring is the ideal season in Extremadura, especially in the countryside, when the valleys and hills bloom with wildflowers. The stunning spectacle of cherry blossom season in the Jerte Valley and La Vera takes place around mid-March (for more information, visit *www.turismovalledeljerte.com*). Fall is also a good time for Extremadura, though there may be rain starting in late October.

Planning Your Time

Madrid is an excellent hub for venturing farther into Spain, but with so many choices, we've divided destinations into must-see stand-alone excursions and worthy pit stops en route to other parts of the country. Some are day trips; others are best overnight.

The top stand-alone destinations from Madrid are **Toledo, Segovia** (add **Sepúlveda** if time allows), **Salamanca,** and **Sigüenza,** in order of importance. Salamanca should be an overnight trip as it's farther and has buzzy nightlife, while the others can be long day-trips.

If you're traveling to other areas in Spain and beyond, we suggest seeing the following destinations along the way:

Visiting Salamanca? Stop in **Ávila** (buses go direct to Salamanca without stopping, but most trains stop in Ávila).

Visiting Santander, San Sebastián, or Bilbao? Stop in **Burgos.**

Visiting Asturias? Stop in **León**.

Visiting Galicia? Stop in **Villafranca del Bierzo** or **Astorga.**

Visiting Córdoba or Granada? Stop in **Almagro.**

Visiting Valencia? Stop in **Cuenca.** Most trains, including the high-speed AVE to Valencia, call there.

Visiting Portugal? Stop in **Extremadura.**

Extremadura is a neglected destination, even for Spanish tourists, but it's a beautiful part of the country with fascinating cities like Cáceres (a UNESCO World Heritage Site) and Trujillo, both of which have been used as filming locations for *Game of Thrones.* You can get a lightning impression of Extremadura in a day's drive from Madrid (or on a pit stop on the way to Lisbon), though overnighting is preferable. It's about 2½ hours from Madrid to **Jerte**; from there, take the A66 south to **Cáceres** before heading east to **Trujillo** on the N521. Split your time evenly between Cáceres and Trujillo. If you have more time, spend a day exploring the Roman monuments in **Mérida** and do some world-famous bird-watching in the **Parque Natural de Monfragüe,** near **Plasencia.** A deeper dive into the region must include a visit the stunning **Monasterio de Yuste,** where Spain's founding emperor, Carlos V, died in 1558.

Getting Here and Around

AIR
The only international airport in central Spain is Madrid's Barajas; Salamanca, León, and Valladolid have domestic airports but receive very few flights. Extremadura's only airport is Badajoz, which receives domestic flights from Madrid and Barcelona.

AIRPORT Madrid–Barajas Adolfo Suárez Airport. ☎ *91/321–1000* ⊕ *www.aena.es.*

BUS
Bus connections between Madrid and the "Castiles" are frequent and cheap; there are several stations and stops in Madrid. Because of unpredictable travel patterns due to COVID-19, some of the below routes may not be fully operational. Double-check all timetables on carriers' websites for up-to-date information.

Buses to Toledo (1 hour) leave every half hour from the southern Plaza Elíptica, and buses to Segovia (1¼ hours) leave every hour from La Sepulvedana's headquarters, near Príncipe Pío. Jiménez Dorado sends buses to Ávila (1¾ hours) from the Estación del Sur. ALSA has service to León (4½ hours), Valladolid (2¼ hours), and Soria (3 hours). Avanza serves Cuenca (2¾ hours), Salamanca (3 hours), and Burgos (2½ hours).

From Burgos, buses head north to the Basque Country; from León, you can press on to Asturias. Service between towns is not as frequent as it is to and from Madrid, so in some cases, you may find it quicker to return to Madrid and make your way from there. Online reservations are rarely necessary but might save you a few bucks and the minutes you'd otherwise spend waiting in line.

Buses to Extremadura's main cities from Madrid leave on time. Some examples of destinations from Madrid are: Cáceres (seven daily), Guadalupe (two daily), Trujillo (12 daily), and Mérida (seven daily). For schedules and prices, check the tourist offices or consult the individual bus lines. Note that it's best to avoid rush hour as journeys can be delayed.

A headache-free way to plan bus travel is on *www.omio.com,* a scheduling and purchasing site that allows you to view different prices and bus companies on one platform.

CONTACTS ALSA. ☎ *90/242–2242* ⊕ *www.alsa.es.***Avanza.** *(Auto-Res)* ☎ *91/272–2832* ⊕ *www.avanzabus. com.***La Sepulvedana.** ☎ *90/211–9699*

⊕ *lasepulvedana.es.***Larrea.** (*Avanza*)
☎ *91/851–5592* ⊕ *larrea.avanzagrupo.*
*com.***Movelia.** ☎ *90/264–6428* ⊕ *www.*
movelia.es.

CAR

Major highways—the A1 through A6—
spoke out from Madrid, making Spain's
farthest corners no more than five- to six-
hour drives. If possible, avoid returning to
Madrid on major highways at the end of a
weekend or a holiday. The beginning and
end of August are notorious for traffic
jams, as is Semana Santa (Holy Week),
which starts on Palm Sunday and ends
on Easter Sunday. National (toll-free)
highways and back roads are slower but
provide one of the great pleasures of
driving around the Castilian countryside:
surprise encounters with castles, quaint
villages, and spectacular vistas.

If you're driving from Madrid to Extremadura, the six-lane A5 moves quickly. The
A66, or Vía de la Plata, which crosses
Extremadura from north to south, is also
effective. The fastest way from Portugal
is the (Portuguese) A6 from Lisbon to
Badajoz (not to be confused with the
Spanish A6, which runs northwest from
Madrid to Galicia). Side roads—particularly those that cross the wilder mountainous districts, such as the Sierra de
Guadalupe—differ in terms of upkeep but
are wonderfully scenic.

Mileage from Madrid:

Madrid to Burgos is 243 km (151 miles).

Madrid to Cáceres is 299 km (186 miles).

Madrid to Cuenca is 168 km (104 miles).

Madrid to Granada is 428 km (266 miles).

Madrid to Léon is 334 km (208 miles).

Madrid to Salamanca is 212 km (132
miles).

Madrid to Segovia is 91 km (57 miles).

Madrid to Toledo is 88 km (55 miles).

Madrid to Ávila is 114 km (71 miles).

RIDESHARE

As slow, right-lane-cruising buses and
clunky old trains make intercity travel in
Castile a nuisance, travelers of all ages
are increasingly taking rideshares, the
most popular of which is Blablacar. Its
free platform allows you to book ahead
via debit or credit card and message
with the driver to set pickup and drop-off
points. It's not only the quickest way
from A to B without a rental car but also
often the cheapest, since drivers aren't
allowed to make a profit on trips (the
amount you pay only offsets costs for
tolls and gas). Check *www.blablacar.
com* for details.

TRAIN

The main towns in Castile and León and
Castile–La Mancha are accessible by
multiple daily trains from Madrid, with
tickets running about €10–€30, depending on train speed (the high-speed
AVE service costs more), the time of
day, and the day of the week. Several
towns make feasible day trips: there are
commuter trains from Madrid to Segovia
(30 minutes), Guadalajara (30 minutes),
and Toledo (30 minutes). Trains to Toledo
depart from Madrid's Atocha station;
trains to Salamanca, Burgos, and León
depart from Chamartín; and both stations
serve Ávila, Segovia, and Sigüenza,
though Chamartín has more frequent
service. Trains from Segovia go only to
Madrid, but you can change at Villalba for
Ávila and Salamanca.

For Extremadura, notoriously rickety
and sluggish trains from Madrid stop at
Monfragüe, Plasencia, Cáceres, Mérida,
Zafra, and Badajoz and run as often as
six times daily. The journey from Madrid
to Cáceres takes about four hours.
Within the province there are services
from Badajoz to Cáceres (three daily, 1
hour 55 minutes), to Mérida (five daily,
40 minutes), and to Plasencia (two daily,
2 hours 40 minutes); from Cáceres to
Badajoz (three daily, 1 hour 55 minutes),
to Mérida (five daily, 1 hour), to Plasencia

(four daily, 1 hour 10 minutes), and to Zafra (two daily, 2 hours 10 minutes); from Plasencia to Badajoz (two daily, 3 hours), to Cáceres (four daily, 1 hour 10 minutes), and to Mérida (four daily, 2 hours 10 minutes). Several cities have separate train stations for normal versus AVE high-speed rail service; the newer AVE stations are often farther from town centers.

⚠ **Expect delays and schedule changes as the government continues to roll out a €20 million project to update the Extremaduran train network.**

CONTACTS RENFE. ☎ 90/232–0320 ⊕ *www.renfe.com.*

Restaurants

This is Spain's rugged heartland, bereft of touristy hamburger joints and filled instead with the country's most traditional *tabernas*, which attract Spanish foodies from across the country. Some of the most renowned restaurants in this region are small and family run, while a few new avant-garde spots in urban areas serve up modern architecture as well as experimental fusion dishes.

Restaurant reviews have been shortened. For full information, visit Fodors. com.

Hotels

Small, independently owned hotels abound in Castile and León, and many of the country's best-reviewed Paradores (*www.paradores.es*) can be found here as well in quiet towns such as Almagro, Ávila, Cuenca, and Sigüenza. Paradores in Toledo, Segovia, and Salamanca are modern buildings with magnificent views and, in the case of Segovia, have wonderful indoor and outdoor swimming pools. Reacting to a spate of bad press and unsatisfactory customer reviews, the Parador brand invested €21 million in its Castile and León properties in 2019, but it came under fire again in 2020 when—despite raking in €14 million in profits the year prior—it cut most workers' salaries by a quarter in the midst of the COVID-19 outbreak. Corporate politics aside, there are plenty of pleasant alternatives to Paradores such as Segovia's Hotel Infanta Isabel, Salamanca's Hotel Rector, and Cuenca's Posada de San José, housed in a 16th-century convent.

In Extremadura, Paradores occupy buildings of great historic or architectural interest; the Extremaduran government also runs a few hospederías , regional offshoots of the Parador chain. Most "high-end" hotels, with a few exceptions (such as the space-age Miluna bubble hotel in Toledo), are modern boxes with little character. You're almost always better off staying in a charming, underrated *hotel rural* or *casa rural* (guesthouse).

Hotel reviews have been shortened; for full information, visit Fodors.com.

What It Costs in Euros

	$	$$	$$$	$$$$
RESTAURANTS				
	under €12	€12–€17	€18–€22	over €22
HOTELS				
	under €90	€90–€125	€126–€180	over €180

Tours

In summer, the tourist offices of Segovia, Toledo, and Sigüenza organize Trenes Turísticos (miniature tourist trains) that glide past all the major sights; contact local tourist offices for schedules.

A great way to get to know Extremadura is by bike (in any season but scorching summer). You can essentially forego maps by following the ancient Roman road, the Vía de la Plata, which runs through Extremadura from north to south along the A66 and passes by Plasencia, Cáceres, Mérida, and Zafra. Note that the region north of the province of Cáceres, including the Jerte Valley, La Vera, and the area surrounding Guadalupe, is mountainous and uneven: be prepared for an invigoratingly bumpy ride. The regional government has also opened four Vías Verdes, or "green way" paths geared toward hiking and biking, along disused railroads; a notable (if rugged) one goes from Logrosán (a couple of miles southwest of Guadalupe) to Villanueva de la Serena (east of Mérida and near Don Benito). Check tourist offices for maps of these and other trails.

Equiberia

Horseback tours, ranging 1–10 days, offer a unique way to experience the gorges, fields, and forests of the Sierra de Guadarrama, Segovia, Ávila, and beyond. ✉ *Camino Cepedamingo, Ávila ✛ in Navarredonda de Gredos* ☎ *68/934–3974* ⊕ *www.equiberia.com* ✉ *From €150.*

Valle Aventura

Hiking, horseback riding, cycling, and kayaking trips in the Jerte Valley can be organized with this company. ✉ *Garganta de los Infiernos Actividades en la Naturaleza* ☎ *63/663–1182* ⊕ *www.valleaventura.com* 🖂 *From €180.*

Toledo

88 km (55 miles) southwest of Madrid.

The spiritual capital of Castile, Toledo sits atop a rocky mount surrounded on three sides by the Río Tajo (Tagus River). When the Romans arrived here in 192 BC, they built their fortress (the Alcázar) on the highest point of the rock. Later, the Visigoths remodeled the stronghold.

In the 8th century, the Moors arrived and strengthened Toledo's reputation as a center of religion and learning. Today, the Moorish legacy is evident in Toledo's strong crafts tradition, the mazelike streets, and the predominance of brick construction (rather than the stone of many of Spain's historical cities). For the Moors—an imprecise catch-all term for Islam-practicing North African settlers of the Iberian Peninsula—beauty was to be savored from within rather than displayed on the surface. Even Toledo's cathedral—one of the most richly endowed in Spain—is hard to see from the outside, largely obscured by the warren of houses around it.

Alfonso VI, aided by El Cid ("Lord Conqueror"), captured the city in 1085 and dubbed himself emperor of Toledo. Under the Christians, the town's strong intellectual life was maintained, and Toledo became famous for its school of translators, who taught Arab medicine, law, culture, and philosophy. Religious tolerance continued, and during the rule of Pedro the Cruel (so named because he allegedly had members of his own family murdered to advance his position), a Jewish banker, Samuel Levi, became the royal treasurer and one of the wealthiest men in the booming city. By the late 1400s, however, hostility toward Jews and Arabs had grown as the ruthlessly intolerant Catholic monarchs established Toledo as a bastion of the Catholic church.

Under Toledo's long line of cardinals—most notably Mendoza, Tavera, and Cisneros—Renaissance Toledo was a center of the humanities. Economically and politically, however, the city began to decline at the end of the 15th century. The expulsion of the Jews from Spain in 1492, as part of the Spanish Inquisition, eroded Toledo's economic and intellectual prowess. Then, when Madrid became the permanent center of the Spanish court in 1561, Toledo lost its political importance too, and the expulsion from Spain of the converted Arabs (Moriscos) in 1601 meant the departure of most of the city's artisans. The years the painter El Greco spent in Toledo—from 1572 to his death in 1614—were those of the city's decline, which is greatly reflected in his works.

In the late 19th century, after hundreds of years of neglect, the works of El Greco came to be widely appreciated, and Toledo was transformed into a major tourist destination—even if the cosmopolitan luxury one might expect from such a hot spot never quite arrived. The winding streets and steep hills can be tough to navigate, especially when you're searching for a specific sight, so take a full day (or three) to absorb the town's medieval trappings—and relish in getting lost from time to time.

A note on COVID-19: Travel restrictions devastated Toledo in 2020 and 2021 as the city lost its main economic engine, the cash flow of 2 million annual tourists. By mid-2021, one in five local businesses was on the brink of permanently closing, and the historical center remained a ghost town. When shopping and making bookings, seek out family-run establishments to help them recover.

GETTING HERE AND AROUND

The best way to get to Toledo from Madrid is the high-speed AVE train, which leaves from Madrid at least nine times daily from Atocha station and gets you there in 30 minutes. From the ornate Neo-Mudejar train station, take a taxi, bus (L61 or L62), or walk the 1½ km (1 mile) to the city center.

ALSA buses leave Madrid every half hour from Plaza Elíptica and take 1¼ hours.

TOURS

Toledo de la Mano

Toledophile Adolfo Ferrero, author of a 200-page guidebook about the town, delves far deeper on his private tours than those run by competitors, touching on the city's history of multiculturalism and its significance in medieval Europe. Groups of up to 55 people can be accommodated. ✉ *Calle Nuncio Viejo 10, Toledo* ☎ *62/917–7810* ⊕ *www.toledodelamano. com* ✉ *From €140.*

Toledo Tours

Self-guided tour packages cater to those interested in the city's gastronomy, art, history, and other aspects, with various mix-and-match "Toledopass" deals including admission to various museums and landmarks. Pick the itinerary that best suits your interests and cut the lines. ✉ *Toledo* ☎ *92/582–6616* ⊕ *www.toledo- turismo.org* ✉ *From €19.*

Toledo Train Vision

This unabashedly touristy "train" chugs past many of Toledo's main sights, departing from the Plaza de Zocodover every hour on the hour during the week, and every 30 minutes on weekends. The tour takes 45–50 minutes and has recorded information in 16 languages (including English, Spanish, and French) plus children's versions in those three languages, too. Buy tickets at the kiosk in Plaza de Zocodover. ✉ *Pl. de Zocodover, Toledo* ☎ *62/530–1890* ✉ *€7.*

VISITOR INFORMATION

CONTACTS Toledo Tourist Office. ✉ *Pl. de Zocodover 8, Toledo* ☎ *92/526–7666, 68/785–4965, 92/523–9121* ⊕ *www. turismo.toledo.es.*

Sights

Alcázar

MILITARY SIGHT | Originally a Moorish citadel (*al-qasr* is Arabic for "fortress") and occupied from the 10th century until the Reconquest, Toledo's Alcázar is on a hill just outside the walled city, dominating the horizon. The south facade—the building's most severe—is the work of Juan de Herrera, of Escorial fame, while the east facade incorporates a large section of battlements. The finest facade is the northern, one of many Toledan works by Miguel Covarrubias, who did more than any other architect to introduce the Renaissance style here. The building's architectural highlight is his Italianate courtyard, which, like most other parts of the building, was largely rebuilt after the Spanish Civil War, when the Alcázar was besieged by the Republicans. Though the Nationalists' ranks were depleted, they held on to the building. Dictator Francisco Franco later turned the Alcázar into a monument to Nationalist bravery. It now houses the Museo del Ejército (Military Museum), which was formerly in Madrid. Hang onto your ticket—it's needed when you exit the museum. ✉ *Cuesta de los Capuchinos, Toledo* ☎ *92/523–8800* ⊕ *www.museo.ejercito.es* ✉ *From €5 (free Sun. 10–3).*

Calle del Comercio

STREET | Near Plaza de Zocodover, this is the town's narrow and busy pedestrian thoroughfare. It's lined with bars and shops and shaded in summer by awnings. It was repaved in 2021, taking advantage of the absence of tourists. ✉ *Calle del Comercio, Toledo.*

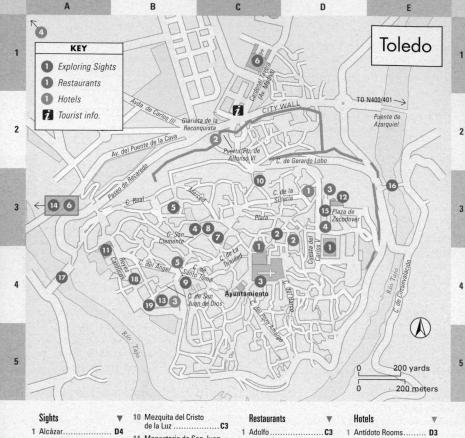

Toledo

KEY
- Exploring Sights
- Restaurants
- Hotels
- Tourist info.

★ **Cathedral**

CHURCH | One of the most impressive structures in all of Spain, this is a must-see on any visit to the city. The elaborate structure owes its impressive Mozarabic chapel, with an elongated dome crowning the west facade, to Jorge Manuel Theotokópoulos. The rest of the facade is mainly early 15th century. Immediately to your right is a beautifully carved plateresque doorway by Covarrubias, marking the entrance to the Treasury, which houses a small crucifixion scene by the Italian painter Cimabue and an extraordinarily intricate late-15th-century monstrance by Juan del Arfe. The ceiling is an excellent example of Mudejar (11th- to 16th-century Moorish-influenced) workmanship. From here, walk around to the ambulatory. In addition to Italianate frescoes by Juan de Borgoña and an exemplary baroque illusionism by Narciso Tomé known as the Transparente, you'll find several El Grecos, including one version of *El Espolio* (*Christ Being Stripped of His Raiment*), the first recorded instance of the painter in Spain. ⊠ *Calle Cardenal Cisneros 1,* ☎ *92/522–2241* ⊕ *www.catedralprimada.es* ⊠ *From €10.*

★ **Convento de San Clemente**

CHURCH | Founded in 1131, this is Toledo's oldest convent—and it's still in use. The handful of nuns who live here produce sweet wine and marzipan. The impressive complex, a bit outside the city center, includes ruins of a mosque on which a chapel was built in the Middle Ages, those of an Islamic house and courtyard (with an ancient well and Arab baths), and those of a Jewish house from the same period. Free tours, offered twice daily (though not dependably—be forewarned), might include a visit to the kitchen where the Mother Superior will let you sample some sweets if she's in a good mood. Skip the touristy marzipan shops and buy the real stuff here. There's also an adjacent cultural center with rotating history exhibits. ⊠ *Calle San Clemente, Toledo* ☎ *92/525–3080*

⊠ *Free* ⊙ *Closed sporadically (call before visiting).*

Convento de Santo Domingo el Antiguo (*Convento de Santo Domingo de Silos; Santo Domingo Convent*)

CHURCH | This 16th-century Cistercian convent houses the earliest of El Greco's Toledo paintings as well as the crypt where the artist is believed to be buried. The friendly nuns at the convent will show you around its odd little museum, which includes decaying bone relics of little-known saints and a life-size model of John the Baptist's decapitated head. ⊠ *Pl. Santo Domingo el Antiguo, Toledo* ☎ *92/522–2930* ⊠ *€2.*

Hospital de Tavera (*Hospital de San Juan Bautista*)

HOSPITAL | Architect Alonso de Covarrubias's last work, this hospital lies outside the city walls, beyond Toledo's main northern gate. A fine example of Spanish Renaissance architecture, the building also houses the **Museo de Duque de Lema** in its southern wing. The most important work in the museum's miscellaneous collection is a painting by the 17th-century artist José Ribera. The hospital's monumental chapel holds El Greco's *Baptism of Christ* and the exquisitely carved marble tomb of Cardinal Tavera, the last work of Alonso de Berruguete. Descend into the crypt to experience some bizarre acoustical effects. A full ticket includes the hospital, museum, old pharmacy, and Renaissance patios; a partial ticket includes everything except the museum. Guided tours are available at 45-minute intervals. ⊠ *Calle Duque de Lerma 2 (aka Calle Cardenal Tavera), Toledo* ☎ *92/522–0451* ⊕ *www.fundacionmedinaceli.org/ monumentos/hospital* ⊠ *€6.*

★ **Iglesia de San Ildefonso** (*San Ildefonso Church, The Jesuits*)

CHURCH | Sometimes called "Los Jesuitas," for the religious order that founded it, the Iglesia de San Ildefonso is named for Toledo's patron saint, a 7th-century bishop. It was consecrated in 1718 after

Did You Know?

The alcázar of Toledo
has dominated the city
since at least the 3rd
century. It is the setting
for an important scene
of Franquist lore: During
the Spanish Civil War,
the Nationalist colonel
Moscardó was defend-
ing the building against
overwhelming Republican
forces. The Republicans
held his son hostage,
demanding the alcázar be
surrendered. To his son's
entreaties to "surrender
or they will shoot me,"
the father replied, "Then
commend your soul to
God and die like a hero."

taking 150 years to build the baroque stone facade with twin Corinthian columns. Its semispherical dome is one of the icons of Toledo's skyline. This impressive building's tower affords some of the best views over Toledo. ⊠ *Pl. Juan de Mariana 1, Toledo* ☎ *92/525–1507* ✍ *€3.*

Iglesia de San Román

CHURCH | Hidden in a virtually unspoiled part of Toledo, this early-13th-century Mudejar church (built on the site of an earlier Visigoth one) is now the **Museo de los Concilios y de la Cultura Visigoda** (Visigoth Museum) with exhibits of statuary, manuscript illustrations, jewelry, and an extensive collection of frescoes. The church tower is adjacent to the ruins of Roman baths. ⊠ *Calle San Román, Toledo* ☎ *92/522–7872* ✍ *€6 (free Fri. and Sat. 4:30–6:30 and Sun. 10–2:30).*

★ Iglesia de Santo Tomé (Santo Tomé Church)

CHURCH | Not to be confused with the marzipan shop bearing the same name, this chapel topped with a Mudejar tower was built specially to house El Greco's most masterful painting, *The Burial of Count Orgaz.* Using vivid colors and splashes of light, he portrays the benefactor of the church being buried with the posthumous assistance of St. Augustine and St. Stephen, who have appeared at the funeral to thank the count for his donations to religious institutions named after the two saints. Though the count's burial took place in the 14th century, El Greco painted the onlookers in contemporary 16th-century costumes and included people he knew; the boy in the foreground is one of El Greco's sons, and the sixth figure on the left is said to be the artist himself. Santo Tomé is Toledo's most visited church besides the cathedral, so to avoid crowds, plan to visit as soon as the building opens. ⊠ *Pl. del Conde 4, Calle Santo Tomé,* ☎ *92/525–6098* ⊕ *www.santotome.org* ✍ *€3.*

Mezquita del Cristo de la Luz (Mosque of Christ of the Light)

MOSQUE | Originally a tiny Visigothic church, the mosque-chapel was transformed into a mosque during the Moorish occupation. The Islamic arches and vaulting survived, making this the most important relic of Moorish Toledo, even if a glaringly out of place sculpture of Jesus on the cross is the centerpiece of the building today. Legend has it that the chapel got its name when Alfonso VI's horse, striding triumphantly into Toledo in 1085, fell to its knees out front (a white stone marks the spot). It was then "discovered" that a candle had burned continuously behind the masonry the whole time the Muslims had been in power. Allegedly, the first Mass of the Reconquest was held here, and later a Mudejar apse was added. There are remnants of a Roman house in the yard nearby. ⊠ *Cuesta de Carmelitas Descalzos 10,* ☎ *92/525–4191* ✍ *€3.*

★ Monasterio de San Juan de los Reyes

CHURCH | This convent church in western Toledo was erected by Ferdinand and Isabella to commemorate their victory at the Battle of Toro in 1476. (It was also intended to be their burial place, but their wish changed after Granada was recaptured from the Moors in 1492, and their actual tomb is in that city's Capilla Real.) The breathtakingly intricate building is largely the work of architect Juan Guas, who considered it his masterpiece and asked to be buried there himself. In true plateresque fashion, the white interior is covered with inscriptions and heraldic motifs. ⊠ *Calle San Juan de los Reyes 2, Toledo* ☎ *92/522–3802* ⊕ *www.sanjuandelosreyes.org* ✍ *€3.*

Museo de Santa Cruz

ART MUSEUM | In a 16th-century Renaissance hospital with a stunning Classical-Plateresque facade, this museum is open all day without a break (unlike many of Toledo's other sights). Works of art have replaced the hospital beds, and among the displays is El Greco's *Assumption* of 1613, the artist's last known work. A small Museo de Arqueología (Archaeology Museum) is in and around the hospital's delightful cloister. ⊠ *Calle Cervantes 3, Toledo* ☎ *92/522–1402* ☞ *€4, free Weds. after 4 and Sun.* ☉ *Closed Sun. after 2:30.*

Museo del Greco (*El Greco Museum*)
ART MUSEUM | This house that once belonged to Peter the Cruel's treasurer, Samuel Levi, is said to have later been El Greco's home, though historians now believe he actually lived across the street. Nevertheless, the interior of the El Greco Museum is decorated to resemble a typical house of the artist's time. The house is now incorporated into a revamped El Greco museum with several of the artist's paintings, including a panorama of Toledo with the Hospital of Tavera in the foreground, and works by several of El Greco's students (including his son) and other 16th- and 17th-century artists. Medieval caves have been excavated at the site, and there's a beautiful garden in which to take refuge from Toledo's often-scorching summer heat. The impressive museum complex has been the centerpiece for Toledo tourism since the "El Greco 2014" festival, marking the 400th anniversary of the artist's death. ⊠ *Paseo del Tránsito, Toledo* ☎ *92/522–3665* ☞ *€3 (free Sat. after 2).*

Museo Ruiz de Luna
ART MUSEUM | Most of the region's pottery is made in Talavera de la Reina, 76 km (47 miles) west of Toledo. At this museum you can watch artisans throw local clay, then trace the development of Talavera's world-famous ceramics, chronicled through some 1,500 tiles, bowls, vases, and plates back to the 14th century. ⊠ *Place de San Augustín, Calle San Agustín el Viejo 13, Talavera de la Reina* ☎ *92/580–0149* ⊕ *cultura.castillala-mancha.es* ☞ *€3* ☉ *Closed Mon.*

Plaza de Zocodover
PLAZA/SQUARE | Toledo's main square was built in the early 17th century as part of an unsuccessful attempt to impose a rigid geometry on the chaotic Moorish streets. Over the centuries, this tiny plaza has hosted bullfights, executions (autos-da-fé) of heretics during the Spanish Inquisition, and countless street fairs. Today it's home to the largest and oldest marzipan store in town, Santo Tomé. You can catch intracity buses here, and the tourist office is on the south side of the plaza. ⊠ *Pl. Zocodover, Toledo.*

Puente de Alcántara
BRIDGE | Roman in origin, this is the city's oldest bridge. Next to it is a heavily restored castle built after the Christian capture of 1085 and, above this, a vast and severe military academy, an eyesore of Francoist architecture. From the other side of the Río Tajo, the bridge offers fine views of Toledo's historic center and the Alcázar. ⊠ *Calle Gerardo Lobo, Toledo.*

Puente de San Martín
BRIDGE | This pedestrian bridge on the western edge of Toledo dates to 1203 and has splendid horseshoe arches. At forty meters long, it was one of the longest bridges in the world at the time of construction. ⊠ *Puente de San Martín, Toledo.*

★ **Sinagoga de Santa María La Blanca**
SYNAGOGUE | Founded in 1203, Toledo's second synagogue—situated in the heart of the Jewish Quarter—is nearly two centuries older than the more elaborate Tránsito, just down the street. Santa María's white interior has a forest of columns supporting capitals with fine filigree work, a wonder of Mudejar architecture. It was a center of study and prayer until the 1355 assault on the Jewish Quarter and subsequent pogroms in 1391. ⊠ *Calle de los Reyes Católicos 4, Toledo* ☎ *92/522–7257* ☞ *€3.*

Toledo's Santa María la Blanca synagogue is a fascinating symbol of cultural cooperation: built by Islamic architects, in a Christian land, for Jewish use.

★ **Sinagoga del Tránsito** (*Museo Sefardí, Sephardic Museum*)
SYNAGOGUE | This 14th-century synagogue's plain exterior belies sumptuous interior walls embellished with colorful Mudejar decoration. There are inscriptions in Hebrew and Arabic glorifying God, Peter the Cruel, and Samuel Levi (the original patron). It's a rare example of architecture reflecting Arabic as the lingua franca of medieval Spanish Jews. It's said that Levi imported cedars from Lebanon for the building's construction, echoing Solomon when he built the First Temple in Jerusalem. This is one of only three synagogues still fully standing in Spain (two in Toledo, one in Córdoba), from an era when there were hundreds—though more are in the process of being excavated. Adjoining the main hall is the **Museo Sefardí,** a small but informative museum of Jewish culture in Spain. ✉ *Calle Samuel Levi 2, Toledo* ☎ *92/522–3665* 🌐 *www.mecd.gob.es/msefardi/home.html* 🎫 *€3 (free Sat. afternoon and Sun.).*

🍴 Restaurants

Adolfo
$$$$ | **SPANISH** | Visit this white-tablecloth restaurant, situated steps from the cathedral, for traditional Toledan recipes with fine-dining twists complemented by some 2,800 wines stored in a 9th-century cave. Don't pass up the hearty partridge stew, deemed the best in Spain by the former Spanish king Juan Carlos I; it sings alongside a glass of Adolfo's proprietary red wine. **Known for:** game dishes; chef's menu; historic building. [$] *Average main: €50* ✉ *Calle del Hombre de Palo 7, Toledo* ☎ *92/522–7321* 🌐 *www.grupoadolfo.com* 🕒 *No dinner Sun.*

Bar Ludeña
$$ | **SPANISH** | Locals and visitors come together at this old-timey tapas bar for steaming cauldrons of *carcamusas toledanas,* a local meat stew studded with peas and chorizo. (Give the rest of the menu a pass.) **Known for:** rustic ambience; free tapa with every drink; hearty carcamusa stew. [$] *Average main:*

€12 ✉ *Pl. de la Magdalena 10, Toledo* ☎ *92/522–3384* ⏱ *Closed Wed.*

★ Cervecería El Trébol

$$ | **SPANISH** | You can't leave Toledo without indulging in one of El Trébol's famous *bombas,* fried fist-size spheres of mashed potato stuffed with spiced meat and anointed with aioli. They're best enjoyed on the twinkly outdoor patio with a locally brewed beer in hand. **Known for:** local craft beers; to-die-for bombas; most pleasant patio in town. Ⓢ *Average main: €15* ✉ *Calle de Santa Fe 1, Toledo* ☎ *92/528–1297* ⊕ *www.cerveceriatrebol. com.*

Cervecería Entrecalles

$ | **SPANISH** | With 10 artisanal beers on tap and 150 available by the bottle— many of them locally brewed—Entrecalles is Toledo's premier craft beer bar. A basic but well-executed bar-food menu (burgers, patatas bravas, croquetas) provides ballast for all the suds; the prix-fixes are a steal. Ⓢ *Average main: €10* ✉ *Calle de la Paz, Toledo* ☎ *92/5041678* ⊕ *www. cerveceriaartesana.es* ⏱ *Closed Mon.*

★ Churrería Santo Tomé

$ | **SPANISH** | **FAMILY** | Recharge at this adorable four-table churro shop , established over a century ago, with hot homemade churros dipped in melted chocolate so thick it's almost spreadable. The 6 am opening time means you can indulge in churros for breakfast like a local. **Known for:** local institution; coffee and hot chocolate; fresh and feather-light churros. Ⓢ *Average main: €5* ✉ *Calle Santo Tomé 27, Toledo* ☎ *92/521–6324.*

★ Restaurante Iván Cerdeño

$$$$ | **SPANISH** | The buzziest opening in Toledo in recent memory, chef Iván Cerdeño's namesake restaurant, inaugurated in 2019, is a beacon of Castilian *alta gastronomía*—think architectural dishes composed of foams, spherified sauces, and edible flowers served in a modern white-tablecloth dining room. The ever-rotating tasting menus almost

always feature a course or two of local wild game such as partridge or roe deer. **Known for:** secluded location across the Tagus; hot new opening; Castilian fine dining. Ⓢ *Average main: €75* ✉ *Cigarral del Ángel, Ctra. de la Puebla, Toledo* ☎ *92/522–3674* ⊕ *www.ivancerdeno.com* ⏱ *Closed Mon. and Tues.*

Hotels

★ Antídoto Rooms

$$ | **HOTEL** | Antídoto is a breath of fresh air in Toledo's mostly staid hotel scene: expect turquoise beamed ceilings, poured-concrete floors, and designer light fixtures. **Pros:** friendly staff; in the heart of the old town; highly Instagrammable rooms. **Cons:** awkward room layout; sheets could be softer; in-room bathrooms with no curtains and transparent doors. Ⓢ *Rooms from: €120* ✉ *Calle Recoletos 2, Toledo* ☎ *68/976–6605* ⊕ *www.antidotorooms.com* ⚲ *10 rooms* ⋈ *No Meals.*

Hacienda del Cardenal

$$ | **HOTEL** | Once a summer palace for Cardinal Lorenzana, who lived in the 1700s, this serene three-star hotel with a pool on the outskirts of the old town hits the sweet spot between rustic and refined. **Pros:** lovely courtyard; spacious rooms; convenient dining. **Cons:** stairs inconvenient for those with heavy

---

Tea Break

Tetería Dar Al-Chai. Rest your legs at this Arabian tea house–bar appointed with plush couches, low tables, and colorful tapestries. Sample specially blended teas incorporating flowers, dried fruit, and spices. **Known for:** peaceful spot; specially blended teas; delicious crepes and cakes. ✉ *Pl. Barrio Nuevo 5, Toledo* ☎ *92/522–5625* ⊕ *www. facebook.com/teteriadaralchai.*

luggage; parking is pricey; restaurant often full. $ *Rooms from: €100* ✉ *Paseo de Recaredo 24, Toledo* ☎ *92/522–4900* ⊕ *www.elhostaldelcardenal.com* ⇆ *27 rooms* ❙◯❙ *Free Breakfast.*

Hotel Sercotel Pintor El Greco

$$$ | HOTEL | Next door to the painter's house, this former 17th-century bakery is a chic, contemporary hotel managed by the Sercotel chain. **Pros:** complimentary wine and olives; cozy decor; parking garage adjacent. **Cons:** elevator goes to the second floor only; street noise in most rooms; bar area sometimes closed for private events. $ *Rooms from: €130* ✉ *Alamillos del Tránsito 13, Toledo* ☎ *92/528–5191* ⊕ *www.hotelpintorelgreco.com* ⇆ *60 rooms* ❙◯❙ *No Meals.*

★ Miluna

$$$$ | HOTEL | Taking a page from the playbook of Aire de Bardenas, Navarra's avant-garde bubble hotel, Miluna opened in 2018 on the outskirts of Toledo. **Pros:** the ideal place to unplug; telescopes in every room; a bubble hotel that won't break the budget. **Cons:** so popular it's difficult to get a reservation; outdoor temperatures can be extreme in winter and summer; no alternate dining options in vicinity. $ *Rooms from: €189* ✉ *C. Valdecarretas, Parcela 364, Toledo* ☎ *92/567–9229* ⊕ *www.miluna.es* ⇆ *4 rooms.*

🛍 Shopping

The Moors established silver, damascene (metalwork inlaid with gold or silver), pottery, embroidery, and marzipan traditions here. A turn-of-the-20th-century art school next to the Monasterio de San Juan de los Reyes keeps some of these crafts alive. For inexpensive pottery, stop at the large stores on the outskirts of town, on the main road to Madrid. Many shops are closed on Sunday.

Confitería Santo Tomé

CANDY | Since 1856, Santo Tomé has been Spain's most famous maker of marzipan, a Spanish confection made from sugar,

honey, and almond paste. Visit the main shop on the Plaza de Zocodover, or take a tour of the old convent-turned-factory where it's actually made at Calle Santo Tomé 3 (advance booking required). ✉ *Pl. de Zocodover 7, Toledo* ☎ *92/522–1168, 92/522–3763* ⊕ *www.mazapan.com.*

El Baúl de la Piker

MIXED CLOTHING | There's no shortage of throwback treasures at this independently owned vintage shop specializing in women's wear. Keep an eye out for retro leather pieces—Toledo has long been known for its fine leather artisanship. ✉ *Calle Trastámara 17, Toledo* ☎ *92/567–2083* ⊕ *www.elbauldelapiker.com* ◷ *Closed Sun.*

★ La Encina de Ortega

FOOD | This is a one-stop-shop for local wines, olive oil, manchego cheese, and—most notably—ibérico pork products (ham, chorizo, dry-cured sausages) made from pigs raised on the family farm. Stick around for charcuterie boards and generously poured glasses of wine. ✉ *Calle La Plata 22, Toledo* ☎ *92/510–2072* ⊕ *www.laencinadeortega.com* ◷ *Closed Sat. afternoon, Sun.*

Almagro

215 km (134 miles) south of Madrid.

The center of this noble town contains the only preserved medieval theater in Europe. It stands beside the ancient Plaza Mayor, where 85 Roman columns form two colonnades supporting green-frame 16th-century buildings. Enjoy casual tapas—such as pickled baby eggplant (*berenjenas de Almagro*), a hyperlocal specialty known the country over—and rustic Manchegan wines in the bars lining the square. Near the plaza are granite mansions emblazoned with the heraldic shields of their former owners and a splendid parador in a restored 17th-century convent.

GETTING HERE AND AROUND

Almagro can be reached by train from Madrid, with one scheduled departure per day departing from Atocha or Chamartín stations for the 2½-hour journey, but it's probably best to rent a car or book a Blablacar rideshare. The drive south from the capital takes you across the plains of La Mancha, where Don Quixote's adventures unfolded.

VISITOR INFORMATION

CONTACTS Almagro. ✉ *Pl. Mayor 1, Almagro* ☎ *92/686–0717* 🌐 *www.ciudad-almagro.com.*

Sights

Corral de Comedias

PERFORMANCE VENUE | Appearing almost as it did in 1628 when it was built, this theater has wooden balconies on four sides and the stage at one end of the open patio. During the golden age of Spanish theater—the time of playwrights Pedro Calderón de la Barca, Cervantes, and Lope de Vega—touring actors came from all over Europe to Almagro, once a burgeoning urban center for its mercury mines and lace industry. Few such theaters stand today. Forego the tourist-oriented spectacles unless you're thoroughly bilingual or a Spanish theater buff: poor acoustics and archaic Spanish scripts make it difficult to understand what's going on. An international classical theater festival takes place here in July. ✉ *Pl. Mayor 18, Almagro* ☎ *92/686–1539* 🌐 *www.corraldecomedias.com* 🎟 *From €4.*

★ Museo Etnográfico Campo de Calatrava

HISTORY MUSEUM | For a window into what agrarian life was like in this area in centuries past, pop into this tiny museum presided over by the passionate historian who amassed the antique curiosities on display. The influence of the Central European "Fúcares" families on the area is especially fascinating. A guided tour, in Spanish, takes a little less than an hour and is well worth it. ✉ *Calle Chile 6, Almagro* ☎ *65/701–0077* 🌐 *www.museodealmagro.com* 🎟 *€5.*

Museo Nacional del Teatro

HISTORY MUSEUM | **FAMILY** | This museum, housed in the ancestral seat of the Calatrava Order of knights, displays models of the Roman amphitheaters in Mérida (Extremadura) and Sagunto (near Valencia), both still in use, as well as costumes, pictures, and documents relating to the history of Spanish theater. Kids love handling the antique instruments previously used for sound effects during productions. ✉ *Calle del Gran Maestre 2, Almagro* ☎ *92/626–1014, 92/626–1018* 🌐 *museoteatro.mcu.es* 🎟 *€3 (free Sat. afternoon and Sun. morning)* ⏲ *Closed Mon.*

Hotels

★ Parador de Almagro

$$$ | **HOTEL** | Five minutes from the Plaza Mayor of Almagro, this parador is a finely restored 16th-century Franciscan convent with cells, cloisters, and patios. **Pros:** ample free parking; pretty indoor courtyards; outdoor pool. **Cons:** double-bed rooms smaller than normal rooms; occasionally untidy public areas; inconsistent restaurant. [$] *Rooms from: €135* ✉ *Ronda de San Francisco 31, Almagro* ☎ *92/686–0100* 🌐 *www.parador.es* 🛏 *54 rooms.*

Cuenca

168 km (105 miles) southeast of Madrid, 150 km (93 miles) northwest of Valencia.

Cuenca is one of the most surreal-looking towns in Spain, built on a sloping escarpment with precipitous sides plunging down to the Huécar and Júcar rivers. When real estate grew scarce a few centuries back, local builders constructed gravity-defying homes that dangle over the abyss. These Casas Colgadas

("Hanging Houses") are a unique architectural attraction. The old town's dramatic setting grants spectacular views of the surrounding countryside, and its cobblestone streets, cathedral, churches, and taverns contrast starkly with the modern town, which sprawls beyond the river gorges. Though somewhat isolated, Cuenca makes a good overnight stop if you're traveling between Madrid and Valencia, or even a worthwhile detour between Madrid and Barcelona.

GETTING HERE AND AROUND

From Madrid, buses leave for Cuenca about every two hours from Conde de Casal. From Valencia, four buses leave every four to six hours, starting at 8:30 am. A high-speed AVE train leaves Madrid approximately every hour and stops in Cuenca (after about 55 minutes) on its way to Valencia. Slower, cheaper trains also run several times daily between Cuenca and Valencia, Madrid, Albacete, and Alicante, on the coast. Rideshares (such as Blablacar) to and from the city are plentiful.

VISITOR INFORMATION

CONTACTS Cuenca. ⊠ *Calle Alfonso VIII 2, Cuenca* ☎ *96/924–1051* ⊕ *www. visitacuenca.es.*

 Sights

Cuenca has a cathedral and more than a dozen churches, but visitors are allowed inside only about half of them. The best views of the city are from the square in front of a small palace at the very top of Cuenca, where the town tapers out to the narrowest of ledges. Here, gorges flank the precipice, and old houses sweep down toward a distant plateau. The lower half of the old town is a maze of tiny streets, any of which will take you up to the Plaza del Carmen. From here the town narrows and a single street, Calle Alfonso VIII, continues the ascent to the Plaza Mayor, which passes under the arch of the town hall.

★ **Casas Colgadas** (*Hanging Houses*)
NOTABLE BUILDING | As if Cuenca's famous Casas Colgadas, suspended impossibly over the cliffs below, were not eye-popping enough, they also house one of Spain's finest and most curious museums, the **Museo de Arte Abstracto Español** (Museum of Spanish Abstract Art)—not to be confused with the adjacent Museo Municipal de Arte Moderno. Projecting over the town's eastern precipice, these houses originally formed a 15th-century palace, which later served as a town hall before falling into disrepair in the 19th century. In 1927 the cantilevered balconies that had once hung over the gorge were rebuilt, and in 1966 the painter Fernando Zóbel decided to create (inside the houses) the world's first museum devoted exclusively to abstract art. The works he gathered—by such renowned names as Carlos Saura, Eduardo Chillida, Lucio Muñoz, and Antoni Tàpies—are primarily by exiled Spanish artists who grew up under Franco's regime. The museum has free smartphone audio guides that can be downloaded from the website. A much-anticipated fine-dining restaurant within one of the historic houses, with local Michelin-starred chef Jesús Segura at the helm, had not yet opened at the time of writing. ⊠ *Calle de los Canónigos, Cuenca* ☎ *96/921–2983* ⊕ *www.march. es/arte/cuenca* ⊠ *Free.*

Catedral de Cuenca

CHURCH | This cathedral looms large and casts an enormous shadow in the evening throughout the adjacent Plaza Mayor. Built during the Gothic era in the 12th century atop ruins of a conquered mosque, the cathedral's massive triptych facade lost its Gothic character in the Renaissance. Inside are the tombs of the cathedral's founding bishops, an impressive portico of the Apostles, and a Byzantine reliquary. There's also a museum in what was once the cellar of the Bishop's Palace containing a jewel-encrusted Byzantine diptych of the 13th century, a Crucifixion by the 15th-century

Cuenca's precarious Casas Colgadas (Hanging Houses) are also home to the well-regarded Museum of Abstract Art.

Flemish artist Gerard David, a variety of carpets from the 16th through 18th centuries, and two small El Grecos. An excellent audio guide is included in the price of admission. ✉ *Pl. Mayor, Cuenca* ☎ *96/922–4626* ⊕ *www.catedralcuenca. es* 🎫 *€5 (free 1st Mon. of month)*.

Ciudad Encantada (*Enchanted City*)
NATURE SIGHT | FAMILY | Not a city at all, the Ciudad Encantada, 35 km (22 miles) north of Cuenca, is a series of large, fantastic mushroom-like rock formations erupting in a landscape of pines. It was formed over thousands of years by the forces of water and wind on limestone rocks, and you can see it in under two hours. See if you can spot formations named "Cara" (Face), "Puente" (Bridge), "Amantes" (Lovers), and "Olas en el Mar" (Waves in the Sea). Rent a car to get here, or arrange a visit with Ecotourism Cuenca (www.ecoturismocuenca. com   61/650–7695). ✉ *Ciudad Encantada, Cuenca* ☎ *63/490–9952* ⊕ *www. ciudadencantada.es* 🎫 *€5*.

★ **Puente de San Pablo**
BRIDGE | The 16th-century stone footbridge over the Huécar gorge was fortified with iron in 1903 for the convenience of the Dominican monks of San Pablo, who lived on the other side. If you don't have a fear of heights, cross the narrow bridge to take in the vertiginous view of the river and equally thrilling panorama of the Casas Colgadas. It's by far the best view of the city. If you've read the popular English novel *Winter in Madrid*, you'll recognize this bridge from the final scene. ✉ *Cuenca*.

 Restaurants

Much of Cuenca's cuisine is based on wild game, but farm-raised lamb, rabbit, and poultry are ubiquitous on menus. Trout from the adjacent river (and, increasingly, from farms) is the fish of choice, and it turns up in entrées and soups. In almost every restaurant you'll find *morteruelo,* Cuenca's pâté of *jabalí* (wild boar), rabbit, partridge, hen, liver, pork loin, and spices, as well as gazpacho *manchego* (aka galiano), a meat stew thickened with dry flatbread—a remnant of the Sephardic culinary canon. For dessert, try *alajú* , a hard sugar candy containing honey, almonds, and lemon that's great with cheese, or the more ubiquitous *torrijas* , bread slices dipped in milk, fried until custardy, and sprinkled with cinnamon-sugar

Figón del Huécar

$$$$ | **SPANISH** | This family-run white-tablecloth restaurant serves updated Castilian classics in an airy dining room set in a medieval stone house overlooking the old city (ask for an outdoor table when booking). Specialty dishes include Manchegan *migas* (fried pork and breadcrumbs), *ajoarriero* (pounded potatoes, garlic, egg, and olive oil), and veal with potatoes *al montón* (fried with garlic). **Known for:** elegant dining room; breathtaking views; scrumptious desserts. $ *Average main: €35* ✉ *Ronda de Julián Romero 6, Cuenca* ☎ *96/924–0062, 62/906–3366* 🌐 *www.figondelhuecar.es* 🕒 *Closed Mon. No dinner Sun.*

★ La Ponderosa

$$ | **TAPAS** | La Ponderosa is a quintessential yet elevated Castilian bar where locals mingle at high volume while tossing back local wine and munching on well-priced seasonal delicacies like griddled wild asparagus, suckling lamb chops, and seared wild mushrooms. It's a standing-room-only joint, so if you want to sit, you'll have to come early and find a place on the terrace. **Known for:** hidden-gem local wines; simple and delicious vegetable dishes; buzzy atmosphere. $ *Average main: €15* ✉ *Calle de San Francisco 20, Cuenca* ☎ *96/921–3214* 🕒 *Closed Sun. and July.*

Trivio

$$$$ | **SPANISH** | The punchy, artfully presented dishes at Trivio—think wild game tartare and house-pickled vegetables—are an anomaly in a region known for its stodgy country fare. Choose from three well-priced tasting menus in the dining room, or opt for a more casual experience in the Bistró-Bar. **Known for:** pretty plating; award-winning croquettes; bold tasting menus. $ *Average main: €30* ✉ *Calle Colón 25, Cuenca* ☎ *96/903–0593* 🌐 *www.restaurantetrivio.com* 🕒 *Closed Mon. No dinner Sun.*

🛏 Hotels

Cueva del Fraile

$ | **HOTEL** | **FAMILY** | Surrounded by dramatic landscapes, this family-friendly three-star lodging occupies a 16th-century building on the outskirts of town. **Pros:** beautiful interior garden terrace; good value; outdoor swimming pool and tennis courts. **Cons:** interiors show their age; no a/c in some rooms; location 7 km (4½ miles) from town. $ *Rooms from: €69* ✉ *Ctra. Cuenca–Buenache, Km 7, Cuenca* ☎ *96/921–1571* 🌐 *www.hotelcuevadelfraile.com* 🕒 *Closed Jan.* 🛏 *75 rooms.*

Hostal Cánovas

$ | **B&B/INN** | **FAMILY** | Near Plaza de España, in the heart of the new town, this quirky inn is one of Cuenca's best bargains, and though the lobby is no stunner, the inviting guest rooms more than compensate. **Pros:** clean rooms; spacious digs; low prices even during high season. **Cons:** thin walls; uphill trek to the old quarter; slightly sunken beds with plastic mattress protectors. $ *Rooms from: €60* ✉ *Calle Fray Luis de León 38, Cuenca* ☎ *96/921–3973* 🌐 *www.hostalcanovas.com* 🛏 *17 rooms.*

★ Parador de Cuenca

$$$ | **HOTEL** | The rooms are luxurious and serene at the exquisitely restored 16th-century convent of San Pablo, pitched on a precipice across a dramatic gorge from Cuenca's city center. **Pros:** consistently good restaurant; spacious rooms; great views of the hanging houses and gorge. **Cons:** secure garage parking not always available; expensive breakfast not always included in room rate; calls to reception sometimes go

unanswered. [$] *Rooms from: €180* ✉ *Subida a San Pablo, Cuenca* ☎ *96/923–2320* 🌐 *www.parador.es* 🛏 *63 rooms* 🍴 *No Meals.*

★ Posada de San José

$ | **B&B/INN** | **FAMILY** | This family-friendly inn, housed in a centuries-old convent, clings to the top of the Huécar gorge in Cuenca's old town. **Pros:** well-prepared local food; cozy historical rooms; stunning views of the gorge. **Cons:** sloping floors can be vertiginous when lying in bed; built to 17th-century proportions, some doorways are low; certain rooms are cramped. [$] *Rooms from: €50* ✉ *Calle Julián Romero 4, Cuenca* ☎ *96/921–1300, 63/981–6825* 🌐 *www.posadasanjose.com* 🛏 *31 rooms.*

Sigüenza

132 km (82 miles) northeast of Madrid.

The ancient university town of Sigüenza dates back to Roman, Visigothic, and Moorish times and still has splendid architecture and an awe-inspiring Gothic cathedral. It's one of the rare Spanish towns that has not surrendered to modern development and sprawl. If you're coming from Madrid via the A2, the approach, through craggy hills and ravines, is dramatic. Sigüenza is an ideal base for exploring the countryside on foot or by bike, thanks to the Ruta de Don Quixote, a network of paths named for Cervantes's literary hero that passes through the town center and nearby villages.

GETTING HERE AND AROUND

There are five train departures daily to Sigüenza from Madrid's Chamartín station, and the journey takes about 1½ hours. Sigüenza's train station is an easy walk from the historic walled center. Buses depart from Madrid's Avenida de América station once a day and take 2 hours. If you arrive by car, park near the train station to avoid the narrow cobblestone streets of the city center. Rideshares, such as Blablacar, are another option, provided there are trips that align with your schedule.

TOURS

Tren Medieval

Leaving from Madrid's Chamartín station, this delightful medieval-theme train service runs to Sigüenza mid-April through mid-November. The (otherwise thoroughly modern) train comes populated with minstrels, jugglers, and other entertainers, and it's a great activity for Spanish-speaking children. The ticket price includes round-trip fare, a guided visit to Sigüenza, entry to the main monuments and museums, and discounts at area restaurants. ✉ *Estación de Sigüenza, Sigüenza* ☎ *90/232–0320* 🌐 *www.renfe.com/es/es/experiencias* 🎫 *€35* 🕒 *Closed winter.*

👁 Sights

Castillo de Sigüenza

CASTLE/PALACE | **FAMILY** | This enchanting castle overlooking wild, hilly countryside from above Sigüenza is now a parador. Nonguests can visit the dining room and common areas. The structure was founded by the Romans and rebuilt at various later periods. Most of the current structure was erected in the 14th century, when it became a residence for the queen of Castile, Doña Blanca de Borbón, who was banished here by her husband, Pedro the Cruel. During the Spanish Civil War (1936–39), the castle was the scene of fierce battles, and much of the structure was destroyed. The parador's lobby has an exhibit on the subsequent restoration with photographs of the bomb damage. If you have a half-hour to spare, there's a lovely walking path around the hilltop castle with a 360-degree view of the city and countryside below. ✉ *Pl. de Castillo, Sigüenza* ☎ *94/939–0100* 🎫 *Free.*

Catedral de Sigüenza
CHURCH | **FAMILY** | Begun around 1150 and completed in the 16th century, Sigüenza's cathedral combines Romanesque and Renaissance architecture. Wander from the late-Gothic cloister to a room lined with 17th-century Flemish tapestries, then onto the north transept, where the 15th-century plateresque sepulchre of Dom Fadrique of Portugal is housed. The Chapel of the Doncel (to the right of the sanctuary) contains Don Martín Vázquez de Arca's tomb, commissioned by Queen Isabella, to whom Don Martín served as *doncel* (page) before an untimely death at the gates of Granada in 1486. In a refurbished early-19th-century house next to the cathedral's west facade, the small **Diocesan Museum** has a prehistoric section and religious art from the 12th to 18th century. It also runs the weekend tours of the burial chambers (catacombs) under the cathedral—a spooky favorite for kids. ✉ *Calle Serrano Sanz 2, Sigüenza* ☎ *94/939–1023* 🌐 *www.catedralsiguenza.es* 🎟 *€6 including museum.*

Plaza Mayor
PLAZA/SQUARE | The south side of the cathedral overlooks this harmonious arcaded Renaissance square that hosts a medieval market on weekends. Legend has it, a group of American tycoons found the plaza so charming that they offered to buy it in order to reconstruct it, piece by piece, stateside. ✉ *Plaza Mayor, Sigüenza.*

🍴 Restaurants

★ Bar Alameda
$$ | **TAPAS** | **FAMILY** | This family-run bar and restaurant punches above its weight with market-driven tapas that reflect a sense of place. Spring for the stuffed foraged mushrooms or seared Sigüenza-style blood sausage. **Known for:** family-friendly atmosphere; local wines by the glass; thoughtfully prepared tapas. [$] *Average main: €15* ✉ *Calle de la Alameda 2, Sigüenza* ☎ *67/727–7773* ⏲ *Closed Wed.*

🛏 Hotels

★ Parador de Sigüenza
$$$$ | **HOTEL** | **FAMILY** | This fairy-tale 12th-century castle has hosted royalty for centuries, from Ferdinand and Isabella right up to Spain's present king, Felipe VI. **Pros:** plenty of parking; sense of history and place; excellent food. **Cons:** bland, modern furniture that doesn't jibe with the space; much of castle is a neo-medieval replica; occasionally surly service. [$] *Rooms from: €185* ✉ *Pl. del Castillo, Sigüenza* ☎ *94/939–0100* 🌐 *www.parador.es* 🛏 *81 rooms* 🍴 *Free Breakfast.*

Segovia

91 km (57 miles) north of Madrid.

Medieval Segovia rises on a steep ridge that juts above a stark, undulating plain. It's defined by its ancient monuments, excellent cuisine, embroideries and textiles, and old-fashioned charm. An important military town in Roman times, Segovia was later established by the Moors as a major textile center. Captured by the Christians in 1085, it was enriched by a royal residence, and in 1474 the half sister of Henry IV, Isabella the Catholic (married to Ferdinand of Aragón), was crowned queen of Castile here. By that time Segovia was a bustling city of about 60,000 (its population hovers around 52,000 today), but its importance soon diminished as a result of its taking the losing side of the Comuneros in the popular revolt against Emperor Carlos V. Though the construction of a royal palace in nearby La Granja in the 18th century somewhat revived Segovia's fortunes, it never recovered its former vitality. Early in the 20th century, Segovia's sleepy charm came to be appreciated by artists and writers, among them painter Ignacio Zuloaga and poet Antonio Machado. Today the streets swarm with day-trippers from Madrid—if you can, visit sometime other than in summer, and

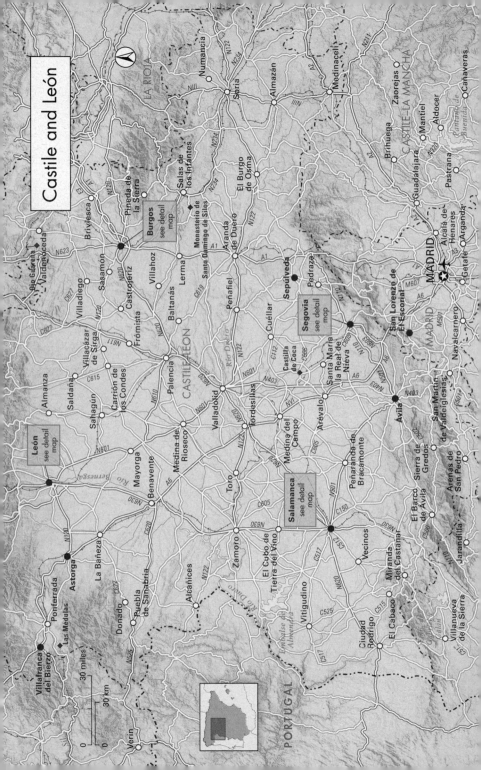

spend the night to have much of the city to yourself.

You'll want to hit the triumvirate of basic sights: the aqueduct, alcázar, and cathedral. Come evening, don't miss the bustling food and nightlife scene around the Plaza Mayor.

GETTING HERE AND AROUND

High-speed AVE trains from Madrid's Chamartín station—the fastest and costliest option—take 30 minutes and drop you at Guiomar station, about 7 km (4 miles) outside Segovia's center. Buses 11 and 12 are timed to coincide with arriving trains. Bus 11 will take you to the foot of the aqueduct after about a 15-minute ride, and Bus 12 drops you near the bus station.

La Sepulvedana buses depart Madrid (Moncloa station) for Segovia some 28 times a day. Direct routes take 55 minutes and cost €8 each way. There are also plentiful Blablacar options. (Check *www.blablacar.com* or the app for details.)

Urbanos de Segovia operates the 13 inner-city bus lines and one tourist line, which are better options for getting around than struggling through the narrow streets (and problematic parking) with a car. Segovia's central bus station is a five-minute walk from the aqueduct along the car-free Paseo de Ezequiel González.

ESSENTIALS

BUS CONTACTS Bus Station. ✉ *Paseo de Ezequiel González, Segovia* ☎ *92/142–7705.* **La Sepulvedana.** ✉ *Pl. la Estación de Autobuses, Segovia* ☎ *90/211–9699* ⊕ *lasepulvedana.es.* **Urbanos de Segovia.** ✉ *Segovia* ☎ *90/233–0080* ⊕ *segovia. avanzagrupo.com.*

VISITOR INFORMATION Segovia Tourist Office. ✉ *Pl. Azoguejo 1, Segovia* ☎ *92/146–6720, 92/146–6721* ⊕ *www. turismodesegovia.com.*

Sights

★ Alcázar

CASTLE/PALACE | FAMILY | It's widely believed that the Walt Disney logo is modeled after the silhouette of this castle, whose crenellated towers appear to have been carved out of icing. Possibly dating to Roman times, this castle was considerably expanded in the 14th century, remodeled in the 15th, altered again toward the end of the 16th, and completely reconstructed after being gutted by a fire in 1862, when it was used as an artillery school. The exterior, especially when seen below from the Ruta Panorámica, is awe-inspiring, as are the superb views from the ramparts. Inside, you can enter the throne room, chapel, and bedroom used by Ferdinand and Isabella as well as a claustrophobia-inducing winding tower. The intricate woodwork on the ceiling is marvelous, and the first room you enter, lined with knights in shining armor, is a crowd pleaser, particularly for kids. There's also a small armory museum, included in the ticket price. ✉ *Pl. de la Reina Victoria, Segovia* ☎ *92/146–0759, 92/146–0452* ⊕ *www.alcazardesegovia.com* 🎫 *€9 for castle, tower, and museum.*

★ Aqueduct of Segovia

RUINS | Segovia's Roman aqueduct is one of the greatest surviving examples of Roman engineering and the city's main sight. Stretching from the walls of the old town to the lower slopes of the Sierra de Guadarrama, it's about 2,952 feet long and rises in two tiers to a height of 115 feet. The raised section of stonework in the center originally carried an inscription, of which only the holes for the bronze letters remain. Neither mortar nor clamps hold the massive granite blocks together, but miraculously, the aqueduct has stood since the end of the 1st century AD. ✉ *Pl. del Azoguejo.*

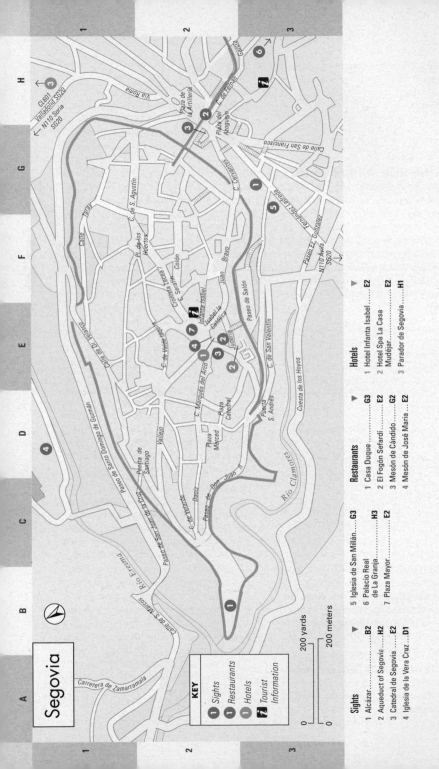

Segovia

KEY

- 1 Sights
- 1 Restaurants
- 1 Hotels
- i Tourist Information

Sights ▶
1 Alcázar................**B2**
2 Aqueduct of Segovia...**H2**
3 Catedral de Segovia **E2**
4 Iglesia de la Vera Cruz **D1**

5 Iglesia de San Millán.....**G3**
6 Palacio Real
   de La Granja.............**H3**
7 Plaza Mayor..............**E2**

Restaurants ▶
1 Casa Duque **G3**
2 El Fogón Sefardí........**E2**
3 Mesón de Cándido **G2**
4 Mesón de José María ...**E2**

Hotels ▶
1 Hotel Infanta Isabel.....**E2**
2 Hotel Spa La Casa
   Mudéjar................**E2**
3 Parador de Segovia.....**H1**

0 ——— 200 yards

0 ——— 200 meters

★ Catedral de Segovia

CHURCH | Segovia's 16th-century cathedral was built to replace an earlier one destroyed during the revolt of the Comuneros against Carlos V. It's one of the country's last great examples of the Gothic style. The designs were drawn up by the leading late-Gothicist Juan Gil de Hontañón and executed by his son Rodrigo, in whose work you can see a transition from the Gothic to the Renaissance style. The interior, illuminated by 16th-century Flemish windows, is light and uncluttered (save for the wooden neoclassical choir). Across from the entrance, on the southern transept, is a door opening into the late-Gothic cloister, the work of architect Juan Guas. Off the cloister, a small museum of religious art, installed partly in the first-floor chapter house, has a white-and-gold 17th-century ceiling, a late example of *Mudejar artesonado* (a type of intricately joined wooden ceiling) work. ✉ *Pl. Mayor, Segovia* ☏ *92/146–2205* ⊕ *www.catedralsegovia. es* ✆ *From €3 (free Sun. Mass).*

Iglesia de la Vera Cruz

CHURCH | This isolated Romanesque church on the outskirts of town was built in 1208 for the Knights Templar. Like other buildings associated with the order, it has 12 sides, inspired by the Church of the Holy Sepulchre in Jerusalem. It's about a 45-minute walk from town (you can see this church on a cliffside from the castle windows), but the trek pays off in full when you climb the bell tower and see the Segovia skyline silhouetted against the Sierra de Guadarrama. Change is not given for bills larger than €20. ✉ *Ctra. de Zamarramia, Segovia* ☏ *92/143–1475* ✆ *€2 (free Tues. 4–6 pm).*

Iglesia de San Millán

CHURCH | Built in the 12th century and a model example of the Segovian Romanesque style, this church, a five-minute walk outside the town walls, may be the finest in town, aside from the cathedral. The exterior is notable for its arcaded porch, where church meetings were once held. The virtually untouched interior is dominated by massive columns, whose capitals carry such carved scenes as the Flight into Egypt and the Adoration of the Magi. The vaulting on the crossing shows the Moorish influence on Spanish medieval architecture. It's open for Mass only. ✉ *Av. Fernández Ladreda 26, Segovia* ☏ *92/146–3876* ⊕ *www.parroquiasanmillansegovia.com* ✆ *Free.*

★ Palacio Real de La Granja (*Royal Palace of La Granja*)

CASTLE/PALACE | If you have a car, don't miss the Palacio Real de La Granja (Royal Palace of La Granja) in the town of La Granja de San Ildefonso, on the northern slopes of the Sierra de Guadarrama. The palace site was once occupied by a hunting lodge and a shrine to San Ildefonso, administered by Hieronymite monks from the Segovian monastery of El Parral. Commissioned by the Bourbon king Felipe V in 1719, the palace has been described as the first great building of the Spanish Bourbon dynasty. The Italian architects Juvarra and Sachetti, who finished it in 1739, were responsible for the imposing garden facade, a late-baroque masterpiece anchored throughout its length by a giant order of columns. The interior was badly gutted by fire, but the collection of 15th- to 18th-century tapestries warrants a visit. Even if you don't go into the palace, walk through the magnificent gardens: terraces, ornamental ponds, lakes, classical statuary, woods, and baroque fountains dot the mountainside. On Wednesday, Saturday, and Sunday evenings in the summer (April–August, 5:30–7 pm), the illuminated fountains are turned on, one by one, creating an effect to rival that of Versailles. The starting time has been known to change on a whim, so call ahead. ✉ *Pl. de España 15,* ✥ *About 11 km (7 miles) southeast of Segovia on N601* ☏ *92/147–0019, 92/147–0020* ⊕ *www.patrimonionacional.es* ✆ *€8.*

Segovia's Roman aqueduct, built more than 2,000 years ago, is remarkably well preserved.

Plaza Mayor

PLAZA/SQUARE | In front of the cathedral, this historic square comes alive every night and especially on weekends, when visiting Madrileños and locals gather at casual cafés that line the perimeter. There's a gazebo in the middle that occasionally hosts live music. (Otherwise it's occupied by children playing while their parents dine nearby.) ✉ *Pl. Mayor, Segovia.*

🍴 Restaurants

Casa Duque

$$$$ | **SPANISH** | **FAMILY** | Segovia's oldest restaurant, founded in 1895 and still run by the same family, has a rustic interior with wood beams and bric-a-brac hanging on the walls. The decor suits the unfussy (if perhaps overpriced) cuisine, which features roast meats and stewed broad beans. **Known for:** no-knife-needed cochinillo asado (roast suckling pig); genial English-language menus and service; back-in-time setting. [$] *Average main: €30* ✉ *Calle Cervantes 12, Segovia* ☎ *92/146–2487, 92/146–2486* 🌐 *www.restauranteduque.es.*

★ El Fogón Sefardí

$$$ | **SPANISH** | This tavern in Segovia's historic Jewish quarter is owned by La Casa Mudéjar Hospedería hotel and has won awards for the region's best tapas. The extensive menu highlights Segovian specialties like cochinillo as well as traditional Sephardic Jewish cuisine (though it's not a kosher kitchen), plus a variety of well-executed *raciones* (shared plates). **Known for:** Sephardic-influenced cuisine; generous salads; great cochinillo. [$] *Average main: €20* ✉ *Calle Judería Vieja 17, Segovia* ☎ *92/146–6250* 🌐 *www.lacasamudejar.com.*

Mesón de Cándido

$$$$ | **SPANISH** | Amid the dark-wood beams and Castilian knickknacks of this restaurant beneath the aqueduct hang photos of celebrities who have dined here, among them Ernest Hemingway, Salvador Dalí, and Princess Grace. The suckling pig (*cochinillo*) is the star; partridge stew and roast lamb are also memorable, especially on cold afternoons. **Known for:** famous former patrons like Ernest Hemingway; wood-fired-oven-roasted cochinillo; historic building. $ *Average main: €30* ✉ *Pl. de Azoguejo 5,* ☎ *92/142–5911* ⊕ *www.mesondecandido.es.*

★ Mesón de José María

$$$$ | SPANISH | According to foodies, this old-timey *mesón* (traditional tavern-restaurant) serves the most delectable cochinillo asado in town, but there are plenty of lighter, fresher dishes to choose from as well. Expect a boisterous mix of locals and tourists. **Known for:** local crowd (a rarity in this touristy town); best cochinillo in town; beamed dining room. $ *Average main: €35* ✉ *Calle Cronista Lecea 11, Segovia* ✛ *off Pl. Mayor* ☎ *92/146–1111, 92/146–6017* ⊕ *www. restaurantejosemaria.com.*

Hotels

Hotel Infanta Isabel

$$ | HOTEL | On the corner of the Plaza Mayor, this classically appointed hotel boasts cathedral views in a bustling shopping area. **Pros:** some rooms have balconies overlooking the plaza; central location; lived-in, cozy ambience. **Cons:** rooms facing the plaza can be noisy on weekends; some rooms are cramped and oddly shaped; decidedly unhip decor. $ *Rooms from: €120* ✉ *Pl. Mayor 12, Segovia* ☎ *92/146–1300* ⊕ *www. hotelinfantaisabel.com* ⬎ *37 rooms* ⦵| *No Meals.*

Hotel Spa La Casa Mudéjar

$$$ | HOTEL | Built in the 15th century as a Mudejar palace, this historical property has spacious rooms and a well-priced spa (€30 per person; adults only) that's extremely popular, even with nonguests. **Pros:** affordable spa; terrific restaurant serving rare Sephardic dishes; historic building with Roman ruins. **Cons:** no nearby parking; forgettable interiors; beds nothing special. $ *Rooms from:*

€134 ✉ *Calle Isabel la Católica 8, Segovia* ☎ *92/146–6250* ⊕ *www.lacasamudejar. com* ⬎ *40 rooms.*

Parador de Segovia

$$ | HOTEL | From the large windows of this modern-style parador, 3 km (2 miles) from the old town, you can take in spectacular views of the cathedral and aqueduct. **Pros:** beautiful views of the city; spacious rooms; sunny, picturesque pool area. **Cons:** lacks antique touches of more historic paradores; uncozy, passé decor; need a car (or €8 taxi) to get here. $ *Rooms from: €120* ✉ *Ctra. de Valladolid, Segovia* ☎ *92/144–3737* ⊕ *www. parador.es* ⬎ *113 rooms.*

Shopping

After Toledo, the province of Segovia is Castile's most important area for traditional artisanry. Glass and crystal are specialties of La Granja, and ironwork, lace, basketry, and embroidery are famous in Segovia. You can buy good lace from the (mostly) Romani vendors in Segovia's Plaza del Alcázar, but prepare for some strenuous bargaining, and never offer more than half the opening price. The area around Plaza San Martín is a good place to buy crafts.

Calle Daoíz

NEIGHBORHOODS | Leading to the Alcázar, this street overflows with locally made (if tourist-oriented) ceramics, textiles, and gift shops. ✉ *Segovia.*

Sepúlveda

58 km (36 miles) northeast of Segovia.

A walled village with a commanding position, Sepúlveda has a charming main square, but the main reasons to visit are its 11th-century Romanesque church and striking gorge with a scenic hiking trail.

Castillo de Coca

Perhaps the most famous medieval site near Segovia—worth the 52 km (32-mile) detour northwest of the city en route to Ávila or Valladolid—is the Castillo de Coca. Built in the 15th century for Archbishop Alonso de Fonseca I, the salmon-hue castle is a turreted Mudejar structure of plaster and red brick surrounded by a deep moat. It looks like a stage set for a fairy tale, and, indeed, it was intended not as a fortress but as a place for the notoriously pleasure-loving archbishop to hold riotous parties. The interior, now occupied by a forestry school, has been modernized, with only fragments of the original decoration preserved. *www.castillodecoca.com*

GETTING HERE AND AROUND

Sepúlveda is about 1 hour north of Madrid on the A1. There are also several buses (and Blablacar rideshares) a day from both Segovia and Madrid. The city is perched atop a hill overlooking a ravine, so you'll likely want transportation to the top. Don't park or get off the bus too soon.

VISITOR INFORMATION

CONTACTS Sepúlveda Tourist Office. ✉ *Pl. del Trigo 6, Sepúlveda* ☎ *92/154–0425* 🌐 *sepulveda.es.*

Sights

★ Ermita de San Frutos

CHURCH | This 11th-century hermitage is in ruins, but its location, on a peninsula jutting out into a bend 100 meters above the Duratón River, is extraordinary. You'll need a car to get there, about 15 minutes' drive west of Sepúlveda. Stay on the marked paths—the surrounding area is a natural park and a protected nesting ground for rare vultures—and try to go at sunset, when the light enhances spectacular views of the sandstone monastery and river below. Inside the monastery, there's a small chapel and plaque describing the life of San Frutos, the patron saint of Segovia. An ancient pilgrimage route stretches 77 km (48 miles) from the monastery to Segovia's cathedral, and pilgrims still walk it each year. As an add-on to the trip, you can rent kayaks from **NaturalTur** (*92/152–1727*) to paddle the river. ✉ *, Sepúlveda* ☎ *No phone* 🎫 *Free.*

Iglesia de San Salvador

CHURCH | This 11th-century church is the oldest Romanesque church in Segovia Province. The carvings on its capitals, probably by a Moorish convert, are quite outlandish. ✉ *Calle Subida a El Salvador 10, Sepúlveda.*

Restaurants

★ Restaurante Fogón del Azogue

$$$ | **SPANISH** | **FAMILY** | The menu at this white-tablecloth aerie, which overlooks rolling farmland, hinges on local delicacies like fried blood sausage, creamy ham croquettes, and—naturally, since we're in Segovia province—crackly roast milk-fed lamb and suckling pig. The spacious venue is well-suited to hosting large groups. **Known for:** brick-oven-roasted pork and lamb; refined Castilian cuisine; wraparound windows with gorgeous views. [$] *Average main: €22* ✉ *Calle de San Millán 6, Sepúlveda* ☎ *69/020–2772* ⏲ *Closed Mon.–Thurs. No dinner Sun.*

San Lorenzo de El Escorial

50 km (31 miles) northwest of Madrid.

An hour from Madrid, and within Madrid province, San Lorenzo de El Escorial makes for a leisurely day trip away from the hustle and bustle of the Spanish capital. The medieval town's main attraction is the Real Sitio de San Lorenzo de El Escorial, the Royal Site of San Lorenzo of El Escorial. A dozen or so trains leave daily from the Madrid Sol train station, or you can take the C3 regional line from Atocha, Chamartín, Nuevos Ministerios, or Recoletos. The journey takes about an hour, and the entrance to El Escorial is about a 15-minute walk from the train station.

 Sights

★ El Escorial

CASTLE/PALACE | A UNESCO World Heritage Site and one of Spain's most visited landmarks, the imposing Monastery and Real Sitio de San Lorenzo de El Escorial (or just El Escorial) was commissioned by Felipe II after the death of his father in the 1500s and remains the most complete and impressive monument of the later Renaissance in Spain. The monastery was built as an eternal memorial for his relatives and the crypt here is the resting place of the majority of Spain's kings, from Charles V to Alfonso XIII. A fantasy land of gilded halls, hand-painted chambers, and manicured French gardens, the gargantuan royal residence also houses an important collection of paintings by Renaissance and baroque artists donated by the crown. The library alone is worth the €12 entry fee—its vibrant frescoes and leather-bound tomes spur the imagination. ⊠ *Pl. de España 1, San Lorenzo de El Escorial* ☎ *91/890–5903* ⊕ *www.sanlorenzoturismo.es* ⊠ *€12* ⊗ *Closed Mon.* Ⓜ *El Escorial.*

🍴 Restaurants

★ Charolés Restaurante

$$$$ | SPANISH | FAMILY | According to Spain's top food critics, this restaurant ladles out the best cocido madrileño in the country. Each component of the multicourse boiled dinner, from the chickpeas to the chorizo to the pickled peppers, is sourced from top-notch producers from around the peninsula. **Known for:** within walking distance of the palace; probably the world's best cocido madrileño; cozy historical decor. Ⓢ *Average main: €35* ⊠ *Calle Floridablanca 24, San Lorenzo de El Escorial* ☎ *91/890–5975* ⊕ *www.charolesrestaurante.com.*

Ávila

114 km (71 miles) northwest of Madrid.

On a windy plateau littered with giant boulders, with the Sierra de Gredos in the background, Ávila is a walled fairy-tale town that wouldn't look out of place in *Game of Thrones*. After it was wrested from the Moors in 1090, soaring crenelated walls were erected around its perimeter—by some 1,900 builders, who allegedly finished the task in just nine years. The walls have nine gates and 88 cylindrical towers bunched together, making them unique to Spain in form—they're quite unlike the Moorish defense architecture that the Christians adapted elsewhere. They're most striking when seen from afar; for the best views (and photos), cross the Adaja River, turn right on the Carretera de Salamanca, and walk uphill about 250 yards to a monument of pilasters surrounding a cross known as the "Four Posts."

Ávila's fame is largely due to St. Teresa. Born here in 1515 to a noble family of Jewish origin, Teresa spent much of her life in Ávila, leaving a legacy of convents and the ubiquitous *yemas* (candied egg yolks), originally distributed free to the

Ávila's city walls, which still encircle the old city, have a perimeter of about 2½ km (1½ miles).

poor and now sold at high prices to tourists. The town comes to life during the Fiestas de la Santa Teresa in October, a weeklong celebration that includes lighted decorations, parades, singing in the streets, and religious observances.

GETTING HERE AND AROUND

Jiménez Dorado (*www.jimenezdorado. com*) and Avanza (*avila.avanzagrupo.com*) serve Ávila and its surrounding villages. Some two dozen trains depart for Ávila each day from Chamartín station, and there are usually plentiful Blablacar rideshares available. The city itself is easily managed on foot.

VISITOR INFORMATION

CONTACTS Ávila Tourist Office. ⊠ *Pl. de la Catedral, Av. de Madrid 39, Ávila* ☎ *92/020–6200* ⊕ *www.turismoavila. com.*

Sights

Basílica de San Vicente (*Basilica of St. Vincent*)

CHURCH | Where this Romanesque basilica stands, it's said that St. Vincent was martyred in 303 AD with his sisters, Sts. Sabina and Cristeta. Construction began in 1130 and continued through the 12th century, and the massive church complex was restored in the late 19th and early 20th centuries. The west front, shielded by a vestibule, displays damaged but expressive carvings depicting the death of Lazarus and the parable of the rich man's table. The sarcophagus of St. Vincent forms the centerpiece of the interior. The extraordinary, Eastern-influenced canopy above the sarcophagus is a 15th-century addition. Combined, these elements form one of Spain's most prized examples of Romanesque architecture. ⊠ *Pl. de San Vicente 1, Ávila* ☎ *92/022–5969* ⊕ *www.basilicasanvicente.es* ⊠ *€3 (free Sun.).*

Casa de los Deanes (*Deans' Mansion*)
HISTORIC HOME | This 15th-century building houses the cheerful **Museo Provincial de Ávila,** full of local archaeology and folklore. Part of the museum's collection is housed in the adjacent Romanesque temple of San Tomé el Viejo, a few minutes' walk east of the cathedral apse. ✉ *Pl. de Nalvillos 3, Ávila* ☎ *92/021–1003* 💰 *€2 (free Sat. and Sun.)* ⊙ *Closed Mon.*

★ **Catedral de Ávila**
CHURCH | The battlement apse of Ávila's cathedral forms the most impressive part of the city's walls. Entering the town gate to the right of the apse, you can reach the sculpted north portal by turning left and walking a few steps. The west portal, flanked by 18th-century towers, is notable for the crude carvings of hairy male figures on each side. Known as "wild men," these figures appear in many Castilian palaces of this period. The Transitional Gothic structure, with its granite nave, is considered to be the first Gothic cathedral in Spain. Look for the early-16th-century marble sepulchre of Bishop Alonso de Madrigal. Known as El Tostado (the Toasted One) for his swarthy complexion, the bishop was a tiny man of enormous intellect. When on one occasion Pope Eugenius IV ordered him to stand—mistakenly thinking him to still be on his knees—the bishop pointed to the space between his eyebrows and hairline, and retorted, "A man's stature is to be measured from here to here!" ✉ *Pl. de la Catedral, Ávila* ☎ *92/021–1641* ⊕ *catedralavila.es* 💰 *€6.*

Centro de Interpretación del Misticismo
(*Mysticism Interpretation Center*)
SCIENCE MUSEUM | The only such museum of its kind in Europe, this center is devoted to mysticism, the practice of religious ecstasy made famous by Ávila's native daughter, St. Teresa—one of Christianity's first female mystics. Exhibits explain the role of mysticism in Judaism, Christianity, and a number of Eastern religions. The exterior of the building, a medieval house, is original, but the giant prism ceiling that reflects light throughout the interior is obviously a new addition. ✉ *Paseo del Rastro, Ávila* ☎ *92/021–2154* ⊕ *www.avilamistica.es* 💰 *€2* ⊙ *Closed Mon.*

Convento de Santa Teresa
CHURCH | This Carmelite convent was founded in the 17th century on the site of the St. Teresa's birthplace. Teresa's account of an ecstatic vision, in which an angel pierced her heart, inspired many baroque artists, most famously the Italian sculptor Giovanni Bernini. There's a small museum with creepy relics including one of Teresa's fingers. You also can see the small and rather gloomy garden where she played as a child. ✉ *Pl. de la Santa 2, Ávila* ☎ *92/021–1030* ⊕ *www.santateresadejesus.com* 💰 *Church and reliquary free, museum €2.*

Real Monasterio de Santo Tomás
CHURCH | In an unlikely location—among apartment blocks a good 10-minute walk from the walls—is one of the most important religious institutions in Castile. The monastery was founded by Ferdinand and Isabella with the backing of the Inquisitor-General Tomás de Torquemada, largely responsible for the expulsion of the Jews per the Alhambra Decree, who is buried in the sacristy. Further funds were provided by the confiscated property of converted Jews who were dispossessed during the Inquisition. Three decorated cloisters lead to the church; inside, a masterful high altar (circa 1506) by Pedro Berruguete overlooks a serene marble tomb by the Italian artist Domenico Fancelli. One of the earliest examples of the Italian Renaissance style in Spain, this work was built for Prince Juan, the only son of Ferdinand and Isabella, who died at 19. After Juan's burial here, his heartbroken parents found themselves unable to return. There are free guided tours at 6 pm on weekends and holidays. ✉ *Pl. de Granada 1, Ávila* ☎ *92/022–0400* 💰 *€4.*

 Restaurants

Las Cancelas

$$$ | SPANISH | Locals flock to this little tavern for the tapas and fat, juicy steaks served in the boisterous barroom or white-tablecloth dining area, set in a covered arcaded courtyard. There are 14 hotel rooms available, too—simple, endearingly well-worn arrangements at moderate prices. **Known for:** good value; quaint, romantic dining room; chuletón de Ávila (gargantuan local steak). Ⓢ *Average main: €20* ✉ *Calle de la Cruz Vieja 6, Ávila* ☎ *92/021–2249* ⊕ *www.lascancelas.com* ⊗ *Closed early Jan.–early Feb. No dinner Sun.*

Restaurante El Molino de la Losa

$$$$ | SPANISH | FAMILY | Sitting at the edge of the serene Adaja River, El Molino, housed in a 15th-century mill, enjoys one of the best views of the town walls. Lamb, the restaurant's specialty, is roasted in a medieval wood oven, and the beans from nearby El Barco de Ávila (*judías de El Barco*) are a local delicacy. **Known for:** refined cuisine; succulent roast lamb; views of the river and city walls. Ⓢ *Average main: €30* ✉ *Calle Bajada de la Losa 12, Ávila* ☎ *92/021–1101, 92/021–1102* ⊕ *www.elmolinodelalosa.com* ⊗ *No dinner.*

Hotels

★ Best Western Premier Sofraga Palacio

$$$ | HOTEL | A breath of fresh air on Ávila's aging hotel scene, this newly inaugurated (2021) property strikes a delicate balance between old and new. **Pros:** sparkling new property; pleasingly mellow decor; historical building with character. **Cons:** popular wedding venue; service still working out some kinks; restaurant is overpriced for the area. Ⓢ *Rooms from: €138* ✉ *López Nuñez 1, Ávila* ☎ *92/025–4080* ⊕ *www.bestwestern.com* ⦿ *Free Breakfast* ⇆ *27 rooms.*

Palacio de los Velada

$$ | HOTEL | This four-star hotel occupies a beautifully restored 16th-century palace in the heart of the city next to the cathedral, an ideal spot if you like to relax between sightseeing. **Pros:** bountiful breakfast buffet; gorgeous glass-covered patio; amiable service. **Cons:** expensive off-site parking; some rooms don't have views because the windows are so high; lack of power outlets. Ⓢ *Rooms from: €100* ✉ *Pl. de la Catedral 10, Ávila* ☎ *92/025–5100* ⊕ *www.hotelpalaciodelosvelada.com* ⇆ *145 rooms.*

Parador de Ávila

$$$ | HOTEL | FAMILY | Post up in a 16th-century medieval castle attached to the massive town walls at this parador whose standout feature is its lush garden containing archaeological ruins. **Pros:** family-friendly rooms and services; gorgeous garden and views; good restaurant. **Cons:** interiors need a refresh; long walk into town; underwhelming breakfast. Ⓢ *Rooms from: €175* ✉ *Marqués de Canales de Chozas 2, Ávila* ☎ *92/021–1340* ⊕ *www.parador.es* ⇆ *61 rooms* ⦿ *No Meals.*

Salamanca

212 km (132 miles) northwest of Madrid.

Salamanca's radiant sandstone buildings, mathematically proportioned Plaza Mayor, and meandering river make it one of the most majestic and beloved cities in Spain. For centuries, its eponymous university has imbued the city with an intellectual verve, a stimulating arts scene, and—in recent decades—raging nightlife to match. You'll see more foreign students here per capita than anywhere else in Spain.

If you approach from Madrid or Ávila, your first glimpse of Salamanca will be the city rising from the wide and winding Tormes River. In the foreground is a 15-arch Roman bridge; soaring above it

Salamanca's Plaza Mayor once hosted bullfights.

is the combined bulk of the old and new cathedrals. Piercing the skyline to their right is the Renaissance monastery and church of San Esteban. Behind these, and largely out of sight from the river, is a medieval warren of palaces, convents, and university buildings that culminates in the Plaza Mayor. Despite enduring considerable damage over the centuries, Salamanca remains one of Spain's greatest cities architecturally, a veritable showpiece of the Spanish Renaissance.

GETTING HERE AND AROUND

You'll probably feel rushed if you try to visit Salamanca from Toledo in an out-and-back day trip. To fully enjoy its splendor, plan on an overnight. Approximately 13 trains depart Madrid for Salamanca daily, several of which are high-speed ALVIA itineraries that take just over an hour and a half. Avanza buses leave from the Estación Sur de Autobuses; Blablacar rideshares (about 2 hours and 15 minutes) are faster and more affordable.

Once in town, Salamanca de Transportes runs 64 municipal buses equipped with

lifts for passengers with disabilities on routes throughout the city of Salamanca. You may opt to take a bus in order to reach the train and bus stations on the outskirts of the city.

CONTACTS Salamanca de Transportes. ✉ *Calle Gran Vía 4, Salamanca* ☎ *92/321–2829* ⊕ *www.salamancadetransportes. com.*

VISITOR INFORMATION
CONTACTS Salamanca Municipal Tourist Office. ✉ *Pl. Mayor 32, Salamanca* ☎ *92/321–8342* ⊕ *www.salamanca.es.*

Sights

Casa de Las Conchas (*House of Shells*)
HISTORIC HOME | This house, whose facade is covered in scallop shell carvings, was built around 1500 for Dr. Rodrigo Maldonado de Talavera, a chancellor of the Order of St. James, whose symbol is the shell. Among the playful plateresque details are the lions over the main entrance, engaged in a fearful tug-of-war with the Talavera crest. The interior

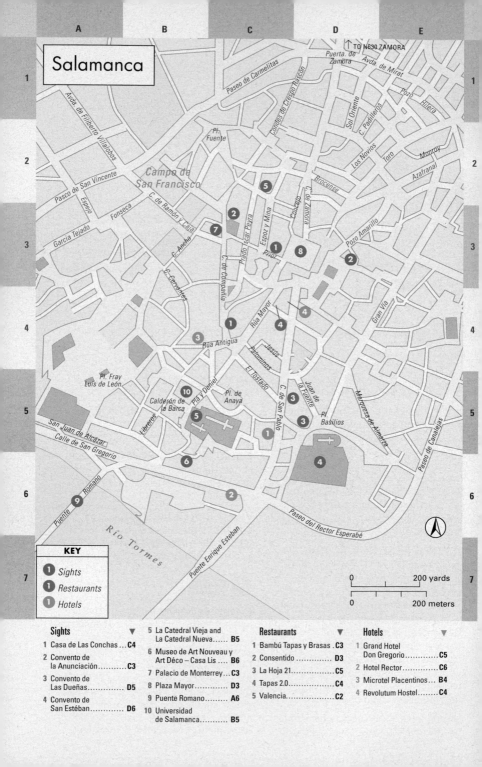

Salamanca

has been converted into a public library. Duck into the charming courtyard, which has an intricately carved upper balustrade that imitates basketwork. ✉ *Calle Compañía 2, Salamanca* ☎ *92/326–9317* ⚞ *Free*.

Convento de la Anunciación (*Convento de la Anunciación*)

CHURCH | Archbishop Alonso de Fonseca I lies here, in this splendid Gothic-style marble tomb created by Diego de Siloe during the early 1500s on the outskirts of the historic center. Magnificent churrigueresque altarpieces depicting scenes in the life of Jesus were restored in 2014. The cloister is closed to the public as the convent, aka "Las Úrsulas," is still active. ✉ *Calle de las Úrsulas 2, Salamanca* ☎ *92/321–9877* ⚞ *€3*.

★ **Convento de Las Dueñas** (*Convent of the Dames*)

CHURCH | Founded in 1419, this convent hides a 16th-century cloister that is the most fantastically decorated in Salamanca, if not in all of Spain. The capitals of its two superimposed Salmantine arcades are crowded with a baffling profusion of grotesques that can absorb you for hours. Don't forget to look down: The interlocking diamond pattern on the ground floor of the cloister is decorated with the knobby vertebrae of goats and sheep. It's an eerie yet perfect accompaniment to all the grinning, disfigured heads sprouting from the capitals looming above you. The museum has a fascinating exhibit on Spain's little-known slavery industry. Seek out the traditional sweets made by the nuns. ✉ *Pl. del Concilio de Trento, Salamanca* ☎ *92/321–5442* ⚞ *€2*.

★ **Convento de San Esteban** (*Convent of St. Stephen*)

CHURCH | The convent's monks, among the most enlightened teachers at the university in medieval times, introduced Christopher Columbus to Isabella (hence his statue in the nearby Plaza de Colón, back toward Calle de San Pablo). The complex was designed by one of the

Fonseca's Mark

Nearly all of Salamanca's outstanding Renaissance buildings bear the five-star crest of the all-powerful and ostentatious Fonseca family. The most famous of them, Alonso de Fonseca I, was the archbishop of Santiago and later of Seville; he was also a notorious womanizer and a patron of the Spanish Renaissance.

monks who lived here, Juan de Álava. The west facade, a thrilling plateresque masterwork in which sculpted figures and ornamentation are piled up to a height of more than 98 feet, is a gathering spot for tired tourists and picnicking locals, but the crown jewel of the structure is a glowing golden sandstone cloister with Gothic arcading punctuated by tall, spindly columns adorned with classical motifs. The church, unified and uncluttered but also dark and severe, allows the one note of color provided by the ornate and gilded high altar of 1692. An awe-inspiring baroque masterpiece by José Churriguera, it deserves five minutes of just sitting and staring. You can book free guided tours on the website. ✉ *Pl. Concilio de Trento 1, Salamanca* ☎ *92/321–5000* ⊕ *www.conventosanesteban.es* ⚞ *€4* ⊙ *Museum closed Mon.*

★ **La Catedral Vieja and La Catedral Nueva**

CHURCH | Nearest the river stands the Catedral Vieja (Old Cathedral), built in the late 12th century and one of the most riveting examples of the Spanish Romanesque. Because the dome of the crossing tower has strange, plumelike ribbing, it's known as the Torre del Gallo (Rooster's Tower). The much larger Catedral Nueva (New Cathedral) went up between 1513 and 1526 under the late-Gothic architect Juan Gil de Hontañón. Controversially, a 1992 restoration added an astronaut carving to the facade as a wink to the modern era—see if you can spot it. Both cathedrals are part of the same complex, though they have different visiting hours, and you need to enter the New to get to the Old. ⊠ *Pl. de Anaya and Calle Cardenal Pla y Deniel, Salamanca* ☎ *92/321–7476, 92/328–1123* ⊕ *www.catedralsalamanca.org* ✉ *Catedral Nueva free, Catedral Vieja €5 (free Tues. 10–noon).*

Museo de Art Nouveau y Art Déco – Casa Lis

ART MUSEUM | Sure, the best thing about this museum is probably the stunning Moderniste building it's housed in, but the collections within—comprising 19th-century paintings and glass, French and German china dolls, Viennese bronze statues, and more—are a welcome reprieve from all the churrigueresque convents and churches. ⊠ *Calle Gibraltar 14, Salamanca* ☎ *92/312–1425* ⊕ *www. museocasalis.org* ✉ *€5 (free Thurs. 11–2)* ⊘ *Closed Mon. Apr.–mid-Oct.*

Palacio de Monterrey

CASTLE/PALACE | Built in the mid-16th century by Rodrigo Gil de Hontañón and one of the most stunning Renaissance palaces in Spain, this lavish abode was meant for an illegitimate son of Alonso de Fonseca I. The building is flanked by towers and has an open arcaded gallery running the length of the upper level. Such galleries—often seen on the ground floor of palaces in Italy—were intended to provide privacy for the women of the house and to cool the floor below during the summer. Following years of renovations and much anticipation, the palace finally opened to the public in 2018; tours, which cost €5 per person, are by appointment only (inconveniently, reservations must be made in person at the Plaza Mayor tourist office). Feast your eyes on seldom-before-seen Titians, Coellós, and other masterpieces presided over by the Alba family. ⊠ *Pl. de las Agustinas, Salamanca* ☎ *92/321–8342* ⊕ *www.fundacioncasadealba.com* ✉ *€5 tour.*

★ Plaza Mayor

PLAZA/SQUARE | Built in the 1730s by Alberto and Nicolás Churriguera, Salamanca's Plaza Mayor is one of the largest and most beautiful squares in Spain. The lavishly elegant, pinkish *ayuntamiento* (town hall) dominates its northern side. The square and its arcades are popular gathering spots for Salmantinos of all ages, and its terrazas are the perfect spot for a coffee break. At night, the plaza swarms with students meeting "under the clock" on the plaza's north side. *Tunas* (roving musicians in traditional garb) often meander among the cafés and crowds, playing for smiles, applause, and tips. ⊠ *Plaza Mayor, Salamanca.*

Puente Romano (*Roman Bridge*)

BRIDGE | Next to this bridge is an Iberian stone bull, and opposite the bull is a statue commemorating the young hero of the 16th-century picaresque novel *The Life of Lazarillo de Tormes and His Fortunes and Adversities,* a masterpiece of Spanish literature. There's also a 300-meter track and a network of trails on the south side of the bridge ideal for jogging. ⊠ *Salamanca.*

Universidad de Salamanca

COLLEGE | The university's walls, like those of the cathedral and other structures in Salamanca, often bear large ocher lettering recording the names of famous university graduates. The earliest names are said to have been written in the blood of the bulls killed to celebrate the successful completion of a doctorate (call it medieval graffiti!). The elaborate facade of the Escuelas Mayores (Upper Schools) dates to the early 16th century; see if you can spy the eroded "lucky" frog that's become the symbol of the city—legend has it that students who spot the frog on their first try will pass all their exams. The interior of the Escuelas Mayores, drastically restored in parts, is disappointing after the splendor of the facade and not worth entering unless you're a diehard Spanish literature buff. But if you

are, the lecture hall of Fray Luis de León, where Cervantes, Pedro Calderón de la Barca, and numerous other luminaries of Spain's golden age once sat, is of interest, as is the grand library. Don't miss the serene courtyard (free entry) of the Escuelas Menores (Lower Schools) that wraps around the patio in front of the Escuelas Mayores. ✉ *Calle Libreros, Salamanca* ☎ *92/329–4400, 95/222–2998* 🌐 *www.usal.es* 🎫 *Free to view facade, €10 to enter (free Mon. morning).*

🍴 Restaurants

Bambú Tapas y Brasas

$$$ | **TAPAS** | Bambú is two restaurants in one: there's a jovial basement tapas bar serving gargantuan tapas and beers, and then there's the far more sedate white-tablecloth dining room, whose *alta cocina*menu is as experimental as it is expensive. Both are worthwhile options; go with the vibe that suits you best. **Known for:** terrific grilled meats; free tapas with every drink at the bar; upscale dining room. [$] *Average main: €20* ✉ *Calle Prior 4, Salamanca* ☎ *92/326–0092* 🌐 *www.bambubrasas.com* 🕑 *No dinner Mon.*

★ Consentido

$$$$ | **MODERN EUROPEAN** | In his mid-30s, Salamanca-born chef Carlos Hernández del Río cut his teeth in such star-studded kitchens as Elkano, Zuberoa, and DiverXO before returning to his roots in 2020 to open this restaurant showcasing the best ingredients, techniques, and wines from his native region—with a few geeky French twists. Expect immaculately prepared appetizers like griddled fresh artichokes with Béarnaise followed by mains including stewed chickpeas with sherry and pork and marinated Tormes river trout, all served in a bright dining room with checkerboard tile floors and designer furniture. **Known for:** rising-star chef; hottest restaurant in town; homemade breads and pâtés. [$] *Average main: €24* ✉ *Plaza del Mercado 8, Salamanca* ☎ *92/370–8261* 🌐 *www.restaurante-consentido.es* 🕑 *Closed Mon. and Tues.*

★ La Hoja 21

$$$ | **SPANISH** | Just off the Plaza Mayor, this upscale restaurant has a glass facade, high ceilings, butter-yellow walls, and minimalist art—a welcome relief from the dime-a-dozen Castilian *mesones*. Savor traditional fare with a twist, such as ibérico pork ravioli and langoustine-stuffed trotters at dinner, or spring for the €16 lunch prix fixe, an absolute steal, served Tuesday through Thursday. **Known for:** nuanced yet unpretentious modern fare; romantic, low-key atmosphere; phenomenally affordable menú del día (prix fixe). [$] *Average main: €21* ✉ *Calle San Pablo 21, Salamanca* ☎ *92/326–4028* 🌐 *www.lahoja21.com* 🕑 *Closed Mon. No dinner Sun.*

★ Tapas 2.0

$$ | **TAPAS** | Decidedly modern, dependably delicious, and shockingly cheap, Tapas 2.0 might pull you back for a second meal. The cool *ensaladilla rusa* (tuna-y potato salad), a specialty, is perhaps one of the best in Spain; then there are more substantial dishes, like "Momofuku-style" fried chicken and saucy lamb meatballs, all complemented by a wine list featuring unexpected pours like German Riesling. **Known for:** best tapas in town; ensaladilla rusa; uncommon wines. [$] *Average main: €14* ✉ *Calle Felipe Espino 10, Salamanca* ☎ *92/321–6448* 🌐 *www.tapastrespuntocero.es.*

Valencia

$$$ | **SPANISH** | Despite its Mediterranean name, this traditional, family-run restaurant serves up Castilian specialties like garlic soup, partridge salad, local river trout, white asparagus, and suckling lamb. The tiny front bar is decorated with black-and-white photos of local bullfighters, and is usually packed with locals (as is the back room). **Known for:** outdoor seating; hidden-gem local hangout; soul-warming Castilian fare. [$] *Average main: €20* ✉ *Calle Concejo 15, Salamanca*

☎ *92/321–7868* 🌐 *www.restaurantevalencia.com* ⏲ *Closed Mon. Nov., Tues. Sept.–May, and Sun. June–Aug.*

Hotels

Grand Hotel Don Gregorio
$$$$ | **HOTEL** | This upscale boutique hotel has spacious, contemporary rooms in a building with roots in the 15th century. **Pros:** spa and in-room massages; quiet and comfortable; complimentary cava upon arrival. **Cons:** no outdoor space for lounging; overpriced restaurant; hodgepodge, passé decor. [$] *Rooms from: €245* ✉ *Calle San Pablo 80–82, Salamanca* ☎ *92/321–7015* 🌐 *www.hoteldongregorio.com* 🛏 *17 rooms* 🍴 *Free Breakfast.*

★ Hotel Rector
$$$$ | **HOTEL** | From the stately entrance to the high-ceiling guest rooms, this charming 13-room hotel offers a fairy-tale European experience. **Pros:** good location; personal service; terrific value for a luxury hotel. **Cons:** no balconies; parking costs extra; breakfast could be more ample. [$] *Rooms from: €210* ✉ *Paseo Rector Esperabé 10, Salamanca* ☎ *92/321–8482* 🌐 *www.hotelrector.com* 🛏 *13 rooms* 🍴 *No Meals.*

★ Microtel Placentinos
$$ | **B&B/INN** | This is a cheap-and-cheerful B&B tucked down a quiet pedestrian street in Salamanca's historic center, near the Palacio de Congresos convention center and a short walk from the Plaza Mayor. **Pros:** some rooms have whirlpool baths; short walk to bus station; quirky decor. **Cons:** boring breakfast buffet; rooms by interior staircase can be noisy; some accommodations are cramped. [$] *Rooms from: €90* ✉ *Calle Placentinos 9, Salamanca* ☎ *92/328–1531* 🌐 *www.microtelplacentinos.com* 🛏 *9 rooms* 🍴 *Free Breakfast.*

Revolutum Hostel
$ | **HOTEL** | What some might call a "designer hostel," that's not all it is; this is the best modern budget hotel in Salamanca. **Pros:** special rates for families and longer stays; all rooms have private bathrooms; breakfast included. **Cons:** you have to make your own bed in some rooms; deposit required for towels; small bathrooms in some rooms. [$] *Rooms from: €49* ✉ *Calle Sánchez Barbero 7, Salamanca* ☎ *92/321–7656* 🌐 *www.revolutumhostel.com* 🛏 *20 rooms.*

Nightlife

Particularly in summer, Salamanca sees the greatest influx of foreign students of any city in Spain. By day they study Spanish, and by night they fill Salamanca's bars and clubs.

BARS AND CAFÉS

★ The Doctor Cocktail
COCKTAIL LOUNGES | This petite, unpretentious *coctelería* off the Plaza Mayor serves an enormous breadth of drinks, from colorful tiki numbers (some with pyrotechnics) to Prohibition-era classics, until 1:30 am daily. ✉ *Calle Doctor Pinuela 5, Salamanca* ☎ *92/326–3151.*

Gran Café Moderno
CAFÉS | After-hours types end the night here, snacking on churros dipped in chocolate to ward off the next day's hangover. Gran Café Moderno is also a fine spot to loosen up before hitting the rowdier nightclubs and to recharge in the afternoon—choose from a wide variety of coffee drinks with or without booze. ✉ *Gran Vía 75–77, Salamanca* ☎ *63/753–8165.*

Mist Cocktail Bar
COCKTAIL LOUNGES | Sip fabulously gaudy cocktails both classic and experimental at this bar that also pulls excellent single-origin espressos. Weather permitting, try to snag a spot on the large outdoor patio. ✉ *Calle Bordadores 14, Salamanca* ☎ *92/321–4530* 🌐 *www.cafenieblabar.com.*

 Performing Arts

Teatro Liceo

MUSIC | This 732-seat theater, 40 yards from Plaza Mayor, is a renovated 19th-century building erected over an 18th-century convent. It hosts classic and modern performances of opera, dance, and flamenco as well as film festivals. ☒ *Calle del Toro 23, Salamanca* ☎ *92/328–1716* ⊕ *www.ciudaddecultura. org.*

Shopping

El Rastro

MARKET | This Sunday flea market— named after the larger one in Madrid—is held just outside Salamanca's historic center. It has some 400 stalls. ☒ *Av. de Aldehuela.*

Isisa Duende

CRAFTS | If you have a car, skip the souvenir shops in Salamanca's center and instead take a joyride 35 km (22 miles) along the SA300 road to Isisa Duende, a wooden crafts workshop run by a charming husband-and-wife team. Their music boxes, photo frames, and other items are carved and painted with local motifs. Call ahead to schedule a free tour; if you're pressed for time, you can buy some of their wares in the tourist office on the Plaza Mayor. ☒ *Calle San Miguel 1, Ledesma* ☎ *62/651–0527, 62/533–6703* ⊕ *www.isisa-duende.es.*

★ Luis Méndez

JEWELRY & WATCHES | Luis and his two brothers are independent third-generation jewelers whose work is distinguished by intricate filigree. The most stunning specimens—costing more than €1,000—are fashioned out of gold and pearls, but there are more affordable options made from silver and semiprecious stones. Visit their boutique, or purchase from the online Etsy catalog. ☒ *Calle Meléndez 8, Bajo 2, Salamanca* ☎ *92/326–0725, 92/344–9111* ⊕ *www. luismendez.net.*

★ Mercado Central

FOOD | **FAMILY** | At Salamanca's most historic market with more than 50 stalls you can stock up on local gourmet specialties—such as farinato sausages, jamón ibérico (acorn-fed ham), and sheep's cheeses—and round out your shopping spree with a glass of wine at any of the traditional tapas counters. ☒ *Pl. del Mercado, Salamanca* ☎ *92/321–3000* ⊕ *www.mercadocentralsalamanca. com* ☯ *Closed Sun.*

Burgos

243 km (151 miles) north of Madrid on A1.

On the banks of the Arlanzón River, this small city boasts some of Spain's most outstanding Gothic architecture. If you approach on the A1 from Madrid, the spiky twin spires of Burgos's cathedral, rising above the main bridge, welcome you to the city. Burgos's second pride is its heritage as the city of El Cid, the part-historical, part-mythical hero of the so-called Reconquest of Spain. For better and for worse, the city has long been synonymous with both militarism and religion; and even today more nuns fill the streets than almost anywhere else in Spain. Burgos was born as a military camp—a fortress built in 884 on the orders of the Christian king Alfonso III, who was struggling to defend the upper reaches of Old Castile from the constant forays of the Arabs. It quickly became vital in the defense of Christian Spain, and its reputation as an early outpost of Christianity was cemented with the founding of the Royal Convent of Las Huelgas, in 1187, and cemented as it became a place of rest and sustenance for Christian pilgrims on the Camino de Santiago. In 1938, as the Spanish Civil War raged on, soon-to-be-dictator

The small city of Burgos is famous for its magnificent Gothic cathedral.

Francisco Franco made Burgos his first seat of government, a testament to the city's conservative leanings. Today Burgos is a modern Spanish city like any other, and happily, its name is more likely to recall its famous *queso fresco* (quark) and *morcilla* (blood sausage) than its fraught political past.

GETTING HERE AND AROUND

Burgos can be reached by train from Madrid, with 13 departures daily from Chamartín (2½ hours on the fast ALVIA train and 4½ on the regional line) and by bus, with hourly service from various Madrid stations. There are usually Blablacar rideshares available as well. Once in town, municipal buses cover 45 routes throughout the city, many of them originating in Plaza de España.

VISITOR INFORMATION

CONTACTS Burgos Tourist Office. ⊠ *Pl. de Alonso-Martínez 7, Burgos* ☎ *94/720–3125* ⊕ *turismo.aytoburgos.es.*

 Sights

Arco de Santa María

NOTABLE BUILDING | Across the Plaza del Rey San Fernando from the cathedral, this is the city's main gate, rebuilt in the 16th century by King Charles V. Walk through toward the river and look above the arch at the 16th-century statues of the first Castilian judges, El Cid, King Carlos I, and Spain's patron saint, James. ⊠ *Burgos.*

Cartuja de Miraflores (*Miraflores Charterhouse*)

CHURCH | The plain facade of this 15th-century Carthusian monastery, some 3 km (2 miles) outside the historic center, belies a richly decorated interior. There's an altarpiece by Gil de Siloe that is said to be gilded with the first gold plundered in the Americas. ⊠ *Ctra. Fuentes Blancas, Burgos* ☎ *94/725–2586* ⊕ *www.cartuja.org* 🎫 *Free.*

★ Catedral de Burgos

CHURCH | Start your tour of the city with the cathedral, which contains such a

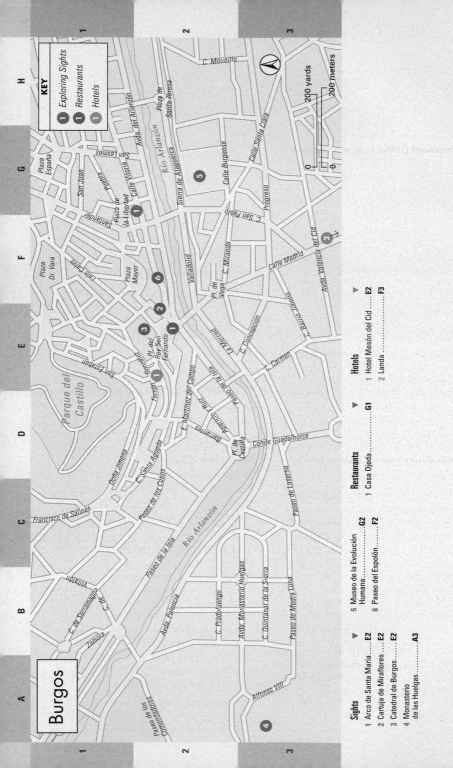

Burgos

200 yards

200 meters

C. Molinillo

Plaza de Santa-Teresa

Avda. del Arlanzón

Río Arlanzón

Calle Burgensa

Calle Santa Clara

Sierra de Atapuerca

5

Progreso

C. San Pablo

Plaza España

San Lesmes

Puente San Juan

Calle Vitoria

Plaza de la Libertad

1

Santander

Gen. Santocildes

Plaza Mayor

6

Valladolid

2

C. Miranda

Pl. de Vega

Calle Madrid

Avda. Valencia del Cid

2

Parque del Castillo

San Esteban

Gen. Gonzalo

Pl. del Rey San Fernando

3

1

Fernán

1

E. Martínez del Campo

C. La Merced

C. Concepción

C. Carmen

Barrio Gimeno

Doña Jimena

C. Santa Águeda

Paseo de los Cubos

Paseo de la Isla

Barrantes

Apuntadores

Pl. de Castilla

Conde Guadalhorce

Río Arlanzón

Paseo de Tasarna

Francisco de Salinas

Villalón

C. de Serramagna

Zamora

C. 2

Avda. Palencia

C. Pradoluengo

Avda. Monasterio Huelgas

C. Quintanar de la Sierra

Paseo de Medra Luna

Afonso VIII

Paseo de los Comendadores

4

Sights

- 1 Arco de Santa María **E2**
- 2 Cartuja de Miraflores **E2**
- 3 Catedral de Burgos **E2**
- 4 Monasterio
  de las Huelgas **A3**
- 5 Museo de la Evolución
  Humana **G2**
- 6 Paseo del Espolón **F2**

Restaurants

- 1 Casa Ojeda **G1**

Hotels

- 1 Hotel Mesón del Cid **E2**
- 2 Landa **F3**

wealth of art and other treasures that the local burghers lynched their civil governor in 1869 for trying to take an inventory of it—the proud citizens feared that the man was plotting to steal their riches. Just as opulent as what's inside is the sculpted flamboyant Gothic facade. The cornerstone was laid in 1221, and the two 275-foot towers were completed by the middle of the 14th century, though the final chapel was not finished until 1731. There are 13 chapels, the most elaborate of which is the hexagonal Condestable Chapel. You'll find the **tomb of El Cid** (1026–99) and his wife, Ximena, under the transept. El Cid (whose real name was Rodrigo Díaz de Vivar) was a feudal warlord revered for his victories over the Moors; the medieval *Song of My Cid* transformed him into a Spanish national hero. At the other end of the cathedral, high above the West Door, is the **Reloj de Papamoscas** (Flycatcher Clock), so named for the sculptured bird that opens its mouth as the hands mark each hour. The grilles around the choir have some of the finest wrought-iron work in central Spain, and the choir itself has 103 delicately carved walnut stalls, no two alike. The 13th-century stained-glass windows that once shed a beautiful, filtered light were destroyed in 1813, one of many cultural casualties of Napoléon's retreating troops. You'll learn all of this and more via the free audio guide, which has a kid-friendly option. ⊠ *Pl. de Santa María, Burgos* 🕾 *94/720–4712* ⊕ *www.catedraldeburgos.es* ⧆ *€7.*

Monasterio de las Huelgas (*Monasterio de las Huelgas*)
CHURCH | This convent on the outskirts of town, founded in 1187 by King Alfonso VIII, is still run by Cistercian nuns. There's a small on-site textile museum, but the building's main attraction is its stained-glass panels, some of the oldest in Spain. Admission includes a guided tour (Spanish only) of the monastery which is the only way to view the monastery. The monastery closes from 2 to

4 pm. ⊠ *Calle de Los Compases, Burgos* 🕾 *94/720–6045* ⊕ *www.patrimonionacional.es* 🕘 *Closed Mon.* ⧆ *€6 (free Wed. and Thurs. afternoon).*

★ **Museo de la Evolución Humana**
SCIENCE MUSEUM | FAMILY | This airy, modern complex is one of the best natural history museums in the world and traces human evolution from primate to the present day. There are life-size replicas of our ancient ancestors, plus hands-on exhibits and in-depth scientific explanations (in English) that will fascinate visitors of all ages. Pair with a museum-led visit to the Atapuerca archaeological site (inquire at reception or online to arrange). ⊠ *Paseo Sierra de Atapuerca, Burgos* 🕾 *94/725–7103* ⊕ *www.museoevolucionhumana.com* ⧆ *€6* 🕘 *Closed Mon.*

Paseo del Espolón
PROMENADE | The Arco de Santa María frames the city's loveliest promenade, the Espolón. Shaded with black poplars, it follows the riverbank. ⊠ *Burgos.*

 **Restaurants**

Casa Ojeda
$$$$ | SPANISH | This restaurant—a Castilian classic—is known for refined Burgos standbys, especially *cochinillo* (suckling pig) and lamb straight from the 200-year-old wood oven. Wines by the glass are local and reasonably priced. **Known for:** tried-and-true Castilian cuisine; fall-off-the-bone lamb; old-school waitstaff. Ⓢ *Average main: €32* ⊠ *Calle Vitoria 5,* 🕾 *94/720–9052* ⊕ *www.restauranteojeda.com* 🕘 *No dinner Sun.*

 Hotels

Hotel Mesón del Cid
$$ | HOTEL | Once home to a 15th-century printing press, this independently owned hotel and restaurant has been hosting travelers for generations in light, airy guest rooms (ask for one facing the cathedral). **Pros:** cathedral views from

upgraded rooms; central location; comfy, clean digs. **Cons:** some rooms are noisy; could use a face-lift; parking is a tight squeeze. [$] *Rooms from: €125* ✉ *Pl. Santa María 8,* ☎ *94/720–8715* 🌐 *www.mesondelcid.es* 🛏 *55 rooms* 🍴 *Free Breakfast.*

★ Landa

$$$ | HOTEL | FAMILY | If you've ever dreamed of holing up in a luxurious castle, consider booking a room at Landa, a converted 14th-century palace some 5 km (3 miles) from the city center surrounded by lush gardens. **Pros:** beautiful lobby; surprisingly affordable for level of luxury; stunning indoor-outdoor swimming pool. **Cons:** inconsistent food quality; you'll need your own transportation to get here; roads to and from town are busy. [$] *Rooms from: €162* ✉ *Ctra. de Madrid–Irún, Km 235, Burgos* ☎ *94/725–7777* 🌐 *www.landa.as* 🛏 *37 rooms* 🍴 *No Meals.*

Nightlife

Due to its student population, Burgos has an energetic *vida nocturna* (nightlife), especially in Las Llanas, near the cathedral. House wines and *cañas* (half-pints) flow freely through the crowded tapas bars along Calles Laín Calvo and San Juan, near the Plaza Mayor. Calle Puebla, a small, dark street off Calle San Juan, also gets constant revelers. Order a drink at any Burgos bar, and the bartender will plunk down a free *pinchito* (small tapa)—a longstanding tradition.

Bardeblás

CAFÉS | This intimate bar stays open until 4:30 am on the weekends, inviting you to stay awhile—and you just might, thanks to its strong and affordable drinks and catchy throwback jams. ✉ *Calle de la Puebla 29, Burgos* ☎ *94/720–1162.*

Cervecería Flandes

PUBS | With 12 beers on tap that run the gamut from Belgian ales to rare Castilian microbrews, this Burgos stalwart for 20 years attracts a diverse crowd of students, travelers, and beer geeks. Just don't expect any fancy food here—potato chips, nachos, and other sundry snacks are the only grub available. ✉ *Pl. Huerto del Rey 21, Burgos* ☎ *65/993–4813* 🌐 *www.cerveceriaflandes.es.*

El Camino de Santiago

West of Burgos, the León-bound N120 crosses the ancient Camino de Santiago, or Way of St. James, revealing lovely old churches, tiny hermitages, ruined monasteries, and medieval villages across rolling fields. West of León, you can follow the well-worn Camino pilgrimage route as it approaches the giant cathedral in Santiago de Compostela.

Shopping

Ribera del Duero reds, bottled south of the city along the eponymous river, might not be as well known as those from Rioja, but they can be equally (if not more) sublime. You also can stock up on Burgos-style *morcilla* (blood sausage) and local cheese. Beyond culinary finds, keep your eye out for small artisan shops specializing in ceramics and textiles.

★ Delicatessen Ojeda

FOOD | A food lover's paradise, this pristine, well-lit store carries all the Castilian delicacies you can imagine, from Burgos-style morcilla and cheese to roasted oil-packed peppers and top-quality dried beans and pulses. ✉ *Calle de Vitoria 5, Burgos* ☎ *94/720–4832* 🌐 *www.delicatessenojeda.com.*

Side Trips from Burgos

Monastery of Santo Domingo de Silos

For a sojourn with masters of the Gregorian chant, head to the monastery where 1994's triple-platinum album *Chant* was recorded in the 1970s and '80s. Located 58 km (36 miles) southeast of Burgos, the monastery has an impressive two-story cloister that's lined with intricate Romanesque carvings. Try to drop in for an evening vespers service. It's a unique experience that's well off the tourist path. Single men can stay here for up to eight days (€42 per night with full board). Guests are expected to be present for breakfast, lunch, and dinner but are otherwise left to their own devices. ⊕ *www.abadiadesilos.es*

Ojo Guareña

If you have a day to spare or are traveling on to Cantabria, stop at this breathtaking hermitage hewn into a karst cliffside surrounded by leafy woodlands situated a mile south of Cueva. A national monument, the cave complex housing the religious structure stretches 90 km (56 miles), and there's rock art throughout the many chambers that depicts the cave as a dwelling for early humans. Archeologists date the site's use from the Middle Paleolithic to the Middle Ages. A worthwhile guided tour of the hermitage lasts 45 minutes; even more scintillating is the tour of nearby Palomera Cave (by appointment only). ⊕ *www.merindaddesotoscueva.es*

León

334 km (208 miles) northwest of Madrid, 184 km (114 miles) west of Burgos.

León, the ancient capital of Castile and León, was built on the banks of the Bernesga River in the high plains of Old Castile; today it's a wealthy and conservative provincial capital and prestigious university town. The wide avenues of western León are lined with boutiques, and the twisting alleys of the half-timber old town hide the bars, bookstores, and *chocolaterías* popular with students.

Historians say that the city was not named for the proud lion that has been its emblem for centuries but rather for the Roman word *legio* (legion), a reference to the fact that the city was camp for the Roman legions in AD 70. The capital of Christian Spain was moved here from Oviedo in 914 as the Reconquest spread south, ushering in the city's most prosperous era.

As you wander the old town, you can see fragments of the 6-foot-thick ramparts that were once part of the Roman walls. Look down and you might notice small brass scallop shells set into the street. The scallop is the symbol of St. James; the town government installed them to mark the path for modern-day pilgrims heading north to Santiago de Compostela.

GETTING HERE AND AROUND

León can be reached by train from Madrid with a dozen or so departures daily from Chamartín station; the journey takes 2 hours 15 minutes on the high-speed lines (ALVIA and AVE) and between three and four on trains making local stops. ALSA has several bus departures daily, and there are generally plentiful Blablacar rideshares available.

VISITOR INFORMATION

CONTACTS León Tourist Office. ⊠ *Plaza Regla 2, León* ☎ *90/220–3030, 98/723–7082* ⊕ *www.turismocastillayleon.com.*

Sights

Antiguo Convento de San Marcos

CHURCH | Originally a home for knights of the Order of St. James, who patrolled the Camino de Santiago, this monastery was begun in 1513 by the head of the order, King Ferdinand. It is now a parador. The plateresque facade is a majestic swath of small, intricate sculptures (many depicting knights and lords) and ornamentation—one of the most impressive Renaissance works in Spain. Inside, a cloister full of medieval statues leads you to the bar, which still has the original defensive arrow slits as windows. As the Anexo Monumental del Museo de León, the convent also displays historic paintings and artifacts. ⊠ *Pl. de San Marcos 7,* ☎ *98/724–5061, 98/723–7300* ⊕ *www. parador.es* ⊠ *Museum €1* ⊗ *Closed Mon.*

Basílica de San Isidoro

CHURCH | This sandstone basilica was built into the side of the city wall in 1063 and rebuilt in the 12th century on the site of an ancient Roman temple. Adjoining the basilica, the **Panteón de los Reyes** (Royal Pantheon), which has been called "the Sistine Chapel of Romanesque art," has vibrant 12th-century frescoes on its pillars and ceiling. Look for the agricultural calendar painted on one archway, showing which farming task should be performed each month. Twenty-three kings and queens were buried here, but their tombs were destroyed by French troops during the Napoleonic Wars. Treasures in the adjacent **Museo de San Isidoro** include a jewel-encrusted agate chalice, a richly illustrated handwritten Bible, and polychrome wood statues of the Virgin Mary. Admission includes a guided tour of the Royal Pantheon and museum. ⊠ *Pl. de San Isidoro 4, León* ☎ *98/787–6161* ⊕ *www.museosanisidorodeleon.com* ⊠ *€5 (free after 4 on last Thurs. of month)* ⊗ *Closed Mon.*

Casa Botines

ART MUSEUM | This Gaudí masterpiece, which previously housed a bank, was converted into an excellent museum dedicated to the Moderniste architect in 2017. Under its conical spires and behind its fish-scale-patterned facade are more than 5,000 works of art spanning eight centuries by such renowned masters as Sorolla, Madrazo, Gutiérrez, and Solana. Given that this is the largest of Gaudí's buildings to be opened as a museum, it's worth ponying up the extra few euros for a guided tour. ⊠ *Calle Legión VII 3, León* ⊕ *www.casabotines.es* ⊠ *From €5* ⊗ *Closed Wed. morning and Sun. afternoon.*

★ Catedral de León

CHURCH | The pride of León is its soaring cathedral, begun in 1205. It is an outstanding example of Gothic architecture complete with gargoyles, flying buttresses, and pointed arches. Its 2,000 square yards of vivid stained-glass panels—second only, perhaps, to those in Chartres, France—depict biblical stories and Castilian landscapes. A glass door to the choir gives an unobstructed view of nave windows and the painted altarpiece, framed with gold leaf. The cathedral also contains the sculpted tomb of King Ordoño II, who moved the capital of Christian Spain to León. The museum's collection boasts giant medieval hymnals, textiles, sculptures, wood carvings, and paintings. Look for the carved-wood Mudejar archive, with a letter of the alphabet above each door—it's one of the world's oldest filing cabinets. Guided tours can be scheduled by phone. ⊠ *Pl. de Regla, León* ☎ *98/787–5770* ⊕ *www. catedraldeleon.org* ⊠ *From €6.*

Fundación Vela Zanetti

ART MUSEUM | This contemporary art museum, constructed using minimalist wood beams and glass panels inside a 15th-century mansion, pays homage to Zanetti, a 20th-century Castilian artist known for his thought-provoking

The colorful panels on León's MUSAC, the Museum of Modern Art, were inspired by the rose window of the city's Gothic cathedral.

murals portraying agrarian life. Some may remind you of works by El Greco for their shimmering luminosity. It's worth the stop, and you can view the exhibit in under an hour. ⊠ *Casona de Villapérez, Calle Pablo Flórez, León* ☎ *98/724–4121* ⊘ *Closed Sun. and Mon.* 🎫 *Free.*

MUSAC (Museo de Arte Contemporáneo de Castilla y León) (*Museum of Modern Art of Castilla y León*)

ART MUSEUM | It's worth detouring to this museum for its facade alone, a modern technicolor masterpiece by famed Spanish architects Mansilla + Tuñón. The endless rainbow of rectangles that encloses the building is an homage to the colorful stained glass of the cathedral. Inside, wander through rooms bearing the latest art and multimedia projects by locally and nationally acclaimed artists. Films and concerts are also shown throughout the year. ⊠ *Av. de los Reyes Leoneses 24, León* ☎ *98/709–0000* ⊕ *www.musac.es* 🎫 *€3 (free Sun. 5–9)* ⊘ *Closed Mon.*

Museo de León

HISTORY MUSEUM | This museum displays artifacts from the region from prehistoric to contemporary times, including sculptures, engravings, paintings, and furniture, but the crown jewel of the collection is the Cristo Carrizo (Carrizo Crucifix), a small 11th-century Romanesque ivory carving distinguished by its lifelike expression and powerful presence. Notice the figure's carefully coiffed hair and beard and the loincloth arranged in sumptuous Byzantine detail. ⊠ *Pl. de Santo Domingo 8, León* ☎ *98/723–6405* ⊕ *www.museodeleon.com* 🎫 *€1* ⊘ *Closed Mon.*

Plaza de Santa María del Camino

PLAZA/SQUARE | This square was once called Plaza del Grano (Grain Square) because it was the site of the city's corn and bread market. Also here is the church of **Santa María del Camino,** where pilgrims stop on their way west to Santiago de Compostela. The fountain in the middle of the plaza depicts two cherubim

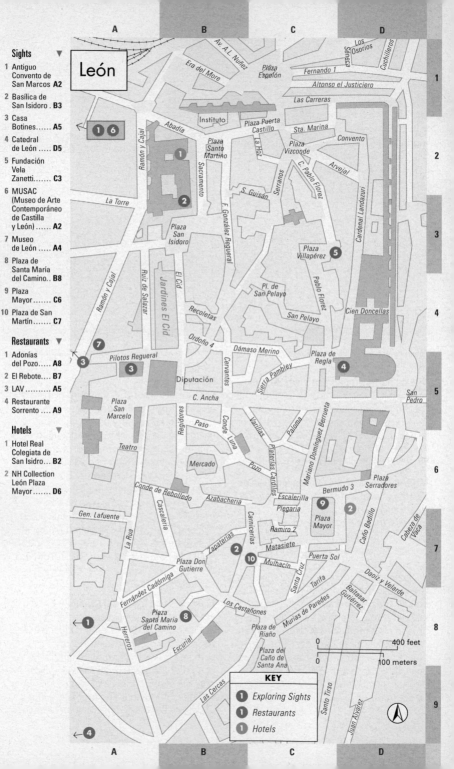

León

Sights ▼

1 Antiguo Convento de San Marcos **A2**
2 Basílica de San Isidoro . **B3**
3 Casa Botines...... **A5**
4 Catedral de León **D5**
5 Fundación Vela Zanetti....... **C3**
6 MUSAC (Museo de Arte Contemporáneo de Castilla y León) **A2**
7 Museo de León **A4**
8 Plaza de Santa María del Camino.. **B8**
9 Plaza Mayor....... **C6**
10 Plaza de San Martín....... **C7**

Restaurants ▼

1 Adonías del Pozo..... **A8**
2 El Rebote.... **B7**
3 LAV **A5**
4 Restaurante Sorrento **A9**

Hotels ▼

1 Hotel Real Colegiata de San Isidoro... **B2**
2 NH Collection León Plaza Mayor **D6**

KEY

1 *Exploring Sights*
1 *Restaurants*
1 *Hotels*

clutching a pillar, symbolizing León's two rivers and the capital.

Plaza Mayor

MARKET | This is the heart of the old town, and on Wednesday and Saturday mornings the arcaded plaza bustles with farmers selling produce and cheeses. ✉ *León.*

Plaza de San Martín

PLAZA/SQUARE | León's busiest tapas bars are in this 12th-century square. The surrounding area is called the Barrio Húmedo, or "Wet Neighborhood," allegedly because of the large amount of wine spilled here late at night. ✉ *León.*

🍴 Restaurants

Adonías del Pozo

$$$$ | **SPANISH** | In this softly lit dining room furnished with rustic tables and colorful ceramics, feast on top-of-the-line cured *cecina* (Leonese air-dried beef "ham"), roasted peppers, and chorizo. Grilled sea bream is a treat for seafood lovers; banana pudding with chocolate sauce is a treat for just about everyone. **Known for:** well-priced menú del día; excellent sausages and roast meats; homey dining room. [$] *Average main: €30* ✉ *Calle Santa Nonia 16, León* ☎ *98/720–6768, 98/725–2665* ⏲ *Closed Sun.*

El Rebote

$ | **TAPAS** | Though every drink comes with a complimentary croqueta at this pocket-size bar frequented by locals, the crisp, gooey orbs are so succulent that you'll want to order a few extra. Be sure to sample the smoky cured beef *cecina* rendition. **Known for:** sardine-can digs; to-die-for croquetas; quirky local wines by the glass. [$] *Average main: €8* ✉ *Pl. San Martín 9, León* ☎ *98/721–3510* ⏲ *Closed Mon.*

LAV

$$$$ | **SPANISH** | The most exciting nueva cocina restaurant on the León dining scene, LAV appeals to all the senses with unexpected flavor combinations, playful plating, and personable service. Tasting menus—a steal at €41—begin with "surprise sandwiches" at the bar and progress into the kitchen for a brief "show cooking" demo before winding up in the dining room. **Known for:** fine dining that doesn't take itself too seriously; terrific-value tasting menu; local ingredients used in ways you've never seen before. [$] *Average main: €39* ✉ *Av. del Padre Isla 1, León* ☎ *98/779–8190* 🌐 *www.restaurantelav.com* ⏲ *Closed Sun.*

★ Restaurante Sorrento

$$$ | **SPANISH** | **FAMILY** | León is a cold, windy town for much of the year, so it's no surprise that the local version of *cocido* (boiled dinner) is heartier than usual with mounds of green cabbage, spoonable blood sausage, and some 10 types of meat (chorizo, beef shanks, pork belly, and chicken, to name a few). Sample the city's best rendition at this spartan yet inviting downstairs restaurant outside the historic center—and be sure to bring an appetite. **Known for:** local crowd; warm service; soul-satisfying cocido leonés. [$] *Average main: €18* ✉ *Calle Bernardo del Carpio 1, León* ☎ *98/707–3270* ⏲ *Closed Mon.*

🛏 Hotels

Hotel Real Colegiata de San Isidoro

$$$ | **HOTEL** | Other hotels around town bill themselves as being steps from the main tourist attractions, but the Hotel Real Colegiata, which houses a Romanesque collegiate library and museum, is located within one. **Pros:** free tour of the grounds; modern Spanish restaurant; gorgeous historic building. **Cons:** no in-room coffee-making facilities; unrenovated rooms lack style; no gym, pool, or spa. [$] *Rooms from: €140* ✉ *Pl. Santo Martino 5, León* ☎ *98/787–5088* 🌐 *www.hotelrealcolegiata.com* 🔑 *32 rooms* 🍽 *Free Breakfast.*

★ NH Collection León Plaza Mayor
$$$ | **HOTEL** | This handsome hotel, housed in a palace overlooking the 17th-century Plaza Mayor, is awash with whites, dark woods, and neutral tones. **Pros:** subdued, elegant interiors; varied breakfasts; parking below building. **Cons:** some furniture could use replacing; maintenance a little inconsistent; parking is a tight squeeze. [$] *Rooms from: €170* ✉ *Pl. Mayor 15–17, León* ☎ *98/734–4357* 🌐 *www.nh-collection.com* 🛏 *51 rooms* 🍴 *No Meals.*

Nightlife

León's most popular hangouts are clustered around the Plaza Mayor, frequented mainly by couples and families, and Plaza San Martín, where the college kids hang. The surrounding streets (Calles Escalerilla, Plegaria, Ramiro II, Matasiete, and Mulhacén) are packed with tapas bars. In the Plaza Mayor, you might want to start at **La Pañería, The Harley,** or **Mishiara.** In Plaza de San Martín, begin your evening with tapas and *cortitos* (local slang for two-gulp glasses of beer) at **Taberna Los Cazurros, El Rebote,** or **Mesón Jabugo.** Then, go clubbing at **Studio 54,** a *discoteca* housed in an old theater whose crowd gets progressively younger (and LGBT friendly) as the night goes on.

Shopping

Tasty regional treats include roasted red peppers, potent brandy-soaked cherries, and candied chestnuts—but León's most prized artisanal product is *cecina*, air-dried beef that packs an umami punch similar to that of good jerky or a dry-aged steak. You can buy all of these items in food shops around the city. Note: Many stores in León are closed on Sunday.

Prada a Tope
FOOD | Prada A Tope has a restaurant, winery, and gourmet store, plus a huge estate in the countryside outside León. It operates this small café and shop in the city whose delicacies include chestnuts in syrup, bittersweet figs and pears in wine, jams, and liqueurs. Not enough room in your suitcase? Order by mail from its website. ✉ *Calle Alfonso IX 9, León* ☎ *98/725–7221, 98/756–3366* 🌐 *www.pradaatope.es.*

Astorga

46 km (29 miles) southwest of León.

Astorga, where the pilgrimage roads from France and Portugal merge, once had 22 hospitals to lodge and care for ailing travelers. Though the city is no longer the bustling crossroads that it once was, plenty of travelers visit this charming town for its eye-popping Gaudí masterpiece, *El Palacio Episcopal,* and its famed *cocido maragato,* a stick-to-your-ribs stew. It gets its name from the historical area Astorga is situated in, La Maragatería, which at one time stood apart from its neighbors for its special dialect, elaborate dress, and distinctive folk music.

GETTING HERE AND AROUND

More than a dozen buses depart daily from León, and the trip takes about 45 minutes. If you're driving, there's ample parking. The city is navigable on foot once you've arrived.

VISITOR INFORMATION

CONTACTS Astorga Tourist Office. ✉ *Pl. Eduardo de Castro 5, Astorga* ☎ *98/761–8222* 🌐 *www.aytoastorga.es.*

Sights

★ Centro de Interpretación del León Romano (*Roman Museum*)
RUINS | **FAMILY** | This hidden-gem museum uses the archaeological record to show what life was like in Astorga during Roman times, when the city was called Asturica Augusta. The most memorable part of the experience is the Ruta Romana, a walking tour of Roman archaeological remains in Astorga (combined

tickets can be bought at the museum). Descriptions are in Spanish only. ✉ Pl. San Bartolomé 2, Astorga ☎ 98/761–6937 ⊕ www.aytoleon.es ✉ From €3 ⊗ Closed Mon.

La Catedral de Santa María de Astorga
CHURCH | The museum within this gothic cathedral displays 10th- and 12th-century chests, religious silverware, and paintings and sculptures by Astorgans through the ages, but the real treasure is the cathedral itself. You'll be especially wowed by the chancel, which contains Spain's most elaborate Romanist (Late Renaissance) retable, and by the choir, sculpted from walnut wood in an exuberant Flemish style. ✉ Pl. de la Catedral, Astorga ☎ 98/761–5820 ⊕ www.catedral-astorga.com ✉ From €6.

★ **Palacio de Gaudí** (Palacio Episcopal)
CASTLE/PALACE | Opposite Astorga's cathedral is this fairy-tale neo-Gothic palace designed for a Catalan cleric by Antoni Gaudí in 1889. Though the humdrum interiors pale in comparison to the eye-popping exteriors, those interested in local ecclesiastical history shouldn't miss visiting the **Museo de Los Caminos** (Museum of the Way). ✉ Pl. de la Catedral, Glorieta Eduardo de Castro, Astorga ☎ 98/761–6882 ⊕ www.palaciodegaudi.es ✉ €5 ⊗ Closed Mon.

🍴 Restaurants

Restaurante Serrano
$$ | SPANISH | This local hangout serves Astorgan dishes that incorporate wild game, foraged mushrooms, and regional meats. For a break from carnivorous Castilian cuisine, tuck into house-made pasta dishes or chickpeas stewed with fresh octopus, a house specialty. **Known for:** wild game; attentive old-school service; dishes using crème-de-la-crème "pico pardal" garbanzos. $ Average main: €17 ✉ Calle Portería 2, Astorga ☎ 98/761–7866, 64/607–1736 ⊕ www.restauranteserrano.es ⊗ Closed Mon.

Hotels

Hotel Vía de la Plata
$$ | HOTEL | FAMILY | A giant slate terrace with views of the countryside is the main draw of this airy, streamlined hotel with a vibe that feels more city than country. **Pros:** free parking; great views and service; gorgeous terrace. **Cons:** small breakfast area; wedding parties can be noisy; spa not included in rate. $ Rooms from: €90 ✉ Calle Padres Redentoristas 5, Astorga ☎ 98/761–9000 for hotel, 98/760–4165 for spa ⊕ www.hotelviadelaplata.es ➯ 38 rooms ⌖ Free Breakfast.

Villafranca del Bierzo

135 km (84 miles) west of León.

After crossing León's grape-growing region, where the funky, floral Bierzo wines are produced, you'll arrive in this medieval village, dominated by a massive (and still-inhabited) feudal fortress. Visit the Romanesque church of Santiago to see the Puerta del Perdón (Door of Pardon), a sort of spiritual consolation prize for exhausted Camino pilgrims who couldn't make it over the mountains. Stroll the streets and seek out the onetime home of the infamous Grand Inquisitor Tomás de Torquemada. If you've made it all the way here, don't leave Bierzo without visiting the area's most famous archaeological site, Las Médulas, whose bizarre stone formations are the remnants of Roman gold mines.

GETTING HERE AND AROUND
A rental car is the best way to access this rural region, though buses from León also service the area. You'll likely want your own transportation once you arrive anyway to visit Las Médulas, several kilometers away; it's also possible to hike or get there by bicycle.

VISITOR INFORMATION

CONTACTS Villafranca del Bierzo Tourist Office. ✉ *Av. Díaz Ovelar 10, Villafranca del Bierzo* ☎ *98/754–0028* 🌐 *www.villafrancadelbierzo.org.*

Sights

★ Las Médulas

RUINS | FAMILY | One of northern Spain's most impressive archaeological sites, this mountainous area of former Roman gold mines—located 24 km (15 miles) south of town—is a UNESCO World Heritage Site. The landscape is the result of an ancient mining technique in which myriad water tunnels were burrowed into a mountain, causing it to collapse. Miners would then sift through the rubble for gold. What's left at Las Médulas are half-collapsed mountains of golden clay with exposed tunnels peeking through lush green forest. Take in the best panorama from the Orellán viewpoint. There are hiking paths, a small archaeology exhibit (open weekends), and a visitor center. You can pay to enter some of the tunnels or browse the larger area for free. The visitor center also organizes 3-km (2-mile) walking tours—call ahead to book. A parking lot was added in summer 2021; the price is €3 per vehicle. ✉ *Carucedo* ☎ *98/742–2848* 🌐 *www.facebook.com/fundacion.lasmedulas* 🎫 *Free, archaeology center €2, Orellán tunnel €2, guided walking tour €3.*

Hotels

★ Casa Rural do Louteiro

$ | B&B/INN | FAMILY | This charming, rustic inn, in a tiny village near the archaeological site of Las Médulas, was lovingly converted from a series of medieval ruins. **Pros:** rustic details; fire pit on winter evenings; friendly staff. **Cons:** no housekeeping service; disorganized front-desk management; plenty of hiking and biking nearby, but you'll need a car to get here. [$] *Rooms from: €70* ✉ *Calle Louteiro 6, Orellán* ☎ *65/293–3419, 65/293–3971* 🌐 *www.casadolouteiro.com* 🛏 *3 cottages* 🍴 *No Meals.*

Parador de Villafranca del Bierzo

$$ | HOTEL | FAMILY | This modern two-story hotel built with local stone looks out over the Bierzo valley. **Pros:** free parking; quiet surroundings; indoor and outdoor swimming pools. **Cons:** rooms are plain and some overlook parking lot; lacks history of other paradores; noisy a/c in some rooms. [$] *Rooms from: €95* ✉ *Av. de Calvo Sotelo 28, Villafranca del Bierzo* ☎ *98/754–0175* 🌐 *www.parador.es* 🛏 *51 rooms.*

Jerte and El Valle del Jerte (Jerte Valley)

220 km (137 miles) west of Madrid.

Every spring, the Jerte Valley in northern Extremadura becomes one of Spain's top attractions for its riot of cherry blossoms. Unsurprisingly, this is where Spain's biggest cherry harvest originates, backed by the snowcapped Gredos mountains. Book ahead for March and April—peak cherry blossom season—and monitor the bloom date estimates on the tourist board's website (www.turismovalledeljerte.com) or local Spanish-language news outlets like El Periódico Extremadura (www.elperiodicoextremadura.com).

GETTING HERE AND AROUND

You will need a car to get here and explore the valley. For a scenic route, follow N110 southwest from Ávila to Plasencia.

VISITOR INFORMATION

CONTACTS Valle del Jerte Tourist Office. ✉ *Paraje Virgen de Peñas Albas (N110), Cabezuela del Valle* ☎ *92/747–2558* 🌐 *www.turismovalledeljerte.com.*

Cherry trees blossom in the Jerte Valley.

Sights

Cabezuela del Valle

TOWN | Full of half-timber stone houses, this is one of the valley's best-preserved villages. Follow N110 to Plasencia, or, if you enjoy mountain scenery, detour from the village of Jerte to Hervás, traveling a narrow road that winds 35 km (22 miles) through forests of low-growing oak trees and over the Honduras Pass. ✉ *Cabezuela del Valle.*

Puerto de Tornavacas (*Tornavacas Pass*)

VIEWPOINT | There's no more striking introduction to Extremadura than the Puerto de Tornavacas—literally, the point "where the cows turn back." Part of the N110 road northeast of Plasencia, the pass marks the border between Extremadura and the stark plateau of Castile. Its elevation of 4,183 feet affords a breathtaking view of the valley formed by the fast-flowing Jerte River. The lower slopes are covered with a dense mantle of ash, chestnut, and cherry trees, whose richness contrasts with the granite cliffs of Castile's Sierra de Gredos, blanketed in garnacha grapevines. But cherries, of course, are the principal crop. Camping is popular in this area (contact the tourist office for more details), and even the most experienced hikers can find some challenging trails. ✉ *Plasencia.*

Restaurants

★ La Cabaña

$$ | **SPANISH** | This homey, sun-drenched restaurant serves honest Extremaduran fare at an excellent price. Unlike at other dining options in the area, cooks here pay special attention to presentation and ingredient quality—attributes on display in the not-too-greasy migas, wonderfully juicy Iberian pork dishes, and refreshing tomato salads. **Known for:** bright, casual dining room; ibérico pork dishes; home-cooked food. [$] *Average main: €15* ✉ *Av. Ramón y Cajal 17, Jerte* ☎ *64/523–3953* 🌐 *www.restaurantelacabañajerte.es.*

Hotels

Finca El Carpintero

$ | **B&B/INN** | **FAMILY** | This restored 150-year-old stone mill and farmhouse makes an ideal base for enjoying the area's great outdoors. **Pros:** picturesque grounds with swimming pool; ideal country escape, especially in spring and fall; cozy atmosphere. **Cons:** spent towels and small TVs; disparity in quality between rooms and suites; need a car. $ Rooms from: €76 ⊠ N110, Km 360.5, Tornavacas ✛ 9 km (5½ miles) northeast of Jerte ☎ 92/717–7089, 65/932–8110 ⊕ www.fincaelcarpintero.com ⤴ 8 rooms ⦿l Free Breakfast.

La Casería

$$ | **B&B/INN** | **FAMILY** | One of Extremadura's first rural guesthouses, this rambling home 10 km (6 miles) southeast of Jerte is on a spectacular 120-acre working farm, once a 16th-century Franciscan convent. **Pros:** privacy in the cottages; views of Jerte Valley; outdoor activities. **Cons:** far from all main sights and national parks; main lodge often rented out to groups; need a car to get here. $ Rooms from: €120 ⊠ N110, Km 378.5, Navaconcejo ☎ 92/717–3141 ⊕ www.lacaseria.es ⤴ 9 rooms ⦿l Free Breakfast.

La Vera and Monasterio de Yuste

45 km (28 miles) east of Plasencia.

In northern Extremadura, the fertile La Vera region sits at the foot of the Gredos mountains, which are usually snowcapped through June. With its wildflowers, mountain vistas, and world-famous Yuste Monastery, the area welcomes hordes of tourists, especially in spring, its most beautiful season. One of the favorite souvenirs to take home is La Vera's famous smoky paprika, or "pimentón," available in three types: *dulce* (mild), *agridulce* (medium), and *picante* (hot). You're likely to see strings of red peppers hanging out to dry on the windowsills of area homes.

GETTING HERE AND AROUND

You'll need a car to get here. Turn left off the C501 at Cuacos and follow signs for the monastery (1 km [½ mile]).

VISITOR INFORMATION

CONTACTS Jaraíz de la Vera Tourist Office. ⊠ Calle Mérida 17, Jaraíz de la Vera ☎ 92/717–0587.

Sights

★ **Monasterio de Yuste** (*Yuste Monastery*)

CHURCH | In the heart of La Vera—a region of steep ravines (*gargantas* in Spanish), rushing rivers, and sleepy villages—lies the Monasterio de San Jerónimo de Yuste, founded by Hieronymite monks in the early 15th century. Badly damaged in the Peninsular War, it was left to decay after the suppression of Spain's monasteries in 1835, but it has since been restored by the Hieronymites. Today it's one of the most impressive monasteries in all of Spain. Carlos V (1500–58), founder of Spain's vast 16th-century empire, spent his last two years in the Royal Chambers, enabling the emperor to attend mass within a short stumble of his bed. The guided tour also covers the church, the crypt where Carlos V was buried before being moved to El Escorial (near Madrid), and a glimpse of the monastery's cloisters. ⊠ Ctra. de Yuste, ☎ 92/717–2197 ⊕ www.patrimonionacional.es ⊠ From €7 ⊗ Closed Mon.

Museo del Pimentón (*Paprika Museum*)

OTHER MUSEUM | Tucked away in a 17th-century row house, this quirky museum tells the history of the locally made paprika, dubbed "red gold," for which Jaraíz de la Vera is best known. The three floors feature audiovisual presentations and examples of grinding tools and recipes. The museum is the centerpiece of the village's annual pepper

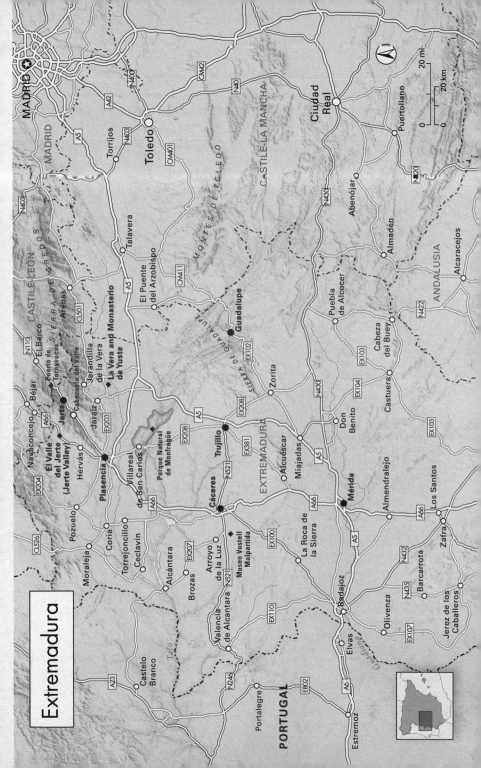

Parque Natural de Monfragüe [eye]

At the junction of the Tiétar and Tajo rivers, 20 km (12 miles) south of Plasencia on the EX208 and 60 km (37 miles) southwest of La Vera via the EX203, lies Extremadura's only national park. This rocky, mountainous wilderness is known for its diverse plant and animal life including lynxes, boars, deer, foxes, black storks, imperial eagles, and the world's largest colony of black vultures, attracting bird-watchers from around the world. Bring binoculars and head for the lookout point called Salto del Gitano (Gypsy's Leap), on the C524 just south of the Tajo River—vultures can often be spotted wheeling in the dozens at close range. The park's visitor center and main entrance is in the hamlet of Villareal de San Carlos. *www.parquedemonfrague.com*

festival, held in August. ✉ *Pl. Mayor 7, Jaraíz de la Vera* ☎ *92/746–0810* 🌐 *museodelpimenton.business.site* 🎟 *Free* 🕒 *Closed Sun. afternoon and Mon.*

Hotels

★ La Posada de los Sentidos

$$ | **B&B/INN** | **FAMILY** | There are five charming, rustic rooms in this rural hotel housed in a 16th-century convent house. **Pros:** views of the Gredos mountains; staff can arrange any number of experiences; private garden with play area. **Cons:** shared kitchen with other guests; soundproofing not ideal; rooms can get chilly on cold nights. $ *Rooms from: €100* ✉ *Calle Machín 19, Jarandilla de la Vera* ☎ *63/542–9779* 🌐 *www.laposadadelossentidos.es* 🍴 *No Meals* 🛏 *5 rooms.*

Cáceres

299 km (186 miles) west of Madrid, 125 km (78 miles) southwest of Monasterio de Yuste.

The provincial capital and one of Spain's oldest cities, Cáceres is known for its UNESCO-protected old town and lively tapeo. The Roman colony called Norba Caesarina was founded in 35 BC, but when the Moors took over in the 8th century, they named the city Quazris, which eventually morphed into the Spanish Cáceres. Amazingly, some 22 Moorish towers survive in the historic center today. Ever since noble families helped Alfonso IX expel the Moors in 1229, the city has prospered; the pristine condition of the medieval and Renaissance quarter is the result of the families' continued occupancy of the palaces erected in the 15th century.

GETTING HERE AND AROUND

Trains from Madrid take about 2½ hours and are the cheapest and easiest way to get to Cáceres. Catch a city bus outside the train station, which takes you to Plaza Mayor in the historic quarter, or walk 15 minutes into town. From Madrid, Blablacar rideshares are an excellent option as well. The city center is walkable. If you drive, park on the outskirts as the winding, narrow medieval streets are difficult to navigate.

TRAIN STATION Cáceres Train Station. ✉ *Av. Juan Pablo II 6, Cáceres* ☎ *92/723–5061, 90/224–0202* 🌐 *www.renfe.com.*

TOURS

Cuenta Trovas de Cordel
✉ *Pl. Mayor, Cáceres* ☎ *66/728–3187, 66/777–6205* 🌐 *www.cuentatrovas.com.*

CONTACTS Cáceres. ✉ *Pl. Mayor, Cáceres*
☎ *92/701–0834, 92/721–7237 tours*
⊕ *turismo.caceres.es.*

 Sights

★ **Cáceres Museum**
HISTORY MUSEUM | The Casa de las
Veletas (House of the Weather Vanes)
is a 12th-century Moorish mansion that
is now used as the city's museum.
Filled with archaeological finds from the
Paleolithic through Visigothic periods,
the museum also includes an art section
with works by El Greco, Picasso, and
Miró. The highlight is the superbly
preserved Moorish cistern—the aljibe—
with horseshoe arches supported by
mildewy stone pillars. ✉ *Pl. de las Veletas
1,* ☎ *92/701–0877* ⊕ *museodecaceres.
juntaex.es* ☞ *€2 (free Sun. and for EU
residents)* ⊙ *Closed Mon.*

★ **Ciudad Monumental**
NEIGHBORHOOD | Travel back a few cen-
turies in Cáceres's Ciudad Monumental
(aka *casco antiguo* or *ciudad vieja*), one
of the best-preserved medieval quarters
in Europe. It's so convincingly ancient
that *Game of Thrones* used it as a filming
location. There isn't a single modern
building to detract from its aura. It's
virtually deserted in winter and occasionally dusted with a light coating of
snow—a fairy-tale sight. Most of the
city's main monuments are located here,
but of Cáceres's approximately 100,000
residents, fewer than 400 reside within
this tiny enclave.

Concatedral de Santa María
CHURCH | This Gothic church, built mainly
in the 16th century, is now the cathedral
and the city's most important religious
site. The elegantly carved wooden
reredos (dating to 1551), left unpainted
according to Extremaduran custom, is
barely visible in the gloom. Follow the
lines of pilgrims to the statue of San
Pedro de Alcántara in the corner; legend
says that touching the stone figure's
shoes brings luck. A small museum in
the back displays religious artifacts. ✉ *Pl.
de Santa María,* ☎ *92/721–5313* ⊕ *www.
concatedralcaceres.com* ☞ *€5.*

Iglesia de San Mateo
CHURCH | Construction on this church
began in the 14th century, purportedly
over the ruins of a mosque, and took
nearly 300 years to finish. The interior is
austere, with a 16th-century choir and
walls lined with the tombs of prominent
Cáceres citizens. The church opens at 10
most mornings, but check with the tourist office in case of changes. ✉ *Pl. de San
Mateo, Cáceres* ☎ *92/724–6329* ☞ *Free.*

Museo de Historia de la Computación
SCIENCE MUSEUM | **FAMILY** | Medieval
Cáceres is about the last place you'd
expect to find an eclectic collection of
more than 150 Apple computers through
the ages, but in this pocket-size space
you can see (and sometimes play around
with) museum curator Carlos's prehis-
toric-looking machines from the '80s,
'90s, and early 2000s. Tours take about
an hour and are well worth the fee. ✉ *Pl.
de San Juan 13, Cáceres* ☎ *92/731–6501*
⊕ *www.museohc.com* ☞ *€7* ⊙ *Closed
Mon.*

★ **Museo Helga de Alvear** (*Visual Arts
Center Foundation Helga de Alvear*)
ART MUSEUM | After a day spent mean-
dering through medieval passageways
and marveling at ancient churches, this
contemporary art museum, presided over
by one of Europe's great modern art collectors, is a breath of fresh air. Highlights
include sculptures by Ai Weiwei and Dan
Graham and paintings by Josef Albers
and John Baldessari. A much-anticipated
renovation by Tuñón Arquitectos (of Atrio
fame), finished in February 2021, added
galleries and multimedia spaces to house
the gallerist's entire collection. ✉ *Calle
Pizarro 8, Cáceres* ☎ *92/762–6414*
⊕ *www.fundacionhelgadealvear.es*
☞ *Free* ⊙ *Closed Mon.*

The San Mateo church, with the Torre de las Cigüeñas (Tower of the Storks) in the background

★ Museo Vostell Malpartida

ART MUSEUM | The first thing that grabs your attention at this museum—located 14 km (9 miles) outside town—is the landscape that surrounds it: the **Los Barruecos** nature reserve. Spanning 800 acres, the park's otherworldly landscape comprises rolling grasslands, lakes, and enormous, peculiarly shaped boulders, which you can explore on foot. These curious natural forms inspired Wolf Vostell, a German artist of the Fluxus and Happening movements (whose wife was Extremeña), to turn a defunct yarn factory located within the park into a museum. Today you can still take in his bizarre, thought-provoking work—including a Cadillac surrounded by dinner plates and a wall of rusty Guardia Civil motorcycles—much as it was when he was alive. ⊠ *Calle Los Barruecos, Cáceres* 🕿 *92/701–0812* ⊕ *www.museovostell.org* 🖃 *€3* ⊗ *Closed Mon.*

Palacio de Carvajal

CASTLE/PALACE | This palace has an imposing granite facade, arched doorway, and tower, and the interior has been restored with period furnishings and art to look as it did when the Carvajal family lived here in the 16th century. Legend has it that King Ferdinand IV ordered the execution of two brothers from the Carvajal family, whom he accused of killing one of his knights. Thirty days later, the king was sued in the Court of God. Judgment was postponed until after the king's death, when the Carvajal brothers were declared innocent. ⊠ *Calle Amargura 1, at Pl. Santa María, Cáceres* 🕿 *92/725–5597* 🖃 *Free.*

Palacio de los Golfines de Abajo

CASTLE/PALACE | Wander the halls of one of Cáceres's great noble homes on a memorable guided tour (English available). Begun in the late 15th century and finished in the late 16th—hence the sumptuous plateresque facade—the palace bears the insignia of the Catholic Monarchs, who greatly enriched the Golfín family. See if you can also spot the coat of arms of the Golfines, situated beneath a gothic double window on the top floor. ✉ *Pl. de los Golfines 1, Cáceres* 🌐 *www.palaciogolfinesdeabajo.com* 🕒 *Closed Mon.* 🎫 *€3.*

Palacio de los Golfines de Arriba

CASTLE/PALACE | After you pass through the gate leading to the old quarter, you'll see this palace, dominated by a soaring tower dating to 1515. Only three of the four corner towers remain, adorned with various coats of arms of the families who once lived here. Inside, there are classical colonnaded courtyards with Renaissance details, but they're no longer open to the public. During the Civil War, soon-to-be-Caudillo Francisco Franco declared this building the seat of his nationalist government before moving it to Burgos and, ultimately, Madrid. Until 2019, the facade bore a plaque memorializing the dictator, but it was removed as part of a larger effort by the city to scrub Cáceres clean of fascist propaganda once and for all. ✉ *Calle Condes.*

Palacio del Capitán Diego de Cáceres

CASTLE/PALACE | The battlement tower of this palace is also known as the Torre de las Cigüeñas (Tower of the Storks) for obvious reasons. It's now a military residence, but rooms are occasionally open for exhibitions. ✉ *Pl. San Mateo.*

Plaza Mayor

PLAZA/SQUARE | This long, inclined, arcaded plaza contains several cafés, the tourist office, and—on breezy summer nights—nearly everyone in town. In the middle of the arcade opposite the old quarter is the entrance to the lively Calle General Ezponda, lined with tapas bars, student hangouts, and discotecas that keep the neighborhood electric with activity until dawn. The city's main Christmas market, selling candles and figurines and sweets, is held here. ✉ *Cáceres.*

Santuario de la Virgen de la Montaña

(*Sanctuary of the Virgin of the Mountain*)

VIEWPOINT | Overlooking Cáceres's Ciudad Monumental is this 18th-century shrine dedicated to the city's patron saint. It's built on a mountain with stunning views of the old town, especially at sunset. The panorama is worth the 15-minute drive—or even the grueling two-hour walk past chalets and farms—despite the rather mundane interior of the church (barring the impressive gilded baroque altar). ✉ *Ctra. Santuario Virgin de la Montaña, Cáceres* 🎫 *Free.*

🍴 Restaurants

★ Atrio Restaurante Hotel

$$$$ | **SPANISH** | This jaw-droppingly elegant award-winning restaurant and hotel, housed in a medieval building redesigned by star architect firm Mansilla + Tuñón, is the crown jewel of Extremaduran hospitality. The ground-floor restaurant specializes in refined contemporary cooking, and the menu changes according to what's in season in chef Toño Pérez's private garden. **Known for:** phenomenal luxury hotel on-site; interiors with bespoke furniture and original works by Warhol et al.; value for a two-Michelin-star restaurant. [$] *Average main: €75* ✉ *Pl. de San Mateo 1, Cáceres* ☎ *92/724–2928* 🌐 *www.restauranteatrio.com.*

El Figón de Eustaquio

$$$$ | **SPANISH** | A fixture on the quiet and pleasant Plaza San Juan, this restaurant has been run by the same family for 70 years and counting. In its jumble of old-fashioned dining rooms with wood-beam ceilings, feast on regional delicacies including *venado de montería* (wild venison) and *perdiz estofada* (partridge stew) complemented by full-bodied local wines. **Known for:** pleasant outdoor patio; old-school Extremaduran cooking; good selection of local wines. [$] *Average main: €30* ✉ *Pl. San Juan 12–14,* ☎ *92/724–4362, 92/724–8194* 🌐 *www.elfigondeeustaquio.com.*

★ La Marina

$$ | **SPANISH** | **FAMILY** | The third-generation owner of this beloved bar keeps endangered Cacereño dishes alive such as eggs scrambled with lamb brains (a delicacy!); spicy stewed pig ear; and *zarangollo*, a garlicky, vinegary salad of blistered roasted peppers and parsley topped with flaked Spanish tuna. There is outdoor seating available. **Known for:** above-and-beyond service; sensational offal dishes; griddled seafood and meats. *[$] Average main: €14 ✉ Av. Virgen de la Montaña 18, Cáceres ☎ 62/938–6238 🌐 www.lamarinacaceres.es ⏲ Closed Sun. No dinner Mon.*

La Tapería

$$ | TAPAS | This tiny taberna, which serves some of the best tapas in town, is always packed with locals. Order a few tostas (open-faced sandwiches on crusty peasant bread) and raciones (shared plates), and pair them with Extremaduran wines. **Known for:** free tapa with every drink; local hangout; fresh, filling tostas. *[$] Average main: €12 ✉ Calle Sánchez Garrido 1, bajo, Cáceres ☎ 92/722–5147 ⏲ Closed Mon.*

Hotels

Hotel Iberia Plaza Mayor

$ | HOTEL | FAMILY | Confusingly, this budget-friendly hotel isn't on the Plaza Mayor but rather 100 yards down a quiet side street. **Pros:** great value; generous breakfast buffet; prime location. **Cons:** dated furniture; no on-site parking; soundproofing could be better. *[$] Rooms from: €50 ✉ Calle Pintores 2, Cáceres ☎ 92/724–7634 🌐 www.iberiahotel.com 🔑 38 rooms 🍴 Free Breakfast.*

★ NH Collection Cáceres Palacio de Oquendo

$$$ | HOTEL | This 16th-century palace, which spans the length of Plaza San Juan on the edge of the old quarter, is now a NH Collection hotel that rivals the city's parador—at much lower rates. **Pros:** quiet area close to Plaza Mayor; excellent value; recent redesign. **Cons:** pricey breakfast and mediocre restaurant; no parking; some rooms have only skylights (no windows). *[$] Rooms from: €135 ✉ Pl. San Juan 11, Cáceres ☎ 92/721–5800 🌐 www.nh-hotels.com 🔑 86 rooms 🍴 No Meals.*

Parador de Cáceres

$$$$ | HOTEL | This 14th-century palace in the old town boasts elegant public spaces filled with antiques. **Pros:** stunning old building; spacious rooms; peaceful outdoor dining area. **Cons:** some bathrooms need updating; unattractive indoor dining room; spartan decor. *[$] Rooms from: €205 ✉ Calle Ancha 6, Cáceres ☎ 92/721–1759 🌐 www.parador.es 🔑 39 rooms 🍴 Free Breakfast.*

Nightlife

El Corral de las Cigüeñas

LIVE MUSIC | There's a hopping nighttime music scene at this charming old-town café with an outdoor patio. In winter months, the club is open evenings Thursday through Sunday. Hours vary depending on events; call ahead or check concert schedules online. Students with a valid ID get a discount. *✉ Cuesta de Aldana 6, ☎ 92/721–6425, 64/775–8245 🌐 www.elcorralcc.com ⏲ Closed Mon. and Tues.*

Shopping

Centro de Artesanía Casa Palacio de los Moraga

CRAFTS | Eschew the usual souvenir shops and instead drop by this art collective that sells wallets, purses, pins, toys, clothes, and other decorative elements in leather and ceramics made by local artisans. *✉ Calle Cuesta de Aldana 1, ☎ 92/722–7453 🌐 www.extremadurartesana.com ⏲ Closed Mon.*

Pastelería Isa

FOOD | The city's premier pastry shop since opening in 1952, "La Isa" is best known for its *mojicón*, an oversized orange-scented muffin native to Extremadura that's the perfect café con leche sidekick. ⊠ *Pl. Mayor 25, Cáceres* ☎ *92/724–8185.*

★ **Sierra de Montánchez**

FOOD | Satisfy your jamón cravings at this gourmet shop specializing in acorn-fed pork products. There are usually baskets of terrific-quality La Dalia pimentón on sale as well; grab one or two tins here as they're hard to find outside Extremadura. ⊠ *Pl. de la Concepción 5, Cáceres* ☎ *92/721–2025* ⊕ *www.sierrademont-anchez.es* ⊗ *Closed Sun.*

Trujillo

45 km (28 miles) east of Cáceres, 256 km (159 miles) southwest of Madrid.

Trujillo rises up from the boulder-strewn fields like a great granite schooner under full sail. From above, the rooftops and towers are worn and medieval-looking. At street level, Renaissance architecture abounds in squares such as the Plaza Mayor, with its elegant San Martín church. As in Cáceres, storks' nests top many towers—the birds have become an emblem of Trujillo. With roots in Roman times, the city was captured from the Moors in 1232 and colonized by a number of leading military families.

GETTING HERE AND AROUND

There is no train service to Trujillo, but Avanza bus offers five departures daily from Madrid's Estacion de Sur (3½ hours). There are usually several Blablacar rideshares available each day as well. Take in Trujillo on foot, as the streets are mostly cobbled or crudely paved with stone (suitable footwear needed; prepare for hills, too). The two main roads into Trujillo leave you at the unattractive bottom end of town. Things get progressively older the farther you climb, but even on the lower slopes—where most of the shops are concentrated—you need walk only a few yards to step into what seems like the Middle Ages.

BUS CONTACTS **Avanza Bus.** ☎ *91/272–2832* ⊕ *www.avanzabus.com.*

ESSENTIALS
VISITOR INFORMATION **Trujillo Tourist Office.** ⊠ *Pl. Mayor, Trujillo* ☎ *92/732–2677.*

 Sights

Iglesia de Santa María La Mayor

CHURCH | Attached to a Romanesque bell tower, this Gothic church is the most beautiful in Trujillo. It's only occasionally used for Mass, and its interior has been virtually untouched since the 16th century. The upper choir has an exquisitely carved balustrade, and the coats of arms at each end indicate the seats Ferdinand and Isabella occupied when they came here to worship. Note the high altar, circa 1480, adorned with great 15th-century Spanish paintings. To see it properly illuminated, place a coin in the box next to the church entrance. Climb the tower for stunning views of the town and vast plains stretching toward Cáceres and the Sierra de Gredos. The optional audio guide is well worth the €1 fee. ⊠ *Pl. de Santa María, Trujillo* 🎫 *From €2.*

★ La Villa

HISTORIC DISTRICT | This is Trujillo's oldest area, enclosed by restored stone walls. Follow them along Calle Almenas, which runs west from the Palacio de Orellana-Pizarro, beneath the **Alcázar de Los Chaves,** a castle-fortress that was converted into a guest lodge in the 15th century and hosted visiting dignitaries including Ferdinand and Isabella. Now a college, the building has seen better days. Passing the alcázar, continue west along the wall to the **Puerta de San Andrés,** one of La Villa's four surviving gates (there were originally seven). Views from the hilltop are particularly memorable at sunset, when spotlights illuminate the old quarter. ⊠ *Trujillo.*

Museo de la Coria (*Fundación Xavier de Salas*)

OTHER MUSEUM | Near the Puerta de la Coria and occupying a former Franciscan convent built in the 15th century, this museum's exhibits on Spain's conquest of Latin America are similar to those in the Casa Museo de Pizarro but with more emphasis on military operations. Even if this doesn't sound like your speed, the museum is worth visiting if only for a look inside the old convent's two-tier central cloister. ✉ *Pl. de Santa María, Trujillo* ☎ *92/765–9032, 92/732–1898* 🌐 *www.fundacionxavierdesalas.com* 🎟 *Free* 🕒 *Closed weekdays.*

Palacio de Orellana-Pizarro

CASTLE/PALACE | The Palacio de Orellana-Pizarro, renovated by Juan Pizarro himself in the 16th century, now serves as a school and has one of the most elegant Renaissance courtyards in town. The ground floor, open to visitors, has a deep, arched front doorway; on the second story is an elaborate Renaissance balcony bearing the crest of the Pizarro family. Miguel de Cervantes, on his way to thank the Virgin of Guadalupe for his release from prison, spent time writing in the palace. ✉ *Trujillo* ✥ *Behind Pl. Mayor* 🎟 *Free.*

Pizarro House Museum

The Pizarro family residence is now a modest museum dedicated to the connection between Spain and Latin America. The first floor emulates a typical home from 15th-century Trujillo, and the second floor is divided into exhibits on Peru and Pizarro's life there. The museum explains the "Curse of the Pizarro," recounting how the conquistador and his brothers were killed in brutal battles with rivals; those who survived never again enjoyed the wealth they had achieved in Peru. Glaringly absent from the museum is any mention of what came after Pizarro's conquests: mass murder of Incas, feudalism and enslavement, forced conversions to Catholicism, and so on. The museum closes from 2 to 4. ✉ *Calleja del Castillo 1, Trujillo* 🎟 *€2.*

★ Plaza Mayor

PLAZA/SQUARE | One of the finest plazas in Spain, this Renaissance gem is dominated by a bronze equestrian statue of Francisco Pizarro—the work of an American sculptor, Charles Rumsey. Notice the Palacio del Marqués de la Conquista, the most dramatic building on the square with plateresque ornamentation and imaginative busts of the Pizarro family flanking its corner balcony. It was built by Francisco Pizarro's half-brother Hernando. ✉ *Pl. Mayor.*

Trujillo Castle

CASTLE/PALACE | For spectacular views, climb this large fortress—a *Game of Thrones*filming location—built by the Moors in the 9th century over older Roman foundations. To the south are silos, warehouses, and residential neighborhoods. To the north are green fields and brilliant flowers, partitioned by a maze of nearly leveled Roman stone walls, and an ancient cistern. The castle's size underscores the historical importance of now-tiny Trujillo. ✉ *Cerro Cabeza de Zorro, Trujillo* ☎ *92/732–2677* 🎟 *€2.*

🍴 Restaurants

★ El 7 de Sillerías

$$$ | **SPANISH** | Ask Trujillo locals for the best food in town, and many will point you here for fresh, reasonably priced tapas and mains including *croquetas* (try the wild mushroom rendition) and *secreto ibérico* (seared Iberian pork shoulder steak). The weekday lunch menú del día—three courses and wine—is a steal. **Known for:** prix fixe weekday lunch deal; pleasant patio out back; secreto ibérico, a specialty pork dish. [$] *Average main: €20* ✉ *Calle Sillerías 7, Trujillo* ☎ *92/732–1856* 🌐 *www.el7desillerias.com* 🕒 *Closed Tues.*

Restaurante Bizcocho Plaza
$$$ | **SPANISH** | A Trujillo institution conveniently located on the Plaza Mayor, Bizcocho specializes in Extramaduran cuisine—think local jamón, cheese, and migas—and the stone-and-tile dining room is cozy and cool even in the summer. Reservations are essential on holiday weekends. **Known for:** well-presented plates; central location; excellent Iberian pork dishes. [$] *Average main: €20* ✉ *Pl. Mayor 11, Trujillo* ☎ *92/732–2017* 🌐 *www.restaurantebizcochoplaza.com.*

Hotels

★ Hotel Boutique Posada Dos Orillas
$ | **HOTEL** | This hotel occupies a 16th-century stagecoach inn on a quiet pedestrian street uphill from the Plaza Mayor. **Pros:** beautiful terrace; good weekend rates; pleasant interiors. **Cons:** small TVs; beds a little basic; no reserved parking. [$] *Rooms from: €75* ✉ *Calle de los Cambrones 6, Trujillo* ☎ *92/765–9079* 🌐 *www.dosorillas.com* 🛏 *13 rooms* 🍴 *Free Breakfast.*

Izán Trujillo
$$ | **HOTEL** | **FAMILY** | Once a 16th-century convent, this dependable four-star hotel is a five-minute walk from the Plaza Mayor. **Pros:** central location; air of calm throughout the property; friendly and efficient staff. **Cons:** rooms vary in size; small swimming pool; inconsistent in restaurant. [$] *Rooms from: €90* ✉ *Pl. del Campillo 1, Trujillo* ☎ *92/745–8900* 🌐 *www.izanhoteles.es* 🛏 *78 rooms* 🍴 *No Meals.*

★ Parador de Trujillo
$$$ | **HOTEL** | **FAMILY** | In another of the region's 16th-century convents, this parador is the essence of peace and tranquility, with rooms that are cozy and serene. **Pros:** homey decor; peace and quiet in the heart of town; swimming pool. **Cons:** rooms are a bit like monastery quarters—on the small side; somewhat overpriced; poor-quality bath products. [$] *Rooms from: €148* ✉ *Calle Santa Beatriz de Silva 1, Trujillo* ☎ *92/732–1350* 🌐 *www.parador.es* 🛏 *50 rooms* 🍴 *Free Breakfast.*

Shopping

Eduardo Pablos Mateos
CRAFTS | This workshop specializes in wood carvings, basketwork, and furniture made from esparto grass. Call ahead to schedule a personal tour. ✉ *Calle de San Judas 3, Trujillo* ☎ *92/732–1066, 60/617–4382 mobile.*

La Despensa
FOOD | This gourmet shop on the corner of Plaza Mayor used to be the wine cellar of a 16th-century palace. Now it sells local products including jamón, cheese, wine, and locally made beer at excellent prices. ✉ *Cuesta de la Sangre 0, Trujillo* ☎ *65/450–3419.*

Guadalupe

200 km (125 miles) southwest of Madrid, 96 km (60 miles) east of Trujillo.

Guadalupe's monastery is one of the most inspiring sights in Extremadura. Its story begins around 1300, when, as the story goes, a local shepherd uncovered a statue of the Virgin, supposedly carved by St. Luke. King Alfonso XI, who often hunted here, had a church built to house the statue and vowed to found a monastery should he defeat the Moors at the battle of Salado in 1340. After his victory, he kept his promise. The monastery's heyday came between the 15th and 18th centuries, when, under the rule of the Hieronymites, it was turned into a pilgrimage center rivaling Santiago de Compostela in importance. Pilgrims have sought out the monastery since the 14th century and, in recent decades, are joined by just as many tourists. Yet Guadalupe's isolation—a good two-hour drive from the nearest town—has protected it from the tourbus crowds.

The surrounding area is known for its copper-ware, crafted here since the 16th century.

GETTING HERE AND AROUND

There's no train to Guadalupe, and bus service is sporadic. It's easiest if you have your own car and park on the outskirts of town. Guadalupe itself is small enough to explore on foot but hilly with cobblestone streets, so wear comfortable shoes.

ESSENTIALS

VISITOR INFORMATION Guadalupe Tourist Office. ✉ *Pl. Santa María de Guadalupe 0, Guadalupe* ☎ *92/715–4128.*

Sights

Plaza Mayor (*Plaza de Santa María de Guadalupe*)

PLAZA/SQUARE | In the middle of this tiny, irregularly shaped plaza—which is transformed during festivals into a bullring—is a 15th-century fountain where Columbus's two Native American servants were baptized in 1496. Here, as is the case across Extremadura, there's a conspicuous lack of reckoning or awareness regarding the region's role in the plunder and annihilation of much of the so-called New World. ✉ *Guadalupe.*

★ **Real Monasterio de Santa María de Guadalupe** (*Royal Monastery of Our Lady of Guadalupe*)

CHURCH | Looming in the background of the Plaza Mayor is the late-Gothic facade of Guadalupe's colossal monastery church, flanked by battlement towers. The (required Spanish-only) guided tour begins in the Muejar cloister and continues on to the chapter house, with hymnals, vestments, and paintings including a series of small panels by Zurbarán. The ornate 17th-century sacristy has a series of eight Zurbarán paintings, from 1638 to 1647. These austere representations of monks of the Hieronymite order and scenes from the life of St. Jerome are the artist's only significant paintings housed in the setting for which they were intended. The tour concludes in the garish, late-baroque Camarín, the chapel where the famous *Virgen Morena* (*Black Virgin*) is housed. Each September 8, the virgin is brought down from the altarpiece and walked around the cloister in a procession with pilgrims following on their knees. Outside, the monastery's gardens have been restored to their original, geometric Moorish style. ✉ *Pl. Santa María de Guadalupe, Guadalupe* ✣ *Entrance on Pl. Mayor* ☎ *92/736–7000* 🌐 *www.monasterioguadalupe.com* 🎟 *€5.*

Hotels

Casa Rural Abacería de Guadalupe

$ | **B&B/INN** | **FAMILY** | For a simple, inexpensive overnight stay, try this small, tidy guesthouse on a quiet side street near the center of the village, around the corner from the parador. **Pros:** plenty of peace and quiet; private location; good for families. **Cons:** cold hallways in the winter; individual rooms are a bit small; no Wi-Fi. [$] *Rooms from: €50* ✉ *Calle Marqués de la Romana, Guadalupe* ☎ *92/715–4282, 65/020–8405* 🌐 *www.airbnb.com* 🛏 *3 rooms* 🍴 *Free Breakfast.*

★ **Hospedería del Real Monasterio**

$ | **HOTEL** | An excellent and considerably cheaper alternative to the town parador, this inn was built around the 16th-century Gothic cloister of the monastery itself. **Pros:** helpful staff; guests get free monastery admission; excellent restaurant. **Cons:** a bit pricey; the monastery's church bells chime around the clock; uncomfortable beds. [$] *Rooms from: €75* ✉ *Pl. Juan Carlos I, Guadalupe* ☎ *92/736–7000* 🌐 *www.hotelhospederiamonasterioguadalupe.com* 🕒 *Closed mid-Jan.–mid-Feb.* 🛏 *47 rooms* 🍴 *No Meals.*

Parador de Guadalupe

$$$ | **HOTEL** | This exquisite estate, once the 15th-century palace of the Marquis de la Romana, now houses one of Spain's finest paradores. **Pros:**

idyllic balconies; stunning architecture; down-home Extremeño cooking. **Cons:** long hike from reception to the farthest rooms; tight parking; old-world property with old-world amenities. $ *Rooms from: €132* ✉ *Calle Marqués de la Romana 12, Guadalupe* ☎ *92/736–7075* ⊕ *www.parador.es* ↪ *41 rooms* ☉ *Free Breakfast.*

Mérida

76 km (47 miles) south of Cáceres, 191 km (119 miles) north of Seville, 347 km (216 miles) southwest of Madrid.

Mérida has some of the most impressive Roman ruins in Iberia. Founded by the Romans in 25 BC on the banks of the Río Guadiana, the city is strategically located at the junction of major Roman roads from León to Seville and Toledo to Lisbon. The glass-and-steel bus station, on the other side of the river from the town center, commands a good view of the exceptionally long Roman bridge. On the bank opposite the ruins is the *alcazaba* (fortress).

Other Roman sites nearby require a drive. Across the train tracks in a modern neighborhood is the *circo* (circus), where chariot races were held. Little remains of the grandstands, which seated 30,000, but the outline of the circus is clearly visible and impressive for its size. Of the existing aqueduct remains, the most impressive is the Acueducto de los Milagros (Aqueduct of Miracles), north of the train station.

GETTING HERE AND AROUND

There are several buses daily to Mérida from Badajoz (1 hour), Sevilla (2½ hours), Cáceres (45 minutes), Trujillo (1½ hours), and Madrid (4½ hours). There are also several daily trains, which take about the same travel time but cost more. Check the RENFE website (*www.renfe.com*) or tourist office for schedules. Alternatively, there are usually several Blablacar

rideshare departures from Madrid and Mérida's neighboring cities each day. Once in Mérida, the city center is navigable on foot or by tourist train.

At the tourist office or via the website *www.turismomerida.org*, you can purchase a €15 combo ticket including entry to six sights: the Roman Theater and Amphitheater, Roman Circus, Alcazaba (Arab Citadel), Morería Archaeological Site, Crypt of the Basilica of Santa Eulalia, and House of Mithraeum and Columbarium.

ESSENTIALS

VISITOR INFORMATION Mérida Tourist Office. ✉ *Calle Santa Eulalia 66, Mérida* ☎ *92/438–0191* ⊕ *www.turismomerida. org.*

TOURS

 Sights

Alcazaba Árabe (*Fortress*)

RUINS | To get to this sturdy square fortress, built by the Romans and strengthened by the Visigoths and Moors, continue west from the Museo Nacional de Arte Romano, down Suarez Somontes toward the river and the city center. Turn right at Calle Baños and you can see the towering columns of the Templo de Diana, the oldest of Mérida's Roman buildings. To enter the *alcazaba*, follow the fortress walls around to the side farthest from the river. Climb up to the battlements for sweeping river views, or go underground to see the *aljibe*, or cistern. ✉ *Calle de Graciano, Mérida* ☎ *No phone* ⊕ *www.turismomerida.org/ what-to-see/arab-citadel* ☞ *€6.*

Basílica de Santa Eulalia

CHURCH | Originally a Visigothic structure, this basilica marks the site of a Roman temple as well as the alleged place where the child martyr Eulalia was burned alive in AD 304 for spitting in the face of a Roman magistrate. The site was a focal point for pilgrimages during

Mérida's excellently preserved Roman amphitheater is the site of a drama festival every July.

the Middle Ages. In 1990, excavations revealed layer upon layer of Paleolithic, Visigothic, Byzantine, and Roman settlements. The popular €15 sightseeing combination ticket sold at the tourist office includes entry only into the underground crypt of the basilica; it's an additional €2 to visit the main structure. ⊠ *Rambla Mártir Santa Eulalia, Av. de Extremadura 3, Mérida* ☎ *92/430–3407* ✉ *€2.*

★ Morería Archaeological Site

RUINS | FAMILY | Mérida's Roman *teatro* (theater) and *anfiteatro* (amphitheater) are set in a verdant park, and the theater—the best preserved in Spain—seats 6,000 and is used for a classical drama festival each July. The amphitheater, which holds 15,000 spectators, opened in 8 BC for gladiatorial contests. Next to the entrance to the ruins is the main tourist office, where you can pick up maps and brochures. You can buy a ticket to see only the Roman ruins or, for a bit more, an *entrada conjunta* (joint admission), which also grants access to the

crypt of the Basílica de Santa Eulalia and to the Alcazaba. To reach the monuments by car, follow signs to the "Museo de Arte Romano." Parking is usually easy to find. ⊠ *Av. de los Estudiantes, Mérida* ☎ *92/431–2530* ✉ *€12 Roman ruins, €16 Joint Ticket including Basílica de Santa Eulalia and Alcazaba.*

Museo de Arte Visigótico

HISTORY MUSEUM | An abandoned 18th-century church contains this easily digestible museum compiling some of the most important Visigothic artworks on the Iberian Peninsula. It's a branch of the Museo Nacional de Arte Romano, in a separate location north of the Plaza de España, in Mérida's old town. If you enjoy this museum and are traveling to Málaga, check out the recently opened (2018) Ifergan Collection, which, according to some scholars, contains the most valuable ensemble of Visigothic art in the world, including figurines recovered from an ancient shipwreck. ⊠ *Calle Santa Eulalia 1, Mérida* ☎ *92/430–0106* ✉ *Free.*

★ **Museo Nacional de Arte Romano**
(*National Museum of Roman Art*)
HISTORY MUSEUM | Across the street from the entrance to the Roman sites and connected by an underground passage is Mérida's superb Roman art museum, in a building designed by the Spanish architect Rafael Moneo. Walk through a series of passageways to the luminous, cathedral-like main exhibition hall, which is supported by arches the same proportion and size (50 feet) as the Roman arch in the center of Mérida, the Arco de Trajano (Trajan's Arch). Exhibits include mosaics, frescoes, jewelry, statues, pottery, household utensils, and other Roman works. The crypt beneath the museum contains the remains of several homes and a necropolis that were uncovered while the museum was being built in 1981. ⊠ *Calle José Ramón Mélida, Mérida* ☎ *92/431–1690, 92/431–1912* ⊕ *www.mecd.gob.es/mnromano/home. html* 🎫 *€3* ⏱ *Closed Mon. (free weekends after 2).*

Plaza de España
PLAZA/SQUARE | Mérida's main square is lively day and night. The plaza's oldest building is a 16th-century palace, now the Hotel Ilunion Mérida Palace. Behind it stretches Mérida's most charming area, with Andalusian-esque white houses shaded by palms, in the midst of which stands the Arco de Trajano, part of a Roman city gate. It's a great place to people-watch over tapas at sunset. ⊠ *Mérida.*

🍴 Restaurants

Vía de la Tapa
$ | **TAPAS** | **FAMILY** | One of the specialties at this local hangout, known for its cheap, thoughtfully prepared tapas, is *morcilla de Guadalupe*, blood sausage made in the nearby town of the same name. Note to diners with time constraints: The service can be slow (and churlish) when the restaurant is packed. **Known for:** worth-the-wait outdoor

seating; budget menú del día; fall-off-the-bone stewed meats. 💲 *Average main: €11* ⊠ *Calle José Ramón Mélida 48, Mérida* ☎ *92/431–5859* ⊕ *www.viadelatapa. es* ⏱ *Closed Mon.*

Hotels

★ **Ilunion Mérida Palace**
$$ | **HOTEL** | **FAMILY** | Dominating the Plaza de España, this five-star luxury hotel has a rooftop pool deck, Roman- and Moorish-theme design elements, and a twinkly central courtyard. **Pros:** outdoor pool, terrace, and solarium; standout breakfast; gym facilities. **Cons:** plaza-facing rooms can be noisy in summer; middling hotel restaurant; a bit far from the Roman ruins. 💲 *Rooms from: €120* ⊠ *Pl. de España 19, Mérida* ☎ *92/438–3800* ⊕ *www.ilunionmeridapalace.com* ⤴ *76 rooms* ○ *No Meals.*

Parador de Mérida (*Parador Vía de la Plata*)
$$$ | **HOTEL** | **FAMILY** | This spacious hotel exudes Andalusian cheerfulness with hints at its Roman and Moorish past—it was built over the remains of a Roman temple, later became a baroque convent, and then served as a prison. **Pros:** dazzling-white interior; serene interior courtyard; central location. **Cons:** erratic Wi-Fi; restaurant not up to snuff; could use a revamp. 💲 *Rooms from: €165* ⊠ *Calle Almendralejo 56, Mérida* ☎ *92/431–3800* ⊕ *www.parador.es* ⤴ *81 rooms* ○ *No Meals.*

Chapter 5

GALICIA, ASTURIAS, AND CANTABRIA

Updated by
Benjamin Kemper

⊙ **Sights** ⬥ **Restaurants** 🏠 **Hotels** ⬥ **Shopping** ⅄ **Nightlife**
★★★★☆   ★★★☆☆   ★★★★☆   ★★★☆☆   ★★★☆☆

WELCOME TO GALICIA, ASTURIAS, AND CANTABRIA

TOP REASONS TO GO

★ **Ascend to food heaven:** Ancient Santiago de Compostela has more restaurants and bars per square mile than any other city around.

★ **Embark on remote mountain hikes:** Explore the spectacular Picos de Europa range on foot, and hole up in far-flung mountain villages.

★ **Clink glasses of local Albariño:** The Rías Baixas vineyards yield some of Spain's finest white wines.

★ **Live your idyllic seaside fantasy:** Watch the fishing boats come and go in busy ports like Vigo.

★ **Discover Santander:** There's enough music, architecture, opera, and theater in the Cantabrian capital to keep you busy for days (and nights).

The misty and mysterious regions of Galicia, Asturias, and Cantabria stretch east above Portugal, along Spain's windswept northern coast. Explorers once called this far-flung corner of the peninsula *finis terrae* (the end of the earth).

1 Santiago de Compostela. The exuberant final destination for Christian and (increasingly) secular pilgrims on the Walk of St. James.

2 Ourense and La Ribeira Sacra. Stunning medieval architecture, dramatic valleys, and natural hot springs.

3 Lugo. Beautifully preserved Roman ramparts.

4 Muxia. A quaint fishing village on a peninsula jutting into the Atlantic.

5 Fisterra. Once the "end of the earth," now an optional add-on finale to the Camino.

6 Muros. Famous for its late-afternoon fish auction.

7 Cambados. Consistently listed as one of Spain's prettiest towns.

8 Pontevedra. Home base for wine-soaked adventures in the Rías Baixas.

9 Vigo. A formidable port, red-roofed fishermen's houses, and a lively old town.

10 Baiona. The site of one of Spain's most popular Paradores.

11 Tui. A fortified old border town.

12 A Coruña. The aristocratic epicenter of Galicia with bountiful shops and chic restaurants.

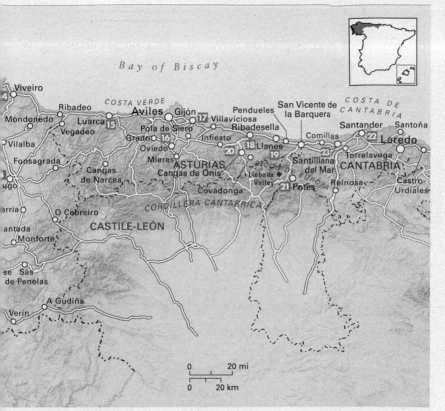

Bay of Biscay

COSTA VERDE

COSTA DE CANTABRIA

ASTURIAS

CANTABRIA

PICOS DE EUROPA

CORDILLERA CANTÁBRICA

CASTILE-LEÓN

| 0 | 20 mi |
| 0 | 20 km |

13 Betanzos. A charming medieval town at the confluence of two rivers.

14 Viveiro. Scenic unspoiled beaches make this a popular summer resort.

15 Luarca. The beloved white town on Asturias's Green Coast.

16 Oviedo. A timeless, stately city with palpable youthful energy.

17 Gijón. An ancient Roman port with uproarious and unpretentious nightlife.

18 Ribadesella. Synonymous with seafood, natural wonders, and canoe-racing.

19 Llanes. The beach town Spaniards love for its colorful houses and mountain backdrop.

20 Cangas de Onís. Unofficial capital of Picos de Europa National Park.

21 Potes. Sigh-worthy cheeses and 9th century monasteries.

22 Santander. Cantabria's tranquil yet culture-packed capital.

23 Santillana del Mar. An architectural treasure trove of 15th- to 17th-century stone houses.

EATING AND DRINKING WELL IN GALICIA, ASTURIAS, AND CANTABRIA

A plethora of seafood delicacies

Galicia, Asturias, and Cantabria are famous for seafood and fish so fresh that chefs frown on drowning the inherent flavors in sauces and seasonings. Inland, the Picos de Europa and the mountain meadows are rich in game, lamb, and beef.

The northern coast of Spain is justly famous for fish and seafood, and specialties include *merluza a la gallega* (steamed hake with paprika sauce) in Galicia and *merluza a la sidra* (hake in a cider sauce) in Asturias. Look also for Galician seafood treasures such as *vieiras* (scallops) and *pulpo a la gallega* (boiled octopus that's drizzled with olive oil and dusted with salt and paprika). The rainy weather means that bracing stews are a favorite form of sustenance, especially *fabada asturiana* (Asturian bean-and-sausage stew) and Galicia's *caldo gallego* (a thick soup of white beans, turnip greens, ham, and potatoes). Cantabria's cooking is part mountain fare, such as roast kid and lamb or *cocidos* (pork-and-bean stews) in the highlands, and part seafood dishes, such as *sorropotún* (a bonito, potato, and vegetable stew) along the coast.

CABRALES CHEESE

Asturias is known for Spain's most pungent cheese, Cabrales, a blue made from raw cow milk (with goat curd added for a softer consistency). Produced in the Picos de Europa mountains of eastern Asturias, the cheese is prized both for the quality of the milk and the dry highland air used to cure it. It's often melted over roast meats or eaten as an appetizer or dessert with a nip of sherry.

BEANS AND LEGUMES

Fabada asturiana is as famous in Spain as Valencia's paella or Andalusia's gazpacho. Not unlike French cassoulet, the hearty white bean stew is ladled out in copious quantities and—don't say we didn't warn you—often necessarily followed by a siesta. The secret to great fabada is the ultra-creamy "de la Granja" bean grown in the region, which you can buy in vacuum-sealed bags as culinary souvenirs at gourmet shops. Fatback, *morcilla* (blood sausage), chorizo, and other regional pork products give fabada its signature smoky flavor. Other bean dishes to try include *verdinas con almejas* (beans with clams) and *pote* (boiled dinner with white beans and cabbage).

VEGETABLES

Bitter and tart turnip greens (*grelos*) are a staple in Galicia, so celebrated that they have their own festival, La Festa do Grelo, held in February and March. As a side, they're often eaten with boiled pork shoulder (*lacón*), boiled potatoes, and chorizo. They make it into soups as well such as *caldo gallego*, which calls for the stalks and greens, *alubias* (white beans), and potatoes—plus pork for ballast and flavor.

The classic octopus-and-potato combination.

PULPO A LA GALLEGA

This Galician delicacy, also known as *polbo á feira*, consists of octopus that's been boiled (traditionally in a copper cauldron), cut into tentacled coins, drizzled with olive oil, sprinkled with salt and smoky paprika, and served on a wooden plate. A common variation adds an understory of boiled potato to soak up the heady brackish juices.

TO DRINK

Wine lovers the world over know Galicia through its Albariño, the citrusy, slate-y white produced in the Rías Baixas that's become a fixture on restaurant menus. But there are plenty of other intriguing wines to try in northern Spain such as Ribeiro, a floral white blend traditionally sipped from shallow white ceramic cups called *cuncas*, and godello, Spain's current golden-boy grape that has somms swooning over its honeyed complexity. By contrast, Asturias makes little wine but over 10 million gallons of *sidra* (hard cider) annually. At Asturian restaurants, waiters dramatically decant ("escanciar") it from overhead to aerate it slightly. Those with a penchant for the hard stuff shouldn't miss Galicia's *queimada*, a potent "witches' brew" of grappa-like *orujo* steeped with lemon peel, coffee beans, and sugar that's set aflame in an earthenware bowl.

The hearty and fortifying caldo gallego

EL CAMINO DE SANTIAGO

Crossing meadows, mountains, and villages across Spain, about 350,000 travelers embark each year on a pilgrimage to Galicia's Santiago de Compostela, the sacred city of St. James. They're not all pious religious types these days, though a spiritual quest is generally the motivation. While some complete the hike alone, many more do it with friends or family.

HISTORY OF THE CAMINO

The surge of spiritual seekers heading to Spain's northwest coast began as early as the 9th century, when news spread that the apostle James's remains were being kept there. By the middle of the 12th century, about 1 million pilgrims were arriving in Santiago de Compostela each year. An entire industry of food hawkers, hoteliers, and trinket sellers awaited their arrival. The pilgrims even had the world's first travel guide, the *Codex Calixtinus* (published in the 12th century), to help them on their way. Some made the journey in response to their conscience, to do penance for their sins against God, while others were sentenced by law to make the trek as payment for crimes against the state. Legend claims that St. James's body was transported secretly to the area by boat after his martyrdom in Jerusalem in AD 44. The idea had stuck by 814, when a hermit claimed to see miraculous lights in the sky, accompanied by the sound of angels singing, on a wooded hillside near Padrón. Human bones were quickly discovered at the site, and immediately—and perhaps somewhat conveniently—declared to be those of the apostle (the bones may actually have belonged to Priscillian, the leader of a 4th-century Christian sect). Word of this important find quickly spread across a relic-hungry Europe. Within a couple of centuries, the road to Santiago had become as popular as the other two major medieval pilgrimages, to Rome and to Jerusalem. After the 12th century, pilgrim numbers declined due to the dangers of robbery along the route, a growing skepticism about the genuineness of St. James's remains, and the rise of science in place of religion.

THE PILGRIMAGE TODAY

The pilgrims follow one of seven main routes, walking about 19 miles per day in a nearly 500-mile journey. Along the way, they encounter incredible local hospitality and trade stories with fellow adventurers. By the late 1980s, there were only about 3,000 pilgrims trickling into Santiago a year, but in 1993 the Galician government launched an initiative to increase the number of visitors to the region, and the popularity of the pilgrimage soared. In holy years, when St. James's Day (July 25) falls on a Sunday, the number of pilgrims usually doubles.

WHO WAS ST. JAMES?

St. James the Great, brother of St. John the Evangelist (author of the Gospel of John and the Book of Revelation), was

The Camino de Santiago passes through the medieval town of Logroño, capital of Spain's Rioja region.

one of Jesus's first apostles. Sent by Jesus to preach that the kingdom of heaven had come, he crossed Europe and ended up in Spain. Along the way, he saved a knight from drowning in the sea. As legend goes, the knight resurfaced covered in scallop shells: This is why Camino pilgrims carry this seashell on their journey. St. James is said to have been beheaded by King Herod Agrippa on his return to Judea in AD 44 but rescued by angels. He was subsequently transported in a rudderless stone boat back to Spain, where his lifeless body was encased in a rock. James is said to have resurfaced to aid the Christians in the Reconquest Battle of Clavijo, gaining him the (rather problematic) title of Matamoros, or Moor Killer. When the body of St. James was "found," people came in droves to see his remains—the Spanish and Portuguese name for St. James is Santiago. The belief arose that sins would be cleansed through the penance of this long walk, an idea encouraged by the Church.

THE PILGRIMAGE EXPERIENCE

Not everyone does the route in one go. Some split it into manageable chunks and take years to complete the whole course. Most, however, walk

Scallop shell symbols mark the routes of the Camino de Santiago.

At the culmination of the Camino de Santiago is the cathedral of Santiago, in the Plaza del Obradoiro. It's named for the "obradoiro" (workshops) of stonemasons that were here while the cathedral was being built.

an average of 30 km (19 miles) per day to arrive in Santiago after a monthlong trek. The route sometimes follows a mountain trail and other times passes through villages and fields. It is generally so well marked that most travelers claim not to need a map (bringing one is highly recommended, however): Simply follow the route markers—scallop shells on blue backgrounds with an arrow beneath, posted on buildings or painted on rocks and trail posts. Walking is not the only option: Bicycles are common and will cut the time needed to complete the pilgrimage in half; horseback riding can also be arranged. Every town along the route has an official Camino albergue , or hostel, often in an ancient monastery or original pilgrim's hospice. They are basic and generally accommodate 40–150 people. You can bunk for free—though a donation is expected—in the company of fellow walkers but may only stay one night, unless severe Camino injuries prevent you from moving on. Be aware that these places fill up fast. Walkers get first priority, followed by cyclists and those on horseback, with organized walking groups at the bottom of the pecking order. If there is no room at the official albergues, there are plenty of paid hostels along the route. Wherever you stay, get your Pilgrims' Passport, or "credencial ," stamped, as proof of how far you've walked.

A TYPICAL DAY

A typical day on the Camino involves walking hard through the morning to the next village in time to get a free bed. The afternoon is for catching up with fellow pilgrims, having a look around town, and doing a bit of washing. The people you meet along the way and the camaraderie with fellow pilgrims is a highlight of the trip for many, regardless of age. Some albergues serve a communal evening meal, but there is always a bar in town that offers a lively atmosphere and a cheap (€8–€12) pilgrim's set menu (quality and fare varies; it consists of three courses plus bread and beverage). Over dinner, walkers compare sore feet, guzzle local wine, and make new walking partners for the following day. Make sure you're back to the albergue by curfew, usually 10 or 11, lest you find a locked door.

THE FINISH LINE

Arriving at the end of the Camino de Santiago is an emotional experience. It is common to see small groups of pilgrims, hands clasped tightly together, tearfully approaching the moss- and lichen-covered cathedral in Santiago's Plaza del Obradoiro. After entering the building through the Pilgrim's Door and hugging the statue of St. James, a special mass awaits at midday, the highlight of which (if you time your arrival correctly) is seeing the *botafumeiro*, a giant incense-filled censer, swinging from the ceiling. Those that have covered more than 100 km (62 miles) on foot, or twice that distance on a bicycle—as shown by the stamped passport—can then collect their Compostela certificate from the pilgrim's office (near the cathedral, at Rúa do Vilar 1).

USEFUL WEBSITES

The official Camino website (*www. caminodesantiago.gal*) has detailed route maps, packing lists, and a tab for booking albergues, though perhaps handier is the (unaffiliated yet well-reviewed) Way of St James app, which is free to download. The following are also treasure troves of information: *www. caminodesantiago.me, www.csj.org.uk,* and *www.caminoadventures.com.*

CAMINO TIPS

The most popular of the seven main routes of the Camino de Santiago is the 791-km (480-mile) **Camino francés** (French Way), which starts in France (in Saint-Jean-Pied-de-Port) and crosses the high *meseta* plains into Galicia. The **Camino norte** (Northern Way), which runs through the woodlands of Spain's rugged north coast, is also gaining in popularity.

The busiest time on the Camino is June–September; busy can mean crowded paths and booked-up albergues, particularly if you start the Camino on the first few days of the month. April, May, and late September are more tranquil. Making the journey in winter is not advised due to soggy and unpredictable weather.

As any seasoned hiker will tell you, the most important piece of equipment is your hiking boots, which should be as professional as your budget allows and broken in before you hit the trail. Other essentials include a good-quality—and waterproof (it rains year round in Galicia)—backpack, sleeping bag, sunscreen, and medical kit including Vaseline and blister remedies for sore feet. Don't forget a set of earplugs as well.

To get your Camino "passport"/credential ahead of time, contact a Camino confraternity group. Or just sort it out upon arrival—you can always snap one up last minute at common starting points, local churches, and popular albergues for about €2. For a complete list of confraternity groups in cities throughout Spain, visit *www. oficinadelperegrino.com/en/preparation/ confraternities-in-spain.*

It's common today for families to walk the Camino de Santiago together.

Spain's green, mountainous north is en route to nowhere, an end in itself. Spaniards who have spent time in the region wax poetic about it and describe it with a palpable sense of nostalgia. Its ruggedness and open-armed hospitality evoke a humbler, simpler Spain of generations past. Galicians have a term for this wistful longing for people and places left behind: *morriña.*

Creeping north and northwest from the lonesome Castilian plains to the rocky seacoast, Galicia, Asturias, and Cantabria take in lush hills and scraggly vineyards, gorgeous *rías* (estuaries), and perhaps the country's wildest mountains, the Picos de Europa. Santander and the entire Cantabrian region are cool summer refuges with sandy beaches, high sierras (including part of the Picos), and tiny highland towns. Santander, once the main seaport for Old Castile, on the Bay of Biscay, is in a mountainous zone wedged between the Basque Country and Asturias.

Northwestern Spain has a Celtic feel with its shamrock-covered hills and oft-overcast skies. Ancient granite buildings wear a blanket of moss, and even the stone *hórreos* (granaries) are built on stilts above the damp ground. Swirling fog and heavy mist help keep local folktales of the supernatural alive. Rather than the usual flamenco guitar, a *gaita* (bagpipe) is the more common choice for buskers here, a legacy of the Celts who settled here in the 5th and 6th centuries BC.

Santiago de Compostela, where the cathedral holds the remains of the apostle James, has drawn pilgrims for 900 years, leaving churches, shrines, and former hospitals in their path. Asturias, north of the main pilgrim trail, has always maintained a separate identity, isolated by the rocky Picos de Europa. This and the Basque Country are the only parts of Spain never conquered by the Moors, so Asturian architecture shows little Moorish influence. According to lore (yet increasingly disputed), it was from a mountain base at Covadonga that the Christians won their first decisive battle against the Moors and launched the so-called Reconquest of Spain. Despite being very much its own region, Cantabria is in spirit much closer to Asturias—with which it shares the Picos de Europa, Castilian Spanish, and similar architecture—than its passionately independent neighbor, the Basque Country.

MAJOR REGIONS

Santiago de Compostela and Eastern Galicia. Santiago isn't only for pilgrims—it's also a vibrant university town with terrific food and a charming old town whose crown jewel is its towering 13th-century cathedral.

The Costa da Morte and Rías Baixas. From the small fishing village of Malpica to Muros, from Fisterra (World's End) down to Vigo and the Portuguese border, this area also takes in the peaceful seaside towns of Cambados and Baiona, the gorgeous beaches of Las Islas Cíes, and the medieval streets of Pontevedra.

A Coruña and Rías Altas. Galicia has more coastline and unspoiled, non-touristy beaches than anywhere else in Spain. There are vast sandy expanses and tiny, tucked-away coves, but take note: The water is colder than the Mediterranean, and the weather more temperamental.

Asturias. The Senda Costera (Coastal Way) nature route between Pendueles and Llanes takes in some of Asturias's most spectacular coastal scenery, including noisy *bufones* (large waterspouts created naturally by erosion) and u-shaped Playa de Ballota. Asturias is bordered to the southeast by the imposing Picos de Europa, which are best accessed via the scenic coastal towns of Llanes or Ribadesella.

Picos de Europa. One of Spain's best-kept secrets, the "Peaks of Europe" straddle Asturias, Cantabria, and Castile and León. In addition to 8,910-foot peaks, there are deep caves, well-kept mountain refuges, and interesting wildlife. The region is also known for its fine cheeses.

Cantabria. Wide beaches, delectable sweets, and summer music-and-dance festival are highlights in this rural region. The Liébana Valley, the Renaissance town at Santillana del Mar, and ports and beaches like San Vicente de la Barquera rank among northern Spain's finest treasures.

Planning

When to Go

Galicia sizzles (think highs of 95°F [35°C]) June–September, even if it's one of Spain's coolest regions. Summer is the best time for swimming, hiking, water sports, and live music. Asturias and Cantabria, in the mountains, are cooler than Galicia, though Galicia is rainier—not for nothing is this region called Green Spain. Avoid these three regions in winter (unless you like moody weather and solitude): The rain, wind, and freezing temperatures make most activities a pain. Spring and fall are safer bets as the weather is calmer and crowds are few.

Planning Your Time

You can take a train, bus, or rideshare to Santiago de Compostela, but flying is most convenient. Budget one week, give or take, to cover Santiago and southern Galicia. From Santiago, you can drive down the PO550 to Cambados, stopping on the way at fishing villages along the Ría de Arousa. If you continue along the coastal road to Pontevedra, pause there to explore the medieval streets lined with tapas bars, then drive down to Vigo for a lunch of oysters on Rúa Pescadería. Continue south and arrive before dark at the Baiona Parador.

Alternatively, travel to A Coruña, and from there head north to some of Spain's loveliest beaches and Viveiro. From here cross into Asturias and post up in Luarca or Gijón. Another attractive option is zipping up the mountain passes into Picos de Europa and staying in a remote village.

Farther east, Santillana del Mar's Renaissance architecture, the Altamira Caves, and the Sardinero Beach at Santander are top spots, while the fishing villages and beaches around Llanes in eastern Asturias and San Vicente de la Barquera in Cantabria have beguiling ports and inlets. If you want to truly delve into the Picos de Europa and the region's rugged coastline, Asturias and Cantabria merit more than a week's exploration.

Getting Here and Around

AIR

There are airports in Santiago de Compostela, Santander, A Coruña, and Vigo, plus one near San Esteban de Pravia, 47 km (29 miles) north of Oviedo, Asturias' only airport. Santiago is the busiest of the bunch. Airport shuttles run by ALSA generally leave from the city bus station.

BIKE

Cycling the Camino de Santiago de Compostela is becoming more popular every year, particularly with international visitors. The official *French Way by Bicycle* PDF is downloadable on *www.caminodesantiago.gal* and available in print at the Santiago tourist office. It advises that the approximately 800-km (500-mile) route from the French border to Santiago is no cake walk—bridle paths, dirt tracks, rough stones, and mountain passes await. The best time of year to tackle it is late spring or early autumn. The Asturias tourist office outlines routes in that region on *www.turismoasturias.es/en/turismo-activo/bici*. For something a little less arduous, try the final leg of the Camino Francés, from Sarria to Santiago, which takes 2–4 days.

BIKE ROUTES

Camino Ways

This tour operator can help you bike the Camino with tailor-made packages for individuals and families, child-friendly accommodations if necessary, meals, luggage transfer, and bike rental. ⊠ *Calle Gomez Ulla 6, Santiago de Compostela* ☎ *923/990672* ⊕ *www.caminoways.com*.

Camino de Santiago

☎ *902/112000, 981/900643* ⊕ *www.caminodesantiago.gal*.

BUS

ALSA runs buses every few hours from Madrid to Galicia and Asturias. On arrival, there is good bus service between cities such as Santiago, Vigo, Pontevedra, Lugo, A Coruña, Gijón, Oviedo, and Santander. However, train travel between the aforementioned is generally faster and more comfortable (and more expensive). Reaching smaller towns and villages by bus is usually possible but time-consuming and inconvenient. Galicia-based Monbus offers quick, inexpensive transportation between major cities like Santiago, A Coruña, Vigo, and Pontevedra, as well as smaller towns that may not be easily accessible by train.

CONTACTS ALSA. ☎ *902/422242* ⊕ *www.alsa.com*.**Monbus.** ☎ *982/292900* ⊕ *www.monbus.es*.

CAR

Driving is the best way to get around. The four-lane A6 expressway links the area with central Spain; it takes about 6½ hours to cover the 650 km (403 miles) from Madrid to Santiago, and from Madrid, it's 240 km (149 miles) on the N1 or the A1 toll road to Burgos, after which you can take the N623 to complete the 162 km (100 miles) to Santander.

The expressway north from León to Oviedo and Gijón is the fastest way to cross the Cantabrian Mountains. The AP9 north–south Galician ("Atlantic") expressway links A Coruña, Santiago, Pontevedra, and Vigo, and the A8 in Asturias links Santander to Luarca and beyond. Local roads along the coast or through the hills are more scenic but slower.

TRAIN

RENFE (*www.renfe.es*) runs several trains a day from Madrid to Santander (4½ hours), Oviedo (5 hours), and Gijón (5½ hours), and a separate line serves Santiago (4½ hours). At the time of writing, the long-awaited high-speed AVE line connecting Ourense and Madrid (2½ hours) was slated to be completed by December 2021. Local RENFE trains connect the region's major cities with most of the surrounding small towns, but there are often dozens of stops on the way. Narrow-gauge RENFE–FEVE trains clatter slowly across northern Spain, connecting Galicia and Asturias with Santander, Bilbao, and Irún (on the French border).

RENFE's Transcantábrico Gran Lujo train tour (*www.renfe.com*) is an eight-day, 1,000-km (600-mile) journey through the Basque Country, Cantabria, Asturias, and Galicia. English-speaking guides narrate, and a private bus takes the group from train stations to natural attractions. Passengers sleep on the train in suites and dine on local specialties. Itineraries run April–October; the all-inclusive cost is around €6,000 for seven nights per person in a deluxe suite.

Restaurants

From the humblest taverns to the haughtiest dining rooms, chefs in Galicia, Asturias, and Cantabria emphasize the use of fresh, local ingredients. Excellent, cheap meals can be found at smaller, family-run eateries, which usually stick to traditional foods and draw mostly local crowds. Restaurants that stray from the culinary norm—those with top-notch service, experimental cuisine, and elegant surroundings—tend to command a higher price tag.

Restaurant reviews have been shortened. For full information, visit Fodors. com.

Hotels

Expect to feel at home in the region's traditional inns: They're usually small, centuries-old, family-owned properties, with pleasing gardens, exposed stone walls, and genuine service. City hotels don't have the same country charm, but they make up for it with modern-day conveniences and (generally) spacious rooms. Chain hotels in the region may resemble their American counterparts, but they don't always come with ample parking, big breakfasts, fitness rooms, and other amenities that we've come to accept as standard. Book ahead for stays in May–September, high season.

Hotel reviews have been shortened. For full information, visit Fodors.com.

What It Costs in Euros			
$	$$	$$$	$$$$
RESTAURANTS			
under €12	€12–€17	€18–€22	over €22
HOTELS			
under €90	€90–€125	€126–€180	over €180

Santiago de Compostela

650 km (403 miles) northwest of Madrid.

Welcome to one of the most beloved and beautiful cities not just in Galicia but in all of Spain. Wander down the cobblestone streets of the old town, and you'll gasp at the gorgeous mix of Romanesque, Gothic, and baroque buildings. Or pop into an art gallery or one of the city's many chic literary cafés to catch some poetry or local music. A large, lively university makes Santiago one of the most electric cities in Spain, and its cathedral makes it one of the most impressive. The building is opulent and awesome, yet its towers create a sense of harmony as a benign St. James, dressed in pilgrim's costume, looks down from his perch. Santiago de Compostela welcomes around 4 million visitors a year, with an extra million during Holy Years, which occur when St. James's Day (July 25) falls on a Sunday.

The scheduled 2021 festivities will carry into 2022 to make up for lost time due to COVID, a first in Santiago history. The subsequent jubilee will be celebrated in 2027.

GETTING HERE AND AROUND

Santiago is connected to Pontevedra (61 km [38 miles]) and A Coruña (57 km [35 miles]) via the AP9 tollway. The N550 is free but slower. Parking anywhere in the city center can be difficult unless you use one of the numerous car parks around the outside edge of the historical quarter.

Bus service out of Santiago's station is plentiful, with eight daily buses to Madrid (7–9 hours) and hourly buses to A Coruña and to the Santiago Airport.

High-speed Talgo trains to Madrid take just over six hours; there is daily service to Irún, on the French border, via León

and Santander. Trains depart every hour for Galicia's other major towns.

Santiago's center is very pedestrian friendly, and the distances between attractions are relatively short, so walking is the best and often the only way around town.

BUS STATION Santiago de Compostela Bus Station. ⊠ *Praza de Camilo Díaz Baliño, Santiago de Compostela* ☎ *981/542416.*

TRAIN STATION Santiago de Compostela Train Station. ⊠ *Rúa do Hórreo 75A, Santiago de Compostela* ☎ *912/320320 RENFE.*

VISITOR INFORMATION

CONTACTS Santiago de Compostela Tourist Office. ⊠ *Rúa do Vilar 63, Santiago de Compostela* ☎ *981/555129* ⊕ *www. santiagoturismo.com.*

TOURS

Cathedral Roof Tours

For a bird's-eye view of the city, join one of the tours arranged by the cathedral museum that takes you across the *cubiertas*, the granite steps of the cathedral roofs. Pilgrims made the same 100-foot climb in medieval times to burn their travel-worn clothes below the Cruz dos Farrapos (Cross of Rags). There is a limited number of English-language tours. ✉ *Catedral de Santiago de Compostela, Praza do Obradoiro, Santiago de Compostela* ☏ *902/557812* ⊕ *www.catedraldesantiago.es* 🎫 *From €12.*

Asociación Profesional de Guías Turísticos de Galicia

Santiago's association of well-informed guides, an offshoot of the tourist office, can arrange walking tours of the city or tours to any place in Galicia. Spanish-language city tours depart Praza de Praterías at 12 and 6 and cost €12; English tours were on hold at the time of writing. Look out for the yellow umbrella at the meeting point. Advance booking is mandatory either by phone or email (info@guiasdegalicia.org). ✉ *Praza de Praterías,* ☏ *606/985185* ⊕ *www.guiasdegalicia.org* 🎫 *From €12.*

Sights

★ Casco Antiguo (*Old Town*)

HISTORIC DISTRICT | The best way to spend your time in Santiago de Compostela is to simply wander the old town, losing yourself in its maze of narrow stone-paved streets and postage-stamp plazas. In the process you'll stumble on old *pazos* (manor houses), convents, and churches. The most beautiful pedestrian thoroughfares are Rúa do Vilar, Rúa do Franco, and Rúa Nova—portions of which are covered by arcaded walkways called *soportales* , designed to keep walkers out of the rain. Don't miss Praza da Quintana, bounded by the majestic walls of the cathedral and the 9th-century Monastery of San Paio de Antealtares, a favorite summer hangout for buskers and young travelers.

★ Catedral de Santiago de Compostela

(*Cathedral of Santiago de Compostela*)
CHURCH | It's a new era for the Catedral: In 2020, the unsightly—and seemingly permanent—scaffolding came down to reveal one of Spain's most impressive (and painstakingly laborious) restorations. What was once a discolored, greenish, and weather-worn facade is now radiant, golden, and spotless—a befittingly grand finale to arduous pilgrimages. Although the facade is baroque, the interior holds one of the finest Romanesque sculptures in the world: the Pórtico de la Gloria, completed in 1188 by Maestro Mateo. It is the cathedral's original entrance, its three arches carved with figures from the Apocalypse, the Last Judgment, and purgatory. Below Jesus is a serene St. James, poised on a carved column. Look carefully and you can see five smooth grooves, formed by the millions of pilgrims who have placed their hands here over the centuries. On the back of the pillar, devotees lean forward to touch foreheads in the hope that his genius be shared. St. James presides over the high altar in a bejeweled cloak, which pilgrims embrace upon arriving at the cathedral. The stairs behind the sculpture are the cathedral's focal point, surrounded by dazzling baroque decoration, sculpture, and drapery. The crypt beneath the altar, which houses the purported remains of James and his disciples St. Theodore and St. Athenasius, is generally closed to the public. A pilgrims' Mass is held daily at noon. ✉ *Praza do Obradoiro,* ☏ *902/044077 museum information and booking* ⊕ *www.catedraldesantiago.es/en* 🎫 *Cathedral free; €12 for museum, portico, and art exhibits.*

Centro Galego de Arte Contemporánea

(*Galician Center for Contemporary Art*)
ART MUSEUM | Santiago's premier contemporary art museum is housed in a stark yet elegant modern building that

Santiago de Compostela's Praza do Obradoiro

contrasts with Santiago's ancient feel. Inside, a lobby of gleaming Italian marble gives way to white-walled, high-ceilinged exhibition halls filled with mind-bending conceptual art—some of which might be a bit "out there" for the uninitiated. The temporary exhibits are excellent. Portuguese designer Álvaro Siza built this museum from smooth, angled granite to mirror the medieval convent of San Domingos de Bonaval next door. ⊠ *Rúa Valle Inclán 2, Santiago de Compostela* ☎ *981/546619* ⊕ *cgac.xunta.gal* ⊠ *Free* ⊗ *Closed Mon.*

Cidade da Cultura

NOTABLE BUILDING | More than a decade in the making, Santiago's City of Culture is a controversial striated-stone-and-glass edifice on Monte Gaiás. It was meant to whisk Galician culture into the future but fell short: Construction was stopped in 2013 due to delays and mismanagement. A pared-down version has since opened with a museum, an archive library, temporary art exhibits, and cultural attractions including concerts and talks. The design of the complex, by the American architect Peter Eisenman, takes inspiration from the shape of a scallop shell, the emblem of St. James. ⊠ *Monte Gaiás, Santiago de Compostela* ☎ *881/997565 museum information* ⊕ *www.cidadedacultura.gal* ⊠ *Museum free, exhibits priced separately* ⊗ *Museum closed Mon.*

Hostal de los Reyes Católicos (*Hostel of the Catholic Monarchs*)

NOTABLE BUILDING | This hostel was built in 1499 by Ferdinand and Isabella to house the pilgrims who previously slept on Santiago's streets. It's the oldest refuge in the world and was converted from a hospital into a parador in 1954. The facade bears two Castilian coats of arms along with Adam, Eve, and various saints; inside, the four arcaded patios have gargoyle rainspouts said to be caricatures of 16th-century townsfolk. Behind the lobby is the building's focal point, a Renaissance chapel in the shape of a cross. Thanks to the Parador Museo initiative, even non-overnight guests can behold these architectural treasures on a guided tour. ⊠ *Praza do Obradoiro 1, Santiago de Compostela* ⊕ *www.civitatis. com/en/santiago-de-compostela/hos- tal-reyes-catolicas-tour* 🖼 *€12.*

★ **Mercado de Abastos de Santiago** (*Santiago City Market*)

MARKET | Designed by architect Joaquín Vaquero Palacios, this charming stone building, built in 1941, houses a bustling traditional food market. It fills up around 11, when locals come to shop, but the operating hours are roughly 8 am to 3 pm. Whether you snap up local cheeses and tinned fish to take home or merely ogle Galicia's wondrous bounty of shell- fish and produce, don't miss this market, one of Spain's most underrated foodie destinations. ⊠ *Rúa Ameás, Santiago de Compostela* 🕾 *981/583438* ⊕ *www. mercadodeabastosdesantiago.com* ⊘ *Closed Sun.*

Museo do Pobo Galego (*Galician Folk Museum*)

HISTORY MUSEUM | Next to the Centro Galego de Arte Contemporánea stands the medieval convent of San Domingos de Bonaval. The museum within holds photos, farm implements, traditional costumes, and other items illustrat- ing aspects of traditional Galician life. The star attraction is the 13th-century self-supporting spiral granite staircase that still connects three floors. ⊠ *San Domingos de Bonaval, Santiago de Com- postela* 🕾 *981/583620* ⊕ *www.museodo- pobo.gal* 🖼 *€4 (free Sun.)* ⊘ *Closed Mon.*

Museum of Pilgrimage and Santiago (*Pil- grimage Museum*)

HISTORY MUSEUM | North of Acibechería (follow Ruela de Xerusalén) is the Museo das Peregrinacións containing Camino de Santiago iconography: sculptures, carvings, *azabache* (compact black coal, or jet) items, and more. For an overview of the history of St. James, the cathe- dral, and the pilgrimage, as well as the Camino's role in the development of the city itself, this is a key visit. ⊠ *Praza das*

Praterías 2, Santiago de Compostela 🕾 *981/566110* ⊕ *museoperegrinacions. xunta.gal* 🖼 *€3 (free Sat. afternoon and Sun.)* ⊘ *Closed Mon. and some holidays.*

Pazo de Xelmírez (*Palace of Archbishop Xelmírez*)

CASTLE/PALACE | Step into this rich 12th-century building to view an unusual example of Romanesque civic architec- ture, with a cool, clean, vaulted dining hall. The little figures carved on the corbels in this graceful, 100-foot-long space are drinking, eating, and listening to music with great medieval gusto. Each is different, so stroll around for a tableau of mealtime merriment. The palace is attached to the cathedral. However, the entrance varies—it's best to ask at the cathedral museum where to enter the Pazo de Xelmírez. ⊠ *Praza do Obradoiro, Santiago de Compostela* 🕾 *981/552985* ⊕ *www.catedraldesantiago.es* 🖼 *€6, includes cathedral museum.*

Praza do Obradoiro

PLAZA/SQUARE | The imposing baroque facade of the cathedral dominates this sprawling square. Look for the stone slab in the center, which indicates "kilometer zero" on the pilgrimage trail. It is also the setting for the spectacular fireworks display on July 24 (the eve of St. James's Day). Traffic-free and flanked on all sides by historical buildings—including the 16th-century Hostal de los Reyes Católi- cos—it is the quintessential place to soak up the city's rich history. ⊠ *Praza do Obradoiro, Santiago de Compostela.*

🍴 Restaurants

A Barrola

$$$ | SEAFOOD | A solid bet on a street packed with middling tourist eateries, this seafood restaurant has polished wood floors and a bustling terrace. The *caldo gallego, santiaguiños* (slipper lobsters), *arroz con bogavante* (rice with lobster), and seafood empanadas are superb—as any of the university-faculty

Santiago de Compostela

Sights ▼

1 Casco Antiguo **B4**
2 Catedral de Santiago de Compostela **B3**
3 Centro Galego de Arte Contemporánea.......... **E1**
4 Cidade da Cultura........ **E7**
5 Hostal de los Reyes Católicos.................. **A3**
6 Mercado de Abastos de Santiago ... **D4**
7 Museo do Pobo Galego . **E1**
8 Museum of Pilgrimage and Santiago............ **D4**
9 Pazo de Xelmirez **B3**
10 Praza do Obradoiro..... **A3**

Restaurants ▼

1 A Barrola **A5**
2 Abastos 2.0.............. **D4**
3 A Tafona by Lucía Freitas.............. **E3**
4 Bierzo Enxebre........... **C2**
5 Carretas................. **A2**
6 Casa Marcelo............. **A3**
7 O Curro da Parra........ **D3**
8 Restaurante Filigrana................. **A7**

Hotels ▼

1 Hotel Costa Vella.......... **C1**
2 Hotel Monumento San Francisco........... **B1**
3 Hotel Spa Relais & Châteaux A Quinta da Auga.................. **A7**
4 Parador Hostal dos Reis Católicos **A3**
5 Pazo Cibrán.............. **E7**

regulars will tell you. **Known for:** local delicacies; raucous atmosphere; seafood feasts. $ *Average main: €20* ✉ *Rúa do Franco 29, Santiago de Compostela* ☎ *981/577999* ⊕ *www.restaurantebarro-la.com* ◷ *Closed Mon.*

A Tafona by Lucía Freitas

$$$ | SPANISH | This upscale restaurant by one of the region's most promising chefs serves elevated Galician cuisine in a bright, modern dining room with exposed stone walls. Menus feature a plethora of hyperlocal ingredients that have "first and last names," as the chef likes to say: Cambados oysters, Fisterra razor clams, Cachena beef, etc. **Known for:** finest Galician ingredients; experimental tasting menus; Michelin-starred dining. $ *Average main: €18* ✉ *Virxe da Cerca 7, Santiago de Compostela* ☎ *981/562314* ⊕ *www.restauranteatafona.com* ◷ *Closed Mon. and Tues. No dinner Sun.*

★ Abastos 2.0

$$$$ | TAPAS |"From market to plate" is this nueva cocina restaurant's philosophy: Chefs start and finish the day with an empty larder and a blank menu. The freshest fish and produce are handpicked at the neighboring Mercado de Abastos and coaxed into exciting dishes that defy tradition. **Known for:** contemporary design; market-fresh ingredients; inventive tapas. $ *Average main: €25* ✉ *Casetas 13–18, Pl. de Abastos, Santiago de Compostela* ☎ *654/015937* ⊕ *www.abastosdouspuntocero.com* ◷ *Closed Sun.*

Carretas

$$$$ | SEAFOOD | This casual seafood spot around the corner from the Hostal de los Reyes Católicos specializes in shellfish ranging from melt-in-your-mouth battered mini-scallops to a take-no-prisoners *variado de mariscos* platter with langoustines, king prawns, crab, and *percebes* (barnacles, a local delicacy). **Known for:** complimentary liqueurs with dessert; lively atmosphere; fresh seafood. $ *Average main: €25* ✉ *Rúa das Carretas 21,* ☎ *981/563111* ⊕ *www.restaurantecarretas.com* ◷ *No dinner Sun. Closed Mon.*

★ Casa Marcelo

$$$$ | FUSION | Fusing traditional Galician cuisine with Japanese, Mexican, and Peruvian, among others, Casa Marcelo whips up creatively plated dishes in an open-plan kitchen. The jovial dining area—always full and always loud—seats guests at long communal tables, a nod to the fact that the dishes are meant to be shared. **Known for:** extremely popular; impress-your-date cuisine; fusion tapas. $ *Average main: €30* ✉ *Rúa das Hortas 1, Santiago de Compostela* ☎ *981/558580* ◷ *Closed Mon. and Tues. No dinner Sun.*

O Curro da Parra

$$ | SPANISH | Across from the market, this lively two-floor restaurant has exposed brick walls, wooden tables, and a menu of modern, seasonally driven dishes ranging from oyster croquetas to saucy local beef meatballs, plus an ever-changing variety of seafood preparations. **Known for:** fantastic wines; market-to-table cuisine; attractive plating. $ *Average main: €17* ✉ *Rúa Travesa 20, Santiago de Compostela* ☎ *981/556059* ⊕ *www.ocurrodaparra.com.*

★ Restaurante Filigrana

$$$$ | SPANISH | Although the eggplant-colored walls, crystal chandeliers, and carefully chosen antique furniture evoke a traditional French dining room, the food at this restaurant—attached to the Hotel Spa Relais & Châteaux A Quinta da Auga—is unmistakably Galician. Try delicacies such as chestnut cream soup, fresh-caught hake, and bay scallops roasted in their shells with garlic-parsley oil. **Known for:** old-school Galician fine dining; weekday lunch prix fixe; bucolic environs. $ *Average main: €25* ✉ *Hotel Spa Relais & Châteaux A Quinta da Auga, Paseo da Amaia 23B, Santiago de Compostela* ☎ *981/534636* ⊕ *www.aquintadaauga.com.*

Hotels

Hotel Costa Vella

$ | **B&B/INN** | **FAMILY** | At this classically Galician inn, there's an idyllic little garden and views of red-tile rooftops, the baroque convent of San Francisco, and the green hills beyond (ask for a garden view). **Pros:** warm, accommodating staff; charming views; ideal location. **Cons:** no elevator; creaky floors; thin walls and noise from other rooms carries. [$] *Rooms from: €85* ✉ *Rúa Porta da Pena 17, Santiago de Compostela* ☎ *981/569530* 🌐 *www.costavella.com* 🛏 *14 rooms* 🍴 *Free Breakfast.*

Hotel Monumento San Francisco

$$$ | **HOTEL** | Contemporary stained-glass windows add pizzazz to the solemn interior of this converted 13th-century convent that adjoins the church of the same name. **Pros:** independently owned; easily accessible by car; indoor pool area with vaulted ceilings. **Cons:** decor a bit corporate and dated; might be too quiet for some; can get chilly at night. [$] *Rooms from: €180* ✉ *Campillo San Francisco 3, Santiago de Compostela* ☎ *981/581634* 🌐 *www.sanfranciscohm.com* 🛏 *81 rooms* 🍴 *Free Breakfast.*

★ Hotel Spa Relais & Châteaux A Quinta da Auga

$$$$ | **HOTEL** | Tastefully converted from a 14th-century printing factory, this restored stone building is set among manicured gardens and beside the burbling Río Sar. Rooms drip with French crystal chandeliers and opulent antique furniture—handpicked by the owner—a level of attention to detail that's mirrored by the above-and-beyond service. **Pros:** destination restaurant; tranquil spa with pool; attentive service. **Cons:** small beds; Wi-Fi spotty in some rooms; 10-minute drive from town. [$] *Rooms from: €300* ✉ *Paseo da Amaia 23B, Santiago de Compostela* ☎ *981/534636* 🌐 *www.aquintadaauga.com* 🛏 *61 rooms* 🍴 *Free Breakfast.*

★ Parador Hostal dos Reis Católicos

$$$$ | **HOTEL** | One of the finest paradores in the country, this 15th-century building was once a royal hostel and hospital for sick pilgrims. **Pros:** collectible antiques and paintings; views of Praza do Obradoiro; excellent cuisine. **Cons:** popular with the tour-bus set; confusing corridors; pricey. [$] *Rooms from: €268* ✉ *Praza do Obradoiro 1, Santiago de Compostela* ☎ *981/582200* 🌐 *www.parador.es* 🛏 *137 rooms* 🍴 *No Meals.*

Pazo Cibrán

$ | **B&B/INN** | This comfortable 18th-century Galician manor house, 7 km (4 miles) from Santiago de Compostela, has an antiques-packed living room that overlooks gardens with magnolias, palms, and a bamboo walk. **Pros:** country hospitality; delightful gardens; picturesque old estate. **Cons:** inaccessible without a car; limited dining nearby; only open for groups November–March. [$] *Rooms from: €70* ✉ *San Xulián de Sales 6, Vedra* ✥ *Take N525 toward Ourense from Santiago and turn right at Km 11, after gas station* ☎ *981/511515* 🌐 *www.pazocibran.es* 🛏 *11 rooms* 🍴 *Free Breakfast.*

Nightlife

Though weekends are always popping, Thursday is just as big a night in Santiago, since many students spend weekends at home with their families. For up-to-date info on concerts, films, and clubs, visit *www.compostelacultura.gal.* Bars and seafood-centric tapas joints line the old streets south of the cathedral, particularly **Rúa do Franco, Rúa da Raiña,** and **Rúa do Vilar.** A great first stop, especially if you haven't eaten dinner, is **Rúa de San Clemente,** off Praza do Obradoiro, where several bars offer hefty free tapas with each drink.

BARS

Casa das Crechas

BARS | Drink to Galicia's Celtic roots here, with live music and Celtic wood carvings hanging from thick stone walls, while dolls of playful Galician witches ride their brooms above the bar. ⊠ *Vía Sacra 3, Santiago de Compostela* ☎ *981/560751* ⊕ *www.facebook.com/casadascrechas.*

★ O Filandón

BARS | Venture forth through the narrow cheese shop and you'll discover a cozy bar in the back, where an inviting log fire burns on chilly evenings and pilgrims gather and swap stories and pin handwritten notes to the walls (there are literally thousands). The pinchos (snacks) that come with drinks are more than generous: hunks of freshly baked bread with assorted charcuterie and cheeses. ⊠ *Rúa da Acibechería 6, Santiago de Compostela* ☎ *981/572738.*

Pub Modus Vivendi

PUBS | Galicia's oldest pub is also one of its most unusual: Modus Vivendi is in a former stable. The old stone feeding trough is now a low table, and instead of stairs you walk on ridged stone inclines designed for the former occupants— horses and cattle. On weekends the bar hosts live music (jazz, Spanish, Celtic) and sometimes storytelling. ⊠ *Praza Feixóo 1, Santiago de Compostela* ☎ *607/804140.*

CAFÉS

With its melancholic and often chilly weather, Santiago is a great city for cozy coffee-drinking and people-watching. There are many cafés clustered around the cathedral—particularly on Rúa Caldería and Rúa do Vilar.

Café Casino

CAFÉS | Upholstered armchairs, mirrors, and wood paneling make this Art Nouveau café in a former casino especially atmospheric. ⊠ *Rúa do Vilar 35, Santiago de Compostela* ☎ *981/577503* ⊕ *www. cafecasino.gal.*

Café Iacobus

CAFÉS | **FAMILY** | Dunk hot churros into melted chocolate at this cheery, snug café with stone walls and white tile

floors. Another branch is at Rúa Caldería 42. ⊠ *Rúa da Senra 24, Santiago de Compostela* ☎ *981/585967.*

Cafe Literarios

CAFÉS | Tranquil by day and lively at night, Cafe Literarios has colorful paintings, large windows, and plenty of outdoor tables. It overlooks the plaza. Stick to booze and coffee here as the food is distinctly underwhelming. ⊠ *Praza da Quintana 1, Santiago de Compostela* ☎ *981/882912.*

Ourense and La Ribeira Sacra

105 km (65 miles) southeast of Santiago de Compostela, 95 km (59 miles) east of Vigo.

Despite the uninspiring backdrop of Ourense's new town, Galicia's third-largest city has bubbling thermal springs and an attractive medieval quarter whose animated streets, tapas bars, and plazas come alive on weekends. A smattering of notable historical monuments includes the colossal arches of the **Ponte Vella** (Roman bridge) spanning the Río Miño and the 13th-century Cathedral of San Martino. Between the cathedral and the Praza do Ferro is the **Os Vinos** area, ideal for tapas-hopping.

Ourense is a good starting point for exploring the dramatic landscapes of the Ribeira Sacra and Canón do Sil (Sil River Canyon), plus charming villages such as Allariz and Ribadavia. Ourense's surroundings brim with vineyards, trails, Romanesque churches, and monasteries.

GETTING HERE AND AROUND

RENFE and Monbus service Ourense from Santiago and Vigo in less than two hours. The A52 links Ourense to Vigo and Pontevedra, and the AG53 with Santiago.

VISITOR INFORMATION

CONTACTS Lugo Tourist Office. ✉ *Praza do Campo 11, Lugo* ☎ *982/251658.*

Sights

Thermal Baths

HOT SPRING | Several hot springs along the Minho River at varying temperatures draw visitors from far and wide and are ideal for soaking weary muscles on the pilgrim trail. Some are free and others charge a small entrance fee. There is a tourist train that stops at the main baths including A Chavasqueira and Outariz. ✉ *A Chavasqueira Thermal Baths, Campo da Feira, Ourense* 🌐 *www.turismode-ourense.gal.*

Restaurants

Fuentefría

$ | SPANISH | The *tostas* (open-faced sandwiches) are the tapa to try here. Whether your chosen toast-topper is smoked salmon, blue cheese, baked ham, or otherwise, you can't go wrong at this down-home bar. **Known for:** terrific tostas with local toppers; house-made empanada gallega; genial service. [$] *Average main: €8* ✉ *Rúa Viriato 6, Ourense* ☎ *697/487868.*

Hotels

Casa Rural Torre Lombarda

$ | B&B/INN | Though this rustic, well-kept inn is a mere 20-minute drive from the city center, its natural surroundings and open-armed hospitality make you feel like you're much farther afield. **Pros:** idyllic country escape not far from the city; free parking; old mill on-site. **Cons:** ill-suited for travelers with limited mobility; creaky floorboards; no breakfast or 24-hour service. [$] *Rooms from: €59* ✉ *Praza Torre Lombarda* ☎ *988/554005* 🌐 *www.torrelombarda.com* 🍴 *No Meals* 🛏 *9 rooms.*

Hotel Carrís Cardenal Quevedo

$$ | HOTEL | Steps from restaurants, shops, and lively tapas bars is this city-center hotel with smartly decorated rooms that exude an urban sensibility—think crisp white bedding and polished wooden floors. **Pros:** prime location; modern bells and whistles; good restaurant. **Cons:** uninspiring views; tight parking space; no in-room coffee. [$] *Rooms from: €105* ✉ *Rúa Cardenal Quevedo 28–30, Ourense* ☎ *988/375523* 🌐 *www.carrishoteles.com* 🛏 *39 rooms* 🍴 *Free Breakfast.*

★ **Parador de Santo Estevo**

$$$ | HOTEL | Clinging to the edge of the Canón do Sil, this parador, carefully built into the colossal 12th-century Benedictine Monasterio de Santo Estevo, stands out for its atmospheric setting and spectacular vistas. **Pros:** magnificent views; spa on site; historical sanctuary surrounded by nature. **Cons:** remote; popular wedding venue; mediocre food. [$] *Rooms from: €130* ✉ *Monasterio de Santo Estevo, Ourense* ✥ *Off CV323 beyond Luintra, 26 km (16 miles) northeast of Ourense* ☎ *988/010110* 🌐 *www.parador.es* ⏲ *Closed Dec.–Feb.* 🛏 *77 rooms* 🍴 *Free Breakfast.*

Lugo

102 km (63 miles) east of Santiago de Compostela.

Off the A6 freeway, Galicia's oldest provincial capital is notable for its 2-km (1½-mile) **Roman wall.** The beautifully preserved ramparts surround the old town. A walkway on top has good views. The baroque *ayuntamiento* (town hall) has a magnificent rococo facade overlooking the tree-lined **Praza Maior.** There's a good view of the Río Miño valley from the **Parque Rosalía de Castro,** outside the Roman walls near the cathedral, which mixes Romanesque, Gothic, baroque, and neoclassical styles.

GETTING HERE AND AROUND

CONTACTS Estación de Autobuses Lugo. ✉ *Prazo da Constitución, Lugo.* **Estación de Tren Lugo.** ✉ *Pl. Conde de Fontao, Lugo* ☎ *912/320320 RENFE* 🌐 *www.renfe.com.*

VISITOR INFORMATION

CONTACTS Lugo Tourist Office. ✉ *Praza do Campo 11, Lugo* ☎ *982/251658.*

Sights

City Walls

PROMENADE | A UNESCO World Heritage Site, the 3rd-century Roman walls encircling Lugo provide a picturesque 2-km (1-mile) walk and the best bird's-eye views of the town. There are 85 towers and 10 gates, and the walls have four staircases and two ramps providing access to the top.

Restaurants

Mesón de Alberto

$$$ | SPANISH | One hundred meters from the cathedral, this smart-casual venue has excellent Galician fare and professional service. The bar and adjoining bodega serve affordable *raciones* (sharable plates) including local cheeses with quince jam and cornbread; up in the dining room, the star menu item is Galician beef. **Known for:** standout shellfish; snug little dining room; fantastic steak. [$] *Average main: €20* ✉ *Rúa de la Cruz 4, Lugo* ☎ *982/228310* 🌐 *www.mesondealberto.com* ⏲ *No dinner Sun. and Mon. Closed Tues.*

Hotels

Fervenza Casa Grande

$ | B&B/INN | This centuries-old manor house situated 14 km (8 miles) south of Lugo is tucked away in a forest by the Río Miño. **Pros:** ideal hideaway for outdoorsy types; intimate feel; restaurant that's a destination in itself. **Cons:** rooms could use a refurb; removed from town; inadequate soundproofing. [$] *Rooms from: €62* ✉ *Ctra. Lugo–Paramo, Km 11, O Corgo, Lugo* ☎ *982/151610* 🌐 *www.fervenza.com* 🛏 *9 rooms* 🍴 *Free Breakfast.*

Muxia

75 km (47 miles) northwest of Santiago de Compostela, 30 km (18 miles) north of Fisterra.

Muxia is a tiny (population: 4,700), far-flung fishing village surrounded by the soaring rocky cliffs and virgin beaches of the Costa da Morte. It's also close to many hiking trails that meander through lush green forests, making it a perfect rural getaway.

Sights

O Camiño dos Faros (*Way of the Lighthouses*)

SCENIC DRIVE | Three lighthouses can be visited by car within an hour and a half on this route. Expect extraordinary views of the vertiginous rocky cliffs and churning waters that earned this part of Galicia its nickname, Costa da Morte. Start at the Faro de Cabo Touriñán, which guards a narrow peninsula marking what was once believed to be the westernmost point of continental Europe. A 20-minute drive away is the Faro da Punta da Barca, a stone lighthouse built in 1926 alongside the 16th-century Virxe da Barca sanctuary. Finish with Faro de Cabo Vilán, which juts dramatically above a red-rock promontory; it was the first in Spain to run by electricity. Alternatively the 200-km (124-mile) route can be hiked on a well-marked trail that runs from Malpica to Finisterre. ✉ *Muxia* 🌐 *www.caminodosfaros.com/en.*

Beaches

Praia de Nemiña

BEACH | A favorite with surfers and sport fisherman, this somewhat undiscovered

The Costa da Morte and Rías Baixas

beach is buffered from the wind by green forested hills on either side. It's a fine place for a midday picnic or romantic stroll at sunset on fine white sand. **Amenities:** showers. **Best for:** sunset; surfing; walking. ✉ *Muxia.*

🛏 Hotels

Casa Fontequeiroso

$ | **B&B/INN** | Surrounded by green hills and pine forests and a five-minute drive from the beaches of Costa da Morte, this bed-and-breakfast has simple yet tasteful rooms with wooden furniture and red-tile floors. **Pros:** owner is a fantastic cook; bicycles available for guests; bucolic surroundings. **Cons:** no amenities nearby; lunch and dinner must be prebooked; remote. [$] *Rooms from: €80* ✉ *Lugar de Queiroso, Nemiña* ☎ *981/748946* 🌐 *www.casafontequeiroso.com* 🛏 *6 rooms* 🍴 *Free Breakfast.*

Fisterra

50 km (31 miles) west of Santiago de Compostela, 75 km (48 miles) southwest of A Coruña.

There was a time when this windswept outcrop over raging waters was thought to be the end of the earth—*finis terrae*—and many Spaniards continue to believe, incorrectly, that Fisterra is the westernmost point of Europe (that point is actually in Portugal). Despite this, many camino pilgrims opt to hike to the "end of the earth" from Santiago de Compostela; indeed, arriving at Fisterra's picturesque lighthouse, beyond which there is nothing but the open Atlantic, is thrilling. The town all but shuts down in winter, but in summer it's a pleasant seaside resort with an attractive harbor.

VISITOR INFORMATION

CONTACTS Fisterra Turismo. ✉ *Rúa Carrumeiro 10, Fisterra* ☎ *627/239731* 🌐 *www.concellofisterra.gal/turismo/oficina_turismo/en.*

Sights

Santa María das Areas

CHURCH | Aside from legends, another draw in this tiny seaside town is its main plaza and the 12th-century church of Santa María das Areas. Romanesque, Gothic, and baroque elements combine in an impressive (if gloomy) facade. ✉ *Rúa Alcalde Fernández 14, Fisterra.*

Hotels

Hotel Naturaleza Mar da Ardora

$$ | HOTEL | A two-minute walk from Mar de Fora Beach, this boutique hotel is surrounded by gardens and boasts stunning beach views. **Pros:** dinner on the terrace; on-site spa; sweeping sea views. **Cons:** dated interiors; noise carries between rooms; relatively pricey. [$] *Rooms from: €110* ✉ *Playa de la Potiña 15, Fisterra* ☎ *667/641304* 🌐 *www.hotelmardaardora.com* 🛏 *6 rooms* 🍴 *Free Breakfast.*

Muros

65 km (40 miles) southwest of Santiago de Compostela, 55 km (34 miles) southeast of Fisterra.

Muros is a popular summer resort with arcaded streets framed by Gothic arches. The quiet alleys of the old town reveal well-preserved Galician granite houses, but the real action takes place when fishing boats return from the mussel-breeding platforms to hawk their wares at the evening fish auction (usually 4 pm), announced by siren. Anyone is welcome, but only wholesalers can buy. Trays overflowing with octopus tendrils and cod carcasses line the floor, which is splattered with squid ink and fish blood (stand far away or wear rubber boots). Good beaches nearby include Praia de San Francisco and Praia da Area.

GETTING HERE AND AROUND

Monbus runs frequent buses between Muros and Santiago de Compostela and A Coruña. By car, take the AP9 north from Vigo and Pontevedra (just under 2 hours away) or the AC550 west from Santiago de Compostela and A Coruña (1½ hours).

VISITOR INFORMATION

CONTACTS Muros Tourist Office. ✉ *Curro da Praza 1, Muros* ☎ *981/826050* 🌐 *www.murosturismo.gal.*

Cambados

34 km (21 miles) north of Pontevedra, 61 km (37 miles) southwest of Santiago de Compostela.

This breezy seaside town has a charming, almost entirely residential old quarter and is ground zero for Albariño winemaking. The impressive main square, **Praza de Fefiñáns,** is bordered by an imposing bodega. Cambados's **cemetery** is one of the most picturesque in Spain: Its tombs surround a mossy medieval church ruin.

GETTING HERE AND AROUND

Cambados is less than an hour from either Santiago de Compostela (to the north), or Vigo and Pontevedra (to the south) all via the AP9.

Sights

Bodegas del Palacio de Fefiñanes

WINERY | Set in a 16th-century stone palace, this illustrious winery has been making wine since the 17th century and crafts textbook Albariños. The 1583 Albariño de Fefiñanes sees five years in

Wine Tasting in Rías Baixas

Albariño Wine

Rías Baixas, in southern Galicia, is the most important Denomination of Origin (D.O.) in the province and the largest global producer of Albariño, a crisp, young, and aromatic varietal that has international prestige. Albariño has been compared to riesling for its vibrant acidity, to Petit Manseng and Viognier for its peach and apricot notes, and to Pinot Gris for its floral bouquet. Its dry, slate-y qualities sing alongside local seafood.

Vineyards and bodegas are spread throughout Pontevedra province and beyond, with a particularly high density in Cambados, a major Albariño-producing area. With more than 7,000 growers and 20,000 individual vineyard plots in Rías Baixas, planning a wine trip to the region can feel overwhelming. Happily, free resources like **Ruta do Viño Rías Baixas** (⊕ www.

rutadelvinoriasbaixas.com/en) and **Rías Baixas Wines** (⊕ www.riasbaixaswines.com) are available to help if you wish to self-guide. Set tours are a safer bet if you have limited time or want to learn as much as possible.

Wine Tours

Guiados Pontevedra. Custom tours of two to three bodegas in the region, including an English-speaking guide, will run you approximately €100 for four hours (minimum two people). ⊠ *Pontevedra* ☎ *654/222081* ⊕ *www. guiadospontevedra.com.*

North West Iberia Wine Tours. One-, three-, and six-day wine tours include transport, admissions, lunch, and wine tasting at two different locations as well as a visit to a local *pazo* (estate) and camellia garden. ⊠ *Rúa Enrique Marinas Romero 30–5H, A Coruña* ☎ *881/879910* ⊕ *www.northwestiberiawinetours.com* ⊠ *From €180.*

Bordeaux barrels. Guided tours including tastings are approximately €10. Reservations recommended. ⊠ *Pl. de Fefiñanes, Cambados* ☎ *986/542204* ⊕ *www. fefinanes.com* ⊠ *From €5.*

Don Olegario

WINERY | This award-winning, family-run winery offers an intimate tour followed by a tasting on the terrace overlooking the vineyards. ⊠ *Refoxos, Corbillón, Cambados* ☎ *986/520886* ⊕ *www.donolegario.com* ⊠ *From €8* ⚲ *Reservations essential.*

Pazo de Rubianes

GARDEN | The jewel of this property is the camellia garden, one of the largest and most impressive collections of flowers in the world. The camellias bloom November–May and peak February–April. The

15th-century manor house is decadently furnished and also worth a visit, as is the attached bodega and chapel. Gourmet picnic baskets with local products can be assembled for a leisurely lunch amid the vines and flowers. There are also guided tours, which last about two hours and include the gardens, winery, *pazo*, chapel, and a tasting. ⊠ *Rúa do Pazo 7, Cambados* ☎ *986/510534* ⊕ *www.pazoderubianes.com* ⊠ *Self-guided tour (by appointment) free, guided tour €16.*

🍴 Restaurants

María José

$$ | SEAFOOD | Across from the parador, this long-established restaurant produces inventive dishes like scallop salad, mango soup with mascarpone ice cream, and salmon with anchovy mayonnaise. Specialties include *arroz de marisco caldoso* (shellfish, stock, and rice). **Known for:** unironic throwback 90s dining room; terrace tables with sea views; abundant portions at economical prices. $ *Average main: €14* ⊠ *C. San Gregorio 2–1, Cambados* ☎ *986/542281* ☾ *No dinner Sun.–Tues.*

Hotels

Parador de Cambados

$$$ | HOTEL | This airy mansion's rooms are warmly furnished with wrought-iron lamps, area rugs, and full-length wood shutters over small-pane windows. **Pros:** easily accessible; excellent dining; outdoor pool. **Cons:** limited parking; rooms showing wear; occasionally surly staff. $ *Rooms from: €130* ⊠ *Paseo Calzada, Cambados* ☎ *986/542250* ⊕ *www.parador.es* ☾ *Closed Jan.* ⊅ *58 rooms* ⫿⊘⫿ *No Meals.*

★ Quinta de San Amaro

$$$ | HOTEL | This quirky rural hotel is a great base for wine tourism, thanks to the gorgeous vineyard views and complimentary visit to a local winery. **Pros:** in the heart of wine country; beautiful views; outstanding service and memorable restaurant. **Cons:** need a car to get here; somewhat remote at a 15-minute drive from Cambados; small swimming pool. $ *Rooms from: €130* ⊠ *Rúa San Amaro 6, Cambados* ☎ *630/877590* ⊕ *www.quintadesanamaro.com* ⊅ *14 rooms* ⫿⊘⫿ *Free Breakfast.*

Shopping

Cucadas

CRAFTS | Head to this crafts shop for its large selection of baskets, shells, copper items, and lace. ⊠ *Praza de Fefiñáns 8, Cambados* ☎ *986/542511* ⊕ *www.facebook.com/CUCADAS.1985.*

Pontevedra

135 km (84 miles) southeast of Fisterra, 59 km (37 miles) south of Santiago de Compostela.

At the mouth of a *ría* (estuary), Pontevedra is a delightful home base for exploring Rías Baixas. Its well-preserved old quarter is a dense warren of pedestrian-only streets and handsome plazas flanked with elegant stone buildings, many of which are festooned with cascading flowers. The city got its start as a Roman settlement (its name comes from an old Roman bridge over the Río Lérez). In the 16th century it became an influential hub of fishing and international trade. Today, its streets and plazas are awash with charming bars and restaurants. Weekends are particularly busy.

GETTING HERE AND AROUND

RENFE and Monbus offer quick, frequent service between Vigo and Pontevedra, a half-hour journey; the same bus and train routes also link Pontevedra to Santiago de Compostela and A Coruña to the north along the AP9.

CONTACTS Estación de Autobuses Pontevedra. ⊠ *Calle de la Estación, Pontevedra* ☎ *986/852408.*

VISITOR INFORMATION

CONTACTS Pontevedra Tourist Office. ⊠ *Ayuntamiento de Pontevedra, Pl. de España 1, Pontevedra* ☎ *986/090890* ⊕ *www.visit-pontevedra.com.*

Sights

Adega Eidos

WINERY | This sleek winery overlooks Sanxenxo harbor and produces a modern, fruit-forward style of albariño harvested from old, ungrafted vines grown on granite slopes. Only natural yeasts are used in the fermentation. Tours including nibbles and a wine tasting cost approximately €5. ⊠ *Padriñán 65, Sanxenxo,*

Pontevedra ☎ *986/690009* ⊕ *www.adegaeidos.com* 🖪 *From €5.*

Museo de Pontevedra

HISTORY MUSEUM | Housed in two 18th-century mansions connected by a stone bridge, this museum includes exquisite Celtic jewelry, silver from all over the world, and several large model ships. The original kitchen, with a stone fireplace, is intact; below, descend steep wooden stairs to the reconstructed captain's chamber on the battleship *Numancia*, which limped back to Spain after the Dos de Mayo battle with Peru in 1866. Complete the loop by going upstairs in the first building, where there are Spanish, Italian, and Flemish paintings. ⊠ *Rúa Padre Amoedo Carballo 3, Pontevedra* ☎ *986/804100* ⊕ *www.museo.depo.gal* 🖪 *Free* ⊙ *Closed Mon.*

Pazo Baión

WINERY | Surrounded by Albariño vineyards, this 15th-century stone manor house stands in pleasant contrast to its 100-year-old boutique wine cellar, built in an art deco style. Winemaker José Hidalgo produces a silky Albariño with notes of citrus and floral aromas here. Reservations are required. ⊠ *Abelleira 6, Vilanova de Arousa,* ☎ *986/543535* ⊕ *www.pazobaion.com* 🖪 *From €15.*

Real Basilica de Santa María la Mayor

CHURCH | The 16th-century seafarers' basilica has lovely, sinuous vaulting and, at the back of the nave, a Romanesque portal. There's also an 18th-century Christ by the Galician sculptor Ferreiro. ⊠ *Av. de Santa María 24, Pontevedra* ☎ *986/866185* 🖪 *Free.*

🍴 Restaurants

Casa Solla

$$$$ | SPANISH | Book a table at this terrace garden restaurant 2 km (1 mile) outside of town toward O Grove for a fine-dining culinary tour of the region. Local mackerel, chorizo, hake, and beef are mainstays here, as are traditional Galician cheeses and wines. **Known for:** eye-popping plating; ideal for special occasions; tasting menu only. Ⓢ *Average main: €94* ⊠ *Av. Sineiro 7, San Salvador de Poio* ☎ *986/872884* ⊙ *Closed Mon. No dinner Thurs. and Sun.*

La Navarra

$ | TAPAS | Join the locals leaning on wine-barrel tables to watch soccer and snack on Galician cheeses and spicy chorizo, which hangs from ceiling racks above the bar. **Known for:** good charcuterie and tostas; raucous sports bar; local hangout. Ⓢ *Average main: €10* ⊠ *Rúa Princesa 13, Pontevedra* ☎ *986/851254* ⊙ *Closed Sun.*

Hotels

Parador de Pontevedra

$$$ | HOTEL | A 16th-century manor house in the heart of the old quarter, this parador has guest rooms with recessed windows embellished with lace curtains and large wooden shutters; some face a small rose garden. **Pros:** free parking; interesting collection of bric-a-brac; tranquil yet central location. **Cons:** confusing corridors; dungeon-y rooms; limited parking. Ⓢ *Rooms from: €140* ⊠ *Rúa Barón 19, Pontevedra* ☎ *986/855800* ⊕ *www.parador.es* ⤧ *47 rooms* ⏹ *No Meals.*

Vigo

31 km (19 miles) south of Pontevedra, 90 km (56 miles) south of Santiago de Compostela.

Vigo's formidable port is choked with trawlers and fishing boats and lined with clanging shipbuilding yards. The city's gritty exterior gives way to a compact and lively center that clings to a tiered hill rising over an ancient Roman settlement. A jumble of modernist buildings and red-roofed fisherman's houses hide the narrow streets of Vigo's appealing *casco vello* (old town). Vigo's highlights can be explored in a few hours.

Fishing is central to the livelihood of thousands who live and work in Vigo, and its fish market handles some of the largest quantities of fresh fish in Europe, which is consumed across the continent. From 10 to 3:30 daily, on **Rúa Pescadería** in the barrio of **La Piedra,** Vigo's famed *ostreras*—a group of rubber-gloved fisherwomen who have been peddling fresh oysters to passersby for more than decades—shuck the bushels of oysters hauled into port that morning. Competition has made them expert hawkers who cheerfully badger all who walk by their pavement stalls. When you buy half a dozen (for around €10), the women plate them and plunk a lemon on top; you can then take your catch into any nearby restaurant and turn it into a meal. A short stroll southwest of the old town brings you to the fishermen's barrio of **El Berbés.** Facing the port, it has several seafood restaurants, most with outdoor tables in summer.

GETTING HERE AND AROUND

A small airport connects Vigo to a handful of destinations, like Madrid and Barcelona, but trains and buses are your best bet for transportation within Galicia. Northbound RENFE trains leave on the hour for Pontevedra, Santiago de Compostela, and A Coruña, making stops at smaller towns in-between. Monbus and ALSA also connect Vigo to the same destinations via the AP9, while AUTNA runs a daily shuttle south to Porto and its international airport, a 2½-hour trip.

CONTACTS Vigo Bus Station. ☒ *Av. de Madrid 57, Vigo* ☏ *986/373411.* **Vigo Train Station.** ☒ *C. Areal s/n, Vigo* ☏ *912/320320 RENFE* ⊕ *www.renfe. com.*

VISITOR INFORMATION

CONTACTS Vigo Tourist Office. ☒ *Estación Marítima de Ría, Rúa Cánovas del Castillo 3, Oficina 4, Vigo* ☏ *986/224757* ⊕ *www. turismodevigo.org.*

Sights

★ Islas Cíes

ISLAND | The Cíes Islands, 35 km (21 miles) west of Vigo, are among Spain's best-kept secrets. They form a pristine nature preserve that's one of the last unspoiled refuges on the Spanish coast. Starting on weekends in May and then daily June–late September, Naviera Mar de Ons *(986/225272, www.mardeons. com)* runs about eight boats from Vigo's harbor (subject to weather conditions), returning later in the day, for the €20 round-trip fare (tickets must be booked in advance on the website). The 45-minute ride brings you to white-sand beaches surrounded by turquoise waters brimming with marine life; there's also great birding. The only way to get around is your own two feet: it takes about an hour to cross the main island. If you want to stay overnight, there's a designated camping area. The tourist office has up-to-date information on timetables and crossings. ■**TIP**→ **It is mandatory for travelers to the Cíes Islands to first obtain authorization from the Xunta de Galicia online portal (autorizacionillasatlanticas. xunta.gal/illasr).** ☒ *Estación Marítima,* ⊕ *www.campingislascies.com* ☒ *€20.*

Museo de Arte Contemporánea de Vigo (MARCO) (*Museum of Contemporary Art*)

ART MUSEUM | Housed in a refurbished prison on Vigo's main shopping drag, this museum doesn't have a permanent collection but hosts intriguing temporary exhibitions and solo shows of featured artists. ☒ *Rúa do Príncipe 54, Vigo* ☏ *986/113900* ⊕ *www.marcovigo.com* ☒ *Free* ⊘ *Closed Mon.*

Parque Monte del Castro

CITY PARK | South of Vigo's old town, this is a quiet, stately park with sandy paths, palm trees, mossy embankments, and stone benches. Atop a series of steps are the remains of an old fort and a *mirador* (lookout) with fetching views of Vigo's coastline and the Islas Cíes. Along its shady western side lies the Castro de Vigo, the remains of Vigo's first Celtic settlement, dating to the 3rd century BC. ✉ *Av. Marqués de Alcedo, between Praza de España and Praza do Rei, Vigo* 🎫 *Free* 🕒 *Castro de Vigo closed Sun. and Mon.* ☞ *Reservations required for Castro de Vigo.*

🍴 Restaurants

Cocedero Bar La Piedra

$ | **SPANISH** | Fancy it ain't, but this jovial tapas bar is where you can devour the freshest catch from the Rúa Pescadería fisherwomen, and it does a roaring lunch trade with Vigo locals. Expect heaping plates of *marisco* (shellfish) and scallops with roe at market prices, plus fresh and fruity Albariño, its trusty sidekick. **Known for:** fresh seafood; simple, down-to-earth atmosphere; front-row seats for oyster hawkers. [$] *Average main: €10* ✉ *Rúa Pescadería 3, Vigo* ☎ *986/431204.*

El Mosquito

$$$$ | **SPANISH** | Signed photos from the likes of King Juan Carlos and Julio Iglesias cover the walls of this elegant stone-wall restaurant opened in 1928. Specialties include *lenguado a la plancha* (grilled sole) and *navajas* (razor clams). **Known for:** caramel flan; extensive wine cellar; dependably good seafood. [$] *Average main: €25* ✉ *Praza da Pedra 4, Vigo* ☎ *616/504544* 🌐 *www.elmosquitorestaurante.com* 🕒 *No dinner Sun.*

Tapas Areal

$$$ | **TAPAS** | This ample and lively bar flanked by ancient stone and exposed redbrick walls is a good spot for tapas and beer as well as albariños and Ribeiros. **Known for:** fresh and modern tapas; buzzing atmosphere; good albariño selection. [$] *Average main: €18* ✉ *Rúa México 36, Vigo* ☎ *986/418643* 🌐 *www.tapasareal.com* 🕒 *Closed Sun.*

🛏 Hotels

Gran Hotel Nagari Boutique and Spa

$$ | **HOTEL** | A short walk from the harbor, this boutique hotel has a glitzy early-aughts aesthetic in public spaces—think colorful plastic swivel chairs and gold brocade curtains—though guest rooms are more neutral, with white linens and sparse wall art; upgrades add in-room jacuzzis. **Pros:** a short stroll from the old town; excellent spa; rooftop pool with city and Atlantic views. **Cons:** confusing panel controls in rooms; spa and pool not complimentary; parking not complimentary. [$] *Rooms from: €120* ✉ *Pl. de Compostela 21, Vigo* ☎ *986/211111* 🌐 *www.granhotelnagari.com* 🔑 *63 rooms* 🍽 *Free Breakfast.*

🍸 Nightlife

The streets around Praza de Compostela and the pedestrian-only Rúa Montero Ríos, down toward the waterfront, come alive in the early evening for drinks and tapas. Night owls should check out the snazzier cocktail bars in the Areal district (along Rúa Areal and Rúa de Rosalía de Castro) or the rock and indie scene in the Churruca neighborhood (Rúa Rogelio Abalde, Rúa Churruca) from midnight onward, where you can often stumble across live music.

La Trastienda del Cuatro

WINE BARS | Around the corner from Praza de Compostela, this trendy wine bar (with a good upscale restaurant in the back) has a wide-reaching wine list complemented by modern tapas with winks to Asian and Latin cuisines. ✉ *Rúa de Pablo Morillo 4, Vigo* ☎ *986/115881* 🌐 *www.latrastiendadelcuatro.com.*

Shopping

There's a large shopping center next to where the cruise ships dock. Close by you'll find Mercado da Pedra, the city's main market, where clothing, food, and a variety of goods are sold. For souvenirs, head to the old town, where there is an abundance of artisanal shops selling locally crafted leather, wood, and ceramics. On the aptly named Rúa Cesteiros (literally "street of basketmakers"), you can check out Vigo's famous handwoven baskets. Vigo's commercial shopping area is centered on Rúa Principe.

Activities

There are several horseback riding clubs in the hills around Vigo. The Galician Equestrian Federation is an excellent source of information.

HORSEBACK RIDING

Granja O Castelo

HORSEBACK RIDING | The rural hotel Granja O Castelo conducts horseback rides along the main pilgrimage routes to Santiago including those departing O Cebreiro and Braga (Portugal). ✉ *Castelo 41,* ☎ *986/425937, 608/381334* 🌐 *www.caminoacaballo.com* 🎫 *from €1,300 for 4 days.*

Baiona

12 km (8 miles) southwest of Vigo.

At the southern end of the AP9 freeway and the Ría de Vigo, Baiona (Bayona in Castilian) is a summer hideaway for affluent Galicians. When Columbus's *Pinta* landed here in 1492, Baiona became the first town to receive the news of the discovery of the so-called New World. Once a castle, **Monte Real** is one of Spain's most popular paradores; walk around the battlements for superb views. Inland from Baiona's waterfront is the jumble of streets that make up Paseo Marítimo; head here for seafood restaurants and lively cafés and bars. Calle Ventura Misa is one of the main drags. On your way into or out of town, check out Baiona's **Roman bridge.** The best nearby beach is Praia de América, north of town toward Vigo.

GETTING HERE AND AROUND

ATSA buses leave every 30 minutes from Vigo, bound for Baiona and Nigrán. By car, take the AG57 from Vigo to the north or the PO340 from Tui to the southeast.

Hotels

★ Parador de Baiona

$$$$ | **HOTEL** | This baronial parador, positioned on a hill within the perimeter walls of a medieval castle, has plush rooms, some with balconies and ocean views toward the Islas Cíes. **Pros:** luxurious bathrooms; views of the ría; stupendous medieval architecture. **Cons:** dark rooms; dinner can be disappointing; especially pricey for rooms with sea views. [$] *Rooms from: €290* ✉ *Av. Arquitecto Jesús Valverde, Baiona* ☎ *986/355000* 🌐 *www.parador.es* 🛏 *122 rooms* 🍴 *Free Breakfast.*

Pazo de Touza

$$ | **HOTEL** | This 16th-century stone manor house is surrounded by manicured gardens and has a terrace that looks out onto a labyrinth of hedges. **Pros:** immaculate gardens; historical manor house; tranquil setting. **Cons:** popular wedding venue; 15-minute drive from Baiona; some traffic noise from nearby road. [$] *Rooms from: €110* ✉ *Rúa dos Pazos* ☎ *986/383047* 🌐 *www.pazodatouza.info* 🛏 *8 rooms* 🍴 *No Meals.*

The coastline of Baiona is one of the first things the crew of Columbus's ship the saw when they returned from their discovery of America.

Tui

14 km (9 miles) southeast of Baiona, 26 km (16 miles) south of Vigo.

The steep, narrow streets of Tui, noble with their emblazoned mansions, are a reminder that this was one of the seven capitals of the Galician kingdom. Today it's an important border town; the mountains of Portugal are visible from the cathedral. Across the river in Portugal, the old fortress town of Valença contains reasonably priced shops, bars, restaurants, and a hotel with splendid views.

GETTING HERE AND AROUND

From Vigo, take the scenic coastal route PO552, which goes up the banks of the Río Miño along the Portuguese border or, if time is short, jump on the inland A55; both routes lead to Tui.

 Sights

Tui Cathedral

CHURCH | A crucial building during the medieval wars between Castile and Portugal, Tui's 12th-century Romanesque cathedral looks like a fortress. Its majestic cloisters surround a lush formal garden. Rooftop ("Cubiertas") tours take place weekdays at 1 pm and 5:15 pm from June to August. ⊠ *Pl. de San Fernando, Tui* ☎ *986/600511* ⊕ *www. catedraldetui.com* 🎫 *Free, €9 for rooftop tour.*

 Hotels

Parador de Tui

$$$ | HOTEL | This stately granite-and-chestnut hotel on the bluffs overlooking the Miño is filled with local art, and the rooms are furnished with antiques including four-poster beds. **Pros:** swimming pool (seasonal); restaurant with excellent seafood; enticing gardens. **Cons:** somewhat pricey; a bit of a walk from

Tui proper; dark rooms. $ *Rooms from: €150* ⊠ *Av. Portugal, Tui* ☎ *986/600300* ⊕ *www.parador.es* ⊘ *Closed Jan.–mid-Feb.* ⊷ *32 rooms* ⊙ *No Meals.*

A Coruña

57 km (35 miles) north of Santiago de Compostela.

One of Spain's busiest ports, A Coruña is often (mistakenly) overlooked by travelers. While the weather can be fierce, wet, and windy, there are frequent bouts of sunshine. The dramatic weather, along with a thriving commercial center and intriguing historic quarter, gives the city and its people a distinctive personality. It is also the wealthiest city in Galicia.

A Coruña takes pride in its gastronomy, and there is a buzzing nightlife scene as well as a host of interesting sights such as the world's oldest still-functioning lighthouse. The city's shining jewel is the city's emblematic row of glass-enclosed, white-paned galleries on the houses that line the harbor—a remarkable sight when the light catches them on a sunny day.

GETTING HERE AND AROUND
The A9 motorway provides excellent access to and from Santiago de Compostela, Pontevedra, Vigo, and Portugal, while Spain's north coast and France are accessible along the N634.

Buses run every hour from A Coruña to Santiago. Trains also operate on an hourly basis to Santiago and Pontevedra from the city's San Cristóbal train station; Madrid can be reached in five hours on the high-speed AVE.

Outside the old town, the city's local buses shuttle between the Dársena de la Marina seafront and more far-flung attractions such as the Torre de Hércules lighthouse.

CONTACTS A Coruña Bus Station. ⊠ *Rúa Caballeros 21, A Coruña* ☎ *981/184335.* **A**

Coruña Train Station. ⊠ *Av. Ferrocaril, A Coruña* ☎ *912/320320* ⊕ *www.renfe. com.*

VISITOR INFORMATION
CONTACTS A Coruña Tourist Office. ⊠ *Oficina de Turismo, Pl. de María Pita 6, A Coruña* ☎ *981/923093* ⊕ *www.turismo-coruna.com.*

 Sights

Aquarium Finisterrae
AQUARIUM | **FAMILY** | Situated next to the Torre de Hércules, this aquarium features interactive exhibits, an underwater hall, and a seal colony. A fitting tribute to Galicia's relationship with the sea, it focuses on the ecosystems of the Atlantic and Galician coast. ⊠ *Paseo Alcalde Francisco Vázquez 34, A Coruña* ☎ *981/189842* ⊡ *€10.*

Castillo de San Antón (Museo Arqueológico e Histórico)
HISTORY MUSEUM | At the northeastern tip of the old town is St. Anthony's Castle, a 16th-century fort that houses A Coruña's Museum of Archaeology. The collection includes remnants of the prehistoric Celtic culture that once thrived in these parts, including silver artifacts as well as ruins from castros, the Celts' stone forts. ⊠ *Paseo Alcalde Francisco Vázquez 2, A Coruña* ☎ *981/189850* ⊡ *€2* ⊘ *Closed Mon.*

Colexiata de Santa María do Campo
CHURCH | Called St. Mary of the Field because the building was once beyond the city's walls, this Romanesque beauty dates to the mid-13th century. The facade depicts the Adoration of the Magi; the celestial figures include St. Peter, holding the keys to heaven. Because of an architectural miscalculation the roof is too heavy for its supports, so the columns inside lean outward and the buttresses outside have been thickened. The interior is often closed but the exterior alone is worth seeing. ⊠ *Calle Santa María 1, A Coruña.*

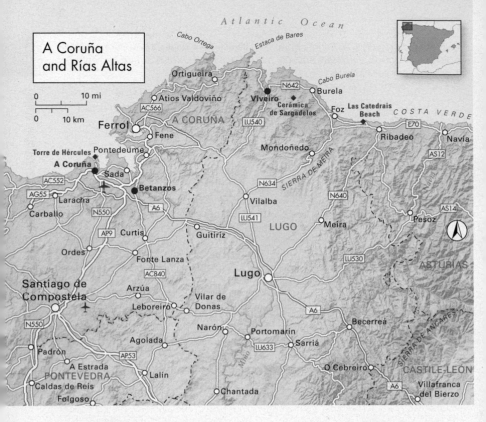

Atlantic Ocean

Cabo Ortega · Estaca de Bares

COSTA VERDE

ASTURIAS

SIERRA DE MEIRA

SIERRA DE ANCARES

CASTILE-LEÓN

PONTEVEDRA

A CORUÑA

LUGO

Cabo Burela

Ortigueira · Burela · N642 · Cabo Burela
Atios · Valdoviño · Viveiro · Cerámica de Sargadelos · Foz · Las Catedrais Beach
AC566 · LU540 · Ribadeo · E70 · Navia
Ferrol · Fene
Torre de Hércules · Pontedeume
A Coruña · Sada · Mondoñedo · AS12
AC552 · Betanzos · N634 · N640 · AS14
AG55 · Laracha · A6 · Vilalba · Meira · Pesoz
Carballo · N550 · LU541 · LU530
AP9 · Curtis · Guitiríz · A6
Ordes · Fonte Lanza · AC840 · Lugo
Santiago de Compostela · Arzúa · Vilar de Donas · Becerreá
Leboreiro · A6 · O Cebreiro
N550 · Narón · Portomarín · Villafranca del Bierzo
Padrón · Agolada · LU633 · Sarriá · A6
A Estrada · AP53 · Lalín · Chantada
Caldas de Reis · Folgoso

0 — 10 mi
0 — 10 km

Iglesia de Santiago

CHURCH | This 12th-century church, the oldest in A Coruña, was the first stop on the Camino Inglés (English route) toward Santiago de Compostela. Originally Romanesque, it's now a hodgepodge that includes Gothic arches, a Baroque altarpiece, and two 18th-century rose windows. ⊠ *Rúa do Parrote 1, A Coruña.*

Paseo Marítimo

PROMENADE | To see why sailors once nicknamed A Coruña "la ciudad de cristal" (the glass city), stroll the Paseo Marítimo, said to be the longest seaside promenade in Europe. Although the congregation of boats is charming, the real sight is across the street: a long, gracefully curved row of houses. Built by fishermen in the 18th century, they face away from the sea—it's said that at the end of a long day, these seafarers were tired of

looking at the water. Nets were hung from the porches to dry, and fish was sold on the street below. When Galicia's first glass factory opened nearby, someone thought to enclose these porches in glass, like the latticed stern galleries of oceangoing galleons, to keep wind and rain at bay. The resulting emblematic glass galleries spread across the harbor and eventually throughout Galicia. The 13 km (8 miles) of flat surface with ocean views make it a wonderful jogging spot. ⊠ *Paseo Marítimo, A Coruña.*

Praza de María Pita

PLAZA/SQUARE | The focal point of the old town, this bustling large plaza has a north side that's given over to the neoclassical Palacio Municipal, or city hall, built 1908–12 with three Italianate domes. The monument in the center, built in 1998, depicts the heroine Maior (María) Pita.

When England's Sir Francis Drake arrived to sack A Coruña in 1589, the locals were only half-finished building the defensive Castillo de San Antón. A 13-day battle ensued. When María Pita's husband died, she took up his lance, slew the Briton who tried to plant the Union Jack, and revived the exhausted Coruñeses, inspiring other women to join the battle. The surrounding streets of the old town are a hive of activity, lined with tapas bars and shops. ⊠ *Pr. de María Pita, A Coruña.*

★ Torre de Hércules

LIGHTHOUSE | Much of A Coruña sits on a peninsula, on the tip of which sits this city landmark and UNESCO World Heritage Site—the oldest still-functioning lighthouse in the world. First installed during the reign of Trajan, the Roman emperor born in Spain in AD 98, the lighthouse was rebuilt in the 18th century and looks strikingly modern; all that remains from Roman times are inscribed foundation stones. Scale the 245 steps for superb views of the city and coastline—if you're here on a summer weekend, the tower opens for views of city lights along the Atlantic. Lining the approach to the lighthouse are sculptures depicting figures from Galician and Celtic legends. ⊠ *Av. de Navarra, A Coruña* ☎ *981/223730* ⊕ *www.torredeherculesa-coruna.com* 🎫 *€3 (free Mon.).*

🏖 Beaches

Orzán and Riazor Beaches

BEACH | A Coruña's Paseo Marítimo winds along two pleasant, well-maintained urban beaches, Playa del Orzán and Playa de Riazor. These long curves of fine golden sand tend to be busy in summer with chattering groups of local families and friends enjoying the milder climate. The area of Playa del Orzán in front of the hotel Meliá María Pita is popular with surfers. Cross the Paseo Marítimo for a choice of cafés and restaurants with animated terraces. Seafront kiosks sell ice cream and snacks. There is no natural shade, but you can rent sun loungers and parasols in summer. **Amenities:** food and drink; lifeguards; showers; toilets. **Best for:** surfing; swimming; walking. ⊠ *Paseo Marítimo, A Coruña.*

🍽 Restaurants

★ Adega O Bebedeiro

$$ | SPANISH | This tiny restaurant is beloved by locals for its dependable Galician food. It feels like an old farmhouse, with stone walls and floors, a fireplace, pine tables and stools, and dusty wine bottles (*adega* is Gallego for bodega, or wine cellar). **Known for:** genial service; postprandial liqueurs on the house; good octopus and seafood. Ⓢ *Average main: €17* ⊠ *Rúa Ángel Rebollo 34, A Coruña* ☎ *981/210609* ⊕ *www.adegaobebedeiro. com* ⊘ *Closed Mon., and 1st wk in Jan. No dinner Sun.*

El De Alberto

$$$ | SPANISH | El De Alberto marries traditional Galician flavors with eye-catching modern presentation. Alberto, the passionate and friendly chef-owner, has no qualms about, say, dolloping kimchi sauce on local octopus or painting truffle butter on baked scallops (instead of the usual squirt of lemon). **Known for:** great value; cheerily decorated dining room; playful nueva cocina dishes. Ⓢ *Average main: €18* ⊠ *Rúa Ángel Rebollo 18, A Coruña* ☎ *981/907411* ⊘ *Closed Mon. No dinner Sun.*

La Penela

$$$ | SEAFOOD | This sophisticated sea-foam-green dining room is the perfect place to feast on fresh fish while sipping Albariño. Don't miss the crabs or mussels with béchamel, a dish that La Penela is locally famous for. **Known for:** terrace dining; French-inflected seafood dishes; views of the harbor and Plaza de María Pita. Ⓢ *Average main: €18* ⊠ *Pl. de María Pita 12, A Coruña* ☎ *981/209200* ⊕ *www. lapenela.com* ⊘ *Closed last 2 wks of Jan. No dinner Sun.*

Hotels

Hotel Lois
$$ | B&B/INN | Steps from the tapas bars of Calle Estrella, Hotel Lois is an excellent choice for its location alone, and its clean, contemporary style and excellent value for money make it all the more appealing. **Pros:** discount at nearby car park; surrounded by restaurants; central location. **Cons:** no access to street with car; no parking on-site; patchy Wi-Fi in some rooms. [$] *Rooms from: €90* ✉ *Estrella 40, A Coruña* ☎ *981/212269* 🌐 *hotel-lois.mydirectstay.com/es/index.html* 🔑 *10 rooms.*

NH Collection A Coruña Finisterre
$$ | HOTEL | A favorite with businesspeople and families, the oldest and busiest of A Coruña's top hotels is a few minutes' walk from the port. **Pros:** big-brand efficiency; port and city views; heated pool. **Cons:** unimpressive breakfast; inconvenient €20/day outdoor parking; some rooms showing wear. [$] *Rooms from: €106* ✉ *Paseo del Parrote 2–4,* ☎ *855/215–4084* 🌐 *www.nh-hotels.com/hotel/nh-collection-a-coruna-finisterre* 🔑 *92 rooms* 🍴 *No Meals.*

Nightlife

Begin your evening in the **Praza de María Pita**: cafés and tapas bars proliferate off its western corners and inland. **Rúas Estrella, Franja, Riego de Agua, Barrera, and Galera** and the **Praza do Humor** have many tapas bars that get progressively busier as the night develops, some of which serve Ribeiro wine in bowls and free tapas with every drink. Start at the top of Calle Estrella (at the farthest end from Pr. María Pita) beginning with A Taberna de Cunqueiro (Rúa Estrella 22) and work your way back. Night owls head for the posh and pricey clubs around **Playa del Orzán** (Orzán Beach), particularly along Rúa Juan Canalejo. For lower-key entertainment, the old town has cozy taverns and plenty of bars that stay open into the early hours.

Taberna da Galera
WINE BARS | This trendy wine bar in the heart of the old town serves Galician *raciones* to a lively crowd. Feast on *tigres* (stuffed mussels), octopus tempura, or delightfully runny tortilla española, and accompany it all with a glass of fresh Ribeiro wine. ✉ *Rúa Galera 32, A Coruña* ☎ *881/923996* 🌐 *www.tabernadagalera.com* 🕒 *Closed Sun.*

Shopping

Rúa Real and **Praza de Lugo** have boutiques with contemporary threads. A stroll down **Rúa San Andrés,** two blocks inland from Calle Real, or **Rúa Juan Flórez,** leading into the newer town, can yield some sartorial treasures. The Mercado Municipal de San Agustín, close to Praza de María Pita, is the place to go to stock up on local produce, tinned fish, and all kinds of charcuterie.

★ Alfarería Aparicio
CRAFTS | The glazed terra-cotta ceramics from Buño, a town 40 km (25 miles) west of A Coruña on the C552, are prized by aficionados. To see where they're made, drive there, then stop in this store to snap up some souvenirs. ✉ *Rúa Nova 4, A Coruña* ☎ *981/711136* 🌐 *www.alfareriaaparicio.es.*

Mundo Galego
FOOD | Stop here for local cheese, wine, liqueur, and other Galician specialties. The shop also organizes tastings. ✉ *Rúa Galera 40, A Coruña* ☎ *981/912038* 🌐 *www.facebook.com/mundogalego* 🕒 *Closed Sun.*

A Coruña is a major port town, but fashionistas might know it as where the first Zara clothing shop opened, back in 1975.

Activities

In A Coruña and the surrounding area, enjoy year-round outdoor activities including sailing, golf, and hiking. Swimmers and surfers can take advantage of the 2 km (1 mile) of beach and coastline in the heart of the city. See Beaches section.

Betanzos

25 km (15 miles) east of A Coruña, 65 km (40 miles) northeast of Santiago de Compostela.

The charmingly frayed-at-the-edges medieval town of Betanzos is surrounded by parts of its old city wall. An important Galician port in the 13th century, the old town straddles the confluence of the Mendo and Mandeo Rivers and is known today for its white galleried houses, stately Gothic monuments, and lively taverns serving tortilla de Betanzos—an ultra-runny rendition of the classic Spanish omelet.

GETTING HERE AND AROUND

From Vigo and other destinations south, head north on the AP9; from A Coruña, head east for half an hour along the same freeway. The medieval center, with its narrow lanes rising up from the Pont Nova, is best explored on foot.

VISITOR INFORMATION

CONTACTS Betanzos Tourist Office. ⊠ *Praza de Galicia 1, Betanzos* ☎ *981/776666* ⊕ *turismo.betanzos.es.*

Sights

Igrexa de San Francisco de Betanzos
CHURCH | The 1292 monastery of San Francisco was converted into a church in 1387 by nobleman Fernán Pérez de Andrade. His magnificent tomb, to the left of the west door, has him lying on the backs of a stone bear and boar, with hunting dogs at his feet and an angel receiving his soul by his head. ⊠ *Pl. de Fernán Pérez Andrade, Betanzos* 🎟 *€2.*

Two Great Detours

A Beach Detour

As Catedrais Beach (Las Catedrais Beach). One of Spain's best-kept secrets, this spectacular stretch of sand, also known as Praia de Augas Santas (Beach of the Holy Waters) features vast rock formations, domes, arches, and caves that were naturally formed by wind and sea. In high season (July–September) it is mandatory to reserve a ticket to access the actual beach via ascatedrais.xunta.gal. The arches are accessible for walks when the tide goes out; otherwise, the beach can be completely covered. **Amenities:** parking. **Best for:** spectacular natural scenery; beach walks; rock formations. ✉ *A8, 516 exit, Ribadeo* 🎟 *Free.*

Shopping Side Trip

Cerámica de Sargadelos. Distinctive blue-and-white-glazed contemporary ceramics are made at Cerámica de Sargadelos, 21 km (13 miles) east of Viveiro. It's usually possible to watch artisans work (weekdays 9–1:15), but call ahead to check. ✉ *Ctra. Paraño,* ☎ *982/557841* 🌐 *www.sargadelos.com.*

Igrexa de Santa María do Azogue de Betanzos

CHURCH | This 15th-century church, a few steps uphill from the church of San Francisco, is a national monument. It has Renaissance statues that were stolen in 1981 but subsequently recovered. ✉ *Pl. de Fernán Pérez Andrade, Betanzos* 🎟 *Free.*

Igrexa de Santiago de Betanzos

CHURCH | The tailors' guild put up the Gothic-style church of Santiago, which includes a Pórtico de la Gloria inspired by that of Santiago's cathedral. Above the door is a carving of St. James as the Slayer of the Moors—a title that hasn't aged particularly well. ✉ *Pl. de Lanzós, Betanzos* 🎟 *Free.*

Viveiro

121 km (75 miles) northeast of Betanzos.

The once-turreted city walls of this popular summer resort are still partially intact. The **Semana Santa** processions, when penitents follow religious processions on their knees, are particularly noteworthy. The beaches in Viveiro Bay are some of the north's finest.

GETTING HERE AND AROUND

Narrow-gauge FEVE trains connect Viveiro to Oviedo, Gijón, and other points east. By car, head east on the AP9 from A Coruña, then take the LU540 to Viveiro.

VISITOR INFORMATION

CONTACTS Viveiro Tourist Office. ✉ *Av. Ramón Canosa 3, Viveiro* ☎ *982/560879* 🌐 *www.viveiroturismo.com.*

🛏 Hotels

Hotel Ego

$$$ | **HOTEL** | The view of the ría from this hilltop hotel outside Viveiro is unbeatable, and every room has one. **Pros:** hilltop views; excellent restaurant; relaxing public areas. **Cons:** small spa; the facade resembles an airport terminal; a little generic. [$] *Rooms from: €143* ✉ *Playa de Area 1, off N642, Faro (San Xiao), Viveiro* ☎ *982/560987* 🌐 *www.hotelego.es* 🛏 *45 rooms* 🍴 *Free Breakfast.*

Luarca

92 km (57 miles) northeast of Oviedo.

The village of Luarca (Lluarca in Asturian) is in a cove at the end of the Río Negro. It has a fishing port and, to the west, a sparkling bay. The town is a maze of cobblestone streets, stone stairways, and whitewashed houses hemmed in by a harborside decorated with painted flowerpots.

GETTING HERE AND AROUND

To get to Oviedo, Gijón, and other destinations east, take a FEVE train or ALSA bus; it's about a two-hour trip. By car, take the A8 west along the coast from Oviedo and Gijón or east from A Coruña.

VISITOR INFORMATION

CONTACTS Luarca Tourist Office. ✉ *Calle Ramón Asenjo 25, Luarca* ☎ *985/640083* 🌐 *www.turismoluarca.com.*

🍴 Restaurants

Barómetro

$$$ | **SEAFOOD** | **FAMILY** | Decorated with an ornate barometer to gauge the famously unpredictable local weather, this family-run seafood spot is in a 19th-century building on the harbor. In addition to an inexpensive *menú del día* (prix fixe), there's outstanding seafood à la carte including fried *calamares* (squid) and uni-stuffed asparagus. **Known for:** seafood noodle soup; excellent-value prix-fixe lunch; popular with locals. [$] *Average main: €18* ✉ *Paseo del Muelle 5, Luarca* ☎ *985/470662* 🕒 *Closed Tues. No dinner Sun.*

Sport

$$$ | SPANISH | This family-run restaurant has been going strong since the 1950s. Its large windows overlook the river, and its kitchen makes a mean *fabada asturiana* (bean-and-sausage stew). **Known for:** riverside dining; rollo de bonito (tuna meatballs in tomato sauce); day-boat seafood. $ *Average main: €22* ✉ *Calle Rivero 9, Luarca* ☎ *985/641078.*

Hotels

★ Hotel Rural 3 Cabos

$$ | B&B/INN | FAMILY | On a grassy hill with spectacular bay views, this cozy yet modern B&B makes for a charming stay. **Pros:** free bike rental; house-made cake at breakfast; stunning views of land and sea. **Cons:** car needed; out of the way (15-minute drive to Luarca); restaurant only open to guests. $ *Rooms from: €105* ✉ *Ctra. de El Vallín, Km 4, Luarca* ☎ *985/924252* ⊕ *www.hotelrural3cabos. com* ۞ *Closed Jan. (can vary)* ➟ *6 rooms* ❯⊘ *Free Breakfast.*

Villa La Argentina

$$ | B&B/INN | Built in 1899 by a wealthy *indiano* (a Spaniard who made his fortune in the Americas and returned), this charming Asturian mansion on the hill above Luarca offers modern apartments in the garden or Belle Époque suites in the main building. **Pros:** peace and quiet; lovely gardens; swimming pool. **Cons:** not central; uphill walk from town; simple breakfast. $ *Rooms from: €118* ✉ *Villar, Luarca* ☎ *985/640102* ⊕ *www.villalaargentina.com* ۞ *Closed Jan. and Feb.* ➟ *12 rooms* ❯⊘ *Free Breakfast.*

Oviedo

92 km (57 miles) southeast of Luarca, 50 km (31 miles) southeast of Cudillero, 30 km (19 miles) south of Gijón.

Inland, the Asturian countryside morphs into rolling green hills punctuated with

Cudillero

The coastal road leads 35 km (22 miles) east of Luarca to this crayon-box fishing village clustered around a tiny port. The peridot hills, the shimmering water, and the pops of color among the white houses—a canny use of leftover boat paint—make this village one of the prettiest and most touristic in Asturias. Seafood and cider restaurants line the central street, which turns into a boat ramp at the bottom of town.

wooden tile-roof *hórreos* (granaries) strung with dried corn. A drive through the mountains and valleys brings you to Asturias' stately capital, Oviedo. Although its periphery is primarily industrial, the city has three of the most famous pre-Romanesque churches in Spain and a large university, giving it both ancient charm and youthful zest. Start your explorations with the two exquisite 9th-century chapels outside the city, on the slopes of Monte Naranco.

GETTING HERE AND AROUND

Oviedo is served by the A66 tollway that links to Gijón and Avilés, where you can get on the A8 west to A Coruña or east toward Santander. Madrid is reached on the N630 south.

There are several buses per day to Gijón (30 minutes) and to Santiago and A Coruña (5 hours). Madrid is 4½ hours away by rail from Oviedo's RENFE station on Calle Uría. The FEVE service operates across the north coast, with Gijón easily reached in a half an hour and Bilbao 7½ hours away.

Local buses operate along the main arteries of Oviedo, between the train station and shopping areas, but most of the action is in the historical center, where Oviedo's oldest buildings are clustered in the labyrinth of streets around the Plaza

Alfonso. Considering the short distances, walking is the best option, though taxis are inexpensive.

CONTACTS Oviedo Bus Station. ✉ *Calle Pepe Cosmen, Oviedo* ⊕ *www.estaciondeautobusesdeoviedo.com.***Oviedo Train Station.** ✉ *Calle Uria,* ☎ *912/320320 Renfe.*

VISITOR INFORMATION
CONTACTS Tourist Information Center of Asturias. ✉ *Pl. de la Constitución 4, Oviedo* ☎ *984/493563* ⊕ *www.visitoviedo.info.*

Sights

Catedral Metropolitana de San Salvador de Oviedo
CHURCH | Oviedo's Gothic cathedral was built between the 14th and 16th centuries around the city's most cherished monument, the **Cámara Santa** (Holy Chamber). King Ramiro's predecessor, Alfonso the Chaste (792–842), built it to hide the treasures of Christian Spain during the struggle with the Moors. Damaged during the Spanish Civil War, it has since been rebuilt. Inside is the gold-leaf **Cross of the Angels,** commissioned by Alfonso in 808 and encrusted with pearls and jewels. On the left is the more elegant **Victory Cross,** actually a jeweled sheath crafted in 908 to cover the oak cross used by Pelayo in the battle of Covadonga. ✉ *Pl. Alfonso II El Casto, Oviedo* ☎ *985/219642* ⊕ *www. catedraldeoviedo.com* 🎟 *€7 (incudes audioguide).*

San Julián de los Prados (*Santullano*)
CHURCH | Older than its more famous pre-Romanesque counterparts on Monte Naranco, the 9th-century church of Santullano has surprisingly well-preserved frescoes inside. Geometric patterns, rather than representations of humans or animals, cover almost every surface, along with a cross containing Greek letters. ✉ *C. Selgas 1,* ☎ *687/052826* 🎟 *€2 (free 1st Mon. of each month)* ☽ *Closed Sun.*

★ Santa María del Naranco and San Miguel de Lillo
CHURCH | These two churches—the first with superb views and its plainer sister 300 yards uphill—are the jewels of an early architectural style called Asturian pre-Romanesque, a more primitive, hulking, defensive line that preceded Romanesque architecture by nearly three centuries. Commissioned as part of a summer palace by King Ramiro I when Oviedo was the capital of Christian Spain, these masterpieces have survived for more than 1,000 years. Tickets for both sites are available in the church of Santa María del Naranco. ✉ *Monte Naranco, Oviedo* ✛ *2 km (1 mile) north of Oviedo* ☎ *638/260163* ⊕ *www.santamariadelnaranco.es* 🎟 *€4, includes guided tour (free Mon., without guide).*

Restaurants

Casa Fermín
$$$$ | **SPANISH** | Skylights, plants, and an air of modernity belie the age of this sophisticated restaurant, which opened in 1924 and is now in its fourth generation. The nueva cocina menu changes seasonally, and there is also a tasting menu. **Known for:** special-occasion dining; exceptional seafood; inventive Asturian cuisine. $ *Average main: €26* ✉ *C. San Francisco 8, Oviedo* ☎ *985/216452* ⊕ *www.casafermin.com* ☽ *Closed Sun.*

La Corte de Pelayo
$$$ | **SPANISH** | Head to this renowned white-tablecloth restaurant and meeting spot on one of Oviedo's main thoroughfares for *cachopo,* a heart-stopping fried veal cutlet stuffed with ham and cheese—an Asturian speciality. If you prefer something a bit lighter, there are salads, fresh fish, and meat dishes. **Known for:** wonderful cachopo; central location; lively atmosphere. $ *Average main: €20* ✉ *Calle San Francisco 21, Oviedo* ☎ *985/213145* ⊕ *www.lacortedepelayo.com* ☽ *No dinner Sun. Closed Mon.*

Tierra Astur

$$ | **SPANISH** | **FAMILY** | This *sidrería* (cider restaurant) is popular among locals and tourists alike, who come to enjoy the lively barroom atmosphere. Cider is poured from a great height, and traditional, family-style Asturian fare like *fabada* and *tablas* (cheese and charcuterie boards) are ideal for sharing. **Known for:** abundant Asturian cider; succulent chuletón (rib-eye steak); platters with over 40 types of meats and cheese. $ *Average main: €15* ⊠ *Calle Gascona 1, Oviedo* ☎ *985/202502* ⊕ *www.tierra-astur.com.*

 ## Hotels

Barceló Oviedo Cervantes

$$ | **HOTEL** | A playful revamp of this townhouse in the city center added a neo-Moorish portico to the original latticed facade and indulgent amenities like entertainment systems in some of the bathrooms. **Pros:** on-site bar and restaurant; central location close to train station; fun '70s design. **Cons:** erratic service; uninteresting views; subpar lighting in rooms. $ *Rooms from: €104* ⊠ *Calle Cervantes 13, Oviedo* ☎ *985/255000* ⊕ *www.barcelo.com* ⇨ *72 rooms* ⦿ *No Meals.*

★ Eurostars Hotel de la Reconquista

$$$ | **HOTEL** | Occupying an 18th-century hospice emblazoned with a huge stone coat of arms, the luxurious Reconquista is by far the most distinguished hotel in Oviedo. **Pros:** good breakfast buffet; spacious rooms; great location. **Cons:** some street noise; some rooms have uninteresting views; decor may be fusty for some. $ *Rooms from: €180* ⊠ *Calle Gil de Jaz 16, Oviedo* ☎ *985/241100* ⊕ *www. eurostarshotels.co.uk* ⦿ *Free Breakfast* ⇨ *142 rooms.*

▼ Nightlife

Oviedo gets a little rowdy after dark on weekends, and there's plenty in the way of loud live music. Most of the bars are concentrated on Calle Mon and its continuation, Calle Oscura. Calle Canóniga, off Calle Mon, also has a number of bars. Calle Gascona is cider row, lined with *sidrerías* that spill out onto the street and serve tapas till late. Bartenders here pour the cider from a great height, which aerates the naturally still cider.

● Shopping

Shops throughout the city carry *azabache* jewelry made of jet.

Joyería Santirso

JEWELRY & WATCHES | This family-run shop has been selling silver jewelry, including Asturias's world-famous azabache, for five generations. ⊠ *Calle Rúa 7, Oviedo* ☎ *985/225304* ⊕ *www.joyeriasantirso. com* ⊗ *Closed Sun.*

Mercado El Fontán

MARKET | Oviedo's main traditional market, built in 1885 in a structural rationalist style, brims with produce, cheeses, meats, and a jaw-dropping variety of fresh seafood. On Sunday morning there's an open-air *rastro* (flea market) on the adjoining square. ⊠ *Pl. 19 de Octubre, Oviedo* ☎ *985/204394* ⊕ *www. mercadofontan.es* ⊗ *Closed Sun.*

 ## Activities

SKIING
Fuentes de Invierno

SKIING & SNOWBOARDING | An hour's drive from Oviedo in the heart of the Cantabrian Mountains, Fuentes de Invierno has five chairlifts and 15 trails of varying difficulty. ⊠ *Ctra. del Puerto de San Isidro, Oviedo* ☎ *985/959106* ⊕ *www. fuentesdeinvierno.com* ⊿ *€27.*

Valgrande Pajares

SKIING & SNOWBOARDING | This resort has two chairlifts, eight slopes, and cross-country trails. ✉ *Estación Invernal y de Montaña Valgrande-Pajares, Brañillín, Pajares ⚐ 60 km (37 miles) south of Oviedo* ☎ *985/957097* ⊕ *www. valgrande-pajares.com* ☜ *€29.*

Gijón

30 km (19 miles) north of Oviedo.

The Campo Valdés baths, dating to the 1st century AD, and other reminders of Gijón's time as an ancient Roman port remain visible downtown. Gijón (Xixón in Asturian) was almost destroyed in a 14th-century struggle over the Castilian throne, but by the 19th century it was a thriving port and industrial city. Today it is part fishing port, part summer resort, and part university town, packed with cafés, restaurants, and sidrerías. It's a bit scruffier than Oviedo but also more down-to-earth.

GETTING HERE AND AROUND

Gijón is 30 minutes away from Oviedo by ALSA bus or FEVE train, both of which run every half hour throughout the day. The A8 coastal highway stretches east from Gijón to Santander, and west to Luarca and eventually A Coruña.

CONTACTS Gijón Bus Station. ✉ *Calle Magnus Blikstad 2, Gijón* ⊕ *www.alsa. com/en/web/bus/bus-stations/gijon-station.***Gijón Train Station.** ✉ *Calle Sanz Crespo, Gijón* ☎ *912/432343* ⊕ *www. renfe.com.*

VISITOR INFORMATION

CONTACTS Gijón Tourist Office. ✉ *Casa Paquet, Calle Fermín García Bernardo, Gijón* ☎ *985/341771* ⊕ *www.gijon.es/es/turismo/informacion-turistica.*

Sights

Cimadevilla

VIEWPOINT | This steep peninsula—the old fishermen's quarter—is now the main nightlife hub. At sunset, the sidewalk in front of bar El Planeta (Tránsito de las Ballenas 4), overlooking the harbor, is a prime spot to join locals drinking Asturian cider. From the park at the highest point on the headland, beside Basque artist Eduardo Chillida's massive sculpture *Elogio del Horizonte* (*In Praise of the Horizon*), there's a panoramic view of the coast and city. ✉ *Gijón.*

★ Museum of the Asturian People (*Museum of the People of Asturias*)

HISTORY MUSEUM | Across the river, on the eastern edge of town, this rustic museum contains traditional Asturian houses, cider presses, a mill, and an exquisitely painted granary. Also here is the Museo de la Gaita (Bagpipe Museum) celebrating the areas centuries-old bagpiping tradition. There are bagpipes from other parts of the world on display as well. ✉ *Paseo del Doctor Fleming 877, La Güelga,* ☎ *985/182960* ⊕ *www.gijon.es/es/directorio/museu-del-pueblu-dasturies* ☜ *Free* ⊘ *Closed Mon.*

Termas Romanas de Campo Valdés (*Roman Baths*)

RUINS | Dating to the time of Augustus, the ruins of Gijón's baths are under the plaza at the end of the beach. Visits take approximately 20 minutes, and there are no English descriptions. ✉ *Campo Valdés,* ☎ *985/185151* ☜ *Free* ⊘ *Closed Mon.*

Beaches

As capital of the Costa Verde, Gijón overlooks two attractive sandy beaches that are large enough to avoid overcrowding in summer.

Playa de Poniente (*Sunset Beach*)

BEACH | Tucked into the city's harbor, this horseshoe-shape curve of fine artificial sand and calm waters is wonderful for an evening stroll. **Amenities:** lifeguards; showers; toilets. **Best for:** sunset; swimming; walking. ⊠ *Calle Rodriguez San Pedro, Gijón.*

Playa de San Lorenzo

BEACH | Gijón's other popular beach, beyond the headland from Playa de Poniente, has golden sand backed by a promenade that extends from one end of town to the other. Across the narrow peninsula and the Plaza Mayor is the harbor, where the fishing fleet comes in with the day's catch. As long as the tide is out, you can sunbathe. The waves are generally moderate, but weather and currents can be unpredictable. **Amenities:** food and drink; lifeguards; showers; toilets; water sports. **Best for:** sunset; swimming; walking. ⊠ *Av. Rufo García Rendueles, Gijón.*

 Restaurants

★ La Galana

$$$ | SPANISH | La Galana is a typical Asturian sidrería, colossal barrels lining the walls, thick wooden tables, and plenty of standing room at the bar, where locals munch on Cabrales cheese. The kitchen serves refined cider-house fare: Expect cheeses with quince jam, *pulpo a la brasa* (grilled octopus), and a range of creative tapas. **Known for:** local cider; lovingly prepared cider-house fare; great-value prix fixe. $ *Average main: €20* ⊠ *Pl. Mayor 10, Gijón* ☎ *985/172429* ⊕ *www. restauranteasturianolagalana.es.*

Restaurante Auga

$$$$ | SPANISH | This upscale, glass-enclosed dining room, housed in what was once Gijón's fish market, overlooks the harbor and serves imaginative seafood and meat dishes. Expect a variety of raw, grilled, smoked, foamed, and roasted

options, all plated with panache. **Known for:** harbor and sea views; alfresco dining; award-winning kitchen. $ *Average main: €34* ⊠ *Calle Claudio Alvargonzález, Gijón* ☎ *985/168186* ⊕ *www.restauranteauga. com* ◉ *Closed Mon. No dinner Sun.*

 Hotels

Hostel Gijón Centro

$ | B&B/INN | Steps from the harbor and Plaza Mayor, this tiny guesthouse offers rooms with large windows affording plenty of natural light, plus simple, modern decor and comfortable beds. **Pros:** excellent value; quiet; central location. **Cons:** simple lodging; no on-site facilities; tiny bathrooms. $ *Rooms from: €70* ⊠ *Calle San Antonio 12, Flat 1, Gijón* ☎ *657/029242* ⊕ *www.hostelgijoncentro. es* ⤳ *6 rooms* ⦿ *No Meals.*

★ Hotel El Mirador de Ordiales

$ | B&B/INN | This cozy hilltop B&B offers exquisite views of the valley below and the snowcapped Picos de Europa in the distance. **Pros:** stunning views; spacious rooms; good base for hiking. **Cons:** breakfast is extra; few dining options in the area; far afield. $ *Rooms from: €85* ⊠ *Camín de Ordiales 545, Siero* ☎ *653/938156, 985/721020* ⊕ *www. elmiradordeordiales.com* ⤳ *3 rooms* ⦿ *No Meals.*

Parador de Gijón

$$$ | HOTEL | This is one of the most dressed-down and inviting paradores in Spain, and most rooms have wonderful views over the lake or park. **Pros:** terrific restaurant; park views; welcoming; down-to-earth staff. **Cons:** expensive for the area; austere guest rooms; some distance from the old town. $ *Rooms from: €130* ⊠ *Av. Torcuato Fernández Miranda 15,* ☎ *985/370511* ⊕ *www.parador.es* ⤳ *40 rooms* ⦿ *Free Breakfast.*

Ribadesella

67 km (40 miles) east of Gijón, 84 km (50 miles) northeast of Oviedo.

The N632 twists around green hills dappled with eucalyptus groves and affords glimpses of the sea, beaches, and snowcapped Picos de Europa. This fishing village and beach resort is famous for its seafood, cave formations, and canoe races (held on the Río Sella the first Saturday in August).

GETTING HERE AND AROUND

FEVE and ALSA connect Ribadesella to Gijón and Oviedo by train and bus, a journey of 1½–2 hours. By car, you can take the A8 from Gijón and Oviedo past Villaviciosa to Ribadesella.

VISITOR INFORMATION

CONTACTS Ribadesella Tourist Office. ✉ *Paseo Princesa Letizia, Ribadesella* ☎ *985/860038* 🌐 *www.ribadesella.es.*

Sights

Rock Art Center of Tito Bustillo

CAVE | Discovered in 1968, the cave here has 20,000-year-old paintings on a par with those in Lascaux, France, and Altamira. Giant horses and deer prance about the walls. To protect the paintings, no more than 375 visitors are allowed inside each day, so reservations are essential. The guided tour is in Spanish. Audioguides are available in English. There's also a museum of Asturian cave finds, open year-round. ✉ *Av. de Tito Bustillo,* ☎ *902/306600* 🌐 *www.centrotitobustillo.com* 🎟 *€5, free Wed.* 🕒 *Closed Mon., Tues., and Jan.*

Beaches

Playa de Santa Marina

BEACH | To the west of the Río Sella estuary, which divides the town, this gentle curve of golden sand is one of the prettiest beaches in Asturias. It's tucked beneath the town's seafront promenade, lined with 20th-century mansions. Moderate waves provide safe swimming conditions, although, as with all of Spain's Atlantic-facing beaches, currents and weather can be unpredictable. In high season (particularly in August) the beach can get very busy. This part of the coast is not called the "dinosaur coast" for nothing; over by the Punta'l Pozu Viewpoint, you can see footprints embedded in the rocks and cliff faces where they left their mark millions of years ago. Amenities listed are only available June–September. **Amenities:** food and drink; lifeguards; showers; toilets. **Best for:** surfing; swimming. ✉ *Paseo Agustin de Argüelles Marina, Ribadesella.*

Restaurants

Arbidel

$$$$ | **SPANISH** | This award-winning, modern Asturian restaurant in the old town is adorned with rustic stone walls and a hand-painted mural. There are also inventive tapas and a tasting menu (approximately €90). **Known for:** good-value tasting menus; apple gazpacho with sardines; experimental Asturian cuisine. [$] *Average main: €28* ✉ *Calle Oscuro 1, Ribadesella* ☎ *985/861440* 🌐 *www.arbidel.com* 🕒 *Closed Mon. No dinner Sun.–Thurs.*

Hotels

Hotel Ribadesella Playa

$$$ | **B&B/INN** | Spending a night in this restored turn-of-the-20th-century mansion on the beach is pleasant and peaceful: It's family run and has a timeless, stately charm that may remind you of black-and-white European art films. **Pros:** good breakfast; lovely views of the Cantabrian sea; proximity to the Tito Bustillo cave and the beach. **Cons:** noise from outside; limited availability in high season; some rooms are small. [$] *Rooms from: €130* ✉ *Calle Ricardo Cangas 3,*

Ribadesella ☎ 985/860715 ⊕ www.hotel-ribadesellaplaya.com ⊗ Closed Nov.–Mar. ⊅ 17 rooms †⊙| Free Breakfast.

Llanes

40 km (25 miles) east of Ribadesella.

This beach town is on a pristine stretch of the Costa Verde. The shores in both directions outside town have vistas of cliffs looming over white-sand beaches and isolated caves. A long canal connected to a small harbor cuts through the heart of Llanes, and along its banks rise colorful houses with glass galleries against a backdrop of the Picos de Europa. At the daily port-side fish market, usually held around 1 pm, vendors display heaps of freshly caught seafood.

GETTING HERE AND AROUND
The scenic A8 coastal route from Gijón continues past Villaviciosa and Ribadesella and then winds through Llanes before heading east toward Santander. FEVE trains and ALSA buses make the trip in 2–3½ hours.

VISITOR INFORMATION
CONTACTS Llanes Tourist Office. ⊠ Antigua Lonja de Pescado, Calle Marqués de Canillejas 1, ☎ 985/400164 ⊕ www.llanes.es.

Sights

Basílica de Santa María del Conceyu
CHURCH | This 13th-century church rising over the main square is an excellent example of Romantic Gothic architecture. ⊠ Pl. Christo Rey, Llanes ⊠ Free.

Mirador Panorámico La Boriza
VIEWPOINT | Dotting the Asturian coast east and west of Llanes are *bufones*, cavelike cavities that expel water when waves are sucked in. These active blowholes shoot streams of water as high as 100 feet at unpredictable intervals. They are clearly marked so you can find

them, and there are barriers to protect you when they expel water. There is one east of Playa Ballota; try to watch it in action from this mirador east of Llanes, between the villages of Cué and Andrin. If you miss the spurt, the view is still worth a stop—on a clear day you can see the coastline all the way east to Santander. ⊠ Llanes ⊠ Free.

Plaza Cristo Rey
PLAZA/SQUARE | Peaceful and well-conserved, this plaza marks the center of the old town, which is partially surrounded by the remains of its medieval walls. ⊠ Llanes.

Beaches

Playa Ballota
BEACH | One km (½ mile) east of Llanes is the pristine and secluded Playa Ballota, with private coves and one of the few stretches of nudist sand in Asturias. **Amenities:** food and drink (seasonal). **Best for:** nudists; swimming; walking. ⊠ Calle Ballota.

Playa de Torimbia
BEACH | Farther west of Llanes is the partially nudist Playa de Torimbia, a wild, virgin beach as yet untouched by development. It is reached only via a footpath—roughly a 15-minute walk. This secluded crescent of fine, white sand and crystal-clear waters is backed by Asturias's green hills, making it one of the region's most picturesque beaches. Winds can be strong, and there is no real infrastructure. **Amenities:** none. **Best for:** nudists; solitude; swimming; walking. ⊠ ⊹ Off C. Niembru, 8 km (5 miles) west of Llanes.

Playa de Toró
BEACH | On the eastern edge of town is Playa de Toró, where fine white sands are peppered with unique rock formations. This pristine beach is ideal for sunbathing and families. **Amenities:** lifeguards; showers; toilets. **Best for:** swimming. ⊠ Av. de Toró.

Hiking in the Picos de Europa

Playa del Sablón

BEACH | **FAMILY** | Steps from the old town is the protected Playa del Sablón (whose name derives from the Asturian word for "sand"), a little swath of beach that gets crowded on weekends. **Amenities:** food and drink; lifeguards; showers; toilets. **Best for:** swimming. ✉ *Calle Sablón, Llanes.*

🍴 Restaurants

La Casa del Mar

$ | **SEAFOOD** | If you feel like rubbing shoulders with Asturian fishermen—and eating their catch cooked just the way they like it—then this spot by the port is for you. The glassed-in terrace has a view of the small harbor bobbing with boats, and the menu offers such local classics as baby squid in ink sauce, spider crab, seafood meatballs, and razor clams, all with minimum fuss and maximum value. **Known for:** popular with locals; down-home seafood; €7 bottles of Albariño. [$] *Average main: €10* ✉ *Calle Muelle 4, Calle Marinero,* ☎ *985/401215.*

🛏 Hotels

Hotel Caeaclaveles

$$$ | **HOTEL** | This ultramodern eco-hotel in the woods is an architectural marvel with its grass-topped roof, sinuous walls, full-length windows, and polished-cement ceiling. **Pros:** quiet and scenic; award-winning architecture; plenty of natural light. **Cons:** decor pales in comparison to the exterior; no children under nine; somewhat remote, car needed. [$] *Rooms from: €130* ✉ *La Pereda, Carretera LLN-6, Km 2, Llanes* ☎ *985/925981* 🌐 *www.caeaclaveles.com* 🕓 *Closed mid-Dec.–mid-Jan.* 🛏 *5 rooms* 🍴 *Free Breakfast.*

La Posada de Babel

$$$ | **B&B/INN** | Outside Llanes, among oak, chestnut, and birch trees, you'll find this charming family-run inn with personalized attention and roaring fires in the public rooms. **Pros:** beautiful grounds; comfy base for hiking; amiable staff. **Cons:** room styles vary; closed in winter; tech could use a revamp. [$] *Rooms from: €130* ✉ *La Pereda, Llanes* ✣ *4*

km (2½ miles) southwest of Llanes ☎ *985/402525* 🌐 *www.laposadadebabel.com* 🕓 *Closed Dec.–Easter* 🛏 *12 rooms* 🍴 *Free Breakfast.*

Cangas de Onís

25 km (16 miles) south of Ribadesella, 70 km (43 miles) east of Oviedo.

The first capital of so-called Christian Spain, Cangas de Onís is also the nerve center of the Picos de Europa National Park. It's tucked into a narrow valley carved by the Sella River and has the feel of a mountain village.

VISITOR INFORMATION

CONTACTS Cangas de Onís Tourist Office. ✉ *Av. Covadonga 1, Cangas de Onís* ☎ *985/848043* 🌐 *www.turismocangasdeonis.com.*

Sights

Picos de Europa Visitor Center

VISITOR CENTER | To help plan your rambles, consult the scale model of the park outside the visitor center; staff inside can advise you on suitable routes. Stores on the same street sell English maps and guidebooks. ✉ *Pedro Pidal Visitor Center, Av. Covadonga 1, Cangas de Onís* ☎ *985/848614* 🌐 *www.parquenacionalpicoseuropa.es/english/visitor-centres.*

Puente Romano de Cangas de Onís

BRIDGE | A high, humpback medieval bridge (also known as the Puente Romano, or Roman Bridge, because of its style) spans the Río Sella gorge with a reproduction of Pelayo's Victory Cross, or La Cruz de la Victoria, dangling underneath. ✉ *Cangas de Onís.*

Restaurants

Restaurante Los Arcos

$$ | **SPANISH** | On one of the town's main squares, this busy smart-casual restaurant decorated in whites and grays serves local cider, fine Spanish wines, and honest regional dishes. The well-priced lunch menu features mouthwatering *revueltos* (scrambled eggs with add-ins), seafood, and stews. **Known for:** scrambled eggs with blood sausage; great value; over 40 local cheeses. [$] *Average main: €15* ✉ *Hotel Los Lagos Nature, Pl. Camila Beceña 3, Cangas de Onís* ☎ *985/849277* 🌐 *www.loslagosnature.com/restauranteLosArcos.*

Hotels

Hotel Posada del Valle

$ | **B&B/INN** | A British couple converted this 19th-century stone farmhouse into an idyllic hillside inn with stunning views of the Picos. **Pros:** surrounded by nature; wealth of local knowledge at your fingertips; views of the Picos. **Cons:** restaurant does not serve lunch; limited breakfast; remote and difficult to find. [$] *Rooms from: €88* ✉ *Collía, Cangas de Onís* ☎ *985/841157* 🌐 *www.posadadelvalle.com* 🕓 *Closed Nov.–Mar.* 🛏 *12 rooms* 🍴 *Free Breakfast.*

★ Parador de Cangas de Onís

$$$ | **HOTEL** | On the banks of the Río Sella just west of Cangas, this friendly parador is made up of an 18th-century Benedictine monastery and a modern wing. **Pros:** grounds steeped in history; gorgeous riverside location and mountain views; notable restaurant. **Cons:** chilly corridors; limited menu not suited to vegetarians; rooms on lower floor can be noisy. [$] *Rooms from: €130* ✉ *Monasterio de San Pedro de Villanueva, Villanueva, Ctra. N625, Cangas de Onís* ✥ *From N634 take right turn for Villanueva* ☎ *985/849402* 🌐 *www.parador.es* 🕓 *Closed Jan.–Mar.* 🛏 *64 rooms* 🍴 *Free Breakfast.*

Activities

The tourist office in Cangas de Onís can help you organize a Picos de Europa trek. The Picos visitor center in Cangas has general information, audiovisual

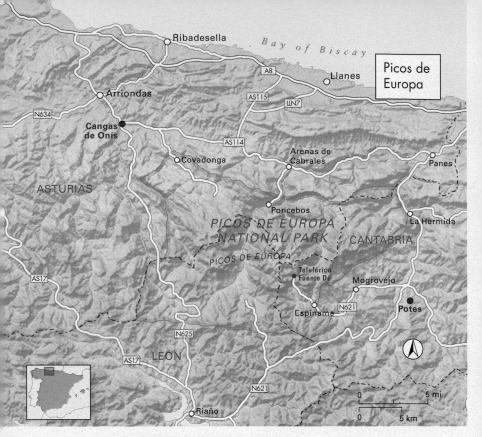

components, route maps, and a useful scale model of the range.

Astursella Aventura

RAFTING | This outdoor adventure company specializes in canoeing, rafting, and canyon rappelling in and around the Río Güeña. ✉ *Ramón Prada Vicente 3, Cangas de Onís* ☎ *985/848370* ⊕ *www. astursellaaventura.com.*

Cangas Aventura Turismo Activo

MOUNTAIN CLIMBING | Rafting, canoeing, jet-skiing, climbing, trekking, horseback riding, paintballing, and snowshoeing packages are all available here. ✉ *Av. Covadonga 17 Bajo, Cangas de Onís* ☎ *985/849261* ⊕ *www.cangasaventura. com.*

Potes

115 km (69 miles) southwest of Santander, 81 km (50 miles) southeast of Cangas de Onís.

Famed for its cheeses, the region of La Liébana is a highland domain whose main city is Potes. Potes is named for its ancient bridges and is known for the stunning 9th-century **monasteries** of Santo Toribio de Liébana, Lebeña, and Piasca that dot its perimeter. The gorges of the Desfiladero de la Hermida pass are 13 km (8 miles) north, and the rustic town of Mogrovejo is on the way to the vertiginous cable car at Fuente Dé, 10 km (6 miles) west of Potes.

GETTING HERE AND AROUND

Potes is just over two hours from Gijón and Oviedo via the A8, and 1½ hours from Santander via the A8 and N621.

VISITOR INFORMATION

CONTACTS Potes Tourist Office. ✉ *Pl. la Serna, Potes* ☎ *942/730787* 🌐 *www.ayuntamientodepotes.es.*

Sights

Teleférico Fuente Dé

VIEWPOINT | As you approach the parador of Fuente Dé, at the head of the valley northwest of the hamlet of Espinama, you'll see a wall of gray rock jutting 6,560 feet into the air. At the top is a tiny hut: El Mirador del Cable (the cable-car lookout point). Get there via a 2,625-foot funicular (€18 round-trip). After you exit the funicular, you can hike along the Ávila Mountain pasturelands, rich in wildlife, between the central and eastern massifs of the Picos. There's an official entrance to Picos de Europa National Park here. ✉ *Potes* ☎ *942/736610* 🌐 *entradas.telefericofuentede.com.*

Restaurants

★ El Bodegón

$$ | **SPANISH** | An invitingly cozy space awaits behind the ancient stone facade of this restaurant, 200 meters from the main plaza. Part of the house is original, but much has been renovated, providing an attractive combination of traditional mountain design and modern construction. **Known for:** affordable mountain cooking; standout wines; popular spot. [$] *Average main: €15* ✉ *Calle San Roque 4, Potes* ☎ *942/730247* 🕒 *Closed Wed.*

Hotels

Hotel del Oso

$$ | **HOTEL** | **FAMILY** | This homey and economical lodge is the perfect base for exploring the Picos de Europa. **Pros:** swimming pool and tennis court; dependably good restaurant; convenient base for hiking. **Cons:** lower floor rooms can be noisy; decor is outdated; some rooms are on the small side. [$] *Rooms from: €92* ✉ *Cosgaya, Potes* ☎ *942/733018* 🌐 *www.hoteldeloso.es* 🕒 *Closed Dec. 15–Feb. 15* 🛏 *49 rooms* 🍴 *Free Breakfast.*

Hotel Valdecoro

$ | **B&B/INN** | In this family-run mountain house, which faces the main road through town, efficient staff tend to guest rooms with modern appointments, making for a pleasant stay. **Pros:** lounge with a fireplace; cozy mountain feel; fine rustic restaurant. **Cons:** rooms are tidy but unremarkable; on the main road; no air conditioning. [$] *Rooms from: €78* ✉ *Rte. Paco Wences, Calle Roscabao, Potes* ☎ *942/730025* 🌐 *www.hotelvaldecoro.es* 🕒 *Closed Jan. and Feb.* 🛏 *41 rooms* 🍴 *Free Breakfast.*

Santander

390 km (242 miles) north of Madrid, 154 km (96 miles) north of Burgos, 116 km (72 miles) west of Bilbao, 194 km (120 miles) northeast of Oviedo.

One of the great ports on the Bay of Biscay, Santander is surrounded by busy beaches, yet it manages to avoid the package-tour feel of many Spanish seaside resorts. A fire destroyed most of the old town in 1941, so the rebuilt city looks relatively modern. It comes to life in summer, when its music-and-dance festival draws students, tourists, and performers.

From the 1st to the 4th century, Roman Santander—then called Portus Victoriae—was a major port. Commercial life accelerated between the 13th and 16th centuries, but the waning of Spain's naval power and a series of plagues during the reign of Felipe II caused its fortunes to plummet. The economy was restarted after 1778, when Seville's monopoly on trade with the Americas was revoked and Santander entered fully into commerce with the so-called New World. In 1910 the Palacio de la Magdalena was built by popular subscription as a gift to Alfonso XIII and his queen, Victoria Eugenia, lending Santander prestige as one of Spain's royal watering holes.

The modern city benefits from several promenades and gardens, most of which face the bay. Walk east along the Paseo de Pereda, the main boulevard, to Puerto Chico, a small yacht harbor. Then follow Avenida Reina Victoria to find the tree-lined park paths above the first of the city's beaches, Playa de la Magdalena. Walk onto the Península de la Magdalena to the Palacio de la Magdalena, today the summer seat of the University of Menéndez y Pelayo. Beyond the Magdalena Peninsula, wealthy locals occupy mansions facing the long stretch of shoreline known as El Sardinero, Santander's best beach.

CRUISE SHIP TRAVEL TO SANTANDER, SPAIN

Ferries dock at the passenger terminal, Estación Marítima, which is downtown. Facilities inside the terminal include a supermarket, café, and tourist information desk. The main tourist office is on Jardines de Pereda. The old town and commercial shopping area are both a short, easy walk away.

There are plenty of hotels close to the port, but consider overnighting in the more scenic Playa del Sardinero beach area; it's 5–10 minutes away from the center via taxi. Metered taxis can be hailed at the entrance of the terminal, and a one-way trip to Playa del Sardinero costs less than €12 (luggage usually costs extra). In Spain it is not customary to tip taxi drivers, but if you want to leave something, rounding up by €1 or €2 is acceptable. The train station (Plaza de las Estaciones) is about a 10-minute walk, and from here you can reach any of Spain's major cities. Local and national buses departing from the Estación de Autobuses (Calle Naveas de Tolosa) run to nearby destinations including Santillana del Mar, a 30-minute drive away.

GETTING HERE AND AROUND
Santander is easily navigated on foot, but if you're looking to get to El Sardinero beach, hail a taxi or take the bus from the central urban transport hub at Jardines de Pereda.

CONTACTS Santander Bus Station. ✉ *Calle Navas de Tolosa,* ☎ *942/211995.* **Santander Train Station.** ✉ *Pl. de las Estaciones, Santander* ☎ *912/320320 Renfe* ⊕ *www.renfe.com.*

VISITOR INFORMATION
CONTACTS Santander Tourist Office. ✉ *Jardines de Pereda,* ☎ *942/203000* ⊕ *turismo.santander.es.*

 ## Sights

Catedral de Santander
CHURCH | The blocky cathedral marks the transition between Romanesque and Gothic. Though largely rebuilt in the neo-Gothic style after serious damage in the town's 1941 fire, the cathedral retained its 12th-century crypt. The chief attraction here is the tomb of Marcelino Menéndez y Pelayo (1856–1912), Santander's most famous literary figure. The cathedral is across Avenida de Calvo Sotelo from the Plaza Porticada. ✉ *Calle de Somorrostro, Santander* 🔊 *€1.*

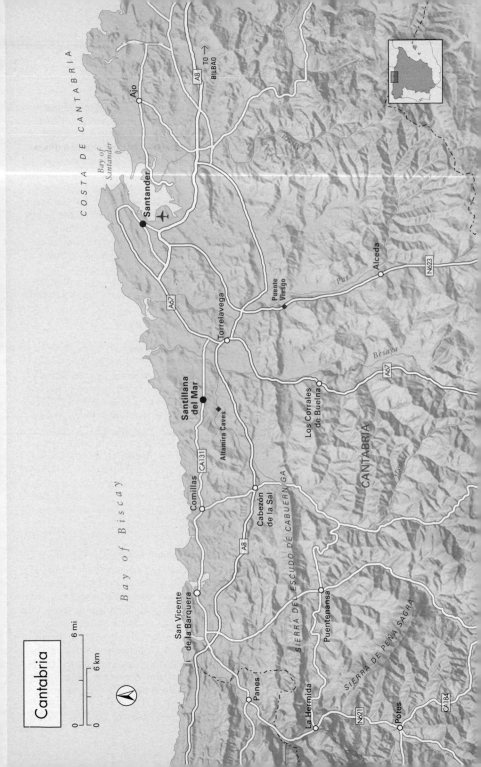

★ Centro Botín

ARTS CENTER | Inaugurated in 2017, this futuristic museum and performance center designed by architect Renzo Piano was the biggest cultural opening in northern Spain in recent memory. It houses contemporary artwork by international artists. Worth a visit for the eye-popping architecture and views alone, the building overlooks the harbor and is surrounded by the Jardines de Pereda. There is a café on-site as well as two viewing decks accessible free of charge. ✉ *Jardines de Pereda, Muelle de Albareda, Santander* ☎ *942/047147* 🌐 *www.centrobotin.org/en* 🎫 *€10, viewpoint free* 🕒 *Closed Mon. (except mid-July–Aug.).*

Gran Casino del Sardinero

CASINO | This elegant Belle Époque casino and restaurant—worth a quick visit even if gambling isn't your thing—is the heart of El Sardinero, the vacationer's quarter west of the old city. You can't miss it with its regal white facade, red awnings, and pleasant tree-shaded park. Around it you'll find expensive hotels and several fine restaurants. ✉ *Pl. de Italia, Santander* ☎ *942/276054* 🌐 *www.grancasinosardinero.es* 🎫 *€3.*

Palacio de la Magdalena

CASTLE/PALACE | Built on the highest point of the Peninsula de Magdalena and surrounded by 62 acres of manicured gardens and rocky beaches, this early-20th-century palace is the most distinctive building in Santander. It was originally a summer home for King Alfonso XIII and Queen Victoria Eugenia, and it has architectural influences from France and England. Today it is a venue for meetings, weddings, and classes. There are also daily guided visits—call in advance to schedule a tour in English. ✉ *Av. Magdalena,* ☎ *942/203084* 🌐 *www.palaciomagdalena.com* 🎫 *€5.*

Beaches

Playa El Sardinero

BEACH | Santander's longest and most popular beach has a full range of amenities and fine, golden sand. Although this northeast-facing stretch is exposed, moderate waves in summer make it fine for bathing—despite the chilly water temperatures. In winter, it is a favorite among surfers, particularly the part of the beach in front of Hotel Chiqui. Enter the beach via the sun-dappled Piquío Gardens, where terraces filled with flowers and trees lead the way down to the beach. **Amenities:** food and drink; lifeguards; showers; toilets; water sports. **Best for:** surfing; swimming; walking. ✉ *Santander.*

Restaurants

Bodega del Riojano

$$$ | **SPANISH** | The paintings on wine-barrel ends that decorate this classic restaurant have given it the nickname "Museo Redondo" (Round Museum). The building dates back to the 16th century, when it was a wine cellar, apparent in the heavy wooden beams overhead and the rough, rustic tables. **Known for:** friendly service; elevated traditional Cantabrian and Riojan fare; historic setting. [$] *Average main: €19* ✉ *Calle Río de la Pila 5, Santander* ☎ *942/216750* 🌐 *www.bodegadelriojano.com* 🕒 *No dinner Sun.*

El Serbal

$$$$ | **SPANISH** | Five blocks from the marina, this white-tablecloth dining room with blue walls and hardwood floors pulls out all the stops: Order the tasting menu, for instance, and you'll sample no fewer than five varieties of olive oil. Mains hinge on Cantabrian seafood and run the gamut from cod *al pil pil* (with an emulsified garlic-oil sauce) to flambéed suckling pig to scallop tartare. **Known for:** elegant dining room; pristine seafood; well-executed tasting menu. [$] *Average main: €25* ✉ *Calle de Andrés del Rio 7, Santander*

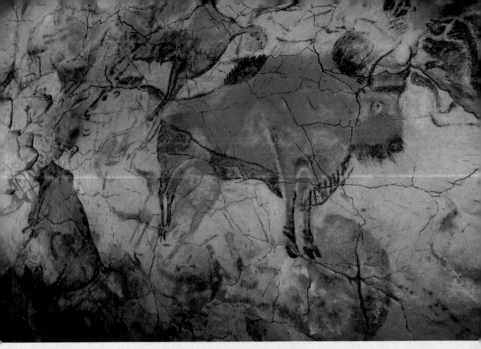

The Altamira Museum's replica of a Paleolithic cave displays paintings of bison.

☎ *942/222515* ⊕ *www.elserbal.com* ⊗ *Closed Mon. No dinner Sun.*

★ La Casona del Judío

$$$$ | **SPANISH** | While the à la carte menu at this tasteful fine-dining establishment is exquisite, the real draw here are the tasting menus (€52 and €68), which offer a whirlwind tour of modern Cantabrian cooking at a phenomenal value. Request a table in the romantically lit brick wine cellar, and savor such delicacies as roast partridge with celery root puree, griddled tiger prawns, and ultra-creamy rice pudding. **Known for:** chatty chef; modern Cantabrian cuisine; tasting menus. $ *Average main: €24* ⊠ *Calle de Repuente 20, Santander* ☎ *942/342726* ⊕ *www.casonadeljudio.com* ⊗ *Closed Mon. No dinner Sun.*

 Hotels

Abba Santander Hotel

$$ | **HOTEL** | Abba Santander is a chain hotel with welcoming staff and modern conveniences. **Pros:** intriguing architectural details; cheerful service; central location. **Cons:** busy part of town; beds may be too firm for some; additional cost for parking. $ *Rooms from: €100* ⊠ *Calle Calderón de la Barca 3, Santander* ☎ *942/212450, 942/091516 bookings* ⊕ *www.abbahoteles.com/en/destinations/abba-santander-hotel/hotel.html* ⇌ *37 rooms* ⫶◯⫶ *Free Breakfast.*

Hotel Bahía

$$ | **HOTEL** | One of Santander's best-rated hotels is this plush, traditional standby overlooking the water and the cathedral. **Pros:** friendly service; great for watching maritime traffic; central location. **Cons:** outdated interiors; bells can be noisy on the cathedral side; no gym. $ *Rooms from: €120* ⊠ *Calle Cádiz 22, Santander* ☎ *902/570627* ⊕ *www.hotelbahias-antander.com* ⇌ *188 rooms* ⫶◯⫶ *No Meals.*

Las Brisas

$$$ | **B&B/INN** | This aparthotel used to be an aristocratic family's mansion by the sea. **Pros:** defiantly un-corporate; close to the shore; charming Old World feel. **Cons:**

some rooms are a bit cramped; mildly disorganized; 30-minute walk from the city center. $ *Rooms from: €139* ✉ *Calle la Braña 14, El Sardinero* ☎ *942/270111* ⊕ *www.hotellasbrisas.net* ⊘ *Closed Dec. 15–Feb. 15* ⇄ *13 rooms* ⦿ *Free Breakfast.*

Nightlife

Most people start their evening in the tapas bars and taverns in and around Plaza de Cañadío, and Calle Hernán Cortés. Night owls continue on to Calle del Sol and Calle de Santa Lucía, which have pleasant spots for late-night drinking, some with live music.

Cañadío

BARS | An after-work favorite, Cañadío draws a lively evening crowd for tempting tapas and chilled beer on tap. ✉ *Calle de Gómez Oreña 15, Santander* ☎ *942/314149* ⊕ *www.restaurantecanadio.com.*

🛍 Shopping

For most items, head to the center: The streets around the *ayuntamiento* (town hall) are good for clothing, shoes, and sportswear. At the bustling Mercado de la Esperanza, just behind the ayuntamiento, you can find fish and shellfish that have been freshly plucked from the Cantabrian Sea as well as locally produced cheeses, cured sausages, and tinned fish. Open-air fruit and vegetable stalls mark the entrance.

Mantequerías Cántabras

FOOD | Local delicacies—including Santander's most famed dessert, *sobaos pasiegos* (fluffy buttery cakes)—are sold here. ✉ *Mercado del Este, Calle Hernán Cortés 4, Santander* ☎ *942/074787* ⊘ *Closed Sun.*

Puente Viesgo

In 1903, four caves were discovered in this 16th-century hamlet in the Pas Valley under the 1,150-foot peak of Monte del Castillo. Two of these—Cueva del Castillo and Cueva de las Monedas—are open to the public. Bison, deer, bulls, and humanoid stick figures are depicted within the caves; the oldest designs are thought to be 35,000 years old. Most arresting are the paintings of 44 hands (35 of them remain). The painters are thought to have blown red pigment around their hands through a hollow bone, leaving the negative image. Reservations are essential via *cuevas.culturadecantabria.com.*

Santillana del Mar

29 km (18 miles) west of Santander.

Santillana del Mar has a thriving tourism industry, thanks to cave art discovered 2 km (1 mile) north of town. The town itself is worth a visit of at least a day. Just as the Altamira Caves have captured the essence of prehistoric life, the streets, plazas, taverns, and manor houses of Santillana del Mar paint a vivid portrait of medieval and Renaissance village life in northern Spain. Its stunning ensemble of 15th- to 17th-century stone houses is one of Spain's greatest architectural collections.

VISITOR INFORMATION

CONTACTS Santillana del Mar Tourist Office. ✉ *Calle Jesús Otero 20, Santillana del Mar* ☎ *942/818812* ⊕ *www.santillanadelmarturismo.com.*

Sights

Altamira Caves

CAVE | These world-famous caves, 3 km (2 miles) southwest of Santillana del Mar, have been called the Sistine Chapel of prehistoric art for the beauty of their drawings, believed to be some 18,000 years old. First uncovered in 1875, the caves are a testament to early mankind's admiration of beauty and surprising technical skill in representing it, especially in the use of rock forms to accentuate perspective. All visitors are entered into a lottery for tickets to enter the actual caves, yet only five are allowed in each week. The reproduction in the museum, however, is open to all. ✉ *Museo de Altamira, Marcelino Sanz de Sautuola, Santillana del Mar* ☎ *942/818005* 🌐 *museodealtamira.mcu.es* 🎟 *€3 (free Sat. afternoon and Sun.)* 🕒 *Closed Mon.*

Colegiata de Santa Juliana

CHURCH | Santillana del Mar is built around the Colegiata, Cantabria's finest Romanesque structure. Highlights include the 12th-century cloister, famed for its sculpted capitals, a 16th-century altarpiece, and the tomb of Santa Juliana, who is the town's patron saint and namesake. ✉ *Pl. las Arenas 1A, Santillana del Mar* ☎ *639/830520* 🎟 *€3.*

Museo Diocesano

OTHER MUSEUM | Inside the 16th-century Regina Coeli convent is a museum devoted to liturgical art including wooden figures of saints, oil paintings of biblical scenes, altarpieces, and a collection of plundered treasures from the so-called New World. ✉ *Calle El Cruce, Santillana del Mar* ☎ *942/840317* 🎟 *€3* 🕒 *Closed Mon.*

Hotels

★ Parador de Santillana Gil Blas

$$$ | **HOTEL** | Built in the 16th century, this imposing stone palace has baronial rooms with heavy wooden beams and splendid antique furnishings. **Pros:** attentive service; storybook surroundings; opulent decor. **Cons:** drafty in winter; expensive; noise carries from the square into the rooms. [$] *Rooms from: €175* ✉ *Pl. Ramón Pelayo 11, Santillana del Mar* ☎ *942/028028* 🌐 *www.parador.es* 🛏 *28 rooms* 🍴 *No Meals.*

Posada La Casa del Organista

$$ | **B&B/INN** | A typical *casona montañesa* (mountain manor) with painstakingly crafted stone and wood details, this intimate, gentlemanly hideaway makes a comfortable base for exploring the town and surrounding countryside. **Pros:** good base; lovely views of tiled roofs and rolling hills; immaculately clean. **Cons:** no elevator; some rooms are small; difficult to book in high season. [$] *Rooms from: €96* ✉ *Calle Los Hornos 4, Santillana del Mar* ☎ *942/840352* 🌐 *www.casadelorganista.com* 🕒 *Closed Dec. 21–Jan. 20* 🛏 *14 rooms* 🍴 *No Meals.*

Chapter 6

THE BASQUE COUNTRY, NAVARRA, AND LA RIOJA

Updated by
Benjamin Kemper

◉ **Sights**
★★★★★

🍴 **Restaurants**
★★★★★

🛏 **Hotels**
★★★★☆

🛍 **Shopping**
★★★★☆

🍸 **Nightlife**
★★★☆☆

WELCOME TO THE BASQUE COUNTRY, NAVARRA, AND LA RIOJA

TOP REASONS TO GO

★ **Explore the Basque coast:** From colorful fishing villages to tawny beaches, the dramatic Basque coast always delights the eye.

★ **Eat *pintxos* (bar snacks) in San Sebastián:** Nothing matches San Sebastián's Parte Vieja, where tavern-hoppers graze at counters heaped with eye-catching morsels.

★ **Appreciate Bilbao's art and architecture:** The gleaming titanium Guggenheim and the Museo de Bellas Artes (Fine Arts Museum) shimmer where steel mills and shipyards once stood, while verdant pastures can be seen in the distance.

★ **Swirl and sip your way through La Rioja:** Spain's most prestigious wine region takes in ancient cobwebbed *bodegas* and architectural wonders.

★ **Splurge on an avant-garde tasting menu:** Few areas on earth boast such a high concentration of renowned chefs making delicious, innovative food.

Inland from the Bay of Biscay, on the border with France, The Basque Country, Navarra, and La Rioja are a Spain apart, a land of dewy green hills, sprawling vineyards, and rocky meadowlands. These regions occupy a fertile slot situated between the Picos de Europa and the Pyrenees mountain ranges and are a cool, rainy reprieve from the sun-scorched Spanish *meseta* (high plain) to the south.

1 Bilbao. Go for the Guggenheim; stay for the pintxos and the quaint old town.

2 Bermeo. Take a peek at the most important fishing port in the Basque Country.

3 Mundaka. Surf with the pros.

4 Axpe Atxondo. Live your Basque rural fantasy in a tiny mountain town.

5 Getaria and Zumaia. Explore Balenciaga's old stomping grounds and taste the grilled turbot that Anthony Bourdain made famous.

6 San Sebastián. Make a pilgrimage to Spain's culinary mecca with more Michelin stars per capita than (almost) any other city on earth.

7 Vitoria-Gasteiz. Experience true-blue Basque culture without a tour bus in sight in the region's gritty industrial capital.

8 Laguardia. Savor world-class wine in ultra-modern tasting rooms.

9 Pasaia. Slow down in a sleepy fishing village just a few minutes' drive from San Sebastián.

10 Hondarribia. Stroll among colorful captains' houses before hopping on a ferry to France.

11 Pamplona. Visit this Hemingway haunt, known for the running of the bulls and its Navarran culture.

12 Logroño. Make this scrappy, food-focused city your home base for enological adventures in La Rioja.

13 La Rioja Alta. Hop from bodega (winery) to bodega in La Rioja's most coveted wine-producing area.

14 Haro. Hole up in La Rioja's most wine-centric town, and feast on local roast lamb.

15 Sierra Rioja Alta. Hike, ski, and discover untamed nature in the Riojan highlands.

6

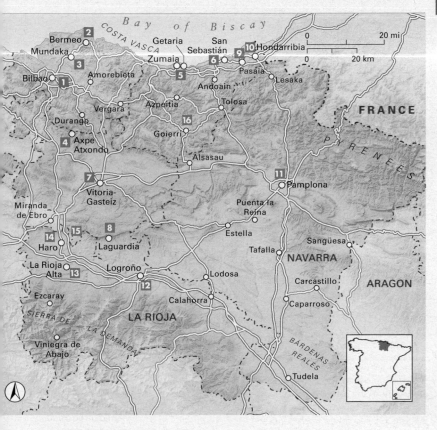

EATING AND DRINKING WELL IN THE BASQUE COUNTRY

A nueva cocina interpretation of the classic bacalao al pil pil.

Basque cuisine, Spain's most prestigious regional gastronomy, incorporates the refined culinary sensibilities of the French and the no-nonsense country cooking of inland Iberia, but it's no hybrid cuisine.

The distinctive seafood, meat, and vegetable dishes served here are often impossible to find elsewhere in Spain, thanks to hyperlocal ingredients and culinary secrets passed down from generation to generation.

The so-called *Nueva Cocina Vasca* (New Basque Cuisine) movement began more than 40 years ago as an echo of the nouvelle cuisine of France. Young chefs like Pedro Subijana and Juan Mari Arzak began deconstructing versions of classic Basque dishes like *marmitako* (tuna and potato stew) and *bacalao al pil pil* (salt cod bathed in emulsified garlic sauce) with the aim to redefine and promote Basque cooking globally. Today the region has the world's second-highest concentration of Michelin stars per capita. Although the core of Basque cooking hinges on the art of preparing fish, there is no dearth of lamb, beef, or pork in the Basque diet.

CIDER

Don't miss a chance to go to a *sagardotegi*, a boisterous cider house where the cider spurts into your glass straight from the barrel to be quaffed in a single gulp. *Txuletas de buey* (juicy rib eyes grilled over coals) and *tortilla de bacalao* (cod omelet) provide ballast for the rustic apple cider. The cider-cod combination is linked to the Basque fishermen and whalers who carried cider, rather than wine, in their galleys.

BABY EELS

Angulas, known as elvers in English, are a Basque delicacy that has become an expensive treat, with prices reaching €1,000 a kilogram. The 3- to 4-inch-long eels look like spaghetti with eyes and are typically served in a small earthenware dish sizzling with olive oil, garlic, and a single slice of chili. A special wooden fork is used to eat them, to avoid any metallic taste and because the wood grips the slippery eels better than metal. Don't be misled by the "gulas" sold in lower-end *tapas* bars and groceries across Spain: They look just like angulas, but they're made from processed whitefish.

BACALAO

Cod, a Basque favorite since the Stone Age, comes in various guises. *Bacalao al pil pil* is a classic Bilbao specialty, simmered—rather than fried—with garlic and olive oil in its own juices. The "pil pil" refers to the sound of the emulsion of cod and olive oil bubbling up from the bottom of the pan. Served with a red chili pepper, this is a beloved Basque delicacy.

BESUGO A LA DONOSTIARRA

Besugo (sea bream) cooked San Sebastián style is baked in the oven, covered with flakes of garlic that look like scales, and enlivened at the last minute with vinegar and parsley.

A colorful bowl of marmitako.

OX

Traditionally the ox was a beast of burden in the Basque Country, fed and maintained with reverence and care, but today the term *buey* (ox) is synonymous with good eating. When slaughtered at the age of 12 or 13, oxen's flesh is tender and marbled with streaks of fat rich with grassy aromas. Nowadays, most steaks marketed as *txuletas de buey* (ox steaks) are in fact cut from beef—inaccurately labeled but delicious nonetheless.

TUNA AND POTATO STEW

Marmitako, the Basque answer to bouillabaisse, is a stick-to-your-ribs potato, yellowfin tuna, and red pepper stew. Beware: it sometimes has a strong fishy taste. One bite, and you'll understand why the dish, named after the French for cooking pot (*marmite*), has long been the preferred restorative for weather-beaten seafarers.

WINE

Basque Txakoli, a simple, zippy white (and, increasingly, rosé) made from tart indigenous grapes, is refreshing with seafood and *pintxos.* Those who prefer a Basque red should spring for a Tempranillo from Rioja Alavesa, the part of Rioja wine country north of the Ebro.

An expensive plate of angulas.

Northern Spain is a misty land of green hills, low russet rooflines, and colorful fishing villages; it's also home to the formerly industrial city of Bilbao, reborn as a center of art and architecture. The semiautonomous Basque Country—which spills over the French border—has a verdant landscape and a rugged coastline, and a distinct national and cultural entity.

The Navarra region is considered Basque in the Pyrenees—indeed, Euskera is spoken in much of the region's north, and Navarran is spoken in the south. La Rioja, tucked between the Sierra de la Demanda (a mountain range that separates La Rioja from the central Castilian steppe) and the Ebro, is Spain's premier wine country.

Called the País Vasco in Castilian Spanish and Euskadi in the linguistically mysterious, non-Indo-European Basque language, Euskera, the Basque region is essentially a country within a country, or a nation within a state (the semantics are much debated). Though a significant portion of Basques still favor independence from Spain, the separatist terrorist organization ETA (Euskadi Ta Askatasuna, meaning "Basque Homeland and Liberty"), which used to cause some travelers pause, officially disbanded on May 2, 2018. There have been no significant politically motivated acts of violence in the region in years.

Basque culture, with its pre-Roman roots, is unlike that of any other region in Spain. In local festivals, locals play such rural sports as chopping mammoth tree trunks and lifting boulders. The Basques' competitive streak carries over into poetry and gastronomy; *bertsolariak* (amateur poets) improvise duels of sharp-witted verse, and gastronomic societies compete in cooking contests to see who can make the best *sopa de ajo* (garlic soup) or *marmitako*.

It's worth noting that the French Basque Country is not covered in this guide; we cover only the Spanish provinces. In addition, although most locales and subjects in this chapter have both Basque and Castilian (Spanish) spellings, we've given preference to what we consider to be the most widely used name (e.g., pintxos, not pinchos, and San Sebastián, not "Donosti").

MAJOR REGIONS

Bilbao and inland Basque Country. Starring the futuristic Museo Guggenheim Bilbao, Frank Gehry's titanium brainchild, Bilbao is one of Spain's artistic hot spots. The Basque capital city of Vitoria, by contrast, has intriguing medieval architecture and is relatively undiscovered by tourists.

San Sebastián and the Basque Coast. East along the Bay of Biscay toward Gipuzkoa province and San Sebastián, colorful fishing villages and beach towns appear one after the other on the snaking BI-3438 coastal highway. Weaving through dewy forests and punctuated with jaw-dropping views of the Atlantic, this is one of the most scenic drives in Spain. After passing the sleepy port of Getaria and a handful of well-to-do resorts, you'll arrive in San Sebastián, Bilbao's aristocratic cousin, a city that invites you to slow down with its elegant boardwalks and leisurely pintxo crawls. East of the city is Pasaia (Spanish: Pasajes), from which the Marquis de Lafayette set off to help the rebel forces in the American Revolution and where Victor Hugo spent a winter writing. Just shy of the French border is Hondarribia, a brightly painted, flower-festooned port town.

Navarra and Pamplona. Bordering the French Pyrenees and populated largely by Basques, Navarra grows progressively less Basque toward its southern and eastern edges. Pamplona, the ancient Navarrese capital, draws crowds with its annual feast of San Fermín. Olite, south of Pamplona, has a storybook castle. The towns of Puente la Reina and Estella are visually indelible stops on the Camino de Santiago.

La Rioja (named for the Río Oja), a rugged compendium of highlands, plains, and vineyards nourished by the Río Ebro, is synonymous with fine wine. Most inhabitants live along the Ebro, in the cities of Logroño and Haro, though the mountains and upper river valleys are arguably more scenic. A mix of Atlantic and Mediterranean climates, and cultures with Basque overtones, La Rioja comprises La Rioja Alta (Upper Rioja), the moist and mountainous western end (where most of the region's great wines come from), and La Rioja Baja (Lower Rioja), the dryer eastern extremity with a more Mediterranean climate and less prestigious wines. Logroño, the scruffy regional capital, straddles the two.

Planning

When to Go

Relatively clear skies and warm temperatures last from mid-April to mid-October, making the warm-weather months the best time of year to visit. Some shops and restaurants close in August.

Pamplona in July is bedlam, though for hard-core party animals it's heaven.

The Basque Country is rainy in the winter, but the bracing Atlantic weather can be invigorating if you're in the right mindset. Basque cuisine's heartiest, richest dishes taste their best when it's cold and damp outside—case in point: the menus at traditional cider houses, which (for the most part) are only available January to mid-May.

The September film festival in San Sebastián coincides with the spectacular whaleboat regattas, while the beaches are still ideal and mostly uncrowded.

When looking for a place to stay, remember that the north is an expensive, well-to-do part of Spain, which is reflected in room rates—though some steals can be found in the off-season (and on Airbnb). San Sebastián is particularly pricey, and Pamplona rates triple during San Fermín in July. Be sure to book far ahead for summer travel.

Planning Your Time

A road trip through the Basque Country, Navarra, and La Rioja requires at least a week, but you can get a good sense of Bilbao and San Sebastián, the region's most essential cities, in two days each.

The Baztán Valley, Pamplona, Laguardia, and La Rioja's capital, Logroño, are other top stops.

If you have a spare day or two, visit Mundaka and the coast of Bizkaia west of Bilbao; Getaria, Pasaia, and Hondarribia near San Sebastián; and the wineries of Haro in La Rioja.

La Rioja's also has some of the finest mountain landscapes in Spain in Sierra de la Demanda, and worthwhile culinary pilgrimages in the "gastronomical hotel" Echaurren in Ezcaray and Venta Moncalvillo in the village of Daroca.

There's also much more to this area's festival scene than the world-famous San Fermín and its running of the bulls in Pamplona. From music and dance festivals to colorful religious processions to quirky food fairs like the Getaria Anchovy Festival, there are lots of events that can be worth planning a trip around (*see "On the Calendar" in Travel Smart*).

Getting Here and Around

AIR
Bilbao's airport serves much of this area, and there are smaller, notoriously expensive airports at Hondarribia (serving San Sebastián), Logroño, and Pamplona, which are generally only used by domestic carriers in high season.

AIRPORTS Aeropuerto de Bilbao. ✉ *48180 Loiu, Bilbao* ⊕ *www.aena.es.*

BICYCLE
Bicycle travel in the Basque Country and across the north of Spain is hilly and often wet, but for the iron-hearted, -lunged, -legged, and-bottomed, this is a scenic way to travel and terrific exercise, albeit somewhat perilous on the region's narrow roads.

BUS
Frequent coach bus service connects the major cities to Madrid, Zaragoza, and Barcelona (with a layover or transfer to Spain's other destinations). The trip between Barcelona and Bilbao takes seven to eight hours.

Public bus service between cities and smaller towns is surprisingly comprehensive—and cheap. Consult Google Maps or visit a local tourist office for route information.

CAR
Even the remotest points are an easy one-day drive from Madrid, and northern Spain is well-connected by freeways.

The drive from Madrid to Bilbao is 397 km (247 miles), about five hours; follow the A1 past Burgos to Miranda del Ebro, where you pick up the AP68. Car rentals are available in the major cities: Bilbao, Pamplona, San Sebastián, Hondarribia, and Vitoria. Note: The Basque word for calle is "kalea." We have standardized our addresses using "Calle" for ease of Google Mapping, but you will see Kalea on road signs in most Basque locales.

TAXI
In cities, taxis can usually be hailed on the street, and drivers are generally amenable to longer trips (say, from San Sebastián to Astigarraga's cider houses).

TRAIN
Currently only snail-speed old RENFE trains connect Madrid to Bilbao, San Sebastián, and Logroño. The much-anticipated "Y Vasca" AVE route—over 20 years in the making and expected to be completed in 2026—will make the trip much quicker. Once you've arrived, a car is the most convenient way to get around, but the regional company FEVE runs a delightful narrow-gauge train that winds through stunning landscapes. From San Sebastián, lines west to Bilbao (the Euskotren) and east to Hendaye, France, depart from Estación de Amara; most long-distance trains use RENFE's Estación del Norte.

See the Travel Smart chapter for more information about train travel.

RIDESHARE

If you don't have a car, the fastest and cheapest way to get from Madrid or Barcelona to major destinations in the Basque Country, Navarra, and La Rioja is via the Blablacar rideshare platform, which boasts more worldwide users than Uber. Simply type your origin and destination into the app, select the itinerary that best suits your schedule, and confirm your booking via credit card. You can then text with the driver to arrange pickup and drop-off locations. Prices remain low because it is a rideshare service as opposed to a taxi-like service and drivers aren't allowed to make a profit (the fee you pay helps offset the cost of gas and tolls). Download the app in your mobile provider's appstore or browse trips on www.blablacar.com.

Restaurants

Foodies may never want to leave the Basque Country, where avant-garde and down-home cooking styles merge seamlessly. Everywhere you look in the region's cities and towns, there are mom-and-pop taverns, pintxo bars, and *asadores*—restaurants specializing in grilled meats and fish. But this area of Spain is also known for its Michelin-starred destination restaurants, venues sequestered in off-the-beaten-path villages that have become dining meccas such as Asador Etxebarri (in Atxondo), Martín Berasategui (in Lasarte), and Mugaritz (in Errenteria).

Restaurant reviews have been shortened. For full information, visit Fodors.com.

Hotels

Ever since the Guggenheim put Bilbao on the map as a design destination, the city's hotel fleet has expanded and reflected (in the case of the Gran Hotel Domine, literally) the glitter and panache of Gehry's museum. Boutique hotels, chic designer properties, and trusted-brand behemoths have made older hotels look small and quaint by comparison.

Hotel reviews have been shortened. For full information, visit Fodors.com.

What It Costs in Euros			
$	$$	$$$	$$$$
RESTAURANTS			
under €12	€12–€17	€18–€22	over €22
HOTELS			
under €90	€90–€125	€126–€180	over €180

Bilbao

102 km (63 miles) west of San Sebastián, 116 km (72 miles) east of Santander, 397 km (247 miles) north of Madrid.

Time in Bilbao (Bilbo in Euskera) may be recorded as BG or AG—Before Guggenheim or After Guggenheim. Never has a single monument of art and architecture so radically changed a city, at least not in Spain. Frank Gehry's stunning museum, plus Norman Foster's sleek subway system, the Santiago Calatrava glass footbridge and airport, the leafy César Pelli Abandoibarra park and commercial complex next to the Guggenheim, and the Philippe Starck Azkuna Zentroa cultural center have breathed unprecedented creative energy and verve into what was once a sooty industrial hub.

Greater Bilbao contains almost 1 million inhabitants, nearly half the total population of the Basque Country. Founded in 1300 by Vizcayan noble Diego López de Haro, the city became an industrial center in the mid-19th century because of the abundance of minerals in the surrounding hills. An affluent industrial class grew up here, as did the working class in suburbs that line the Margen Izquierda (Left Bank) of the Nervión estuary.

Bilbao's newer attractions get more press, but the city's old treasures still quietly line the banks of the silty Nervión. The Casco Viejo (Old Quarter)—also known as Siete Calles (Seven Streets)— is a charming jumble of shops, bars, and restaurants on the river's right bank, near the Puente del Arenal bridge. This elegant proto-Bilbao nucleus was carefully restored after devastating floods in 1983. Throughout the Casco Viejo are ancient mansions emblazoned with family coats of arms, wooden doors, and fine ironwork balconies. The most interesting square is the 64-arch Plaza Nueva, where an outdoor market is pitched every Sunday morning.

Walking the banks of the Nervión is a satisfying jaunt. After all, this was how—while out on a morning jog—Guggenheim director Thomas Krens first discovered the perfect spot for his project, nearly opposite the right bank's Deusto University. From the Palacio de Euskalduna upstream to the colossal Mercado de la Ribera, parks and green zones line the river. César Pelli's Abandoibarra project fills in the half mile between the Guggenheim and the Euskalduna bridge with a series of parks, the Deusto University library, the Meliá Bilbao Hotel, and a major shopping center.

On the left bank, the wide, late-19th-century boulevards of the Ensanche neighborhood, such as Gran Vía (the main shopping artery) and Alameda de Mazarredo, are the city's more formal face. Bilbao's cultural institutions include, along with the Guggenheim, the Museo de Bellas Artes, and an opera society (Asociación Bilbaína de Amigos de la Ópera, or ABAO) whose program includes 47 performances attended by over 90,000 spectators. In addition, epicureans have long ranked Bilbao's culinary offerings among the best in Spain. Don't miss a chance to ride the trolley line, the Euskotren, for a trip along the river from Atxuri Station to Basurto's San Mamés soccer stadium, reverently dubbed the "Catedral del Fútbol" (the Cathedral of Football).

GETTING HERE AND AROUND

Euskotren's Tranvía Bilbao, running up and down the Ría de Bilbao (aka Nervión Estuary) past the Guggenheim to the Mercado de la Ribera, is an attraction in its own right: silent, swift, and panoramic as it glides up and down its grassy runway. The Euskotren that leaves from Atxuri Station north of the Mercado de la Ribera runs along a spectacular route through Gernika and the Urdaibai Biosphere Preserve to Mundaka and Bermeo, probably the best way short of a boat to see this lovely wetlands preserve.

Bilbobus provides local bus service 6:15 am–10:55 pm. Plaza Circular and Plaza Moyua are the principal hubs for all lines. Once the metro and normal bus routes stop service, take a night bus, known as a Gautxori ("night bird"). Six lines run every 30 minutes between Plaza Circular and Plaza Moyúa and the city limits on Friday 11:30 pm–2 am and on Saturday overnight until 7 am.

Metro Bilbao is linear, running down the Nervión estuary from Basauri, above, or east of, the Casco Viejo, all the way to the mouth of the Nervión at Getxo, before continuing to the beach town of Plentzia. The Moyúa station is the most central stop and lies in the middle of Bilbao's Ensanche, or modern part. The second subway line runs down the left bank of the Nervión to Santurtzi. The fare is approximately €2 for a one-way ticket and around €1 with the Barik travel card (see below).

The reusable Barik card is good for metro and bus travel and for the Artxanda Funicular, RENFE, and Euskotren trains and trams, and costs €3, plus a minimum additional value of €5. Cards can be purchased at Barik vending machines in the Bilbao metro stations and from any of the four Bilbao metro help offices (Atención al Cliente de Metro Bilbao), located in or near several main stations including Areeta, San Mamés, Casco Viejo, and Ansio. Hours are weekdays 8:30–7:30. One card can be used by up to 10 people. Transfers cost extra.

For up to 24, 48, or 72 hours, the Bilbao Bizkaia Card (www.bilbaobizkaiacard. com) allows for unlimited use of the metro, buses, train, tram, and Artxanda funicular railway all around the Bizkaia region; discounts on certain restaurants, bars, and shops; and free entry to a variety of cultural activities including more than 25 sights such as the Guggenheim, Museo de Bellas Artes de Bilbao, and Museo de Reproducciones Artísticas de Bilbao. The card costs €10 for 24 hours, €15 for 48 hours, and €20 for 72 hours.

BUS AND SUBWAY INFORMATION
Bilbobus. ☎ 94/445–3471 ⊕ www.bilbobus.com. **Metro Bilbao.** ☎ 94/425–4025 ⊕ www.metrobilbao.eus.

STATIONS Bilbao-Abando Railway Station. ✉ Edificio Terminus, Pl. Circular 2, El Ensanche ☎ 94/479–5760 ⊕ www.adif. es. **Euskotren.** ☎ 90/254–3210 ⊕ www. euskotren.es. **Termibus Bilbao.** ✉ Gurtubay 1, San Mamés ☎ 94/439–5077.

VISITOR INFORMATION
CONTACTS Bilbao Tourism Office. ✉ Plaza Biribila 1, El Ensanche ☎ 94/479–5760 ⊕ www.bilbaoturismo.net Ⓜ Abando.

TOURS

Bilbao Paso a Paso
Bilbao Paso a Paso organizes walking tours, guided visits to the Guggenheim, hot-air-balloon rides, gastronomical tours around the city, LGBT+ itineraries, and excursions to nearby sites. ✉ San Nicolás de Olabeaga 62B, Casco Viejo ☎ 94/415–3892 ⊕ www.bilbaopasoapaso. com From €175 Ⓜ Olabeaga.

Bilbao Turismo
Weekend guided tours, in English and Spanish, are conducted by the tourist office (reservations required). ✉ Pl. Circular 1, El Ensanche ☎ 94/479–5760 ⊕ www.bilbaoturismo.net Ⓜ Abando.

Bilboats
One- and two-hour boat tours take you downstream from Plaza Pío Baroja the city center, passing some of Bilbao's iconic buildings and bridges. Customized day trips can also be arranged. ✉ Pl. Pío Baroja, Bilbao ☎ 94/642–4157 ⊕ www. bilboats.com From €13 Ⓜ Moyúa.

 Sights

Azkuna Zentroa
NOTABLE BUILDING | In the early 20th century, this was a municipal wine-storage facility used by Bilbao's Rioja wine barons. Now, the city-block-size, Philippe Starck–designed civic center is filled with shops, cafés, restaurants, movie theaters, swimming pools, fitness centers, and nightlife opportunities at the very heart of the city. Conceived as a hub for entertainment, culture, wellness, and civic coexistence, it added another star to Bilbao's cosmos of architectural and cultural offerings when it opened. The complex regularly hosts film festivals and art exhibitions, and it's a cozy place to take refuge on a rainy afternoon. ✉ Pl. Arriquibar 4, El Ensanche ☎ 94/401–4014 ⊕ www.azkunazentroa.eus Ⓜ Moyúa.

Begoñako Basilika
CHURCH | Bilbao's most cherished religious sanctuary, dedicated to the patron saint of Vizcaya, can be reached by the 313 stairs from Plaza de Unamuno or by the gigantic elevator (the Ascensor de Begoña) looming over Calle Esperanza 6 behind the San Nicolás church. The church's Gothic nave was begun in 1519 on the site of an early hermitage, where the Virgin Mary was alleged to have appeared long before. Finished in 1620, the basilica was completed with

the economic support of the shipbuilders and merchants of Bilbao, many of whose businesses are commemorated on the inner walls of the church. The high ground the basilica occupies was strategically important during the Carlist Wars of 1836 and 1873, and as a result La Begoña suffered significant damage that was not restored until the beginning of the 20th century. It's comparable in importance to Barcelona's Virgen de Montserrat. ⊠ *Calle Virgen de Begoña 38, Begoñalde* ☎ *94/412–7091* ⊠ *Free* Ⓜ *Casco Viejo.*

Biblioteca de Bidebarrieta

LIBRARY | This historic library and intellectual club was originally called El Sitio (The Siege) in memory of Bilbao's successful resistance to the Carlist siege of 1876. (Carlists were supporters of Fernando VII's brother, Don Carlos, over his daughter Isabella II as rightful heir to the Spanish throne.) Now a municipal library, the Bidebarrieta has a music auditorium that is one of Bilbao's most beautiful venues and a spot to check for the infrequent performances held there. The reading rooms are open to the public, and are a good place to read newspapers, make notes, or just enjoy the historical echoes of the place. ⊠ *Calle Bidebarrieta 4, Casco Viejo* ☎ *94/415–0915* ⊗ *Closed Sun.* ⊠ *Free* Ⓜ *Casco Viejo.*

Catedral de Santiago de Bilbao (*St. James's Cathedral*)

CHURCH | Bilbao's oldest church was a pilgrimage stop on the coastal route to Santiago de Compostela. Work on the structure began in 1379, but fire delayed completion until the early 16th century. The florid Gothic style with Isabelline elements features a nave in the form of a Greek cross, with ribbed vaulting resting on cylindrical columns. The notable outdoor arcade was used for public meetings of the early town's governing bodies. ⊠ *Pl. de Santiago 1, Casco Viejo* ☎ *94/415–3627* ⊕ *www.catedralbilbao. com* ⊠ *€6* Ⓜ *Casco Viejo.*

Convento de la Encarnación

CHURCH | The Basque Gothic architecture of this early-16th-century convent, church, and museum gives way to Renaissance and baroque ornamentation high on the main facade. The Museo Diocesano de Arte Sacro (Diocesan Museum of Sacred Art) occupies a carefully restored 16th-century cloister. The inner patio, ancient and intimate, is alone worth the visit. On display are religious silverwork, liturgical garments, sculptures, and paintings dating back to the 12th century. The convent is across from the Atxuri station just upstream from the Puente de San Antón. ⊠ *Pl. de la Encarnación, Casco Viejo* ☎ *94/432–0125* ⊕ *www.eleizmuseoa.com* ⊠ *€3* ⊗ *Closed Mon.* Ⓜ *Casco Viejo.*

Doña Casilda Iturrizar Park

CITY PARK | FAMILY | Bilbao's main park, stretching east toward the river from the Museo de Bellas Artes, is a lush collection of exotic trees, ducks and geese, fountains, falling water, and great expanses of lawns usually dotted with lovers. It's a sanctuary from the hard-edged Ensanche, Bilbao's modern, post-1876 expansion. Doña Casilda de Iturrizar was a well-to-do 19th-century Bilbao matron who married a powerful banker and used his wealth to support various cultural and beneficent institutions in the city, including this grassy refuge. ⊠ *El Ensanche* Ⓜ *San Mamés.*

Euskal Museoa Bilbao Museo Vasco (*Basque Museum of Bilbao*)

HISTORY MUSEUM | This be-all-end-all museum on Basque ethnography and Bilbao's cultural history occupies a 16th-century convent. Highlights include El Mikeldi, a pre-Christian, Iron Age stone animal representation that may be 4,000 years old; the room dedicated to Basque shepherds and the pastoral way of life; and the exhibit "Mar de los Vascos" ("Sea of the Basques") about whaling, fishing, and maritime activities. Placards are in Spanish and Basque only. ⊠ *Pl. Unamuno*

4, Casco Viejo ☎ 94/415–5423 ⊕ www.
euskalmuseoa.eus ⊠ €3 (free Thurs.)
🕐 Closed Tues. Ⓜ Casco Viejo.

Funicular de Artxanda

VIEWPOINT | Take a five-minute spin on
the Artxanda Funicular, the railway that
joins downtown Bilbao with the summit
of Artxanda Mountain. The panorama
from the hillsides of Artxanda is the most
scenic in Bilbao, and the summit also has
a park, hotel, sports complex, and several
restaurants. The asadores, in particular,
are excellent. ⊠ Pl. de Funicular, Matiko
☎ 94/445–4966 ⊕ funicularartxanda.
bilbao.eus ⊠ €5 round-trip Ⓜ Casco Viejo.

Iglesia de San Nicolás

CHURCH | Honoring the patron saint of
mariners, San Nicolás de Bari, the city's
early waterfront church was built over
an earlier hermitage and consecrated in
1756. With a striking baroque facade over
the Arenal, originally a sandy beach, the
church weathered significant damage at
the hands of French and Carlist troops
in the 19th century. Sculptures by Juan
Pascual de Mena adorn the interior. Look
for the oval plaque to the left of the door
marking the high-water mark of the flood
of 1983. ⊠ Pl. de San Nicolás 1, Casco
Viejo ☎ 94/416–3424 ⊠ Free Ⓜ Casco
Viejo.

La Casa de la Villa (City Hall) (Casa
Consistorial)

GOVERNMENT BUILDING | Architect Joaquín
de Rucoba built this city hall in 1892,
on the site of the San Agustín convent
destroyed during the 1836 Carlist War.
It shares the Belle Époque style of de
Rucoba's Teatro Arriaga. The Salón Árabe,
the highlight of the interior, was designed
by the same architect who built Bilbao's
Café Iruña, as their neo-Mudejar motifs
suggest. ⊠ Pl. de Ernesto Erkoreka 1,
El Arenal ☎ 94/420–4200, 94/420–5298
⊠ Free Ⓜ Abando.

Los Jardines de Albia

GARDEN | Bilbaínos wax poetic about
this welcoming town green surrounded

by concrete jungle. Overlooking the
square is the Basque Gothic **Iglesia de
San Vicente Mártir,** whose amply robed
sculpture of the Virgin—located on the
main facade—had to be sculpted a
second time after the original version
was deemed too scantily clad, according
to local legend. The Jardines de Albia are
centered on the bronze effigy of writer
Antonio de Trueba, by the famous Spanish sculptor Mariano Benlliure (1866–
1947). ⊠ Calle Colón de Larreátegui, El
Ensanche Ⓜ Abando.

★ Mercado de la Ribera

MARKET | This renovated triple-decker
ocean liner, with its prow facing down
the estuary toward the open sea, is
one of the best markets of its kind in
Europe—and one of the biggest, with
more than 400 retail stands (covering
37,950 square feet) that run the gamut
from fish markets to pintxo bars to wine
shops. Like the architects of the Guggenheim and the Palacio de Euskalduna
nearly 75 years later, the architect here
was playful with this epicurean mecca in the river. From the stained-glass
entryway over Calle de la Ribera to the
tiny catwalks over the river and the
bustling pintxo stalls on the ground floor,
the market is an inviting—if increasingly overtouristed—place. ⊠ Calle de la
Ribera 22, Casco Viejo ☎ 94/602–3791
⊕ mercadodelaribera.biz 🕐 Closed Sun.
Ⓜ Casco Viejo.

★ Museo de Bellas Artes (Museum of
Fine Arts)

ART MUSEUM | Considered one of the
top five museums in a country that has
a staggering number of museums and
great paintings, the Museo de Bellas
Artes is like a mini Prado, with representatives from every Spanish school and
movement from the 12th through 20th
centuries. The museum's fine collection
of Flemish, French, Italian, and Spanish
paintings includes works by El Greco,
Francisco de Goya y Lucientes, Diego
Velázquez, José Ribera, Paul Gauguin,

and Antoni Tàpies. One large and excellent section traces developments in 20th-century Spanish and Basque art alongside works by better-known European contemporaries, such as Fernand Léger and Francis Bacon. Look especially for Zuloaga's famous portrait of La Condesa Mathieu de Moailles and Joaquín Sorolla's portrait of Basque philosopher Miguel de Unamuno. ⊠ *Parque de Doña Casilda de Iturrizar, Pl. Museo 2, El Ensanche* ☎ *94/439–6060* ⊕ *www. museobilbao.com* ⊘ *Closed Tues.* ⊠ *€7* Ⓜ *Moyúa.*

★ Museo Guggenheim Bilbao

ART MUSEUM | With its eruption of light in the ruins of Bilbao's scruffy shipyards and steelworks, the Guggenheim has dramatically reanimated this onetime industrial city. At once suggestive of a silver-scaled fish and a mechanical heart, Frank Gehry's sculpture in titanium, limestone, and glass is the perfect habitat for the 250 Contemporary and Postmodern artworks it contains. Artists whose names are synonymous with the art of the 20th century (Kandinsky, Picasso, Miró, Pollock, Calder, and Malevich) and European artists of the 1950s and 1960s (Eduardo Chillida, Antoni Tàpies, Jose Maria Iglesias, Francesco Clemente, and Anselm Kiefer) are joined by contemporary figures (Bruce Nauman, Juan Muñoz, Julian Schnabel, Miquel Barceló, and Jean-Michel Basquiat). The ground floor is dedicated to large-format and installation work, some of which—like Richard Serra's *Serpent*—was created specifically for the space. Recent exhibitions have spotlighted social issues and integrated AR components. Buy tickets in advance online and from Servicaixa ATMs or, in the Basque Country, the BBK bank machines. ⊠ *Abandoibarra Etorbidea 2, El Ensanche* ☎ *94/435–9080* ⊕ *www. guggenheim-bilbao.eus* ⊠ *€13* ⊘ *Closed Mon. Sept.–June* Ⓜ *Moyúa.*

Museo Marítimo Ría de Bilbao (*Maritime Museum of Bilbao*)

OTHER MUSEUM | **FAMILY** | This carefully researched nautical museum on the left bank of the Ría de Bilbao reconstructs the history of the Bilbao waterfront and shipbuilding industry beginning from medieval times. Temporary exhibits range from visits by extraordinary seacraft such as tall ships or traditional fishing vessels to thematic displays on 17th- and 18th-century clipper ships or the sinking of the *Titanic.* ⊠ *Muelle Ramón de la Sota 1, San Mamés* ☎ *94/608–5500* ⊕ *www.itsasmuseum.eus* ⊠ *€6 (free Tues. Sept.–June)* ⊘ *Closed Mon.* Ⓜ *San Mamés.*

Plaza Miguel de Unamuno (*Plaza Unamuno*)

PLAZA/SQUARE | This roomy square at the upper edge of the Casco Viejo honors Bilbao's greatest intellectual, Miguel de Unamuno (1864–1936), the philosopher, novelist, professor, and public figure. Unamuno wrote some of Spain's most seminal works including *Del sentimiento trágico de la vida en los hombres y los pueblos* (*The Tragic Sense of Life in Men and Nations*). His *Niebla* (*Mist*) has been generally accepted as the first existentialist novel, published in 1914 when Jean-Paul Sartre was but nine years old. ⊠ *Casco Viejo* Ⓜ *Casco Viejo.*

Plaza Nueva (*Plaza Barria*)

PLAZA/SQUARE | This 64-arch neoclassical plaza, built in 1851, is known for its Sunday-morning flea market, December 21 Santo Tomás festivities, and permanent tapas and restaurant offerings. Note the size of the houses' balconies (the bigger the balcony, the richer the original proprietor) and the tiny windows near the top of the facades, where servants' quarters would've been. The building behind the coat of arms at the head of the square was once a government office but is now the **Academia de la Lengua Vasca** (Academy of the Basque Language). The coat of arms shows the tree of Guernica

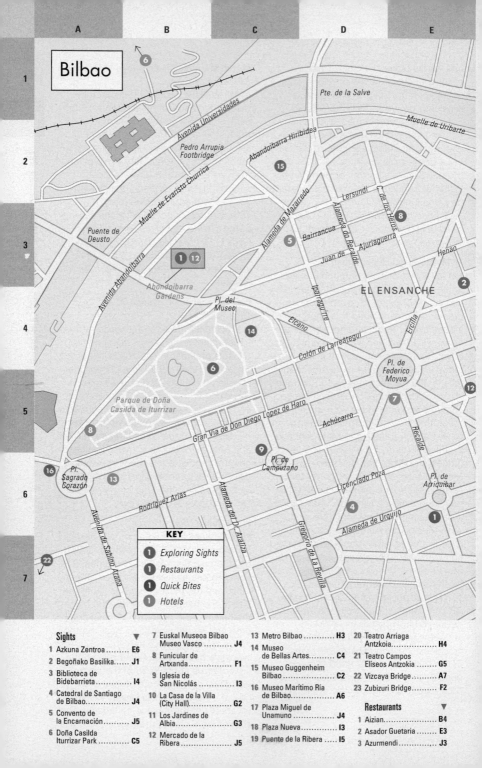

Bilbao

Pte. de la Salve

Muelle de Uribarte

Avenida Universidades

Pedro Arrupia Footbridge

Muelle de Evaristo Churrita

Abandoibarra Hiribidea

Puente de Deusto

Avenida Abandoibarra

Abandoibarra Gardens

Pl. del Museo

Alameda de Mazarredo

Bairrancua

Juan de

Ajuriaguerra

Lersundi

Alameda de Recalde

de los Heros

Ercilla

Henao

EL ENSANCHE

Etcano

Colón de Larreátegui

Pl. de Federico Moyua

Parque de Doña Casilda de Iturrizar

Gran Via de Don Diego Lopez de Haro

Iparraguirre

Achúcarro

Recalde

Pl. de Campuzano

Licenciado Poza

Pl. de Arriquibar

Pl. Sagrado Corazón

Rodríguez Arias

Avenida de Sabino Arana

Alameda del Dr Araliza

Gregorio de la Revilla

Alameda de Urquijo

KEY

- 1 Exploring Sights
- 1 Restaurants
- 1 Quick Bites
- 1 Hotels

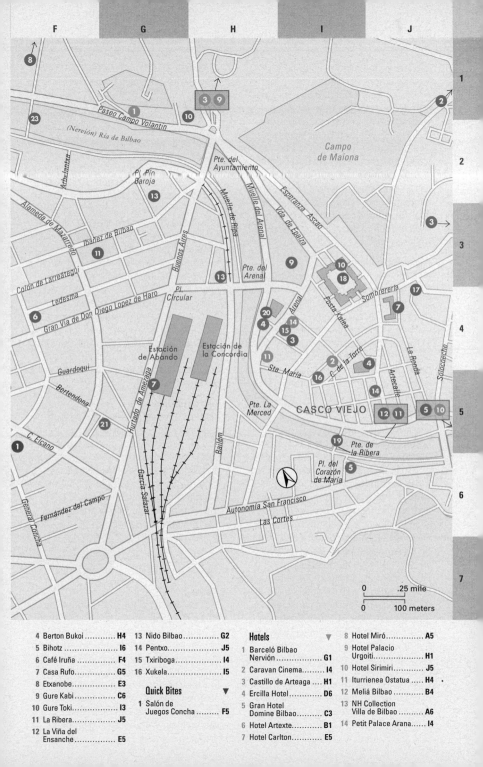

(or Gernika in Basque), symbolic of Basque autonomy, and two wolves, which represent Don Diego López de Haro (López derives from *lupus,* meaning wolf). The bars and shops around the arcades include two **Victor Montes** establishments, one for pintxos at Plaza Nueva 8 and the other for sit-down dining at No. 2. **Café Bar Bilbao** (No. 6), aka Casa Pedro, has Belle Époque interiors accented by photos of early Bilbao, while **Argoitia** (No. 15), across the square, has a nice angle on the midday sun. ✉ *Casco Viejo* Ⓜ *Casco Viejo.*

Puente de la Ribera

BRIDGE | This footbridge just downriver from the prow of the Mercado de la Ribera was traditionally known as the Puente del Perro Chico for the 25-cent coin once charged as a toll for crossing. Until Calatrava's Zubizuri was built, this was the only pedestrian bridge of Bilbao's nine river crossings. The bridge is officially named the Puente-Pasarela Conde Mirasol for the street it leads into. ✉ *Casco Viejo* Ⓜ *Casco Viejo.*

Teatro Arriaga Antzkoia

PERFORMANCE VENUE | This 1,500-seat theater was once as exciting a source of Bilbao pride as the Guggenheim is today. Built between 1886 and 1890, when Bilbao's population was a mere 35,000, the Teatro Arriaga represented a gigantic per-capita cultural investment. The original "Nuevo Teatro" (New Theater) de Bilbao was a lavish Belle Époque, Neo-Baroque jewel modeled after the Paris Opéra, by architect Joaquín Rucoba (1844–1909); it was renamed in 1902 for the Bilbaíno musician considered "the Spanish Mozart," Juan Crisóstomo de Arriaga (1806–26). After a 1914 fire, the new version of the theater opened in 1919. Although now largely upstaged by the sprawling, modern Palacio de Euskalduna, the Arriaga still hosts its fair share of opera, theater, concerts, and dance events September–June. ✉ *Pl.*

Arriaga 1, Casco Viejo ☎ *94/479–2036* ⊕ *www.teatroarriaga.eus* Ⓜ *Casco Viejo.*

★ **Vizcaya Bridge** (*Hanging Bridge*)
BRIDGE | One of Bilbao's most extraordinary sights since it was built in 1893, this transporter bridge suspended from cables ferries cars and passengers across the Nervión, uniting two distinct worlds: the exclusive, bourgeois Arenas and Portugalete, a staid, working-class town. Portugalete is a 15-minute walk from Santurce, where the quayside Mandanga Hogar del Pescador serves simple fish specialties. *Besugo* is the traditional choice, but the grilled sardines are equally sublime at a fraction of the price. ✉ *Barria 3, Las Arenas* ✛ *To reach bridge, take subway to Areeta, or drive across Puente de Deusto, turn left on Av. Lehendakari Aguirre, and follow signs for Las Arenas; it's a 10- or 15-min drive from downtown* ☎ *94/480–1012* ⊕ *www.puente-colgante.com* 🎫 *From €1* Ⓜ *Areeta.*

Zubizuri Bridge

BRIDGE | Santiago Calatrava's seagull-shaped bridge (the name means "white bridge" in Euskera) connects Campo Volantín on the right bank with El Ensanche on the left and is located just a few minutes from the Guggenheim. Other Calatrava creations in the area include the airport west of Bilbao at Loiu and the bridge at Ondarroa. ✉ *El Ensanche* Ⓜ *Moyúa.*

🍴 Restaurants

Aizian

$$$$ | SPANISH | Chef José Miguel Olazabalaga's Aizian is anything but a "hotel restaurant," even if it's situated inside the Meliá Bilbao. Sure, his dishes err on the safe side—you won't find tweezed microgreens and dry-ice displays here—but they're dependably delicious: think sautéed wild mushrooms topped with foie gras and a runny egg or seared venison loin with beets and smoked

chestnut puree. **Known for:** old-school Basque with a twist; good value for fine dining; dreamy torrija (Spanish "French" toast). $ *Average main: €40* ✉ *Meliá Bilbao, Calle Lehendakari Leizaola 29, El Ensanche* ☎ *94/428–0039* ⊕ *www. restaurante-aizian.com* ⊘ *Closed Sun.* Ⓜ *San Mamés.*

Asador Guetaria
$$$$ | **BASQUE** | With a wood-paneled dining room decorated with antiques, this family operation is a longtime local favorite for top-quality fish and meats cooked over coals. The kitchen, open to view, cooks *lubina* (sea bass), *besugo* (red sea bream), *dorada* (gilthead bream), *txuletas de buey*, and *chuletas de cordero* (lamb chops) to perfection in a classic asador setting. **Known for:** homey, old-timey dining room; masterful grilled dishes; familial atmosphere. $ *Average main: €50* ✉ *Colón de Larreátegui 12, El Ensanche* ☎ *94/424–3923, 94/423–2527* ⊕ *www.guetaria.com* Ⓜ *Moyúa.*

★ Azurmendi
$$$$ | **BASQUE** | The experience at this envelope-pushing restaurants starts as you enter the spacious indoor garden, are led on a tour of the kitchen, and then perhaps visit the sunny greenhouse to nibble on gourmet appetizers or a have a "picnic" in the lobby with dishes like truffled eggs "cooked inside out." The culinary climax takes place in the dining room with dishes like lemongrass mushroom pie or lobster out of the shell sluiced with charred pepper juice. **Known for:** a 10-minute drive out of town; three-Michelin-star dining; most innovative restaurant experience in Bilbao. $ *Average main: €250* ✉ *Legina Auzoa, Bilbao* ☎ *94/455–8866* ⊕ *www.azurmendi. restaurant* ⊘ *Closed Mon. and Tues.*

Berton Bukoi
$$ | **BASQUE** | Dinner is served until midnight in this sleek yet casual pintxo spot in the Casco Viejo. The industrial design—think wood tables with a green-tint polyethylene finish and exposed

ventilation pipes—belies a comfort-food-heavy menu with star dishes like grilled octopus brochettes and juicy grilled steaks. **Known for:** knockout pintxos; terrific value; top-quality steaks. $ *Average main: €15* ✉ *Calle Jardines 8, Casco Viejo* ☎ *94/416–7035* ⊕ *www.berton.eus* Ⓜ *Casco Viejo.*

★ Bihotz
$ | **CAFÉ** | When your feet need a rest, unwind at this third-wave coffeehouse that uses a sleek La Marzocco machine and is furnished with cushy armchairs and floor lamps. There are also small-production vermouths and local craft beers to try alongside soups, sandwiches, and other snacks. **Known for:** homey, inviting ambience; best cafés con leche in town; excellent craft beer selection. $ *Average main: €8* ✉ *Calle Arechaga 6, Casco Viejo* ☎ *94/471–9674* ⊕ *www.facebook. com/bihotzsanfrancisco* ⊘ *Closed Mon.* Ⓜ *Casco Viejo.*

★ Café Iruña
$$ | **CAFÉ** | This essential Bilbao haunt (est. 1903) in El Ensanche's most popular garden and square is a favorite for its interior design, boisterous ambience, and tried-and-true classics like Basque steak frites or bacalao al pil pil. The neo-Mudejar dining room overlooking the square is the place to be—if they try to stuff you in the back dining room, resist or come back another time. **Known for:** intricate neo-Mudejar dining room; no-nonsense Basque comfort food; packed with locals. $ *Average main: €15* ✉ *Los Jardines de Albia, Calle Berástegui 4, El Ensanche* ☎ *94/423–7021* ⊕ *www.cafeirunabilbao. net* Ⓜ *Moyúa.*

★ Casa Rufo
$$$ | **BASQUE** | Charming and cozy, this centenarian Bilbao institution is essentially a series of nooks and crannies tucked into a fine food, wine, olive oil, cheese, and ham emporium. Leave it to the affable owners to recommend a house specialty such as the oversize *txuleton de buey* (beef chop), which

pairs wonderfully with the house Rioja *crianza* (two years in oak, one in bottle) and any number of other options from the 1,000-pour-strong wine list. **Known for:** homey dining room; deep wine list with hard-to-find selections; delectable txuleton de buey. [$] *Average main: €20* ✉ *Calle Hurtado de Amézaga 5, El Ensanche* ☎ *94/443–2172* 🌐 *www.casarufo.com* 🕓 *Closed Sun.* [M] *Abando.*

Etxanobe

$$$$ | **BASQUE** | This legendary Nueva Cocina Vasca ("new Basque cuisine") restaurant relocated to a larger space in 2018 to accommodate its two distinct concepts: La Despensa and El Atelier. La Despensa is sleek and informal (yet still pricey), with dim lighting, neon signage, and look-at-me plating, while the white-tablecloth Atelier features even more refined, seafood-centric cuisine. **Known for:** pristine seafood; two restaurants under one roof—one casual and the other refined; impeccable designer decor. [$] *Average main: €35* ✉ *Calle de Juan de Ajuriaguerra 8, El Ensanche* ☎ *94/442–1071* 🌐 *www.atelieretxanobe.com* 🕓 *Closed Tues.* [M] *Uribitarte.*

Gure Kabi

$$$ | **SPANISH** | **FAMILY** | This family-friendly restaurant off the tourist track serves a wide range of unfussy, lovingly prepared dishes ranging from creamy squid *croquetas* to griddled European lobster. The best value is the €14 weekday *menú del día* (prix fixe). **Known for:** killer prix fixe lunch; Basque home cooking; locals-only vibe. [$] *Average main: €22* ✉ *Calle Particular de Estraunza 4–6, El Ensanche* ☎ *94/600–4843* 🌐 *www.gurekabi.com* 🕓 *Closed Sun.* [M] *Indautxu.*

★ Gure Toki

$$ | **BASQUE** | You'd be hard-pressed to find a more pleasant outdoor lunch in Bilbao than at this chic little pintxo bar with sunlit tables smack on the charming Plaza Nueva (the name means "Our Place" in English). Fried *rabas* (squid strips), croquetas, and locally made *txistorra* (smoky chorizo sausage) never come off the menu, for a good reason. **Known for:** efficient service; unbeatable location for people-watching; knockout pintxos. [$] *Average main: €16* ✉ *Plaza Nueva 12, Casco Viejo* ☎ *94/415–8037* 🌐 *www.guretoki.com* 🕓 *Closed Wed.* [M] *Zazpi Kaleak.*

La Ribera

$$$ | **BASQUE** | **FAMILY** | Make a beeline to this gastro bar on the ground floor of the eponymous *mercado* to satisfy your Basque food cravings after you've ogled all the shimmering fresh fish, plump *jamones ibéricos* (Iberian hams), and sweet-smelling fruit. The €15 menú del día is a terrific deal, and the highbrow pintxos are consistently tasty. **Known for:** wide selection of sweet and savory snacks; hip, young vibe; good prix fixe lunch. [$] *Average main: €20* ✉ *Mercado de la Ribera, Calle de la Ribera 20, Casco Viejo* ☎ *94/657–5474* 🌐 *www.laribera-bilbao.com* 🕓 *Closed Mon. and Tues.* [M] *Casco Viejo.*

★ La Viña del Ensanche

$$$ | **BASQUE** | Littered with used napkins and furnished with simple wood tables beneath hams hanging from the rafters, this lively, deceptively simple bar attracts locals and tourists alike for its exceptional pintxos. Don't pass up the deconstructed Galician-style octopus on a bed of mashed potatoes laced with *pimentón* (paprika) or the appetizer of house-made foie gras with three preserves. **Known for:** house-made foie gras; croquetas flecked with top-shelf Joselito jamón; loud, convivial atmosphere. [$] *Average main: €20* ✉ *Diputazio 10, El Ensanche* ☎ *94/415–5615* 🌐 *www.lavinadelensanche.com* 🕓 *Closed Sun.* [M] *Moyúa.*

Nido Bilbao

$$$ | **BASQUE** | Even the bread is housemade at this wildly popular Basque restaurant on the Left Bank that's renowned for dishes like goose foie gras with raspberry coulis, dry-aged T-bone steaks, and house-made *morcilla* (blood sausage). A list of small-production and organic

wines rounds out the hyperlocal dining experience. **Known for:** natural wines; market-driven cuisine; house-made everything, from sausages to breads and ice creams. $ *Average main: €22* ✉ *Calle Barroeta Aldamar 3, El Ensanche* ☎ *94/436–0643* ⊕ *www.nidobilbao.com* ⊘ *Closed Sun.* Ⓜ *Abando.*

★ Pentxo

$$ | **BASQUE** | **FAMILY** | Consistently delicious, shockingly affordable, and unapologetically old-school, Pentxo is the sort of restaurant Bilbaínos like to keep to themselves. Whether you pop in for a pintxo at the bar (the flash-fried *antxoas rellenas*, or stuffed anchovies, are a must) or come for a €15 prix fixe lunch (opt for whatever seafood main is listed), you'll leave wishing you could be a regular. **Known for:** unbeatable lunch deal; local crowd; outstanding pintxos and coffee drinks. $ *Average main: €15* ✉ *Calle Belostikale 20, Casco Viejo* ☎ *94/416–9472* ⊕ *www.restaurantepentxo.com* ⊘ *Closed Sun.* Ⓜ *Casco Viejo.*

Txiriboga

$ | **TAPAS** | Locals flock to this hole-in-the-wall for what might be the city's best croquetas—choose from jamón, chicken, bacalao, or wild mushroom. The *rabas* (fried calamari) also stand out for their non-greasy, ultra-crisp exterior. **Known for:** terrific calamari; quintessential Basque taberna; burst-in-your-mouth croquetas. $ *Average main: €9* ✉ *Calle Santa Maria 13, Casco Viejo* ☎ *94/415–7874* ⊘ *Closed Mon.* Ⓜ *Casco Viejo.*

Xukela

$$ | **TAPAS** | The main draw at this quirky tavern is the pintxos—imaginative, internationally inflected bites ranging from smoked Cantabrian anchovies to mushroom-foie-gras toasts. The interior feel like a professor's study, with books and magazines scattered about, and there's a sign on the wall that says, "This is an Atheist establishment." **Known for:** varied wine list; nueva cocina tapas at taberna prices; cozy interior. $ *Average*

main: €14 ✉ *Calle de El Perro 2, Casco Viejo* ☎ *94/415–9772* Ⓜ *Casco Viejo.*

☕ Coffee and Quick Bites

Salón de Juegos Concha

$ | **SPANISH** | Forget the name—locals know that this slightly seedy *salón de juegos* (literally "gambling hall") is worth a visit not for its slot machines but for its gloriously runny potato omelets, which are made fresh nonstop from 8 am to midnight and boast a gloriously gushy center. The basic potato-and-onion rendition will set you back less than €2; more deluxe versions (with crab, *jamón ibérico*, etc.) are a tad pricier. *Minors are not allowed entry, but the staff will happily wrap your food to go.* **Known for:** secret local spot; hot Spanish omelet served around the clock; shockingly affordable. $ *Average main: €4* ✉ *Calle General Concha 1, Bilbao* ☎ *94/410–1971* Ⓜ *Moyúa.*

🛏 Hotels

Barceló Bilbao Nervión

$$$ | **HOTEL** | Sandwiched between the Casco Viejo and the industrial area surrounding the Guggenheim, this corporate hotel soars seven stories over the Nervión, and its best rooms boast semicircular windows that make you feel like you're hovering over it. **Pros:** supremely comfortable; stylish modern decor; great location. **Cons:** lacks local flavor; not terribly homey; no river views from interior rooms. $ *Rooms from: €175* ✉ *Paseo Campo de Volantín 11, Casco Viejo* ☎ *94/445–4700* ⊕ *www.barcelo.com* ⤳ *350 rooms* ⦿ *No Meals* Ⓜ *Uribitarte.*

★ Caravan Cinema

$$$ | **B&B/INN** | This cozy, cinema-themed pension with in-room Nespresso machines and huge TVs is a great value. **Pros:** independently owned; cheerful staff; convenient to main sights. **Cons:** contact proprietor to schedule check-in time; inadequate soundproofing; some rooms overlook a gritty little courtyard. $ *Rooms from: €160* ✉ *Calle Correo 11, Casco Viejo* ☎ *68/886–0907* ⊕ *www. caravan-cinema.com* �'*11 rooms* ⦿ *No Meals* Ⓜ *Arriaga.*

★ Castillo de Arteaga
$$$$ | **HOTEL** | Built in the mid-19th century for Empress Eugenia de Montijo, wife of Napoléon III, this neo-Gothic limestone castle with rooms in the watchtowers and defensive walls is one of the most extraordinary lodging options in or around Bilbao (and Relais & Châteaux agrees). **Pros:** views over the wetlands; palatial interiors; market-driven restaurant worth a trip in itself. **Cons:** restaurant is pricey and there aren't many inexpensive alternatives in the area; spotty Wi-Fi in some rooms; isolated from the village and 30 minutes from Bilbao. $ *Rooms from: €200* ✉ *Calle Gaztelubide 7, Gautegiz de Arteaga* ✛ *40 km (25 miles) northwest of Bilbao* ☎ *94/627–0440* ⊕ *www.castillodearteaga.com* ⊗ *Closed late Dec.–early Jan.* �'*13 rooms* ⦿ *Free Breakfast.*

Ercilla Hotel
$$ | **HOTEL** | A prim business crowd fills this modern hotel that's known for its streamlined rooms and professional service. **Pros:** views from rooftop bar; a Bilbao nerve center for journalists, politicians, and businesspeople; steps from pintxo hot spots. **Cons:** room keys deactivate easily; not the place for a quiet getaway; lots of stairs. $ *Rooms from: €95* ✉ *Calle Ercilla 37, Endantxu* ☎ *94/470–5700* ⊕ *www.ercilladebilbao.com* ➡ *325 rooms* ⦿ *Free Breakfast* Ⓜ *Moyúa.*

Gran Hotel Domine Bilbao
$$$ | **HOTEL** | This sleek art hotel across from the Guggenheim showcases the conceptual wit of Javier Mariscal, creator of Barcelona's 1992 Olympic mascot Cobi, and the structural know-how of Bilbao architect Iñaki Aurrekoetxea. **Pros:** emblematic of Bilbao's architectural renaissance; spacious, updated rooms; breakfast on the rooftop terrace. **Cons:**

hard on the wallet; a little full of its own glamour; soundproofing could be better. $ *Rooms from: €175* ✉ *Alameda de Mazarredo 61, El Ensanche* ☎ *94/425–3300* ⊕ *www.granhoteldominebilbao.com* ➡ *145 rooms* ⦿ *No Meals* Ⓜ *Moyúa.*

Hotel Artetxe
$ | **B&B/INN** | **FAMILY** | With rooms overlooking Bilbao from the heights of Artxanda, this Basque farmhouse with renovated interiors and eager young owners offers excellent value. **Pros:** peace and quiet on the outskirts of town; plenty of space for children to play; great service. **Cons:** far from the center; BYOB; no evening restaurant service. $ *Rooms from: €65* ✉ *Calle de Berriz 112, Bilbao* ✛ *Off Ctra. Enékuri–Artxanda, Km 7* ☎ *94/474–7780* ⊕ *www.hotelartetxe.com* ➡ *12 rooms* ⦿ *Free Breakfast.*

Hotel Carlton
$$ | **HOTEL** | This grande dame, equidistant from the Casco Viejo and the Abandoibarra neighborhood, exudes old-world grace and charm along with a sense of history—which it has aplenty: Orson Welles, Ava Gardner, Ernest Hemingway, and Lauren Bacall are but a few of the luminaries who once stayed here. **Pros:** spacious rooms; luxury gym and business center; historic, old-world surroundings. **Cons:** occasionally grumpy personnel; some "modern" design touches come across as tacky; surrounded by concrete and urban frenzy. $ *Rooms from: €120* ✉ *Pl. Federico Moyúa 2, El Ensanche* ☎ *94/416–2200* ⊕ *www.hotelcarlton.es* ➡ *142 rooms* ⦿ *Free Breakfast* Ⓜ *Moyúa.*

Hotel Miró
$$$$ | **HOTEL** | Between the Guggenheim and the Museo de Bellas Artes, this boutique hotel refurbished by Barcelona fashion designer Toni Miró competes with the reflecting facade of Javier Mariscal's Domine Bilbao hotel just up the street. **Pros:** pleasingly muted decor; views of the Guggenheim; free coffee, tea, and

popcorn in the lobby. **Cons:** staff can be snooty; overpriced; uncozy. [$] *Rooms from: €230* ✉ *Alameda de Mazarredo 77, El Ensanche* ☎ *94/661–1880* 🌐 *www.mirohotelbilbao.com* 🛏 *50 rooms* 🍴 *No Meals* [M] *Moyúa.*

Hotel Palacio Urgoiti

$$$ | HOTEL | FAMILY | This majestic hotel occupying a reconstructed 17th-century country palace out toward the airport, is a peaceful country retreat with a 9-hole pitch-and-putt in the hotel gardens and other activities nearby. **Pros:** convenient to the airport; elegant environment with easy access to outdoor activities; handy train service into Bilbao. **Cons:** 15-minute drive to Bilbao; freezing indoor pool; teeth-rattling flights overhead. [$] *Rooms from: €135* ✉ *Calle Arritugane, Mungia* ✣ *13 km (8 miles) west of Bilbao, 2 km (1 mile) from airport* ☎ *94/674–6868* 🌐 *www.palaciourgoiti.com* 🛏 *43 rooms* 🍴 *Free Breakfast.*

Hotel Sirimiri

$ | HOTEL | A small, attentively run hotel near the Atxuri station, this modest spot has modern rooms with views of some of Bilbao's oldest architecture. **Pros:** steps from tram; excellent buffet-style breakfast; handy to the Mercado de la Ribera, Casco Viejo, and the Atxuri train station. **Cons:** lacks character of surrounding buildings; tight quarters; thin walls. [$] *Rooms from: €80* ✉ *Pl. de la Encarnación 3, Casco Viejo* ☎ *94/433–0759* 🌐 *www.hotelsirimiri.es* 🛏 *28 rooms* 🍴 *Free Breakfast* [M] *Casco Viejo.*

★ Iturrienea Ostatua

$ | B&B/INN | This quirky, cozy hotel occupies a traditional Basque town house overlooking Bilbao's Casco Viejo. **Pros:** budget-friendly; comfy interiors; attentive personnel. **Cons:** slow Wi-Fi; no on-site parking and the closest lot is expensive; exterior-facing rooms can be noisy. [$] *Rooms from: €76* ✉ *Calle Santa María 14, Casco Viejo* ☎ *94/416–1500* 🌐 *www.iturrieneaostatua.com* 🛏 *19 rooms* 🍴 *No Meals* [M] *Casco Viejo.*

Meliá Bilbao

$$$ | HOTEL | Designed by architect Ricardo Legorreta and inspired by the work of Basque sculptor Eduardo Chillida (1920–2002), this high-rise hotel was built over what was once the nerve center of Bilbao's shipbuilding industry; fittingly, it recalls a futuristic ocean liner. **Pros:** creature comforts, top-notch dining; some rooms face the Guggenheim. **Cons:** inconsistent service; maintenance issues; a high-rise colossus. [$] *Rooms from: €157* ✉ *Calle Lehendakari Leizaola 29, El Ensanche* ☎ *94/428–0000* 🌐 *www.melia.com* 🛏 *213 rooms* 🍴 *No Meals* [M] *San Mamés.*

NH Collection Villa de Bilbao

$$ | HOTEL | The Bilbao outpost of this trusted chain is a great value and offers choice extras—morning newspapers at your door, exceptional breakfasts, comfortable rooms, and professional service. **Pros:** scenic walk to the Bellas Artes and Guggenheim museums; near San Mamés stadium; spacious rooms. **Cons:** a bit cold and corporate; disorganized reception staff; poor bathroom maintenance. [$] *Rooms from: €115* ✉ *Gran Vía 87, El Ensanche* ☎ *94/441–6000* 🌐 *www.nh-hoteles.com* 🛏 *139 rooms* 🍴 *No Meals* [M] *San Mamés.*

Petit Palace Arana

$$ | HOTEL | Across from the Teatro Arriaga in the Casco Viejo, this design hotel has a blended style of contemporary and antique. **Pros:** oldest hotel in the city; excellent breakfast; in the heart of traditional Bilbao. **Cons:** brisk service; bathrooms lack privacy; can be noisy at night on the street side of the building. [$] *Rooms from: €93* ✉ *Bidebarrieta 2, Casco Viejo* ☎ *94/415–6411* 🌐 *www.petitpalace.com/es* 🛏 *64 rooms* 🍴 *Free Breakfast* [M] *Casco Viejo.*

🛍 Shopping

The main stores for clothing are found around Plaza Moyúa in El Ensanche, along streets such as Iparraguirre and Rodríguez Arias. The Casco Viejo has dozens of smaller shops, many of them in handsomely restored early houses with gorgeous wooden beams and ancient stones, specializing in an endless variety of products from crafts to antiques. Wool items, gourmet products, and wood carvings from around the Basque Country can be found throughout Bilbao. Basque *txapelas* (berets, or boinas in Spanish) are famous worldwide and make fine gifts.

Ganboa Jewellery
JEWELRY & WATCHES | Try on handmade, one-of-a-kind jewelry at this tranquil boutique, whose Basque owner finds inspiration for her organic designs in nature. Prices range from approximately €40 to €300 per piece. ⊠ *Arechaga Kalea 5, Casco Viejo* ☎ *94/652–7989* ⊕ *www. ganboajewellery.com* ⦾ *Closed Sat. at 2 pm and Sun.* Ⓜ *Casco Viejo.*

★ La Bendita
FOOD | This pocket-size gourmet shop tucked beside the cathedral sells the finest sweets, wines, and *conservas* (preserves) the region has to offer. Slender green Txakoli bottles and vintage-label Cantabrian anchovies make wonderful souvenirs. ⊠ *Calle Bidebarrieta 16, Casco Viejo* ☎ *94/652–3623* ⦾ *Closed Sun.* Ⓜ *Arriaga.*

From Bilbao, drive northwest down the Nervión to Neguri and Getxo and follow the coast road through Baquio, Bermeo, and Mundaka to Gernika before proceeding east—this is the scenic route but well worth the extra time. Depending on stops for lunch or sprawling on a breezy beach, plan for a two- to six-hour drive, all of it spectacularly picturesque. The other choice is to pick up the A8 toll road east toward San Sebastián and France, exiting for Gernika and the BI635 coast road through Bizkaia's hills.

★ Proyecto Hemen
CRAFTS | Embodying Bilbao's envelope-pushing urban pulse, this Casco Viejo concept store sells ceramics, textiles, and accessories designed by its three young owners, who partnered to open the storefront in 2017. ⊠ *Erronda Kalea 12, Casco Viejo* ☎ *94/657–8494* ⊕ *www. proyectohemen.com* ⦾ *Closed Sat. at 2 pm and Sun.* Ⓜ *Atxuri.*

🏃 Activities

MULTISPORT
Bilbobentura
KAYAKING | There's perhaps no better way to take in Bilbao's intriguing urban landscape than on a kayak ride down the estuary. Bilbobentura offers ski packages, hiking tours, and bicycle, kayak, and SUP rentals. Rental rates begin at €8 for bicycles, €11 for single-person kayaks, and €14 for stand-up paddle boards. ⊠ *Ramón de la Sota 1, San Mamés* ☎ *66/073–4953* ⊕ *www.bilbobentura. com.*

SOCCER
Soccer is religion in Bilbao, even if the scrappy Athletic Club has been on a decades-long losing streak. "The Lions" are often in the top half of the league standings and take special pleasure in tormenting powerhouses Madrid and Barcelona. The local rivalry with San Sebastián's Real Sociedad is as bitter as baseball's Yankees–Red Sox feud.

San Mamés Stadium
SOCCER | Athletic Bilbao calls this decade-old €213 million stadium on the Nervión its home turf. It seats over 53,000 and has a retractable roof that keeps spectators dry, rain or shine. ⊠ *Rafael Moreno Pitxitxi, San Mamés* ☎ *94/441–3954* ⊕ *www.bilbaostadium. com* Ⓜ *San Mamés.*

Bermeo

34 km (21 miles) northeast of Bilbao, 9 km (5 miles) east of San Juan de Gaztelugatxe.

Walk from the old town down to the port to get a sense of Bermeo's charm. Before the town became synonymous with commercial fishing (it once boasted the largest fishing fleet in Spain), it was a booming whaling center. In the 16th century, Bermeo whalers reportedly donated the tongue of every whale to raise money for the Church. Bermeo has one of only two wooden-boat shipyards on the northern coast, and the boats docked in its busy harbor make a colorful picture. Drive to the top of the windswept hill above town, where a cemetery overlooks the crashing waves below, then head west on the coastal road to explore the breathtaking island hermitage of San Juan de Gaztelugatxe, a must-see sight.

Mundaka

37 km (23 miles) northeast of Bilbao.

Tiny Mundaka, famous among surfers all over the world for its left-breaking roller at the mouth of the Ría de Gernika, has much to offer nonsurfers as well. The town's elegant summer homes and stately houses bearing family coats of arms compete for pride of place with the hermitage on the Santa Catalina peninsula and the parish church's Renaissance doorway.

VISITOR INFORMATION

CONTACTS Mundaka. ✉ *Calle Josepa Deuna, Mundaka* ☎ *94/617–7201* 🌐 *www.mundakaturismo.com.*

Sights

Bosque de Oma (*Painted Forest*)
FOREST | FAMILY | Outside of town, about 5 km (3 miles) from Gernika, lies the Urdaibai Natural Reserve. Stop here for a stroll through the Bosque de Oma, featuring rows of trees vividly painted by Basque artist Agustín Ibarrola. It's a striking and successful marriage of art and nature. The nearby **Cuevas de Santimamiñe** have important prehistoric cave paintings that can be accessed virtually at a visitor center. ✉ *Barrio Basondo, Kortezubi* ☎ *94/465–1657* 🌐 *www.bosquedeoma.com* 🎟 *Free.*

Beaches

Mundaka Beach
BEACH | This beach is said to have the longest surf break in Europe and among the best in the world, making it a magnet for surfers. In summer and fall this beach is off-limits to families who just want to splash around. Inland from the beach is the Urdaibai Natural Preserve, a UNESCO-designated biosphere. **Amenities:** lifeguards; water sports. **Best for:** surfing. ✉ *Calle Matadero.*

Restaurants

Baserri Maitea
$$$$ | **BASQUE** | Eleven km (7 miles) south of Mundaka and 1 km (½ mile) northwest of Gernika, you'll find this restaurant in an idyllic 18th-century *caserío.* Garlands of red peppers and garlic hang from wooden beams in the cathedral-like interior, and the kitchen pumps out hearty yet refined fish and meats cooked over a wood-fire grill. **Known for:** personable waitstaff; spectacular ambience in a Basque farmhouse; bacalao dishes. [$] *Average main: €25* ✉ *Calle Atxondoa, Mundaka* ☎ *94/625–3408* 🌐 *www.baserrimaitea.com* 🕒 *No dinner Sun.–Thurs.*

Restaurante Portuondo
$$$$ | **BASQUE** | Sweeping beach views through picture windows, aromas of fresh fish cooking over hot coals, a sophisticated country dining room—these are just a few reasons Portuondo, a 15-minute walk outside town, is a

Basque Culture

Nobody knows where the Basques came from or when they arrived in this windswept corner of the Iberian Peninsula. Though the first written records of the Basques are from Roman times, studies indicate that this "tribe" of proto-Europeans has inhabited the area for at least 7,000 years and perhaps reached North America before Columbus. A combination of impenetrable geography and a fierce warrior class kept the Basques somewhat isolated from the rest of the continent for hundreds, if not thousands, of years—enough time to establish and preserve their distinctive mythology, sports, food, and language.

Basque Language

Although all Basques speak French north of the border and Spanish south of the border, many (approximately one-quarter of the population on the Spanish side) consider **Euskera** their first language. The mother tongue is so vital to the Basque identity that the cultural signifier "Basque" in Euskera is "Euskalduna," literally "Speaker of Basque." As Europe's only non-Indo-European language, Euskera is one of the great enigmas of linguistic scholarship. To the nonspeaker, Euskera sounds like rough, consonant-heavy Spanish, though its highly complex grammar has no relation to the Romance languages.

Basque Cuisine

Traditional Basque cuisine combines vegetables, Atlantic fish, beef, and lamb with a love of sauces that is rare south of the Pyrenees. Today the *Nueva Cocina Vasca* movement has painted Basque food as highly innovative and slightly precious, even if most everyday Basques still eat as they always have—simply, from the land and sea. With the seemingly eternal trendiness of pintxos (the Basque equivalent of tapas), Basque cuisine solidified itself as part of the international culinary zeitgeist.

Basque Sports

A Basque village without a frontón (pelota court) is as unimaginable as an American town without a baseball diamond. *Pelota*, or **jai alai** in Euskera, is the fastest-moving ball sport, according to Guinness World Records, with ball speeds reaching 150 mph. The game is played on a three-walled court 175 feet long and 56 feet wide with 40-foot side walls, and the object is to angle the ball along or off of the side wall so that it cannot be returned. Betting is popular.

Herrikirolak (rural sports) are based on farming and seafaring. Stone lifters (*harrijasotzaileak* in Euskera) heft weights up to 700 pounds. *Aizkolari* (axe men) chop wood in various contests, and the *gizon proba* (man trial) pits three-man teams moving weighted sleds. Then there are the *estropadak*, whaleboat rowers who compete in spectacular regattas (culminating in the September competition off La Concha beach in San Sebastián).

When it comes to **soccer**, Basque goaltenders have developed special fame in Spain, where Bilbao's Athletic Club and San Sebastián's Real Sociedad have won national championships with budgets far inferior to those of Real Madrid or FC Barcelona.

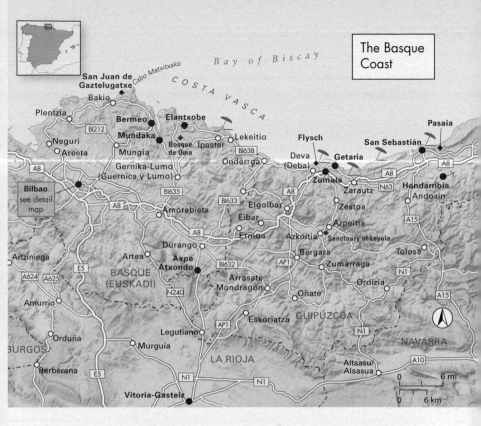

stalwart Mundaka restaurant. If you're in the mood for something informal, post up at the downstairs pintxo bar. **Known for:** buzzy tapas area; meats and fish grilled to perfection; beautiful setting. $ *Average main: €30* ⊠ *Portuondo Auzoa 1, Mundaka* ✛ *Ctra. Gernika–Bermeo BI2235, Km 47* ☎ *94/687–6050* ⊕ *www. restauranteportuondo.com* ⊙ *No dinner Mon.–Thurs.*

 ## Hotels

Atalaya

$$ | HOTEL | Tastefully converted from a private house, this 1911 landmark on the shore has become a favorite for quick overnight rail getaways from Bilbao, and scenery along the 37-km (23-mile) train ride is spectacular. **Pros:** free parking; well-maintained sauna; intimate retreat from Bilbao's sprawl and bustle. **Cons:** limited menu in the restaurant; tight quarters in some rooms; outdated tech. $ *Rooms from: €115* ⊠ *Calle Itxaropen 1, Mundaka* ☎ *94/687–6899* ⊕ *www. atalayahotel.es* ⇌ *13 rooms.*

Kurutziaga Jauregia

$$ | HOTEL | Basque for Palacio de la Cruz, this elegant 18th-century town house is a perfect alternative to the Atalaya for an overnight getaway from Bilbao. **Pros:** quiet retreat in downtown Mundaka; nice terrace; steps from the harbor. **Cons:** parking can be difficult; tight streets; small and basic rooms. $ *Rooms from: €95* ⊠ *Calle Kurtzio 1, Mundaka* ☎ *94/687–6925* ⊕ *mundakahotelkurutzia-ga.com* ⇌ *23 rooms* ⦿ *Free Breakfast.*

Embattled Gernika

On Monday, April 26, 1937—market day—Gernika, 33 km (20 miles) east of Bilbao, was attacked by German and Italian air brigades at the behest of the Nationalist forces in what would be history's second terror bombing against a civilian population. (The first, much less famous, was against neighboring Durango, about a month earlier.) Gernika, a rural town, had been one of the symbols of Basque identity since the 14th century. As early as the Middle Ages, Spanish sovereigns had sworn under the ancient oak tree of Gernika to respect Basque *fueros*, local courts with the sort of autonomy that was anathema to Generalísimo Francisco Franco's Madrid-centered "National Movement," which promoted Spanish unity over local identity. The planes of the Nazi Luftwaffe were sent with the blessings of Franco to experiment with saturation bombing of civilian targets and to decimate the traditional seat of Basque autonomy.

When the raid ended, between 153 and 1,654 civilians—the exact number of casualties is unclear—lay dead or dying in the ruins, and today Gernika remains a symbol of the atrocities of war, largely thanks to Picasso's famous canvas *Guernica*. The city was destroyed (although the oak tree miraculously emerged unscathed), and has been rebuilt as a modern if architecturally uninteresting town. Not until the 60th anniversary of the event did Germany officially apologize for the bombing.

When Spain's Second Republic commissioned Picasso to create a work for the Paris 1937 International Exposition, little did he imagine that his grim canvas protesting the bombing of a Basque village would become one of the most famous paintings in history.

Picasso's painting had its own struggle. The Spanish Pavilion in the International Exposition nearly substituted a more upbeat work, using *Guernica* as a backdrop. In 1939, Picasso ceded *Guernica* to New York's Museum of Modern Art, stipulating that the painting should return only to a democratic Spain. Over the next 30 years, as Picasso's fame grew, so did *Guernica*'s—as a work of art and a symbol of Spain's captivity.

When Franco died in 1975, two years after Picasso, negotiations with Picasso's heirs for the painting's return to Spain were already underway. Now on display at Madrid's Centro de Arte Reina Sofía, *Guernica* is home for good.

Axpe Atxondo

47 km (29 miles) east of Bilbao, 45 km (28 miles) south of Mundaka, 44 km (28 miles) south of Elantxobe.

The village of Axpe, in the valley of Atxondo, sits in the shadow of 4,777-foot Mt. Anboto—one of the highest peaks in the Basque Country outside the Pyrenees.

According to local lore, the Basque nature goddess Mari lives in a cave close to the summit. Amboto, with its spectral gray rock face, is a sharp contrast to the soft green meadows running up to the very foot of the mountain. In his *Mitología Vasca* (*Basque Mythology*), ethnologist José María de Barandiarán describes the goddess as "a beautiful woman, well constructed in all ways except for one foot, which was like that of a goat."

GETTING HERE AND AROUND

From Bilbao, drive east on the A8/E70 freeway toward San Sebastián. Get off at the Durango exit, 40 km (24 miles) from Bilbao, and take the BI632 toward Elorrio. At Apatamonasterio turn right onto the BI3313 and continue to Axpe.

🍴 Restaurants

★ Asador Etxebarri

$$$$ | BASQUE | Of all the three-Michelin-star Basque temples, Victor Arguinzoniz's Etxebarri may be the most exclusive, since it only opens for lunch (except for Saturday) and reservations are limited. Here, grilling is elevated to an art form, with various types of woods, coals, and tools carefully selected for the preparation of each dish. **Known for:** surprisingly unpretentious, laid-back atmosphere; No. 10 spot on "World's 50 Best" restaurants list; temple of open-hearth cuisine. [$] *Average main: €60* ✉ *Pl. San Juan 1, Axpe* ☎ *94/658–3042* 🌐 *www.asadoretxebarri.com* 🕓 *Closed Mon. Dinner Sat. only. Closed Aug.*

🛏 Hotels

★ Mendi Goikoa Bekoa

$ | HOTEL | This handsome hillside estate is among the province's most exquisite hideaways. **Pros:** smart and attentive service; sweet, sweet silence; gorgeous setting. **Cons:** reservations via online form; not open year-round; need a car to get here. [$] *Rooms from: €80* ✉ *Barrio San Juan 33, Axpe* ☎ *94/682–0833* 🌐 *www.mendigoikoabekoa.com* 🕓 *Closed Nov.–Easter* 🛏 *11 rooms* 🍽 *Free Breakfast.*

Getaria and Zumaia

80 km (50 miles) east of Bilbao, 22 km (14 miles) west of San Sebastián.

Getaria (Guetaria in Castilian) is known as *la cocina de Guipúzcoa* (the kitchen of the Guipúzcoa province) for its many restaurants and taverns. It was also the birthplace of Juan Sebastián Elcano (1487–1526), the first circumnavigator of the globe and Spain's most emblematic naval hero. Elcano took over and completed Magellan's voyage after Magellan was killed in the Philippines in 1521. The town's galleonlike church has sloping wooden floors resembling a ship's deck. From Getaria you can walk an hour to Zarautz, the next town east, which has a wide family-friendly beach and plenty of taverns and cafés, plus a 12-km (7-mile) trail called the Anillo Verde Azul (EBU) that encircles the town.

Zumaia, the town west of Getaria, is a snug little port and summer resort with the Urola River flowing—back and forth, according to the tide—through town. It is best-known for a dramatic sedimentary rock formation called the Flysch. Zumaia and Getaria are connected along the coast road and by several good footpaths.

VISITOR INFORMATION

CONTACTS Getaria Tourist Office. ✉ *Parque Aldamar 2, Getaria* ☎ *94/314–0957* 🌐 *www.getariaturismo.eus.* **Zumaia Tourist Office.** ✉ *Pl. de Kantauri 13, Zumaia* ☎ *94/314–3396* 🌐 *www.zumaia.eus.*

👁 Sights

Cristóbal Balenciaga Museum

OTHER MUSEUM | The haute-couture maestro Cristóbal Balenciaga (1895–1972) was born in Getaria, and the impressive museum created in his honor is a must-see, regardless of your fashion sensibilities. The collection and interactive exhibits are distributed between two buildings, the mansion where Balenciaga was born and a starkly geometric monolith inaugurated in 2011. Feast your eyes on couture relics from the foundation's 1,200-item collection, from suits to gowns and accessories that represent his life's work. "Balenciaga is a couturier in the truest sense of the word," said Coco Chanel of her rival. "The others are simply fashion designers." ✉ *Aldamar Parkea 6, Getaria* ☎ *94/300–8840* 🌐 *www.cristobalbalenciagamuseoa.com* 🎫 *€10* 🕒 *Closed Mon. in Sept.–June.*

★ Flysch

NATURE SIGHT | FAMILY | The Flysch is the crown jewel of the Basque Coast Geopark, a 13-km (8-mile) stretch of coastline distinguished by spectacular cliffs and rock formations. Taking its name from the German for "slippery"—a reference to the slipping of tectonic plates that thrust the horizontal rock layers into vertical panels—the Flysch contains innumerable layers of sedimentary rock displaying some 20 million years of geological history. One such layer is black and devoid of fossils; it was identified by scientists as marking the Cretaceous–Paleogene extinction event, which caused the extinction of the dinosaurs. ✉ *Playa de Itzurun, Zumaia* 🎫 *Free.*

Sanctuary of Loyola

RELIGIOUS BUILDING | This sanctuary, about 20 km (12 miles) south of Zumaia in Cestona, is an exuberant Churrigueresque-Baroque structure erected in honor of Íñigo Lopez de Oñaz y Loyola (1491–1556) after he was canonized in 1622 for his defense of the Catholic Church against the tides of Martin Luther's Reformation. Almost two centuries later, Roman architect Carlos Fontana designed the basilica that memorializes the saint. The ornate construction contrasts with the austere lifestyle of St. Ignatius, who took vows of poverty and chastity after his conversion. Polychrome marble, flamboyant altar work, and a huge but delicate dome decorate the interior. The fortresslike tower house has the room where Ignatius (Eneko in Euskera) experienced conversion while recovering from a wound received in an intra-Basque battle. ✉ *Loiola Auzoa 16, Cestona* ✥ *from Bilboa, take Exit 48 toward Zestoa-Azpeitia* 🌐 *loyola.global* 🎫 *€4.*

🍴 Restaurants

Asador Bedua

$$$$ | BASQUE | This rustic (if perhaps overpriced) fourth-generation asador draws the crowds for its excellent *tortilla de bacalao, txuleta de buey*, and fish of all kinds, especially the classic besugo cooked "*a la donostiarra*" (roasted and finished with garlic-vinegar sauce). Txakoli from nearby Getaria is the beverage of choice. **Known for:** farmhouse-chic ambience; top-quality txuleton; pristine seafood and home-grown vegetables. [$] *Average main: €30* ✉ *Cestona, Barrio Bedua,* ✥ *Up Urola, 3 km (2 miles) from Zumaia* ☎ *94/386–0551* 🌐 *www.bedua.eus.*

★ Elkano

$$$$ | SEAFOOD | Ever since Anthony Bourdain waxed poetic about award-winning Elkano's grilled turbot on *Parts Unknown*, the dish has become something of a holy grail among in-the-know foodies. Order the famous flatfish (at its fatty prime in May and June), and you'll receive what Bourdain called an "anatomy lesson" as the maître d' extols the virtues of each separate cut, culminating with the gelatinous fins—which you're encouraged to suck between your fingers, caveman style. **Known for:** grilled turbot; reputation as an Anthony Bourdain favorite; rare, quirky wines. [$] *Average main: €45* ✉ *Calle Herrerieta 2, Getaria* ☎ *94/314–0024* 🌐 *www.restauranteelkano.com* 🕒 *Closed Tues.*

★ Segore Etxe-Berri

$$$ | BASQUE | FAMILY | Hidden in the lush, hilly countryside southwest of Tolosa—and many miles off the tourist track—is this idyllic agroturismo comprised of a restaurant and five-room bed-and-breakfast housed in a traditional *caserío* (Basque farmhouse) perched on a hilltop. After snapping a few pics of the jaw-dropping views, tuck into a soul-satisfying Basque feast of roast chicken (raised on the property), stewed game meats, or fresh fish. **Known for:** meats and vegetables from the estate; culinary gem in the middle of nowhere; outdoor playground for kids. $ *Average main: €18* ✉ *Calle Valle Santa Marina, Albiztur* ☎ *94/358–0976* 🌐 *www.segore.com* 🕑 *Closed Tues. No dinner Mon., Wed., and Thurs.*

Hotels

Landarte

$$ | **B&B/INN** | **FAMILY** | Kick back in this restored 16th-century country manor house 1 km (½ mile) from Zumaia and an hour's walk from Getaria. **Pros:** warm, family-friendly atmosphere; unusual wall art; traditional cuisine on request. **Cons:** can't go far without a car; €9 breakfast; some top-floor rooms under the low eaves could be tricky for taller guests. $ *Rooms from: €95* ✉ *Ctra. Artadi Anzoa 1, Zumaia* ☎ *94/386–5358* 🌐 *www.landarte.net* 🕑 *Closed mid-Dec.–Feb.* 🛏 *6 rooms.*

★ **Saiaz Getaria**

$$ | **HOTEL** | For an idyllic beach escape and panoramic views over the Bay of Biscay, this renovated 15th-century house on Getaria's uppermost street is a no-brainer. **Pros:** historic property; discounts at nearby spa and gym; waves lull you to sleep. **Cons:** only two (first-come, first-served) parking spaces; spotty Wi-Fi; soundproofing could be better. $ *Rooms from: €115* ✉ *Roke Deuna 25, Getaria* ☎ *94/314–0143* 🌐 *www.saiazgetaria.com* 🕑 *Closed Dec. 20–Jan. 6* 🛏 *17 rooms.*

Shopping

Getaria, Zumaia, and the surrounding villages are great places to pick up locally canned anchovies, tuna, and sardines as well as bottles of *txakoli*, pickled piparra peppers, and *sagardoa* (Basque cider). Of note is the *ventresca de bonito del norte* (oil-cured albacore tuna belly), so veined with delicious omega-3-rich fat that it's almost spreadable—the best canned tuna money can buy.

Salanort

FOOD | This highly regarded *conservas* company might be most famous for its anchovies, which are always plump and expertly packed, but you can also stock up on local wines and liqueurs here such as *patxaran* , a digestif made with sloe berries. ✉ *Nagusia 22, Getaria* ☎ *94/314–0036* 🌐 *www.salanort.com.*

San Sebastián

100 km (62 miles) northeast of Bilbao.

San Sebastián (Donostia in Euskera) is a majestic city arched around one of the finest urban beaches in the world, **La Concha**, so named for its shell-like shape, with Ondarreta and Zurriola beaches at the southwestern and northeastern ends. The promontories of Monte Urgull and Monte Igueldo serve as bookends for La Concha, while Zurriola has Monte Ulía rising over its far end. The best way to take in San Sebastián is on foot: Promenades and pathways twist up the hills that surround the city and afford postcard-perfect views. The first records of San Sebastián date to the 11th century. A backwater for most of Spain's history, the city had the good fortune in 1845 to woo Queen Isabella II, who was seeking relief from a skin ailment in the icy Atlantic waters. Isabella was followed by much of the aristocracy of the time, and San Sebastián became—and remains—a favored summer retreat for Madrid's well-to-do.

The city is bisected by the **Urumea River,** which is crossed by three ornate bridges inspired by late-19th-century French architecture. At the mouth of the Urumea, the incoming surf smashes the rocks with such force that white foam erupts, and the sound is wild and Wagnerian. The city is laid out with wide streets on a grid pattern, thanks mainly to the dozen times it has been all but destroyed by fire. The last conflagration came after the French were expelled in 1813; English and Portuguese forces occupied the city, abused the population, and torched the place. Today, San Sebastián is a seaside resort on par with Nice and Monte Carlo. It becomes one of Spain's most expensive cities in the summer, when French vacationers descend in droves. It is also, like Bilbao, a center of Basque nationalism.

Neighborhoods include the scenic, touristy La Parte Vieja, tucked under Monte Urgull north of the mouth of the Urumea River; hip-and-happening Gros (so named for a corpulent Napoleonic general), across the Urumea to the north; commercial Centro, the main city nucleus around the cathedral; residential Amara, farther east toward the Anoeta sports complex; glitzy La Concha, at center stage around the beach; and stately El Antiguo, at the western end of La Concha. Igueldo is the high promontory over the city at the southwestern side of the bay. Alto de Miracruz is the high ground to the northeast toward France; Errenteria is inland east of Pasaia; Oiartzun is a village farther north; Astigarraga is in apple-cider country to the east of Anoeta.

GETTING HERE AND AROUND

San Sebastián is a very walkable city, though local buses (€1.75) are also convenient. Buses for Pasajes (Pasaia), Errenteria, Astigarraga, and Oiartzun originate in Calle Okendo, one block west of the Urumea River behind the Hotel Maria Cristina. Bus A-1 goes to Astigarraga; A-2 is the bus to Pasajes.

The Euskotren's Metro Donostialdea, the city train, is popularly known as El Topo (The Mole) for the amount of time it spends underground. It originates at the Amara Viejo station in Paseo Easo and tunnels its way to Hendaye, France, every 30 minutes (€5.80; 45 minutes). Euskotren also serves Bilbao by way of

Lasarte–Oria, but buses and Blablacar rideshares will get you there in about half the time. It recently opened new stations that connect the neighboring towns of Lasarte-Oria (€1.19; 12 minutes), Pasaia (€1.19; 12 minutes) and Irun (€1.73; 30 minutes) to San Sebastián.

For the funicular up to Monte Igueldo (☎ 943/213525 ⊕ www.monteigueldo. es; €3.15), the station is just behind Ondarreta beach at the western end of La Concha.

BUS CONTACTS Estación de Autobuses. ✉ Paseo de Federico García Lorca 1, San Sebastián ☎ 94/347–5150 ⊕ www. estaciondonostia.com.

CAR RENTAL Europcar. ✉ Aeropuerto de San Sebastián, Calle Gabarrari 22, Hondarribia ☎ 94/366–8530 ⊕ www.europcar. com.

TRAIN CONTACTS Estación de Amara. (Estación de Easo) ✉ Pl. Easo 9, San Sebastián ☎ 90/254–3210 ⊕ www.renfe. com.**Estación de San Sebastián–Donostia.** (Estación del Norte) ✉ Paseo de Francia 22, San Sebastián ☎ 90/224–3402 ⊕ www.renfe.com.

VISITOR INFORMATION
CONTACTS San Sebastián–Donostia Tourist Office. ✉ Alameda del Blvd. 8, San Sebastián ☎ 94/348–1166 ⊕ www. sansebastianturismoa.eus.

 Sights

Every corner of Spain champions its culinary identity, but San Sebastián is especially proud of its varied food scene. Many of the city's restaurants and pintxo bars are in the **Parte Vieja** (Old Quarter), on the east end of the bay beyond the elegant **Casa Consistorial** (City Hall) and formal **Alderdi Eder** gardens. The building that now houses city hall opened as a casino in 1887; after gambling was outlawed early in the 20th century, the town council moved here from the Plaza de la Constitución, the Parte Vieja's main square.

Aquarium Donostia-San Sebastián

AQUARIUM | FAMILY | For a stroll through and under some 6,000 marine animals—ranging from tiger sharks to sea turtles, with one participative pool where kids are encouraged to touch and try to pick up fish—the aquarium is a great rainy-day activity. The illustrated history of Basque whaling and boatbuilding is also fascinating. ⊠ Pl. Carlos Blasco de Imaz 1, Parte Vieja ☎ 94/344–0099 ⊕ www. aquariumss.com ☎ €13.

Catedral del Buen Pastor (Cathedral of the Good Shepherd)

CHURCH | You can see the facade of this 19th-century cathedral from the river, across town. With the tallest church spire in the province, the Catedral del Buen Pastor was constructed in the neo-Gothic style. It's worth a glimpse inside for its beautiful stained-glass windows. ⊠ Pl. del Buen Pastor, Calle Urdaneta 12, Centro ☎ 94/346–4516 ☎ Free ⊙ Closed weekends.

Chillida Leku Museum

ART MUSEUM | In the Jáuregui section of Hernani, 10 minutes south of San Sebastián (close to both Martín Berasategui's restaurant in nearby Lasarte and the cider houses of the Astigarraga neighborhood, like Sidrería Petritegi), the Eduardo Chillida Sculpture Garden and Museum, in a 16th-century farmhouse, got a face-lift to finally reopen in April 2019. It is a treat for anyone interested in contemporary art. ⊠ Caserío Zabalaga, Barrio Jáuregui 66, Lasarte ☎ 94/333–6006 ⊕ www.museochillidaleku.com ☎ €12 ⊙ Closed Tues.–Thurs.

Iglesia de Santa María del Coro

CHURCH | Just in from the harbor, in the shadow of Monte Urgull, is this baroque church with a stunning carved facade of an arrow-riddled St. Sebastian flanked by two towers. The interior is strikingly restful considering the bustling area.

Note the sculptures The Harmony of Sound, by Maximilian Peizmann, to the right of the entrance, and By the Cross to the Light, by Eduardo Chillida, in the baptistery. ⊠ Calle Mayor 12, Parte Vieja ☎ 94/342–3124 ☎ €3.

Isla de Santa Clara

ISLAND | FAMILY | You can visit the uninhabited Isla de Santa Clara, which rises from the center of the bay and shields La Concha from high swells. Ferries (around €7 round trip) run from the mainland every 30 minutes and are packed on summer weekends, and reaching the island from the beach is a fun challenge for experienced swimmers. There's a small bar at the ferry dock and lifeguard service at a beach that reveals itself only at low tide. Bring sturdy sandals as the coastline is rocky. In June 2021, a 15-ton bronze fountain called Hondalea ("Sea Floor"), by Basque sculptor Cristina Iglesias, was unveiled within the lighthouse; its whooshing flows are meant to mimic the tides.   ⊠ San Sebastián ⊕ www. motorasdelaisla.com.

Kursaal

PERFORMANCE VENUE | Designed by the world-renowned Spanish architect Rafael Moneo and located at the mouth of the Urumea River, the Kursaal is San Sebastián's postmodern concert hall, film society, and convention center. The gleaming cubes of glass that make up this bright complex were conceived as a perpetuation of the site's natural geography, an attempt to underline the harmony between the natural and the artificial and to create a visual stepping-stone between the heights of Monte Urgull and Monte Ulía. Home of the Basque Country's symphony orchestra, this venue is also a favorite for ballet, opera, theater, and jazz performances. It has two auditoriums, a gargantuan banquet hall, meeting rooms, exhibition space, a set of terraces overlooking the estuary, and a nueva cocina restaurant called Ni Neu. For guided tours of the building,

San Sebastián's famed, curving beach La Concha

make arrangements in advance. ✉ *Av. de Zurriola 1, Gros* ☎ *94/300–3000* ⊕ *www. kursaal.eus.*

⭐ Monte Igueldo

VIEWPOINT | On the western side of the bay, this promontory is a must-visit. You can walk or drive up or take the funicular (around €4 round trip), with departures every 15 minutes. From the top, you get a bird's-eye view of San Sebastián's gardens, beaches, parks, wide tree-lined boulevards, and Belle Époque buildings. There's also a small amusement park. ✉ *Igueldo* ☎ *94/321–3525 for funicular* ⊕ *www.monteigueldo.es* ⊗ *Closed most of Jan. and Wed. Nov.–Feb.*

Tabakalera

ARTS CENTER | Occupying a century-old tobacco factory, this vibrant cultural center, inaugurated in 2015, epitomizes the creative, forward-thinking verve of San Sebastián. Check the website to see what performances, exhibitions, and screenings are planned ahead of your visit, and drop by to steep yourself in the city's here and now. The roof deck (free admission) affords pleasing views of the river directly below. ✉ *Pl. Andre Zigarrogileak 1, Amara* ☎ *94/311–8855* ⊕ *www. tabakalera.eus.*

Beaches

⭐ La Concha

BEACH | **FAMILY** | San Sebastián's shell-shaped main beach is one of the most famous urban beaches in the world. Night and day, rain or shine, it's filled with locals and tourists alike, strolling and taking in the city's skyline and the uninhabited Isla de Santa Clara just offshore. Several hotels line its curved expanse including the grande dame Hotel de Londres y de Inglaterra. The beach has clean, pale sand and few rocks or seaweed, but only a bit of shade, near the promenade wall. Lounge chairs are available for rent. The calm surf makes it a favorite pick for families. **Amenities:** lifeguards; showers; toilets. **Best for:** sunrise; sunset; walking. ✉ *Calle de la Concha Ibilbidea, La Concha.*

Zurriola

BEACH | Just across the Urumea River from La Concha lies this sprawling, less touristy beach. Exposed to the open Atlantic, the beach boasts waves that are sometimes big enough to surf—and occasionally too dangerous for kids. **Amenities:** lifeguards; water sports. **Best for:** surfing. ✉ *Zurriola Ibilbidea, Gros.*

🍴 Restaurants

★ Antonio Bar

$$ | **TAPAS** | Tuna carpaccio with pickled Basque peppers, battered hake cheeks, tripe and pork jowl stew—these are some of the classics you'll find on the menu at Antonio, a neighborhood standby that serves unpretentious pintxos at fair prices. Ask about nightly specials, which vary depending on what's in season. **Known for:** regional beers and wines; no-nonsense pintxo bar; packed with locals. [$] *Average main: €17* ✉ *Calle Bergara 3, Centro* 🌐 *www.antoniobar.com* 🕒 *Closed Sun.*

★ Arzak

$$$$ | **BASQUE** | One of the world's great culinary meccas, award-winning Arzak embodies the prestige, novelty, and science-driven creativity of the Basque culinary zeitgeist. The restaurant and its high-tech food lab—both helmed by founder Juan Mari Arzak's daughter Elena these days—are situated in the family's 19th-century home on the outskirts of San Sebastián, and though the space might not be much to look at, the ever-changing dishes are downright thrilling for their trompe l'oeil presentations, unexpected flavor combinations, and rare ingredients. **Known for:** fresh flavors and eye-popping plating; old-school hospitality; thrilling culinary experience. [$] *Average main: €242* ✉ *Av. Alcalde Jose Elosegui 273, Alto de Miracruz* ☎ *94/327–8465, 94/328–5593* 🌐 *www.arzak.es* 🕒 *Closed Sun. and Mon., June 15–July 2, and 3 wks in early Nov.*

Bar La Cepa

$$$$ | **TAPAS** | This boisterous tavern established in 1948 has ceilings lined with dangling *jamónes*, walls covered with old photos of San Sebastián, and a dining room packed with locals and tourists in equal measure. Everything from the Iberian ham to the little olive-pepper-and-anchovy combos called "*penaltis*" will whet your appetite, but those who opt for a full meal shouldn't overlook the dry-aged *txuleton.* **Known for:** amicable staff; hand-cut Iberian ham; melt-in-your-mouth steak. [$] *Average main: €25* ✉ *Calle 31 de Agosto 7, Parte Vieja* ☎ *94/342–6394* 🌐 *www.barlacepa.com* 🕒 *Closed Tues. and second half of Nov.*

Bergara

$$$ | **TAPAS** | Winner of many a miniature cuisine award (don't miss the prawn-filled *txalupa* tartlet), this Gros neighborhood standby offers outside-the-box takes on traditional tapas and pintxos. It also serves more substantial dishes for sit-down meals. **Known for:** trendy atmosphere; heavenly foie gras; variety of newfangled and traditional pintxos. [$] *Average main: €20* ✉ *Calle General Arteche 8, Gros* ☎ *94/327–5026* 🌐 *www.pinchosbergara.es.*

Bodegón Alejandro

$$$$ | **BASQUE** | Hiding in the basement of a timber building in the heart of the parte vieja, this restaurant—where world-renowned chef Martín Berasategui cut his teeth—toes the line between traditional and contemporary Basque cuisine. Its dishes include hake in citrus sauce, locally sourced pork with mashed potatoes, and hazelnut soufflé for dessert. **Known for:** seasonal vegetable delicacies like de lágrima peas and white asparagus; top-quality meats and fish; affordable and delectable tasting menus. [$] *Average main: €24* ✉ *Calle de Fermín Calbetón 4, Parte Vieja* ☎ *94/342–7158* 🌐 *www.bodegonalejandro.com.*

★ Casa Urola

$$$$ | BASQUE | FAMILY | Don't be put off by the slightly outdated decor of this Parte Vieja stalwart—the kitchen at Casa Urola is easily one of the city's most adroit. Savor appetizers made with hard-to-find regional vegetables like cardoon, borage, and tiny de lágrima peas before moving onto entrées like seared squab, presented with a pâté of its own liver, and roasted hake loin, served with white wine and clams. **Known for:** signature torrija; repuation as restaurant industry favorite; flawless Basque cuisine. $ Average main: €28 ⊠ Calle de Fermín Calbetón 20, Parte Vieja ☎ 94/344–1371 ⊕ www. casaurolajatetxea.es ⊗ Closed Tues.

★ Ganbara

$$ | TAPAS | This busy bar and restaurant near Plaza de la Constitución is now run by the third generation of the same family. Specialty morsels range from shrimp and asparagus to acorn-fed Iberian ham on croissants and anchovies, sea urchins, and—the house specialty—wild mushrooms topped with an egg yolk. **Known for:** lively and loud atmosphere; traditional Basque pintxos; to-die-for wild mushrooms. $ Average main: €14 ⊠ Calle San Jerónimo 21, Parte Vieja ☎ 94/342–2575 ⊕ www.ganbarajatetxea.com ⊗ Closed Mon.–Weds. No dinner Sun.

Goiz Argi

$ | TAPAS | The specialty of this tiny bar—and the reason locals flock here in droves—is the garlicky seared-shrimp brochette. **Known for:** juicy shrimp skewers; cheerful bartenders; good value. $ Average main: €9 ⊠ Calle de Fermín Calbetón 4, Parte Vieja ☎ 94/342–5204.

Gorriti

$ | TAPAS | Next to the open-air Brecha Market, this traditional little pintxos bar is a well-priced neighborhood standby filled with good cheer and delicious tapas. **Known for:** simple, well-prepared Basque bites; fabulous tortilla de bacalao; casual local crowd. $ Average main: €11 ⊠ Calle

San Juan 3, Parte Vieja ☎ 94/342–8353 ⊕ www.bargorriti.com ⊗ Closed Sun.

★ La Viña

$$ | TAPAS | FAMILY | This centrally located, no-frills bar is almost always crowded, drawing busloads of tour groups as well as locals, who come to try the viral "burnt" cheesecake with an oozy core. This silky, creamy dessert pairs perfectly with a cup of coffee, while, on the savory side, the underrated pintxos—red peppers stuffed with bacalao, croquetas, veal meatballs, what have you—sing alongside a glass of Rioja. **Known for:** world-famous cheesecake with a cult following; wide variety of classic pintxos; old-timey ambience. $ Average main: €15 ⊠ Calle 31 de Agosto 3, Parte Vieja ☎ 94/342–7495 ⊕ www.lavinarestau-rante.com ⊗ Closed Mon.

★ Martín Berasategui

$$$$ | CONTEMPORARY | Basque chef Martín Berasategui has more Michelin stars than any other chef in Spain, and at his flagship in the dewy village of Lasarte-Oria, it's easy to see why. Dishes are Basque at heart but prepared with exacting, French-inflected technique that comes through in dishes like artfully composed salads, elegant caviar preparations, and eel-and-foie-gras mille-feuilles—a Berasategui signature. **Known for:** artful mix of classic and avant-garde; once-in-a-lifetime dining experience; idyllic, white-tablecloth outdoor terrace. $ Average main: €88 ⊠ Calle Loidi 4, Lasarte ✛ 8 km (5 miles) south of San Sebastián ☎ 94/336–6471, 94/336–1599 ⊕ www.martinberasategui.com ⊗ Closed Sun.–Tues. and mid-Dec.–mid-Jan.

Maun Grill Bar

$$ | BASQUE | Opened in 2019 in Mercado de San Martín, Maun is not your typical no-frills "bar de mercado" but rather a gastronomical food counter whose mouthwatering dishes—such as fish stew, squid in ink sauce, and heirloom tomato salad—are made with ultra-fresh ingredients sourced right there

at the market. **Known for:** market-fresh cuisine; promising young chef; terrific value. $ *Average main: €16* ✉ *Mercado San Martín, Urbieta Kalea 9, Centro* ☎ *60/323–4761* 🌐 *www.maungrillbar.com* 🕓 *Closed Mon.*

Mugaritz

$$$$ | **ECLECTIC** | This bucolic farmhouse in the hills above Errenteria, 8 km (5 miles) northeast of San Sebastián, is a veritable laboratory of modern cooking techniques helmed by (arguably) the most experimental chef in Spain today, Andoni Aduriz. The obligatory three-hour, 20-course experience—which might be too abstract for some—includes dishes like "don't search, find" and "tradition: onion and squid," all complemented by zany wild-card wines. **Known for:** long, immersive dining experience; being a bit "out there"; abstract dishes. $ *Average main: €231* ✉ *Otzazulueta Baserria, Aldura Aldea 20, Errenteria, San Sebastián* ☎ *94/352–2455, 94/351–8343* 🌐 *www.mugaritz.com* 🕓 *Closed Mon.–Wed. and mid-Jan.–mid-Apr.*

Ni Neu

$$$ | **CONTEMPORARY** | Ni Neu ("Me, Myself" in Euskera), defined by its experimental comfort-food cuisine, occupies a bright corner of Rafael Moneo's dazzling Kursaal complex at the mouth of the Urumea. Cobble together a meal out of the pintxos (croquetas, fried anchovies, etc.), or spring for a tasting menu centered on rice dishes. **Known for:** traditional Basque fare with a modern twist; €36 tasting menu (a steal); riverside dining. $ *Average main: €20* ✉ *Av. Zurriola 1, Gros* ☎ *94/300–3162* 🌐 *www.restaurantenineu.com* 🕓 *Closed Mon.–Wed.*

Restaurante Astelena 1997

$$$$ | **BASQUE** | Chef Ander González transformed the narrow stone rooms of a defunct banana warehouse into one of the finest spots for modern Basque dining—at a great price. The €55 weekend *menú degustación* (tasting menu) hinges on what's in season, though dishes like seared *txuleton* and hake in white wine sauce with clams never come off the menu for a reason. At the time of writing, the restaurant was open for lunch only. **Known for:** surprisingly good value for this part of town; unpretentious yet elegant Basque cuisine; fantastic seafood dishes. $ *Average main: €24* ✉ *Euskal Herria 3, Parte Vieja* ☎ *94/342–5867* 🌐 *www.restauranteastelena.com* 🕓 *Closed Mon. and Tues. No dinner.*

Restaurante Kokotxa

$$$$ | **INTERNATIONAL** | The menu at this award-winning restaurant in the heart of the Parte Vieja hinges on chef Daniel López's clean, innovative cuisine, which plays on traditional Basque and Spanish flavors and often adds an Asian twist. Opt for a market-driven *degustación* or López's classic tasting menu, which includes signature dishes like whole langoustine with Navarrese white beans and Sichuan-spiced squab in liver ragout. **Known for:** surprisingly casual atmosphere; Asian-inflected Basque cuisine; only Michelin-starred dining in the city center. $ *Average main: €88* ✉ *Calle del Campanario 11, Parte Vieja* ☎ *94/342–1904* 🌐 *www.restaurantekokotxa.com* 🕓 *Closed Sun.–Tues.*

Topa Sukalderia

$$ | **LATIN AMERICAN** | **FAMILY** | This buzzy Latin-Spanish fusion restaurant is the brainchild of Andoni Luis Aduriz of two-Michelin-star Mugaritz. A breath of fresh air on the local dining scene serving colorful cocktails and saucy dishes to the backdrop of Cuban jazz, Topa prides itself on making everything from scratch, from its nixtamalized tortillas to its "thousand-day" mole (originally a gift of Enrique Olvera of Pujol). **Known for:** best margs and guac in town; Basque-Latin fusion cuisine; latest project by Mugaritz chef. $ *Average main: €15* ✉ *Calle Agirre Miramon 7, Gros* ☎ *94/356–9143* 🌐 *www.topasukalderia.com* 🕓 *Closed Mon.–Wed.*

★ Zelaia Sagardotegia

$$$$ | **BASQUE** | This traditional *sagardotegi*, located 7 km (4 miles) south of San Sebastián, is where the region's top chefs—Juan Mari Arzak, Martín Berasategui, and Pedro Subijana, to name a few—ring in every cider season with a resounding *¡txotx!* ("cheers" in Basque). Removed from the tourist track and open from mid-January to late April, Zelaia invites guests into its barrel-lined warehouses to chow down on a set menu of bacalao-centric dishes, thick-cut steaks, and—for dessert—local sheep's-milk cheese with quince preserves and walnuts. **Known for:** being an authentic cider house; unlimited cider drinking; food that's an echelon above other sagardotegis. [$] *Average main: €30* ✉ *B0 Martindegi 29* ☎ *94/355–5851* 🌐 *www.zelaia.eus* 🕒 *Closed late Apr.–mid-Jan. and Sun.*

Zuberoa

$$$$ | **BASQUE** | This is the kind of restaurant where the chef greets every table and meals start with an amuse-bouche of foie gras—in other words, a slice of old-school heaven. Market-driven meals (think roasted wild game, tiny *de lágrima* peas, and strawberry gazpacho) unfold to the backdrop of a 15th-century farmhouse with an ivy-lined patio (the latter is open in summer only). **Known for:** dining room in a 15th-century caserío; Michelin-starred old-world Basque cuisine; wonderfully hospitable chef. [$] *Average main: €40* ✉ *Araneder Bidea, Barrio Iturriotz, San Sebastián* ☎ *94/349–1228* 🌐 *www.zuberoa.com* 🕒 *Closed Wed. year-round, and Sun. June–Oct. No dinner Sun. year-round, and Tues. Nov.–May.*

Hotels

Arrizul Congress Hotel

$$$ | **HOTEL** | This clean-cut urban hotel, located steps from the river and Zurriola Beach, opened in early 2017 and is a dependable option for families and business travelers alike. **Pros:** within walking distance of all the main sights; feels fresh and modern; triples are available. **Cons:** occasionally unprofessional front-desk staff; so-so soundproofing means noisy mornings; architectural foibles make some rooms awkward. [$] *Rooms from: €180* ✉ *Calle Ronda 3, Gros* ☎ *94/332–7026* 🌐 *www.hotelarrizulcongress.com* 🛏 *46 rooms.*

Astoria7 Hotel

$$$$ | **HOTEL** | Set in the renovated Astoria Cinema, this movie-themed hotel has a spacious lobby adorned with autographed photos of the many movie stars who have attended the famous San Sebastián Film Festival over the years. **Pros:** spacious rooms; varied, good-quality breakfast; fun and campy cinematographic decor. **Cons:** 20-minute walk (or short bus ride) to beach and the Parte Vieja; not for non-cinephiles; ugly high-rise building. [$] *Rooms from: €254* ✉ *Calle de la Sagrada Família 1, Centro* ☎ *94/344–5000* 🌐 *www.astoria7hotel.com/en* 🛏 *102 rooms* 🍴 *No Meals.*

Hotel de Londres y de Inglaterra

$$$$ | **HOTEL** | On the main beachfront promenade overlooking La Concha, this stately hotel has a regal, old-world feel and Belle Époque aesthetic that starts in the elegant marble lobby, with its shimmering chandeliers, and continues throughout the hotel. **Pros:** professional service; best hotel views in town; cozy and comfortable rooms. **Cons:** unremarkable and unkempt breakfast area; street side can be noisy on weekends; noticeable wear and tear. [$] *Rooms from: €330* ✉ *Zubieta 2, La Concha* ☎ *94/344–0770* 🌐 *www.hlondres.com* 🛏 *148 rooms* 🍴 *Free Breakfast.*

★ Hotel María Cristina

$$$$ | **HOTEL** | The graceful beauty of the Belle Époque is embodied here, in San Sebastián's most luxurious hotel on the west bank of the Urumea, which has hosted countless movie stars and dignitaries since opening in 1912. **Pros:** grand historic building; old-world elegance with

new-world amenities; elaborate white-tablecloth breakfasts. **Cons:** views aren't as dramatic as other top hotels'; staff can be a bit stiff; wildly expensive. [$] *Rooms from: €415* ✉ *Paseo República Argentina 4, Centro* ☎ *94/343–7600* 🌐 *www.hotel-mariacristina.com* 🛏 *136 rooms* 🍴 *No Meals.*

Hotel Parma

$$$ | **HOTEL** | Overlooking the Kursaal concert hall and the Zurriola beach at the mouth of the Urumea River, this small but inviting two-star is situated at the edge of the Parte Vieja, San Sebastián's prime grazing area for tapas and vinos. **Pros:** Parte Vieja location; you can hear the crashing of the waves; river views. **Cons:** digs are a bit cramped and cluttered; interiors could use a face-lift; some rooms look out onto a scuzzy courtyard. [$] *Rooms from: €170* ✉ *Paseo de Salamanca 10, Parte Vieja* ☎ *94/342–8893* 🌐 *www.hotelparma.com* 🛏 *27 rooms* 🍴 *Free Breakfast.*

★ One Shot Tabakalera House

$$$ | **HOTEL** | Locals call this four-star newcomer a "hotel within a museum" because of its location inside the Tabakalera cultural center, a hotbed of art and innovation inaugurated in 2015. **Pros:** close to the RENFE train station; located within the city's cultural center; avant-garde design. **Cons:** 10-minute walk into town; no room service; no coffeemakers in most rooms. [$] *Rooms from: €180* ✉ *Paseo Duque de Mandas 52, Amara* ☎ *94/393–0028* 🌐 *www.hotelone-shottabakalerahouse.com* 🛏 *33 rooms* 🍴 *No Meals.*

Pensión Nuevas Artes

$$ | **B&B/INN** | This tidy 10-room hotel four blocks east of San Sebastián's cathedral stands out for its rock-bottom (at least by San Sebastian standards) prices. **Pros:** steps from the Buen Pastor Cathedral and top sights; cozy atmosphere; terrific value. **Cons:** bad soundproofing; no check-in between 2 and 5 pm; no a/c. [$] *Rooms from: €110* ✉ *Urbieta 64, Centro* ☎ *94/347–4905* 🌐 *www.pension-nuevasartes.com* 🛏 *10 rooms* 🍴 *No Meals.*

Villa Soro

$$$$ | **HOTEL** | The open lobby of this mansion-cum-hotel has vaulted ceilings and curved Victorian stairs that lead to a sunny, stained-glassed sitting area and opulent guest rooms. **Pros:** free on-site parking and loaner bikes; historic mansion away from the tourist fray; more than a dozen Spanish wines by the glass at the bar. **Cons:** basement rooms are a bit dreary; front-desk staff harried at times; 10-minute taxi or bus ride from the center of town. [$] *Rooms from: €305* ✉ *Av. de Ategorrieta 61, Gros* ☎ *94/329–7970* 🌐 *www.villasoro.es* 🍴 *Free Breakfast* 🛏 *25 rooms.*

Nightlife

BARS AND PUBS

Gu

COCKTAIL LOUNGES | The renovated Gu, with its floor-to-ceiling windows overlooking La Concha, is a glitzy indoor-outdoor cocktail bar and nightclub housed in a futuristic building resembling a cruise ship. ✉ *Ijentea 9, Centro* ☎ *84/398–0775* 🌐 *www.gusansebastian.com.*

DANCE CLUBS

Bataplán

DANCE CLUBS | San Sebastián's top dance club is near the western end of La Concha. Guest DJs and events determine the vibe, although you can count on high-energy dance music and enthusiastic drinking. ✉ *Paseo de la Concha 10, Centro* ☎ *94/346–0439* 🌐 *www.bataplan-disco.com.*

MUSIC CLUBS

Akerbeltz

LIVE MUSIC | This feel-good dive bar is a perfect late-night refuge for music and drinks. ✉ *Calle Mari 19, Parte Vieja* ☎ *94/346–0934, 94/345–1452.*

★ ¡BE! Club

LIVE MUSIC | Formerly known as Bebop, this San Sebastián classic—which eschews the usual Top 40 in favor of Latin, jazz, and unconventional dance tunes—got a major face-lift in 2018 and is all the better for it. ⊠ *Paseo de Salamanca 3, Parte Vieja* ☎ *94/347–8505* ⊕ *www.beclubss.com.*

Shopping

San Sebastián is a busy shopping town. Wander Calle San Martín and the surrounding pedestrian-only streets to see what's in the windows.

Alboka Artesanía

CRAFTS | This is the best city-center shop for Basque-made artisan items such as patterned tablecloths and linens, goatskin jai alai balls, ceramics, and traditional dress. ⊠ *Pl. Constitución 8, Parte Vieja* ☎ *94/342–6300* ⊕ *albokaartesania.com* ⊘ *Closed Sun.*

Casa Ponsol

HATS & GLOVES | This is the best place to buy a *boina*, or traditional felt hat. The Leclerq family has been hatting (and clothing) the local male population for four generations, since 1838. ⊠ *Calle Narrica 4, at Calle Sarriegui 3, Parte Vieja* ☎ *94/342–0876* ⊕ *www.casaponsol.com* ⊘ *Closed Sun.*

Mimo

FOOD | This posh gourmet food and wine shop also hosts Basque cooking classes and the city's best food tours. ⊠ *Calle Okendo 1, Centro* ☎ *94/342–1143* ⊕ *www.mimo.eus.*

Vitoria-Gasteiz

62 km (39 miles) south of Bilbao, 100 km (62 miles) west of Pamplona.

The capital of the Basque Country, and the region's second-largest city after Bilbao, Vitoria-Gasteiz might be Euskadi's least "Basque" city, at least from a foreigner's perspective, since it's neither a seafaring port nor a mountain enclave. It sprawls, instead, over the steppe-like meseta de Álava (Álava plain) and functions as a modern industrial center with plentiful cultural events, fine restaurants, and museums—in other words, it's a Basque city for Basques.

It takes in a strikingly well-preserved Casco Medieval (Medieval Quarter). Founded by Sancho el Sabio (the Wise) in 1181, the urban center was built largely of granite, so Vitoria's oldest streets and squares seem especially weathered and ancient. **Calle Cuchillería** ("La Kutxi" to locals) is the old town's main tapas drag with over 40 establishments packed into a 500-meter (1/3-mile) stretch.

GETTING AROUND
Take the A1 and the PA34 from Pamplona, which takes one hour by car; buses also run regularly between the two cities. From Bilbao, hop on the AP68 and N622, which takes 44 minutes. Vitoria is a spread-out city, but the area you'll spend your time in is small, only about 1 km (½ mile) square, and easily covered on foot.

BUS STATION Estación de Autobuses de Vitoria–Gasteiz. ⊠ *Pl. de Euskaltzaindia, Vitoria* ☎ *94/516–1666.*

CAR RENTALS Europcar. ⊠ *Calle Adriano VI 29, Vitoria* ☎ *94/520–0433* ⊕ *www.europcar.com.*

VISITOR INFORMATION
CONTACTS Vitoria–Gasteiz. ⊠ *Pl. España 1, Vitoria* ☎ *94/516–1598* ⊕ *www.vitoria-gasteiz.org.*

Sights

★ Artium Museum

ART MUSEUM | Officially named the Centro-Museo Vasco de Arte Contemporáneo, this former bus station is regarded as the third corner of the Basque art triangle, along with the Bilbao Guggenheim and San Sebastián's

Chillida–Leku. The museum's permanent collection—including 20th- and 21st-century paintings and sculptures by Jorge Oteiza, Chillida, Agustín Ibarrola, and Nestor Basterretxea, among others—makes it one of Spain's finest treasuries of contemporary art. ⊠ *Calle Francia 24, Vitoria* ☎ *94/520–9020* ⊕ *www.artium. eus* 🎟 *Free (donation recommended)* ⊙ *Closed Mon.*

Bibat Museum

HISTORY MUSEUM | **FAMILY** | The 1525 Palacio de Bendaña and adjoining bronze-plated building are home to one of Vitoria's main attractions, the Bibat, which combines the Museo Fournier de Naipes (Playing-Card Museum) with the Museo de Arqueología. The *palacio* houses the 15,000 playing-card sets of Don Heraclio Fournier, who founded a famous playing-card factory in 1868. One of the largest and finest such collections in the world, it features hand-painted cards from Japan, round cards from India, and other ancient specimens dating to the 12th century. The Museo de la Arqueología, in the newest building, has Paleolithic dolmens, Roman art and artifacts, medieval objects, and the famous Stele del Jinete (Stele of the Horseback Rider), an early Basque tombstone. ⊠ *Calle Cuchillería 54, Vitoria* ☎ *94/520–3700* ⊕ *www.fourniermuseoabibat.eus* 🎟 *Free* ⊙ *Closed Mon.*

★ Catedral de Santa María

CHURCH | Dating to the 14th century, this crumbling cathedral is currently being restored—but it's still open to visitors, which, in fact, is what makes the experience stand out. Tour guides hand out hard hats and show you around the restoration site. It's a unique opportunity to study the building's architecture from the foundation up. A prominent and active supporter of the project is British novelist Ken Follett, whose novel *World Without End* is about the construction of the cathedral. A statue of the author has been placed on one side of the cathedral.

⊠ *Pl. Santa Maria, Vitoria* ☎ *94/525–5135* ⊕ *www.catedralvitoria.eus* 🎟 *From €9.*

Museo de Armería de Álava

OTHER MUSEUM | Just south of the park, this weaponry museum has prehistoric hatchets, 20th-century pistols, and a sand-table reproduction of the 1813 battle between the Duke of Wellington's troops and the French. ⊠ *Paseo Fray Francisco 3, Vitoria* ☎ *94/518–1925* ⊕ *www.armamuseoa.eus* 🎟 *Free* ⊙ *Closed Mon.*

Museo de Bellas Artes de Álava (*Museum of Fine Arts*)

ART MUSEUM | Paintings by Ribera, Picasso, and the Basque painter Zuloaga adorn the walls of this exuberant baroque building, whose collection spans from the 18th to the 20th century. ⊠ *Paseo Fray Francisco 8, Vitoria* ☎ *94/518–1918* ⊕ *www.arteederrenmuseoa.eus* 🎟 *Free* ⊙ *Closed Mon.*

Plaza de España

PLAZA/SQUARE | Across Virgen Blanca, past the monument and the handsome Victoria Café stands this arcaded neoclassical square with the austere elegance typical of 19th-century municipal architecture. ⊠ *Pl. de España, Vitoria.*

Plaza de la Virgen Blanca

PLAZA/SQUARE | In the southwest corner of old Vitoria, this plaza is ringed by noble houses with covered arches and white-trim glass galleries. The monument in the center commemorates the Duke of Wellington's victory over Napoléon's army here in 1813. ⊠ *Pl. de la Virgen Blanca, Vitoria.*

Street Art

PUBLIC ART | In a city as noble and staid as Vitoria, you don't expect to find world-class street art, but that's precisely what's been drawing more and more tourists and artsy types to the parallel streets of Anorbin and Carnicerías in the old town. Feast your eyes on multistory, thought-provoking murals depicting family scenes, landscapes, and political issues. ✉ *Cantón Anorbin, Vitoria.*

Torre de Doña Ochanda

CASTLE/PALACE | FAMILY | This 15th-century tower houses Vitoria's Museo de Ciencias Naturales, which contains botanical, zoological and geological collections along with the museum's most prized items: pieces of amber from the nearby archaeological site at Peñacerrada-Urizaharra. ✉ *Calle Siervas de Jesús 24, Vitoria* ☎ *94/518–1924* 🎫 *Free* 🕒 *Closed Mon.*

Torre de los Anda

HISTORIC HOME | This is the oldest house and defensive tower in Vitoria, constructed in the 15th century beside the cathedral. Though it's closed to the public, the courtyards and winding streets that surround it are worth exploring. ✉ *Plaza de la Burullería, Vitoria.*

🍴 Restaurants

Bar El Toloño

$$ | TAPAS | This deceptively simple-looking bar resembles an American diner with shiny white plastic chairs and a sleek wood bar top. But these unassuming interiors belie a real culinary jewel of a restaurant that has won a plethora of awards for its knockout pintxos including *txangurro gratinado* (crab gratin) and rabbit ravioli. **Known for:** hidden-gem bar; pristine seafood dishes; worth-the-wait creative pintxos. [$] *Average main: €15* ✉ *Cuesta San Francisco 3, Vitoria* ☎ *94/523–3336* 🌐 *www.tolonobar.com.*

★ El Portalón

$$$$ | SPANISH | With creaky wood floors, bare brick walls, and ancient beams and coats of arms, this 15th-century inn turns out classical Castilian and Basque specialties reflective of the region. Try the *cochinillo lechal* (roast suckling pig) or any of the monkfish preparations. **Known for:** deep wine list; historical building; Basque comfort food. [$] *Average main: €23* ✉ *Calle Correría 147, Vitoria* ☎ *94/514–2755* 🌐 *www.restauranteelportalon.com* 🕒 *No dinner Sun.*

★ La Bodeguilla Lanciego

$$$ | BASQUE | This inviting white-tablecloth taberna established in 1959 serves soul-satisfying cuisine in a cabin-like dining room decorated with taupe curtains, blond-wood chairs, and original artwork. Steak frites are the go-to here with roast turbot coming in a close second. **Known for:** peppy staff; excellent txuletas; subtle, tasteful decor. [$] *Average main: €19* ✉ *Calle Olagibel 60, Vitoria* ☎ *94/525–0073* 🌐 *www.labodeguillalanciego.com* 🕒 *Closed Sun.*

Zaldiarán

$$$$ | BASQUE | Don't be put off by the outdated plating (think sorbet served in martini glasses); book a meal here for contemporary interpretations of Basque classics, such as tempura-battered artichokes and razor clams with yuzu vinaigrette. The tasting menu (approximately €70) changes seasonally. **Known for:** impress-your-date ambience; heavenly steak tartare; good-value tasting menus. [$] *Average main: €25* ✉ *Av. Gasteiz 21, Vitoria* ☎ *94/513–4822* 🌐 *www.restaurantezaldiaran.com* 🕒 *Closed Mon.–Wed. No dinner Thurs. and Fri.*

🛏 Hotels

Etxegana Hotel and Spa

$$$ | HOTEL | FAMILY | On top of a mountain in the heart of Basque country's "little Switzerland," 20 minutes north of Vitoria-Gasteiz and 40 minutes south of Bilbao, this relaxing retreat features breathtaking views of the surrounding mountains and an excellent restaurant and spa. **Pros:** stunning views; family-run and welcoming; surrounded by nature. **Cons:** Wi-Fi could be better in some rooms; popular wedding venue; half-hour drive to town. [$] *Rooms from: €145* ✉ *Ipiñaburu 38,* ☎ *94/633–8448* 🌐 *www.etxegana.com* 🛏 *18 rooms* 🍴 *Free Breakfast.*

★ La Casa de los Arquillos

$$ | B&B/INN | Brightly lit, with clean Scandi-minimal design, this adorable B&B is steps from Plaza de España. **Pros:** unbeatable location; independently owned; good breakfast. **Cons:** some rooms don't have blackout drapes; no parking or 24-hour reception; rooms are up two flights of stairs. $ *Rooms from: €120* ✉ *Paseo los Arquillos 1, Vitoria* ☎ *94/515–1259* ⊕ *www.lacasadelosarquillos.com* ☞ *8 rooms* ⦿ *Free Breakfast.*

Parador de Argómaniz

$$ | HOTEL | This 17th-century palace has panoramic views over the Álava plains and feels like a time warp with its long stone hallways decorated with bulky, opulent antiques. **Pros:** excellent restaurant; gorgeous details and surroundings; contemporary rooms and comforts. **Cons:** no patio furniture on guest-room balconies; isolated at a 15-minute drive from Vitoria; noisy radiators might wake you up. $ *Rooms from: €110* ✉ *Calle del Parador 14, (N1, Km 363), Argómaniz* ✛ *East of Vitoria off N104 toward Pamplona* ☎ *94/529–3200* ⊕ *www.parador.es* ☞ *53 rooms* ⦿ *No Meals.*

Nightlife

★ Dazz

LIVE MUSIC | Drop by this kitschy bar for live music and Basque comfort food in the evenings; there's usually an impressively smooth band playing rock, blues, or jazz. Lunch on the outdoor picnic tables is wonderful when the weather is nice. ✉ *Calle Cuchillería 60, Vitoria* ☎ *94/556–1642* ⊕ *www.facebook.com/benat.lasa.3.*

Shopping

Victofer Conservas Artesanas

FOOD | This century-old purveyor that supplies top restaurants in the area is a great place to stock up on top-shelf vegetable conservas (preserved and canned foods). The piquillo peppers and white asparagus tips are especially heavenly—and make terrific souvenirs. ✉ *Calle Cuchillería 14, Vitoria* ☎ *94/525–5305* ⊕ *www.victofer.com* ⊙ *Closed Sun.*

Laguardia

45 km (28 miles) south of Vitoria

Founded in 908 AD to stand guard—as its name suggests—over Navarra's southwestern flank, Laguardia is situated on a promontory overlooking the Río Ebro and the vineyards of La Rioja Alavesa wine country. The peaceful medieval town is an ideal outpost for vineyard-hoppers.

VISITOR INFORMATION

CONTACTS Laguardia Tourist Office. ✉ *Casa Garcetas, Calle Mayor 52, Laguardia* ☎ *94/560–0845* ⊕ *www.laguardia-alava.com.*

Sights

Starting from the 15th-century Puerta de Carnicerías, or Puerta Nueva, the central portal off the parking area on the east side of town, the first landmark is the 16th-century **Ayuntamiento,** with its imperial shield of Carlos V. Farther into the square is the current town hall, built in the 19th century. A right turn down Calle Santa Engracia takes you past impressive facades—the floor inside the portal at No. 25 is a lovely stone mosaic, and a walk behind the triple-emblazoned 17th-century facade of No. 19 reveals a stagecoach, floor mosaics, wood beams, and an inner porch. The Puerta de Santa Engracia, with an image of the saint in an overhead niche, opens out to the right, and on the left, at the entrance to Calle Víctor Tapia, No. 17 bears a coat of arms with the Latin phrase "Laus Tibi" (Praise Be to Thee).

Bodega el Fabulista

WINERY | This family-run bodega is famed for its down-to-earth, approachable tours, which take place in the 16th-century caves below Laguardia and are followed by a tasting of three wines for €15. ✉ *Pl. San Juan, Laguardia* ☎ *94/562–1192* 🌐 *www.bodegaelfabulista.com* 🎫 *From €15* 🕒 *Closed Sun.*

Bodegas Baigorri

WINERY | This sleek, modern winery is an architectural wonder of glass and steel with floor-to-ceiling windows that overlook the vineyards and a state-of-the-art multilevel wine cellar. The two-hour morning tour ends around 2 pm—the perfect time to book lunch at the upstairs restaurant. The tasting menu pairs the three-course menu with four signature wines for around €50 and is highly recommended. ✉ *Ctra. Vitoria–Logroño, Km 53, Logroño* ☎ *94/560–9420* 🌐 *www.bodegasbaigorri.com* 🎫 *€15* 🕒 *Closed Sun. and Mon.*

Casa de la Primicia

NOTABLE BUILDING | Laguardia's oldest civil structure, the 15th-century Casa de la Primicia is where tithes of fresh fruit were collected in medieval times. Visit the restored underground bodega, where tours include wine tastings. ✉ *Calle Páganos 78, Laguardia* ☎ *94/562–1266, 94/560–0296* 🌐 *www.bodegascasaprimicia.com* 🎫 *€12.*

Eguren Ugarte

WINERY | The family behind this majestic winery has been in the business for five generations. Surrounded by vineyards on all sides, Eguren Ugarte offers a variety of pre-bookable tours and tastings on foot, horseback, and Segway. ✉ *Ctra. A124, Km 61, Páganos, Laguardia* ☎ *94/560–0766* 🌐 *www.egurenugarte.com* 🎫 *From €15.*

Galería Juanjo San Pedro

ART GALLERY | This gallery is filled with colorful abstract paintings of landscapes and rural life by a local artist. ✉ *Calle Mayor 11, Laguardia* ☎ *65/892–8580* 🌐 *www.juanjosanpedro.es* 🕒 *Closed Sun.*

★ **Herederos de Marqués de Riscal**

WINERY | The village of Elciego, 6 km (4 miles) southeast of Laguardia, is the site of the historic Marqués de Riscal winery. Tours of the vineyards and cellars—among the most legendary in La Rioja—are conducted in English. Reservations are required. The estate also includes the stunning Frank Gehry–designed Hotel Marqués de Riscal, crafted out of waves of metal reminiscent of his Guggenheim Bilbao. ✉ *Calle Torrea 1,* ☎ *94/560–6000* 🌐 *www.marquesderiscal.com* 🎫 *From €19.*

★ **Santa María de los Reyes**

CHURCH | Laguardia's architectural masterpiece is this church's Gothic polychrome portal—the only of its kind in Spain. Protected by a posterior Renaissance facade, the door centers on a lovely, lifelike effigy of La Virgen de los Reyes (Virgin of the Kings), sculpted in the 14th century and painted in the 17th by Ribera. Guided tours can be arranged at the tourist office; be sure to specify your language upon purchasing. ✉ *Calle Mayor 52, Laguardia* ☎ *94/560–0845* 🎫 *Tours €3* ✍ *Reservations via the tourist office only.*

Hotels

Hospedería de los Parajes

$$$ | **HOTEL** | Amenities at this traditional hotel in a restored stone building include a complimentary glass of wine at check-in, to be taken in a 16th-century wine cave. **Pros:** cozy, grandmotherly digs; charming wine cellar; centrally located. **Cons:** Wi-Fi spotty in some rooms; poor natural light; expensive and remote parking. [$] *Rooms from: €180* ✉ *Calle Mayor 46–48, Laguardia* ☎ *94/562–1130* 🌐 *www.hospederiadelosparajes.com* 🛏 *18 rooms* 🍴 *Free Breakfast.*

Hotel Castillo El Collado

$$$$ | **HOTEL** | Guests are treated like royalty in this castle-like 18th-century manor house. **Pros:** website features every room (so ask for the one you want); close to the heart of town; old-world European feel. **Cons:** underwhelming breakfast; spotty Wi-Fi in some rooms; maintenance could be improved.
[$] *Rooms from: €192* ✉ *Paseo El Collado 1, Laguardia* ☎ *94/562–1200* 🌐 *www.castillocollado.com* 🛏 *10 rooms* 🍴 *Free Breakfast.*

★ **Hotel Marqués de Riscal, A Luxury Collection Hotel**

$$$$ | **HOTEL** | Frank Gehry's post-Guggenheim hotel looks like an extraterrestrial colony in the middle of one of La Rioja's oldest vineyards. **Pros:** superb dining; dazzling architecture; dependable big-brand (Marriott) luxury. **Cons:** service isn't always five-star; phenomenally expensive; interiors pale in comparison to the exterior. [$] *Rooms from: €550* ✉ *Calle Torrea 1, Elciego* ✥ *6 km (4 miles) southwest of Laguardia* ☎ *94/518–0880* 🌐 *www.hotel-marquesderiscal.com* 🛏 *43 rooms* 🍴 *Free Breakfast.*

Hotel Viura

$$$$ | **HOTEL** | The sharp angles and bright colors of this architecturally avant-garde luxury hotel cut a striking contrast to the vernacular architecture surrounding it, and the location—12 km (7 miles) west of Laguardia in the sleepy village of Villabuena de Álava—makes it a good base for exploring La Rioja Alavesa and neighboring Rioja Alta. **Pros:** quirky, Instagrammable architecture; king-size beds; rooftop gym and bar. **Cons:** not much to do in the village; no spa; soundproofing could be improved. [$] *Rooms from: €202* ✉ *Calle Mayor, Villabuena de Álava* ☎ *94/560–9000* 🌐 *www.hotelviura.com* 🛏 *33 rooms* 🍴 *Free Breakfast.*

★ **Mayor de Migueloa**

$$ | **HOTEL** | With its stone floors and rough-hewn ceiling beams, this 17th-century palace transports you back in time, but it features thoroughly modern comforts: a terrific on-site tavern (get the Riojana potatoes), cushy beds, framed prints, and flower-fringed wrought-iron balconies. **Pros:** quaint countrified rooms; restaurant that's a destination in itself; off-season specials. **Cons:** no Wi-Fi in some rooms; exterior-facing rooms are noisy on weekends; parking is far.
[$] *Rooms from: €110* ✉ *Calle Mayor de Migueloa 20,* ☎ *94/560–0187* 🌐 *www.mayordemigueloa.com* ⏲ *Closed Jan. 8–Feb. 8* 🛏 *8 rooms* 🍴 *No Meals.*

Pasaia

7 km (4 miles) east of San Sebastián.

Three towns make up the busy little port of Pasaia (Rentería in Spanish): **Pasai Antxo** (Pasajes Ancho), an industrial area; **Pasai de San Pedro** (Pasajes de San Pedro), a large fishing harbor; and historic **Pasai Donibane** (Pasajes de San Juan), a colorful cluster of 16th- and 17th-century buildings. The most scenic way in is via Pasai de San Pedro, on the San Sebastián side of the strait: Catch a five-minute launch across the mouth of the harbor (approximately €2 round trip).

Pasaia has lots of history. In 1777, a 20-year-old General Lafayette set out from Pasai Donibane to aid the American Revolution. Victor Hugo spent the summer of 1843 here writing his *Voyage aux Pyrénées*; in fact, the **Victor Hugo House** is now the tourist office, though its walls still feature drawings and documents that belonged to the writer. **Albaola Factory,** a center of maritime culture, is directed by Xabier Agote, who taught boatbuilding in Rockland, Maine.

🍴 Restaurants

★ **Casa Cámara**

$$$$ | **SEAFOOD** | Four generations ago, Pablo Cámara turned this 19th-century fishing wharf on the Pasaia narrows into

a first-class seafood restaurant with lovely views over the shipping lane. A steaming *sopa de pescado* (fish soup) on a wet Atlantic day is a memorable event, or try *cangrejo del mar* (spider crab with vegetable sauce) or the superb hake with salsa verde. **Known for:** quaint, old-timey ambience; pristine shellfish; pier-side dining. [$] *Average main: €46* ✉ *Calle San Juan 79, Pasai Donibane* ☎ *94/352–3699* 🌐 *www.casacamara.com* 🕓 *Closed Mon.–Wed. No dinner.*

Hondarribia

20 km (13 miles) east of Pasaia.

Hondarribia is the last fishing port before the French border and a wonderful day trip from San Sebastián. Lined with fishermen's homes and small fishing boats, the harbor is a scenic if slightly touristy spot. If you have a taste for history, follow signs up the hill to the medieval bastion and onetime castle of Carlos V, now a Parador, and keep your eye out for coats of arms emblazoned on the corners of old buildings (as opposed to above entryways)—an Hondarribia peculiarity.

VISITOR INFORMATION

CONTACTS Hondarribia Tourist Office. ✉ *Pl. de Armas 9, Hondarribia* ☎ *94/364–3677* 🌐 *www.hondarribia.eus.*

🍴 Restaurants

Alameda

$$$$ | BASQUE | The Txapartegi brothers—Mikel, Kepa, and Gorka—are the decorated chefs behind this restaurant. The elegantly restored house and its sunny terrace in upper Hondarribia are a delight, as are the seasonally rotated combinations of carefully chosen ingredients, from fish and duck to vegetables. **Known for:** scenic seaside environs; Michelin-starred dining; freshest seafood and meats. [$] *Average main: €36* ✉ *Calle Minasoroeta 1, Hondarribia* ☎ *94/364–2789* 🌐 *www.restaurantealameda.net* 🕓 *Closed Mon.–Wed. No dinner.*

★ Hermandad de Pescadores

$$$ | SEAFOOD | One of the Basque country's most historic and typical fishermen's guilds, this central restaurant exudes tradition. At simple wooden tables and a handsome mahogany bar, local volunteers serve straight-forward, hearty fare—think *sopa de pescado*, mussels, and clams *a la marinera* (in a thick, garlicky sauce)—at better-than-reasonable prices. **Known for:** homey, unfussy dining room; dayboat fish; affordable top-quality seafood—a rarity in the region. [$] *Average main: €20* ✉ *Calle Zuloaga 12, Hondarribia* ☎ *94/364–2738* 🌐 *www.hermandaddepescadores.com* 🕓 *Closed Mon. No dinner weekdays.*

🛏 Hotels

Casa Artzu

$ | B&B/INN | FAMILY | Better hosts than this warm, friendly clan are hard to find, and their 13th-century family house and renovated barn offer modern accommodations overlooking the Bidasoa estuary and the Atlantic. **Pros:** good value; free parking; family-friendly. **Cons:** need a car to get to the beach; breakfast €3 extra; credit cards not accepted. [$] *Rooms from: €52* ✉ *Barrio Montaña,* ☎ *94/364–0530* 🌐 *www.casa-artzu.com* 🛏 *6 rooms.*

★ Parador de Hondarribia

$$$$ | HOTEL | FAMILY | You can live like a medieval lord in this 10th-century bastion, home in the 16th century to Spain's founding emperor, Carlos V—hence its alternative name: Parador El Emperador. **Pros:** great sea views; terrific breakfasts; cozy old-fashioned rooms. **Cons:** expensive parking; no a/c (but ceiling fans); no restaurant. [$] *Rooms from: €283* ✉ *Pl. de Armas 14,* ☎ *94/364–5500* 🌐 *www.parador.es* 🛏 *36 rooms* 🍽 *No Meals.*

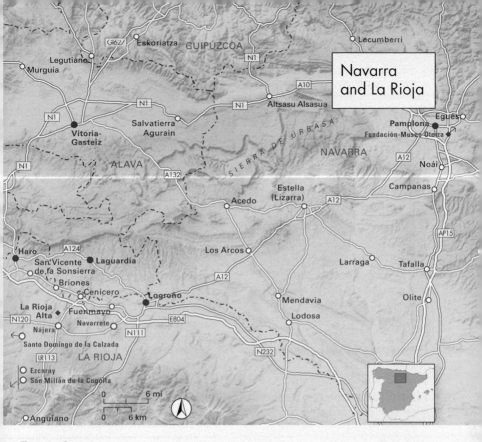

Pamplona

79 km (47 miles) southeast of San Sebastián.

Pamplona (Iruña or Iruñea in Euskera) is known worldwide for its running of the bulls, made famous by Ernest Hemingway in his 1926 novel, *The Sun Also Rises*. The occasion is the festival of San Fermín, July 6–14, when Pamplona's population triples (along with its hotel rates), so reserve rooms months in advance. Every morning of the festival, a rocket is shot off at 8 sharp, and the bulls kept overnight in the corrals at the edge of town are run through a series of closed-off streets leading to the bullring, an 850-meter (1/2-mile) dash. Running among them are Spaniards and foreigners feeling audacious (or perhaps foolhardy) enough to risk getting gored.

The degree of peril in the thrilling *encierro* (running) is difficult to gauge. Serious injuries occur nearly every day during the festival; deaths are rare but do occur. After the bulls' desperate gallop through town, every one of them is killed in the bullring, realities that draw ire from many anti-bullfighting Spaniards and animal rights groups. Indeed, the festival comes under more scrutiny with each passing year. Running is free, but tickets to *corridas* (bullfights) are pricey and can be difficult to finagle.

Founded by the Roman emperor Pompey as Pompaelo, or Pampeiopolis, Pamplona was successively taken by the Franks, the Goths, and the Moors. In 750, the Pamplonians put themselves under the protection of Charlemagne and managed to expel their Arab rulers temporarily. But the foreign commander took advantage of this trust to destroy the city walls; when he was driven out once more by the Moors, the Navarrese took their revenge, ambushing and slaughtering the retreating Frankish army as it fled over the Pyrenees through the mountain pass of Roncesvalles in 778. This is the episode depicted in the 11th-century *Song of Roland,* although its anonymous French poet cast the Moors as the aggressors. For centuries after that, Pamplona was a collection of three rival towns until they were forcibly incorporated into one city by Carlos III (the Noble, 1387–1425) of Navarra.

GETTING HERE AND AROUND

BUS STATION Estación de Autobuses de Pamplona. ✉ *Av. de Yanguas y Miranda 2, Pamplona* ☎ *90/202–3651* ⊕ *www.estaciondeautobusesdepamplona.com.*

CAR RENTALS Europcar. ✉ *Blanca de Navarra Hotel, Av. Pio XII 43, Pamplona* ☎ *94/817–2523* ⊕ *www.europcar.com.*

TRAIN INFORMATION Estación de Pamplona. ✉ *Pl. de la Estación 1, Pamplona* ☎ *90/232–0320, 90/243–2343* ⊕ *www.renfe.com.*

VISITOR INFORMATION

CONTACTS Pamplona Tourist Office. ✉ *Calle San Saturnino 2, Pamplona* ☎ *94/842–0700* ⊕ *www.pamplona.es.*

 Sights

Archivo Real y General de Navarra
HISTORIC SIGHT | This Rafael Moneo-designed monolith of glass and stone, ingeniously contained within a Romanesque palace, is Pamplona's architectural pièce de résistance. With papers and parchments dating to the 9th century, the archive holds more than 75,000 linear feet of documents and has room for more than 55,500 feet more. The library and reading rooms are lined with cherrywood and crowned with a gilded ceiling. ✉ *Calle Dos de Mayo, Pamplona*

☎ *84/842–4667, 84/842–4623* ⊕ *www.navarra.es* ✉ *Free* ⊘ *Closed weekends.*

Catedral de Pamplona
CHURCH | The fragile gabled Gothic arches of this 14th-century cloister make it one of the finest of its type in the country. Inside are the tombs of Carlos III and his wife, marked by an alabaster sculpture. The well-preserved kitchen is one of just three surviving Gothic kitchens of Spain. The Museo Catedralicio Diocesano (Diocesan Museum) houses religious art from the Middle Ages and the Renaissance. Call in advance for guided tours in English. ✉ *Calle Curia, Pamplona* ☎ *94/821–2594* ⊕ *www.catedraldepamplona.com* ✉ *€5* ⊘ *Museum closed Sun.*

Ciudadela
CITY PARK | Take an evening paseo with locals through this central park with promenades and pools on the site of an ancient fortress. ✉ *Pamplona.*

Fundación-Museo Oteiza
ART MUSEUM | East of Pamplona on the road toward France, this museum dedicated to the father of modern Basque art is a must-visit. Jorge Oteiza (1908–2003), in his seminal treatise, *Quosque tandem,* called for Basque artists to find an aesthetic of their own instead of attempting to become part of the Spanish canon. Rejecting ornamentation in favor of essential form and a noninvasive use of space, Oteiza created a school of artists from which the sculptor Eduardo Chillida (1924–2002) was the most famous. The building itself, Oteiza's home for more than two decades, is a large cube of earth-color concrete designed by Oteiza's longtime friend, Pamplona architect Francisco Javier Sáenz de Oiza. The sculptor's living quarters, his studio and laboratory, and the workshop used for teaching divide the museum into three sections. ✉ *Calle de la Cuesta 7, Pamplona* ✛ *From town, take Ctra. N150 east for 8 km (5 miles) to Alzuza* ☎ *94/833–2074* ⊕ *www.museooteiza.org* ✉ *€4 (free Fri.)* ⊘ *Closed Mon.*

Museo de Navarra

HISTORY MUSEUM | In a 16th-century building once used as a hospital for pilgrims on their way to Santiago de Compostela, this museum has a collection of regional archaeological artifacts and historical costumes. Placards are Spanish-only. ✉ *Cuesta de Santo Domingo 47,* ☎ *94/842–6492* 🌐 *www.museodenavarra.navarra.es* 🎫 *€2 (free Sat. afternoon and Sun.)* 🕓 *Closed Mon.*

Museo Universidad de Navarra

ART MUSEUM | Designed by local celebrity architect Rafael Moneo, this contemporary art museum opened in 2014 on the University of Navarra campus. It has an exceptional photograph collection dating to the birth of photography as an art form, and the permanent art collection features classic works by Rothko, Picasso, Kandinsky, and Tàpies. ✉ *Calle Universidad, Pamplona* ☎ *94/842–5700* 🌐 *www.museo.unav.edu* 🎫 *€5.*

Plaza del Castillo

PLAZA/SQUARE | One of Pamplona's greatest charms is the warren of narrow streets near the Plaza del Castillo (especially Calle San Nicolás) filled with restaurants and bars. ✉ *Pamplona.*

🍴 Restaurants

Café Iruña

$$ | **CAFÉ** | Pamplona's gentry have been flocking to this ornate, French-style café since 1888, but in 1926 Ernest Hemingway made it part of world literary lore in *The Sun Also Rises.* You can have a drink with a bronze version of the author in his favorite perch at the far end of the bar, or enjoy views of the plaza from a table on the terrace. **Known for:** grand, ornate dining area; chocolate con churros; long waits. [$] *Average main: €14* ✉ *Pl. del Castillo 44, Pamplona* ☎ *94/822–2064* 🌐 *www.cafeiruna.com.*

Errejota

$$$$ | **SPANISH** | Previously called Josetxo, this warm, family-run restaurant in a stately mansion with a classically elegant interior is one of Pamplona's foremost addresses for refined cuisine. There's something for everyone on the diverse, internationally inflected menu, whose highlights include baby artichokes with langoustine tails and monkfish with black-olive vinaigrette and soy-anchovy mayonnaise. **Known for:** standout artichokes; white-tablecloth dining room; modern Navarrese cuisine. [$] *Average main: €26* ✉ *Pl. Príncipe de Viana 1,* ☎ *94/822–2097* 🌐 *www.errejota.es* 🕓 *Closed Sun. (except during San Fermín), Easter wk, and Aug.*

Europa Restaurante

$$$$ | **SPANISH** | Pamplona's finest restaurant, in the hotel of the same name, the Europa offers refined, Michelin-starred Navarrese cooking with reasonably priced à la carte dining as well as excellent tasting menus available. The small and light first-floor dining room offers the perfect backdrop to dishes like slow-cooked lamb and pork or the best bacalao al pil pil you may try on your trip. **Known for:** affordable tasting menus; nicest restaurant in town; seasonal vegetable dishes. [$] *Average main: €27* ✉ *Calle Espoz y Mina 11, Pamplona* ☎ *94/822–1800* 🌐 *www.hreuropa.com* 🕓 *Closed Sun.*

★ Gaucho

$ | **TAPAS** | This legendary tavern, which remains surprisingly calm even during San Fermín, serves some of the best tapas in Pamplona. Opt for classics like garlicky mushroom brochettes and jamón-filled croquetas, or spring for more modern creations such as seared goose liver on toast or almond-encrusted morcilla. **Known for:** old-timey atmosphere; delectable foie gras; delicious tapas for all budgets. [$] *Average main: €9* ✉ *Calle Espoz y Mina 7, Pamplona* ☎ *94/822–5073* 🌐 *www.cafebargaucho.com.*

Running with the Bulls

In *The Sun Also Rises*, Hemingway describes the Pamplona encierro in anything but romantic terms. Jake Barnes hears the rocket, steps out onto his balcony, and watches the crowd run by: men in white with red sashes and neckerchiefs. "One man fell, rolled to the gutter, and lay quiet." It's a textbook move—an experienced runner who falls remains motionless (bulls respond to movement)—and first-rate observation and reporting. In the next chapter, a man is gored and dies. The waiter at Café Iruña mutters, "You hear? Muerto. Dead. He's dead. With a horn through him. All for morning fun."

The Running Course

At daybreak, six fighting bulls are guided through the streets by 8–10 *cabestros*, or steers (also known as *mansos*, meaning "tame ones"), to the holding pens at the bullring, from which they will emerge later to fight. The course covers 902 yards. The short distance from Cuesta de Santo Domingo down to the corrals is the most dangerous part of the run. The walls are sheer, and the bulls pass quickly. The fear here is of a bull hooking along the wall of the Military Hospital on his way up the hill, forcing runners out in front of the speeding pack in a classic hammer-and-anvil movement. Mercaderes is next, cutting

left for about 300 feet by the town hall, then right up Calle Estafeta. The outside of each turn and the centrifugal force of 22,000 pounds of bulls and steers is very dangerous. Calle Estafeta is the longest (about 1,200 feet), straightest, and least complicated part of the course.

The Classic Run

At the end of Estafeta the course descends left through the *callejón*, or narrow tunnel, into the bullring. The bulls move more slowly here, allowing runners to stay close and even to touch them as they glide down into the tunnel. The only uncertainty is whether there will be a pileup in the tunnel. The most dramatic photographs of the encierro have been taken here, as the pack slams through what occasionally turns into a solid wall of people. If all goes well, the bulls will have arrived in the ring in less than three minutes.

Legal Issues

It is illegal to attempt to attract a bull, thus removing him from the pack and creating a deadly danger. It's also illegal to participate while intoxicated or while taking photos. Sexual assault among the onlookers and partygoers has become an increasing problem. Every year more women report being attacked or inappropriately touched in the crowds.

Hotels

★ Gran Hotel La Perla

$$$$ | HOTEL | The oldest hotel in Pamplona (and the spot where Ernest Hemingway first conceived of his first novel, *The Sun Also Rises*) underwent several years of refurbishing before it reinvented itself as a high-end lodging option. **Pros:** staff are well-versed in history of the property; good soundproofing; even entry-level rooms are spacious. **Cons:** round-the-clock mayhem during San Fermín; prices triple during San Fermín; no pool, gym, or spa. Ⓢ *Rooms from: €214* ⊠ *Pl. del Castillo 1, Pamplona* ☎ *94/822–3000* ⊕ *www.granhotellaperla.com* ⇨ *44 rooms* ⏺ *Free Breakfast.*

Hotel Maisonnave

$$$ | HOTEL | FAMILY | This modern four-star hotel has a nearly perfect location, tucked away on a relatively quiet pedestrian street yet steps from the action on Plaza del Castillo and Calle Estafeta. **Pros:** friendly, multilingual staff; lively bar and restaurant; great location. **Cons:** corporate feel; more three- than four-star; modern interior design lacks local character. Ⓢ *Rooms from: €134* ⊠ *Calle Nueva 20, Pamplona* ☎ *94/822–2600* ⊕ *www.hotel-maisonnave.es* ⇨ *138 rooms* ⏺ *Free Breakfast.*

Pamplona Catedral Hotel

$$$ | HOTEL | Set in a renovated convent, this contemporary hotel offers a great value and one of the most convenient locations in Pamplona, steps from the cathedral. **Pros:** above-and-beyond service; convenient location; exceptional breakfasts. **Cons:** somewhat seedy area; heating and a/c are not central; bleak interiors. Ⓢ *Rooms from: €152* ⊠ *Calle Dos de Mayo 4, Pamplona* ☎ *94/822–6688* ⊕ *www.pamplonacatedralhotel.com* ⇨ *49 rooms* ⏺ *Free Breakfast.*

Sercotel Restaurante Hotel Europa

$ | HOTEL | More famous for its world-class Michelin-starred restaurant on the ground floor, this modestly priced hotel is one of Pamplona's best-kept secrets, just a block and half from the bullring and within shouting distance of party central, Plaza del Castillo. **Pros:** central location; good value; special restaurant offers for hotel guests. **Cons:** noisy during the fiesta unless you score an interior room; prices can double during San Fermín; rooms on the small side. Ⓢ *Rooms from: €78* ⊠ *Calle Espoz y Mina 11, Pamplona* ☎ *94/822–1800* ⊕ *www.hoteleuropa-pamplona.com* ⇨ *25 rooms* ⏺ *Free Breakfast.*

Nightlife

Canalla

DANCE CLUBS | Dress up, or you might flunk the bouncer's inspection at this lounge-y nightclub, filled until dawn with young singles and couples. Cover charge depends on visiting DJs and events, and Fridays are popular student nights. ⊠ *Av. Bayona 2, Pamplona* ☎ *67/921–9871* ⊕ *www.canalla.es* ⊘ *Closed Sun.–Wed.*

Ozone

DANCE CLUBS | This techno haven is one of the most popular dance clubs in town. Cover charge depends on visiting DJs and events; check the website for lineups and prices. ⊠ *Calle Monasterio de Velate 5, Pamplona* ☎ *94/826–1593* ⊕ *www.ozonepamplona.com* ⊘ *Closed Sun.–Wed.*

Performing Arts

Edificio Baluarte

MUSIC | The Congress Center and Auditorium, built in 2003 by local architectural star Patxi Mangado, is a sleek assemblage of black Zimbabwean granite. It contains a concert hall of exquisite acoustical perfection utilizing beechwood from upper Navarra's famed Irati *haya* (beech) forest. Performances and concerts, from opera to ballet, are held in this modern venue, built on the remains of one of the five bastions of Pamplona's 16th-century

Ciudadela. ✉ *Pl. del Baluarte, Pamplona* ☎ *94/806–6066* ⊕ *www.baluarte.com.*

★ Zentral

CONCERTS | A self-proclaimed "gastro club," with food and live music offerings, this venue hosts events ranging from Lindy Hop dance parties to lectures on food science. It morphs into a DJ-driven *discoteca* most nights after 1 am. ✉ *Mercado de Santo Domingo, Calle de Santo Domingo, 1st fl., Pamplona* ☎ *94/822–0764* ⊕ *www.zentralpamplona.com.*

Shopping

Botas are the leather wineskins from which Basques typically drink at bullfights or during fiestas, and the most iconic bota manufacturer, ZZZ, is from Pamplona. The art lies in drinking a stream of wine from a bota held at arm's length without spilling a drop.

Caminoteca Pamplona

SPORTING GOODS | Owned by a former Camino pilgrim, this small store stocks everything and anything a hiker embarking on the Camino de Santiago could need, from backpacks, boots, hiking socks, and walking sticks to smaller but equally necessary items like blister ointment, rain ponchos, and sporks. ✉ *Calle de Curia 15,* ☎ *94/821–0316* ⊕ *www.caminoteca.com.*

★ Fragment Store

HOUSEWARES | This well-curated boutique run by young designers is the city's top spot to buy handmade jewelry and accessories, kitchenware, couture garments, and eye-catching stationery. ✉ *Calle Nueva 4, Pamplona* ☎ *84/841–0430* ⊕ *karlotalaspalas.com/fragment* ⊘ *Closed Sun.*

Gurgur Delicias de la Estafeta

FOOD | Come here to buy delicacies from across Navarra, including wines, sweets, cured meats, and cheeses, as well as a variety of bull-themed T-shirts and paraphernalia. ✉ *Calle Estafeta 21, Pamplona* ☎ *94/820–7992* ⊕ *www.gurgurestafeta. es.*

Javier (*Xabier, Xavier*)

CASTLE/PALACE | This gorgeous Navarran hamlet 54 km (33½ miles) southeast of Pamplona, perched atop a lush riverbed and gorge, is the birthplace of the 16th-century Roman Catholic missionary Francis Xavier, cofounder of the Jesuit order. There's a fine castle, cathedral, and monastery, comfortable hotels, a couple of restaurants, and an impressive visitor center with rotating exhibits. Whatever your religious persuasion, it's a beautiful stop on your travels in the Pamplona area. ✉ *Javier* ☎ *94/888–4024* ⊕ *www. javier.es* 🎟 *Castle €3.*

Manterola

FOOD | Here you can buy some toffee called La Cafetera, a local *café con leche* sweet. The shop also sells Navarran wine and other delicacies. ✉ *Calle Tudela 5, Pamplona* ☎ *94/822–3174* ⊕ *www.manterola.es* ⊘ *Closed Sun.*

Olentzero

SOUVENIRS | You can buy *botas* in most Navarrese towns, but Pamplona's Olentzero gift shop sells the best brand, Las Tres Cetas, written "ZZZ." ✉ *Calle de la Estafeta 42, Pamplona* ☎ *94/882–0245* ⊕ *www.olentzeroa.com.*

Olite

TOWN | FAMILY | An unforgettable glimpse into the Kingdom of Navarra of the Middle Ages is the reward for journeying to this town. The 11th-century church of San Pedro is revered for its finely worked Romanesque cloisters and portal, but it's the town's castle—restored by Carlos III in the French style and brimming with ramparts, crenellated battlements, and watchtowers—that most captures the imagination. You can walk the ramparts, and should you get tired or hungry, part of the castle has been converted into a parador, making a fine place to grab a snack or catch a few z's. ✉ *41 km*

(25 miles) south of Pamplona, Olite
☎ *94/874–0000* ⊕ *www.olite.es.*

Torrens Alimentación
FOOD | Navarran favorites such as piquillo peppers and chistorra sausages are sold here. ✉ *Calle San Miguel 12, Pamplona* ☎ *94/822–4286* ⊕ *www.torrensaliment-acion.com* ⊗ *Closed Sat. afternoon and Sun.*

Logroño

85 km (53 miles) southwest of Pamplona.

A busy industrial city of 153,000, Logroño has a lovely old quarter bordered by the Ebro and medieval walls, with **Bretón de los Herreros** and **Muro Francisco de la Mata** being its principal streets. Wine-loving travelers who prefer the bustle of a city to the quiet of the country should hole up here and take day trips to the outlying vineyards.

Near Logroño, the Roman bridge and the *mirador* (lookout) at **Viguera** are the main sights in the lower Iregua Valley. According to legend, Santiago (St. James) helped the Christians defeat the Moors at the **Castillo de Clavijo,** another panoramic spot. **Río Leza** is La Rioja's most dramatic canyon.

GETTING HERE AND AROUND
BUS STATION Estación de Autobuses de Logroño. ✉ *Av. España 1, Logroño* ☎ *94/123–5983* ⊕ *www.logroño.es.*

TRAIN STATION Estación de Logroño. ✉ *Av. de Colón 83, Logroño* ☎ *90/243–2343* ⊕ *www.adif.es.*

VISITOR INFORMATION
CONTACTS Oficina de Turismo de Logroño. ✉ *Escuelas Trevijano, Calle Portales 50, Logroño* ☎ *94/127–7000* ⊕ *www.logroño. es.*

⊙ Sights

Church of San Bartolomé
CHURCH | The oldest still-standing church in Logroño, San Bartolomé was built between the 13th and 14th centuries in a French Gothic style. Highlights include the 11th-century Mudejar tower and an elaborate 14th-century Gothic doorway. Some carvings on the stone facade depict scenes from the Bible. This is also a landmark on the Camino de Santiago pilgrimage path. ✉ *Pl. San Bartolomé 2, Logroño* ☎ *94/125–2254* ⊠ *Free.*

Concatedral de Santa María de la Redonda
CHURCH | Noted for its twin baroque towers, the present-day cathedral was rebuilt in the 16th century in a Gothic style atop ruins of a 12th-century Romanesque church. ✉ *Calle Portales 14, Logroño* ☎ *94/125–7611* ⊕ *www.laredonda.org* ⊠ *Free.*

Puente de Piedra (*Stone Bridge*)
BRIDGE | Many of Logroño's monuments, such as this elegant bridge, were built as part of the Camino de Santiago pilgrimage route. ✉ *Av. de Navarra 1.*

Santa María del Palacio
CHURCH | This 11th-century church is known as La Aguja (The Needle) for its pyramid-shaped 135-foot Roman-esque-Gothic tower. ✉ *Calle del Marqués de San Nicolás 30, Logroño* ⊠ *Free.*

Santiago el Real (*Royal St. James's Church*)
CHURCH | Reconstructed in the 16th century, this church is noted for its equestrian statue of the saint (also known as Santiago Matamoros, or St. James the Moorslayer) presiding over the main door. ✉ *Calle Barriocepo 6, Logroño* ☎ *94/120–9501* ⊕ *www.santiagoelreal.org* ⊠ *Free.*

⊙ Restaurants

For tapas, you'll find bars with signature specialties on the connecting streets **Calle del Laurel** and **Travesía de Laurel,** the

The fertile soil and fields of the Ebro River Valley make some of Spain's most colorful landscapes.

latter also known as El Sendero de los Elefantes (Path of the Elephants)—an allusion to *trompas* (trunks), Spanish for a snootful. Try Bar Soriano for "champis" (*champiñones*, or mushrooms), Blanco y Negro for *matrimonio* ("wedded" white and salt-cured anchovies on a mini-baguette), and Bar Travesía for *tortilla de patata*. If you're ordering wine, a young "cosecha" or "clarete" comes in squat *chato* glasses, a crianza brings out the crystal, and a reserva or gran reserva (selected grapes aged over three years in oak and bottle) usually elicits goblets for proper swirling, nosing, and tasting.

Cachetero

$$$$ | **SPANISH** | A Calle del Laurel standby, this refined taberna with wood-paneled walls serves Riojan specialties like *cochinillo asado* (roast suckling pig) and pimentón-laced potatoes *a la riojana* (potato and chorizo stew) as well as risottos and excellent seafood dishes. **Known for:** butter-soft cochinillo asado; personable waitstaff; refined Riojan cuisine. [$] *Average main: €25* ✉ *Calle del Laurel 3, Logroño* ☎ *94/122–8463* 🌐 *www.cachetero.com* 🕒 *Closed Tues., and first 2 wks of Aug. No dinner Sun.*

★ La Taberna de Baco

$$ | **SPANISH** | This bright, modern bar is a great spot to try seasonal, market-fresh tapas like heirloom tomato salad with chilies and raw onion or cheesy mushroom "carpaccio," but locals flock here for one dish in particular: *oreja a la plancha*, griddled pig's ear swimming in punchy *brava* (spicy) sauce. Shatteringly crisp and unapologetically rich, it's one of the best versions you'll have in Spain. **Known for:** amiable bartenders; offal even the squeamish can learn to love; wide selection of small-production wines. [$] *Average main: €12* ✉ *Calle de San Agustín 10, Logroño* ☎ *94/121–3544* 🌐 *tabernadebaco.com.*

★ Tondeluna

$$ | **SPANISH** | Tondeluna has six communal tables (with 10 seats each), and all have views into the kitchen, where cooks plate dishes both novel and familiar like glazed beef cheeks with apple puree and

Getaria-style hake with *panadera* (thinly sliced and sautéed) potatoes. **Known for:** value prix fixes; good balance of experimental and classic dishes; lively dining room. [$] *Average main: €16* ✉ *Calle Muro de la Mata 9,* ☎ *94/123–6425* 🌐 *www.tondeluna.com* 🕓 *No dinner Sun.*

Hotels

Eurostars Marqués de Vallejo

$$$ | **HOTEL** | Close to—but not within earshot of—the raucous food fight that is Calle del Laurel, this hotel by the cathedral is within walking distance of all the major sights. **Pros:** pleasant public areas with art; central location; clean, homey rooms. **Cons:** no longer independently owned; street-side rooms can be noisy in summer; breakfast spread could use some love. [$] *Rooms from: €142* ✉ *Calle Marqués de Vallejo 8, Logroño* ☎ *94/124–8333* 🌐 *www.eurostarshotels.com* 🛏 *50 rooms* 🍴 *Free Breakfast.*

NH Logroño Herencia Rioja

$$$ | **HOTEL** | This modern four-star hotel near the old quarter has contemporary, comfortable rooms, first-rate facilities, a well-trained staff, and a businesslike buzz about it. **Pros:** clean, corporate comfort; excellent breakfast; two steps from Calle del Laurel's tapas bonanza. **Cons:** undistinguished modern building; cheerless interiors; tight, white-knuckle parking. [$] *Rooms from: €141* ✉ *Calle Marqués de Murrieta 14, Logroño* ☎ *94/121–0222* 🌐 *www.nh-hoteles.com* 🛏 *83 rooms* 🍴 *No Meals.*

La Rioja Alta

The Upper Rioja, the most prized subregion of La Rioja's wine country, extends from the Río Ebro to the Sierra de la Demanda. La Rioja Alta has the most fertile soil, the best vineyards and agriculture, the most impressive castles and monasteries, a ski resort at Ezcaray, and the historic economic advantage of being on the Camino de Santiago.

Sights

Ezcaray

TOWN | Enter the Sierra de la Demanda by heading south from Santo Domingo de la Calzada on LR111. Your first stop is the town of Ezcaray, with its aristocratic houses emblazoned with family crests, of which the Palacio del Conde de Torremúzquiz (Palace of the Count of Torremúzquiz) is the most distinguished. Good excursions from here are the Valdezcaray ski station; the source of the Río Oja at Llano de la Casa; La Rioja's highest point, the 7,494-foot Pico de San Lorenzo; and the Romanesque church of Tres Fuentes, at Valgañón. The hamlet is famous for its wild mushrooms—and the resulting tapas, too. ✉ *Ezcaray* ☎ *94/135–4679 tourist office* 🌐 *www.ezcaray.org.*

Nájera

TOWN | This town was the capital of Navarra and La Rioja until 1076, when the latter became part of Castile and the residence of the Castilian royal family. The monastery of Santa María la Real (www.santamarialareal.net), the "pantheon of kings," is distinguished by its 16th-century Claustro de los Caballeros (Cavaliers' Cloister), a flamboyant Gothic structure with 24 lacy, plateresque Renaissance arches overlooking a grassy patio. The sculpted 12th-century tomb of Doña Blanca de Navarra is the monastery's best-known sarcophagus, while the 67 Gothic choir stalls dating from 1495 are among Spain's best. ✉ *Nájera* ☎ *94/136–1083 tourist office* 🌐 *www.najera.es.*

Navarrete

TOWN | This town, 14 km (9 miles) west of Logroño via the A12, has noble houses and the 16th-century Santa María de la Asunción church. The village is also famous for ceramics; shop at any of the artisan shops in the town center.

☎ *94/144–1062 tourist office* ⊕ *www. navarrete.es/turismo.*

★ **San Millán de la Cogolla**

TOWN | This town, southeast of Santo Domingo de la Calzada, has two jaw-dropping monasteries on the UNESCO World Heritage sites list. There's **Monasterio de Yuso**, where a 10th-century manuscript on St. Augustine's *Glosas Emilianenses* contains handwritten notes in what is considered the earliest example of the Spanish language, the vernacular Latin dialect known as Roman Paladino. And then there's the Visigothic **Monasterio de Suso** (www.monasteriodesanmillan.com), where Gonzalo de Berceo, recognized as the first Castilian poet, wrote and recited his 13th-century verse in the Castilian tongue, now the language of nearly 600 million people around the world. ⊠ *San Millán de la Cogolla* ☎ *94/137–3259 tourist office* ⊕ *www.sanmillandelacogolla.es/oficina-de-turismo-san-millan* ⊠ *€4 for Suso Monastery, €7 for Yuso Monastery* ☾ *monasteries closed Mon.*

Santo Domingo de la Calzada

TOWN | A stop on the Camino de Santiago, this town is named after an 11th-century saint who built roads and bridges for pilgrims and founded the hospital that is now a parador. The cathedral (Calle Cristo 94/134–0033) is a Romanesque-Gothic pile containing the saint's tomb, choir murals, and a walnut altarpiece carved by Damià Forment in 1541. The live hen and rooster in a plateresque stone chicken coop commemorate a legendary local miracle in which a pair of roasted fowl came back to life to protest the innocence of a pilgrim hanged for theft. Be sure to stroll through the town's beautifully preserved medieval quarter. ⊠ *Nájera* ✛ *On N120 20 km (12 miles) west of Nájera* ⊕ *www.santodomingodelacalzada.org.*

Hotels

★ **Echaurren**

$$$ | HOTEL | Rioja's renowned "gastro hotel," Echaurren is a food lover's paradise with two envelope-pushing restaurants and Relais & Châteaux–certified digs. **Pros:** Rioja's gastronomical mecca, highly personal service; comfortable beds. **Cons:** no bathtubs in most rooms; entry-level rooms are cramped; loud church bells. $ *Rooms from: €180* ⊠ *Calle Padre José García 19, Ezcaray* ☎ *94/135–4047* ⊕ *www.echaurren.com* ⌖ *25 rooms* ⎮⊙⎮ *Free Breakfast.*

Hostal Nuestra Señora de Valvanera

$ | HOTEL | FAMILY | Housed in a monastery atop a 9th-century hermitage, this rural hotel run by a Benedictine community is an ideal base for hiking. **Pros:** rooms of varying sizes for families; simplicity and silence; cool for the summer. **Cons:** decidedly unhip; limited dining choices; spartan accommodations. $ *Rooms from: €65* ⊠ *Monasterio de Valvanera, Ctra. LR435, Ezcaray* ☎ *94/137–7044* ⊕ *www.monasteriodevalvanera.es/hospederia* ⌖ *28 rooms* ⎮⊙⎮ *No Meals.*

Hostería San Millan

$$ | HOTEL | This magnificent inn occupies a wing of the historic Monasterio de Yuso. **Pros:** graceful building; good breakfasts; historic site. **Cons:** popular among the tour-bus set; somewhat isolated; monastic interiors. $ *Rooms from: €100* ⊠ *Monasterio de Yuso, San Millán de la Cogolla* ☎ *94/137–3277* ⊕ *www.hosteriasanmillan.com* ⎮⊙⎮ *Free Breakfast* ⌖ *25 rooms.*

Hotel Venta de Goyo

$ | B&B/INN | A favorite with anglers and hunters, this cheery inn across from the confluence of the Urbión and Najerilla Rivers has spartan wood-trimmed bedrooms with red-checked bedspreads and an excellent restaurant specializing in venison, wild boar, partridge, woodcock, and game of all kinds. **Pros:** unforgettable house-made jams; excellent game and mountain cooking; charming rustic bar. **Cons:** hot in the summer; next to the road; a bit isolated. $ *Rooms from: €40* ✉ *Puente Río Neila 2, (Ctra. LR113, Km 24.6), Viniegra de Abajo* ☎ *94/137–8007* 🌐 *www.ventadegoyo.es* 🛏 *22 rooms* 🍴 *No Meals.*

Haro

49 km (30 miles) west of Logroño.

Haro is the wine capital of La Rioja. Its Casco Viejo (Old Quarter) and best taverns are concentrated along the loop known as La Herradura (the Horseshoe), with the Santo Tomás church at the apex of its curve and Calle San Martín and Calle Santo Tomás leading down to the upper left-hand (northeast) corner of Plaza de la Paz. Up the left side of the horseshoe, Bar La Esquina is the first of many tapas bars. Bar Los Caños, behind a stone archway at San Martín 5, is built into the vaults and arches of the former church of San Martín and serves excellent local crianzas and reservas and a memorable pintxo of quail egg, anchovy, hot pepper, and olive.

VISITOR INFORMATION

CONTACTS Haro Tourist Office. ✉ *Pl. de la Paz 1, Haro* ☎ *94/130–3580* 🌐 *www.haroturismo.org.*

Sights

Bodegas (*Wineries*)
NEIGHBORHOOD | Haro's century-old bodegas have been headquartered in the Barrio de la Estación (Train Station District) since the railroad opened in 1863 and are a fantastic place to go winery-hopping, since they're within walking distance of one another. Guided tours and tastings, some in English, can be arranged at the facilities themselves or through the tourist office. ✉ *Barrio de la Estación.*

★ Bodegas López de Heredia Viña Tondonia
WINERY | Call or email the historic López de Heredia Viña Tondonia winery—known for its vintage-release wines—to reserve a spot on one of the tours, or drop into the Zaha Hadid–designed tasting room for an informal glass or two. No photography allowed. ✉ *Av. Vizcaya 3, Haro* ☎ *94/131–0244* 🌐 *www.lopezdeheredia.com* 🎟 *€40 for tour.*

Bodegas Muga
WINERY | This sprawling, prestigious bodega offers visits, tours, and tastings as well as a wine bar and restaurant. Segway and hot air balloon tours can also be arranged ahead of time. ✉ *Barrio de la Estación, Haro* ☎ *94/130–6060* 🌐 *www.bodegasmuga.com* 🎟 *€15* 🕒 *Closed Sun.*

Santo Tomás
CHURCH | The architectural highlight of Haro, this single-nave Renaissance and late-Gothic church was completed in 1564. It has an intricately sculpted plateresque portal on the south side and a gilded baroque organ facade towering over the choir loft. ✉ *Calle Santo Tomás 5,* ☎ *94/131–1690.*

Restaurants

★ Terete
$$$$ | **SPANISH** | A perennial local favorite, this rustic spot has been roasting lamb in wood ovens since 1877 and serves a hearty *menestra de verduras* (vegetables stewed with bits of ham) that is justly revered as a mandatory sidekick. With rough hand-hewn wooden tables distributed around dark stone and wood-beam dining rooms, the medieval stagecoach-inn environment matches the traditional roasts. **Known for:** stock of some of La Rioja's best reservas and crianzas; 19th-century wood-burning oven; succulent roast lamb and suckling pig. $ *Average main: €30* ✉ *Calle Lucrecia Arana 17, Haro* ☎ *94/131–0023* 🌐 *www.terete.es* 🕒 *Closed Mon., 1st 2 wks in July, and last 2 wks in Nov. No dinner Sun.*

THE PYRENEES

Updated by
Benjamin Kemper

⊙ Sights	🍴 Restaurants	🏨 Hotels	💼 Shopping	🍸 Nightlife
★★★★☆	★★★☆☆	★★★☆☆	★☆☆☆☆	★☆☆☆☆

WELCOME TO THE PYRENEES

TOP REASONS TO GO

★ **Revel in the Romanesque:** Feast your eyes on 900-year-old religious architecture in Taüll and marvel at the mural paintings of the Noguera de Tor Valley.

★ **Explore Spain's Grand Canyon:** The Parque Nacional de Ordesa y Monte Perdido has stunning scenery, along with marmots and mountain goats.

★ **Hike the highlands:** Trek the verdant highlands of the Basque Country's Baztán Valley, then hug the Bidasoa River down to colorful Hondarribia and the Bay of Biscay.

★ **Venture deep into rural Aragón:** The enchanting medieval town of Alquézar winds up to a 9th-century citadel that keeps watch over the Parque Natural de la Sierra y los Cañones de Guara, famous for prehistoric cave paintings.

★ **Ride the cogwheel train at Ribes de Freser, near Ripoll:** Ascend the gorge to the sanctuary and ski station at Vall de Núria, then hike to the remote highland valley and refuge of Coma de Vaca.

1 **Camprodon.** A stylish little mountain hub.

2 **Beget.** Perhaps Catalonia's cutest town.

3 **Sant Joan de les Abadesses.** Known for the important 12th-century Romanesque church of Sant Joan.

4 **Ripoll.** Home of 9th-century Benedictine Monastery of Santa Maria.

5 **Ribes de Freser and Vall de Núria.** The starting point of the famous cogwheel train.

6 **Puigcerdà.** A base for skiers and hikers from both sides of the border.

7 **Llívia.** A small Spanish exclave surrounded on all sides by France.

8 **Bellver de Cerdanya.** The dictionary definition of a perfect Pyrenean mountain village.

9 **La Seu d'Urgell.** Ancient town facing the snowy rock wall of the Sierra del Cadí.

10 **Sort.** Home base for skiers and anglers.

11 **Parc Nacional d'Aigüestortes i Estany de Sant Maurici.** One of Spain's finest and wildest national parks.

12 **Taüll.** A Romanesque treasure box.

13 **Vielha.** A small Pyrenean city near the French border.

14 **Arties.** Lvely mountain town with hiking, nature, and Romanesque art.

15 **Salardú.** A convenient base with steep streets and a fortified bell tower.

16 **Zaragoza.** Home to the famous La Pilarica.

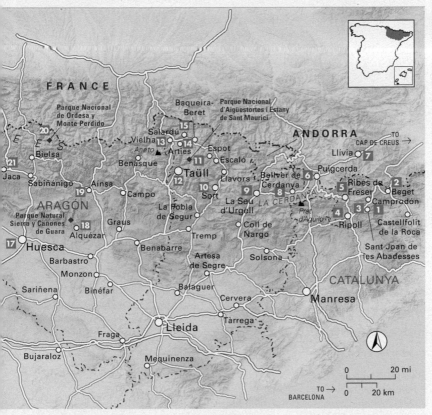

17 Huesca. There's plenty of charm in the hilly medieval quarter.

18 Alquézar. A fortified town that tops lists of Spain's most picturesque villages.

19 Aínsa. Walled village with cobblestone streets and sweeping views.

20 Parque Nacional de Ordesa y Monte Perdido. A stunning national park with well-marked trails and intriguing fauna.

21 Jaca. Known for 11th-century cathedral and fortress and lively eateries.

22 Monasterio de San Juan de la Peña. Popular with Holy Grail seekers.

23 Hecho and Ansó Valleys. Idyllic mountain villages dot dramatic gorges.

24 Roncal Valley. Known for farmland and sheep milk cheese.

25 Roncesvalles (Orreaga). The first stop for pilgrims on the Camino de Santiago.

26 Burguete (Auritz). Made famous in Hemingway's *The Sun Also Rises*.

27 Baztán Valley. Scenic point between the central Pyrenees and the Atlantic.

EATING AND DRINKING WELL IN THE PYRENEES

T-bone steak, chorizo and longaniza sausages with peppers.

Pyrenean cuisine is hearty mountain fare characterized by thick soups, stews, roasts, and local game. Ingredients are prepared with slightly different techniques and recipes in each valley, village, and kitchen.

The culinary traditions of the Pyrenees match the area's three main cultural identities—Catalan, Aragonese, and Basque, from east to west. Within these, there are more niche local specialties, particularly in La Garrotxa, La Cerdanya, Ribagorça, Vall d'Aran, Benasque, Alto Aragón, Roncal, and Baztán. Game is common throughout. Trout, mountain goat, deer, boar, partridge, rabbit, duck, and quail are roasted over coals or cooked in aromatic stews called *civets* in Catalonia and *estofados* in Aragón and the Basque Pyrenees. Fish and meat are sometimes seared on white-hot slate (*a la llosa* in Catalan, *a la piedra* in Spanish). Sheep, goat, and cow cheeses vary from valley to valley, along with types of sausages and charcuterie.

WILD MUSHROOMS

Wonderfully aromatic wild mushrooms plucked from the mountainsides are available year-round but are particularly abundant and varied in autumn. They're a constant in Pyrenean meat and egg dishes—particularly in non-breakfast scrambled egg dishes called *remenats* (*revueltos* in Spanish, *nahasiak* in Basque)—though they're equally divine on their own simply sautéed with garlic, parsley, and olive oil. Seek out varieties like *rovellons* (saffron milk caps), and *camagrocs* (a type of chanterelle).

HEARTY STEWS

Cool climes and grueling farm work made filling meat-and-vegetable stews a mainstay of the Pyrenean table. The Pyrenees has its own rendition of French *garbure* with legumes, vegetables, potatoes, pork, chicken, and sometimes lamb or wild boar, all floating in a rich beef stock. *Olha aranesa* (Aranese soup)—a cousin to Catalan *escudella* and central Spain's *cocido madrileño*—is another Pyrenean power soup with pasta, chickpeas, white beans, and several cuts of pork that's served in multiple courses.

Wild black trumpet mushrooms

PYRENEAN STEWS

Wild boar stew is known by different names in the various languages of the Pyrenees, but it's a gloriously gamy treat no matter where you try it. Wild boar is prepared in many different ways between Catalonia, Aragón, and the Basque Country, but most recipes include onions, carrots, mushrooms, peppers, sherry, and sweet paprika. *Civet d'isard* (mountain-goat stew), known as *estofado de ixarso* in the Pyrenees of Aragón, is another favorite, prepared in much the same way but with a more delicate taste.

TRINXAT

The Catalan verb *trinxar* means to chop or shred, and *trinxat* is winter cabbage, previously softened by frost, chopped fine and mixed with mashed potato and fatback or bacon. A quintessential high-altitude comfort food, trinxat plays the acidity of the cabbage against the saltiness of the pork and the butteriness of boiled potatoes.

DUCK WITH TURNIPS

The Pyrenean dish *tiró amb naps* (duck with turnips) has its roots in pre-Columbian Europe, as do nearly all European recipes that use turnips instead of potatoes, an import from the Americas. The frequent use of duck (*pato* in Spanish, *anec* in Catalan, *tiró* in La Cerdanya) in the Cerdanya Valley two hours north of Barcelona is a taste acquired from French Catalunya, just over the Pyrenees.

Spring duckling with potatoes

The soaring mountain range that stretches from the Mediterranean to the Atlantic is striated by some three dozen gorgeous valleys, which were all but completely isolated from one another until around the 10th century. The region has retained much of its distinctive cultural identities as well as a palpably unbridled highland spirit. Local languages abound across the range, with Spanish and Euskera (Basque) spoken in upper Navarra; Aragonese (and its local varieties) in Aragón; and Catalan at the eastern end of the chain from Ribagorça to the Mediterranean. Spanish is spoken fluently by all, though often as a second language.

As the gateway between the Iberian Peninsula and the rest of Europe, the Pyrenees were always a strategic barrier—and a stronghold to be reckoned with: The Romans never subdued the "Vascones" (as Greek historian Strabo [63–21 BC] called the Basques) in the western Pyrenean highlands; Charlemagne lost Roland and his rear guard at Roncesvalles in 778, and his Frankish heirs lost all of Catalonia in 988; and Napoléon Bonaparte never completed his conquest of the peninsula, largely because of communications and supply problems posed by the Pyrenees. Hitler, whether for geographical or political reasons, decided not to use post–Civil War Spain to launch his African campaign in 1941. In fact, following the Spanish Civil War and World War II, the Pyrenees were a corridor to freedom for downed pilots, Jewish refugees, and POWs fleeing the Nazis and Franco's dictatorship.

MAJOR REGIONS
Eastern Catalan Pyrenees. Catalonia's easternmost Pyrenean valley, the Vall de Camprodon, is still hard enough to reach that, despite pockets of Barcelona

summer colonies, it has retained much of its farm culture and mountain wildness. It has several exquisite towns and churches and—more stunning still—dramatic mountains in the Sierra de Catllar. Start from Cap de Creus in the Empordà to get the full experience of the Pyrenean cordillera's rise from the sea; then move west through Beget, Camprodon, the Ter Valley, Sant Joan de les Abadesses, and Ripoll before heading north through Ribes de Freser and Vall de Nuria. Vallter 2000, La Molina, and Núria are ski resorts at either end of the Pyrenean heights on the north side of the valley.

La Cerdanya. Said to be in the shape of the handprint of God, this high pastureland is bordered north and south by snow-covered peaks. La Cerdanya starts in France, at Col de la Perche (near Mont Louis) and ends in the Spanish province of Lleida, at Martinet. Being split between two countries, and subdivided into two more provinces on each side, gives the valley an identity all its own. Puigcerdà is the largest town and is a lively base for skiers and hikers, while the Spanish enclave of Llívia is easily reached across the border. Bellver de Cerdanya showcases examples of traditional Pyrenean architecture, surrounded by refreshing mountain views, while the ancient town of La Seu d'Urgell houses the 11th-century chapel of Sant Miquel and the 14th-century convent of Sant Domenec—now a converted parador. Residents on both sides of the border speak Catalan, a Romance language derived from early Provençal French, and regard the valley's political border with undisguised hilarity. Unlike any other valley in the upper Pyrenees, this one runs east–west and thus has a record annual number of sunlight hours.

Western Catalan Pyrenees. "The farther from Barcelona, the wilder" is the rule of thumb, and this is true of the rugged countryside and fauna in the western part of Catalonia. Sort, the capital of the Pallars Sobirà (Upper Pallars Valley), is the area's epicenter for skiing, fishing, and white-water kayaking. Three of the greatest destinations in the Pyrenees are in this region: the harmonious, Atlantic-influenced Vall d'Aran with its capital, Vielha; the Noguera de Tor Valley (aka Vall de Boí), with its matching set of gemlike Romanesque churches in Taüll; and Parc Nacional d'Aigüestortes i Estany de Sant Maurici, which has a network of pristine lakes and streams. The main geographical units in this section are the valley of the Noguera Pallaresa River, the Vall d'Aran headwaters of the Atlantic-bound Garonne, and the Noguera Ribagorçana River Valley (Catalonia's western limit).

Aragón and Central Pyrenees. The highest, remotest, and most spectacular range of the Pyrenees is the middle section, farthest from sea level. From Benasque on Aragón's eastern side to Jaca at the western edge are the great heights and most dramatic landscapes of Alto Aragón (Upper Aragón), including the Maladeta (11,165 feet), Posets (11,070 feet), and Monte Perdido (11,004 feet) peaks, the three highest points in the chain. The oft-bypassed cities of Zaragoza and Huesca and are useful Pyrenean gateways and historic destinations in themselves. Both are charmingly provincial. Drive east out of Huesca into the Sierra de Guara, declared a World Heritage Site by UNESCO in 1998, whose crown jewel is the historic village of Alquézar; hiking and other outdoor activities abound here. Farther north, stop at Aínsa for its 11th-century citadel and castle. The Parque Nacional de Ordesa y Monte Perdido was declared a world heritage site by UNESCO in 1997 and boasts some of the region's best trails. Deep in Alto Aragón, Jaca has a fine 11th-century cathedral and fortress, and a lively personality all its own. The Hecho and Ansó Valleys are the westernmost valleys in Aragón and rank among the wildest and most unspoiled reaches of the Pyrenees. With only cross-country skiing available, it doesn't see hordes of winter tourists (unlike its neighbors).

The Navarran and Basque Pyrenees. Beginning in the Roncal Valley, the language you hear may be Euskera, the pre-Indo-European tongue of the Basques. The highlands of Navarra, from Roncesvalles and Burguete down through the Baztan Valley to Hondarribia, are a magical realm of rolling hillsides, folklore, and emerald pastures.

Planning

When to Go

If you're a hiker, stick to the summer (June–September, especially July), when the weather is better and there's less chance of a serious snowfall—not to mention blizzards or lightning storms at high altitudes.

October, with comfortable daytime temperatures and chillier evenings, is ideal for enjoying the still-green Pyrenean meadows and valleys and hillside hunts for wild mushrooms. November brings colorful leaves, the last mushrooms, and the first frosts.

For skiing, come December–March. The green springtime thaw, mid-March–mid-April, is spectacular for skiing on the snowcaps and trout fishing or golfing on the verdant valley floors.

August is the only crowded month, when all of Europe is on summer vacation and the cooler highland air is at its best.

Planning Your Time

You could hike all the way from the Atlantic to the Mediterranean in 43 days, but not many have that kind of vacation time. A week is ideal for a single area—La Cerdanya and the Eastern Catalan Pyrenees, easily accessed from Barcelona; the Western Catalan Pyrenees and Vall d'Aran in the Lleida province of Catalonia; Jaca and the central Pyrenees, north of Zaragoza; or the Basque Pyrenees north of Pamplona.

A day's drive up through Figueres (in Catalonia) and Olot will bring you to the town of **Camprodón.** The picturesque villages dotted around this area—in particular **Beget, Sant Joan de les Abadesses,** and **Ripoll**—are all worthy stops, especially for the famous monastery of Santa Maria de Ripoll with its 13th-century Romanesque portal. La Cerdanya's sunny wide plains are popular for walkers and mountain bikers year-round and skiing in La Molina and Masella in winter. **Puigcerdà, Llívia,** and **Bellver de Cerdanya** are must-visits, too.

To the west, the historic town of **La Seu d'Urgell** is an important stop on the way to the **Parc Nacional d'Aigüestortes i Estany de Sant Maurici,** the **Vall d'Aran,** and the winter-sports center Baqueira-Beret. Stop at **Taüll** and the **Noguera de Tor Valley** for Romanesque churches.

The central Aragonese Pyrenees reveal the most dramatic scenery and Aneto, the highest peak in the Pyrenees. The **Parque Nacional de Ordesa y Monte Perdido** is Spain's most majestic canyon—reminiscent of North America's Grand Canyon. **Alquézar** and **Ainsa** are upper Aragón's best-preserved medieval towns, while **Zaragoza, Huesca,** and **Jaca** are the most important cities.

Farther west, the lower Navarran Pyrenees give way to rolling pasturelands. **Roncesvalles** is the first stop off for pilgrims on the life-affirming **Camino de Santiago,** and the peaceful **Baztán Valley** guards a land of ancient traditions.

Getting Here and Around

AIR

Barcelona's international airport, El Prat, is the main gateway to the Catalan Pyrenees from the east. From the north, the Pyrenees can be reached via Toulouse Blaqnac; from the west, your best bet for international flights is Biarritz Airport in France. Smaller airports at Zaragoza, Pamplona, and San Sebastián's Hondarribia are useful for domestic flights.

BUS

Bus travel in the Pyrenees is the only way to cross from east to west (or vice versa), other than hiking or driving, but requires some zigzagging up and down valleys. In most cases, four daily buses run by ALSA *(www.alsa.com)* or Avanza *(www.avanzabus.com)* connect the main pre-Pyrenean cities (Barcelona, Zaragoza, Huesca, and Pamplona) and the main highland distributors (Puigcerdà, La Seu d'Urgell, Vielha, Benasque, and Jaca). The time lost waiting for buses makes this option inefficient if you're crunched for time.

CAR

The easiest way (and in many cases, the *only* way) to tour the Pyrenees is by car—and it comes with the best scenery. The Eje Pirenaico (Pyrenean Axis, or N260) is a carefully engineered, safe cross-Pyrenean route that connects Cap de Creus, the Iberian Peninsula's easternmost point on the Mediterranean Costa Brava (east of Girona and Cadaqués), with Cabo de Higuer, the lighthouse west of Hondarribia at the edge of the Atlantic Bay of Biscay.

The Collada de Toses (Tosses Pass) to Puigcerdà is the most difficult route into the Cerdanya Valley, but it's toll-free, has spectacular scenery, and you get to include Camprodón, Olot, and Ripoll in your itinerary. Safer and faster but more expensive (tolls total more than €22 from Barcelona to Bellver de Cerdanya) is the E9 through the Tuñel del Cadí. Once you're there, most of the Cerdanya Valley's two-lane roads are wide and well paved. As you go west, roads can be more difficult to navigate, winding dramatically through mountain passes.

TRAIN

There are three small train stations deep in the Pyrenees: Ribes de Freser in the eastern Catalan Pyrenees; Puigcerdà, in the Cerdanya Valley; and La Pobla de Segur, in the Noguera Pallaresa Valley. The larger gateways are Zaragoza, Huesca, and Lleida. From Madrid, connect through Barcelona for the eastern Pyrenees, Zaragoza and Huesca for the central Pyrenees, and Pamplona or San Sebastián for the Navarran and Basque Pyrenees. For information on timetables and routes, consult *www.renfe.com*. 2021 saw the addition of two new low-cost train routes to Barcelona in Ouigo *(www.ouigo.com)* and Avlo *(www.avlorenfe.com)*.

Hiking the Pyrenees

There are many reasons to visit the Pyrenees—skiing, food, art, and architecture, to name a few—but hiking is the region's biggest draw. No matter how spectacular the mountains seem from the road, they are exponentially more dazzling from upper hiking trails that are accessible only on foot. The natural splendor is best enjoyed on day hikes or overnight two-day treks to mountain huts (*refugios*, or *refugis* in Catalan) in the Ordesa or Aigüestortes national parks, in the Alberes range, or on the hike from Col de Núria to Ulldeter.

Local tourist offices provide maps and can recommend day hikes.

Download the Wikiloc app (www.wikiloc.com) to track your hike, access offline topographic base maps, and share photos of your trek. It's a popular app locally, so you can download other users' hikes.

A live-tracking feature allows you to share your location with family as a safety precaution.

Hiking in the Pyrenees should always be undertaken carefully: proper footwear, headwear, water supply, and weather-forecast awareness are essential. High-altitude climbs are not recommended for first-timers unless you hire a guide. There can be unexpected snowstorms even in summer.

Restaurants

In the high Pyrenees, cozy stone inns, with their hearty cuisine and comfortable interiors, are a welcome sight after a day of hiking or sightseeing. Often family-run and relaxed, they rarely have any kind of dress code, and nourishing meals frequently close with a complimentary *chupito* (shot) of local liqueur. Down in the main cities, restaurants tend to be more contemporary and slightly more expensive yet equally hospitable.

Restaurant reviews have been shortened. For full information, visit Fodors.com.

Hotels

Most hotels in the Pyrenees are informal and outdoorsy, with a large fireplace in one of the public rooms. They are usually built of wood, glass, and stone and have steep slate roofs that blend in with the surrounding mountains. There's a high concentration of family operations passed down from generation to generation, though chain options also abound.

Hotel reviews have been shortened. For full information, visit Fodors.com.

What It Costs in Euros			
$	$$	$$$	$$$$
RESTAURANTS			
under €12	€12–€17	€18–€22	over €22
HOTELS			
under €90	€90–€125	€126–€180	over €180

Tours

Trekking, horseback riding, adventure sports such as canyoning and ballooning, and more contemplative outings like bird-watching and botanical tours, are a few of the activities available at the main Pyrenean resorts.

Populated with trout, the Pyrenees' cold streams provide excellent angling from mid-March to the end of August. Notable places to cast a line are the Segre, Aragón, Gállego, Noguera Pallaresa, Arga, Esera, and Esca Rivers. Pyrenean ponds and lakes also tend to be rich in trout.

Pyrenean Experience
British expat Georgina Howard specializes in showcasing Basque-Navarran culture, walking, and gastronomy. The walking tours include accommodations and meals. ✉ *Iaulin Borda, Ameztia, Ituren* ☎ *650/713759* ⊕ *www.pyrenean-experience.com* ✉ *From €1,000.*

Skiing

Skiing is the main winter attraction in the Pyrenees, and the range holds over half of Spain's ski resorts. Baqueira-Beret, in Vall d'Aran, is the most renowned ski resort. According to the Pyrenean Observatory of Climate Change (OPCC), the climate crisis is heating up the Pyrenees alarmingly fast, but thanks to snow machines, there is usually fine skiing December–March here and at more than 20 resorts including Vallter 2000 at Setcases in the Camprodon Valley and La Molina and Masella in La Cerdanya. Although weekend skiing can be crowded in the eastern valleys, Catalonia's western Pyrenees have more breathing room; same goes for Aragón, whose main resorts are Cerler-Benasque, Panticosa, Formigal, Astún, and Candanchú. Numerous resorts offer heliskiing and cross-country skiing. Leading areas for the latter include Lles, in the Cerdanya; Salardú and Beret, in Vall d'Aran; and Panticosa, Benasque, and Candanchú, in Aragón. Jaca, Puigcerdà, and Vielha also offer winter activities such as public skating sessions, figure-skating classes, and ice-hockey programs.

A good resource for up-to-date ski conditions and information is On the Snow *(www.onthesnow.com/spain/skireport.html).* Tourist offices also provide insight.

Camprodon

127 km (79 miles) northwest of Barcelona, 80 km (50 miles) west of Girona.

Camprodon, the capital of its *comarca* (county), is at the junction of the Ter and Ritort Rivers—both excellent trout streams. The rivers flow by, through, and under much of the town, giving it a highland waterfront character (as well as a long history of flooding). Its best-known symbol is the elegant 12th-century stone bridge that broadly spans the Ter River in the center of town. Camprodon owes much of its opulence to the summer residents from Barcelona who built mansions along **Passeig Maristany,** the leafy promenade at its northern edge.

GETTING HERE AND AROUND

The C38 runs into the center of town from both north (France) and south (Barcelona, Vic, or Ripoll) directions. If coming from France, the southbound D115 changes into the C38 once over the Spanish border. The best way to explore is on foot, as the streets are narrow and can be tricky to navigate by car.

VISITOR INFORMATION

CONTACTS Camprodon Tourist Office. ✉ *Carrer Sant Roc 22, Camprodón* ☎ *972/740010* 🌐 *www.valldecamprodon.org.*

🛏 Hotels

★ Fonda Rigà

$$ | B&B/INN | FAMILY | A highland inn with comfortable modern rooms and spectacular mountain views, this perch is an excellent base for hiking, horseback riding, and viewing Pyrenean flora and fauna. **Pros:** outstanding restaurant; stunning views and quiet surroundings; complimentary house wine and bottled water. **Cons:** remote from Camprodon; a serious 5-km (3-mile) drive above the valley floor; bookings only by email or phone. [$] *Rooms from: €114* ✉ *Ctra. de Tregurà de Dalt, Km 4.8* ✥ *At end of Tregurà route, 10 km (6 miles) up Ter Valley from Camprodón* ☎ *972/136000* 🕒 *Closed Nov. 1–15 and 2 wks in late June/early July (dates can vary)* 🛏 *16 rooms* 🍴 *Free Breakfast.*

Hotel Camprodon

$$$ | HOTEL | This elegant Moderniste building has rooms over the bustling Plaça Dr. Robert on one side and over the river on the other. **Pros:** central location; wonderful views over the river; charming Art Nouveau style and preserved features throughout. **Cons:** five-night minimum stay in summer; rooms on the square can be noisy in summer; no parking. [$] *Rooms from: €166* ✉ *Pl. Dr. Robert 3, Camprodón* ☎ *972/740013* 🌐 *www.hotelcamprodon.com* 🛏 *50 rooms* 🍴 *No Meals.*

Hotel Maristany

$$$ | HOTEL | A stately old chalet on Camprodón's grandest promenade, this lovely family-owned hotel offers a chance to live like the 19th- and 20th-century Barcelona aristocracy who spent their summers

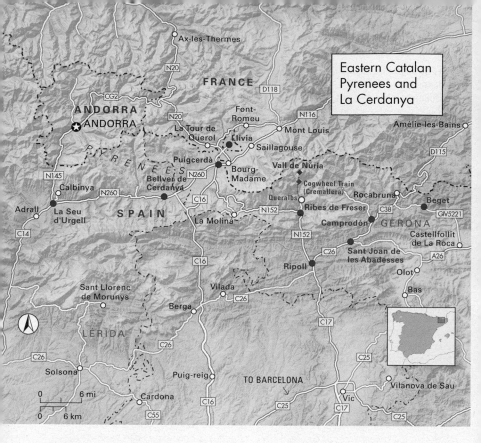

Eastern Catalan Pyrenees and La Cerdanya

here. **Pros:** private parking; tranquil location outside the center; excellent restaurant. **Cons:** so-so soundproofing; rooms and baths are somewhat cramped; not in the heart of the action. $ *Rooms from: €135* ✉ *Av. Maristany 20, Camprodón* ☎ *972/130078* ⊕ *www.hotelmaristany. com* ⊗ *Closed Dec. 11–Easter* ⤳ *10 rooms* ⊓⊙⊦ *Free Breakfast.*

🎭 Performing Arts

Festival de Música de Isaac Albéniz

MUSIC | Camprodon's most famous son is composer Isaac Albéniz (1860–1909), who spent more than 20 years in exile in France, where he became friends with musical luminaries such as Pablo Casals, Claude Debussy, and Gabriel Fauré. His celebrated classical guitar piece *Asturias* is one of Spain's best-known works. In July and August, during the Isaac Albéniz Music Festival, a series of concerts by renowned artists and young talent from the European classical music scene is held in the monastery of Sant Pere. For an up-to-date concert schedule, contact the tourist office or visit the website. ✉ *Sant Pere de Camprodón, Carrer Monestir 2, Camprodón* ⊕ *www.albeniz.cat.*

🛍 Shopping

Cal Xec

FOOD | This legendary sausage and cheese store also sells the much-prized, vanilla-flavored Birbas cookies. It's at the end of the Camprodon Bridge. ✉ *Carrer Isaac Albéniz 1, Camprodón* ☎ *972/740084* ⊕ *www.calxec.com.*

Mercat Setmanal
CRAFTS | Held every Sunday 9–2, this market sells all manner of artisanal food, crafts, clothing, antiques, and bric-a-brac. ✉ *Pl. Dr. Robert, Camprodón.*

Beget

17 km (10 miles) east of Camprodón.

The village of Beget, considered Catalonia's *més bufó* (cutest), was inaccessible by car until the mid-1960s, when a *pista forestal* (jeep track) was laid down. In 1980, Beget was finally fully connected to the rest of the world by an asphalt roadway, which can be hazardous when mist descends, as it often does. The GIV5223 road to Castellfollit de la Roca, 12 km (7 miles) away, winds scenically among the formerly volcanic peaks of the Alta Garrotxa. Beget's 30-some houses are eccentric stone structures with heavy wooden doors and a golden color particular to the Vall de Camprodón. Archaic stone bridges span the stream where protected trout swim in clear mountain water.

GETTING HERE AND AROUND

Drive northeast out of Camprodon on Carrer Molló (C38) for 2 km (1 mile) before turning right onto the Carretera Camprodon–Beget (GIV5223) for 14 km (9 miles) to Beget. Cars are not allowed to enter the village, but there is parking just outside. When leaving, head toward Oix, which leads to Castellfollit de la Roca and the N260, to avoid having to retrace your steps back up the mountain.

Sights

Sant Cristòfol
CHURCH | The 12th-century Romanesque church of Sant Cristòfol (St. Christopher) has a diminutive bell tower and a rare 6-foot Majestat—a polychrome wood carving of the risen Christ in head-to-foot robes that dates to the 12th century. The church is usually closed, but ask in the bar-restaurant behind the church, or in El Forn de Beget, and someone may direct you to the keeper of the key. A euro or two is collected for church upkeep. ✉ *Pl. Major, Beget* ☎ *No phone* 🎟 *€2.*

Restaurants

Can Po
$ | **CATALAN** | This ancient, ivy-covered, Pyrenean stone-and-mortar farmhouse perched over a deep gully in nearby Rocabruna is famed for carefully prepared local dishes like *vedella amb crema de ceps* (veal in wild mushroom sauce) and the Catalan classic *oca amb peres* (goose stewed with pears). Try the *civet de porc senglar* (stewed wild boar) in winter, or any of the many varieties of wild mushrooms that find their way into the kitchen at this rustic mountain retreat. **Known for:** rich and delicious stews; hearty mountain cuisine; cozy setting. [$] *Average main: €11* ✉ *Ctra. de Beget, Rocabruna* ☎ *972/741045* 🕒 *Closed Mon.–Thurs. (except public holidays). Call ahead to check in low season.*

Hotels

El Forn de Beget
$$ | **B&B/INN** | Perched above the Trull River in the upper part of the village, this little stone hotel and restaurant has panoramic views over Alta Garrotxa. **Pros:** classic mountain food; a true hideaway in the Pyrenees; wonderful river views from the dining room. **Cons:** remote location; rooms are small and close together; need a car to get here. [$] *Rooms from: €100* ✉ *Carrer Josep Duñach "En Feliça" 9, Beget* ☎ *972/741230* 🌐 *www.elfornde-beget.com* 🛏 *4 rooms* 🍴 *Free Breakfast.*

Did You Know?

Trekking in the Pyrenees can be a very serious endeavor—it's possible to walk the entire way from the Atlantic Coast to the Mediterranean in about six weeks, but shorter one- or two-day hikes can be just as stunning.

Sant Joan de les Abadesses

14 km (9 miles) southwest of Camprodón.

The site of an important church, Sant Joan de les Abadesses is named for the 9th-century abbess Emma and her successors. Emma was the daughter of Guifré el Pilós (Wilfred the Hairy), a hero of the Christian Reconquest of Ripoll who some regard as the founder of Catalonia. The town's arcaded Plaça Major offers a glimpse of its medieval past, as does the broad, elegant 12th-century bridge over the Ter.

GETTING HERE AND AROUND
Exit southwest of Camprodon on Carrer Molló (C38) for 9 km (6 miles), passing through Sant Pau de Segúries. At the rotary, take the first exit onto the N260 for 4 km (2½ miles) to Sant Joan de les Abadesses. If you're coming from Ripoll, take the northbound N260 for 10 km (6 miles). Once here, it's an easy stroll.

VISITOR INFORMATION
CONTACTS Sant Joan de les Abadesses Tourist Office. ✉ *Pl. de la Abadía 9, Sant Joan de les Abadesses* ☎ *972/720599* ⊕ *www.santjoandelesabadesses.cat.*

Sights

Monastery of Sant Joan de les Abadesses
CHURCH | In the 12th-century Romanesque church of Sant Joan, the altarpiece—a 13th-century polychrome wood sculpture of the Descent from the Cross—is one of the most expressive and human of that epoch. Wilfred the Hairy gifted this church to his daughter, Emma, and did the same for his son Radulfo with the Monastery of Santa Maria de Ripoll.   See Ripoll sights. ✉ *Pl. de la Abadía, Sant Joan de les Abadesses*

☎ *972/722353* ⊕ *www.monestirsant-joanabadesses.cat* ✉ *€3* ☞ *No credit cards.*

Ripoll

10 km (6 miles) southwest of Sant Joan de los Abadesses, 105 km (65 miles) north of Barcelona.

One of Catalonia's first Christian strongholds of the so-called Reconquest and a center of religious erudition during the Middle Ages, Ripoll is known as the *bressol* (cradle) of Catalonia's liberation from Moorish domination and the spiritual home of Guifré el Pilós (Wilfred the Hairy), the count of Barcelona who some historians claim founded the Catalan nation in the late 9th century. A dark, mysterious country town built around a 9th-century **Benedictine monastery** , Ripoll was a focal point of culture throughout French Catalonia and the Pyrenees, from the monastery's 879 founding until the mid-1800s, when Barcelona began to eclipse it.

GETTING HERE AND AROUND
The C17 northbound from Vic heads into the center of Ripoll. From Camprodon and Sant Joan de les Abadesses, head southwest on the C38, which turns into the N260 to the town center. There are direct trains from Barcelona (2 hours; line R3 on the Cercanías commuter rail) and approximately two daily bus connections (1½ hours, ⊕ *www.teisa-bus.com*). It's a 10-minute walk from the station to the center, and the small town is easy to explore on foot.

VISITOR INFORMATION
CONTACTS Ripoll Tourist Office. ✉ *Pl. de l'Abat Oliva, Ripoll* ☎ *972/702351* ⊕ *www.visit.ripoll.cat.*

👁 Sights

Monastery of Santa Maria de Ripoll

CHURCH | Decorated with a pageant of biblical figures, the 12th-century doorway to the church is one of Catalonia's great works of Romanesque art. It was crafted as a triumphal arch by stonemasons and sculptors of the Roussillon school, which was centered on French Catalonia and the Pyrenees. You can pick up a guide to the figures surrounding the portal in the nearby Centro de Interpretación del Monasterio, in Plaça de l'Abat Oliva. The center has an interactive exhibition that explains the historical, cultural, and religious relevance of this so-called cradle of Catalonia. It also provides information about guided tours. ⊠ Pl. Monasterio, Ripoll ☎ 972/704203 ⌑ €6.

Ribes de Freser and Vall de Núria

14 km (9 miles) north of Ripoll.

The small town of Ribes de Freser is the starting point of the famous *cremallera* (cogwheel) train, which connects passengers with Núria, a small mountaintop ski resort and pilgrimage site, via a spectacular ascent through the Gorges of Núria.

GETTING HERE AND AROUND

The N260 north of Ripoll goes straight to Ribes de Freser. Continue farther north on the GIV5217 to reach Queralbs by car. Queralbs and Ribes de Freser are easily explored on foot.

VISITOR INFORMATION

CONTACTS **Vall de Ribes Tourist Office.**
⊠ Ctra. de Bruguera 2, Ribes de Freser ☎ 972/727728 ⊕ www.vallderibes.cat.

👁 Sights

Camí dels Enginyers

TRAIL | With a trailhead at the ski area of Núria, at an altitude of 6,562 feet, the dramatic—and occasionally heart-stopping—"engineers' path" is best done in summer. The three-hour trek, aided at one point by a cable handrail, leads to the remote highland valley of Coma de Vaca, where a cozy refuge and hearty replenishment await. Phone ahead to make sure there's space, and check weather conditions. In the morning you can descend along the riverside Gorges de Freser trail, another three-hour walk, to Queralbs, where there are connecting trains to Ribes de Freser. ⊠ Refugi de Coma de Vaca, Termino Municipal de Queralbs dentro del Espacio protegido Ter Freser, Queralbs ☎ 649/229012 ⊕ www.comadevaca.cat/index.php/en ⊙ Closed Sept.–May.

Queralbs

TOWN | The three-hour walk down the mountain from Vall de Núria to the sleepy village of Queralbs follows the course of the cogwheel train on a rather precipitous but fairly easy route (provided there's no snow). The path overlooks gorges and waterfalls overshadowed by sheer peaks before exiting into the quaint village of Queralbs, where houses made of stone and wood cling to the side of the mountain. There is a well-preserved Romanesque church, notable for its six-arch portico, marble columns, single nave, and pointed vault. ⊠ Queralbs

Santuari de la Mare de Déu de Núria

CHURCH | The legend of this Marian religious retreat is based on the story of Sant Gil of Nîmes, who did penance in the Núria Valley during the 7th century. The saint left behind a wooden statue of the Virgin Mary, a bell he used to summon shepherds to prayer, and a cooking pot; 300 years later, a pilgrim found these treasures in this sanctuary. The bell and the pot came to have special importance to unfertile women, who, according to local lore, would be blessed with as many children as they wished after placing their heads in the pot and ringing the bell. ✉ *Vall de Núria* ✣ *26 km (16 miles) north of Ripoll* 🎟 *Free.*

★ **Vall de Núria Rack Railway (Cremallera)**
TRAIN/TRAIN STATION | **FAMILY** | The 45-minute train ride from the town of Ribes de Freser up to Núria provides one of Catalonia's most eclectic excursions—in few other places in Spain does a train make such a precipitous ascent. The cogwheel train, nicknamed *La Cremallera* ("The Zipper" in English), was completed in 1931 to connect Ribes with the Santuari de la Mare de Déu de Núria (Mother of God of Núria) and with hiking trails and ski runs. ✉ *Estación de Ribes-Enllaç, Ribes de Freser* ☎ *972/732020* 🌐 *www.valldenuria.cat/en/summer/rack-railway/presentation* 🎟 *€26 round-trip* ⏰ *Closed weekdays in Nov.*

Hotels

Hostal Les Roquetes
$ | **B&B/INN** | A short walk from the cogwheel train and in the center of the village, this *hostal* has cheerful rooms and spectacular views. **Pros:** good base for walks in the area; fantastic views; friendly service. **Cons:** only accessible by local road or cogwheel train, and those times are limited; limited food options outside of weekends; simple lodging. [$] *Rooms from: €78* ✉ *Ctra. de Ribes 5, Queralbs* ☎ *972/727369* ⏰ *Closed Nov.* 🛏 *8 rooms* 🍴 *No Meals.*

Hotel Vall de Núria
$$$ | **HOTEL** | **FAMILY** | A mountain refuge and hotel run by the government of Catalonia, this family-oriented base camp has double, triple, and quadruple rooms. **Pros:** clean and simple; convenient location in the heart of the Pyrenees; pristine mountain air. **Cons:** minimum two-night stay in high season; hotel feels institutional and austere; high rates for basic lodging. [$] *Rooms from: €140* ✉ *Estación de Montaña Vall de Núria, Queralbs* ☎ *972/732020* 🌐 *www.valldenuria.cat/en* ⏰ *Closed Nov.* 🛏 *65 rooms, 12 apartments* 🍴 *Free Breakfast.*

Puigcerdà

65 km (40 miles) northwest of Ripoll, 170 km (106 miles) northwest of Barcelona.

Puigcerdà ("poo-cher-DA") is the largest town in the valley; in Catalan, *puig* means "hill," and *cerdà* derives from "Cerdanya." From the promontory upon which it stands, the views down across the meadows of the valley floor and up into the craggy peaks of the surrounding Pyrenees are dramatic. The 12th-century **Romanesque bell tower**—all that remains of the town church of Santa Maria, destroyed in 1936 at the outset of the Spanish Civil War—and the sunny sidewalk cafés facing it are among Puigcerdà's prettiest spots, as is the Gothic church of **Sant Domènec.** A prime base for skiers and hikers from both sides of the border, Puigcerdà has lively restaurants and a bustling shopping promenade. On Sunday, markets sell clothes, cheeses, fruits, vegetables, and wild mushrooms.

GETTING HERE AND AROUND

From Ripoll take the northwest-bound N260 for 63 km (39 miles) toward Ribes de Freser. There are several commuter trains a day (they are less frequent on weekends) connecting Barcelona Sants to Puigcerdà (line R3). Buses go from Barcelona Estación del Nord (www.alsa.com). Once you reach the center, there is ample parking, and the easiest way to get around town is on foot.

VISITOR INFORMATION

CONTACTS Puigcerdà Tourist Office. ✉ *Bell tower, Pl. Santa Maria, Puigcerdà* ☎ *972/880542* 🌐 *www.puigcerda.cat.*

> ## Tip
>
> The tourist office on the outskirts of Puigcerdà (*Oficina de Turisme del Consell Comarcal de la Cerdanya, corner of Ctra. N260 and N152* 972/880542) has up-to-date information on the best hiking trails in La Cerdanya. If you're planning a long-distance hiking trip, local bus connections will get you to your starting point and retrieve you at the finish line.

Sights

Ligne de Cerdagne

TRAIN/TRAIN STATION | FAMILY | Affectionately called *le petit train jaune* ("the little yellow train"), this line runs from Bourg-Madame and La Tour de Querol, both easy hikes over the border into France from Puigcerdà (Bourg-Madame is the closest). The border at La Tour, a pretty hour-long hike from Puigcerdà, is marked by a stone painted with the Spanish and French flags. The *carrilet* (narrow-gauge railway) is the last in the Pyrenees and is used for tours as well as transportation; it winds slowly through La Cerdanya to the medieval walled town of Villefranche-de-Conflent, where it can also be picked up. The 63-km (39-mile) tour can take most of the day, especially if you stop to browse in Mont-Louis or Villefranche. The last section, between La Cabanasse and Villefranche, is the most picturesque. In low season the trains have infrequent and unpredictable timetables. ✉ *Oficina de Turisme de la Cerdanya, Ctra. Cruïlla N152 N260, Puigcerdà* ☎ *972/140665 Cerdanya tourist office (Spain), 046/8041547 Pyrenées Cerdagne tourist office (France)* 🌐 *www.pyrenees-cerdagne.com/en/le-train-jaune-english/the-schedules* 🎫 *€10 round trip.*

Plaça Cabrinetty

PLAZA/SQUARE | With its porticoes and covered walks, this square named for a hero of the Carlist Wars is protected from the gusty mountain wind. It is ringed by pastel-painted Renaissance houses, some with decorative sgraffito designs and all with balconies. ✉ *Puigcerdà*

Santa Maria Bell Tower

VIEWPOINT | The 12th-century Santa Maria church in the center of town was largely destroyed in 1936 during the Spanish Civil War. The bell tower remains and is open to visitors. At the top, take in a 360-degree panorama of La Cerdanya's towns, bucolic farmlands, and snowy peaks. ✉ *Pl. Santa Maria, Puigcerdà* ☎ *972/880542* 🎫 *€2.*

Restaurants

Tap de Suro

$$ | CATALAN | Named for the classic bottle stopper (*tap*) made of cork (*suro*), this wine store-cum-gastrobar is the perfect place to unwind over local cheeses, duck and goose liver, and other delicacies. Expect a varied and affordable tapas menu and an ever-rotating wine selection with labels from Spain and France. **Known for:** cozy; intriguing wines from near and far; top-notch cheeses and charcuterie. [$] *Average main: €14* ✉ *Carrer Querol 21, Puigcerdà* ☎ *678/655928* 🕓 *Closed Mon.*

Hotels

Hotel del Lago

$$ | HOTEL | A comfortable old favorite near Puigcerdà's emblematic lake, this spa hotel with old-fashioned decor consists of several salmon-pink spire-topped mansions arranged around a grassy central garden. **Pros:** short walk to the center; lakeside real estate; spa with hot tub and pool. **Cons:** pricey for its services; showing wear in spots; no restaurant (only breakfast). $ *Rooms from: €115* ✉ *Av. Dr. Piguillem 7, Puigcerdà* ☎ *972/881000* ⊕ *www.hotellago.com* ⇨ *24 rooms* ⦿| *Free Breakfast.*

Villa Paulita

$$$ | HOTEL | This stately town-house complex at the edge of Puigcerdà's famous lake has some of the most sought-after rooms and food in the Cerdanya Valley. **Pros:** right on the lake; renowned restaurant with good breakfast; close to activity. **Cons:** underwhelming pool and spa; cramped entry-level rooms with outdated technology; overpriced for what it offers. $ *Rooms from: €145* ✉ *Av. Pons i Gasch 15, Puigcerdà* ☎ *972/884622* ⊕ *www. villapaulitahotel.com* ⇨ *38 rooms* ⦿| *Free Breakfast.*

Shopping

Puigcerdà is one big shopping mall—one that's long been a center for contraband clothes, cigarettes, and other items smuggled across the French border for as long as anyone can remember.

Carrer Major

NEIGHBORHOODS | This is an uninterrupted row of stores selling books, jewelry, fashion, sports equipment, and more. ✉ *Puigcerdà.*

Mercat Setmanal del Diumenge

MARKET | On Sunday morning (9–2), walk over to this lively weekly market that, like those in most Cerdanya towns, features local crafts and specialties such as herbs, goat cheese, wild mushrooms, honey, and baskets. ✉ *Paseo 10 de Abril, Puigcerdà.*

★ Pastisseria Confiteria Cosp

FOOD | For the best *margaritas* in town (no, not those—these are crunchy-edged madeleines made with almonds), head to the oldest commercial establishment in Catalonia, founded in 1806. ✉ *Carrer Major 20, Puigcerdà* ☎ *972/880103.*

Llívia

6 km (4 miles) northeast of Puigcerdà.

A Spanish exclave in French territory, Llívia was marooned by the 1659 Peace of the Pyrenees treaty, which ceded 33 villages to France. Incorporated as a *vila* (town) by royal decree of Carlos V—who spent a night here in 1528 and was impressed by the town's beauty and hospitality—Llívia managed to remain Spanish. In the middle of town, look for the mosaic commemorating Lampègia, *princesa de la paul i de l'amor* (princess of peace and of love), erected in memory of the red-haired daughter of the Duke of Aquitania and lover of Munuza, a Berber governor who ruled La Cerdanya in the 8th century in Islamic Spain.

GETTING HERE AND AROUND

From Puigcerdà you could basically walk to Llívia, 6 km (4 miles) north just across the French border, but there are also buses from the Puigcerdà train station. By car, follow the Camí Vell de Llívia to the N154, which goes directly to Llívia.

VISITOR INFORMATION

CONTACTS Llívia Tourist Office. ✉ *Carrer dels Forns 10, Llívia* ☎ *972/896313.*

Sights

Mare de Déu dels Àngels

CHURCH | At the upper edge of town, this fortified church has wonderful acoustics; check to see if any classical music events are on—especially in August, when it hosts a classical music festival. Information about the festival's concerts is generally released in June. ✉ *Carrer dels Forns 13, Llívia* ☒ *Free.*

Museu de la Farmacia

NOTABLE BUILDING | Across from the Mare de Déu dels Àngels church, this ancient pharmacy, housed within the Museo Municipal, was founded in 1415 and has been certified as the oldest working pharmacy in Europe. ✉ *Carrer dels Forns 10, Llívia* ☎ *972/896313* 🎟 *€4* ⏲ *Closed Mon.*

🍴 Restaurants

★ Can Ventura

$$$ | **CATALAN** | In a flower-festooned 17th-century stone house is one of La Cerdanya's finest restaurants, which serves elevated Catalan fare with French touches. Beef a la llosa and duck with orange and spices are house specialties, and the wide selection of *entretenimientos* (hors d'oeuvres or tapas) is the perfect way to begin. **Known for:** additional bar area for drinks and tapas; beef seared on hot slate; cozy mountain lodge setting. [$] *Average main: €20* ✉ *Pl. Major 1, Llívia* ☎ *972/896178* 🌐 *www.canventura.com* ⏲ *Closed Mon. and Tues.*

La Formatgeria de Llívia

$$$$ | **SPANISH** | This restaurant on the eastern edge of town is inside a former cheese factory, and the proprietors continue the tradition by producing fresh cheese on the premises while you watch. In the restaurant, fine local cuisine and fondues come with panoramic views looking south toward Puigmal and across the valley. **Known for:** open fire in winter; fondues and raclettes; homemade cheese. [$] *Average main: €25* ✉ *Pl. de Ro, Gorguja, Llívia* ☎ *972/146279* 🌐 *www.laformatgeria.com* ⏲ *Closed Tues. and Wed. (except during Aug. and public holidays).*

Bellver de Cerdanya

18 km (11 miles) southwest of Puigcerdà, 31 km (19 miles) southwest of Llívia.

Bellver de Cerdanya has preserved its slate-roof-and-fieldstone Pyrenean architecture more successfully than many of La Cerdanya's larger towns. Perched on a promontory over the **Río Segre,** which winds around much of the town, Bellver is essentially a fishing village plopped in the mountains, with trout as the protagonist. The town's Gothic church of **Sant Jaume** and the arcaded **Plaça Major,** in the upper part of town, are exquisite examples of traditional Pyrenean mountain-village design.

GETTING HERE AND AROUND

Take the southwest-bound N260 from Puigcerdà; once here, it's easily explored on foot.

VISITOR INFORMATION

CONTACTS Bellver de Cerdanya Tourist Office. ✉ *Pl. Major 12, Bellver de Cerdanya* ☎ *973/510016.*

🛏 Hotels

Aparthotel Bellver

$$ | **B&B/INN** | Rustic terra-cotta tiles, arresting mountain views, and stone rooms warmed by fireplaces lure tranquility-loving travelers to this unfussy inn in the town center. **Pros:** on-site parking; snug common area with fireplace; open year-round. **Cons:** no a/c; two-night minimum stay in July and August; books up quickly. [$] *Rooms from: €100* ✉ *Carrer de la Batllia 61–63, Bellver de Cerdanya* ☎ *973/510627* 🌐 *www.aparthotelbellver.com* ⏲ *Sometimes closes 10 days in May or June (check ahead)* 🔑 *12 apartments* 🍽 *Free Breakfast.*

La Seu d'Urgell

20 km (12 miles) south of Andorra la Vella (in Andorra), 45 km (28 miles) west of Puigcerdà, 200 km (120 miles) northwest of Barcelona.

La Seu d'Urgell is an ancient town facing the snowy rock wall of the Sierra del Cadí. As the seat (*seu*) of the regional archbishopric since the 6th century, it has a rich legacy of art and architecture. The Pyrenean feel of the streets, with their

Did You Know?

The Catedral de Santa Maria is the focal point of the historic part of La Seu d'Urgell. The town was also the site of the kayak contest of the 1992 Olympics, and it's still a popular site for kayakers.

dark balconies and porticoes, overhanging galleries, and colonnaded porches—particularly **Carrer dels Canonges**—makes Seu mysterious and memorable. Look for the medieval **grain measures** at the corner of Carrer Major and Carrer Capdevila. The tiny food shops on the arcaded Carrer Major are good places to assemble lunch for a hike.

GETTING HERE AND AROUND

Take the N260 southwest from Puigcerdà via Bellver de Cerdanya. From the direction of Lleida, head north on the C13 for 63 km (39 miles), then take the C26 after Balaguer, before joining the C14 for 32 km (20 miles) and then the N260 into the center. There are buses daily from Barcelona. The town is compact and can be explored on foot.

CONTACTS ALSA. ✉ *Estación de Autobuses, Calle Bisbe de Bell-Loch 1, La Seu d'Urgell* ☎ *902/422242* 🌐 *www.alsa.com.*

VISITOR INFORMATION

CONTACTS La Seu d'Urgell Tourist Office. ✉ *Carrer Major 8, La Seu d'Urgell* ☎ *973/351511* 🌐 *www.turismeseu.com.*

Sights

★ Catedral de Santa Maria

CHURCH | This 12th-century cathedral is the finest in the Pyrenees, and the sunlight casting the rich reds and blues of Santa Maria's southeastern rose window into the deep gloom of the transept is a moving sight. The 13th-century cloister is famous for the individually hewn, often whimsical capitals on its 50 columns, crafted by the same Roussillon school of masons who carved the doorway on the church of Santa Maria in Ripoll. Don't miss the haunting 11th-century chapel of Sant Miquel or the Diocesan Museum, which has a collection of striking medieval murals from various Pyrenean churches and a colorfully illuminated 10th-century Mozarabic manuscript of the monk Beatus de Liébana's commentary on the apocalypse. ✉ *Pl. del Deganat, La Seu d'Urgell* ☎ *973/353242* 🌐 *www.museudiocesaurgell.org* 🎫 *€4, includes museum* 🕒 *Closed Sun.*

Hotels

★ Cal Serni

$$$ | **B&B/INN** | Ten minutes north of La Seu d'Urgell in the Pyrenean village of Calbinyà, this enchanting 15th-century farmhouse and inn exudes rustic charm with its stone-walled rooms and traditional wooden furnishings. **Pros:** incredible views; mountain solitude minutes from La Seu; window into local country cooking. **Cons:** tight public spaces; small guest rooms; simple lodgings. [$] *Rooms from: €140* ✉ *Ctra. de Calbinyà, Valls de Valira, Calbinyà* ☎ *973/352809* 🌐 *www.calserni.com* 🛏 *6 rooms* 🍴 *Free Breakfast.*

El Castell de Ciutat

$$$$ | **HOTEL** | Outside town, the idyllic mountain setting of this wood-and-slate Relais & Château-approved property beneath La Seu's castle makes it one of the finest places to stay in the Pyrenees. **Pros:** on-site spa; best restaurant for many miles; magnificent Pyrenean panoramas. **Cons:** next to a busy highway; standard upper-floor rooms feel slightly cramped; misses out on the feel of the town. [$] *Rooms from: €200* ✉ *Ctra. de Lleida (N260), Km 229, La Seu d'Urgell* ☎ *973/350000* 🌐 *www.hotelelcastell.com* 🛏 *33 rooms, 5 suites* 🍴 *Free Breakfast.*

Parador de la Seu d'Urgell

$$ | **HOTEL** | These comfortable quarters in the center of town are built into the 14th-century convent of Sant Domènec. **Pros:** historic building; next to the Santa Maria cathedral; handy for wandering town. **Cons:** mediocre restaurant; some rooms are small; no parking. [$] *Rooms from: €120* ✉ *Calle Sant Domènec 6, La Seu d'Urgell* ☎ *973/352000* 🌐 *www.parador.es* 🛏 *79 rooms* 🍴 *No Meals.*

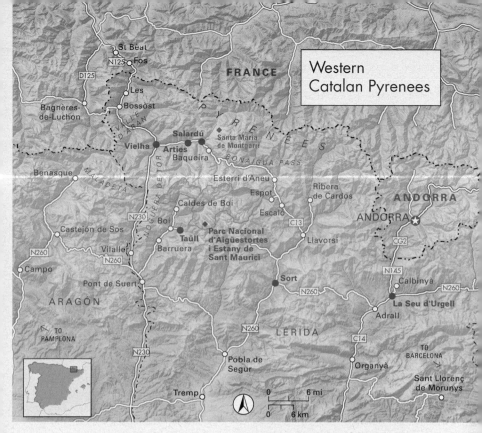

Sort

*59 km (37 miles) west of La Seu d'Urgell,
136 km (84 miles) north of Lleida, 259
km (161 miles) northwest of Barcelona.*

The capital of the Pallars Sobirà (Upper
Pallars Valley) is the area's epicenter for
skiing, fishing, and white-water kayaking.
The word *sort* is Catalan for "luck," and
its local lottery shop, La Bruixa d'Or (The
Gold Witch), became a tourist attraction
by living up to the town's name and
selling more than an average number of
winning tickets. Don't be fooled by the
modern town you see from the main
road. One block back, Sort is honey-
combed with tiny streets and protected
corners built to stave off harsh winter
weather.

GETTING HERE AND AROUND
Heading west from La Seu d'Urgell, take
the N260 toward Lleida, then head west
again at Adrall, staying on the N260, and
drive 53 km (33 miles) over the Cantó
Pass to Sort.

VISITOR INFORMATION
**CONTACTS Pallars Sobirà Tourist
Office.** ⊠ Camí de la Cabanera 1, Sort
☎ 973/621002 ⊕ turisme.pallarssobira.
cat.

 Restaurants

★ Fogony
$$$$ | **SPANISH** | Come here for seasonal
and contemporary creations from an
acclaimed chef and supporter of the
slow-food movement, with a prix fixe
menu that may include dishes such as

pollo a la cocotte con trufa (organic blue-foot chicken with truffle) and *solomillo de ternera de los Pirineos con ligero escabeche de verduras y setas* (fillet of Pyrenean veal with marinated vegetables and mushrooms). This restaurant is one of the best of its kind in the Pyrenees and, if you hit Sort at lunchtime, it makes an excellent reason to stop. **Known for:** award-winning menu; part of the slow food movement; family run. $ *Average main: €38* ⊠ *Av. Generalitat 45, Sort* ☎ *973/621225* ⊕ *www.fogony.com* ⊘ *Closed Mon. and Tues. and 2 wks in Jan. No dinner Sun.*

Parc Nacional d'Aigüestortes i Estany de Sant Maurici

33 km (20 miles) north of Sort, 168 km (104 miles) north of Lleida, 292 km (181 miles) northwest of Barcelona.

Catalonia's only national park, which translates to "twisted waters" in Catalan, is the undisputed jewel of the Catalan Pyrenees. Its dramatic unspoiled landscape was shaped over 2 million years of glacial activity. Hikers can reach the park from the Noguera Pallaresa and Ribagorçana valleys, from the villages of Espot to the east, and from Taüll and Boí to the west. There are several visitor centers with maps and information on hiking routes and accommodation in the villages that border the park such as Espot and Boí.

GETTING HERE AND AROUND

The C13 north up the Noguera Pallaresa Valley covers 34 km (21 miles) from Sort to Espot. One of the main entrances to the park is 4 km (2 miles) west of Espot, where there is also a parking lot. No cars are allowed inside the park (except official taxis/transport).

VISITOR INFORMATION

CONTACTS Casa del Parc Nacional de Boí (Park Information Center - Boí). ⊠ *Ca de Simamet, Carrer de les Graieres 2, Boí* ☎ *973/696189* ⊕ *www.vallboi.cat/en.***Casa del Parc Nacional d'Espot (Park Information Center).** ⊠ *Carrer de Sant Maurici 5, Espot* ☎ *973/624036.*

 Sights

★ Parc Nacional d'Aigüestortes i Estany de Sant Maurici

NATIONAL PARK | Barring Ordesa to the west, this is without a doubt the most jaw-dropping park in the Pyrenees, with some of the most arresting mountain scenery in Europe. The terrain is formed by jagged peaks, steep rock walls, and deep glacial depressions filled with crystalline water, all of which lie in the shadow of the twin peaks of Els Encantats. Until the turn of the last century, this area was one of the remotest in Europe, known only to shepherds and hunters. Its 200-some streams, lakes, and lagoons intersperse with fir and birch forests and empty into the Noguera River water-courses: the Pallaresa to the east and the Ribagorçana to the west. Rain and snow are notably frequent in all areas. The land range sweeps from wildflower-blanketed meadows below 5,000 feet to rocky crests at nearly double that height; it's inhabited by Pyrenean chamois, golden eagles, capercaillies, and other fauna in great abundance. The twin Encantats measure more than 9,000 feet, and the surrounding peaks of Beciberri, Peguera, Montarto, and Amitges hover between 8,700 feet and a little less than 10,000 feet. The park offers an abundance of walking trails. The most popular is a one-day scenic traverse across the park from east to west, starting at the village

Hiking in the Pyrenees

Walking the Pyrenees, with one foot in France and the other in Spain, is exhilarating. Though the Alps are taller, the Pyrenees are less known and more remote, which has kept them comparatively pristine and untouristed.

In fall and winter, the Alberes Mountains between Cap de Creus, the Iberian Peninsula's easternmost point, and the border with France at Le Perthus are a grassy runway between the Côte Vermeille's curving beaches to the north and the green patchwork of the Empordá to the south. The well-marked GR (Gran Recorrido) 11 is a favorite two-day spring or autumn hike, with an overnight at the Refugi de la Tanyareda, just below Puig Neulós, the highest point in the Alberes.

The eight-hour walk from Coll de Núria to Ulldeter over the Sierra Catllar, above Setcases, is another grassy corridor in good weather, April–October. The luminous Cerdanya Valley is a hiker's paradise year-round, while the summertime Andorra hike is a scenic 360-degree tour of the tiny country.

The Parc Nacional d'Aigüestortes i Estany de Sant Maurici is superb for trekking from spring through fall. The ascent of the highest peak in the Pyrenees, the 11,168-foot Aneto peak above Benasque, is a long day's round-trip best approached in summer and only by fit and experienced hikers. Much of the hike is over the Maladeta Glacier, from the base camp at the Refugio de La Renclusa. There are also plenty of day hikes suitable for beginners here.

In the Parque Nacional de Ordesa y Monte Perdido, you can take day trips up to the Cola de Caballo waterfall and back around the southern rim of the canyon or, for true mountain goats, longer hikes via the Refugio de Góriz to La Brèche de Roland and Gavarnie or to Monte Perdido, the parador at La Pineta, and the village of Bielsa. Another prized walk involves bed and dinner in the base-camp town of Torla or a night up at the Refugio de Góriz at the head of the valley.

The section of the Camino de Santiago walk from Saint-Jean-Pied-de-Port to Roncesvalles is a marvelous 8- to 10-hour trek any time of year, though check weather reports October–June.

Local *excursionista* (outing) clubs can help you get started; local tourist offices may also have brochures and rudimentary trail maps. Note that the higher reaches are safely navigable only in summer.

Some useful contacts for hiking are **Cercle d'Aventura** (972/881017), **Giroguies Senderisme** (636/490830), and **Guies de Meranges** (616/855535).

of Espot and finishing in Boí. Although driving inside the park is not permitted, it is possible to organize taxis to help you on your way from Boí or Espot, and, in summer, buses also provide transportation in and around the park. ✉ *Espot* ☎ *973/696189* ⊕ *parcsnaturals. gencat.cat/en/xarxa-de-parcs/aiguest-ortes/inici/index.html* ♿ *Free.*

7

The Pyrenees PARC NACIONAL D'AIGÜESTORTES I ESTANY DE SANT MAURICI

Vielha

79 km (49 miles) northwest of Sort, 297 km (185 miles) northwest of Barcelona, 160 km (99 miles) north of Lleida.

Vielha (Viella in Spanish), capital of the Vall d'Aran, is a lively crossroads at the center of a movement to defend and reconstruct the valley's architectural, institutional, and linguistic heritage. At first glance, the town looks like a typical ski-resort base, but the compact and bustling old quarter has a Romanesque church and narrow streets filled with a good selection of restaurants, shops, and a couple of late-night bars. Hiking and climbing are popular around Vielha; guides are available year-round and can be arranged through the tourist office.

GETTING HERE AND AROUND

From the direction of Taüll, head south on the L500 for 15 km (9 miles) toward El Pont de Suerte. At Campament de Tor, turn right onto the northbound Carretera Lleida–Vielha (N230). Vielha's center is fairly compact and everything can be reached on foot, but you'll need a car to get to Salardú, Arties, and the ski station of Baqueira-Beret.

VISITOR INFORMATION

CONTACTS Vielha Tourist Office. ✉ *Carrer Sarriulera 10, Vielha* ☎ *973/640688* ⊕ *www.visitvaldaran.com.*

Sights

Sant Miquel

CHURCH | Vielha's octagonal 14th-century bell tower on the Romanesque parish church of Sant Miquel is one of the town's key sights, as is its 15th-century Gothic altar. The partly damaged 12th-century wood carving called *Cristo de Mig Aran*, displayed under glass, evokes a sense of mortality and humanity with a power unusual in medieval sculpture. ✉ *Pl. de la Iglesia, Vielha* ☎ *973/640021.*

🍴 Restaurants

El Molí

$$$ | SPANISH | A picturesque riverside location, knotty pine walls, wood beams, and a rustic menu that highlights regional specialties make this a lovely spot for a meal. There is a ground-floor dining room with large windows that frame a broad sweep of the river and a second, smaller dining room tucked up in the attic. **Known for:** flame-licked calçots (Catalan green onions) in season; aged Pyrenean beef cooked over coals; river views. $ *Average main: €20* ✉ *Carrèr Sarriulèra 26, Vielha* ☎ *973/641718* ⊕ *www.hotelelmoli. es/en* ⊗ *No dinner Tues. Closed Wed. and Dec. 18–Jan. 18.*

Nightlife

DeVins

WINE BARS | This popular wine bar has a prime location overlooking the river and gets busy in the early evening serving tapas, cheese boards, and wine. Later on, it becomes a bar dedicated mainly to gin and tonics, but other spirits and a decent wine list are also available. ✉ *Carrèr Major 23, Vielha* ☎ *647/511146* ⊗ *Closed Tues.*

Saxo Blu

PUBS | This is one of the most popular late-night hangouts for all ages. ✉ *Carrèr Marrec 6, Vielha.*

🛍 Shopping

Eth Galin Reiau

FOOD | On the same square as the church, this shop has its own line of gourmet products ranging from locally produced pâté de foie gras and cheese to liqueurs, marmalades, and honey. ✉ *Pl. de la Gleisa 2, Vielha* ☎ *973/641941* ⊕ *www.tiendagalinreiau.com* ⊗ *Closed Sun.*

Activities

Skiing, white-water rafting, hiking, climbing, horseback riding, and fly-fishing are a few of the sports available in the Vall d'Aran. There are terrific walks through the wooded valleys of the Río Garona, and mountain climbers can relish steep, well-marked hikes up the surrounding peaks: Maubermé (9,450 feet), Besiberri Nord (9,885 feet), and Tuc de Mulleres (9,873 feet).

SKIING

★ Baqueira-Beret Estación de Esquí
(*Baqueira-Beret Ski Station*)
SKIING & SNOWBOARDING | **FAMILY** | This ski center offers Catalonia's most varied and reliable skiing. Its 87 km (54 miles) of *pistes* (slopes), spread over 53 runs, range from the gentle Beret slopes to the vertical chutes of Baqueira. The Bonaigua area is a mixture of steep and gently undulating trails, with some of the longest, most varied runs in the Pyrenees. A dozen or so restaurants and four children's areas are scattered about the facilities, and the thermal baths at Tredós are 4 km (2½ miles) away. ☎ *973/639025* 🌐 *www.baqueira.es.*

Arties

7 km (4 miles) east of Vielha, 3½ km (2 miles) west of Salardú.

The village of Arties is a lively village with Romanesque, Gothic, and Renaissance architecture that straddles a clear river presided over by Montarto Peak.

GETTING HERE AND AROUND

The C28 east out of Vielha reaches Arties in 7 km (4 miles). The village is small and best explored on foot. Cross the bridge over the river to hit the main square.

Restaurants

Tauèrna Urtau Arties
$$ | **TAPAS** | **FAMILY** | The area's beloved tapas chain is friendly, fun, and always busy with customers helping themselves to some 40 mouthwatering types of *pinchos* (dainty bar-side tapas ranging from mini hamburgers to fried king prawns to sautéed mushrooms). You can also have larger portions in the sit-down dining area. **Known for:** rollicking atmosphere; Basque-style "help yourself at the bar" pinchos; cider and local products. [$] *Average main: €16* ✉ *Pl. Urtau 12, Arties* ☎ *973/640926* 🌐 *www.urtau.com* 🕒 *Closed 2 wks in Oct. or Nov.*

Hotels

★ Casa Irene
$$$ | **B&B/INN** | A rustic haven, Casa Irene exudes an old-fashioned elegance that's never over the top. **Pros:** individualized attention from staff; free shuttle to the slopes; understated yet tasteful decor. **Cons:** often booked up; nothing hip about it; street-facing rooms can be noisy on summer nights. [$] *Rooms from: €180* ✉ *Carrer Major 22, 6 km (4 miles) east of Vielha, Arties* ☎ *973/644364* 🌐 *www.hotelcasairene.com* 🕒 *Closed May, June, Oct., and Nov.* 🛏 *22 rooms* 🍴 *Free Breakfast.*

Parador de Arties
$$$ | **HOTEL** | Built around the Casa de Don Gaspar de Portolà, once home to the military officer who colonized California, this modern parador with friendly staff and an outdoor pool (seasonal) has views of the Pyrenees and is handy for exploring the Romanesque sights in nearby villages. **Pros:** marvelous panoramas from cozy public areas; free parking; quiet and personal for a parador. **Cons:** feels old-fashioned; requires driving; neither at the foot of the slopes nor in the thick of the Vielha après-ski vibe. [$] *Rooms from: €160*

Santa Maria de Montgarri

Partly in ruins, this 11th-century chapel was once an important way station on the route into the Vall d'Aran from France. The beveled hexagonal bell tower and the rounded stones, which look as if they came from a brook bottom, give the structure a curious stippled appearance. The Romería de Nuestra Señora de Montgarri (Feast of Our Lady of Montgarri), on July 2, is a country fair with food, games, music, and dance. The sanctuary can be reached by following the C142 road until Beret and then walking 6 km (4 miles) along a dirt track that can also be accessed by off-road vehicles. It is difficult to get there during the winter snow season.

✉ Calle San Juan 1, Arties ☎ 973/640801 ⊕ www.parador.es ⊘ Closed 40 days after Easter wk (dates vary) ⇴ 54 rooms, 3 suites ⏹ No Meals.

Salardú

9 km (6 miles) east of Vielha.

Salardú is a key crossroads in the Vall d'Aran, convenient to Baqueira-Beret, Montarto Peak, the lakes and Circ de Colomers, and Parc Nacional d'Aigüestortes as well as the villages of Tredós, Unha, and Montgarri. The town itself, with some 700 inhabitants, is known for its steep streets and octagonal fortified bell tower.

GETTING HERE AND AROUND

The C28 east out of Vielha goes straight to Salardú and Tredós in 9 km (6 miles) and on to Baqueira-Beret in 13 km (8 miles).

 Restaurants

Casa Rufus

$$$ | SPANISH | Pine walls and floors, red-and-white-check curtains, and flowy white tablecloths furnish this stuck-in-time restaurant in the gray-stone village of Gessa, between Vielha and Salardú.

Try the *conejo relleno de ternera y cerdo* (rabbit stuffed with veal and pork). *Civets* (stews) of mountain goat or venison, though not on the menu, can be requested in advance. **Known for:** wide selection of local meat dishes; good stop-off on way to or from the Baqueira ski slopes; one of the best restaurants in the area. ⓢ *Average main: €18* ✉ *Carrer Sant Jaume 8, Gessa* ☎ *973/645246* ⊘ *Closed May and June, weekdays in Oct. and Nov., and Sun. Oct.–Apr.*

★ Taberna Eth Bot

$$ | SPANISH | FAMILY | You can feast where the farm animals once grazed in this converted 16th-century stable, where the fixed-price menu features local dishes such as *olha aranesa* (a multicourse meat-and-legume feast), *patatas rellenas* (potato stewed with a choice of meat or vegetables), or *estofado de jabalí y arroz* (wild boar stew served with rice). A bottle of wine, water, and bread—and a shot of local liqueur at the end—are thrown in for good measure. **Known for:** value prix fixe; atmospheric building; hearty Aranese cuisine. ⓢ *Average main: €17* ✉ *Pl. Mayor 1, Salardú* ☎ *973/644212* ⊕ *www.ethbot.es.*

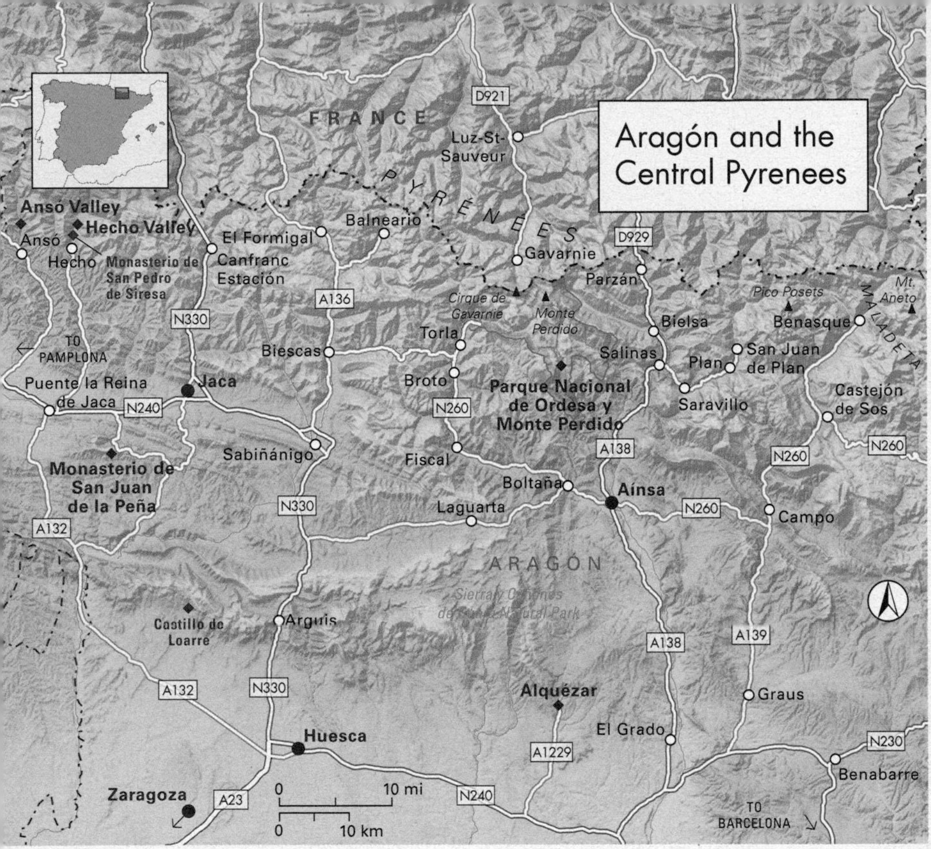
Aragón and the Central Pyrenees
FRANCE
PYRÉNÉES
ARAGÓN
Ansó Valley
Hecho Valley
Ansó
Hecho
Monasterio de San Pedro de Siresa
El Formigal
Canfranc Estación
Balneario
Luz-St-Sauveur
D921
Gavarnie
D929
Parzán
Cirque de Gavarnie
Monte Perdido
Pico Posets
Mt. Aneto
MALADETA
Benasque
A136
N330
TO PAMPLONA
Biescas
Torla
Bielsa
Salinas
San Juan de Plan
Plan
Broto
Parque Nacional de Ordesa y Monte Perdido
Saravillo
Castejón de Sos
Puente la Reina de Jaca
N240
Jaca
N260
A138
Sabiñánigo
Fiscal
Monasterio de San Juan de la Peña
Boltaña
Aínsa
Campo
Laguarta
A132
Sierra y Cañones de Guara Natural Park
Castillo de Loarre
Arguis
A139
Alquézar
Graus
El Grado
Huesca
A1229
N230
Benabarre
Zaragoza
A23
0
10 mi
0
10 km
TO BARCELONA

Hotels

Hotel Val de Ruda

$$$$ | HOTEL | For rustic surroundings—light on luxury but long on comfort—only a two-minute walk from the ski lift, this modern-traditional construction of glass, wood, and stone is a good choice. **Pros:** pleasant and outdoorsy; friendly family service; terrific breakfasts. **Cons:** not cheap; only open during ski season; some upstairs rooms are cozy but tiny. [$] *Rooms from: €255* ✉ *Ctra. Baqueira-Beret Cota 1500, Salardú* ☎ *973/645258* 🌐 *www.hotelvalderudabaqueira.com* 🕑 *Closed after Easter wk–Nov.* 🛏 *35 rooms* 🍴 *Free Breakfast.*

Zaragoza

138 km (86 miles) west of Lleida, 307 km (191 miles) northwest of Barcelona, 164 km (102 miles) southeast of Pamplona, 322 km (200 miles) northeast of Madrid.

Despite its sizable population of 710,000, this sprawling provincial capital midway between Barcelona, Madrid, Bilbao, and Valencia retains a laidback feel. It is a worthwhile detour from the tourist track yet still accessible via the AVE, Spain's high-speed railroad, with both Madrid and Barcelona only 90 minutes away. The first decade of this century were major boom years here, and it's been rated one of Spain's most desirable places to live because of its air quality, affordability, and low population density.

Straddling the Ebro, Zaragoza (pronounced tha-ra-GO-tha) was originally named Caesaraugusta after Roman emperor Augustus. It was a thriving river port by 25 BC, and its rich history is exemplified in its Roman ruins, Jewish baths, and umpteen architectural styles: Moorish, Romanesque, Gothic-Mudejar, Renaissance, baroque, neoclassical Art Nouveau, and more. Parts of the **Roman walls** are visible near the city's landmark **Basílica de Nuestra Señora del Pilar.** Nearby, the medieval **Puente de Piedra** (Stone Bridge) spans the Ebro. Key sights include the **Lonja** (Stock Exchange), **La Seo cathedral,** the Moorish **Aljafería** (Fortified Palace and Jewel Treasury), **Mercado de Lanuza** (Produce Market), and many **Mudejar churches** in the old town.

Worthwhile excursions from Zaragoza include Goya's birthplace in **Fuendetodos,** 44 km (27 miles) to the southeast, and **Monasterio de Piedra,** an hour's drive southwest. Founded in 1195 by Alfonso II of Aragón, this lush oasis of caves, waterfalls, and suspended walkways surrounds a 12th-century Cistercian monastery and a 16th-century Renaissance section that is now a hotel (www.monasteriopiedra. com).

GETTING HERE AND AROUND

Several trains per day link Zaragoza and Barcelona, Lleida, and Huesca (www. renfe.com). Buses link Zaragoza, Huesca, and Jaca (aragon.avanzagrupo.com). By car, travel west from Barcelona on the E90 motorway. Zaragoza's sights are accessible on foot.

BUS STATION Estación Central de Autobuses. ⊠ *Calle Miguel Roca i Junyent 7, Zaragoza* ☎ *976/700599* ⊕ *www.estacion-zaragoza.es.*

VISITOR INFORMATION

CONTACTS Zaragoza Tourist Office. ⊠ *Pl. Nuestra Señora del Pilar, Zaragoza* ☎ *902/142008* ⊕ *www.zaragoza.es/ turismo.*

Sights

Alma Mater Museum

ART MUSEUM | Portraits of archbishops (one by Goya), Flemish tapestries, Renaissance and medieval paintings, and the remains of the Romanesque door of Zaragoza's church of Santiago form parts of this museum's collection. ⊠ *Pl. de la Seo 5, Zaragoza* ☎ *976/399488* ⊕ *www. almamatermuseum.com* ☎ *€3* ⊗ *Closed Mon.*

★ Catedral–Basílica de Nuestra Señora del Pilar (*Basilica of Our Lady of the Pillar*)

CHURCH | This basilica on the banks of the Ebro, often shortened to La Pilarica or El Pilar, is Zaragoza's symbol and pride. An immense baroque structure with 11 vivid tile-topped cupolas, La Pilarica is home to the Virgen del Pilar, patron saint of peninsular Spain and the entire Hispanic world. The fiestas honoring this most Spanish of saints, held in mid-October, are ushered in with processions, street concerts, bullfights, and traditional *jota* dancing. Among the basilica's treasures are two frescoes by Goya—one of them, *El Coreto de la Vírgen,* painted when he was young and the other, the famous *Regina Martirum,* after his studies in Italy. The bombs displayed to the right of the altar of La Pilarica chapel fell through the roof of the church in 1936 and miraculously failed to explode. Behind La Pilarica's altar is the tiny opening where the devout line up to kiss the rough marble pillar where La Pilarica is said to have been discovered. ⊠ *Pl. del Pilar, Zaragoza* ☎ *Basilica free, tower €4, museum €2* ⊗ *Museum closed Sun. Tower closed Mon. in winter.*

Catedral del Salvador de Zaragoza (La Seo)

(*Catedral de San Salvador*)
CHURCH | Zaragoza's main cathedral, at the eastern end of Plaza del Pilar, is the city's bishopric, or diocesan *seo* (seat). It was built in many architectural styles: Mudejar (the brick-and-tile exterior),

Gothic (the altarpiece), churrigueresque (the doorways), and baroque (the facade). The Museo de Tapices within contains medieval tapestries. The nearby medieval Casa y Arco del Deán form one of the city's favorite corners. ✉ *Pl. de la Seo 4, Zaragoza* ☎ *976/291231* 💳 *€4, includes museum.*

EMOZ (Escuela Museo Origami Zaragoza)

ART MUSEUM | Within Zaragoza's Centro de Historias, EMOZ houses one of the finest collections of origami in the world. These eye-popping exhibitions change themes seasonally and reveal the surprising story of Zaragoza's historical connection to the art of paper-folding. ✉ *Centro de Historias, Pl. San Agustín 2, Zaragoza* ☎ *876/034569* ⊕ *www.emoz.es* 💳 *€6* ⊙ *Closed Mon.*

IAACC Pablo Serrano

ART MUSEUM | A collection of works by the famous 20th-century sculptor Pablo Serrano (1908–85) and his wife, Juana Francés, are on display in this museum. ✉ *Paseo María Agustín 20, Zaragoza* ☎ *976/280659* ⊕ *www.iaacc.es* 💳 *Free* ⊙ *Closed Mon.*

Iglesia de San Pablo

CHURCH | After the basilica and La Seo, this church, with examples of Mudejar architecture in its brickwork, is considered by Zaragozanos to be the "third cathedral."✉ *Carrer San Pablo 42, Zaragoza* ☎ *976/446296* 💳 *Free* ⊙ *Closed Sun.*

Museo de Zaragoza

ART MUSEUM | This museum contains a treasure trove of works by Zaragoza's emblematic painter, Goya, including his portraits of Fernando VII and his best graphic works: *Desastres de la Guerra, Caprichos,* and *La Tauromaquia.* ✉ *Pl. de los Sitios 6, Zaragoza* ☎ *976/222181* ⊕ *www.museodezaragoza.es* 💳 *Free* ⊙ *Closed Mon.*

Museo del Foro de Caesaraugusta

RUINS | FAMILY | Remains of the Roman forum and elaborate sewage system can be seen here. Two more Roman sites, the thermal baths at Calle de San Juan y San Pedro and the river port at Plaza San Bruno, are also open to the public. You can organize in advance to see the presentation videos in English through the Museo del Teatro Romano (976/726075). English-language audio guides are also available. ✉ *Pl. de la Seo 2, Zaragoza* ☎ *976/721221* 💳 *€3* ⊙ *Closed Mon.*

Museo del Teatro de Caesaraugusta

RUINS | In addition to the restored Roman amphitheater here, built in the 1st century AD, you can see objects recovered in the excavation including theatrical masks, platters, and even hairpins. ✉ *Calle San Jorge 12, Zaragoza* ☎ *976/726075* 💳 *€4* ⊙ *Closed Mon.*

Museo Goya Colección Ibercaja

ART MUSEUM | A fine collection of Goya's works, particularly engravings, are on view here. ✉ *Carrer Espoz y Mina 23, Zaragoza* ☎ *976/397387* ⊕ *museogoya.ibercaja.es* 💳 *€6.*

Museo Pablo Gargallo

ART MUSEUM | This is one of Zaragoza's sightseeing treasures, both for the palace in which it is housed and for its collection: Gargallo, born near Zaragoza in 1881, was one of Spain's greatest modern sculptors. ✉ *Pl. de San Felipe 3, Zaragoza* ☎ *976/724922* 💳 *€4* ⊙ *Closed Mon.*

Palacio de La Aljafería

CASTLE/PALACE | This is one of Spain's three greatest Moorish palaces. If Córdoba's Mezquita shows the energy of the 10th-century Caliphate and Granada's Alhambra is the crowning 14th-century glory of Al-Andalus (the 789-year Moorish empire on the Iberian Peninsula), then the late-11th-century Aljafería is the middle child. Originally a fortress and royal residence, and later a seat of the Spanish

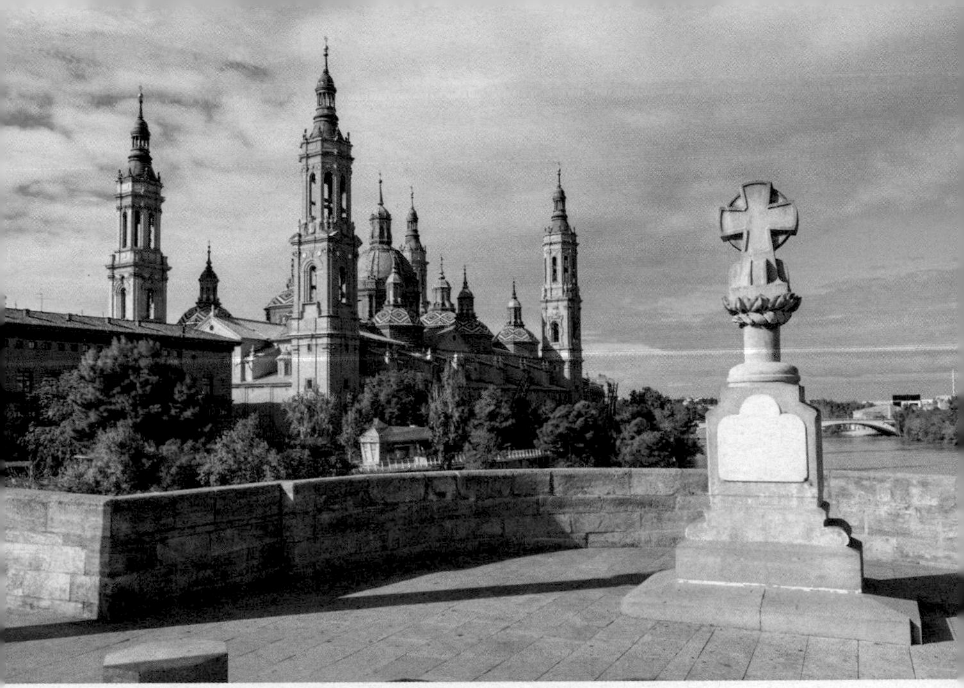

Overlooking the Río Ebro and Zaragoza's Basílica de Nuestra Señora del Pilar

Inquisition, the Aljafería is now the home of the Cortes (Parliament) de Aragón. The 9th-century Torre del Trovador (Tower of the Troubadour) appears in Giuseppe Verdi's opera *Il Trovatore.* Visits by online reservation only. ✉ *Diputados, Zaragoza* ☎ *976/289528* 🌐 *reservasonline.aljaferia.com* 🎫 *€5* 🕒 *Closed Thurs. and Fri. if parliament is in session.*

🍴 Restaurants

★ El Tubo Neighborhood

$$ | SPANISH | El Tubo, the area surrounding the intersection of Calle Estébanes and Calle Libertad, is tapas central. Try to stick to one tapa per bar so you can sample as many spots as possible. **El Champi** (Calle Libertad 16) isn't much to look at, but this tiny establishment serves killer griddled mushrooms stacked on bread to soak up the garlic-infused oil. **Bodegas Almau** (Calle Estébanes 10) has shelves heaving with wine bottles and a bar stacked with gargantuan pinchos, which regulars gobble down in the standing-room-only barroom. **Known for:** packed pedestrianized streets; variety of tapas bars; lively atmosphere. [$] *Average main: €15* ✉ *Calle Estébanes, Zaragoza.*

Los Victorinos

$$ | TAPAS | Named after a much-feared and respected breed of fighting bull, this rustic tavern, located behind La Seo, is dripping with taurine paraphernalia. It offers an elaborate and inventive selection of pinchos and tapas. *Jamón ibérico de bellota* (acorn-fed Iberian ham), Spain's culinary crown jewel, is a no-brainer, though quail eggs or the classic *gilda*—olives, green peppers, and anchovies on a toothpick—are also on the bar and hard to resist. **Known for:** lively old-school atmosphere; zippy one-bite gildas (pickled brochettes); melt-on-your-tongue Iberian ham. [$] *Average main: €15* ✉ *Calle José de la Hera 6, Zaragoza* ☎ *976/394213* 🕒 *Closed Mon. and 2 wks in May. No lunch weekdays. No dinner Sun.*

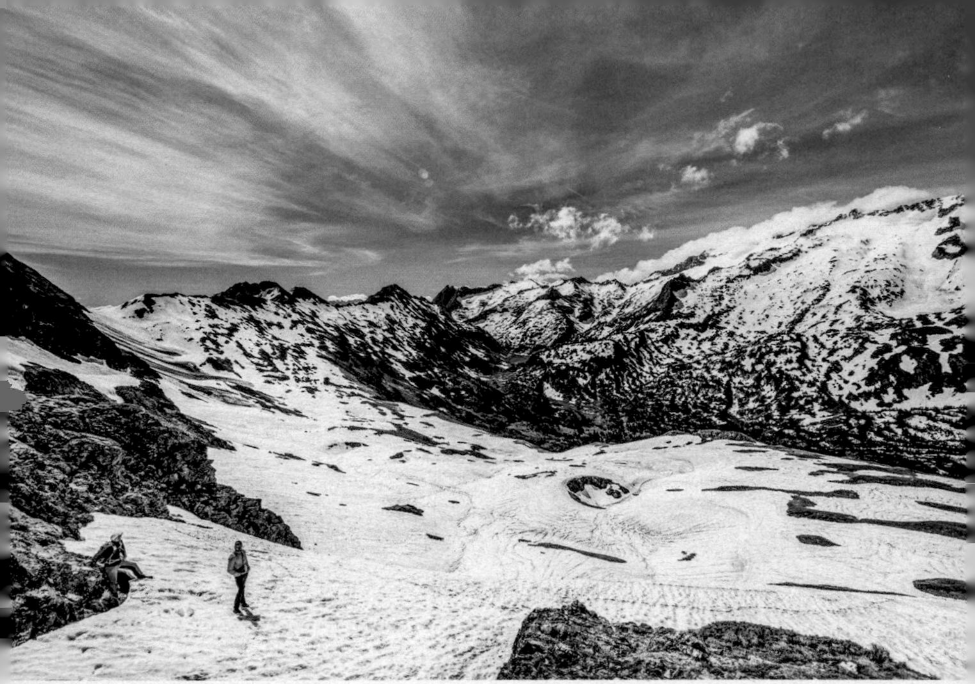

Mountain trekking in the Huesca province

★ Palomeque

$$$ | **TAPAS** | For upscale tapas, sharable *raciones*, and a more sedate restaurant atmosphere, step into Palomeque. Dishes hinge on market produce and fuse traditional recipes with playful modern plating. **Known for:** charmingly dated decor; hidden gem; dishes with local produce and meats. [$] *Average main: €20* ✉ *Calle Agustín Palomeque 11, Zaragoza* ☎ *976/214082* 🌐 *www.restaurantepalomeque.es* 🕒 *Closed Sun.*

Tragantúa

$$$ | **SPANISH** | This rollicking wood-paneled dining room serves surprisingly sublime seafood, cooked *a la plancha* (on the griddle), *al horno* (in the oven), or folded into a variety of rice dishes. The beer is fresh and cold, and the house wines, largely from Upper Aragón's envelope-pushing Somontano D.O., are big and bold—and dangerously economical. **Known for:** comfy dining room; excellent house wines; seafood so fresh you might as well be on the coast. [$] *Average main: €21* ✉ *Pl. Santa Marta, Zaragoza* ☎ *976/299174* 🌐 *www.grupoloscabezudos.es* 🕒 *Closed last 2 wks in June and 2nd wk in Jan.*

Hotels

★ Hotel Sauce

$ | **HOTEL** | Hotel Sauce might be the perfect budget hotel—it has quirky wall art, mid-century modern furniture, bright and uncluttered rooms, and a location that can't be beat. **Pros:** excellent value; central location; modern facilities and café on-site. **Cons:** rooms are too small for long stays; reception service can be erratic; not many rooms. [$] *Rooms from: €60* ✉ *Espoz y Mina 33, Zaragoza* ☎ *976/205050* 🌐 *www.hotelsauce.com* 🛏 *40 rooms* 🍴 *No Meals.*

Hotel Palafox Zaragoza

$$$ | **HOTEL** | One of Zaragoza's top hotels, Palafox combines contemporary design with traditional urban service and elegance. **Pros:** top comfort and service;

good restaurant; private parking for guests. **Cons:** decor could use a revamp; modern and somewhat antiseptic; rooms not as impressive as the public spaces. [$] *Rooms from: €130* ✉ *Calle Marqués Casa Jiménez, Zaragoza* ☎ *976/237700* 🌐 *www.palafoxhoteles.com* 🛏 *179 rooms* 🍴 *Free Breakfast.*

Huesca

68 km (42 miles) northeast of Zaragoza, 123 km (76 miles) northwest of Lleida.

Once a Roman colony, Huesca was the capital of Aragón until the royal court moved to Zaragoza in 1118. The town's university was founded in 1354 and has a rigorous Aragonese studies department.

GETTING HERE AND AROUND

From Zaragoza there are several trains a day (www.renfe.com). Avanza (www.avanzabus.com) runs buses between Huesca and Zaragoza, Lleida, and Jaca. By car from Zaragoza, head northwest toward Huesca on the A23. The center is small and best managed on foot.

CONTACTS Bus Station. ✉ *Calle José Gil Cávez 10, Huesca.*

VISITOR INFORMATION

CONTACTS Huesca Tourist Office. ✉ *Pl. Luis López Allué, Huesca* ☎ *974/292170* 🌐 *www.huescaturismo.com.*

Sights

Huesca Cathedral
CHURCH | An intricately carved gallery tops the eroded facade of Huesca's 13th-century Gothic cathedral. Damián Forment, a protégé of the 15th-century Italian master sculptor Donatello, created the alabaster altarpiece, which has scenes from the Crucifixion. ✉ *Pl. de la Catedral, Huesca* ☎ *974/231099* 🎟 *€4* 🕒 *Museum closed Sun.*

Castillo de Loarre

This walled 11th-century monastery, 36 km (22 miles) west of Huesca off Route A132 on A1206, is nearly indistinguishable from the rock outcroppings that surround it. Inside the walls are a church, a tower, a dungeon, and even a medieval toilet. The complex affords views of almond and olive groves in the Ebro basin. www.castillodeloarre.es

Museo de Huesca
HISTORY MUSEUM | This museum occupies parts of the former royal palace of the kings of Aragón and holds paintings by Aragonese primitives, including *La Virgen del Rosario* by Miguel Jiménez, and several works by the 16th-century Maestro de Sigena. The eight chambers of the gallery, set around an octagonal patio, include the Sala de la Campana (Hall of the Bell), where, in the 12th century, beheadings of errant nobles took place. ✉ *Pl. de la Universidad, Huesca* ☎ *974/220586* 🌐 *www.museodehuesca.es* 🎟 *Free* 🕒 *Closed Mon.*

San Pedro el Viejo
CHURCH | This church has an 11th-century cloister. Ramiro II and his father, Alfonso I, the only Aragonese kings not entombed at San Juan de la Peña, rest in a side chapel. ✉ *Pl. de San Pedro, Huesca* ☎ *No phone* 🌐 *www.sanpedroelviejo.com* 🎟 *€3.*

Restaurants

★ Las Torres
$$$$ | **SPANISH** | Huesca's top restaurant makes inventive use of first-rate local ingredients like wild mushrooms, wild boar, venison, and lamb. The glass-walled

kitchen is as inviting as the food that emerges from it, and the wine list is strong on Somontano, Huesca's own D.O. **Known for:** excellent value; Aragonese dishes with a modern twist; terrific tasting menus. [$] *Average main: €25* ✉ *Calle María Auxiliadora 3, Huesca* ☎ *974/228213* 🌐 *www.lastorres-restaurante.com* 🕒 *No dinner Sun. or Mon. Closed 2 wks over Easter and last 2 wks of Aug.*

Hotels

Hostal San Marcos

$ | **B&B/INN** | This elegant building dates to the late 19th century, though the public spaces have been updated for comfort. **Pros:** good value; central location; historic and elegant building. **Cons:** simple lodgings; rooms can seem cluttered and somewhat cramped; noise from the street. [$] *Rooms from: €62* ✉ *Calle San Orencio 10, Huesca* ☎ *974/222931* 🌐 *www.hostalsanmarcos.es* 🛏 *29 rooms* 🍴 *Free Breakfast.*

Hotel Abba Huesca

$$ | **HOTEL** | This modern hotel in Huesca has comfortable rooms and a buzzing contemporary bar where guests and locals mingle. **Pros:** on-site bar, restaurant, and outdoor pool; excellent value; understated elegance. **Cons:** surrounded by unattractive buildings; slightly outside the center of town; decor lacks pizzazz. [$] *Rooms from: €90* ✉ *Calle de Tarbes 14, Huesca* ☎ *974/292900* 🌐 *www.abbahuescahotel.com* 🛏 *84 rooms* 🍴 *No Meals.*

Shopping

Ultramarinos La Confianza

FOOD | Founded in 1871, La Confianza may be the oldest grocery store in Spain. It's in the porticoed Plaza Mayor in the old town and worth popping into to see the tiled floors and hand-painted ceiling, and to browse the shelves stacked high with local products, from dried fruit and nuts to specialty chocolates and salt cod. ✉ *Pl. Mayor (Pl. López Allué), Huesca* ☎ *974/222632* 🌐 *www.ultramarinoslaconfianza.com* 🕒 *Closed Sun.*

Alquézar

51 km (32 miles) northeast of Huesca, 123 km (76 miles) northeast of Zaragoza.

As though carved from the ocher rock itself, Alquézar looms over the Parque Natural Sierra y Cañones de Guara and is one of Spain's prettiest towns. Its maze of winding cobbled streets and low archways coil around a central square, which stands out for its oblong shape and porched area that was built to provide shelter from the sun and rain. Look up as you walk—many facades bear coats of arms that date to the 16th century.

GETTING HERE AND AROUND

From Huesca, take the A22 or N240 east for 29 km (18 miles) before merging onto the A1229 toward Alquézar. Cars cannot enter the old quarter, so the only way to see the town is on foot.

VISITOR INFORMATION

CONTACTS Alquézar Tourist Office. ✉ *Calle Arrabal 14, Alquézar* ☎ *974/318940* 🌐 *www.alquezar.es.*

Sights

Bodegas Lalanne

WINERY | A 20-minute drive south of Alquézar drops you at this family-run wine estate that's been in business for over a century. Plan to spend about two hours here between the winery tour and tasting, in which you'll sample bold New World-style wines—Gewürztraminer, Cabernet Sauvignon, etc.—that are a hallmark of the Somontano D.O. Be sure to call ahead or book online. ✉ *Ctra. A1232, Km 3.8, Alquézar* ☎ *974/310689* 🌐 *www.bodegaslalanne.eu* 🎟 *from €38.*

Colegiata de Santa María la Mayor

CHURCH | The Colegiata, originally a 9th-century Moorish citadel, was conquered by the Christians in 1067. An interesting mix of Gothic, Mudejar, and Renaissance details are found in the shaded cloister, and there are biblical murals that date to the Romanesque era. The church, built in the 16th century, contains an almost life-size Romanesque figure of Christ, but restoration has taken away some of the building's charm—its interior brickwork is now only a painted representation. Visits are conducted via guided tour (Spanish only) and depart every 30 minutes. ⊠ *Diseminado Afueras, off Calle la Iglesia, Alquézar* ☎ *974/318940* ⊕ *www.patrimoniocul-turaldearagon.es/bienes-culturales/ colegiata-de-santa-maria-alquezar* ⊠ *€3* ⊘ *Closed Jan. 6–Feb. 7.*

Parque Cultural del Río Vero

RUINS | FAMILY | A UNESCO World Heritage Site, this park within the Sierra de Guara contains more than 60 limestone caves with prehistoric paintings. Some date to around 22,000 BC, though most are from between 12,000 and 4,000 BC. Information and guided tours are available through the interpretation center in Colungo; check the monthly schedule on the home page. Hours vary, so call ahead. ⊠ *Calle Las Braules 2, Colunga* ✛ *9½ km (6 miles) east of Alquézar* ☎ *974/306006* ⊕ *www.parquecultural-riovero.com/en* ⊠ *Free, €4 for some exhibits.*

★ Pasarelas de Alquézar

TRAIL | FAMILY | Take a breathtaking riverside hike (1½ hours) on the Ruta de las Pasarelas loop, which hugs near-sheer cliffs that plunge into rushing turquoise waters. There's a waterfall, a cave, and plenty of placards with information on the surrounding nature and historical buildings. Be sure to bring plenty of water and to arrive early, since parking (follow the signs) is limited. Certain stretches are on metal pathways with steep drops, so those with limited mobility or a fear of heights should skip this one. The trail starts at Plaza de Rafael Ayerbe beside the ayuntamiento (town hall). No bikes or pets allowed. ⊠ *Pl. Rafael Ayerbe, Alquézar* ☎ *682/932809* ⊕ *www.pasarelasdealquezar.com* ⊠ *€4.*

Restaurants

Casa Pardina

$$$$ | SPANISH | Romantic dining at a reasonable price is the main draw at this restaurant with two fixed-price menus offering dozens of dishes to choose from. The cuisine is distinctly Aragonese with a few modern twists (think local venison stewed with dates, plums, and honey), and the wine hails from nearby Somontano. **Known for:** locally sourced ingredients and local olive oil; outdoor dining with sweeping views; set menu only. $ *Average main: €29* ⊠ *Calle Medio, Alquézar* ☎ *974/318425* ⊕ *www. casapardina.com* ⊘ *Closed Tues. No lunch weekdays Oct.–Easter.*

Hotels

Hotel Santa María de Alquézar

$$ | B&B/INN | FAMILY | Just outside the old town walls, this hotel has the best views around—overlooking the Río Vero canyon and the Colegiata de Santa María. **Pros:** phenomenal views; bright rooms; relaxed ambience. **Cons:** some street noise; not inside the old town; parking is tricky in high season. $ *Rooms from: €95* ⊠ *Calle Arrabal, Alquézar* ☎ *974/318436* ⊕ *www. hotel-santamaria.com* ⊘ *Closed Jan.–mid-Feb. Call ahead for other seasonal closures* ⇆ *21 rooms* ⦿| *Free Breakfast.*

Activities

The Sierra de Guara is one of Europe's best places for canyoning (descending mountain gorges, usually in or near streams and other water sources).

Avalancha

ADVENTURE TOURS | **FAMILY** | There are several agencies in Alquézar that specialize in guided private or group trips for all levels and ages. Avalancha is our top pick for canyoning and other adventure activities and provides equipment, including wet suits and helmets. ✉ *Paseo San Hipolito, Alquézar* ☎ *974/318299* 🌐 *www.avalancha.org.*

Aínsa

66 km (41 miles) southwest of Benasque, 113 km (70 miles) northeast of Huesca, 214 km (133 miles) northeast of Zaragoza.

Aínsa's uninspiring new town belies one of Aragón's most impressive walled medieval quarters, where houses are jammed together along narrow cobbled streets. A stroll here affords sweeping views of the surrounding mountains and Parque Nacional de Odesa.

GETTING HERE AND AROUND

Head north out of Huesca on the E7, then take the N260 for a total of 98 km (61 miles) before hopping on the A2205 for 15 km (9 miles). Aínsa can only be explored on foot once you're through the old city walls.

VISITOR INFORMATION

CONTACTS Aínsa Tourist Office. ✉ *Av. Ordesa 5, Aínsa* ☎ *974/500767* 🌐 *www.villadeainsa.com.*

Sights

Castillo de Aínsa

CASTLE/PALACE | The citadel and castle, originally built by the Moors in the 11th century, was conquered by the Christians and reconstructed in the 16th century. ✉ *Pl. Mayor 1, Aínsa* ☎ *974/318940* 🌐 *www.patrimonioculturaldearagon.es/bienes-culturales/castillo-de-ainsa* 🎫 *€4.*

Iglesia de Santa María

CHURCH | This 12th-century Romanesque church, with its quadruple-vaulted door and 13th-century cloister, is in the corner of the attractive, porticoed Plaza Mayor. ✉ *Calle Santa Cruz, Aínsa* 🎫 *Free.*

Hotels

Hotel Casa de San Martín

$$$ | **HOTEL** | Situated on a remote and wonderfully scenic stretch of the Eje Pirenaico (Pyrenean Axis Highway), midway between medieval Aínsa and the Parque Nacional de Ordesa y Monte Perdido, is this tasteful mountaintop B&B with verdant valley views, stone-wall rooms, and standout down-home cuisine. The owner knows the surrounding trails through pine and oak forests like the back of his hand, and you can explore many of them without leaving the property, which spans over 200 acres. **Pros:** in a converted monastery; secluded eden in the mountains; noteworthy food and local wine. **Cons:** entry via 5-km (3-mile) gravel driveway; no pool; few nearby restaurants. [$] *Rooms from: €170* ✉ *Calle Única 1, Aínsa* ☎ *974/338349* 🌐 *https://casadesanmartin.com/* 🍴 *Free Breakfast* 🛏 *9 rooms.*

Hotel Los Arcos

$$ | **B&B/INN** | This intimate (there are only six bedrooms) hotel welcomes guests with exposed stone walls, comfortable furnishings, and warm tones throughout. **Pros:** central location on the main square; excellent service; comfortable furnishings. **Cons:** no elevator; noise from the square; no parking. [$] *Rooms from: €118* ✉ *Pl. Mayor 23, Aínsa* ☎ *974/500016* 🌐 *www.hotellosarcosainsa.com* 🛏 *6 rooms* 🍴 *Free Breakfast.*

Hotel Los Siete Reyes

$$ | **B&B/INN** | One of two boutique hotels in Aínsa's Plaza Mayor, Los Siete Reyes occupies a handsome restored mansion with ample stone-walled bedrooms overlooking the square. **Pros:** good views

Did You Know?

The Parque Nacional de Ordesa y Monte Perdido is sometimes called a junior version of the Grand Canyon. The region was designated a national park partly to protect the Pyrenean ibex, which nevertheless became extinct in 2000.

of the mountain or village; central location; charming and atmospheric. **Cons:** dark painted walls make rooms gloomy; noise from the square; patchy Wi-Fi. [$] *Rooms from: €120* ✉ *Pl. Mayor, Aínsa* ☎ *974/500681* 🌐 *www.lossietereyes.com* 🛏 *6 rooms* 🍴 *Free Breakfast.*

En Route: Broto

Broto is a typical Aragonese mountain town with a notable 16th-century Gothic church. Nearby villages, such as **Oto**, have stately manor houses with classic local features: baronial entryways, conical chimneys, and wooden galleries. **Torla** is Parque Nacional de Ordesa y Monte Perdido's main entry point, with regular buses that go up to the park entrance during summer; it is a popular base for hikers.

Parque Nacional de Ordesa y Monte Perdido

79 km (49 miles) west of Bielsa, 45 km (30 miles) west of Aínsa, 92 km (57 miles) north of Huesca.

This splendid but often overlooked park was founded by royal decree in 1918 to protect the natural integrity of the central Pyrenees. It expanded from 4,940 to 56,810 acres when provincial and national authorities added the Monte Perdido massif, the head of the Pineta Valley, and the Escuain and Añisclo Canyons.

VISITOR INFORMATION

CONTACTS Centro de Visitantes de Torla. ✉ *Av. Ordesa, Torla* ☎ *974/486472* 🌐 *www.ordesa.net.*

Sights

★ Ordesa and Monte Perdido National Park

NATIONAL PARK | Welcome to the wildest, most unspoiled corner of the Pyrenees. The three main valleys of this national park—Ordesa, Pineta, and Añisclo—are carved out by the Ara River and its tributaries, the Arazas. They culminate in the majestic massif of Monte Perdido, which stands at 11,000 feet on the Franco-Spanish border; it's the highest of the park's three main mountains. The remote yet worthwhile valley of Las Gargantas de Escuaín is famous for its dolmen and soaring rock walls. Throughout the park, you'll find lakes; waterfalls; high mountain meadows; and forests of pine, fir, larch, beech, and poplar. Protected wildlife includes trout, boar, chamois, lammergeier, and the *sarrio*mountain goat (*Rupicapra pyrenaica*). Well-marked mountain trails lead to waterfalls, caves, and spectacular observation points. The standard tour, a full-day's hike (eight hours), runs from the parking area in the Pradera de Ordesa, 8 km (5 miles) northeast of Torla, up the Arazas River, past the Gradas de Soaso (Soaso Risers, a natural stairway of waterfalls) to the Cola de Caballo (Horse's Tail), a fan of falling water at the head of the Cirque de Cotatuero, a dramatic natural amphitheater. There is one refuge, Refugio Góriz, north of the Cola de Caballo. A return walk on the south side of the valley, past the Cabaña de los Cazadores (Hunters' Hut), offers a breathtaking view followed by a two-hour descent back to the parking area. ✉ *Torla* ☎ *974/486472* 🌐 *www.ordesa.net* 🎟 *Free.*

Restaurants

A'Borda Samper

$ | **SPANISH** | At this wood-beamed barroom, you can dine on comfort-food tapas and mains like battered zucchini, meatballs bobbing in tomato sauce, fried eggs with sausage, and juicy steaks.

Known for: genial service; hearty country cooking; house-made desserts. $ *Average main: €11* ✉ *Calle Travecinal, Torla* ☎ *619/321757.*

Hotels

Villa de Torla

$$ | **B&B/INN** | **FAMILY** | This classic mountain refuge, with sundecks, flower-festooned terraces, and a private dining room, rents rooms of various shapes and sizes. **Pros:** restaurant on-site; in a postcard-perfect Pyrenean village; graet amenities. **Cons:** not all rooms have a private bathroom; street noise in summer; some rooms on the small side. $ *Rooms from: €120* ✉ *Pl. Aragón 1, Torla* ☎ *974/486156* ⊕ *www.hotelvilladetorla. com* ⤸ *38 rooms* ⑪ *Free Breakfast.*

Jaca

24 km (15 miles) southwest of Biescas, 164 km (102 miles) north of Zaragoza.

Jaca, the most important municipal center in Alto Aragón, is anything but sleepy with plenty of standing-room tapas bars and cafés. Founded in 1035 as the kingdom of Jacetania, it was an important stronghold during the so-called Reconquest of the Iberian Peninsula and was never overtaken by the Moors. On the first Friday of May, the town still commemorates the decisive battle in which the appearance of a battalion of women, their hair and jewelry flashing in the sun, intimidated the Moorish cavalry into beating a headlong retreat. Avoid the industrial-looking outskirts and head straight to the atmospheric old town, where there's a splendid 11th-century cathedral and fortress and bustling restaurants and bars.

Sights

Canfranc International Railway Station

TRAIN/TRAIN STATION | **FAMILY** | In July and August a guided train tour departs from the Jaca RENFE station, heading to the valley and Canfranc's magnificent Belle Époque train station, abandoned since 1970 and slowly falling to pieces. Surely the largest and most ornate building in the Pyrenees, the station has a bewitching history and was used as a location in the 1965 film *Doctor Zhivago.* Ask at the tourist office for schedules. In addition, a nontourist train runs year-round between Jaca and Canfranc. Reservations are essential; call ahead or reserve your spot online. ✉ *Estación Internacional de Canfranc, Jaca* ☎ *974/373141* ⊕ *www. canfranc.es/venta-online.php* ✎ *From €4.*

Ciudadela de Jaca

MILITARY SIGHT | The massive pentagonal Ciudadela is an impressive example of 17th-century military architecture. It has a display of more than 35,000 military miniatures, arranged to represent different periods of history. Check the website to confirm hours, which vary by month. ✉ *Av. del Primer Viernes de Mayo, Jaca* ☎ *974/357157* ⊕ *www.ciudadeladejaca. es* ✎ *From €8.*

Jaca Cathedral

CHURCH | An important stop on the pilgrimage to Santiago de Compostela, Jaca's 11th-century Romanesque Catedral de San Pedro has lovely carved capitals and was the first French-Romanesque cathedral in Spain, paving the way for later Spanish Romanesque architecture. Inside the cathedral and near the cloisters, the Museo Diocesano has excellent Romanesque and Gothic frescoes and artifacts. ✉ *Pl. de San Pedro 1, Jaca* ✎ *Cathedral free, museum €6.*

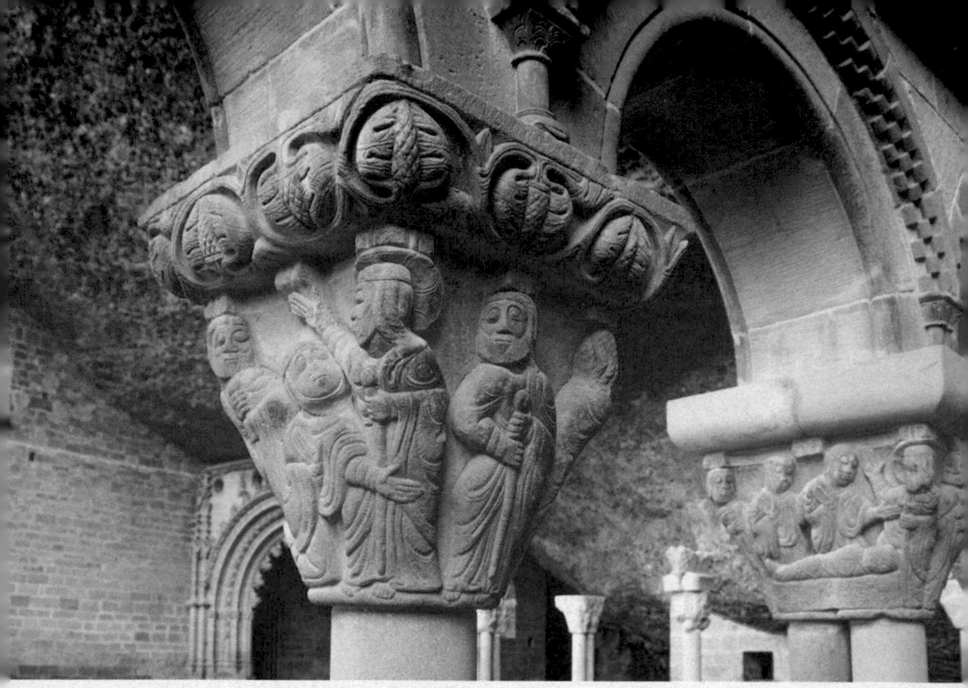

The Monasterio de San Juan de la Peña near Jaca

🍴 Restaurants

La Tasca de Ana

$ | **TAPAS** | One of the best tapas bars in town, La Tasca de Ana is boisterous and filled with locals. With only a handful of tables and standing room by the bar, it's not the setting for a quiet romantic dinner, but it's a fine place to kick-start the evening with local wine and tapas like *rodolfitos* (battered langoustines) and stuffed piquillo peppers. **Known for:** delectable langoustines; lively atmosphere; quick and efficient service. [$] *Average main: €9* ✉ *Calle Ramiro I 3, Jaca* ☎ *974/363621* 🌐 *www.latascadeana.com* ⏲ *Closed Mon., 2 wks in May, and 2 wks in Sept. No lunch weekdays.*

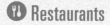

🛏 Hotels

Gran Hotel

$ | **HOTEL** | This rambling hotel—Jaca's old grande dame—has seen better days, but its central location makes it a practical base. **Pros:** within walking distance of sights; good value; quiet location. **Cons:** no frills; needs renovation; charmless for the Pyrenees. [$] *Rooms from: €80* ✉ *Paseo de la Constitución 1, Jaca* ☎ *974/360900* 🌐 *www.granhoteljaca.com* 🔑 *165 rooms* 🍽 *Free Breakfast.*

★ **Hotel Barosse**

$$$ | **B&B/INN** | In a village on the outskirts of Jaca, this intimate adults-only bed-and-breakfast is worth sacrificing city-center conveniences. **Pros:** friendly service; peaceful rural setting; boutique-style accommodations. **Cons:** not in the center of Jaca; a car is necessary; not suited to families with kids. [$] *Rooms from: €138* ✉ *Calle de Estirás 4, Jaca* ☎ *974/360582, 638/845992* 🌐 *www.barosse.com* ⏲ *Closed Nov.* 🔑 *5 rooms* 🍽 *Free Breakfast.*

Hotel Rural El Mirador de los Pirineos

$$$ | **B&B/INN** | On the way to the Monasterio de San Juan de la Peña, 10 km (6 miles) from Jaca, this tranquil, homey hotel has a spa and pool, making it a pleasant retreat. **Pros:** perfect for R&R; a peaceful and charming alternative to urban Jaca; idyllic setting. **Cons:** staff not

always on hand; only two restaurants nearby; not luxurious. $ *Rooms from: €147* ✉ *Calle Ordana 8, Santa Cruz de la Serós* ☎ *974/355593, 609/470 231 reservations* ⊕ *www.elmiradordelospiri-neos.com* ☾ *Closed Apr. and May (dates depend on Easter, so call ahead to check) and 2 wks in Nov.* ⇨ *7 rooms* ⦿ *Free Breakfast*

Nightlife

Jaca's music bars are concentrated in the Casco Antiguo, on Calle Ramiro I, and along Calle Gil Bergés and Calle Bellido. In the porticoed Plaza de la Catedral, there are a number of bars with terraces, in the shade of the cathedral, to be enjoyed day or evening.

Bar Casa Fau

CAFÉS | This busy bar with front-row seats to the cathedral serves coffee and soft drinks, a good selection of wine by the glass, and beer on tap—all of which can be accompanied by tapas and light snacks. ✉ *Pl. de la Catedral 3, Jaca* ☎ *974/361594.*

🛍 Shopping

Bodegas Langa

WINE/SPIRITS | This charming local bar-meets- *bodega* (winery) stocks regional wines and artisanal products. Be sure to allow time for the tapas menu while you sip and shop. ✉ *Pl. San Pedro 5, Jaca* ☎ *974/360494* ⊕ *www.bodegaslanga.es.*

Activities

Ski areas

SKIING & SNOWBOARDING | On the road to Somport and the French border, the ski areas of Candanchú and Astún are 32 km (20 miles) north of Jaca. ✉ *Jaca* ⊕ *www.astun.com.*

Monasterio de San Juan de la Peña

23 km (14 miles) southwest of Jaca, 185 km (115 miles) north of Zaragoza, 90 km (56 miles) east of Pamplona.

South of the Aragonese valleys of Hecho and Ansó is the Monastery of San Juan de la Peña, a site connected to the legend of the Holy Grail and one of the centers of Christian resistance during the 700-year Islamic reign of the Iberian Peninsula.

GETTING HERE AND AROUND
From Jaca, drive 11 km (7 miles) west on the N240 toward Pamplona to a left turn clearly signposted for San Juan de la Peña. From there it's another 11 km (7 miles) on the A1603 to the monastery.

◉ Sights

★ Monasterio de San Juan de la Peña

CHURCH | The origins of this mysterious cliffside sanctuary can be traced to the 9th century, when a hermit monk named Juan settled here on the *peña* (cliff). A monastery was founded on the spot in 920, and in 1071, Sancho Ramírez, son of King Ramiro I, made use of the structure, which was built into the mountain's rock wall, to found this Benedictine monastery. The cloister, tucked under the cliff, dates to the 12th century and contains intricately carved capitals depicting biblical scenes. The church of the New Monastery contains the Kingdom of Aragon Interpretation Centre, where audio guides in English are available. ✉ *Jaca* ✛ *Off N240 on A1603* ☎ *974/355119* ⊕ *www.monasteriosanjuan.com* 🎟 *From €9.*

Hecho and Ansó Valleys

The Hecho Valley is 49 km (30 miles) northwest of Jaca. The Ansó Valley is 25 km (15 miles) west of Hecho, 118 km (73 miles) east of Pamplona.

The Ansó Valley is Aragón's western limit. Rich in fauna (mountain goats, wild boar, and even a bear or two), it follows the Veral River up to Zuriza. Towering over the head of the valley is Navarra's highest point, the 7,989-foot **Mesa de los Tres Reyes** (Plateau of the Three Kings), named not for the Magi but for the kings of Aragón, Navarra, and Castile, whose 11th-century kingdoms bordered one another here, allowing them to meet without leaving their respective realms. The **Selva de Oza** (Oza Forest), at the head of the Hecho Valley, is above the **Boca del Infierno** (Mouth of Hell), a tight draw that road and river barely squeeze through.

It's worth stopping at the pretty villages of **Ansó** and **Hecho,** where a preserved collection of stone houses are tightly bunched together along narrow cobbled streets overlooking the valley. In Ansó, on the last Sunday in August, residents don traditional medieval costumes and perform ancestral dances.

GETTING HERE AND AROUND

You can reach the Hecho Valley from Jaca by heading west on the N240 and then north on the A176.

VISITOR INFORMATION

CONTACTS Hecho Tourist Office. ✉ *Paseo Ctra. de Oza 38, Hecho* ☎ *974/375505* 🌐 *www.valledehecho.es.*

Sights

Monasterio de San Pedro de Siresa

CHURCH | The area's most important monument, the 9th-century retreat Monasterio de San Pedro de Siresa, presides over the village of Siresa, 2 km (1 mile) north of Hecho. Only the 11th-century church remains, but it is a marvelous example of Romanesque architecture. Cheso, a medieval Aragonese dialect descended from the Latin spoken by the Siresa monks, is thought to be the closest to Latin of all Romance languages and dialects. It has been kept alive in the Hecho Valley, especially in the works of local poet Veremundo Méndez Coarasa. ✉ *Calle San Pedro, Siresa* 🎫 *€3* 🕓 *Closed Mon.*

En Route

From Ansó, head west to Roncal on the narrow and winding but panoramic 17-km (11-mile) road through the Sierra de San Miguel. To enjoy this route fully, count on taking a good 45 minutes to reach the Esca River and the Roncal Valley.

Hotels

Casa Blasquico

$ | **B&B/INN** | This pleasantly kitsch inn with bright painted walls is a typical mountain chalet with flowered balconies and a plethora of memorabilia inside. **Pros:** friendly service; two cute dormered rooms; fine mountain cuisine. **Cons:** public rooms cluttered; rooms lack space; no elevator. [$] *Rooms from: €60* ✉ *Pl. la Fuente 1, Hecho* ☎ *974/375007, 657/892128* 🌐 *www.casablasquico.es* 🕓 *Closed weekdays Nov.–Mar.* 🛏 *6 rooms* 🍴 *Free Breakfast.*

Hotel de Montaña Usón

$ | **B&B/INN** | For an eco-friendly (solar-powered) base for exploring the upper Hecho Valley or the Oza Forest, look no further than this adorable Pyrenean inn situated 7 km (4 miles) north of Hecho. **Pros:** friendly service; great value for the area; stunning views into the mountains. **Cons:** no elevator; remote setting; reception closes at 10 pm. [$] *Rooms from: €63* ✉ *Ctra. Selva de Oza*

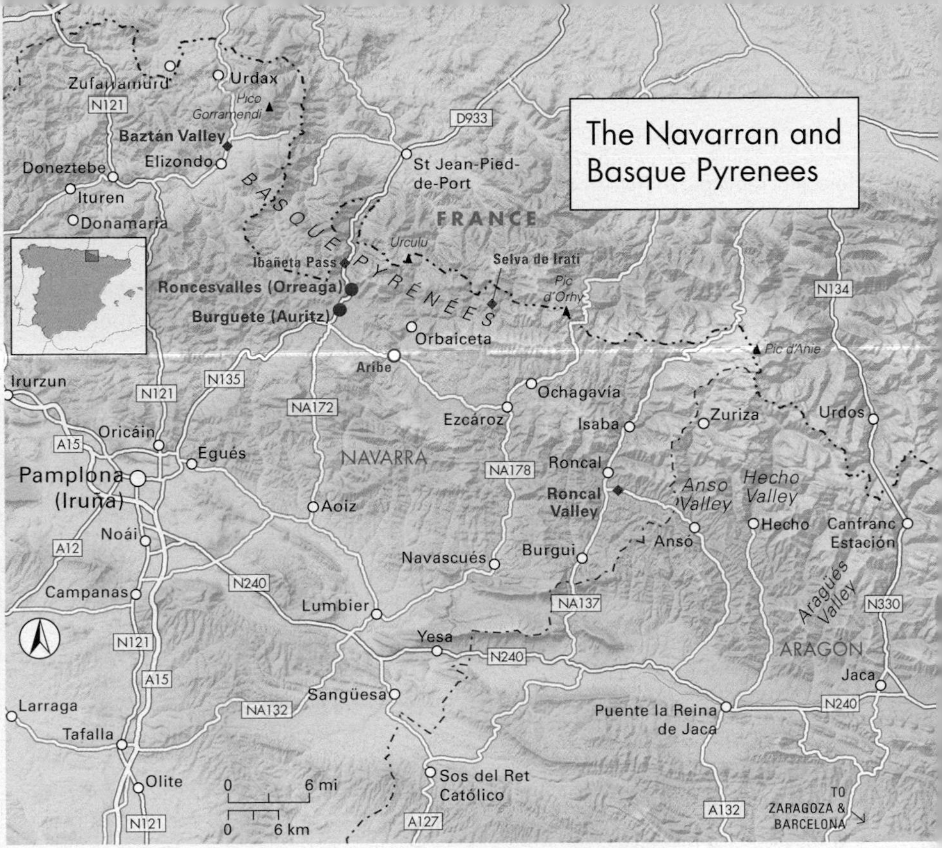

The Navarran and Basque Pyrenees
Zufarramurdi
Urdax
Pico Gorramendi
N121
D933
Baztán Valley
Elizondo
Doneztebe
Ituren
Donamaria
BASQUE PYRENEES
St Jean-Pied-de-Port
FRANCE
Urculu
Ibañeta Pass
Selva de Irati
Roncesvalles (Orreaga)
Burguete (Auritz)
Pic d'Orhy
N134
Orbaiceta
Pic d'Anie
Aribe
Irurzun
N135
N121
NA172
Ochagavía
Ezcároz
Isaba
Zuriza
Urdos
Oricáin
A15
Egués
NAVARRA
NA178
Roncal
Pamplona (Iruña)
Roncal Valley
Anso Valley
Hecho Valley
Aoiz
Noái
Hecho
Canfranc Estación
A12
Ansó
Navascués
Burgui
Campanas
N240
Aragüés Valley
Lumbier
NA137
N330
N121
Yesa
N240
ARAGON
A15
Jaca
Sangüesa
Larraga
NA132
Puente la Reina de Jaca
N240
Tafalla
Olite
0 6 mi
0 6 km
Sos del Ret Católico
N121
A127
A132
TO ZARAGOZA & BARCELONA

(HU2131), Km 7, Usón ⊕ From Hecho follow signs for Siresa. From there it's about 5 km (3 miles) north ☎ 608/729369 🌐 www.hoteluson.com ⏰ Closed Nov.–Mar. 🛏 8 rooms, 4 apartments 🍴 No Meals.

Posada Magoria

$ | **B&B/INN** | All guest rooms in this carefully restored Art Nouveau house, now an eco-friendly B&B, have splendid views and are furnished with knickknacks from the 1920s and have pristine bedding and modern comforts. **Pros:** healthy retreat; homey, relaxed atmosphere; cozy ambience in beautiful surroundings. **Cons:** scant restaurants in the area; thin walls—choose a room on a higher floor; small rooms and bathrooms. [$] *Rooms from: €60* ✉ *Calle Milagro 32A, Ansó* ☎ *974/370049* 🌐 *www.posadamagoria.com* 🛏 *7 rooms* 🍴 *Free Breakfast.*

Roncal Valley

17 km (11 miles) west of Ansó Valley, 72 km (45 miles) west of Jaca, 86 km (53 miles) northeast of Pamplona.

The Roncal Valley, the eastern edge of the Basque Pyrenees, is known across Spain for its eponymous sheep's-milk cheese. Roncal is also the birthplace of Julián Gayarre (1844–90), the leading tenor of his time. The 34-km (21-mile) drive through the towns of **Burgui** and **Roncal** to **Isaba** winds through green hillsides past *caseríos,* traditional Basque farmhouses covered by long, sloping roofs that were designed to house animals on the ground floor and the family up above to take advantage of the body heat of the livestock. Burgui's red-tile roofs backed by rolling pastures contrast with the vertical rock and steep slate roofs of the

Aragonese and Catalan Pyrenees. Isaba's wide-arch bridge across the Esca is a graceful reminder of Roman aesthetics and engineering.

GETTING HERE AND AROUND

To get to the valley from Jaca, take the N240 west along the Aragón River; a right turn north on the A137 follows the Esca River from the head of the Yesa Reservoir up the Roncal Valley.

VISITOR INFORMATION

CONTACTS Roncal Tourist Office. ⊠ *Ctra. del Roncal, Roncal* ☎ *948/475256* ⊕ *www.vallederoncal.es.*

◉ Sights

Aribe

TOWN | Two kilometers (1 mile) south of Ochagavía, at Escároz, a small secondary roadway winds 22 km (14 miles) over the Abaurrea heights to Aribe, known for its triple-arch medieval bridge, ancient *hórreo* (granary), Zamariain viewpoint, and Zubi Esekia suspension bridge.

El Tributo de las Tres Vacas (*The Tribute of the Three Cows*)

FAIRGROUND | Try to be in the Roncal Valley for this event, celebrated every July 13 with few exceptions since 1375. The mayors of the valley's villages, dressed in traditional gowns, gather near the summit of San Martín to receive the symbolic payment of three cows from their French counterparts, in memory of the settlement of ancient border disputes. Feasting and celebrating follow. ⊠ *Roncal.*

Ochagavía (Otsagabia)

TOWN | The road west (NA140) to Ochagavía (Otsagabia in Basque) through the Portillo de Lazar (Lazar Pass) has views of the Anie and Orhi peaks, which tower over the French border. The village itself, with original cobblestone streets and riverside promenade, makes for a pleasant spot to stretch the legs. ⊠ *Roncal.*

Selva de Irati (*Irati Forest*)

FOREST | A 15-km (9-mile) detour north through the town of Orbaizeta up to the headwaters of the Irati River, at the Irabia Reservoir, gets you a good look at the Selva de Irati, one of Europe's major beech forests and the source of much of the lumber for the Spanish Armada. ⊠ *Roncal.*

Roncesvalles (Orreaga)

64 km (40 miles) northwest of Isaba in the Roncal Valley, 48 km (30 miles) north of Pamplona.

Roncesvalles (Orreaga in Basque) is a small village and the site of the Battle of Roncesvalles (or Battle of Roncevaux Pass), when Charlemagne's army, under the command of Roland, was attacked and overcome by Basque soldiers in AD 778. The battle became the inspiration for one of France's most revered literary poems, *Le Chanson de Roland* (*The Song of Roland*), written in the 11th century.

The village's strategic position, 23 km (14 miles) from the original starting line of Saint-Jean-Pied-de-Port in France, has made it the first stop-off point for pilgrims on the Camino de Santiago since the 10th century. Its Gothic Colegiata (built in the style of the Notre-Dame Cathedral in Paris), hospital, and 12th-century chapel have provided shelter since then. Mountains in this area rarely reach higher than 4,900 feet. This part of the Camino offers some of the trail's best scenery.

GETTING HERE AND AROUND

The N135 northbound out of Pamplona goes straight to Roncesvalles.

VISITOR INFORMATION

CONTACTS Orreaga-Roncesvalles Tourist Office. ⊠ *Antiguo Molino, Calle de Nuestra Señora de Roncesvalles, Orreaga* ☎ *948/760301* ⊕ *www.roncesvalles. es.*

Sights

Ibañeta Pass

SCENIC DRIVE | This 3,468-foot pass, above Roncesvalles, is a gorgeous route into France. A menhir (monolith) marks the traditional site of the legendary battle in *The Song of Roland*, during which Roland fell after calling for help on his ivory battle horn. The well-marked eight-hour walk to or from Saint-Jean-Pied-de-Port (which does *not* follow the road) is the first and one of the most beautiful and dramatic sections of the Santiago pilgrimage. ⊠ *Orreaga.*

Real Colegiata de Santa María de Roncesvalles

CHURCH | Built on the orders of King Sancho VII el Fuerte (the Strong), the Collegiate Church houses the king's tomb, which measures more than 7 feet long. ⊠ *Calle de Nuestra Señora de Roncesvalles, Orreaga* ☎ *948/760000* ⬚ *€5.*

Hotels

Casa de Beneficiados

$$ | **HOTEL** | Whether you're embarking on the pilgrimage or not, this hotel in a restored 18th-century building adjoining the Colegiata provides warm, low-lit, stone-walled common areas and modern, comfortable rooms. **Pros:** oozes pilgrim-trail ambience; historic building with lots of character; friendly service. **Cons:** simple food; apartments lack the charm of the common areas; take caution arriving by car in bad weather. Ⓢ *Rooms from: €90* ⊠ *Calle Nuestra Señora de Roncesvalles, Orreaga* ☎ *948/760105* ⊕ *www.hotelroncesvalles.com* ☾ *Closed mid-Nov.–mid-Mar.* ⇆ *16 rooms* ⦿⦿ *No Meals.*

Burguete (Auritz)

2 km (1 mile) south of Roncesvalles.

Burguete (Auritz in Basque) lies between two mountain streams forming the headwaters of the Urobi River and is surrounded by meadows and forests. The town was immortalized in Ernest Hemingway's *The Sun Also Rises* with an evocative description of trout fishing here in an ice-cold stream. Hemingway himself spent time here doing just that.

GETTING HERE AND AROUND
The N135 northbound out of Pamplona goes to Burguete in 44 km (27 miles). From Roncesvalles, it's 2 km (1 mile) south on the N135.

Hotels

Hotel Loizu

$$ | **B&B/INN** | **FAMILY** | An inn for pilgrims since the 18th century, the Loizu is now a country-style hotel that makes an excellent base for exploring the Selva de Irati. **Pros:** comfortable and ample rooms; family-run; friendly service. **Cons:** basic breakfast; bathrooms are a bit cramped; noise from other rooms. Ⓢ *Rooms from: €90* ⊠ *Calle San Nicolás 13, Auritz* ☎ *948/760008* ⊕ *www.loizu.com* ☾ *Closed mid-Dec.–Mar.* ⇆ *27 rooms* ⦿⦿ *Free Breakfast.*

Baztan Valley

62 km (38 miles) northwest of Roncesvalles, 80 km (50 miles) north of Pamplona.

Tucked between the Bidasoa River headwaters and the 3,545-foot peak of Gorramendi Mountain on the border with France lies the Baztan Valley. These rounded green hills are a scenic halfway stop-off point between the central

Pyrenees and the Atlantic. Roads here meander through picture-perfect villages of geranium-covered white stone houses with red-tile roofs grouped around a central *frontón* (handball court).

This once-isolated pocket of the Basque-Navarran Pyrenees is peppered with smugglers' trails and is the site of the Camino de Baztanas, the oldest stretch of the Camino de Santiago. You can follow the ancient footsteps of pilgrims starting from the historic village of **Urdax.** Nearby, close to the village of **Zugarramurdi,** you can visit a collection of limestone caves, otherwise knowns as Las Cuevas de las Brujas (Witches' Caves), which bore witness to so-called witches' covens and their pagan rituals before their eventual and brutal persecution in the 1600s. In the valley's main town, **Elizondo,** stately homes and ancestral mansions, built by nobles returning with their fortunes from the Americas, straddle the banks of the Baztan River.

Try to be in the village of Ituren in late September for its Carnival, the Day of the Joaldunak, which has been recognized as one of the oldest celebrations in Europe. Here you can see striking costumes hung with clanging cowbells as participants parade from farm to farm and house to house paying homage to their ancestors; some anthropologists argue that the rituals go back to pagan times. Check the exact dates of the event with the tourist office as each year's schedule depends on the phases of the moon.

VISITOR INFORMATION
CONTACTS Baztan Valley Tourist Office.
(*Centro de Turismo Rural de Bértiz*) ✉ *Pl. Erlategi 6, Elizondo* ☎ *608/012050* ⊕ *www.valledebaztan.com.*

 **Restaurants**

★ Donamaria'ko Benta
$$$$ | BASQUE | FAMILY | This family-run restaurant and B&B in a former 19th-century residence has a crackling fire in winter and a willow-shaded patio in summer. Prix fixe menus change seasonally and center on well-executed classics like *secreto de cerdo ibérico con crema de hongos* (Iberian pork steak with wild mushroom cream) and *txangurro a la Donostiarra* (baked crab). **Known for:** friendly service; riverside dining in summer; traditional Navarran recipes. ⓢ *Average main: €30* ✉ *Barrio de las Ventas 4, Donamaria* ☎ *948/450708* ⊕ *www.donamariako.com* ⊗ *Closed Mon. and Dec. 10–Jan. 5. No dinner Sun.*

Galarza
$$ | BASQUE | Stop here for Basque and Navarran comfort food served in an old stone house on the river, with a Navarran emphasis on vegetables. Try the *txuritabel* (roast lamb with a special stuffing of egg and vegetables), which is best in the spring (though available year-round), or *txuleta de ternera* (grass-fed veal raised in the valley), good any time of year. *Brocheta de rape y langostinos* (monkfish and king prawns served on skewers) is another favorite here; the desserts feature delicious homemade *cuajada* (tangy sheep milk custard). **Known for:** wood-beam dining room; old-school Basque cooking; house-made desserts. ⓢ *Average main: €15* ✉ *Calle Santiago 1, Elizondo* ☎ *948/580101* ⊗ *Closed Tues., 2 wks in Feb., last wk of Sept., and 1st wk of Oct. No dinner Mon.–Thurs. in Nov.–June.*

BARCELONA

Updated by
Isabelle Kliger

◉ Sights	🍴 Restaurants	🛏 Hotels	🛍 Shopping	🍸 Nightlife
★★★★★	★★★★★	★★★★★	★★★★★	★★★★★

WELCOME TO BARCELONA

TOP REASONS TO GO

★ **Explore La Boqueria:** Barcelona's produce market may be the most exciting cornucopia in the world.

★ **Visit Santa Maria del Mar:** The early Mediterranean Gothic elegance, rhythmic columns, and unbroken spaces make this church peerless.

★ **See La Sagrada Família:** Gaudí's unfinished masterpiece is the city's most iconic treasure.

★ **Experience El Palau de la Música Catalana:** This Art Nouveau tour de force is alive with music.

★ **Shop for fashion and design:** How could a city famous for its architecture not offer an abundance of innovative clothing, furniture, and design shops as well?

★ **Watch *castellers* and *sardanas*:** Human castles and Catalonia's national dance are two fun ways to appreciate Catalan culture.

1 La Rambla. This busy thoroughfare passes the Boqueria market and other key sights.

2 Barri Gòtic. The Gothic Quarter surrounds Catedral de al Seu and the medieval Jewish quarter.

3 El Raval. A funky multicultural sprawl.

4 Sant Pere and La Ribera. The cobblestone streets of La Ribera are filled with interesting shops and restaurants and the Picasso Museum.

5 La Ciutadella and Barceloneta. Waterfront neighborhoods with great seafood restaurants.

6 The Eixample. This post-1860 grid of city blocks is home to the Sagrada Familia and other Gaudí buildings.

7 Gràcia. A once outlying village is now a trendy neighborhood that includes Gaudí's Park Güell.

8 Upper Barcelona. Old-school Sarrià has gourmet shops and fine restaurants; Pedralbes is upscale and residential.

9 Montjuïc and Poble Sec. Montjuïc is a sprawling neighborhood of parks and museums; Poble Sec is known for its multiethnic vibe and up-and-coming food scene.

Pl. de Francesc Macià
Travessera de Gràcia
Avda. Diagonal
TO TIBIDABO
Park Güell
7
GRÀCIA
Sant Antoni Maria Claret
C. de Verdi
C. de Indústria
C. Menéndez Pelayo
C. Gran de Gràcia
Paris
C. del Comte d'Urgell
Plaça de Joan Carles I
C. del Rosselló
C. de Provença
Avda. Diagonal
C. de Mallorca
Passeig de S. Joan
C. de Corsega
C. de Roger de Flor
C. de Bailèn
C. de Nàpoles
C. de Sicília
C. de Sardenya
C. de Marina
6 EIXAMPLE
C. de València
La Sagrada Família
C. de València
C. d'Aragó
C. d'Aragó
Consell de Cent
C. de la Diputació
C. de la Diputació
C. de Vilamós
C. del Comte Borrell
C. de Villarroel
C. de Casanova
C. de Muntaner
C. d'Aribau
C. de Balmes
Rambla de Catalunya
Passeig de Gràcia
C. de Pau Claris
C. de Roger Lluria
C. del Bruc
C. de Girona
C. de Bailèn
Plaça Tetuán
Corts Catalanes
Plaça Universitat
Gran Via de les
Corts Catalanes
C. de Sepúlveda
Ronda S. Pere
C. de Casp
C. de Floridablanca
Plaça de Catalunya
Rda. de Sant Antoni
Pl. Urquinaona
C. d'Ausias Marc
C. de Ribes
MACBA
SANT PERE
Arc del Triomf
C. de Tamarit
Joaquim Costa
Fontanella
3
El Palau de la Música Catalana
S. Pere Més Alt
C. de Manso
BARRI GÒTIC
RAVAL
Hospital de la Santa Creu
C. del Carme
2
S. Pere Més Baix
4
C. dels Almogàvers
La Rambla
Jonqueres
Passeig de Lluís Companys
Avda. de la Meridiana
P. de Carles I
C. de Sant Pau
Carretes
C. de Hospital
Avda. Catedral
1
LA RAMBLA
La Boqueria Market
Santa Maria del Mar
LA RIBERA
Passeig Pujades
Pg. Picasso
Parc de la Ciutadella
C. de Sant Pau
C. la Unió
C. Ferran
Pl. St. Jaume
Plaça Reial
C. Princesa
Passeig del Born
C. del Comerç
C. de Nou de la Rambla
Pg. de Montjuïc
Plaça Portal de la Pau
Pg. de Colom
C. Ample
Pl. d'Antoni López
Via Laietana
C. Ciutat
CIUTADELLA
C. de Wellington
Vila Olímpica
Passeig de Carles I
Moll de Sant Bertrán
Rambla de Mar
Moll d'Espanya
Passeig Joan de Borbó
Avda. d'Icària
Estació de França
5
Avda. d'Icària
PORT OLÍMPIC
BARCELONETA

EATING AND DRINKING WELL IN BARCELONA

A stew of broad beans and black and white botifarra sausage.

Barcelona cuisine draws from Catalonia's rustic country cooking and uses ingredients from the Mediterranean, the Pyrenees, and inland farmlands. Cosmopolitan influences and experimental contemporary innovation have combined to make Barcelona, historically linked to France and Italy, an important food destination.

The Mediterranean diet of seafood, vegetables, olive oil, and red wine comes naturally to Barcelona. Fish of all kinds, shrimp, shellfish, and rice dishes combining them are common, as are salads of seafood and Mediterranean vegetables. Vegetable and legume combinations are standard. Seafood and upland combinations, the classic *mar i muntanya* (surf and turf) recipes, join rabbit and prawns or cuttlefish and meatballs, while salty and sweet tastes—a Moorish legacy—are found in recipes such as duck with pears or goose with figs.

CAVA

Order champagne in Barcelona and you'll get anything from French bubbly to dirty looks. Ask, instead, for *cava*, sparkling wine from the Penedès region just southwest of the city. The first cava was produced in 1872 after the phylloxera plague wiped out most of Europe's vineyards. Cava (from the "cave" or wine cellar where it ferments) has a drier, earthier taste than champagne, and slightly larger bubbles.

SALADS

Esqueixada is a cold salad consisting of strips of raw, shredded, salt-cured cod marinated in oil and vinegar with onions, tomatoes, olives, and red and green bell peppers. Chunks of dried tuna can also be included, as well as chickpeas, roasted onions, and potatoes, too. *Escalibada* is another classic Catalan salad of red and green bell peppers and eggplant that have been roasted over coals, cut into strips, and served with onions, garlic, and olive oil.

Esqueixada, or raw codfish salad

LEGUMES

Botifarra amb mongetes (sausage with white beans) is the classic Catalan sausage made of pork and seasoned with salt and pepper, grilled and served with stewed white beans and *allioli* (an olive oil and garlic emulsion); botifarra can also be made with truffles, apples, eggs, wild mushrooms, and even chocolate. *Mongetes de Sant Pau amb calamarsets* (tiny white beans from Santa Pau with baby squid) is a favorite *mar i muntanya*.

VEGETABLES

Espinaques a la catalana (spinach with pine nuts, raisins, and garlic) owes a debt to the Moorish sweet-salt counterpoint and to the rich vegetable-growing littoral along the Mediterranean coast north and south of Barcelona. Bits of

A dessert of mel i mató (honey with fresh cheese)

bacon, fatback, or *jamón ibérico* may be added; some recipes use fine almond flakes as well. *Albergínies* (eggplant or aubergine) are a favorite throughout Catalonia, whether roasted, stuffed, or stewed, while *carxofes* (artichokes) fried to a crisp or stewed with rabbit is another staple.

FISH

Llobarro a la sal (sea bass cooked in salt) is baked in a shell of rock salt that hardens and requires a tap from a hammer or heavy knife to break and serve. The salt shell keeps the juices inside the fish and the flesh flakes off in firm chunks, while the skin of the fish prevents excessive saltiness from permeating the meat. *Suquet* is a favorite fish stew, with scorpion fish, monkfish, sea bass, or any combination thereof, cooked with potatoes, onions, and tomatoes.

DESSERTS

Crema catalana (Catalan cream) is the most popular dessert in Catalonia, a version of the French crème brûlée, custard dusted with cinnamon and confectioner's sugar and burned with a blowtorch (traditionally, a branding iron was used) before serving. The less sweet and palate-cleansing *mel i mató* (honey and fresh cheese) runs a close second in popularity.

The infinite variety and throb of street life, the nooks and crannies of the medieval Barri Gòtic, the ceramic tile and stained glass of Moderniste facades, the art and music, the food (ah, the food!)— one way or another, Barcelona will find a way to get your full attention.

The Catalonian capital greeted the new millennium with a cultural and industrial rebirth comparable only to the late-19th-century Renaixença (Renaissance) that filled the city with its flamboyant Moderniste (Art Nouveau) buildings. An exuberant sense of style—from hip new fashions to cutting-edge interior design, to the extravagant visions of star-status postmodern architects—gives Barcelona a vibe like no other place in the world. Barcelona is Spain's most visited city, and it's no wonder: it's a 2,000-year-old master of the art of perpetual novelty.

Barcelona's present boom began on October 17, 1987, when Juan Antonio Samaranch, president of the International Olympic Committee, announced that his native city had been chosen to host the 1992 Olympics. This single masterstroke allowed Spain's so-called second city to throw off the shadow of Madrid and its 40-year "internal exile" under Franco, and resume its rightful place as one of Europe's most dynamic destinations. The Catalan administration lavished millions in subsidies from the Spanish government for the Olympics, then used the Games as a platform to broadcast the news about Catalonia's cultural and national identity from one end of the planet to the other. More Mediterranean than Spanish, historically closer and more akin to Marseille or Milan than to Madrid, Barcelona has always been ambitious, decidedly modern (even in the 2nd century), and quick to accept the latest innovations. (The city's electric light system, public gas system, and telephone exchange were among the first in the world.) Its democratic form of government is rooted in the so-called Usatges Laws instituted by Ramon Berenguer I in the 11th century, which amounted to a constitution. This code of privileges represented one of the earliest known examples of democratic rule; Barcelona's Consell de Cent (Council of 100), constituted in 1274, was Europe's first parliament and one of the cradles of Western democracy. The center of an important seafaring commercial empire with colonies spread around the Mediterranean as far away as Athens, when Madrid was still a Moorish outpost on the arid Castilian steppe—it was Barcelona that absorbed new ideas and styles first. It borrowed navigation techniques from the Moors. It embraced the ideals of the French Revolution. It nurtured artists like Picasso and Miró, who blossomed in the city's air of freedom and individualism. Barcelona, in short, has always been ahead of the curve.

Planning

Planning Your Time

The best way to get around Barcelona is on foot; the occasional resort to subway, taxi, or tram will help you make the most of your visit. The comfortable FGC (Ferrocarrils de la Generalitat de Catalunya) trains that run up the center of the city from Plaça de Catalunya to Sarrià put you within 20- to 30-minute walks of nearly everything. The metro and the FGC close just short of midnight Monday–Thursday and Sunday, and at 2 am on Friday; on Saturday, the metro runs all night. The main attractions you need a taxi or the metro to reach are Montjuïc (Miró Foundation, MNAC, Mies van der Rohe Pavilion, CaixaFòrum, and Poble Espanyol), most easily accessed from Plaça Espanya; Park Güell above Plaça Lesseps; and the Auditori at Plaça de les Glòries. You can reach Gaudí's Sagrada Família by two metro lines (Nos. 2 and 5), but you may prefer the walk from the FGC's Provença stop, as it's an enjoyable half-hour jaunt that passes by three major Moderniste buildings: Palau Baró de Quadras, Casa Terrades (Casa de les Punxes), and Casa Macaia.

Sarrià and Pedralbes are easily explored on foot. The Torre Bellesguard and the Col.legi de les Teresianes are uphill treks; you might want to take a cab. It's a pleasant stroll from Sarrià down through the Jardins de la Vil.la Cecilia and Vil.la Amèlia to the Cátedra Gaudí (the pavilions of the Finca Güell, with Gaudí's amazing wrought-iron dragon gate); from there, you can get to the Futbol Club Barcelona through the Jardins del Palau Reial de Pedralbes and the university campus, or catch a two-minute taxi.

All of the Ciutat Vella (Barri Gòtic, Born-Ribera, La Rambla, El Raval, and Barceloneta) is best explored on foot. If you stay in Barceloneta for dinner, have the restaurant call you a taxi to get back to your hotel (usually not more than €15).

The city bus system is also a viable option—you get a better look at the city as you go—but the metro is faster and more comfortable. The tramway offers a quiet ride from Plaça Francesc Macià out Diagonal to the Futbol Club Barcelona, or from behind the Parc de la Ciutadella out to Glòries and the Fòrum at the east end of Diagonal.

When to Go

For optimal weather and marginally fewer tourists, the best times to visit Barcelona and the rest of Catalonia are April–June and mid-September–mid-December. Catalans and Basques vacation in August, causing epic traffic jams at both ends of the month.

Discounts and Deals

The very worthwhile **Barcelona Card** (www.barcelona-card.com) comes in three-, four-, and five-day versions (€46, €56, and €61). You get unlimited travel on public transport, free admission at numerous museums, and discounts on restaurants, leisure sights, and stores. Meanwhile, the two-day "Express" gives you free public transport and a discount on admissions. You can get the cards in Turisme de Barcelona offices in Plaça de Catalunya and Plaça Sant Jaume and at the Casa Batlló, the Aquarium, and the Poble Espanyol, among other sites; buy in advance online for a 10% discount.

Getting Here and Around

AIR
Most flights arriving in Spain from the United States and Canada pass through Madrid's Barajas (MAD), but the major gateway to Catalonia and other nearby regions is Spain's second-largest airport,

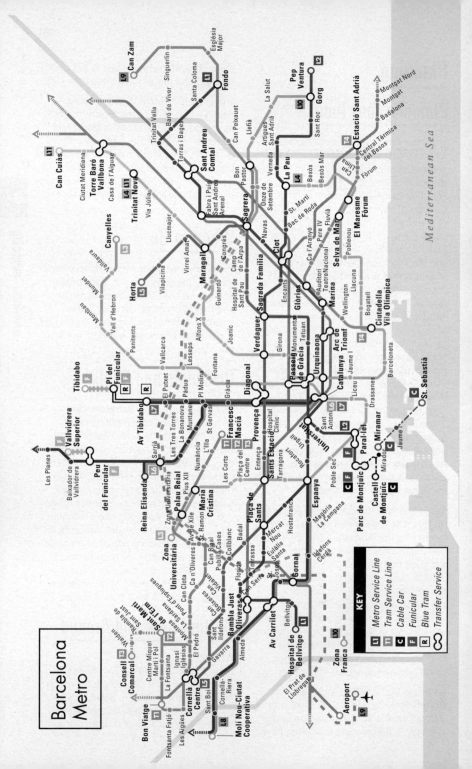

Barcelona Metro

Barcelona's spectacular glass, steel, and marble Prat del Llobregat (BCN). The T1 terminal is a sleek, ultramodern facility that uses solar panels for sustainable energy and offers a spa, a fitness center, restaurants and cafés, and VIP lounges. This airport is served by numerous international carriers, but Catalonia also has two other airports that handle passenger traffic, including charter flights. One is just south of Girona, 90 km (56 miles) north of Barcelona and convenient to the resort towns of the Costa Brava. Bus and train connections from Girona to Barcelona work well and cheaply, provided you have the time. The other Catalonia airport is at Reus, 110 km (68 miles) south of Barcelona, a gateway to Tarragona and the beaches of the Costa Daurada. Flights to and from the major cities in Europe and Spain also fly into and out of Bilbao's Loiu (BIL) airport.

AIRPORT INFORMATION Aeroport de Girona–Costa Brava. (GRO) ✉ 17185 Vilobi de Onyar, Girona ☎ 902/404704 general info on Spanish airports ⊕ www.aena. es.**Aeropuerto de Madrid (Adolfo Suárez Madrid-Barajas).** (MAD) ✉ Av. de la Hispanidad s/n, Madrid ☎ 902/404704 general info on Spanish airports ⊕ www. aeropuertomadrid-barajas.com/eng.**Aeropuerto de Reus.** (REU) ✉ Autovía Tarragona–Reus, Reus ☎ 902/404704 general info on Spanish airports ⊕ www.aena.es/ en/reus-airport/reus.html.**Aeropuerto Internacional de Bilbao.** (BIO) ✉ Loiu 48180, Bilbao ☎ 902/404704 general info on Spanish airports ⊕ www.aeropuertodebilbao.net/en.**Barcelona El Prat de Llobregat.** (BCN) ✉ C–32B s/n ☎ 902/404704 general info on Spanish airports ⊕ www.aena. es/en/barcelona-airport/index.html.

GROUND TRANSPORTATION

Check first to see if your hotel in Barcelona provides airport-shuttle service. If not, visitors typically get into town by train, bus, taxi, or rental car.

Cab fare from the airport into town is €30–€40, depending on traffic, the part of town you're heading to, and the amount of baggage you have (there's a €4.30 surcharge for airport pickups/drop-offs). If you're driving your own car, follow signs to the Centre Ciutat, from which you can enter the city along Gran Vía. For the port area, follow signs for the Ronda Litoral. The journey to the center of town can take 25–45 minutes, depending on traffic.

The Aerobus leaves Terminal 1 at the airport for Plaça de Catalunya every 10 minutes 5:35–7:20 am and 10:25 pm–1:05 am, and every 5 minutes 7:30 am–10:20 pm. From Plaça de Catalunya the bus leaves for the airport every 5 or 10 minutes between 5 am and 12:30 am. The fare is €5.90 one-way and €10.20 round-trip. Aerobuses for Terminals 1 and 2 pick up and drop off passengers at the same stops en route, so if you're outward bound make sure that you board the right one. The A1 Aerobus for Terminal 1 is two-tone light and dark blue; the A2 Aerobus for Terminal 2 is dark blue and yellow.

The train's only drawback is that it's a 10- to 15-minute walk from your gate through Terminal 2 over the bridge. From Terminal 1 a shuttle bus drops you at the train. Trains leave the airport every 30 minutes between 5:42 am and 11:38 pm, stopping at Estació de Sants, for transfer to the Arc de Triomf, then at Passeig de Gràcia and finally at El Clot–Aragó. Trains going to the airport begin at 5:21 am from El Clot, stopping at Passeig de Gràcia at 5:27 am, and Sants at 5:32 am. The trip takes about half an hour, and the fare is €4.60. Add an extra hour if you take the train to or from the airport.

CITY BUS, SUBWAY, AND TRAM

In Barcelona the underground metro, or subway, is the fastest, cheapest, and easiest way to get around. Metro lines run Monday–Thursday and Sunday 5 am–midnight, Friday to 2 am, Saturday and holiday evenings all night. The FGC trains run 5 am to just after midnight on weekdays and to 1:52 am on weekends and the eves of holidays. Sunday trains run on weekday schedules. Single-fare tickets cost €2.40 (€4.60 to the airport); a 10-ride pass called "T Casual" costs €11.35.

Transfers from a metro line to the FGC (or vice versa) are free within an hour and 15 minutes. Note that in many stations, you need to validate your ticket at both ends of your journey. Maps showing bus and metro routes are available free from the tourist information office in Plaça de Catalunya.

CONTACTS Transports Metropolitans de Barcelona. (*TMB*) ☎ *93/214–8000, 93/298–7000* ⊕ *www.tmb.cat/en/home.*

TAXI
In Barcelona taxis are black and yellow and show a green rooftop sign on the front right corner when available for hire. The meter currently starts at €2.25 and rises in increments of €1.18 every kilometer. These rates apply 8 am–10 pm weekdays. At hours outside of these, the rates rise 20%.

Trips to or from a train station entail a supplemental charge of €2.50; a cab to or from the airport, or the Barcelona Cruise Terminal, adds a supplemental charge of €4.30, as do trips to or from a football match. The minimum price for taxi service to or from the Barcelona airport is €20 for terminals T1, T2, and T3, and €39 from T4. There are cabstands (*parades,* in Catalan) all over town, and you can also hail cabs on the street, though if you are too close to an official stand they may not stop. You can call for a cab by phone 24 hours a day. Drivers do not expect a tip, but rounding up the fare is standard.

CONTACTS Barna Taxi. ✉ *Barcelona* ☎ *93/322222* ⊕ *www.barnataxi.com.* **Radio Taxi 033.** ✉ *Barcelona* ☎ *93/303–3033* ⊕ *radiotaxi033.com.***Taxi Class Rent.** ✉ *Barcelona* ☎ *93/307–0707* ⊕ *www. taxiclassrent.com/en.*

TRAIN
International overnight trains to Barcelona arrive from many European cities, including Paris, Grenoble, Geneva, Zurich, and Milan; the four-a-day high-speed trains to and from Paris take about 5½ hours, and advance-purchase tickets online are competitive with flight prices. Almost all long-distance trains arrive at and depart from Estació de Sants, though many make a stop at Passeig de Gràcia that comes in handy for hotels in the Eixample or in the Ciutat Vella. Estació de França, near the port, handles only a few regional trains within Catalonia. Train service connects Barcelona with most other major cities in Spain; in addition a high-speed Euromed route connects Barcelona to Tarragona and Valencia.

Spain's intercity services (along with some of Barcelona's local train routes) are the province of the government-run railroad system—RENFE (Red Nacional de Ferrocarriles Españoles). The high-speed AVE train now connects Barcelona and Madrid (via Lleida and Zaragoza) in less than three hours. (Spain has more high-speed tracks in service than any other country in Europe.) The fast TALGO and ALTARIA trains are efficient, though local trains remain slow and tedious. The Catalan government's FGC (Ferrocarrils de la Generalitat de Catalunya) also provide train service, notably to Barcelona's commuter suburbs of Sant Cugat, Terrassa, and Sabadell.

Information on the local/commuter lines (*rodalies* in Catalan, *cercanias* in Castilian) can be found at rodalies.gencat.cat/en/inici/index.html. Rodalies go, for example, to Sitges from Barcelona, whereas you would take a regular RENFE train to, say, Tarragona. It's important to know whether you are traveling on RENFE or on rodalies (the latter distinguished by a stylized C), so you don't end up in the wrong line.

Both Catalonia and the Basque Country offer scenic railroad excursions. The day train from Barcelona to Madrid runs through bougainvillea-choked towns before leaping out across Spain's central *meseta* (plateau) via Zaragoza, with most trains arriving at Atocha Station in Madrid in about 2½ hours. The train from Barcelona's Plaça de Catalunya north to Sant Pol de Mar and Blanes runs along the edge of the beach.

First-class train service in Spain, with the exception of the *coche-cama* (Pullman) overnight service, barely differs from second class or *turista*. The TALGO or the AVE trains, however, are much faster than second-class carriers like the slow-poke Estrella overnight from Barcelona to Madrid, both with limited legroom and general comforts. The AVE is the exception: these sleek, comfortable bullet trains travel between Barcelona and Madrid or between Madrid and Seville. Some 30 AVE trains a day connect Barcelona and Madrid, with departures from 5:50 am to 9:15 pm. Trips take from 2 hours 30 minutes to 3 hours 10 minutes.

STATIONS Estació de França. ⊠ *Av. Marquès de l'Argentera 1, Born-Ribera* ☎ *912/320320 RENFE station info* ⊕ *www.renfe.com* Ⓜ *L4 Barceloneta.* **Estació de Passeig de Gràcia.** ⊠ *Passeig de Gràcia/Carrer Aragó, Eixample* ☎ *912/432343 station info, 912/320320 RENFE general info* ⊕ *www.renfe.com* Ⓜ *L2/L3/L4 Passeig de Gràcia.* **Estació de Sants.** ⊠ *Pl. dels Països Catalans s/n, Les Corts* ☎ *912/432343 station info, 902/320320 RENFE general info* ⊕ *www.renfe.com* Ⓜ *L3/L5 Sants Estació.* **Ferrocarrils de la Generalitat de Catalunya (FGC).** ⊠ *Carrer Vergos 44, Sarrià* ☎ *93/366–3000* ⊕ *www.fgc.cat/en* Ⓜ *Sarrià (FGC).* **RENFE.** ☎ *912/320320* ⊕ *www.renfe.com.*

INFORMATION AND PASSES Eurail. ⊕ *www.eurail.com.* **Rail Europe.** ⊕ *www. raileurope.com.*

Tours

ART TOURS

The Ruta del Modernisme (Moderniste Route), a self-guided tour, provides an excellent guidebook (available in English) that interprets 120 Moderniste sites from the Sagrada Família and the Palau de la Música Catalana to Art Nouveau building facades, lampposts, and paving stones. The €18 Guide, sold at the Pavellons Güell and the Institut Municipal del Paisatge Urbà (*Av. Drassanes 6*), comes with a book of vouchers good for discounts up to 50% on admission to most of the Moderniste buildings and sites in the Guide in Barcelona and 13 other towns and cities in Catalonia, as well as free guided tours in English at selected Moderniste sites. Check when buying the guide what is on and when, as availability may vary.

The Palau de la Música Catalana offers guided tours in English every hour on the hour from 10 to 3:30. Sagrada Família guided tours cost extra. Casa Milà offers a selection of private experiences, including a guided tour before the house opens to the public and a night tour with dinner. Architect Dominique Blinder of Urban Cultours project specializes in Barcelona's Jewish heritage and explorations of the Barcelona Jewish Quarter but can also provide tours of virtually any architectural aspect of Barcelona.

Recinte Modernista de Sant Pau. ⊠ *Carrer Sant Antoni Maria Claret 167, Eixample* ☎ *93/553–7801* ⊕ *www.santpaubarcelona.org/en* ☎ *From €15* Ⓜ *L5 Sant Pau/Dos de Maig.*

CULINARY TOURS

Barcelona's cooking classes have upped their game of late, with traditional, mass-tourism-focused cooking schools making way for a new generation of "slow food" favorites like The Paella Club and Bear on Bike. Jane Gregg, founder of Epicurean Ways, offers gourmet and wine tours of Barcelona and Catalonia. Teresa Parker of Spanish Journeys organizes cooking classes, seasonal specials, custom cultural or culinary tours, corporate cooking retreats, or off-the-beaten-path travel. Canadian-born Marwa Preston of Wanderbeak offers food experiences ranging from Michelin-starred splurges to tapas walks, with just the right mix of food, wine, and local culture.

CONTACTS Epicurean Ways. ☎ 434/738–2293 in U.S., 93/802–2688 in Spain ⊕ www.epicureanways.com.**Wanderbeak.** ⊠ Carrer del Comerç, 29 ☎ 93/220-6101 ⊕ www.wanderbeak.com.

BIKE TOURS

Bike Tours Barcelona

This company offers a three-hour bike tour (in English) for €25 (or €35 for an e-Bike on request), with a drink included. Just look for the guide with a bike and a blue flag at the northeast corner of the Casa de la Ciutat in Plaça Sant Jaume, outside the Tourist Information Office. Tours depart at 11 am daily; there is an additional tour at 4:30 pm Friday–Monday, April 1–September 15. The company will also organize private guided tours through the Barri Gòtic, parks, the Port Olímpic and Barceloneta, the Ruta Moderniste, and other itineraries on request. Touring on your own? The company also rents bikes by the hour or the day, at its shop in Carrer Esparteria. ⊠ Carrer Esparteria 3, Barri Gòtic ☎ 932/682105 ⊕ biketoursbarcelona.com Ⓜ Jaume I.

BOAT TOURS

Golondrina harbor boats make short trips from the Portal de la Pau, near the Columbus monument. The fare is €7.70 for a 40-minute "Barcelona Port" tour of the harbor and €15.50 for the "Barcelona Sea" 90-minute ride out past the beaches and up the coast to the Fòrum at the eastern end of Diagonal. Frequency and departure times may vary depending on the season, but the Port tour typically runs hourly from 12:15 am–5:15 pm

in spring and summer, and every 30 minutes in July, August, and September, while the Sea tour departs at 12:30 pm daily, all year-round; three times daily (at 12:30, 1:30 and 3:30) in spring and fall, and hourly from 12:30 to 6:30 pm from April to September.

CONTACTS Las Golondrinas. ⊠ Pl. Portal de la Pau s/n, Moll de les Drassanes, La Rambla ☎ 93/442–3106 ⊕ lasgolondrinas.com/en Ⓜ L3 Drassanes.

BUS TOURS

The Bus Turístic (9 or 9:30 am to 7 or 8 pm every 5–25 minutes, depending on the season), sponsored by the tourist office, runs on three circuits with stops at all the major sights. The blue route covers upper Barcelona; the red route tours lower Barcelona; and the green route runs from the Port Olímpic along Barcelona's beaches to the Fòrum at the eastern end of Diagonal (April through September only). A one-day ticket can be bought online (with a 10% discount) for €30 (a two-day ticket is €40).

The product and prices are all but identical, though the Bus Turístic is the official tourist office tour, offering discount vouchers and superior service. In the event of long lines or delays on the Bus Turístic, Hop On Hop Off Tours is a good alternative.

CONTACTS Barcelona Hop On Hop Off Tours. ☎ 871/180–005 ⊕ www.hop-on-hop-off-bus.com/barcelona-bus-tours.**Bus Turístic.** ⊠ Pl. de Catalunya 3, Eixample ☎ 93/285–3832 ⊕ www.barcelonabusturistic.cat Ⓜ Catalunya.**Julià Travel.** ⊠ Carrer Balmes 5, Eixample ☎ 93/402–6900 ⊕ www.juliatravel.com/destinations/barcelona Ⓜ Catalunya, L1/L2 Universitat.

BALLOON AND HELICOPTER TOURS

Baló Tours S.L

Baló Tours S.L. runs balloon tours north of Barcelona around Vic (in the foothills of the Pyrenees, and along the Costa Brava) for up to 12 passengers at a time. ⊠ *Carrer Bisbe Morgades 49, Entresol 2a, Vic* ☎ *938/894443, 93/414–4774* ⊕ *www.balotour.com* ✉ *€150.*

Cat Helicopters

Cat Helicopters circles Barcelona for €79 per person for 6 minutes, €139 for 10 minutes, and €369 for a 35-minute flight that takes in the nearby Montserrat Mountains. ⊠ *Helipuerto de Barcelona, Passeig de l'Escullera, Moll Adossat s/n, Port Olímpic* ☎ *93/224–0710* ⊕ *www.cathelicopters.com* ✉ *From €79* Ⓜ *L3 Drassanes.*

PRIVATE GUIDES

Guides from the organizations listed below are generally competent, though the quality of language skills and general showmanship may vary.

Barcelona Guide Bureau

Daily walking tours of the major sites in Barcelona are available, as well as tours to Montserrat, the Dalí Museum in Figueres and beautiful nearby Girona. Some tours offer fast-track entrance to museums and popular venues like the Sagrada Família. ⊠ *Via Laietana 54, 2–2, Born-Ribera* ☎ *93/268–2422, 667/419-140 on weekends* ⊕ *www.barcelonaguidebureau.com* ✉ *From €15* Ⓜ *Urquinaona.*

WALKING TOURS

Turisme de Barcelona offers weekend walking tours of the Barri Gòtic, the Waterfront, Picasso's Barcelona, Modernisme, and a shopping circuit, in English. Prices range from €18 to €25, with 10% discounts for purchases online. For private tours, Julià Travel leads walks around Barcelona. Tours leave from their offices, but you may be able to arrange a pickup at your hotel. Prices range from around €69 for a private half-day tour, to €239 for a full day, including lunch.

For the best English-language walking tour of the medieval Jewish Quarter, Dominique Tomasov Blinder, of Urbancultours is an architect with many years'

experience in Jewish heritage. Her tour of Jewish Barcelona, past and present, is a unique combination of history, current affairs, and personal experience; learn more at www.urbancultours.com.

CONTACTS Urbancultours. ✉ *info@urbancultours.com* ⊕ *www.urbancultours.com.*

SEGWAY TOURS

Barcelona Segway Tours, with an office near Arc de Triomf, puts you up on one of its futuristic two-wheelers for a two-hour tour (€49) of the Barri Gòtic, La Rambla, and the seafront; its longer three-hour excursion (€69) starts at Arc de Triomf and takes you to the top of the green mountain of Montjuic. Tours depart daily at 10 am, 12:30, and 4pm. Helmets are provided; children must be more than 10 years of age; learn more at www.barcelonasegwaytour.com.

Visitor Information

Turisme de Barcelona

In addition to being a useful resource for information, tickets, and bookings, Turisme de Barcelona offers daily walking tours of the Barri Gòtic, Picasso's Barcelona, Modernisme, and more. There is also an Easy Walking Tour of the Barri Gòtic, which has been adapted for people with reduced mobility: Departure times for tours in English depend on which of the tours you choose. Book online for a 10% discount. The Picasso tour, which includes the entry fee for the Museu Picasso, is a great bargain. All tours depart from the Plaça de Catalunya tourist office, except for the Easy Walking Tour, which starts at The Tourist Office in Plaça Sant Jaume. ⊠ *Pl. de Catalunya 17, soterrani, Eixample* ☎ *93/285–3834* ⊕ *bcnshop.barcelonaturisme.com/shopv3* ✉ *From €18* Ⓜ *Pl. de Catalunya.*

Restaurants and Hotels

Restaurant and hotel reviews have been shortened. For full information, visit Fodors.com.

What It Costs in Euros			
$	$$	$$$	$$$$
RESTAURANTS			
under €16	€16–€22	€23–€29	over €29
HOTELS			
under €125	€125–€174	€175–€225	over €225

La Rambla

The promenade in the heart of premodern Barcelona was originally a watercourse, dry for most of the year, that separated the walled Ciutat Vella from the outlying Raval. In the 14th century, the city walls were extended and the arroyo was filled in, so it gradually became a thoroughfare where peddlers, farmers, and tradesmen hawked their wares. (The watercourse is still there, under the pavement. From time to time a torrential rain will fill it, and the water rises up through the drains.) The poet-playwright Federico García Lorca called this the only street in the world he wished would never end— and in a sense, it doesn't.

Down the watercourse now flows a river of humanity, gathered here and there around the mimes, acrobats, jugglers, musicians, puppeteers, portrait artists, break dancers, rappers, and rockers competing for the crowd's attention. Couples sit at café tables no bigger than tea trays while nimble-footed waiters dodge traffic, bringing food and drink from kitchens. With the din of taxis and motorbikes in the traffic lanes on either side of the promenade, the revelers and rubberneckers, and the Babel of languages, the scene is as animated at 3 am as it is at 3 pm.

Barcelona's most famous boulevard boasts a generous pedestrian strip down the middle and it is a tourist magnet. Much as you may want to avoid the crowds and the tacky, touristy shops and eateries that now cater to the crush of visitors, a stroll here is essential to your Barcelona experience. From the rendezvous point at the head of La Rambla at Café Zurich to La Boqueria produce market, the Liceu opera house, or La Rambla's lower reaches, there are crowds but also gems along this spinal column of Barcelona street life. Keep a close eye on your valuables, as this part of the city is sadly teeming with pickpockets.

Sights

Casa Bruno Cuadros

NOTABLE BUILDING | Like something out of an amusement park, this former umbrella shop was whimsically designed (assembled is more like it) by Josep Vilaseca in 1885. A Chinese dragon with a parasol, Egyptian balconies and galleries, and a Peking lantern all reflect the Eastern style that was very much in vogue at the time of the Universal Exposition of 1888. Now housing a branch office of the Banco Bilbao Vizcaya Artentaria (BBVA), this prankster of a building is much in keeping with Art Nouveau's eclectic playfulness, though it has never been taken very seriously as an expression of Modernisme and is generally omitted from most studies of Art Nouveau architecture. ⊠ *La Rambla 82, La Rambla* Ⓜ *L3 Liceu.*

★ Gran Teatre del Liceu

NOTABLE BUILDING | Barcelona's opera house has long been considered one of the most beautiful in Europe, a rival to La Scala in Milan. First built in 1848, this cherished cultural landmark was torched in 1861, later bombed by anarchists in 1893, and once again gutted by an accidental fire in early 1994. During that

Visit La Boqueria market early (it opens at 8 am) to avoid the crowds as you discover all this colorful institution has to offer.

most recent fire, Barcelona's soprano Montserrat Caballé stood on La Rambla in tears as her beloved venue was consumed. Five years later, a restored Liceu, equipped for modern productions, opened anew. Even if you don't see an opera, you can take a tour of the building. Some of the Liceu's most spectacular halls and rooms, including the glittering foyer known as the Saló dels Miralls (Room of Mirrors), were untouched by the fire of 1994, as were those of Spain's oldest social club, El Círculo del Liceu—established in 1847 and restored to its pristine original condition after the fire. Hour-long guided tours are available in Spanish or English for €19, while backstage tours can be arranged on request. ⊠ *La Rambla 51–59, La Rambla* ☎ *93/485–9931 premium visit reservations, 93/485–9914 express and guided tour information and reservations* ⊕ *www.liceubarcelona.cat* ☜ *Variety of tours from €19* Ⓜ *L4 Liceu.*

★ La Boqueria

MARKET | Barcelona's most spectacular food market, also known as the Mercat de Sant Josep, is an explosion of life and color with small tapas bar-restaurants. A solid polychrome wall of fruits, herbs, vegetables, nuts, candied fruits, cheeses, hams, fish, and poultry greets you as you turn in from La Rambla. Under a Moderniste hangar of wrought-iron girders and stained glass, the market occupies a Neoclassical square built in 1840. Highlights include the sunny greengrocer's market outside, along with Pinotxo (Pinocchio), just inside to the right, which serves some of the best food in Barcelona. The Kiosko Universal and Quim de la Boqueria both offer delicious alternatives. Don't miss the *fruits del bosc* (fruits of the forest) stand at the back of La Boqueria, with its display of wild mushrooms, herbs, nuts, and berries. To avoid crowds, go before 8 am or after 5 pm. ⊠ *La Rambla 91, La Rambla* ☎ *93/318–2017 information desk, Tues.–Thurs. 8–3, Fri. and Sat. 8–5, 93/318–2584* ⊕ *www.boqueria.info* ☉ *Closed Sun.* Ⓜ *Liceu.*

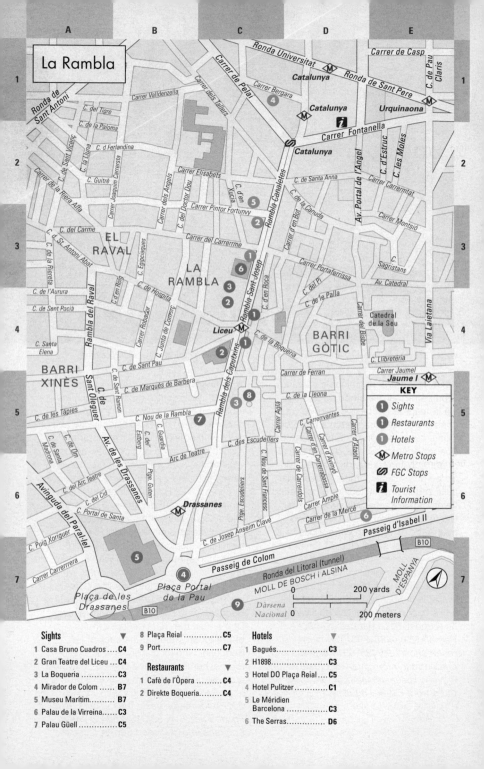

La Rambla

Sights ▼
1 Casa Bruno Cuadros **C4**
2 Gran Teatre del Liceu ... **C4**
3 La Boqueria **C3**
4 Mirador de Colom **B7**
5 Museu Marítim.......... **B7**
6 Palau de la Virreina...... **C3**
7 Palau Güell **C5**

8 Plaça Reial **C5**
9 Port....................... **C7**

Restaurants ▼
1 Cafè de l'Òpera **C4**
2 Direkte Boqueria........ **C4**

Hotels ▼
1 Bagués................... **C3**
2 H1898................... **C3**
3 Hotel DO Plaça Reial **C5**
4 Hotel Pulitzer............ **C1**
5 Le Méridien
  Barcelona **C3**
6 The Serras............... **D6**

Mirador de Colom (*Columbus Monument*)
VIEWPOINT | This Barcelona landmark to Christopher Columbus sits grandly at the foot of La Rambla along the wide harbor-front promenade of Passeig de Colom, not far from the very shipyards (Drassanes Reials) that constructed two of the ships of his tiny but immortal fleet. Standing atop the 150-foot-high iron column—the base of which is aswirl with gesticulating angels—Columbus seems to be looking out at "that far-distant shore" he discovered; in fact he's pointing, with his 18-inch-long finger, in the general direction of Sicily. For a bird's-eye view of La Rambla and the port, take the elevator to the small viewing platform (*mirador*) at the top of the column. The entrance is on the harbor side. ⊠ *Pl. Portal de la Pau s/n, Port Olímpic* ☎ *93/285–3832* ⌨ *€6* Ⓜ *L3 Drassanes.*

★ **Museu Marítim**
HISTORY MUSEUM | FAMILY | The superb Maritime Museum is housed in the 13th-century Drassanes Reials (Royal Shipyards), at the foot of La Rambla adjacent to the harbor front. This vast covered complex launched the ships of Catalonia's powerful Mediterranean fleet directly from its yards into the port. Today, these are the world's largest and best-preserved medieval shipyards. On the Avinguda del Paral·lel side of Drassanes is a completely intact section of the 14th- to 15th-century walls—Barcelona's third and final ramparts—that encircled El Raval along the Paral·lel and the Rondas de Sant Pau, Sant Antoni, and Universitat. Though the shipyards seem more like a cathedral than a naval construction site, the Maritime Museum is filled with vessels, including a spectacular collection of ship models. Headphones and infrared pointers provide a first-rate self-guided tour. The cafeteria-restaurant Norai, open daily 9 am to 8 pm offers dining in a setting of medieval elegance, and has a charming terrace. ⊠ *Av. de les Drassanes s/n, La Rambla* ☎ *93/342–9920* ⊕ *www.mmb.cat/en*

⌨ *€10 (includes admission to Santa Eulàlia clipper); free Sun. after 3* ☉ *Santa Eulàlia closed Mon.* Ⓜ *L3 Drassanes.*

Palau de la Virreina (*La Virreina Centre de la Imatge*)
CASTLE/PALACE | The baroque Virreina Palace, built by a viceroy to Peru in the late 18th century, is now a major center for themed exhibitions of contemporary art, film, and photography. The **Tiquet Rambles** office on the ground floor, run by the city government's Institut del Cultura (ICUB), open daily 10–8:30, is the place to go for information and last-minute tickets to concerts, theater and dance performances, gallery shows, and museums. The portal to the palace, and the pediments carved with elaborate floral designs, are a must-see. ⊠ *Rambla de les Flors 99, La Rambla* ☎ *93/316–1000* ⊕ *ajuntament. barcelona.cat/lavirreina/ca* ⌨ *Free; €3 charge for some exhibits* ☉ *Closed Mon.* Ⓜ *Liceu.*

★ **Palau Güell**
HISTORIC HOME | Gaudí built this mansion in 1886–90 for textile baron Count Eusebi de Güell Bacigalupi, his most important patron. The dark facade is a dramatic foil for the brilliance of the inside, where spear-shape Art Nouveau columns frame the windows, rising to support a series of detailed and elaborately carved wood ceilings. The basement stables are famous for the "fungiform" (mushroom-like) columns carrying the weight of the whole building. Don't miss the figures of the faithful hounds, with the rings in their mouths for hitching horses, or the wooden bricks laid down in lieu of cobblestones in the entryway upstairs. The dining room is dominated by an Art Nouveau fireplace in the shape of a deeply curving horseshoe arch and walls with floral and animal motifs. Gaudí is most himself on the roof, where his playful, polychrome ceramic chimneys seem like preludes to later works like the Park Güell and La Pedrera. ⊠ *Nou de la Rambla 3–5, La Rambla* ☎ *93/472–5771,*

A shipshape collection of nautical wonders is on display at the Museu Marítim.

93/472–5775 ⊕ www.palauguell.cat/
en ✉ €12 (€11 online); free 1st Sun.
of month for tickets purchased online
⊘ Closed Mon. ☞ Guided tours (1 hr) in
English Fri. at 10:30 am and Sat. at 2:30
pm at no additional cost Ⓜ L3 Drassanes,
Liceu.

★ Plaça Reial

PLAZA/SQUARE | Nobel Prize–winning
novelist Gabriel García Márquez, architect
and urban planner Oriol Bohigas, and
Pasqual Maragall, former president of
the Catalonian Generalitat, are among
the many famous people said to have
acquired apartments overlooking this elegant square, a chiaroscuro masterpiece
in which neoclassical symmetry clashes
with big-city street funk. Plaça Reial is
bordered by stately ocher facades with
balconies overlooking the wrought-iron
Fountain of the Three Graces, and an
array of lampposts designed by Gaudí
in 1879. Cafés and restaurants line the
square. Plaça Reial is most colorful on
Sunday morning, when collectors gather
to trade stamps and coins; after dark it's
a center of downtown nightlife for the
jazz-minded, the young, and the adventurous (it's best to be streetwise touring
this area in the late hours). ⊠ Plaça Reial,
La Rambla Ⓜ L3 Liceu.

Port

MARINA/PIER | Beyond the Columbus
monument—behind the ornate Duana (now the Barcelona Port Authority
headquarters)—is La Rambla de Mar, a
boardwalk with a drawbridge designed
to allow boats into and out of the inner
harbor. La Rambla de Mar extends out to
the Moll d'Espanya, with its ultra-touristy
Maremagnum shopping center (open
on Sunday, unusual for Barcelona) and
the excellent Aquarium. Next to the
Duana you can board a Golondrina boat
for a tour of the port and the waterfront or, from the Moll de Barcelona on
the right, take a cable car to Montjuïc
or Barceloneta. Trasmediterránea and
Baleària passenger ferries leave for Italy
and the Balearic Islands from the Moll
de Barcelona; at the end of the quay is
Barcelona's World Trade Center and the

Eurostars Grand Marina Hotel. ✉ *Port Olímpic* [M] *Drassanes.*

🍴 Restaurants

Cafè de l'Òpera

$ | **CAFÉ** | Directly across from the Liceu opera house, this high-ceiling Art Nouveau café has welcomed operagoers and performers for more than 100 years. It's a central point on the Rambla tourist traffic pattern, so locals are increasingly hard to find, but the café has hung onto its atmosphere of faded glory nonetheless. **Known for:** late-night hours; Art Nouveau decor; good for a drink. [$] *Average main: €12* ✉ *La Rambla 74, La Rambla* ☎ *93/317–7585* 🌐 *www.cafeoperabcn.com* [M] *Liceu.*

Direkte Boqueria

$$$$ | **CATALAN** | Local gourmands pilgrimage to this tiny, unassuming-looking bar on the edge of the famous Boquería market, where Catalan chef Arnau Muñío flexes his culinary chops in full view of the diners at his chef's-table-style counter. There are two tasting menus, one long, one short, both of which showcase Muñío's unique approach to Catalan-Asian fusion food. **Known for:** need to book ahead; accessible fine dining; Asian-Catalan fusion. [$] *Average main: €45* ✉ *Cabres 14, La Rambla* ☎ *93/114–6939* 🌐 *www.direkte.cat* ⏲ *Closed Mon., Tues.* [M] *Liceu L3.*

🛏 Hotels

Bagués

$$$ | **HOTEL** | The luxury of the Eixample has worked its way down to La Rambla, as this boutique gem (formerly the shop and atelier of the well-known Art Nouveau jeweler of the same name) bears ample witness. **Pros:** free entrance to the Egyptian Museum of Barcelona; view of the cathedral and port from the rooftop terrace; steps from the opera house. **Cons:** hectic location; rooms a bit small for the price; street-facing rooms can be noisy. [$] *Rooms from: €210* ✉ *La Rambla 105, La Rambla* ☎ *93/343–5000* 🌐 *www.hotelbagues.com* 🛏 *28 rooms, 3 suites* 🍴 *No Meals* [M] *Pl. Catalunya, L3 Liceu.*

H1898

$$$ | **HOTEL** | Overlooking La Rambla, this imposing mansion (once the headquarters of the Compañiá General de Tabacos de Filipinas) couldn't be better located for anyone who likes to be right in the thick of things—especially for opera fans, with the Liceu just around the corner. **Pros:** ideal location for exploring the Barri Gòtic; historic spaces plus modern amenities like a spa and roof deck; impeccable service. **Cons:** some street noise from the Rambla in lower rooms; some guests complain about water pressure; subway rumble discernible in lower rooms on the Rambla side. [$] *Rooms from: €220* ✉ *La Rambla 109, La Rambla* ☎ *93/552–9552* 🌐 *www.hotel1898.com* 🛏 *169 rooms* 🍴 *No Meals* [M] *Catalunya, Liceu.*

Hotel DO Plaça Reial

$$$$ | **HOTEL** | Just at the entrance to the neoclassical Plaça Reial, this charming boutique hotel—with its three restaurants, La Terraza (under the arcades on the square), El Terrat, and La Cuina (downstairs under graceful brick vaulting)—is a find for lovers of food and tasteful design. **Pros:** 24-hour room service; very central location; helpful multilingual staff. **Cons:** area can get busy; neighborhood can be rowdy at night; street noise discernible in lower rooms. [$] *Rooms from: €245* ✉ *Pl. Reial 1, La Rambla* ☎ *93/481–3666* 🌐 *sonder.com* 🍴 *No Meals* 🛏 *18 rooms* [M] *L3 Liceu.*

Hotel Pulitzer

$$ | **HOTEL** | Hotel Pulitzer is like a breath of fresh air in a neighborhood with very little else going for it. **Pros:** rooftop is a Barcelona hot spot; hidden gem in an unfashionable location; excellent value. **Cons:** no gym, pool, or spa; soulless part of town; some rooms could do with an upgrade. [$] *Rooms from: €130* ✉ *Bergara 8, La Rambla* ☎ *93/481–6767* 🌐 *www.*

hotelpulitzer.es/en 🍴 *No Meals* 🛏 *92 rooms* [M] *Catalunya L1, L3.*

Le Méridien Barcelona
$$$$ | HOTEL | There's no dearth of hotels along La Rambla in the heart of the city, but few rival the upscale Le Méridien, popular with businesspeople and tourists alike for its suites overlooking the promenade and cozy amenities. **Pros:** Mediterranean suites have large private terraces; central location; soaker tubs in deluxe rooms. **Cons:** no pool; slightly sketchy location; rooms small for the price. [$] *Rooms from: €239* ✉ *La Rambla 111, La Rambla* ☎ *93/318–6200* 🌐 *www.marriott.com/hotels/travel/bcnmd-le-meridien-barcelona* 🛏 *231 rooms* 🍴 *No Meals* [M] *Catalunya L3 Liceu.*

🍸 Nightlife

The liveliest pedestrian promenade in the city bustles with a dizzying array of tourist-baiting shops, eateries, and arched paths to Plaça Reial's euphoric nightlife scene. Casual and unpretentious, the scene erupts nightly with a parade of rambunctious crowds of expats, curious interlopers, and assorted celebrations.

BARS

Boadas
COCKTAIL LOUNGES | Barcelona's oldest cocktail bar opened its doors in 1933 and quickly gained a reputation as the only place to enjoy a genuine mojito. The faithful—who still include a few of the city's luminaries—have been flocking ever since, despite the bar's decidedly lackluster decor. The space has the look and feel of an old-fashioned private club and is still the spot to watch old-school barmen in dapper duds mixing drinks the way tradition dictates. ✉ *Tallers 1, La Rambla* ☎ *93/318–9592* 🌐 *boadascocktails.com* 🕒 *Closed Sun.* [M] *Catalunya.*

Jamboree-Jazz and Dance-Club
LIVE MUSIC | This legendary nightspot has hosted some of the world's most influential jazz musicians since its opening in 1960. Decades later, the club continues to offer two nightly shows and remains a notable haven for new generations of jazz and blues aficionados. After the last performance, the spot transforms into a late-night dance club playing soul, hip-hop, and R&B. ✉ *Pl. Reial 17, La Rambla* ☎ *93/304–1210* 🌐 *www.jamboreejazz.com/en* [M] *Liceu.*

Barri Gòtic

A labyrinth of medieval buildings, squares, and narrow cobblestone streets, the Barri Gòtic comprises the area around the Catedral de la Seu, built over Roman ruins you can still visit and filled with the Gothic structures that marked the zenith of Barcelona's power in the 15th century. On certain corners you feel as if you're making a genuine excursion back in time.

The Barri Gòtic rests squarely atop the first Roman settlement. Sometimes referred to as the *rovell d'ou* (the yolk of the egg), this high ground the Romans called Mons Taber coincides almost exactly with the early 1st- to 4th-century fortified town of Barcino. Sights to see here include the Plaça del Rei, the remains of Roman Barcino underground beneath the Museum of the History of the City, the Plaça Sant Jaume and the area around the onetime Roman Forum, the medieval Jewish Quarter, and the ancient Plaça Sant Just.

👁 Sights

Ajuntament de Barcelona
HISTORIC SIGHT | The 15th-century city hall on Plaça Sant Jaume faces the Palau de la Generalitat, with its mid-18th-century neoclassical facade, across the square once occupied by the Roman Forum. The Ajuntament is a rich repository of sculpture and painting by the great Catalan masters, from Marès to Gargallo to Clarà, from Subirachs to Miró and

Llimona. Inside is the famous Saló de Cent, from which the Consell de Cent, Europe's oldest democratic parliament, governed Barcelona between 1373 and 1714. The Saló de les Croniques (Hall of Chronicles) is decorated with Josep Maria Sert's immense black-and-burnished-gold murals (1928) depicting the early-14th-century Catalan campaign in Byzantium and Greece under the command of Roger de Flor. The city hall is open to visitors on Sunday 10–2, with self-guided visits in English available without prior booking; on local holidays; and for occasional concerts or events in the Saló de Cent. ⊠ Pl. Sant Jaume 1, Barri Gòtic ☎ 93/402–7000 ⊕ ajuntament.barcelona.cat/en ☑ Free Ⓜ L4 Jaume I, L3 Liceu.

Baixada de Santa Eulàlia
RELIGIOUS BUILDING | Down Carrer Sant Sever from the side door of the cathedral cloister, past Carrer Sant Domènec del Call and the Esglèsia de Sant Sever, is a tiny shrine, in an alcove overhead, dedicated to the 4th-century martyr Santa Eulàlia, former patron saint of the city (before she was replaced by current patron saint Mare de Deu de la Mercè). Down this hill, or baixada (descent), Eulàlia was rolled in a barrel filled with— as the Jacint Verdaguer verse in ceramic tile on the wall reads—glavis i ganivets de dos talls (swords and double-edged knives), the final of the 13 tortures to which she was subjected before her crucifixion at Plaça del Pedró. ⊠ Carrer Sant Sever s/n, Barri Gòtic Ⓜ Liceu, Jaume I.

Casa de l'Ardiaca (Archdeacon's House)
NOTABLE BUILDING | The interior of this 15th-century building, home of the Municipal Archives (upstairs), has superb views of the remains of the 4th-century Roman watchtowers and walls. Look at the Montjuïc sandstone carefully, and you will see blocks taken from other buildings carved and beveled into decorative shapes, proof of the haste of the Romans to fortify the site as the

Visigoths approached from the north, when the Pax Romana collapsed. In the center of the lovely courtyard here, across from the Santa Llúcia chapel, is a fountain; on the day of Corpus Christi in June the fountain impressively supports l'ou com balla, or "the dancing egg," a Barcelona tradition in which eggs are set to bobbing atop jets of water in various places around the city. ⊠ Carrer de Santa Llúcia 1, Barri Gòtic ☎ 93/256–2255 ⊕ ajuntament.barcelona.cat/arxiumunicipal/arxiuhistoric/ca ☉ Closed Sun. Ⓜ L3 Liceu, L4 Jaume I.

Catedral de la Seu
CHURCH | Barcelona's cathedral is a repository of centuries of the city's history and legend—although as a work of architecture visitors might find it a bit of a disappointment. Don't miss the beautifully carved choir stalls of the Knights of the Golden Fleece; the intricately and elaborately sculpted organ loft over the door out to Plaça Sant Iu; the series of 60-odd wood sculptures of evangelical figures along the exterior lateral walls of the choir; and, in the crypt, the tomb of Santa Eulàlia. The leafy, palm tree–shaded **cloister** surrounds a tropical garden and a pool populated by 13 snow-white geese, one for each of the tortures inflicted upon St. Eulàlia in an effort to break her faith. In front of the cathedral is the grand square of **Plaça de la Seu,** where on Saturday from 6 pm to 8 pm, Sunday morning, and occasional evenings, barcelonins gather to dance the sardana, the circular folk dance. ⊠ Pl. de la Seu s/n, Barri Gòtic ☎ 93/342–8262 ⊕ www.catedralbcn.org ☑ Free for worshippers, cultural/tourist visits €9. Ⓜ L4 Jaume I.

Columnes del Temple d'August (Columns of the Temple of Augustus)
RUINS | The highest point in Roman Barcelona is marked with a circular millstone at the entrance to the Centre Excursionista de Catalunya, a club dedicated to exploring the mountains and highlands of Catalonia on foot and on skis. Inside

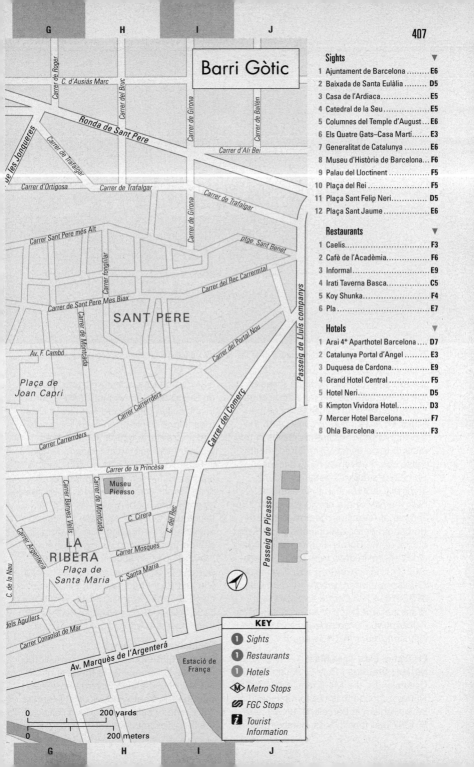

Barri Gòtic

Sights ▼

Restaurants ▼

Hotels ▼

The ornate Gothic interior of the Catedral de la Seu is always enclosed in shadows, even at high noon.

the entryway on the right are some of the best-preserved 1st- and 2nd-century Corinthian Roman columns in Europe. Massive, fluted, and crowned with the typical Corinthian acanthus leaves in two distinct rows under eight fluted sheaths, these columns remain only because Barcelona's early Christians elected, atypically, not to build their cathedral over the site of the previous temple. The Temple of Augustus, dedicated to the Roman emperor, occupied the northwest corner of the Roman Forum, which coincided approximately with today's Plaça Sant Jaume. ✉ *Centre Excursionista de Catalunya, Carrer Paradís 10, Barri Gòtic* ☎ *93/256–2122 Centre Excursionista* ⊕ *ajuntament.barcelona.cat/museuhistoria/ca/muhba-temple-daugust* ⊘ *Closed Mon. afternoon* Ⓜ *L4 Jaume I.*

Els Quatre Gats–Casa Martí
NOTABLE BUILDING | Built by Josep Puig i Cadafalch for the Martí family, this Art Nouveau house was the fountainhead of bohemianism in Barcelona. It was here in 1897 that four friends, notable dandies all—Ramon Casas, Pere Romeu, Santiago Russinyol, and Miguel Utrillo—started a café called the Quatre Gats (Four Cats), meaning to make it *the* place for artists and art lovers to gather. (One of their wisest decisions was to mount a show, in February 1900, for an up-and-coming young painter named Pablo Picasso.) The exterior was decorated with figures by sculptor Eusebi Arnau (1864–1934). Inside, Els Quatre Gats hasn't changed one iota: pride of place goes to the Casas self-portait, smoking his pipe, comically teamed up on a tandem bicycle with Romeu. Drop in for a café con leche and you just might end up seated in Picasso's chair. ✉ *Carrer Montsió 3 bis, Barri Gòtic* ☎ *93/302–4140* ⊕ *www.4gats.com* Ⓜ *Pl. Catalunya, L4 Jaume I, L4 Urquinaona.*

Generalitat de Catalunya
NOTABLE BUILDING | Opposite city hall, the Palau de la Generalitat is the seat of the autonomous Catalan government. Seen through the front windows of this ornate 15th-century palace, the gilded ceiling of the Saló de Sant Jordi (St. George's Hall),

named for Catalonia's dragon-slaying patron saint, gives an idea of the lavish decor within. Carrer del Bisbe, running along the right side of the building from the square to the cathedral, offers a favorite photo op: the ornate gargoyle-bedecked Gothic bridge overhead, connecting the Generalitat to the building across the street. The Generalitat opens to the public on the second and fourth weekends of the month, with free one-hour guided tours in English (request in advance), through the Generalitat website. There are carillon concerts here on Sunday at noon, another opportunity to see inside. ⌂ *Pl. de Sant Jaume 4, Barri Gòtic* ☎ *9393/402–4600* ⊕ *www.gencat. cat* Ⓜ *L4 Jaume I, L3 Liceu.*

★ Museu d'Història de Barcelona
(*Museum of the History of Barcelona [MUHBA]*)

HISTORY MUSEUM | This fascinating museum just off Plaça del Rei traces Barcelona's evolution from its first Iberian settlement through its Roman and Visigothic ages and beyond. The Romans took the city during the Punic Wars, and you can tour underground remains of their Colonia Favencia Iulia Augusta Paterna Barcino (Favored Colony of the Father Julius Augustus Barcino) via metal walkways. Some 43,000 square feet of archaeological artifacts, from the walls of houses, to mosaics and fluted columns, workshops (for pressing olive oil and salted fish paste), and street systems, can be found in large part beneath the plaça. See how the Visigoths and their descendants built the early medieval walls on top of these ruins, recycling chunks of Roman stone and concrete, bits of columns, and even headstones. In the ground-floor gallery is a striking collection of marble busts and funerary urns discovered in the course of the excavations. Guided tours are available in English at 10:30 am daily, but have to be reserved in advance. ⌂ *Palau Padellàs, Pl. del Rei s/n, Barri Gòtic* ☎ *93/256–2100* ⊕ *ajuntament. barcelona.cat/museuhistoria/en* 🚊 *From*

€7; free with Barcelona Card, Sat. and the first Sun. of month ☉ *Closed Mon.* Ⓜ *L4 Jaume I, L3 Liceu.*

Palau del Lloctinent (*Lieutenant's Palace*)

CASTLE/PALACE | The three facades of the Palau face Carrer dels Comtes de Barcelona on the cathedral side, the Baixada de Santa Clara, and Plaça del Rei. Typical of late Gothic–early Renaissance Catalan design, it was constructed by Antoni Carbonell between 1549 and 1557, and remains one of the Gothic Quarter's most graceful buildings. The heavy stone arches over the entry, the central patio, and the intricately coffered wooden roof over the stairs are all good examples of noble 16th-century architecture. The door on the stairway is a 1975 Josep Maria Subirachs work portraying scenes from the life of Sant Jordi and the history of Catalonia. The Palau del Lloctinent was inhabited by the king's official emissary or viceroy to Barcelona during the 16th and 17th centuries; it now houses the historical materials of the Archivo de la Corona de Aragón (Archive of the Crown of Aragon), and offers an excellent exhibit on the life and times of Jaume I, one of early Catalonia's most important figures. The patio also occasionally hosts early-music concerts, and during the Corpus Christi celebration is one of the main venues for the ou com balla, when an egg "dances" on the fountain amid an elaborate floral display. ⌂ *Carrer dels Comtes de Barcelona 2, Barri Gòtic* ☎ *93/485–4285 archives office* Ⓜ *L4 Jaume I.*

★ Plaça del Rei

PLAZA/SQUARE | This little square is as compact a nexus of history as anything the Barri Gòtic has to offer. Long held to be the scene of Columbus's triumphal return from his first voyage to the New World—the precise spot where Ferdinand and Isabella received him is purportedly on the stairs fanning out from the corner of the square—the **Palau Reial Major** (admission included in the €7 entrance fee for the Museu d'Història de Barcelona; closed Monday) was the official royal residence in Barcelona. The main room is the **Saló del Tinell,** a magnificent banquet hall built in 1362. To the left is the **Palau del Lloctinent** (Lieutenant's Palace); towering overhead in the corner is the dark 15th-century **Torre Mirador del Rei Martí** (King Martin's Watchtower). ⊠ *Pl. del Rei s/n, Barri Gòtic* Ⓜ *L3 Liceu, L4 Jaume I.*

★ Plaça Sant Felip Neri

PLAZA/SQUARE | A tiny square just behind Plaça de Garriga Bachs off the side of the cloister of the Catedral de la Seu, this was once a burial ground for Barcelona's executed heroes and villains, before all church graveyards were moved to the south side of Montjuïc, the present site of the municipal cemetery. The church of San Felip Neri here is a frequent venue for classical concerts. On January 30th, 1938, one of Franco's bombs fell in the square, taking the lives of 42 people, most of whom were children from the School of Sant Philip Neri. Fragments of a bomb made the pockmarks that are still visible on the walls of the church. These days, the schoolchildren still play in the square, which is cherished by locals for its silence and serenity (at least when the children are indoors), despite its tragic history. ⊠ *Pl. Sant Felip Neri, Barri Gòtic* Ⓜ *L3 Liceu, L4 Jaume I.*

Plaça Sant Jaume

PLAZA/SQUARE | Facing each other across this oldest epicenter of Barcelona (and often on politically opposite sides as well) are the seat of Catalonia's regional government, the Generalitat de Catalunya, in the **Palau de La Generalitat,** and the City Hall, the Ajuntament de Barcelona, in the **Casa de la Ciutat.** This square was the site of the Roman forum 2,000 years ago, though subsequent construction filled the space with buildings. The square was cleared in the 1840s, but the two imposing government buildings are actually much older: the Ajuntament dates from

the 14th century, and the Generalitat was built between the 15th and mid-17th century. ⊠ *Pl. Sant Jaume, Barri Gòtic* Ⓜ *Jaume I.*

Restaurants

★ Caelis

$$$$ | CATALAN | In the Hotel Ohla Barcelona, Caelis keeps its Michelin-starred, fine-dining style and adds the pizzazz of open-kitchen show cooking. The two tasting menus (€92 and €135) change regularly and there is also a 15-course vegetarian menu for €92. **Known for:** Michelin star; lunchtime menu option; tasting menus for carnivores and vegetarians. Ⓢ *Average main: €92* ⊠ *Via Laietana 49, Barri Gòtic* ✦ *Inside Hotel Ohla Barcelona* ☎ *93/510–1205* ⊕ *www.caelis.com* ⊘ *Closed Sun. and Mon. No lunch Tues.* Ⓜ *Urquinaona.*

Cafè de l'Acadèmia

$$ | CATALAN | With wicker chairs, stone walls, and classical music, this place is sophisticated-rustic in style. Contemporary Mediterranean cuisine specialties such as roast vegetable "timbale" with black sausage and Parmesan or eggplant terrine with goat cheese, make it more than just a café. **Known for:** politician crowd; lively terrace; great set lunch. Ⓢ *Average main: €17* ⊠ *Lledó 1, Barri Gòtic* ☎ *93/319–8253* ⊘ *Closed weekends, and 3 wks in Aug.* Ⓜ *Jaume I.*

★ Informal

$$$ | CATALAN | Discreetly tucked away on the ground floor of the impeccable The Serras hotel, local star chef Marc Gascons has outdone himself with this superb bistro-style restaurant. With upscale takes on tapas and modern twists on traditional Catalan food, the menu here is like a hip, contemporary version of what a Barcelona grandma would serve for Sunday dinner. **Known for:** Michelin-starred chef; creative patatas bravas; contemporary twist on Catalan classics. Ⓢ *Average main: €25* ⊠ *Passeig*

El Call: The Jewish Quarter

Barcelona's Jewish Quarter, El Call (a name derived from the Hebrew word *qahal*, or "meeting place"), is just to the Rambla side of the Palau de la Generalitat. Carrer del Call, Carrer de Sant Domènec del Call, Carrer Marlet, and Arc de Sant Ramón del Call mark the heart of the medieval ghetto. Confined by law to this area at the end of the 7th century (one reason the streets in Calls or Aljamas were so narrow was that their inhabitants could only build into the streets for more space), Barcelona's Jews were the private bankers to Catalonia's sovereign counts (only Jews could legally lend money). The Jewish community also produced many leading physicians, translators, and scholars in medieval Barcelona, largely because the Jewish faith rested on extensive Talmudic and textual study, thus promoting a high degree of literacy. The reproduction of a plaque bearing Hebrew text on the corner of Carrer Marlet and Arc de Sant Ramón del Call was the only physical reminder of the Jewish presence here until the medieval synagogue reopened as a historical site in 2003.

The **Sinagoga Major de Barcelona** (*Carrer Marlet 2, Barri Gòtic, Standard summer opening hours are weekdays 10:30–6:30, Sunday 10:30–3 [closed Saturday], but this may vary due to religious and other holidays so best to verify online at* ⊕ *www.sinagogamayor.com*), the restored original synagogue at the corner of Marlet and Sant Domènec del Call, is virtually all that survives of the Jewish presence in medieval Barcelona. Tours are given in English, Hebrew, and Spanish; admission costs €3.50 and includes a booklet in English explaining the history of the community.

The story of Barcelona's Jewish community came to a bloody end in August 1391, when during a time of famine and pestilence a nationwide outbreak of anti-Semitic violence reached Barcelona, with catastrophic results: nearly the entire Jewish population was murdered or forced to convert to Christianity. This resulted in a centuries-long end to public Jewish life in the city.

8

Barcelona   BARRI GÒTIC

de Colom 9, Barri Gòtic ☎ 93/169–1869 ⊕ *restauranteinformal.com/en* ⊗ *Closed Mon., Tues.* Ⓜ *Barceloneta L4.*

Irati Taverna Basca

$$ | BASQUE | There's only one drawback to this lively Basque bar between Plaça del Pi and La Rambla: it's narrow at the street end, and harder to squeeze into than the Barcelona metro at rush hour. Skip the tapas on the bar and opt for the plates brought out piping-hot from the kitchen. **Known for:** txakoli sparkling wine; quick bites; Basque specialties. Ⓢ *Average main: €22* ⊠ *Cardenal Casañas 17,*

Barri Gòtic ☎ 93/302–3084 ⊕ *gruposagar-di.com/restaurante/irati-taverna-basca* Ⓜ *Liceu.*

Koy Shunka

$$$$ | JAPANESE | Two blocks away from their mothership Shunka, partners Hideki Matsuhisa and Xu Zhangchao have done it again. This time, with more space to work with, the Japanese-Chinese team of master chefs has been awarded a Michelin star for their tribute to Asian fusion cooking, based on products from the Catalan larder. **Known for:** inventive fusion cuisine; contemporary

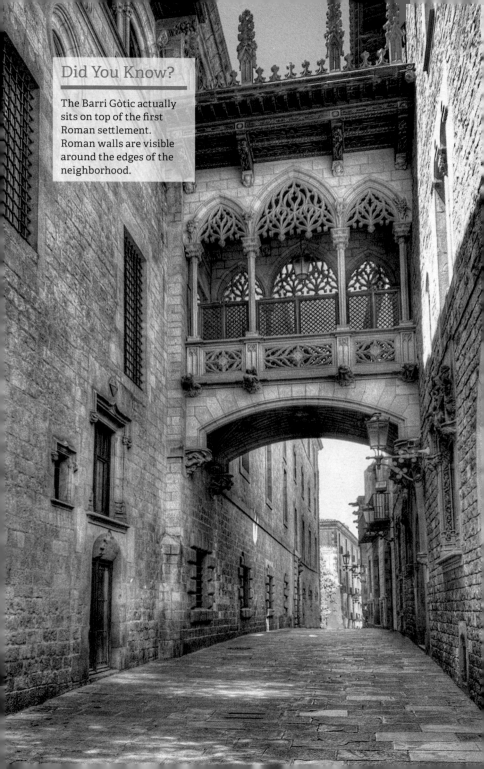

Did You Know?

The Barri Gòtic actually sits on top of the first Roman settlement. Roman walls are visible around the edges of the neighborhood.

atmosphere; scrumptious cerdo ibérico. [$] *Average main: €95* ✉ *Copons 7, Barri Gòtic* ☎ *93/412–7939* 🌐 *www.koyshunka.com* ⏲ *Closed Mon., Tues., 3 wks in Aug., and 2 wks at Christmas. No dinner Sun.* [M] *Urquinaona.*

Pla

$ | **CATALAN** | Filled with couples night after night, this dining spot is candle-lit and sleekly designed in glass over ancient stone, brick, and wood. The cuisine is light and contemporary, featuring inventive salads and fresh seafood, as well as options for vegetarians and vegans. **Known for:** vegetarian options; extensive wine list; romantic ambience. [$] *Average main: €15* ✉ *Bellafila 5, Barri Gòtic* ☎ *93/412–6552* 🌐 *www.restaurant-pla.cat* ⏲ *No lunch weekdays* [M] *Jaume I.*

Hotels

Arai 4* Aparthotel Barcelona (*Arai-Palau Dels Quatre Rius Monument*)

$$$ | **HOTEL** | **FAMILY** | You couldn't ask for a better location from which to explore Barcelona's Barri Gòtic—or for a bivouac more elegant—than one of the aparthotel suites in this stunning restoration. **Pros:** warm and attentive service; free admission to Egyptian Museum of Barcelona; historic character retained in former palace. **Cons:** seedy area; on busy street; rooms on the top floor lack historic charm. [$] *Rooms from: €200* ✉ *Avinyó 30, Barri Gòtic* ☎ *93/320–3950* 🌐 *www.hotelarai.com* 🍴 *No Meals* 🛏 *31 rooms* [M] *L3 Liceu.*

Catalunya Portal d'Angel

$ | **HOTEL** | Converted in 1998 from a historic stately home dating back to 1825, the Catalunya Portal d'Angel beckons with its neoclassic facade and original grand marble staircase. **Pros:** pleasant breakfast pavilion in the garden; includes walking tours of the Old City and the Eixample; great location. **Cons:** faces busy pedestrian mall; small rooms; lighting needs improvement. [$] *Rooms from: €90* ✉ *Av. Portal d'Angel 17, Barri Gòtic* ☎ *93/318–4141* 🌐 *www.cataloniahotels.com/en/hotel/catalonia-portal-del-angel* 🛏 *82 rooms, 1 suite* 🍴 *No Meals* [M] *Pl. Catalunya.*

Duquesa de Cardona

$$ | **HOTEL** | A refurbished 16th-century town house, built when the Passeig de Colom in front was lined with the summer homes of the nobility, this hotel on the waterfront is a five-minute walk from everything in the Barri Gòtic and Barceloneta, and no more than a 30-minute walk to the Eixample. **Pros:** dreamy location; glass of cava on check-in; 24-hour room service. **Cons:** pricey for a four-star; no spa; rooms on the small side. [$] *Rooms from: €150* ✉ *Passeig de Colom 12, Barri Gòtic* ☎ *93/268–9090* 🌐 *www.hduquesadecardona.com* 🛏 *51 rooms* 🍴 *No Meals* [M] *L4 Barceloneta, L3 Drassanes.*

Grand Hotel Central

$$$$ | **HOTEL** | **FAMILY** | At the edge of the Gothic Quarter, very near the Barcelona cathedral, this fashionable midtown hotel is popular with business and pleasure travelers alike, with contemporary decor and upscale amenities. **Pros:** Mediterranean City Bar and Restaurant on-site; infinity pool with breath-taking city views; excellent location between the Gothic Quarter and the Born. **Cons:** busy thoroughfare outside; sometimes seems very business-y; pricey breakfast. [$] *Rooms from: €280* ✉ *Via Laietana 30, Barri Gòtic* ☎ *93/295–7900* 🌐 *www.grandhotelcentral.com* 🛏 *147 rooms* 🍴 *No Meals* [M] *L4 Jaume I.*

★ Hotel Neri

$$$$ | **HOTEL** | Just steps from the cathedral, in the heart of the city's old Jewish Quarter, this elegant, upscale, boutique hotel, part of the prestigious Relais & Chateaux hotel group, marries ancient and avant-garde designs. **Pros:** set in a restored medieval palace; ideal, central location (in the middle of Barri Gòtic); barbecue and occasional live music on the

rooftop terrace. **Cons:** limited loungers by the rooftop pool; noisy on summer nights and school days; very pricey. [$] *Rooms from: €260* ✉ *Carrer Sant Sever 5, Barri Gòtic* ☎ *93/304–0655* 🌐 *www.hotelneri.com/en* 🛏 *22 rooms, 6 apartments* 🍴 *No Meals* [M] *L3 Liceu, L4 Jaume I.*

★ Kimpton Vividora Hotel

$$$ | **HOTEL** | Every Kimpton hotel is designed to reflect the character of the city it inhabits and, in the case of Kimpton Vividora, that means deep blues and earthy terra-cotta hues mixed with bright splashes of color and a rooftop terrace with views that are guaranteed to make you swoon. **Pros:** stunning rooftop bar with views; a design-lover's dream; great food at Café Got and Fauna restaurant. **Cons:** no parking available; small rooftop pool; touristy location. [$] *Rooms from: €175* ✉ *Duc 15, Barri Gòtic* ☎ *93/548–4611* 🌐 *kimptonvividorahotel.com/en* 🍴 *No Meals* 🛏 *166 rooms* [M] *Catalunya L1, L3.*

Mercer Hotel Barcelona

$$$$ | **HOTEL** | On a narrow side street near Plaça Sant Jaume, this romantic boutique hotel, a medieval town house, is among the most spectacular examples of Barcelona's signature genius for the redesign and rebirth of historical properties. **Pros:** breakfast in glassed-in patio; in the heart of the Old City; comfortable rooftop terrace with a plunge pool and (in season) a bar-café. **Cons:** no gym or spa; very pricey; expensive breakfast. [$] *Rooms from: €300* ✉ *Carrer dels Lledó 5, Barri Gòtic* ☎ *93/310–7480* 🌐 *www.mercerbarcelona.com/en* 🛏 *28 rooms* 🍴 *No Meals* [M] *L4 Jaume I.*

★ Ohla Barcelona

$$$ | **HOTEL** | One of Barcelona's top design hotels (also with incredible food), the Ohla has a neoclassical exterior (not counting the playful eyeballs stuck to the facade) that belies its avant-garde interior, full of witty, design-conscious touches. **Pros:** high-end wines at Vistro49; rooftop terrace and pool; remarkable restaurant Caelis on-site. **Cons:** uncomfortable furniture in lobby; adjacent to noisy Via Laietana; some rooms are small. [$] *Rooms from: €221* ✉ *Via Laietana 49, Barri Gòtic* ☎ *93/341–5050* 🌐 *www.ohlabarcelona.com* 🛏 *74 rooms* 🍴 *Free Breakfast* [M] *L4 Urquinaona.*

★ The Serras

$$$$ | **HOTEL** | If you're looking for an ultra-exclusive boutique hotel that offers superb comfort, discretion, excellent facilities, and outstanding, personalized service, this is it. **Pros:** excellent restaurant Informal; dreamy "El Sueño" rooftop terrace with show-stopping views; outstanding, personalized service. **Cons:** hard on the budget; no sauna or spa; rooms on the smaller side. [$] *Rooms from: €350* ✉ *Passeig Colom 9, Barri Gòtic* ☎ *93/169–1868* 🌐 *www.hoteltheserrasbarcelona.com* 🛏 *28 rooms* 🍴 *No Meals* [M] *L4 Barceloneta.*

🍸 Nightlife

Medieval Barri Gòtic is a wanderer's paradise filled with ancient winding streets, majestic squares, and myriad period-perfect wine bars and dimly lighted pubs found in the hidden corners of labyrinthine alleyways.

BARS

El Paraigua

COCKTAIL LOUNGES | This eatery's stunning Moderniste facade—intricately carved wood, an exquisite vintage register, and other delicate reminders of its former incarnation as a turn-of-the-20th-century umbrella shop—is usually enough to lure newcomers inside for a closer look. But for fiesta-loving night owls, the real attraction is downstairs in the arched, exposed-brick cocktail club, a former convent basement offering first-rate cocktails and weekend jazz concerts in a note-perfect setting. ✉ *Carrer del Pas de l'Ensenyança 2, Barri Gòtic* ☎ *93/317–1479* 🌐 *www.elparaigua.com* [M] *Jaume I.*

Harlem Jazz Club

LIVE MUSIC | Located on a rare tree-lined street in the Barri Gòtic, this club attracts patrons of all ages and musical tastes. Listen to live Cuban salsa, swing, and reggae while enjoying killer cocktails in a relaxed and friendly atmosphere. Most concerts start around 10 or 11 pm and finish around 1 am, and many people linger until closing time. ⊠ Comtessa de Sobradiel 8, Barri Gòtic ☎ 93/310–0755 ⊕ www.harlemjazzclub.es Ⓜ Jaume I, Liceu.

La Vinateria del Call

WINE BARS | Located in the heart of Barcelona's former Jewish Quarter, this rustic charmer serves a wide variety of hearty national wines paired with regional cheeses, meats, and tapas. Popular with wine-loving romantics for its antique carved-wood furnishings and candlelit setting, the venue also attracts visitors and regulars looking for a respite from the area's chaotic pace. ⊠ Salomó ben Adret, 9, Barri Gòtic ☎ 93/302–6092 ⊕ www.lavinateriadelcall.com Ⓜ Liceu, Jaume I.

Milk

BARS | Resembling a prim parlor lounge with touches of kitsch, this cozy bar bistro with plush sofas, gilded mirrors, handmade knickknacks, and tastefully worn tapestry wallpaper has been a favorite hangout for young expats for more than a decade. Best known for its legendary brunch, night time here tends to be less crowded and more intimate. Try the Michelada, a dramatic alternative Bloody Mary reserved for the strongest constitutions: Corona beer mixed with hot sauce, Worcestershire, and tomato juice. ⊠ Gignas 21, Barri Gòtic ☎ 93/268–0922 ⊕ www.milkbarcelona.com Ⓜ Jaume I.

★ Ocaña

DANCE CLUBS | Located in a trio of ancient mansions on buzzy Plaça Reial's southern flank, this venue is dedicated to Jose Peréz Ocaña, a cross-dressing artist, LGBTQ activist and proud bohemian, and a dominating figure of Barcelona's decadent post-Franco explosion of alternative culture. With an adjoining Mediterranean restaurant, as well as a sizable café bar, club, and cocktail lounge, Ocaña also has the fiercest drag queen hostesses on the square. ⊠ Pl. Reial 13–15, Barri Gòtic ☎ 93/676–4814 ⊕ www.ocana.cat Ⓜ Drassanes.

Sidecar Factory Club

DANCE CLUBS | A mainstay of the decadent nightlife centered on Plaça Reial, this long-running music club has never fallen out of fashion—in fact, it attracts new fans just as the old ones bow out. With a firm focus showcasing up-and-coming indie talent, the venue offers a way to discover new favorites in moody neon red surroundings. ⊠ Pl. Reial 7, Barri Gòtic ☎ 93/317–7666 ⊕ www.sidecar.es Ⓜ Drassanes.

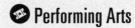 Performing Arts

FLAMENCO

Barcelona's flamenco scene is surprisingly vibrant for a culture so far removed from Andalusia. Los Tarantos, in Plaça Reial, is a must for its authentic flamenco performances.

Los Tarantos

FOLK/TRADITIONAL DANCE | This small basement boîte spotlights some of Andalusia's best flamenco in 30-minute shows of dance, percussion, and song. These shows are a good intro to the art and feel much less touristy than most standard flamenco fare. Shows are daily at 7:30, 8:30, and 9:30 pm. ⊠ Pl. Reial 17, Barri Gòtic ☎ 93/304–1210 ⊕ www.tarantos-barcelona.com/en Ⓜ Liceu.

Shopping

The Barri Gòtic was built on trade and cottage industries, and there are plenty of nimble fingers producing artisan goods in the old-world shops along its stone streets. Start at the cathedral and work your way outward.

ART GALLERIES

Sala Parès

ART GALLERIES | The dean of Barcelona's art galleries, this place is the oldest art gallery in Barcelona. It opened in 1840 as an art-supplies shop; as a gallery, it dates to 1877 and has shown every Barcelona artist of note since then. Picasso and Miró exhibited their work here, as did Casas and Rossinyol before them. Nowadays, Catalan artists like Perico Pastor and Carlos Morago get pride of place. ✉ *Petritxol 5, Barri Gòtic* ☎ *93/318–7020* ⊕ *salapares.com* ⊘ *Closed Sun. and Mon.* Ⓜ *Liceu, Catalunya.*

CERAMICS AND GLASSWARE

★ Art Escudellers

CERAMICS | Ceramic pieces from all over Spain are on display at this large store across the street from the restaurant Los Caracoles; more than 140 different artisans are represented, with maps showing what part of Spain the work is from. Wine, cheese, and ham tastings are held downstairs, and you can even throw a pot yourself in the workshop. There are four other branches of Art Escudellers in the old city, including one on the Carrer Avinyó. ✉ *Escudellers 23, Barri Gòtic* ☎ *93/412–6801* ⊕ *www.artescudellers. com* Ⓜ *Liceu, Drassanes.*

CLOTHING

Sombrereria Obach

HATS & GLOVES | This *sombrerería* (hat shop) is as much part of the Barri Gòtic's landscape as any of its medieval churches. Occupying a busy corner in El Call—the old Jewish district—curved glass windows displays the sort of hats, caps, and berets that have been dressing heads in Barcelona since 1924. Styles are classic and timeless, from traditional Basque berets to Stetsons and panamas. ✉ *Call 2, Barri Gòtic* ☎ *93/318–4094* ⊕ *www. sombrereriaobach.com* ⊲ *Closed Sun.* Ⓜ *Jaume I, Liceu.*

Catalan Flamenco

Barcelona has a burgeoning and erudite flamenco scene, even if the dance is imported from Andalusia. For the best flamenco in Barcelona, consult listings and concierges and don't be put off if the venue seems touristy—these venues often book the best artists. Barcelona-born *cantaors* include Mayte Martín and Miguel Poveda. Keep an eye on the billboards for such names as Estrella Morente (daughter of the late, great Enrique Morente) and Chano Domínguez (who often appears at the Barcelona Jazz Festival).

FOOD

Caelum

FOOD | At the corner of Carrer de la Palla and Banys Nous, this café and shop sells wines and foodstuffs such as honey, biscuits, chocolates, and preserves made in convents and monasteries all over Spain. You can pop in to pick up an exquisitely packaged pot of jam, or linger over pastries and coffee in the tearoom, part of which is housed in an old medieval bathhouse in the candlelit basement. ✉ *De la Palla 8, Barri Gòtic* ☎ *93/302–6993* ⊘ *Closed Sun.* Ⓜ *Liceu, Jaume I.*

La Casa del Bacalao

FOOD | This cult store decorated with cod-fishing memorabilia specializes in salt cod and books of codfish recipes. Slabs of salt and dried cod, used in a wide range of Catalan recipes (such as esqueixada, in which shredded strips of raw salt cod are served in a marinade of oil and vinegar) can be vacuum-packed for portability. ✉ *Moles 11, just off Portal de l'Àngel, Barri Gòtic* ☎ *93/301–6539* ⊕ *lacasadelbacalao.es* ⊲ *Closed Sun.* Ⓜ *Catalunya.*

GIFTS AND SOUVENIRS
Artesania Catalunya – CCAM
CRAFTS | In 2010 the Catalan government created the registered trademark Empremtes de Catalunya to represent Catalan artisans and to make sure that visitors get the real deal when buying what they believe to be genuine products. The official shop now sells jewelry re-created from eras dating back to pre-Roman times, Gaudí-inspired sculptures, traditional Cava mugs, and some bravely avant-garde objects from young artisans—all officially sanctioned as fit to represent the city. ⊠ *Banys Nous 11, Barri Gòtic* ☎ *93/467–4660* ⊕ *ccam.gencat.cat/ca/inici* ☉ *Closed Sun. afternoon* Ⓜ *Jaume I, Liceu.*

Cereria Subirà
CRAFTS | Known as the city's oldest shop, having remained open since 1761 (though it was not always a candle store), this "waxery" (*cereria*) offers candles in all sizes and shapes, ranging from wild mushrooms to the Montserrat massif, home of the Benedictine abbey dear to the heart of every barcelonin. ⊠ *Baixada Llibreteria 7, Barri Gòtic* ☎ *93/315–2606* ⊕ *www.cereriasubira.cat/en* ☞ *Closed Sun.* Ⓜ *Jaume I.*

MARKETS
Mercat Gòtic
MARKET | A browser's bonanza, this interesting if somewhat pricey Thursday (9 am–8 pm) market for antique clothing, jewelry, and art objects occupies the plaza in front of the cathedral. ⊠ *Av. Plaça de la Catedral, Barri Gòtic* ⊕ *www.mercatgoticbcn.com* ☉ *Closed Fri.–Wed. and Aug.* Ⓜ *Jaume I, Urquinaona.*

Plaça del Pi
MARKET | On random days, this little square fills with the interesting tastes and aromas of a natural-produce market (honeys, cheeses) throughout the month, while neighboring Plaça Sant Josep Oriol holds a painter's market every Sunday. ⊠ *Pl. del Pi, Barri Gòtic* Ⓜ *Catalunya, Liceu.*

SHOES
★ La Manual Alpargatera
SHOES | If you appreciate old-school craftsmanship in footwear and reasonable prices, visit this boutique just off Carrer Ferran. Handmade rope-sole sandals and espadrilles are the specialty, and this shop has sold them to everyone—including the pope. The flat, beribboned espadrilles model used for dancing the *sardana* is available, as are fashionable wedge heels with peep toes and comfy slippers. The cost of a pair of espadrilles here might put you back about $50, which is far less than the same quality shoes in the United States. They offer free express shipping worldwide for orders over €150. ⊠ *Avinyó 7, Barri Gòtic* ☎ *93/301–0172* ⊕ *www.lamanual.com* Ⓜ *Liceu, Jaume I.*

El Raval

El Raval (from *arrabal,* meaning "suburb" or "slum") is the area to the west of La Rambla, on the right as you walk toward the port. Originally a rough quarter outside the second set of city walls that ran down the left side of La Rambla, El Raval was once notorious for its Barri Xinès (or Barrio Chino) red-light district, the lurid attractions of which are known to have fascinated a young Pablo Picasso.

Gypsies, acrobats, prostitutes, and *saltimbanques* (clowns and circus performers) who made this area their home soon found immortality in the many canvases Picasso painted of them during his Blue Period. It was the ladies of the night on Carrer Avinyó, not far from the Barri Xinès, who may have inspired one of the 20th-century's most famous paintings, Picasso's *Les Demoiselles d'Avignon,* an important milestone on the road to Cubism. Not bad for a city slum.

El Raval, though still rough-and-tumble, has been gentrified and much improved since 1980, largely as a result of the construction of the Museu d'Art Contemporani de Barcelona (MACBA) and other cultural institutions nearby, such as the Centre de Cultura Contemporània (CCCB), Filmoteca, and the Convent dels Àngels. La Rambla del Raval has been opened up between Carrer de l'Hospital and Drassanes, bringing light and air into the streets of the Raval for the first time in a thousand years. The medieval Hospital de la Santa Creu, Plaça del Pedró, the Mercat de Sant Antoni, and Sant Pau del Camp are highlights of this funky, rough-edged part of Barcelona.

Sights

★ Antic Hospital de la Santa Creu i Sant Pau

HISTORIC SIGHT | Founded in the 10th century as one of Europe's earliest medical facilities, the mostly 15th- and 16th-century complex contains some of Barcelona's most impressive Gothic architecture. From the grand entrance, the first building on the left is the 18th-century **Reial Acadèmia de Cirurgia i Medicina** (Royal Academy of Surgery and Medicine); the surgical amphitheater is kept just as it was in the days when students learned by observing dissections. Through a gate to the left of the Casa de Convalescència is the garden-courtyard of the hospital complex, the **Jardins de Rubió i Lluc,** centered on a baroque cross and lined with orange trees. On the right is the **Biblioteca Nacional de Catalunya,** Catalonia's national library. The library is spectacular: two parallel halls—once the core of the hospital—230 feet long, with towering Gothic arches and vaulted ceilings, designed in the 15th century by the architect of the church of Santa Maria del Pi, Guillem Abiell. This was the hospital where Antoni Gaudí was taken, unrecognized and assumed to be a pauper, after he was struck by a trolley on June 7, 1926. ⊠ *Carrer Hospital 56 (or Carrer del Carme 45), El Raval* ☎ *93/327–0125 Reial Acadèmia de Medicina, 93/270–2300 Biblioteca de Catalunya* ⊕ *www.bnc. cat* 🖾 *From €8* ⊙ *Royal Academy of Medicine: closed Sun.–Tues., Thurs., and Fri; Biblioteca de Catalunya and Capella: closed Sun.* Ⓜ *L3 Liceu.*

Centre de Cultura Contemporànea de Barcelona (*CCCB*)

ARTS CENTER | Just next door to the MACBA, this multidisciplinary gallery, lecture hall, and concert and exhibition space offers a year-round program of cultural events and projects. The center also has a remarkable film archive of historic shorts and documentaries, free to the public. Housed in the restored and renovated Casa de la Caritat, a former medieval convent and hospital, the CCCB, like the Palau de la Música Catalana, is one of the city's shining examples of contemporary flare added to traditional architecture and design. A smoked-glass wall on the right side of the patio, designed by architects Albert Villaplana and Helio Piñon, reflects out over the rooftops of El Raval to Montjuïc and the Mediterranean beyond. ⊠ *Carrer Montalegre 5, El Raval* ☎ *93/306–4100* ⊕ *www.cccb.org* 🖾 *Exhibitions €6; Sun. 3–8, free. Admission to CCCB Film Archive is free* ⊙ *Closed Mon.* Ⓜ *L1/L2 Universitat, Catalunya.*

Hotel España

NOTABLE BUILDING | Just off La Rambla behind the Liceu opera house on Carrer Sant Pau is the Hotel España, remodeled in 1904 by Lluís Domènech i Montaner, architect of the Moderniste flagship Palau de la Música Catalana. Completely refurbished in 2010, the interior is notable for its Art Nouveau decor. The sculpted marble Eusebi Arnau fireplace in the bar, the Ramon Casas undersea murals in the salon (mermaids singing each to each), and the lushly ornate dining room are the hotel's best artistic features. The España is so proud of its place in the cultural history of the city—and justly so—it opens to the public for 40-minute guided tours, usually once a week on Thursdays. Check their website for times. (Note that

One of the earliest medical complexes in Europe is the Antic Hospital de la Santa Creu i Sant Pau.

tours are usually in Spanish or Catalan, but English can be requested.) ⊠ *Carrer Sant Pau 9–11, El Raval* ☏ *93/550–0000* ⊕ *www.hotelespanya.com* ✉ *Tour €5 (free for hotel and restaurant guests)* Ⓜ *L3 Liceu.*

Mercat de Sant Antoni

MARKET | A mammoth hangar at the junction of Ronda de Sant Antoni and Comte d'Urgell, designed in 1882 by Antoni Rovira i Trias, the Mercat de Sant Antoni is considered the city's finest example of wrought-iron architecture. The Greek-cross-shaped market covers an entire block on the edge of the Eixample, and some of the best Moderniste stall facades in Barcelona distinguish this exceptional space. Fully functioning as of 2017 after years of painstaking restoration to incorporate medieval archaeological remains underneath, the market is a foodie paradise of fruit, vegetables, fish, cheeses, and more. On Sunday morning, visit Sant Antoni, and wander the outdoor stalls of the weekly flea market full of stamps and coins, comic books and trading cards, VHS, CDs, vinyl, and vintage clothing. ⊠ *Carrer Comte d'Urgell s/n, El Raval* ☏ *93/426–3521* ⊕ *www. mercatdesantantoni.com* ⊘ *Closed Sun.* Ⓜ *L2 Sant Antoni.*

★ Museu d'Art Contemporani de Barcelona
(*Barcelona Museum of Contemporary Art, MACBA*)

ART MUSEUM | **FAMILY** | Designed by American architect Richard Meier in 1992, this gleaming explosion of light and geometry in El Raval houses a permanent collection of contemporary art, and also regularly mounts special temporary exhibitions. Meier gives a nod to Gaudí (with the Pedrera-like wave on one end of the main facade), but his minimalist building otherwise looks unfinished. That said, the MACBA is unarguably an important addition to the cultural capital of this once-shabby neighborhood. The MACBA's 20th-century art collection (Calder, Rauschenberg, Oteiza, Chillida, Tàpies) is excellent, while the free app offers a useful introduction to the philosophical foundations of contemporary art as well

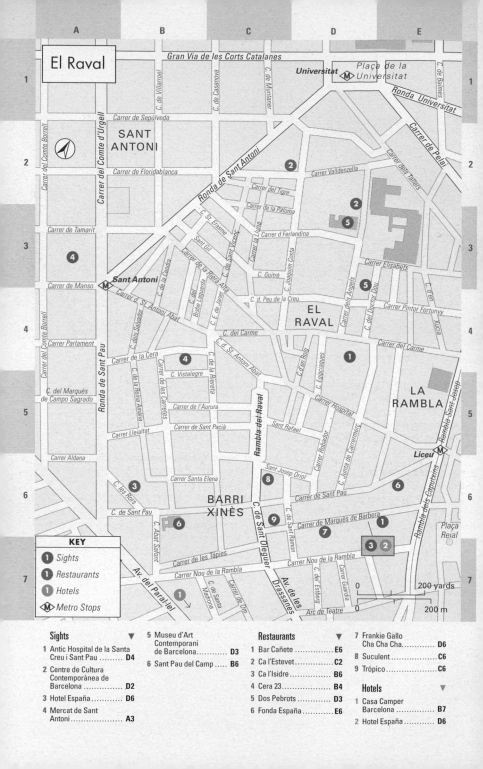

El Raval

SANT ANTONI

EL RAVAL

LA RAMBLA

BARRI XINÈS

KEY

- **1** Sights
- **1** Restaurants
- **1** Hotels
- **M** Metro Stops

0   200 yards

0   200 m

Sights ▼

1 Antic Hospital de la Santa Creu i Sant Pau **D4**

2 Centre de Cultura Contemporània de Barcelona **D2**

3 Hotel España **D6**

4 Mercat de Sant Antoni **A3**

5 Museu d'Art Contemporani de Barcelona............ **D3**

6 Sant Pau del Camp **B6**

Restaurants ▼

1 Bar Cañete **E6**

2 Ca l'Estevet............... **C2**

3 Ca l'Isidre **B6**

4 Cera 23 .... **B4**

5 Dos Pebrots **D3**

6 Fonda España **E6**

7 Frankie Gallo Cha Cha Cha............ **D6**

8 Suculent **C6**

9 Trópico.................... **C6**

Hotels ▼

1 Casa Camper Barcelona **B7**

2 Hotel España **D6**

as the pieces themselves. The museum also offers wonderful workshops and activities for kids. ✉ *Pl. dels Àngels 1, El Raval* ☎ *93/412–0810* ⊕ *www.macba.cat* ✆ *€11 (€10 online), free Sat. after 4 p.m.* ⊘ *Closed Tues.* Ⓜ *L1/L2 Universitat, L1/L3 Catalunya.*

★ Sant Pau del Camp

CHURCH | Barcelona's oldest church was originally outside the city walls (*del camp* means "in the fields") and was a Roman cemetery as far back as the 2nd century, according to archaeological evidence. What you see now was built in 1127 and is the earliest Romanesque structure in Barcelona. Elements of the church—the classical marble capitals atop the columns in the main entry— are thought to be from the 6th and 7th centuries. The hulking, mastodonic shape of the church is a reminder of the church's defensive posture in the face of intermittent Roman persecution and, later, Moorish invasions and sackings. Check for musical performances here, as the church is an acoustical gem. The tiny cloister is Sant Pau del Camp's best feature and one of Barcelona's semisecret treasures. ✉ *Carrer de Sant Pau 101, El Raval* ☎ *93/441–0001* ⊕ *stpaudelcamp.blogspot.com* ✆ *Free when Masses are celebrated; guided tour Sun. at 12:45, €5* ⊘ *Cloister closed Sun. during Mass; no tours Sun. in mid-Aug.* Ⓜ *L3 Paral.lel.*

🍽 Restaurants

★ Bar Cañete

$$ | TAPAS | A superb tapas and *platillos* (small plates) emporium, this spot just around the corner from the Liceu opera house is arguably one of Barcelona's best tapas restaurants. The interior is loud and bright, with a long bar overlooking the burners and part of the kitchen that leads down to the 20-seat communal tasting table at the end of the room. **Known for:** superb tapas; fresh seafood; Spanish ham specialists. Ⓢ *Average main: €18*

✉ *Unió 17, El Raval* ☎ *93/270–3458* ⊕ *www.barcanete.com/en* Ⓜ *Liceu.*

Ca l'Estevet

$$ | CATALAN | This restaurant has been serving up old-school Catalan cuisine to local and loyal customers since 1940 (and under a different name for 50 years before that), and the practice has been made perfect. Tuck into the likes of botifarra sausage with spinach and chickpeas, meatballs with squid and shrimp, or veal stew with wild mushrooms. **Known for:** historic location; Catalan specialties; large, hearty portions. Ⓢ *Average main: €16* ✉ *Valldonzella 46, El Raval* ☎ *93/301–2939* ⊕ *www.restauranteestevet.com* ⊘ *Closed Mon.* Ⓜ *Universitat.*

Ca l'Isidre

$$$$ | CATALAN | A throwback to an age before foams and food science took over the gastronomic world, this restaurant has elevated simplicity to the level of the spectacular since the early 1970s. Isidre and Montserrat share their encyclopedic knowledge of local cuisine with guests, while their daughter Núria cooks traditional Catalan dishes. **Known for:** art collection; once frequented by Miró and Dalí; locally sourced produce. Ⓢ *Average main: €32* ✉ *Flors 12, El Raval* ☎ *93/441–1139* ⊕ *www.calisidre.com* ⊘ *Closed Tues. and 1st 2 wks of Aug.* Ⓜ *Paral.lel.*

Cera 23

$ | SPANISH | A hidden gem among a crop of modern restaurants putting the razzle back into the run-down Raval, Cera 23 offers a winning combination of great service and robust cooking in a fun, friendly setting; stand at the bar and enjoy a blackberry mojito while you wait for your table. The open kitchen is in the dining area, so guests can watch the cooks create contemporary presentations of traditional Spanish dishes. **Known for:** exceptional service; volcano black rice; open kitchen viewable to diners. Ⓢ *Average main: €15* ✉ *Cera 23, El Raval* ☎ *93/442–0808* ⊕ *www.cera23.com* ⊘ *Closed Mon.–Wed.* Ⓜ *Sant Antoni.*

Dos Pebrots

$$ | **MEDITERRANEAN** | Albert Raurich of Dos Palillos has transformed his favorite neighborhood haunt into a cutting-edge tapas bar that explores the history of Mediterranean cuisine. Everything from the Roman condiment *garum* to 10th-century Xarab fruit salad gets reinvented in a contemporary context. **Known for:** restored original exterior; unique tapas; unusual ingredients. [$] *Average main: €20* ✉ *Doctor Dou 19, El Raval* ☎ *93/853–9598* 🌐 *www.dospebrots.com* 🕓 *Closed Mon. and Tues., and 2 wks at Christmas* [M] *Catalunya.*

★ **Fonda España**

$$$ | **CATALAN** | The sumptuous glory of this restored late-19th-century Art Nouveau dining room now has food to match, courtesy of superstar chef Martín Berasategui. Go for broke with the "gastronomic voyage" tasting menu or feast à la carte on updated period dishes such as "the mermaids"—a smooth cod pil pil (a Basque sauce)—and pigeon with a liver pâté heart, rhubarb, and green apple. **Known for:** excellent set lunches; Art Nouveau decor; satisfying traditional dishes. [$] *Average main: €23* ✉ *Sant Pau 9, El Raval* ☎ *93/550–0010* 🌐 *www.hotelespanya.com* 🕓 *Closed Mon. and Tues. No dinner Sun. No lunch in Aug.* [M] *Liceu.*

Frankie Gallo Cha Cha Cha

$ | **PIZZA** | There are days when only a pizza will do and nowhere in Barcelona does them better than Frankie Gallo Cha Cha Cha. And while the name may not roll off the tongue, Frankie Gallo Cha Cha Cha's winning combination of wood-fired sourdough pizzas, craft beer, top-notch artisanal ingredients and buzzing atmosphere is guaranteed to go down well. **Known for:** best pizza joint in town; eggplant parmigiana pizza; great atmosphere. [$] *Average main: €13* ✉ *Marquès de Barberà, 15, El Raval* ☎ *93/159–4250* 🌐 *frankiegallochachacha.com* [M] *Drassanes L3.*

★ **Suculent**

$$ | **CATALAN** | This is a strong contender for the crown of Barcelona's best bistro, as chef Toni Romero continues to turn out Catalan tapas and dishes that have roots in rustic classics but reach high modern standards of execution. The name is a twist on the Catalan *sucar lent* (to dip slowly), and excellent bread is duly provided to soak up the sauces. **Known for:** big, bold flavors; must-try steak tartare on marrow bone; set menus or à la carte. [$] *Average main: €18* ✉ *Rambla del Raval 45, El Raval* ☎ *93/443–6579* 🌐 *www.suculent.com* 🕓 *Closed Mon. and Tues.* [M] *Liceu.*

★ **Trópico**

$ | **LATIN AMERICAN** | This lively brunch spot is a breath of fresh air in an otherwise somewhat sketchy neighborhood. The name "trópico" (or tropical) refers to both the bright decor and the menu that takes inspiration from the tastes of the tropics—from Colombian *arepas*, to Brazilian chicken *coxinhas*, Thai dragon fruit smoothies, Peruvian *ají*, and Indian-style curries. **Known for:** Colombian arepas; food from the tropics; vibrant decor and atmopshere. [$] *Average main: €14* ✉ *Marquès de Barberà 24, El Raval* ☎ *93/667–7552* 🌐 *www.tropicobcn.com* [M] *Drassanes L3.*

Hotels

Casa Camper Barcelona

$$$ | **HOTEL** | A marriage between the Camper footwear empire and the (now defunct) Vinçon design store produced this 21st-century hotel halfway between La Rambla and the MACBA (Museum of Contemporary Art), with a focus on sustainability (think solar panels and water recycling) and a unique "one big family" feel. **Pros:** complimentary 24-hour snack bar; just steps from MACBA and the Boqueria; great breakfast with dishes cooked to order. **Cons:** extra per person charge for children over three years old; expensive for what you get; no in-room

minibar. $ *Rooms from: €180* ✉ *Carrer Elisabets 11, El Raval* ☎ *93/342–6280* ⊕ *www.casacamper.com* ⇆ *40 rooms* ⦿ *Free Breakfast* Ⓜ *Catalunya, L3 Liceu.*

★ Hotel España

$ | **HOTEL** | This beautifully renovated Art Nouveau gem is the second oldest (after the nearby Sant Agustí) and among the best of Barcelona's smaller hotels. **Pros:** lavish breakfast; alabaster fireplace in the bar lounge; near Liceu opera house and La Rambla. **Cons:** bed lighting could be improved; lower rooms facing Carrer Sant Pau get some street noise; no views. $ *Rooms from: €117* ✉ *Carrer Sant Pau 9–11, El Raval* ☎ *93/550–0000* ⊕ *www. hotelespanya.com* ⇆ *82 rooms* ⦿ *No Meals* Ⓜ *L4 Liceu.*

▶ Nightlife

El Raval has slowly evolved from a forgotten, seedy no-man's-land into one of the choicest districts to enjoy provocative modern art and a pulsating, boho-glam party scene. Though not to everyone's taste, hippie students, tattooed misfits, artists, and more recently trend-seeking nomads routinely bar crawl up and down a stretch of nightlife-friendly streets (Joaquin Costa is one) featuring a wide assortment of divey dens, music bars, pubs, and funky *coctelerias*.

BARS

Ambar

BARS | Right off the tree-lined Rambla del Raval, the clientele at this popular watering hole is as colorful as the snazzy, red-quilted bar and moody green-blue lighting: expat students and pierced young artists rub shoulders with visiting rabble-rousers warming up for a wild night out. With its basic menu of classic cocktails and long drinks, the main attraction is arguably the space itself—the epitome of shabby chic (with an emphasis on shabby) with its calculated mix of modern and retro. ✉ *Sant Pau 77, El Raval* ☎ *3/626587044* ⊕ *www.facebook.com/ ambaraval.*

Casa Almirall

BARS | The twisted wooden fronds framing the bar's mirror, an 1888 vintage bar-top iron statue of a muse, and Art Nouveau touches such as curvy door handles make this one of the most authentic bars in Barcelona. It's also the second oldest, dating from 1860. (The oldest is the Marsella, another Raval favorite.) It's a good spot for evening drinks after hitting the nearby MACBA (Museu d'Art Contemporani de Barcelona) or for a prelunch *vermut* (vermouth) on weekends. ✉ *Joaquín Costa 33, El Raval* ☎ *93/318–9917* ⊕ *www.casaalmirall.com/en* ⊗ *Closed Sun. and Mon.* Ⓜ *Universitat.*

La Confitería

BARS | Located in a former pastry shop, this vintage bar has retained so much of the 19th-century Moderniste facade and interior touches (onetime cake display cases are now filled with period memorabilia) that visitors undoubtedly experience the sensation of time standing still. Divided into two equally inviting spaces and open unconventionally late for a bar (3 am), the front is usually packed with regulars, while the granite-and-metal tables in the back are popular with couples. ✉ *Sant Pau 128, El Raval* ☎ *93/140–5435* ⊕ *www.confiteria.cat* Ⓜ *Paral.lel.*

Manchester

BARS | There's no doubt about what the name of this laid-back Raval hangout pays tribute to: that of the early '80s Manchester scene, with the Joy Division and Happy Mondays and the Stone Roses. The sheer number of people (both locals and foreigners) crowding around the wood tables and dancing in the spaces in between suggest that a tribute is welcome. ✉ *Valldonzella 40, El Raval* ☎ *627/733081* ⊕ *www.manchesterbar. com* Ⓜ *Catalunya.*

Marsella

BARS | Inaugurated in 1820, this historic venue, a favored haunt for artistic notables such as Gaudí, Picasso, and Hemingway, has remained remarkably unchanged since its celebrated heyday. The chipped paint on the walls and ceiling, cracked marble tables, and elaborate spiderwebs on chandeliers and bottles all add to the charm, but the main reason patrons linger is one special shot: Marsella is one of few establishments serving homemade absinthe (*absenta* in Spanish), a potent aniseed-flavored spirit meant to be savored and rumored to enhance productivity. ⊠ *Sant Pau 65, El Raval* ☎ *93/442–7263* ⊕ *www.facebook. com/Bar-Marsella-148097715525039* Ⓜ *Liceu.*

Sala Apolo

DANCE CLUBS | Set across three levels and multiple rooms, Sala Apolo offers a variety of house/techno nights and intimate live music concerts. Two Sunday afternoons a month, it turns into Barcelona's hottest LGBTQ destination, playing host to the immensely popular Churros con Chocolate and VenTú! tea dances. ⊠ *Nou de la Rambla, 113, El Raval* ☎ *93/441–4001* ⊕ *www.sala-apolo.com* Ⓜ *Paral·lel.*

33/45

BARS | From the street, this indie-cool hipster haven seems too brightly lighted for gritty-glam Raval. But its mismatched sofas with oversize pillows and eclectic selection of flavored gins, tequila blends, and imported beer attracts a steady flow of lounge lizards. ⊠ *Joaquin Costa 4, El Raval* ☎ *93/187–4138* ⊕ *www.3345.es* Ⓜ *Sant Antoni.*

Two Schmucks

COCKTAIL LOUNGES | One of only two Barcelona cocktail bars currently listed among The World's 50 Best Bars (debuting at an impressive 26th spot in 2020), Two Schmucks is that fun-filled neighborhood bar we all crave. Laid-back, but never boring, don't be surprised if you find founders Moe Aljaff and AJ White shaking and stirring until the early hours. ⊠ *Joaquín Costa 52, El Raval* ☎ *63/539–6088* ⊕ *www.facebook.com/schmuckordie* Ⓜ *Universitat L1, L2.*

MUSIC CLUBS: JAZZ AND BLUES

Jazz Sí Club

LIVE MUSIC | Run by the Barcelona contemporary music school next door, this workshop and (during the day) café is a forum for musicians, teachers, and fans to listen to and debate their art. Most weeks, the schedule offers jazz on Monday and Wednesday; pop, blues, and rock jam sessions on Tuesday; Cuban salsa on Thursday; flamenco on Friday; and rock and pop on weekends. The small cover charge (€6–€10, depending on which night you visit) includes a drink. Gigs start between 6:30 and 8:45 pm. ⊠ *Requesens 2, El Raval* ☎ *93/443-4346* ⊕ *tallerdemusics.com/en/jazzsi-club* Ⓜ *Sant Antoni.*

🛍 Shopping

Shopping in El Raval reflects the district's multicultural and bohemian vibe. Around MACBA (Barcelona Museum of Contemporary Art) you'll find dozens of designer-run start-ups selling fashion, crafts, and housewares, while the edgier southernmost section has an abundance of curious establishments chock-full of ethnic foods (along Calles Hospital and Carme) and vintage clothing (on Calle Riera Baixa).

BOOKS

La Central del Raval

BOOKS | This luscious bookstore in the former chapel of the Casa de la Misericòrdia sells books amid stunning architecture and holds regular cultural events. ⊠ *Elisabets 6, El Raval* ☎ *900/802109* ⊕ *www.lacentral.com* ⊗ *Closed Sun.* Ⓜ *Catalunya.*

MARKETS

Flea Market BCN

MARKET | Barcelona's current rage for retro and vintage reaches its pinnacle once a month on a little square behind the medieval shipyards. Flea Market BCN sees hipsters and hippies, dads and dealers empty out their wardrobes and garages so that you can walk away with art-deco wall clocks or a 1970s hand mixer. Flea Market BCN is held on the second Sunday of every month. ⊠ *Pl. Blanquerna* ⊕ *fleamarketbcn.com* Ⓜ *Drassanes.*

Mercat de Sant Antoni

MARKET | Just outside El Raval at the end of Ronda Sant Antoni, this steel hangar colossus is an old-fashioned food and secondhand clothing and books (many in English) market. Although the indoor food market is closed on Sunday, Sunday morning is the most popular time to browse the used-book and video game market outside. ⊠ *Comte d'Urgell 1, El Raval* ☎ *93/426–3521* ⊕ *www.mercatde-santantoni.com* Ⓜ *Sant Antoni.*

Sant Pere and Born/La Ribera

Sant Pere, Barcelona's old textile neighborhood, is centered on the church of Sant Pere. A half mile closer to the port, the Barri de la Ribera and the former market of El Born, now known as the Born-Ribera district, were at the center of Catalonia's great maritime and economic expansion of the 13th and 14th centuries. Surrounding the basilica of Santa Maria del Mar, the Born-Ribera area includes Carrer Montcada, lined with 14th- to 18th-century Renaissance palaces; Passeig del Born, where medieval jousts were held; Carrer Flassaders and the area around the early mint; the antiques shop- and restaurant-rich Carrer Banys Vells; Plaça de les Olles; and Pla del Palau, where La Llotja, Barcelona's early maritime exchange, housed the fine-arts school where Picasso, Gaudí, and Domènech i Montaner all studied,

as did many more of Barcelona's most important artists and architects.

Long a depressed neighborhood, La Ribera began to experience a revival in the 1980s; now replete with intimate bars, cafés, and trendy boutiques, it continues to enjoy the blessings of gentrification. An open excavation in the center of El Born, the onetime market restored as a multipurpose cultural center, offers a fascinating view of pre-1714 Barcelona, dismantled by the victorious troops of Felipe V at the end of the War of the Spanish Succession. The Passeig del Born, La Rambla of medieval Barcelona, is once again a pleasant leafy promenade.

◉ Sights

Capella d'en Marcús (*Marcús Chapel*)
CHURCH | This Romanesque hermitage looks as if it had been left behind by some remote order of hermit-monks who meant to take it on a picnic in the Pyrenees. The tiny chapel, possibly—along with Sant Llàtzer—Barcelona's smallest religious structure, and certainly one of its oldest, was originally built in the 12th century on the main Roman road into Barcelona, the one that would become Cardo Maximo just a few hundred yards away as it passed through the walls at Portal de l'Àngel. Bernat Marcús, a wealthy merchant concerned with public welfare and social issues, built a hospital here for poor travelers; the hospital chapel that bears his name was dedicated to the Mare de Déu de la Guia (Our Lady of the Guide). As a result of its affiliation, combined with its location on the edge of town, the chapel eventually became the headquarters of the Confraria del Correus a Cavall (Brotherhood of the Pony Express), also known as the *troters* (trotters), that made Barcelona the key link in overland mail between the Iberian Peninsula and France. ⊠ *Carrer Carders 2 (Placeta d'en Marcús), Born-Ribera* ☎ *93/310–2390* Ⓜ *Jaume I.*

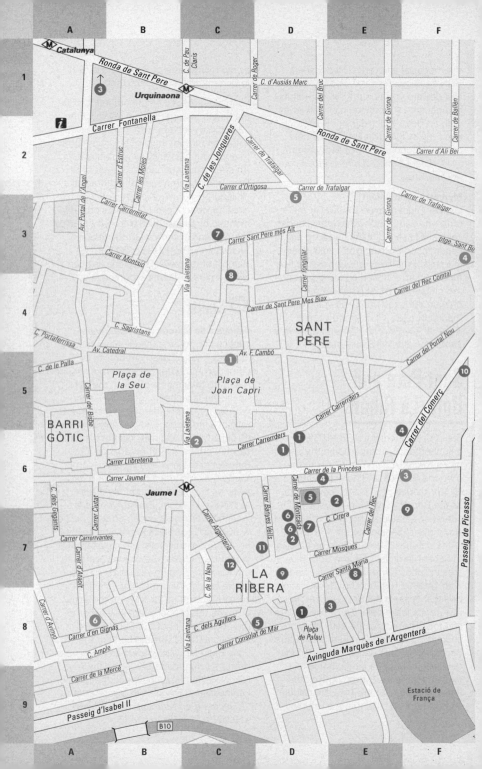

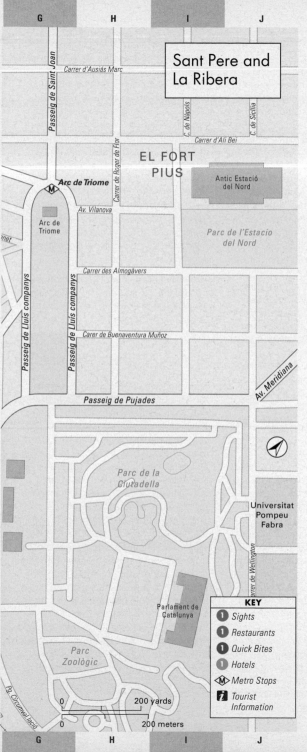

Sant Pere and La Ribera

EL FORT PIUS

Arc de Triome

Arc de Triome

Antic Estació del Nord

Parc de l'Estacio del Nord

Parc de la Ciutadella

Parc Zoològic

Universitat Pompeu Fabra

Parlament de Catalunya

Passeig de Sant Joan · Carrer d'Ausiàs Marc · C. de Nàpols · C. de Sicília · Carrer d'Ali Bei · Carrer de Roger de Flor · Av. Vilanova · Carrer des Almogàvers · Carer de Buenaventura Muñoz · Passeig de Lluis companys · Passeig de Lluis companys · Passeig de Pujades · Av. Meridiana · Carrer de Wellington · Pg. Circumval·lació

KEY

- 1 Sights
- 1 Restaurants
- 1 Quick Bites
- 1 Hotels
- Ⓜ Metro Stops
- 🛈 Tourist Information

0 — 200 yards
0 — 200 meters

Sights ▼

1 Capella d'en Marcús D6
2 Carrer Flassaders................... E6
3 La Llotja............................. A1
4 Museu de la Xocolata............. F6
5 Museu Picasso D6
6 Palau Dalmases.................... D7
7 Palau de la Música Catalana......C3
8 Passeig del Born.................... E7
9 Santa Maria del Mar............. D7

Restaurants ▼

1 Bar del Pla.......................... D6
2 Bodega La Puntual D7
3 Cal Pep.............................. E8
4 Cremat 11........................... D6
5 El Passadís d'en Pep D8
6 El Xampanyet...................... D7
7 Euskal Etxea....................... D7
8 Le Cucine Mandarosso C4
9 Llamber F7
10 Picnic F5
11 Proper.............................. D7
12 Sagardi............................. C7

Quick Bites ▼

1 Gocce di Latte..................... D8

Hotels ▼

1 The Barcelona EDITION C5
2 H10 Montcada Boutique Hotel....................................C6
3 Hotel chic&basic Born............. F6
4 Hotel Rec F3
5 Hotel Yurbban Trafalgar.......... D3
6 The Wittmore...................... A8

Carrer Flassaders

STREET | Named for the weavers and blanket makers whom this street belonged to in medieval times, Carrer Flassaders begins on Carrer Montcada opposite La Xampanyet, one of La Ribera's most popular bars for tapas and cava. Duck into the short, dark Carrer Arc de Sant Vicenç; at the end you'll find yourself face to face with La Seca, the Royal Mint, where money was manufactured until the mid-19th century. Turn left on Carrer de la Seca to Carrer de la Cirera; overhead to the left is the image of Santa Maria de Cervelló, one of the patron saints of the Catalan fleet. Turn right on Carrer de la Cirera, and arrive at the corner of Carrer dels Flassaders. Wander through Flassaders' boutiques. Look up to your right at the corner of the gated Carrer de les Mosques, famous as Barcelona's narrowest street. The mustachioed countenance peering down at you was once a medieval advertisement for a brothel. Hofmann, at No. 44, is the excellent pastry shop of famous Barcelona chef Mey Hofmann; don't pass up the mascarpone croissants. ⊠ Flassaders, Born-Ribera Ⓜ Jaume I.

La Llotja (Maritime Exchange)

NOTABLE BUILDING | Barcelona's maritime trade center, the Casa Llotja de Mar, was designed to be the city's finest example of civil architecture, built in the Catalan Gothic style between 1380 and 1392. At the end of the 18th century the facades were (tragically) covered in the neoclassical uniformity of the time, but the interior, the great Saló Gòtic (Gothic Hall), remained unaltered, and was a grand venue for balls throughout the 19th century. The hall, with its graceful arches and columns and floors of light Carrara and dark Genovese marble, has now been brilliantly restored. The building, which is not typically open to the general public, now houses the Barcelona Chamber of Commerce. The **Reial Acadèmia Catalana de Belles Arts de Sant Jordi** (Royal Catalan Academy of Fine Arts of St. George) still has its seat in the Llotja, and its museum is one of Barcelona's semisecret collections of art, from medieval paintings by unknown artists to modern works by members of the Academy itself. To slip into the Saló Gòti, walk down the stairs from the museum to the second floor, then take the marble staircase down and turn right. ⊠ Casa Llotja, Passeig d'Isabel II 1, Born-Ribera ☎ 93/319–2432 Reial Acadèmia, 670/466260 guided visits to museum ⊕ www.racba.org ⊠ €12 ⊂⊃ Mostly closed to the public. Tours priced at €12 available in Catalan. Group tours in English can be booked in advance. Ⓜ L4 Barceloneta.

Museu de la Xocolata (Museum of Chocolate)

OTHER MUSEUM | FAMILY | The elaborate, painstakingly detailed chocolate sculptures, which have included everything from La Sagrada Família to Don Quixote's windmills, delight both youthful and adult visitors to this museum, set in an imposing 18th-century former monastery and developed by the Barcelona Provincial Confectionery Guild. Other exhibits here touch on Barcelona's centuries-old love affair with chocolate, the introduction of chocolate to Europe by Spanish explorers from the Mayan and Aztec cultures in the New World, and both vintage and current machinery and tools used to create this sweet delicacy. The 'Bean To Bar' experience showcases the full production process for making artisanal chocolate using traceable cocoa from different parts of the world. The end product can be bought in the museum shop. The beautiful shop and café offers rich hot and cold chocolate drinks, boxes and bars of artisanal chocolate, and house-made cakes and pastries. Classes on making and tasting chocolate are offered, too. ⊠ Carrer del Comerç 36, Born-Ribera ☎ 93/268–7878 ⊕ www. museuxocolata.cat ⊠ €6 Ⓜ L4 Jaume 1, L1 Arc de Triomf.

★ **Museu Picasso** (*Picasso Museum*)
ART MUSEUM | The Picasso Museum is housed in five adjoining palaces on Carrer Montcada, a street known for Barcelona's most elegant medieval mansions. Picasso spent his key formative years in Barcelona (1895–1904), and although this collection doesn't include a significant number of the artist's most famous paintings, it is strong on his early work, showcasing the link between Picasso and Barcelona. Displays include childhood sketches, works from Picasso's Rose and Blue periods, and the many famous 1950s Cubist variations on Velázquez's *Las Meninas* (in Rooms 12–16). The lower-floor sketches, oils, and schoolboy caricatures and drawings from Picasso's early years in A Coruña are perhaps the most fascinating part, showing the facility the artist seemed to possess almost from the cradle. On the second floor are works from his Blue Period in Paris, a time of loneliness, cold, and hunger for the artist. Admission is free the first Sunday of the month and every Thursday from 4 p.m.. Book online or arrive early to avoid the long lines and crowds. ⊠ *Carrer Montcada 15–19, Born-Ribera* ☎ *93/256–3000, 93/256–3022 guided tour and group reservations* ⊕ *www.museupicasso.bcn.cat* ☎ *€12; free Thurs. from 4 pm, and 1st Sun. of month. Tours €6* ⊘ *Closed Mon. after 5 pm* ☞ *Guided tours of permanent collection (in English) Tues. and Wed. at 3, Thurs. at 7, and Sun. at 11 (except Aug.)* Ⓜ *L4 Jaume I, L1 Arc de Triomf.*

Palau Dalmases

NOTABLE BUILDING | If you can get through the massive wooden gates that open onto Carrer Montcada (at the moment, the only opportunity is when the first-floor café-theater Espai Barroc is open) you'll find yourself in Barcelona's best 17th-century Renaissance courtyard, built into a former 15th-century Gothic palace. Note the door knockers up at horseback level; then take a careful look at the frieze of "The Rape of Europa" running up the stone railing of the elegant stairway at the end of the patio. It's a festive abduction: Neptune's chariot, cherubs, naiads, dancers, tritons, and musicians accompany Zeus, in the form of a bull, as he carries poor Europa up the stairs and off to Crete. The stone carvings in the courtyard, the 15th-century Gothic chapel, with its reliefs of angelic musicians, and the vaulting in the reception hall and salon, are all that remain of the original 15th-century palace. ⊠ *Carrer Montcada 20, Born-Ribera* ☎ *93/310–0673 Espai Barroc* ⊕ *palaudalmases.com* ☎ *Shows €30 (includes 1 drink)* Ⓜ *L4 Jaume I.*

★ Palau de la Música Catalana

NOTABLE BUILDING | One of the world's most extraordinary music halls, with facades that are a riot of color and form, the Music Palace is a landmark of Carrer Amadeus Vives, set just across Via Laietana, a 10-minute walk from Plaça de Catalunya. The Palau is a flamboyant tour de force designed in 1908 by Lluís Domènech i Montaner. Originally conceived by the Orfeó Català musical society as a vindication of the importance of music at a popular level—as opposed to the Liceu opera house's identification with the Catalan aristocracy—the Palau was for many decades an opposing crosstown force with the Liceu. The exterior is remarkable in itself. The Miquel Blay sculptural group is Catalonia's popular music come to life, with everyone included from St. George the dragonslayer to women and children, fishermen, and every strain and strata of popular life and music. The Palau's over-the-top decor overwhelms the senses even before the first note of music is heard. ⊠ *Carrer Palau de la Música 4–6, Born-Ribera* ☎ *93/295–7200, 93/295–7207 box office* ⊕ *www.palaumusica.cat/en* ☎ *Guided tour €14* Ⓜ *L1/L4 Urquinaona.*

★ Passeig del Born

PLAZA/SQUARE | Once the site of medieval jousts and autos-da-fé of the Inquisition, the passeig, at the end of Carrer

Montcada behind the church of Santa Maria del Mar, was early Barcelona's most important square. Late-night cocktail bars and miniature restaurants with tiny spiral stairways now line the narrow, elongated plaza. Walk down to the Born—a great iron hangar, once a produce market designed by Josep Fontseré, in the Plaça Comercial, across the street from the end of the promenade. The initial stages of the construction of a public library in the Born uncovered the remains of the lost city of 1714, complete with blackened fireplaces, taverns, wells, and the canal that brought water into the city. The streets of the 14th- to 18th-century Born-Ribera lie open in the sunken central square of the old market; around it, on the ground level, are a number of new multifunctional exhibition and performance spaces; these give the city one of its newest and liveliest cultural subcenters. ✉ *Passeig del Born, Born-Ribera* ☎ *93/256–6851 El Born Centre de Cultura i Memòria* 🌐 *elbornculturaimemoria.barcelona.cat* 🎫 *Free to upper galleries, €4 to the archaeological site* 🕒 *Closed Mon.* [M] *L4 Jaume I/Barceloneta.*

★ Santa Maria del Mar

CHURCH | The most beautiful example of early Catalan Gothic architecture, Santa Maria del Mar is extraordinary for its unbroken lines and elegance, and the lightness of the interior is especially surprising considering the blocky exterior. The site was home to a Christian cult from the late 3rd century. Built by mere stonemasons who chose, fitted, and carved each stone hauled down from a Montjuïc quarry, the church is breathtakingly and nearly hypnotically symmetrical. The medieval numerological symbol for the Virgin Mary, the number eight (or multiples thereof) runs through every element of the basilica: the 16 octagonal pillars are 2 meters in diameter and spread out into rib vaulting arches at a height of 16 meters; the painted keystones at the apex of the arches are 32 meters from the floor; and the central nave is twice as wide as the lateral naves (8 meters each). Although anticlerical anarchists burned the basilica in 1936, it was restored after the end of the Spanish Civil War by Bauhaus-trained architects. ✉ *Pl. de Santa Maria 1, Born-Ribera* ☎ *93/310–2390* 🌐 *www.santamariadelmarbarcelona.org* 🎫 *From €5* [M] *L4 Jaume I.*

🍴 Restaurants

★ Bar del Pla

$ | **CATALAN** | Specializing in Catalan bar food and local, organic, biodynamic, and natural wine, this sometimes-rowdy bar may not look like much from the outside but the hordes of people waiting to be seated give it away. Top choices include the mushroom carpaccio with wasabi vinaigrette and strawberries, the black squid-ink croquettes and the spicy *patatas bravas*. Everything about Bar del Pla is on trend despite its old-school appearance. **Known for:** mushroom carpaccio with wasabi vinaigrette and strawberries; Catalan natural wines; excellent tapas. [$] *Average main: €15* ✉ *Montcada 2, Born-Ribera* ☎ *93/268–3003* 🌐 *www.bardelpla.cat* 🕒 *Closed Sun.* [M] *Jaume I L4.*

★ Bodega La Puntual

$$ | **CATALAN** | Just down the road from the Picasso Museum, Bodega La Puntual might look like a tourist trap, but it's a classic, specializing in hearty portions of Catalan fare, made from seasonal, locally sourced produce. Top menu choices include the fresh marinated anchovies, the plate of premium hand-cut Iberian *jamón*, and *trinxat*: a traditional Catalan dish made with potatoes, cabbage, and pork meat, served with a fried egg. **Known for:** great for lunch after the Picasso Museum; seasonal, locally sourced ingredients; traditional Catalan food. [$] *Average main: €22* ✉ *Montcada 22, Born-Ribera* ☎ *93/310–3545* 🌐 *grupovarela.es/bodega-la-puntual-barcelona* [M] *Jaume I L4.*

Did You Know?

The imposing Gothic
church of Santa Maria
del Mar stands out in
Barcelona as a dramatic
counterpoint to the city's
exuberant Moderniste
architecture.

★ Cal Pep

$$ | TAPAS | A two-minute walk east of Santa Maria del Mar, Cal Pep has been in a permanent feeding frenzy for more than 30 years, intensified even further by the hordes of tourists who now flock here. Pep serves a selection of tapas, cooked and served hot over the counter in his loud, hectic bar that somehow manages to keep delivering the very highest quality tapas, year in year out. **Known for:** lively counter scene; excellent fish fry; delicious tortilla de patatas. $ *Average main: €22* ✉ *Pl. de les Olles 8, Born-Ribera* ☎ *93/310–7961* ⊕ *www.calpep.com* ⊘ *Closed Sun. and 3 wks in Aug. No lunch Mon.* Ⓜ *Jaume I, Barceloneta.*

Cremat 11

$ | FRENCH FUSION | Brunch spots may be ten a penny these days but few can compete with the superb, French-owned Cremat 11, almost hidden down this tiny street behind the Picasso Museum. The dining room is small but cozy, and there is also a shady outdoor patio on what is arguably one of the prettiest squares in the city. **Known for:** killer cocktails; leafy patio on a pretty square; steak and eggs. $ *Average main: €12* ✉ *Cremat Gran 11, Born-Ribera* ☎ *682/038377* ⊕ *cremat11. business.site* Ⓜ *Jaume I L4.*

El Passadís d'en Pep

$$$$ | SEAFOOD | Hidden away at the end of a narrow unmarked passageway off the Pla del Palau, near the Santa Maria del Mar church, this restaurant is a favorite with well-heeled and well-fed gourmands who tuck in their napkins before devouring some of the city's best traditional seafood dishes. Sit down and waiters will begin serving delicious starters of whatever's freshest that day in the market in rapid-fire succession. **Known for:** no menu, but you can prebook a set menu online; tapas served in rapid-fire succession; fresh seafood and Iberian ham. $ *Average main: €50* ✉ *Pl. del Palau 2, Born-Ribera* ☎ *93/310–1021* ⊕ *www.passadis.com* ⊘ *Closed public holidays and 3 wks in Aug.* Ⓜ *Jaume I.*

El Xampanyet

$ | TAPAS | Just down the street from the Museu Picasso, dangling *botas* (leather wineskins) announce one of Barcelona's liveliest and most visually appealing taverns, with marble-top tables and walls decorated with colorful ceramic tiles, some of which may look like they've been here since the joint opened in 1929. It's usually packed to the rafters with a rollicking mob of local and out-of-town celebrants. **Known for:** real cava; perfect Iberian ham; mouthwatering pa amb tomàquet. $ *Average main: €12* ✉ *Montcada 22, Born-Ribera* ☎ *93/319–7003* ⊘ *Closed Mon. and 2 wks in Aug. No dinner Sun.* Ⓜ *Jaume I.*

Euskal Etxea

$$ | BASQUE | An elbow-shaped, pine-paneled space, this bar-restaurant (one of the Sagardi group of Basque restaurants) is one of the better grazing destinations in the Born, with a colorful array of tapas and *pintxos* (bite-sized snacks typical of the Basque country, served on a toothpick) on the bar, ranging from the olive-pepper-anchovy "*Gilda*" to chunks of tortilla on bread. Other good bets include the *pimientos de piquillo* (red piquillo peppers) stuffed with codfish paste. **Known for:** excellent Euskal Txerria confit; Basque pintxos; art gallery on-site. $ *Average main: €20* ✉ *Placeta de Montcada 1–3, Born-Ribera* ☎ *93/310–2185* ⊕ *www. gruposagardi.com* Ⓜ *Jaume I.*

Le Cucine Mandarosso

$ | ITALIAN | This no-frills, big-flavor southern-Italian restaurant near the Via Laietana is a favorite with locals. Like Naples itself, it's cheap, charming, and over-full, with generous portions of burrata, lasagne, ragù, carbonara, and so on, featuring authentic ingredients from the in-store deli. **Known for:** great homemade pastas; hidden gem; always packed. $ *Average main: €15* ✉ *Verdaguer i Callís 4, Born-Ribera* ☎ *93/269–0780*

🌐 *www.lecucinemandarosso.com* ⏲ *Closed Mon.* [M] *Urquinaona.*

Llamber

$$ | **TAPAS** | It may look like one of the stylish, tourist-trap tapas restaurants that have sprung up recently, but Llamber's culinary pedigree sets it apart from the competition; chef Francisco Heras earned his chops in Spain's top restaurants. This dapper, friendly space attracts a mixed crowd with its excellent wine list and well-crafted tapas based on classic Catalan and Asturian recipes. **Known for:** well-crafted tapas; pig's trotters with rice; good late-night option. [$] *Average main: €18* ✉ *Fusina 5, Born-Ribera* ☎ *93/319–6250* 🌐 *www.llamber.com* [M] *Jaume 1.*

★ Picnic

$ | **LATIN AMERICAN** | There's a reason why Picnic has reigned supreme on the Barcelona brunch scene for more than a decade. Between the buzzing indoor dining room, the breezy outdoor patio, and the strongest Bloody Mary game in town, there's a reason why locals and visitors can't stay away. **Known for:** top brunch choice in town; breezy outdoor patio; excellent Bloody Marys. [$] *Average main: €12* ✉ *Comerç 1, Born-Ribera* ☎ *93/511–6661* 🌐 *www.picnic-restaurant.com* [M] *Arc de Triomf L1.*

Proper

$$ | **ARGENTINE** | Argentinian chef Augusto Mayer has brought the "gastronomic tavern" concept from his home country to Barcelona. The menu is simple and affordable: unfussy dishes of local, seasonal produce, mostly prepared in the wood-fired oven, and meant for sharing. **Known for:** wood-fired oven; Argentinian-style steak; local produce. [$] *Average main: €20* ✉ *Banys Vells 20, Born-Ribera* ☎ *93/295–5307* 🌐 *www.properbcn.com* ⏲ *Closed Sun. and Mon.* [M] *Jaume I L4.*

Sagardi

$$ | **BASQUE** | **FAMILY** | An attractive wood-and-stone cider-house replica, Sagardi piles the counter with a dazzling variety of cold Basque-style pintxos served on toothpicks; even better, though, are the hot offerings straight from the kitchen. The restaurant in back serves Basque delicacies like veal sweetbreads with artichokes and *txuletas de buey* (beef steaks) grilled over coals. **Known for:** veal sweetbreads and steak; Basque pintxos; multiple locations, all equally good. [$] *Average main: €22* ✉ *Argenteria 62, Born-Ribera* ☎ *93/319–9993* 🌐 *www.gruposagardi.com* [M] *Jaume I.*

☕ Coffee and Quick Bites

★ Gocce di Latte

$ | **ICE CREAM** | If you're looking to freshen up after a long, sweaty day of sightseeing, this artisanal Italian-owned *gelateria* is just the ticket. In addition to a broad range of dairy-based flavors, there are plant-based options and fresh-fruit sorbets, plus gluten-free cones. The vegan dark chocolate gelato is a particular favorite. **Known for:** vegan dark chocolate gelato; Italian-style gelato; dairy-free options. [$] *Average main: €6* ✉ *Pla de Palau 4, Born-Ribera* ☎ *61/798–6186* 🌐 *www.facebook.com/heladeriagoccedilatte* [M] *Barceloneta L4.*

🛏 Hotels

The Barcelona EDITION

$$$$ | **HOTEL** | The Edition hotels are known for their sleek, minimalist design and top-notch food and drink options and the Barcelona outpost adds a breezy 10th-floor terrace with sweeping views. The sights of El Born, Barri Gòtic, and the Eixample are within walking distance, though the hotel restaurant and bar—the Mediterranean restaurant Bar Veraz and the Punch Room cocktail bar—are destinations in their own rights. **Pros:** great food and drink options; dreamy views from the rooftop; excellent service. **Cons:** only upgraded rooms have balconies; pricey; tiny swimming pool. [$] *Rooms*

from: €420 ⊠ Av. de Francesc Cambó 14, Born-Ribera ☎ 93/626–3330 ⊕ www. editionhotels.com/es/barcelona ⤳ 100 rooms ⦾ No Meals Ⓜ Jaume I L4.

H10 Montcada Boutique Hotel

$$ | HOTEL | A short walk from the attractions of the Gothic Quarter and the Born-Ribera district, the Montcada is a good choice for comfort and convenience. **Pros:** pleasant breakfast room; inviting rooftop deck with Jacuzzi; great location. **Cons:** bed lighting could improve; wardrobes a tight fit by the bed; no pool or spa. Ⓢ *Rooms from: €160* ⊠ *Via Laietana 24, Born-Ribera* ☎ *93/268–8570* ⊕ *www.h10hotels.com* ⤳ *80 rooms* ⦾ *No Meals* Ⓜ *Jaume I.*

Hotel chic&basic Born

$ | HOTEL | The lobby of this hip little boutique hotel in the Born, with its leather sofa and banquettes, might remind you of a Starbucks, but the rooms tell a different story: the concept for chic&basic was whimsical, edgy accommodations at affordable prices, and designer Xavier Claramunt rose to the occasion. **Pros:** excellent price-quality for this location; superb location for Born/Ribera and Ciutadella; free bicycle rentals for guests. **Cons:** no children under 12; no room service or minibars; clothing storage limited, on open racks. Ⓢ *Rooms from: €84* ⊠ *Princesa 50, Born-Ribera* ☎ *93/295–4652* ⊕ *www.chicandbasic.com* ⤳ *31 rooms* ⦾ *No Meals* Ⓜ *L4 Jaume I.*

Hotel Rec

$ | HOTEL | Within an easy stroll of many of Barcelona's best restaurants and top sights, this is an affordable urban lodging in an unbeatable location. **Pros:** great location; great value; top restaurant downstairs. **Cons:** area can be sketchy at night; noisy street outside; rooms on the small side. Ⓢ *Rooms from: €120* ⊠ *Rec Comtal 17–19, Sant Pere* ☎ *93/556–9960* ⊕ *www.hotelrecbarcelona.com* ⦾ *No Meals* ⤳ *99 rooms* Ⓜ *Arc de Triomf L1.*

★ Hotel Yurbban Trafalgar

$ | HOTEL | Guests and locals alike rave about the rooftop terrace at the Yurbban Trafalgar, and with good reason: the panoramic view is hands down one of the best in the city at this hip, casual hotel, which offers some of the best value accommodation in the city. **Pros:** superb rooftop terrace; outstanding breakfast; spa access at next-door property. **Cons:** small shower stalls; room service ends at 11 pm; small, basic rooms. Ⓢ *Rooms from: €95* ⊠ *Carrer Trafalgar 30, Born-Ribera* ☎ *93/268–0727* ⊕ *yurbban.com/ en* ⦾ *No Meals* ⤳ *56 rooms* Ⓜ *L1/L3 Urquinaona.*

The Wittmore

$$$$ | HOTEL | The Wittmore is an adults-only romantic hideaway par excellence, tucked away in a tiny cul-de-sac in one of the Barri Gòtic's prettiest mazes of streets, just north of the marina and a short walk from Passeig de Colom. **Pros:** plunge pool and bar on rooftop terrace; ultra chic; cocktail bar with fireplace. **Cons:** budget-busting rates; no spa or gym; decor on the dark side. Ⓢ *Rooms from: €260* ⊠ *Riudares 7, Barri Gòtic* ☎ *93/550–0885* ⊕ *www.thewittmore. com* ⤳ *21 rooms* ⦾ *No Meals* Ⓜ *L3 Drassanes/L4 Jaume 1.*

▾ Nightlife

Nightlife in La Ribera tends to be laid-back, in keeping with the rather tranquil, medieval architectural surroundings. El Born is more eclectic, with bars and lounge spots specializing in everything from craft beer to organic wines.

BARS

Ale&Hop

BREWPUBS | A slick microbrewery with exposed brick walls and indie beats, Ale&Hop was a trailblazer in the city's craft-beer-bar invasion. There are plenty of artisanal brews, plus wine and vegetarian snacks. ⊠ *Basses de Sant Pere*

10, Sant Pere ☎ 93/126–9094 ⊕ www.
facebook.com/aleandhop Ⓜ Arc de
Triomf.

Eldiset
WINE BARS | Specializing in local wine
from Catalonia, this charming wine bar—
an escape from the rowdy watering holes
in nearby Passeig del Born and Plaça
Comercial—also has an impressive food
menu. ⊠ Antic de Sant Joan 3, Born-Ribera ☎ 93/268–1987 ⊕ www.facebook.
com/eldiset Ⓜ Barceloneta L4.

La Vinya del Senyor
WINE BARS | Ambitiously named "The
Lord's Vineyard," this romantic wine bar
directly across from the entrance to the
Santa Maria del Mar has an extensive
wine list featuring more than 350 wines
by the bottle, and a rotating selection
of 20 by the glass. Watch your step on
the rickety ladder leading to the pint-
size mezzanine or head to the terrace.
⊠ Pl. de Santa Maria 5, Born-Ribera
☎ 93/310–3379 ⊕ www.lavinyadelsenyor.
es Ⓜ Jaume I.

Paradiso
COCKTAIL LOUNGES | Hidden behind the
fridge door in an unassuming-looking
pastrami bar, this speakeasy is one of the
city's worst-kept secrets. Cocktail maes-
tro Giacomo Giannotti's creations are
works of art, bursting with fire, smoke,
and dry ice. And they taste absolutely
delicious. ⊠ Rera Palau 4, Born-Ribera
☎ 93/360–7222 ⊕ paradiso.cat/en Ⓜ Barceloneta L4.

Paspartú
COCKTAIL LOUNGES | Dark and inviting,
the bar stocks 25 gin flavors and has
plenty of comfortable seating in which
to try them. ⊠ Basses de Sant Pere 12
☎ 699/546252 ⊕ www.facebook.com/
paspartubar Ⓜ Arc de Triomf.

Rubí Bar
BARS | The whimsical apothecary-like
spirits cabinet, exposed-stone wall, and
dramatic red lighting will be the first

things to catch your eye, but the relaxed
atmosphere and inventive selection of
cocktails bring locals and expats back
again and again. Check out the choice of
home-brewed flavored gins tantalizingly
displayed on the bar shelves in hand-labe-
led bottles. ⊠ Banys Vells 6, Born-Ribera
☎ 93697/673802 Ⓜ Jaume I.

🎭 Performing Arts

La Puntual (Putxinel·lis de Barcelona)
THEATER | FAMILY | As one of the city's
pioneering puppet (in Catalan, putxinel·li)
theaters, this beloved venue features
entertaining marionette, puppet, and
shadow puppet performances. Weekend
matinee performances are major kid
magnets and tend to sell out fast, so
arrive early or reserve a ticket in advance
online. ⊠ Allada Vermell 15, Born-Ribera
☎ 93697/673802 ⊕ www.lapuntual.info
💲 From €9.10 Ⓜ Jaume I.

🛍 Shopping

The Ribera and Born neighborhoods have
some of Barcelona's best shopping.
Interior design and clothing shops are
the main draw, especially along Carrer
Argenteria, Plaça de Santa Maria, and
Carrer Banys Vells.

CERAMICS AND GLASSWARE
Baraka
CRAFTS | Barcelona's prime purveyor of
Moroccan goods, ceramics chief among
them, the wares here are generally
of good price and great quality. Other
African countries are represented, such
as spectacular busts covered in tiny
beads from Camaroon. ⊠ Canvis Vells 2,
Born-Ribera ☎ 93616/268-4220
⊕ www.barakaweb.com ⌣ Closed Sun.
Ⓜ Jaume I.

CLOTHING
Custo Barcelona
WOMEN'S CLOTHING | Ever since Custo Dal-
mau and his brother David returned from
a round-the-world motorcycle tour with

visions of California surfing styles dancing in their heads, Custo Barcelona has been a runaway success with its clingy cotton tops in bright and cheery hues. Now with three branches in Barcelona (including an outlet shop at Plaça del Pi 2, in the Barri Gòtic) and many more across the globe, Custo is scoring even more acclaim by expanding into coats, dresses, and kids' wear. ✉ *Pl. de les Olles 7, Born-Ribera* ☎ *93/268–7893* ⊕ *www.custo.com* ❂ *Closed Sun.* Ⓜ *Barceloneta.*

El Ganso

MIXED CLOTHING | Who would have thought that two Madrid-born brothers could out-Brit the Brits? One of Spain's more recent fashion success stories, El Ganso makes very appealing preppy-inspired men's, women's, and children's wear—striped blazers, pleated skirts, and tailored suits made for upper-class frolics. ✉ *Rambla de Catalunya, 116, Eixample* ☎ *93932/368–2069* ⊕ *www.elganso.com* ❂ *Closed Sun.* Ⓜ *Diagonal.*

FOOD

★ Casa Gispert

FOOD | This shop is one of the most aromatic and picturesque in Barcelona, bursting with teas, coffees, spices, saffron, chocolates, and nuts. The star is an almond-roasting stove in the back of the store—purportedly the oldest in Europe, dating from 1851 like the store itself, so make sure to pick up a bag of freshly roasted nuts to take with you. ✉ *Sombrerers 23, Born-Ribera* ☎ *93/319–7535* ⊕ *www.casagispert.com* ❂ *Closed Sun.* Ⓜ *Jaume I.*

Demasié

FOOD | The shop's motto, "galetes Exageradament Bones" (biscuits that are exaggeratedly good) may seem like a bit of hype, but these rich colorful cookies are exceptionally tasty. They are best enjoyed with a cup of coffee at the bar inside, or you can have them wrapped up in a pretty duck-egg-blue box to take home with you. ✉ *Princesa 28, Born-Ribera*

☎ *93/269–1180* ⊕ *www.demasie.es* Ⓜ *Jaume I.*

★ El Magnífico

FOOD | Just up the street from Santa Maria del Mar, this coffee emporium is famous for its sacks of coffee beans from all over the globe and is said to serve the best cup of coffee in Barcelona, also available to go. El Magnífico's best-kept secret is its nearby "Mag by El Magnífico" coffee shop (Carrer de Grunyí 10), open Fri.–Sun. only. ✉ *Carrer Argenteria 64, Born-Ribera* ☎ *93/319–3975* ⊕ *www.cafeselmagnifico.com* ❂ *Closed Sun.* Ⓜ *Jaume I.*

La Botifarreria de Santa Maria

FOOD | This busy emporium next to the church of Santa Maria del Mar stocks excellent cheeses, hams, pâtés, and homemade *sobrassadas* (pork pâté with paprika). Catalan botifarra sausage is the main item here, with a wide range of varieties, including egg sausage for meatless Lent and sausage stuffed with spinach, asparagus, cider, cinnamon, and Cabrales cheese. ✉ *Santa Maria 4, Born-Ribera* ☎ *93/319–9123* ⊕ *www.labotifarreria.com* ❂ *Closed Sun.* Ⓜ *Jaume I.*

★ Vila Viniteca

WINE/SPIRITS | Near Santa Maria del Mar, this is perhaps the best wine treasury in Barcelona, with a truly massive catalog, tastings, courses, and events, including a hugely popular street party to welcome in new-harvest wines (usually late October or early November). Under the same ownership, the tiny grocery store next door offers exquisite artisanal cheeses ranging from French goat cheese to Extremadura's famous *Torta del Casar*. There are a few tables inside, and, for a corkage fee, you can enjoy a bottle of wine together with a tasting platter. ✉ *Agullers 7-9, Born-Ribera* ☎ *9390/777–7017* ⊕ *www.vilaviniteca.es* ❂ *Closed Sun.* Ⓜ *Jaume I.*

GIFTS AND SOUVENIRS

Natura

CRAFTS | The Spanish Natura chain has branches around the city and stocks a good selection of global crafts, including incense, clothing, tapestries, candles, shoes, gadgets, and surprises of all kinds. ⊠ *Argenteria 78, Born-Ribera* ☎ *93/268–2525* ⊕ *www.naturaselection. com* ⊙ *Closed Sun.* Ⓜ *Jaume I.*

La Ciutadella and Barceloneta

Barceloneta and La Ciutadella fit together historically. In the early 18th century, some 1,000 houses in the Barrio de la Ribera, then the waterfront neighborhood around Plaça del Born, were ordered torn down, to create fields of fire for the cannon of La Ciutadella, the newly built fortress that kept watch over the rebellious Catalans. Barceloneta, then a marshy wetland, was filled in and developed almost four decades later, in 1753, to house the families who had lost homes in La Ribera.

Open water in Roman times, and gradually silted in only after the 15th-century construction of the port, it became Barcelona's fishermen's and stevedores' quarter. Eventually it became a sort of a safety valve, a little fishing village next door where locals could go to escape the formalities and constraints of city life, for a Sunday seafood lunch on the beach and a stroll through what felt like a freer world. With its tiny original apartment blocks, and its checkered history, Barceloneta maintains its spontaneous, carefree flavor.

Sights

Arc de Triomf

NOTABLE BUILDING | This exposed-redbrick arch was built by Josep Vilaseca as the grand entrance for the 1888 Universal Exhibition. Similar in size and sense to the traditional triumphal arches of ancient Rome, this one refers to no specific military triumph anyone can recall. In fact, Catalonia's last military triumph of note may have been Jaume I el Conqueridor's 1229 conquest of the Moors in Mallorca—as suggested by the bats (always part of Jaume I's coat of arms) on either side of the arch itself. The Josep Reynés sculptures adorning the structure represent Barcelona hosting visitors to the exhibition on the western side (front), while the Josep Llimona sculptures on the eastern side depict the prizes being given to its outstanding contributors. ⊠ *Passeig de Sant Joan, La Ciutadella* Ⓜ *L1 Arc de Triomf.*

El Transbordador Aeri del Port (*port cable car*)

VIEWPOINT | FAMILY | This hair-raising cable-car ride over the Barcelona harbor from Barceloneta to Montjuïc (with a midway stop in the port) is an adrenaline rush with a view. The rush comes from being packed in with 18 other people (standing-room only) in a tiny gondola swaying a hundred feet or so above the Mediterranean. The cable car leaves from the tower at the end of Passeig Joan de Borbó and connects the Torre de San Sebastián on the Moll de Barceloneta, the tower of Jaume I in the port boat terminal, and the Torre de Miramar on Montjuïc. The Torre de Altamar restaurant in the tower at the Barceloneta end serves excellent food and wine. ⊠ *Passeig Joan de Borbó 88, Barceloneta* ☎ *93/441–4820* ⊕ *www.telefericodebarcelona.com* 🎟 *From €11* Ⓜ *L4 Barceloneta.*

Estació de França

NOTABLE BUILDING | Barcelona's main railroad station until about 1980, and still in use, the elegant Estació de França is outside the west gate of the Ciutadella. Rebuilt in 1929 for the International Exhibition and restored in 1992 for the Olympics, this mid-19th-century building overshadows Estació de Sants, the city's main intercity and international terminus. The marble and bronze, the Moderniste decorative details, and the delicate tracery of its wrought-iron roof girders make this one of the most beautiful buildings of its kind. Stop in for a sense of the bygone romance of European travel. ⊠ *Av. Marquès de l'Argentera s/n, La Ciutadella* ☎ *902/320230 RENFE office, 90/232–0320 ticket sales and reservations* Ⓜ *L4 Barceloneta.*

Museu d'Història de Catalunya

HISTORY MUSEUM | Established in what used to be a port warehouse, this state-of-the-art interactive museum makes you part of Catalonian history, from prehistoric times to the contemporary democratic era. After centuries of "official" Catalan history dictated from Madrid (from 1714 until the mid-19th century Renaixença, and from 1939 to 1975), this offers an opportunity to revisit Catalonia's autobiography. Explanations of the exhibits appear in Catalan, Castilian, and English. The rooftop restaurant has excellent views over the harbor and is open to the public (whether or not you visit the museum itself) during museum hours. ⊠ *Pl. de Pau Vila 3, Barceloneta* ☎ *93/225–4700* ⊕ *www.mhcat.cat/enmhc* ⊠ *€6 (free on the first Sun. of every month, 10 am–2:30 pm)* ⊗ *Closed Sun. afternoon and Mon.* Ⓜ *L4 Barceloneta.*

★ Parc de la Ciutadella (*Citadel Park*)

CITY PARK | FAMILY | Once a fortress designed to consolidate Madrid's military occupation of Barcelona, the Ciutadella is now the city's main downtown park. The clearing dates from shortly after the War of the Spanish Succession in the early 18th century, when Felipe V demolished some 1,000 houses in what was then the Barri de la Ribera to build a fortress and barracks for his soldiers and a *glacis* (open space) between rebellious Barcelona and his artillery positions. The fortress walls were pulled down in 1868 and replaced by gardens laid out by Josep Fonseré. In 1888 the park was

the site of the Universal Exposition that put Barcelona on the map as a truly European city. ⊠ *Passeig de Picasso 21, La Ciutadella* Ⓜ *L4 Barceloneta, Ciutadella–Vila Olímpica, L1 Arc de Triomf.*

Parlament de Catalunya

NOTABLE BUILDING | Once the arsenal for the Ciutadella—as evidenced by the thickness of the building's walls—this is the only surviving remnant of Felipe V's fortress. For a time it housed the city's museum of modern art, before it was repurposed to house the unicameral Catalan Parliament. Under Franco, the Generalitat—the regional government—was suppressed, and the Hall of Deputies was shut fast for 37 years. Book a free 45-minute guided tour of the building; it includes the grand "Salon Rose," which is worth a visit in itself. ⊠ *Pl. de Joan Fiveller, Parc de la Ciutadella s/n, La Ciutadella* ☎ *93/304–6500* ⊕ *www.parlament.cat* ⊠ *Free* Ⓜ *L4 Ciutadella/Vila Olímpica.*

Port Olímpic

MARINA/PIER | Filled with yachts, restaurants, tapas bars, and mega-restaurants serving tourist fare continuously from 1 pm to 1 am, the Olympic Port is 2 km (1 mile) up the beach from Barceloneta, marked by the mammoth shimmering goldfish sculpture in its net of girders by starchitect Frank Gehry. In the shadow of Barcelona's first real skyscraper, the Hotel Arts, the Olympic Port draws thousands of young people of all nationalities on Friday and Saturday nights, especially in summer, to the beach at Nova Icària, generating a buzz redolent of spring break in Cancún. ⊠ *Port Olímpic, Port Olímpic* Ⓜ *L4 Ciutadella/Vila Olímpica.*

Port Vell (*Old Port*)

MARINA/PIER | FAMILY | From Pla del Palau, cross to the edge of the port, where the Moll d'Espanya, the Moll de la Fusta, and the Moll de Barceloneta meet (*Moll* means docks). Just beyond the colorful Roy Lichtenstein sculpture in front of the post office, the modern Port Vell complex—an IMAX theater, aquarium, and

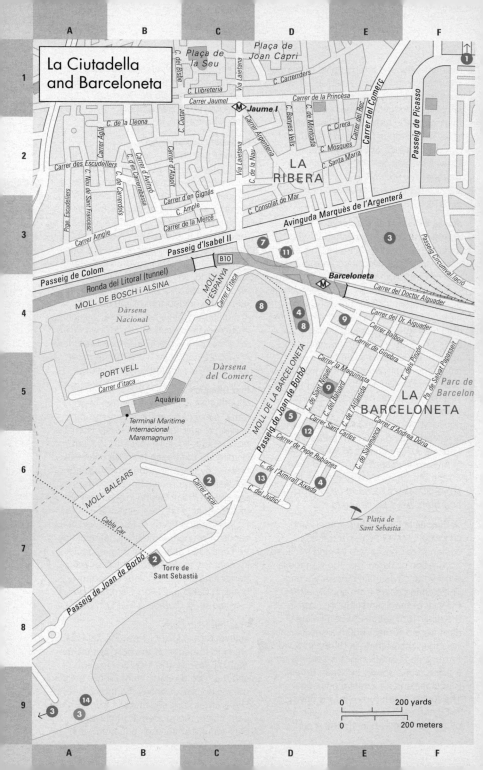

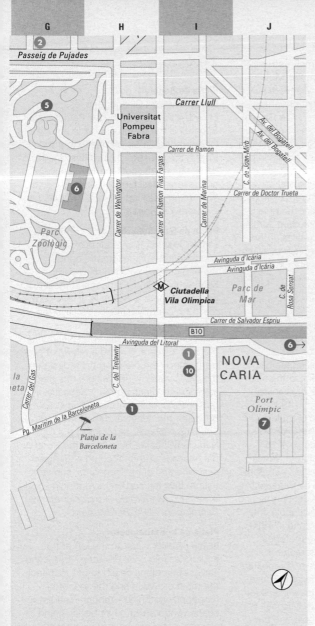

Sights ▼

Restaurants ▼

Hotels ▼

Maremagnum shopping mall—stretches seaward to the right on the Moll d'Espanya. The Palau de Mar, with rows of somewhat pricey, tourist-oriented quayside terrace restaurants (La Gavina or Merendero de la Mari are okay if you must), stretches down along the Moll de Barceloneta to the left. Key points in the rather soulless Maremagnum complex (noteworthy if only for being one of very few shopping options that remains open on Sunday in Barcelona) are the grassy hillside (popular on April 23, Sant Jordi's Day) and the *Ictineo II*, a replica of the world's first submarine created by Narcis Monturiol (1819–85), launched in the Barcelona port in 1862. ⊠ *Port Vell, Barceloneta* Ⓜ *L4 Barceloneta.*

Sant Miquel del Port

CHURCH | Have a close look at this baroque church with its modern (1992), pseudo-bodybuilder version of the winged archangel Michael himself, complete with sword and chain, in the alcove on the facade. (The figure is a replica; the original was destroyed in 1936.) One of the first buildings to be completed in Barceloneta, Sant Miquel del Port was begun in 1753 and finished by 1755 under the direction of architect Damià Ribes. Due to strict orders to keep Barceloneta low enough to fire La Ciutadella's cannon over, Sant Miquel del Port had no bell tower and only a small cupola until Elies Rogent added a new one in 1853. Interesting to note are the metopes: palm-sized gilt bas-relief sculptures around the interior cornice and repeated outside at the top of the facade. These 74 Latin-inscribed allegories each allude to different attributes of St. Michael. For example, the image of a boat and the Latin inscription "iam in tuto" (finally safe), alludes to the saint's protection against the perils of the sea. ⊠ *Carrer de Sant Miquel 39, Barceloneta* ☎ *93/221–6550* Ⓜ *L4 Barceloneta.*

 ## Beaches

Platja de Bogatell

BEACH | FAMILY | Cleaner and less crowded than tourist-heavy Barceloneta, Bogatell is the beach of choice among locals, though it's a bit of a longer trek from the city center. **Amenities:** food and drink; lifeguards; parking (fee); showers; toilets. **Best for:** partiers; sunrise; swimming; walking. ⊠ *Av. de Litoral, La Ciutadella* Ⓜ *Bogatell.*

Platja de Sant Sebastià

BEACH | FAMILY | Barceloneta's most southwestern platjas (to the right at the end of Passeig Joan de Borbó), Sant Sebastià is the oldest and most historic of the city beaches; it was here that 19th-century barcelonins cavorted in bloomers and bathing costumes. Neglected (and a bit disreputable) during the Franco years, it's had a rebirth of popularity since the pre-Olympic redesign of the city's waterfront. Despite repeated attempts to "clean up" Sant Sebastià, it remains a popular unofficial nudist spot. Between the beach and the Torre Sant Sebastia cable car terminus is the Club Natació Atlètic de Barcelona; the Hotel W Barcelona is at the far south end. **Amenities:** food and drink; lifeguards; showers; toilets. **Best for:** partiers; swimming. ⊠ *Passeig Maritim de la Barceloneta s/n, Barceloneta* Ⓜ *L4, Barceloneta.*

Platja de la Barceloneta

BEACH | FAMILY | Just to the left at the end of Passeig Joan de Borbó, this is the easiest Barcelona beach to get to, hence the most crowded and the most fun for people-watching—though itinerant beach vendors can be a nuisance, and pickpocketing has become increasingly problematic in recent years. Never leave your belongings unattended on any of Barcelona's beaches. Along with swimming, there are windsurfing and kitesurfing rentals to be found just up behind the beach at the edge of La Barceloneta. Rebecca Horn's sculpture

Formerly an obsolete harbor, Port Vell is a modern yacht-basin and lively entertainment center.

L'Estel Ferit, a rusting stack of cubes, expresses nostalgia for the beach-shack restaurants that lined the beach here until 1992. Surfers trying to catch a wave wait just off the breakwater in front of the beachfront Agua restaurant. **Amenities:** food and drink; lifeguards; showers; toilets; water sports. **Best for:** partiers; surfing; swimming; walking; windsurfing. ✉ *Passeig Marítim de la Barceloneta s/n, Barceloneta* Ⓜ *Ciutadella/Vila Olímpica.*

Platja de la Mar Bella

BEACH | Closest to the Poblenou metro stop near the eastern end of the beaches, this is a thriving gay enclave and the unofficial nudist beach of Barcelona (although clothed bathers are welcome, too). The water-sports center Base Nàutica de la Mar Bella rents equipment for sailing, surfing, and windsurfing. Outfitted with showers, safe drinking fountains, and a children's play area, La Mar Bella also has lifeguards who warn against swimming near the breakwater. **Amenities:** food and drink; lifeguards; showers; toilets; water sports. **Best**

for: partiers; nudists; LGBTQ beachgoers; swimming; windsurfing. ✉ *Passeig Marítim del Bogatell, Poblenou* Ⓜ *Poblenou.*

Platja de la Nova Icària

BEACH | FAMILY | One of Barcelona's most popular beaches, this strand is just east of Port Olímpic, with a full range of entertainment and refreshment venues close at hand. (Xiringuito Escribà is one of the most popular restaurants overlooking neighboring Bogatell beach.) The wide beach is directly across from the neighborhood built as the residential Olympic Village for Barcelona's 1992 Olympic Games, an interesting housing project that has now become a popular residential neighborhood. Vendors prowl the sand, offering everything from sunglasses to cold drinks to massages. Pickpocketing has been an issue here, too, so keep an eye on your belongings. **Amenities:** food and drink; lifeguards; showers; toilets; water sports. **Best for:** partiers; swimming; walking; windsurfing. ✉ *Passeig*

Marítim del Port Olímpic s/n, Port Olímpic. Ⓜ *Ciutadella/Vila Olímpic.*

Restaurants

Barceloneta and the Port Olímpic (Olympic Port) have little in common beyond their seaside location. Port Olímpic is a massive-scaled, modern environment, while Barceloneta has retained its traditional character as a blue-collar neighborhood, even if few fishermen live here now. Decades-old family restaurants and tourist traps can look similar from the street; a telltale sign of unreliable establishments is the presence of hard-selling waiters outside, aggressively courting passing customers.

East of the Eixample and extending to the sea just beyond Port Olímpic, Poblenou's formerly rough-around-the-edges neighborhood with a historical heart has lately seen an influx of edgy art studios, design shops, and a few hip restaurants—many of these spaces are installed in converted warehouses.

Agua

$$ | MEDITERRANEAN | Hit Agua's terrace on warm summer nights and sunny winter days, or just catch rays inside the immense windows. Either way you'll have a prime spot for beachside people-watching and seafood-eating. **Known for:** popular tourist spot; must reserve in advance; fresh seafood. Ⓢ *Average main: €22* ⊠ *Passeig Marítim de la Barceloneta 30, Port Olímpic* ☎ *93/225–1272* ⊕ *www.grupotragaluz.com* Ⓜ *Ciutadella–Vila Olímpica.*

Barceloneta

$$$ | SEAFOOD | This restaurant in an enormous riverboat-like building at the end of the yacht marina in Barceloneta is geared for high-volume business. The food—paellas and grilled fish dishes are the specialties—is delicious, and the hundreds of fellow diners make the place feel like a cheerful New Year's Eve celebration. **Known for:** fresh grilled fish; lively waterside spot; excellent rice and paella. Ⓢ *Average main: €27* ⊠ *Escar 22, Moll de Pescadors, Barceloneta* ☎ *93/221–2111* ⊕ *www.restaurantbarceloneta.com* Ⓜ *Barceloneta.*

Camping Mar

$$ | CATALAN | Slightly hidden in the exclusive yachting marina behind the W Barcelona hotel, this is a restaurant that only attracts those in the know, which might explain why it is largely devoid of tourists. Specialties here include the grilled avocado and tamarind vinaigrette, the grilled, spicy mussels and the brothy lobster rice. **Known for:** lobster rice; hidden gem; healthy food and paellas. Ⓢ *Average main: €21* ⊠ *Pg. Joan de Borbó 103, Marina Vela, Barceloneta* ☎ *93/408–8901* ⊕ *www.encompaniadelobos.com/en/camping-mar* ⊘ *Closed Mon. and Tues.* Ⓜ *Barceloneta L4.*

★ Can Fisher

$$ | CATALAN | This is the restaurant that the Barcelona locals flock to when they want their fix of fresh seafood, served on a sun-kissed terrace with a generous side of sea views. Top menu choices include the mouthwatering shrimp croquettes, and the black rice with baby squid, *Padrón* peppers and garlicky *allioli*. **Known for:** garlicky black rice with baby squid; good service; local favorite on the beach. Ⓢ *Average main: €22* ⊠ *Av. del Litoral 64, Port Olímpic* ☎ *93/597–1840* ⊕ *www.canfisher.com* Ⓜ *Ciutadella Vila Olímpica L4.*

Can Majó

$$ | SEAFOOD | FAMILY | One of Barcelona's best-known seafood restaurants is by the beach in Barceloneta and specializes in such house favorites as *caldero de bogavante* (a cross between paella and lobster bouillabaisse) and *suquet* (fish stewed in its own juices). Can Majó doesn't consistently reach the standards that once made it famous, but the cooking is still a notch above most of the touristy haunts nearby. **Known for:** excellent paella; terrace overlooking the Mediterranean;

Spanish rice and fish dishes. $ *Average main: €22* ✉ *Emília Llorca Martín 23, Barceloneta* ☎ *93/221–5455* ⊕ *www.canmajo.es* ⊗ *Closed Mon.* Ⓜ *Barceloneta.*

Can Solé

$$$$ | SEAFOOD | With no sea views or touts outside to draw in diners, Can Solé has to rely on its reputation as one of Barceloneta's best options for seafood for more than 100 years. Faded photos of half-forgotten local celebrities line its walls, but there's nothing out-of-date about the food. **Known for:** open kitchen; fresh fish daily; traditional Spanish rice dishes. $ *Average main: €30* ✉ *Sant Carles 4, Barceloneta* ☎ *93/221–5012* ⊕ *restaurantcansole.com* ⊗ *Closed Mon. and 2 wks in Aug. No dinner Sun.* Ⓜ *Barceloneta.*

★ Carballeira

$$$ | SEAFOOD | Locals have been coming here for the finest Galician shellfish since 1944, and on weekends, it is not uncommon to see four generations of a family gathered around a table in the maritime-theme dining room. There's everything from oysters to octopus, scallops, shrimp, razor clams, and many kinds of fish. **Known for:** exemplary service; fresh fish and shellfish; Galician specialties like black baby scallops. $ *Average main: €25* ✉ *Reina Cristina 3, Barceloneta* ☎ *93/310–1006* ⊕ *www. carballeira.com* Ⓜ *Barceloneta L4.*

1881 Per Sagardi

$$$ | BASQUE | Views of yachts sailing out into the glittering Mediterranean sea and the aroma of a wood-fired grill that turns out classic Basque cuisine are a compelling combination here. The Sagardi group's most stylish establishment is perched atop a handsomely renovated former warehouse, which now houses the Catalan History Museum. **Known for:** spectacular sea views; all-day kitchen; pleasant terrace. $ *Average main: €24* ✉ *Pl. de Pau Vila 3, Barceloneta* ☎ *93/221–0050* ⊕ *www.gruposagardi. com* Ⓜ *Barceloneta.*

★ El Vaso de Oro

$ | TAPAS | A favorite with visiting gourmands, this often overcrowded little counter serves some of the best beer and tapas in town. The house-brewed artisanal draft beer—named after the Fort family who owns and runs the bar—is drawn and served with loving care by veteran epauletted waiters who have it down to a fine art. **Known for:** beef fillet is a favorite; old-school service; stand-up dining. $ *Average main: €15* ✉ *Balboa 6, Barceloneta* ☎ *93/319–3098* ⊕ *www. vasodeoro.com* ⊗ *Closed first 3 wks of Sept.* Ⓜ *Barceloneta.*

★ Enoteca

$$$$ | CATALAN | In the Hotel Arts, Enoteca is the Barcelona outlet for the talents of award-winning chef Paco Pérez. His creative and technically accomplished cooking uses peerless Mediterranean and Pyrenean products, transforming them into astonishing dishes that are both surprising and satisfying. À la carte choices are excellent, but the real fun is to be found in the tasting menu, which changes with the seasons and focuses on freshly caught fish and seafood and *mar i muntanya* (Catalan surf and turf) flavor combinations, equally pleasing to the eye and the palate. **Known for:** two Michelin stars; superstar chef; tasting menus. $ *Average main: €40* ✉ *Hotel Arts, Marina 19, Port Olímpic* ☎ *93/483–8108* ⊕ *enotecapacoperez.com/en* ⊗ *Closed Sun., Mon., 2 wks in Mar., and 2 wks at Christmas. No lunch Tues.–Fri.* Ⓜ *Ciutadella–Vila Olímpica.*

Green Spot

$$ | VEGETARIAN | The vegan and vegetarian options in Barcelona have improved remarkably in recent years, led by the likes of Green Spot, with its extensive menu of flavor-packed vegetarian and vegan dishes designed to please vegetarians and carnivores alike. The dining room's pale oak paneling elegantly frames an open kitchen and airy dining room serving fun, fresh fusion food that

everyone will like. **Known for:** delicious black pizza with activated charcoal; craft beer; stylish space. $ *Average main: €16* ✉ *Reina Cristina 12, Barceloneta* ☎ *93/802–5565* 🌐 *www.encompaniadelobos.com* [M] *Barceloneta.*

La Cova Fumada

$ | **TAPAS** | There's no glitz, no glamour, and not even a sign on the wall, but the battered wooden doors of this old, family-owned tavern hide a tapas bar to be treasured. Loyal customers and hordes of tourists queue for the market-fresh seafood, served hot from the furiously busy kitchen. **Known for:** erratic opening times; the original "bomba" fried potato croquette; blink and you will miss it. $ *Average main: €12* ✉ *Baluard 56, Barceloneta* ☎ *93/221–4061* 🕒 *Closed Sun. No dinner Mon.–Wed. and Sat.* [M] *Barceloneta.*

La Mar Salada

$$ | **SEAFOOD** | This restaurant stands out by offering creative twists on classic dishes at comparatively affordable prices. Traditional favorites such as paella, black rice, and *fideuà* (a paella-like pasta dish) are reinvigorated, and freshness is assured as ingredients come directly from the lonja fish quay across the street, a lively auction where Barcelona's small fishing fleet sells its wares. **Known for:** fixed-price lunch menu; good-value seafood; creative desserts. $ *Average main: €20* ✉ *Passeig Joan de Borbó 58, Barceloneta* ☎ *93/221–1015* 🌐 *www.lamarsalada.cat* [M] *Barceloneta.*

★ Pez Vela

$$ | **SPANISH** | The quality of beachside dining in Barcelona has surged in recent years, and this pseudo- *chiringuito* (beach bar) beneath the towering W Hotel is a top choice for paella with a perfect view of the sea. Rice dishes are better than at many better-known seafood specialists. **Known for:** Galician-style octopus; great selection of paellas; beachside location and views. $ *Average main: €22* ✉ *Passeig del Mare Nostrum 19–21, Barceloneta* ☎ *93/221–6317* 🌐 *www.grupotragaluz.com* [M] *Barceloneta.*

🛏 Hotels

Hotel Arts Barcelona

$$$$ | **HOTEL** | This luxurious Ritz-Carlton-owned, 44-story skyscraper overlooks Barcelona from the Port Olímpic, providing stunning views of the Mediterranean, the city, the Sagrada Família, and the mountains beyond. **Pros:** excellent pool area with plush loungers; superb restaurant on-site; fine art throughout hotel. **Cons:** very pricey; a 20-minute hike or more from central Barcelona; no free Wi-Fi. $ *Rooms from: €320* ✉ *Carrer de la Marina 19–21, Port Olímpic* ☎ *93/221–1000* 🌐 *www.hotelartsbarcelona.com* 🔑 *483 rooms* 🍴 *No Meals* [M] *L4 Ciutadella–Vila Olímpica.*

Motel One

$ | **HOTEL** | More like a sleekly designed boutique hotel than a roadside guest house, Motel One fits the bill for well-designed no-frills accommodation in a great location. **Pros:** optimal location for exploring the city; great value; private underground parking. **Cons:** no minibars; rooms are very small; no pool, gym, or spa. $ *Rooms from: €99* ✉ *Passeig de Pujades 11-13, La Ciutadella* ☎ *93/626–1900* 🌐 *www.motel-one.com/en/hotels/barcelona/hotel-barcelona-ciutadella* 🍴 *No Meals* [M] *Arc de Triomf L1.*

W Barcelona

$$$$ | **HOTEL** | This towering sail-shape monolith dominates the skyline on the Barcelona waterfront and is more of a self-contained urban resort, geared for romantic escapes and special events than for city breaks. **Pros:** unrivaled views; private beach and multiple pools create a resort feel; excellent restaurants on-site. **Cons:** loud music in public areas; far from public transportation (20-minute hike); extra amenities can get pricey. $ *Rooms from: €331* ✉ *Pl. de la Rosa del Vents 1, Moll de Llevant, Barceloneta*

☎ 93/295–2800 ⊕ www.marriott.com/ hotels/travel/bcnwh-w-barcelona ⇌ 473 rooms ⏵⏵ No Meals Ⓜ L4 Barceloneta.

Nightlife

The stretch of seaside between Port Vell and Port Olímpic is bursting with Barceloneta's lively *chiringuitos* (beach snacks), laid-back bars, and terraced seafood restaurants. In sharp contrast, Port Olímpic's posh nightclub scene caters to a mixed international bag of partygoers, ages 21 and over.

Once the city's central industrial hub, Poblenou's contrasting faces—a quaint tree-lined rambla surrounded by vast warehouse spaces and ultramodern edifices—has become Barcelona's hippest enclave. Once-abandoned spaces have been renovated into chic artists' lofts, while vintage shops and nondescript restaurants are now enjoying new lives as retro bars and lounges.

BARS
Balius Bar
COCKTAIL LOUNGES | Named after the historic hardware store that once stood here, Balius Bar has retro-chic decor, great music (check out the live jazz sessions on Sunday), and excellent cocktails. ⊠ Pujades 196, Poblenou ☎ 93/315–8650 ⊕ baliusbar.com Ⓜ Poblenou.

La Cervecita Nuestra de Cada Día
BREWPUBS | For craft beer lovers, this modern high-ceilinged bar and shop is a must. Filled to the brim with more than 200 international craft brands plus several local artisanal beers on tap, the venue solidifies its devotion to everything cerveza with organized tastings, pairings, and courses. Claim your spot early as regulars routinely dominate the seating at the long bar or the cozy corner tables up front. ⊠ Llull 184, Poblenou ☎ 616/318430 ☽ Closed Sun. Ⓜ Llacuna.

La Barceloneta, Land of Paella

Paella is Valencian, not Catalan, but it's typical for Barcelona families to go out for paella in La Barceloneta on Sunday. Paella marinera is rice boiled in fish stock and seasoned with clams, mussels, prawns, and jumbo shrimp, while the more traditional paella valenciana omits seafood but includes chicken, rice, and snails. *Arròs negre* (black rice) is cooked in squid ink. *Fideuá* is made with vermicelli noodles mixed with the standard ingredients. Paella is for a minimum of two diners—it's usually enough for three.

Madame George
COCKTAIL LOUNGES | Everything about this stylish bar is a happy contradiction: the chandeliered space has large gilded mirrors and polished chocolate brown stools that curiously complement the rickety antiques and quirky touches (check out the bathtub sofa in the back room). Cocktails run the full gamut from classic to creative (the piscopolitan, a perfect marriage of Peruvian pisco and the classic cosmo cocktail, is a triumph). ⊠ Pujades 179, Poblenou ☎ 93/500–5151 ⊕ www. madamegeorgebar.com ☽ Closed Mon. and Tues. Ⓜ Poble Nou.

Més de Vi
WINE BARS | The brainchild of two Catalan sommeliers, Més de Vi is a chic wine bar with a purpose: to educate visitors on the art of Spanish wines, with a particular focus on regional vintages. There are plenty of seating options: a tasting table for serious aficionados, romantic tête-à-tête tables, and a bar area for socializing. ⊠ Marià Aguiló 123, Poblenou ☎ 93/007–9151 ⊕ www.restaurantemesdevi.es/en ☽ Closed Mon. Ⓜ Poble Nou.

The Eixample

The Eixample (ay-shompla) is an open-air Moderniste museum. Designed as a grid, in the best Cartesian tradition, the Eixample is oddly difficult to find your way around in; the builders seldom numbered the buildings and declined to alphabetize the streets, and even Barcelona residents can get lost in it. The easiest orientation to grasp is the basic division between the well-to-do Dreta, to the right of Rambla Catalunya looking inland, and the more working-class Ezquerra to the left. Eixample locations are also either *mar* (on the ocean side of the street) or *muntanya* (facing the mountains). Another useful rule of thumb is that a downhill slant generally leads to the sea, while an uphill slant will take you to the mountains.

 Sights

Casa Amatller

HISTORIC HOME | The neo-Gothic Casa Amatller was built by Josep Puig i Cadafalch in 1900, when the architect was 33 years old. Puig i Cadafalch's architectural historicism sought to recover Catalonia's proud past, in combination with eclectic elements from Flemish and Dutch architectural motifs. Note the Eusebi Arnau sculptures—especially his St. George and the Dragon, and the figures of a drummer with his dancing bear. The first-floor apartment, where the Amatller family lived, is a museum, with the original furniture and decor (guided tours are offered in English daily at 11 am). Admission is discounted if booked online. ⊠ *Passeig de Gràcia 41, Eixample* ☎ *93/216–0175* ⊕ *amatller.org/en* 🚇 *From €24* Ⓜ *L2/L3/ L5 Passeig de Gràcia, FGC Provença.*

★ Casa Batlló

HISTORIC HOME | **FAMILY** | Gaudí at his most spectacular, the Casa Batlló is actually a makeover: it was originally built in 1877 by one of Gaudí's teachers, Emili Sala Cortés, and acquired by the Batlló family in 1900. Batlló wanted to tear down the undistinguished Sala building and start over, but Gaudí persuaded him to remodel the facade and the interior, and the result is astonishing. The facade—with its rainbow of colored glass and *trencadís* (polychromatic tile fragments) and the toothy masks of the wrought-iron balconies projecting outward toward the street—is an irresistible photo op. Nationalist symbolism is at work here: the scaly roof line represents the Dragon of Evil impaled on St. George's cross, and the skulls and bones on the balconies are the dragon's victims, allusions to medieval Catalonia's code of chivalry and religious piety. On summer evenings, you can listen to a concert (starts at 8 pm) and enjoy a drink on the terrace, as part of the "Magic Night" program. ⊠ *Passeig de Gràcia 43, Eixample* ☎ *93/216–0306* ⊕ *www.casabatllo.es* 🚇 *From €35* Ⓜ *L2/ L3/L4 Passeig de Gràcia, FGC Provença.*

Casa Calvet

HISTORIC HOME | This exquisite but more conventional town house (for Gaudí, anyway) was the architect's first commission in the Eixample (the second was the dragon-like Casa Batlló, and the third, and last—he was never asked to do another—was the stone quarry–esque Casa Milà). Peaked with baroque scroll gables over the unadorned (no ceramics, no color, no sculpted ripples) Montjuïc sandstone facade, Casa Calvet compensates for its structural conservatism with its Art Nouveau details, from the door handles to the benches, chairs, vestibule, and spectacular glass-and-wood elevator. The only part of the building accessible to visitors is the ground-floor China Crown restaurant, originally the suite of offices for Calvet's textile company, with its exuberant Moderniste decor. ⊠ *Carrer Casp 48, Eixample* ◷ *No dinner Sun.* Ⓜ *L1/L4 Urquinaona.*

Casa de les Punxes (*House of the Spikes*)

HISTORIC HOME | Also known as Casa Terrades for the family that owned the house and commissioned Puig i Cadafalch to build it, this extraordinary cluster of six conical towers ending in impossibly sharp needles is another of Puig i Cadafalch's inspirations, this one rooted in the Gothic architecture of northern European countries. One of the few freestanding Eixample buildings, visible from 360 degrees, this ersatz Bavarian or Danish castle in downtown Barcelona is composed entirely of private apartments, some of them built into the conical towers themselves on three circular levels, connected by spiral stairways. The ground floor, first level, terrace, and towers are now open to the public; check the website for the schedule of guided tours in English. ⊠ *Av. Diagonal 416–420, Eixample* ☎ *93/018–5242* ⊕ *www.casadelespunxes.com* ⊠ *From €13* Ⓜ *L4/L5 Verdaguer, L3/L5 Diagonal.*

Casa Golferichs (*Golferichs Civic Center*)
HISTORIC HOME | Gaudí disciple Joan Rubió i Bellver built this extraordinary house, known as El Xalet (The Chalet), for the Golferichs family when he was not yet 30. The rambling wooden eaves and gables of the exterior enclose a cozy and comfortable dark-wood-lined interior with a pronounced verticality. The top floor, with its rich wood beams and cerulean walls, is often used for intimate concerts; the ground floor exhibits paintings and photographs. The building serves now as the quarters of the Golferichs Centre Civic, which offers local residents a range of conferences and discussions, exhibitions and adult education courses, and organizes various thematic walking tours of the city. ⊠ *Gran Via 491, Eixample* ☎ *93/323–7790* ⊕ *www.golferichs.org* ⊙ *Closed weekends* Ⓜ *L1 Rocafort, Urgell.*

★ Casa Milà

NOTABLE BUILDING | Usually referred to as *La Pedrera* (The Stone Quarry), with a curving stone facade that undulates around the corner of the block, this building, unveiled in 1910, is one of Gaudí's most celebrated yet initially reviled designs. Seemingly defying the laws of gravity, the exterior has no straight lines, and is adorned with winding balconies covered with wrought-iron foliage sculpted by Josep Maria Jujol. Gaudí's rooftop chimney park, alternately interpreted as veiled Saharan women or helmeted warriors, is as spectacular as anything in Barcelona, especially in late afternoon when the sunlight slants over the city into the Mediterranean. Inside, the handsome **Espai Gaudí** (Gaudí Space) in the attic has excellent critical displays of Gaudí's works from all over Spain. The Pis de la Pedrera apartment is an interesting look into the life of a family that lived in La Pedrera in the early 20th century. Entrance lines can be long; book ahead for tours. ⊠ *Passeig de Gràcia 92, Eixample* ☎ *93/214–2576* ⊕ *www.lapedrera.com/en* ⊠ *From €24* Ⓜ *L2/L3/L5 Diagonal, FGC Provença.*

★ Disseny Hub

ARTS CENTER | This eye-catching center of activity is home to no less than four museum collections: the Museu de Arts Tèxtil i Indumentària (Textiles and Clothing Museum) of fashion, embroidery, jewelry, and accessories from ancient times to modern haute couture; the Museu de Ceràmica (Ceramics Museum), tracing the evolution of ceramic arts from 13th-century Moorish influences to the present, with a number of pieces by Miró and Picasso; the Museu de les Arts Decoratives (Museum of Decorative Arts), devoted mainly to the historical high arts of furniture and furnishings; and the Gabinet de les Arts Gràfiques (Graphic Arts Collection) of posters, packaging, typographic styles, and printed papers. ⊠ *Edific DHUB, Pl. de les Glòries Catalans 37–8, Eixample* ☎ *93/256–6700* ⊕ *www.museudeldisseny.cat* ⊠ *€6, valid for 2 days; free Sun. 3–8 and all day 1st Sun. every month; 30% discount with Bus Turistic tickets* ⊙ *Closed Mon.* Ⓜ *L1 Glòries.*

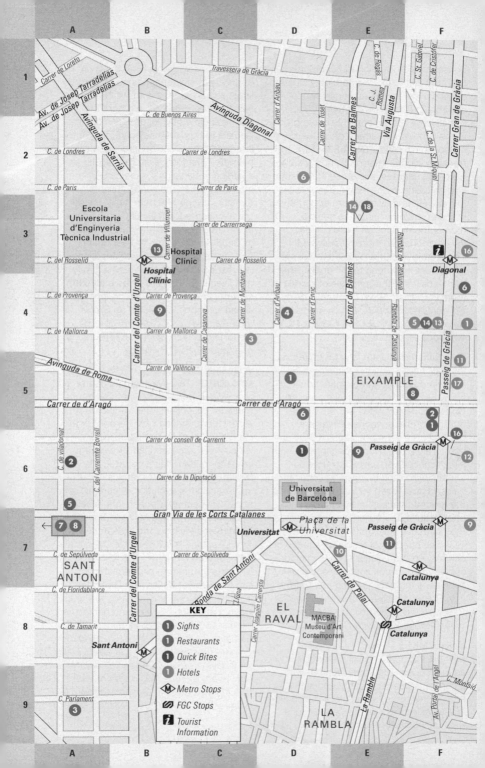

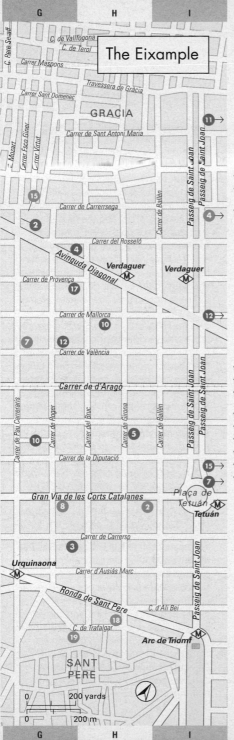

The Eixample

Sights ▼

1 Casa Amatller **F5**
2 Casa Batlló **F5**
3 Casa Calvet.............. **G7**
4 Casa de les Punxes..... **G3**
5 Casa Golferichs......... **A6**
6 Casa Milà **F4**
7 Disseny Hub...............**I6**
8 Fundació Antoni Tàpies. **F5**
9 Museu del Modernisme de Barcelona............. **E6**
10 Passatge Permanyer... **G6**
11 Recinte Modernista de Sant Pau **I2**
12 Temple Expiatori de la Sagrada Família...........**I4**

Restaurants ▼

1 The Alchemix............ **D5**
2 Bar Mut **G3**
3 Benzina **A9**
4 Besta **D4**
5 Betlem **H6**
6 Boa-Bao **D5**
7 Cinc Sentits............. **A7**
8 Cruix..................... **A7**
9 Disfrutar **B4**
10 Embat **H4**
11 Honest Greens........... **E7**
12 La Real Hamburguesería........ **G5**
13 La Taverna Del Clínic... **B3**
14 Lasarte................... **F4**
15 Manairó...................**I6**
16 Moments **F6**
17 Sartoria Panatieri....... **G4**
18 Xerta **E3**

Quick Bites ▼

1 DeLaCrem **D6**
2 L'Atelier **A6**

Hotels ▼

1 Alma Hotel Barcelona **F4**
2 Casa Bonay.............. **H7**
3 The Corner Hotel......... **C4**
4 Hotel 1882..................**I3**
5 Hotel Alexandra Barcelona **F4**
6 Hotel Astoria **D2**
7 Hotel Claris Grand Luxe Barcelona **D0**
8 Hotel El Palace Barcelona **G7**
9 Hotel Granvía............. **F7**
10 Hotel Jazz................. **E7**
11 Majestic Hotel & Spa ... **F5**
12 Mandarin Oriental Barcelona **F6**
13 Monument Hotel......... **F4**
14 Ohla Eixample............ **E3**
15 Seventy Barcelona **G3**
16 Sir Victor Hotel........... **F3**
17 SixtyTwo Hotel **F5**
18 yök Casa + Cultura...... **H8**
19 Yurbban Passage Hotel & Spa.............. **G8**

Fundació Antoni Tàpies

ART MUSEUM | This foundation created in 1984 by Catalonia's then-most important living artist, Antoni Tàpies, continues to promote the work of important Catalan artists and writers. Tàpies, who died in 2012, was an abstract painter who was influenced by surrealism, and his passion for art and literature still echoes in the halls of this enchanting Modernist building by esteemed architect Domènech i Montaner. There are thought-provoking temporary exhibitions, a comprehensive lecture series, and film screenings. The modern split-level gallery also has a bookstore that's strong on Tàpies, Asian art, and Barcelona art and architecture. ⊠ Carrer Aragó 255, Eixample ☎ 93/487–0315 ⊕ www.fundaciotapies.org ⊠ €8 ⊗ Closed Sun. afternoon and Mon. Ⓜ L2/L3/L4 Passeig de Gràcia.

Museu del Modernisme de Barcelona

(Museum of Catalan Modernism: MMBCN)

ART MUSEUM | Unjustly bypassed in favor of rival displays in the Casa Milà, Casa Batlló, and the DHUB Design Museum in Plaça de les Glòries, this museum houses a small but rich collection of Moderniste furnishings, paintings and posters, sculpture (including works by Josep Limona), and decorative arts. Don't miss the section devoted to Gaudí-designed furniture. ⊠ Carrer Balmes 48, Eixample ☎ 93/272–2896 ⊕ www.gothsland.com ⊠ €12 ⊗ Closed Sun. Ⓜ L1/L2 Universitat.

Passatge Permanyer

STREET | Cutting through the middle of the block bordered by Pau Claris, Roger de Llúria, Consell de Cent, and Diputació, this charming, leafy mid-Eixample sanctuary is one of 46 passatges (alleys or passageways) that cut through the blocks of this gridlike area. Once an aristocratic enclave and hideaway for pianist Carles Vidiella and poet, musician, and illustrator Apel·les Mestre, Passatge Permanyer is, along with the nearby Passatge Méndez Vigo, the best of these through-the-looking-glass downtown Barcelona alleyways. ⊠ Passatge Permanyer, Eixample Ⓜ L2/L3/L4 Passeig de Gràcia.

★ Recinte Modernista de Sant Pau

NOTABLE BUILDING | Set in what was one of the most beautiful public projects in the world—the Hospital de Sant Pau—the Sant Pau Art Nouveau Site is, sadly, no longer a hospital, but it is a UNESCO World Heritage site that's extraordinary in its setting, style, and the idea that inspired it. Architect Lluis Domènech i Montaner believed that trees, flowers, and fresh air were likely to help people recover from what ailed them more than anything doctors could do in emotionally sterile surroundings. The hospital wards were set among gardens, their brick facades topped with polychrome ceramic tile roofs in extravagant shapes and details. Domènech also believed in the therapeutic properties of form and color, and decorated the hospital with Eusebi Arnau sculptures and colorful mosaics, replete with motifs of hope and healing and healthy growth. The center offers self-guided tours with audio guides in the form of an app that can be downloaded to your personal devices, for maximum safety and hygiene. ⊠ Carrer Sant Antoni Maria Claret 167, Eixample ☎ 93/553–7801 ⊕ www.santpaubarcelona.org/en ⊠ From €15; free 1st Sun. of month Ⓜ L5 Sant Pau/Dos de Maig.

★ Temple Expiatori de la Sagrada Família

NOTABLE BUILDING | Barcelona's most emblematic architectural icon, Antoni Gaudí's Sagrada Família, is still under construction close to 140 years after it was begun. This striking and surreal creation was conceived as a gigantic representation of the entire history of Christianity. Begun in 1882 under architect Francisco de Paula del Villar and passed on in 1883 to Gaudí (until his death in 1926), the church is now in the final stage of construction. No building in Barcelona and few in the world are more deserving of the investment of a few hours to the better part of a day. The apse of the basilica, consecrated by Pope Benedict XVI in 2010, has space for close to 15,000 people and a choir loft for 1,500. The towers include those dedicated to the four evangelists—Matthew, Mark, Luke, and John—the Virgin Mary, and the highest of all, dedicated to Christ the Savior. By 2022, the 170th anniversary of the birth of Gaudí, the great central tower and dome, resting on four immense columns of Iranian porphyry, considered the hardest of all stones, will soar to a height of 564 feet, making the Sagrada Família Barcelona's tallest building. Prior to the outbreak of the COVID-19 pandemic, the Sagrada Familia was due to be completed by 2026, the 100th anniversary of Gaudí's death, after 144 years of construction. A new official date is yet to be announced. Take an elevator up the bell towers for spectacular views. The museum displays Gaudí's scale models and photographs showing the progress of construction. The architect is buried to the left of the altar in the crypt. Lines to enter the church can stretch around the block. Buy your tickets online, with a reserved time of entry, and jump the queue. ⊠ *Pl. de la Sagrada Família, Carrer Mallorca 401, Eixample* ☎ *93/207–3031, 93/208–0414 visitor info* ⊕ *sagradafamilia.org* ⊠ *From €20* Ⓜ *L2/L5 Sagrada Família.*

🍴 Restaurants

The sprawling blocks of the Eixample contain Barcelona's finest selection of restaurants, from upscale and elegant traditional cuisine in Modernist houses to high-concept fare in sleek minimalist-experimental spaces.

The Alchemix

$ | **ASIAN** | Purists tempted to run screaming from The Alchemix's blend of creative cocktails and Asian-influenced, avant-garde gastonomy should think again. Against the odds, this strange brew is a transformative triumph, as with the umami-poached king oyster mushroom, with prawns and pork rinds, paired with Uni Mead, a cocktail made from sea urchin, mead, soy milk, tobacco bitters, and lemon juice. Tapas and à la carte dishes, such as steamed cockles with green curry, also impress. **Known for:** expert bar staff; original cocktails; imaginative cuisine. Ⓢ *Average main: €14* ⊠ *València 212, Eixample* ☎ *933/833–7678* ⊕ *www.thealchemix.com* ⊗ *Closed Tues.* Ⓜ *Universitat.*

★ Bar Mut

$$$ | **CATALAN** | Just above Diagonal, this elegant retro space serves first-rate products ranging from wild sea bass to the best Ibérico hams. Crowded, noisy, chaotic, delicious—it's everything a great tapas bar or restaurant should be. **Known for:** snacks at nearby spin-off Entrepanes Diaz; great wine list; upmarket tapas. Ⓢ *Average main: €26* ⊠ *Pau Claris 192, Eixample* ☎ *93/217–4338* ⊕ *www.bar-mut.com* ⊗ *Closed Mon.* Ⓜ *Diagonal.*

★ Benzina

$$ | **ITALIAN** | Named for the car-mechanic shop that once stood here, Benzina blends industrial-chic elements with splashes of color and excellent music (on vinyl, naturally) to create a hip but cozy Italian restaurant that would not look out of place in New York. The food, however, is center stage: the freshly made pasta is among the best in the city. **Known for:** best spaghetti carbonara in the city; chic decor; creative Italian cuisine. Ⓢ *Average main: €18* ⊠ *Passatge Pere Calders 6, Eixample* ☎ *93/659–5583* ⊕ *www.benzina.es* Ⓜ *Poble Sec.*

Continued on page 459

TEMPLE EXPIATORI DE LA
SAGRADA FAMÍLIA

Antoni Gaudí's striking and surreal masterpiece was conceived as nothing short of a Bible in stone, an arresting representation of the history of Christianity. Today this Roman Catholic church is Barcelona's most emblematic architectural icon, looming over Barcelona like a mid-city massif of grottoes and peaks. Construction is ongoing and continues to stretch toward the heavens.

CONSTRUCTION, PAST AND PRESENT

"My client is not in a hurry," was Gaudí's reply to anyone curious about his project's timetable . . . good thing, too, because the Sagrada Família was begun in 1882 under architect Francesc Villar, passed on in 1883 to Gaudí, and is still thought to be several years from completion. Gaudí added Art Nouveau touches to the crypt and in 1891 started the Nativity facade. Conceived as a symbolic construct encompassing the complete story and scope of the Christian faith, the church was intended by Gaudí to impress the viewer with the full sweep and force of the Gospel. At the time of his death in 1926 only one tower of the Nativity facade had been completed.

Initially scheduled for completion in 2026, the 100th anniversary of Gaudí's death and what would be 144 years of construction in the tradition of the great medieval and Renaissance cathedrals of Europe, the Sagrada Familia project has been further delayed due to the Covid-19 pandemic. In 2012, architect Jordi Faulí took over from Jordi Bonet, who had continued in the footsteps of his father, architect Lluís Bonet, to make Gaudí's vision complete.

(left) Sagrada Família interior. (top) Shepherds gather to witness the birth of Christ in the Nativity facade.

DETAILS TO DISCOVER: THE EXTERIOR

GAUDÍ IN THE PASSION FACADE

Subirachs pays double homage to the great Moderniste master in the Passion facade: Gaudí himself appears over the left side of the main entry making notes or drawings, the evangelist in stone, while the Roman soldiers are modeled on Gaudí's helmeted, Star Wars–like warriors from the roof of La Pedrera.

Gaudí in the Passion facade

TOWER TOPS

Break out the binoculars and have a close look at the pinnacles and peaks of the Sagrada Família's towers. Sculpted by Japanese artist Etsuro Sotoo, these clusters of grapes and different kinds of fruit are symbols of fertility, of rebirth, and of the Resurrection of Christ.

Sotoo's ornamental fruit

SUBIRACHS IN THE PASSION FACADE

At Christ's feet in the entombment sculpture is a blocky figure with a furrowed brow, thought to be a portrayal of the agnostic's anguished search for certainty. This figure is generally taken as a self-portrait of Subirachs, characterized by the sculptor's giant hand and an "S" on his massive right arm.

DONKEY ON THE NATIVITY FACADE

On the left side of the Nativity facade over the Portal of Hope is a *burro*, a small donkey, known to have been modeled from a donkey that Gaudí saw near the work site. The *ruc català* (Catalan donkey) is a beloved and iconic symbol of Catalonia, often displayed on Catalonian bumpers as a response to the Spanish fighting bull.

The donkey in the Nativity facade

THE ROSE TREE DOOR

The richly sculpted Rose Tree Door, between the Nativity facade and the cloisters, portrays Our Lady of the Rose Tree with the infant Jesus in her arms, St. Dominic and St. Catherine of Siena in prayer, with three angels dancing overhead. The sculptural group on the wall known as "The Death of the Just" portrays the Virgin and child comforting a moribund old man, the Spanish prayer "Jesús, José, y María, asistidme en mi última agonía" (Jesus, Joseph, and María, help me in my final agony). The accompanying inscriptions in English, "Pray for us sinners now and at the hour of our death, Amen" are the final words of the Ave María prayer.

The heavily embelished Rose door

COLUMN FROM THE PORTAL OF CHARITY

The column, dead center in the Portal of Charity, is covered with the genealogy of Christ going back through the House of David to Abraham. At the bottom of the column is the snake of evil, complete with the apple of temptation in his mouth, closed in behind an iron grate, symbolic of Christianity's mission of neutralizing the sin of selfishness.

The column in the Portal of Charity

FACELESS ST. VERONICA

Because her story is considered legendary, not historical fact, St. Veronica appears faceless in the Passion facade. Also shown is the veil she gave Christ to wipe his face with on the way to Calvary that was said to be miraculously imprinted with his likeness. The veil is torn in two overhead and covers a mosaic that Subirachs allegedly disliked and elected to conceal.

STAINED-GLASS WINDOWS

The stained-glass windows of the Sagrada Família are work of Joan Vila-Grau. The windows in the west central part of the nave represent the light of Jesus and a bubbling fountain in a bright chromatic patchwork of shades of blue with green and yellow reflections. The main window on the Passion facade represents the Resurrection. Gaudí left express instructions that the windows of the central nave have no color, so as not to alter the colors of the tiles and trencadis (mosaics of broken tile) in green and gold representing palm leaves. These windows will be clear or translucent, as a symbol of purity and to admit as much light as possible.

St. Veronica with the veil

TORTOISES AND TURTLES

Nature lover Gaudí used as many elements of the natural world as he could in his stone Bible. The sea tortoise beneath the column on the Mediterranean side of the Portal of Hope and the land turtle supporting the inland Portal of Faith symbolize the slow and steady stability of the cosmos and of the church.

Stained-glass windows

SAINT THOMAS IN THE BELL TOWER

Above the Passion facade, St. Thomas demanding proof of Christ's resurrection (thus the expression "doubting Thomas") and perched on the bell tower is pointing to the palm of his hand asking to inspect Christ's wounds.

CHRIST RESURRECTED ABOVE PASSION FACADE

High above the Passion facade, a gilded Christ sits resurrected, perched between two towers.

Christ resurrected

MAKING THE MOST OF YOUR VISIT

The Nativity facade

WHEN TO VISIT

To avoid crowds, come first thing in the morning. Or, plan to visit during mid-morning and mid to late-afternoon when golden light streams through the stained glass windows.

TIMING

If you're just walking around the exterior, an hour or two is plenty of time. If you'd like to go inside to the crypt, visit the museum, visit the towers, and walk down the spiraling stairway, you'll need three to four hours.

BONUS FEATURES

The **museum** displays Gaudí's scale models and shows photographs of the construction. The **crypt** holds Gaudí's remains. The excellent gift shop has a wide selection of Gaudi-related articles including, sculptures, jewelry, miniature churches, and beautiful books.

BUYING TICKETS

Tickets, with a set entry time, can only be purchased online. Advance reservations (available up to two months in advance) are essential to avoid disappointment. It's a good idea to book a private tour for more context.

VISITOR INFORMATION

✉ Pl. de la Sagrada Família, Eixample
☎ 93/207–3031 ⊕ www.sagradafamilia.org
💶 €20, with audio guide €26, with guided tour €27, with towers (depending if access is per-mitted at the time) €33 ⊘ Oct.–Mar., daily 9–6; Apr.–Sept., daily 9–8 Ⓜ Sagrada Família.

WHAT TO WEAR AND BRING

Visitors are encouraged not to wear shors and to cover bare shoulders. It's a good idea to bring binoculars to absorb details all the way up.

WHICH TOWER?

We do not recommend visiting the towers while construction is ongoing but if you must, choose the Nativity Façade. These are the oldest of the Sagrada Família's towers and the only ones that Gaudí worked on. Also, there's a small bridge which affords better views and a close-up of parts of the façade.

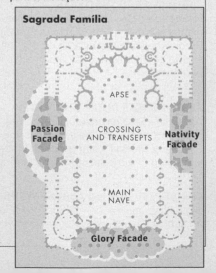

Sagrada Família

APSE

Passion Facade

CROSSING AND TRANSEPTS

Nativity Facade

MAIN NAVE

Glory Facade

Besta

$$ | CATALAN | The atmosphere is relaxed but sophisticated and the menu is a melting pot of Catalan and Galician cuisines. Fresh fish and seafood take pride of place, as do the local, seasonal vegetables. **Known for:** cosmopolitan vibe; seafood dishes; Catalan-Galician cuisine. [$] *Average main: €20* ✉ *Aribau 106, Eixample* ☎ *93/019–8294* 🌐 *bestabarcelona.com* [M] *Universitat L1, L2.*

★ Betlem

$ | CATALAN | Set In a charming Moderniste space dating back to 1892, this bar hits the perfect balance of quality, price, service, and ambiance. The menu mixes classic dishes like deep-fried calamari and spicy *patatas bravas,* with house specials like the steak tartare and show-stopping omelet with black pudding (or *butifarra negra*) and seasonal mushrooms. **Known for:** Moderniste interior; omelet with black pudding and mushrooms; sunny terrace. [$] *Average main: €15* ✉ *Girona 70, Eixample* ☎ *93/265–5105* [M] *Girona L4.*

Boa-Bao

$ | ASIAN FUSION | Blending food from across Asia (think bao buns, dim sum, pho, noodles, and curries) with a strong cocktail game and on-point design, Boa-Bao has the trend-conscious barcelonins convinced. There's a small patio if you prefer to dine outdoors, but that would mean missing out on the impressive redesign of a former two-story art gallery that now serves as a restaurant. **Known for:** strong cocktails; on-point design; not to be confused with Bao Bao chain. [$] *Average main: €15* ✉ *Pl. Dr. Letamendi 1, Eixample* ☎ *67/609–2974* 🌐 *www.boabao.es* ⏲ *Closed Mon. and Tues.* [M] *Passeig de Gràcia L2, L3, L4.*

★ Cinc Sentits

$$$$ | CATALAN | Obsessively local, scrupulously sourced, and masterfully cooked, the dishes of Catalan-Canadian chef Jordi Artal put the spotlight on the region's finest ingredients in an intimate, sophisticated setting. It's hard to believe that this garlanded restaurant is Jordi's first, but there's no arguing with the evidence of your *cinc sentits* (five senses). **Known for:** tasting menu only; excellent chef; awarded two Michelin stars. [$] *Average main: €109* ✉ *Entença 60, Eixample* ☎ *93/323–9490* 🌐 *cincsentits.com* ⏲ *Closed Mon. and Tues.* [M] *Provença.*

★ Cruix

$$$ | CATALAN | With two tasting menus priced at €28 (for nine courses) and €35 (for 12), Cruix is the fine-dining restaurant for people who don't want to blow 200 bucks on fine dining. Everything here is laid-back and unpretentious, including the exposed-brick interior, but the quality speaks to the Chef Miquel Pardo's pedigree: he worked under Spanish superstar chefs like Albert Adrià and Jordi Cruz before opening Cruix in 2017. **Known for:** excellent rice with shrimp and garlic; fine dining on a budget; affordable tasting menus. [$] *Average main: €28* ✉ *Entença 57, Eixample* ☎ *93/525–2318* 🌐 *www.cruixrestaurant.com* ⏲ *Closed Mon. and Tues. No dinner Sun.* [M] *Rocafort L1.*

★ Disfrutar

$$$$ | ECLECTIC | Three former head chefs from the now-closed "World's Best Restaurant" El Bulli have combined their considerable talents to create this roller-coaster ride of culinary fun. Sun streams into the gorgeous interior through skylights, spotlighting tasting menus of dazzling inventiveness and good taste. **Known for:** surprisingly affordable wine list; inventive food; tasting menus only. [$] *Average main: €160* ✉ *Villarroel 163, Eixample* ☎ *93/348–6896* 🌐 *www.disfrutarbarcelona.com* ⏲ *Closed weekends* [M] *Hospital Clínic.*

Embat

$$ | CATALAN | An *embat* is a puff of wind in Catalan, and this little bistro is a breath of fresh air in the sometimes stuffy Eixample. The highly affordable market cuisine is always impeccably fresh and freshly conceived, from flavorful brunches to a bargain lunch selection and a more elaborate evening menu. **Known for:** stylish minimalist interior; market-fresh Catalan dishes; modern, unfussy fare. [$] *Average main: €17* ✉ *Mallorca 304, Eixample* ☎ *93/458–0855* 🌐 *embatrestaurant.com* 🕒 *Closed Sun.* [M] *Verdaguer.*

Honest Greens

$ | **VEGETARIAN** | There are a few fish and meat options on the menu but most visitors skip the animal proteins and opt for the impressive selection of plant-based foods. Delicious salads, tasty vegetarian curries, and fresh grilled vegetables are a hit with the health-conscious and the vegan desserts are even tastier than regular versions. **Known for:** lots of vegan options; healthy but delicous food; great desserts. [$] *Average main: €18* ✉ *Rambla de Catalunya 3, Eixample* ☎ *93/122–7664* 🌐 *honestgreens.com/en* [M] *Catalunya L1, L3.*

★ La Real Hamburguesería

$ | **BURGER** | If you're jonesing for a burger, this laid-back, Venezuelan-owned fast-food spot is the place to go. The burgers are great, of course, but so are sides like deep-fried cheese sticks (*tequeños*) with sweet chili sauce. [$] *Average main: €14* ✉ *València 285, Tienda 03, Eixample* ☎ *93/832–8694* 🌐 *larealbcn.com* [M] *Girona L4.*

La Taverna Del Clínic

$$ | **SPANISH** | This is the kind of place you would never stumble upon by accident and, as a result, it is only really known to discerning locals and serious food lovers. The bar spills out onto a sunny street-side terrace where customers can enjoy truffle cannelloni and an excellent variation on patatas bravas, paired with selections from the excellent wine list. **Known for:** superb cheese selection; contemporary tapas; excellent patatas bravas. [$] *Average main: €20* ✉ *Rosselló 155, Eixample* ☎ *93/410–4221* 🌐 *www.latavernadelclinic.com* [M] *Hospital Clinic.*

★ Lasarte

$$$$ | **BASQUE** | While Martin Berasategui, one of San Sebastián's corps of master chefs, may not run the day-to-day operations of this Barcelona kitchen (it's in the capable hands of chef Paolo Casagrande) the restaurant continues to be a culinary triumph. Expect an eclectic selection of Basque, Mediterranean, and off-the-map creations, a hefty bill, and fierce perfectionism apparent in every dish. **Known for:** heavenly grilled pigeon; inventive cuisine at one of the best restaurants in Barcelona; magnificent tasting menu. [$] *Average main: €70* ✉ *Mallorca 259, Eixample* ☎ *939393/445–3242* 🌐 *www.restaurantlasarte.com* 🕒 *Closed Sun., Mon., 2 wks in Jan., 1 wk at Easter, and 3 wks in Aug./Sept.* [M] *Diagonal, Passeig de Gràcia, Provença (FGC).*

Manairó

$$$ | **CATALAN** | A *manairó* is a mysterious Pyrenean elf, and Jordi Herrera may be the culinary version: his ingenious meat-cooking methods—such as filet mignon *al faquir* (heated from within on red-hot spikes) or blowtorched on a homemade centrifuge—may seem eccentric but produce diabolically good results. Melt-in-your-mouth meat dishes form the centerpiece of Manairó's menus, but they are ably supported by a bonanza of bold and confident creations that aren't frightened of big flavors. **Known for:** sculptures and artworks by the chef; innovative contemporary cuisine; delicious meat dishes. [$] *Average main: €26* ✉ *Diputació 424, Eixample* ☎ *9393/231–0057* 🌐 *www.manairo.com* 🕒 *Closed Sun. and 1st wk of Jan.* [M] *Monumental.*

★ Moments

$$$$ | **CATALAN** | Inside the ultrasleek Hotel Mandarin Oriental Barcelona, this restaurant, with food by Raül Balam and his mother—the legendary Carme

Ruscalleda—lives up to its stellar pedigree, with original preparations that draw on deep wells of Catalan culinary traditions. Dishes display a masterful lightness of touch and come to the table so exquisitely presented that putting a fork into them feels almost like wanton vandalism. **Known for:** elaborate tasting menus; outstanding wine list; chef's table. $ *Average main: €150* ✉ *Passeig de Gràcia 38–40, Eixample* ☎ *9393/151–8781* 🌐 *www.mandarinoriental.com* 🕒 *Closed Sun., Mon., and 2 wks in Jan.* [M] *Passeig de Gràcia.*

Sartoria Panatieri

$ | **PIZZA** | "Farm to pizza" is the tagline at this urban chic pizzeria specializing in home-cured artisanal charcuteries and pizzas made in a wood-fired oven. The dough for the Neapolitan-style pizzas is made with organic hand-milled flour, and all the ingredients are fresh, organic, seasonal, and local (some are grown on-site at the restaurant). **Known for:** home-cured artisanal charcuteries; chic crowd; Neapolitan-style pizza made in a wood-fired oven. $ *Average main: €14* ✉ *Provença 330, Eixample* ☎ *93/105–5795* 🌐 *www.sartoriapanatieri.com* [M] *Diagonal L3, L5.*

★ Xerta

$$$$ | **CATALAN** | Much of Xerta's menu is the expected swanky fine-dining fare, but it stands out for its unique produce from the deltas and rivers of the Terres de l'Ebre region, such as sweet miniature *canyuts* (razor clams), oysters, and fresh eel. The superb weekday four-course lunch menu is a steal at €42. **Known for:** superb midweek lunch; produce from Terres de l'Ebre region; outstanding seafood and rice dishes. $ *Average main: €55* ✉ *Ohla Eixample hotel, Còrsega 289, Eixample* ☎ *9393/737–9080* 🌐 *www.xertarestaurant.com* 🕒 *Closed Sun. and Mon.* [M] *Provença.*

Coffee and Quick Bites

★ DeLaCrem

$ | **ICE CREAM** | For a cool pick-me-up on a hot Barcelona afternoon, you can't beat the seasonal, locally sourced, Italian-style ice cream from DeLaCrem. From the classics like vanilla, chocolate, and dulce de leche to more unconventional combinations like mandarin and orange blossom yogurt, pear and Parmesan, or pumpkin and toasted butter. **Known for:** pumpkin and toasted butter gelato; Italian-style ice cream; unconventional flavors. $ *Average main: €5* ✉ *Enric Granados, 15, Eixample* ☎ *93/004–1093* 🌐 *delacrem.cat* [M] *Universitat L1, L2.*

★ L' Atelier

$ | **BAKERY** | This superb café, bakery, and pastry school has set a new standard for sweet treats in the city. The boundless creativity of undisputed pastry genius and chef Eric Ortuño, has barcelonins pilgrimaging here from all over the city for their morning pastries. **Known for:** Catalan specialties during Easter; outstanding pastries; outstanding croissants. $ *Average main: €10* ✉ *Viladomat 140, Eixample* ☎ *93/828–7373* 🌐 *latelierbarcelona.com* 🕒 *Closed Sun. afternoon* [M] *Urgell L1.*

Hotels

★ Alma Hotel Barcelona

$$$$ | **HOTEL** | Only the facade is left to recall the Moderniste origins of the building; the inside spaces were completely redesigned in 2011, and the Alma emerged as Barcelona's sleekest mid-Eixample hotel. **Pros:** complementary minibar; British afternoon tea served daily (open to the public); gorgeous garden with sushi bar. **Cons:** no outdoor pool; budget-stretching room rates; pricey buffet breakfast. $ *Rooms from: €300* ✉ *Carrer Mallorca 271, Eixample* ☎ *93/216–4490* 🌐 *www.almahotels.com* 🛏 *72 rooms* 🍴 *No Meals* [M] *L3/L5 Diagonal, L4 Girona, FGC Provença.*

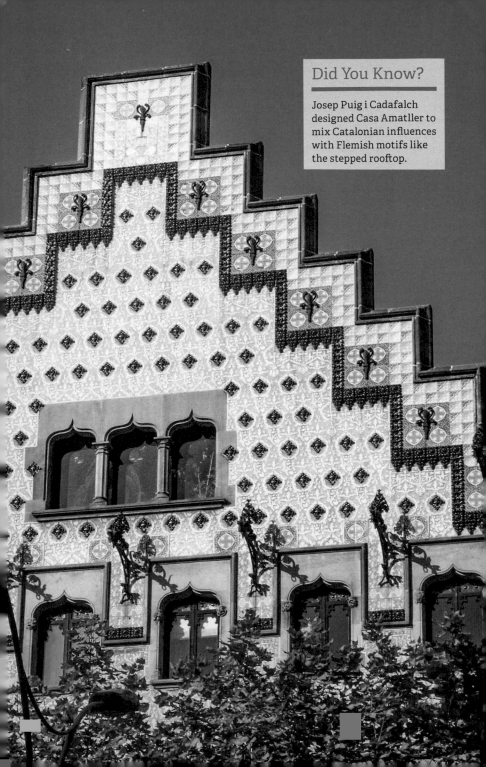

Casa Bonay

$$ | **HOTEL** | Fans of Barcelona's Modern-iste architecture will fall for this boutique hotel in a restored mansion dating back to 1869. There are plenty of places to relax, including the ultra-trendy Libertine cocktail bar, the cozy rooftop, and the guest rooms with original 19th-century design details such as the Modern-iste-style floor tiles with their colorful geometric shapes. **Pros:** stunning Mod-erniste design; contemporary Catalan food from Bodega Bonay; affordable. **Cons:** soundproofing could be better; no spa or pool; most rooms don't have balconies. $ *Rooms from: €153* ✉ *Gran Via de les Corts Catalanes 700, Eixample* ☎ *93/545–8070* ⊕ *www.casabonay.com* ⊠ *No Meals* ⟿ *67 rooms* Ⓜ *Tetuan L2.*

The Corner Hotel

$$$ | **HOTEL** | This hip hotel, positioned (yep, you guessed it) on a corner, has been fashioned from a handsome, turn-of-the-century building in Barcelona's stylish Eixample district, within a few blocks of Gaudí's key sights on Passeig de Gràcia. **Pros:** cool decor; walking distance to Passeig de Gràcia; rooms include complimentary bottle of water plus coffee and tea. **Cons:** interior-facing rooms lack natural light; some traffic noise; breakfast expensive for what you get. $ *Rooms from: €185* ✉ *Mallorca 178, Eixample* ☎ *93/554–2400* ⊕ *www. thecornerhotel-barcelona.com* ⟿ *72 rooms* ⊠ *No Meals* Ⓜ *FGC Provença; L5 Hospital Clinic.*

Hotel Alexandra Barcelona

$$ | **HOTEL** | **FAMILY** | Part of Hilton's upscale Curio Collection, Hotel Alexandra delivers a boutique hotel experience at a reasonable price. **Pros:** free private parking; affordable; suites have terraces and outdoor tubs. **Cons:** standard rooms on the small side; interior is rather dark; lower floors can be noisy. $ *Rooms from: €151* ✉ *Mallorca 251, Eixample* ☎ *93/467–7166* ⊕ *www.hilton.com/en/ hotels/bcnmaqq-alexandra-barcelona-ho-tel* ⊠ *No Meals* Ⓜ *Diagonal L3, L5.*

Hotel Astoria

$$ | **HOTEL** | Three blocks west of Rambla Catalunya, near the upper middle of the Eixample, this renovated classic property, part of the cutting-edge Derby Hotels Collection group of brilliant artistic restorations, is a treasure for the budget-minded. **Pros:** free entrance to the Egyptian Museum of Barcelona; prime location; excellent value for price. **Cons:** rooms on lower floors on the street side can be noisy; limited gym facilities; rooftop terrace pool is small. $ *Rooms from: €105* ✉ *Carrer Paris 203, Eixample* ☎ *9393/209–8311* ⊕ *www.derbyhotels. es/en/hotels/astoria-hotel* ⟿ *117 rooms* ⊠ *No Meals* Ⓜ *Provença (FGC), L3/L5 Diagonal.*

★ Hotel Claris Grand Luxe Barcelona

$$$$ | **HOTEL** | The legendary Hotel Claris, with its vast collection of antiques, is an icon of design, tradition, and connois-seurship. **Pros:** first-rate restaurant La Ter-raza; rooms in a variety of styles; Mayan Secret Spa with temazcal and pure chocolate skin treatment. **Cons:** capacity bookings can sometimes overwhelm the staff; rooftop terrace noise at night can reach down into sixth-floor rooms; basic ("Superior") rooms small for the price. $ *Rooms from: €250* ✉ *Carrer Pau Claris 150, Eixample* ☎ *9393/487–6262* ⊕ *www. hotelclaris.com* ⊠ *No Meals* ⟿ *124 rooms* Ⓜ *L2/L3/L4 Passeig de Gràcia.*

★ Hotel 1882

$$ | **HOTEL** | Just a few minutes' walk from Gaudí's unfinished masterpiece, la Sagrada Família, this hotel may be named for the year in which work on that project began but the feel is distinctly contemporary. **Pros:** strong sustaina-bility profile; private parking (at a cost); affordable designer hotel. **Cons:** no res-taurant (except breakfast); quite far from downtown attractions and beaches; no bar on the rooftop. $ *Rooms from: €125* ✉ *Còrsega 482, Eixample* ☎ *93/347–8486*

🌐 www.hotelbarcelona1882.com 🛏 182 rooms 🍴 No Meals [M] Sagrada Familia L2, L5.

★ Hotel El Palace Barcelona

$$$$ | HOTEL | Founded in 1919 by Caesar Ritz, the original Ritz (the grande dame of Barcelona hotels) was renamed in 2005 but kept its lavish, timeless style intact. **Pros:** Mayan-style sauna in the award-winning spa; historic grand-dame luxury; legendary cocktail bar. **Cons:** painfully pricey; may feel slightly intimidating; formal atmosphere. [$] *Rooms from: €320* ✉ *Gran Vía de les Corts Catalanes 668, Eixample* ☎ *9393/510–1130* 🌐 *www.hotelpalacebarcelona.com* 🛏 *120 rooms* 🍴 *No Meals* [M] *L2/L3/L4 Passeig de Gràcia.*

Hotel Granvía

$ | HOTEL | A 19th-century palatial home (built for the owner of the Bank of Barcelona), the Granvía opened as a hotel in 1935, and reopened in 2013 after a lengthy renovation, with its original features still intact: an art deco cupola in the entrance, coffered ceilings, pillared arches, and a marble grand staircase. **Pros:** pleasant terrace; historical setting; central location. **Cons:**; bathrooms a bit cramped; no pool, gym, or spa; most standard rooms have twin beds yoked together rather than doubles. [$] *Rooms from: €120* ✉ *Gran Vía de les Corts Catalanes 642, Eixample* ☎ *93/318–1900* 🌐 *www.hotelgranvia.com* 🛏 *58 rooms* 🍴 *Free Breakfast* [M] *L2/L3/L4 Passeig de Gràcia.*

Hotel Jazz

$$ | HOTEL | Bright colors, clean lines, and contemporary artwork give this hotel (dead center in the heart of Barcelona) a hip, fashionable feel. **Pros:** elevators work only on room keys, for added security; rooftop bar serves tapas and cocktails; central location. **Cons:** can get noisy; a bit pricey; no gym or spa. [$] *Rooms from: €170* ✉ *Carrer Pelai 3, Eixample* ☎ *93/552–9696* 🌐 *www.hoteljazz.com* 🛏 *108 rooms* 🍴 *No Meals* [M] *L1/L2 Universitat, Catalunya.*

★ Majestic Hotel & Spa

$$$$ | HOTEL | With an unbeatable location on Barcelona's most stylish boulevard—steps from Gaudí's La Pedrera and near the area's swankiest shops—and a stunning rooftop terrace with killer views of the city's landmarks, this hotel is a near-perfect place to stay. **Pros:** superb, personalized service; very good restaurant and spa; beloved city landmark with interesting history. **Cons:** pricey but excellent buffet breakfast; some standard rooms a bit small for the price; not easy on the wallet. [$] *Rooms from: €280* ✉ *Passeig de Gràcia 68, Eixample* ☎ *93/488–1717* 🌐 *majestichotelgroup.com/en/barcelona/hotel-majestic* 🛏 *275 rooms* 🍴 *No Meals* [M] *L2/L3/L4 Passeig de Gràcia, Provença (FGC).*

★ Mandarin Oriental Barcelona

$$$$ | HOTEL | A carpeted ramp leading from the elegant Passeig de Gràcia (flanked by Tiffany and Brioni boutiques) lends this hotel the air of a privileged—and pricey—inner sanctum. **Pros:** outstanding Moments restaurant; breathtaking views and Peruvian food on the roof; babysitters and parties for the kids, on request. **Cons:** rooms relatively small for a five-star accommodation; Wi-Fi free in rooms only if booked online; very pricey. [$] *Rooms from: €420* ✉ *Passeig de Gràcia 38–40, Eixample* ☎ *93/151–8888* 🌐 *www.mandarinoriental.com/barcelona* 🛏 *120 rooms* 🍴 *No Meals* [M] *L2/L3/L4 Passeig de Gràcia, L3/L5 Diagonal, Provença (FGC).*

★ Monument Hotel

$$$$ | HOTEL | Originally the home of Enric Battló, a brother of the textile magnate who commissioned Gaudí to redesign the Moderniste masterpiece Casa Battló, and a minute's walk away on the Passeig de Gràcia, the historic 1898 building that houses the Monument went through several incarnations before it was transformed into the elegant upmarket hotel it is today. **Pros:** superbly professional multilingual staff; outstanding dining options; ideal mid-Eixample location. **Cons:** pricey breakfast; hard on the budget; most "junior suites" are in effect large doubles with seating areas. $ *Rooms from: €340 ⊠ Passeig de Gràcia 73, Eixample ☎ 93/548–2000 ⊕ www.monumenthotel. com ⟿ 158 rooms* †○¶ *No Meals* Ⓜ *L3/L5 Diagonal, Provença (FGC).*

Ohla Eixample
$$$ | HOTEL | With its location just off Passeig de Gràcia and Rambla de Catalunya, Ohla Eixample is ideally situated for designer shopping and gawking at Gaudí, but it's still within easy reach of the Ciutat Vella and the beach. **Pros:** sleek design; outstanding food; well located for shopping and Gaudí. **Cons:** more modern than cozy; a bit far from the Old Town; lack of privacy with open plan room/shower. $ *Rooms from: €189 ⊠ Còrsega 289, Eixample ☎ 93/737–7977 ⊕ www. ohlaeixample.com/en* †○¶ *No Meals ⟿ 94 rooms* Ⓜ *Diagonal L3, L5.*

★ Seventy Barcelona
$$ | HOTEL | In a residential neighborhood two blocks from the top of Passeig de Gràcia, this boutique hotel is in an ideal spot for travelers who like to be close to the action, without being in the thick of it. **Pros:** excellent quality for the price; thoughtful, helpful staff; affordable boutique hotel. **Cons:** outdoor pool is adults only; few rooms with patios or balconies; busy street outside. $ *Rooms from: €160 ⊠ Còrsega 344-352, Eixample ☎ 93/012–1270 ⊕ www.seventybarcelona.com* †○¶ *No Meals* Ⓜ *Diagonal L3, L5.*

Sir Victor Hotel
$$$$ | HOTEL | Named after Catalan poet and playwright Caterina Albert i Paradís, who became a prominent member of the Modernisme movement under her pseudonym Victor Català, the uptown, upmarket Sir Victor Hotel will appeal to design lovers with its modern, ultra-elegant design. **Pros:** rooftop overlooking La Pedrera; on point design; excellent food

and drinks. **Cons:** standard rooms on the small side; quite pricey; expensive public parking. $ *Rooms from: €252 ⊠ Rosselló 265, Eixample ☎ 93/271–1244 ⊕ www. sirhotels.com/en/victor* †○¶ *No Meals ⟿ 91 rooms* Ⓜ *Diagonal L3, L5.*

SixtyTwo Hotel
$$$ | HOTEL | Across from Gaudí's Casa Batlló and just down Passeig de Gràcia from his Casa Milà (La Pedrera), this boutique hotel is surrounded by Barcelona's top shopping addresses and leading restaurants. **Pros:** free coffee, tea, and snacks in the lounge, 24/7; good deals on parking; ideal location. **Cons:** good breakfast buffet; no pool, gym, or spa; some rooms a bit small. $ *Rooms from: €225 ⊠ Passeig de Gràcia 62, Eixample ☎ 93/272–4180 ⊕ www.sixtytwohotel. com ⟿ 44 rooms* †○¶ *No Meals* Ⓜ *L2/L3/ L4 Passeig de Gràcia.*

yök Casa + Cultura
$$ | APARTMENT | Ideally located at the edge of the Eixample and Sant Pere neighborhoods, yök is named after the Catalan word "lloc," meaning "place" or "location." The property is comprised of three renovated boutique apartments that date back to 1900 and the time of the Catalan Moderniste movement, with a rooftop terrace that has sweeping views of Barcelona. **Pros:** great option for families or groups; sleek design; stunning rooftop. **Cons:** no pool or spa; no restaurant; minimum two-night stay. $ *Rooms from: €130 ⊠ Carrer de Trafalgar 39, Eixample ☎ 64/062–5313 ⊕ www.helloyok. com* †○¶ *No Meals ⟿ 3 apartments* Ⓜ *Arc de Triomf L1.*

Yurbban Passage Hotel & Spa
$$ | HOTEL | On the edge of the hip Sant Pere neighborhood, right where it meets the more upmarket Eixample, you're never far from anything when you choose to stay here. **Pros:** rooftop with views and a pool; great value; outstanding spa. **Cons:** area can be a bit sketchy at night; no parking; small rooftop pool. $ *Rooms from: €138 ⊠ Trafalgar 26, Eixample*

93/882–8977 ⊕ www.yurbbanpassage.com ⌾❘ No Meals ⇥ 60 rooms Ⓜ Urquinaona L1, L4.

ⓨ Nightlife

Barcelona's vast L'Eixample district is the largest and most diverse nightlife destination in town.

BARS

★ Banker's Bar

COCKTAIL LOUNGES | With decor details from its past life as a bank (like the safety deposit boxes on the wall), the swank cocktail bar of the Mandarin Oriental Hotel lounge is an atmospheric spot for an opulent night out. There's an "East meets West" menu for classic cocktail favorites—the Banker's Martini is the house specialty—and light food. DJs play mellow jazz, swing, and blues tunes on weekends. ✉ Hotel Mandarin Oriental, Passeig de Gràcia 38–40, Eixample 93/151–8782 ⊕ www.mandarinoriental.es/barcelona Ⓜ Passeig de Gràcia.

Dry Martini

COCKTAIL LOUNGES | An homage to the traditional English martini bar of decades past, this stately spot by local mixology maestro Javier de las Muelas is paradise for cocktail aficionados seeking expertly mixed drinks. ✉ Aribau 162, Eixample 93/217–5072 ⊕ www.drymartiniorg.com Ⓜ Provença.

Jonny Aldana

BARS | This cheery technicolor bar-resto, featuring a tiled facade and open-window bar with stools inside and out, is bursting with 1950s iconography. Wines are sold by the glass and beer is served from the tap, but it's the superb vermouths and cocktails combined with vegetarian tapas that keep patrons coming back. ✉ Aldana 9, Eixample 93/174–2083 ⊕ www.jonnyaldana.com ⊘ Closed Mon. Ⓜ Paral.lel.

La Vinoteca Torres

WINE BARS | In a space ideally located on Barcelona's exclusive shopping avenue, Passeig de Gràcia, the acclaimed Torres wine dynasty offers an ample selection of their international wines and spirits to accompany delectable Mediterranean fish or meat dishes such as the signature oxtail in Sangre de Toro red wine sauce. The dark, modern space is adorned with walls of stacked wine bottles, and strategic lighting illuminates the natural wood tables. ✉ Passeig de Gràcia 78, Eixample 93/272–6625 ⊕ www.lavinotecatorres.com Ⓜ Passeig de Gràcia, Diagonal.

Les Gens que J'aime

COCKTAIL LOUNGES | Bohemia meets the Moulin Rouge at this intimate, below-street-level bordello-inspired bar with turn-of-the-20th-century memorabilia like fringed lampshades, faded period portraits, and comfy wicker sofas cushioned with lush red velvet. There's usually jazz playing in this laid-back spot where guests linger over cocktails (whiskey sours are popular). ✉ València 286, bajos, Eixample 93/215–6879 ⊕ www.lesgensquejaime.com Ⓜ Passeig de Gràcia.

Milano

LIVE MUSIC | For more than a decade, this "secret" basement bar, in an area otherwise dominated by student pubs and tourist traps, has had a rotating lineup of international acts including blues, soul, jazz, flamenco, swing, and pop. The space resembles a 1940s cabaret, with a brass bar, spot-lit photos of previous acts, and red banquette-style seating. ✉ Ronda Universitat 35, Eixample 93/112–7150 ⊕ www.camparimilano.com/en Ⓜ Catalunya, Universitat.

★ Morro Fi

BARS | Opened by a trio of vermouth aficionados, Morro Fi (loosely translates as "refined palate") began as a food blog that morphed into a bar determined to educate people about enjoying vermouth (they even produce their own brand) with select tapas. The result? Locals and the odd expat routinely spilling out into the streets, drink in hand while indie music blares. ✉ *Consell de Cent 171, Eixample* ⊕ *www.morrofi.cat* Ⓜ *Urgell.*

★ Pepa Bar a Vins

WINE BARS | When it comes to wine, the team at Pepa really know their grapes, and they excel with natural wines, though there's also vermouth and artisanal beer if you're in the mood for that. The food is excellent, too, and it's all served in an old converted library. ✉ *Aribau 41, Eixample* ☎ *93/611–1885* ⊙ *Closed Mon. and Tues.* Ⓜ *Universitat L1, L2.*

Senyor Vermut

BARS | This snazzy, high-ceilinged *vermuteria* has guests lining up to sample a generous selection of more than 40 *vermuts* served with traditional tapas. From bitter to earthy or aged in a barrel, the classic aperitif is the star attraction though other offerings include wine, beer, and juices. ✉ *Carrer de Provença 85, Eixample* ☎ *93/532–8865* Ⓜ *Entença.*

SIPS

COCKTAIL LOUNGES | Perhaps more akin to a laboratory than a cocktail bar, SIPS draws from a menu influenced by seasonal ingredients and uses state-of-the-art techniques to mix a range of classic recipes and signature concoctions. ✉ *Muntaner 108, Eixample* ☎ *6193/964–1402* ⊕ *sips.barcelona* Ⓜ *Hospital Clínic L5.*

★ Solange Cocktails and Luxury Spirits

COCKTAIL LOUNGES | This sleek, luxurious lounge space is named after Solange Dimitrios, 007's original Bond girl, and the homage includes signature cocktails that reference Bond films, characters, and even a "secret mission" concoction for the more daring. ✉ *Carrer Aribau 143, Eixample* ☎ *93/164–3625* ⊕ *www.solangecocktail.com* Ⓜ *Hospital Clínic, Diagonal.*

Xixbar

COCKTAIL LOUNGES | The interior of this Alice in Wonderland–like venue of checkered half-walls, a marble bar, and contemporary objets d'art rarely seen on ceilings is the first clue that you've landed somewhere special. Beyond that, with 50-plus flavors of gins and infusions, and a lounge-friendly 3 am last call on weekends, Xix turns conventional cocktail drinkers into card-carrying gin lovers. ✉ *Carrer de Rocafort 19, Eixample* ☎ *93/423–4314* ⊕ *www.xixbar.com* ⊙ *Closed Sun. and Mon.* Ⓜ *Poble Sec.*

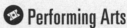 **Performing Arts**

FLAMENCO

Palacio del Flamenco

FOLK/TRADITIONAL DANCE | This Eixample music hall showcases some of the city's best flamenco. Prices start at €35 for a drink and a show, up to €110. (Save money by purchasing tickets online in advance.) Late shows are slightly cheaper. ✉ *Balmes 139, Eixample* ☎ *93/218–7237* ⊕ *www.palaciodelflamenco.com* 🎫 *€35-€110* Ⓜ *Provença, Diagonal.*

THEATER

Teatre Nacional de Catalunya

THEATER | This grandiose glass-enclosed classical temple was designed by Ricardo Bofill, architect of Barcelona's airport and the sail-shaped W Barcelona hotel. Programs cover everything from Shakespeare to avant-garde theater. Most productions, as the name suggests, are in Catalan but beautiful to witness all the same. ✉ *Plaça de les Arts 1, Eixample* ☎ *93/306–5700* ⊕ *www.tnc.cat* Ⓜ *Glóries, Monumental.*

Teatre Tívoli

THEATER | One of the city's most beloved traditional theater and dance venues, the Tívoli has staged timeless classics and has hosted everyone from the Ballet Nacional de Cuba to flamenco and teeny-bopper treats. ✉ *Casp 8, Eixample* ☎ *93/215–9570* ⊕ *www.grupbalana.com* Ⓜ *Catalunya.*

Gràcia

Once it's own village, Gràcia has become Barcelona's bohemian neighborhood, filled with trendy bars and restaurants, outdoor cafés, gourmet shops, artists studios, and designer boutiques. This is where Barcelona's young, creative crowd comes to party and hang out. The area begins at Gaudí's playful Park Güell and continues past his first commissioned house, Casa Vicens.

 Sights

Casa-Museu Gaudí

HISTORIC HOME | Up the steps of Park Güell and to the right is the whimsical Alice-in-Wonderland-esque house where Gaudí lived with his niece from 1906 until 1925. Now a small museum, exhibits include Gaudí-designed furniture and decorations, drawings, and portraits and busts of the architect. Stop by if you are in the area, but the museum is not worth traveling far for. ✉ *Park Güell, Carretera del Carmel 23A, Gràcia* ☎ *93/219–3811* ⊕ *www.casamuseugaudi.org* ✆ *€5.50* ☞ *Not included in the admission fee for Park Güell* Ⓜ *L3 Lesseps, Vallcarca.*

★ Casa Vicens

HISTORIC HOME | Antoni Gaudí's first important commission as a young architect began in 1883 and finished in 1885. For this house Gaudí still used his traditional architect's tools, particularly the T square. The historical eclecticism (that is, borrowing freely from past architectural styles around the world) of the early Art Nouveau movement is evident in the Orientalist themes and Mudejar (Moorish-inspired) motifs lavished throughout the design. The client, Don Manuel Vicens Montaner, a stock and currency broker, entrusted the young architect with designing his summer garden home in the former village of Gràcia. Casa Vicens stands out for its polychromatic façade, made with green and white checkered tiles, in combination with tiles with floral patterns. ✉ *Carrer de les Carolines 20–26, Gràcia* ⊕ *www.casavicens.org* ✆ *€16* Ⓜ *L3 Fontana, Lesseps.*

Gran de Gràcia

STREET | This highly trafficked central artery up through Gràcia is lined with buildings of great artistic and architectural interest, beginning with the hotel **Can Fuster**. Built between 1908 and 1911 by Palau de la Música Catalana architect Lluís Domènech i Montaner in collaboration with his son Pere Domènech i Roure, the building shows a clear move away from the chromatically effusive heights of Art Nouveau. More powerful, and somehow less superficial, than much of that style of architecture, it uses the winged supports under the balconies and the floral base under the corner tower as important structural elements instead of as pure ornamentation, as Domènech i Montaner the elder might have. As you move up Gran de Gràcia, probable Francesc Berenguer buildings can be identified at No. 15; No. 23, with its scrolled cornice; and Nos. 35, 49, 51, 61, and 77. ✉ *Gran de Gràcia, Gràcia* Ⓜ *L3 Fontana, Lesseps; FGC Gràcia.*

Mercat de la Llibertat

MARKET | This uptown version of the Rambla's Boqueria market is one of Gràcia's coziest spaces, a food market big enough to roam in and small enough to make you feel at home. Built by Francesc Berenguer between 1888 and 1893, the Llibertat market reflects, in its name alone, the revolutionary and democratic sentiment strong in Gràcia's traditionally blue-collar residents. Look for Berenguer's decorative swans swimming along the roof line and the snails surrounding Gràcia's coat of arms. ✉ *Pl. Llibertat 27, Gràcia* ☎ *93/217–0995* ⊕ *www.bcn.es/mercatsmunicipals* ⊘ *Closed Sun.* Ⓜ *FGC Gràcia.*

★ Park Güell

CITY PARK | **FAMILY** | Alternately shady, green, floral, or sunny, this park is one of

Gaudí's, and Barcelona's, most visited venues. Named for and commissioned by Gaudí's main patron, Count Eusebi Güell, it was originally intended as a gated residential community based on the English Garden City model, with a covered marketplace. The pillars of the market support the main public square above it, where impromptu dances and plays were performed. Gaudí highlights include the gingerbread gatehouses; the **Casa-Museu Gaudí,** where the architect lived; the Room of a Hundred Columns; and the fabulous serpentine polychrome bench that snakes along the main square by Gaudí assistant Josep Maria. Visitors must pay an entrance fee to the "monumental area," where the main attractions are located; the rest of the park remains free to enter. Tickets should be booked online up to three months in advance. ⊠ *Carrer d'Olot s/n, Gràcia* ☎ *93/409–1831* ⊕ *parkguell.barcelona* 🎫 *From €10* ⌕ *Book online to skip the lines* Ⓜ *L3 Lesseps, Vallcarca.*

Plaça de la Vila de Gràcia

PLAZA/SQUARE | Originally named Plaça Rius i Taulet (until 2009) for the memorable Gràcia mayor Francesc Rius i Taulet, this is the town's most emblematic and historic square, marked by the handsome clock tower in its center. The tower, unveiled in 1864, is just over 110 feet tall. It has water fountains around its base, royal Bourbon crests over the fountains, and an iron balustrade atop the octagonal brick shaft stretching up to the clock and belfry. The symbol of Gràcia, the clock tower was bombarded by federal troops when Gràcia attempted to secede from the Spanish state during the 1870s. ⊠ *Pl. de la Vila de Gràcia, Gràcia* Ⓜ *L3 Fontana, Gràcia (FGC).*

Plaça de la Virreina

PLAZA/SQUARE | The much-damaged and oft-restored church of Sant Joan de Gràcia in this square stands where the Palau de la Virreina once stood, the mansion of the same *virreina* (wife, or in this case, widow of a viceroy) whose 18th-century palace, the Pallau de la Virreina, stands on the Rambla. (The Palau is now a prominent municipal museum and art gallery.) The story of La Virreina, a young noblewoman widowed at an early age by the death of the elderly viceroy of Peru, is symbolized in the bronze sculpture in the center of the square: it portrays Ruth of the Old Testament, represented carrying the sheaves of wheat she was gathering when she learned of the death of her husband, Boaz. Ruth is the Old Testament paradigm of wifely fidelity to her husband's clan, a parallel to La Virreina—who spent her life doing good deeds with her husband's fortune. ⊠ *Pl. de la Virreina, Gràcia* Ⓜ *L3 Fontana.*

Plaça del Diamant

PLAZA/SQUARE | This little square is of enormous sentimental importance in Barcelona as the site of the opening and closing scenes of 20th-century Catalan writer Mercé Rodoreda's famous 1962 novel *La Plaça del Diamant.* Translated by the late American poet David Rosenthal as *The Time of the Doves,* it is the most widely translated and published Catalan novel of all time: a tender yet brutal story of a young woman devoured by the Spanish Civil War and, in a larger sense, by life itself. The bronze birds represent the pigeons that Colometa spent her life obsessively breeding; the male figure on the left pierced by bolts of steel is Quimet, her first love and husband, whom she met at a dance in this square and later lost in the war. ⊠ *Pl. del Diamant* Ⓜ *L3 Fontana.*

🍴 Restaurants

This lively and intimate neighborhood is home to many of Barcelona's artists, musicians, and actors. The bohemian atmosphere is reflected in an eclectic collection of restaurants encompassing everything from street food and affordable ethnic cuisine to thoroughly sophisticated dining.

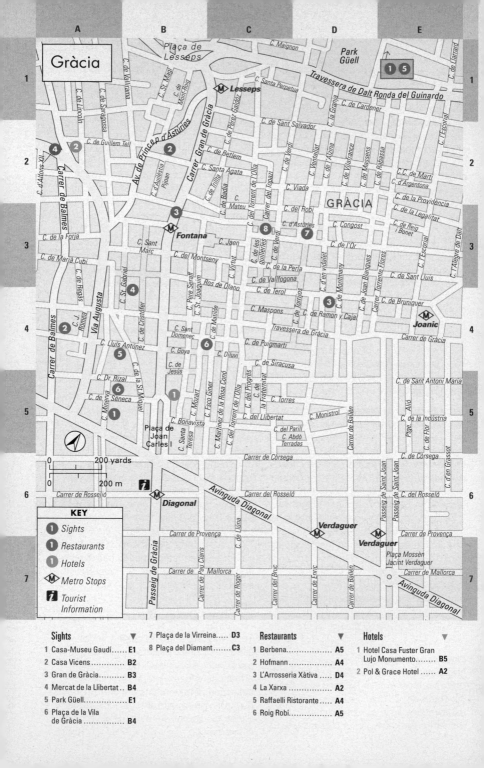

Gràcia

KEY

- Sights
- Restaurants
- Hotels
- Metro Stops
- Tourist Information

0 — 200 yards
0 — 200 m

Sights ▼
1 Casa-Museu Gaudí...... **E1**
2 Casa Vicens............. **B2**
3 Gran de Gràcia.......... **B3**
4 Mercat de la Llibertat.. **B4**
5 Park Güell............... **E1**
6 Plaça de la Vila
   de Gràcia **B4**
7 Plaça de la Virreina..... **D3**
8 Plaça del Diamant........ **C3**

Restaurants ▼
1 Berbena.................. **A5**
2 Hofmann................. **A4**
3 L'Arrosseria Xàtiva **D4**
4 La Xarxa **A2**
5 Raffaelli Ristorante **A4**
6 Roig Robí................ **A5**

Hotels ▼
1 Hotel Casa Fuster Gran
   Lujo Monumento........ **B5**
2 Pol & Grace Hotel **A2**

Berbena

$$ | **CATALAN** | One of the first things you'll notice here is the scent of freshly baked bread, then you'll take in the cozy, ultra-contemporary interior. Take a seat at one of the oversized windows facing the street and your taste buds will get in on the action, appreciating the natural wine, craft beer, and variety of healthy, seasonal Catalan dishes made almost exclusively from locally sourced organic produce. **Known for:** local "secret"; seasonal, organic food; natural wine. $ *Average main: €18* ✉ *Minerva 6, Gràcia* ☎ *93/801–5987* ⊕ *berbenabcn.com* ⊗ *Closed Mon. and Tues.* Ⓜ *Diagonal L3, L5.*

Hofmann

$$$$ | **MEDITERRANEAN** | The late Mey Hofmann, German-born and Catalonia-trained, was revered for decades for her creative Mediterranean and international cuisine based on carefully selected raw materials prepared with unrelenting quality. Her team carries on her legacy in this graceful designer space with a glassed-in kitchen as center stage. **Known for:** adjoining Racó Hofmann café; great value set menu at lunch time; sardine tart. $ *Average main: €30* ✉ *La Granada del Penedès 14, Gràcia* ☎ *93/218–7165* ⊕ *www.hofmann-bcn.com* ⊗ *No lunch Sat., Closed Sun.* Ⓜ *Gràcia, Diagonal.*

L'Arrosseria Xàtiva

$$ | **SPANISH** | **FAMILY** | This rustic dining room in Gràcia, a spin-off from the original in Les Corts, is a great spot to savor some of Barcelona's finest paellas and rice dishes. What's more, they can be ordered as individual helpings (as opposed to that standard minimum-two-person serving)—meaning you don't have to eat the same dish as your companion. Fish, seafood, and grilled meats round out a complete menu prepared with loving care and using top ingredients. **Known for:** all-day kitchen on weekends; individual rice portions; traditional paella. $ *Average main: €18* ✉ *Torrent d'en Vidalet 26, Gràcia*

☎ *93/284–8502* ⊕ *www.grupxativa.com* Ⓜ *Joanic.*

★ La Xarxa

$$ | **CATALAN** | This beautifully restored, historic wine bar doesn't get much tourist traffic but the focus on local produce and outstanding service means that the cozy patio stays busy from lunchtime on. Don't miss the veal cheek macaroni or the anchovies marinated in sherry vinegar. **Known for:** local gem; anchovies marinated in sherry vinegar; beautifully restored historic wine bar. $ *Average main: €18* ✉ *Pl. Molina 2, Gràcia* ☎ *93/200–1348* ⊕ *grupovarela.es/la-xarxa* ⊗ *Closed Mon., No dinner Sun.* Ⓜ *Plaça Molina FGC.*

★ Raffaelli Ristorante

$$ | **ITALIAN** | For authentic-but-sophisticated home-cooked Italian cuisine, this is the go-to spot in the Catalan capital. Sisters Greta and Gioia Raffaelli and their father Sandro, originally from Lucca, Italy, serve Neapolitan-style fried pizza, steaming dishes of seafood spaghetti, mouthwatering veal *alla Milanesa*, and a light-as-air tiramisú to finish it all off. **Known for:** Neapolitan fried pizza; authentic, home-cooked Italian food; Italian wine list. $ *Average main: €17* ✉ *Luis Antúnez 11, Gràcia* ☎ *65/256–0729* ⊕ *raffaelliristorante.com/en* Ⓜ *Gràcia FGC.*

Roig Robí

$$$ | **CATALAN** | A polished dining spot with a garden terrace, Roig Robí ("ruby red" in Catalan, as in the color of certain wines) maintains a high level of culinary excellence, serving traditional Catalan market cuisine with original touches directed by chef Mercé Navarro. Top-value prix fixe menus of seasonal specialties are available at both lunch and dinner. **Known for:** helmed by excellent chef; top-notch Catalan market cuisine; seasonal specials. $ *Average main: €26* ✉ *Sèneca 20, Gràcia* ☎ *93/218–9222* ⊕ *www.roigrobi.com* ⊗ *Closed Sun. and 2 wks in Aug. No lunch Sat.* Ⓜ *Diagonal, Gràcia (FGC).*

8

Barcelona GRÀCIA

Hotels

Hotel Casa Fuster Gran Lujo Monumento

$$$$ | HOTEL | Though there's much to recommend about this hotel, one of the key recommendations is the opportunity to stay in an Art Nouveau building designed by Lluís Domènech i Montaner, architect of the sumptuous Palau de la Música Catalana. **Pros:** all the Moderniste details you could want; ample rooms with luxury-level amenities; well situated for exploring both Gràcia and the Eixample. **Cons:** rooms facing Passeig de Gràcia could use better soundproofing; service can be a bit stiff; maybe too much Modernism for some. $ *Rooms from: €270* ✉ *Passeig de Gràcia 132, Gràcia* ☎ *93/255–3000* ⊕ *www.hotelcasafuster. com* ⬑ *105 rooms* ❤️| *No Meals* Ⓜ *L3/L5 Diagonal.*

Pol & Grace Hotel

$ | HOTEL | Named for the young owners who renovated and opened this hotel, the Pol & Grace is strategically located for exploring Gràcia. **Pros:** book exchange and DVD collection in the lobby; fun and laid-back atmosphere; children under 10 stay free. **Cons:** building of no particular architectural interest; no restaurant on-site; no gym or pool. $ *Rooms from: €85* ✉ *Guillem Tell 49, Gràcia* ☎ *93/415–4000* ⊕ *www.polgracehotel.es* ⬑ *64 rooms* ❤️| *No Meals* Ⓜ *Sant Gervasi, Pl. Molina (FGC).*

Shopping

Anna Povo

WOMEN'S CLOTHING | Look for an elegant and innovative selection of relaxed knits, coats, and dresses at this stylish boutique. Anna Povo's designs tend to sleek and minimalist, in cool tones of gray and beige. ✉ *Providència 75, Gràcia* ☎ *93/319–3561* ⊕ *www.annapovo.com* ◔ *Closed Sun.* Ⓜ *Joanic.*

Upper Barcelona: Sarrià and Pedralbes

Sarrià was originally a country village, overlooking Barcelona from the foothills of the Collserola. Eventually absorbed by the westward-expanding city, the village, 15 minutes by FGC commuter train from Plaça de Catalunya, has become a unique neighborhood made up of old-timers who speak only Catalan; writers, artists, and other creatives; gourmet shops and upscale restaurants; and expats, who prize the neighborhood for its proximity to the international schools.

Cross Avinguda Foix from Sarrià and you're in Pedralbes—the wealthiest residential neighborhood in the city. (Many of the F.C. Barcelona superstars have their multimillion-euro homes here, and the exclusive Real Club de Tenis de Barcelona is close by.) The centerpiece of this district is the 14th-century Monestir (Monastery) de Pedralbes; other points of interest include Gaudí's Pavellons de la Finca Güell, and the gardens of the Palau Reial de Pedralbes, a 20-minute walk downhill from the monastery.

Sights

Col·legi de les Teresianes

COLLEGE | Built in 1889 for the Reverend Mothers of St. Theresa, when Gaudí was still occasionally using straight lines, the upper floors of this former school are reminiscent of those in Berenguer's apartment at Carrer de l'Or 44, with its steep peaks and verticality. Hired to take over for another architect, Gaudí found his freedom of movement somewhat limited in this project. The dominant theme here is the architect's use of steep, narrow catenary arches and Mudejar exposed-brick pillars. The most striking effects are on the second floor, where two rows of a dozen catenary arches run the width of the building, each of

A quiet space for reflection: the courtyard of the Monestir de Pedralbes

them unique; as Gaudí explained, no two things in nature are identical. The brick columns are crowned with T-shaped brick capitals (for St. Theresa). ✉ *Ganduxer 85, Sant Gervasi* ☎ *93/212–3354* ⊕ *ganduxer. escolateresiana.com* Ⓜ *La Bonanova, Les Tres Torres (FGC).*

★ Monestir de Pedralbes
RELIGIOUS BUILDING | This marvel of a monastery, named for its original white stones (*pedres albes, from the Latin petras albas*), is really a convent, founded in 1326 for the Franciscan order of Poor Clares by Reina (Queen) Elisenda. The three-story Gothic cloister, one of the finest in Europe, surrounds a lush garden. The day cells, where the nuns spend their mornings praying, sewing, and studying, circle the arcaded courtyard. The Capella de Sant Miquel, just to the right of the entrance, has murals painted in 1346 by Catalan master Ferrer Bassa. Look for the letters spelling out " *No m'oblidi/ digui-li a Joan/ a quatre de setembre de 1415"* ("Do not forget me / tell John / September 4, 1415") scratched between the figures of St. Francis and St. Clare (with book and quill). While the true meaning of the message is unknown, one theory is that it was written by a brokenhearted novice. The nuns' upstairs dormitory contains the convent's treasures: paintings, liturgical objects, and seven centuries of artistic and cultural patrimony. ✉ *Baixada del Monestir 9, Pedralbes* ☎ *93/256–3434* ⊕ *mone-stirpedralbes.bcn.cat/en* 🎟 *€5; free Sun. after 3 pm, and 1st Sun. of every month* ⊘ *Closed Mon.* Ⓜ *Reina Elisenda (FGC).*

Pavellons de la Finca Güell–Càtedra Gaudí
GARDEN | Work on the Finca began in 1883 as an extension of Count Eusebi Güell's family estate. Gaudí, the count's architect of choice, was commissioned to do the gardens and the two entrance pavilions (1884–87); the rest of the project was never finished. The Pavellons (pavilions) now belong to the University of Barcelona, which has handed them over to the Municipal Institute for Urban Landscape (IMPUiQV) for ten years (2015-2024). During this period,

Upper Barcelona: Sarrià and Pedralbes

KEY

- **1** Sights
- **1** Restaurants
- **1** Hotels
- Ⓜ Metro Stops
- Ⓕ FGC Stops

IMPUiQV will carry out a comprehensive restoration of Gaudí's work. Depending on the state of the renovation work, the complex may be open for heritage visits, as well as cultural and educational activities but will largely remain closed. The fierce wrought-iron dragon gate is Gaudí's reference to the Garden of the Hesperides, as described by national poet Jacint Verdaguer's epic poem *L'Atlàntida* (1877)—the *Iliad* of Catalonia's historic-mythic origins. ⊠ *Av. Pedralbes 7, Pedralbes* ☎ *9393/317–7652 guided tours* ⊕ *www.rutadelmodernisme.com* Ⓜ *L3 Palau Reial.*

Sarrià

NEIGHBORHOOD | The village of Sarrià was originally a cluster of farms and country houses overlooking Barcelona from the hills. Once dismissively described as nothing but "winds, brooks, and convents," this quiet enclave is now a prime residential neighborhood at the upper edge of the city. Start an exploration at the square—the locus, at various times, of antique and bric-a-brac markets, book fairs, artisanal food and wine fairs, sardana dances (Sunday morning), concerts, and Christmas pageants. The 10th-century Romanesque **Church of Sant Vicenç** dominates the main square, the Plaça de Sarrià; the bell tower, illuminated on weekend nights, is truly impressive. Across Passeig de la Reina Elisenda from the church (50 yards to the left) is the 100-year-old Moderniste **Mercat de Sarrià.** Allow a few hours to wander the surrounding streets and to stop at Sarrià's famous **Foix** pastry shops. ⊠ *Sarrià* Ⓜ *Sarrià (FGC Line L6).*

Tibidabo

VIEWPOINT | FAMILY | One of Barcelona's two promontories, this hill bears a distinctive name, generally translated as "To Thee I Will Give." It refers to the Catalan legend that this was the spot from which Satan tempted Christ with all the riches of the earth below (namely, Barcelona). On a clear day, the views from this 1,789-foot peak are legendary. Tibidabo's skyline is marked by a neo-Gothic church, the work of Enric Sagnier in 1902, and—off to one side, near the village of Vallvidrera—the 854-foot communications tower, the **Torre de Collserola,** designed by Sir Norman Foster. If you're with kids, take the San Francisco–style Tramvía Blau (Blue Trolley) from Plaça Kennedy to the overlook at the top, and transfer to the funicular to the 100-year-old **amusement park** at the summit. ⊠ *Pl. Tibidabo 3–4, Tibidabo* ☎ *93/211–7942 amusement park* ⊕ *www.tibidabo.cat* ⊠ *Amusement park €28.50* Ⓜ *FGC L7 Tibidabo, then Tramvía Blau.*

★ Torre Bellesguard

HISTORIC HOME | For an extraordinary Gaudí experience, climb up above Plaça de la Bonanova to this private residence built between 1900 and 1909 over the ruins of the summer palace of the last of the sovereign count-kings of the Catalan-Aragonese realm, Martí I l'Humà (Martin I the Humane), whose reign ended in 1410. In homage to this medieval history, Gaudí endowed the house with a tower, gargoyles, and crenellated battlements. The rest—the catenary arches, the trencadís in the facade, the stained-glass windows—is pure Art Nouveau. Look for the red and gold Catalan *senyera* (banner) on the tower, topped by the four-armed Greek cross Gaudí often used. Guided tours in English available every day at 11 am and 1 pm. The visit includes access to the roof, which Gaudí designed to resemble a dragon, along with the gardens, patio, and stables. Reservations are required for the highly recommended guided tour (reserva@bellesguardgaudi.com). ⊠ *Calle Bellesguard 16–20, Sant Gervasi* ☎ *93/250–4093* ⊕ *www.bellesguardgaudi.com* ⊠ *From €10* ⊙ *Closed Mon.* ⟲ *Guided tours in English available every day at 11 am and 1 pm* Ⓜ *Av. Tibidabo (FGC).*

🍴 Restaurants

Take an excursion to the upper reaches of town for an excellent selection of bars, cafés, and restaurants, along with cool summer evening breezes and a sense of well-heeled village life.

ABaC

$$$$ | **CATALAN** | The only choice here is between the two tasting menus, but chef Jordi Cruz is a culinary phenom in Spain, so you can trust that you'll be wowed. The hypercreative sampling varies wildly from season to season, but no expense or effort is ever spared. **Known for:** elegant setting in elegant boutique hotel; celebrity chef; creative in-season dishes. $ *Average main:* €195 ⊠ *Av. del Tibidabo 1–7, Tibidabo* ☎ *93/319–6600* ⊕ *www.abacrestaurant. com/en* Ⓜ *Tibidabo.*

Bar Tomás

$ | **TAPAS** | Famous for its *patatas bravas amb allioli* (potatoes with fiery hot sauce and allioli, an emulsion of crushed garlic and olive oil), accompanied by freezing mugs of San Miguel beer, this old-fashioned Sarrià classic is worth seeking out. You'll have to elbow your way to a tiny table and shout to be heard over the hubbub, but you'll get an authentic taste of local bar life. **Known for:** San Miguel beer in frozen mugs; excellent patatas bravas; traditional tavern atmosphere. $ *Average main:* €8 ⊠ *Major de Sarrià 49, Sarrià* ☎ *93/203–1077* ⊕ *www.eltomasdesarria. com* ⏱ *Closed Sun. and Aug.* Ⓜ *Sarrià.*

Coure

$$ | **MEDITERRANEAN** | *Cuina d'autor* is a Catalan phrase for chef-led original cooking, and that is exactly what you get in this smart subterranean space on restaurant-centric Passatge Marimón, just above the Diagonal thoroughfare. The upstairs bar gets busy with a post-work crowd of food-loving locals, but downstairs is a cool, minimalist restaurant. **Known for:** seasonal veggies; interesting wine list; great local fish. $ *Average main:* €22 ⊠ *Passatge Marimón 20, Sant Gervasi* ☎ *93/200–7532* ⏱ *Closed Sun. and Mon., and 3 wks in Aug.* Ⓜ *Diagonal.*

Gouthier

$$ | **SEAFOOD** | This Paris-style oyster bar spills out onto a pretty square in the former village of Sarrià. Oysters of all kinds are shucked and served fresh alongside rye bread and creamy pats of French butter. **Known for:** quiet location; supplies oysters to leading restaurants; pleasant terrace. $ *Average main:* €20 ⊠ *Mañé i Flaquer 8, Sarrià* ✛ *Located on Pl. Vicenç de Sarrià* ☎ *93/205–9969* ⊕ *www.gouthier.es* ⏱ *Closed Sun. and Mon.* Ⓜ *Sarrià.*

Hisop

$$$ | **CATALAN** | The minimalist interior design of Oriol Ivern's small restaurant is undistinguished, but his cooking is stellar. This is budget-conscious fine dining that avoids exotic ingredients but lifts local dishes to exciting new heights. **Known for:** local, seasonal ingredients; great-value tasting menu; Michelin star. $ *Average main:* €27 ⊠ *Passatge de Marimón 9, Sant Gervasi* ☎ *93/241–3233* ⊕ *www. hisop.com* ⏱ *Closed Sun. and 1st wk of Jan.* Ⓜ *Diagonal.*

Tram-Tram

$$$ | **CATALAN** | At the end of the old tram line above the village of Sarrià, this restaurant is a Barcelona classic, serving straightforward but delicious food. Try the *menú de degustació* and you might get an organic tomato, prawn, and green bean salad, followed by cod medallions and venison filet mignon. **Known for:** pleasant interior garden patio; menú de degustació (tasting menu); excellent Spanish omelet. $ *Average main:* €24 ⊠ *Major de Sarrià 121, Sarrià* ☎ *93/204–8518* ⊕ *tram-tram.com* ⏱ *Closed Mon. and 2 wks in Aug. No dinner Sun. and Tues.* Ⓜ *Sarrià.*

★ Via Veneto

$$$$ | CATALAN | Open since 1967, this elegant, family-owned temple of fine Catalan dining was a favorite of Salvador Dalí and now attracts local sports stars and politicians. The menu is a mix of contemporary offerings punctuated by old-school classics, and you can trust the expert sommelier to guide you through the daunting 10,000-bottle-strong wine list. **Known for:** Michelin star; incredible roast duck; celebrity crowd. $ Average main: €38 ⊠ Ganduxer 10, Sant Gervasi ☎ 93/200–7244 ⊕ www.viavenetobarcelona.com ⊘ Closed Sun. and Aug. No lunch Sat. Ⓜ La Bonanova (FGC), Maria Cristina.

Hotels

ABaC Hotel

$$$$ | HOTEL | This classy boutique hotel with a Michelin-starred restaurant is located in the environs of Gràcia, at the base of Avenida Tibidado, and provides a complete respite from the bustle of the city. **Pros:** high-end dining; oasis-style rooms, completely soundproofed; a respite from the busy city. **Cons:** layout of hotel can be disorientating; far from the city center and beaches; only 15 rooms, so it's easily booked up. $ Rooms from: €260 ⊠ Av. Tibidabo 1, Sant Gervasi ☎ 93/319–6600 ⊕ www.abacbarcelona.com/en ⇆ 15 rooms ⦿ No Meals Ⓜ FGC L7 Avinida Tibidabo.

Primero Primera

$$ | HOTEL | FAMILY | The Perez family converted their apartment building on a leafy side street in the quiet, upscale, residential neighborhood of Tres Torres and opened it as an exquisitely designed, homey boutique hotel. **Pros:** 24-hour free snack bar; private parking; retro-modern ambience. **Cons:** service can be uneven; bit of a distance from downtown; very small pool. $ Rooms from: €202 ⊠ Doctor Carulla 25–29, Sant Gervasi ☎ 93/417–5600 ⊕ www.primeroprimera.com ⇆ 30 rooms ⦿ Free Breakfast Ⓜ Tres Torres (FGC).

Activities

SOCCER

Futbol Club Barcelona

SOCCER | Founded in 1899, FC Barcelona won its third European Championship in 2009, the Liga championship, and its 27th Copa del Rey (King's Cup)—Spain's first-ever *triplete*—and did it again in 2015. Even more impressive was its razzle-dazzle style of soccer, rarely seen in the age of cynical defensive lockdowns and muscular British-style play. Barça, as the club is known, is Real Madrid's nemesis (and vice versa) and a sociological and historical phenomenon of deep significance in Catalonia. Ticket windows at Access 14 to the Camp Nou stadium are open Monday–Thursday 9–5, Friday 9–2:30, and Saturday 9–1:30 (if there's a match at home). You can also buy tickets online through the FC Barcelona website, or from Ticketmaster (www.ticketmaster.es) or Entradas (www.entradas.es). Tours of the stadium and museum can also be organized through the FC Barcelona website. ⊠ Aristides Maillol 12, Les Corts ☎ 902/189900 ⊕ www.fcbarcelona.com Ⓜ Collblanc, Palau Reial.

Montjuïc and Poble Sec

A bit remote from the hustle and bustle of Barcelona street life, Montjuïc more than justifies a day or two of exploring. It's easy to take buses within Montjuïc to get from sight to sight.

Sights

★ CaixaForum (Casaramona)

ARTS CENTER | FAMILY | This 1911 neo-Mudejar Art Nouveau masterpiece, originally built to house a factory by Josep Puig i Cadafalch (architect of Casa de les Punxes, Casa Amatller, Casa Martí, and Casa Quadras) is a center for art exhibits, concerts, lectures, and cultural events, and well worth keeping an eye

Find replicas of buildings from all over Spain and see craftspeople at work in the Spanish village, at the foot of Montjuïc.

on in newspaper and magazine leisure listings for special exhibitions. The Caix-aForum also regularly lays on a whole range of films, concerts, and hands-on learning activities for kids. The original brickwork is spectacular; the restoration is a brilliant example of the fusion of ultramodern design techniques with traditional (even Art Nouveau) architecture. ⊠ *Av. Francesc Ferrer i Guàrdia 6–8, Montjuïc* ☎ *93/476–8600* ⊕ *caixaforum. org/es/barcelona/home* ⊠ *€6* Ⓜ *L1/L3 Pl. d'Espanya.*

Castell de Montjuïc
CASTLE/PALACE | Built in 1640 by rebels against Felipe IV, the castle has had a dark history as a symbol of Barcelona's military domination by foreign powers, usually the Spanish army. The fortress was stormed several times, most famously in 1705 by Lord Peterborough for Archduke Carlos of Austria. In 1808, during the Peninsular War, it was seized by the French under General Dufresne. Later, during an 1842 civil disturbance, Barcelona was bombed from its heights

by a Spanish artillery battery. After the 1936–39 civil war, the castle was used as a dungeon for political prisoners. Lluís Companys, president of the Generalitat de Catalunya during the civil war, was executed by firing squad here on October 14, 1940. In 2007 the fortress was formally ceded back to Barcelona. A popular weekend park and picnic area, the moat contains attractive gardens, with one side given over to an archery range, and the various terraces have panoramic views over the city and out to sea. ⊠ *Ctra. de Montjuïc 66, Montjuïc* ☎ *93/256–4440, 93/302–3553 for Sala Montjuic* ⊕ *ajuntament.barcelona.cat/castelldemontjuic/en* ⊠ *€5 (free Sun. from 3 pm); Sala Montjuic tickets €7* Ⓜ *L2/L3 Paral.lel and Funicular.*

Estadi Olímpic Lluís Companys (*Olympic Stadium*)
HISTORIC SIGHT | Open for visitors, the Olympic Stadium was originally built for the International Exhibition of 1929, with the idea that Barcelona would then host the 1936 Olympics (ultimately staged

in Hitler's Berlin). After failing twice to win the nomination, the city celebrated the attainment of its long-cherished goal by renovating the semi-derelict stadium—preserving the original facade and shell—in time for 1992, providing seating for 60,000. The nearby Museu Olímpic i de l'Esport, a museum about the Olympic movement in Barcelona, shows audiovisual replays from the 1992 Olympics, and provides interactive simulations for visitors to experience the training and competition of Olympic athletes. An information center traces the history of the modern Olympics from Athens in 1896 to the present. ⊠ *Passeig Olímpic, 15-17, Montjuïc* ☎ *93/426–2089 Estadi Olímpic, 93/292–5379 Museu Olímpica* ⊕ *www.estadiolimpic.cat/en* ☞ *Free* ⊘ *Museum closed Mon.* Ⓜ *L1/L3 Espanya.*

★ Fundació Joan Miró

ART MUSEUM | The Miró Foundation, a gift from the artist Joan Miró to his native city, is one of Barcelona's most exciting showcases of modern and contemporary art. The airy white building, with panoramic views north over Barcelona, was designed by the artist's close friend and collaborator Josep Lluís Sert and opened in 1975; and extensions were added by Sert's pupil Jaume Freixa in 1988 and 2000. Miró's playful and colorful style, filled with Mediterranean light and humor, seems a perfect match for its surroundings, and the exhibits and retrospectives that open here tend to be progressive and provocative. Look for Alexander Calder's Mercury Fountain while you're here. ⊠ *Parc de Montjuïc s/n, Parc de Montjuïc, Montjuïc* ☎ *93/443–9470* ⊕ *www.fmirobcn.org* ☞ *€13* ⊘ *Closed Mon.* Ⓜ *L1/L3 Pl. Espanya; L3 Paral.lel, then Funicular de Montjuïc.*

Mies van der Rohe Pavilion

NOTABLE BUILDING | One of the masterpieces of the Bauhaus School, the legendary Pavelló Mies van der Rohe—the German contribution to the 1929

International Exhibition, reassembled between 1983 and 1986—remains a stunning "less is more" study in interlocking planes of white marble, green onyx, and glass. In effect, it is Barcelona's aesthetic opposite (in company with Richard Meier's Museu d'Art Contemporani and Rafael Moneo's Auditori) to the flamboyant Art Nouveau/Modernisme of Gaudí and his contemporaries. Note the mirror play of the black carpet inside the pavilion with the reflecting pool outside, and the iconic Barcelona chair designed by Ludwig Mies van der Rohe (1886–1969) and Lilly Reich (1885-1947); reproductions have graced modern interiors around the world for decades. ⊠ *Av. Francesc Ferrer i Guàrdia 7, Montjuïc* ☎ *93/215–1011* ⊕ *miesbcn.com* ☞ *€8* Ⓜ *L1/L3 Pl. Espanya.*

Museu d'Arqueologia de Catalunya

HISTORY MUSEUM | Just downhill to the right of the Palau Nacional, the Museum of Archaeology holds important finds from the Greek ruins at Empúries, on the Costa Brava. These are shown alongside fascinating objects from, and explanations of, megalithic Spain. ⊠ *Passeig Santa Madrona 39–41, Montjuïc* ☎ *93/423–2149* ⊕ *www.mac.cat* ☞ *€6; free first Sun. of month and June 12–28* ⊘ *Closed Sun. afternoon and Mon.* Ⓜ *L1/L3 Pl. Espanya.*

★ Museu Nacional d'Art de Catalunya (*Catalonian National Museum of Art, MNAC*)

ART MUSEUM | Housed in the impossingly domed, towered, frescoed, and columned Palau Nacional, built in 1929 as the centerpiece of the International Exposition, this superb museum was renovated between 1985 and 1992 by Gae Aulenti, architect of the Musée d'Orsay in Paris. In 2004, the museum's four holdings (Romanesque, Gothic, the photography collection and the Cambó Collection—an eclectic trove, including a Goya, donated by Francesc Cambó) were joined by the 19th- and 20th-century collection of Catalan Impressionist

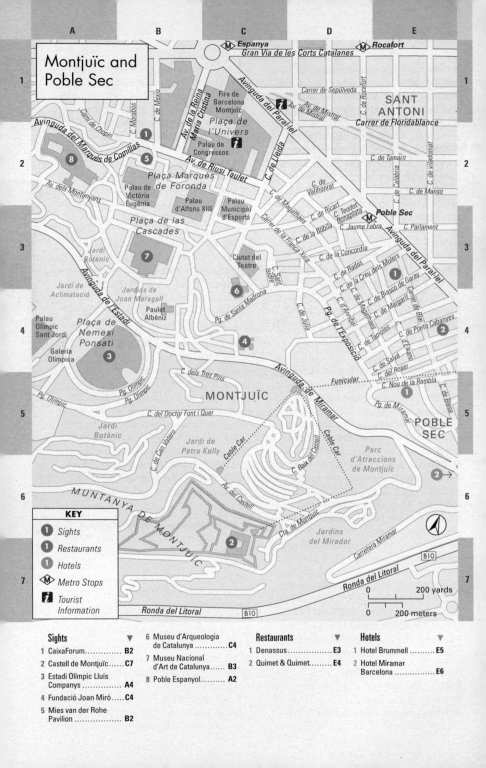

Montjuïc and Poble Sec

KEY

- 1 Sights
- 1 Restaurants
- 1 Hotels
- Ⓜ Metro Stops
- 𝑖 Tourist Information

0 ___ 200 yards

0 ___ 200 meters

and Moderniste painters. With this influx of artistic treasure, the Museu Nacional has become Catalonia's grand central museum. The central hall of the museum contains an enormous pillared and frescoed cupola. ✉ *Palau Nacional, Parc de Montjuïc s/n, Montjuïc* ☎ *93/622–0360* 🌐 *www.museunacional.cat* 🎫 *From €12 (valid for day of purchase and 1 other day in same month); free Sat. after 3 pm and 1st Sun. of month* ⏲ *Closed Mon.* [M] *L1/L3 Pl. Espanya.*

Poble Espanyol (*Spanish Village*)
MUSEUM VILLAGE | **FAMILY** | Created for the 1929 International Exhibition, the Spanish Village is a sort of open-air architectural museum, with faithful replicas to scale of building styles, from an Aragonese Gothic-Mudejar bell tower to the tower walls of Ávila, drawn from all over Spain; the ground-floor spaces are devoted to boutiques, cafés and restaurants, workshops, and studios. The liveliest time to come is at night, and a reservation at one of the half dozen restaurants gets you in for free, as does the purchase of a ticket for either of the two discos or the Tablao del Carmen flamenco club. ✉ *Av. Francesc Ferrer i Guàrdia 13, Montjuïc* ☎ *93/508–6300* 🌐 *www.poble-espanyol.com* 🎫 *€14 (€13 online); after 8 pm €7 (€6 online)* [M] *L1/L3 Pl. Espanya.*

🍴 Restaurants

★ Denassus
$$ | **CATALAN** | The jury's out as to whether Denassus is a wine bar with fabulous food or a restaurant with spectacular wine, but everyone agrees it's a hit. Put together by two experienced sommeliers, the wine list is carefully selected, and mainly natural Catalan wine, paired with top-notch tapas. **Known for:** Peking duck croquettes; Catalan natural wine; unpretentious vibe. [$] *Average main: €16* ✉ *Blai 53, Poble Sec* ☎ *93/387–7645* 🌐 *denassus.com* ⏲ *Closed Tues.* [M] *Poble Sec L3.*

Quimet & Quimet
$ | **TAPAS** | At this tiny tapas spot, fourth-generation chef-owner Quim and his family improvise ingenious canapés and innovative canned and tinned foods. All you have to do is orient them toward cheese, anchovies, or whatever it is you might crave, and they masterfully do the rest—and recommend the wine to go with it. **Known for:** arrive early to avoid disappointment; local wines; classic foodie haunt. [$] *Average main: €15* ✉ *Poeta Cabanyes 25, Poble Sec* ☎ *93/442–3142* 🌐 *www.quimetquimet.com* ⏲ *Closed Sun. and Aug. No dinner Sat.* [M] *Paral.lel.*

🛏 Hotels

Hotel Brummell
$$ | **HOTEL** | The rustic-chic lobby with work by local artists sets the tone at this hotel that has propelled the once-scruffy neighborhood of Poble Sec into a trendier era. Behind reception is a small brick-and-paving stone patio, and beyond that, a comfortable bar; one flight up is the chill-out deck, with a long narrow plunge pool, a sauna, and an herb garden. **Pros:** chic design; fun wellness and fitness program; young, friendly international staff. **Cons:** vending machines in lieu of in-room minibars; slightly off the beaten track; storage is limited. [$] *Rooms from: €160* ✉ *Nou de la Rambla 174, Poble Sec* ☎ *93/125–8622* 🌐 *www.hotelbrummell.com* 🛏 *20 rooms* 🍴 *No Meals* [M] *L3 Paral.lel.*

Hotel Miramar Barcelona
$$$ | **HOTEL** | **FAMILY** | Only the facade remains of this imposing "palace," built in 1929 for Barcelona's second Universal Expositionas and later transformed by architect Oscar Tusquets into an elegant, romantic hillside resort. **Pros:** free parking and spa access when you book online; romantic retreat away from the buzz of the city; complimentary glass of cava on check-in. **Cons:** pricey breakfast; quite far from the city center; feels a bit dated.

$ *Rooms from: €250* ✉ *Pl. Carlos Ibáñez 3, Montjuïc* ☎ *93/281–1600* 🌐 *www.hotelmiramarbarcelona.com* 🛏 *74 rooms* 🍴 *No Meals* [M] *L3 Drassanes.*

Nightlife

Poble Sec, a stone's throw from L'Eixample district, has an eclectic collection of fashionable cafés, bars, and eateries.

BARS

Celler Cal Marino

WINE BARS | Rustic and charming with an arched, brick-wall in the center, barrel tables, and rows of multicolor *sifón* fizzy-water bottles, this homey venue serves wine by the glass or liter (for takeaway) from the wine cellar, artisanal beers, and vermouth paired with homemade tapas. Tuesday through Friday the special is three drinks matched with three tapas, while Sunday is often dedicated to live jazz concerts and vermouth aperitifs. ✉ *Margarit 54, Poble Sec* 🌐 *calmarino.tumblr.com* 🕒 *Closed Sun. evening* [M] *Poble Sec, Paral.lel.*

★ Lilith & Sons

BARS | A favorite meeting point for the local creative, progressive crowd, the bar is named after Lilith, the feminist icon who is Jewish mythology's favorite female demon and alleged first wife of Adam. Expect excellent service, loud music and strong drinks. ✉ *Fontrodona 23, Poble Sec* ☎ *63/372–2120* 🌐 *www.lilithandsons.com* [M] *Poble Sec L3.*

Performing Arts

FLAMENCO

El Tablao de Carmen

FOLK/TRADITIONAL DANCE | Large tour groups come to this venerable flamenco dinner-theater venue in the Poble Espanyol named after, and dedicated to, the legendary dancer Carmen Amaya. Diehard flamenco aficionados might dismiss the ensembles that perform here as a tad touristy, but the dancers, singers, and guitarists are pros. Visitors can enjoy one of the two nightly performances over a drink or over their choice of a full-course, prix fixe meal, with prices ranging from €45 to €154. Reservations are recommended. Dinner shows are held daily at 6 pm and 8:30 pm. ✉ *Poble Espanyol, Av. Francesc Ferrer i Guàrdia 13, Montjuïc* ☎ *93/325–6895* 🌐 *www.tablaodecarmen.com* 🎟 *Starting from €45 for a flamenco show and a drink* [M] *Espanya.*

CATALONIA, VALENCIA, AND THE COSTA BLANCA

Updated by
Elizabeth Prosser

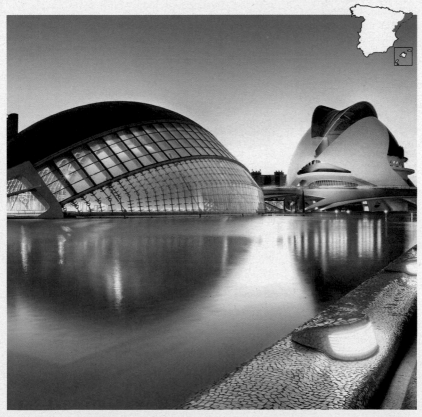

◉ Sights	🍴 Restaurants	🛏 Hotels	🛍 Shopping	🍸 Nightlife
★★★★☆	★★★★☆	★★★☆☆	★★★☆☆	★★★☆☆

WELCOME TO CATALONIA, VALENCIA, AND THE COSTA BLANCA

TOP REASONS TO GO

★ **Girona:** Explore a city where monuments of Christian, Jewish, and Islamic cultures have coexisted for centuries and are just steps apart.

★ **Valencia reborn:** The city has seen a transformation of the Turia River into a treasure trove of museums, concert halls, parks, and architectural wonders.

★ **Great restaurants:** Foodies argue that the fountainhead of creative gastronomy has moved from France to Spain— and in particular to the great restaurants of the Empordà and Costa Brava.

★ **Dalí's home and museum:** "Surreal" doesn't begin to describe the Teatre-Museu Dalí in Figueres or the wild coast of the artist's home at Cap de Creus.

★ **Las Fallas festival:** Valencia's Las Fallas in mid-March, a week of fireworks and solemn processions with a finale of spectacular bonfires, is one of the best festivals in Europe.

Year-round, Catalonia is the most visited of Spain's autonomous communities. The rugged Costa Brava in the north and the Costa Daurada to the south are havens for sun-seekers. Excellent rail, air, and highway connections link Catalonia to the beach resorts of Valencia, its neighbor to the south.

1 Girona

2 Figueres

3 Besalú

4 Olot

5 Tossa de Mar

6 Sant Feliu de Guixols

7 S'Agaró

8 Calella de Palafrugell and Around

9 Begur and Around

10 Cadaqués and Around

11 Montserrat

12 Sitges

13 Santes Creus

14 Santa Maria de Poblet

15 Tarragona

16 Valencia

17 Albufera Nature Park

18 Dénia

19 Calpe

20 Altea

21 Alicante

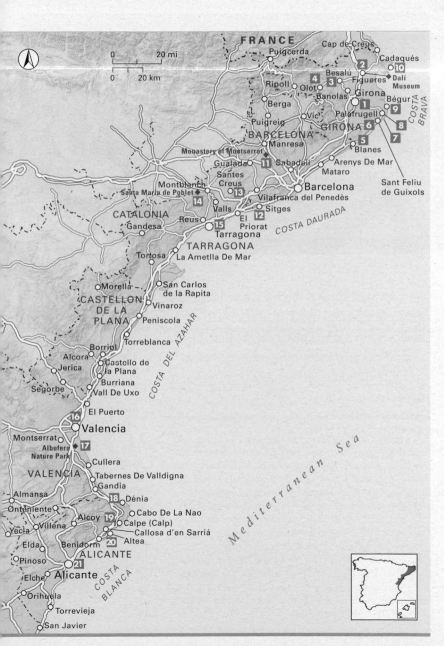

FRANCE

Cap de Creus

Puigcerda

Cadaqués

2 **10**

Besalú

4 **3** Dalí Museum

Ripoll Figueres

Olot

Banolas Girona

Berga

Bégur

9

COSTA BRAVA

Puigreig

Vic Palafrugell

8

BARCELONA GIRONA **6**

Manresa **5** Blanes

Monastery of Montserrat

Gualada Sabadell Arenys De Mar

Santes **11** Mataro

Creus

Montblanch **13** Barcelona Sant Feliu

Santa Maria de Poblet de Guixols

Valls Vilafranca del Penedès

14 **12** Sitges

CATALONIA Reus El COSTA DAURADA

Gandesa **15** Priorat

Tarragona

TARRAGONA

Tortosa La Ametlla De Mar

San Carlos

Morella de la Rapita

CASTELLON Vinaroz

DE LA Peniscola

PLANA

Torreblanca

Borriol

Alcora Castello de COSTA DEL AZAHAR

Jerica la Plana

Burriana

Segorbe Vall De Uxo

El Puerto

16 Valencia

Montserrat

Albufera **17**

Nature Park

Cullera

VALENCIA Tabernes De Valldigna

Almansa Gandia

Onteniente **18** Dénia

Alcoy **19** Cabo De La Nao

Yecla Villena Calpe (Calp)

Elda Callosa d'en Sarriá

Benidorm **20** Altea

Pinoso ALICANTE

21

Elche Alicante

Orihuela COSTA BLANCA

Torrevieja

San Javier

Mediterranean Sea

0   20 mi

0   20 km

EATING AND DRINKING WELL IN CATALONIA

Paella valenciana in a classic paella pan.

Food in both Catalonia and Valencia runs the gamut of classic Mediterranean dishes, and Catalans feel right at home with *paella valenciana* (Valencian paella). Fish preparations are similar along the coast, though inland favorites vary from place to place.

The grassy inland meadows of Catalonia's northern Alt Empordà region put quality beef on local tables; from the Costa Brava comes fine seafood, such as anchovies from L'Escala and *gambas* (prawns) from Palamós, both deservedly famous. *Romesco*—a blend of almonds, peppers, garlic, and olive oil—is used as a vegetable, fish, and seafood sauce in Tarragona, especially during the *calçotadas* (spring onion feasts) in February. *Allioli*, garlicky mayonnaise, is another popular topping. The Ebro Delta is renowned for fresh fish, oysters, and eels, as well as *rossejat* (fried rice in a fish broth). Valencia and the Mediterranean coast are the homeland of paella valenciana. *Arròs a banda* is a variant in which the fish and rice are cooked separately.

CALÇOTS

The *calçot* is a sweet spring onion developed by a 19th-century farmer who discovered how to extend the edible portion by packing soil around the base. It is grilled on a barbecue, then peeled and dipped into romesco sauce. In January, the town of Valls holds a *calçotada* where upward of 30,000 people gather for meals of onions, sausage, lamb chops, and red wine.

RICE

Paella valenciana is one of Spain's most famous gastronomic contributions. A simple country dish dating to the early 18th century, "paella" refers to the wide frying pan with short, sturdy handles that's used to cook the rice. Anything fresh from the fields that day, along with rice and olive oil, traditionally went into the pan, but paella valenciana has particular ingredients: short-grain rice, chicken, rabbit, *garrofó* (a local legume), tomatoes, green beans, sweet peppers, olive oil, and saffron. *Paella marinera* (seafood paella) is a different story: rice, cuttlefish, squid, mussels, shrimp, prawns, lobster, clams, garlic, olive oil, sweet paprika, and saffron, all stewed in fish broth. Other paella variations include *paella negra,* a black rice dish made with squid ink; *arròs a banda* made with peeled seafood; and *fideuà,* paella made with noodles.

SEAFOOD STEWS

Sèpia amb pèsols is a vegetable and seafood *mar i muntanya* ("surf and turf") beloved on the Costa Brava: cuttlefish and peas are stewed with potatoes, garlic, onions, tomatoes, and a splash of wine. The *picadillo*—the finishing touches of flavors and textures—includes parsley, black pepper, fried bread, pine nuts, olive oil, and salt. *Es niu* ("the nest") of game fowl, cod, tripe,

Fresh calçots

cuttlefish, pork, and rabbit is another Costa Brava favorite. Stewed for a good five hours, this is a much-celebrated wintertime classic. You'll also find *suquet de peix,* the Catalan fish stew, at restaurants along the Costa Brava.

FRUITS AND VEGETABLES

Valencia and the eastern Levante region have long been famous as Spain's *huerta,* or garden. The alluvial soil of the littoral produces an abundance of everything from tomatoes to asparagus, peppers, chard, spinach, onions, artichokes, cucumbers, and the whole range of Mediterranean bounty. Catalonia's Maresme and Empordà regions are also fruit and vegetable centers, making this coastline a cornucopia of fresh produce.

WINES

The Penedès wine region west of Barcelona has been joined by new wine Denominations of Origin from all over Catalonia. Alt Camp, Tarragona, Priorat, Montsant, Costers del Segre, Pla de Bages, Alella, and Empordà all produce excellent reds and whites to join Catalonia's sparkling cava on local wine lists. The rich, full-bodied reds of Montsant and Priorat, especially, are among the best in Spain.

Suquet of fish, potatoes, onions, and tomatoes

The long curve of the Mediterranean from the French border to Cabo Cervera below Alicante encompasses the two autonomous communities of Catalonia and Valencia, with the country's second- and third-largest cities (Barcelona and Valencia, respectively). Rivals in many respects, the two communities share a language, history, and culture that set them apart from the rest of Spain.

Girona is the gateway to Northern Catalonia's attractions—the Pyrenees, the volcanic region of La Garrotxa, and the beaches of rugged Costa Brava. Northern Catalonia is memorable for the soft, green hills of the Empordà farm country and the Alberes mountain range at the eastern end of the Pyrenees. Across the landscape are *masías* (farmhouses) with staggered-stone roofs and square towers that make them look like fortresses. Even the tiniest village has its church, arcaded square, and *rambla,* where villagers take their evening *paseo* (stroll).

Salvador Dalí's deep connection to the Costa Brava is enshrined in the Teatre-Museu Dalí in Figueres: he's buried in the crypt beneath it. His wife Gala is buried in his former home, a castle in Púbol. His summer home in Port Lligat Bay, north of Cadaqués, is now a museum of his life and work.

The province of Valencia was incorporated into the Kingdom of Aragón, Catalonia's medieval Mediterranean empire, when it was conquered by Jaume I in the 13th century. Along with Catalonia, Valencia became part of the united Spanish state in the 15th century, but defenders of its separate cultural and linguistic identity still resent the centuries of Catalan domination. The Catalan language prevails in Tarragona, a city and province of Catalonia, but Valenciano—a dialect of Catalan—is spoken and used on street signs in the Valencian provinces.

The coastal farmland and beaches that attracted the ancients now call to modern-day tourists, though in parts, a number of "mass-tourism" resorts have marred the shore. Inland, however, local culture survives intact. The rugged and beautiful territory is dotted with small fortified towns, several of which bear the name of Spain's 11th-century national hero, El Cid, commemorating the battles he fought here against the Moors some 900 years ago.

MAJOR REGIONS

For many, **Northern Catalonia** is one of the top reasons to visit Spain. The historic center of Girona, its principal city, is a labyrinth of climbing cobblestone streets and staircases, with remarkable Gothic and Romanesque buildings at every turn. El Call, the Jewish Quarter, is one of the best-preserved areas of its kind in Europe, and the Gothic cathedral is an architectural masterpiece. Streets in the modern part of the city are lined with smart shops and boutiques, and the overall quality of life in Girona is considered among the best in Spain. Nearby towns Besalú and Figueres are vastly different. Figueres is an unremarkable town made exceptional by the Dalí Museum. Besalú is a picture-perfect Romanesque village on a bluff overlooking the Riu Fluvià. Lesser known are the medieval towns in and around the volcanic (now extinct) area of La Garrotxa: Vic, Rupit, and Olot boast the best produce in the region.

The Costa Brava (Wild Coast) is a nearly unbroken series of sheer rock cliffs dropping down to clear blue-green waters, punctuated by innumerable coves and tiny beaches on narrow inlets, called *calas*. It basically begins at Blanes and continues north along 135 km (84 miles) of coastline to the French border at Portbou. Although the area does have spots of real-estate excess, the rocky terrain of many pockets (Tossa de Mar, Begur, and Cadaqués) has discouraged overbuilding. On a good day here, the luminous blue of the sea contrasts with red-brown headlands and cliffs, and the distant lights of fishing boats reflect on wine-color waters at dusk. Small stands of umbrella pine veil the footpaths to many of the secluded coves and little patches of white sand—often, the only access is by boat.

The **Southern Catalonia** area is home to Montserrat, home to the shrine of La Moreneta (the Black Virgin of Montserrat), the lively coastal town of Sitges, the Cistercian monasteries of Santes Creus and Santa Maria de Poblet, and the region's principal town of Tarragona. Farther south lies Valencia, Spain's third-largest city and the capital of its region and province, equidistant from Barcelona and Madrid. For a day trip there's the Albufera, a scenic coastal wetland teeming with native wildlife, especially migratory birds.

The Costa Blanca (White Coast) begins at Dénia, south of Valencia, and stretches down roughly to Torrevieja, below Alicante. It's best known for its magical vacation combo of sand, sea, and sun, with popular beaches and more secluded coves and stretches of sand. Alicante itself has two long beaches, a charming old quarter, and mild weather most of the year.

Planning

When to Go

Come for the beaches in the hot summer months, but expect crowds and serious heat—in some places up to 40°C (104°F). The Mediterranean coast is more comfortable in May and September.

February and March are the peak months for skiing in the Pyrenees. Winter travel in the region has other advantages: Valencia still has plenty of sunshine, and if you're visiting villages and wineries in the countryside, you might have the place all to yourself. Note that many restaurants and hotels outside the major towns may close on weekdays or longer in winter, so call ahead. Many museums and sites close early in winter (6 pm).

The Costa Brava and Costa Blanca beach areas get hot and crowded in summer, and accommodations are at a premium. In contrast, spring is mild and an excellent time to tour the region, particularly the rural areas, where blossoms infuse the air with pleasant fragrances and wildflowers dazzle the landscape.

Planning Your Time

Not far from Barcelona, the beautiful towns of Vic, Girona, and Cadaqués are easily reachable from the city by bus or train in a couple of hours. Figueres is a must if you want to see the Teatre-Museu Dalí. Girona makes an excellent base from which to explore La Garrotxa—for that, you'll need to rent a car.

Valencia is three hours by express train from Barcelona. Historic Valencia and the Santiago Calatrava–designed City of Arts and Sciences complex can be covered in two days, but stay longer and indulge in the city's food and explore the nightlife in the Barrio del Carmen.

FESTIVALS

In Valencia, **Las Fallas** fiestas begin March 1 and reach a climax between March 15 and El Día de San José (St. Joseph's Day) on March 19, Father's Day in Spain. Las Fallas originated from St. Joseph's role as patron saint of carpenters; in medieval times, carpenters' guilds celebrated the arrival of spring by cleaning out their shops and making bonfires with scraps of wood. These days it's a 19-day celebration ending with fireworks, floats, carnival processions, and bullfights. On March 19, huge wood and papier-mâché effigies of political figures and other personalities (the result of a year's work by local community groups) are torched to end the fiestas.

Getting Here and Around

AIR

El Prat de Llobregat in Barcelona is the main international airport for the Costa Brava; Girona is the closest airport to the region, with bus connections directly into the city and to Barcelona. Valencia has an international airport with direct flights to London, Paris, Brussels, Lisbon, Zurich, and Milan as well as regional flights from Barcelona, Madrid, Málaga, and other cities in Spain. There is a regional airport in Alicante serving the Valencian region and Murcia.

BOAT AND FERRY

Many short-cruise lines along the coast offer the chance to view the Costa Brava from the sea. Visit the port areas in the main towns and you'll quickly spot several tourist cruise lines. Plan to spend around €15–€27, depending on the length of the cruise. Many longer cruises include a stop en route for a swim. The glass-keel Nautilus boats for observation of the Medes Islands underwater park cost around €20 and run daily April–October and weekends November–March.

The shortest ferry connections to the Balearic Islands originate in Dénia. Balearia sails from there to Ibiza, Formentera, and Mallorca.

BOAT AND FERRY INFORMATION Balearia. ☎ 912/660215, 084/35087312 From abroad ⊕ www.balearia.com/en.**Nautilus.** ✉ Passeig Marítim 23, L'Estartit ☎ 972/751489 ⊕ www.nautilus.es.

BUS

Private companies run buses down the coast and from Madrid to Valencia, and to Alicante. ALSA is the main bus line in this region; check local tourist offices for schedules. Sarfa operates buses from Barcelona to Blanes, Lloret, Sant Feliu de Guixols, Platja d'Aro, Palamos, Begur, Roses, L'Escala, and Cadaqués.

CONTACTS ALSA. ☎ 902/422242 ⊕ www.alsa.es.**Moventis Sarfa.** ✉ Estació del Nord, Alí Bei 80, Barcelona ☎ 902/302025 ⊕ compras.moventis.es/en-GB Ⓜ Arc de Triomf.**Sagalés.** ✉ Alí Bei 80, Barcelona ☎ 902/130014 tickets ⊕ www.sagales.com Ⓜ Arc de Triomf.**Sagalés AirportLine.** ☎ 902/130014 ⊕ www.sagalesairportline.com.

CAR

A car is necessary for explorations inland and convenient for reaching locations on the coast, where drives are smooth and scenic. Catalonia and Valencia have excellent roads; the only drawbacks are the high cost of fuel and the high tolls on the *autopistas* (highways, usually designated by the letters "AP"). The national roads (starting with the letter N) can get clogged, however, so you're often better off on toll roads if your time is limited.

TRAIN
Most of the Costa Brava is not served directly by railroad. A local line runs up the coast from Barcelona to Blanes, then turns inland and connects at Maçanet-Massanes with the main line up to France. Direct trains stop only at major connections, such as Girona, Flaçà, and Figueres. To visit one of the smaller towns in between, you can take a fast direct train from Barcelona to Girona, for instance, then get off and wait for a local to come by.

Express intercity trains reach Valencia from all over Spain, arriving at the new Joaquin Sorolla station; from there, a shuttle bus takes you to the Estación del Norte, the terminus in the center of town, for local connections. From Barcelona there are 15 trains a day, including the fast train TALGO, which takes 3½ hours. There are 22 daily trains to Valencia from Madrid; the high-speed train takes about 1 hour 40 minutes.

For the Costa Blanca, the rail hub is Alicante.

CONTACTS RENFE. ☎ *912/320320* ⊕ *www.renfe.com.*

Farmhouse Stays in Catalonia

Dotted throughout Catalonia are farmhouses (*casas rurales* in Spanish, and *cases de pagès* or *masíes* in Catalan), where you can spend a weekend or longer. Accommodations vary from small rustic homes to spacious luxurious farmhouses with fireplaces and pools. Stay in a guest room at a bed-and-breakfast, or rent an entire house and do your own cooking. Most tourist offices, including the main Catalonia Tourist Office, have information and listings. Several organizations in Spain have detailed listings and descriptions of Catalonia's farmhouses.

CONTACTS Agroturisme.org. ☎ *932/680900* ⊕ *www.agroturisme.cat.* **Cases Rurals.** ☎ *660/576834* ⊕ *www. casesrurals.com.*

Restaurants

Catalonia's eateries are deservedly famous. Girona's El Celler de Can Roca was voted Best Restaurant in the World multiple times in recent years in the annual critics' poll conducted by British magazine *Restaurant,* and a host of other first-rate establishments continue to offer inspiring fine dining in Catalonia. Yet you needn't go to an internationally acclaimed restaurant to dine well. Superstar chef Ferran Adrià of the former foodie paradise elBulli dines regularly at dives in Roses, where straight-up fresh fish is the attraction. Northern Catalonia's Empordà region is known for seafood and a rich assortment of inland and upland products. Beef from Girona's verdant pastureland is prized throughout Catalonia, while wild mushrooms from the Pyrenees and game from the Alberes range offer seasonal depth to menus across the region. From a simple beachside paella or *llobarro* (sea bass) at a *chiringuito* (beach shack) with tables on the sand, to the splendor of a meal at El Celler de Can Roca, playing culinary hopscotch through Catalonia is a good way to get to know the region.

Restaurant reviews have been shortened. For full information, visit Fodors. com.

Hotels

Lodgings on the Costa Brava range from the finest hotels to spartan pensions. The better accommodations have splendid views of the seascape. If you plan to visit during the high season (July and August), be sure to book reservations well in advance at almost any hotel in the area; the Costa Brava remains one of the most popular summer resort areas in Spain. Many Costa Brava hotels close down in the winter season (November–March).

Hotel reviews have been shortened. For full information, visit Fodors.com.

What It Costs in Euros			
$	$$	$$$	$$$$
RESTAURANTS			
under €12	€12–€17	€18–€22	over €22
HOTELS			
under €90	€90–€125	€126–€180	over €180

Girona

97 km (60 miles) northeast of Barcelona.

At the confluence of four rivers, Northern Catalonia's Girona (population: 97,000) keeps intact the magic of its historic past; with its brooding hilltop castle, soaring Gothic cathedral, and dreamy riverside setting, it resembles a vision from the Middle Ages. Today, as a university center, Girona combines past and vibrant present: art galleries, chic cafés, and trendy boutiques have set up shop in many of the restored buildings of the old quarter, known as the Força Vella (Old Fortress), which is on the east side of the Riu Onyar. Built on the side of the mountain, it presents a tightly packed labyrinth of medieval buildings and monuments on narrow cobblestone streets with connecting stairways. You can still see vestiges of the Iberian and Roman walls in the cathedral square and in the patio of the old university. In the central quarter is El Call, one of Europe's best-preserved medieval (12th- to 15th-century) Jewish communities and an important center of Kabalistic studies.

The main street of the Força Vella is Carrer de la Força, which follows the old Via Augusta, the Roman road that connected Rome with its provinces.

Explore Girona on foot to discover many of its delights. One of Girona's treasures is its setting, high above where the Onyar merges with the Ter; the latter flows from a mountain waterfall that can be glimpsed in a gorge above the town. Walk first along the west bank of the Onyar, between the train trestle and the Plaça de la Independència, to admire the classic view of the old town, with its pastel waterfront facades. Many of the windows and balconies are adorned with fretwork grilles of embossed wood or delicate iron tracery. Cross Pont de Sant Agustí over to the old quarter from under the arcades in the corner of Plaça de la Independència and find your way to the Punt de Benvinguda tourist office, to the right at Rambla Llibertat 1. Work your way up through the labyrinth of steep streets, using the cathedral's huge baroque facade as a guide. Try to be in Girona during the second week of May, when the streets of the old quarter are festooned with the flowers of spring during the Girona Festival of Flowers.

GETTING HERE AND AROUND

There are more than 20 daily trains from Barcelona to Girona (continuing on to the French border). Regional trains can take between one and two hours, and can be picked up from a number of stations in Barcelona, while the high-speed AVE train service is a convenient option, running from Barcelona Sants station to Girona in under 40 minutes (it's advisable to prebook the AVE). The train station is about a 20-minute walk from the old

Northern Catalonia and the Costa Brava

quarter; alternatively, taxis can be picked up in front of the train station on arrival. There are frequent Sagales buses to Girona Airport; they take an average of 75 minutes and cost €16 one-way, €25 round-trip. The Sagales 602 and 603 buses run from Barcelona's El Prat de Llobregat airport and Estació del Nord, in the city center of Barcelona, to Girona city bus station. Getting around the city is easiest on foot or by taxi; several bridges connect the historic old quarter with the more modern town across the river.

CONTACTS Sagalés. ⊠ *Girona* ☎ *902/130014* ⊕ *www.sagales.com.*

DISCOUNTS AND DEALS

The GironaMuseums discounts admission to all the city's museums.

Some are free on the first Sunday of every month.

Check the tourist office or at the Punt de Benvinguda welcome center, which can also arrange guided tours.

TOURS
Bike Breaks

In recent times, Girona has developed a passion for all things bike related. Bike Breaks provides bike rentals and tours so that you can get to know the city and its surroundings on two wheels. ⊠ *Carrer Nou 14, Girona* ☎ *972/205465* ⊕ *www. gironacyclecentre.com* ⊠ *Tours from €25.*

VISITOR INFORMATION Girona Office of Tourism. ⊠ *Rambla de la Llibertat 1, Girona* ☎ *972/010001* ⊕ *www.girona.cat/ turisme.***Punt de Benvinguda.** ⊠ *Berenguer Carnicer 3, Girona* ☎ *972/011669* ⊕ *www. turismegirones.cat.*

Beaches of the Costa Brava and Costa Blanca

Costa Brava Beaches

The beaches on the Costa Brava range from stretches of fine white sand to rocky coves and inlets; summer vacationers flock to **Tossa de Mar, Roses, Begur** and **Calella de Palafrugell**; in all but the busiest weeks of July and August, the tucked-away coves of **Cap de Creus National Park** are oases of peace and privacy. **Valencia** has a long beach that's wonderful for sunning and a promenade lined with paella restaurants; for quieter surroundings, head farther south to **El Saler.**

Costa Blanca Beaches

The southeastern coastline of the Costa Blanca varies from the long stretches of sand dunes north of **Dénia** and south of **Alicante** to the coves and crescents in between. The benign climate permits lounging on the beach at least eight months of the year. **Altea,** popular with families, is busy and pebbly, but the old town has retained a traditional pueblo feel with narrow cobbled streets and attractive squares. **Calpe's** beaches have the scenic advantage of the sheer outcrop Peñón de Ifach (Cliff of Ifach), which stands guard over stretches of sand to either side. Dénia has family-friendly beaches to the north, where children paddle in relatively shallow waters, and rocky inlets to the south.

◉ Sights

Banys Arabs (*Arab Baths*)

HOT SPRING | A misnomer, the Banys Arabs were actually built by Morisco craftsmen (workers of Moorish descent) in the late 12th century, long after Girona's Islamic occupation (714–797) had ended. Following the old Roman model that had disappeared in the West, the custom of bathing publicly may have been brought back from the Holy Land with the Crusaders. These baths are sectioned off into three rooms in descending order: a *frigidarium*, or cold bath, a square room with a central octagonal pool and a skylight with cupola held up by two stories of eight fine columns; a *tepidarium*, or warm bath; and a *caldarium*, or steam room, beneath which is a chamber where a fire was kept burning. Here the inhabitants of old Girona came to relax, exchange gossip, or do business. It is known from another public bathhouse in Tortosa, Tarragona, that the various social classes came to bathe by sex and religion on fixed days of the week: Christian men on one day, Christian women on another, Jewish men on still another, Jewish women (and prostitutes) on a fourth, Muslims on others. ⊠ *Carrer Ferran el Catòlic s/n, Girona* ☎ *972/190969* ⊕ *www.banysarabs.org* ⊠ *€3.*

Basilica of Sant Feliu

CHURCH | One of Girona's most beloved churches and its first cathedral until the 10th century, Sant Feliu was repeatedly rebuilt and altered over four centuries and stands today as an amalgam of Romanesque columns, a Gothic nave, and a baroque facade. The vast bulk of this structure is landmarked by one of Girona's most distinctive belfries, topped by eight pinnacles. The basilica was founded over the tomb of St. Felix of Africa, a martyr under the Roman emperor Diocletian. ⊠ *Pujada de Sant Feliu 29, Girona* ☎ *972/201407* ⊠ *From €7.*

There's more to Girona's cathedral than the 90 steps to get to it; inside there's much to see, including the Treasury.

★ Cathedral

NOTABLE BUILDING | At the heart of the Força Vella, the cathedral looms above 90 steps and is famous for its nave—at 75 feet, the widest in the world and the epitome of the spatial ideal of Catalan Gothic architects. Since Charlemagne founded the original church in the 8th century, it has been through many fires and renovations. Take in the rococo-era facade, "eloquent as organ music" and impressive flight of 17th-century stairs, which rises from its own *plaça*. Inside, three smaller naves were compressed into one gigantic hall by the famed architect Guillermo Bofill in 1416. The change was typical of Catalan Gothic "hall" churches, and it was done to facilitate preaching to crowds. Note the famous silver canopy, or *baldaquí* (baldachin). The oldest part of the cathedral is the 11th-century Romanesque **Torre de Carlemany** (Charlemagne Tower) ⊠ *Pl. de la Catedral s/n, Girona* ☎ *972/427189* ⊕ *www.catedraldegirona. cat* ⊠ *From €7 (includes Basilica de Sant Feliu).*

★ El Call

HISTORIC DISTRICT | Girona is especially noted for its 13th-century Jewish Quarter, El Call, which branches off Carrer de la Força, south of the Plaça Catedral. The quarter is a network of lanes that crisscross above one another, and houses built atop each other in disorderly fashion along narrow stone medieval streets. With boutique shopping, artsy cafés, and lots of atmospheric eateries and bars, there is plenty to explore. ⊠ *Girona.*

Monestir de Sant Pere de Galligants

CHURCH | The church of St. Peter, across the Galligants River, was finished in 1131, and is notable for its octagonal Romanesque belfry and the finely detailed capitals atop the columns in the cloister. It now houses the **Museu Arqueològic** (Museum of Archaeology), which documents the region's history since Paleolithic times and includes some artifacts from Roman times. ⊠ *Carrer Santa Llúcia 8, Girona* ☎ *972/202632* ⊕ *www.macgirona.cat* ⊠ *€5* ⊙ *Closed Mon.*

Museu d'Art

ART MUSEUM | The Episcopal Palace near the cathedral contains the wide-ranging collections of Girona's main art museum. On display is everything from superb Romanesque *majestats* (carved wood figures of Christ) to reliquaries from Sant Pere de Rodes, illuminated 12th-century manuscripts, and works of the 20th-century Olot school of landscape painting. ⊠ *Pujada de la Catedral 12, Girona* ☎ *972/203834* ⊕ *museuart.cat* ⊠ *€6* ⊘ *Closed Mon.*

Museu d'Història de la Ciutat

HISTORY MUSEUM | From pre-Roman objects to paintings and drawings from the notorious siege at the hands of Napoleonic troops, to the early municipal lighting system and the medieval printing press, artifacts from Girona's long and embattled past are exhibited in this fascinating museum. Rooms organized chronologically and by theme educate visitors on the ways the city has developed. ⊠ *Carrer de la Força 27,* ☎ *972/222229* ⊕ *www.girona.cat/museuhistoria* ⊠ *€4; free 1st Sun. of month* ⊘ *Closed Mon.*

Museum of Jewish History

HISTORY MUSEUM | Housed in a former synagogue and dedicated to the preservation of Girona's Jewish heritage, this center organizes conferences, exhibitions, and seminars and contains 21 stone tablets, one of the finest collections in the world of medieval Jewish funerary slabs. These came from the old Jewish cemetery of Montjuïc, revealed when the railroad between Barcelona and France was laid out in the 19th century. Its exact location, about 1½ km (1 mile) north of Girona on the road to La Bisbal and known as La Tribana, is being excavated. The center also holds the **Institut d'Estudis Nahmànides,** with an extensive library of Judaica. ⊠ *Carrer de la Força 8, Girona* ☎ *972/216761* ⊕ *www.girona.cat/call/eng/museu.php* ⊠ *€4.*

Passeig Arqueològic

GARDEN | The landscaped gardens of this stepped archaeological walk are below the restored walls of the Força Vella (which you can walk, in parts) and enjoy superlative views of the city from belvederes and watchtowers. From there, climb through the Jardins de la Francesa to the highest ramparts for a view of the cathedral's 11th-century Torre de Carlemany. ⊠ *Girona.*

Restaurants

Cal Ros

$$$$ | CATALAN | Tucked under the arcades just behind the north end of Plaça de la Llibertat, this restaurant combines ancient stone arches with crisp, contemporary furnishings and cheerful lighting. The menu changes regularly, featuring organically raised local produce in season, and fresh fish in updated versions of traditional Catalan cuisine. **Known for:** updated traditional cuisine; rice dishes; atmospheric setting. Ⓢ *Average main: €24* ⊠ *Carrer Cort Reial 9, Girona* ☎ *972/219176* ⊘ *Closed Mon. and Tues. No dinner Sun.*

★ El Celler de Can Roca

$$$$ | CONTEMPORARY | Anointed twice (in 2013 and 2015) by an international panel of food critics and chefs as the best restaurant in the world, El Celler de Can Roca is a life-changing culinary experience, helmed by the Roca brothers—Joan, Josep, and Jordi. There are two tasting menus, at €190 and €215, and you can consider your visit blessed if yours includes signature dishes like lobster *parmentier* with black trumpet mushrooms, suckling Iberian pig with pepper sauce and quince terrine, or Dublin Bay prawns with curry smoke (the Rocas pioneered the technique of roasting in the aromas of spices during the cooking process). **Known for:** one of the best restaurants in the world; reservations required many months or even a year ahead; extensive wine selection.

$ *Average main: €190* ✉ *Can Sunyer 48, Girona* ☎ *972/222157* ⊕ *cellercanroca. com* ☉ *Closed Sun. and Mon., Easter wk, 1 wk in Aug., and Dec. 19–Jan. 11. No lunch Tues.*

La Fabrica

$ | CAFÉ | Christian, a professional cyclist, and his wife, Amber, opened this inviting space, serving brunch and superb coffee, in an old carpentry factory (La Fabrica means "the factory" in Spanish). There are raw concrete floors, exposed brick walls, high ceilings, and an abundance of bike memorabilia—not to mention cyclists themselves. **Known for:** cycle memorabilia; excellent coffee; interesting crowd. $ *Average main: €9* ✉ *Carrer de la Llebre 3, Girona* ☎ *872/000273* ⊕ *www.lafabricagirona.com* ☉ *No dinner.*

Mimolet

$$$ | CATALAN | Contemporary architecture and cuisine in the old part of Girona make for interesting dining at this sleek, streamlined restaurant. *Vieira con alcachofas, sanguina y huevo de codorniz* (scallop with artichokes, blood orange, and quail egg) or *cochinillo con jamón ibérico, parmentier y brotes* (suckling pig with Iberian ham) are typical dishes on the frequently changing, fixed-price seasonal menu. **Known for:** tasting menu of seasonal dishes; weekday lunchtime menus; local wines. $ *Average main: €22* ✉ *Pou Rodó 12, Girona* ☎ *972/297973* ⊕ *www.mimolet.cat* ☉ *Closed Mon.*

Rocambolesc

$ | CAFÉ | FAMILY | Couldn't get a table at El Celler de Can Roca? Keep trying, but in the meantime there's Rocambolesc, the latest of the Roca family culinary undertakings. **Known for:** ice cream and sorbet; popsicles; fun toppings. $ *Average main: €5* ✉ *Carrer Santa Clara 50, Girona* ☎ *972/416667* ⊕ *www.rocambolesc.com.*

Hotels

★ Alemanys 5

$$$$ | APARTMENT | FAMILY | Award-winning architect Anna Noguera and her partner Juan-Manuel Ribera transformed a 16th-century house steps from the cathedral into two extraordinary apartments: one for up to five people, the other for six. **Pros:** perfect for families or small groups; superb architectural design; ideal location. **Cons:** needs booking in advance; minimum stay required; difficult to navigate the small streets by car (instructions provided). $ *Rooms from: €300* ✉ *Carrer Alemanys 5, Girona* ☎ *649/885136* ⊕ *www.alemanys5.com* ⇗ *2 apartments* ❘❍❘ *No Meals.*

Hotel Peninsular

$$ | HOTEL | In a handsomely restored early-20th-century building across the Riu Onyar, with views into Girona's historic Força Vella, this modest but useful hotel occupies a strategic spot at the end of the Pont de Pedra (Stone Bridge), a Girona landmark in the center of the shopping district. **Pros:** near the stop for the bus from Girona airport; friendly staff; good location at the hub of Girona life. **Cons:** smallish rooms; basic decor; no frills. $ *Rooms from: €90* ✉ *Carrer Nou 3, Av. Sant Francesc 6, Girona* ☎ *972/203800* ⊕ *www.hotelpeninsulargirona.com* ⇗ *48 rooms* ❘❍❘ *No Meals.*

▼ Nightlife

Girona is a university town, so the night scene is especially lively during the school year. In the labyrinth of small streets throughout the pedestrianized Barri Vell (Old Town), several *vermuterias* (vermouth-focused bars), wine bars, and affable taverns provide entertainment as night falls.

Sunset Jazz Club

LIVE MUSIC | As the evening develops, drop into the Sunset Jazz Club to catch some live jazz by national and

With its picturesque rivers, Girona is often called the Spanish Venice.

international artists in a softly lit, buzzing venue with exposed brick walls and dark furnishings. ⊠ *Calle Jaume Pons i Martí, Girona* ☎ *872/080145* ⊕ *www.sunset-jazz-club.com.*

Shopping

FOOD, CANDY, AND WINE
Gluki

CHOCOLATE | This chocolatier and confectioner has been in business since 1870. ⊠ *Carrer Nou 9, Girona* ☎ *972/201989* ⊕ *www.gluki.cat* ⊙ *Closed Sun. and Mon.*

La Simfonia

WINE/SPIRITS | At this relaxed wine shop that has a small restaurant, you can get a tour through a stellar range of regional wines (and cheeses)—and sample before you buy. ⊠ *Pl. de l'Oli 6, Girona* ☎ *972/411253* ⊕ *www.lasimfonia.com* ⊙ *Closed Sun. and Mon.*

Torrons Victoria Candela

FOOD | Tasty nougat is the specialty here. ⊠ *Carrer de Argenteria, 8, Girona* ☎ *972/220938* ⊕ *www.turronescandela.com.*

JEWELRY
Baobab

JEWELRY & WATCHES | A lot of designer Anna Casal's original jewelry seems at first sight to be rough-hewn; it takes a second careful look to realize how sophisticated it really is. This shop doubles as her studio. ⊠ *Carrer de les Hortes 18, Girona* ☎ *972/410227* ⊙ *Closed Sun.*

Figueres

37 km (23 miles) north of Girona.

Figueres is the capital of the *comarca* (county) of the Alt Empordà, the bustling county seat of this predominantly agricultural region. Local people come from the surrounding area to shop at its many stores and stock up on farm equipment and supplies. Thursday is market day, and farmers gather at the top of La Rambla to do business and gossip, taking refreshments at cafés and discreetly pulling

Figueres's Famous Son

With a painterly technique that rivaled that of Jan van Eyck, a flair for publicity so aggressive it would have put P. T. Barnum to shame, and a penchant for the shocking (he loved telling people Barcelona's historic Barri Gòtic should be knocked down), artist Salvador Dalí, whose most lasting image may be the melting watches in his iconic 1931 painting *The Persistence of Memory*, enters art history as one of the foremost proponents of surrealism, the movement launched in the 1920s by André Breton. The artist, who was born in Figueres and died there in 1989, decided to create a museum-monument to himself during the last two decades of his life. Dalí often frequented the Cafeteria Astòria at the top of La Rambla (still the center of social life in Figueres), signing autographs for tourists or just being Dalí: he once walked down the street with a French omelet in his breast pocket instead of a handkerchief.

out and pocketing large rolls of bills, the result of their morning transactions. What brings the tourists to Figueres in droves, however, has little to do with agriculture and everything to do with Salvador Dalí's jaw-droppingly surreal "theater-museum"—one of the most visited museums in Spain.

GETTING HERE AND AROUND
Figueres is one of the stops on the regular train service from Barcelona to the French border. Local buses are also frequent, especially from nearby Cadaqués, with more than eight scheduled daily. If you're driving, take the AP7 north from Girona. The town is small enough to explore on foot.

VISITOR INFORMATION
CONTACTS Figueres. ✉ *Pl. de l'Escorxador 2, Figueres* ☎ *972/503155* ⊕ *en. visitfigueres.cat.*

Sights

Castell de Sant Ferran
CASTLE/PALACE | Just a minute's drive northwest of Figueres is this imposing 18th-century fortified castle, one of the largest in Europe—only when you start exploring can you appreciate how immense it is. The parade grounds extend for acres, and the arcaded stables can hold more than 500 horses; the perimeter is roughly 4 km (2½ miles around). This castle was the site of the last official meeting of the Republican parliament (on February 1, 1939) before it surrendered to Franco's forces. Ironically, it was here that Lieutenant Colonel Antonio Tejero was imprisoned after his failed 1981 coup d'état in Madrid. Call ahead and arrange for the two-hour Catedral de l'Aiguas guided tour in English (€15), which includes a trip through the castle's subterranean water system by Zodiac pontoon boat. ✉ *Pujada del Castell s/n, Figueres* ☎ *972/506094* ⊕ *www.castillosanfernando.org/en* ☞ *€4* ⊗ *Closed Mon. (except public holidays).*

Museu del Joguet de Catalunya
OTHER MUSEUM | FAMILY | Hundreds of antique dolls and toys are on display here—including collections owned by, among others, Salvador Dalí, Federico García Lorca, and Joan Miró. The museum also hosts Catalonia's only *caganer* exhibit. These playful little figures answering nature's call have long had a special spot in the Catalan

The Dalí Museum in Figueres is itself a work of art. Note the eggs on the exterior: they're a common image in the artist's work.

pessebre (Nativity scene). Farmers are the most traditional figures, squatting discreetly behind the animals, but these days you'll find Barça soccer players and politicians, too. ✉ *Carrer de Sant Pere 1,* ☎ *972/504585* ⊕ *www.mjc.cat* 🎟 *€7* 🕐 *Closed Mon. Oct.–May.*

★ Teatre-Museu Dalí

ART MUSEUM | "Museum" was not a big enough word for Dalí, so he christened his monument a theater. In fact, the building was once the Força Vella theater, reduced to a ruin in the Spanish Civil War. Now topped with a glass geodesic dome and studded with Dalí's iconic egg shapes, the multilevel museum pays homage to his fertile imagination and artistic creativity. It includes gardens, ramps, and a spectacular drop cloth Dalí painted for Les Ballets de Monte Carlo. Don't look for his greatest paintings here, although there are some memorable images, including *Gala at the Mediterranean,* which takes the body of Gala (Dalí's wife) and morphs it into the image of Abraham Lincoln once you

look through coin-operated viewfinders. The sideshow theme continues with other coin-operated pieces, including *Taxi Plujós* (*Rainy Taxi*), in which water gushes over the snail-covered occupants sitting in a Cadillac once owned by Al Capone, or *Sala de Mae West,* a trompe-l'oeil vision in which a pink sofa, two fireplaces, and two paintings morph into the face of the onetime Hollywood sex symbol. Fittingly, another "exhibit" on view is Dalí's own crypt. ✉ *Pl. Gala-Salvador Dalí 5, Figueres* ☎ *972/677500* ⊕ *www. salvador-dali.org* 🎟 *€14* 🕐 *Closed Mon. Oct.–May (except public holidays).*

🍴 Restaurants

★ Hotel Empordà

$$$$ | **CATALAN** | Just 1½ km (1 mile) north of town, this restaurant run by Jaume Subirós—housed within a rather nondescript, 42-room hotel—has been hailed as the birthplace of modern Catalan cuisine and has become a beacon for gourmands. The menu changes seasonally and may contain dishes such

Dali's Castle

Castell Gala Dalí - Púbol. The third point of the Dalí triangle (along with the Teatre-Museu Dalí and Casa Salvador Dalí - Portlligat, his summer house) is the medieval castle of Púbol, where the artist's wife and perennial model, Gala, is buried in the crypt. During the 1970s this was Gala's residence, though Dalí also lived here in the early 1980s. It contains paintings and drawings, Gala's haute-couture dresses, and other objects chosen by the couple. It's also a chance to wander through another Daliesque landscape, with lush gardens, fountains decorated with masks of Richard Wagner (the couple's favorite composer), and distinctive elephants with giraffe's legs and claw feet. Púbol, a small village roughly between Girona and Figueres, is near the C66. If you are traveling by train, get off at the Flaçà station on RENFE's Barcelona–Portbou line; walk or take a taxi 4 km (2½ miles) to Púbol. The Sarfa bus company also has a stop in Flaçà and on the C66 road, some 2 km (1¼ miles) from Púbol. ⊠ *Púbol-la Pera, Púbol* ☎ *972/488655* ⊕ *www.salvador-dali.org* ⊗ *Best to call ahead or check website. Reduced hours and opening days vary month to month* ⚠ *Reservations currently essential* ⚐ *€8.*

as *cordero lechal al romero, cebollitas, pera, y boniato* (suckling lamb with rosemary, onion, pear, and sweet potato) or *espárragos de Riumors, al perfume de trufa blanca y pecorino* (asparagus from Riumors, with white truffle parfum and pecorino). **Known for:** impeccable service; historic culinary destination; birthplace of modern Catalan cuisine. $ *Average main: €27* ⊠ *Av. Salvador Dalí i Domènech 170, Figueres* ☎ *972/500562* ⊕ *www.elmotel-restaurant.com.*

 Hotels

Hotel Duràn

$$ | HOTEL | Dalí had his own private dining room in this former stagecoach relay station, though the guest rooms, refurbished in bland pale-wood tones and standard contemporary furnishings, offset the hotel's historic 19th-century exterior. **Pros:** family-friendly; good central location; dining room has pictures of Dalí. **Cons:** parking inconvenient and an extra charge; rooms lack character; somewhat erratic service. $ *Rooms from: €100* ⊠ *Carrer Lasauca 5, Figueres* ☎ *972/501250* ⊕ *www.hotelduran.com* ⇗ *65 rooms* ⦿ *No Meals.*

Besalú

34 km (21 miles) northwest of Girona, 25 km (15 miles) west of Figueres.

Besalú is one of the best-preserved medieval towns in Catalonia. Among its main sights are the 12th-century Romanesque fortified bridge over the Riu Fluvià; two churches—Sant Vicenç (set on an attractive, café-lined plaza) and Sant Pere; and the ruins of the convent of Santa Maria on the hill above town.

GETTING HERE AND AROUND

With a population of less than 2,500, the village is easily small enough to stroll through—restaurants and sights are within walking distance of each other. There is bus service to Besalú from Figueres and the surrounding Costa Brava resorts.

VISITOR INFORMATION

CONTACTS Besalú Tourist Office. ✉ *Carrer del Pont 1, Besalú* ☎ *972/591240* 🌐 *www.besalu.cat.*

Sights

Convent de Santa Maria
RUINS | The ruins of the Santa Maria Convent, on a hill just outside of town, make a good walk and offer a panoramic view over Besalú. ✉ *Besalú.*

Església de Sant Pere
CHURCH | This 12th-century Romanesque church is part of a 10th-century monastery, still in an excellent state of preservation. ✉ *Pl. de Sant Pere s/n, Besalú.*

Església de Sant Vicenç
CHURCH | Founded in 977, this pre-Romanesque gem contains the relics of St. Vincent as well as the tomb of its benefactor, Pere de Rovira. La Capella de la Veracreu (Chapel of the True Cross) displays a reproduction of an alleged fragment of the True Cross brought from Rome by Bernat Tallafer in 977 and stolen in 1899. ✉ *Pl. Sant Vicenç s/n, Besalú.*

Jewish ritual baths
RUINS | The remains of this 13th-century *mikvah,* or Jewish ritual bath, were discovered in the 1960s; it's one of the few surviving in Spain. A stone stairway leads down into the chamber where the water was drawn from the river, but little else indicates the role that the baths played in the medieval Jewish community. Access is by guided tour only (organized through the tourist office). ✉ *Calle de Pont Vell 1, Besalú* ☎ *972/591240 tourist office* 🕓 *Admission by guided tour only* ✍ *Reservations essential* 🎟 *€3.*

Pont Fortificat
BRIDGE | The town's most emblematic feature is this Romanesque 11th-century fortified bridge with crenellated battlements spanning the Riu Fluvià. ✉ *Carrer del Pont, Besalú.*

Restaurants

★ Els Fogons de Can Llaudes
$$$$ | CATALAN | A faithfully restored 10th-century Romanesque chapel holds proprietor Jaume Soler's outstanding restaurant—one of Catalonia's best. A typical dish could be *confitat de bou i raïm glacejat amb el seu suc* (beef confit au jus with glacé grapes), but the menu changes weekly. **Known for:** wonderful decor; Romanesque chapel; rotating fixed-price menu only. [$] *Average main: €80* ✉ *Pl. de Prat de Sant Pere 6, Besalú* ☎ *972/590858* 🕓 *Closed Tues., and last 2 wks of Nov.*

Olot

21 km (13 miles) west of Besalú, 55 km (34 miles) northwest of Girona.

Capital of the *comarca* (administrative region) of La Garrotxa, Olot is famous for its 19th-century school of landscape painters and has several excellent Art Nouveau buildings, including the Casa Solà-Morales, which has a facade by Lluís Domènech i Montaner, architect of Barcelona's Palau de la Música Catalana. The Sant Esteve church at the southeastern end of Passeig d'en Blay is famous for its El Greco painting *Christ Carrying the Cross* (1605).

The villages of Vall d'En Bas lie south of Olot, off the C153. A freeway cuts across this countryside to Vic, but you'll miss a lot by taking it. The twisting old road leads you through rich farmland past farmhouses with dark wooden balconies bedecked with bright flowers. Turn off for Sant Privat d'En Bas and Els Hostalets d'En Bas. Farther on, the picturesque medieval village of Rupit has excellent restaurants serving the famous *patata de Rupit,* potato stuffed with duck and beef, while the rugged Collsacabra mountains offer some of Catalonia's most pristine landscapes.

Besalú contains astonishingly well-preserved medieval buildings.

🍽 Restaurants

Ca l'Enric

$$$$ | CATALAN | Chefs Jordi and Isabel Juncà have become legends in the town of La Vall de Bianya, just north of Olot, with exquisite cuisine that's firmly rooted in local products. Dishes star game of all sorts, truffles, and wild mushrooms, and are served in a historic stone-walled 19th-century inn. **Known for:** fixed-price menus; local ingredients; truffles and wild mushrooms, in season. $ *Average main: €34 ⊠ Ctra. de Camprodon s/n, La Vall de Bianya, Olot ⊹ Nacional 260, Km 91 ☎ 972/290015 ⊕ www.restaurant-calenric.cat ⊗ Closed Mon., Dec. 27–Jan. 17, and 1st 2 wks of July (can vary). No dinner Sun.–Wed.*

Les Cols

$$$$ | CATALAN | Chef Fina Puigdevall has made this sprawling 18th-century *masia* (Catalan farmhouse) a triumph. The cuisine on the prix fixe menu (no à la carte option) is seasonal and based on locally grown products, from wild mushrooms to the extraordinarily flavorful legumes and vegetables produced by the rich, volcanic soil of La Garrotxa. **Known for:** incredible decor; also five rooms for overnight stays; seasonal fixed-price menu. $ *Average main: €135 ⊠ Mas les Cols, Ctra. de la Canya s/n, Olot ☎ 972/269209 ⊕ www.lescols.com ⊗ Closed Mon. and Tues. No dinner Sun.*

Tossa de Mar

80 km (50 miles) northeast of Barcelona, 41 km (25 miles) south of Girona.

Christened "Blue Paradise" by painter Marc Chagall, who summered here for four decades, Tossa's pristine beaches are among Catalonia's best. Set around a gorgeous bay, it's comprised of the the Vila Vella (Old Town) and the Vila Nova (New Town). The Vila Vella is a lovely district open to the sea and threaded by steep cobblestone streets with many restored buildings.

Ava Gardner filmed the 1951 British drama *Pandora and the Flying Dutchman* here (a statue dedicated to her stands on a terrace on the medieval walls). Things may have changed since those days, but this beautiful village retains much of the unspoiled magic of its past. The primary beach at Tossa de Mar is the Platja Gran (Big Beach) in front of the town beneath the walls, and just next to it is Mar Menuda (Little Sea), where the small, colorfully painted fishing boats—maybe the same ones that caught your dinner—pull up onto the beach.

The beaches and town are a magnet for vacationers in July and August. Out of season, it's far more sedate, but the mild temperatures make it an ideal stop for coastal strolls.

GETTING HERE AND AROUND

By car, the fastest way to Costa Brava's Tossa de Mar from Barcelona is to drive up the inland C-33 tollway toward Girona, then take Sortida 10 (Exit 9A). The C-32 can also get you there in a similar length of time. The main bus station (as well as the local tourist office inside the station) is on Plaça de les Nacions Sense Estat.

Sights

Museu Municipal

ART MUSEUM | In a lovingly restored 14th-century house, this museum is said to be Catalonia's first dedicated to modern art. It is home to one of the only three Chagall paintings in Spain, *Celestial Violinist*. ⊠ *Pl. Pintor Roig i Soler 1, Tossa de Mar* ☎ *972/340709* ⊙ *Closed Mon.* ᴁ €3.

Vila Vella and Castillo de Tossa de Mar

HISTORIC DISTRICT | Listed as a national artistic-historic monument in 1931, Tossa de Mar's Vila Vella (Old Town) is the only remaining example of a fortified medieval town in Catalonia. Set high above the town on a promontory, the Old Town is presided over by the ramparts and towers of the 13th-century Castillo de Tossa

de Mar, and is a steep yet worthy climb up from the main town, accessed from the western side of Platja Gran Tossa de Mar (Playa Grande). The cliff-top views, particularly at sunset, are remarkable, and the labyrinth of narrow, cobblestone lanes lined with ancient houses (some dating back to the 14th century) is a delight to explore at a leisurely pace. Bar del Far del Tossa (Carrer del Far 14), near the lighthouse, has some of the best views in town, plus drinks, snacks, and light meals. ⊠ *Passeig de Vila Vella 1, Tossa de Mar.*

🏖 Beaches

Mar Menuda (*Little Sea*)

BEACH | FAMILY | Just north of the town center, this small sandy crescent is a pleasant Blue Flag beach that's popular with local families. The sand is coarse, but the calm, shallow waters make it ideal for children. Fishing boats bob peacefully in the water nearby after completing their morning's work. At the top of the beach there is a second cove called La Banyera de Ses Dones (the women's bathtub), which provides ideal conditions for diving, though if the sea is not calm, it is dangerous for swimmers. By day there is little natural shade, so bring adequate sunblock and an umbrella if you plan a long beach session. It gets extremely busy in high season. **Amenities:** none. **Best for:** snorkeling; sunset; swimming. ⊠ *Av. Mar Menuda, Tossa de Mar.*

Platja Gran (*Big Beach*)

BEACH | FAMILY | Sweeping past the Vila Vella, this well-maintained, soft-sand beach runs along the front of town to meet the base of the Cap de Tossa. One of the most photographed coastlines in this area of Spain, it is also, at the height of summer, one of the busiest. Conditions are normally fine for swimming (any warnings are announced via loudspeaker). A rising number of motorboats is impacting the water quality, but for now it retains its Blue Flag status. Running behind the beach, there is no shortage of cafés and kiosks selling ice cream and snacks. There is no natural shade, but you can rent deck chairs and umbrellas. **Amenities:** food and drink; lifeguards; showers; toilets; water sports. **Best for:** snorkeling; sunset; swimming. ✉ *Av. de sa Palma, Tossa de Mar.*

🍴 Restaurants

La Cuina de Can Simon
$$$$ | **CATALAN** | Elegantly rustic, this restaurant beside Tossa de Mar's medieval walls serves a combination of classical Catalan cuisine with up-to-date, innovative touches. Two tapas tasting menus (€75 and €90) provide more than enough to sample, and you can also order à la carte. **Known for:** welcoming tapa and cava upon entrance; seasonal menu; top-notch service. [$] *Average main: €28* ✉ *Carrer del Portal 24,* ☎ *972/341269* 🌐 *www.restaurantcansimon.com* 🕓 *Closed Mon. No dinner Sun.*

🛏 Hotels

Hotel Capri
$$ | **HOTEL** | **FAMILY** | Located on the beach, this hotel is in hailing distance of the old quarter in the medieval fortress; rooms are simple, and those with sea views have private terraces. **Pros:** family-friendly option; good value; great location. **Cons:** no private parking; minimal amenities; rooms are small. [$] *Rooms from: €110* ✉ *Passeig del Mar 17, Tossa de Mar* ☎ *972/340358* 🌐 *www.hotelcapritossa.com* 🕓 *Closed Nov.–Feb.* 🛏 *22 rooms* 🍴 *Free Breakfast.*

★ Hotel Diana
$$$$ | **HOTEL** | Built in 1906 by architect Antoni de Falguera i Sivilla, disciple of Antoni Gaudí, this Moderniste gem sits on the square in the heart of the Vila Vella, steps from the beach. **Pros:** Moderniste touches; attentive service; ideal location, with sea views. **Cons:** room rates unpredictable; minimal amenities; some rooms are small. [$] *Rooms from: €250* ✉ *Pl. de Espanya 6, Tossa de Mar* ☎ *972/341886* 🌐 *www.hotelesdante.com* 🕓 *Closed Nov.–Mar.* 🛏 *21 rooms* 🍴 *Free Breakfast.*

Hotel Sant March
$$ | **HOTEL** | **FAMILY** | This family hotel in the center of town is two minutes from the beach, with guest rooms that open onto a pleasant interior garden that serve as an oasis of tranquility in a sometimes hectic town. **Pros:** warm personal touch; central location; good value. **Cons:** few exterior views; rooms a bit small; no elevator. [$] *Rooms from: €120* ✉ *Av. Pelegrí 2,* ☎ *972/340078* 🌐 *www.hotelsantmarch.com* 🕓 *Closed Oct. 15–Mar.* 🛏 *29 rooms* 🍴 *Free Breakfast.*

Sant Feliu de Guixols

23 km (14 miles) northeast of Tossa de Mar.

The little fishing port of Sant Feliu de Guixols is set on a small bay; Moderniste mansions line the seafront promenade, recalling a time when the cork industry made this one of the wealthier towns on the coast. In front of them, a long crescent beach of fine white sand leads around to the fishing harbor at its north end. Behind the promenade, a well-preserved old quarter of narrow streets and squares leads to a 10th-century gateway with horseshoe arches (all that remains of a pre-Romanesque monastery); also here is a church that combines Romanesque, Gothic, and baroque styles. Nearby, the iron-structured indoor market, which dates back to the 1930s, sells the freshest and finest local produce, with colorful stalls often overflowing onto the Plaça del Mercat in front.

GETTING HERE AND AROUND

To get here, take the C65 from Tossa de Mar—though adventurous souls might prefer the harrowing hairpin curves of the G1682 coastal corniche.

Sights

Museu d'Història de Sant Feliu de Guíxols

HISTORY MUSEUM | Inside the Romanesque Benedictine monastery is this museum, which contains interesting exhibits about the town's cork and fishing trades, and displays local archaeological finds. ⊠ Pl. del Monestir s/n, Sant Feliu de Guixols ☎ 972/821575 ⊕ www.museu.guixols.cat ☜ Free (until further notice).

🍴 Restaurants

Can Segura

$$ | CATALAN | Half a block in from the beach at Sant Feliu de Guixols, this restaurant serves house-cooked seafood and upland specialties. The dining room is always full, with customers waiting their turn in the street, but the staff is good at finding spots at the jovially long communal tables. Known for: excellent rice dishes; first-rate seafood specialties; communal dining. $ Average main: €15 ⊠ Carrer de Sant Pere 11, Sant Feliu de Guixols ☎ 972/321009.

🛏 Hotels

Hostal del Sol

$$ | HOTEL | FAMILY | Once the summer home of a wealthy family, this Moderniste hotel has a grand stone stairway and medieval-style tower, as well as a garden and a lawn where you can relax by the pool. Pros: good breakfast; good value; family-friendly option. Cons: far from the beach; bathrooms a bit claustrophobic; on a busy road. $ Rooms from: €120 ⊠ Ctra. a Palamós 194, Sant Feliu de Guixols ☎ 972/320193 ⊕ www.hostaldel-sol.cat/en ⍩ Free Breakfast ۞ Closed mid-Oct.–Easter ➴ 41 rooms.

S'Agaró

3 km (2 miles) north of Sant Feliu de Guixols.

S'Agaró is an elegant gated community on a rocky point at the north end of the cove. The 30-minute walk along the **sea wall** from Hostal de La Gavina to Sa Conca Beach is a delight, and the one-hour hike from Sant Pol Beach over to Sant Feliu de Guixols offers views of the Costa Brava at its best.

🍴 Restaurants

Villa Mas

$$$$ | CATALAN | This Moderniste villa on the coast road from Sant Feliu to S'Agaró, with a lovely turn-of-the-20th-century zinc bar, serves typical Catalan and seasonal Mediterranean dishes like *arròs a la cassola* (deep-dish rice) with shrimp brought fresh off the boats in Palamos, just up the coast. The terrace is a popular and shady spot just across the road from the beach. **Known for:** fresh seafood catches; dining on terrace; across from beach. $ *Average main:* €28 ⊠ *Passeig de Sant Pol 95, S'Agaró* ☎ 972/822526 ⊕ *www.restaurantvilla-mas.com* ۞ *Closed Mon.; no dinner Sun. or Tues.–Thurs.*

🛏 Hotels

★ L'Hostal de la Gavina

$$$$ | HOTEL | Opened in 1932 by farmer-turned-entrepreneur Josep Ensesa, the original hotel grew from a cluster of country villas into a sprawling complex of buildings of extraordinary splendor that have attracted celebrity guests from Orson Welles and Ava Gardner to Sean Connery. **Pros:** sea views, including from pool and terrace; in a gated community; impeccable service and amenities. **Cons:** walls are thin; hard on the budget; expensive restaurant. $ *Rooms from:* €490 ⊠ *Pl. Roserar s/n, S'Agaró* ☎ 972/321100

🌐 *www.lagavina.com* ⏲ *Closed Nov.–Easter* 🛏 *74 rooms* 🍴 *Free Breakfast.*

Calella de Palafrugell and Around

25 km (15½ miles) north of S'Agaró.

Up the coast from S'Agaró, the C31 brings you to Palafrugell and Begur; to the east are some of the prettiest, least developed inlets of the Costa Brava. One road leads to **Llafranc,** a small port with waterfront hotels and restaurants, and forks right to the fishing village of **Calella de Palafrugell,** known for its July habaneras festival. (The *habanera* is a form of Cuban dance music brought to Europe by Catalan sailors in the late 19th century; it still enjoys a nostalgic cachet here.) Just south is the panoramic promontory of **Cap Roig,** with views of the barren Formigues Isles.

North along the coast lie **Tamariu, Aiguablava, Fornell, Platja Fonda,** and (around the point at Cap de Begur) **Sa Tuna** and **Aiguafreda.** There's not much to do in any of these hideaways, but you can luxuriate in wonderful views, some of the Costa Brava's best beaches and coves, and the soothing quiet. Tamariu, a largely unspoiled former fishing village backed by simple whitewashed houses and a small strip of seafood restaurants that hug the shoreline, is reached by descending a vertiginous road set between mountains and pine forests. Farther north, toward Begur, the small, sheltered Aiguablava beach sets the stage for memorable sunsets. Its restaurant, Toc Al Mar, is a favorite with barcelonins (Barcelona residents) on weekend coastal jaunts and offers picture-perfect views.

🍴 Restaurants

★ Pa i Raïm

$$$ | **CATALAN** | "Bread and Grapes" in Catalan, Pa i Raïm is an excellent restaurant set in writer Josep Pla's ancestral family home in Palafrugell. It has one rustic dining room as well as another in a glassed-in winter garden, plus a leafy terrace, which is the place to be in summer. **Known for:** standout prawns tempura; contemporary fare; traditional country cuisine. [$] *Average main: €20* ✉ *Torres i Jonama 56, Palafrugell* ☎ *972/447278* 🌐 *www.pairaim.com* ⏲ *Closed Mon. No dinner Sun.–Thurs.*

🛏 Hotels

Hotel-Restaurant El Far

$$$$ | **B&B/INN** | **FAMILY** | Rooms in this 17th-century hermitage attached to a 15th-century watchtower have original vaulted ceilings, hardwood floors, and interiors accented with floral prints; the larger doubles and the suite can accommodate extra beds for children. **Pros:** spectacular views of bay; friendly service; graceful architecture. **Cons:** pricey for what you get; a bit of a distance from the beach; need car. [$] *Rooms from: €330* ✉ *Muntanya de Sant Sebastia, Carrer Uruguai s/n,* ☎ *972/301639* 🌐 *www.hotelelfar.com/en* 🛏 *9 rooms* 🍴 *Free Breakfast.*

Begur and Around

11 km (7 miles) north of Calella de Palafrugell.

From Begur, go east through the calas or take the inland route past the rose-color stone houses and ramparts of the restored medieval town of **Pals.** Nearby **Peratallada** is another medieval fortified town with an 11th-century castle, tower, and palace. The name is derived from *pedra tallada,* meaning "carved stone," and behind the town's well-preserved walls is a maze of narrow streets and ivy-covered houses built from stone that was carved from the moat, which still encircles the town. In the center, the arcaded Plaça de les Voltes is alive with restaurants, shops, and cafés. North of Pals there are signs for **Ullastret,** an Iberian village dating to the 5th century BC. **L'Estartit** is the jumping-off point for the spectacular natural park surrounding the Medes Islands, famous for its protected marine life and consequently for diving and underwater photography.

Sights

Empúries
RUINS | The Greco-Roman ruins here are Catalonia's most important archaeological site, and this port is one of the most monumental ancient engineering feats on the Iberian Peninsula. As the Greeks' original point of arrival in Spain, Empúries was also where the Olympic Flame entered Spain for Barcelona's 1992 Olympic Games. ✉ *Puig i Cadafalch s/n* ☎ *972/770208* 🌐 *www.macempuries.cat* 🎟 *€6* 🕒 *Closed Mon. mid-Nov.–mid-Feb.*

Medes Islands (*Underwater Natural Park*)
NATURE SIGHT | The marine reserve around the Medes Islands, an archipelago of several small islands, is just off the coastline of L'Estartit, and is touted as one of the best places in Spain to scuba dive. Thanks to its protected status, the marine life—eels, octopus, starfish, and grouper—is tame, and you can expect high visibility unless the weather is bad. If diving doesn't appeal, you can take one of the glass-bottomed boats that frequent the islands from the mainland and view from above. ✉ *L'Estartit.*

Restaurants

Restaurant Ibèric
$$$ | **CATALAN** | This excellent pocket of authentic Costa Brava cuisine serves everything from snails to wild boar in season. Wild mushrooms scrambled with eggs or stewed with hare are specialties, as are complex and earthy red wines made by enologist Jordi Oliver (of the Oliver Conti vineyard in the Alt Empordà's village of Capmany). **Known for:** lovely terrace; traditional setting; eclectic cuisine. [$] *Average main: €20* ✉ *Carrer Valls 11, Ullastret* ☎ *972/757108* 🌐 *www.restaurantiberic.com* 🕒 *Closed Mon. No dinner.*

Hotels

El Convent Hotel and Restaurant
$$$$ | **HOTEL** | Built in 1730, this elegant former convent is a 10-minute walk to the beach at the Cala Sa Riera—the quietest and prettiest inlet north of Begur. **Pros:** terrace for dining; quiet and private; appealing architecture. **Cons:** rooms are not soundproofed; minimum three-night stay in summer; need car. [$] *Rooms from: €275* ✉ *Ctra. de la Platja del Racó 2, Begur* ☎ *972/623091* 🌐 *www.hotel-conventbegur.com* 🛏 *25 rooms* 🍴 *Free Breakfast.*

★ **Hotel Aigua Blava**
$$$$ | **HOTEL** | **FAMILY** | What began as a small hostel in the 1920s is now a sprawling luxury hotel, run by the fourth generation of the same family. **Pros:** impeccable service; private playground; gardens and pleasant patios at every turn. **Cons:** expensive restaurant; no beach in the inlet; no elevator. [$] *Rooms from: €371* ✉ *Platja de Fornells s/n,* ☎ *972/622058* 🌐 *www.aiguablava.com* 🍴 *Free Breakfast* 🕒 *Closed Nov.–Mar.* 🛏 *85 rooms.*

Cadaqués and Around

Sights

★ Cap de Creus

NATURE SIGHT | North of Cadaqués, Spain's easternmost point is a fundamental pilgrimage, if only for the symbolic geographical rush. The hike out to the lighthouse—through rosemary, thyme, and the salt air of the Mediterranean—is unforgettable. The Pyrenees officially end (or rise) here. New Year's Day finds mobs of revelers awaiting the first emergence of the "new" sun from the Mediterranean. Gaze down at heart-pounding views of the craggy coast and crashing waves with a warm mug of coffee in hand or fine fare on the table at **Bar Restaurant Cap de Creus,** which sits on a rocky crag above the Cap de Creus. On a summer evening, you may be lucky and stumble upon some live music on the terrace. ✉ *Carrer de Cadaqués al Cap de Creus.*

Casa Salvador Dalí - Portlligat

HISTORIC HOME | This was Dalí's summerhouse and a site long associated with the artist's notorious frolics with everyone from poets Federico García Lorca and Paul Eluard to filmmaker Luis Buñuel. Filled with bits of the surrealist's daily life, it's an important point in the "Dalí triangle," completed by the castle at Púbol and the Teatre-Museu Dalí in Figueres. You can get here by a 3-km (2-mile) walk north along the beach from Cadaqués. Only small groups of visitors are admitted at any given time, and reservations in advance are required. ✉ *Portlligat s/n,* ☎ *972/251015* 🌐 *www.salvador-dali.org* 🎫 *€14; advance reservations required* 🕒 *Closed Jan.–Mar., Mon. June–Dec., and Mon. and Tues. Apr.–May* ✍ *Reservations essential.*

★ Sant Pere de Rodes

VIEWPOINT | The monastery of Sant Pere de Rodes, 7 km (4½ miles) by car (plus a 20-minute walk) above the pretty fishing village of El Port de la Selva, is a spectacular site. Built in the 10th and 11th centuries by Benedictine monks—and sacked and plundered repeatedly since—this restored Romanesque monolith commands a breathtaking panorama of the Pyrenees, the Empordà plain, the sweeping curve of the Bay of Roses, and Cap de Creus. (Topping off the grand trek across the Pyrenees, Cap de Creus is a spectacular six-hour walk from here on the well-marked GR11 trail.) In July and August, the monastery is the setting for the annual Festival Sant Pere (www.festivalsantpere.com), drawing top-tier classical musicians from all over the world. Find event listings online (in Catalan); phone for reservations or to book a post-concert dinner in the monastery's refectory-style restaurant (972/194–233, 610/310–0730). ✉ *Camí del Monestir s/n, El Porte de la Selva* ☎ *972/387559* 🌐 *www.festivalsantpere.com* 🎫 *€6* 🕒 *Closed Mon.*

Restaurants

★ Casa Anita

$$$$ | **SEAFOOD** | Simple, fresh, and generous dishes are the draw at this informal little eatery, an institution in Cadaqués. Tables are shared, and there is no menu; the staff recite the offerings of the day, which might include wonderful local prawns and sardines *a la plancha* (grilled), mussels, and sea bass. **Known for:** famous clientele; no menu; regional wines. [$] *Average main: €25* ✉ *Carrer Miquel Rosset 16,* ☎ *972/258471* 🕒 *Closed Mon., and mid-Oct.–1st wk in Dec.*

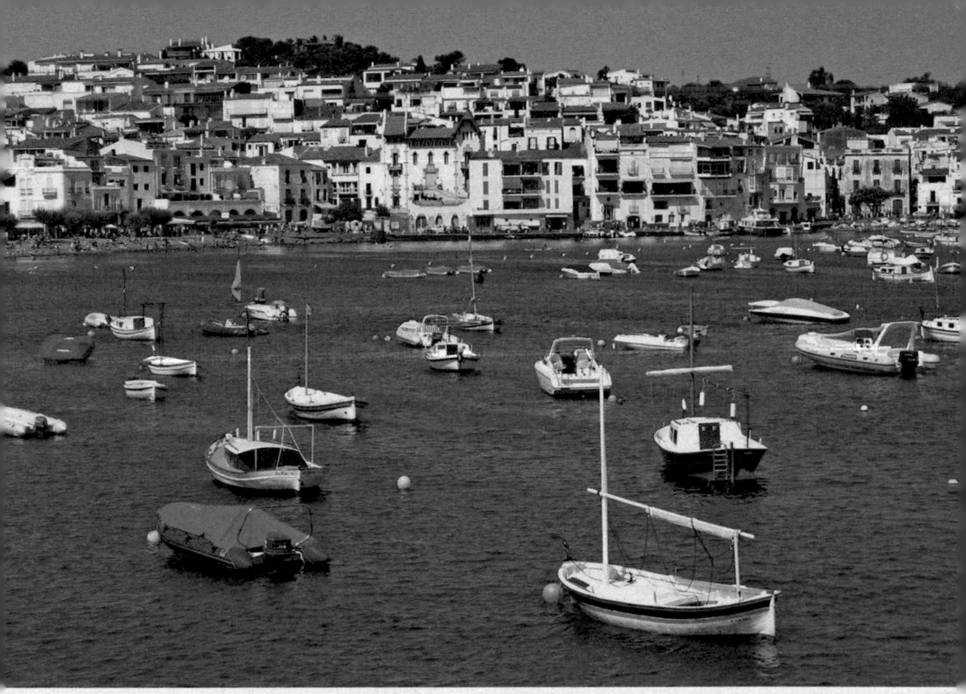

The popular harbor of Cadaqués

Compartir

$$$$ | **CATALAN** | The word "compartir" means "to share" and this excellent restaurant bases its menu on a small-plate sharing approach that has been taken to another level by the culinary team of Mateu Casañas, Oriol Castro, and Eduard Xatruch (all former elBulli chefs). Each dish is served by attentive staff within an 18th-century courtyard. **Known for:** beautiful courtyard setting; sharing plates; creative gastronomy. [$] *Average main: €24* ✉ *Riera Sant Vicenç s/n, Cadaqués* ☎ *972/258482* 🌐 *www.compartircadaques.com* 🕓 *Closed Mon., and Jan.–early Feb.*

Hotels

Hotel Llané Petit

$$$$ | **HOTEL** | This intimate, typically Mediterranean, bay-side hotel caters to people who want to make the most of their stay in the village and don't want to spend too much time in their hotel. **Pros:** good breakfast; semiprivate beach next to hotel; free Wi-Fi. **Cons:** somewhat lightweight beds and furnishings; small rooms; some soundproofing issues. [$] *Rooms from: €197.50* ✉ *Pl. Llane Petit s/n, Cadaqués* ☎ *972/251020* 🌐 *www.llanepetit.com* 🕓 *Closed Nov.–Mar.* 🛏 *37 rooms* 🍴 *Free Breakfast.*

Hotel Playa Sol

$$$$ | **HOTEL** | **FAMILY** | In business for more than 50 years, this hotel on the cove of Es Pianc is just a five-minute walk from the village center and is a good option for families, due to its connecting rooms, swimming pool, and bike rental. **Pros:** great views; attentive, friendly service; family-friendly. **Cons:** rooms with balcony and sea views are harder to book; decor could be more colorful; small rooms. [$] *Rooms from: €250* ✉ *Riba Es Pianc 3,* ☎ *972/258100* 🌐 *www.playasol.com* 🕓 *Closed Nov.–mid-Feb.* 🛏 *48 rooms* 🍴 *No Meals.*

Montserrat

50 km (31 miles) west of Barcelona.

A popular side trip from Barcelona is a visit to the dramatic, sawtooth peaks of Montserrat, where the shrine of La Moreneta (the Black Virgin of Montserrat) sits. Montserrat is as memorable for its strange topography as it is for its religious treasures. The views over the mountains that stretch all the way to the Mediterranean and, on a clear day, to the Pyrenees, are breathtaking, and the rugged, boulder-strewn terrain makes for exhilarating walks and hikes.

GETTING HERE AND AROUND

By car from Barcelona, follow the A2/A7 autopista on the upper ring road (Ronda de Dalt), or from the western end of the Diagonal as far as Salida 25 to Martorell. Bypass this industrial center and follow signs to Montserrat. You can also take the FGC train from the Plaça d'Espanya metro station (hourly 7:36 am–5:41 pm), connecting with either the cable car at Aeri Montserrat or with the rack railway (Cremallera) at Monistrol Montserrat. Both the cable car and rack railway take 15 minutes and depart every 20 minutes and 15 minutes, respectively. Once you arrive at the monastery, several funiculars can take you farther up the mountain.

 ## Sights

★ La Moreneta

RELIGIOUS BUILDING | The shrine of La Moreneta, one of Catalonia's patron saints, resides in a Benedictine monastery high in the Serra de Montserrat, surrounded by—and dwarfed by the grandeur of—sheer, jagged peaks. The crests above the monastic complex bristle with chapels and hermitages. The shrine and its setting have given rise to countless legends about what happened here: St. Peter left a statue of the Virgin Mary carved by St. Luke, Parsifal found the Holy Grail, and Wagner (who wrote the opera *Parsifal*) sought musical inspiration. The shrine is world famous and one of Catalonia's spiritual sanctuaries, and not just for the monks who reside here—honeymooning couples flock here by the thousands seeking La Moreneta's blessing on their marriages, and twice a year, on April 27 and September 8, the diminutive statue of Montserrat's Black Virgin becomes the object of one of Spain's greatest pilgrimages. Only the basilica and museum are regularly open to the public. The famous Escolania de Montserrat boys' choir sings the Salve and Virulai from the liturgy weekdays at 1 pm and Sunday at noon. ⊠ *Montserrat* ☎ *No phone* ⊕ *www.montserratvisita. com* 🎫 *€16 sanctuary, audio guide, museum, and audiovisual presentation.*

Sitges

43 km (27 miles) southwest of Barcelona.

Sitges is the prettiest and most popular resort in Barcelona's immediate environs, with an excellent beach and a whitewashed and flowery old quarter. It's also one of Europe's premier gay resorts. From April through September, the fine white sand of the Sitges beach is elbow-to-elbow with sun worshippers. On the eastern end of the strand is an alabaster statue of the 16th-century painter El Greco, usually associated with Toledo, where he spent most of his professional career. The artist Santiago Rusiñol is responsible for this surprise; he was such a Greco fan that he not only installed two of his paintings in his Museu del Cau Ferrat but also had this sculpture planted on the beach.

Sitges and the two nearby Cistercian monasteries to the west of it, Santes Creus and Santa Maria de Poblet, are a trio of attractions that can be seen in a day.

Whitewashed buildings dominate the landscape in Sitges.

GETTING HERE AND AROUND

By car from Barcelona, head southwest along Gran Vía or Passeig Colom to the freeway that passes the airport on its way to Castelldefels. From here, the freeway and tunnels will get you to Sitges in 20–30 minutes. En route, the small village of Garraf is a worthwhile pit stop, with narrow lanes flanked by whitewashed houses that cling to a promontory looking out to sea. It has a small beach backed by colorful beach huts, providing a quieter refuge from the crowds in Sitges (although it too gets busy in high season).

Just over 30 minutes by train (€4 each way), there's regular service from all three Barcelona stations. Buses, roughly the same price, run at least hourly from Plaza Espanya and take about 45 minutes, depending how many stops they make. If you're driving head south on the C32.

Sights

Bodegas Torres

WINERY | This family vineyard-winery provides tours and tastings of some excellent Penedès wines. There are also pairings on offer—wine with cheese or wine and Ibérico ham, and a restaurant amongst the vines with superlative views of Montserrat mountain. ⊠ *Finca "El Maset", Ctra. BP2121 (direction Sant Martí Sarroca), Vilafranca del Penedès* ⊹ *From Sitges, make straight for the AP–2 autopista by way of Vilafranca del Penedès* ☎ *938/177400* ⊕ *www.torres. es.*

Museu del Cau Ferrat

ART MUSEUM | This is the most interesting museum in Sitges, established by the bohemian artist and cofounder of the Quatre Gats café in Barcelona, Santiago Rusiñol (1861–1931), and containing some of his own paintings together with two by El Greco. Connoisseurs of wrought iron will love the beautiful collection of *cruces terminales*, crosses that once marked town boundaries. Next door is the Museu de Maricel, with more artistic treasures. ✉ *Carrer Fonollar 6,* ☎ *938/940364* 🌐 *www.museusdesitges.com* 🎟 *€10, includes Museu del Maricel* 🕒 *Closed Mon.*

Passeig Maritim
PROMENADE | A focal point of Sitges life, this long esplanade is an iconic pedestrianized promenade that sweeps past the bay of Sitges. It's backed by upmarket villas, mountain vistas, and ocean views. ✉ *Passeig Maritim, Sitges.*

Vinseum (*Museu de les Cultures del Vi de Catalunya*)
OTHER MUSEUM | This interesting wine museum in the Royal Palace has exhibits describing wine-making history in Catalonia. ✉ *Pl. Jaume I 5, Vilafranca del Penedès* ☎ *938/900582* 🌐 *www.vinseum.cat* 🎟 *€7, includes tasting and audio guide* 🕒 *Closed Mon.*

Beaches

Playa de la Ribera
BEACH | **FAMILY** | In the heart of Sitges, Playa de la Ribera is one of the town's largest and most popular beaches. Its soft, golden sand and calm waters make it perennially popular with families, especially. It's backed by a promenade lined with numerous bars and restaurants. **Amenties:** food and drink; lifeguards; showers; toilets. **Best for:** swimming; walking; sunbathing.

✉ *Sitges*

Restaurants

Vivero
$$$ | **SEAFOOD** | Perched on a rocky point above the bay at Playa San Sebastián, Vivero specializes in paellas and seafood; try the *mariscada*, a meal-in-itself ensemble of lobster, mussels, and prawns. Weather permitting, the best seats in the house are on the terraces, with wonderful views of the water. **Known for:** wonderful water views; excellent mariscada; outdoor dining. [$] *Average main: €22* ✉ *Passeig Balmins s/n, Playa San Sebastián,* ☎ *938/942149* 🌐 *www.elviverositges.com.*

Santes Creus Monastery and Around

95 km (59 miles) west of Barcelona.

Sitges, with its beach and its summer festivals of dance and music, film and fireworks, is anything but solemn. Head inland, however, some 45 minutes' drive west, and you discover how much the art and architecture—the very tone of Catalan culture—owes to its medieval religious heritage. Monolithic Romanesque architecture and beautiful cloisters characterize the Cistercian monasteries at Santes Creus and Poblet.

GETTING HERE AND AROUND

It takes about 45 minutes to drive to Santes Creus from Sitges. Take the C32 west, then get onto the C51 and TP2002, or drive inland toward Vilafranca del Penedès and the AP-7 freeway, followed by the AP-2 (Lleida).

Regular trains leave Sants and Passeig de Gràcia stations for Sitges, Garraf, and Vilafranca del Penedès; the ride takes a half hour to an hour. To get to Santes Creus or Poblet from Sitges, take a Lleida-bound train to L'Espluga de Francolí, 4 km (2½ miles) from Poblet; there's one direct train in the morning at 7:37 and four more during the day with transfers at Sant Vicenç de Calders. From L'Espluga, take a cab to the monastery.

Sights

Montblanc
TOWN | The ancient gates are too narrow for cars, and a walk through its tiny streets reveals Gothic churches with stained-glass windows, a 16th-century

hospital, and medieval mansions. ✉ *Off AP-2, Salida 9 (Exit 9).*

Santes Creus

RELIGIOUS BUILDING | Founded in 1157, Santes Creus is the first of the monasteries you'll come upon as the A2 branches west toward Lleida; take Exit 11 off the highway. Three austere aisles and an unusual 14th-century apse combine with the restored cloisters and the courtyard of the royal palace. ✉ *Pl. Jaume el Just s/n* ☎ *977/638329* ✉ *€6* ⊗ *Closed Mon.*

Santa Maria de Poblet

8 km (5 miles) west of Santes Creus.

This splendid Cistercian monastery, located at the foot of the Prades Mountains, is one of the great masterpieces of Spanish monastic architecture. Declared a UNESCO World Heritage site, the cloister is a stunning combination of lightness and size, and on sunny days the shadows on the yellow sandstone are extraordinary.

GETTING HERE AND AROUND
The Barcelona–Lleida train can drop you at L'Espluga de Francolí, from where it's a 4-km (2½-mile) walk to the monastery. Buses from Tarragona or Lleida will get you a little closer, with a 2¾-km (1½-mile) walk. The drive from Sitges takes about an hour, via the C32 and AP-2 (Exit 9 when coming from Sitges).

⊙ Sights

★ Monasterio de Santa María de Poblet
RELIGIOUS BUILDING | Founded in 1150 by Ramón Berenguer IV in gratitude for the Christian Reconquest, the monastery first housed a dozen Cistercians from Narbonne. Later, the Crown of Aragón used Santa Maria de Poblet for religious retreats and burials. The building was damaged in an 1836 anticlerical revolt, and monks of the reformed Cistercian Order have managed the difficult task of

Celebrated Onions

Valls. This town, famous for its early spring *calçotada* (onion feast) held on the last Sunday of January, is 10 km (6 miles) from Santes Creus and 15 km (9 miles) from Poblet. Even if you miss the big day, calçots are served November through April at rustic farmhouses such as Cal Ganxo in nearby Masmolets (✉ *Carrer de la Font F 14* ☎ *977/605960*).

restoration since 1940. Today, a community of monks and novices still pray before the splendid retable over the tombs of Aragonese rulers, restored to their former glory by sculptor Frederic Marès; they also sleep in the cold, barren dormitory and eat frugal meals in the stark refectory. ✉ *Off AP-2 (Exit 9 from Barcelona, Exit 8 from Lleida), Pl. Corona de Aragón 11* ☎ *977/870089* ⊕ *www. poblet.cat* ✉ *€8.*

Tarragona

98 km (61 miles) southwest of Barcelona, 251 km (156 miles) northeast of Valencia.

Tarragona, the principal town of southern Catalonia, today is a vibrant center of culture and art, a busy fishing and shipping port, and a natural jumping-off point for the towns and pristine beaches of Sitges and the Costa Daurada, 216 km (134 miles) of coastline north of the Costa del Azahar. However, in Roman times, Tarragona was one of the finest and most important outposts of the Roman Empire, and was famous for its wine even before that. The town's population was the first *gens togata* (literally, the toga-clad people) in Spain, which conferred on them equality with the citizens of Rome. Its vast Roman remains, chief among them the Circus Maximus, bear witness to Tarragona's grandeur, and to this the Middle Ages added wonderful city walls and citadels. Due to its Roman remains and medieval Christian monuments, Tarragona has been designated a UNESCO World Heritage site.

Though modern, Tarragona has preserved its heritage superbly. Stroll along the town's cliff-side perimeter and you'll see why the Romans set up shop here: Tarragona is strategically positioned at the center of a broad, open bay, with an unobstructed view of the sea. As capital of the Roman province of Hispania Tarraconensis (from 218 BC), Tarraco (as it was then called) formed the empire's principal stronghold in Spain. St. Paul preached here in AD 58, and Tarragona became the seat of the Christian church in Spain until it was superseded by Toledo in the 11th century.

If you're entering the city en route from Barcelona, you'll pass the **Triumphal Arch of Berà**, dating from the 3rd century BC, 19 km (12 miles) north of Tarragona; and from the Lleida (Lérida) autopista, you can see the 1st-century **Roman aqueduct** that helped carry fresh water 32 km (20 miles) from the Gaià River. Tarragona is divided clearly into old and new by Rambla Vella; the old town and most of the Roman remains are to the north, while modern Tarragona spreads out to the south. Start your visit at acacia-lined Rambla Nova, at the end of which is a balcony overlooking the sea, the **Balcó del Mediterràni.** Then walk uphill along Passeig de les Palmeres; below it is the ancient amphitheater, the curve of which is echoed in the modern, semicircular Imperial Tarraco hotel on the promenade.

GETTING HERE AND AROUND

Tarragona is well connected by train. There are half-hourly express trains from Barcelona (1 hour 20 minutes; prices from €8.05) and regular train service from other major cities, including Madrid.

Buses are frequent between Barcelona and Tarragona—7 to 10 leave Barcelona's Estació del Nord for Tarragona every day. Connections between Tarragona and Valencia are frequent too. There are also bus connections with the main Andalusian cities, plus Alicante and Madrid.

Tours of the cathedral and archaeological sites are conducted by the tourist office, located just below the cathedral.

VISITOR INFORMATION

CONTACTS Visitor Information Tarragona. ⊠ *Carrer Major 37, Tarragona* ☎ *977/250795* ⊕ *www.tarragonaturisme. cat/en.*

 ## Sights

Amphitheater

RUINS | Tarragona, the Emperor Augustus's favorite winter resort, had arguably the finest amphitheater in Roman Iberia, built in the 2nd century AD for gladiatorial and other contests. The remains have a spectacular view of the sea. You're free to wander through the access tunnels and along the tiers of seats. In the center of the theater are the remains of two superimposed churches, the earlier of which was a Visigothic basilica built to mark the bloody martyrdom of St. Fructuós and his deacons in AD 259. At the time of writing the arena and stands are currently closed, but the upper part is still open, free of charge. ⊠ *Parc de l'Amphiteatre Roma s/n, Tarragona* ☎ *977/242579* ⊙ *Closed Mon.*

Casa Castellarnau

HISTORY MUSEUM | The headquarters of the city's Museu d'Història (History Museum), with plans showing the evolution of the city, this Gothic *palauet* (town house) built by Tarragona nobility in the 18th century includes stunning furnishings from the 18th and 19th centuries. The last member of the Castellarnau family vacated the house in 1954. The museum's highlight is the Hippolytus Sarcophagus, which bears a bas-relief depicting the legend of Hippolytus and Fraeda. ⊠ *Carrer dels Cavallers 14, Tarragona* ☎ *977/242220* 🖥 *€3.30* ۞ *Closed Mon.*

Catedral

RELIGIOUS BUILDING | Built between the 12th and 14th century on the site of a Roman temple and a mosque, this cathedral shows the transition from Romanesque to Gothic style. The initial rounded placidity of the Romanesque apse gave way to the spiky restlessness of the Gothic—the result is somewhat confusing. The main attraction here is the 15th-century Gothic alabaster altarpiece of Sant Tecla by Pere Joan, a richly detailed depiction of the life of Tarragona's patron saint. ⊠ *Pl. Pla de la Seu s/n, Tarragona* ☎ *977/226935* ⊕ *www.catedraldetarragona.com* 🖥 *€5 (cathedral and museum)* ۞ *Closed Sun. and Mon.*

El Serrallo

MARKET | The always-entertaining fishing quarter and harbor are below the city near the bus station and the mouth of the Francolí River. Attending the afternoon fish auction is a golden opportunity to see how choice seafood starts its journey toward your table in Barcelona or Tarragona. Restaurants in the port, such as the popular El Pòsit del Serrallo (Moll des Pescadors 25), offer fresh fish in a rollicking environment. ⊠ *Tarragona.*

Gaudí Centre

ART MUSEUM | This small museum in Reus (a 20-minute drive from Tarragona) showcases the life and work of the city's most illustrious son, including copies of the models Gaudí made for his major works and a replica of his studio. His original notebook—with English translations—is filled with his thoughts on structure and ornamentation, complaints about clients, and calculations of cost-and-return on his projects. A pleasant café on the third floor overlooks the main square of the old city and the bell tower of the Church of Sant Pere. The Centre also houses the Tourist Office; pick up information here about visits to one of Lluís Domènech i Montaner's most important buildings, the Casa Navàs (by appointment, €10). ⊠ *Pl. del Mercadal 3, Reus* ☎ *977/010670* ⊕ *www.gaudicentre.cat/en* 🖥 *€10.*

Museu Paleocristià i Necròpolis (*Early-Christian Museum and Necropolis*)

RUINS | Just uphill from the fish market are this early Christian necropolis and museum. In 1923, the remains of a burial ground were discovered during the construction of a tobacco factory. The excavations on display—more than 2,000 tombs, sarcophagi, and funeral objects—allow visitors a fascinating insight into Roman funeral practices and rituals. ⊠ *Av. Ramon y Cajal 84, Tarragona* ☎ *977/251515* 🖥 *€4* ۞ *Closed Mon.*

Passeig Arqueològic

PROMENADE | A 1½-km (1-mile) circular path skirting the surviving section of the 3rd-century-BC Ibero-Roman ramparts, this walkway was built on even earlier walls of giant rocks. On the other side of the path is a glacis, a fortification added by English military engineers in 1707 during the War of the Spanish Succession. Look for the rusted bronze of Romulus and Remus. ⊠ *Access from Via de l'Imperi Romà, Tarragona.*

Praetorium

RUINS | This towering building was Augustus's town house, and is reputed to be the birthplace of Pontius Pilate. Its Gothic appearance is the result of extensive alterations in the Middle Ages, when it housed the kings of Catalonia and Aragón during their visits to Tarragona. ⊠ *Pl. del Rei, Tarragona* ☎ *977/221736, 977/242220* 🖥 *€3.30 (includes Roman Circus)* ۞ *Closed Mon.*

Roman Circus

RUINS | Students have excavated the vaults of the 1st-century AD Roman arena, near the amphitheater. The plans just inside the gate show that the vaults now visible formed only a small corner of a vast space (350 yards long), where 23,000 spectators gathered to watch chariot races. As medieval Tarragona grew, the city gradually engulfed the circus. ✉ *Pl. del Rei, Rambla Vella s/n, Tarragona* ☎ *977/221736* 🎟 *€3.30 (includes Praetorium)* 🕒 *Closed Mon.*

🍴 Restaurants

Les Coques

$$$ | **CATALAN** | If you have time for only one meal in the city, take it at this elegant little restaurant in the heart of historic Tarragona. The menu is bursting with both mountain and Mediterranean fare, and the prix fixe lunch is a bargain at €19. **Known for:** good wine list; mountain fare; good-value prix fixe lunch. [$] *Average main: €22* ✉ *Carrer Sant Llorenç 15, Tarragona* ☎ *977/228300* 🌐 *www.les-coques.com* 🕒 *Closed Mon. No dinner.*

Les Voltes

$$ | **CATALAN** | Built into the vaults of the Roman Circus, this unique spot serves a hearty cuisine within one of the oldest sites in Europe. You'll find Tarragona specialties, mainly fish dishes, as well as international recipes, with *calçots* (spring onions, grilled over a charcoal fire) in winter. (For the calçots when in season, you need to reserve a day—preferably two or more—in advance.) **Known for:** historic setting; calçots (reserve a day or more in advance); Tarragona specialties. [$] *Average main: €15* ✉ *Carrer Trinquet Vell 12, Tarragona* ☎ *977/230651* 🌐 *www.restaurantlesvoltes.cat* 🕒 *Closed Mon. No dinner Tues. and Sun.*

🛏 Hotels

Hotel Plaça de la Font

$ | **HOTEL** | The central location and the cute rooms at this budget choice just off the Rambla Vella in the Plaça de la Font make for a practical base in downtown Tarragona. **Pros:** easy on the budget; nearby public parking lot; comfortable, charming rooms. **Cons:** basic facilities; rooms with balconies can be noisy on weekends; rooms are on the small side. [$] *Rooms from: €78* ✉ *Pl. de la Font 26, Tarragona* ☎ *977/240882* 🌐 *www.hotelpdelafont.com* 🍽 *No Meals* 🛏 *20 rooms.*

🍸 Nightlife

Nightlife in Tarragona takes two forms: older and quieter in the upper city, younger and more raucous down below. There are some lovely rustic bars and wine bars in the *casco antiguo*, the upper section of Old Tarragona, around Plaça del Forum and Carrer de Santa Anna. Port Esportiu, a pleasure-boat harbor separate from the working port, has another row of dining and dancing establishments; young people flock here on weekends and summer nights.

El Korxo

WINE BARS | This popular, cozy wine bar, with chunky wooden tables, subdued lighting, and quirky creative details, offers its clientele a taste of different wines from around Spain, as well as craft beers, charcuterie and cheeses, and other light snacks. ✉ *Santa Anna 6, Tarragona* ☎ *692/460018.*

🛍 Shopping

Carrer Major

ANTIQUES & COLLECTIBLES | You have to bargain hard but Carrer Major has some exciting antiques stores. They're worth a thorough rummage, as the gems tend to be hidden. ✉ *Carrer Major, Tarragona.*

Valencia

351 km (218 miles) southwest of Barcelona, 357 km (222 miles) southeast of Madrid.

Valencia, Spain's third-largest municipality, is a proud city with a thriving nightlife and restaurant scene, quality museums, and spectacular contemporary architecture, juxtaposed with a thoroughly charming historic quarter. During the civil war, it was the last seat of the Republican Loyalist government (1935–36), holding out against Franco's National forces until the country fell to 40 years of dictatorship. Today it represents the essence of contemporary Spain—daring design and architecture along with experimental cuisine—but remains deeply conservative and proud of its traditions. Although it faces the Mediterranean, Valencia's history and geography have been defined most significantly by the Turia River and the fertile huerta that surrounds it.

The city has been fiercely contested ever since it was founded by the Greeks. El Cid captured Valencia from the Moors in 1094 and won his strangest victory here in 1099: he died in the battle, but his corpse was strapped into his saddle and so frightened the besieging Moors that it caused their complete defeat. In 1102 El Cid's widow, Jimena, was forced to return the city to Moorish rule; Jaume I finally drove them out in 1238. Modern Valencia was best known for its frequent disastrous floods until the Turia River was diverted to the south in the late 1950s. Since then the city has been on a steady course of urban beautification. The lovely bridges that once spanned the Turia look equally graceful spanning a wandering municipal park, and the spectacularly futuristic Ciutat de les Arts i les Ciències (City of Arts and Sciences), most of it designed by Valencia-born architect Santiago Calatrava, has at last created an exciting architectural link between this river town and the Mediterranean.

If you're in Valencia, an excursion to Albufera Nature Park (which is in the area said to be the birthplace of paella) is a worthwhile day trip.

GETTING HERE AND AROUND

By car, Valencia is about 3½ hours from Madrid via the A3 motorway, and about the same from Barcelona on the AP-7 toll road. Valencia is well connected by bus and train, with regular service to and from cities throughout the country, including nine daily AVE high-speed express trains from Madrid, making the trip in 1 hour 40 minutes, and six Euromed express trains daily from Barcelona, taking about 3½ hours. Valencia's bus station is across the river from the old town; frequent buses make the four-hour trip from Madrid and the five-hour trip from Barcelona. Dozens of airlines, large and small, serve Valencia airport, connecting the city with dozens of cities throughout Spain and the rest of Europe.

Once you're here, the city has an efficient network of bus, tram, and metro service. For timetables and more information, stop by the local tourist office. The double-decker Valencia Bus Turístic runs daily 9:30–7:45 (until 9:15 in summer) and departs every 20–30 minutes from the Plaza de la Reina. It travels through the city, stopping at most of the main sights: 24- and 48-hour tickets (€17 and €19, respectively) let you get on and off at eight main boarding points, including the Institut Valencià d'Art Modern, the Museo de Bellas Artes, and the Ciutat de les Arts i les Ciències. The same company also offers a two-hour guided trip (€17) to Albufera Nature Park, including an excursion by boat through the wetlands, departing from the Plaza de la Reina. In summer (and sometimes during the rest of the year) Valencia's tourist office organizes tours of Albufera. You see the port area before continuing south to the lagoon itself, where you can visit a traditional *barraca* (thatch-roof farmhouse). At the time of writing Valencia Bus Turistic

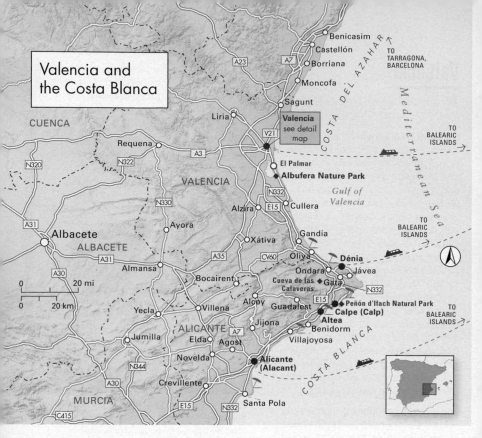

Valencia and the Costa Blanca

service had been temporarily suspended due to COVID, but the website has the latest updates.

BUS CONTACT Valencia Bus Station.
✉ *Carrer de Menendez Pidal 11, Valencia* ☎ *963/466266.*

FESTIVALS

Gran Fira de València (Great Valencia Fair)
Valencia's monthlong festival, in July, celebrates theater, film, dance, and music. Check the website for the latest updates. ✉ *Valencia* ⊕ *www.granfiravalencia.com.*

Las Fallas
If you want nonstop nightlife at its frenzied best, come during the climactic days of Las Fallas, March 15–19 (the festival begins March 1), when revelers throng the streets to see the gargantuan *ninots*, effigies made of wood, paper, and plaster depicting satirical scenes and

famous people. Last call at many bars and clubs isn't until the wee hours, if at all. On the last night, all the effigies but one (the winner is spared) are burned to the ground during La Crema, and it seems as though the entire city is ablaze. ✉ *Valencia* ⊕ *www.visitvalencia.com/en/ events-valencia/festivities/the-fallas.*

TOURS

Valencia Bus Turístic
Valencia's tourist bus allows you to hop on and hop off as you please, while audio commentary introduces the city's history and highlights. ✉ *Pl. de la Reina s/n, Valencia* ☎ *699/982514* ⊕ *www.valencia-busturistic.com* 🎫 *From €17.*

VISITOR INFORMATION
CONTACTS Valencia Tourist Office.
✉ *Pl. del Ayuntamiento 1, Valencia* ☎ *963/524908* ⊕ *www.visitvalencia.com/ en.*

👁 Sights

Casa Museo José Benlliure

ART MUSEUM | The modern Valencian painter and sculptor José Benlliure (1858–1937) is known for his intimate portraits and massive historical and religious paintings, many of which hang in Valencia's Museo de Bellas Artes (Museum of Fine Arts). Here in his elegant house and studio are 50 of his works, including paintings, ceramics, sculptures, and drawings. Also on display are works by his son, Pepino, who painted in the small, flower-filled garden in the back of the house, and iconographic sculptures by Benlliure's brother, the well-known sculptor Mariano Benlliure. ⊠ *Calle Blanquerías 23, Valencia* ☎ *963/911662* 🖥 *€2; free Sun.* ⊙ *Closed Mon.*

★ Catedral de Valencia

RELIGIOUS BUILDING | Valencia's 13th- to 15th-century cathedral is the heart of the city. The building has three portals—Romanesque, Gothic, and rococo. Inside, Renaissance and baroque marble were removed to restore the original Gothic style, as is now the trend in Spanish churches. The Capilla del Santo Cáliz (Chapel of the Holy Chalice) displays a purple agate vessel purported to be the Holy Grail (Christ's cup at the Last Supper) and thought to have been brought to Spain in the 4th century. Behind the altar is the left arm of St. Vincent, martyred in Valencia in 304. Stars of the cathedral museum are Goya's two famous paintings of St. Francis de Borja, Duke of Gandia. Left of the entrance is the octagonal tower El Miguelete, which you can climb (207 steps) to the top: the roofs of the old town create a kaleidoscope of orange and brown terra-cotta, with the sea in the background. ⊠ *Pl. de l'Almoina, s/n, Ciutat Vella* ☎ *963/918127* ⊕ *www.catedraldevalencia.es* 🖥 *€8, includes audio guide.*

★ Ciutat de les Arts i les Ciències

SCIENCE MUSEUM | FAMILY | Designed mainly by native son Santiago Calatrava, this sprawling futuristic complex is the home of Valencia's **Museu de les Ciències Príncipe Felipe** (Prince Philip Science Museum), **L'Hemisfèric** (Hemispheric Planetarium), **L'Oceanogràfic** (Oceanographic Park), and **Palau de les Arts** (Palace of the Arts, an opera house and cultural center). With resplendent buildings resembling combs and crustaceans, the Ciutat is a favorite of architecture buffs and curious kids. The Science Museum has soaring platforms filled with lasers, holograms, simulators, hands-on experiments, and a swell "zero gravity" exhibition on space exploration. The eye-shape planetarium projects 3-D virtual voyages on its huge IMAX screen. At l'Oceanogràfic (the work of architect Felix Candela), the largest marine park in Europe, you can take a submarine ride through a coastal marine habitat. Other attractions include an amphitheater, an indoor theater, and a chamber-music hall. ⊠ *Av. del Profesor López Piñero 7,* ☎ *961/974686* ⊕ *www.cac.es* 🖥 *Museu de les Ciències from €8, L'Oceanogràfic from €30, L'Hemisfèric from €8. Combined ticket €39.*

Institut Valencià d'Art Modern (IVAM)

ART MUSEUM | Dedicated to modern and contemporary art, this blocky, uninspired building on the edge of the old city—where the riverbed makes a loop—houses a permanent collection of 20th-century avant-garde painting, European Informalism (including the Spanish artists Antonio Saura, Antoni Tàpies, and Eduardo Chillida), pop art, and photography. ⊠ *Carrer de Guillem de Castro 118, Ciutat Vella* ☎ *963/176600* ⊕ *www.ivam.es* 🖥 *€6; free Fri. 7:30 pm–9 pm, Sat. 3–7 pm, and Sun.* ⊙ *Closed Mon.*

★ Lonja de la Seda (Silk Exchange)

NOTABLE BUILDING | On the Plaza del Mercado, this 15th-century building is a product of Valencia's golden age, when the city's prosperity as one of the capitals of

Valencia

Sights

1 Casa Museo José Benlliure **B1**
2 Catedral de Valencia **C3**
3 Ciutat de les Arts i les Ciències................. **E7**
4 Institut Valencià d'Art Modern (IVAM)... **A1**
5 Lonja de la Seda **B3**
6 Mercado Central (Central Market) **B4**
7 Museo de Belles Artes **D1**
8 Palacio del Marqués de Dos Aguas **C4**
9 Palau de la Generalitat................ **C2**
10 Palau de la Música **E6**
11 Real Colegio del Corpus Christi **D4**
12 San Nicolás **B2**

Restaurants ▼
1 La Casa Montaña........ **E6**
2 La Pepica **E6**
3 La Riuà **D3**

Hotels ▼
1 Ad Hoc Monumental ... **D2**
2 Hostal Antigua Morellana........ **C3**
3 Palau de la Mar........... **E6**
4 Rooms Ciencias.......... **E7**
5 Westin Valencia **E6**

the Corona de Aragón made it a leading European commercial and artistic center. The Lonja was constructed as an expression of this splendor and is widely regarded as one of Spain's finest civil Gothic buildings. Its facade is decorated with ghoulish gargoyles, complemented inside by high vaulting and slender helicoidal (twisted) columns. Opposite the Lonja stands the Iglesia de los Santos Juanes (Church of the St. Johns), gutted during the 1936–39 Spanish Civil War, and, next door, the Moderniste Mercado Central), with its wrought-iron girders and stained-glass windows. ⊠ Lonja 2, Ciutat Vella ☎ 962/084153 ☎ €2. Free Sun.

★ **Mercado Central (Central Market)**

MARKET | This bustling food market (at nearly 88,000 square feet, one of the largest in Europe) is open from 7:30 am to 3 pm, Monday through Saturday. Locals and visitors alike line up at the 1,247 colorful stalls to shop for fruit, vegetables, meat, fish, and confectionery. Hop on a stool at The Central Bar, located in the heart of the throng, and taste award-winning chef Ricard Camarena's casual yet no less tasty take on tapas and *bocadillos* (sandwiches), while enjoying front-row-seat viewing of the action. ⊠ Pl. Ciudad de Brujas s/n, Valencia ☎ 963/829100 ⊕ www.mercadocentralvalencia.es ☉ Closed Sun.

★ **Museo de Bellas Artes** (*Museum of Fine Arts*)

ART MUSEUM | Valencia was a thriving center of artistic activity in the 15th century—one reason that the city's Museum of Fine Arts, with its lovely palm-shaded cloister, is among the best in Spain. To get here, cross the old riverbed by the Puente de la Trinidad (Trinity Bridge) to the north bank; the museum is at the edge of the **Jardines del Real** (Royal Gardens; open daily 8–dusk), with its fountains, rose gardens, tree-lined avenues, and small zoo. The permanent collection of the museum includes many of the finest paintings by Jacomart and

Juan Reixach, members of the group known as the Valencian Primitives, as well as work by Hieronymus Bosch—or El Bosco, as they call him here. The ground floor has a number of brooding, 17th-century Tenebrist masterpieces by Francisco Ribalta and his pupil José Ribera, a Diego Velázquez self-portrait, and a room devoted to Goya. ⊠ Calle Sant Pius V 9, Trinitat ☎ 963/870300 ⊕ www. museobellasartesvalencia.gva.es ☎ Free ☉ Closed Mon.

Palacio del Marqués de Dos Aguas (*Ceramics Museum*)

HISTORY MUSEUM | Since 1954, this palace has housed the Museo Nacional de Cerámica, with a magnificent collection of local and artisanal ceramics. Look for the Valencian kitchen on the second floor. The building itself, near Plaza Patriarca, has gone through many changes over the years and now has elements of several architectural styles, including a fascinating baroque alabaster facade. Embellished with carvings of fruits and vegetables, the facade was designed in 1740 by Ignacio Vergara. It centers on the two voluptuous male figures representing the Dos Aguas (Two Waters), a reference to Valencia's two main rivers and the origin of the noble title of the Marqués de Dos Aguas. The museum's collection centers around traditional Valencian ceramics, textiles, furniture, and clothing as well as a section on antique pottery from Greek, Iberian, and Roman times through the 20th century. ⊠ Rinconada Federico García Sanchiz 6, Valencia ☎ 963/516392 ☎ Palace and museum €3; free Sat. 4–8 and Sun. ☉ Closed Mon.

Palau de la Generalitat

NOTABLE BUILDING | On the left side of the Plaza de la Virgen, fronted by orange trees and box hedges, is this elegant facade. The Gothic building was once the home of the Cortes Valencianas (Valencian Parliament), until it was suppressed by Felipe V for supporting the losing side during the 1700–14 War of the Spanish

Succession. The two *salones* (reception rooms) in the older of the two towers have superb woodwork on the ceilings. Don't miss the Salon de los Reyes, a long corridor lined with portraits of Valencia's kings through the ages; call in advance for permission to enter it. ✉ *Calle Caballeros 2, Valencia* ☎ *963/424636* ⏲ *Closed weekends.*

Palau de la Música

PERFORMANCE VENUE | On one of the nicest stretches of the Turia riverbed is this huge glass vault, Valencia's main concert venue. Home of the Orquesta de Valencia, the main hall also hosts touring performers from around the world, including chamber and youth orchestras, opera, and an excellent concert series featuring early, baroque, and classical music. It's worth popping in to see the building even without concert tickets, and there is also an art gallery, which hosts free changing exhibitions by renowned modern artists. ✉ *Passeig de l'Albereda 30, Valencia* ☎ *963/375020* 🌐 *www.palauvalencia.com.*

Real Colegio del Corpus Christi (*Iglesia del Patriarca*)

RELIGIOUS BUILDING | This seminary, with its church, cloister, and library, is the crown jewel of Valencia's Renaissance architecture. Founded by San Juan de Ribera in the 16th century, it has a lovely Renaissance patio and an ornate church, and its museum—Museum of the Patriarch—holds artworks by Juan de Juanes, Francisco Ribalta, and El Greco. ✉ *Calle de la Nave 1, Casco Antiguo* ☎ *963/514176* 🌐 *www.seminariocorpuschristi.org* 🎫 *€5.*

San Nicolás

CHURCH | A small plaza contains Valencia's oldest church (dating to the 13th century), once the parish of the Borgia Pope Calixtus III. The first portal you come to, with a tacked-on, rococo bas-relief of the Virgin Mary with cherubs, hints at what's inside: every inch of the originally Gothic church is covered with exuberant ornamentation. ✉ *Calle Caballeros 35, Casco Antiguo* ☎ *963/913317* 🌐 *www.sannicolasvalencia.com* ⏲ *Closed Mon.* 🎫 *€7.*

Beaches

Playa las Arenas

BEACH | This wide (nearly 450 feet) and popular grand municipal beach stretches north from the port and the America's Cup marina more than a kilometer (½ mile) before it gives way to the even busier and livelier Platja de Malvarossa. The Paseo Marítimo promenade runs the length of the beach and is lined with restaurants and small hotels, including the **Neptuno** and the upscale **Las Arenas Balneario** resort. There's no shade anywhere, but the fine golden sand is kept pristine and the water is calm and shallow. **Amenities:** food and drink; lifeguards; showers; toilets; water sports. **Best for:** sunset; swimming; walking; windsurfing. ✉ *Valencia* 🌐 *www.playadelasarenas.com/en.*

Restaurants

La Casa Montaña

$$$ | **TAPAS** | The walls are lined with rotund wine barrels at this welcoming bodega with a Moderniste facade, tucked down a side street in the city's old fishermen's quarter. Established in 1836, the restaurant serves a large and varied selection of tapas, from melt-in-your-mouth jamón to rustic stews and grilled seafood, all well accompanied by a superlative, regularly updated selection of wines. **Known for:** quality wine list; loads of character; good tapas and shared plates. [$] *Average main: €21* ✉ *Carrer de Josep Benlliure 69, Valencia* ☎ *963/672314* 🌐 *www.emilianobodega.com* ⏲ *No dinner Sun.*

La Pepica

$$$ | **SPANISH** | Locals regard this bustling, informal restaurant, on the promenade at El Cabanyal beach, as the best in town

Valencia's L'Oceanogràfic (Ciutat de les Arts i les Ciènces) has amazing exhibits, as well as an underwater restaurant.

for seafood paella. Founded in 1898, the walls of the establishment are covered with signed pictures of appreciative visitors, from Ernest Hemingway to King Juan Carlos and the royal family. **Known for:** fruit tarts; historic locale; locally revered seafood paella. $ *Average main: €20* ⊠ *Av. Neptuno 6, Valencia* ☎ *963/710366* ⊕ *www.lapepica.com* ⊙ *Closed last 2 wks in Nov. and last 2 wks in Jan. No dinner Sun.–Thurs.*

La Riuà

$$ | SPANISH | A favorite of Valencia's well connected and well-to-do since 1982, this family-run restaurant a few steps from the Plaza de la Reina specializes in seafood dishes like *anguilas* (eels) prepared with *all i pebre* (garlic and pepper), *parrillada de pescado* (selection of freshly grilled fish), and traditional paellas. Lunch begins at 2 and not a moment before. **Known for:** longtime family-run establishment; specialty eel dish; award-winning dining. $ *Average main: €16* ⊠ *Calle del Mar 27, bajo, Valencia* ☎ *963/914571*

⊕ *www.lariua.com* ⊙ *Closed Mon.–Wed. No dinner.*

Hotels

Ad Hoc Monumental

$$ | HOTEL | This nicely designed 19th-century town house sits on a quiet street at the edge of the old city, a minute's walk from the Plaza Almoina and the cathedral in one direction, and steps from the Turia gardens in the other. **Pros:** great value; courteous, helpful staff; close to sights but quiet. **Cons:** not especially family-oriented; parking can be a nightmare; small rooms. $ *Rooms from: €90* ⊠ *Carrer Boix 4, Ciutat Vella* ☎ *963/919140* ⊕ *www.adhochoteles.com* ⇌ *28 rooms* ⦿ *No Meals.*

★ Hostal Antigua Morellana

$ | B&B/INN | Run by four convivial sisters, this 18th-century town house provides the ultimate no-frills accommodation in the heart of the old city. **Pros:** complimentary tea in the lounge; friendly service; excellent location. **Cons:** simple amenities; no parking; small rooms. [$] *Rooms from: €65* ✉ *Carrer d´En Bou 2, Ciutat Vella* ☎ *963/915773* 🌐 *www.hostalam.com* 🛏 *18 rooms.*

Palau de la Mar

$$$$ | **HOTEL** | In a restored 19th-century palace, this boutique hotel looks out at the Porta de La Mar, which marked the entry to the old walled quarter of Valencia. **Pros:** big bathrooms with double sinks; great location near the sights and shops; courtyard and garden. **Cons:** top-floor rooms have low, slanted ceilings; small gym; rooms overlooking road can be noisy. [$] *Rooms from: €240* ✉ *Av. Navarro Reverter 14, Ciutat Vella* ☎ *963/162884* 🌐 *www.hospes.com/en/palau-mar* 🛏 *66 rooms* 🍴 *Free Breakfast.*

Rooms Ciencias

$$ | **HOTEL** | **FAMILY** | A good choice if you're traveling with family or friends, these budget accommodations are easy on the wallet. **Pros:** private parking (additional charge); friendly staff; near the Ciutat de les Arts i les Ciències. **Cons:** a bit far from city center and beaches; rooms on street can be noisy; rooms can be cramped. [$] *Rooms from: €115* ✉ *Av. Instituto Obrero de Valencia 20, Eixample* ☎ *960/627462* 🌐 *www.roomsciencias.com* 🛏 *28 rooms* 🍴 *No Meals.*

Westin Valencia

$$$$ | **HOTEL** | Built in 1917 as a cotton mill, with successive recyclings as a fire station and a stable for the mounted National Police Corps, this classic property was transformed in 2006 into a luxury hotel. **Pros:** interior garden; attentive, professional, multilingual staff; location steps from the metro that connects directly to the airport. **Cons:** some rooms could use refreshing; rates rise to astronomical during special events; patchy Wi-Fi. [$] *Rooms from: €200* ✉ *Av. Amadeo de Saboya 16, Pl. del Reial* ☎ *963/625900* 🌐 *www.westinvalencia.com* 🛏 *135 rooms* 🍴 *No Meals.*

🍸 Nightlife

Valencianos have perfected the art of doing without sleep. Nightlife in the old town centers on Barrio del Carmen, a lively web of streets that unfolds north of Plaza del Mercado. Popular bars and pubs dot Calle Caballeros, starting at Plaza de la Virgen; the Plaza del Tossal also has some popular cafés, as does Calle Alta, off Plaza San Jaime.

Some of the funkier, newer places are in and around Plaza del Carmen. Across the river, look for appealing hangouts along Avenida Blasco Ibáñez and on Plaza de Cánovas del Castillo. Out by the sea, Paseo Neptuno and Calle de Eugenia Viñes are lined with clubs and bars, lively in summer. The monthly English-language nightlife and culture magazine *24/7 Valencia* (www.247valencia.com) is free at tourist offices and various bars and clubs; leisure guides in Spanish include *Hello Valencia* (www.hellovalencia.es) and *La Guía Go* (www.laguiago.com/valencia).

BARS AND CAFÉS

Café de las Horas

BARS | This surreal bordello-style bar is an institution for Valencia's signature cocktail, Agua de Valencia (a syrupy blend of cava or champagne, orange juice, vodka, and gin). The bar's warm atmosphere and convivial vibe are perfect for whiling away the hours at the start (or end) of the night. ✉ *Calle del Conde de Almodóvar 1, Valencia* ☎ *963/917336.*

Tyris On Tap

BREWPUBS | Valencia's first craft-beer brewery, Cerveza Tyris, has a popular bar opposite the Mercado Central where visitors can sample a smorgasbord of locally brewed beers on tap. ✉ *Carrer de la Taula de Canvis 6, El Carmen* ☎ *961/132873* 🌐 *www.cervezatyris.com.*

MUSIC CLUBS

Jimmy Glass Jazz Bar

LIVE MUSIC | Aficionados of modern jazz gather at this bar (check website for details as opening hours vary according to performances booked), which books an impressive range of local and international combos and soloists. ⊠ *Carrer Baja 28, El Carmen* ⊕ *www.jimmyglassjazz. net.*

Radio City

LIVE MUSIC | The airy, perennially popular, bar–club–performance space at Radio City offers eclectic nightly shows featuring music from flamenco to Afro-jazz fusion. ⊠ *Carrer Santa Teresa 19, El Carmen* ☎ *963/914151* ⊕ *www.radiocity-valencia.com.*

Shopping

Plaza Redonda

MARKET | A few steps from the cathedral, off the upper end of Calle San Vicente Mártir, the restored Plaza Redonda ("Round Square") is lined with stalls selling all sorts of souvenirs and traditional crafts. ⊠ *Pl. Redonda, El Carmen.*

Albufera Nature Park

11 km (7 miles) south of Valencia.

South of Valencia, Albufera Nature Park is one of Spain's most spectacular wetland areas. Home to the largest freshwater lagoon on the peninsula, this protected area and bird-watcher's paradise is bursting with unusual flora and fauna, such as rare species of wading birds. Encircled by a tranquil backdrop of rice fields, it's no surprise that the villages that dot this picturesque place have some of the best options in the region for trying classic Valencian paella or *arròs a banda* (rice cooked in fish stock).

GETTING HERE AND AROUND

From Valencia, buses 24 and 25 depart for the Centre d'Interpretació Raco de l'Olla 7 am–9 pm daily (schedule varies between summer and winter and can be checked on: www.emtvalencia.es/ciudadano/index.php). However the Centre d'Interpretació Raco de l'Olla is currently only open 9 am–2 pm.

Sights

★ Albufera Nature Park

NATURE PRESERVE | This beautiful freshwater lagoon was named by Moorish poets—*albufera* means "the sun's mirror." The park is a nesting site for more than 250 bird species, including herons, terns, egrets, ducks, and gulls. Bird-watching companies offer boat rides all along the Albufera. For maps, guides, and tour arrangements, start your visit at the park's information center, the Centre d'Interpretació Raco de l'Olla in El Palmar. ⊠ *Ctra. de El Palmar s/n, El Palmar* ✛ *Carrer de Vicente Baldoví s/n* ☎ *963/868050* ⊕ *www.albufera.com* 🎫 *Free.*

El Palmar

TOWN | This is the major village in the area, with streets lined with restaurants specializing in various types of paella. The most traditional kind is made with rabbit or game birds, though seafood is also popular in this region because it's so fresh. ⊠ *El Palmar.*

🍴 Restaurants

Maribel Arroceria

$$ | SPANISH | So tasty is the paella here that even Valencianos regularly travel out of the city to Maribel Arroceria, off the main drag in El Palmar. While you sit surrounded by the rice fields of Albufera Nature Park, during the week you can devour a fixed-price lunchtime *menu del dia* (€25) of three starters to share, a paella, and dessert, served in the contemporary, air-conditioned dining room

Dénia's massive fort overlooks the harbor and provides a dramatic element to the skyline, with the Montgü mountains in the background.

or outside at pavement tables overlooking the canal. **Known for:** seating by the canal; highly prized paellas; reasonable prix fixe lunch menus. $ *Average main: €17* ✉ *Carrer de Francisco Monleón 5, El Palmar* ☎ *961/620060* ⊕ *www.arroceria-maribel.com* ☉ *Closed Wed. No dinner.*

Dénia

The stretch of coastline known as the Costa Blanca (White Coast) begins at Dénia, south of Valencia. Dénia is the port of departure on the Costa Blanca for the ferries to Ibiza, Formentera, and Mallorca—but if you're on your way to or from the islands, stay a night in the lovely little town in the shadow of a dramatic cliff-top fortress. Or, spend a few hours wandering in the Baix la Mar, the old fishermen's quarter with its brightly painted houses, and exploring the historic town center. The town has become something of a culinary hot spot and is home to award-winning restaurants, which

for its compact size is something of an achievement.

GETTING HERE AND AROUND
Dénia is linked to other Costa Blanca destinations via Line 1of the Alicante–Benidorm narrow-gauge TRAM train. There's also regular bus service from major towns and cities, including Madrid (7¼–9 hours) and Valencia (1¾–2½ hours). Local buses can get you around all of the Costa Blanca communities.

The Playa del Arenal, a tiny bay cut into the larger one, is worth a visit in summer. You can reach it via the coastal road (CV736) between Dénia and Jávea.

VISITOR INFORMATION
CONTACTS Visitor Information Dénia. ✉ *Pl. Oculista Buigues 9, Dénia* ☎ *966/422367* ⊕ *www.denia.net.*

 Sights

Castillo de Dénia
CASTLE/PALACE | The most interesting architectural attraction here is the castle

overlooking the town, and the **Palau del Governador** (Governor's Palace) inside. On the site of an 11th-century Moorish fortress, the Renaissance-era palace was built in the 17th century and was later demolished. A major restoration project is under way. The fortress has an interesting archaeological **museum** as well as the remains of a Renaissance bastion and a Moorish portal with a lovely horseshoe arch. ✉ *Av. del Cid–Calle San Francisco s/n, Dénia* ☎ *966/422367* 🎟 *€3 (includes entrance to archaeological museum).*

Cueva de las Calaveras (*Cave of the Skulls*)
CAVE | **FAMILY** | About 15 km (9 miles) inland from Dénia, this 400-yard-long cave was named for the 12 Moorish skulls found here when it was discovered in 1768. The cave of stalactites and stalagmites has a dome rising to more than 60 feet and leads to an underground lake. ✉ *Ctra. Benidoleig–Pedreguera, Km 1.5, Benidoleig* ☎ *966/404235* 🌐 *www.cuevadelascalaveras.com* 🎟 *€4.*

🍴 Restaurants

El Raset
$$$ | **SEAFOOD** | Across the harbor, this Valencian favorite has been serving traditional cuisine with a modern twist for more than 30 years. From a terrace with views of the water you can choose from an array of excellent seafood dishes, including house specialties such as *arroz en caldero* (rice with monkfish, lobster, or prawns) and *gambas rojas* (local red prawns). À la carte dining can be expensive, while set menus are easier on your wallet. **Known for:** excellent seafood dishes; tasty paella; reasonably priced set menus. [$] *Average main: €20* ✉ *Calle Bellavista 7, Dénia* ☎ *965/785040* 🌐 *www.grupoelraset.com.*

🛏 Hotels

★ Art Boutique Hotel Chamarel
$$$ | **B&B/INN** | Ask the staff and they'll tell you that *chamarel* means a "mixture of colors," and this hotel brimming with charm, built as a grand family home in 1840, is certainly an eccentric blend of styles, cultures, periods, and personalities. **Pros:** interior courtyard; individual attention; friendly, helpful staff. **Cons:** not on the beach; no pool; rooms over the street are noisy. [$] *Rooms from: €150* ✉ *Calle Cavallers 3,* ☎ *966/435007* 🌐 *www.hotelchamarel.com* 🔑 *15 rooms* 🍴 *Free Breakfast.*

★ Hostal Loreto
$ | **HOTEL** | Travelers on tight budgets will appreciate this basic yet impeccable lodging, on a central pedestrian street in the historic quarter just steps from the Town Hall. **Pros:** broad, comfy roof terrace; good value; great central location in former nunnery. **Cons:** no amenities; no elevator; rooms can be dark. [$] *Rooms from: €82* ✉ *Calle Loreto 12, Dénia* ☎ *966/435419* 🌐 *www.hostalloreto.com* 🔑 *43 rooms* 🍴 *Free Breakfast.*

★ Hotel El Raset
$$$ | **B&B/INN** | Just across the esplanade from the port, where the Balearia ferries depart for Mallorca and Ibiza, this upscale boutique hotel has amenities that few lodgings in Dénia offer. **Pros:** good restaurant from same owners down the street; staff is friendly, attentive, and multilingual; good location. **Cons:** dim overhead lighting in rooms; no pool; pricey private parking. [$] *Rooms from: €160* ✉ *Calle Bellavista 1, Port* ☎ *965/786564* 🌐 *www.hotelelraset.com* 🔑 *20 rooms* 🍴 *Free Breakfast.*

★ La Posada del Mar
$$$$ | **HOTEL** | A few steps across from the harbor, this hotel in the 13th-century customs house has inviting rooms with seafront views; there's a subtle nautical theme, most evident in the sailor's-knot ironwork along the staircase. **Pros:**

lovely sea views; close to center of town; serene environment. **Cons:** pricey parking; no pool; rooms overlooking the main road can be noisy. [$] *Rooms from: €208* ✉ *Puerto de Denia, Pl. de les Drassanes 2, Port* ☎ *966/432966* 🌐 *www.laposadadelmar.com* 🛏 *31 rooms* 🍴 *Free Breakfast.*

Calpe (Calp)

35 km (22 miles) south of Dénia.

Calpe has an ancient history, as it was chosen by the Phoenicians, Greeks, Romans, and Moors as a strategic point from which to plant their Iberian settlements. The real-estate developers were the latest to descend upon it: much of Calpe today is overbuilt with high-rise resorts and *urbanizaciónes*. But the old town is a delightful maze of narrow streets and small squares, archways and cul-de-sacs, with houses painted in Mediterranean blue, red, ocher, and sandstone; wherever there's a broad expanse of building wall, you'll likely discover a mural. Calpe is a delightful place to wander.

GETTING HERE AND AROUND

The narrow-gauge TRAM railway from Dénia to Alicante also serves Calpe, as do local buses.

VISITOR INFORMATION

CONTACTS Visitor Information Calpe. ✉ *Av. Ejércitos Españoles 44, Calp* ☎ *965/836920* 🌐 *www.calpe.es.*

Sights

Fish Market

MARKET | The fishing industry is still very important in Calpe, and every evening the fishing boats return to port with their catch. The subsequent auction at the fish market can be watched from the walkway of La Lonja de Calpe. ✉ *Port, Calp* 🕒 *Closed weekends.*

Peñón d'Ifach Natural Park

NATURE SIGHT | The landscape of Calpe is dominated by this huge calcareous rock more than 1,100 yards long, 1,090 feet high, and joined to the mainland by a narrow isthmus. The area is rich in flora and fauna, with more than 300 species of plants and 80 species of land and marine birds. A visit to the top is not for the fainthearted; wear shoes with traction for the hike, which includes a trip through a tunnel to the summit. The views are spectacular, reaching to the island of Ibiza on a clear day. Check with the local visitor information center about guided tours for groups. ✉ *Calp.*

Restaurants

Patio de la Fuente

$$$ | MEDITERRANEAN | In an intimate little space with wicker chairs and pale mauve walls, this restaurant in the old town serves a bargain Mediterranean three-course prix fixe dinner, wine included; you can also order à la carte. In summer, dine on the comfortable patio out back. **Known for:** outdoor dining; good-value three-course dinner; divine Scotch egg. [$] *Average main: €18* ✉ *Carrer Dos de Mayo 16, Calp* ☎ *965/831695* 🌐 *www.patiodelafuente.com* 🕒 *Closed Mon. and Tues.*

Hotels

Pensión el Hidalgo

$ | B&B/INN | This family-run pension near the beach has small but cozy rooms with a friendly, easygoing feel, and several have private balconies overlooking the Mediterranean. **Pros:** beachfront location; breakfast terrace with sea views; reasonable prices. **Cons:** weak Wi-Fi connection in some rooms; you must book far ahead in summer; basic design. [$] *Rooms from: €70* ✉ *Av. Rosa de los Vientos 19, Calp* ☎ *965/839862* 🌐 *www.pensionelhidalgo.com* 🛏 *9 rooms* 🍴 *No Meals.*

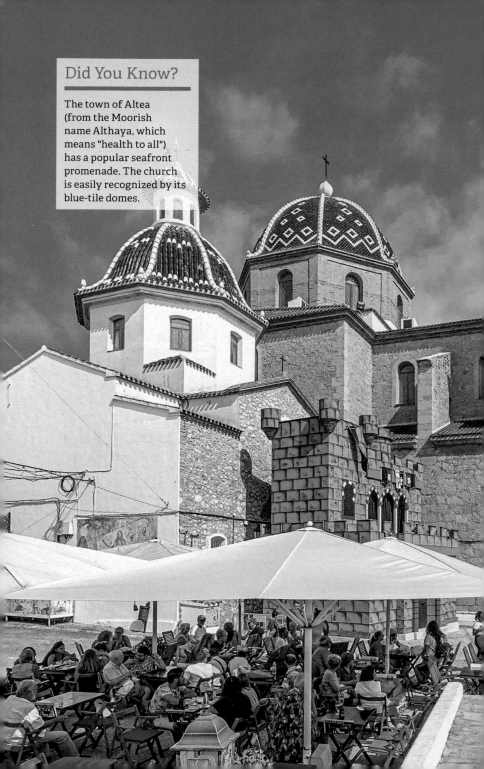

Activities

Mundo Marino

BOATING | FAMILY | Choose from a wide range of sailing trips, including cruises up and down the coast, and sunset trips with a glass of cava. Glass-bottom boats make it easy to observe the abundant marine life. ✉ *Puerto Pesquero, Calp* ☎ *966/423066* 🌐 *www.mundomarino.es.*

Altea

11 km (7 miles) southwest of Calpe.

Perched on a hill overlooking a bustling beachfront, Altea (unlike some of its neighboring towns) has retained much of its original charm, with an atmospheric old quarter laced with narrow cobblestone streets and stairways, and gleaming white houses. At the center is the striking church of Nuestra Señora del Consuelo, with its blue ceramic-tile dome, and the Plaza de la Iglesia in front.

GETTING HERE AND AROUND

Also on the Dénia–Alicante narrow-gauge TRAM train route, Altea is served by local buses, with connections to major towns and cities. The old quarter is mainly pedestrianized.

VISITOR INFORMATION

CONTACTS Visitor Information Altea. ✉ *Calle Sant Pere 14, Altea* ☎ *965/844114* 🌐 *www.visitaltea.es.*

Restaurants

La Costera

$$$ | FRENCH | This popular restaurant focuses on fine French fare, with such specialties as house-made foie gras (simply called foie), fillet of turbot, and beef entrecôte. There's also a variety of game in season, including venison and partridge. **Known for:** French specialties; in-season game; bucolic outdoor terrace. [$] *Average main: €22* ✉ *Costera Mestre de Música 8, Altea* ☎ *965/840230* 🌐 *www.altealacostera.com* 🕓 *Closed Mon. No lunch Tues.–Thurs. No dinner Sun.*

Oustau de Altea

$$ | EUROPEAN | In one of the prettiest corners of Altea's old town, this eatery was formerly a cloister and a school. Today the dining room and terrace combine contemporary design gracefully juxtaposed with a rustic setting, and the restaurant is known for serving polished international cuisine with French flair. **Known for:** contemporary artwork; cuisine with French style; dishes named after classic films. [$] *Average main: €15* ✉ *Calle Mayor 5, Casco Antiguo* ☎ *965/842078* 🌐 *www.oustau.com* 🕓 *Closed Mon. and Feb.*

Hotels

Hostal Fornet

$ | HOTEL | The pièce de résistance at this simple, pleasant hotel, at the highest point of Altea's historic center, is the roof terrace with its stunning view; from here, you look out over the church's distinctive blue-tiled cupola and the surrounding tangle of streets, with a Mediterranean backdrop. **Pros:** lovely views; top value; multilingual owners. **Cons:** door is locked when reception is not staffed, and you have to call to be let in; small rooms; no pool or beach. [$] *Rooms from: €55* ✉ *Calle Beniardá 1, Casco Antiguo* ☎ *965/843005* 🌐 *www.hostalfornetaltea.com* 🛏 *23 rooms* 🍴 *No Meals.*

Alicante (Alacant)

183 km (114 miles) south of Valencia, 52 km (32 miles) south of Altea.

The Greeks called it Akra Leuka (White Summit) and the Romans named it Lucentum (City of Light). A crossroads for inland and coastal routes since ancient times, Alicante has always been known for its luminous skies. The city is dominated by the 16th-century grande dame castle, **Castillo de Santa Bárbara,** a top attraction. The best approach is via the elevator cut deep into the mountainside. Also memorable is Alicante's grand **Esplanada,** lined with date palms. Directly under the castle is the city beach, the Playa del Postiguet, but the city's pride is the long, curved Playa de San Juan, which runs north from the Cap de l'Horta to El Campello.

GETTING HERE AND AROUND

Alicante has two train stations: the main Estación de Madrid and the local Estación de la Marina, from which the local FGV line runs along the Costa Blanca from Alicante to Dénia. Playa Postiguet can be reached by several buses from downtown, including 21 and 22.

The slower narrow-gauge TRAM train goes from the city center on the beach to El Campello. From the same open-air station in Alicante, the Line 1 train departs to Benidorm, with connections on to Altea, Calpe, and Dénia.

VISITOR INFORMATION

CONTACTS Tourist Information Alicante. ⊠ *Marina Deportiva, Muelle Levante 6, Alicante* ☎ *965/177201* ⊕ *www.alicante-turismo.com.***TRAM.** ⊠ *Alicante-Luceros, Alicante* ☎ *900/720472* ⊕ *www.tramalicante.es.*

 Sights

Ayuntamiento

NOTABLE BUILDING | Constructed between 1696 and 1780, the town hall is a beautiful example of baroque civic architecture. Inside, a gold sculpture by Salvador Dalí of San Juan Bautista holding the famous cross and shell rises to the second floor in the stairwell. Ask gate officials for permission to explore the ornate halls and rococo chapel on the first floor. Look for the plaque on the first step of the staircase that indicates the exact sea level, used to define the rest of Spain's altitudes "above sea level." ⊠ *Pl. de Ayuntamiento, Alicante* ☎ *966/900886* ⊘ *Closed weekends.*

Basílica de Santa María

RELIGIOUS BUILDING | Constructed in a Gothic style over the city's main mosque between the 14th and 16th century, this is Alicante's oldest house of worship. The main door is flanked by beautiful baroque stonework by Juan Bautista Borja, and the interior highlights are the golden rococo high altar, a Gothic image in stone of St. Mary, and a sculpture of Sts. Juanes by Rodrigo de Osona. ⊠ *Pl. de Santa María s/n, Alicante* ☎ *965/177201 tourist office (for information)* ⊘ *Closing times can vary due to religious services.*

★ Castillo de Santa Bárbara (*St. Barbara's Castle*)

CASTLE/PALACE | One of the largest existing medieval fortresses in Europe, Castillo de Santa Bárbara sits atop 545-foot-tall Monte Benacantil. From this strategic position you can gaze out over the city, the sea, and the whole Alicante plain for many miles. Remains from civilizations dating from the Bronze Age onward have been found here; the oldest parts of the castle, at the highest level, are from the 9th through 13th century. The castle also houses the Museo de la Ciudad de Alicante (MUSA), which uses audiovisual presentations and archaeological finds to tell the story of Alicante, its people, and the city's enduring relationship with the sea. ⊠ *Monte Benacantil s/n, Alicante* ☎ *965/152969* ⊕ *www.castillodesantabarbara.com* 🎫 *Castle and museum free.*

Concatedral of San Nicolás de Bari

RELIGIOUS BUILDING | Built between 1616 and 1662 on the site of a former mosque, this church (called a *con*catedral because it shares the seat of the bishopric with the Concatedral de Orihuela) has an austere facade designed by Agustín Bernardino, a disciple of the great Spanish architect Juan de Herrera. Inside, it's dominated by a dome nearly 150 feet high, a pretty cloister, and a lavish

Alicante's Esplanada de España, lined with date palms, is the perfect place for a stroll. The municipal brass band offers concerts on the bandstand of the Esplanada on Sunday evenings in July and August.

baroque side chapel, the Santísima Sacramento, with an elaborate sculptured stone dome of its own. Its name comes from the day that Alicante was reconquered (December 6, 1248) from the Moors, the feast day of St. Nicolás. ⊠ *Pl. Abad Penalva 2, Alicante* ☎ *965/212662* 🆓 *Free* 🕙 *Closed Sun. except services.*

Museo Arqueológico Provincial

HISTORY MUSEUM | Inside the old hospital of San Juan de Dios, the MARQ has a collection of artifacts from the Alicante region dating from the Paleolithic era to modern times, with a particular emphasis on Iberian art. ⊠ *Pl. Dr. Gómez Ulla s/n, Alicante* ☎ *965/149000* ⊕ *www.marqalicante.com* 🆓 *€3* 🕙 *Closed Mon.*

🍽 Restaurants

El Portal

$$$$ | **SPANISH** | Blending tradition with novelty is not always an easy task, but it is what draws people back to El Portal in droves. Chef Sergio Sierra runs a slick operation, from the restaurant's extravagant decor (think modern interpretation of Roaring '20s) to a menu that is committed to offering the best flavors of the region—from the freshest seafood to premium cuts of meat to seasonal produce. **Known for:** cocktails, wine, and dinner all in one place; montadito de solomillo de vacuno con trufa (steak sandwich with truffle oil); unique decor and DJ soundtrack. $ *Average main: €26* ⊠ *C. Bilbao 2, Alicante* ☎ *965/144444* ⊕ *www.elportaltaberna.es.*

La Taberna del Gourmet

$$$ | **TAPAS** | This wine bar and restaurant in the heart of the *casco antiguo* (old town) earns high marks from locals and international visitors alike. A bar with stools and counters offers a selection of fresh seafood tapas—oysters, mussels, razor clams—to complement a well-chosen list of wines from La Rioja, Ribera del Duero, and Priorat, and the two dining rooms are furnished with thick butcher-block tables and dark brown leather chairs. **Known for:** fresh seafood tapas; reservations essential; excellent

wine list. $ *Average main: €20* ⊠ *Calle San Fernando 10, Alicante* ☎ *965/204233* ⊕ *www.latabernadelgourmet.com.*

Nou Manolín

$$$$ | SPANISH | An Alicante institution, this inviting exposed-brick and wood-lined restaurant is very popular with locals, who come for the excellent-value tapas and daily menu. It's a superb place to tuck into fish freshly caught that afternoon, a tribute to the city's enduring relationship with the sea. **Known for:** a favorite of culinary superstar Ferran Adrià; market-fresh produce; authentic local vibe. $ *Average main: €25* ⊠ *Calle Villegas 3, Alicante* ☎ *965/616425* ⊕ *www. grupogastronou.com.*

Hotels

Hostal Les Monges Palace

$ | HOTEL | In a restored 1912 building, this family-run hostal in Alicante's central *casco antiguo* features lovingly preserved exposed stone walls, ceramic tile floors, and rooms furnished with eccentric artwork and quirky charm. **Pros:** lots of character; personalized service; ideal location with rooftop terrace. **Cons:** the newer, modern part is not as atmospheric; bathrooms in standard rooms are small; must book well in advance. $ *Rooms from: €75* ⊠ *Calle San Agustín 4, Alicante* ☎ *965/215046* ⊕ *www.lesmonges.es* ⤶ *24 rooms* ⦿ *Free Breakfast.*

Nightlife

El Barrio, the old quarter west of Rambla de Méndez Núñez, is the prime nightlife area of Alicante, with music bars and discos every couple of steps. In summer, or after 3 am, the liveliest places are along the water, on Ruta del Puerto and Ruta de la Madera.

Shopping

Mercado Central

MARKET | Bulging with fish, vegetables, and other local items, this is the place to stop by and discover Alicante's fresh produce, traded from this Moderniste-inspired building since 1921. ⊠ *Av. Alfonso el Sabio 10, Alicante* ⊙ *Closed Sun.*

Chapter 10

IBIZA AND THE BALEARIC ISLANDS

Updated by
Isabelle Kliger

⊙ **Sights**
★★★☆☆

🍴 **Restaurants**
★★★★☆

🛏 **Hotels**
★★★★☆

🛍 **Shopping**
★★★☆☆

🍸 **Nightlife**
★★★☆☆

WELCOME TO
IBIZA AND THE BALEARIC ISLANDS

TOP REASONS TO GO

★ **Pamper yourself:** Luxurious boutique hotels on restored and redesigned rural estates are *the* hip places to stay in the Balearics. Many have their own holistic spas: restore and redesign yourself at one of them.

★ **Enjoy seafood delicacies:** Seafood specialties come straight from the boat to portside restaurants all over the islands.

★ **Party hard:** Ibiza's summer club scene is the biggest, wildest, and glitziest in the world.

★ **Take in the gorgeous views:** The *miradores* (viewpoints) of Mallorca's Tramuntana, along the road from Valldemossa to Sóller, highlight the most spectacular seacoast in the Mediterranean.

★ **Discover Palma:** Capital of the Balearics, Palma is one of the great unsung cities of the Mediterranean—a showcase of medieval and modern architecture, a venue for art and music, a mecca for sailors, and a killer place to shop for shoes.

The Balearic Islands lie 80–305 km (50–190 miles) off the Spanish mainland, roughly between Valencia and Barcelona. In the center, Mallorca, with its rolling eastern plains and mountainous northwest, is the largest of the group. Menorca, its closest neighbor, is virtually flat; but like Ibiza and tiny Formentera to the west, it has a rugged coastline of small inlets and sandy beaches.

1 Ibiza. Sleepy from November to May, the island is Party Central in midsummer for retro hippies and nonstop clubbers. Dalt Vila, the medieval quarter of Eivissa, the capital, on the hill overlooking the town, is a UNESCO World Heritage Site.

2 Formentera. Day-trippers from Ibiza chill out on this (comparatively) quiet little island with long stretches of protected beach.

3 Mallorca. Palma, the island's capital, is a trove of art and architectural gems. The Tramuntana, in the northwest, is a region of forested peaks and steep sea cliffs that few landscapes in the world can match.

4 Menorca. Mahón, the capital city, commands the largest and deepest harbor in the Mediterranean. Many of the houses above the port date to the 18th-century occupation by the British Navy.

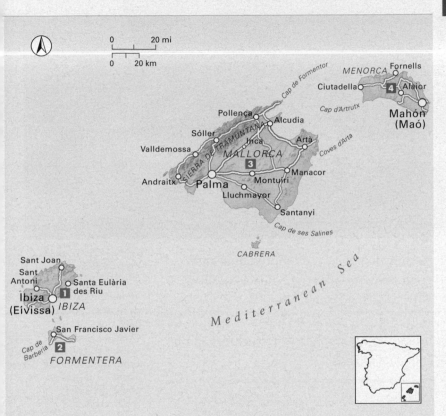

EATING AND DRINKING WELL IN THE BALEARIC ISLANDS

Tumbet is a traditional vegetable dish, served in a clay pot

Mediterranean islands should guarantee great seafood—and the Balearics deliver, with superb products from the crystalline waters surrounding the archipelago. Inland farms supply free-range beef, lamb, goat, and cheese.

Ibiza's fishermen head out to the tiny inlets for sea bass and bream, which are served in beach shacks celebrated for *bullit de peix* (fish casserole), *guisat* (fish and shellfish stew), and *burrida de ratjada* (ray with almonds). Beyond the great seafood, there are traditional farm dishes that include *sofrit pagès* (lamb or chicken with potatoes and red peppers), *botifarron* (blood sausage), and *rostit* (oven-roasted pork). Mallorcans love their *sopas de peix* (fish soup) and their *panades de peix* (fish-filled pastries), while Menorca's harbor restaurants are famous for *llagosta* (spiny lobster), grilled or served as part of a *caldereta*—a soupy stew. Interestingly, mayonnaise is widely believed to have been invented by the French in Mahón, Menorca, after they took the port from the British in 1756.

BALEARIC ALMONDS

Almonds are omnipresent in the Balearics, used in sweets as well as seafood recipes. Typically used in the *picada*—the ground nuts, spices, and herbs on the surface of a dish—almonds are essential to the Balearic economy. After a 19th-century phylloxera plague decimated Balearic vineyards, almond trees replaced vines and the almond crop became a staple.

VEGETABLES

The *tumbet mallorquin* is a classic Balearic dish made of layers of fried zucchini, bell peppers, potatoes, and eggplant with tomato sauce between each layer. It's served piping hot in individual earthenware casseroles.

SEAFOOD

There are several seafood dishes to look out for in the Balearics. *Burrida de ratjada* is boiled ray baked between layers of potato with almonds. The *picada* covering the ray during the baking includes almonds, garlic, egg, a slice of fried bread, parsley, salt, pepper, and olive oil. *Caldereta de llagosta* (spiny lobster soup) is a quintessential Menorcan staple sometimes said to be authentic only if the Menorcan spiny lobster is used. *Guisat de marisc* (shellfish stew) is an Ibiza stew of fish and shellfish cooked with a base of onions, potatoes, peppers, and olive oil. Nearly any seafood from the waters around Ibiza may well end up in this staple.

PORK

Rostit is baked in the oven with liver, eggs, bread, apples, and plums. *Sobrasada* (finely ground pork seasoned with sweet red paprika and stuffed in a sausage skin) is one of Mallorca's two most iconic food products (the other is the *ensaimada,* a

Clams are one of the many seafood options you'll find in the Balearics.

sweet spiral pastry made with *saim,* or lard). Sobrasada originated in Italy but became popular in Mallorca during the 16th century.

MENORCAN CHEESE

Mahón cheese is a Balearic trademark, and Menorca has a Denominación de Origen (D.O.), one of the 12 officially designated cheese-producing regions in Spain. The *curado* (fully cured) cheese is the tastiest.

WINE

With just 2,500 acres of vineyards (down from 75,000 in 1891), Mallorca's two D.O. wine regions—Binissalem, near Palma, and Pla i Llevant on the eastern side of the island—will likely remain under the radar to the rest of the world. While you're here, though, treat yourself to a Torre des Canonge white, a fresh, full, fruity wine, or a red Ribas de Cabrera from the oldest vineyard on the island, Hereus de Ribas in Binissalem, founded in 1711. Viticulture on Menorca went virtually extinct with the reversion of the island to Spain after its 18th-century British occupation, but since the last half of the 20th century, a handful of ambitious, serious winemakers—mainly in the area of Sant Lluís—have emerged to put the local product back on the map.

Local cheese from Menorca

BEST BEACHES OF THE BALEARICS

Ibiza is "Party Island," and its beaches get crowded.

When it comes to oceanfront property, the Balearic Islands have vast and varied resources: everything from long sweeps of beach on sheltered bays to tiny crescents of sand in rocky inlets and coves called *calas*—some so isolated you can reach them only by boat.

Not a few of the Balearic beaches, like their counterparts on the mainland coasts, have become destinations for communities of holiday chalets and retirement homes, usually called *urbanizaciónes*, their waterfronts lined with the inevitable shopping centers and pizza joints—skip these and head to the simpler and smaller beaches in or adjoining the Balearics' admirable number of nature reserves. Granted you'll find few or no services, and be warned that smaller beaches mean crowds in July and August, but these are the Balearics' best destinations for sun and sand. The local authorities protect these areas more rigorously, as a rule, than they do those on the mainland, and the beaches are gems.

BEACH AMENITIES

Be prepared: services at many of the smaller Balearic beaches are minimal or nonexistent. If you want a deck chair or something to eat or drink, bring it with you or make sure to ask around to see if your chosen secluded inlet has at least a *chiringuito*: a waterfront shack where the food is likely to feature what the fisherman pulled in that morning.

SES SALINES, IBIZA

Easy to reach from Eivissa, Ibiza's capital, this is one of the most popular beaches on the island, but the setting—in a protected natural park area—has been spared overdevelopment. The beach is relatively narrow, but the fine golden sand stretches more than a kilometer along the curve of Ibiza's southernmost bay. Two other great choices, on the east coast, are Cala Mastella, a tiny cove tucked away in a pine woods where a kiosk on the wharf serves the fresh catch of the day, and Cala Llenya, a family-friendly beach in a protected bay with shallow water.

The benefits of the popular beaches are their ample amenities.

BENIRRÁS, IBIZA

Benirrás is a small cove tucked away on Ibiza's northern coast backed by pine-clad hills. Known for its sunsets and laid-back vibe, it's popular with artists and hippies. Every Sunday at sunset, drummers gather to form ritualistic drum circles, one of the island's most popular events. On other days, it's a peaceful stretch of soft sand with calm water to spend a few hours.

PLAYA DE SES ILLETES, FORMENTERA

The closest beach to the port at La Sabina, where the ferries come in from Ibiza, Ses Illetes is Formentera's preeminent party scene: some 3 km (2 miles) of fine white sand with beach bars and snack shacks, and jet skis and windsurfing gear for rent.

ES TRENC, MALLORCA

One of the few long beaches on the island that's been spared resort development, this pristine 3-km (2-mile) stretch of soft, white sand southeast of Palma, near Colònia Sant Jordi, is a favorite with nude bathers—who stay mainly at the west end—and day-trippers who arrive by boat. The water is crystal-clear blue and shallow for some distance out. The 10-km (6-mile) walk along the beach from Colònia Sant Jordi to the Cap Salines lighthouse is one of Mallorca's treasures.

CALA MACARELLA/CALA MACARELLETA, MENORCA

This pair of beautiful, secluded coves edged with pines is about a 20-minute walk through the woods from the more developed beach at Santa Galdana, on Menorca's south coast. Macarella is the larger and busier of the two; Macarelleta, a few minutes farther west along the path, is popular with nude bathers and boating parties. Cala Pregonda, on the north coast, is a lovely crescent cove with pine and tamarisk trees behind and dramatic rock formations at both ends.

For peace and quiet, head to Macarella on Mallorca.

Could anything go wrong in a destination that gets, on average, 300 days of sunshine a year? True, the water is only warm enough for a dip May–October, but the climate does seem to give the residents of the Balearics a sunny disposition year-round. They are a remarkably hospitable people, not merely because tourism accounts for such a large chunk of their economy, but because history and geography have combined to put them in the crossroads of so much Mediterranean trade and traffic.

The Balearic Islands were outposts, successively, of the Phoenician, Carthaginian, and Roman empires before the Moors invaded in 902 and took possession for some 300 years. In 1235, Jaume I of Aragón ousted the Moors, and the islands became part of the independent kingdom of Mallorca until 1343, when they returned to the Crown of Aragón under Pedro IV. With the marriage of Isabella of Castile to Ferdinand of Aragón in 1469, the Balearics were joined to a united Spain. Great Britain occupied Menorca in 1704, during the War of the Spanish Succession, to secure the superb natural harbor of Mahón as a naval base, but returned it to Spain in 1802 under the Treaty of Amiens.

During the Spanish Civil War, Menorca remained loyal to Spain's democratically elected Republican government, while Mallorca and Ibiza sided with Francisco Franco's insurgents. Mallorca then became a base for Italian air strikes against the Republican holdouts in Barcelona. This topic is still broached delicately on the islands; they remain fiercely independent of one another in many ways. Even Mahón and Ciutadella, at opposite ends of Menorca—all of 44 km (27 miles) apart—remain estranged over differences dating to that war.

The tourist boom, which began during Franco's regime (1939–75), turned great stretches of Mallorca's and Ibiza's coastlines into strips of high-rise hotels, fast-food restaurants, and discos.

Planning

When to Go

July and August are peak season in the Balearics; it's hot, and even the most secluded beaches are crowded. Weatherwise, May and October are ideal, with June and September just behind. Winter is quiet; it's too cold for the beach but fine for hiking, golfing, and exploring— though on Menorca the winter winds are notoriously fierce. The clubbing season on Ibiza begins in June.

Note: between November and March or April many hotels and restaurants are closed for their own vacations or seasonal repairs.

Planning Your Time

Most European visitors to the Balearics pick one island and stick with it, but you could easily see all three. Start in Mallorca with **Palma.** Begin early at the cathedral and explore the Llotja, the Almudaina palace, and the Plaça Major. The churches of Santa Eulàlia and Sant Francesc and the Arab Baths are a must. Staying overnight in Palma means you can sample the nightlife and have time to visit the museums.

Take the old train to **Sóller** and rent a car for a trip over the Sierra de Tramuntana to **Deià, Son Marroig,** and **Valldemossa.** The roads are twisty, so give yourself a full day. Spend the night in Sóller, and you can drive from there in less than an hour via **Lluc** and **Pollentia** to the Roman and Moorish ruins at **Alcúdia.**

By fast ferry it's just over three hours from Port d'Alcúdia to **Ciutadella,** on Menorca; the port, the **cathedral,** and the narrow streets of the old city can be explored in half a day. Make your way across the island to **Mahón,** and devote an afternoon to the highlights there.

From Mahón, you can take a 30-minute interisland flight to **Eivissa.** On Ibiza, plan a full day for the UNESCO World Heritage Site **Dalt Vila** and the shops of **Sa Penya,** and the better part of another for **Santa Gertrudis** and the north coast. If you've come to Ibiza to party, of course, time has no meaning.

Getting Here and Around

AIR

The easiest way to reach Mallorca, Menorca, and Ibiza is to fly. Each of the three islands is served by an international airport, all of them within 15–20 minutes by car or bus from their respective capital cities. There are daily domestic connections to each from Barcelona (about 50 minutes), Madrid, and Valencia: no-frills and charter operators fly to Eivissa, Palma, and Mahón from many European cities, especially during the summer. There are also flights between the islands. Book early in high season.

BIKE

The Balearic Islands—especially Ibiza and Formentera—are ideal for exploration by bicycle. Ibiza is relatively flat and easy to negotiate, though side roads can be in poor repair. Formentera is level, too, with bicycle lanes on all connecting roads. Parts of Mallorca are quite mountainous, with challenging climbs through spectacular scenery; along some country roads, there are designated bike lanes. Bicycles are easy to rent, and tourist offices have details of recommended routes. Menorca is relatively flat, with lots of roads that wander through pastureland and olive groves to small coves and inlets.

BOAT AND FERRY

From Barcelona: The Acciona Trasmediterránea and Balearia car ferries serve Ibiza, Mallorca, and Menorca from Barcelona. The most romantic way to get to the Balearic Islands is by overnight ferry from Barcelona to Palma, sailing (depending on the line and the season) between 11 and 11:30 pm; you can watch the lights of Barcelona sinking into the horizon for hours—and when you arrive in Palma, around 7 am, see the spires of the cathedral bathed in the morning sun. Overnight ferries have lounges and private cabins. Round-trip fares vary with the line, the season, and points of departure and destination but from Barcelona start from as low as €45 for lounge seats or €150 per person for a double cabin (tax included).

Faster ferries operated by Balearia, with passenger lounges only, speed from Barcelona to Eivissa (Ibiza), to Palma and Alcúdia (Mallorca), and to Mahón (Menorca). Depending on the destination, the trip takes between three and six hours.

From Valencia: Acciona Trasmediterránea ferries leave Valencia late at night for Ibiza, arriving early in the morning. Balearia fast ferries (no vehicles) leave Valencia for Sant Antoni on Ibiza in the late afternoon, making the crossing in about 2½ hours. Acciona Trasmediterránea and Balearia have services from Valencia to Mallorca, and Trasmediterránea also runs a service to Mahón (Menorca). Departure days and times vary with the season, with service more frequent in summer.

From Dénia: Balearia runs a daily three-hour fast ferry service for passengers and cars between Dénia and Ibiza, another between Dénia and Formentera, and a similar eight-hour service between Dénia and Palma on weekends.

Interisland: Daily fast ferries connect Ibiza and Palma; one-way fares run €66–€81, depending on the type of accommodations. The Pitiusa and Trasmapi lines offer frequent fast ferry and hydrofoil service between Ibiza and Formentera (€22.50 one-way, €40–€50 round-trip). Daily ferries connect Alcúdia (Mallorca) and Ciutadella (Menorca) in three to four hours, depending on the weather; a hydrofoil makes the journey in about an hour.

BOAT AND FERRY CONTACTS Acciona Trasmediterránea. ☎ *90202/454645* ⊕ *www.trasmediterranea.es/en.***Balearia.** ☎ *991202/660215* ⊕ *www.balearia. com.***Mediterranea Pitiusa.** ✉ *Eivissa* ☎ *609/741067 reservations, 971/314461 Eivissa ticket office* ⊕ *www.mediterraneapitiusa.com.***Trasmapi.** ✉ *Eivissa* ☎ *971/314433 information, 971/310711 Eivissa ticket office* ⊕ *www.trasmapi. com.*

BUS
There is bus service on all the islands, though it's not extensive, especially on Formentera. ⇨ *Check each island's Getting Here and Around section for details.*

CAR
Ibiza is best explored by car or motor scooter: many of the beaches lie at the end of rough, unpaved roads. Tiny Formentera can almost be covered on foot, but renting a car or a scooter at La Sabina is a time saver. A car is essential if you want to beach-hop on Mallorca or Menorca and explore beyond the main cities and resorts.

TAXI
On Ibiza, taxis are available at the airport and in Eivissa, Figueretas, Santa Eulàlia, and Sant Antoni. On Formentera, there are taxis in La Sabina and Es Pujols. Legal taxis on Ibiza and Formentera are metered, but it's a good idea to get a rough estimate of the fare from the driver before you climb aboard. Taxis in Palma are metered. For trips beyond the city, charges are posted at the taxi stands. On Menorca, you can pick up a taxi at the airport or in Mahón or Ciutadella.

TRAIN
The public Ferrocarriles de Mallorca railroad track connects Palma and Inca, with stops at about half a dozen villages en route.

A journey on the privately owned Palma–Sóller railroad is a must: completed in 1912, it still uses the carriages from that era. The train trundles across the plain to

Bunyola, then winds through tremendous mountain scenery to emerge high above Sóller. An ancient tram connects the Sóller terminus to Port de Sóller, leaving every hour on the hour 8–5; the Palma terminal is near the corner of the Plaça d'Espanya, on Calle Eusebio Estada next to the Inca train station.

Restaurants

On the Balearic Islands many restaurants tend to have short business seasons. This is less true of Mallorca, but on Menorca, Ibiza, and especially on Formentera, it might be May (or later) before the shutters are removed from that great seafood shack you've heard so much about. Really fine dining experiences are in limited supply on most of the islands, although this tide is turning, especially in cosmopolitan Palma de Mallorca; in the popular beach resorts, the promenades can seem overrun with paella and pizza joints. Away from the water, however, there are exceptional meals to be had—and the seafood couldn't be any fresher.

Restaurant reviews have been shortened. For full information, visit Fodors.com.

Hotels

Many hotels on the islands include a continental or full buffet breakfast in the room rate.

IBIZA

Ibiza's high-rise resort hotels and holiday apartments are mainly in Sant Antoni, Talamanca, Ses Figueretes, and Playa d'en Bossa. Overbuilt Sant Antoni has little but its beach to recommend it. Playa d'en Bossa, close to Eivissa, is prettier but lies under a flight path. To get off the beaten track and into the island's largely pristine interior, look for *agroturismo* lodgings in Els Amunts (the Uplands)

and in villages such as Santa Gertrudis or Sant Miquel de Balanzat.

FORMENTERA

If July and August are the only months you can visit, reserve well in advance. Accommodations on Formentera, the best of them on the south Platja de Mitjorn coast, tend to be small private properties converted to studio apartment complexes, rather than megahotels.

MALLORCA

Mallorca's large-scale resorts—more than 1,500 of them—are concentrated mainly on the southern coast and primarily serve the package-tour industry. Perhaps the best accommodations on the island are the number of grand old country estates and town houses that have been converted into boutique hotels, ranging from simple and relatively inexpensive *agroturismos* to stunning outposts of luxury. Palma also boasts an excellent selection of thoughtfully designed boutique hotels.

MENORCA

Aside from a few hotels and hostels in Mahón and Ciutadella, almost all of Menorca's tourist lodgings are in beach resorts. As on the other islands, many of these are fully reserved by travel operators in the high season and often require a week's minimum stay, so it's generally most economical to book a package that combines airfare and accommodations. Or inquire at the tourist office about boutique and country hotels, especially in and around Sant Lluís.

Hotel reviews have been shortened. For full information, visit Fodors.com.

WHAT IT COSTS in Euros

	$	$$	$$$	$$$$
RESTAURANTS				
	under €12	€12–€17	€18–€22	over €22
HOTELS				
	under €90	€90–€125	€126–€180	over €180

Tours

Ibiza resorts run trips to neighboring beaches and to smaller islands. Trips from Ibiza to Formentera include an escorted bus tour. In Sant Antoni, there are a number of tour organizers to choose from.

Most Mallorca hotels and resorts offer guided tours. Typical itineraries are the Caves of Artà or Drac, on the east coast, including the nearby Auto Safari Park and an artificial-pearl factory in Manacor; the Chopin museum in the old monastery at Valldemossa, returning through the writers' and artists' village of Deià; the port of Sóller and the Arab gardens at Alfàbia; the Thursday market and leather factories in Inca; Port de Pollença; Cap de Formentor; and the northern beaches.

Excursions a Cabrera

Several options are available for visits to Cabrera, from a three-hour sunset tour, including sparkling wine and dessert, to a daylong tour, with time to explore independently. One option for this is to take a self-guided tour of the island's underwater ecosystem—using a mask and snorkel with their own sound system; the recording explains the main points of interest as you swim. Boats generally depart from Colònia Sant Jordi, 47 km (29 miles) southeast of Palma. You can buy tickets on the dock at Carrer Babriel Roca or online. ⊠ *Carrer de Dofi 11, Colònia de Sant Jordi* ☎ *971/649034* ⊕ *www.excursionsacabrera.es* ⊠ *From €40.*

Yellow Catamarans

On Menorca, sightseeing trips on glass-bottom catamarans leave Mahón's harbor from the quayside near the Xoriguer gin factory. Departure times vary; check with the tourist information office on the Moll de Ponent, at the foot of the winding stairs from the old city to the harbor. ⊠ *Moll de Llevant 12, Mahón* ☎ *971/352307, 639/676351 for reservations* ⊕ *www.yellowcatamarans.com* ⊠ *From €12.50* ⊗ *Closed Sun. mid-July–mid Sept.*

Ibiza

Tranquil countryside, secluded coves, and intimate luxury lodging to the north; sandy beaches and party venues by the score to the south; a capital crowned with a historic UNESCO World Heritage Site, and laid-back (and English-speaking) hospitality islandwide—Ibiza is a vacation destination not to be missed. Settled by the Carthaginians in the 5th century BC, Ibiza has seen successive waves of invasion and occupation, the latest of which began in the 1960s, when it became a tourist destination. With a full-time population of barely 140,000, it now gets some 2 million visitors a year. It's blessed with beaches—56 of them, by one count—and also has the world's largest nightclub. About a quarter of the people who live on Ibiza year-round are expats.

October through April, the pace of life here is decidedly slow, and many of the island's hotels and restaurants are closed. In the 1960s and early 1970s, Ibiza was discovered by sun-seeking hippies and eventually emerged as an icon of counterculture chic. Ibizans were—and still are—friendly to and tolerant of their eccentric visitors. In the late 1980s and 1990s, club culture took over. Young ravers flocked here from all over the world to dance all night and pack the sands of built-up beach resorts like Sant

Antoni. That party-hearty Ibiza is still alive and well, but a new wave of luxury rural hotels, offering oases of peace and privacy, with spas and high-end restaurants, marks the most recent transformation of the island into a venue for more upscale tourism. In fact, it is entirely feasible to spend time on Ibiza and not see any evidence of the clubbing and nightlife scene for which it is so famous.

GETTING HERE AND AROUND

Ibiza is a 55-minute flight or a nine-hour ferry ride from Barcelona.

Ibizabus serves the island. Buses run to Sant Antoni every 15–30 minutes 7:30 am–midnight (until 10:30 pm November–May) from the bus station on Avenida d'Isidor Macabich in Eivissa, and to Santa Eulàlia every half hour 6:50 am–11:30 pm Monday–Saturday (until 10:30 November–April), with late buses on Saturday in the summer party season at midnight, 1, and 2 am; Sunday service is hourly 7:30 am–11:30 pm (until 10:30 pm November–April). Buses to other parts of the island are less frequent, as is the cross-island bus between Sant Antoni and Santa Eulàlia.

On Ibiza, a six-lane divided highway connects the capital with the airport and Sant Antoni. Traffic circles and one-way streets make it a bit confusing to get in and out of Eivissa, but out in the countryside driving is easy and in most cases is the only way of getting to some of the island's smaller coves and beaches.

BUS CONTACT Ibizabus. ⊠ *Eivissa* ☎ *971/340382, 600/482972 for Discobus* ⊕ *www.ibizabus.com.*

TAXI CONTACTS Cooperativa Limitada de Taxis de Sant Antoni. ⊠ *Carrer del Progrés, Sant Antoni* ☎ *971/343764.* **Radio-Taxi.** ⊠ *Eivissa* ☎ *971/398483.*

Eivissa (Ibiza Town)

Hedonistic and historic, Eivissa (Ibiza, in Castilian) is a city jam-packed with cafés, nightspots, and trendy shops; looming over it are the massive stone walls of **Dalt Vila**—the medieval city declared a UNESCO World Heritage Site in 1999—and its Gothic cathedral. Squeezed between the north walls of the old city and the harbor is **Sa Penya**, a long labyrinth of stone-paved streets with some of the city's best offbeat shopping, snacking, and exploring.

TOURS

Dalt Vila Tours

This 75-minute dramatized tour of Dalt Vila departs from the Portal de Ses Taules, at the foot of the walls. Three performers in period costume enact a legendary 15th-century love story as they move through the medieval scenes. Reservations are essential. The tour is in Spanish, though English speakers can be accommodated for groups of 10 or more. Confirm timetables at the Tourist Office. ⊠ *Portal de Ses Taules, Dalt Vila* ☎ *971/399232* ⛵ *From €10.*

VISITOR INFORMATION

Ibiza Tourist Office

⊠ *La Cúria, Pl. de la Catedral s/n, Dalt Vila* ☎ *971/399232* ⊕ *tourism.eivissa.es.*

 Sights

Bastió promenade

PROMENADE | The Bastio Sant Bernat stone edifice is one of the oldest bastions in the Balearic Islands, harkening back to when inhabitants feared attacks from pirates. From here a promenade with stunning sea views runs west to the bastions of Sant Jordi and Sant Jaume, past the Castell—a fortress formerly used as an army barracks. In 2007 work began to transform the fortress into a luxury parador, but archaeological discoveries under the work site have delayed the reconstruction indefinitely.

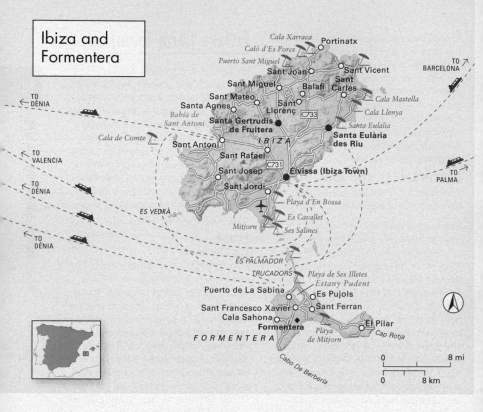

Ibiza and Formentera

The promenade ends at the steps to the Portal Nou (New Gate). ⊠ *Portal Nou, Eivissa.*

Cathedral
CHURCH | Built on a site used for temples and other religious buildings since the time of the Phoenicians, Ibiza's cathedral has a Gothic tower and a baroque nave, and a small museum of religious art and artifacts. It was built in the 13th and 14th centuries and renovated in the 18th century. ⊠ *Pl. de la Catedral s/n, Dalt Vila* ☎ *971/312773* ☜ *Museum €1.*

Centre d'Interpretació Madina Yabisa
HISTORY MUSEUM | A few steps from the cathedral, this small center has a fascinating collection of audiovisual materials and exhibits on the period when the Moors ruled the island. ⊠ *Major 2, Dalt Vila* ☎ *971/392390* ☜ *€2* ⊘ *Closed Mon.*

Museu d'Art Contemporani
ART MUSEUM | Just inside the old city portal arch, this museum houses a collection of paintings, sculpture, and photography from 1959 to the present. The scope of the collection is international, but the emphasis is on artists who were born or lived in Ibiza during their careers. There isn't much explanatory material in English, however. There is also an underground archaeological site in the basement, some of which dates back as far as the 6th century BC. ⊠ *Ronda Narcís Puget s/n, Dalt Vila* ☎ *971/302723* ⊕ *www.mace.eivissa.es* ☜ *Free* ⊘ *Closed Mon.*

Sant Domingo
CHURCH | The roof of this 17th-century church is an irregular arrangement of tile domes. It is worth visiting for the fresco paintings on the main nave, created by

the Majorcan painter Matas in 1884, and for the chapels. The nearby *ajuntament* (town hall) is housed in the former monastery of the church. ✉ *Carrer General Balanzat 6, Dalt Vila* 🕒 *Closed Mon.*

Beaches

Es Cavellet Beach

BEACH | This wild stretch of white sand hugged by turquoise waves is popular with nudist sunbathers and can be reached on foot from Ses Salines beach (20-minute walk). By car it's a 10-km (6-mile) drive from Eivissa, through the salt flats. Parts are backed by sand dunes, and on a clear day it serves up views of Eivissa and Formentera. El Chiringuito bar and restaurant, one of Ibiza's favorite waterfront beach bars, is known for its relaxed vibe, good food and cocktails, and its lively season-opening and season-closing parties. **Amenities:** food and drink; parking (fee); showers. **Best for:** nudists; swimming. ✉ *Sant Josep de sa Talaia.*

Ses Salines

BEACH | Very much a place to see and be seen, the beach at Ses Salines is a mile-long narrow crescent of golden sand about 10 minutes' drive from Eivissa, in a wildlife conservation area. Trendy restaurants and bars, like the Jockey Club and Malibu, bring drinks to you on the sand and have DJs for the season, keeping the beat in the air all day long. The beach has different areas: glitterati in one zone, naturists in another, gay couples in another. There are no nearby shops, but the commercial vacuum is filled by vendors of bags, sunglasses, fruit drinks, and so on, who can be irritating. The sea is shallow, with a gradual drop-off, but on a windy day breakers are good enough to surf. **Amenities:** food and drink; lifeguards; parking (fee); showers; toilets; water sports. **Best for:** nudists; partiers; swimming; windsurfing. ✉ *Eivissa* ✥ *10 km (6 miles) west on E20 ring road from Eivissa toward airport, then south on PM802 local road to beach.*

Restaurants

Es Boldado

$$$$ | **MEDITERRANEAN** | The real magic of Ibiza can only be discovered when you head off the beaten track, and Es Boldado proves it. Getting here requires a bumpy ride down a dirt track off the main road that links Sant Josep de la Talaia with the beautiful beaches at Cala d'Hort, but the reward more than makes up for it. **Known for:** seafood paella; off the beaten path; incredible views of the Es Vedra islands. [$] *Average main: €28* ✉ *Playa Cala d'Hort, 07830* ☎ *626/494537* 🌐 *esboldadoibiza.com.*

Restaurante Jardín La Brasa

$$$$ | **MEDITERRANEAN** | A perennial favorite, La Brasa is tucked down a side street close to the walls of the Dalt Vila. Here you can dine on traditional Ibizan cuisine, such as barbecued entrecôte steak, lamb chops, or grilled squid, within a tree-filled courtyard lit by fairy lights and candles—a haven from the bustling surroundings. **Known for:** reservations needed in high season; courtyard setting; grilled meat. [$] *Average main: €25* ✉ *Carrer de Pere Sala 3, Eivissa* ☎ *971/301202* 🌐 *www.labrasaibiza.com.*

Hotels

Boutique Hostal Salinas

$$$$ | **B&B/INN** | The rooms might be a bit basic for the price but this bed-and-breakfast with a gem of a restaurant is ideally situated near the beach. **Pros:** minutes' walk to the beach; excellent buffet breakfast; family-friendly. **Cons:** small armoires; rooms need soundproofing; pricey in high season, with a five-day minimum stay May 20–October. [$] *Rooms from: €242* ✉ *Ctra. Sa Canal, Km 5, Ses Salinas, Sant Josep de sa Talaia* ☎ *971/308899, 647/912906* 🌐 *www.*

An evening stroll among the shops in Eivissa

boutiquehostalsalinas.com ⏲ *Closed late Oct.–Apr. (dates can vary)* 🛏 *11 rooms* 🍴 *Free Breakfast.*

La Ventana

$$ | B&B/INN | Inside the medieval walls, this intimate hillside hotel has fine views of the old town and the harbor from some of the rooms. **Pros:** roof terrace; historic setting; good value. **Cons:** lots of stairs to climb, especially if you want a room with a view; rooms are small; surroundings can be noisy until late. [$] *Rooms from: €91* ✉ *Sa Carrossa 13, Eivissa* ☎ *971/390857* 🌐 *en.laventanaibiza.com* 🛏 *12 rooms, 2 suites* 🍴 *No Meals.*

MIM Ibiza Es Vivé

$$$$ | HOTEL | Owned by F.C. Barcelona soccer superstar Leo Messi, MIM has a stylish, upbeat vibe and a location convenient to both Eivissa old town and Figueretas beach. The pool features a so-called "constellation effect" that allows guests to listen to music while underwater. Other facilities include a restaurant serving Mediterranean cuisine, a cocktail bar, and a terrace bar with DJs and panoramic views. **Pros:** well located for the old town and the beach; great pool area; views from the roof terrace. **Cons:** rooms on the small side; some balconies don't have any views; adults only. [$] *Rooms from: €269* ✉ *Carrer de Carles Roman Ferrer 8, Dalt Vila* ☎ *971/301902* 🌐 *mimhotels.com/es/ibiza/hotel-mim-ibiza* 🍴 *Free Breakfast* 🛏 *53 rooms.*

🍸 Nightlife

Ibiza's discos are famous throughout Europe. Keep your eyes open during the day for free invitations handed out on the street—these can save you expensive entry fees. Between June and September, an all-night "Discobus" service (600/482972) runs between Eivissa, Sant Antoni, Santa Eulàlia/Es Canar, Playa d'En Bossa, and the major party venues. The cost is €3 for one ride, €12 for a five-trip ticket.

BARS AND GATHERING PLACES

Calle Santa Creu

GATHERING PLACES | FAMILY | Hidden behind the walls of the Dalt Vila, this narrow lane is lined with bustling eateries. It's at its most atmospheric in the evening, when you can enjoy a candlelit dinner on the cobblestones as the world slowly saunters past. ⊠ *Santa Creu, Dalt Vila.*

Carrer de la Mare de Déu (Calle de la Virgen) (*Calle de la Virgen*)

GATHERING PLACES | Gay nightlife converges on this street in Sa Penya. ⊠ *Mare de Déu, Eivissa.*

Sunset Ashram

BARS | There are many places to take in a spectacular sunset in Ibiza, but this one ranks as one of the White Isle's top spots. Set above a beautiful stretch of unspoiled coastline, boho Sunset Ashram mixes beach casual with ambient music, tasty cocktails, and unobstructed panoramic views of the golden hour. Dinner is also served here (reservations essential). ⊠ *Cala Conta s/n, San Agustin des Vedra* ☎ *661/347222* ⊕ *www.sunsetashram. com/en.*

DANCE CLUBS

Amnesia

DANCE CLUBS | This popular club in San Rafael opened in 1980 and it's still going strong, with several ample dance floors that throb to house and funk. Like most of the clubs on the island, it opens for the season at the end of May, with a gala bash. ⊠ *Ctra. Eivissa–Sant Antoni, Km 5, San Rafael* ☎ *971/198041* ⊕ *www. amnesia.es.*

Keeper

DANCE CLUBS | Clubbers start the evening here, where there's no cover and the action starts at 11 pm. The indoor space at Keeper can get a bit cramped, but out on the terrace freedom reigns. ⊠ *Marina Botafoch, Paseo Juan Carlos I s/n, Ibiza Nueva* ☎ *971/310509.*

Pacha

DANCE CLUBS | A young, international crowd gathers after 2 am at the flagship venue of this club empire, where each of the five rooms offers a different style, including techno, house music, R&B, and hip-hop. ⊠ *Av. 8 de Agosto s/n, Eivissa* ☎ *971/313600* ⊕ *www.pacha.com.*

Privilege

DANCE CLUBS | Billing itself as the largest club in the world, the long-running center of Ibiza's nightlife has a giant dance floor, a swimming pool, and more than a dozen bars. ⊠ *Urbanización San Rafael s/n, San Rafael* ☎ *971/198161* ⊕ *privilegeibiza. com.*

🛍 Shopping

Although the Sa Penya area of Eivissa still has a few designer boutiques, much of the area is now given over to the so-called hippie market, with stalls selling clothing and crafts of all sorts May–October. Browse Avenida Bartolomeu Rosselló and the main square of Dalt Vila for casual clothes and accessories.

Divina

MIXED CLOTHING | With no shortage of shops in Eivissa selling clothing in the classic white Ibiza style, Divina stands out for its range of clothes for kids and its modest selection of real Panama hats. ⊠ *Pl. de la Vila 17, Dalt Vila* ☎ *971/301157.*

Enotecum

WINE/SPIRITS | This store has a good range of wines, including labels produced in the Balearics, and spirits. ⊠ *Av. d'Isidoro Macabich 36, Eivissa* ☎ *971/399167* ⊕ *www.enotecum.com* ☉ *Closed Sun.*

🏃 Activities

BOATING

Coral Yachting

BOATING | You can charter all sorts of power craft, sailboats (small and large), and catamarans here, by the day or by the week, with or without a skipper.

✉ *Marina Botafoc, Local 323–324, Eivissa* ☎ *971/313926* ⊕ *www.coralyachting. com.*

IbizAzul Charters

BOATING | A variety of motorized craft and sailboats are available for rent here for weekend or weeklong charters. Daytrips are also available, departing from Santa Eulalia Port. ✉ *Ctra. Ibiza–Portinatx, Km 16.5, Sant Joan* ☎ *971/325264* ⊕ *www. ibizazul.com.*

HORSEBACK RIDING
Can Mayans

HORSEBACK RIDING | Hire horses here for rides along the coast and inland. Can Mayans has a riding school and a gentle touch with beginners. ✉ *Ctra. Santa Gertrudis–Sant Lorenç, Km 4, San Lorenzo de Balafia* ☎ *690/922144* ⊕ *canmayans. es.*

SCUBA DIVING
Active Dive

DIVING & SNORKELING | Instruction and guided dives, as well as kayaking, parasailing, and boat rentals are available here. ✉ *Surf Lounge Ibiza, Calle des Molí 10, Sant Antoni* ☎ *618/796358* ⊕ *www. active-dive.com.*

Arenal Diving

SCUBA DIVING | Book lessons and dives here, from beginner level to advanced, with PADI-trained instructors and guides. ✉ *Av. Doctor Fleming 16, Sant Antoni* ☎ *633/078412* ⊕ *arenaldiving.com.*

Sea Horse Scuba Diving Centre

SCUBA DIVING | A short distance from Sant Antoni, this aquatic center offers basic scuba training as well as excursions to spectacular nearby dive sites, especially the Cala d'Hort Marine Nature Reserve and the Pillars of Hercules underwater caves. ✉ *Edificio Yais 5, Calle Vizcaya 8, Playa Port des Torrent, Sant Josep de sa Talaia* ☎ *629/349499, 678/717211* ⊕ *www.seahorsedivingibiza.com.*

TENNIS
Ibiza Club de Campo

TENNIS | With six clay courts, seven courts for padel tennis (a racquet sport that's like a mix between tennis and squash and typically played in doubles), a 25-meter pool, and a gym, this is the best-equipped club on the island. Nonresidents and nonmembers can play tennis for €10 or padel from €7 per hour per person. ✉ *Ctra. Ibiza–Sant Josep, Km 2.5, Sant Josep de sa Talaia* ☎ *971/303030* ⊕ *www.ibizaclubdecampo.es* 🎫 *From €7/hr.*

Santa Eulària des Riu

15 km (9 miles) northeast of Eivissa.

At the edge of this town on the island's eastern coast, to the right below the road, a Roman bridge crosses what some claim is the only permanent river in the Balearics (hence *des Riu*, or "of the river"). The town itself follows the curve of a long sandy beach, a few blocks deep with restaurants, shops, and vacation apartments. From here it's a 10-minute drive to Sant Carles and the open-air hippie market, Las Dalias, held there every Saturday and Sunday. The popular Las Dalias night market offers shopping with live music, food, and drinks and runs from June to September, every Sunday, Monday, and Tuesday.

GETTING HERE AND AROUND

By car, take the C733 from Eivissa. From May to October, buses run from Eivissa more or less every half hour Monday–Saturday and every hour on Sunday. Service is less frequent the rest of the year.

VISITOR INFORMATION

CONTACTS Santa Eularia des Riu. ✉ *Carrer Mariano Riquer Wallis 4,* ☎ *971/330728* ⊕ *www.visitsantaeulalia.com.*

Restaurants

Hoyo 19

$$$ | MEDITERRANEAN | FAMILY | Hoyo 19 (or Hole 19) overlooks the golf course, but locals come here to enjoy the serenity and beautiful green setting, just a ten-minute drive from Santa Eularia. Open all year-round, from breakfast on, the menu focuses on Mediterranean haute cuisine, with superb rice dishes cooked over a wood fire and excellent locally sourced meat and fish options. **Known for:** patios overlooking the golf course; peaceful setting; rice dishes cooked over a wood fire. $ *Average main: €18* ✉ *Golf Ibiza, Ctra. Jesús a Cala Llonga, s/n, Santa Eulària des Riu* ☎ *971/196052* ⊕ *www.golfibiza.com/restaurante*.

Oleoteca Ses Escoles

$$$ | MEDITERRANEAN | Chef-owner Miguel Llabres honed his craft at starred restaurants in Mallorca and opened here in 2014, to local acclaim. He keeps the menu short and focuses on garden-fresh seasonal vegetables and free-range local meats. **Known for:** Ibizan potato salad; free-range local meats; gourmet shop. $ *Average main: €22* ✉ *Crtra Ibiza-Portinatx, Sant Joan de Labritja* ☎ *871/870229* ⊕ *www.sesescoles.com* ⊘ *Closed Jan., and Mon. Oct.–Apr.*

🛏 Hotels

Can Curreu

$$$$ | B&B/INN | The traditional architecture here, reminiscent of a Greek island village, features a cluster of low, whitewashed buildings—and each room has one of these buildings to itself, with a private patio artfully separated from its neighbors. **Pros:** friendly, efficient staff; luxurious spa; horseback riding stables. **Cons:** patchy Wi-Fi; bit of a drive to the nearest beaches; pricey. $ *Rooms from: €295* ✉ *Ctra. de Sant Carles, Km 12,* ☎ *971/335280* ⊕ *www.cancurreu.com* ⤳ *18 rooms* ⦿| *Free Breakfast.*

★ Can Gall

$$$$ | B&B/INN | Santi Marí Ferrer remade his family's *finca* (farmhouse), with its massive stone walls and native *savina* wood beams, into one of the island's friendliest and most comfortable country inns. **Pros:** poolside pergola for events and yoga sessions; oasis of quiet; family friendly. **Cons:** some private terraces a bit small; 15-minute drive to beaches; often booked out for weddings. $ *Rooms from: €220* ✉ *Ctra. Sant Joan, Km 17.2, San Lorenzo de Balafia* ☎ *971/337031, 670/876054* ⊕ *cangall.com* ⤳ *2 rooms, 9 suites* ⦿| *Free Breakfast.*

Hostal Yebisah

$ | HOTEL | Longtime residents and civic boosters Toni and Tanya Molio are the owners of this simple lodging on the promenade in the heart of town. **Pros:** good value; ideal location; friendly service. **Cons:** best rates only for minimum booking of four nights; minimal amenities; bathrooms a bit cramped. $ *Rooms from: €86* ✉ *Paseo S'Alamera 13, Santa Eulària des Riu* ☎ *971/330160* ⊕ *www.hostalyebisah.com* ⊘ *Closed Nov.–Apr.* ⤳ *26 rooms* ⦿| *No Meals.*

W Ibiza

$$$$ | HOTEL | Bright, vibrant, and bursting with color, the W Ibiza encapsulates the lively, hedonistic spirit of Ibiza. **Pros:** ultra-plush signature W beds; beachfront location; excellent spa and wellness center. **Cons:** rather pricey; attracts the party crowd and can get noisy; more modern than cozy. $ *Rooms from: €530* ✉ , *Santa Eulària des Riu* ☎ *871/556888* ⊕ *www.marriott.com/hotels/travel/ibzwh-w-ibiza* ⦿| *No Meals* ⤳ *162 rooms.*

Activities

BICYCLING

Kandani

BIKING | Bicycle rentals start at €15 for one day or €10 per day for weeklong rentals, and accessories are also available, as are guided cycling tours. ✉ *Carrer*

César Puget Riquer 27, Santa Eulària des Riu ☎ *971/339264* ⊕ *www.kandani.es* 🖪 *from €15.*

DIVING
Divestar Ibiza
SCUBA DIVING | This is one of the best-equipped and best-staffed diving centers on the island, for beginners and experienced PADI-qualified divers alike. ⊠ *Playa Cala Martina s/n, Santa Eulària des Riu* ☎ *971/336726* ⊕ *www.divestar-ibiza.com.*

Subfari
SCUBA DIVING | This is one of the best places to come for diving off the north coast of the island. ⊠ *Puerto de Portinatx s/n, Sant Joan de Labritja* ✛ *22 km (14 miles) north via C733* ☎ *971/337558, 677/466040* ⊕ *www.subfari.es.*

GOLF
Club de Golf Ibiza
GOLF | Ibiza's only golf club combines the 9 holes at the Club Roca Llisa resort complex (Course II) with the newer and more challenging 18-hole Course I nearby. Fairway maintenance on Course II leaves a bit to be desired. ⊠ *Ctra. Jesús–Cala Llonga s/n, Santa Eulària des Riu* ☎ *971/196052* ⊕ *www.golfibiza.com* 🖪 *Course I, €98; Course II, €65* 🏌 *Course I: 18 holes, 6561 yards, par 72; Course II: 9 holes, 6265 yards (2 rounds), par 71.*

Santa Gertrudis de Fruitera

15 km (9 miles) north of Eivissa.

Blink and you miss it: that's true of most of the small towns in the island's interior and especially so of Santa Gertrudis. It's not much more than a bend in the road, but it's worth a look. The brick-paved town square is closed to vehicle traffic—perfect for the sidewalk cafés and boutique stores. From here, you are only a few minutes' drive from some of the island's best resort hotels and spas and the most beautiful secluded northern coves and beaches: **S'Illa des Bosc,**

Benirrás (where they have drum circles to salute the setting sun), **S'Illot des Renclí, Portinatx,** and **Caló d'En Serra.** Artists and expats like it here: they've given the town an appeal that now makes for listings of half a million dollars or more for a modest two-bedroom house.

GETTING HERE AND AROUND
By car, take the C733 from Eivissa. Buses run from Eivissa more or less seven times a day on weekdays and less frequently on weekends (check ibiza-bus.com).

🍴 Restaurants

Can Caus
$$ | SPANISH | FAMILY | Ibiza might pride itself on its seafood, but there comes a time for meat and potatoes. When that time comes, take the 20-minute drive to the outskirts of Santa Gertrudis to this family-style roadside restaurant where you can feast on skewers of barbecued *sobrasada* (sausage), goat chops, and lamb kebabs. **Known for:** Ibizan home cooking; grilled meats; local vibe. 💲 *Average main: €16* ⊠ *Ctra. Sant Miquel, Km 3.5, Santa Gertrudis* ☎ *971/197516* ⊕ *www.cancaus.com* ☉ *Closed Mon. and in low season (varies).*

La Paloma
$$$ | MEDITERRANEAN | Channeling that Ibiza-boho vibe, La Paloma feels like a refuge for artists and hippies, nestled amid the shady overhang of orange and lemon trees. The eclectic menu often features crunchy salads, Middle Eastern- and North African–inspired dishes, fish, and homemade pasta (the chef is Italian and many of the ingredients come directly from there). **Known for:** large shaded terrace amid a lemon and orange grove; peaceful setting with beautiful views; organic dishes and fresh salads. 💲 *Average main: €22* ⊠ *Calle Emili Pou 4, Sant Joan de Labritja* ✛ *7 km (4½ miles) from Santa Gertrudis de Fruitera* ☎ *971/325543* ⊕ *www.palomaibiza.com.*

🛏 Hotels

Atzaró

$$$$ | **HOTEL** | Ibiza may be best known as a magnet for the international jet set, but there's also a quieter, more sophisticated side to the island, which can be found at this hotel on a thirteen-hectare orange farm. There are sprawling gardens, two restaurants, a spa, and a generous outdoor swimming pool, as well as plentiful fragrant orange groves and an on-site vegetable garden. The food in La Veranda and The Orange Tree restaurants is local and seasonal and packed with flavor—a true celebration of the farm-to-table movement. Guest rooms are rustic-chic, with solid teak four-poster beds, cool white linens, and quality natural materials. Many have their own private gardens, balconies, terraces, or pools. **Pros:** 140-foot outdoor freshwater pool; exclusive rural hideaway; farm-to-table dining. **Cons:** service can be a tad slow; very pricey; minimum stay five nights in high season. $ *Rooms from: €545* ⊠ *Ctra. Sant Joan Km 15, Santa Gertrudis* ☏ *971/338838* ⊕ *www.atzaro. com* ⇗ *24 rooms* ⊙ *Closed Nov.–Mar.* ⦿ *Free Breakfast.*

★ Cas Gasi

$$$$ | **B&B/INN** | A countryside setting on a hillside overlooking a valley makes this lovely late-19th-century manor house a quiet escape in a lively destination, with photo-ready views of Ibiza's only mountain (1,567-foot Sa Talaiassa). **Pros:** attentive personal service; peace and quiet; excellent breakfast. **Cons:** minimum stay required in July and August; not geared to families; very expensive. $ *Rooms from: €575* ⊠ *Cami Vell a Sant Mateu s/n, Santa Gertrudis* ☏ *971/197700* ⊕ *www. casgasi.com* ⇗ *9 rooms, 1 suite* ⦿ *Free Breakfast.*

🛍 Shopping

te Cuero

LEATHER GOODS | This store specializes in hand-tooled leather bags and belts with great designer buckles, boots, and sandals. ⊠ *Pl. de la Iglesia 6, Santa Gertrudis* ☏ *971/197100* ⊙ *Closed weekends and Dec.–Mar.*

Formentera

Environmental protection laws shield much of Formentera, making it a calm respite from neighboring Ibiza's dance-until-you-drop madness. Though it does get crowded in the summer, the island's long, white-sand beaches are among the finest in the Mediterranean; inland, you can explore quiet country roads by bicycle in relative solitude.

From the port at La Savina, it's only 3 km (2 miles) to Formentera's capital, **Sant Francesc Xavier,** a few yards off the main road. There's an active hippie market in the small plaza in front of the church. At the main road, turn right toward Sant Ferran, 2 km (1 mile) away. Beyond Sant Ferran the road continues for 7 km (4 miles) along a narrow isthmus, staying slightly closer to the rougher northern side, where the waves and rocks keep yachts—and thus much of the tourist trade—away.

The plateau on the island's east side ends at the lighthouse **Faro de la Mola.** Nearby is a **monument to Jules Verne,** who set part of his 1877 novel *Hector Servadac* (published in English as *Off on a Comet*) in Formentera. The rocks around the lighthouse are carpeted with purple thyme and sea holly in spring and fall.

Back on the main road, turn right at Sant Ferran toward Es Pujols. The few hotels here are the closest Formentera comes to beach resorts, even if the beach is not the best. Beyond Es Pujols the road skirts **Estany Pudent,** one of two lagoons that almost enclose La Savina. Salt was once extracted from Pudent, hence its name, which means "stinking pond," although the pond now smells fine. At the northern tip of Pudent, a road to the right leads to a footpath that runs the length of **Trucadors,** a narrow sand spit. The long, windswept beaches here are excellent.

GETTING HERE AND AROUND

Formentera is a one-hour ferry ride from Ibiza or 25 minutes on the jet ferry. Balearia operates ferry services to Formentera from Ibiza and Dénia, the nearest landfall on the Spanish mainland.

On Ibiza, you can also take ferries from Santa Eulària and Sant Antoni to La Savina, as well as numerous ferries to the coves and calas on the east and west coasts of the island. Day-trippers can travel to Formentera for a few hours in the sun before heading back to Ibiza to plug into the nightlife.

A very limited bus service connects Formentera's villages, shrinking to one bus each way between San Francisco and Pilar on Saturday and disappearing altogether on Sunday and holidays.

FERRY CONTACTS Baleària. 🌐 *www.balearia.com.*

TAXI CONTACTS Parada de Taxis La Savina. ✉ *Carretera Savina-es Pujols, KM 3, La Savina* ☎ *971/322002.*

VISITOR INFORMATION

CONTACTS Formentera Tourist Office. ✉ *Estación Maritima s/n,* ☎ *971/322057.*

Beaches

★ Playa de Ses Illetes

BEACH | The closest beach to the port at La Savina is an exquisitely beautiful string of dunes stretching to the tip of the Trucador Peninsula at Es Pau. Collectively called Ses Illetes, they form part of a national park and are consistently voted by travel site contributors as among the five best beaches in the world. Ibiza clubbers like to take the fast ferry over from Eivissa after a long night and chill out here, tapping the sun for the energy to party again. The water is fairly shallow and the meadows of seagrass in it shelter colorful varieties of small fish; the fairly constant breezes are good for windsurfing. Nude and topless sunbathing raises no eyebrows anywhere along the dunes. Be warned: there's no shade here at all, and rented umbrellas fetch premium prices. **Amenities:** food and drink; lifeguards; showers; toilets; water sports. **Best for:** nudists; snorkeling; swimming; windsurfing. ✉ *La Savina* ✣ *4 km (2½ miles) north of La Savina.*

Hotels

Can Aisha

$$$$ | **B&B/INN** | With only five apartments, this converted stone farmhouse can feel like a family compound, especially when everyone is gathered on the sundeck or around the communal barbecue. **Pros:** kitchenettes with basic equipment; all apartments have private terraces; shops and restaurants nearby. **Cons:** often booked out; no kids and no pets; short season. [$] *Rooms from: €260* ✉ *Venda de Sa Punta 3205, Es Pujols* ☎ *616/654982* 🌐 *www.canaisha.com* 🕒 *Closed roughly Oct.–May* 🛏 *5 apartments* 🍴 *Free Breakfast.*

Casa Pacha

$$$$ | **HOTEL** | Legendary nightlife brand Pacha's hotel brings "barefoot simplicity and understated comfort" to Ibiza's laid-back sister island of Formentera. Situated right on Cala Migjorn—one of Europe's most beautiful beaches—this ultra-sophisticated spot seeks to capture the carefree spirit of the Balearics, encouraging visitors to unwind and recharge. The spacious rooms and suites have pared back, stylish interiors in neutral tones, with polished concrete floors and natural materials like wood and linen, creating a sense of tranquility. All have breath-taking sea views and feature either private ter-races or balconies. The beach restaurant invites guests to dine and drink with their toes in the sand, seated around wooden tables designed for sharing, connecting, and bringing people together. **Pros:** yoga classes overlooking the sea; unbeatable beachfront location; free parking. **Cons:** rather expensive; limited facilities nearby; minimum two-night stay in high season. $ *Rooms from: €510* ✉ *Camí es Arenals, Km.11, Formentor* ☎ *971/199366* ⊕ *casa-pacha.com* ⊙ *Closed Oct–May* ⦿ *Free Breakfast* ⇦ *14 rooms.*

🛍 Shopping

The island of Formentera has three main crafts markets: El Pilar, San Françesc Xavier, and Es Pujols. Stores and work-shops sell handmade items, including ceramics, jewelry, and leather goods. El Pilar's crafts market draws shoppers on Sunday and Wednesday from May to mid-October. May through mid-October, crafts are sold in the morning at the San Françesc Xavier market and in the evening in Es Pujols.

🏃 Activities

DIVING
Vell Marí

SCUBA DIVING | With more than 25 years' experience, Vell Marí is known for its diving courses ranging from beginners to advanced. ✉ *Puerto de la Savina, Marina de Formentera, Local 14–16, La Savina* ☎ *971/322105.*

Mallorca

Saddle-shape Mallorca is more than five times the size of Menorca or Ibiza. The Sierra de Tramuntana, a dramatic mountain range soaring to nearly 5,000 feet, runs the length of its northwest coast, and a ridge of hills borders the southeast shores; between the two lies a flat plain that in early spring becomes a sea of almond blossoms, the so-called snow of Mallorca. The island draws close to 14 million visitors a year, many of them bound for summer vacation packages in the coastal resorts. The beaches are beautiful, but save time for the charms of the northwest and the interior: caves, bird sanctuaries, monasteries and medie-val towns, local museums, outdoor cafés, and village markets.

GETTING HERE AND AROUND

From Barcelona, Palma de Mallorca is a 50-minute flight, an 8-hour overnight ferry, or a 4½-hour catamaran journey.

If you're traveling by car, Mallorca's main roads are well surfaced, and a four-lane, 25-km (15-mile) motorway penetrates deep into the island between Palma and Inca. The Vía Cintura, an efficient beltway, rings Palma. For destinations in the north and west, follow the "Andratx" and "Oeste" signs on the beltway; for the south and east, follow the "Este" signs. Driving in the mountains that parallel the northwest coast and descend to a cor-niche (cliff-side road) is a different matter; you'll be slowed not only by the narrow winding roads but also by tremendous views, tourist traffic, and groups of cyclists.

VISITOR INFORMATION

CONTACTS **Oficina de Turismo de Mallorca.** ✉ *Aeropuerto de Mallorca, Son Sant Joan s/n, Palma* ☎ *971/789556* ⊕ *www.infomallorca.net.*

Palma de Mallorca

If you look north of the cathedral (La Seu, or the seat of the bishopric, to Mallor-cans) on a map of the city of Palma, you can see around the Plaça Santa Eulàlia a jumble of tiny streets that made up the earliest settlement. Farther out, a ring of wide boulevards traces the fortifications built by the Moors to defend the larger city that emerged by the 12th century.

The zigzags mark the bastions that jutted out at regular intervals. By the end of the 19th century, most of the walls had been demolished; the only place where you can still see the massive defenses is at Ses Voltes, along the seafront west of the cathedral.

A *torrent* (streambed) used to run through the middle of the old city, dry for most of the year but often a raging flood in the rainy season. In the 17th century it was diverted to the east, along the moat that ran outside the city walls. Two of Palma's main arteries, La Rambla and the Passeig des Born, now follow the stream's natural course. The traditional evening paseo takes place on the bustling Born.

If you come to Palma by car, park in the garage beneath the Parc de la Mar (the ramp is just off the highway from the airport, as you reach the cathedral) and stroll along the park. Beside it run the huge bastions guarding the Palau Reial de l'Almudaina; the cathedral, golden and massive, rises beyond. Where you exit the garage, there's a **ceramic mural** by the late Catalan artist and Mallorca resident Joan Miró, facing the cathedral across the pool that runs the length of the park.

If you begin early enough, a walk along the ramparts at Ses Voltes from the mirador beside the cathedral is spectacular. The first rays of the sun turn the upper pinnacles of La Seu bright gold and then begin to work their way down the sandstone walls. From the Parc de la Mar, follow Avinguda Antoni Maura past the steps to the palace. Just below the Plaça de la Reina, where the **Passeig des Born** begins, turn left on Carrer de la Boteria into the Plaça de la Llotja. (If the Llotja itself is open, don't miss a chance to visit—it's the Mediterranean's finest Gothic-style civic building.) From there stroll through the Plaça Drassana to the **Museu d'Es Baluard,** at the end of Carrer Sant Pere. Retrace your steps to Avinguda Antoni Maura. Walk up the Passeig des Born to Plaça Joan Carles I, then right on Avenida de La Unió.

GETTING HERE AND AROUND

Palma's Empresa Municipal de Transports (EMT) runs 65 bus lines and a tourist train in and around the Mallorcan capital. Most buses leave from the Intermodal station, next to the Inca railroad terminus on the Plaça d'Espanya; city buses leave from the ground floor, while intercity buses leave from the underground level. The tourist office on the Plaça d'Espanya has schedules. Bus A1 connects the airport with the city center and the port; No. 2 circumnavigates the historic city center; No. 20 connect the city center with the Porto Pi commercial center; No. 46 goes to the Fundació Pilar i Joan Miró, and Bus A2 connects S'Arenal with the airport. The fare for a single local ride is €2; to the airport it's €5.

You can hire a horse-drawn carriage with driver at the bottom of the Born, and also on Avinguda Antonio Maura, in the nearby cathedral square, and on the Plaça d'Espanya, at the side farthest from the train station. A tour of the city costs €1 per hour (€30 for a half hour, €45 for 45 minutes, €60 for an hour).

Haggle firmly, and the driver might come down a bit off the posted fare.

Boats from Palma to neighboring beach resorts leave from the jetty opposite the Auditorium, on the Passeig Marítim. The tourist office has a schedule.

BUS INFORMATION Empresa Municipal de Transports. ⊠ *Calle Josep Anselm Clavé 5, Palma* ☎ *971/214444* ⊕ *www.emtpalma. cat.*

BUS STATION Estació Intermodal. ⊠ *Pl. d'Espanya s/n, Palma* ☎ *971/177777* ⊕ *www.tib.org.*

TAXI INFORMATION Radio-Taxi Ciutat. ⊠ *Francesc Sancho 7, Palma* ☎ *971/201212* ⊕ *www.radiotaxiciutat. com.*

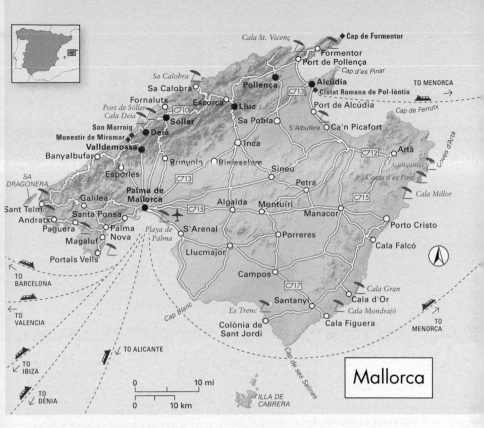

Mallorca

VISITOR INFORMATION

CONTACTS Oficine d'Informació Turística.
✉ *Pl. de la Reina 2, Palma* ☎ *971/173990*
🌐 *www.infomallorca.net.*

TOURS

City Sightseeing

The open-top City Sightseeing bus leaves
from behind the Palau de la Aludaina
every 20–25 minutes starting at 9:30
am and makes 20 stops throughout the
town, including La Rambla, the Passeig
Marítim, and the Castell de Bellver.
Tickets are valid for 24 or 48 hours, and
you can get on and off as many times as
you wish. All Palma tourist offices have
details. ✉ *Passeig Maritim 16, Palma*
🌐 *city-sightseeing-spain.com/en/25/pal-
ma-de-mallorca* 🎫 *From €18.*

👁 Sights

Ajuntament (*Town Hall*)
GOVERNMENT BUILDING | Along Carrer
Colom is the 17th-century *ajuntament*.
Stop in to see the collection of *gigantes*,
the huge painted and costumed manne-
quins paraded through the streets during
festivals, which are on display in the
lobby. The olive tree on the right side of
the square is one of Mallorca's so-called
olivos milenarios—purported to be
more than 1,000 years old. The adjacent
building is the Palau del Consell, the
headquarters of the island's government,
a late-19th-century building on the site
of a medieval prison. The *palau* (palace)
has its own collection of *gigantes* and
an impressive stained-glass window
over the ornate stone staircase; visits
inside can be arranged by appointment

Cathedral of Palma de Mallorca

(*visites@conselldemallorca.net*). ⊠ *Pl. Cort 1, Centro* ☎ *971/225900* ⊕ *www. palma.cat.*

Banys Arabs (*Arab Baths*)

RUINS | One of Palma's oldest monuments, the 10th-century public bathhouse has a wonderful walled garden of palms and lemon trees. In its day, it was not merely a place to bathe but a social institution where you could soak, relax, and gossip with your neighbors. ⊠ *Carrer Can Serra 7, Centro* ☎ *637/046534* ⊠ *€3.*

Bodega Antonio Nadal Ros (*Viñas de Son Roig*)

WINERY | Binissalem, about a half-hour drive (25 km [15 miles]) from Palma, is the center of one of the island's two D.O. registered wine regions and has a riotous harvest festival in mid-September, when surplus grapes are dumped by the truckload for participants to fling at each other. Some of Mallorca's best wineries are here, many of them open for tastings and tours. This winery is hard to find, but it's worth a detour, especially for its award-winning red Tres Uvas, a rich blend of Cabernet Sauvignon and Tempranillo, easy on the palate. It's open for tours and tastings, but call ahead on weekends. ⊠ *C. de Son Roig s/n, Binissalem* ☎ *630/914511* ⊕ *www.antonionadalros. com* ⊠ *From €25.*

Bodegas José Ferrer

WINERY | One of the largest of Mallorca's wineries, Bodegas José Ferrer can be visited for tastings. Ferrer wines consistently do well at international competitions in France and Germany; Pedra de Binissalem, their ecological red, is a subtle blend of Cabernet Sauvignon and the local varietal Manto Negro—well worth a try. ⊠ *Carrer del Conquistador 103, Binissalem* ☎ *971/151–1050* ⊕ *www. vinosferrer.com* ۞ *Closed Sun. Nov.–Feb.* ⊠ *From €11.*

Caixa Forum (*Grand Hotel*)

NOTABLE BUILDING | Built between 1901 and 1903 by Luis Domènech i Montaner, originator of Barcelona's Palau de la Música Catalana, this former hotel has an alabaster facade sculpted like a wedding cake, with floral motifs, angelic heads, and coats of arms. The original interiors are gone, however. The building is owned and used by the Fundació La Caixa, a cultural and social organization funded by the region's largest bank. Don't miss the permanent exhibit of paintings by the Mallorcan impressionist Hermenegildo Anglada Camarasa. ⊠ *Pl. Weyler 3, Centro* ☎ *971/178512* ⊕ *caixaforum.org/es/palma* 🖃 *€6* ⊘ *Closed Dec. 25–Jan. 6.*

Can Corbella
NOTABLE BUILDING | On the corner of Carrer de Jaume II is this gem of Palma's early Moderniste architecture, designed in the 1890s by Nicolás Lliteras. ⊠ *Pl. Cort, Centro.*

Can Forteza Rei
NOTABLE BUILDING | Designed by Lluís Forteza Rei in 1909, this Art Nouveau delight has twisted wrought-iron railings and surfaces inlaid with bits of polychrome tile which are signature touches of Antoni Gaudí and his contemporaries. A wonderful carved stone face in a painful grimace, flanked by dragons, ironically frames the stained-glass windows of a third-floor dental clinic. There's a chocolate shop on the ground floor. ⊠ *Pl. Marqués Palmer 1, Centro.*

Castell de Bellver (*Bellver Castle*)
NOTABLE BUILDING | Overlooking the city and the bay from a hillside, the castle was built at the beginning of the 14th century in Gothic style but with a circular design—the only one of its kind in Spain. It houses an archaeological museum of the history of Mallorca and a small collection of classical sculpture. The Bus Turistic 50 and the EMT municipal buses Nos. 4, 20, and 46 all stop a 20-minute walk from the entrance. In summer, there are classical music concerts in the courtyard, performed by the Ciutat de Palma Symphony Orchestra. ⊠ *Carrer de Camilo José Cela s/n, Palma* ☎ *971/735065, 971/225900 concerts box office* ⊕ *castelldebellver.palma.cat* ⊘ *Closed Mon.* 🖃 *€4 (free Sun.).*

★ Catedral de Majorca (*La Seu*)
CHURCH | Palma's cathedral is an architectural wonder that took almost 400 years to build. Begun in 1230, the wide expanse of the nave is supported by 14 70-foot-tall columns that fan out at the top like palm trees. The nave is dominated by an immense rose window, 40 feet in diameter, dating to 1370. Over the main altar (consecrated in 1346) is the surrealistic *baldoquí* (baldachin) by Antoni Gaudí, completed in 1912. This enormous canopy, with lamps suspended from it like elements of a mobile, rises to a Crucifixion scene at the top. To the right, in the Chapel of the Santísimo, is an equally remarkable 2007 work by the sculptor Miquel Barceló: a painted ceramic tableau covering the walls like a skin. Based on the New Testament account of the miracle of the loaves and fishes, it's a bizarre composition of rolling waves, gaping cracks, protruding fish heads, and human skulls. The **bell tower** above the cathedral's Plaça Almoina door holds nine bells, the largest of which is called N'Eloi, meaning "Praise." The 5-ton N'Eloi, cast in 1389, requires six men to ring it and has shattered stained-glass windows with its sound. From April through October you can take a guided tour of the bell tower and the cathedral's terraces overlooking panoramic views of the city. Reservations must be made in advance on the website. ⊠ *Pl. Almoina s/n, Centro* ☎ *971/723133* ⊕ *www.catedraldemallorca.org* 🖃 *€8* ⊘ *Closed for cultural visits all afternoons, Sun.*

★ Museu d'Es Baluard (*Museum of Modern and Contemporary Art of Palma*)
ART MUSEUM | West of the city center, this museum rises on a long-neglected archaeological site, parts of which date back to the 12th century. The building itself is an outstanding convergence of old and new: the exhibition space uses the surviving 16th-century perimeter walls of the fortified city, including a stone courtyard facing the sea and a promenade along the ramparts. There are

Illa de Cabrera

Off the south coast of Mallorca, this verdant isle is one of the last unspoiled places in the Mediterranean—the largest of the 19 islands that make up the Cabrera Archipelago. To protect its dramatic landscape, varied wildlife, and lush vegetation, it was declared a national park in 1991. Throughout its history, Cabrera has had its share of visitors, from the Romans to the Arabs. Today, the only intact historical remains are those of a 14th-century castle overlooking the harbor. Tours are operated daily by the Marcabrera company (www.marcabrera.com). Boats depart from Colònia Sant Jordi, 47 km (29 miles) southeast of Palma. Full-day trips, starting at 10 and returning at 3, with a stop to swim or snorkel in the Cueva Azul (Blue Cave), start from €450; two-hour excursions by speedboat, leaving three times a day, are €49.

three floors of galleries, and the collection includes work by Miró, Picasso, and Antoni Tàpies, among other major artists. The courtyard café–terrace Es Baluard (no dinner Sunday–Wednesday October–mid-June) affords a fine view of the marina. To get here, take the narrow Carrer de Sant Pere through the old fishermen's quarter, from Plaça de la Drassana. ⊠ *Pl. Porta de Santa Catalina 10, Palma* ☎ *971/908200* ⊕ *www.esbaluard.org/en* ✉ *€6* ⊘ *Closed Mon.*

Museu Fundació Pilar y Joan Miró (*Pilar and Joan Miró Foundation Museum*)
ART MUSEUM | The permanent collection here includes a great many drawings and studies by the Catalan artist, who spent his last years on Mallorca, but it exhibits far fewer finished paintings and sculptures than the Fundació Miró in Barcelona. While the exhibits are fairly limited, the setting and views of Palma alone are worth taking the detour. ⊠ *Saridakis 29, Palma* ☎ *971/701420* ⊕ *www.miromallorca.com* ✉ *€9* ⊘ *Closed Mon.*

Museu Fundación Juan March
ART MUSEUM | A few steps from the north archway of the Plaça Major is the Museu Fundación Juan March. This fine little museum was established to display what had been a private collection of modern Spanish art. The building itself was a sumptuous private home built in the 18th century. The second and third floors were redesigned to accommodate a series of small galleries, with one or two works at most—by Pablo Picasso, Joan Miró, Juan Gris, Salvador Dalí, Antoni Tàpies, and Miquel Barceló, among others—on each wall. ⊠ *Sant Miquel 11, Centro* ☎ *971/713515* ⊕ *www.march.es/arte/palma* ✉ *Free* ⊘ *Closed Sun.*

Palau Reial de l'Almudaina (*Royal Palace of La Almudaina*)
CASTLE/PALACE | Opposite Palma's cathedral, this palace was originally an Arab citadel, then became the residence of the ruling house during the Middle Ages. It's now a military headquarters and the king's official residence when he is in Mallorca. Guided tours generally depart hourly during open hours and cost €2. Try to catch the changing of the Honor Guard ceremony, which takes place in front of the palace at noon on the last Saturday of the month (except July and August). ⊠ *Carrer Palau Reial s/n, Centro* ☎ *97/121–4134* ⊕ *www.patrimonionacional.es/visita/palacio-real-de-la-almudaina* ⊘ *Closed Mon.* ✉ *€7 (Free Wed. and Sun. afternoons).*

Passeig des Born
PROMENADE | While it's known as one of the best streets in Palma to hit the shops, this tree-lined promenade is also a favored place to *pasear* (stroll), lined with palatial-style stone residences (most of which have now been converted into hotels and shops) and busy café-terraces. Bar Bosch, straddling Passeig des Born and Plaça Rei Joan Carles I, has been a key gathering point for locals since 1936. ⊠ *Palma.*

Plaça Major
PLAZA/SQUARE | A crafts market fills this elegant neoclassical space 10–2 on Monday, Tuesday, Friday, and Saturday mornings during most of the year. Until 1838, this was the local headquarters of the Inquisition. A flight of steps on the east side of the Plaça Major leads down to Las Ramblas, a pleasant promenade lined with flower stalls. ⊠ *Centro.*

Sa Llotja (*Exchange*)
NOTABLE BUILDING | On the seafront west of the Plaça de la Reina, the 15th-century Llotja connects via an interior courtyard to the Consolat de Mar (Maritime Consulate). With its decorative turrets, pointed battlements, fluted pillars, and Gothic stained-glass windows—part fortress, part church—it attests to the wealth Mallorca achieved in its heyday as a Mediterranean trading power. The interior (the Merchants' Chamber) often hosts free art exhibitions. ⊠ *Pl. Llotja 5, Palma* 🖼 *Free* ⊙ *Closed Mon.*

Sant Francesc
CHURCH | The 13th-century monastery church of Sant Francesc was established by Jaume II when his eldest son took monastic orders and gave up rights to the throne. Fra Junípero Serra, the missionary who founded San Francisco, California, was later educated here; his statue stands to the left of the main entrance. The basilica houses the tomb of eminent 13th-century scholar Ramón Llull. The cloisters (enter via the side door, on the right) are especially

Cuevas del Drach

Mallorca's "Dragon Caves" are four large caves that reach a depth of 80 feet below the surface, one of the largest underground lakes in the world, and a dazzling array of stalagmites and stalactites that form identifiable shapes such as the Virgin of the Cave, the Buddha, and the Valley of Montserrat. The hour-long tour includes a visit to the caves, an optional boat trip across Lake Martel, and a short classical music concert performed on the lake by musicians in an illuminated boat. For more info check ⊕ *www.cuevasdeldrach.com/en.*

beautiful and peaceful. The €5 entrance fee includes entrance to five other churches. ⊠ *Pl. Sant Francesc 7, Centro* ☎ *971/712695* ⊕ *www.spiritualmallorca.com* 🖼 *€5* ⊙ *Closed Sun.*

Santa Eulàlia
CHURCH | Carrer de la Cadena leads to this imposing Gothic church, where, in 1435, 200 Jews were forced to convert to Christianity after their rabbis were threatened with being burned at the stake. ⊠ *Pl. Santa Eulalia 2, Centro* ☎ *971/714625* 🖼 *Free.*

Teatre Principal
NOTABLE BUILDING | Take time to appreciate the neoclassical symmetry of this theater, Palma's chief venue for classical music. The opera season here usually runs mid-March–June. ⊠ *Carrer de la Riera 2, Centro* ☎ *971/219700 information, 971/219696 tickets* ⊕ *teatreprincipal.com* 🖼 *Performances vary.*

Beaches

Es Trenc

BEACH | FAMILY | Even though it's nearly an hour's drive from Palma, this pristine 2-km (1-mile) stretch of fine white sand on Mallorca's southern coast, much longer than it is wide, is one of the most popular beaches on the island—arrive late on a Saturday or Sunday in summer, and you'll be hard-pressed to find a space to stretch out. At times the water can be a bit choppy, and there are occasional patches of seaweed—but otherwise the clear, clean water slopes off gently from the shore for some 30 feet, making it ideal for families with younger kids. Es Trenc is in a protected natural area free of hotels and other developments, which makes for good bird-watching. Naturists lay their claim to part of the beach's eastern end. **Amenities:** food and drink; lifeguards; parking (fee); toilets. **Best for:** nudists; partiers; swimming; walking. ✉ *MA6040, Colònia de Sant Jordi* ✥ *10 km (6 miles) south of Campos, 6½ km (4 miles) east of Colònia Sant Jordi.*

Restaurants

★ Adrian Quetglas Restaurant

$$$$ | SPANISH | Adrián Quetglas, an Argentinian-born chef of Mallorcan descent, cooked in some of the finest kitchens in London, Paris, and Moscow, before he returned to Mallorca in 2015 to launch this solo venture. Despite having been awarded a Michelin star, Quetglas remains committed to the "democratization" of fine dining, and to deliver the pleasure of high-end gastronomy to a wider audience. **Known for:** lunchtime tasting menu only €35; emerging Michelin-starred chef; accessible fine dining. [$] *Average main: €60* ✉ *Passeig de Mallorca 20, Centro* ☎ *971/781119* 🌐 *adrianquetglas.es* 🕒 *Closed Sun. and Mon.*

Botànic

$$$ | MEDITERRANEAN | In the leafy garden of the Can Bordoy boutique hotel, Botànic is a plant-forward restaurant that also features locally sourced meat and fish. The menu is inspired by the cuisines of Southeast Asia, the Middle East, and Mexico, but firmly rooted in Mediterranean flavors. **Known for:** lovely patio; seasonal, local produce; healthy and flavor-packed dishes. [$] *Average main: €18* ✉ *Forn de la Glória 14, Centro* ☎ *871/871202* 🌐 *canbordoy.com/botanic.*

★ DINS Santi Taura

$$$$ | CATALAN | Local culinary wunderkind Santi Taura is using his eponymous restaurant in the El Llorenç Parc de la Mar hotel to explore historical recipes of the island, served in an ultra-chic, contemporary setting. Some of the most emblematic dishes include *p anada de peix de roca*, a "Mallorcan dim sum" of rock fish pie believed to be one of the oldest recipes on the island, and a dish of rabbit with lobster , which combines the sea and the mountains. **Known for:** traditional Mallorcan rock fish pie; local Michelin-starred chef; bar seating lets you see the chef at work. [$] *Average main: €30* ✉ *Pl. de Llorenç Villalonga 4, Centro* ☎ *656/738214* 🌐 *www.dinssantitaura.com.*

Forn de Sant Joan

$$$$ | MEDITERRANEAN | This former bakery turned restaurant (*forn* means "bakery" or "oven" in Mallorquin) dates back to the 19th century and features exposed brick walls, colorful floor tiles, modern art on the walls, and picture-perfect Mediterranean-style tapas. There's a cocktail bar on the ground floor that overlooks the street, and one of the three distinct dining areas is the area where bread dough was once prepared. **Known for:** cocktail bar; elevated tapas and Mediterranean dishes; former 19th-century bakery. [$] *Average main: €25* ✉ *Carrer de Sant Joan 4, Palma* ☎ *971/728422* 🌐 *www.forndesantjoan.com.*

Coffee and Quick Bites

Café La Lonja (*Sa Llotja*)

$ | TAPAS | A great spot for hot chocolate or a unique tea or coffee, this is a classic spot in the old fishermen's neighborhood. Both the sunny terrace in front and the bar inside are excellent places for drinks and sandwiches. **Known for:** coffee and snacks; a great pit stop; terrace with views of the Llotja. $ *Average main: €9* ✉ *Carrer Sa Lonja del Mar 2, Palma* ☎ *971971/722799* ⊕ *cafelalonja.com* ⊘ *Closed Mon.*

🛏 Hotels

★ Calatrava

$$$$ | HOTEL | FAMILY | In a 19th-century building on a quiet square in the Old Town, Calatrava is one of the many historic buildings that have been converted into elegant boutique hotels in recent years. **Pros:** drinks and breakfast served on the rooftop with sea views; great Old Town location; spacious rooms. **Cons:** arriving by car is tricky and parking is expensive; no pool or gym; limited breakfast options. $ *Rooms from: €320* ✉ *Pl. de Llorenç Villalonga 8, Centro* ☎ *971/728110* ⊕ *www.boutiquehotelcalatrava.com/en* ⍢ *Free Breakfast* ⍩ *16 rooms.*

★ Cap Rocat

$$$$ | HOTEL | What was once a 19th-century military fortress has been converted into one of Mallorca's—and arguably Europe's—most distinctive hotels, on a rocky outcrop some 25 minutes from Palma. **Pros:** impeccable service; stunning backdrop; superb cuisine. **Cons:** isolated from the bustle—and nightlife; sky-high prices; lacks a sandy beach. $ *Rooms from: €500* ✉ *Ctra. de Enderrocat s/n, Cala Blava* ☎ *971/747878* ⊕ *www.caprocat.com* ⊘ *Closed Nov.–mid-Mar.* ⍩ *30 rooms* ⍢ *Free Breakfast.*

Castillo Hotel Son Vida

$$$$ | HOTEL | This lovely hotel in a 13th-century estate is about a 10-minute drive from Palma, with a number of golf courses in the vicinity. **Pros:** outstanding service; set in a quiet green area but still close to Palma; heaven for golfers. **Cons:** eating off-site requires a cab ride or a rental car; rooms are a little dated; adults only. $ *Rooms from: €345* ✉ *Carrer de Raixa 2, Urbanización Son Vida, Ponent* ☎ *971/493493* ⊕ *www.castillohotelsonvida.com* ⍩ *164 rooms* ⍢ *Free Breakfast.*

★ El Llorenç Parc de la Mar

$$$$ | HOTEL | Recent years have seen a number of high-end boutique hotels opening in Palma de Mallorca, none more fabulous than El Llorenç Parc de la Mar. The setting, on a quiet square in the historic Calatrava neighborhood, is ideal for exploring the prettiest parts of Palma on foot. **Pros:** personalized service; incredible split-level rooftop terrace; Michelin-starred restaurant. **Cons:** adults only; tricky to get to by car; rooms on the small side. $ *Rooms from: €325* ✉ *Pl. de Llorenç Villalonga 4, Centro* ☎ *971/677770* ⊕ *www.elllorenc.com/en* ⍢ *No Meals* ⍩ *33 rooms.*

Finca Serena

$$$$ | HOTEL | Rural retreats don't get much more chic or more beautiful than Finca Serena. **Pros:** very relaxing; rural-chic charm; lovely pool area. **Cons:** service can be a bit wobbly; extremely pricey; watch out for creepy-crawlies. $ *Rooms from: €620* ✉ *Ma-3200, Km 3, Manacor* ☎ *971/181858* ⊕ *www.fincaserenamallorca.com/en* ⍢ *Free Breakfast* ⍩ *25 rooms.*

Hostal Apuntadores

$$ | HOTEL | A favorite among budget travelers, this lodging in the heart of the old town, within strolling distance of the bustling Passeig des Born, has a rooftop terrace with what is arguably the city's best view—overlooking the cathedral and the sea. **Pros:** some rooms have balconies; rooms have a/c and heat; good

value. **Cons:** the cheapest rooms share bathrooms; can be noisy; basic decor. [$] *Rooms from: €105* ✉ *Carrer Apuntadores 8, Centro* ☎ *971/713491* 🌐 *www.apuntadoreshostal.com* 🛏 *28 rooms* 🍴 *No Meals.*

★ M House

$$$$ | HOTEL | With an enviable location in Palma's old town, close to the cathedral and some of the best shopping in the city, M House is a true urban oasis. **Pros:** private parking available for €12/day; trendy vibe; personalized service. **Cons:** very tight parking spots; small swimming pool; not all rooms have a terrace. [$] *Rooms from: €245* ✉ *Carrer de Can Maçanet 1A, Centro* ☎ *971/214848* 🌐 *www.mhousehotel.com* 🛏 *37 rooms.*

🍸 Nightlife

Mallorca's nightlife is never hard to find. Many of the hot spots are concentrated 6 km (4 miles) west of Palma at **Punta Portals,** in Portals Nous, where the royal yacht is moored when former king Juan Carlos I comes to Mallorca in early August for the Copa del Rey international regatta. Another major area is **Avinguda Gabriel Roca.** This section of the Passeig Marítim holds many taverns, pubs, and clubs. The network of streets in the old town, around Carrer Apuntadores, is also prime barhopping territory.

BARS AND CAFÉS

★ Bar Abaco

BARS | The over-the-top baroque exuberance of this bar sets it far apart from its setting in an otherwise unfunky, old neighborhood. There are urns and baskets of fresh flowers and fruit tumbling out on to the floor, stone pillars and vaulted ceilings, tall candles, and ambient opera music. Be warned: Abaco's signature cocktails are pricey. ✉ *Carrer de Sant Joan 1, Palma* ☎ *971/714939* 🌐 *www.bar-abaco.es.*

Carrer Apuntadores

GATHERING PLACES | On the west side of Passeig des Born in the old town, this street is lined with casual bars and cafés that appeal to night owls in their twenties and thirties. On the weekend, you can often come across impromptu live rock and pop acts performed on small stages. ✉ *Palma.*

Plaça de la Llotja

GATHERING PLACES | This square, along with the surrounding streets, is the place to go for *copas* (drinking, tapas sampling, and general carousing). ✉ *Palma.*

★ Wineing

WINE BARS | Tucked down Calle Apuntadores, Wineing is a great place to try wines from across the island and beyond. There's a credit-card-operated system that dispenses small tastings (or larger glasses, if you feel inclined), plus a menu of tapas, cheese platters, and grilled meats for sharing. ✉ *Calle Apuntadores 24, Palma* ☎ *971/214011* 🌐 *www.wineing.es.*

DANCE CLUBS

Tito's

DANCE CLUBS | Outdoor elevators transport you from the street to the dance floor at the sleek and futuristic Tito's. ✉ *Passeig Marítim, Av. Gabriel Roca 31, Palma* ☎ *971/730017* 🌐 *www.titosmallorca.com.*

🛍 Shopping

Mallorca's specialties are shoes and leather clothing, utensils carved from olive wood, porcelain and handblown glass, and artificial pearls. Look for designer fashions on the **Passeig des Born** and for antiques on **Costa de la Pols,** a narrow little street near the Plaça Riera. The **Plaça Major** has a modest crafts market on Monday, Tuesday, Friday, and Saturday 10–2. During summer, there's a crafts market on the seafront at Sa Llotja. Palma has a range of food markets, including Mercat Oliva, where you can browse stalls piled high with local produce, meat, and fish. At the San Juan Gastronomic Market there is street-style food, cocktails, and wine in an impressive Moderniste building, constructed in the 1900s.

Many of Palma's best shoe shops are on Avenida Rei Jaime III, between the Plaça Joan Carles I and the Passeig Mallorca.

FOOD
Colmado Santo Domingo

FOOD | This is a wonderful little shop for the artisanal food specialties of Mallorca: sobrasada of black pork, sausages of all sorts, cheeses, jams, and honeys and preserves. ✉ *Carrer Santo Domingo 1, Centro* ☎ *971/714887* ⊕ *www.colmadosantodomingo.com* ⊙ *Closed Fri.–Sun.*

GLASS AND CERAMICS
Gordiola

GLASSWARE | Glassmakers since 1719, Gordiola has a factory showroom in Algaida, on the Palma–Manacor road, where you can watch the glass being blown and even try your hand at making a piece. ✉ *Ctra. Palma–Manacor, Km 19, Algaida* ☎ *971/665046* ⊕ *www.gordiola.com* ⊙ *Closed Sun.*

MARKETS
Mercat de Sineu

MARKET | The island's biggest market takes place every Wednesday, 8 am to 1:30 pm, in the town of Sineu, 34 km (21 miles) east of Palma. The market, among the island's oldest, dates back to the 14th century, when livestock was auctioned—a practice that continues to this day. Come early if you want to see the auction, which takes place in and around the main square. Local crafts and produce, plants and flowers, clothing, and leather goods are traded throughout the village along the labyrinth of narrow streets, which can get very busy. ✉ *Pl. Es Fossar.*

SHOES AND LEATHER GOODS
Alpargatería La Concepción

SHOES | Mallorca's most popular footwear is the simple, comfortable slip-on espadrille (usually with a leather front over the first half of the foot and a strap across the back of the ankle). Look for a pair here. ✉ *Carrer de la Concepción 17, Palma* ☎ *971/710709* ⊕ *www.zapateriamallorca.com* ⊙ *Closed Sun.*

Lottusse

LEATHER GOODS | Shop here for high-end shoes, leather coats, and accessories. ✉ *Av. Jaume III 2, Palma* ☎ *971/710203* ⊕ *www.lottusse.com* ⊙ *Closed Sun.*

 Activities

BALLOONING
Majorca Balloons

BALLOONING | For spectacular views of the island, float up in a hot-air balloon, which lifts off daily, weather permitting, at sunrise and sunset. Call for a reservation. ✉ *C. Farallo 4, Manacor* ☎ *971/596969* ⊕ *www.mallorcaballoons.com* ✈ *1-hr flights from €165 per person.*

BICYCLING

With long, flat stretches and heart-pounding climbs, Mallorca's 675 km (420 miles) of rural roads adapted for cycling make the sport the most popular on the island; many European professional teams train here. Tourist-board offices have excellent leaflets on bike routes with maps, details about the terrain, sights, and distances. The companies below can rent you bikes for exploring Palma and environs.

Embat Ciclos

BIKING | Some 10 km (6 miles) from the city center, on the beach in Platja de Palma, Embat has everything from standard touring bikes to mountains bikes, tandem bikes, and electric bikes for rent and can assist with organizing tours of the island. ✉ *Bartolomé Riutort 27, Can Pastilla* ☎ *971/492358* ⊕ *www.embatciclos.com.*

Palma on Bike

BIKING | This bike-rental shop, just below the Plaça de la Reina in Palma, is open daily and also organizes tours. ✉ *Av. Antoni Maura 10, Centro* ☎ *971/718062* ⊕ *www.palmaonbike.com.*

BIRD-WATCHING

Mallorca has two notable nature reserves: Sa Dragonera and S'Albufera de Mallorca.

Sa Dragonera

BIRD WATCHING | This island and its large colony of sea falcons are accessible by boat from Sant Elm, at the western tip of Mallorca. The boats, run by the operator Cruceros Margarita, leave from the port of Sant Elm with several sailings a day, mainly in the mornings. ✉ *Sant Elm* ☎ *639/617545 for Cruceros Margarita* ⊕ *www.crucerosmargarita.com* ✉ *Boat €15.*

S'Albufera de Mallorca

BIRD WATCHING | This is the largest wetlands zone in Mallorca. ✉ *Ctra. Port d'Alcúdia–Ca'n Picafort, Alcúdia* ☎ *97171/177639* ⊕ *en.balearsnatura. com/parque_natural/parc-natural-de-sal-bufera-de-mallorca* ☞ *Stop at Centre de Recepció (Reception Center) sa Roca for permission to enter park.*

GOLF

Mallorca has more than 20 18-hole golf courses, among them PGA championship venues of fiendish difficulty. The Federación Balear de Golf (Balearic Golf Federation) can provide more information.

Canyamel Golf

GOLF | This club, some 64 km (40 miles) from Palma, at the far eastern tip of the island, has wonderful views of the sea. Fans of the club say the 475-yard 13th hole (par 5) is a heartbreaker. ✉ *Av. d'Es Cap Vermell s/n, Capdepera* ☎ *971/841313* ⊕ *www.canyamelgolf.com* ✉ *€83–€105 for 18 holes, depending on the season* ⚐ *18 holes, 6562 yards, par 73.*

★ Golf Alcanada

GOLF | This 18-hole course, designed by Robert Trent Jones Jr., is widely regarded as the best club on the island, with spectacular views of the bay and lighthouse. ✉ *Ctra. del Faro s/n, Alcúdia* ☎ *971/549560* ⊕ *www.golf-alcanada. com/en* ✉ *From €105 for 18 holes, from €62 for 9 holes (depending on season)* ⚐ *18 holes, 7107 yards, par 72.*

HIKING

Mallorca is excellent for hiking. In the Sierra de Tramuntana, you can easily arrange to trek one way and take a boat, bus, or train back. Ask the tourist office for the free booklet *20 Hiking Excursions on the Island of Mallorca*, with detailed maps and itineraries.

Grup Excursionista de Majorca (*Mallorcan Hiking Association*)

HIKING & WALKING | This association can provide hiking information. ✉ *Carrer dels Horts 1,* ☎ *971/718823* ⊕ *www. gemweb.org.*

SAILING

Cruesa Majorca Yacht Charter

SAILING | A wide range of yachts, cruisers, and catamarans are available for rent here, by the day or the week. In high season, only full-week rentals from Saturday to Friday are available. ✉ *Avenida Antonio Maura 18, Palma* ☎ *971/282821* ⊕ *www. cruesa.com/en* ✉ *From €900 per week.*

Federación Balear de Vela (*Balearic Sailing Federation*)

SAILING | For information on sailing, contact the federation. ✉ *Edificio Palma Arena, Av. Uruguay s/n, Palma* ☎ *971/402412* ⊕ *www.federacionbalearvela.org.*

SCUBA DIVING

Big Blue

SCUBA DIVING | This dive center, next to the Alua Hawaii hotel on the beach boardwalk in Palmanova, offers PADI-certified courses for beginners (€269), including two dives with full equipment (tanks, wet suits, regulators, masks, and fins). ✉ *Carrer Martin Ros Garcia*

Mallorca is a popular place for cyclists, and many European professionals train here.

6, Palmanova ☎ *971/681686* ⊕ *www.bigbluediving.net.*

TENNIS

Tennis is very popular here—the more so for world champion Rafael Nadal being a Mallorcan. There are courts at many hotels and private clubs, and tennis schools as well. The Federació de Tennis de les Illes Balears (Balearics Tennis Federation) can provide information about playing in the area.

Federació de Tennis de les Illes Balears
(*Balearic Tennis Federation*)
TENNIS | The Balearic Tennis Federation (FTIB) provides information about tennis in Mallorca, Menorca, Ibiza, and Formentera, where a wide range of clubs combine tennis and leisure activities for everything from beginners to professional players, as well as for families.
⊠ *Edificio Palma Arena, Calle Uruguay s/n, Palma* ☎ *971/720956* ⊕ *www.ftib.es/es/welcome.*

Valldemossa

18 km (11 miles) north of Palma.

The jumping-off point for a drive up the spectacular coast of the Tramuntana, this pretty little town, north of Palma, is famous for the vast complex of the Reial Cartuja monastery. Surrounded by natural beauty and stunning views, it was also here where Chopin spent the winter of 1838 with George Sand. As most tourists tend to bus in during the day for a few hours and leave, it is worth spending an evening in Valldemossa to soak up the true atmosphere of this beautiful village. At sundown, the quiet streets and *plaças* are a delight to wander through, flanked by sandy stone houses with green shutters and overflowing plant pots. A classical music festival paying tribute to Chopin (among other composers) is held every August, with most performances taking place in the Reial Cartuja monastery.

GETTING HERE AND AROUND
Valldemossa is a 20-minute drive from Palma on the MA1130. Regular bus service from the Plaça d'Espanya in Palma gets you to Valldemossa in about a half hour.

VISITOR INFORMATION
CONTACTS Valldemossa Tourist Office. ✉ *Av. de Palma 7, Valldemossa* ☎ *971/612019.*

Sights

★ **Cartoixa de Valldemossa** (*Royal Carthusian Monastery*)
NOTABLE BUILDING | Originally built as a palace in 1309, the monastery was founded in 1399, but after the monks were expelled in 1835, it acquired a new lease on life by offering apartments to travelers. The most famous lodgers were Frédéric Chopin and his lover, the Baroness Amandine Dupin, the French novelist better known by her pseudonym, George Sand. The two spent three difficult months here in the cold, damp winter of 1838–39. In the church, note the frescoes above the nave—the monk who painted them was Goya's brother-in-law. The pharmacy, made by the monks in 1723, is almost completely preserved. A long corridor leads to the apartments, furnished in period style, occupied by Chopin and Sand (the piano is original). Nearby, another set of apartments houses the local museum, with mementos of Archduke Luis Salvador and a collection of old printing blocks. From here you return to the ornately furnished King Sancho's palace, a group of rooms originally built by King Jaume II for his son. The tourist office, in Valldemossa's main plaza, sells a ticket good for all of the monastery's attractions. ✉ *Pl. de la Cartuja s/n, Valldemossa* ☎ *971/612106* 🌐 *www.cartoixadevalldemossa.com/en* 🎫 *€9.50* 🕒 *Closed Sun.*

Hotels

★ **Mirabó de Valldemossa**
$$$$ | **B&B/INN** | At the far end of a winding dirt road in the hills overlooking the Reial Cartuja, across the valley of Valldemossa, this luxurious little agroturismo is a romantic hideaway that's hard to reach and even harder to tear yourself away from. **Pros:** incredible views; friendly personal service; peace and quiet. **Cons:** no gym or spa; no restaurants nearby; those low stone doorways can be a headache. [$] *Rooms from: €330* ✉ *Ctra. Valldemossa, Km 16, Valldemossa* ☎ *661/285215* 🌐 *mirabo.es/en* 🛏 *9 rooms* 🍴 *Free Breakfast.*

Deià

9 km (5½ miles) southwest of Sóller.

Deià is perhaps best known as the adopted home of the English poet and writer Robert Graves, who lived here off and on from 1929 until his death in 1985. His grave can be found in the small cemetery at the top of the village. Deià is still a favorite haunt of writers and artists, including Graves's son Tomás, author of *Pa amb Oli* (*Bread and Olive Oil*), a guide to Mallorcan cooking, and British painter David Templeton. Ava Gardner lived here for a time; so, briefly, did Picasso. The setting is unbeatable—all around Deià rise the steep cliffs of the Sierra de Tramuntana. There's live jazz on summer evenings, and on warm afternoons literati gather at the beach bar in the rocky cove at Cala de Deià, 2 km (1 mile) downhill from the village. Walk up the narrow street to the village church; the small **cemetery** behind it affords views of mountains terraced with olive trees and of the coves below. It's a fitting spot for Graves's final resting place, in a quiet corner.

About 4 km (2½ miles) west of Deià is **Son Marroig,** a former estate of Austrian archduke Luis Salvador (1847–1915), which is now preserved as a museum, with a lovely garden and stunning coastal views. If you're driving, the best way to reach Son Marroig is the twisty MA10.

GETTING HERE AND AROUND

The Palma–Port de Sóller bus (€4.35) passes through Deià six times daily in each direction Monday–Saturday, five times on Sunday. Taxis to Deià from Palma cost €45 by day, €50 at night; from the airport the fares are €50/€55, and from Sóller €22/€24. Intrepid hikers can walk from Deià through the mountains to Sóller, on a trail of moderate difficulty, in about 2½ hours.

◉ Sights

Ca N'Alluny (*La Casa de Robert Graves*)

HISTORIC HOME | The Fundació Robert Graves opened this museum dedicated to Deià's most famous resident in the house he built in 1932. The seaside house is something of a shrine: Graves's furniture and books, personal effects, and the press he used to print many of his works are all preserved. ✉ *Ctra. Deià-Sóller s/n, Deià* ☎ *971/636185* ⊕ *www.lacasaderobertgraves.org/en* ✉ *€7* ⊗ *Closed Sun.*

Monestir de Miramar

VIEWPOINT | On the road south from Deià to Valldemossa, this monastery was founded in 1276 by Ramón Llull, who established a school of Asian languages here. It was bought in 1872 by the Archduke Luis Salvador and restored as a mirador. Explore the garden and the tiny cloister, then walk through the olive groves to a spectacular lookout. ✉ *Diseminado Miramar 1, Ctra. Deià-Valldemossa (MA10), Km 67, Deià* ☎ *971/616073* ⊕ *www.monestirdemiramar.es* ✉ *€4* ⊗ *Closed Sun.*

Son Marroig

HISTORIC HOME | This estate belonged to Austrian archduke Luis Salvador, who arrived here as a young man and fell in love with the place. He acquired huge tracts of land along the northwestern coast, building miradores at the most spectacular points but otherwise leaving the pristine beauty intact. Below the mirador, you can see Sa Foradada, a rock peninsula pierced by a huge archway, where the archduke moored his yacht. Now a museum, the estate house contains the archduke's collections of Mediterranean pottery and ceramics, Mallorcan furniture, and paintings. The garden is especially fine. From May through September, the Deià International Festival holds classical concerts here. ✉ *Ctra. Deià–Valldemossa (MA10), Km 65, Deià* ☎ *971/639158* ⊕ *www.sonmarroig.com* ✉ *€4* ⊗ *Closed Sun.*

Beaches

Cala Deia

BEACH | Encircled by high pine-topped cliffs, this rocky cove connects to various coastal walking paths as well as a narrow road that twists its way down from the village. Year-round, clear turquoise water makes it great for snorkeling and swims. The popular Ca's Patro March restaurant, hewn into the rocks, overhangs the sea and stirring views. Book a table at the water's edge well in advance; it's often booked out days or even weeks in advance. There is also a simple beach bar. **Best for:** swimming, snorkeling. ✉ *Cala Deia, Deià.*

🛏 Hotels

★ Belmond La Residencia

$$$$ | **HOTEL** | **FAMILY** | Built around two 16th-century manor houses, with additional buildings blending with the lush surroundings, this exceptional hotel is superbly furnished with

Mallorcan antiques, modern canvases, and canopied four-poster beds. **Pros:** in-house art gallery; impossibly picturesque surroundings; private shuttle to the beach. **Cons:** tricky to navigate for those with reduced mobility; extremely pricey; quite far from the beach. [$] *Rooms from: €944* ✉ *Son Canals s/n, Deià* ☎ *971/639011* 🌐 *www.belmond.com* 🛏 *71 rooms, 1 villa* 🍴 *Free Breakfast.*

★ Hotel Es Molí

$$$$ | **HOTEL** | A converted 17th-century manor house in the hills above the valley of Deià, this peaceful hotel is known for its traditional sense of luxury. **Pros:** chamber music concerts twice a week during the summer; attentive service; heated pool with spacious terrace. **Cons:** short season; steep climb to annex rooms; three-night minimum for some stays in high season. [$] *Rooms from: €297* ✉ *Ctra. Valldemossa–Deià s/n, Deià* ☎ *971/639000* 🌐 *www.esmoli.com* 🕒 *Closed Nov.–Mar.* 🛏 *87 rooms* 🍴 *Free Breakfast.*

s'Hotel D'es Puig

$$ | **B&B/INN** | **FAMILY** | This family-run "hotel on the hill" has a back terrace with a lemon-tree garden and a wonderful view of the mountains. **Pros:** private parking for guests; peaceful setting; two pools (one heated). **Cons:** three-night minimum in high season; public spaces can feel a bit cramped; books out quickly. [$] *Rooms from: €99* ✉ *Carrer d'es Puig 4, Deià* ☎ *971/639409, 637/820805* 🌐 *www.hoteldespuig.com* 🕒 *Closed Dec. and Jan.* 🛏 *14 rooms* 🍴 *Free Breakfast.*

Sóller

13 km (8 miles) north of Jardins d'Alfàbia, 30 km (19 miles) north of Palma.

All but the briefest visits to Mallorca should include at least an overnight stay in Sóller, one of the most beautiful towns on the island, with palatial homes built in the 19th and early 20th centuries by the landowners and merchants who thrived on the export of the region's oranges, lemons, and almonds. Many of the buildings here, like the **Church of Sant Bartomeu** and the **Bank of Sóller,** on the Plaça Constitució, and the nearby **Can Prunera,** are gems of the Moderniste style, designed by contemporaries of Antoni Gaudí. The tourist information office in the **town hall,** next to Sant Bartomeu, has a walking-tour map of the important sites.

GETTING HERE AND AROUND

You can travel in retro style from Palma to Sóller on one of the six daily trains (four daily in February, March, November, and December; €25 round-trip) operated by Ferrocarril de Sóller, which depart from Plaça d'Espanya. With a string of wooden rail cars with leather-covered seats dating to 1912, the train trundles along for about an hour, making six stops along the 27-km (17-mile) route; the scenery gets lovely—especially at Bunyola and the Mirador Pujol—as you approach the peaks of the Tramuntana. From the train station in Sóller, a charming old trolley car, called the Tranvía de Sóller, threads its way down through town to the Port de Sóller. The fare is €7 each way. You can also buy a combination round-trip ticket for the train and the trolley for €32. The mountain road between Palma and Sóller is spectacular—lemon and olive trees on stone-walled terraces, farmhouses perched on the edges of forested cliffs—but demanding.

If you're driving to Sóller, take the tunnel at Alfabía instead. Save your strength for even better mountain roads ahead.

TRAIN AND TROLLEY CONTACT Ferrocarril de Sóller. ✉ *Eusebio Estada 1, Palma* ☎ *971/752051 in Palma, 971/752028 in Palma* 🌐 *www.trendesoller.com.*

VISITOR INFORMATION CONTACTS Sóller Tourist Office. ✉ *Pl. Espanya s/n, Sóller* ☎ *971/638008.*

Sights

Can Prunera

HISTORIC HOME | A minute's walk or so from the Plaça de la Constitució, along Sóller's main shopping arcade, brings you to this charming museum, where Moderniste style comes to life. In the lovingly restored family rooms on the first floor of this imposing town house you can see how Sóller's well-to-do embraced the art deco style: the ornate furniture and furnishings, the stained glass and ceramic tile, and the carved and painted ceilings all helped announce their status in turn-of-the-century Mallorcan society. Upstairs, Can Prunera also houses a small collection of paintings by early modern masters, among them Man Ray, Santiago Rusiñol, Paul Klee, and Joan Miró; the garden is an open-air museum in its own right, with sculptures by José Siguiri, Josep Sirvent, and other Mallorcan artists. ✉ *Carrer de la Lluna 86–90, Sóller* ☎ *971/638973* 🌐 *www.canprunera.com* 🎫 *€5* 🕒 *Closed Mon. Nov.–Feb.*

Station Building Galleries

ART MUSEUM | Maintained by the Fundació Tren de l'Art, these galleries have two small but remarkable collections—one of engravings by Miró, the other of ceramics by Picasso. ✉ *Soller Railway Station, Pl. Espanya 6, Sóller* 🎫 *Free.*

Restaurants

Neni

$$ | **ISRAELI** | This Israeli restaurant specializes in healthy bites like hummus and falafel, along with more elaborate dishes like the excellent lamb ribs with feta. It's all served on a breezy patio overlooking the bay of Sóller. **Known for:** sharing plates; terrace with views; communal tables. [$] *Average main: €14* ✉ *Carrer de Migjorn 2, Port de Sóller* ☎ *971/631700* 🌐 *www.bikini-hotels.com/eat-and-drink/neni-mallorca.*

Hotels

Ca'n Abril

$$ | **B&B/INN** | About a minute's walk from the main square, this family-friendly boutique hotel is an oasis of quiet in summer, when Sóller gets most of its tourist traffic. **Pros:** excellent value; friendly service; honesty bar. **Cons:** no pool or gym; no elevator; parking off-site (€10 per day). [$] *Rooms from: €99* ✉ *Carrer Pastor 26, Sóller* ☎ *971/633579* 🌐 *www.hotelcanabril.com* 🕒 *Closed Nov.–mid-Mar.* 🛏 *10 rooms* 🍴 *Free Breakfast.*

Ca'n Isabel

$$$ | **B&B/INN** | Just across the tram tracks from the train station, this former home still feels much like a family hideaway. **Pros:** pretty gardens; convenient location; good value. **Cons:** no elevator; rooms on the small side; no private parking. [$] *Rooms from: €132* ✉ *Carrer Isabel II 13, Sóller* ☎ *971/638097* 🌐 *www.canisabel.com* 🕒 *Closed Nov.–Feb.* 🛏 *6 rooms* 🍴 *Free Breakfast.*

Gran Hotel Sóller

$$$$ | **HOTEL** | A former private estate with an imposing Moderniste facade, this is the largest hotel in town. **Pros:** friendly and efficient service in at least five languages; convenient to trams; short walk from town center. **Cons:** functional decor; small pools; pricey for what you get. [$] *Rooms from: €215* ✉ *Carrer Romaguera 18, Sóller* ☎ *971/638686* 🌐 *www.granhotelsoller.com* 🛏 *40 rooms* 🍴 *Free Breakfast.*

Activities

Ten minutes or so from the center of Sóller on the trolley, the beachfront at Port de Sóller offers all sorts of water-based fun.

Nautic Sóller

WATER SPORTS | On the northwest coast at Port de Sóller, this place has sea kayaks and motorboats available for rent.

Mallorca's Sierra de Tramuntana provides excellent views for hikers.

✉ *Calle de la Marina 4, Port de Sóller* ☎ *609/354132* ⊕ *www.nauticsoller.com.*

Alcúdia

54 km (34 miles) northeast of Palma.

Nothing if not strategic, Alcúdia is the ideal base for exploring Mallorca's north coast, with the 13-km-long (8-mile-long) beach from Port d'Alcúdia to C'an Pica-fort and the adjacent Playa de Muro, the bird-watchers' paradise in the S'Albufera wetlands, and the spectacular drive along the corniche to Cap de Formentor. The charming little walled town itself is a capsule version of Mallorcan history: the first city here was a Roman settlement, in 123 BC. The Moors reestablished a town here, and after the Reconquest it became a feudal possession of the Knights Templar; the first ring of city walls dates to the early 14th century. Begin your visit at the **Church of Sant Jaume** and walk through the maze of narrow streets inside to the **Porta de Xara,** with its twin crenellated towers.

GETTING HERE AND AROUND
Porta de Alcúdia, where the ferry arrives from Ciutadella, is a 3-km (2-mile) taxi ride from the center of Alcúdia. There is also direct bus service from Palma.

VISITOR INFORMATION CONTACTS Alcúdia Tourist Office.
✉ *Passeig de Pere Ventayol s/n, Alcúdia* ☎ *971/549022* ⊕ *www.alcudiamallorca. com.*

 Sights

Ciutat Romana de Pol·lèntia

RUINS | Archaeological remains of the ancient city of Pollentia, which dates to about 100 BC, include La Portella residential area, the Forum, and the 1st-century-AD Roman theater. The Museu Monogràfic de Pollentia has a small collection of statuary and artifacts from the nearby excavations of the Roman capital of the island. ✉ *Av. dels Prínceps d'Espanya s/n, Alcúdia* ☎ *971/547004* ⊕ *www.pollentia. net* ☼ *Oct.-Apr. Closed Sat. and Sun.;*

May–Sept. Closed Mon. ✆ €4, includes museum and archaeological site.

Pollença

8 km (5 miles) from Alcúdia, 50 km (31 miles) from Palma.

This is a pretty little place, with a history that goes back at least as far as the Roman occupation of the island; the only trace of that period is the stone **Roman Bridge** at the edge of town. In the 13th century, Pollença and much of the land around it was owned by the Knights Templar, who built the imposing church of **Nuestra Senyora de Los Ángeles** on the west side of the present-day Plaça Major. The church looks east to the 1,082-foot peak of the Puig de Maria, with the 15th-century sanctuary at the top. The **Calvari** of Pollença is a flight of 365 stone steps to a tiny chapel and a panoramic view as far as Cap de Formentor. There's a colorful weekly market at the foot of the steps on Sunday mornings.

GETTING HERE AND AROUND

Pollença is a fairly easy drive from Palma on the MA013. A few buses each day connect Pollença with Palma and Alcúdia.

VISITOR INFORMATION

CONTACTS Pollença Tourist Office.
✉ *Guillen Cifre de Colonya s/n, Pollença* ☎ *971/535077.*

FESTIVALS

Festival de Pollença
An acclaimed international music event, this festival is held every year in August. Since its inception, in 1961, it has attracted such performers as Mstislav Rostropovich, Jessye Norman, the St. Petersburg Philharmonic, the Camerata Köln, and the Alban Berg Quartet. Concerts are held in the cloister of the Convent of Sant Domingo. ✉ *Pollença* ☎ *971/530108 ext. 154* ⊕ *www.festivalpollenca.com.*

Fornalutx

This pretty little mountain village nestled amid lemon and orange groves, 4 km (2½ miles) north of Sóller, is a worthy scenic detour. Much of its appeal emanates from the narrow pedestrianized streets, blond-stone houses speckled with bougainvillea and topped with red-tiled roofs, and the views over the Sóller valley.

Sights

Cap de Formentor
SCENIC DRIVE | The winding road north from Port de Pollença to the tip of the island is spectacular. Stop at the Mirador de la Cruete, where the rocks form deep, narrow inlets of multishaded blue. A stone tower called the Talaia d'Albercutx marks the highest point on the peninsula. Continue on, around hairpin bends—and past superb coastal views—to reach Cala Formentor beach. The drive is certainly not for the fainthearted, but the beach at the end is one of Mallorca's best, with fine white sand and calm turquoise water, backed by a forest of pine trees that offer shade. ✉ *Formentor.*

🛏 Hotels

Agroturisme Can Beneït
$$$$ | **HOTEL** | Local hospitality expert Toni Duran converted this 200-acre farm, complete with a converted medieval farmhouse and a century-old olive oil mill, into a cozy boutique hotel. The property features three rooms and seven suites, spread across the farmhouse, the converted stables, and the various buildings that belong to the estate. Expect plenty of natural Mallorcan materials, farm-to-table food, and all the sounds, flavors, and smells of the Mediterranean countryside.

Pros: olive oil made on-site; pure relaxation in Mallorca's rural heartland; farm-to-table restaurant. **Cons:** quite isolated; books up quickly; three-night minimum stay in high season. [$] *Rooms from: €285* ✉ *Camí de Binibona s/n, Pollença* ☎ *871/811871* 🌐 *fincacanbeneit.com* 🍴 *Free Breakfast* 🛏 *10 rooms.*

Hotel Juma

$$ | B&B/INN | This little hotel, which opened in 1907, is on Pollença's main square, making it a good choice for a weekend stay because of the Sunday market that takes place there. **Pros:** good value; tasty breakfast in the bar; great location. **Cons:** rooms overlooking square can be noisy; parking can be a problem; basic decor and amenities. [$] *Rooms from: €108* ✉ *Pl. Major 9, Pollença* ☎ *971/535002* 🌐 *www.pollensahotels.com* 🕒 *Closed mid-Nov.–mid-Mar.* 🛏 *7 rooms* 🍴 *Free Breakfast.*

★ Son Brull Hotel and Spa

$$$$ | RESORT |"Oasis" is what springs to mind when driving up through family vineyards to this lovingly restored medieval monastery, reborn as a deluxe resort hotel. **Pros:** charm and sophistication; excellent breakfast included; strategic location for exploring Pollença, Alcúdia, and the S'Albufereta wildlife reserve. **Cons:** no sea view might disappoint some; minimum booking for some arrivals in high season; pricey. [$] *Rooms from: €600* ✉ *Ctra. Palma–Pollença, Km 49.8,* ☎ *971/535353* 🌐 *www.sonbrull.com* 🕒 *Closed Dec. and Jan.* 🛏 *13 rooms, 10 suites* 🍴 *Free Breakfast.*

Lluc

20 km (12 miles) southwest of Pollença.

The Santuari de Lluc, which holds the Black Virgin and is a major pilgrimage site, is widely considered Mallorca's spiritual heart.

GETTING HERE AND AROUND

The Santuari is about midway between Sóller and Pollença on the hairpin route over the mountains (MA10). Two buses daily connect these towns, stopping in Lluc. Taxi fare from either town is about €35.

👁 Sights

Santuari de Lluc

RELIGIOUS BUILDING | La Moreneta, also known as La Virgen Negra de Lluc (the Black Virgin of Lluc), is a votary statue of the Virgin Mary that's held in a 17th-century church, the center of this sanctuary complex. The museum has an eclectic collection of prehistoric and Roman artifacts, ceramics, paintings, textiles, folk costumes, votive offerings, Nativity scenes, and work by local artists. Between September and June, a children's choir sings psalms in the chapel daily at 1:15 pm, Monday–Saturday, and at 11 am for Sunday Mass. The Christmas Eve performance of the "Cant de la Sibila" ("Song of the Sybil"), based on a medieval prophecy of the end of the world, is an annual choral highlight. ✉ *Pl. dels Pelegrins 1, Lluc* ☎ *971/871525* 🌐 *www.lluc.net/en* 🎟 *€5.*

Menorca

Menorca, the northernmost of the Balearics, is a knobby, cliff-bound plateau with some 193 km (120 miles) of coastline and a central hill called El Toro, from the 1,100-foot summit of which you can see the whole island. Prehistoric monuments—*taulas* (huge stone T-shapes), *talayots* (spiral stone cones), and *navetes* (stone structures shaped like overturned boats)—left by the first Neolithic settlers are all over the island.

Tourism came late to Menorca, which aligned with the Republic in the Spanish Civil War; Franco punished the island by discouraging the investment in infrastructure that fueled the Balearic boom on Mallorca and Ibiza. Menorca has avoided many of the problems of overdevelopment: there are still very few high-rise hotels, and the herringbone road system, with a single central highway, means that each resort is small and separate. There's less to see and do on Menorca, and more unspoiled countryside than on the other Balearics. The island, home to some 220 species of birds and more than 1,000 species of plants, was designated a Biosphere Reserve in 1993. Menorca is where Spanish mainlanders tend to take their families on vacation.

GETTING HERE AND AROUND

To get to Menorca from Barcelona take the overnight ferry, or a 40-minute flight. It's around a one-hour ferry ride from Palma.

Several buses a day run the length of Menorca between Mahón and Ciutadella, stopping en route at Alaior, Mercadal, and Ferreries. The bus line Autos Fornells serves the northeast; Transportes Menorca connects Mahón with Ciutadella and with the major beaches and calas around the island. From smaller towns there are daily buses to Mahón and connections to Ciutadella. In summer, regular buses shuttle beachgoers from the west end of Ciutadella's Plaça Explanada to the resorts to the south and west; from Mahón, excursions to Menorca's most remote beaches leave daily from the jetty next to the Nuevo Muelle Comercial.

If you want to beach-hop in Menorca, it's best to have your own transportation, but most of the island's historic sights are in Mahón or Ciutadella, and once you're in town everything is within walking distance. You can see the island's archaeological remains in a day's drive, so you may want to rent a car for just that part of your visit.

BUS CONTACTS Autocares Torres. ✉ Ciutadella ☎ 902/075066 ⊕ www.bus.e-torres.

net/en.**Autos Fornells.** ✉ Mercadal ☎ 971/154390 ⊕ www.autosfornells. com.**Transportes Menorca.** ✉ Mahón ☎ 971/360475 ⊕ www.tmsa.es.

Mahón (Maó)

Established as the island's capital in 1722, when the British began their nearly 80-year occupation, Mahón still bears the stamp of its former rulers. The streets nearest the port are lined with four-story Georgian town houses; the Mahónese drink gin and admire Chippendale furniture; English is widely spoken. The city is quiet for much of the year, but between June and September the waterfront pubs and restaurants swell with foreigners.

GETTING HERE AND AROUND

There's ferry service here from Mallorca, but it's much less frequent than to Ciutadella. Within Mahón, Autocares Torres has three bus routes around the city and to the airport.

BUS STATION Estació Autobuses. ✉ Carrer Moll de Llevant 1, Mahón ☎ 971/356050.

TAXI CONTACT Radio-Taxi. ✉ Mahón ☎ 971/367111, 971/482222 ⊕ www. taxismenorca.com.

VISITOR INFORMATION

CONTACTS Aeropuerto de Menorca Tourist Office. ✉ Arrivals terminal, Menorca Airport, Mahón ☎ 971/356944 ⊕ www. menorca.es.**Mahón Tourist Office (Port).** ✉ Moll de Llevant 2, Mahón ☎ 971/355952 ⊕ www.menorca.es.

 ## Sights

Carrer Isabel II

STREET | This street is lined with many Georgian homes. To get here, walk up Carrer Alfons III and turn right at the ajuntament. ✉ Carrer Isabel II, Mahón.

Mercat Des Claustre

MARKET | This church has a fine painted and gilded altarpiece. Adjoining the

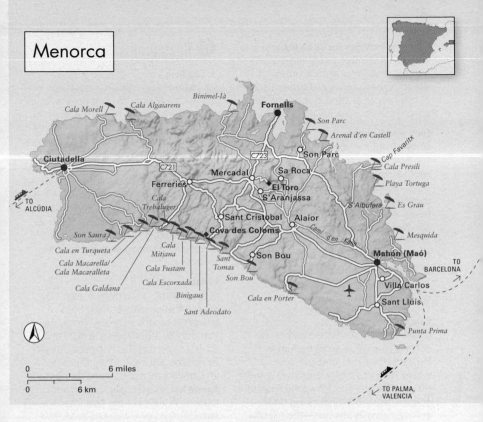

Menorca

church are the cloisters, now a **market,** with stalls selling fresh produce and a variety of local cheeses and sausages. The central courtyard is a venue for a number of cultural events throughout the year. ⊠ *Pl. del Carme,* ☎ *638/920259* ⊕ *mercatdesclaustre.com.*

Santa María

CHURCH | Dating to the 13th century, this church was rebuilt in the 18th century, during the British occupation, and then restored again after being sacked during the Spanish Civil War. The church's pride is its 3,006-pipe Baroque organ, imported from Austria in 1810. Organ concerts are given here Monday to Saturday at 11 am, from May to October. The altar, and the half-domed chapels on either side, have exceptional frescoes. ⊠ *Pl. de la Constitució s/n, Mahón.*

Teatre Principal

NOTABLE BUILDING | Opera companies from Italy en route to Spain made the Teatre Principal in Mahón their first port of call; if the maonesos gave a production a poor reception, it was cut from the repertoire. Built in 1829, it has five tiers of boxes, red plush seats, and gilded woodwork: La Scala in miniature. Lovingly restored, it still hosts a brief opera season. If you're visiting in the first week of December or the last week of May, buy tickets well in advance. ⊠ *Carrer Costa Deià 40, Mahón* ☎ *971/355603* ⊕ *www. teatremao.com.*

Torralba

RUINS | Puzzle over Menorca's prehistoric past at this megalithic site with a number of stone constructions, including a massive taula. Behind it, from the top of a stone wall, you can see, in a nearby field, the monolith **Fus de Sa Geganta** (the Giantess's Spindle). ✉ *Mahón* ⊹ *From Mahón, drive west and turn south at Alaior on road to Cala en Porter; it's 2 km (1 mile) ahead at bend in road, marked by an information kiosk on left.*

Torre d'en Gaumés

RUINS | This Talaiotic site between Alaior and Son Bouis comprises a complex set of stone constructions—fortifications, monuments, deep pits of ruined dwellings, huge vertical slabs, and taulas. ✉ *Alaior* ⊹ *Head south toward Son Bou on west side of Alaior and, after about 1 km (½ mile), the 1st fork left leads to ruins* ☎ *971/157800* ✉ *€3 (Free Mondays).*

 ## Beaches

Cala Galdana

BEACH | FAMILY | A smallish horseshoe curve of fine white sand, framed by almost vertical pine-covered cliffs, is where Menorca's only river, the Agendar, reaches the sea through a long limestone gorge. The surrounding area is under environmental protection—the handful of resort hotels and chalets above the beach (usually booked solid June–September by package-tour operators) were grandfathered in. Cala Galdana is family friendly in the extreme, with calm, shallow waters, and a nearby water park–playground for the kids. A favorite with Menorcans and visitors alike, it gets really crowded in high season, but a 20-minute walk through the pine forest leads to the otherwise inaccessible little coves of Macarella and Macarelleta, remote beaches popular with naturists and boating parties. **Amenities:** food and drink; lifeguards; showers; water sports. **Best for:** swimming; walking. ✉ *35 km (21 miles) from Mahón, Ferreries* ⊹ *Take ME1 to Ferreries, then head south from there on local ME22.*

 ## Restaurants

★ Cap Roig

$$$ | SEAFOOD | A Menorca institution set above Cala Mesquida, Cap Roig owes its well-deserved fame to the quality of its seafood and the splendor of its views. The mussels from the port of Mahón are excellent, as is the lobster, which can be served grilled, in a stew, or as part of one of the restaurant's celebrated rice dishes or paellas. **Known for:** lobster rice; ultra-fresh fish and seafood; splendid views. Ⓢ *Average main: €21* ✉ *Carrer Gran de sa Mesquida 15, Maó* ☎ *971/188383* ⊕ *restaurantcaproig.com* ⊗ *No dinner weekends.*

El Rais

$$$$ | ECLECTIC | Rice dishes reign supreme at upscale El Rais, but that doesn't mean it's all paella. There are starters like Japanese-style nigiri and a Caesar salad rolled in rice paper, as well as risottos, soups, traditional paella, and, of course, rice pudding for dessert. **Known for:** excellent shrimp carpaccio; lunch with views of the port; rice in every form. Ⓢ *Average main: €25* ✉ *Moll de Llevant 314, Maó* ☎ *971/362345.*

★ Es Molí de Foc

$$$$ | SPANISH | Originally a flour mill, this is the oldest building in the village of Sant Climent, and both the atmosphere and the food are exceptional. Taste seasonal dishes, which can include prawn carpaccio with cured Mahón cheese and guacamole, black paella with monkfish and squid, and *carrilleras de ternera* (beef cheeks) with potato. **Known for:** rustic local food with style; summer terrace; brewery on-site. Ⓢ *Average main: €24* ✉ *Carrer Sant Llorenç 65, Sant Climent* ⊹ *4 km (2½ miles) southwest of town* ☎ *971/153222* ⊕ *www.esmolidefoc. es* ⊗ *Closed Mon. Oct.–June. No lunch Mon. July and Aug., and Tues.–Sun. Oct.–June.*

Hotels

Can Alberti

$$$$ | **HOTEL** | Built in 1740, during the British occupation, this former private residence has been turned into an upscale boutique hotel. **Pros:** beautiful design; walking distance to the port; great location. **Cons:** no swimming pool; parking costs €12 per day; no pets. $ *Rooms from: €300* ✉ *Carrer Isabel II 9, Mahón* ☎ *971686/354210* 🌐 *www.casalberti.com* 🛏 *15 rooms* 🍴 *Free Breakfast.*

★ Cristine Bedfor

$$$$ | **HOTEL** | Set around a pretty swimming pool and a lush garden in the historic center of Mahón, this boutique hotel is named after the owner, Cristine Bedfor. **Pros:** plastic-free ethic; gorgeous gardens; good on-site restaurant. **Cons:** only junior suites have private terraces; small swimming pool; parking costs extra. $ *Rooms from: €260* ✉ *Carrer de la Infanta 17, Maó* ☎ *971/635502* 🌐 *cristinebedforhotel.com* 🍴 *Free Breakfast* 🛏 *21 rooms.*

Hotel Port Mahón

$$$ | **HOTEL** | This standby may not win many prizes for imaginative design, but it's a solid choice, with rooms with hardwood floors, generic but comfortable furniture, and plenty of closet space. **Pros:** some rooms have private terraces with impressive views; decent value; good buffet breakfast. **Cons:** no a/c; pool and garden front on the Passeig Marítim; uninspired design. $ *Rooms from: €175* ✉ *Av. Port de Maó s/n, Mahón* ☎ *971/362600* 🌐 *www.sethotels.com* 🛏 *82 rooms* 🍴 *Free Breakfast.*

Hotel Rural y Restaurante Biniarroca

$$$$ | **B&B/INN** | Antique embroidered bed linens, shelves with knickknacks, and comfy chairs—this is an English vision of a peaceful and secluded rural retreat, and its glory is the garden of irises, lavender, and flowering trees. **Pros:** excellent food on-site; peaceful surroundings; some suites have private terraces. **Cons:** adults only; some low ceilings; bit of a drive to the beach. $ *Rooms from: €200* ✉ *Cami Vell 57, Sant Lluís* ☎ *971/150059* 🌐 *www.biniarroca.com* 🕓 *Closed Nov.–Easter* 🛏 *18 rooms* 🍴 *Free Breakfast.*

★ Jardi de Ses Bruixes Boutique Hotel

$$$$ | **B&B/INN** | Built in 1811 by a Spanish ship captain, this *casa señorial* (town house) in the heart of Mahón was lovingly restored by architect and co-owner Fernando Pons as a boutique hotel. **Pros:** amiable, eager-to-please staff; at-home atmosphere; strategic location. **Cons:** thin walls; bathtubs in the bedrooms sacrifice privacy to design; difficult to reach by car, though there is free public parking a few minutes' walk away. $ *Rooms from: €240* ✉ *Carrer de San Fernando 26, Mahón* ☎ *971/363166* 🌐 *www.hotelsesbruixes.com* 🛏 *16 rooms* 🍴 *Free Breakfast.*

Sant Joan de Binissaida

$$$$ | **B&B/INN** | An avenue lined with chinaberry and fig trees leads to this lovely restored farmhouse with environmental credentials, including some solar power and organic produce from the farm. **Pros:** excellent restaurant; vistas clear to the port of Mahón; huge pool. **Cons:** rooms in the annex lack privacy; bit of a drive to the nearest beach; short season, with three-night minimum stay in summer. $ *Rooms from: €240* ✉ *Camí de Binissaida 108, Es Castell* ☎ *971/355598* 🌐 *www.binissaida.com* 🕓 *Closed Nov.–Apr.* 🛏 *15 rooms* 🍴 *Free Breakfast.*

Nightlife

Akelarre Jazz and Dance Club

LIVE MUSIC | This stylish bar near the port has a café-terrace downstairs and live jazz and blues on Thursday and Friday nights. It's open year-round 10:30 am–4 am and serves tapas and snacks to share in the evening. ✉ *Moll de Ponent 41–43, Mahón* ☎ *971/368520.*

Casino Sant Climent

LIVE MUSIC | From May to October, catch live jazz on Tuesday evening at the Casino bar and restaurant. Book ahead for tables on the terrace. ⊠ *Sant Jaume 4,* ⊕ *4 km (2½ miles) southwest of Mahón* ☎ *971/153418* ⊕ *www.casinosantcliment.com.*

Cova d'en Xoroi

DANCE CLUBS | This might be the hottest spot in Menorca to catch the sun going down, drink in hand, and is actually a 20-minute drive from Mahón in the beach resort of Cala en Porter. This dance-until-dawn club is in a series of caves in a cliff high above the sea, which, according to local legend, was once the refuge of a castaway Moorish pirate. In addition to the nighttime DJs, there are afternoon chill-out events with live music. ⊠ *Carrer de Sa Cova s/n, Cala en Porter* ☎ *971/377236* ⊕ *www.covadenxoroi.com.*

Es Cau

LIVE MUSIC | Dug like a cave into the bluff of the little cove of Cala Corb, this is where locals gather (Thursday–Saturday 10 pm–2 am) to sing and play guitar. It's hard to find, but anybody in Es Castell can point the way. ⊠ *Cala Corb s/n, Es Castell* ☎ *No phone.*

🛍 Shopping

Menorca is known for shoes and leather goods, as well as cheese, gin, and wine. Wine was an important part of the Menorcan economy as long ago as the 18th century: the British, who knew a good place to grow grapes when they saw one, planted the island thick with vines. Viticulture was abandoned when Menorca returned to the embrace of Spain, and it has reemerged only in the past few years.

Boba's

SHOES | Duck into the little alley between Carrer Nou and Carrer de l'Angel, and discover the atelier where Llorenç Pons makes his *espardenyes d'autor* (traditional rope-sole sandals) in original and surprising designs. ⊠ *Pont de l'Angel 4, Mahón* ☎ *647/587456* ⊕ *www.facebook.com/bobasmenorca* ⊙ *Closed Sun.*

★ Bodegas Binifadet

WINE/SPIRITS | This is the most promising of the handful of the local wineries, with robust young reds and whites on store shelves all over Menorca. The owners have expanded their product line into sparkling Chardonnay (sold only on the premises), olive oil, jams and conserves, and wine-based soaps and cosmetics. It's well worth a visit, not merely for tastings and guided tours (the website has details), but—weather permitting—for a meal on the terrace. The kitchen puts an international touch on traditional Menorcan recipes and products; the prix fixe menu is a great value at €28 for three courses. In midsummer, reservations are a must. You can also simply drop by for a glass of wine on the terrace; the surroundings are picturesque and peaceful. ⊠ *Ctra. Sant Lluís–Es Castell, Km 0.5, Sant Lluís* ☎ *971/150715* ⊕ *www.binifadet.com* ⊙ *Closed Tues.*

Pons Quintana

SHOES | This showroom has a full-length window overlooking the factory where its very chic women's shoes are made. ⊠ *Carrer Sant Antoni 120, Alaior* ⊕ *13 km (8 miles) northeast of Mahón* ☎ *971/371050* ⊕ *www.ponsquintana.com/en* ⊙ *Closed Sun.*

Xoriguer

WINE/SPIRITS | One gastronomic legacy of the British occupation is gin. At this distillery on Mahón's quayside near the ferry terminal, you can sample various types of gin, and buy some to take home. ⊠ *Moll de Ponent 91, Mahón* ☎ *971/362197* ⊕ *www.xoriguer.es* ⊙ *Closed Sun. and Nov.–Apr.*

🏃 Activities

BICYCLING

Asociación Cicloturista de Menorca

BIKING | Ask here about organized bike tours of the island. ✉ *Moll de Llevant 173, Mahón* ☎ *971971/364816, 610610/464816* ⊕ *www.menorcaciclotur-ista.com/en.*

Bike Menorca

BIKING | You can rent a road bike, mountain bike, or electric bike by the day (from €15) from this full-service outfitter. ✉ *Av. Francesc Femenías 44, Mahón* ☎ *971/353798* ⊕ *www.bikemenorca.com.*

DIVING

The clear Mediterranean waters here are ideal for diving. Equipment and lessons are available at Cala En Bosc, Son Parc, Fornells, Ciutadella, and Cala Tirant, among others.

Blue Islands Diving

DIVING & SNORKELING | Established 2009, Blue Islands Diving is dive center in Cala Galdana that offers diving for all certification levels, including SSI programs and courses, night dives, and snorkeling tours. ✉ *Passatge Riu 7, Serpentona, Cala Galdana* ☎ *633/563526* ⊕ *www.blueislandsdiving.com.*

GOLF

Golf Son Parc

GOLF | Menorca's sole golf course, designed by Dave Thomas, is 9 km (6 miles) east of Mercadal, about a 20-minute drive from Mahón. Rocky bunkers, and the occasional stray peacock on the fairways, make this an interesting and challenging course. The club, open year-round, also has two composition tennis courts and a restaurant. ✉ *Urbanització Son Parc s/n, Mercadal* ☎ *971/188875* ⊕ *golfsonparcmenorca.com* ⅃. *18 holes, 5947 yards, par 71* ☜ *€30–€50 for 9 holes, €49–€80 for 18 holes, depending on season.*

WALKING

In the south, each cove is approached by a *barranca* (ravine or gully), often from several miles inland. The head of **Barranca Algendar** is down a small, unmarked road immediately on the right of the Ferreries–Cala Galdana road; the barranca ends at the local beach resort, and from there you have a lovely walk north along the sea to an unspoiled half moon of sand at **Cala Macarella.** Extend your walk north, if time allows, through the forest along the riding trail to **Cala Turqueta,** where you'll find some of the island's most impressive grottoes.

Ciutadella

44 km (27 miles) west of Mahón.

Ciutadella was Menorca's capital before the British settled in Mahón, and its history is richer. Settled successively by the Phoenicians, Greeks, Carthaginians, and Romans, Ciutadella fell to the Moors in 903 and became a part of the Caliphate of Córdoba until 1287, when Alfonso III of Aragón reconquered it. He gave estates in Ciutadella to nobles who aided him in the battle, and to this day the old historic center of town has a distinctly aristocratic tone. In 1558 a Turkish armada laid siege to Ciutadella, burning the city and enslaving its inhabitants. It was later rebuilt but never quite regained its former stature.

As you arrive via the ME1, the main artery across the island from Mahón, turn left at the second traffic circle and follow the ring road to the Passeig Marítim; at the end, near the **Castell de Sant Nicolau** is a **monument to David Glasgow Farragut,** the first admiral of the U.S. Navy, whose father emigrated from Ciutadella to the United States. From here, take Passeig de Sant Nicolau to the **Plaëa de s'Esplanada** and park near the Plaça d'es Born. Navigate your way from the cathedral through the narrow, medina-like streets of the old town to the 19th century

Mahon's harbor, just below the main square and lined with restaurants, is perfect for a summer evening stroll.

wrought iron Mercat de Peix speckled in green and white tiles—and a hive of activity. Bar Ulisses does a roaring trade day and night, while providing the perfect people-watching perch.

GETTING HERE AND AROUND

Autocares Torres has various bus lines (61, 62 64, 65, 66, 68, 69) running between Ciutadella and the beaches and calas near the city.

BUS CONTACT Autocares Torres. ✉ ☎ *902/075066* ⊕ *www.bus.e-torres.net/ en.*

BUS STATION Estación de Autobuses de Ciutadella. ✉ *Pl. dels Pins 47, Ciutadella* ☎ *93/075066.*

TAXI CONTACT Radio Taxi Menorca. ✉ *Ciutadella* ☎ *971/367111* ⊕ *www. taxismenorca.com/en/home.*

VISITOR INFORMATION

CONTACTS Ciutadella Tourist Office. ✉ *Pl. d'es Born 15, Ciutadella* ☎ *971/383724* ⊕ *www.menorca.es.*

 Sights

Cathedral

CHURCH | Carrer Major leads to this Gothic edifice, which has some beautifully carved choir stalls. The side chapel has round Moorish arches, remnants of the mosque that once stood on this site; the bell tower is a converted minaret. ✉ *Av Carrer Cal Bisbe Torres 8, Ciutadella* ☎ *971/380739* ⊕ *bisbatdemenorca.org/ parroquia-de-ntra-senyora-del-roser-la-cat-edral* 💶 *€6* 🕐 *Closed Sun.*

Convento de Sant Agustí (*El Socorro*)

NOTABLE BUILDING | Carrer del Seminari is lined on the west side with some of the city's most impressive historic buildings. Among them is this 17th-century convent, which hosts Ciutadella's summer festival of classical music (contact *admin@jjmmciutadella.com* for details) in its lovely cloister, and the Diocesan Museum collection of paintings, archaeological finds, and liturgical objects. The room housing the historical library and archives is especially impressive.

✉ *Carrer del Seminari at Carrer Obispo Vila, Ciutadella* ☎ *971/481297* 🎫 *€6 (includes cathedral).*

Mirador d'es Port

VIEWPOINT | From a passage on the left side of Ciutadella's columned and crenellated ajuntament on the west side of the Born, steps lead up to this lookout. From here you can survey the harbor. ✉ *Carrer de Portal de Mar 16, Ciutadella.*

Museu Municipal

HISTORY MUSEUM | The museum houses artifacts of Menorca's prehistoric, Roman, and medieval past, including records of land grants made by Alfons III to the local nobility after defeating the Moors. It occupies an ancient defense tower, the Bastió de Sa Font (Bastion of the Fountain), at the east end of the harbor. ✉ *Pl. de Sa Font s/n, Ciutadella* ☎ *971/380297* 🌐 *www.ajciutadella.org* 🎫 *€2.50 (free Wed.).*

Palau Salort

HISTORIC HOME | This is the only noble house in Ciutadella that's open to the public, albeit at limited times, and you can view five rooms of the palace and the interior garden. The coats of arms on the ceiling are those of the families Salort (*sal* and *ort,* a salt pit and a garden) and Martorell (a marten). Opening hours are irregular so best to check in advance. ✉ *Carrer Major des Born 15, Ciutadella* 🎫 *€3.*

Port

PROMENADE | Ciutadella's port is accessible from steps that lead down from Carrer Sant Sebastià. The waterfront here is lined with seafood restaurants, some of which burrow into caverns far under the Born. ✉ *Ciutadella.*

Beaches

Cala Macarella and Cala Macaralleta

SWIMMING | **FAMILY** | What just might be the two most beautiful of Menorca's small beaches are reachable three ways: by boat, by car from the Mahón–Ciutadella highway (ME1), or, if you're feeling robust and ambitious, on foot from the little resort town of Cala Galdana. Cala Macarella is a little crescent of white sand lapped by breathtakingly turquoise and blue waters that are calm and shallow, and sheltered by rocks on both sides. Remote as it is, it's popular with locals as well as vacationers. A 10-minute walk along the cliffs brings you to the even smaller and more tranquil Cala Macaralleta, where there are no amenities and fewer sunseekers. **Amenities:** food and drink; lifeguards; parking (no fee); toilets. **Best for:** swimming; walking. ✉ *Urbanització Serpentona, Ciutadella.*

🍴 Restaurants

Cafe Balear

$$$$ | **SEAFOOD** | Seafood doesn't get much fresher than here, as the owners' boat docks nearby every day except Sunday. The relaxed atmosphere welcomes either a quick bite or a full dining experience. **Known for:** port-side location; fresh-off-the-boat catches; lobster caldereta. [$] *Average main: €25* ✉ *Pl. de San Juan 15, Ciutadella* ☎ *971/380005* 🕒 *Closed Mon., and Nov. and Dec.*

S'Amarador

$$$$ | **SEAFOOD** | At the foot of the steps that lead down to the port, this restaurant has a café-terrace out front that's perfect for people-watching, drinks, and tapas. Fresh seafood in any form is a sure bet here: try the local John Dory, baked, grilled, or fried with garlic—or splurge on the *caldereta* (€42 per person). **Known for:** good-value fixed-price lunch menu; bustling terrace; flavorsome lobster stew. [$] *Average main: €24* ✉ *Pere Capllonch 42, Ciutadella* ☎ *971/383524* 🌐 *www.samarador.com.*

Smoix

$$$ | **MEDITERRANEAN** | Creative, contemporary Menorcan cuisine is the draw here, in an industrial-style setting with

a small leafy courtyard and low-key cosmopolitan vibe. Start things off with a local gin, and choose from two tasting menus (€38 or €45) or from a small list of à la carte dishes that change according to the season. **Known for:** local gin; crayfish ravioli; brochette with chicken, prawns, shiitake mushrooms and lime. [$] *Average main: €21* ✉ *Av. Jaume I el Conqueridor 38, Ciutadella* ☎ *971/382808* 🌐 *www.smoix.com.*

Hotels

★ Can Faustino

$$$$ | HOTEL | Occupying several renovated and restored 16th-century palace buildings, Can Faustino has a simple yet elegant aesthetic. **Pros:** lovely architecture; ideally located in Ciutadella; outstanding service. **Cons:** street-facing rooms can be noisy; rather pricey; pool area on the small side. [$] *Rooms from: €315* ✉ *Carrer de sa Muradeta 22, Ciutadella* ☎ *971/489191* 🌐 *canfaustino.com/en* 🍴 *Free Breakfast* 🛏 *46 rooms.*

Hotel Rural Sant Ignasi

$$$$ | B&B/INN | FAMILY | About 10 minutes by car from the central square, and set in a centuries-old oak forest, this comfortable manor house dates to 1777 and is a favorite with young Spanish families. **Pros:** decent value; friendly staff; tennis and paddle tennis courts. **Cons:** kids in the pool all day; two-night minimum stay in summer; short season. [$] *Rooms from: €200* ✉ *Ronda Norte s/n, Ciutadella* ✣ *Take Ronda Norte to 2nd traffic circle at Polígono Industrial; just past traffic circle turn left on Son Juaneda and follow signs* ☎ *971/385575* 🌐 *www.santignasi.com* ⏲ *Closed Oct.–Apr.* 🛏 *25 rooms* 🍴 *Free Breakfast.*

★ Hotel Tres Sants

$$$$ | B&B/INN | This chic boutique hotel is in the heart of Ciutadella, on a narrow cobblestone street behind the cathedral, and has killer views from the rooftop terrace, extending over the old city and (in good weather) across the ocean as far as Mallorca. **Pros:** suites for families; ideal location for exploring the city; on-site spa access 24 hours. **Cons:** no parking; no elevator; communal breakfasts don't suit everyone. [$] *Rooms from: €250* ✉ *Carrer Sant Cristofol 2, Ciutadella* ☎ *689626/171731* 🌐 *florderosassa.com/es/hotel-tres-sants/hotel* 🛏 *8 rooms* 🍴 *Free Breakfast.*

Shopping

The *polígono industrial* (industrial complex) on the right as you enter Ciutadella has a number of shoe factories, each with a shop. Prices may be the same as in stores, but the selection is wider. In Plaça d'es Born, a market is held on Monday and Friday.

For the best shopping, try the Ses Voltes area, the Es Rodol zone near Plaça Artrutx, and along the Camí de Maó between Plaça Palmeras and Plaça d'es Born.

Hort Sant Patrici

FOOD | This is a good place to buy the tangy, Parmesan-like Mahón cheese. There's a shop, beautiful grounds with a small vineyard, a sculpture garden and botanical garden, and a display of traditional cheese-making techniques and tools. Most week days, you can watch the cheese being made and guided tours (by reservation; €8) are available in English every Monday at 10 am. Hort Sant Patrici has its own vineyards and olive trees. ✉ *Camí Sant Patrici s/n, Ferreries* ✣ *18 km (11 miles) east of Ciutadella; exit ME1 at 2nd traffic circle after Ferreries onto Camí Sant Patrici* ☎ *971/374512* 🌐 *www.santpatrici.com* ⏲ *Closed Sun. in summer, weekends in winter.*

Maria Juanico

JEWELRY & WATCHES | Interesting plated and anodized silver jewelry and accessories are created by Maria at a workshop in the back of her store. ✉ *Carrer Seminari 38, Ciutadella* ☎ *971/480879* ⊘ *Closed Sat. afternoon and Sun.*

Nadia Rabosio
JEWELRY & WATCHES | This inventive designer has created an original selection of jewelry and hand-painted silks. ✉ *Carrer Santissim 4, Ciutadella* ☎ *971/384080* ⊕ *www.nadiarabosio.com* ⊘ *Closed Sun.*

 Activities

HORSEBACK RIDING
Horseback riding, breeding, and dressage have been traditions on the island for hundreds of years, and the magnificent black Menorcan horses play an important role, not only as work animals and for sport, but also in shows and colorful local festivals. There are 17 riding clubs on the island, a number of which offer excursions on the rural lanes of the unspoiled countryside. The Camí de Cavalls is a riding route in 20 stages that completely circumnavigates the island. Cavalls Son Angel in Ciutadella and Menorca a Cavall in Cala Galdana organize excursions for adults and children. Son Martorellet, on the road to the beach at Cala Galdana, is a ranch where you can visit the stables and watch dressage training exhibitions every Tuesday and Thursday afternoon; there's an equestrian show in traditional costume on Saturday.

Cavalls Son Àngel
HORSEBACK RIDING | FAMILY | This equestrian center specializes in excursions along the Cami de Cavalls, the horseback route that circumnavigates the island, with rides that range from one to two hours for beginners (€25–€50) to three- or five-day trips (all year round except July and August). Riders on the longer excursions need to arrange their own overnight accommodations. ✉ *Camí d'Algaiarens s/n, Ciutadella* ☎ *609/833902, 649/488098* ⊕ *www.cavallssonangel.com* 🍴 *From €25.*

Menorca a Cavall
HORSEBACK RIDING | FAMILY | Hour-and-a-half-long excursions, along portions of the Camí de Cavalls, are €30 in autumn and winter, €40 in spring and summer. Longer rides run €60–€100, depending on the season. Single- and two-day routes along the south coast of Menorca can also be organized autumn through spring. ✉ *Finca Es Calafat, Ctra. Ferreries–Cala Galdana (ME22), Km 4.3, Ferreries* ☎ *971/374637, 685/990545* ⊕ *www.menorcaacavall.com* 🍴 *From €30.*

Son Martorellet
HORSEBACK RIDING | FAMILY | The equestrian performances at the Son Martorellet stables, featuring demonstrations of dressage with the famed Menorcan horses, are offered Tuesday and Thursday afternoons. ✉ *Ctra. Ferreries–Cala Galdana, Km 1.7, Ferreries* ☎ *971/373406, 639/156851* ⊕ *www.sonmartorellet.com.*

El Toro

24 km (15 miles) northwest of Mahón.

The peak of El Toro is Menorca's highest point, at all of 1,175 feet. From the monastery on top you can see the whole island and across the sea to Mallorca.

GETTING HERE AND AROUND
Follow signs in Es Mercadal, the crossroads at the island's center.

 Restaurants

Es Molí d'es Recó
$$$ | CATALAN | A great place to stop for a lunch of typical local cuisine, this restaurant is in an old windmill at the west end of Es Mercadal, on the ME1 about halfway between Mahón and Ciutadella and about 4 km (2½ miles) from El Toro. Menorcan specialties here include squid stuffed with anglerfish and shrimp, and chicken with *centollo* (spider crab). **Known for:** sopa menorquina (vegetable

soup); Menorcan specialties; pretty terrace. [$] *Average main: €21* ✉ *Carrer Major 53, Mercadal* ☎ *971/375392.*

Fornells

35 km (22 miles) northwest of Mahón.

A little village (full-time population: 500) of whitewashed houses with red-tile roofs, Fornells comes alive in the summer high season, when Spanish and Catalan families arrive in droves to open their holiday chalets at the edge of town and in the nearby beach resorts. The bay—Menorca's second largest and deepest—is good for windsurfing, sailing, and scuba diving. The first fortifications built here to defend the Bay of Fornells from pirates date to 1625.

GETTING HERE AND AROUND

Buses leave the Estació Autobusos on Calle José Anselmo Clavé in Mahón for the 50-minute, 40-km (25-mile) trip to Fornells five times daily. By car, it's an easy half-hour drive north on the PM710.

🍴 Restaurants

Ca Na Marga

$$ | **STEAKHOUSE** | On an island known for its excellent paellas and fresh fish and seafood, Ca Na Marga is famed for its top-quality steak, served with a choice of sauce, including green peppercorn or Mahón cheese sauce. Balearic specialties such as lamb shank with thyme and grilled rabbit are also a good bet. **Known for:** rustic dining room; Mediterranean barbecue; "Chuletón" steak. [$] *Average main: €16* ✉ *Carrer de sa Barrera 24, Fornells* ☎ *971/376410* 🌐 *canamarga.com.*

🏃 Activities

SAILING

Several miles long and a mile wide but with a narrow entrance to the sea and virtually no waves, the Bay of Fornells gives the beginner a feeling of security and the expert plenty of excitement.

Wind Fornells

SAILING | Here, on the beach just off Carrer del Rosari, you can rent windsurfing boards and dinghies and take lessons, individually or in groups. It's open April–October. ✉ *Ctra. Es Mercadal–Fornells s/n, Mercadal* ☎ *664/335801* 🌐 *www.windfornells.com* 🎫 *Windsurfing boards from €37 for 2 hrs.*

Cova des Coloms

35 km (22 miles) northwest of Mahón.

There are caverns and grottoes all over the Balearics, some of them justly famous because of their size, spectacular formations, and subterranean pools. This one is well worth a visit.

GETTING HERE AND AROUND

Take the road from Ferreries to Es Migjorn Gran, park by the cemetery, and follow the signs on the footpath, about 30 minutes' walk toward the beach at Binigaus. Signs direct you to the gully, where you descend to the cave.

👁 Sights

Cova des Coloms (*Cave of Pigeons*)

CAVE | This massive cave is the most spectacular on Menorca, with eerie rock formations rising up to a 77-foot-high ceiling. When planning your visit, bear in mind that it's a 30-minute walk each way from the nearest parking place. ✉ *Ferreries* ✣ *On eastern side of ravine from Es Migjorn Gran to beach.*

Chapter 11

SEVILLE AND AROUND

11

Updated by
Joanna Styles

👁 **Sights**
★★★★★

🍴 **Restaurants**
★★★★★

🛏 **Hotels**
★★★★★

🛍 **Shopping**
★★★★★

🍸 **Nightlife**
★★★★☆

WELCOME TO SEVILLE AND AROUND

TOP REASONS TO GO

★ **The Real Alcázar:** Drink in the sumptuously decorated patios and halls, the heavenly gold ceiling, ornate tile, and lush gardens dotted with pools, palms, and peacocks.

★ **Tour Catedral de Sevilla:** Tour Spain's biggest cathedral (there are 80 chapels) to see Christendom's largest altarpiece.

★ **Live and breathe flamenco:** Tune into Andalusia's soundtrack at one of Seville's many flamenco *tablaos* or spontaneously on any corner in Santa Cruz or Triana.

★ **Feast on tapas:** Make small plates your staples at myriad taverns, traditional and modern, where fine dining comes paired with local wines including sherry.

★ **Shop for tiles:** Learn about the history and process of making Sevillian ceramics in a former factory at the Centro de Cerámica Triana, and shop for beautiful souvenirs.

★ **Linger in the Plaza de España:** Take a leisurely stroll at this magnificent semicircular plaza located in María Luisa Park.

1 Centro. The heart of the city's commercial life.

2 Santa Cruz. Home to the Real Alcázar and a glorious labyrinth of whitewashed alleys.

3 El Arenal. This area includes the Parque Maria Luisa, the Torre de Oro on the river, and many picturesque taverns.

4 La Macarena. The city's best churches and convents, pleasant squares, and excellent restaurants are here.

5 Triana. Home to the main workshop for Seville's renowned tile ceramicists.

6 Italica. Known for the ruins of its Roman city.

7 Córdoba. Home to the stunning Mezquita—a must-visit.

8 Ronda. Famous for its dramatic escarpments, views, and gorge.

9 Around Ronda. Caves, mountain villages, and gorges.

10 Arcos de la Frontera. A classic Andalusian pueblo blanco.

11 Jerez de la Frontera. The capital of horse culture and sherry.

12 Cádiz. So old that Julius Caesar once held public office here.

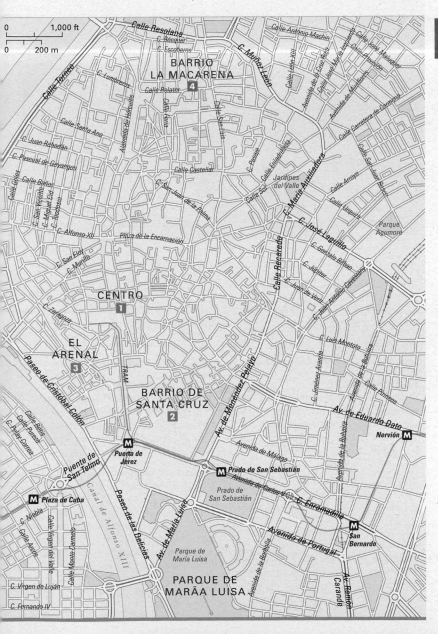

0   1,000 ft
0   200 m

Calle Resolana
C. Béequel
C. Escoberns

Calle Antonio Machin

C. Muñoz León

BARRIO
LA MACARENA 4

Calle León XIII

Calle José Malladez

Calle Pleurión

C. Lumbreras

Calle Relator

Calle Torneo

C. Santa Ana

Calle Feria

Avenida de la Cruz Roja

Avenida de Miraflores

Avenida José María de Izquierda

C. Juan Rabadán

Calle San Luis

Calle Carretera de Carmona

C. Pascual de Gayangos

Calle Castellar

C. Pasale

Calle Estadillala

C. Colés

Calle Baños

C. San Vicente

C. Miguel Cid

C. Bodosia

C. Alfonso XII

C. San Juan de la Palma

Calle Sol

Jardines
del Valle

Calle María Auxiliadora

C. José Laguillo

Calle Arroyo

Calle San Juan Bosco

Calle Urquira

Parque
Agumore

Plaza de la Encarnación

C. Gonzalo Bilbao

C. San Eloy

C. Murillo

C. Júpiter

Calle Recaredo

Calle Juan de Vera

Juan Antonio Cavestany

CENTRO 1

C. Zaragoza

C. Luis Montoto

EL
ARENAL 3

Paseo de Cristóbal Colón

TRAM

BARRIO DE
SANTA CRUZ 2

Av. de Martínez Pelayo

C. Jiménez Aranda

Avenida Calle Pirineos

Av. de la Buhaira

Av. de Eduardo Dato

Nervión M

Avenida de Málaga

M Puerta de
Jerez

M Prado de San Sebastián

Calle Bétis

Calle Pureza

C. Pelay Correa

Puente de
San Telmo

Avenida de Carlos V

Prado de
San Sebastián

C. Enramadilla

Av. de la Buhaira

M Plaza de Cuba

C. Niebla

Canal de Alfonso XIII

Paseo de las Delicias

Av. de María Luisa

M San
Bernardo

Calle Acoro

Calle Virgen del Valle

Calle Marta Carmelo

Parque de
María Luisa

Avenida de Portugal

Av. Ramón
Caranda

C. Virgen de Luján

PARQUE DE
MARÍA LUISA

Avenida de la Borbolla

C. Fernando IV

FLAMENCO

Rule one about flamenco: You don't see it. You feel it. The pain and yearning on the dancers' faces and the eerie voices are real. If the dancers manage to summon the *duende* and allow this soulful state of emotion to take over, then they have done their jobs well.

FLAMENCO 101

Origins: The music is largely Arabic in its beginnings, but you'll detect echoes of Greek dirges and Jewish chants, with healthy doses of Flemish and traditional Castilian thrown in. Hindu sways, Roman mimes, and other movement informs the dance, but we may never know the specific origins of flamenco. The dance, along with the nomadic Gypsies, spread throughout Andalusia and within a few centuries had developed into many variations and styles, some of them named after the city where they were born (such as *malaguenas* and *sevillanas*) and others taking on the names after people,

emotions, or bands. In all, there are more than 50 different styles (or *palos*) of flamenco, four of which are the stylistic pillars others branch off from—differing mainly in rhythm and mood: *toná, soleá, fandango*, and *seguidilla*.

Clapping and castanets: The sum of its parts are awe-inspiring, but if you boil it down, flamenco is a combination of music, singing, and dance. Staccato hand-clapping almost sneaks in as a fourth part—the sounds made from all the participants' palms, or *palmas*, is part of the duende—but this element remains more of a connector that all in the performance take part in when their hands are free. Hand-clapping was likely flamenco's original key instrument before the guitar, *cajón* (wooden box used for percussion), and other instruments arrived on the scene. Perhaps the simplest way to augment the clapping is to add a uniquely designed six-string guitar, in which case you've got yourself a *tablao*, or people seated around a singer and clapping. Dance undoubtedly augments the experience, but isn't necessary for a tablao. These exist all throughout Andalusia and are usually private affairs with people who love flamenco. Castanets (or *palillos*) were absorbed by the Phoenician culture and adopted by the Spanish, now part of their own folklore. They accompany other traditional folk dances in Spain and are used pervasively throughout flamenco (though not always present in some forms of dance).

Flamenco now: Flamenco's enormous international resurgence has been building for the past few decades. Much of this revival can be attributed to pioneers like legendary singer Camarón de la Isla, guitarist Paco de Lucía, or even outsiders like Miles Davis fusing flamenco with other genres like jazz and rock. Today the most popular flamenco fusion artists include Rosalía and Fuel Fandango.

FLAMENCO HEAD TO TOE

Wrists rotate while hands move, articulating each finger individually, curling in and out. The trick is to have it appear like an effortless flourish. Facial expression is considered another tool for the dancer, and it's never plastered on but projected from some deeper place. For women, the hair is usually pulled back in touring flamenco performances in order to give the back row a chance to see more clearly the passionate expressions. In smaller settings like tablaos, hair is usually let down and is supposed to better reveal the beauty of the female form overall. The dancer carries the body in an upright and proud manner: the chest is out, shoulders back. Despite this position, the body should never carry tension—it needs to remain pliable and fluid. With professional dancers, the feet can move so quickly, they blur like hummingbird wings in action. When they move slowly, you can watch the different ways a foot can strike the floor. A *planta* is when the whole foot strikes the floor, as opposed to when the ball of the foot or the heel (*taco*) hits. Each one must be a "clean" strike or the sound will be off.

An exploration of Andalusia must begin with Seville, Spain's fourth-largest city and the place where all romantic images of Andalusia, and Spain, spring vividly to life. Known for its steamy-hot summers, delightfully mild winters, its operatic heroine, Carmen, and stunning *Game of Thrones* settings, Seville is an enchanting city whose fabulous food, extraordinary Mudejar, Gothic, and Renaissance architecture, and exotic flamenco rhythms never fail to seduce and charm.

Seville's whitewashed houses, bright with bougainvillea, ocher-color palaces, and baroque facades, have long enchanted both sevillanos and travelers. It's a city for the senses—the fragrance of orange blossom (orange trees line many streets) suffuses the air in spring, the sound of flamenco echoes through the alleyways in Triana and Santa Cruz, and views of the great Guadalquivir River accompany you at every turn. This is also a fine city for handsome people—stroll down the swankier pedestrian shopping streets and you can't fail to notice just how good looking everyone is. Aside from being blessed with even features and flashing dark eyes, sevillanos exude a cool sophistication that seems more Catalan than Andalusian.

Seville offers a bewitching mosaic of flamenco, matadors, horses, refreshingly cool patios, and religious fervor. Add to this fine architecture (rich baroque and Renaissance monuments, colonial palaces and the sumptuous Real Alcázar), plus fine wining and dining, and this city brings very vibrant color to any holiday.

At the top of your must-see list sit the Real Alcázar (fortress), a Mudejar delight whisking you straight to the land of Scheherazade, and the Cathedral, the largest in Spain and topped with the Giralda minaret tower. Continue your architectural feast with one of the city's splendid palaces, excellent museums, and fine churches while taking in Seville's nod to modernity in the Gaudí-style Metropol Parasol, lofty Torre Seville, and the elegant contemporary bridges.

The layout of the historic center of Seville makes exploring easy. The central zone—Centro—around the cathedral, Calle Sierpes, and Plaza Nueva, is splendid and monumental, but it's not where you'll find Seville's greatest charm. El Arenal, home of the Maestranza bullring, the Teatro de la Maestranza concert hall, and a concentration of picturesque taverns, still buzzes the way it must have when stevedores loaded and unloaded ships from the New World. Just southeast of Centro, the medieval Jewish quarter, Barrio de Santa Cruz, is home to the Real Alcázar and a lovely, whitewashed tangle of alleys. The Barrio de la Macarena to the northeast is rich in sights and authentic Seville atmosphere. The fifth and final neighborhood to explore, on the far side of the Río Guadalquivir, is in many ways the best of all: Triana, the traditional habitat for sailors, bullfighters, and flamenco artists, as well as the main workshop for Seville's renowned ceramicists.

Like all Andalusians, the sevillanos know how to party. Highlights of the year come in the Feria de abril, a week of colorful and musical festivities to welcome spring, quickly followed by celebrations marking Pentecost when locals take a pilgrimage to El Rocío on the Atlantic Ocean. Religious fervor comes into their own during Holy Week when thousands of devout locals take part in some of Spain's most famous processions.

Side trips from Seville range from half-day excursions to the Roman Itálica to longer visits to some of Andalusia's finest towns and cities. Nearby Jerez, celebrated for sherry and horses, and Cádiz, a maritime jewel, are both must-sees. Ronda, one of Spain's most beautiful towns, merits a full day, as does Córdoba, whose Moorish mosque ranks as one of the country's most treasured monuments.

Planning

When to Go

Visit Seville between October and November or between April and May. It's blisteringly hot in the summer, so spend time in the Pedroches of northern Córdoba province if you plan to visit then. Autumn catches the cities going about their business, the temperatures are moderate, and you will rarely see a line form.

December through March tends to be cool, uncrowded, and quiet, but come spring, it's fiesta time, with Seville's Semana Santa (Holy Week, between Palm Sunday and Easter) the most moving and multitudinous. April showcases whitewashed Andalusia at its floral best, with every patio and facade covered with flowers from bougainvillea to honeysuckle.

Getting Here and Around

AIR

Seville's airport is about 7 km (4½ miles) east of the city. There's a bus from the airport to the center of town every half hour daily (5:20 am–1:15 am; €4 one-way, €6 return). Taxi fare from the airport to the city center is around €23 during the day and €26 at night and on Sunday. A number of private companies operate private airport-shuttle services.

BUS

Seville has two intercity bus stations: Estación Plaza de Armas, the main one, with buses serving Córdoba, Granada, Huelva, and Málaga in Andalusia, plus Madrid and Portugal and other international destinations; and the smaller Estación del Prado de San Sebastián, serving Cádiz and nearby towns and villages.

Certain routes operate limited night service from midnight to 2 am Monday through Thursday, with services until 5 am Friday through Sunday. Single rides cost €1.40, but if you're going to be busing a lot, it's more economical to buy a rechargeable multitravel pass, which works out to €0.69 per ride. Special Tarjetas Turísticas (tourist passes) valid for one or three days of unlimited bus travel cost (respectively) €5 and €10. Tickets are sold at newsstands and at the main bus station, Prado de San Sebastián.

CONTACTS Estación del Prado de San Sebastián. ✉ *Calle Vázquez Sagastizábal, El Arenal* ☎ *955/479290.* **Estación Plaza de Armas.** ✉ *Puente Cristo de la Expiración, Centro* ☎ *955/038665* ⊕ *www.autobus-esplazadearmas.es.*

CAR

Getting in and out of Seville by car isn't difficult, thanks to the SE30 ring road, but getting around in the city by car is problematic. We advise leaving your car at your hotel or in a lot while you're here.

TAXI

CONTACTS Radio Taxi Sevilla. ☎ *954/580000.*

TRAIN

Train connections include the high-speed AVE service from Madrid, with a journey time of less than 2½ hours.

CONTACTS Estación Santa Justa. ✉ *Av. Kansas City, El Arenal* ☎ *912/320320.*

VISITOR INFORMATION

CONTACTS City of Seville. ✉ *Paseo Marqués de Contadero s/n, Barrio de Santa Cruz* ✛ *On waterfront, by Torre de Oro* ☎ *955/471232* ⊕ *www.visitasevilla.es.*

Restaurants

Eating out is an intrinsic part of the Andalusian lifestyle. Whether it's sharing some tapas with friends over a prelunch drink or a three-course à la carte meal, many Andalusians eat out at some point during the day. Unsurprisingly, there are literally thousands of bars and restaurants throughout the region catering to all budgets and tastes.

At lunchtime, check out the *menús del día* (daily menus) offered by many restaurants, usually three courses and excellent value (expect to pay €8–€15,

depending on the type of restaurant and location). Roadside restaurants, known as *ventas,* usually provide good food in generous portions and at reasonable prices. Be aware that many restaurants add a service charge (*cubierto*), which can be as much as €3 per person, and some restaurant prices don't include value-added tax (*impuesto sobre el valor añadido/I.V.A.*) at 10%. Note also that restaurants with tasting menus (*menús de degustación*) usually require everyone at the table to have the menu.

Andalusians tend to eat later than their fellow Spaniards: lunch is 2–4 pm, and dinner starts at 9 pm (10 pm in the summer). In cities, many restaurants are closed Sunday night, and fish restaurants tend to close on Monday; in inland towns and cities, some restaurants close for all of August.

Restaurant reviews have been shortened. For full information, visit Fodors.com.

Hotels

Seville has grand old hotels, such as the Alfonso XIII, and a number of converted former palaces.

In Córdoba, several hotels occupy houses in the old quarter, close to the mosque. Other than during Holy Week and the Festival de los Patios in May, it's easy to find a room in Córdoba.

Rental accommodations bookable on portals such as Airbnb are popular in large towns and cities; double-check reviews before you book.

Not all hotel prices include value-added tax (I.V.A.) and the 10% surcharge may be added to your final bill. Check when you book.

Hotel reviews have been shortened. For full information, visit Fodors.com.

What It Costs in Euros			
$	$$	$$$	$$$$
RESTAURANTS			
under €12	€12–€17	€18–€22	over €22
HOTELS			
under €90	€90–€125	€126–€180	over €180

Tours

annie b's Spanish Kitchen
Based in Vejer de la Frontera (Cádiz), Scottish-born Annie B offers food and wine experiences, including sherry tours, tuna *almadraba* (an age-old way of trapping) trips, and cooking classes. ⊠ *Calle Viñas, 11, Vejer de la Frontera* ☏ *620/560649* ⊕ *www.anniebspain.com* ✉ *From €155.*

Azahar Sevilla Tapas Tours
Local food and wine expert, and certified sherry educator, Shawn Hennessey leads intimate guided tours around Seville's best tapas bars (traditional and gourmet). Choose from several different options, lunch or evening. ⊕ *azahar-sevilla.com/ sevilletapas* ✉ *From €85.*

Glovento Sur
Up to five people at a time are taken on balloon trips above Granada, Ronda, and Seville. ⊠ *Placeta Nevot 4, #1A, Granada* ☏ *958/290316* ⊕ *www.gloventosur.com* ✉ *From €165.*

History and Tapas Tour
Glean local, historical, and culinary knowledge on a variety of tours around sights and tapas bars. ⊕ *www.sevilleconcierge. com* ✉ *From €60.*

Sevilla Bike Tour
Guided tours, leaving from the Makinline Shop on Calle Arjona at 10:30 am, take in the major sights of the city and offer interesting stories and insider information along the way. You'll cover about 10 km (6 miles) in three hours. Reservations are required on weekends and recommended on weekdays. ⊠ *Calle Arjona 8, Centro* ☏ *954/562625* ⊕ *www.sevillabike-tour.com* ✉ *From €25.*

Sevilla Walking Tours
Choose one of three walking tours conducted in English: the City Walking Tour, leaving Plaza Nueva from the statue of San Fernando; the Alcázar Tour, leaving Plaza del Triunfo from the central statue; and the Cathedral Tour, also leaving from the Plaza del Triunfo central statue. ⊠ *Seville* ☏ *616/501100* ⊕ *sevillawalkingtours. com* ✉ *From €12.*

Your First Flamenco Experience
Local dancer Eva Izquierdo from Triana teaches you how to clap in time, and take your first dance steps, in authentic costume, all in an hour. ⊠ *Seville* ☏ *626/007868* ⊕ *www.ishowusevilla. com* ✉ *From €18.*

Centro

The Centro area is the heart of Seville's commercial life. It has bustling shopping streets—several of which are pedestrianized—and leafy squares lined with bars and cafés. The residential streets contain some of the best examples of colonial architecture; noteworthy features include fine facades and roof gables topped with local ceramic tiles. Centro is also home to several of the city's most beautiful churches.

Sights

Ayuntamiento (*City Hall*)
GOVERNMENT BUILDING | This Diego de Riaño original, built between 1527 and 1564, is in the heart of Seville's commercial center. A 19th-century plateresque facade overlooks the Plaza Nueva. The other side, on the Plaza de San Francisco, is Riaño's work. Visits must be prebooked via the website. ⊠ *Pl. Nueva 1, Centro* ☏ *955/470243*

Seville's cathedral is the largest and tallest cathedral in Spain, the largest Gothic building in the world, and the third-largest church in the world, after St. Peter's in Rome and St. Paul's in London.

⊕ *casaconsistorialsevilla.sacatuentrada. es* ✉ *€4 (free Sat.)* ⊙ *Closed Fri. and Sun.*

Calle Sierpes

STREET | This is Seville's classy main shopping street. Near the southern end, at No. 85, a plaque marks the spot where the Cárcel Real (Royal Prison) once stood. Miguel de Cervantes began writing *Don Quixote* in one of its cells. ✉ *Calle Sierpes, Centro.*

★ Catedral de Sevilla

CHURCH | Seville's cathedral can be described only in superlatives: it's the largest and highest cathedral in Spain, the largest Gothic building in the world, and the world's third-largest church, after St. Peter's in Rome and St. Paul's in London. After Ferdinand III captured Seville from the Moors in 1248, the great mosque begun by Yusuf II in 1171 was used as a Christian cathedral. In 1401, Seville pulled down the old mosque, leaving only its minaret and outer courtyard, and built a new cathedral in just over a century. The magnificent *retablo* (altarpiece) in the Capilla Mayor (Main Chapel) is the largest in Christendom. The Capilla Real (Royal Chapel) is concealed behind a curtain, but duck in if you're quick, quiet, and properly dressed (no shorts or sleeveless tops). Don't forget the Patio de los Naranjos (Courtyard of Orange Trees), where the fountain in the center was used for ablutions before people entered the original mosque. ✉ *Pl. Virgen de los Reyes, Centro* ☎ *954/214971* ⊕ *www.catedraldesevilla.es* ✉ *€10.*

Metropol Parasol

PLAZA/SQUARE | This huge square, at the west end of Calle Cuna, is home to the world's largest wooden structure, 492 feet long by 230 feet wide. Known in the city as "Las Setas" (The Mushrooms), the piece is actually meant to represent giant trees, and walkways run through the "tree tops" affording great views of the city, especially at sunset. Although it's reminiscent of Gaudí, it was built in 2011. At ground level, there are interesting archaeological remains (mostly Roman) and a large indoor food market. ✉ *Pl. de la Encarnación, Centro* 🎫 *€5.*

★ Palacio de la Condesa de Lebrija

CASTLE/PALACE | This lovely palace has three ornate patios, including a spectacular courtyard graced by a Roman mosaic taken from the ruins in nearby Itálica, surrounded by Moorish arches and fine *azulejos* (painted tiles). The side rooms house a collection of archaeological items. The second floor contains the family apartments and visits are by guided tour only. It's well worth paying for the second-floor tour, which gives an interesting insight into the collections and the family. ✉ *Calle Cuna 8, Centro* ☎ *954/227802* 🎫 *€12 (free Mon. 6–6:30 pm, 1st floor only).*

Palacio de las Dueñas

HISTORIC HOME | The 15th-century home and official residence of the late 18th Duchess of Alba in Seville is an oasis of peace and quiet in the bustling city. Set around an ornate patio with Mudejar arches and a central fountain, the house includes antiques and paintings, as well as memorabilia relating to the duchess herself. Revered in the city and one of Spain's most important noblewomen and society figures, Cayetana de Alba loved bullfighting, flamenco, and ceramics. The visit (first floor only) also includes the stables, gardens (said to have inspired some of the poet Antonio Machado's most famous early verses), and a Gothic chapel. ✉ *Calle Dueñas 5, Centro* ☎ *954/214828* 🌐 *www.lasduenas.es* 🎫 *€10 (free Mon. beginning at 4).*

🍴 Restaurants

Cañabota

$$$$ | **SPANISH** | If you fancy treating yourself to some of the best fish in town, head for this modern-styled restaurant just down the road from the Palacio de la Condesa de Lebrija. Seasonal fish and seafood take center stage on the menu, whose ingredients you can see in the window displaying the catch of the day. **Known for:** efficient service; daily specials like marinated sardines; fresh fish and seafood. [$] *Average main: €30* ✉ *Calle Orfila 3, Centro* ☎ *954/870 298* 🌐 *canabota.es* 🕒 *Closed Sun. and Mon.*

Casa Morales

$ | **TAPAS** | Down a side street off the Avenida de la Constitución, this historic bar (formerly a wine store) takes you back to 19th-century Seville, and it is still run by descendents of the same family that established it in 1850. Locals pack the place at lunchtime, when popular dishes include *menudo con garbanzos* (tripe with chickpeas) and *albóndigas de choco* (cuttlefish croquettes). **Known for:** tripe with chickpeas; local atmosphere; wine list. [$] *Average main: €8* ✉ *Calle García de Vinuesa 11, Centro* ☎ *954/221242* 🕒 *No dinner Sun.*

Castizo

$$ | **SPANISH** | True tradition (castizo itself) comes into its own at this busy venue serving regional dishes such as *jabalí con judiones, setas y foie* (braised wild boar with beans, mushrooms, and foie) alongside more modern plates like the popular *coliflor tostada con holandesa trufada* (cauliflower cheese with truffle oil), plus daily fish specials and the rice dish of the day. The open kitchen gives you a frontline view of your meal in the making. **Known for:** open kitchen; authentic traditional cooking; daily fish and rice specials. [$] *Average main: €12* ✉ *Calle Zaragoza 6, Centro* ☎ *955/180562* 🌐 *www.barracastizo.es* 🕒 *Closed Wed. No dinner Sun.*

El Pintón

$$ | **FUSION** | With a privileged spot a block north from the cathedral, this central restaurant offers two dining spaces: on the traditional inside patio, where wood, mirrors, and tasteful lighting create an intimate but airy space, or outside on the pleasant terrace. The cuisine combines Andalusian dishes with a modern touch, with menu items such as

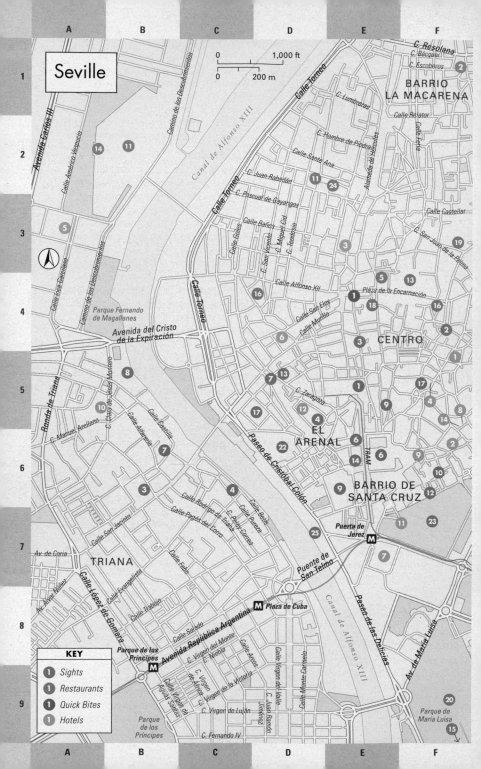

Sights ▼

1 Ayuntamiento E5
2 Basílica de la
   Macarena F1
3 Calle Sierpes E4
4 Capilla de los
   Marineros C6
5 Casa de Pilatos G5
6 Catedral de Sevilla E6
7 Centro de Cerámica
   Triana B6
8 Convento de
   Santa Paula G3
9 Hospital de la Caridad... E6
10 Hospital de los
   Venerables F6
11 Isla de La Cartuja B2
12 Judería
   (Jewish Quarter)......... F6
13 Metropol Parasol F4
14 Monasterio de
   Santa María de las
   Cuevas A2
15 Museo de Artes y
   Costumbres
   Populares................ F9
16 Museo de
   Bellas Artes D4
17 Museo del
   Baile Flamenco F5
18 Palacio de la
   Condesa de Lebrija...... E4
19 Palacio de las
   Dueñas................... F3
20 Parque de
   María Luisa.............. F9
21 Plaza de España G8
22 Plaza de Toros
   Real Maestranza........ D6
23 Real Alcázar............. F7
24 San Lorenzo y
   Jesús del Gran Poder ... E2
25 Torre del Oro D7

Restaurants ▼

1 Abantal.................. H5
2 Bache San Pedro........ F4
3 Bar Las Golondrinas.... B6
4 Bodeguita Romero...... D5
5 Cañabota E4
6 Casa Morales E6
7 Castizo D5
8 De la O B5
9 El Pintón F5
10 El Rinconcillo............ G4
11 Espacio Eslava.......... D2
12 Ispal G7
13 La Azotea D5
14 La Moneda Casa
   Inchausti.................. E6
15 La Sal Bar................ G6
16 Palo Cortao.............. F4
17 Veganitessen............ D5
18 Vineria San Telmo G6

Quick Bites ▼

1 La Campana E4

Hotels ▼

1 Aguilas 5 Sevilla
   Suites F5
2 Casa del Poeta........... F6
3 Casa Romana
   Hotel Boutique E3
4 Corral del Rey F5
5 Eurostars Torre
   Sevilla A3
6 Gran Meliá Colón D4
7 Hotel Alfonso XIII E7
8 Hotel Amadeus
   Sevilla F5
9 Hotel Casa 1800.......... F6
10 Hotel Monte Triana A5
11 Legado Alcázar E7
12 Mercer................... D5
13 Palacio de
   Villapanés Hotel......... G4
14 Pensión Córdoba F5

bloody gazpacho, *huevo en tempura con parmentier trufado* (egg in batter with truffled potato puree), red tuna tartare, and *solomillo ibérico relleno de setas* (Iberian pork steak filled with mushrooms). **Known for:** Mediterranean dishes; value quick bites; attractive interior. Ⓢ *Average main: €13* ✉ *Calle Francos 42, Centro* ☎ *955/075153* ⊕ *elpinton.com.*

★ Espacio Eslava

$$ | **TAPAS** | The crowds gathered outside this local favorite off the Alameda de Hercules may be off-putting at first, but the creative, inexpensive tapas (from €3) are well worth the wait—and so is the house specialty, the Basque dessert *sokoa*. Try delicacies like the *solomillo de pato con pan de queso y salsa de peras al vino* (duck fillet with cheesy bread and pears in wine sauce). Tables at the tapas bar can't be booked (a call will get you a reservation at the next-door Eslava restaurant); to help avoid a wait, visit between 12:30 and 1:30 pm or between 5 and 8 pm. **Known for:** sokoa, a Basque dessert; vegetable strudel; tapas. Ⓢ *Average main: €12* ✉ *Calle Eslava 3, Centro* ☎ *954/906568* ◷ *Closed Mon. No dinner Sun.*

La Azotea

$$ | **SPANISH** | With a young vibe and a vast and inventive menu (which changes seasonally), this tiny restaurant offers a welcome change from Seville's typical fried fare. The owners' haute-cuisine ambitions are reflected in excellent service and lovingly prepared food—but not in the prices. **Known for:** local vibe; creative tapas; seasonal menu. Ⓢ *Average main: €15* ✉ *Calle Conde de Barajas 13, Centro* ☎ *955/116748* ◷ *Closed Sun. and Mon.*

☕ Coffee and Quick Bites

★ La Campana

$ | **CAFÉ** | Under the gilt-edged ceiling at Seville's most celebrated pastry outlet (founded in 1885), you can enjoy the

flanlike *tocino de cielo,* or "heavenly bacon." For breakfast, enjoy a traditional feed of toasted bread with tomato and a strong coffee, served at a standing bar. Prices are reasonable despite its popularity. **Known for:** variety of pastries and desserts; traditional atmosphere; tempting window displays. Ⓢ *Average main: €5* ✉ *Calle Sierpes 1, Centro* ☎ *954/223570* ⊕ *confiterialacampana.com.*

Hotels

Casa Romana Hotel Boutique

$$$ | **HOTEL** | Tucked away down a quiet side street in the heart of the Centro district but just 15 minutes' walk from the main sights, this restored 18th-century town house pays homage, decor-wise, to the Roman Emperor the street is named for. **Pros:** rooftop pool and cocktail bar; classical decor; good location for tapas bars and restaurants. **Cons:** rooms facing patio lack privacy; sights some distance away; standard doubles on the small side. Ⓢ *Rooms from: €150* ✉ *Calle Trajano 15, Centro* ☎ *954/915170* ⊕ *www.hotelcasaromana.com* ⇗ *26 rooms.*

★ Mercer

$$$$ | **HOTEL** | Housed in a 19th-century mansion, Mercer is one of the city's top boutique hotels, featuring a lofty patio with a fountain, a stunning marble staircase, and a striking geometric chandelier atop a glass gallery. **Pros:** rooftop terrace with plunge pool; spacious rooms; luxury lodging. **Cons:** pricey; patio rooms have no views; a little too prim. Ⓢ *Rooms from: €440* ✉ *Calle Castelar 26, Centro* ☎ *954/223004* ⊕ *www.mercersevilla.com* ⇗ *10 rooms.*

★ Palacio de Villapanés Hotel

$$$$ | **HOTEL** | An 18th-century palace with elegant updates and stylish contemporary furnishings, marble-columned patios, high ceilings, and a rooftop with terra-cotta-rooftop views, a pool, and bar, makes this one of the most chic converted-palace accommodations in Seville.

Pros: tall windows and high ceilings; local, off-the-beaten path feel; oozes style and character. **Cons:** small gym; small spa; not the most central location. Ⓢ *Rooms from: €350* ✉ *Calle Santiago 31, Centro* ☎ *650/722265* ⊕ *palaciovillapanes.com/ en* ⏎ *50 rooms.*

Shopping

Ángela y Adela Taller de Diseño
OTHER SPECIALTY STORE | Come to this shop for privately fitted and cus-tom-made flamenco dresses. ✉ *Calle Chapineros 1, Centro* ☎ *954/227186.*

Buffna
HATS & GLOVES | This shop carries hand-made hats and caps for all occasions, especially fancy ones. ✉ *Calle Don Alonso el Sabio 8, Centro* ☎ *954/537824* ⊕ *patriciabuffuna.com.*

Lola Azahares
OTHER SPECIALTY STORE | For flamenco wear, this is one of Seville's most highly regarded stores. ✉ *Calle Cuna 31, Centro* ☎ *954/222912* ⊕ *www.lolaazahares.es.*

Luisa Perez y Riu
OTHER SPECIALTY STORE | Flamenco dresses and all the accessories, designed with a modern touch, are sold at this shop. ✉ *Calle Rivero 9, Centro* ☎ *607/817624* Ⓜ *Puerta de Jerez.*

Plaza del Duque
CRAFTS | A few blocks north of Plaza Nue-va, Plaza del Duque has a crafts market Thursday through Saturday. ✉ *Centro.*

Barrio de Santa Cruz

The most romantic neighborhood in the city, Santa Cruz offers the visitor quin-tessential Seville: whitewashed houses with colorful geraniums and bougainvillea cascading down their facades, winding alleyways, and intimate squares scented with orange blossoms in the spring, all lit by old-style lamps at night. This

Where's Columbus?

Christopher Columbus knew both triumph and disgrace, yet he found no repose—he died, bitterly disil-lusioned, in Valladolid in 1506. No one knows for certain where he's buried; he was reportedly laid to rest for the first time in the Domini-can Republic and then moved over the years to other locations. A portion of his remains can be found in Seville's cathedral.

neighborhood is also the busiest and most touristic part of Seville—so stray from the main thoroughfares and lose yourself in the side streets to discover a place where time seems to have stopped and all you hear is birdsong.

◉ Sights

★ Casa de Pilatos
HISTORIC HOME | With its fine patio and superb azulejo decorations, this palace is a beautiful blend of Spanish Mudejar and Renaissance architecture and is considered a prototype of an Andalu-sian mansion. It was built in the first half of the 16th century by the dukes of Tarifa, ancestors of the present owner, the Duke of Medinaceli. It's known as Pilate's House because Don Fadrique, first marquis of Tarifa, allegedly modeled it on Pontius Pilate's house in Jerusalem, where he had gone on a pilgrimage in 1518. The upstairs apartments, which you can see on a guided tour, have frescoes, paintings, and antique furniture. Admis-sion includes an audio guide in English. ✉ *Pl. de Pilatos 1, Barrio de Santa Cruz* ☎ *954/225298* 🎫 *From €10.*

Hospital de los Venerables
HISTORIC SIGHT | Once a retirement home for priests, this baroque building has a

splendid azulejo patio with an interesting sunken fountain (designed to cope with low water pressure) and an upstairs gallery, but the highlight is the chapel, featuring frescoes by Valdés Leal and sculptures by Pedro Roldán. The building also houses a cultural foundation that organizes on-site art exhibitions. ✉ *Pl. de los Venerables 8, Barrio de Santa Cruz* ☎ *954/562696* 🎟 *€10, includes audio guide (free Mon. and Tues. 9–9.30am if you book online)* 🕓 *Closed Wed.*

★ Juderia (Jewish Quarter)

HISTORIC DISTRICT | The twisting alleyways and traditional whitewashed houses add to the tourist charm of this *barrio*. On some streets, bars alternate with antiques and souvenir shops, but most of the quarter is quiet and residential. On the Plaza Alianza, pause to enjoy the antiques shops and outdoor cafés. In the Plaza de Doña Elvira, with its fountain and azulejo benches, young sevillanos gather to play guitars. Just around the corner from the hospital, at Callejón del Agua and Jope de Rueda, Gioacchino Rossini's Figaro serenaded Rosina on her Plaza Alfaro balcony. Adjoining the Plaza Alfaro, in the Plaza Santa Cruz, flowers and orange trees surround a 17th-century filigree iron cross, which marks the site of the erstwhile church of Santa Cruz, destroyed by Napoléon's general Jean-de-Dieu Soult. ✉ *Barrio de Santa Cruz.*

Museo del Baile Flamenco

OTHER MUSEUM | This private museum in the heart of Santa Cruz (follow the signs) was opened in 2007 by the legendary flamenco dancer Cristina Hoyos and includes audiovisual and multimedia displays briefly explaining the history, culture, and soul of Spanish flamenco. There are also regular classes and shows. ✉ *Calle Manuel Rojas Marcos 3, Barrio de Santa Cruz* ☎ *954/340311* 🌐 *museodelbaileflamenco.com* 🎟 *€10 museum only; €26 museum and show.*

★ Real Alcázar

CASTLE/PALACE | The Plaza del Triunfo forms the entrance to the Mudejar palace built by Pedro I (1350–69) on the site of Seville's former Moorish alcázar. Though the alcázar was designed and built by Moorish workers brought in from Granada, it was commissioned and paid for by a Christian king more than 100 years after the Reconquest of Seville. Highlights include the oldest parts of the building, the 14th-century Sala de Justicia (Hall of Justice) and, next to it, the intimate Patio del Yeso (Courtyard of Plaster); Pedro's Mudejar palace, arranged around the beautiful Patio de las Doncellas (Court of the Damsels); the Salón de Embajadores (Hall of the Ambassadors), the most sumptuous hall in the palace; the Renaissance Palacio de Carlos V (Palace of Carlos V), endowed with a rich collection of Flemish tapestries; and the Estancias Reales (Royal Chambers), with rare clocks, antique furniture, paintings, and tapestries. ✉ *Pl. del Triunfo, Santa Cruz* ☎ *954/502324* 🌐 *www.alcazarsevilla.org* 🎟 *€13; Cuarto Real €5.*

🍴 Restaurants

Abantal

$$$$ | SPANISH | Slightly off the beaten path but worth seeking, chef Julio Fernández's tasting menu takes you on a journey of the senses featuring seemingly ordinary local produce and traditional recipes elevated with unusual textures and preparations. The menu changes with the seasons, but always has 10 dishes (€80) or 13 (€100) as well as extra-virgin-olive-oil menus. **Known for:** innovative take on dishes; long wine list; excellent service. [$] *Average main: €80* ✉ *Calle Alcalde José de la Bandera 7, Barrio de Santa Cruz* ☎ *954/540000* 🌐 *www.abantalrestaurante.es* 🕓 *Closed Sun., Mon., and Aug.*

Seville's grand alcázar is a UNESCO World Heritage Site and an absolute must-see.

Ispal

$$$$ | SPANISH | At this fine-dining venue near the Prado de San Sebastián bus station, you can taste some of the city's most exciting and innovative menus, using ingredients only from the province of Seville. The tapas tasting menu (€59, €89 paired with wine) includes dishes such as *papas con choco* (potatoes and cuttlefish), and *bacalao con tomate* (cod with tomato). **Known for:** suckling pig; regional wine list; exceptional tapas. $ *Average main: €59* ⊠ *Pl. de San Sebastián 1, Barrio de Santa Cruz* ☎ *954/547127* ⊕ *restauranteispal.com* ⊙ *Closed Mon. No dinner Sun.*

La Sal Bar

$$ | SPANISH | An offshoot of the larger Restaurante La Sal around the corner, this tapas bar offers an excellent selection of fish and meat dishes. The venue is renowned for its Almadraba tuna (traditionally hand-lined and caught in Zahara de los Atunes on the Cadiz coast) cooked any which way and always delicious. **Known for:** great choice of tapas; tuna dishes; sea anemone risotto. $ *Average main: €12* ⊠ *Paseo Catalina de Ribera 4, Santa Cruz* ☎ *954/412412* ⊕ *www. lasalzahara.com* ⊙ *Closed Sun.*

★ Vineria San Telmo

$$ | SPANISH | Offering dining in a dimly lit dining room or on the street-level terrace, this popular Argentinean-owned restaurant near the touristy *alcázar* has a menu full of surprises. All dishes—which come as tapas, half portions, or full portions (ideal for sharing)—are superb and sophisticated, especially the eggplant stew with tomato, goat cheese, and smoked salmon; the Iberian pork with potato; and the roast lamb with basil and tarragon. It can get very crowded and noisy at times, thus it's not always the ideal place for a romantic meal for two. **Known for:** Iberian pork with potato; creative tapas; extensive choice of Spanish vinos. $ *Average main: €14* ⊠ *Paseo Catalina de Ribera 4, Santa Cruz* ☎ *954/410600* ⊕ *vineriasantelmo.com/en.*

Hotels

Aguilas 5 Sevilla Suites

$$$$ | **HOTEL** | If you're looking for a self-catering option in the heart of Santa Cruz, you can't go wrong at this comfortable town house. **Pros:** central location; good value for families; home-away-from-home vibes. **Cons:** on pricey side for just 2 people; some rooms are dark; street can be a little noisy. $ *Rooms from: €250* ✉ *Calle Aguilas 5, Barrio de Santa Cruz* ☎ *658/628129* ⊕ *www.aguilas5.com* ⇘ *9 rooms* ❌ *No Meals.*

Casa del Poeta

$$$$ | **HOTEL** | Up a narrow alleyway, behind an ordinary facade, a 17th-century palace that was the haunt of Seville's poets at the end of the 19th century is now an oasis of calm. **Pros:** rooftop with a view; peaceful, central location; authentic palatial atmosphere. **Cons:** could be too traditional for some; difficult to reach by car (call shortly before arrival for staff to meet you); service can be a little slow. $ *Rooms from: €275* ✉ *Calle Don Carlos Alonso Chaparro 3, Santa Cruz* ☎ *954/213868* ⊕ *www.casadelpoeta.es* ⇘ *17 rooms.*

Corral del Rey

$$$$ | **HOTEL** | Southeast Asian and Moroccan decor fuse to perfection throughout this carefully restored 17th-century palace in the heart of Santa Cruz. **Pros:** rooftop terrace with plunge pool; private and peaceful setting but easy walk to sights; meticulously restored 17th-century palace with contemporary updates. **Cons:** based on both sides of small street and some guests have to cross street for breakfast; no direct car access; some rooms on the small side. $ *Rooms from: €300* ✉ *Calle Corral del Rey 12, Barrio de Santa Cruz* ☎ *954/227116* ⊕ *www.corraldelrey.com* ⇘ *17 rooms* ❌ *Free Breakfast.*

★ Hotel Amadeus Sevilla

$$$ | **HOTEL** | With regular classical concerts, a music room off the central patio, and instruments for guests to use, including pianos in some of the sound-proofed rooms, this 18th-century manor house is ideal for touring professional musicians and music fans in general. **Pros:** friendly service; roof terrace; small but charming rooms. **Cons:** ground-floor rooms can be dark; no direct car access; layout slightly confusing. $ *Rooms from: €150* ✉ *Calle Farnesio 6, Santa Cruz* ☎ *954/501443* ⊕ *www.hotelamadeussevilla.com* ⇘ *43 rooms.*

★ Hotel Casa 1800

$$$$ | **B&B/INN** | This classy boutique hotel, in a refurbished 19th-century mansion, is a refuge in bustling Santa Cruz. **Pros:** central location; top-notch amenities; great service. **Cons:** no restaurant; rooms facing the patio can be noisy; on noisy side street. $ *Rooms from: €275* ✉ *Calle Rodrigo Caro 6, Santa Cruz* ☎ *954/561800* ⊕ *www.hotelcasa1800sevilla.com* ⇘ *33 rooms.*

Legado Alcázar

$$$$ | **HOTEL** | Nestled next to the *alcázar*—the monument and hotel share walls—this 17th-century noble house offers a tasteful boutique experience in a very quiet corner. **Pros:** views of the alcázar; very quiet but central location; historic features. **Cons:** room size varies; no restaurant on-site; could be too traditional for some. $ *Rooms from: €195* ✉ *Calle Mariana de Pineda 18, Barrio de Santa Cruz* ☎ *954/091818* ⊕ *www.legadoalcazarhotel.com* ⇘ *18 rooms.*

Pensión Córdoba

$ | **HOTEL** | Just a few blocks from the cathedral, nestled in the heart of Santa Cruz, this small, family-run inn is an excellent value. **Pros:** rooms have a/c; quiet, central location; friendly staff. **Cons:** no breakfast; no entry after 3 am; no elevator to second floor. $ *Rooms from: €85* ✉ *Calle Farnesio 12, Santa Cruz* ☎ *954/227498* ⊕ *www.pensioncordoba.com* ⇘ *11 rooms.*

Nightlife

EME Catedral Hotel

CAFÉS | This rooftop terrace has some of the best views of the cathedral in town. Sip your cocktail to the sound of resident DJs most nights. The terrace is open daily beginning at 1 pm. ✉ *Calle Alemanes 27, Barrio de Santa Cruz* ☎ *954/560000* ⊕ *www.emecatedralhotel.com* Ⓜ *Puerta de Jerez.*

Performing Arts

FLAMENCO

★ **La Casa del Flamenco**

FOLK/TRADITIONAL DANCE | Catch an authentic professional performance in the heart of Santa Cruz on the atmospheric patio of a 15th-century house where the excellent acoustics mean there's no need for microphones or amplifiers. Shows start daily at 7 pm (Nov.–Mar.) or 8:45 pm (Apr.–Oct.). ✉ *Calle Ximénez de Enciso 28, Barrio de Santa Cruz* ☎ *954/029999* ⊕ *www.lacasadelflamencosevilla.com* ☞ *€20.*

Los Gallos

FOLK/TRADITIONAL DANCE | This intimate club in the heart of Santa Cruz attracts mainly tourists. Flamenco performances are entertaining and reasonably authentic. Shows at 8 pm and 10 pm daily. ✉ *Pl. Santa Cruz 11, Santa Cruz* ☎ *954/216981* ⊕ *www.tablaolosgallos.com.*

El Arenal and Parque María Luisa

Parque María Luisa is part shady, mid-city forestland and part monumental esplanade. El Arenal, named for its sandy riverbank soil, was originally a neighborhood of shipbuilders, stevedores, and warehouses. The heart of El Arenal lies between the Puente de San Telmo, just upstream from the Torre de Oro, and the Puente de Isabel II (Puente de Triana). El Arenal extends as far north as Avenida Alfonso XII to include the Museo de Bellas Artes. Between the park and El Arenal is the university.

◉ Sights

Hospital de la Caridad

HISTORIC SIGHT | Behind the Teatro de la Maestranza is this former almshouse for the sick and elderly, where six paintings by Murillo (1617–82) and two gruesome works by Valdés Leal (1622–90), depicting the Triumph of Death, are displayed. The baroque hospital was founded in 1674 by Seville's original Don Juan, Miguel de Mañara (1626–79). A nobleman of licentious character, Mañara was returning one night from a riotous orgy when he had a vision of a funeral procession in which the partly decomposed corpse in the coffin was his own. Accepting the apparition as a sign from God, Mañara devoted his fortune to building this hospital and is buried before the high altar in the chapel. Admission includes an audio guide (available in English). You can also book guided tours and Gregorian chant concerts. ✉ *Calle Temprado 3, El Arenal* ☎ *954/223232* ⊕ *www.santa-caridad.es/en* ☞ *From €8 (free Mon. 3:30–7.30).*

Museo de Artes y Costumbres Populares

(*Museum of Arts and Traditions*)

HISTORY MUSEUM | FAMILY | Among the fascinating items of mainly 19th- and 20th-century Spanish folklore in this museum, in the Mudejar pavilion opposite the Museo Arqueológico, is an impressive Díaz Velázquez collection of lace and embroidery—one of the finest in Europe. There's a reconstruction of a typical late-19th-century Sevillian house on the first floor, while upstairs, exhibits include 18th- and 19th-century court dress, stunning regional folk costumes, religious objects, and musical instruments. In the basement, you can see ceramics, pottery, furniture, and household items from bygone ages. ✉ *Pl. de América 3, El Arenal* ☎ *954/721391*

⊕ *www.museosdeandalucia.es* ✉ *€2* ⊙ *Closed Mon.*

★ **Museo de Bellas Artes** (*Museum of Fine Arts*)

ART MUSEUM | This museum—one of Spain's finest for Spanish art—is in the former convent of La Merced Calzada, most of which dates from the 17th century. The collection includes works by Murillo (the city celebrated the 400th anniversary of his birth in 2018) and the 17th-century Seville school, as well as by Zurbarán, Diego Velázquez, Alonso Cano, Valdés Leal, and El Greco. You will also see outstanding examples of Sevillian Gothic art and baroque religious sculptures in wood (a quintessentially Andalusian art form). In the rooms dedicated to Sevillian art of the 19th and 20th centuries, look for Gonzalo Bilbao's *Las Cigarreras*, a group portrait of Seville's famous cigar makers. An arts-and-crafts market is held outside the museum on Sunday morning. ✉ *Pl. del Museo 9, El Arenal* ☎ *954/786498* ⊕ *www.museosdeandalucia.es* ✉ *€2* ⊙ *Closed Mon.*

★ **Parque de María Luisa**

CITY PARK | Formerly the garden of the Palacio de San Telmo, this park blends formal design and wild vegetation. In the burst of development that gripped Seville in the 1920s, it was redesigned for the 1929 World's Fair, and the impressive villas you see now are the fair's remaining pavilions, many of them consulates or schools. The old casino holds the Teatro Lope de Vega, which puts on mainly musicals. Note the Anna Huntington **statue of El Cid** (Rodrigo Díaz de Vivar, 1043–99), who fought both for and against the Muslim rulers during the Reconquest. The statue was presented to Seville by the Massachusetts-born sculptor for the 1929 World's Fair. ✉ *Main entrance, Glorieta San Diego, Parque Maria Luisa.*

Plaza de España

PLAZA/SQUARE | FAMILY | This grandiose half-moon of buildings on the eastern edge of the Parque de María Luisa was Spain's centerpiece pavilion at the 1929 World's Fair. The brightly colored azulejo pictures represent the provinces of Spain, while the four bridges symbolize the medieval kingdoms of the Iberian Peninsula. In fine weather you can rent small boats to row along the arc-shape canal. To escape the crowds and enjoy views of the square from above, pop upstairs. ✉ *Parque Maria Luisa.*

Plaza de Toros Real Maestranza (*Royal Maestranza Bullring*)

PLAZA/SQUARE | Sevillanos have spent many a thrilling evening in this bullring, one of the oldest and loveliest *plazas de toros* in Spain, built between 1760 and 1763. The 20-minute tour (in English) takes in the empty arena, a museum with elaborate costumes and prints, and the chapel where matadors pray before the fight. Bullfights take place in the evening Thursday–Sunday from April through July and in September. Tickets can be booked online or by phone; book well in advance to be sure of a seat. ✉ *Paseo de Colón 12, El Arenal* ☎ *954/210315 for visits, 954/560759 for bullfights* ⊕ *realmaestranza.com for tours, plazadetorosdelamaestranza.com for tickets* ✉ *Tours €8 (free Mon. 3–7).*

Torre del Oro (*Tower of Gold*)

HISTORIC SIGHT | Built by the Moors in 1220 to complete the city's ramparts, this 12-sided tower on the banks of the Guadalquivir served to close off the harbor when a chain was stretched across the river from its base to a tower on the opposite bank. In 1248, Admiral Ramón de Bonifaz broke through the barrier, and Ferdinand III captured Seville. The tower houses a small naval museum. ✉ *Paseo Alcalde Marqués de Contadero s/n, El Arenal* ☎ *954/222419* ✉ *€3 (free Mon.).*

🍴 Restaurants

Bodeguita Romero
$$ | **SPANISH** | A couple of blocks west of the Cathedral lies one of the city's best-loved tapas venues, usually jam-packed with locals enjoying an aperitif. Established in 1939 and now in its third generation, the bar is most famous for its meat dishes including the *pringá* sandwich (slow-cooked pork, chorizo, and black pudding, in a bun) and pork cheeks. **Known for:** friendly service; traditional tapas; delicious house-marinated potatoes. [$] *Average main: €12* ✉ *Calle Harinas 10, El Arenal* ☎ *954/229556* 🌐 *bodeguitaromero.es* 🕒 *Closed Mon., no dinner Sun.*

La Moneda Casa Inchausti
$$ | **SPANISH** | Almost within stone's throw of the Giralda, this family-run restaurant has been making a name for itself with fresh fish dishes for over two decades. The owners hail from Sanlúcar de Barrameda downriver and the ingredients come from their hometown and always include swordfish, sea bass, and anchovies. **Known for:** value; fresh fish; traditional soups and stews. [$] *Average main: €14* ✉ *Calle Almirantazgo 5, El Arenal* ☎ *954/223642* 🕒 *Closed Sun. and August. No dinner Sat.*

Veganitessen
$ | **VEGETARIAN** | If you're a vegan, vegetarian, or flexitarian and finding the meat and fish scene in Seville a bit heavy, head for this bar inside the Mercado del Arenal. It started life as Spain's first vegan bakery in 2009 and since then the menu has grown to encompass breakfast and brunch, plus a long list of 100%-animal-free options to make into burgers, nachos, or wraps. **Known for:** vegan-friendly; cakes and pastries; good value daily lunch menu. [$] *Average main: €8* ✉ *Calle Pastor y Landero, Mercado del Arenal, Puesto 32, El Arenal* ☎ *611/690463* 🌐 *veganitessen.es* 🕒 *Closed Sun.*

🛏 Hotels

Gran Meliá Colón
$$$$ | **HOTEL** | Originally opened for 1929's Ibero-American Exposition, this classic hotel retains many original features, including a marble staircase leading up to a central lobby crowned by a magnificent stained-glass dome and crystal chandelier. **Pros:** some great views; good central location; excellent restaurant. **Cons:** on a busy and noisy street; some rooms overlook air shaft; pricey. [$] *Rooms from: €350* ✉ *Calle Canalejas 1, El Arenal* ☎ *954/505599* 🌐 *www.melia.com* 🔑 *189 rooms.*

★ **Hotel Alfonso XIII**
$$$$ | **HOTEL** | Inaugurated by King Alfonso XIII in 1929 when he visited the World's Fair, this grand hotel next to the university is a splendid, historic, Mudejar-style palace, built around a central patio and surrounded by ornate brick arches. **Pros:** historic surroundings; both stately and hip; impeccable service. **Cons:** expensive; a tourist colony; too sophisticated for some. [$] *Rooms from: €450* ✉ *Calle San Fernando 2, El Arenal* ☎ *954/917000* 🌐 *www.hotel-alfonsoxiii-seville.com* 🔑 *148 rooms.*

🎭 Performing Arts

Teatro de la Maestranza
OPERA | Long prominent in the opera world, Seville is proud of its opera house. Tickets go quickly, so book well in advance (online is best). ✉ *Paseo de Colón 22, El Arenal* ☎ *954/223344 for info, 954/226573 for tickets* 🌐 *www.teatrodelamaestranza.es.*

Teatro Lope de Vega
ARTS CENTERS | Classical music, ballet, and musicals are performed here. Tickets are best booked online. ✉ *Av. María Luisa s/n, Parque Maria Luisa* ☎ *954/472828 for info, 955/472822 for tickets* 🌐 *www.teatrolopedevega.org.*

Shopping

Artesanía Textil

CRAFTS | You can find blankets, shawls, and embroidered tablecloths woven by local artisans at this textile shop. Their products are also available online. ⊠ *Calle García de Vinuesa 33, El Arenal* ☎ *954/215088* ⊕ *artesania-textil.com.*

El Postigo

CRAFTS | This permanent arts-and-crafts market just around the corner from the Cathedral has over 20 stalls and workshops. ⊠ *Calle Arfe s/n, El Arenal.*

Barrio de la Macarena

This immense neighborhood covers the entire northern half of historic Seville and deserves to be walked many times. Most of the best churches, convents, markets, and squares are concentrated around the center in an area delimited by the Arab ramparts to the north, the Alameda de Hercules to the west, the Santa Catalina church to the south, and the Convento de Santa Paula to the east. The area between the Alameda de Hercules and the Guadalquivir is known to locals as the Barrio de San Lorenzo, a section that's ideal for an evening of tapas grazing.

◉ Sights

Basílica de la Macarena

CHURCH | This church holds Seville's most revered image, the Virgin of Hope—better known as La Macarena. Bedecked with candles and carnations, her cheeks streaming with glass tears, the Macarena steals the show at the procession on Holy Thursday, the highlight of Seville's Semana Santa pageant. The patron of Gypsies and the protector of the matador, her charms are so great that young sevillano bullfighter Joselito spent half his personal fortune buying her emeralds. When he was killed in the ring in 1920,

---

Fiesta Time!

Seville's color and vivacity are most intense during Semana Santa, when lacerated Christs and bejeweled, weeping Mary statues are paraded through town on floats borne by often-barefoot penitents. Two weeks later, sevillanos throw Feria de Abril, featuring midday horse parades with men in broad-brim hats and Andalusian riding gear astride prancing steeds, and women in ruffled dresses riding sidesaddle behind them. Bullfights, fireworks, and all-night singing and dancing complete the spectacle.

La Macarena was dressed in widow's weeds for a month. The adjacent museum tells the history of Semana Santa traditions through processional and liturgical artifacts amassed by the Brotherhood of La Macarena over four centuries. ⊠ *Calle Bécquer 1, La Macarena* ☎ *954/901800* 🎟 *Basilica free, museum €5.*

★ Convento de Santa Paula

CHURCH | This 15th-century Gothic convent has a fine facade and portico, with ceramic decoration by Nicolaso Pisano. The chapel has some beautiful azulejos and sculptures by Martínez Montañés. It also contains a small museum and a shop selling delicious cakes and jams made by the nuns. ⊠ *Calle Santa Paula 11, La Macarena* ☎ *954/536330* 🎟 *€4* ⊗ *Closed Mon.*

San Lorenzo y Jesús del Gran Poder

CHURCH | This 17th-century church has many fine works by such artists as Martínez Montañés and Francisco Pacheco, but its outstanding piece is Juan de Mesa y Velasco's *Jesús del Gran Poder* (*Christ Omnipotent*). ⊠ *Pl. San Lorenzo 13, La Macarena* ☎ *954/915686* 🎟 *Free.*

🍴 Restaurants

Bache San Pedro

$$ | SPANISH | Barack Obama's chosen spot for tapas when he visited the city in April 2019 has outside seating on a small terrace with views of the square or spots inside, where traditional Seville tiles blend perfectly into the sleek industrial vibe. Bringing the taste of Cádiz to Seville, dishes here come as tapas or sharing plates (€3.50–€15) and include *croquetas de puchero* (stew croquettes), a taco of *chicharrones* (pork crackling) with Payoyo goat's cheese, and possibly the spiciest *patatas bravas* (fried potatoes) in town. **Known for:** delicious desserts; friendly service; innovative cuisine. ⓢ *Average main: €13* ✉ *Pl. Cristo de Burgos 23, Seville* ☎ *954/502934* ⊕ *www.bachesanpedro.com* ⊘ *Closed Mon.*

El Rinconcillo

$$ | SPANISH | Founded in 1670, this lovely spot serves a classic selection of dishes, such as the *pavía de bacalao* (fried breaded cod), a superb *salmorejo* (a puree consisting of tomato and bread), and *espinacas con garbanzos*, all in generous portions. The views of Iglesia de Santa Catalina out the front window upstairs are unbeatable, and your bill is chalked up on the wooden counters as you go (tapas are attractively priced from €2.50). **Known for:** views of Iglesia de Santa Catalina; tapas; crowds of locals. ⓢ *Average main: €12* ✉ *Calle Gerona 40, La Macarena* ☎ *954/223183* ⊕ *www.elrinconcillo.es.*

Palo Cortao

$ | SPANISH | Down an uninspiring side street but with a very quiet terrace with views of San Pedro Church, this bar with stool seating around high tables offers tranquil dining and, most notably, one of the best sherry menus in town. Known as an *abacería* (grocer's store), it serves more than 30 finos, amontillados, and olorosos, plus house-made vermouth on the drinks menu, and each pairs perfectly with a food choice. **Known for:** ajoblanco (cold garlic soup); excellent sherry; pairing menu. ⓢ *Average main: €6* ✉ *Calle Mercedes de Velilla 4, La Macarena* ☎ *649/446120* ⊕ *www.palo-cortao.com* ⊘ *Closed Mon. and Tues.*

Triana

Triana used to be Seville's Gypsy quarter. Today, it has a tranquil, neighborly feel by day and a distinctly flamenco feel at night. Cross over to Triana via the **Puente de Isabel II,** an iron bridge built in 1852 and the first to connect the city's two sections. Start your walk in the **Plaza del Altozano,** the center of the Triana district and traditionally the meeting point for travelers from the south crossing the river to Seville. Admire the facade of the Murillo pharmacy here before walking up **Calle Jacinto.** Look out for the fine **Casa de los Mensaque** (now the district's administrative office and usually open on weekday morning), home to some of Triana's finest potters and housing some stunning examples of Seville ceramics. To reach attractions in La Cartuja, take Bus C1.

👁 Sights

Capilla de los Marineros

HISTORIC SIGHT | This seamen's chapel, built in 1759, is one of Triana's most important monuments and home to the Brotherhood of Triana, whose Semana Santa processions are among the most revered in the city. There's also a small museum dedicated to the Brotherhood. ✉ *Calle Pureza 2, Triana* ☎ *954/332645* 💷 *Free, museum €4.*

Centro de Cerámica Triana (*Ceramics Center*)

ARTS CENTER | With none of the 40 original ceramists remaining in Triana, this restored factory complete with its original kilns provides an interesting insight into the neighborhood's tile-making past.

Downstairs, an exhibition explains the manufacturing process and the story of ceramics while upstairs, there's a selection of tiles on show. Free guided tours in English. ✉ *Calle Callao 16, Triana* ☎ *954/474293* 🌐 *ceramicatriana.com* 🎟 *€3. Free with regular Alcázar ticket.*

Isla de La Cartuja

ISLAND | Named after its 14th-century Carthusian monastery, this island in the Guadalquivir River across from northern Seville was the site of the decennial Universal Exposition (Expo) in 1992. The island has the Teatro Central, used for concerts and plays; Parque del Alamillo, Seville's largest and least-known park; and the Estadio Olímpico, a 60,000-seat covered stadium. The best way to get to La Cartuja is by walking across one or both (one each way) of the superb Santiago Calatrava bridges spanning the river. The Puente de la Barqueta crosses to La Cartuja, and downstream the Puente del Alamillo connects the island with Seville. Buses C1 and C2 also serve La Cartuja. ✉ *Triana.*

Monasterio de Santa María de las Cuevas
(*Monasterio de La Cartuja*)

ART MUSEUM | The 14th-century monastery was regularly visited by Christopher Columbus, who was also buried here for a few years. Part of the building houses the **Centro Andaluz de Arte Contemporáneo,** which has an absorbing collection of contemporary art. ✉ *Isla de la Cartuja, Av. Américo Vespucio, Triana* ☎ *955/037070* 🕓 *Closed Mon.* 🎟 *Free.*

🍴 Restaurants

Bar Las Golondrinas

$$ | **SPANISH** | Run by the same family for more than 50 years and lavishly decorated in the colorful tiles that pay tribute to the neighborhood's potters, Las Golondrinas is a fixture of Triana life. The staff never change, and neither does the menu—the recipes for the *punta de solomillo* (sliced sirloin), *chipirones* (fried baby squid), and *caballito de jamón* (ham on bread) have been honed to perfection, and they're served as tapas (€3), or *raciones*, that keep everyone happy. **Known for:** good value; vibrant atmosphere; traditional tapas. [$] *Average main: €12* ✉ *Calle Antillano Campos 26, Triana* ☎ *954/332616.*

De la O

$$ | **SPANISH** | Tucked away on the riverfront in Triana next to Puente Cristo de la Expiración, this modern venue advocates local produce in traditional Andalusian recipes along with a long wine list of Andalusian wines. The long, narrow interior has striking wood-paneled walls with a verdant vertical garden in the middle, while outside dining takes in panoramic views of the river on the intimate terrace. **Known for:** dishes presented artistically; quality local produce; house-made sausages. [$] *Average main: €14* ✉ *Paseo de Nuestra Señora de la O 29, Triana* ☎ *954/339000* 🌐 *www.delaorestaurante.com* 🕓 *No dinner Sun.–Thurs.*

🛏 Hotels

Eurostars Torre Sevilla

$$$$ | **HOTEL** | Andalusia's tallest building, with a 180-meter tower, designed by Cesar Pelli, rises high above the Cartuja area and makes a controversial sight on the city skyline while delivering spectacular views over Seville, Triana, and the river. **Pros:** modern amenities; spectacular views of the city; spacious accommodations. **Cons:** limited spa hours during week; some distance from sights and attractions; indifferent service at times. [$] *Rooms from: €190* ✉ *Calle Gonzalo Jiménez de Quesada 2, Triana* ☎ *954/466022* 🌐 *www.eurostarshotels.com* 🛏 *244 rooms* 🍽 *No Meals.*

Hotel Monte Triana

$$ | **HOTEL** | Comfortable, squeaky-clean facilities and excellent value for the cost are two key reasons for choosing this hotel to the north of the heart of Triana.

Pros: friendly and helpful staff; good value; private parking. **Cons:** decor too basic for some; 20-minute walk into city center; no on-site restaurant. $ *Rooms from: €110* ✉ *Calle Clara de Jesús Montero 24, Triana* ☎ *954/343111* ⊕ *www.hotelesmonte.com* 🛏 *114 rooms.*

Performing Arts

FLAMENCO
Lola de los Reyes
FOLK/TRADITIONAL DANCE | This venue in Triana presents reasonably authentic shows and hosts "flamenco afternoons" on Friday and Saturday—check the website for details. Entrance is free, but there's a one-drink minimum. Booking advised. ✉ *Calle Pureza 107, Triana* ☎ *667/631163* ⊕ *www.loladelosreyes.es* Ⓜ *Blas Infante/Parque de los Príncipes.*

Teatro Central
ARTS CENTERS | This modern venue on the Isla de la Cartuja stages theater, dance (including flamenco), and classical and contemporary music. Tickets can be bought online or at the ticket office. ✉ *Calle José de Gálvez 6, Triana* ☎ *955/542155 for information* ⊕ *www.teatrocentral.es.*

🛍 Shopping

Potters' District
CERAMICS | Look for traditional azulejo tiles and other ceramics in the Triana potters' district, on Calle Alfarería, Calle Antillano Campos, and Calle Callao such as Cerámica Triana (Calle Callao 14) selling a selection of traditional ceramic items. ✉ *Triana*

Itálica

12 km (7 miles) north of Seville, 1 km (½ mile) beyond Santiponce.

Neighboring the small town of Santiponce, Itálica is Spain's oldest Roman

site and one of its greatest, and it is well worth a visit when you're in Seville. If you're here during July, try to get tickets for the Performing Arts Festival held in the ruins.

GETTING HERE AND AROUND
The M170A bus route runs frequently (daily 9 am–3:30 pm) between the Plaza de Armas bus station in Seville and Itálica. The journey time is 20 minutes. If you have a rental car, you could include a visit to the ruins on your way to Huelva. Allow at least two hours for your visit.

👁 Sights

★ Itálica
RUINS | One of Roman Iberia's most important cities in the 2nd century, with a population of more than 10,000, Itálica today is a monument of Roman ruins. Founded by Scipio Africanus in 205 BC as a home for veteran soldiers, Itálica gave the Roman world two great emperors: Trajan (AD 52–117) and Hadrian (AD 76–138). You can find traces of city streets, cisterns, and the floor plans of several villas, some with mosaic floors, though all the best mosaics and statues have been removed to Seville's Museum of Archaeology. Itálica was abandoned and plundered as a quarry by the Visigoths, who preferred Seville. It fell into decay around AD 700. The remains include the huge, elliptical **amphitheater,** which held 40,000 spectators, a **Roman theater,** and **Roman baths.** The finale for season 7 of *Game of Thrones* was filmed here in 2018. The small visitor center offers information on daily life in the city. ✉ *Av. Extremadura 2,* ☎ *600/141767* ⊕ *www.museosdeandalucia.es* 🎫 *€2* ⊘ *Closed Mon.*

Córdoba

166 km (103 miles) northwest of Granada, 407 km (250 miles) southwest of Madrid, 239 km (143 miles) northeast of Cádiz, 143 km (86 miles) northeast of Seville.

Strategically located on the north bank of the Guadalquivir River, Córdoba was the Roman and Moorish capital of Spain, and its old quarter, clustered around its famous Mezquita, remains one of the country's grandest and yet most intimate examples of its Moorish heritage. Once a medieval city famed for the peaceful and prosperous coexistence of its three religious cultures—Islamic, Jewish, and Christian—Córdoba is also a perfect analogue for the cultural history of the Iberian Peninsula.

Córdoba today, with its modest population of a little more than 330,000, offers a cultural depth and intensity—a direct legacy from the great emirs, caliphs, philosophers, physicians, poets, and engineers of the days of the caliphate—that far outstrips the city's current commercial and political power. Its artistic and historical treasures begin with the Mezquita-Catedral (mosque-cathedral), as it is generally called, and continue through the winding, whitewashed streets of the Judería (the medieval Jewish quarter); the jasmine-, geranium-, and orange-blossom-filled patios; the Renaissance palaces; and the two dozen churches, convents, and hermitages, built by Moorish artisans directly over former mosques.

GETTING HERE AND AROUND

BIKE

Never designed to support cars, Córdoba's medieval layout is ideal for bicycles, and there's a good network of designated bicycle tracks.

CONTACTS Rent a Bike Córdoba. ⊠ *Calle Maria Cristina 5* ☎ *957/943700* ⊕ *rentabikecordoba.com.*

BUS

Córdoba is easily reached by bus from Granada, Málaga, and Seville. The city has an extensive public bus network with frequent service. Buses usually start running at 6:30 or 7 am and stop around midnight. You can buy 10-trip passes at newsstands and the bus office in Plaza de Colón. A single-trip fare is €1.30.

Córdoba has organized open-top bus tours of the city that can be booked via the tourist office.

CONTACTS Córdoba. ⊠ *Glorieta de las Tres Culturas* ☎ *957/404040* ⊕ *www.estacionautobusescordoba.es.*

CAR

The city's one-way system can be something of a nightmare to navigate, and it's best to park in one of the signposted lots outside the old quarter.

TAXI

CONTACTS Radio Taxi. ⊠ *Córdoba* ☎ *957/764444.*

TRAIN

The city's modern train station is the hub for a comprehensive network of regional trains, with regular high-speed train service to Granada, Seville, Málaga, Madrid, and Barcelona.

CONTACTS Train Station. ⊠ *Glorieta de las Tres Culturas* ☎ *912/320320.*

VISITOR INFORMATION

CONTACTS Tourist Office. ⊠ *Pl. de las Tendillas 5, Centro* ☎ *957/471577* ⊕ *www.turismodecordoba.org.*

 # Sights

Alcázar de los Reyes Cristianos (*Fortress of the Christian Monarchs*)

CASTLE/PALACE | Built by Alfonso XI in 1328, the *alcázar* in Córdoba is a Mudejar-style palace with splendid gardens. (The original Moorish *alcázar* stood beside the Mezquita, on the site of the present Bishop's Palace.) This is where, in the 15th century, the Catholic monarchs held court and launched their conquest of Granada. Boabdil was imprisoned here in 1483, and for nearly 300 years this *alcázar* served as the Inquisition's base. The most important sights here are the Hall of the Mosaics and a

Córdoba's History

The Romans invaded Córdoba in 206 BC, later making it the capital of Rome's section of Spain. Nearly 800 years later, the Visigoth king Leovigildus took control, but the tribe was soon supplanted by the Moors, whose emirs and caliphs held court here from the 8th to the early 11th century. At that point Córdoba was one of the greatest centers of art, culture, and learning in the Western world; one of its libraries had a staggering 400,000 volumes. Moors, Christians, and Jews lived together in harmony within Córdoba's walls. In that era, it was considered second in importance only to Constantinople; but in 1009, Prince Muhammad II and Omeyan led a rebellion that broke up the caliphate, leading to power flowing to separate Moorish kingdoms.

Córdoba remained in Moorish hands until it was conquered by King Ferdinand in 1236 and repopulated from the north of Spain. Later, the Catholic monarchs used the city as a base from which to plan the conquest of Granada. In Columbus's time, the Guadalquivir was navigable as far upstream as Córdoba, and great galleons sailed its waters. Today, the river's muddy water and marshy banks evoke little of Córdoba's glorious past, but an old Arab waterfall and the city's bridge—of Roman origin, though much restored by the Arabs and successive generations, most recently in 2012—recall a far grander era.

Roman stone sarcophagus from the 2nd or 3rd century. ⊠ *Pl. Campo Santo de los Mártires, Judería* ✛ *Next to Guadalquivir River* ⊕ *alcazardelosreyescristianos. cordoba.es* 🖼 *€5* ⊘ *Closed Mon.*

★ Calleja de las Flores

STREET | A few yards off the northeastern corner of the Mezquita, this tiny street has the prettiest patios, many with ceramics, foliage, and iron grilles. The patios are key to Córdoba's architecture, at least in the old quarter, where life is lived behind sturdy white walls—a legacy of the Moors, who honored both the sanctity of the home and the need to shut out the fierce summer sun. Between the first and second week of May—right after the early May Cruces de Mayo (Crosses of May) competition, when neighborhoods compete at setting up elaborate crosses decorated with flowers and plants—Córdoba throws a Patio Festival, during which private patios are filled with flowers, opened to the public, and judged in a municipal competition. Córdoba's tourist office publishes an itinerary of the best patios in town (downloadable from *patios. cordoba.es/en*)—note that most are open only in the late afternoon on weekdays but all day on weekends. ⊠ *Judería.*

★ Madinat Al-Zahra (*Medina Azahara*)

RUINS | Built in the foothills of the Sierra Morena by Abd ar-Rahman III for his favorite concubine, al-Zahra (the Flower), this once-splendid summer pleasure palace was begun in 936. Historians say it took 10,000 men, 2,600 mules, and 400 camels 25 years to erect this fantasy of 4,300 columns in dazzling pink, green, and white marble and jasper brought from Carthage. A palace, a mosque, luxurious baths, fragrant gardens, fish ponds, an aviary, and a zoo stood on three terraces here, until, in 1013, it was sacked and destroyed by Berber mercenaries. In 1944, the Royal Apartments were rediscovered, and the throne room carefully reconstructed. The outline of the mosque has also been excavated.

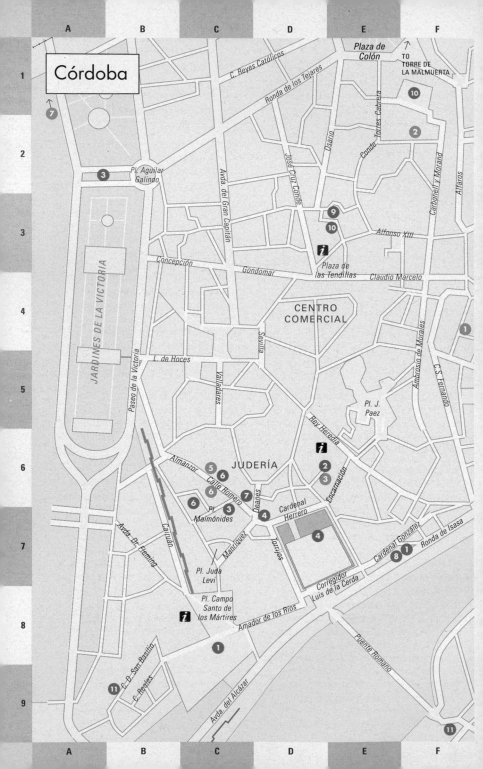

KEY

1 Sights
1 Restaurants
1 Hotels
i Tourist Information

Sights ▼

1 Alcázar de los
  Reyes Cristianos......... **C8**
2 Calleja de las Flores..... **E6**
3 Madinat Al-Zahra....... **A2**
4 Mezquita................ **D7**
5 Museo de
  Bellas Artes **G6**
6 Museo Taurino........... **C6**
7 Palacio de Viana........ **G1**
8 Plaza de los Dolores.... **Q1**
9 Plaza de San Miguel **E3**
10 Plaza Santa Marina **F1**
11 Torre Calahorra **F9**

Restaurants ▼

1 Amaltea.................. **F7**
2 Bodegas Campos....... **H6**
3 Casa Mazal.............. **C7**
4 Casa Pepe de la
  Judería.................. **D7**
5 El Choco **I4**
6 El Churrasco............. **C6**
7 El Rincón de Carmen **C6**
8 La Regadera............. **E7**
9 noor **I2**
10 Taberna de
  San Miguel **E3**
11 Taberna La Viuda **B9**

Hotels ▼

1 Casa de los Azulejos **F4**
2 Hospes Palacio
  del Bailío................. **F2**
3 Hotel Balcón
  de Córdoba **E6**
4 Hotel Maestre........... **G6**
5 La Llave de la Judería... **C6**
6 NH Collection
  Amistad Córdoba **C6**
7 Parador de Córdoba.... **A1**
8 Viento 10.................. **I5**

The only covered part is the Salon de Abd ar-Rahman III (restoration work is due to finish in 2021); the rest is a sprawl of foundations and arches that hint at the original splendor. First visit the nearby museum and then continue with a walk among the ruins. ⊠ *Ctra. de Palma del Río, Km 5.5* ✛ *8 km (5 miles) west of Córdoba on C431* ☎ *957/104933* ⊕ *www. museosdeandalucia.es* ✆ *€2* ⊙ *Closed Mon.*

★ **Mezquita** (*Mosque*)
HISTORIC SIGHT | Built between the 8th and 10th centuries, Córdoba's mosque is one of the earliest and most beautiful examples of Spanish Islamic architecture. Inside, some 850 columns rise before you in a forest of jasper, marble, granite, and onyx. The mezquita has served as a cathedral since 1236, but it was founded as a mosque in 785 by Abd ar-Rahman I. The beautiful **mihrab** (prayer niche) is the mezquita's greatest jewel. In front of the mihrab is the **maksoureh**, a kind of anteroom for the caliph and his court; its mosaics and plasterwork make it a masterpiece of Islamic art. In the 13th century, Christians had the **Capilla de Villaviciosa** built by Moorish craftsmen, its Mudejar architecture blending with the lines of the mosque. Not so the heavy, incongruous Baroque structure of the cathedral, sanctioned in the heart of the mosque by Carlos V in the 1520s. ⊠ *Calle de Torrijos, Judería* ☎ *957/470512* ⊕ *mezquita-catedraldecordoba.es/en* ✆ *Mezquita €11, free Mon.-Sat. 8.30-9.30am, Torre del Alminar €2.*

★ **Museo de Bellas Artes**
ART MUSEUM | Hard to miss because of its deep-pink facade, Córdoba's Museum of Fine Arts, in a courtyard just off the Plaza del Potro, belongs to a former Hospital de la Caridad (Charity Hospital). It was founded by Ferdinand and Isabella, who twice received Columbus here. The collection, which includes paintings by Murillo, Valdés Leal, Zurbarán, Goya, and Joaquín Sorolla y Bastida, concentrates on local artists. Highlights are altarpieces from the 14th and 15th centuries and the large collection of prints and drawings, including some by Fortuny, Goya, and Sorolla. ⊠ *Pl. del Potro 1, San Francisco* ☎ *957/103659* ⊕ *www.museosdeandalucia.es* ⊙ *Closed Mon.* ✆ *€2.*

Museo Taurino (*Museum of Bullfighting*)
OTHER MUSEUM | Two adjoining mansions on the Plaza Maimónides (or Plaza de las Bulas) house this museum, and it's worth a visit, as much for the chance to see a restored mansion as for the posters, Art Nouveau paintings, bulls' heads, suits of lights (bullfighting outfits), and memorabilia of famous Córdoban bullfighters, including the most famous of all, Manolete. To the surprise of the nation, Manolete, who was considered immortal, was killed by a bull in the ring at Linares in 1947. ⊠ *Pl. de Maimónides 1, Judería* ☎ *957/201056* ✆ *€4* ⊙ *Closed Mon.*

Palacio de Viana
CASTLE/PALACE | This 17th-century palace is one of Córdoba's most splendid aristocratic homes. Also known as the **Museo de los Patios,** it contains 12 interior patios, each one different; the patios and gardens are planted with cypresses, orange trees, and myrtles. Inside the building are a carriage museum, a library, embossed leather wall hangings, filigree silver, and grand galleries and staircases. As you enter, note that the corner column of the first patio has been removed to allow the entrance of horse-drawn carriages. ⊠ *Pl. Don Gomé 2, Centro* ☎ *957/496741* ⊕ *palaciodeviana.com* ⊙ *Closed Mon.* ✆ *From €6.*

Plaza de los Dolores
PLAZA/SQUARE | The 17th-century Convento de Capuchinos surrounds this small square north of Plaza San Miguel. The square is where you feel most deeply the city's languid pace. In its center, a statue of **Cristo de los Faroles** (Christ of the Lanterns) stands amid eight lanterns hanging

from twisted wrought-iron brackets. ⊠ *Centro.*

Plaza de San Miguel

PLAZA/SQUARE | The square and café terraces around it, and its excellent tavern, Taberna San Miguel–Casa El Pisto, form one of the city's finest combinations of art, history, and gastronomy. The San Miguel church has an interesting facade with Romanesque doors built around Mudejar horseshoe arches, and a Mudejar dome inside. ⊠ *Centro.*

Plaza Santa Marina

PLAZA/SQUARE | At the edge of the Barrio de los Toreros, a quarter where many of Córdoba's famous bullfighters were born and raised, stands a statue of the famous bullfighter Manolete (1917–47) opposite the lovely church of Santa Marina de Aguas Santas (St. Marina of Holy Waters), built by Ferdinand III when he conquered the city in 1236. Not far from here, on the Plaza de la Lagunilla, is a bust of Manolete. ⊠ *Centro.*

Torre Calahorra

NOTABLE BUILDING | The tower on the far side of the Puente Romano (Roman Bridge), which was restored in 2008, was built in 1369 to guard the entrance to Córdoba. It now houses the **Museo Vivo de Al-Andalus** ("al-Andalus" is Arabic for "Land of the West"), with films and audiovisual guides (in English) on Córdoba's history. Climb the narrow staircase to the top of the tower for the view of the Roman bridge and city on the other side of the Guadalquivir. ⊠ *Av. de la Confederación s/n, Sector Sur* ☎ *957/293929* ⊕ *www.torrecalahorra.es* ⊠ *From €5, includes audio guide.*

🍴 Restaurants

Amaltea

$$ | **INTERNATIONAL** | Satisfying vegetarians, vegans, and their meat-eating friends, this organic restaurant includes some meat and fish on the menu. There's a healthy mix of Mexican, Asian,

Spanish, and Italian-influenced dishes, including salmon steamed in banana leaves, chicken curry with mango and apricots, and couscous. **Known for:** organic options; inviting interior with relaxed vibe; vegetarian food. **$** *Average main: €15* ⊠ *Ronda de Isasa 10, Centro* ☎ *957/491968* 🕙 *No dinner Sun. Closed Sun. in summer.*

★ Bodegas Campos

$$$ | **SPANISH** | A block east of the Plaza del Potro, this traditional old bodega with high-quality service is the epitome of all that's great about Andalusian cuisine. The dining rooms are in barrel-heavy rustic rooms and leafy traditional patios (take a look at some of the signed barrels—you may recognize a name or two, such as the former U.K. prime minister Tony Blair). **Known for:** excellent tapas bar; bodega setting; regional dishes. **$** *Average main: €22* ⊠ *Calle Los Lineros 32, San Pedro* ☎ *957/497500* ⊕ *www. bodegascampos.com.*

Casa Mazal

$$$ | **ECLECTIC** | In the heart of the Judería, this pretty little restaurant serves a modern interpretation of Sephardic cuisine, with organic dishes that are more exotic than the usual Andalusian fare. The many vegetarian options include gazpacho with mango, and the *confitura de cordero con espárragos trigueros* (caramelized lamb with baby asparagus) and *siniya* (trout baked in vine leaves with pomegranate and mint) are delicious. **Known for:** vegetarian dishes; traditional Sephardic cuisine; romantic ambience. **$** *Average main: €18* ⊠ *Calle Tomás Conde 3, Judería* ☎ *957/246304.*

Casa Pepe de la Judería

$$$ | **SPANISH** | Geared toward a tourist clientele, this place is always packed, noisy, and fun, and there is live Spanish guitar music on the roof terrace most summer nights. Antiques and some wonderful old oil paintings fill this three-floor labyrinth of rooms just around the corner from the mosque, near the Judería. **Known**

for: live music on the roof terrace in summer; croquetas de jamón; traditional Andalusian food. [$] *Average main: €20* ✉ *Calle Romero 1, off Deanes, Judería* ☎ *957/200744.*

★ El Choco

$$$$ | SPANISH | The city's most exciting restaurant, which has renewed its Michelin star annually since 2012, El Choco has renowned chef Kisko Garcia at the helm whipping up innovative dishes based on his 10 Commandments to preserve good cooking. One of them is that taste always comes first, and that plays out well during a meal at this minimalist restaurant with charcoal-color walls, glossy parquet floors, and dishes offering new sensations and amazing presentations. **Known for:** innovative presentation; creative Andalusian cooking; good value Michelin-star tasting menu. [$] *Average main: €95* ✉ *Compositor Serrano Lucena 14, Centro* ☎ *957/264863* 🌐 *www.restaurantechoco.es* 🕒 *Closed Mon. and Aug. No dinner Sun.*

El Churrasco

$$$ | SPANISH | The name suggests grilled meat, but this restaurant in the heart of the Judería serves much more than that. In the colorful bar try tapas (from €3.50) such as the *berenjenas crujientes con salmorejo* (crispy fried eggplant slices with thick gazpacho), while in the restaurant, opt for the supremely fresh grilled fish or the steak, which is the best in town, particularly the namesake *churrasco ibérico* (grilled pork, served here in a spicy tomato-based sauce). **Known for:** alfresco dining; grilled meat; tapas. [$] *Average main: €20* ✉ *Calle Romero 16, Judería* ☎ *957/290819* 🕒 *Closed Aug.*

El Rincón de Carmen

$$ | MEDITERRANEAN | With the sights of the Judería on the doorstep, this is a good, central spot for a quick bite in a typical Córdoba patio setting that's particularly pretty at night. Tapas and sharing plates make up the menu where star turns come from the *magret de pato* (duck breast) and *saquitos de bacalao con salsa dulce de pimientos* (cod pastries with sweet pepper sauce). **Known for:** saquitos de bacalao (cod pastries); generous portions; attractive patio setting. [$] *Average main: €14* ✉ *Calle Romero 4, Judería* ☎ *957/291055* 🌐 *restauranterincondecarmen.es* 🕒 *Closed Mon. No dinner Tues. and Sun.*

La Regadera

$$ | SPANISH | It feels as if you could be outside at this bright venue on the river whose fresh interior comes with miniature wall gardens and lots of watering cans (*regaderas*)—there's even a fresh herb garden in the middle. Local produce takes center stage on the menu, where you'll find a mix of traditional and modern dishes including house specials such as wild sea bass ceviche, suckling pig, and cream of lemon. **Known for:** tuna tartare; gardenlike interior; good wine list. [$] *Average main: €16* ✉ *Ronda de Isasa 10, Judería* ☎ *957/101400* 🌐 *www.regadera.es* 🕒 *Closed Mon.*

★ noor

$$$$ | SPANISH | One of the few two Michelin-starred venues in Andalusia, noor offers Andalusí cuisine made exclusively with ingredients that predate the discovery of the New World, so don't expect any potatoes, tomatoes, or chocolate on the menu. Local chef Paco Morales and team create in the open kitchen while diners sit at very modern tables under a dramatic Arabian nights' ceiling. **Known for:** Arabian nights ambience; creative, authentic cuisine; destination dining. [$] *Average main: €95* ✉ *Calle Pablo Ruiz Picasso 8, Centro* ☎ *957/964055* 🌐 *noorrestaurant.es* 🕒 *Closed Sun.–Tues. and July and Aug.*

Taberna de San Miguel

$$ | TAPAS | Just a few minutes' walk from the Plaza de las Tendillas and opposite the lovely San Miguel Church, this popular tapas spot—also known as the Casa el Pisto (Ratatouille House)—was established in 1880. You can choose to

Córdoba's stunning Mezquita charts the evolution of Western and Islamic architecture over a 1,300-year period.

squeeze in at the bar and dine on tapas (from €3) or spread out a little more on the patio decked with ceramics and bullfighting memorabilia, where half and full portions are served. **Known for:** patio with bullfighting memorabilia; historic ambience; tapas, including pisto. $ *Average main: €12* ⌧ *Pl. San Miguel 1, Centro* ☎ *957/470166* ⊕ *www.casaelpisto.com* ⊘ *Closed Sun. and Aug.*

Taberna La Viuda

$ | SPANISH | Slightly off the beaten tourist trail and with a lively, local vibe, this tavern-style venue specializes in traditional local cuisine such as *salmorejo* (cold tomato soup), *flamenquín*, (bacon-wrapped pork loin that's breaded and fried), and oxtail, but you'll also find creative touches on the menu in the form of tuna marinated in ginger and venison cold cuts. Most dishes are available as tapas, half, or full plates, and all can be paired with local wines. **Known for:** wine pairings; traditional local food; warm welcome. $ *Average main: €10* ⌧ *Calle San Basilio 52, Judería* ☎ *957/296905.*

Hotels

Casa de los Azulejos

$$ | B&B/INN | This 17th-century house still has original details like the majestic vaulted ceilings and, with the use of stunning azulejos—hence the name—it mixes Andalusian and Latin American influences. **Pros:** tropical central patio; interesting architecture; generous breakfast buffet. **Cons:** limited privacy; hyperbusy interior design; plunge pool is only open in summer. $ *Rooms from: €100* ⌧ *Calle Fernando Colón 5, Centro* ☎ *957/470000* ⊕ *www.casadelosazulejos.com* ⤴ *9 rooms.*

★ Hospes Palacio del Bailío

$$$$ | HOTEL | One of the city's top lodging options, this tastefully renovated 17th-century mansion is built over the ruins of a Roman house (visible beneath glass floors) in the historic center of town. **Pros:** central location; dazzling interiors; impeccable comforts. **Cons:** pricey; not easy to access by car; parking is limited. $ *Rooms from: €250* ⌧ *Calle*

A typical Córdoba patio, filled with flowers

Ramírez de las Casas Deza 10–12, Plaza de la Corredera ☎ *957/498993* 🌐 *www.hospes.com/palacio-bailio* 🛏 *53 rooms* 🍴 *No Meals.*

★ Hotel Balcón de Córdoba

$$$$ | **HOTEL** | In a tastefully restored 17th-century convent, this boutique hotel has spacious, quiet rooms, and the Mezquita is almost within arm's reach from the rooftop terrace. **Pros:** central location; historic building; rooftop views of the Mezquita. **Cons:** small breakfast area; very quiet; difficult to access by car. [$] *Rooms from: €250* ✉ *Calle Encarnación 8, Judería* ☎ *957/498478* 🌐 *balcondecordoba.com* 🛏 *10 rooms* 🍴 *Free Breakfast.*

Hotel Maestre

$ | **HOTEL** | Around the corner from the Plaza del Potro, this is an affordable hotel in which Castilian-style furniture, gleaming marble, and high-quality oil paintings add elegance to excellent value. **Pros:** helpful reception staff; good location; great value. **Cons:** ancient plumbing; no elevator and lots of steps; could be too basic for some. [$] *Rooms from: €65* ✉ *Calle Romero Barros 4–6, San Pedro* ☎ *957/472410* 🌐 *www.hotelmaestre.com* 🛏 *26 rooms.*

★ La Llave de la Judería

$$$ | **B&B/INN** | This small hotel, occupying a collection of houses just a stone's throw from the mezquita, combines enchanting antique furnishings with modern amenities, but its greatest asset is its exceptionally helpful staff. **Pros:** beautiful interiors; close to the Mezquita; rooms are equipped with computers. **Cons:** dark reception area; direct car access is difficult; rooms facing street can be noisy. [$] *Rooms from: €175* ✉ *Calle Romero 38, Judería* ☎ *957/294808* 🌐 *www.lallavedelajuderia.es* 🛏 *9 rooms.*

NH Collection Amistad Córdoba

$$$ | **HOTEL** | Two 18th-century mansions overlooking Plaza de Maimónides in the heart of the Judería have been melded into a modern business hotel with a cobblestone Mudejar courtyard, carved-wood ceilings, and a plush lounge. **Pros:** central location; pleasant and efficient service; large rooms. **Cons:** main access via steep steps with no ramp; parking is difficult; a little impersonal. ⓢ *Rooms from: €140 ⊠ Pl. de Maimónides 3, Judería* ☎ *957/420335* ⊕ *www.nh-hoteles. com* ⏎ *108 rooms.*

Parador de Córdoba

$$$ | **HOTEL** | On the slopes of the Sierra de Córdoba, on the site of Abd ar-Rahman I's 8th-century summer palace, this modern parador has sunny rooms and nice views. **Pros:** quality traditional cuisine; sleek interiors; wonderful views from south-facing rooms. **Cons:** characterless modern building; far from main sights; not all rooms have views. ⓢ *Rooms from: €140 ⊠ Av. de la Arruzafa 39, El Brillante* ⊹ *5 km (3 miles) north of city* ☎ *957/275900* ⊕ *www.parador.es* ⏎ *94 rooms* � *No Meals.*

Viento 10

$$ | **HOTEL** | Tucked away to the east of the old quarter, but within just 10 minutes' walk of the Mezquita is a quiet, romantic haven, once part of the 17th-century Sacred Martyrs Hospital. **Pros:** Jacuzzi and sauna; quiet location; pillow menu. **Cons:** a little plain; some walking distance to the main monuments; not easy to find. ⓢ *Rooms from: €120 ⊠ Calle Ronquillo Briceño 10, San Pedro* ☎ *957/764960* ⊕ *www.hotelviento10.es* ⊗ *Closed Jan.* ⏎ *8 rooms* ⍾ *No Meals.*

 Nightlife

Bodega Guzman

BARS | For some traditional tipple, check out this atmospheric bodega near the old synagogue. Its sherries are served straight from the barrel in a room that doubles as a bullfighting museum. ⊠ *Calle de los Judios 6, Judería* ☎ *No phone.*

Café Málaga

LIVE MUSIC | A block from Plaza de las Tendillas, this is a laid-back hangout for jazz and blues aficionados. There's live music most days and occasional flamenco nights. ⊠ *Calle Málaga 3, Centro* ☎ *957/474107.*

 Performing Arts

FLAMENCO

Tablao El Cardenal

FOLK/TRADITIONAL DANCE | Córdoba's most famous flamenco club offers performances by established artists on a pleasant open-air patio. Admission is €23 (including a drink), and the 90-minute shows take place Monday through Thursday at 8:15 pm and on Friday and Saturday at 9. Book by phone or the website (in Spanish only). ⊠ *Calle Buen Pastor 2, Judería* ☎ *619/217922* ⊕ *www.tablaocardenal.es.*

 **Shopping**

Meryan

LEATHER GOODS | This is one of Córdoba's best workshops for embossed leather. ⊠ *Calleja de las Flores 2, Judería* ☎ *957/475902* ⊕ *www.meryancor.com.*

Ronda

147 km (91 miles) southeast of Seville, 61 km (38 miles) northwest of Marbella.

Ronda, one of the oldest towns in Spain, is known for its spectacular position and views. Secure in its mountain fastness on a rock high over the Río Guadalevín, the town was a stronghold for the legendary Andalusian bandits who held court here from the 18th to the early 20th century. Ronda's most dramatic element is its ravine (360 feet deep and 210 feet across)—known as **El Tajo**—which divides La Ciudad, the old Moorish town, from El Mercadillo, the "new town," which sprang up after the Christian Reconquest of 1485. Tour buses roll in daily with sightseers from the coast 49 km (30 miles) away, and on weekends affluent sevillanos flock to their second homes here. Stay overnight midweek to see this noble town's true colors.

In the lowest part of town, known as El Barrio, you can see parts of the old walls, including the 13th-century Puerta de Almocobar and the 16th-century Puerta de Carlos V. From here, the main road climbs past the Iglesia del Espíritu Santo (Church of the Holy Spirit) and up into the heart of town.

GETTING HERE AND AROUND

The most attractive approach is from the south. The winding but well-maintained A376 from San Pedro de Alcántara, on the Costa del Sol, travels north up through the mountains of the Serranía de Ronda. But you can also drive here from Seville via Utrera; it's a pleasant drive of a little less than two hours. At least six daily buses run here from Marbella, six from Málaga, and seven from Seville.

VISITOR INFORMATION

CONTACTS Ronda. ⊠ *Paseo de Blas Infante s/n* ☎ *951/152961* ⊕ *www.turismo-deronda.es.*

Sights

Alameda del Tajo

CITY PARK | Beyond the bullring in El Mercadillo, you can relax in these shady gardens, one of the loveliest spots in Ronda. At the end of the gardens, a balcony protrudes from the face of the cliff, offering a vertigo-inducing view of the valley below. Stroll along the cliff-top walk to the Reina Victoria hotel, built by British settlers from Gibraltar at the turn of the 20th century as a fashionable rest stop on the Algeciras–Bobadilla rail line. ⊠ *Paseo Hemingway.*

Baños Arabes (*Arab Baths*)

RUINS | The excavated remains of the Arab Baths date from Ronda's tenure as capital of a Moorish *taifa* (kingdom). The star-shape vents in the roof are an inferior imitation of the ceiling of the beautiful bathhouse in Granada's Alhambra. The baths are beneath the Puente Árabe (Arab Bridge) in a ravine below the Palacio del Marqués de Salvatierra. ⊠ *Calle*

San Miguel ☎ *656/950937* ⊠ *€4 (free Tues. from 3 pm).*

Juan Peña El Lebrijano

BRIDGE | Immediately south of the Plaza de España, this is Ronda's most famous bridge (also known as the Puente Nuevo, or New Bridge), an architectural marvel built between 1755 and 1793. The bridge's lantern-lit parapet offers dizzying views of the awesome gorge. Just how many people have met their ends here nobody knows, but the architect of the Puente Nuevo fell to his death while inspecting work on the bridge. During the civil war, hundreds of victims were hurled from it.

Palacio de Mondragón (*Palace of Mondragón*)

HISTORY MUSEUM | This stone palace with twin Mudejar towers was probably the residence of Ronda's Moorish kings. Ferdinand and Isabella appropriated it after their victory in 1485. Today, it's the museum of Ronda and you can wander through the patios, with their brick arches and delicate Mudejar-stucco tracery, and admire the mosaics and *artesonado* (coffered) ceiling. The second floor holds a small museum with archaeological items found near Ronda, plus the reproduction of a dolmen, a prehistoric stone monument. ⊠ *Pl. Mondragón* ☎ *952/870818* ⊠ *€3.*

Plaza de Toros

SPORTS VENUE | The main sight in Ronda's commercial center, El Mercadillo, is the bullring. Pedro Romero (1754–1839), the father of modern bullfighting and Ronda's most famous native son, is said to have killed 5,600 bulls here during his career. In the museum beneath the plaza you can see posters for Ronda's very first bullfights, held here in 1785. The plaza was once owned by the late bullfighter Antonio Ordóñez, on whose nearby ranch Orson Welles's ashes were scattered (as directed in his will)—indeed, the ring has become a favorite of filmmakers. Every September, the bullring is the scene of

Ronda's *corridas goyescas,* named after Francisco Goya, whose *tauromaquias* (bullfighting sketches) were inspired by Romero's skill and art. The participants and the dignitaries in the audience don the costumes of Goya's time for the occasion. ✉ *Calle Virgen de la Paz* ☎ *952/871539* 🌐 *www.rmcr.org* 🎫 *€8 for entry and museum.*

Santa María la Mayor

CHURCH | This collegiate church, which serves as Ronda's cathedral, has roots in Moorish times: originally the Great Mosque of Ronda, the tower and adjacent galleries, built for viewing festivities in the square, retain their Islamic design. After the mosque was destroyed (when the Moors were overthrown), it was rebuilt as a church and dedicated to the Virgen de la Encarnación after the Reconquest. The naves are late Gothic, and the main altar is heavy with baroque gold leaf. A visit to the rooftop walkway offers lovely views of the town and surroundings. The church is around the corner from the remains of a mosque, Minarete Arabe (Moorish Minaret) at the end of the Marqués de Salvatierra. ✉ *Pl. Duquesa de Parcent* 🎫 *€4.*

🍴 Restaurants

★ Entre Vinos

$ | **TAPAS** | Just off the main road opposite the Hotel Colón, this small and cozy bar has established itself as one of Ronda's best for tapas, wine, and artisan beer. Local Ronda wines are a specialty here—in fact, they're the only ones available, although with more than 100 on the wine list, you'll be spoiled for choice; ask the waiter for recommendations and which tapas to pair them with. **Known for:** Ronda wines; gourmet tapas; bodega (winery) atmosphere. [$] *Average main: €5* ✉ *Calle Pozo 2* ☎ *658/582976* 🕒 *Closed Sun. and Mon.*

Pedro Romero

$$$ | **SPANISH** | Named for the father of modern bullfighting, this restaurant opposite the bullring is packed with bullfight paraphernalia and photos of previous diners who include Ernest Hemingway and Orson Welles. Mounted bulls' heads peer down at you as you eat *choricitos al vino blanco de Ronda* (small sausages in Ronda white wine), *rabo de toro Pedro Romero* (slow-cooked oxtail stew with herbs), or *magret de pato con pera asada* (duck breast with baked pear). **Known for:** friendly service; bullfighting decor; traditional Ronda cooking. [$] *Average main: €18* ✉ *Calle Virgen de la Paz 18* ☎ *952/871110* 🌐 *www.rpedroromero.com.*

🛏 Hotels

Alavera de los Baños

$$ | **B&B/INN** | Fittingly, given its location next to the Moorish baths, this small, German-run hotel—which was used as a backdrop for the film classic *Carmen*—has an Arab theme throughout. **Pros:** atmospheric and historic; first-floor rooms have their own terraces; owners speak several languages. **Cons:** small bathrooms; steep climb into town; rooms vary in size. [$] *Rooms from: €100* ✉ *Calle San Miguel s/n* ☎ *952/879143* 🌐 *www.alaveradelosbanos.com* 🕒 *Closed Dec.–mid-Feb.* 🛏 *11 rooms* 🍴 *Free Breakfast.*

Hotel Montelirio

$$$ | **B&B/INN** | The 18th-century mansion of the Count of Montelirio, perched over the deep plunge to El Tajo, has been carefully refurbished, maintaining some original features, but the highlight is the breathtaking view over the valley. **Pros:** valley views; Turkish bath and open fireplace make it great for winter; historic building. **Cons:** could be too stuffy for some; parking limited; some rooms have windows to the street. [$] *Rooms from: €135* ✉ *Calle Tenorio 8* ☎ *952/873855* 🌐 *www.hotelmontelirio.com* 🛏 *15 rooms.*

Andalusia's classic pueblos blancos look like Picasso paintings come to life.

Around Ronda: Caves, Romans, and Pueblos Blancos

This area of spectacular gorges, remote mountain villages, and ancient caves is fascinating to explore and a dramatic contrast to the clamor and crowds of the nearby Costa del Sol.

Public transportation is very poor in these parts. Your best bet is to visit by car—the area is a short drive from Ronda.

Sights

★ Acinipo

RUINS | Old Ronda, 20 km (12 miles) north of Ronda, is the site of this old Roman settlement, a thriving town in the 1st century AD that was abandoned for reasons that still baffle historians. Today it's a windswept hillside with piles of stones, the foundations of a few Roman houses, and what remains of a theater. Views across the Ronda plains and to the surrounding mountains are spectacular. The site's opening hours vary depending on staff availability and excavations—check with the Ronda tourist office by phone before visiting. ⊠ *Ronda* ✛ *Take A376 toward Algodonales; turnoff for ruins is 9 km (5 miles) from Ronda on MA449* ☎ *951/041452* ⬚ *Free.*

Cueva de la Pileta (*Pileta Cave*)

CAVE | At this site 20 km (12 miles) west of Ronda, a Spanish guide (who speaks some English) will hand you a paraffin lamp and lead you on a roughly 60-minute walk that reveals prehistoric wall paintings of bison, deer, and horses outlined in black, red, and ocher. One highlight is the Cámara del Pescado (Chamber of the Fish), whose drawing of a huge fish is thought to be 15,000 years old. Tours take place on the hour and last around an hour. To book, phone between 10 am and 1 pm only. ⊠ *Benaoján* ✛ *Drive west from Ronda on A374 and take left exit for* *village of Benaoján from where caves are well signposted ☎ 677/610500 ☞ €10.*

Olvera

TOWN | Here, 13 km (8 miles) north of Setenil, two imposing silhouettes dominate the crest of the hill: the 11th-century castle Vallehermoso, a legacy of the Moors, and the neoclassical church of La Encarnación, reconstructed in the 19th century on the foundations of the old mosque. ✉ *Cádiz.*

Setenil de las Bodegas

TOWN | This small city, in a cleft in the rock cut by the Río Guadalporcín, is 8 km (5 miles) north of Acinipo. The streets resemble long, narrow caves, and on many houses the roof is formed by a projecting ledge of heavy rock. ✉ *Cádiz.*

Zahara de la Sierra

TOWN | A solitary watchtower dominates a crag above this village, its outline visible for miles around. The tower is all that remains of a Moorish castle where King Alfonso X once fought the emir of Morocco; the building remained a Moorish stronghold until it fell to the Christians in 1470. Along the streets you can see door knockers fashioned like the hand of Fatima: the fingers represent the five laws of the Koran and are meant to ward off evil. ✉ ⊕ *From Olvera, drive 21 km (13 miles) southwest to the village of Algodonales, then south on A376 for 5 km (3 miles).*

Arcos de la Frontera

31 km (19 miles) east of Jerez.

Its narrow and steep cobblestone streets, whitewashed houses, and finely crafted wrought-iron window grilles make Arcos the quintessential Andalusian *pueblo blanco.* Make your way to the main square, the **Plaza de España,** the highest point in the village; one side of the square is open, and a balcony at the edge of the cliff offers views of the Guadalete Valley. On the opposite end is

the church of **Santa María de la Asunción,** a fascinating blend of architectural styles—Romanesque, Gothic, and Mudejar—with a plateresque doorway, a Renaissance retablo, and a 17th-century baroque choir. The *ayuntamiento* (town hall) stands at the foot of the old castle walls on the northern side of the square; across is the Casa del Corregidor, onetime residence of the governor and now a parador. Arcos is the westernmost of the 19 *pueblos blancos* dotted around the Sierra de Cádiz.

GETTING HERE AND AROUND

Arcos is best reached by private car, but there are frequent bus services here from Cádiz, Jerez, and Seville on weekdays. Weekend services are less frequent.

VISITOR INFORMATION

CONTACTS Arcos de la Frontera. ✉ *Cuesta de Belén 5* ☎ *956/702264* ⊕ *www. turismoarcos.com.*

🍴 Restaurants

Gastrobar El Retablo

$$ | **SPANISH** | Traditional Andalusian cuisine comes in generous portions (tapas and sharing plates) at this popular venue with a small terrace opposite the Iglesia de Santa María. Stars on the menu include *carrillada de cerdo* (pork cheeks), *bacalao con puré de guisantes* (cod with pea puree), *pulpo asado* (octopus) served with fluffy potato. **Known for:** generous portions; octopus; friendly service. $ *Average main: €12* ✉ *Calle Dean Espinosa 6* ☎ *856/041614* ⊗ *Closed Tues.*

Restaurante Aljibe

$$ | **FUSION** | Local cooking meets Moroccan cuisine on one of the best fusion menus in the province at this venue with small dining spaces and an Arabian theme. White prawns, *ensalada de higos y payoyo* (fig and goat cheese salad) and *alcachofas con almejas* (artichokes with clams) sit perfectly next to *pastela* (game pie) and couscous dishes. **Known for:**

Riders fill the streets during Jerez's Feria del Caballo (Horse Fair) in early May.

Moroccan sweets for dessert; Andalusian-Moroccan fusion; good service with a smile. $ *Average main: €14* ✉ *Cuesta del Belén 10* ☎ *622/836527* 🕒 *Closed Mon.–Wed.*

Hotels

★ El Convento

$ | **B&B/INN** | Perched atop the cliff behind the town parador, this tiny hotel in a former 17th-century convent shares the amazing view of another hotel in town, its swish neighbor (La Casa Grande). **Pros:** intimacy; value; picturesque location. **Cons:** no restaurant; small spaces; lots of stairs. $ *Rooms from: €65* ✉ *Calle Maldonado 2* ☎ *956/702333* 🌐 *www.hotelelconvento.es* 🕒 *Closed Jan. and Feb.* 🛏 *13 rooms* 🍴 *No Meals.*

★ La Casa Grande

$ | **B&B/INN** | Built in 1729, this extraordinary 18th-century mansion encircles a central patio with lush vegetation and is perched on the edge of the 400-foot cliff to which Arcos de la Frontera clings. **Pros:** attentive owner; amazing views; impeccable aesthetics. **Cons:** inconvenient parking; long climb to the top floor; interior is a little dark. $ *Rooms from: €80* ✉ *Calle Maldonado 10* ☎ *956/703930* 🌐 *www.lacasagrande.net* 🍴 *No Meals* 🛏 *7 rooms.*

Parador Casa del Corregidor

$$$ | **HOTEL** | Expect a spectacular view from the terrace, as this parador clings to the cliffside, overlooking the rolling valley of the Río Guadalete. **Pros:** gorgeous views from certain rooms; elegant interiors; good restaurant. **Cons:** public areas a little tired; expensive bar and cafeteria; not all rooms have views. $ *Rooms from: €165* ✉ *Pl. del Cabildo s/n* ☎ *956/700500* 🌐 *www.parador.es* 🛏 *24 rooms* 🍴 *No Meals.*

Jerez de la Frontera

97 km (60 miles) south of Seville.

Jerez, world headquarters for sherry, is surrounded by vineyards of chalky soil, producing palomino and Pedro Ximénez grapes that have funded a host of churches and noble mansions. Names such as González Byass, Domecq, Harvey, and Sandeman are inextricably linked with Jerez. The word "sherry," first used in Great Britain in 1608, is an English corruption of the town's old Moorish name, Xeres. Both sherry and thoroughbred horses (the city was European Capital of Horses in 2018) are the domain of Jerez's Anglo-Spanish aristocracy, whose Catholic ancestors came here from England centuries ago. At any given time, more than half a million barrels of sherry are maturing in Jerez's vast aboveground cellars.

GETTING HERE AND AROUND

Jerez is a short way from Seville with frequent daily trains (journey time is around an hour) and buses (1 hour 15 minutes), fewer on weekends. If you're traveling to the city-center by car, park in one of the city-center lots or at your hotel as street parking is difficult. Jerez Airport is small and served by a number of flights to destinations in northern Europe and within Spain.

AIRPORT Jerez de la Frontera Airport. ✉ *Ctra. N-IV, Km 628.5* ☎ *956/150000* ⊕ *www.aena.es.*

BUS STATION Jerez de la Frontera. ✉ *Pl. de la Estación* ☎ *956/149990.*

TAXI CONTACT Tele Taxi. ✉ ☎ *956/344860, 956/350537.*

TRAIN STATION Jerez de la Frontera. ✉ *Pl. de la Estación s/n, off Calle Diego Fernández Herrera* ☎ *912/320320.*

VISITOR INFORMATION

CONTACTS Jerez de la Frontera. ✉ *Edificio Los Arcos, Pl. del Arenal* ☎ *956/338874* ⊕ *www.turismojerez.com.*

Sights

Alcázar

CASTLE/PALACE | Once the residence of the caliph of Seville, the 12th-century *alcázar* in Jerez de la Frontera and its small, octagonal mosque and baths were built for the Moorish governor's private use. The baths have three sections: the *sala fría* (cold room), the larger *sala templada* (warm room), and the *sala caliente* (hot room) for steam baths. In the midst of it all is the 17th-century Palacio de Villavicencio, built on the site of the original Moorish palace. A camera obscura, a lens-and-mirrors device that projects the outdoors onto a large indoor screen, offers a 360-degree view of Jerez. ✉ *Calle Alameda Vieja* ☎ *956/149955* 🔁 *From €5.*

Álvaro Domecq

WINERY | This is Jerez's oldest *bodega* (winery), founded in 1730. Aside from sherry, Domecq makes the world's best-selling brandy, Fundador. Harveys Bristol Cream is also part of the Domecq group. Visits must be booked in advance by phone or email. ✉ *Calle San Ildefonso 3* ☎ *956/339634* ⊕ *www.alvarodomecq.com* 🔁 *From €15.*

★ Bodegas Tradición

WINERY | Tucked away on the north side of the old quarter and founded in 1998, this is one of the youngest bodegas, but it has the oldest sherry. The five types sit in the casks for at least 20 years and most are older. Visits (book in advance by phone or email) include a tour of the winery, a lesson in how to pair each sherry type, and a tour of the unique Spanish art collection that includes works by El Greco, Zurburán, Goya, and Velázquez. ✉ *Pl. de los Cordobeses 3* ☎ *956/168628* ⊕ *www.bodegastradicion.es* 🔁 *€35.*

Catedral de Jerez

CHURCH | Across from the *alcázar* and around the corner from the González Byass winery, the cathedral has an octagonal cupola and a separate bell tower, as well as Zurbarán's canvas *La Virgen Niña Meditando* (*The Virgin as a Young Girl*). ⊠ *Pl. de la Encarnación* ☎ *956/169059* 🖃 *From €6.*

González Byass

WINERY | Home of the famous Tío Pepe, this is one of the most commercial bodegas. The tour, which is in English, is well organized and includes La Concha, an open-air aging cellar designed by Gustave Eiffel. ⊠ *Calle Manuel María González* ☎ *956/357016* ⊕ *www.gonzalezbyass. com* 🖃 *From €19.*

Museo Arqueológico

HISTORY MUSEUM | Diving into the maze of streets that form the scruffy San Mateo neighborhood east of the town center, you come to one of Andalusia's best archaeological museums. The collection is strongest on the pre-Roman period, and the star item, found near Jerez, is a Greek helmet dating from the 7th century BC. ⊠ *Pl. del Mercado s/n* ☎ *956/149560* ⊘ *Closed Sun. and Mon.* 🖃 *Free.*

★ Plaza de la Asunción

PLAZA/SQUARE | Here on one of Jerez's most intimate squares you can find the Mudejar church of **San Dionisio,** patron saint of the city, (open 10–noon Monday–Thursday) and the ornate *cabildo municipal* (city hall), with a lovely plateresque facade dating to 1575. ⊠ *Jerez de la Frontera* 🖃 *Church free* ⊘ *Church closed for touring Fri.–Sun.*

★ Real Escuela Andaluza del Arte Ecuestre

(*Royal Andalusian School of Equestrian Art*)

SPORTS VENUE | **FAMILY** | This prestigious school operates on the grounds of the Recreo de las Cadenas, a 19th-century palace. The school was masterminded by Álvaro Domecq in the 1970s, and every Tuesday and Thursday (Thursday only in January and February) as well as each Friday in August through October, the Cartujana horses—a cross between the native Andalusian workhorse and the Arabian—and skilled riders in 18th-century riding costume demonstrate intricate dressage techniques and jumping in the spectacular show *Cómo Bailan los Caballos Andaluces* (roughly, *The Dancing Horses of Andalusia*). Reservations are essential. The price of admission depends on how close to the arena you sit; the first two rows are the priciest. At certain other times you can visit the museum, stables, and tack room and watch the horses being schooled. ⊠ *Av. Duque de Abrantes* ☎ *956/318008 for information* ⊕ *www.realescuela.org* 🖃 *From €21.*

San Miguel

CHURCH | One block from the Plaza del Arenal, near the *alcázar*, stands the church of San Miguel. Built over the 15th and 16th centuries, its interior illustrates the evolution of Gothic architecture, with various styles mixed into the design. ⊠ *Pl. de San Miguel* ☎ *956/343347* ⊘ *Closed Sun.* 🖃 *€4.*

Sandeman

WINERY | The Sandeman brand of sherry is known for its dashing man-in-a-cape logo. Tours of the sherry bodegas in Jerez give you some insight into his history and let you visit the cellars. Some visitors purchase tapas to have with their sherry tastings. There is also a museum and shop on-site. ⊠ *Calle Pizarro 10* ☎ *675/647177* ⊕ *www.sandeman.com/ visit-us/jerez/sherry-bodegas* 🖃 *From €10.*

Yeguada de la Cartuja

FARM/RANCH | This farm just outside Jerez de la Frontera specializes in Carthusian horses. In the 15th century, a Carthusian monastery on this site started the breed for which Jerez and the rest of Spain are now famous. Visits include a full tour of the stables and training areas and a show. Book ahead. ⊠ *Finca Fuente El Suero, Ctra. Medina–El Portal, Km 6.5* ☎ *956/162809* ⊕ *www.yeguadacartuja. com* 🖃 *From €17.*

Winery Tours in Jerez 🍴

On a bodega visit, you'll learn about the *solera* method of blending old wine with new, and the importance of the *flor* (yeast that forms on the wine as it ages) in determining the kind of sherry.

Phone ahead for an appointment to make sure you join a group that speaks your language. Admission fees start at €10 (more for extra wine tasting or tapas), and tours, which last 60–90 minutes, go through the aging cellars, with their endless rows of casks. (You won't see the actual fermenting and bottling, which take place in more modern, less romantic plants outside town.) Finally, you'll be invited to sample generous amounts of pale, dry fino, nutty amontillado, rich, deep oloroso, and sweet Pedro Ximénez and, of course, to purchase a few robustly priced bottles in the winery shop.

🍴 Restaurants

★ Albores
$$ | SPANISH | Opposite the city hall, this busy restaurant with swift service has pleasant outdoor seating under orange trees and a modern interior with low lighting, and serves innovative, modern dishes with a traditional base. The menu is extensive and changes often, although must-try staples include *barriga de atún con salsa de soja y mermelada de tomate* (tuna belly with soy sauce and tomato jam) and *Retinta* beef. **Known for:** generous portions (sharing is encouraged; half portions also available); tuna cooked any which way; desserts. [$] *Average main: €15* ✉ *Calle Consistorio 12* ☎ *956/320266* 🌐 *www.restaurantealbores.com.*

Atuvera
$ | FUSION | Some of the most colorful meals in Andalusia are served inside what were once the stables of a 16th-century palace. Fresh local produce is used to fuse Asian and Mexican flavors in what locals describe as a vibrant explosion of taste. **Known for:** friendly service; fusion cooking; nice terrace. [$] *Average main: €9* ✉ *Calle Ramón de Cala 13* ☎ *675/548584* 🌐 *atuverajerez.com.*

Bar Juanito
$ | SPANISH | Traditional bars don't come more authentic than Bar Juanito, which has been serving local dishes for more than 70 years and pairs everything, of course, with sherry. You can eat standing at the bar or seated in the pleasant patio restaurant, where there's often live music on Saturday. **Known for:** wide range of sharing plates; artichoke dishes in season (early spring); pork-based stew. [$] *Average main: €10* ✉ *Calle Pescadería Vieja 8–10* ☎ *956/334838.*

★ La Carboná
$$$ | SPANISH | In a former bodega, this eatery has a rustic atmosphere with arches, wooden beams, and a fireplace for winter nights, and in summer you can often enjoy live music and sometimes flamenco dancing while you dine. The chef has worked at several top restaurants, and his menu includes traditional grilled meats as well as innovative twists on classic dishes, such as Iberian ham croquettes with curry and Amontillado mayo or *rodaballo con velouté de palo cortado* (skate with sherry velouté).

Known for: innovative dishes; multiple-course sherry-tasting menu; bodega setting. [$] *Average main: €22* ✉ *Calle San Francisco de Paula 2* ☎ *956/347475* ⏲ *Closed Tues. and July.*

Venta Esteban

$$ | SPANISH | FAMILY | This restaurant is slightly off the beaten track, but well worth seeking out for traditional Jerez cuisine in a pleasant setting. Choose tapas in the bar or à la carte in the spacious and airy dining rooms. **Known for:** homemade custard; traditional stews; seafood. [$] *Average main: €16* ✉ *Colonia de Caulina C.11–03* ✣ *Just off Seville hwy. exit* ☎ *956/316067* 🌐 *www.restauranteventaesteban.es.*

Hotels

★ Casa Palacio Maria Luisa

$$$$ | HOTEL | Once home to Jerez's gentlemen's club (known as the Casino) and something of a symbol of the city's sherry heyday, this restored 19th-century mansion is arguably the most comfortable luxurious hotel in town and the only five-star grand-luxe one. **Pros:** beautifully designed, uber-comfortable rooms; lovely outside terrace; excellent service. **Cons:** might be too grandiose for some; expensive breakfast; small pool. [$] *Rooms from: €300* ✉ *Calle Tornería 22* ☎ *956/926263* 🌐 *casapalaciomarialuisa.com* 🛏 *21 rooms* 🍴 *No Meals.*

Hotel Doña Blanca

$ | HOTEL | Slightly off the main tourist route but still within easy walking distance to attractions, this traditional townhouse hotel offers spacious accommodations with some of the best prices in the city. **Pros:** generously sized rooms; great value; private terrace in some rooms. **Cons:** not right in the city center; might be too basic for some; cold breakfast choices only. [$] *Rooms from: €60* ✉ *Calle Bodegas 11* ☎ *956/348761* 🌐 *www.hoteldonablanca.com* 🛏 *30 rooms* 🍴 *No Meals.*

Hotel Jerez & Spa

$$ | B&B/INN | Tastefully furnished, this hacienda-style hotel offers luxury on the outskirts of town. **Pros:** saltwater swimming pool; Italian restaurant on-site; elegant gardens. **Cons:** outside of town center; breakfast is average; some areas need updating. [$] *Rooms from: €100* ✉ *Av. de la Cruz Roja 7* ☎ *956/153100* 🌐 *www.hace.es* 🛏 *15 rooms* 🍴 *No Meals.*

Hotel YIT Casa Grande

$ | HOTEL | This cozy hotel, right in the city center with all the main attractions on its doorstep, comes complete with its original 1920s Art Nouveau design and period antiques. **Pros:** central location; roof terrace; personalized service. **Cons:** no pool; decor might not appeal to everyone; some rooms have street noise. [$] *Rooms from: €80* ✉ *Pl. de las Angustias 3* ☎ *956/345070* 🌐 *www.hotelcasagrande-jerez.com* 🛏 *15 rooms* 🍴 *No Meals.*

La Fonda Barranco

$ | HOTEL | A block away from the cathedral and behind the police station, this typical Jerez town house has been restored to its full bourgeois glory, preserving original tiled floors, beamed ceilings, and a central patio. **Pros:** good value; central location; personalized attention. **Cons:** some rooms are dark; no elevator; no breakfast available. [$] *Rooms from: €60* ✉ *Calle Barranco 12* ☎ *956/332141* 🌐 *www.lafondabarranco.com* 🛏 *8 rooms, 2 apartments* 🍴 *No Meals.*

Cádiz

32 km (20 miles) southwest of Jerez, 149 km (93 miles) southwest of Seville.

With the Atlantic Ocean on three sides, Cádiz is a bustling town that's been shaped by a variety of cultures and has the varied architecture to prove it. Founded as Gadir by Phoenician traders in 1100 BC, Cádiz claims to be the oldest

Just about the whole city turns out for Jerez's Feria del Caballo, and traditional Andalusian costumes are a common sight.

continuously inhabited city in the Western world. Hannibal lived in Cádiz for a time, Julius Caesar first held public office here, and Columbus set out from here on his second voyage, after which the city became the home base of the Spanish fleet. In the 18th century, when the Guadalquivir silted up, Cádiz monopolized New World trade and became the wealthiest port in Western Europe. Most of its buildings—including the cathedral, built in part with wealth generated by gold and silver from the New World—date from this period. The old city is African in appearance and immensely intriguing—a cluster of narrow streets opening onto charming small squares. The golden cupola of the cathedral looms above low white houses, and the whole place has a slightly dilapidated air. Spaniards flock here in February to revel in the carnival celebrations, and ever more cruise ships visit the harbor, but in general it's not too touristy.

GETTING HERE AND AROUND

Every day, around 15 local trains connect Cádiz with Seville, Puerto de Santa María, and Jerez. The city has two bus stations. The main one, run by Comes, serves most destinations in Andalusia and farther afield; the other, run by Socibus, serves Córdoba and Madrid. There are buses to and from Sanlúcar de Barrameda (14 on weekdays), Arcos de la Frontera (9 daily), and the Costa del Sol (via Seville, 4 daily). Cádiz is easy to get to and navigate by car. Once there, the old city is easily explored by foot.

BUS STATION Cádiz–Estación de Autobuses Comes. ✉ Pl. de Sevilla ☎ 956/807059. **Cádiz-Estación de Autobuses Socibus.** ✉ Av. Astilleros s/n ☎ 956/257415.

TAXI CONTACT Radiotaxi. ✉ Cádiz ☎ 956/212121.

TRAIN STATION Cádiz. ✉ Pl. de Sevilla s/n ☎ 912/320320.

Cádiz's majestic cathedral, as seen from the Plaza de la Catedral

VISITOR INFORMATION

CONTACTS Local Tourist Office. ✉ *Paseo de Canalejas* ☎ *956/241001* ⊕ *turismo. cadiz.es.* **Regional Tourist Office.** ✉ *Av. Ramón de Carranza s/n* ☎ *956/203191* ⊕ *www.cadizturismo.com.*

 ## Sights

Cádiz Cathedral

CHURCH | Five blocks southeast of the Torre Tavira are the gold dome and baroque facade of Cádiz's cathedral, which offers history as well as views from atop the Clock Tower (*Torre del Reloj*)—making the climb to the top worth it. The building's structure was begun in 1722, when the city was at the height of its power. The Cádiz-born composer Manuel de Falla, who died in 1946 at the age of 70, is buried in the crypt. The museum, on Calle Acero, displays gold, silver, and jewels from the New World, as well as Enrique de Arfe's processional cross, which is carried in the annual Corpus Christi parades. The cathedral is known as the New Cathedral because it supplanted the original, neighboring, 13th-century structure, which was destroyed by the British in 1592, rebuilt, and rechristened the church of Santa Cruz when the New Cathedral came along. ✉ *Pl. Catedral* ☎ *956/286154* 🖾 *€6, includes crypt, museum, tower, and church of Santa Cruz.*

Gran Teatro Manuel de Falla

HISTORIC SIGHT | Four blocks west of Santa Inés is the Plaza Manuel de Falla, overlooked by this amazing neo-Mudejar redbrick building. The classic interior is impressive as well—try to attend a performance. ✉ *Pl. Manuel de Falla* ☎ *956/220828.*

Museo de Cádiz (*Provincial Museum*)

HISTORY MUSEUM | On the east side of the Plaza de Mina is Cádiz's provincial museum. Notable pieces include works by Murillo and Alonso Cano as well as the *Four Evangelists* and a set of saints by Zurbarán. The archaeological section contains two extraordinary marble Phoenician sarcophagi from the time of this ancient city's birth. ✉ *Pl. de Mina*

☎ 856/105023 ✆ €2 ⊙ Closed Sun. afternoon and Mon.

Museo de las Cortes
HISTORY MUSEUM | Next door to the Oratorio de San Felipe Neri, this small but pleasant museum has a 19th-century mural depicting the establishment of the Constitution of 1812. Its real showpiece, however, is a 1779 ivory-and-mahogany model of Cádiz, with all of the city's streets and buildings in minute detail, looking much as they do now. ⊠ Calle Santa Inés 9 ☎ 956/221788 ⊙ Closed weekends ✆ Free.

Oratorio de la Santa Cueva
RELIGIOUS BUILDING | A few blocks east of the Plaza de Mina, next door to the Iglesia del Rosario, this oval 18th-century chapel has three frescoes by Goya. On Good Friday, the Sermon of the Seven Words is read and Haydn's Seven Last Words played. ⊠ Calle Rosario 10 ☎ 956/222262 ✆ €4 (free Sun.) ⊙ Closed Mon.

Oratorio de San Felipe Neri
RELIGIOUS BUILDING | A walk up Calle San José from the Plaza de Mina will bring you to this church, where Spain's first liberal constitution (known affectionately as La Pepa) was declared in 1812. It was here, too, that the Cortes (Parliament) of Cádiz met when the rest of Spain was subjected to the rule of Napoléon's brother, Joseph Bonaparte (more popularly known as Pepe Botella, for his love of the bottle). On the main altar is an Immaculate Conception by Murillo, the great sevillano artist who in 1682 fell to his death from a scaffold while working on his Mystic Marriage of St. Catherine in Cádiz's Chapel of Santa Catalina. You can hear Mass in Latin on Sunday at 1 pm. ⊠ Calle Santa Inés 38 ☎ 662/642233 ✆ €4 (free Sun.) ⊙ Closed Mon.

Roman Theater
RUINS | Next door to the church of Santa Cruz are the remains of a 1st-century-BC Roman theater, one of the oldest and largest in Spain. The stage remains unexcavated (it lies under nearby houses), but you can visit the entrance and large seating area as well as the visitor center. ⊠ Calle Mesón 11-13, Barrio del Pópulo ✆ Free ⊙ Closed 1st Mon. of month.

★ Torre Tavira
NOTABLE BUILDING | FAMILY | At 150 feet, this watchtower is the highest point in the old city. More than a hundred such structures were used by Cádiz ship owners to spot their arriving fleets. A camera obscura gives a good overview of the city and its monuments; the last show is a half hour before closing time. ⊠ Calle Marqués del Real Tesoro 10 ☎ 956/212910 ⊕ www.torretavira.com/en ✆ €7.

Yacimiento Arqueológico Gadir
RUINS | Few Phoenician settlements have survived intact, but excavations underneath the Puppet Museum revealed some of the best-preserved ruins in southern Europe. You can visit the 9th-century BC remains and discover eight houses along two cobbled streets complete with animal hoofprints encased in mud and clay. The site also has the remains of a Roman fish-preserving factory with saltwater pools. ⊠ Calle San Miguel 15 ☎ 956/226 337 ✆ Free.

🍴 Restaurants

★ Casa Manteca
$ | SPANISH | Cádiz's most quintessentially Andalusian tavern is in the neighborhood of La Viña, named for the vineyard that once grew here. Chacina (Iberian ham or sausage) and chicharrones de Cádiz (cold pork) served on waxed paper and washed down with manzanilla (sherry from Sanlúcar de Barrameda) are standard fare at the low wooden counter that has served bullfighters and flamenco singers, as well as dignitaries from around the world, since 1953. The walls are covered with colorful posters and other memorabilia from the annual

carnival, flamenco shows, and ferias. **Known for:** manzanilla sherry; atmospheric interior; delicious cold cuts. $ *Average main: €10 ⊠ Corralón de los Carros 66 ☎ 956/213603.*

Código de Barra

$$$$ | SPANISH | Local produce comes under the Dutch microscope at one of the most innovative dining venues in Cádiz, under the direction of chef Léon Griffioen. With only a few tables, and in minimalist surroundings, the restaurant, decked in black and gray, offers a tasting menu (€50 for 7 dishes, €60 for 10; pairing options available) that comes with several surprises including an "olive" and 'deconstructed' *tortillitas de camarones*—it is one explosion of flavor after another. **Known for:** good and long wine list (ask the staff for pairing suggestions); excellent-value tasting menu; creative take on traditional local cuisine. $ *Average main: €50 ⊠ Pl. Candelaria 12 ☎ 635/533303 ⊘ Closed Tues.*

El Faro

$$$ | SPANISH | This famous fishing-quarter restaurant near Playa de la Caleta is deservedly known as one of the best in the province. From the outside, it's one of many whitewashed houses with ocher details and shiny black lanterns; inside, it's warm and inviting, with half-tile walls, glass lanterns, oil paintings, and photos of old Cádiz. **Known for:** tapas; rice dishes; fresh fish. $ *Average main: €22 ⊠ Calle San Felix 15 ☎ 956/211068 ⊕ www.elfarodecadiz.com.*

La Candela

$ | SPANISH | A block north of Plaza Candelaria and on one of Cádiz's narrow pedestrian streets, La Candela is a good place to try local fare with a modern twist. The *salmorejo* (tomato and bread soup) comes baked with pork loin tartare, the duck ravioli with mushrooms, and several dishes come tempura-style or have South American touches such as the sea bass ceviche with tiger's milk and mango. **Known for:** tapas; homemade cheesecake; Spanish-Asian fusion food. $ *Average main: €10 ⊠ Calle Feduchy 1 ☎ 956/221822 ⊕ www.lacandelatapasbar.com.*

Hotels

Hotel Argantonio

$$ | HOTEL | This small, family-run hotel in the historic center of town combines traditional style and modern amenities. **Pros:** great location; good-size bathrooms; friendly and helpful staff. **Cons:** not easy to find; street-facing rooms can be noisy; rooms in the original building on the small side. $ *Rooms from: €120 ⊠ Calle Argantonio 3 ☎ 956/211640 ⊕ www.hotelargantonio.com ⌿ 17 rooms ◯| No Meals.*

Hotel Patagonia Sur

$$ | HOTEL | With a handy central location just two blocks from the cathedral, this modern hotel offers functional and inexpensive lodging, especially during low season. **Pros:** top-floor rooms have a private terrace; good value; central location. **Cons:** small rooms; five-night minimum stay in summer; street noise can be intrusive. $ *Rooms from: €120 ⊠ Calle Cobos 11 ☎ 856/174647 ⊕ www.hotelpatagoniasur.es ⌿ 16 rooms ◯| No Meals.*

Parador de Cádiz

$$$$ | HOTEL | With a privileged position overlooking the bay, this parador has spacious public areas and large modern rooms, most with balconies facing the sea. **Pros:** great views of the bay; bright and cheerful; pool. **Cons:** lacks historic appeal of other paradores; very quiet in the off season; expensive parking. $ *Rooms from: €250 ⊠ Av. Duque de Nájera 9 ☎ 956/226905 ⊕ www.parador.es/en/paradores/parador-de-cadiz ⌿ 124 rooms ◯| No Meals.*

Chapter 12

GRANADA AND AROUND

12

Updated by
Joanna Styles

👁 **Sights**
★★★★★

🍴 **Restaurants**
★★★★☆

🛏 **Hotels**
★★★★☆

💼 **Shopping**
★★★★☆

🍸 **Nightlife**
★★★★☆

WELCOME TO GRANADA AND AROUND

TOP REASONS TO GO

★ **Be seduced by the Alhambra:** Marvel at this extraordinary Moorish delight, a fortress-palace whose patios, courtyards, halls, baths, and gardens rank among the most magnificent in the world.

★ **Lose yourself in time:** Stroll the cobbled alleyways of the Albayzín, the ancient Arab quarter, with its whitewashed facades, churches, convents, and simply stunning views to the Alhambra and the snow-capped Sierra Nevada beyond.

★ **Admire their resting places:** Visit the Capilla Real with the tombs of Spain's greatest monarchs, Isabella and Ferdinand, under whose watch modern day Spain was born and the New World discovered.

★ **Experience the real thing:** Tour the colorful Gypsy caves in Sacromonte and take in a finger-clicking, foot-tapping flamenco show.

★ **Taste the tapas:** Enjoy a complimentary tapa with your drink at any bar in Granada, often more of a mini-meal than a mere mouthful.

Granada is compact and easy to navigate, with the exception of the Albayzín, whose charm lies in losing yourself in the maze of alleyways. Outside the center, prepare for some serious walking in hilly terrain (often on cobbled streets) or take taxis or buses.

1 La Alhambra. Perched on a verdant hill and home to Spain's greatest monument, La Alhambra stands tall over the city, offering panoramic views plus some fine hotels.

2 Realejo. Beneath La Alhambra, narrow cobbled streets and pleasant squares are home to fine palaces and mansions as well as bustling bars and restaurants.

3 Sacromonte. Hilly and riddled with caverns, Sacromonte is the heart of Granada's Gypsy community and its flamenco spirit.

4 Albayzín. Occupying the hillside opposite La Alhambra, the ancient Moorish quarter offers a labyrinth of white-washed alleyways, churches, squares with panoramic views, and boutique hotels and restaurants.

5 Centro. Flat and bustling, the center houses commercial Granada with its main shopping streets, leafy squares and fine architecture including the Cathedral and Capilla Real.

6 Priego de Córdoba. An olive farming town famous for its mansions and baroque churches.

7 Baeza. One of the best-preserved old towns in Spain.

8 Ubeda. Slightly larger than Baeza, this town is known for its architecture, artisan crafts, and olive groves. Shop for all your souvenirs here.

9 The Sierra Nevada. You'll find stunning mountain views and Europe's southernmost ski resort about 45 minutes from Granada.

10 The Alpujarras. The southern slopes of the Sierra Nevada have long been loved by artists and writers for their remoteness and stunning views.

11 Huerta de San Vicente. Lorca's summer home is now a museum and a must-visit for fans of the poet.

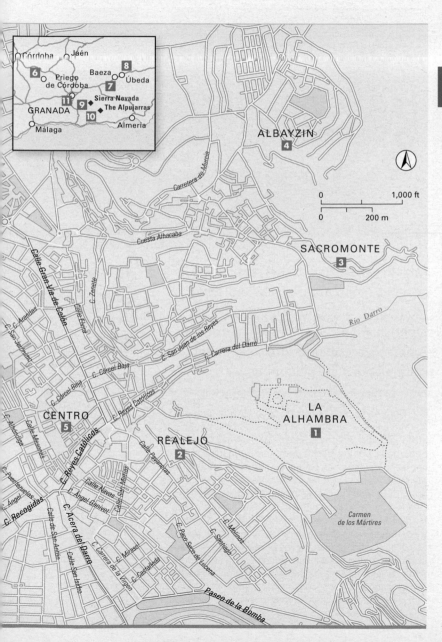

EATING AND DRINKING WELL IN ANDALUSIA

A cool bowl of gazpacho, with accompaniments.

Andalusian cuisine, as diverse as the geography of seacoast, farmland, and mountains, is held together by its Moorish aromas. Cumin seed and other Arabian spices, along with salty-sweet combinations, are ubiquitous.

The eight Andalusian provinces cover a wide geographical and culinary spectrum. Superb seafood is center stage in Cádiz, Puerto de Santa María, and Sanlúcar de Barrameda. *Jamón ibérico de bellota* (Iberian acorn-fed ham) and other Iberian pork products rule from the Sierra de Aracena in Huelva to the Pedroches Mountains north of Córdoba. In Seville look for products from the Guadalquivir estuary, the Sierra, and the rich Campiña farmland, all prepared with great creativity. In Córdoba try *salmorejo cordobés* (a thick gazpacho), *rabo de toro* (oxtail stew), or representatives of the salty-sweet legacy from Córdoba's Moorish heritage such as *cordero con miel* (lamb with honey). Spicy *crema de almendras* (almond soup) is a Granada favorite along with *habas con jamón* (broad beans with ham) from the Alpujarran village of Trevélez.

SHERRY

Dry sherry from Jerez de la Frontera (fino) and from Sanlúcar de Barrameda (manzanilla) share honors as favorite tapas accompaniments. Manzanilla, the more popular choice, is fresher and more delicate, with a slight marine tang. Both are the preferred drinks at Andalusian *ferias* (fairs), particularly in Seville in April and Jerez de la Frontera in May.

COLD VEGETABLE SOUPS

Spain's most popular contribution to world gastronomy after paella may well be gazpacho, a simple peasant soup served cold and filled with scraps and garden ingredients. Tomatoes, cucumber, garlic, oil, bread, and chopped peppers are the ingredients, and side plates of chopped onion, peppers, garlic, tomatoes, and croutons accompany, to be added to taste. *Salmorejo cordobés*, a thicker cold vegetable soup with the same ingredients but a different consistency, is used to accompany tapas.

MOORISH FLAVORS

Andalusia's 781-year sojourn at the heart of Al-Andalus, the Moorish empire on the Iberian Peninsula, left as many tastes and aromas as mosques and fortresses. Cumin-laced *boquerones en adobo* (marinated anchovies) or the salty-sweet *cordero con miel* are two examples, along with coriander-spiked *espinacas con garbanzos* (spinach with garbanzo beans) and *perdiz con dátiles y almendras* (partridge stewed with dates and almonds). Desserts especially reflect the Moorish legacy in morsels such as *pestiños,* cylinders or twists of fried dough in anise-honey syrup.

Crispy fried fish are an Andalusian delicacy.

FRIED FISH

Andalusia is famous for its fried fish, from *pescaito frito* (fried whitebait) to *calamares fritos* (fried squid rings). Andalusians are masters of deep-frying techniques using very hot olive and vegetable oils that produce peerlessly crisp, dry *frituras* (fried seafood); much of Andalusia's finest tapas repertory is known for being served piping hot and crunchy. Look for *tortillita de camarones,* a delicate lacework of tiny fried shrimp.

STEWS

Guisos are combinations of vegetables, with or without meat, cooked slowly over low heat. *Rabo de toro* is a favorite throughout Andalusia, though Córdoba claims the origin of this dark and delicious stew made from the tail of a fighting bull. The segments of tail are cleaned, browned, and set aside before leeks, onions, carrots, garlic, and bay leaves are stewed in the same pan. Cloves, salt, pepper, a liter of wine, and a half liter of beef broth are added to the stew with the meat, and they're all simmered for two to three hours until the meat is falling off the bone and thoroughly tenderized. *Alboronía,* also known as *pisto andaluz,* is a traditional stew of eggplant, bell peppers, and zucchini.

Fried calamari with lemon.

Nestling below the perennially snow-capped Sierra Nevada and rising majestically from a vast fertile place, Granada proudly offers visitors two jewels in Andalusia's crown: the Alhambra and the tomb of the Catholic Monarchs. The two aesthetics, Moorish and Christian, pervade the entire city in its architecture, cuisine, handicrafts, and people.

The kingdom of Granada dates back to 1013, when it was founded by the Moorish Nasrid dynasty, under whose reign the city prospered as one of the richest in Spain for over four centuries. In 1491, split by internal squabbles, Boabdil, the "Rey Chico" (Boy King) gave Ferdinand of Aragón his opportunity to claim Granada for Castille. Spurred by Isabella's religious fanaticism, he laid siege to the city for seven months, and on January 2, 1492, Boabdil was forced to surrender the keys of the city.

Granada perches on three hills: the reddish Alhambra palace dominates the trio and the city skyline; on the opposite side across the small Darro River sprawls the Albayzín, Granada's historic Moorish quarter where time seems to have come to a standstill; and on the third hill sits the Sacromonte, studded with ancient caves and home to the city's Gypsies and flamenco.

All three areas are well worth exploring. The Alhambra ranks as the top must-see and merits a whole day of your visit. If your stay is longer, aim to tour the palace at night too. The Albayzín is an area best appreciated by a leisurely stroll

and Sacromonte is an interesting detour before you descend the hills to the historic center below.

The maze of streets that make up the center harbor a bustling hub of commercial activity, yet another legacy of Granada's Moorish past. The main shopping streets, centering on the Puerta Real, are the Gran Vía de Colón, Reyes Católicos, Zacatín, and Recogidas. Most antiques shops are on Cuesta de Elvira and Alcaicería—off Reyes Católicos. Cuesta de Gomérez, on the way up to the Alhambra, also has several handicrafts shops and guitar workshops. Handicrafts have a distinct Moorish air, present in the ceramics, marquetry (especially the *taraceas*, wooden boxes with inlaid tiles on their lids), woven textiles, and silver-, brass-, and copper-ware.

Side trips from Granada give you the chance to experience some of the finest towns in eastern Andalusia. In the rolling olive groves and high mountains, you'll find gems such as Priego de Córdoba, home to some of the region's most impressive Baroque churches; Baeza and Úbeda, both with exceptional examples of Renaissance architecture; the Sierra

Nevada, a paradise for mountain walkers and climbers; and the Alpujarras, one of Andalusia's most scenic mountain regions, dotted with white villages.

Planning

When to Go

The best months to go are October and November and April and May. It's blisteringly hot in the summer; if that's your only chance to come, plan on visiting Granada's Sierra Nevada to beat the heat. Autumn catches the cities going about their business, the temperatures are moderate, and you will rarely see a line form.

Getting Here and Around

AIR

Four daily flights connect Granada with Madrid and three connect it with Barcelona.

CONTACTS Aeropuerto de Granada. (*Aeropuerto Federico García Lorca*) ✉ *Granada* ☎ *902/404704.*

BUS

Granada's main bus station is at Carretera de Jaén, 3 km (2 miles) northwest of the center of town beyond the end of Avenida de Madrid. Most buses operate from here, except for buses to nearby destinations such as Fuentevaqueros, Viznar, and some buses to Sierra Nevada, which leave from the city center's Plaza del Triunfo near the RENFE station. Luggage lockers (*la consigna*) are available at the main bus and train stations, and you can also leave your luggage at City Locker (Carrera del Darro 3) and Locker in the City (Pasaje Conde Alcalá 1).

Autocares Bonal operates buses between Granada and the Sierra Nevada. ALSA buses run to and from Las Alpujarras (3 times daily), Córdoba (9 times daily), Seville (9 times daily), Málaga (20 times daily), and Jaén, Baeza, Úbeda, Cazorla, Almería, Almuñécar, and Nerja (several times daily).

In Granada, airport buses (€3) run between the center of town and the airport, leaving roughly every hour 7 am–8:45 pm from the Palacio de Congresos and making a few other stops along the way to the airport. Times are listed at the bus stop.

Granada has an extensive public bus network within the city. You can buy 5-, 10-, and 20-trip discount passes on the buses and at newsstands. The single-trip fare is €1.40. Granada Cards include bus trips plus guaranteed tickets for the Alhambra and other main monuments (without having to wait in lines). The card costs from €37, saving at least a third on regular prices. You can purchase the cards online via (*www.granadatur.com/granada-card*) or by phone (*858/889990, daily 9–8*) in advance of your visit; you can download them on your cell phone, or print at home or at the tourist office.

CONTACTS ALSA. ☎ *902/422242* ⊕ *www.alsa.es.* **Granada Bus Station.** ✉ *Ctra. Jaén, Granada* ☎ *902/422242.*

CAR

With the exception of parts of the Alpujarras, most roads in this region are smooth, and touring by car is one of the most enjoyable ways to see the countryside. Local tourist offices can advise about scenic drives. One good route heads northwest from Seville on the A66 passing through stunning scenery; turn northeast on the A461 to Santa Olalla de Cala to the village of Zufre, dramatically set at the edge of a gorge. Backtrack and continue on to Aracena. Return via the Minas de Riotinto (signposted from Aracena), which will bring you back to the A66 heading east to Seville.

TAXI

Taxis are plentiful and may be hailed on the street or from specified taxi stands. Fares are reasonable, and meters are strictly used; the minimum fare is about €4. You are not required to tip taxi drivers, although rounding off the amount is appreciated. Uber is available in Granada and Baeza.

Expect to pay around €20–€25 for cab fare from the airport to the city center.

CONTACTS Taxi Genil. ⊠ *Granada* ☏ *958/132323.* **Tele Radio Taxi.** ⊠ *Granada* ☏ *958/280654.*

TRAIN

There are regular trains from Seville and Almería, but service from Málaga and Córdoba is less convenient, necessitating a change at Antequera. A new AVE high-speed fast track enters operation in 2022; it will reduce journey times considerably (50 minutes to Málaga and 90 minutes to Seville). There are a couple of daily trains from Madrid, Valencia, and Barcelona.

CONTACTS Train Station. ⊠ *Av. de los Andaluces, Granada* ☏ *912/320320.*

Restaurants

Eating out is an intrinsic part of the Andalusian lifestyle. Whether it's sharing some tapas with friends over a prelunch drink or a three-course à la carte meal, many Andalusians eat out at some point during the day. Unsurprisingly, there are literally thousands of bars and restaurants throughout the region catering to all budgets and tastes.

At lunchtime, check out the *menús del día* (daily menus) offered by many restaurants, usually three courses and excellent value (expect to pay €8–€15, depending on the type of restaurant and location). Roadside restaurants, known as *ventas,* usually provide good food in generous portions and at reasonable prices. Be aware that many restaurants add a service charge (*cubierto*), which can be as much as €3 per person, and some restaurant prices don't include value-added tax (*impuesto sobre el valor añadido/I.V.A.*) at 10%. Note also that restaurants with tasting menus (*menús de degustación*) usually require everyone at the table to have the menu.

Andalusians tend to eat later than their fellow Spaniards: lunch is 2–4 pm, and dinner starts at 9 pm (10 pm in the summer). In cities, many restaurants are closed Sunday night, and fish restaurants tend to close on Monday; in inland towns and cities, some restaurants close for all of August.

Restaurant reviews have been shortened. For full information, visit Fodors. com.

Hotels

The Parador de Granada, next to the Alhambra, is a magnificent way to enjoy Granada. Hotels on the Alhambra hill, especially the parador, must be reserved far in advance. Lodging establishments in Granada's city center, around the Puerta Real and Acera del Darro, can be unbelievably noisy, so if you're staying there, ask for a room toward the back. Though Granada has plenty of hotels, it can be difficult to find lodging during peak tourist season (Easter through late October).

Rental accommodations bookable on portals such as Airbnb are popular in large towns and cities, although quality varies so double-check reviews before you book.

Not all hotel prices include value-added tax (I.V.A.) and the 10% surcharge may be added to your final bill. Check when you book.

Hotel reviews have been shortened. For full information, visit Fodors.com.

What It Costs in Euros			
$	$$	$$$	$$$$
RESTAURANTS			
under €12	€12–€17	€18–€22	over €22
HOTELS			
under €90	€90–€125	€126–€180	over €180

Tours

Cabalgar Rutas Alternativas
This is an established Alpujarras equestrian agency that organizes horseback riding in the Sierra Nevada. ✉ *C. Ermita, Bubión* ☎ *958/763135* ⊕ *www.ridingandalucia.com* ✎ *Rides from €25, tours from €795.*

Cycling Country
For information about cycling tours around Granada (Andalusia and Spain), 1–10 days long, contact this company, run by husband-and-wife team Geoff Norris and Maggi Jones in a town about 55 km (33 miles) away. ✉ *Calle Salmerones 18, Alhama de Granada* ☎ *958/360655* ⊕ *www.cyclingcountry.com* ✎ *From €50.*

Glovento Sur
Up to five people at a time are taken on balloon trips above Granada, Ronda, and Seville. ✉ *Placeta Nevot 4, #1A, Granada* ☎ *958/290316* ⊕ *www.gloventosur.com* ✎ *From €165.*

Granada Tapas Tours
Long-time British resident Gayle Mackie offers a range of tapas tours lasting up to three hours. ✉ ☎ *619/444984* ⊕ *www.granadatapastours.com* ✎ *From €40, including 6 tapas.*

Nevadensis
Based in the Alpujarras, Nevadensis leads guided hiking, climbing, and skiing tours of the Sierra Nevada. Note that prices are per group. ✉ *Pl. de la Libertad, Pampaneira* ☎ *958/763127* ⊕ *www.nevadensis.com* ✎ *From €150.*

Visitor Information

CONTACTS Municipal Tourist Office. ✉ *Pl. del Carmen 9, Centro* ☎ *958/248280* ⊕ *www.granadatur.com.* **Provincial Tourist Office.** ✉ *Calle Cárcel Baja 3, Centro* ☎ *958/247128* ⊕ *www.turgranada.es.*

La Alhambra

Sights

★ Alhambra
CASTLE/PALACE | With more than 2.7 million visitors a year, the Alhambra is Spain's most popular attraction. This sprawling palace-fortress was the last bastion of the 800-year Moorish presence on the Iberian Peninsula. Composed of royal residential quarters, court chambers, baths, and gardens, surrounded by defense towers and massive walls, the Alhambra is an architectural gem. The courtyards, patios, and halls offer an ethereal maze of Moorish arches, columns, and domes containing intricate stucco carvings and patterned ceramic tiling. The heart of the Alhambra, the Palacios Nazaríes contain delicate apartments, lazy fountains, and tranquil pools, and are divided into three sections: the *mexuar*, where business, government, and palace administration were headquartered; the *serrallo*, state rooms where the sultans held court; and the harem. The beautiful Sala de los Abencerrajes (Hall of the Moors) has a fabulous, ornate ceiling and star-shape cupola reflected in the pool below. ✉ *Cuesta de Gomérez, Alhambra* ☎ *858/889002 tickets, 958/027900 information* ⊕ *www.alhambra-patronato.es/en* ✎ *From €2, Museo de la Alhambra and Palacio de Carlos V free* ⏱ *Museo de Bellas Artes and Museo de la Alhambra closed Mon.*

Carmen de los Mártires
HISTORIC HOME | Up the hill from the Hotel Alhambra Palace, this

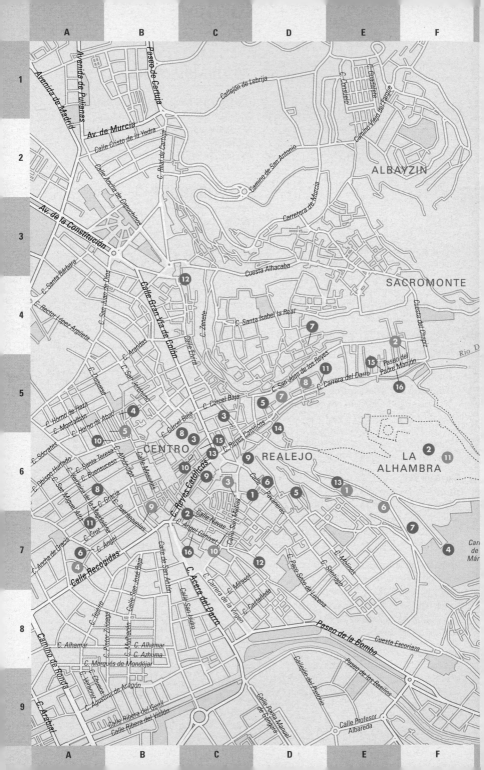

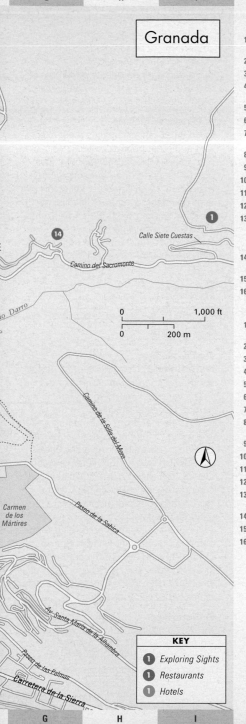

Granada

Sights ▼

1 Abadía del
  Sacromonte **I3**
2 Alhambra **F6**
3 Capilla Real.............. **C6**
4 Carmen de los
  Mártires.................. **F7**
5 Casa de los Pisa **D5**
6 Casa de los Tiros........ **D6**
7 Casa-Museo de
  Manuel de Falla.......... **F7**
8 Cathedral **C6**
9 Centro José Guerrero... **C6**
10 Corral del Carbón........ **C6**
11 El Bañuelo **D5**
12 El Cuarto Real **D7**
13 Fundación
  Rodríguez-Acosta/
  Instituto
  Gómez-Moreno **E6**
14 Museo Cuevas del
  Sacromonte **G3**
15 Palacio Madraza......... **C6**
16 Paseo Padre Manjón.... **E5**

Restaurants ▼

1 Alacena de las
  Monjas.................. **D6**
2 Bar Los Diamantes **C7**
3 Bodegas Castañeda..... **C5**
4 Café Botánico........... **B5**
5 Damasqueros **D6**
6 El Quinteto **A7**
7 El Trillo **D4**
8 La Bodega de
  Antonio.................. **A6**
9 La Brujidera **C6**
10 Oliver.................... **B6**
11 Om-Kalsum.............. **A6**
12 Paprika.................. **C4**
13 Pastelería
  López-Mezquita.......... **C6**
14 Pilar del Toro **D5**
15 Ruta del Azafrán **E5**
16 Tinta Fina **C7**

Hotels ▼

1 Carmen de la
  Alcubilla del Caracol **E6**
2 Casa Morisca **F4**
3 Gar Anat Hotel
  Boutique **C6**
4 Hospes Palacio
  de los Patos **A7**
5 Hostal Rodri **B5**
6 Hotel Alhambra
  Palace..................... **E6**
7 Hotel Casa 1800......... **D5**
8 Hotel Palacio
  Santa Inés **D5**
9 Hotel Párraga Siete **B7**
10 Palacio de los Navas.... **C7**
11 Parador de Granada..... **F6**

Calle Siete Cuestas

Camino del Sacromonte

io Darro

Camino de la Silla del Moro

Carmen
de los
Mártires

Paseo de la Sabica

Av. Santa María de la Alhambra

Paseo de los Palmas

Carretera de la Sierra

0 ———————— 1,000 ft
0 ———————— 200 m

KEY

1 *Exploring Sights*
1 *Restaurants*
1 *Hotels*

turn-of-the-20th-century *carmen* (private villa) and its gardens—the only area open to tourists—are like a Generalife (the Alhambra summer palace) in miniature. ✉ *Paseo de los Mártires, Alhambra* ☎ *958/849103* 🎟 *Free.*

Casa-Museo de Manuel de Falla

HISTORIC HOME | The composer Manuel de Falla (1876–1946) lived and worked for many years in this rustic house tucked into a charming hillside lane with lovely views of the Alpujarras. In 1986 Granada paid homage to him by naming its new concert hall (down the street from the Carmen de los Mártires) the Auditorio Manuel de Falla—from this institution, fittingly, you have a view of his little white house. Note the bust in the small garden: it's placed where the composer once sat to enjoy the sweeping vista. ✉ *Calle Antequeruela Alta 11, Alhambra* ☎ *958/222189* 🌐 *museomanueldefalla.com* 🎟 *€3* ⏲ *Closed Mon.*

Hotels

★ Carmen de la Alcubilla del Caracol

$$$ | **B&B/INN** | In a traditional granadino villa on the slopes of the Alhambra, this privately run lodging is one of Granada's most stylish hotels. **Pros:** great views; bright, airy rooms; walking distance to the Alhambra. **Cons:** tough climb in hot weather; slightly out of town; parking difficult. [$] *Rooms from: €150* ✉ *Calle Aire Alta 12, Alhambra* ☎ *958/215551* 🌐 *www.alcubilladelcaracol.com* ⏲ *Closed mid-July–Aug.* 🛏 *7 rooms* 🍴 *No Meals.*

Hotel Alhambra Palace

$$$$ | **HOTEL** | Built by a local duke in 1910, this neo-Moorish hotel is on leafy grounds at the back of the Alhambra hill, and has a very *Arabian Nights* interior (think orange-and-brown overtones, multicolor tiles, and Moorish-style arches and pillars). **Pros:** bird's-eye views; large, warmly decorated rooms; location near the Alhambra. **Cons:** steep climb up from Granada; often packed with business people (it doubles as a convention center); might be too grandiose for some. [$] *Rooms from: €200* ✉ *Pl. Arquitecto García de Paredes 1, Alhambra* ☎ *958/221468* 🌐 *www.h-alhambrapalace.es* 🛏 *126 rooms* 🍴 *No Meals.*

★ Parador de Granada

$$$$ | **HOTEL** | This is Spain's most expensive and most popular parador, right within the walls of the Alhambra. **Pros:** good location for the Alhambra; garden restaurant; lovely interiors. **Cons:** very expensive; removed from city life; no views in some rooms. [$] *Rooms from: €350* ✉ *Calle Real de la Alhambra, Alhambra* ☎ *958/221440* 🌐 *www.paradorsofspain.com* 🛏 *40 rooms* 🍴 *No Meals.*

Realejo

Sights

Casa de los Tiros

HISTORIC HOME | This 16th-century palace, adorned with the coat of arms of the Grana Venegas family who owned it, was named House of the Shots for the musket barrels that protrude from its facade. The stairs to the upper-floor displays are flanked by portraits of miserable-looking Spanish royals, from Ferdinand and Isabella to Felipe IV. The highlight is the carved wooden ceiling in the Cuadra Dorada (Hall of Gold), adorned with gilded lettering and portraits of royals and knights. Old lithographs, engravings, and photographs show life in Granada in the 19th and early 20th centuries. ✉ *Calle Pavaneras 19, Realejo-San Matías* ☎ *600/143175* 🌐 *www.museosdeandalucia.es/* 🎟 *€2* ⏲ *Closed Mon.*

El Cuarto Real

NOTABLE BUILDING | Just a block away from Casa de los Tiros is the beautifully restored El Cuarto Real, a 13th-century Nasrid palace which has decorations

Continued on page 658

ALHAMBRA: PALACE-FORTRESS

 Floating mirage-like on its promontory overlooking Granada, the mighty and mysterious Alhambra shimmers vermilion in the clear mountain air, with the white peaks of the Sierra Nevada rising behind it. This sprawling palace-fortress, named from the Arabic for "red citadel" (*al-Qal'ah al-Hamra*), was the last bastion of the 800-year Moorish presence on the Iberian Peninsula. Composed of royal residential quarters, court chambers, baths, and gardens, surrounded by defense towers and massive walls, the Alhambra is an architectual gem where Moorish kings worked and played—and murdered their enemies.

LOOK UP

Among the stylistic elements you can see in the Alhambra are **Arabesque** geometrical designs, and elaborate **Mocárabe** arches.

Built of perishable materials, the Alhambra was meant to be forever replenished and replaced by succeeding generations. The Patio de los Leones' (above) has recently been restored to its original appearance.

INSIDE THE FORTRESS

More than 3 million annual visitors come to the Alhambra today, making it Spain's top attraction. Vistors revel in the palace's architectural wonders, most of which had to be restored after the alterations made after the Christian reconquest of southern Spain in 1492 and the damage from an 1821 earthquake. Incidentally, Napoléon's troops commandeered the site in 1812 with intent to level it but their attempts were foiled.

The courtyards, patios, and halls offer an ethereal maze of Moorish arches, columns, and domes containing intricate stucco carvings and patterned ceramic tiling. The intimate arcades, fountains, and light-reflecting pools throughout are identified in the ornamental inscriptions as physical renderings of paradise taken from the Koran and Islamic poetry. The contemporary visitor to this dreamlike space feels the fleeting embrace of a culture that brought its light to a world emerging from medieval darkness.

ARCHITECTURAL TERMS

Arabesque: An ornament or decorative style that employs flower, foliage, or fruit, and sometimes geometrical, animal, and figural outlines to produce an intricate pattern of interlaced lines.

Mocárabe: A decorative element of carved wood or plaster based on juxtaposed and hanging prisms resembling stalactites. Sometimes called *muquarna* (honeycomb vaulting), the impression is similar to a beehive and the "honey" has been described as light.

Mozárabe: Sometimes confused with Mocárabe, the term Mozárabe refers to Christians living in Moorish Spain. Thus, Christian artistic styles or recourses in Moorish architecture (such as the paintings in the Sala de los Reyes) are also identified as *mozárabe*, or, in English, mozarabic.

Mudéjar: This word refers to Moors living in Christian Spain. Moorish artistic elements in Christian architecture, such as horseshoe arches in a church, also are referred to as Mudéjar.

ALHAMBRA'S ARCHITECTURAL HIGHLIGHTS

The **columns** used in the construction of the Alhambra are unique, with extraordinarily slender cylindrical shafts, concave base moldings, and carved rings decorating the upper extremities. The capitals have simple cylindrical bases under prism-shaped heads decorated in a variety of vegetal motifs. Nearly all of these columns support false arches constructed purely for decorative purposes. The 124 columns surrounding the Patio de los Leones (Court of the Lions) are the best examples.

Court of the Lions

Cursive epigraphy is used to quote the Koran and Arabic poems. Considered the finest example of this are the Ibn-Zamrak verses that decorate the walls of the Sala de las Dos Hermanas.

Cursive epigraphy

Glazed ceramic tiles covered with geometrical patterns in primary colors cover the walls of the Alhambra with a profusion of styles and shapes. Red, blue, and yellow are the colors of magic in Sufi tradition, while green is the life-giving color of Islam.

Ceramic tiles

The **horseshoe arch**, widening before rounding off with lower ends extending around the circle until they begin to converge, was the quintessential Moorish architectural innovation, used not only for aesthetic and decorative purposes but because it allowed greater height than the classical, semicircular arch inherited from the Greeks and Romans. The horseshoe arch also had a mystical significance in recalling the shape of the *mihrab*, the prayer niche in the *qibla* wall of a mosque indicating the direction of prayer and suggesting a door to Mecca or to paradise. Horseshoe arches and arcades are found throughout the Alhambra.

Gate of Justice

The Koran describes paradise as "gardens underneath which rivers flow," and **water** is used as a practical and ornamental architectural element throughout the Alhambra. Whether used musically, as in the canals in the Patio de los Leones or visually, as in the reflecting pool of the Patio de los Arrayanes, water is used to enhance light, enlarge spaces, or provide musical background for a desert culture in love with the beauty and oasis-like properties of hydraulics in all its forms.

Alhambra fountains

The Alcazaba was built chiefly by Nasrid kings in the 1300s.

LAY OF THE LAND

The complex has three main parts: the Alcazaba, the Palacio Nazaríes (Nasrid Royal Palace), and the Generalife. Across from the main entrance is the original fortress, the **Alcazaba**. Here, the watchtower's great bell was once used to announce the opening and closing of the irrigation system on Granada's great plain.

A wisteria-covered walkway leads to the heart of the Alhambra, the **Palacios Nazaríes**. Here, delicate apartments, lazy fountains, and tranquil pools contrast vividly with the hulking fortifications outside. It is divided into three sections: the *mexuar*, where business, government, and palace administration were headquartered; the *serrallo*, a series of state rooms where the sultans held court and entertained their ambassadors; and the *harem*, which in its time was entered only by the sultan, his family, and their most trusted servants, most of them eunuchs. Nearby is the Renaissance **Palacio de Carlos V** (Palace of Charles V), featuring a perfectly square exterior but a circular interior courtyard. Designed by Pedro Machuca, a pupil of Michelangelo, it is where the sultan's private apartments once stood. Part of the building houses the free **Museo de la Alhambra**, devoted to Islamic art. Upstairs is the more modest **Museo de Bellas Artes**.

Over on Cerro del Sol (Hill of the Sun) is **Generalife**, the ancient summer palace of the Nasrid kings.

TIMELINE

1238 First Nasrid king, Ibn el-Ahmar, begins Alhambra.

1391 Nasrid Palaces is completed.

1492 Boabdil surrenders Granada to Ferdinand and Isabella, parents of King Henry VIII's first wife, Catherine of Aragon.

1524 Carlos V begins Renaissance Palace.

1812 Napoléonic troops arrive with plans to destroy Alhambra.

1814 The Duke of Wellington sojourns here to escape the pressures of the Peninsular War.

1829 Washington Irving lives on the premises and writes Tales of the *Alhambra*, reviving interest in the crumbling palace.

1862 Granada municipality begins Alhambra restoration that continues to this day.

ALHAMBRA'S PASSAGES OF TIME

From Columbus's commissioning to a bloody murder, historic events as well as everyday affairs happened between these walls.

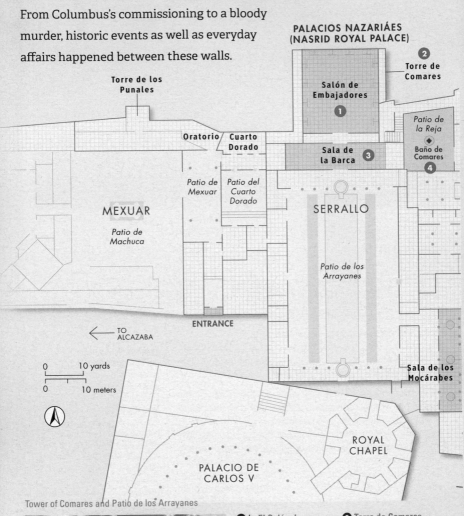

PALACIOS NAZARIÁES (NASRID ROYAL PALACE)

Torre de los Punales

Salón de Embajadores ❶

Torre de Comares ❷

Oratorio / Cuarto Dorado

Sala de la Barca ❸

Patio de la Reja

Baño de Comares ❹

Patio de Mexuar

Patio del Cuarto Dorado

MEXUAR

Patio de Machuca

SERRALLO

Patio de los Arrayanes

TO ALCAZABA

ENTRANCE

0   10 yards
0   10 meters

Sala de los Mocárabes

ROYAL CHAPEL

PALACIO DE CARLOS V

Tower of Comares and Patio de los Arrayanes

❶ In **El Salón de Embajadores**, Boabdil drew up his terms of surrender, and Christopher Columbus secured royal support for his historic voyage in 1492. The carved wooden ceiling is a portrayal of the seven Islamic heavens, with six rows of stars topped by a seventh-heaven cupulino or micro-cupola.

❷ **Torre de Comares**, a lookout in the corner of this hall is where Carlos V uttered his famous line, "Ill-fated the man who lost all this."

❸ Mistakenly named from the Arabic word *baraka* (divine blessing), **Sala de la Barca** has a carved wooden ceiling often described as an inverted boat.

Sala de los Reyes

7 Shhh, don't tell a secret here. In the **Sala de los Ajimeces**, a whisper in one corner can be clearly heard from the opposite corner.

8 In the **Sala de las Dos Hermanas**, twin slabs of marble embedded in the floor are the "sisters," though Washington Irving preferred the story of a pair of captive Moorish beauties.

9 In the **Patio de Los Leones** (Court of the Lions), a dozen crudely crafted lions (restored to their former glory in 2012) support the fountain at the center of this elegant courtyard, representing the signs of the zodiac sending water to the four corners.

10 In the **Sala de los Abencerrajes**, Muley Hacen (father of Boabdil) murdered the male members of the Abencerraje family in revenge for their chief's seduction of his daughter Zoraya. The rusty stains in the fountain are said to be bloodstains left by the pile of Abencerraje heads.

The star-shaped cupola, reflected in the pool, is considered the Alhambra's most beautiful example of stalactite or honeycomb vaulting. The octagonal dome over the room is best viewed at sunset when the 16 small windows atop the dome admit sharp, low sunlight that refracts kaleidoscopically through the beehive-like prisms.

11 In the **Sala de los Reyes**, the ceiling painting depicts the first 10 Nasrid rulers. It was painted by a Christian artist since Islamic artists were not allowed to usurp divine power by creating human or animal figures.

The overhead painting of the knight rescuing his lady from a savage man portrays chivalry, a concept introduced to Europe by Arabic poets.

12 The terraces of **Generalife** grant incomparable views of the city.

Generalife gardens

4 The **Baño de Comares** is where the sultan's favorites luxuriated in brightly tiled pools beneath star-shape pinpoints of light from the ceiling above.

5 **El Peinador de la Reina**, a nine-foot-square room atop a small tower was the Sultana's boudoir. The perforated marble slab was used to infiltrate perfumes while the queen performed her toilette. Washington Irving wrote his *Tales of the Alhambra* in this romantic tree-house-like perch.

6 Sultana Zoraya often found refuge in this charming little balcony (**Mirador de Daraxa**) overlooking the Lindaraja garden.

Map labels:
Peinador de la Reina 5
Apartamientos de Carlos V
Patio de Lindaraja
HAREM
Mirador de Daraxa 6
Sala de las Dos Hermanas 8
Sala de los Ajimeces 7
Patio de los Leones 9
Sala de los Reyes 11
Cistern
Sala de los Abencerrajes 10
TO JARDINES DEL PARTAL, GENERALIFE 12

almost identical to the Alhambra. Only the fortified tower remains standing with its exquisite *qubba* (reception room) with stunning walls and ceiling motifs. The adjoining modern extension houses temporary art exhibitions, and the formal gardens make a peaceful place to rest. ✉ *Pl. de los Campos 6, Realejo-San Matías* ☎ *958/849111* 🎟 *€2* 🕙 *Sun. afternoon and Mon.*

Fundación Rodríguez-Acosta/Instituto Gómez-Moreno

ARTS CENTER | This nonprofit organization was founded at the behest of the painter José Marí Rodríguez-Acosta. Inside a typical *carmen*, it houses works of art, archaeological finds, and a library collected by the Granada-born scholar Manuel Gómez-Moreno Martínez. Other exhibits include valuable and unique objects from Asian cultures and the prehistoric and classical eras. ✉ *Callejón Niños del Rollo 8, Realejo-San Matías* ☎ *958/227497* ⊕ *www.fundacionrodriguezacosta.com* 🎟 *From €5.*

 Restaurants

Alacena de las Monjas

$$$ | **SPANISH** | Just as popular with locals as visitors, this restaurant in the heart of the Realejo district is on the first floor and basement of a 14th-century convent—you can see the original clay vats that supplied the water downstairs. The house special is red tuna, on the menu in a variety of guises, and meat lovers won't want to miss the steaks, about as tender as they come. **Known for:** steak; red tuna dishes; historic setting. 💲 *Average main: €20* ✉ *Pl. del Padre Suarez 5, Realejo-San Matías* ☎ *958/229519* ⊕ *www.alacenadelasmonjas.com* 🕙 *Closed Tues. No dinner Mon.*

★ Damasqueros

$$$$ | **SPANISH** | The modern, wood-paneled dining room and warm lighting form the perfect setting for the creative Andalusian cuisine cooked here by local chef Lola Marín, who learned her trade with some of Spain's top chefs, such as Martín Berasategui. The tasting menu changes weekly and always includes in-season produce in its five courses (cold and hot starters, fish, meat, and dessert). **Known for:** service; fresh local produce; wine pairing. 💲 *Average main: €45* ✉ *Calle Damasqueros 3, Realejo-San Matías* ☎ *958/210550* ⊕ *www.damasqueros.com* 🕙 *Closed Mon. No dinner Sun.*

Hotels

Gar Anat Hotel Boutique

$$ | **HOTEL** | Once a humble hostel on the Granada leg of the Camino de Santiago pilgrimage route, the 17th-century restored palace now offers stylish boutique accommodation. **Pros:** generous breakfast; central location; eclectic decor. **Cons:** some rooms small and dark; street noise can be intrusive; slight challenge to find by car. 💲 *Rooms from: €110* ✉ *Placeta de Peregrinos 2, Realejo-San Matías* ☎ *958/225528* ⊕ *www.hotelgaranat.com* 🛏 *15 rooms* ⭕ *No Meals.*

Sacromonte

The third of Granada's three hills, the Sacromonte rises behind the Albayzín and is covered with prickly pear cacti and riddled with caverns. The Sacromonte has long been notorious as a domain of Granada's Gypsies and thus a den of thieves and scam artists, but its reputation is largely undeserved. The quarter is more like a quiet Andalusian *pueblo* (village) than a rough neighborhood.

Many of the quarter's colorful *cuevas* (caves) have been restored as middle-class homes, and some of the old spirit lives on in a handful of *zambras* (flamenco performances in caves, which are garishly decorated with brass plates and cooking utensils). These shows differ from formal flamenco shows in that the performers mingle with you, usually dragging one or two onlookers onto the floor for an improvised dance lesson. Ask your hotel to book you a spot on a *cueva* tour, which usually includes a walk through the neighboring Albayzín and a drink at a tapas bar in addition to the zambra.

Sights

Abadía de Sacromonte
CAVE | The caverns on Sacromonte are thought to have sheltered early Christians. In the 15th century, treasure hunters found bones inside and assumed they belonged to San Cecilio, the city's patron saint. Thus, the hill was sanctified—*sacro monte* (holy mountain)—and this abbey was built on its summit. Tours in English are at 2 and 5:30. ⊠ *C. del Sacromonte, Sacromonte* ☎ *958/221445* ⊕ *sacromonteabbey.com* ✇ *From €5.*

Museo Cuevas del Sacromonte
OTHER MUSEUM | The ethnographical museum here shows how people lived in this area, and elsewhere in this interesting complex looks at Granada's flora and fauna. During the summer months, there are live flamenco concerts. It's a steep walk to reach the center, even if you take Bus No. C2 (from Plaza Nueva) to shorten the distance. ⊠ *Barranco de los Negros, Sacromonte* ☎ *958/215120* ⊕ *http://sacromontegranada.com/* ✇ *€5.*

Albayzín

Covering a hill of its own, across the Darro ravine from the Alhambra, this ancient Moorish neighborhood is a mix of dilapidated white houses and immaculate *carmenes* (private villas). It was founded in 1228 by Moors who had fled Baeza after Ferdinand III captured the city. Full of cobblestone alleyways and secret corners, the Albayzín guards its old Moorish roots jealously, though its 30 mosques were converted to baroque churches long ago. A stretch of the Moors' original city wall runs beside the ridge called the **Cuesta de la Alhacaba.**

If you're walking—the best way to explore—you can enter the Albayzín from either the Cuesta de Elvira or the Plaza Nueva. Alternatively, on foot or by taxi (parking is impossible), begin in the Plaza Santa Ana and follow the Carrera del Darro, Paseo Padre Manjón, and Cuesta del Chapíz. One of the highest points in the quarter, the plaza in front of the church of San Nicolás (€2; *open mornings only*)— the **Mirador de San Nicolás**—has one of the finest views in all of Granada: on the hill opposite, the turrets and towers of the Alhambra form a dramatic silhouette against the snowy peaks of the Sierra Nevada. The sight is most magical at dawn, dusk, and on nights when the Alhambra is floodlighted. Take note of the mosque just next to the church— views of the Alhambra from the mosque gardens are just as good as those from the Mirador de San Nicolás and a lot less crowded. Interestingly, given the area's Moorish history, the two sloping, narrow streets of Calderería Nueva and Calderería Vieja that meet at the top by the Iglesia San Gregorio have developed into something of a North African bazaar, full of shops and vendors selling clothes, bags, crafts, and trinkets. The numerous little teahouses and restaurants here have a decidedly Moroccan flavor.

Many of the streets are cobbled so wear sturdy footwear with thick soles.

Sights

Casa de los Pisa
HISTORIC HOME | Originally built in 1494 for the Pisa family, the claim to fame of this house is its relationship to San Juan de Dios, who came to Granada in 1538 and founded a charity hospital to take care of the poor. Befriended by the Pisa family, he was taken into their home when he fell ill in February 1550. A month later, he died there, at the age of 55. Since that

time, devotees of the saint have traveled from around the world to this house with a stone Gothic facade, now run by the Hospital Order of St. John. Inside are numerous pieces of jewelry, furniture, priceless religious works of art, and an extensive collection of paintings and sculptures depicting St. John. ✉ *Calle Convalecencia 1, Albaicín* ☎ *958/222144* 🎟 *€3* 🕒 *Closed Sun.*

El Bañuelo (*Little Bath House*)
HISTORIC SIGHT | These 11th-century Arab steam baths might be a little dark and dank now, but try to imagine them some 900 years ago, filled with Moorish beauties. Back then, the dull brick walls were backed by bright ceramic tiles, tapestries, and rugs. Light comes in through star-shape vents in the ceiling, à la the bathhouse in the Alhambra. ✉ *Carrera del Darro 31, Albaicín* ☎ *958/229738* 🎟 *€5 (ticket includes admission to Dar al-Horra), free Sun.*

Paseo Padre Manjón
STREET | Along the Río Darro, this paseo is also known as the Paseo de los Tristes (Promenade of the Sad Ones) because funeral processions once passed this way. The cafés and bars here are a good place for a coffee break. The park, dappled with wisteria-covered pergolas, fountains, and stone walkways, has a stunning view of the Alhambra's northern side. ✉ *Albaicín.*

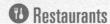

🍴 Restaurants

★ El Trillo
$$$ | **SPANISH** | Tucked away in the warren of alleyways in a restored Albayzín villa, this lovely restaurant offers perhaps the best food in the area. There's a formal dining room, outside garden with pear and quince trees, plus a roof terrace with Alhambra views. **Known for:** rice with wild boar; fine dining; views of the Alhambra. [$] *Average main: €20* ✉ *Callejón del Aljibe del Trillo 3, Albaicín* ☎ *958/225182* 🌐 *www.restaurante-eltrillo.com* 🕒 *No dinner Tues. and Wed.*

Paprika
$$ | **VEGETARIAN** | Inside a pretty brick building and with an informal terrace sprawling over the wide steps of the Cuesta de Abarqueros, Paprika offer unpretentious vegan food. Most ingredients and wines are organic, and dishes include salads, stir-fries, and curries, such as Thai curry with tofu, coconut, and green curry sauce. **Known for:** organic ingredients; value plate of the day; choice of vegan food. [$] *Average main: €12* ✉ *Cuesta de Abarqueros 3, Albaicín* ☎ *958/804785* 🌐 *www.paprika-granada.com.*

Pilar del Toro
$$$ | **SPANISH** | This bar and restaurant, just off Plaza Nueva, is in a 17th-century palace with a stunning patio (complete with original marble columns) and peaceful garden. The menu emphasizes meat dishes such as *cochinillo confitado* (suckling pig confit) and the house specialty, braised *rabo de toro* (oxtail stew) and *salmorejo* (cold tomato soup). **Known for:** oxtail; elegant upstairs restaurant; atmospheric patio. [$] *Average main: €20* ✉ *Calle Hospital de Santa Ana 12, Albaicín* ☎ *958/225470* 🌐 *pilardeltoro.es.*

Ruta del Azafrán
$$ | **SPANISH** | A charming surprise nestled at the foot of the Albayzín by the Darro—this sleek contemporary space in the shadow of the Alhambra offers a selection of specialties. The menu is interesting and diverse and includes dishes like tuna *tataki* (a method of pounding fish in Japanese cuisine) with pineapple and several different couscous dishes. **Known for:** tasting menus; international dishes; views of the Alhambra, especially at night. [$] *Average main: €16* ✉ *Paseo de los Tristes 1, Albaicín* ☎ *958/226882* 🌐 *rutadelazafran.com.*

Hotels

★ Casa Morisca

$$$ | B&B/INN | The architect who owns this 15th-century building transformed it into a hotel so distinctive that he received Spain's National Restoration Award for his preservation of original architectural elements, including barrel-vaulted brickwork, wooden ceilings, and the original pool. **Pros:** easy parking; award-winning design; historic location. **Cons:** no restaurant on-site; stuffy interior rooms; slightly out of the town center. [$] *Rooms from: €140* ✉ *Cuesta de la Victoria 9, Albaicín* ☎ *958/221100* 🌐 *www.hotelcasamorisca.com* 🛏 *14 rooms* 🍴 *No Meals.*

Hotel Casa 1800

$$$ | HOTEL | A stone's throw from the Paseo de los Tristes, this restored 17th-century mansion has a fine, tiered patio. **Pros:** historic building; walking distance to most sights; deluxe suite has balcony with views of the Alhambra. **Cons:** no bar; rooms are small (but comfortable); on a street that doesn't permit cars. [$] *Rooms from: €165* ✉ *Calle Benalua 11, Albaicín* ☎ *958/210700* 🌐 *www.hotelcasa1800granada.com* 🛏 *25 rooms* 🍴 *No Meals.*

Hotel Palacio Santa Inés

$$$ | HOTEL | It's not often you get to stay in a 16th-century palace—and this one has a stunning location in the heart of the Albayzín. **Pros:** perfect location for exploring the Albayzín; some rooms have Alhambra views; quirky interiors. **Cons:** breakfast is average; some rooms rather dark; can't get there by car. [$] *Rooms from: €140* ✉ *Cuesta de Santa Inés 9, Albaicín* ☎ *958/222362* 🌐 *www.palaciosantaines.es* 🛏 *35 rooms* 🍴 *No Meals.*

Performing Arts

FLAMENCO

Cueva de la Rocío

FOLK/TRADITIONAL DANCE | This is a good spot for authentic flamenco shows, staged nightly at 9, 10, and 11. ✉ *C. del Sacromonte 70, Albaicín* ☎ *958/227129* 🌐 *cuevalarocio.es* 🎟 *From €23.*

El Tabanco

FOLK/TRADITIONAL DANCE | In the heart of the Albayzín, this small venue is an art gallery by day and live music venue (mostly flamenco and jazz) by night. Book in advance to be sure of a seat. ✉ *Cuesta de San Gregorio 24, Albaicín* ☎ *662/137046* 🌐 *www.eltabanco.com.*

El Templo del Flamenco

FOLK/TRADITIONAL DANCE | Slightly off the beaten track (take a taxi to get here) and less touristy because of it, this venue has shows at 8 and 10 daily. ✉ *Calle Parnaleros Alto 41, Albaicín* ☎ *622/500052 Tickets, 654/373136 Information* 🌐 *eltemplodelflamenco.com/en.*

Jardines de Zoraya

FOLK/TRADITIONAL DANCE | This show doesn't take place in a cave, but the music and dance are some of the most authentic available. Daily flamenco shows are at 8 and 10:30 pm. ✉ *Calle Panaderos 32, Albaicín* ☎ *958/206266* 🌐 *www.jardinesdezoraya.com* 🎟 *From €20.*

Centro

Sights

Capilla Real (*Royal Chapel*)

RELIGIOUS BUILDING | Catholic monarchs Isabella of Castile and Ferdinand of Aragón are buried at this shrine. When Isabella died in 1504, her body was first laid to rest in the Convent of San Francisco. The architect Enrique Egas began work on the Royal Chapel in 1506 and completed it 15 years later, creating a masterpiece of the ornate Gothic style now known in Spain as Isabelline. In 1521, Isabella's body was transferred to the Royal Chapel crypt, joined by that of her husband, Ferdinand, and later her daughter, Juana la Loca (Joanna the Mad); son-in-law, Felipe el Hermoso (Philip the Handsome); and Prince Felipe of Asturias. The **crypt** containing the coffins is simple, but it's topped by elaborate marble tombs showing Ferdinand and Isabella lying side by side. The **altarpiece** comprises 34 carved panels depicting religious and historical scenes. The **sacristy** holds Ferdinand's sword, Isabella's crown and scepter, and a fine collection of Flemish paintings once owned by Isabella. ✉ *Calle Oficios, Centro* ☎ *958/227848* 🌐 *www.capillareal-granada.com* 🎟 *€5.*

Cathedral

RELIGIOUS BUILDING | Carlos V commissioned the cathedral in 1521 because he considered the Capilla Real "too small for so much glory" and wanted to house his illustrious late grandparents someplace more worthy. Carlos undoubtedly had great intentions, as the cathedral was created by some of the finest architects of its time: Enrique Egas, Diego de Siloé, Alonso Cano, and sculptor Juan de Mena. Alas, his ambitions came to little, for the cathedral is a grand and gloomy monument, not completed until 1714 and never used as the crypt for his grandparents (or parents). Enter through a small door at the back, off the Gran Vía. Old hymnals are displayed throughout, and there's a museum, which includes a 14th-century gold-and-silver monstrance given to the city by Queen Isabella. ✉ *Gran Vía, Centro* ☎ *958/222959* 🎟 *€5 (including audio guide)* 🕑 *Closed Sun. morning.*

Centro José Guerrero

ART GALLERY | Just across a lane from the cathedral and Capilla Real, this building houses colorful modern paintings by José Guerrero. Born in Granada in 1914, Guerrero traveled throughout Europe and lived in New York in the 1950s before returning to Spain. The center also runs excellent temporary contemporary art shows. ✉ *Calle Oficios 8, Centro* ☎ *958/225185* 🌐 *www.centroguerrero.es* 🎟 *Free* 🕑 *Closed Sun. afternoon and Mon.*

Corral del Carbón (*Coal House*)

HISTORIC SIGHT | This building was used to store coal in the 19th century, but its history is much longer. Dating to the 14th century, it was used by Moorish merchants as a lodging house, and then by Christians as a theater. It's one of the oldest Moorish buildings in the city and the only Arab structure of its kind in Spain. ✉ *Calle Mariana Pineda, Centro* 🎟 *Free.*

Palacio Madraza

CASTLE/PALACE | This building conceals the Islamic seminary built in 1349 by Yusuf I. The intriguing baroque facade is elaborate; inside, across from the entrance, an octagonal room is crowned by a Moorish dome. It hosts occasional free art and cultural exhibitions. ✉ *Calle Zacatín, Centro* ☎ *958/241299* 🎟 *€2.*

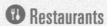

🍴 Restaurants

Bar Los Diamantes

$$ | **TAPAS** | This spit and sawdust bar is a big favorite with locals and draws crowds whatever the time of year. Specialties include fried fish and seafood—try the *surtido de pescado* (assortment of fried fish) to sample the best—as well as *sesos* (fried lambs' brains). **Known for:** busy atmosphere; fried fish; communal tables. [$] *Average main: €14* ✉ *Calle Navas 28, Centro* ☎ *958/222572* 🌐 *www.barlosdiamantes.com.*

Bodegas Castañeda

$$$ | **SPANISH** | A block from the cathedral across Gran Vía, this is a delightfully typical Granada bodega with low ceilings and dark wood furniture. In addition to the wines, specialties here are plates of cheese, pâté, and *embutidos* (cold meats). **Known for:** Spanish tortilla with creamy aioli; atmospheric bar; tapas. [$] *Average main: €18* ✉ *Calle Almireceros 1–3, Centro* ☎ *958/215464.*

★ Café Botánico

$$ | TAPAS | Southeast of Granada's cathedral, this is modern hot spot is a world apart from Granada's usual traditional tapas bar. It attracts an eclectic crowd of students, families, and businesspeople for a diverse, international menu, including Mexican fajitas, Italian risottos, and Thai red curries all sitting side by side. **Known for:** homemade desserts; international menu; good-value lunch deal. [$] *Average main: €15* ✉ *Calle Málaga 3, Centro* ☎ *958/271598.*

El Quinteto

$$ | SPANISH | Don't let the rather impersonal modern exterior put you off because behind the bland-coffeeshop-doors lies one of the city's best eateries. It's known for several dishes on the menu although the *cochinillo confitado* (glazed suckling pig) and braised oxtail are established local favorites. **Known for:** traditional and modern tapas; gluten-free choices; suckling pig. [$] *Average main: €15* ✉ *Calle Solarillo de Gracia 4, Centro* ☎ *958/264815* 🌐 *elquinteto.com* 🕒 *Closed Sun. and Mon.*

La Bodega de Antonio

$$ | SPANISH | Just off Calle Puentezuelas, this authentic patio complete with original pillars provides a cozy vibe. Specials include the house cod (with prawns and clams) and Galician-style octopus, best enjoyed with a *cerdito* (a "little pig" ceramic jug of sweet white wine, so named for its snout pourer). **Known for:** Galician-style octopus; choice of croquettes; generous portions. [$] *Average main: €12* ✉ *Calle Jardines 4, Centro* ☎ *958/252275* 🕒 *Closed Aug.*

★ La Brujidera

$$ | TAPAS | Also known simply as Casa de Vinos (Wine House), this place, up a pedestrian street just behind Plaza Nueva, is a must for Spanish wine lovers. The cozy interior is reminiscent of a ship's cabin, with wood paneling lining the walls, along with bottles of more than 150 Spanish wines. **Known for:** vermouth and sherries on tap; meat and cheese boards; long wine list. [$] *Average main: €12* ✉ *Monjas del Carmen 2, Centro* ☎ *687/851507* 🕒 *Closed 1 wk in Feb.*

Oliver

$$ | SPANISH | The interior may look a bit bare, but whatever this fish restaurant lacks in warmth it makes up for with the food. It serves simple but high-quality dishes like grilled mullet, dorado baked in salt, prawns with garlic, and monkfish in saffron sauce. **Known for:** fresh fish; tapas bar; migas (fried bread crumbs). [$] *Average main: €15* ✉ *Pl. Pescadería 12, Centro* ☎ *958/262200* 🌐 *restauranteoliver.com* 🕒 *Closed Sun.*

Om-Kalsum

$ | MOROCCAN | The Moroccan tapas at this small and bustling venue make a pleasant change from the traditional local fare. Tagine, couscous, and kefta are all menu staples where you'll also find a selection of Middle Eastern dishes, also available in vegetarian versions. **Known for:** lively atmosphere; Moroccan tapas; selection of tapas. [$] *Average main: €8* ✉ *Calle Jardines 17, Centro.*

Pastelería López-Mezquita

$ | SPANISH | Sweet and savory treats come into their own at this family-owned business in the city center. Top of the specialty list are *piononos* (sponge bites filled with caramel and custard) and *pastela* (Moroccan chicken pie). **Known for:** pastela; piononos (sponge bites with custard); cakes and cookies. [$] *Average main: €5* ✉ *Calle Reyes Católicos 39, Centro* ☎ *958/221205* 🕒 *No lunch Sun.*

Tinta Fina

$$$ | SPANISH | Underneath the arches just off Puerta Real, this modern bar and restaurant has a reputation for being one of Granada's most chic venues. It's known for fresh seafood, including oysters and red shrimp, though generous portions of char-grilled steaks, steak tartare, and fresh foie gras are a hit with carnivores. **Known for:** chic atmosphere; cocktail and G&T menus; seafood. $ *Average main: €20* ⊠ *Calle Angel Ganivet 5, Centro* ☎ *958/100041* ⊕ *www.tintafinarestaurante.com.*

Hotels

Hospes Palacio de los Patos

$$$$ | HOTEL | This beautifully restored palace is unmissable, sitting proudly on its own in the middle of one of Granada's busiest shopping streets. **Pros:** central location; great spa and restaurant; historic setting. **Cons:** basement rooms are dark; some street noise; expensive parking. $ *Rooms from: €250* ⊠ *Calle Solarillo de Gracia 1, Centro* ☎ *958/535790* ⊕ *www.hospes.es* 🔑 *42 rooms* ⭐ *No Meals.*

★ Hostal Rodri

$ | HOTEL | This comfortable and quiet hostel lies conveniently off Plaza de la Trinidad near the cathedral and is a good option for cheaper lodging in a city with so many upscale accommodations. **Pros:** central location; value; clean, comfortable rooms. **Cons:** some rooms on small side; no direct car access; could be too basic for some. $ *Rooms from: €55* ⊠ *Calle Laurel de las Tablas 9, Centro* ☎ *958/288043* ⊕ *www.hostalrodri.com* ⭐ *No Meals* 🔑 *10 rooms.*

Hotel Párraga Siete

$ | HOTEL | This family-run hotel in the heart of the old quarter within easy walking distance of sights and restaurants offers excellent value and amenities superior to its official two-star rating. **Pros:** good on-site restaurant; easy nearby parking; central, quiet location. **Cons:** no historic character; difficult to access by car; interiors might be too sparse for some. $ *Rooms from: €80* ⊠ *Calle Párraga 7, Centro* ☎ *958/264227* ⊕ *www.hotelparragasiete.com* 🔑 *20 rooms* ⭐ *No Meals.*

Palacio de los Navas

$$ | B&B/INN | In the center of the city, this palace was built by aristocrat Francisco Navas in the 16th century and it later became the Casa de Moneda (the Mint); its original architectural features blend well with modern ones. **Pros:** great location; peaceful oasis during the day; rooms are set around a beautiful interior patio. **Cons:** can be noisy at night; parking difficult; breakfast uninspiring. $ *Rooms from: €100* ⊠ *Calle Navas 1, Centro* ☎ *958/215760* ⊕ *www.hotelpalaciodelosnavas.com* 🔑 *19 rooms* ⭐ *No Meals.*

Nightlife

Bohemia Jazz Café

LIVE MUSIC | This atmospheric jazz bar has piano performances and occasional live bands. ⊠ *Pl. de los Lobos 11, Centro.*

Shopping

Artesanías González

CRAFTS | Not far from La Alhambra, this is one of the best and longest-established places to buy inlaid wood *taracea* on handmade chessboards, boxes, side tables, and coasters. ⊠ *Cuesta de Gomérez 12, Centro* ☎ *657/987239.*

Espartería San José

CRAFTS | For wicker baskets and esparto-grass mats and rugs, head to this shop off the Plaza Pescadería. ⊠ *Calle Jáudenes 3, Centro* ☎ *958/267415* ⊕ *esparteriasanjose.es.*

Outskirts of Granada

Sights

Casa-Museo Federico García Lorca
HISTORIC HOME | Granada's most famous native son, the poet Federico García Lorca, gets his due here, in the middle of a park devoted to him on the southern fringe of the city. Lorca's onetime summer home, **La Huerta de San Vicente,** is now a museum (guided tours only)—run by his niece Laura García Lorca—with such artifacts as his beloved piano and changing exhibits on specific aspects of his life. ✉ *Parque García Lorca, Virgen Blanca, Arabial* ☎ *958/258466* 🌐 *www.huertadesanvicente.com* 🎫 *€3 (free Wed.)* 🕓 *Closed Mon.*

Monasterio de la Cartuja
RELIGIOUS BUILDING | The exterior of this Carthusian monastery in northern Granada is sober and monolithic, but inside are twisted, multicolor marble columns; a profusion of gold, silver, tortoiseshell, and ivory; intricate stucco; and the extravagant sacristy—it's easy to see why it has been called the Christian answer to the Alhambra. Among its wonders are the trompe l'oeil spikes, shadows and all, in the Sanchez Cotan cross over the *Last Supper* painting at the west end of the refectory. It was begun in 1506 and moved to its present site in 1516, though construction continued for the next 300 years. If you're lucky, you may see small birds attempting to land on these faux perches. You can reach it by Bus No. N7. ✉ *C. de Alfacar, Cartuja* ☎ *958/161932* 🎫 *€5.*

Parque de las Ciencias (*Science Park*)
SCIENCE MUSEUM | **FAMILY** | Across from Granada's convention center and easily reached on Bus No. C4, this science museum is one of the most visited in museums Andalusia. It has a planetarium and interactive demonstrations of scientific experiments. The 165-foot observation tower has views to the south and west. ✉ *Av. del Mediterráneo s/n, Zaidín* ☎ *958/131900* 🌐 *www.parqueciencias.com* 🕓 *Closed Mon.* 🎫 *From €7.*

Restaurants

Restaurante Arriaga
$$$$ | **BASQUE** | Run by Basque chef Álvaro Arriaga, this restaurant sits on the top floor of the Museo de la Memoria de Andalucía just outside the city (it's well worth the taxi drive) and has panoramic views of Granada with the Sierra Nevada behind. Choose from two tasting menus (€65 for six dishes and €80 for nine dishes), both with one surprise after another. **Known for:** panoramic views of Granada; culinary surprises (the menu starts with dessert!); tasting menus. [$] *Average main: €65* ✉ *Av. de las Ciencias 2, Armilla* ☎ *958/132619* 🌐 *www.restaurantearriaga.com* 🕓 *Closed Mon., no dinner Sun. or Tues.*

Priego de Córdoba

103 km (64 miles) southeast of Córdoba, 25 km (15 miles) southeast of Zuheros.

The jewel of Córdoba's countryside is Priego de Córdoba, a town of 23,500 inhabitants at the foot of Monte Tinosa. Wander down Calle del Río, opposite the town hall, to see 18th-century mansions, once the homes of silk merchants. At the end of the street is the Fuente del Rey (King's Fountain), with some 130 water jets, built in 1803. Don't miss the lavish baroque churches of La Asunción and La Aurora or the Barrio de la Villa, an old Moorish quarter with a maze of narrow streets of white-walled buildings. If you plan to visit several monuments, buy the Bono turístico (€5) to save on admission prices.

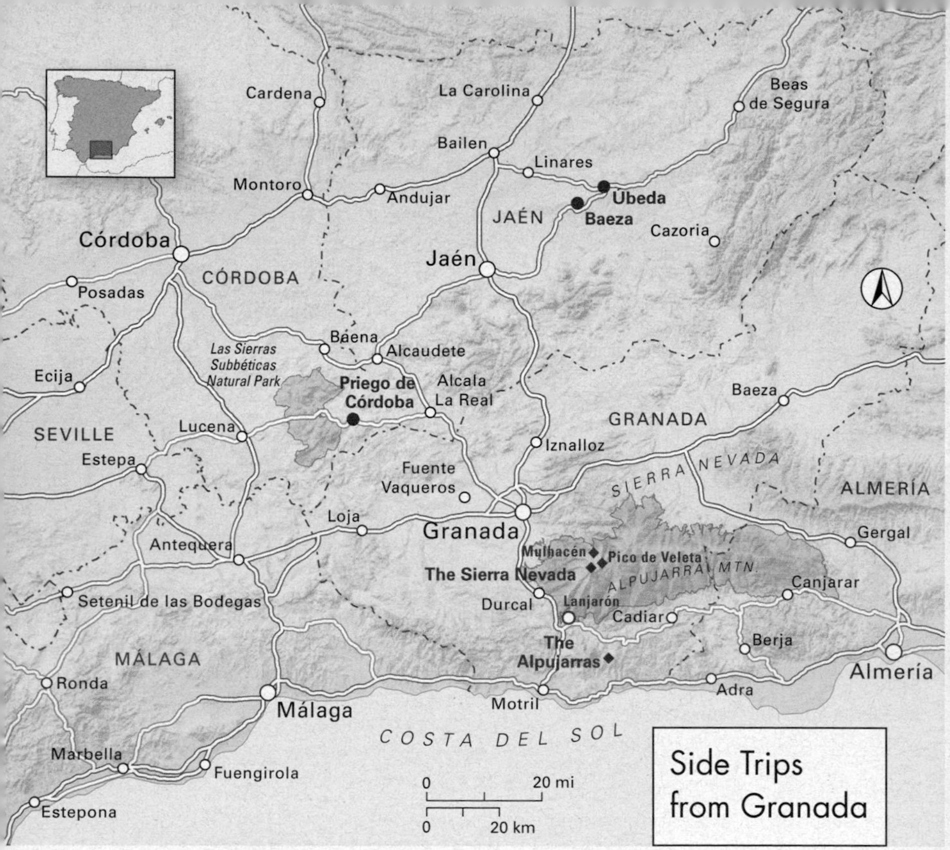
Cardena
La Carolina
Beas de Segura
Bailen
Linares
Montoro
Andujar
Ubeda
JAÉN
Baeza
Cazoria
Córdoba
Jaén
CÓRDOBA
Posadas
Baena
Alcaudete
Las Sierras Subbéticas Natural Park
Ecija
Priego de Córdoba
Alcala La Real
Baeza
GRANADA
SEVILLE
Lucena
Iznalloz
Estepa
Fuente Vaqueros
SIERRA NEVADA
ALMERÍA
Loja
Granada
Gergal
Antequera
Mulhacén
Pico de Veleta
The Sierra Nevada
ALPUJARRA MTN.
Canjarar
Setenil de las Bodegas
Durcal
Lanjarón
Cadiar
Berja
MÁLAGA
The Alpujarras
Almería
Ronda
Málaga
Motril
Adra
COSTA DEL SOL
Marbella
Fuengirola
Estepona
0
20 mi
0
20 km

Side Trips from Granada

GETTING HERE AND AROUND

Priego has reasonable bus service from Córdoba (2½ hours) and Granada (1½ hours), although your best bet is to visit by car en route to either of these cities. Once there, it's perfect for pedestrian exploration.

VISITOR INFORMATION

CONTACTS Priego de Córdoba. ✉ *Pl. de la Constitución 3* ☎ *957/700625* 🌐 *www.turismodepriego.com.*

🍴 Restaurants

La Pianola (*Casa Pepe*)
$ | **SPANISH** | Expect cheap, cheerful, and lively dining at this small venue, a couple of blocks south of the castle and usually packed with locals. On the menu are usual Córdoba staples including oxtail, but the specialties here are the *saquito de boletus* (mushroom pastry) and *carrillada de cerdo* (roast pork cheek). **Known for:** delicious French toast for dessert; good tapas; value dining. [$] *Average main: €9* ✉ *Calle Obispo Caballero 6* ☎ *957/700409* 🕒 *Closed Mon.*

🛏 Hotels

Casa Baños de la Villa
$$ | **HOTEL** | Tucked at the heart of Priego's bright white center, this boutique hotel offers an oasis of peace and quiet, plus the chance to enjoy the in-house spa pool and Turkish bath. **Pros:** in-house spa; central location; friendly hosts. **Cons:** some might find the decor a little brash; monotonous breakfast; no exterior views from rooms. [$] *Rooms from: €120* ✉ *Calle Real 63* ☎ *957/547274* 🌐 *www.casabanosdelavilla.com* 🍽 *Free Breakfast* 🛏 *9 rooms.*

Hotel-Museo Patria Chica

$$ | HOTEL | This charming hotel in a fully restored 19th-century mansion has so many antiques and memorabilia that the term "hotel-museum" really does live up to its name. **Pros:** pool and restaurant on-site; period furnishings; central location. **Cons:** some rooms face the street; slightly out of the town center; quiet. $ *Rooms from: €120* ✉ *Carrera de las Monjas 47* ☎ *957/058385* ⊕ *www.hotelpatriachica.com* ⇥ *15 rooms* ⑪ *No Meals.*

Baeza

48 km (30 miles) northeast of Jaén on N321.

The historic town of Baeza, nestled between hills and olive groves, is one of the best-preserved old towns in Spain. Founded by the Romans, it later housed the Visigoths and became the capital of a Moorish taifa, one of some two dozen mini-kingdoms formed after the Ummayad Caliphate was subdivided in 1031. Ferdinand III captured Baeza in 1227, and for the next 200 years it stood on the frontier of the Moorish kingdom of Granada. In the 16th and 17th centuries, local nobles gave the city a wealth of Renaissance palaces.

GETTING HERE AND AROUND

Frequent buses (16 per day on weekdays, 10 per day on weekends; *ALSA* 902/422242) connect Baeza with Jaén (45 minutes) and Úbeda, although a private car is the best option given the remoteness of the town and that you may want to explore nearby Úbeda on the same day. Baeza is small and flat, and with its sights clustered around the very center it's very easy to explore on foot.

TOURS

Semer Guided Tours

Two-and-a-half-hour guided tours around Baeza (in English, minimum two people, Tuesday–Sunday) recount the history, culture, and traditions of the town. Tours of Úbeda are also available, with a discount for combined tours of both towns. ✉ *Baeza* ☎ *053/757010* ⊕ *visitasguiadas-ubedaybaeza.com* ⇥ *From €11.*

VISITOR INFORMATION

CONTACTS Baeza. ✉ *Pl. del Pópulo* ☎ *953/779982.*

 Sights

Ayuntamiento (*Town Hall*)

GOVERNMENT BUILDING | Baeza's town hall was designed by cathedral master Andrés de Vandelvira. The facade is ornately decorated with a mix of religious and pagan imagery. Look between the balconies for the coats of arms of Felipe II, the city of Baeza, and the magistrate Juan de Borja. Ask at the tourist office about visits to the *salón de plenos,* a meeting hall with painted, carved woodwork. ✉ *Pl. Cardenal s/n.*

Baeza Cathedral

CHURCH | Originally begun by Ferdinand III on the site of a former mosque, the cathedral was largely rebuilt by Andrés de Vandelvira, architect of Jaén's cathedral, between 1570 and 1593, though the west front has architectural influences from an earlier period. A fine 14th-century rose window crowns the 13th-century Puerta de la Luna (Moon Door). Don't miss the baroque silver monstrance (a vessel in which the consecrated Host is exposed for the adoration of the faithful), which is carried in Baeza's Corpus Christi processions—the piece is kept in a concealed niche behind a painting, but you can see it in all its splendor by putting a coin in a slot to reveal the hiding place. Next to the monstrance is the entrance to the clock tower, where a small donation and a narrow spiral staircase take you to one of the best views of Baeza. The remains of the original mosque are in the cathedral's Gothic cloisters. ✉ *Pl. de Santa María* ☎ *953/744157* 🎫 *€4.*

Casa del Pópulo

HISTORIC HOME | Located in the central paseo—where the Plaza del Pópulo (or Plaza de los Leones) and Plaza de la Constitución (or Plaza del Mercado Viejo) merge to form a cobblestone square—this graceful town house was built around 1530. The first Mass of the Reconquest was supposedly celebrated on its curved balcony; it now houses Baeza's tourist office. ✉ *Pl. del Pópulo.*

Convento de San Francisco

HISTORIC SIGHT | This 16th-century convent is one of Vandelvira's religious architectural masterpieces. The building was damaged by the French army and partially destroyed by a light earthquake in the early 1800s, but you can see its restored remains. ✉ *Calle de San Francisco.*

Museo de Baeza

HISTORY MUSEUM | Tucked away behind the tourist office, the Baeza Museum is in itself a museum piece. Housed in a 15th-century noble palace, the facade and interiors are home to an interesting display of Baeza's history, from Roman remains to more recent religious paintings. ✉ *Calle Casas Nuevas* ☎ *953/741582* 🎫 *€2* 🕒 *Closed Mon.*

🍴 Restaurants

Palacio de Gallego

$$$ | **SPANISH** | Located next to the cathedral, this is one of the best restaurants in town, known for its barbecue and roasted dishes. If you're not too hungry, enjoy tapas in the bar. **Known for:** barbecue; red tuna steak; outdoor terrace. [$] *Average main: €20* ✉ *Calle Santa Catalina* ☎ *695/117175* 🕒 *Closed Tues. No lunch Wed.*

🛏 Hotels

Hotel Puerta de la Luna

$$ | **HOTEL** | This restored 17th-century palace, one of Baeza's best accommodation options, is centered on two patios—one with a pond and views of the cathedral tower, the other with a small pool. **Pros:** lovely architecture; good food on-site; central location. **Cons:** difficult to find; basic breakfast; a bit too quiet. [$] *Rooms from: €125* ✉ *Calle Canónigo Melgares Raya 7* ☎ *953/747019* 🌐 *www.hotel-puertadelaluna.com* 🔑 *44 rooms* 🍽 *No Meals.*

Úbeda

9 km (5½ miles) northeast of Baeza on N321.

Úbeda's *casco antiguo* (old town) is one of the most outstanding enclaves of 16th-century architecture in Spain. It's a stunning surprise in the heart of Jaén's olive groves, set in the shadow of the wild Sierra de Cazorla mountain range. For crafts enthusiasts, this is Andalusia's capital for many kinds of artisan goods. Follow signs to the Zona Monumental, where there are countless Renaissance palaces and stately mansions, though most are closed to the public.

GETTING HERE AND AROUND

Frequent buses (16 weekdays, 10 weekends; *ALSA* 902/422242) connect Úbeda with Jaén (one hour) and Baeza, although a private car is the best option given the remoteness of the town and that you may want to explore nearby Baeza in the same day. Úbeda's sights are all within easy reach of the center so exploring on foot is easy.

TOURS

Semer Guided Tours

✉ *Calle Juan Montilla 3* ☎ *953/757916* 🌐 *https://visitasguiadasubedaybaeza.com/.*

Sights

Ayuntamiento Antiguo (*Old Town Hall*)
NOTABLE BUILDING | Begun in the early
16th century but restored as a beautiful
arcaded baroque palace in 1680, the
former town hall is now a conservatory of
music. From the hall's upper balcony, the
town council watched celebrations and
autos-da-fé ("acts of faith"—executions
of heretics sentenced by the Inquisition)
in the square below. You can't enter
the town hall, but on the north side you
can visit the 13th-century church of San
Pablo, with an Isabelline south portal.
⊠ *Pl. Primero de Mayo* ✢ *Off Calle María
de Molina* ☎ *953/750637* ✉ *Church free*
🕐 *Closed Mon.*

Hospital de Santiago
NOTABLE BUILDING | Sometimes joking-
ly called the Escorial of Andalusia (in
allusion to Felipe II's monolithic palace
and monastery outside Madrid), this is
a huge, angular building in the modern
section of town and yet another one of
Vandelvira's masterpieces in Úbeda. The
plain facade is adorned with ceramic
medallions, and over the main entrance
is a carving of Santiago Matamoros (St.
James the Moorslayer) in his traditional
horseback pose. Inside are an arcaded
patio and a grand staircase. Now a cultural center, it holds many of the events at
the International Spring Dance and Music
Festival (www.festivaldeubeda.com).
⊠ *Av. Cristo Rey* ☎ *953/750842* ✉ *Free*
🕐 *Closed Sun. in July, and weekends in
Aug.*

Sacra Capilla de El Salvador
RELIGIOUS BUILDING | The Plaza Vázquez
de Molina, in the heart of the *casco
antiguo*, is the site of this building,
which is photographed so often that it's
become the city's unofficial symbol. It
was built by Vandelvira, but he based his
design on some 1536 plans by Diego de
Siloé, architect of Granada's cathedral.
Considered one of the masterpieces
of Spanish Renaissance religious art,

the chapel was sacked in the frenzy of
church burnings at the outbreak of the
civil war, but it retains its ornate western
facade and altarpiece, which has a rare
Berruguete sculpture. ⊠ *Pl. Vázquez de
Molina* ☎ *609/279905* ✉ *€5 (free Mon.–
Sat. 9:30–10, Sun. 6–7).*

★ **Sinagoga del Agua**
RELIGIOUS BUILDING | This 13th-century
synagogue counts among Úbeda's most
amazing discoveries. Entirely underground and known as the Water Synagogue for the wells and natural spring
under the mikvah, it comprises seven
areas open to visitors, including the main
area of worship, mikvah, women's gallery, and rabbi's quarters. During summer
solstice the sun's rays illuminate the
stairway, providing the only natural light
in the synagogue. ⊠ *Calle Roque Rosas*
☎ *953/758150* ⊕ *www.sinagogadelagua.
com* ✉ *€5.*

Restaurants

Asador de Santiago
$$$ | SPANISH | At this adventurous restau-
rant just off the main street, the chef pre-
pares both Spanish classics, like white
shrimp from Huelva and slow-roasted
local lamb and goat, as well as innovative
dishes like *ensalada de queso de cabra
en hojaldre con calabaza* (salad with goat
cheese pastry and pumpkin) and *lomo
de ciervo en escabeche* (venison steak in
pickled sauce). The candle-filled interior
is more traditional than the bar and has
terra-cotta tiles, dark wood furnishings,
and crisp white linens. **Known for:** roast
meats; fine dining; Spanish classics.
$ *Average main: €20* ⊠ *Av. Cristo Rey 4*
☎ *953/750463* ⊕ *asadordesantiago.com*
🕐 *No dinner Sun.*

Cantina La Estación
$$$ | SPANISH | Meals here, one of
Úbeda's top restaurants, are served in
a train-carriage interior decorated with
railway memorabilia, while tapas reign
at an outside terrace and at the bar. This

distinctive eatery serves creative dishes like *humus con berenjenas, pimientos rojos y anchoas* (eggplant hummus with red peppers and anchovies), fillet of wild boar, and *bacalao confitado* (caramelized cod). **Known for:** value tasting menu; extensive and reasonably priced wine menu; fun interior. $ *Average main: €18* ⊠ *Cuesta de la Rodadera 1* ☎ *687/777230* ⊘ *Closed Wed. No dinner Tues.*

Taberna Misa de 12

$$$ | **SPANISH** | This small bar has the best position on the leafy square, one block from the Plaza del Ayuntamiento, and the pleasant outside terrace is the best place to enjoy the tapas. Despite the tiny kitchen, the menu stretches long and includes homemade croquettes in a selection of flavors and roasted peppers, red tuna tartare, and Iberian pork cuts. **Known for:** outdoor dining; wine list; tapas. $ *Average main: €18* ⊠ *Pl. Primero de Mayo 7* ☎ *622/480049* ⊕ *www.misade12.com* ⊘ *No dinner Mon.*

Hotels

★ Palacio de la Rambla

$$ | **B&B/INN** | In old Úbeda, this stunning 16th-century mansion has been in the same family since it was built—it still hosts the Marquesa de la Rambla when she's in town—and eight of the rooms are available for overnighters. **Pros:** all rooms have access to the garden; elegant style; central location. **Cons:** not much parking; some areas a little tired; grandiosity not for everyone. $ *Rooms from: €125* ⊠ *Pl. del Marqués 1* ☎ *953/750196* ⊕ *www.palaciodelarambla. com* ⊘ *Closed July and Aug.* ⊅ *8 rooms* ⊘⊘ *No Meals.*

★ Parador de Úbeda

$$$ | **HOTEL** | This splendid parador is in a 16th-century ducal palace in a prime location on the Plaza Vázquez de Molina, next to the Capilla del Salvador. **Pros:**

excellent restaurant; perfect location; elegant surroundings. **Cons:** church bells in the morning; parking is difficult; could be too formal for some. $ *Rooms from: €150* ⊠ *Pl. Vázquez de Molina s/n* ☎ *953/750345* ⊕ *www.parador.es* ⊅ *36 rooms* ⊘⊘ *No Meals.*

Shopping

Alfarería Góngora

CERAMICS | All kinds of ceramics are sold here. ⊠ *Calle Cuesta de la Merced 32* ☎ *953/754605.*

Alfarería Tito

CERAMICS | The extrovert Juan Tito can often be found at the potter's wheel in his rambling shop, which is packed with ceramics of every size and shape. ⊠ *Pl. del Ayuntamiento 12* ☎ *953/751302* ⊕ *www.alfareriatito.com.*

Melchor Tito

CERAMICS | You can see classic green-glazed items—the focus of Melchor Tito's work—being made in his workshops in Calle Valencia and Calle Fuenteseca 17, which also both sell the wares. ⊠ *Calle Valencia 44* ☎ *953/753692.*

Pablo Tito

CERAMICS | Clay sculptures of characters from *Don Quixote*, fired by Pablo Tito in an old Moorish-style kiln, are the specialty of this studio and shop (also online). There is also a museum (Monday through Saturday 8–2 and 4–8, Sunday 10–2) on the premises. ⊠ *Calle Valencia 22* ☎ *953/751496* ⊕ *pablotito.es/tienda.*

The Sierra Nevada

Sights

Mulhacén

MOUNTAIN | To the east of Granada, the mighty Mulhacén, the highest peak in mainland Spain, soars to 11,427 feet.

Legend has it that it came by its name when Boabdil, the last Moorish king of Granada, deposed his father, Abul Hassan Ali, and had the body buried at the summit of the mountain so that it couldn't be desecrated. For more information on trails to the two summits, check the National Park Service's site (⊕ www.novadon3is.com). ⊠ *Sierra Nevada.*

Pico de Veleta

MOUNTAIN | Peninsular Spain's second-highest mountain is 11,125 feet high. The view from its summit across the Alpujarras to the sea at distant Motril is stunning, and on a very clear day you can see the coast of North Africa. When the snow melts (July and August) you can drive or take a minibus from the Albergue Universitario (Universitario Mountain Refuge) to within around 400 yards of the summit—a trail takes you to the top in around 45 minutes. It's cold up there, so take a warm jacket and scarf, even if Granada is sizzling hot. ⊠ *Sierra Nevada*

Activities

SKIING

Estación de Esquí Sierra Nevada
SNOW SPORTS | FAMILY | Europe's southernmost ski resort is one of its best equipped. At the Pradollano and Borreguiles stations, there's good skiing from December through April or May; each has a special snowboarding circuit, floodlighted night slopes, a children's ski school, and après-ski sun and swimming in the Mediterranean less than an hour away. In winter, buses to Pradollano leave Granada's bus station three times a day on weekdays and four times on weekends and holidays. Tickets are €9 round-trip. As for Borreguiles, you can get there only on skis. There's an information center (⊕ www.sierranevada.es) at Plaza de Andalucía 4. ⊠ *Sierra Nevada.*

The Alpujarras

Village of Lanjarón: 46 km (29 miles) south of Granada.

A trip to the Alpujarras, on the southern slopes of the Sierra Nevada, takes you to one of Andalusia's highest, most remote, and most scenic areas, home for decades to painters, writers, and a considerable foreign population. The Alpujarras region was originally populated by Moors fleeing the Christian Reconquest (from Seville after its fall in 1248, then from Granada after 1492). To this day, the Galicians' descendants continue the Moorish custom of weaving rugs and blankets in the traditional Alpujarran colors of red, green, black, and white, and they sell their crafts in many of the villages. Be on the lookout for handmade basketry and pottery as well.

Houses here are squat and square; they spill down the southern slopes of the Sierra Nevada, bearing a strong resemblance to the Berber homes in the Rif Mountains, just across the Mediterranean in Morocco. If you're driving, the road as far as Lanjarón and Orgiva is smooth sailing; after that come steep, twisting mountain roads with few gas stations. Beyond sightseeing, the area is a haven for outdoor activities such as hiking and horseback riding. Inquire at the **Information Point** at Plaza de la Libertad, at Pampaneira.

◉ Sights

Lanjarón and Nearby Villages

TOWN | The western entrance to the Alpujarras is some 46 km (29 miles) from Granada at Lanjarón. This spa town is famous for its mineral water, collected from the melting snows of the Sierra Nevada and drunk throughout Spain. Orgiva, the next and largest town in the Alpujarras, has a 17th-century castle.

Here you can leave the A348 and follow signs for the villages of the Alpujarras Altas (High Alpujarras), including Pampaneira, Capileira, and especially Trevélez, which lies on the slopes of the Mulhacén at 4,840 feet above sea level. Reward yourself with a plate of the local *jamón serrano*. Trevélez has three levels—the Barrio Alto, Barrio Medio, and Barrio Bajo—and the butchers are concentrated in the lowest section (Bajo). The higher levels have narrow cobblestone streets, whitewashed houses, and shops. ✉ *Lanjarón.*

Hotels

Hotel Alcadima

$ | **HOTEL** | **FAMILY** | One of the best-value hotels in the area, this pleasant if unfancy hotel in the rustic spa town of Lanjarón makes a good base for exploring the lower part of the Alpujarras. **Pros:** two-bedroom suites are ideal for families; excellent restaurant; swimming pool. **Cons:** could be too plain for some; Lanjarón isn't the prettiest village in the area; down an unattractive side street. [$] *Rooms from: €60* ✉ *Calle Francisco Tarrega 3, Lanjarón* ☎ *958/770809* 🌐 *www.alcadima.com* 🛏 *45 rooms* 🍴 *No Meals.*

Los Tinaos

$ | **APARTMENT** | Located on the way to Trevélez, in the pretty whitewashed village of Bubión that almost clings to the mountainside, these comfortable apartments (for two or four people) come squeaky-clean, with open log fires as well as central heating, and sweeping views across the valley. **Pros:** valley views; a short walk from Pitres; bar serving locally produced wine. **Cons:** steep walk down; could be too basic for some; apartments on the small side. [$] *Rooms from: €60* ✉ *Calle Parras 2, Bubión* ☎ *958/763217* 🌐 *www.lostinaos.com* 🛏 *10 rooms* 🍴 *No Meals.*

COSTA DEL SOL AND COSTA DE ALMERÍA

Updated by
Joanna Styles

◉ Sights	🍴 Restaurants	🛏 Hotels	💼 Shopping	🍸 Nightlife
★★★★☆	★★★★★	★★★★☆	★★★★☆	★★★☆☆

WELCOME TO COSTA DEL SOL AND COSTA DE ALMERÍA

TOP REASONS TO GO

★ **Enjoy the sun and sand:** Relax at any of the beaches; they're all free, though in summer there isn't much towel space.

★ **Soak up the atmosphere:** Spend a day in Málaga, Picasso's birthplace, visiting the museums, exploring the old town, and strolling the Palm Walkway in the port.

★ **Check out Puerto Banús:** Wine, dine, and celebrity-watch at the Costa del Sol's most luxurious and sophisticated port town.

★ **Visit Cabo de Gata:** This protected natural reserve is one of the wildest and most beautiful stretches of coast in Spain.

★ **Shop for souvenirs:** Check out the weekly market in one of the Costa resorts to pick up bargain-price souvenirs, including ceramics.

The towns and resorts along the southeastern Spanish coastline vary considerably according to whether they lie to the east or to the west of Málaga. To the east are the Costa de Almería and the Costa Tropical, less developed stretches of coastline. Towns like Nerja act as a gateway to the dramatic mountainous region of La Axarquía. West from Málaga along the Costa del Sol proper, the strip between Torremolinos and Marbella is the most densely popu-lated. Seamless though it may appear, as one resort merges into the next, each town has a distinctive character, with its own sights, charms, and activities.

1 The Cabo de Gata Nature Reserve. Wild nature and unspoiled beaches in Spain's most southeasterly corner.

2 Agua Amarga. Pictur-esque fishing resort at the heart of the Cabo de Gata.

3 Almería. A vibrant city and one of Spain's top spots for gastronomy.

4 Almuñécar. A tradi-tional seaside town with two lovely beaches.

5 Nerja. Pretty white town perched on the cliffs and home to the famous Nerja Caves.

6 The Axarquía. High mountains dotted with pretty white villages.

7 Málaga. The capital of the Costa del Sol and Spain's Museum City.

8 Antequera. A historic town with an impressive list of ancient monuments.

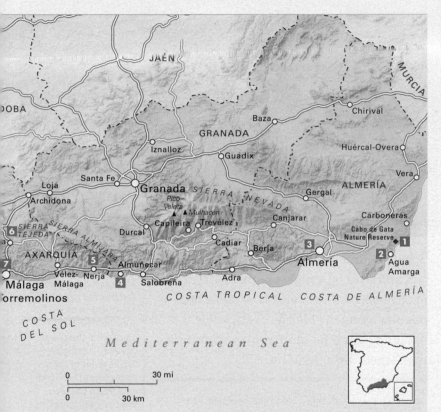

9 The Guadalhorce Valley. Home to a spectacular river gorge and the Caminito del Rey walkway.

10 Torremolinos. Bustling resort with excellent beaches.

11 Fuengirola. Family-friendly seaside town, popular with expat residents.

12 Mijas. Stunning white village with panoramic views over the coastline.

13 Marbella. A favorite with the international jet set and a center for glitz and glamour.

14 Ojén. Pretty white village and the gateway to some excellent mountain walking.

15 Estepona. Attractive resort town famous for its murals and orchids.

16 Casares. Spectacular white village perched on a rocky outcrop.

17 Tarifa. Europe's kitesurf capital and home to miles of sandy beaches.

18 Gibraltar. "The Rock" is an extraordinary combination of Spain and Great Britain, with a fascinating history.

EATING AND DRINKING WELL ALONG SPAIN'S SOUTHERN COAST

Beachside dining on the Costa del Sol

Spain's southern coast is known for fresh fish and seafood, grilled or quickly fried in olive oil. Sardines roasted on spits are popular along the Málaga coast, while upland towns offer more robust mountain fare, especially in Almería.

Chiringuitos, small shanties along the beaches, are summer-only Costa del Sol restaurants that serve fish fresh off the boats. Málaga is known for seafood restaurants serving *fritura malagueña de pescaíto* (fried fish). In mountain towns, you'll find superb *rabo de toro* (oxtail), goat and sheep cheeses, wild mushrooms, and game dishes. Almería shares Moorish aromas of cumin and cardamom with its Andalusian sisters to the west but also turns the corner toward its northern neighbor, Murcia, where delicacies such as *mojama* (salt-dried tuna) and *hueva de maruca* (ling roe) have been favorites since Phoenician times. Almería's wealth of vegetables and legumes combine with pork and game products for a rougher, more powerful culinary canon of thick stews and soups.

TO DRINK

Málaga has long been famous for the sweet Muscatel wine that Russian empress Catherine the Great loved so much she imported it to Saint Petersburg duty-free in 1792. In the 18th century, Muscatel was sold medicinally in pharmacies for its curative powers and is still widely produced and often served as accompaniment to dessert or tapas.

COLD ALMOND AND GARLIC SOUP

Ajoblanco, a summer staple in Andalusia, is a refreshing salty-sweet combination served cold. Exquisitely light and sharp, the almond and garlic soup has a surprisingly creamy and fresh taste. Almonds, garlic, hard white bread, olive oil, water, sherry vinegar, and a topping of muscat grapes are standard ingredients.

FRIED FISH MÁLAGA STYLE

A popular dish along the Costa del Sol and the Costa de Almería, *fritura malagueña de pescaíto* is basically any sort of very small fish—such as anchovies, cuttlefish, baby squid, whitebait, and red mullet—fried in oil so hot that the fish end up crisp and light as a feather. The fish are lightly dusted in white flour, cooked quickly, and drained briefly before arriving piping hot and bone-dry on your plate. For an additional Moorish aroma, fritura masters add powdered cumin to the flour.

ALMERÍA STEWS

Almería is known for heartier fare than neighboring Málaga. *Puchero de trigo* (wheat and pork stew) is a fortifying winter comfort stew of boiled whole grains of wheat cooked with chickpeas, pork, black sausage, fatback, potatoes, saffron, cumin, and fennel. *Ajo*

A classic potato-based stew

Sardines being roasted over glowing logs

colorao (also known as *atascaburras*) is another popular stew, which consists of potatoes, dried peppers, vegetables, and fish that are simmered into a thick red-orange stew *de cuchara* (eaten with a spoon). Laced with cumin and garlic and served with thick country bread, it's a stick-to-your-ribs mariner's soup.

ROASTED SARDINES

Known as *moraga de sardinas,* or *espeto de sardinas,* this method of cooking sardines is popular in the summer along the Pedregalejo and Carihuela beaches east and west of Málaga: the sardines are skewered and extended over logs at an angle so that the fish oils run back down the skewers instead of falling into the coals and causing a conflagration. Fresh fish and cold white wine or beer make this a beautiful and relaxing sunset beach dinner.

A THOUSAND AND ONE EGGS

In Andalusia and especially along the Costa del Sol, *huevos a la flamenca* (eggs flamenco style) is a time-tested dish combining peppers, potatoes, ham, and peas with an egg broken over the top and baked sizzling hot in the oven. Other musts: *Revuelto de setas y gambas* (scrambled eggs with wild mushrooms and shrimp) and the universal Iberian potato omelet, the *tortilla de patatas.*

BEST BEACHES OF THE SOUTHERN COAST

One of the many resorts in Torremolinos

Tourists have been coming to the Costa del Sol since the 1950s, attracted by its magical combination of brochure-blue sea, miles of beaches, and reliably sunny weather.

The beaches here range from the gravel-like shingle in Almuñécar, Nerja, and Málaga to fine, gritty sand from Torremolinos westward. The best (and most crowded) beaches are east of Málaga and those flanking the most popular resorts of Nerja, Torremolinos, Fuengirola, and Marbella. For more secluded beaches, head west of Estepona and past Gibraltar to Tarifa and the Cádiz coast. The beaches change when you hit the Atlantic, becoming appealingly wide with fine golden sand. The winds are usually quite strong here, which means that although you can't read a newspaper while lying out, the conditions for windsurfing and kiteboarding are near perfect.

Beaches are free, and busiest in July, August, and on Sunday May through October when malagueño families arrive for a full day on the beach and lunch at a chiringuito.

OVER THE TOPLESS

In Spain, as in many parts of Europe, it is perfectly acceptable for women to go topless on the beach, although covering up is the norm at beach bars. There are several nude beaches on the Costas; look for the *playa naturista* sign. The most popular are in Maro (near Nerja), Benalnatura (Benalmádena Costa), Cabo Pino (Marbella), and near Tarifa.

LA CARIHUELA, TORREMOLINOS

This former fishing district of Torremolinos has a wide stretch of beach. The chiringuitos here are some of the best on the Costa, and the promenade, which continues until Benalmádena port, with its striking Asian-inspired architecture and great choice of restaurants and bars, is delightful for strolling.

CARVAJAL, FUENGIROLA

Backed by low-rise buildings and greenery, the beach here is unspoiled and refreshingly low-key. East of Fuengirola center, the Carvajal beach bars have young crowds, with regular live music in summer. It's also an easily accessible beach on the Málaga–Fuengirola train, with a stop within walking distance of the sand.

PLAYA LOS LANCES, TARIFA

This white sandy beach is one of the least spoiled in Andalusia. Near lush vegetation, lagoons, and the occasional campground and boho-chic hotel, Tarifa's main beach is famed throughout Europe for its windsurfing and kiteboarding, so expect some real winds: *levante* from the east and *poniente* from the west.

Tarifa is known for its wind: great for windsurfing, kiteboarding, and kite flying.

CABO DE GATA, ALMERÍA

Backed by natural parkland, with volcanic rock formations creating dramatic cliffs and secluded bays, Almería's stunning Cabo de Gata coastline includes superb beaches and coves within the protected UNESCO Biosphere Reserve. The fact that most of the beaches here are only accessible via marked footpaths adds to their off-the-beaten-track appeal.

PUERTO BANÚS, MARBELLA

Looking for action? Some great beach scenes flank the world-famous luxurious port. Puerto Banús is known for its excellent, laid-back Caribbean-style seafood restaurants, good music, and hip, good-looking crowd. Another superb sandy choice are the coves west of the marina, so-called boutique beaches, with club areas and massages available, as well as attractive beaches and tempting shallow waters.

EL SALADILLO, ESTEPONA

Between Marbella and Estepona (take the Cancelada exit off the A7), this relaxed and inviting beach is not as well known as its glitzier neighbors. It's harder to find, so mainly locals in the know frequent it. There are two popular seafood restaurants here, plus a volleyball net, showers, and sun beds and parasols for rent.

Crashing waves at Cabo de Gata

With roughly 320 days of sunshine a year, the Costa del Sol well deserves its nickname, "the Sunshine Coast." It's no wonder much of the coast has been built up with resorts and high-rises. Don't despair, though: you can still find some classic Spanish experiences, whether in the old city of Marbella or one of the smaller villages like Casares. And despite the hubbub of high season, visitors can always unwind here, basking or strolling on mile after mile of sandy beach.

Technically, the stretch of Andalusian shore known as the Costa del Sol runs west from the Costa Tropical, near Granada, to the tip of Tarifa, the southernmost point in Europe, just beyond Gibraltar. For most of the Europeans who have flocked here over the past 50 years, though, the Sunshine Coast has been largely restricted to the 70-km (43-mile) sprawl of hotels, vacation villas, golf courses, marinas, and nightclubs between Torremolinos, just west of Málaga, and Estepona, down toward Gibraltar. Since the late 1950s this area has mushroomed from a group of impoverished fishing villages into an overdeveloped seaside playground and retirement haven. The city of Almería and its coastline, the Costa de Almería, is southwest of Granada's Alpujarras region and due east of the Costa Tropical (around 147 km [93 miles] from Almuñécar).

MAJOR REGIONS

South of Spain's Murcia Coast lie the shores of Andalusia, beginning with the **Costa de Almería.** Several of the coastal towns here, including **Agua Amarga,** have a laid-back charm, with miles of sandy beaches and a refreshing lack of high-rise developments. The mineral riches of the surrounding mountains gave rise to Iberia's first true civilization, whose capital can still be glimpsed in the 4,700-year-old ruins of Los Millares, near the village of Santa Fe de Mondújar. The small towns of Níjar and Sorbas maintain an age-old tradition of pottery making and other crafts, and the western coast of **Almería** has tapped unexpected wealth from a parched land, thanks to modern techniques of growing produce in plastic greenhouses. In contrast to the inhospitable landscape of the mountain-fringed Andarax Valley, the area east of Granada's Alpujarras, near Alhama, has a cool climate and gentle landscape, both conducive to making fine wines.

East of Málaga and west of Almería lies the **Costa Tropical.** Housing developments resemble buildings in Andalusian villages rather than the bland high-rises elsewhere, and its tourist onslaught has been mild. A flourishing farming center, the area earns its keep from tropical fruit, including avocados, mangoes, and pawpaws (also known as custard apples). You may find packed beaches and traffic-choked roads at the height of the season, but for most of the year the Costa Tropical is relatively free of other tourists, if not also devoid of expatriates.

The Málaga Province, with the city of **Málaga** and the provincial towns of the upland hills and valleys to the north, creates the kind of contrast that makes travel in Spain so tantalizing. The region's Moorish legacy—tiny streets honeycombing the steamy depths of Málaga, the layout of the farms, and the crops themselves, including olives, grapes, oranges, and lemons—is a unifying visual theme. Ronda and the whitewashed villages of Andalusia behind the Costa del Sol make for one of Spain's most scenic and emblematic driving routes.

To the west of Málaga, along the coast, the sprawling outskirts of **Torremolinos** signal that you're entering the Costa del Sol, with its beaches, high-rise hotels, and serious numbers of tourists. On the far west, you can still discern Estepona's fishing village and Moorish old quarter amid its booming coastal development. Just inland, **Casares** piles whitewashed houses over the bright-blue Mediterranean below.

Planning

When to Go

May, June, and September are the best times to visit this coastal area, when there's plenty of sunshine but fewer tourists than in the hottest season of July and August. Winter can have bright sunny days, but you may feel the chill, and many hotels in the lower price bracket have heat for only a few hours a day; you can also expect several days of rain. Holy Week, the week before Easter Sunday, is a fun time to visit to see the religious processions.

Planning Your Time

Travelers with their own wheels who want a real taste of the area in just a few days could start by exploring the relatively unspoiled villages of the Costa Tropical: wander around quaint Salobreña, then hit the larger coastal resort of Nerja and head inland for a look around pretty Frigiliana.

Move on to Málaga next; it has lots to offer, including several top art museums, excellent restaurants, and some of the best tapas bars in the province. It's also easy to get to stunning, mountaintop Ronda (⇨ *see Chapter 11*), which is also on a bus route.

Hit the coast at Marbella, the Costa del Sol's swankiest resort, and then take a leisurely stroll around Puerto Banús. Next, head west to Gibraltar for a day of shopping and sightseeing before returning to the coast and Torremolinos for a night on the town.

Choose your base carefully, as the various areas here make for very different experiences. Málaga is a vibrant Spanish city, virtually untainted by mass tourism, while Torremolinos is a budget destination catering mostly to the mass market. Fuengirola is quieter, with a large population of middle-aged expatriates; farther west, the Marbella–San Pedro de Alcántara area is more exclusive and expensive.

Getting Here and Around

AIR

All flights from the United States to Málaga connect in Madrid. British Airways flies several times daily from London (City, Gatwick, and Heathrow) to Málaga, and the budget airlines easyJet and Ryanair also link the two cities. There are direct flights to Málaga from most other major European cities on Iberia or other airlines. Iberia Express/Vueling has five flights daily from Madrid (1 hour 15 minutes), five flights daily from Barcelona (1½ hours), and regular flights from other Spanish cities.

Málaga's Costa del Sol airport is 10 km (6 miles) west of town and is one of Spain's most modern. Trains from the airport into town run every 20 minutes 6:44 am–12:54 am (12 minutes, €1.80) and from the airport to Fuengirola every 20 minutes 5:32 am–11:42 pm (34 minutes, €2.70), stopping at several resorts en route, including Torremolinos and Benalmádena.

From the airport there's also bus service to Málaga every half hour 7 am–midnight and then three buses between midnight and 6 am (€4). At least 10 daily buses (more frequently July–September) run between the airport and Marbella (45 minutes, from €6.15). Taxi fares from the airport to Málaga, Torremolinos, and other resorts are posted inside the terminal: from the airport to Marbella is about €65, to Torremolinos €20, and to Fuengirola €35. Many of the better hotels and all tour companies will arrange for pickup at the airport. Uber operates from Málaga Airport to Costa del Sol resorts and Cabify from the airport to Málaga city center. Both services are slightly cheaper than

taxis and available via their respective online apps.

AIRPORT CONTACT Aeropuerto Costa del Sol (AGP). (*Aeropuerto de Málaga*) ✉ *Av. Comandante García Morato s/n, Málaga* ☎ *913/211000* ⊕ *www.aena.es.*

BIKE

The Costa del Sol is famous for its sun and sand, but many people supplement their beach time with mountain-bike forays into the hilly interior, particularly around Ojén, near Marbella, and along the mountain roads around Ronda. One popular route, which affords sweeping vistas, follows the mountain road from Ojén west to Istán. The Costa del Sol's temperate climate is ideal for biking, though it's best not to exert yourself on the trails in July and August, when temperatures soar. There are numerous bike-rental shops in the area, particularly in Marbella, Ronda, and Ojén; many shops also arrange bike excursions. The cost to rent a mountain bike for the day is around €20. Guided bike excursions, which include bikes, support staff, and cars, generally start at about €50 a day.

BIKE RENTAL CONTACT Bike Tours Malaga. ✉ *Calle Vendeja 6, Málaga* ☎ *650/677063* ⊕ *www.biketoursmalaga. com.* **Marbella Rent a Bike.** ✉ *Marbella* ☎ *952/811062* ⊕ *www.marbellarentabike. com.*

BUS

Until the high-speed AVE train line opens between Antequera and Granada in late 2019, buses are the best way to reach the Costa del Sol from Granada, and, aside from the train service from Málaga to Fuengirola, the best way to get around once you're here. During holidays it's wise to reserve your seat in advance for long-distance travel.

On the Costa del Sol, bus services connect Málaga with Cádiz (two daily), Córdoba (four daily), Granada (20 daily), and Seville (seven daily). In Fuengirola you can catch buses for Mijas, Marbella,

Estepona, and Algeciras. The Avanzabus bus company serves most of the Costa del Sol. ALSA serves Granada, Córdoba, Seville, and Nerja. Los Amarillos serves Jerez and Ronda, and Comes runs services to Cádiz. There are also daily buses between Málaga airport and Granada and Seville.

BUS CONTACTS ALSA. ☎ *902/422242* ⊕ *www.alsa.es.***Avanzabus.** ☎ *912/722832* ⊕ *www.avanzabus.com.***Comes.** ☎ *956/807059* ⊕ *www.tgcomes. es.***Damas.** ✉ *Seville* ☎ *959/256900* ⊕ *damas-sa.es.*

CAR

A car allows you to explore Andalusia's mountain villages. Mountain driving can be hair-raising but is getting better as highways are improved.

Málaga is 536 km (333 miles) from Madrid, taking the A4 to Córdoba, then the A44 to Granada, the A92 to Antequera, and the A45; 162 km (101 miles) from Córdoba via Antequera; 220 km (137 miles) from Seville; and 131 km (81 miles) from Granada by the shortest route of the A92 to Loja, then the A45 to Málaga.

To take a car into Gibraltar you need, in theory, an insurance certificate and a logbook (a certificate of vehicle ownership). In practice, all you need is your passport as well as a valid driving license. Head for the well-signposted multistory parking garage, as street parking on the Rock is scarce.

NATIONAL CAR-RENTAL AGENCIES Helle Hollis. ☎ *952/245544* ⊕ *www.hellehollis. com.*

TAXI

Taxis are plentiful throughout the Costa del Sol and may be hailed on the street or from specified taxi ranks marked "Taxi." Restaurants are usually happy to call a taxi for you, too. Fares are reasonable, and meters are strictly used. You are not required to tip taxi drivers, though

rounding up the amount will be appreciated. Uber operates throughout the Costa del Sol, and Cabify services are available in Málaga city and Marbella.

TRAIN

Málaga is the main rail terminus in the area, with 13 high-speed trains per day from Madrid (2 hours 30 minutes to 3 hours, depending on the train). Málaga is also linked by high-speed train with Barcelona (six daily, 5 hours 45 minutes to 6 hours 35 minutes, depending on the train). Six daily trains also link Seville with Málaga in just under two hours.

High-speed AVE trains from Granada to Málaga begin operation in late 2021 and will reduce the journey time to 50 minutes. Málaga's train station is a 15-minute walk from the city center, across the river.

RENFE connects Málaga, Torremolinos, and Fuengirola, stopping at the airport and all resorts along the way. The train leaves Málaga every 20 minutes 5:20 am–11:30 pm, and Fuengirola every 20 minutes 6:10 am–12:20 am. For the city center, get off at the last stop. A daily train connects Málaga and Ronda via the dramatic Chorro gorge (2 hours 30 minutes).

Restaurants

Málaga is best for traditional Spanish cooking, with a wealth of bars and seafood restaurants serving *fritura malagueña*, the city's famous fried seafood. Torremolinos's Carihuela district is also a good destination for lovers of Spanish seafood. The area's resorts serve every conceivable foreign cuisine, from Thai to the Scandinavian smorgasbord. For delicious cheap eats, try the *chiringuitos*. Strung out along the beaches, these summer-only restaurants serve seafood fresh off the boats. Because there are so many foreigners here, meals on the coast are served earlier than elsewhere in Andalusia; most restaurants open at 1 or 1:30 for lunch and 7 or 8 for dinner.

Restaurant reviews have been shortened. For full information, visit Fodors. com.

Hotels

Most hotels on the developed stretch between Torremolinos and Fuengirola offer large, functional rooms near the sea at competitive rates, but the area's popularity as a budget destination means that most such hotels are booked in high season by package-tour operators. Finding a room at Easter, in July and August, or over holiday weekends can be difficult if you haven't reserved in advance. In July and August many hotels require a stay of at least three days. Málaga is an increasingly attractive base for visitors to this corner of Andalusia and has some good hotels. Marbella, meanwhile, has more than its fair share of grand lodgings, including some of Spain's most expensive rooms. Gibraltar's handful of hotels tends to be more expensive than most comparable lodgings in Spain.

There are also apartments and villas for short- or long-term stays, ranging from traditional Andalusian farmhouses to luxury villas. One excellent source for apartment and villa rentals is **Spain Holiday** *(951/204601)*. For Marbella, you can also try **Nordica Rentals** *(952/811552)*, and, for high-end rentals, **The Luxury Villa Collection** *(44/208 224 1285 in the UK)*. Our local writers vet every hotel to recommend the best overnights in each price category, from budget to expensive. Unless otherwise specified, you can expect a private bath, phone, and TV in your room.

Hotel reviews have been shortened. For full information, visit Fodors.com.

What It Costs in Euros

	$	$$	$$$	$$$$
RESTAURANTS				
	under €12	€12–€17	€18–€22	over €22
HOTELS				
	under €90	€90–€125	€126–€180	over €180

Golf in the Sun

Nicknamed the "Costa del Golf," the Sun Coast has over 70 golf courses within putting distance of the Mediterranean. Most of the courses are between Rincón de la Victoria (east of Málaga) and Gibraltar. The best time for golfing is October–June; greens fees are lower in high summer. Check out the comprehensive website ⊕ *www.golfinspain.com* for up-to-date information.

Tours

Several companies run one- and two-day excursions from Costa del Sol resorts. You can book with local travel agents and hotels; excursions leave from Málaga, Torremolinos, Fuengirola, Marbella, and Estepona, with prices varying by departure point. Most tours last half a day, and in most cases you can be picked up at your hotel. Popular tours include Málaga, Gibraltar, the Cuevas de Nerja, Mijas, Tangier, and Ronda. The Costa del Sol's varied landscape is also wonderful for hiking and walking, and several companies offer walking or cycling tours.

TOUR OPERATORS
John Keo Walking Tours
This company provides guided walks and hikes around the eastern Costa del Sol, weekdays only. Reservations are essential. ☎ *647/273502* ⊕ *www.hikingwalking-spain.com* ✉ *From €15.*

Sierra MTB

A good range of rural and urban guided cycling tours suit all levels. Weekend and weeklong packages, including accommodations and a different bike ride every day, are available in addition to day trips. ✉ *Málaga* ☎ *616/295251* ⊕ *www.sierra-cycling.com* ✉ *From €80.*

Viajes Rusadir

This local firm specializes in Costa del Sol excursions and private tours. ☎ *952/463458* ⊕ *www.viajesrusadir.com* ✉ *From €35.*

Wild Andalucia

Seven-day birdwatching tours around the province of Málaga at different inland and coastal locations. Prices are per person based on a group of four. ✉ *Málaga* ☎ *650/785926* ⊕ *www.wildandalucia.com* ✉ *From €1,200.*

Visitor Information

The official website for the Costa del Sol is ; it has good information on sightseeing and events, guides to towns and villages, and contact details for the regional and local tourist offices, which are listed under their respective towns and cities. Tourist offices are generally open Monday through Saturday 10–7 (until 8 in summer) and Sunday 10–2.

The Cabo de Gata Nature Reserve

40 km (25 miles) east of Almería, 86 km (53 miles) south of Mojácar.

The southeast corner of Spain is one of the country's last unspoiled wildernesses, and much of the coastline is part of a highly protected nature reserve. San José, the largest village, has a pleasant bay, though these days the village has rather outgrown itself and can be very busy in summer. Those preferring smaller, quieter destinations should look farther north, at places such as Agua Amarga, Rodalquilar, and the often-deserted beaches nearby.

GETTING HERE AND AROUND

You need your own wheels to explore the nature reserve and surrounding villages, including San José. When it's time to hit the beach, Playa de los Genoveses and Playa Monsul, to the south of San José, are some of the best. A rough road follows the coast around the spectacular cape, eventually linking up with the N332 to Almería. Alternatively, follow the signs north for the towns of Níjar (approximately 20 km [12 miles] north) and Sorbas (32 km [20 miles] northeast of Níjar); both towns are famed for their distinctive green-glazed pottery, which you can buy directly from workshops.

👁 Sights

Parque Natural Marítimo y Terrestre Cabo de Gata–Níjar

NATURE PRESERVE | Birds are the main attraction at this nature reserve just south of San José; it's home to several species native to Africa, including the *camachuelo trompetero* (large-beaked bullfinch), which is not found anywhere else outside Africa. Check out the Punto de Información visitor center in Rodalquilar, which has an exhibit and information on the region and organizes guided walks and tours of the area. It's open afternoons from Thursday to Sunday. ✉ *Calle Fundición, San José* ⊹ *Rodalquilar* ☎ *671/594419* ⊗ *Closed Mon.–Wed.*

🏖 Beaches

El Playazo

BEACH | *Playazo* literally means "one great beach," and this sandy cove is certainly one of the gems in the Cabo de Gata nature reserve. Just a few minutes' drive from the village of Rodalquilar (once home to Spain's only gold mine), the yellow-sand beach is surrounded by

Dramatic views of the coastline from the Cabo de Gata natural park

ocher-color volcanic rock; an 18th-century fortress stands at one end. These are sheltered waters, so bathing is safe and warm, and the offshore rocks make for great snorkeling. This beach is deserted during most of the year, and its isolation and lack of amenities mean that even in the summer months you won't come across too many other beachgoers. Although nude bathing isn't officially allowed here, it is tolerated. **Amenities:** none. **Best for:** snorkeling; solitude; sunrise. ✉ *Rodalquilar, San José.*

Playa de los Genoveses

BEACH | Named after the Genovese sailors who landed here in 1127 to aid King Alfonso VII, this beach is one of the area's best known and most beautiful. The long, sandy expanse is backed by pines, eucalyptus trees, and low-rising dunes. The sea is shallow, warm, and crystal clear here—snorkeling is popular around the rocks at either end of the cove. Free parking is available mid-September–mid-June; in July and August, you must park in nearby San José and take a free shuttle bus to the beach. The beach can also be reached via an easy coastal walk from San José, a 7-km (4½-mile) round-trip. The beach has no amenities to speak of, so take plenty of water if it's hot. **Amenities:** parking. **Best for:** snorkeling; solitude; sunset; walking. ✉ *San José.*

Hotels

El Faro de los Genoveses

$$$$ | **APARTMENT** | With panoramic views of San José and the wide bay, these modern self-catering apartments make the most of their elevated position at the far west end of the village. **Pros:** friendly and flexible owners; stunning sea and mountain views; clean and comfortable accommodations. **Cons:** 2-night minimum stay; slightly out of the village; some noise from the bar. [$] *Rooms from: €200* ✉ *Calle La Morra 4, San José* ☎ *679/443934* 🌐 *elfarodelosgenoveses.com* 🍴 *No Meals* 🛏 *8 apartments.*

Agua Amarga

22 km (14 miles) north of San José, 55 km (34 miles) east of Almería.

Like other coastal hamlets, Agua Amarga started out in the 18th century as a tuna-fishing port. These days, as perhaps the most pleasant village on the Cabo de Gata coast, it attracts lots of visitors, although it remains much less developed than San José. One of the coast's best beaches is just to the north: the dramatically named Playa de los Muertos (Beach of the Dead), a long stretch of fine gravel bookended with volcanic outcrops.

GETTING HERE AND AROUND

If you're driving here from Almería, follow signs to the airport, then continue north on the A7; Agua Amarga is signposted just north of the Parque Natural Cabo de Gata. The village itself is small enough to explore easily on foot.

🍴 Restaurants

La Palmera

$$ | **SPANISH** | At the far eastern end of the beach, the terrace at this hotel restaurant sits right on the sand; get a table here rather than inside the less impressive dining room. Fresh fish, locally caught and grilled, is the highlight of the menu, which also includes simple salads and plates of fried fish. **Known for:** locally caught fish; arroz a banda (rice with fish and aioli); beachfront dining. [$] *Average main: €16 ✉ Calle Aguada 4, Agua Amarga ☎ 676/726819 🌐 hostalrestaurantelapalmera.net/en 🕒 Closed for 6 wks in winter. Call to check.*

🛏 Hotels

Hotel El Tío Kiko

$$$ | **HOTEL** | On a hill to the west of the village, this modern luxury hotel has commanding sea views and is close enough to the main beach to walk (but far enough to enjoy peace and quiet). **Pros:** varied breakfast; sea views; rooms have balconies, some with hot tubs. **Cons:** could be too quiet for some; up a hill; adults-only mid-June–mid-September. [$] *Rooms from: €180 ✉ Calle Embarque 12, Agua Amarga ☎ 950/138080 🌐 www.eltiokiko.com 🛏 27 rooms 🍴 Free Breakfast.*

Almería

183 km (114 miles) east of Málaga.

Warmed by the sunniest climate in Andalusia, Almería is a youthful Mediterranean city, basking in sweeping views of the sea from its coastal perch and close to several excellent beaches. It's also a capital of the grape industry, thanks to its wonderfully mild climate in spring and fall. Rimmed by tree-lined boulevards and some landscaped squares, the city's core is a maze of narrow, winding alleys formed by flat-roofed, distinctly Mudejar houses. Now surrounded by modern apartment blocks, these dazzlingly white older homes continue to give Almería an Andalusian flavor. Barely touched by tourism, this compact city is well worth a visit—allow an overnight stay to take in the main sights en route to or from Cabo de Gata or Málaga. Almería was Gastronomic Capital of Spain in 2019 so be sure to try the local fare and tapas bars, where you'll be offered a free (and usually elaborate) tapa with your drink.

GETTING HERE AND AROUND

Bus No. 30 (€1.05) runs roughly every 35 minutes 7 am–11 pm from Almería airport to the center of town (Calle del Doctor Gregorio Marañón).

The city center is compact, and most of the main sights are within easy strolling distance of each other.

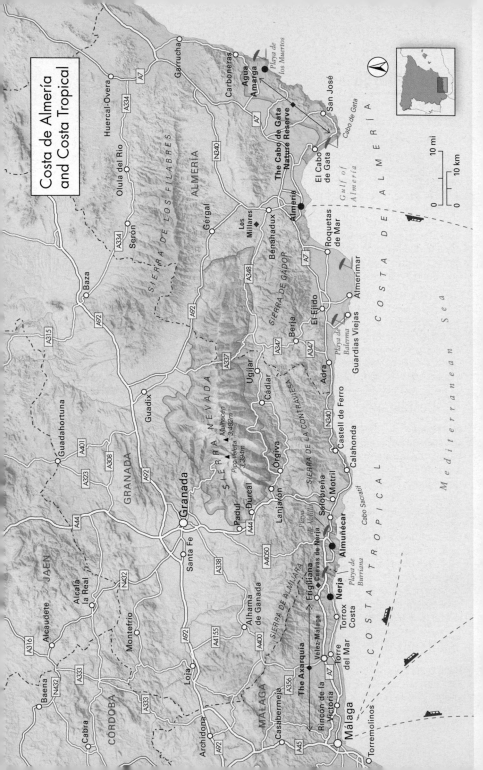

Costa de Almería
and Costa Tropical

VISITOR INFORMATION

CONTACTS Almería Visitor Information. ✉ *Pl. de la Constitución, Almería* ☎ *950/210538* 🌐 *www.turismodealmeria.org.*

👁 Sights

Alcazaba

MILITARY SIGHT | Dominating the city is this fortress, built by Caliph Abd ar-Rahman I and given a bell tower by Carlos III. From here you have sweeping views of the port and city. Among the ruins of the fortress, which was damaged by earthquakes in 1522 and 1560, are landscaped gardens of rock flowers and cacti. ✉ *Calle Almanzor, Almería* ☎ *950/801008* 🎫 *Free* 🕐 *Closed Mon.*

Cathedral

CHURCH | Below the *alcazaba* (citadel) is the local cathedral, with buttressed towers that give it the appearance of a castle. It's in Gothic style, but with some classical touches around the doors. Guided tours are available, and admission includes a visit to the ecclesiastical museum. ✉ *Pl. de la Catedral, Almería* ☎ *950/234848* 🎫 *€5* 🕐 *Closed Mon.–Thurs.*

Mercado Central de Almería

MARKET | Built in 1892 in a Modernist style, Almería's main market provides a colorful insight into the province's long list of fresh produce. The iron structure, characteristic of late 19th-century buildings, is enclosed by a pretty tiled facade. Don't miss the plaque marking Marie Curie's visit here in 1931. ✉ *Calle Aguilar de Campo s/n,* 🕐 *Closed Sun.*

★ Refugios de la Guerra Civil (*Civil War Shelters*)

TUNNEL | Almería, the last bastion of the Republican government during the Spanish Civil War, was hit by 754 bombs launched via air and sea by Nationalist forces. To protect civilians, 4½ km (2¾ miles) of tunnels were built under the city to provide shelter for more than 34,000 people. About 1 km (½ mile) can now be visited on a guided tour that covers the food stores, sleeping quarters, and an operating theater for the wounded, with its original medical equipment. ✉ *Pl. Manuel Pérez García s/n, Almería* ☎ *950/268696* 🎫 *€3* 🕐 *Closed Mon.*

Los Millares 👁

This important archaeological site is nearly 2½ km (1½ miles) southwest from the village of Santa Fe de Mondújar and 19 km (12 miles) from Almería. This collection of ruins scattered on a windswept hilltop was the birthplace of civilization in Spain nearly 5,000 years ago. Large tombs show that the community had an advanced society, and the formidable defense walls indicate it had something to protect. A series of concentric fortifications shows that the settlement grew, eventually holding some 2,000 people. The town was inhabited from 2700 to 1800 BC.

🍴 Restaurants

La Encina

$$$ | **SPANISH** | This justly popular restaurant is housed in an 1860s building that also incorporates an 11th-century Moorish well. Time may have stood still with the setting, but the cuisine reflects a modern twist on traditional dishes, including seafood mains like *bacalao con cebolla, miel y pasas con cruijiente de espinacas* (cod with onion, honey, and raisins) or *rabo de novillo con almendras* (oxtail stew with almonds). **Known for:** creative tapas; bacalao; wine list. [$] *Average main: €18* ✉ *Calle Marín 3, Almería* ☎ *950/273429* 🕐 *Closed Mon.*

Valentín

$$$ | SPANISH | This popular, central spot serves fine regional specialties, such as *arroz de marisco* (rice with seafood), *cazuela de rape en salsa de almendras* (monkfish stew with almond sauce), and the delicious *kokotxas de bacalao en salsa de ostras* (cod cheeks in oyster sauce). The surroundings recently had a facelift and are rustic-yet-elegant Andalusian: whitewashed walls, dark wood, and exposed brick. **Known for:** can be hard to get a table; rice dishes; rustic-chic setting. $ *Average main: €21* ✉ *Calle Tenor Iribarne 10, Almería* 🕾 *950/264475* ☾ *Closed Jan.*

Hotels

Aire Hotel

$$$ | HOTEL | In the heart of the old quarter, early-19th-century architecture is paired with comfortable and up-to-date amenities in this boutique hotel with strong design features. **Pros:** central location; underground Arab baths are included in the rate; terrace with great views. **Cons:** in-room showers offer no privacy; street noise in some rooms; some rooms have no views. $ *Rooms from: €140* ✉ *Pl. de la Constitución 4, Almería* 🕾 *950/282096* ⊕ *www.airehotelalmeria.com* ⌨ *10 rooms* ⏀ *No Meals.*

Hotel Catedral

$$ | HOTEL | In full view of the cathedral, this small hotel combines traditional charm (it has kept many of its original mid-19th-century features, including a stunning arched entryway) with modern elegance. **Pros:** cathedral views; good breakfast; rooftop terrace with plunge pool. **Cons:** cathedral church bells not for everyone; hotel events can be noisy; reception staff could be friendlier. $ *Rooms from: €120* ✉ *Pl. de la Catedral 8, Almería* 🕾 *950/278178* ⊕ *www.hotelcatedral.net* ⌨ *20 rooms* ⏀ *No Meals.*

Nuevo Torreluz Hotel

$ | HOTEL | Value is the overriding attraction at this comfortable and elegant modern hotel, which has slick, bright rooms and the kind of amenities you'd expect to come at a higher price. **Pros:** good value; great central location; large rooms. **Cons:** breakfast served in hotel next door; rooms in the main building are more expensive; no pool. $ *Rooms from: €60* ✉ *Pl. Flores 10, Almería* 🕾 *950/234399* ⊕ *www.torreluz.com* ⌨ *98 rooms* ⏀ *No Meals.*

🎭 Performing Arts

In Almería, the action is on **Plaza Flores,** moving down to the beach in summer.

★ Peña El Taranto

ARTS CENTERS | Founded in 1963, this excellent venue (home to the city's Arab water deposits) has been one of the main centers for flamenco in Andalusia, and foot-stomping live flamenco and concerts are performed every two weeks. Check in advance for exact times and dates. ✉ *Calle Tenor Iribame 20, Almería* 🕾 *950/235057* ⊕ *www.eltaranto.com.*

Almuñécar

85 km (53 miles) east of Málaga.

This small-time resort with a shingle beach is popular with Spanish and Northern European vacationers. It's been a fishing village since Phoenician times, 3,000 years ago, when it was called Sexi; later, the Moors built a castle here for the treasures of Granada's kings. The road west from Motril and Salobreña passes through what was the empire of the sugar barons, who brought prosperity to Málaga's province in the 19th century: the cane fields now give way to lychees, limes, mangoes, pawpaws, and olives.

The village is actually two, separated by the dramatic rocky headland of Punta de

A religious procession in Almuñécar

la Mona. To the east is Almuñécar proper, and to the west is **La Herradura,** a quiet fishing community. Between the two is the Marina del Este yacht harbor, which, along with La Herradura, is a popular diving center. A renowned jazz festival (www.jazzgranada.es) takes place annually in July, often showcasing big names.

GETTING HERE AND AROUND

The A7 runs north of town. There is an efficient bus service to surrounding towns and cities, including Málaga, Granada, Nerja, and, closer afield, La Herradura. Almuñécar's town center is well laid out for strolling, and the local tourist office has information on bicycle and scooter rental.

VISITOR INFORMATION

CONTACTS Almuñécar. ⊠ *Palacete de la Najarra, Av. de Europa, Almuñécar* ☎ *958/631125* ⊕ *www.turismoalmunecar. es.*

👁 Sights

Castillo de San Miguel (*St. Michael's Castle*)

CASTLE/PALACE | A Roman fortress once stood here, later enlarged by the Moors, but the castle's present aspect, crowning the city, owes more to 16th-century additions. The building was bombed during the Peninsular War in the 19th century, and what was left was used as a cemetery until the 1990s. You can wander the ramparts and peer into the dungeon; the skeleton at the bottom is a reproduction of human remains discovered on the spot. ⊠ *Calle San Miguel Bajo, Almuñécar* ☎ *958/838623* ⊗ *Closed Mon.* ⊡ *€4, includes admission to Cueva de Siete Palacios.*

Cueva de Siete Palacios (*Cave of Seven Palaces*)

OTHER MUSEUM | Beneath the Castillo de San Miguel is this large, vaulted stone cellar of Roman origin, now Almuñécar's archaeological museum. The collection is small but interesting, with Phoenician, Roman, and Moorish artifacts. ✉ *Calle San Miguel Bajo, Almuñécar* ☎ *958/838623* 🕙 *Closed Mon.* 🎫 *€4, includes admission to Castillo de San Miguel.*

Restaurants

FIRMVM
$$$ | SPANISH | One of the eastern Costa del Sol's foodie treats sits in a pleasant central square with its signature ruby-red feature wall. Chef Sergio González combines the best of local produce with more exotic touches to perfection: the venison comes with Jack Daniel's bacon jam, and local shrimp goes into a Vietnamese roll. **Known for:** good-value tasting menu; creative fusion dishes; attentive and friendly service. 💲 *Average main: €18* ✉ *Pl. Damasco 2, Almuñécar* ☎ *958/633565* ⊕ *restaurantefirmvm.com* 🕙 *Closed Mon. No dinner Sun.*

Hotels

Casablanca
$$ | HOTEL | This quaint, family-run hotel comes with a pink-and-white neo-Moorish facade, a choice location next to the beach and near the botanical park, and comfortable rooms that are all different. **Pros:** intimate, family-run atmosphere; all rooms have private balconies or views; great location. **Cons:** only some rooms have sea views; parking can be difficult; rooms vary, and some are small. 💲 *Rooms from: €100* ✉ *Pl. San Cristóbal 4, Almuñécar* ☎ *958/635575* ⊕ *www. hotelcasablancaalmunecar.com* 🛏 *39 rooms* 🍽 *No Meals.*

Nerja

52 km (32 miles) east of Málaga, 22 km (14 miles) west of Almuñécar.

Nerja—the name comes from the Moorish word *narixa*, meaning "abundant

Salobreña

About 13 km (8 miles) east of Almuñécar, this unspoiled village of near-perpendicular streets and old white houses on a steep hill beneath a Moorish fortress is a true Andalusian *pueblo* (village), separated from the beachfront restaurants and bars in the newer part of town. It's great for a quick visit, and the pebbly beach makes a nice walk. You can reach Salobreña by descending through the mountains from Granada or by continuing west from Almería on the A7.

springs"—has a large community of expats, who live mainly outside town in *urbanizaciones* ("village" developments). The old village is on a headland above small beaches and rocky coves, which offer reasonable swimming despite the gray, gritty sand. In July and August, Nerja is packed with tourists, but the rest of the year it's a pleasure to wander the old town's narrow streets.

GETTING HERE AND AROUND
Nerja is a speedy hour's drive east from Málaga on the A7. If you're driving, park in the underground lot just west of the Balcón de Europa (it's signposted) off Calle La Cruz. The town is small enough to explore on foot.

VISITOR INFORMATION
CONTACTS Nerja. ✉ *Calle Carmen 1, Nerja* ☎ *952/521531* ⊕ *turismo.nerja.es.*

Sights

★ Balcón de Europa
PROMENADE | FAMILY | The highlight of Nerja, this tree-lined promenade is on a promontory just off the central square, with magnificent views of the mountains and sea. You can gaze far off into the horizon using the strategically placed

telescopes, or use this as a starting point for a horse-and-carriage clip-clop ride around town. Open-air concerts are held here in July and August. ⊠ *Nerja.*

Cuevas de Nerja (*Nerja Caves*)
CAVE | Between Almuñécar and Nerja, these caves are on a road surrounded by giant cliffs and dramatic seascapes. Signs point to the cave entrance above the village of Maro, 4 km (2½ miles) east of Nerja. Its spires and turrets, created by millennia of dripping water, are now floodlit for better views. One suspended pinnacle, 200 feet long, is the world's largest known stalactite. The cave painting of seals discovered here may be the oldest example of art in existence—and the only one known to have been painted by Neanderthals. The awesome subterranean chambers create an evocative setting for concerts and ballets during the Nerja Festival of Music and Dance, held annually during June to July. There is also a bar-restaurant near the entrance with a spacious dining room that has superb views. Afternoon visits are by guided tour only, September–June. They take around 45 minutes so arrive at least an hour before closing time. Private tours in English are available (€15, bookable online). All ticket prices are cheaper online. ⊠ *Maro* ☎ *952/529520* ⊕ *www. cuevadenerja.com* 🎫 *€10.*

🏖 Beaches

Las Alberquillas
BEACH | One of the string of coves on the coastline west of Nerja, this beach of gray sand mixed with shingle is backed by pine trees and scrub that perfume the air. Reachable only via a stony track down the cliffs, this protected beach is one of the few on the Costa del Sol to be almost completely untouched by tourism. Its moderate waves mean you need to take care when bathing. The snorkeling around the rocks at either end of the beach is among the best in the area. This spot's seclusion makes the beach

Frigiliana

On an inland mountain ridge overlooking the sea, this pretty village has spectacular views and an old quarter of narrow, cobbled streets and dazzling white houses decorated with pots of geraniums. It was the site of one of the last battles between the Christians and the Moors. Frigiliana is a short drive from the highway to the village; if you don't have a car, you can take a bus here from Nerja, which is 8 km (5 miles) away.

a favorite with couples and nudists—it's reasonably quiet even at the height of summer. Limited parking is available off the N340 highway, but there are no amenities, so take plenty of water. **Amenities:** none. **Best for:** nudists; snorkeling; solitude. ⊠ *N340, Km 299, Nerja.*

🍽 Restaurants

★ **Oliva**
$$$$ | **MEDITERRANEAN** | Mediterranean cuisine based on fresh, local produce takes center stage at this restaurant, which has both a minimalist, intimate dining room and a pleasant terrace that's heated in winter. Highlights on the seasonal menu (it changes four times a year) include the sole mille-feuille, baby garlic, and ginger mayo, and pistachio falafel. **Known for:** Iberian pork; the best innovative cuisine in town; wine list. $ *Average main: €25* ⊠ *Pl. de España 2, Nerja* ☎ *952/522988* ⊕ *www.restauranteoliva.com* 🕐 *Closed Mon.*

🛏 Hotels

★ **Hotel Carabeo**
$$ | **B&B/INN** | Down a side street near the center of town but still near the sea, this British-owned boutique hotel combines

a great location and views with comfortable, pleasant rooms. **Pros:** sea views; excellent restaurant; great location. **Cons:** rooms are comfortable but compact; difficult to get a room in high season; not open out of season. $ *Rooms from: €90 ⊠ Calle Hernando de Carabeo 34, ☎ 952/525444 ⊕ www.hotelcarabeo.com ⇥ 7 rooms ⏐◯⏐ Free Breakfast ⊘ Closed Dec.–Feb.*

The Axarquía

Vélez-Málaga: 36 km (22 miles) east of Málaga.

The Axarquía region stretches from Nerja to Málaga, and the area's charm lies in its mountainous interior, peppered with pueblos, vineyards, and tiny farms. Its coast consists of narrow, pebbly beaches and drab fishing villages on either side of the high-rise resort town of Torre del Mar.

GETTING HERE AND AROUND

Although bus routes are fairly comprehensive throughout the Axarquía, reaching the smaller villages may involve long delays; renting a car is convenient and lets you get off the beaten track and experience some of the beautiful unspoiled hinterland in this little-known area. The four-lane A7 highway cuts across the region a few miles in from the coast; traffic on the old coastal road (N340) is slower.

TOURS

La Rosilla
Experience local food and culture at a traditional *finca* (traditional estate or ranch) in the heart of the Axarquía. ☎ 659/734401 ⊕ larosilla-catering.com ▱ *From €65.*

VISITOR INFORMATION

CONTACTS Cómpeta. ⊠ *Av. de la Constitución, Cómpeta* ☎ *952/553685* ⊕ *www.competa.es.*

Sights

Ruta del Sol y del Vino and Ruta de la Pasa
TRAIL | The Axarquía has a number of tourist trails that take in the best of local scenery, history, and culture. Two of the best are the Ruta del Sol y del Vino (Sunshine and Wine Trail), through Algarrobo, Cómpeta (the main wine center), and Nerja; and the Ruta de la Pasa (Raisin Trail), which goes through Moclinejo, El Borge, and Comares. The trails are especially spectacular during the late-summer grape harvest or in late autumn, when the leaves of the vines turn gold. A visit to nearby Macharaviaya (7 km [4 miles] north of Rincón de la Victoria) might lead you to ponder this sleepy village's past glory: in 1776 one of its sons, Bernardo de Gálvez, became the Spanish governor of Louisiana and later fought in the American Revolution (Galveston, Texas, is named for him). Macharaviaya prospered under his heirs and for many years enjoyed a lucrative monopoly on the manufacture of playing cards for South America. Gálvez was named Honorary Citizen of the United States in December 2014 and his portrait now hangs in the Foreign Affairs Committee room in the Capitol. A sculpture of the family now stands next to Málaga train station. ⊠ *Ruta del Sol y del Vino.*

Vélez-Málaga
TOWN | The capital of the Axarquía is a pleasant agricultural town of white houses, mango and avocado orchards, and vineyards. It's worth a half-day trip to see the Thursday market, Contemporary Art Centre (CAC), the ruins of a Moorish castle, and the church of Santa María la Mayor, built in the Mudejar style on the site of a mosque that was destroyed when the town fell to the Christians in 1487. The town also has a thriving flamenco scene with regular events (www.flamencoabierto.com). ⊠ *Vélez-Málaga.*

Restaurants

El Convento

$$ | SPANISH | Housed in a restored convent, this cozy restaurant offers atmospheric dining inside and a pleasant terrace outside. Excellent tapas and *tostas* (toppings on toasted bread) are available at the bar in addition to an extensive menu of local and international dishes in the restaurant. **Known for:** good value dining; tostas; croquettes. **$** *Average main: €12* ✉ *Calle de los Moros 5, Vélez-Málaga* ☎ *951/250100.*

🛏 Hotels

Hotel Palacio Blanco

$$ | HOTEL | This light and airy boutique hotel is housed in a charmingly restored 18th-century mansion just a short distance from the castle. **Pros:** rooftop terrace with pool; central location; spacious rooms. **Cons:** few facilities; first-floor rooms are a little dark; no on-site parking. **$** *Rooms from: €95* ✉ *Calle Felix Lomas 4, Vélez-Málaga* ☎ *952/549174* ⊕ *www. palacioblanco.com* ⤴ *9 rooms* ⏐○⏐ *Free Breakfast.*

Málaga

175 km (109 miles) southeast of Córdoba.

Málaga is one of southern Spain's most welcoming and happening cities, and it more than justifies a visit. Visitor figures soared after the Museo Picasso opened in 2003 and again after a new cruise-ship terminal opened in 2011, and the city has had a well-earned face-lift, with many of its historic buildings restored or undergoing restoration. The area between the river and the port has been transformed into the Soho art district, and since the arrival of three new art museums in 2015, the city has become one of southern Europe's centers for art. Alongside all this rejuvenation, some great shops and lively bars and restaurants have sprung up all over the center.

True, the approach from the airport certainly isn't that pretty, and you'll be greeted by huge 1970s high-rises that march determinedly toward Torremolinos. But don't give up: in its center and eastern suburbs, this city of about 550,000 people is a pleasant port, with ancient streets and lovely villas amid exotic foliage. Blessed with a subtropical climate, it's covered in lush vegetation and averages some 324 days of sunshine a year.

Central Málaga lies between the Río Guadalmedina and the port, and the city's main attractions are all here. The Centro de Arte Contemporáneo (CAC) sits next to the river; to the east lies the Soho district, hoisted from its former seedy red-light reputation to a vibrant cultural hub with galleries and up-and-coming restaurants. Around La Alameda Boulevard (mostly pedestrianized in 2019), with its giant weeping fig trees, is old-town Málaga: elegant squares, pedestrian shopping streets such as Calle Marqués de Larios, and the major monuments, which are often tucked away in labyrinthine alleys.

Eastern Málaga starts with the pleasant suburbs of El Palo and Pedregalejo, once traditional fishing villages. Here you can eat fresh fish in the numerous chiringuitos and stroll Pedregalejo's seafront promenade or the tree-lined streets of El Limonar. A few blocks west is Málaga's bullring, La Malagueta, built in 1874, and Muelle Uno (port-front commercial center), whose striking glass cube is home to the Centre Pompidou. It's great for a drink and for soaking up views of the old quarter.

GETTING HERE AND AROUND

If you're staying at one of the coastal resorts between Málaga and Fuengirola, the easiest way to reach Málaga is via the train (every 20 minutes). If you're

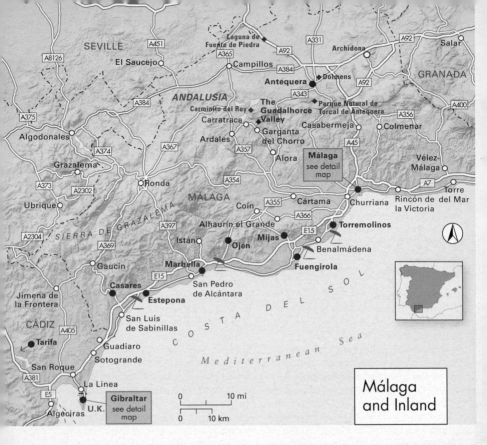

Málaga and Inland

driving, there are several well-signposted underground parking lots, and it's not that daunting to negotiate by car. Málaga has two metro lines from the west, and both reach central train and bus stations.

Málaga is mostly flat, so the best way to explore it is on foot or by bike via the good network of designated bike paths. To get an overview of the city in a day, hop on the Málaga Tour City Sightseeing Bus. There is a comprehensive bus network, too, and the tourist office can advise on routes and schedules. Taxis are readily available and Cabify and Uber both operate in Málaga city.

BIKE RENTAL CONTACT Bike Tours Malaga. ⊠ *Calle Vendeja 6, Málaga* ☎ *650/677063* ⊕ *www.biketoursmalaga. com.*

BUS CONTACT Málaga Bus Station. ⊠ *Paseo de los Tilos, Málaga* ☎ *952/350061.*

CAR RENTAL CONTACTS Europcar. ⊠ *Málaga Costa del Sol Airport, Málaga* ☎ *911/505000* ⊕ *www.europcar.es.* **Niza Cars.** ⊠ *Málaga Costa del Sol Airport, Málaga* ☎ *952/236179* ⊕ *www.nizacars. es.*

TAXI COMPANY Unitaxi. ⊠ *Málaga* ☎ *952/320000.*

TRAIN INFORMATION Málaga Train Station. ⊠ *Esplanada de la Estación, Málaga* ☎ *912/320320* ⊕ *www.renfe.com.*

TOURS

Málaga Tour City Sightseeing Bus

This open-top, hop-on hop-off tour bus gives you an overview of Málaga's main sites in a day, including the Gibralfaro. Buy tickets online ahead of your trip or when you board the bus. ⊠ *Málaga*

⊕ *www.city-sightseeing.com* ⊡ *From €22.*

Spain Food Sherpas
Eat your way around Málaga with the Taste of Tapas Tour or the evening Wine and Tapas Tour with local guides who know their stuff when it comes to the city's culinary culture. ⊠ *Málaga* ⊟ ⊕ *www.spainfoodsherpas.com* ⊡ *From €58.*

VISITOR INFORMATION
CONTACTS Guide to Malaga. ⊠ *Málaga* ⊕ *www.guidetomalaga.com* .**Málaga Turismo.** ⊠ *Pl. de la Marina, Paseo del Parque, Málaga* ⊠ *951/926620* ⊕ *www. malagaturismo.com.*

 Sights

Alcazaba
RUINS | Just beyond the ruins of a Roman theater on Calle Alcazabilla stands Málaga's greatest monument. This fortress was begun in the 8th century, when Málaga was the principal port of the Moorish kingdom, although most of the present structure dates to the 11th century. The inner palace was built between 1057 and 1063, when the Moorish emirs took up residence; Ferdinand and Isabella lived here for a while after conquering the city in 1487. The ruins are dappled with orange trees and bougainvillea and include a small museum; from the highest point you can see over the park and port. ⊠ *Málaga* ✛ *Entrance on Calle Alcazabilla* ⊡ *From €4 (free Sun. from 2 pm).*

Centre Pompidou Málaga
ART MUSEUM | The only branch outside France of the Centre Pompidou in Paris opened in March 2015 in the striking glass cube designed by Daniel Buren at Muelle Uno on Málaga port. Housing more than 80 paintings and photographs, the museum showcases 20th- and 21st-century modern art, with works by Kandinsky, Chagall, Scurti, Miró, and Barceló on permanent display. There are

also regular temporary exhibitions each year. ⊠ *Pasaje Doctor Carrillo Casaux s/n, Málaga* ⊠ *951/926200* ⊕ *www.centre-pompidou-malaga.eu* ⊡ *From €7 (free Sun. from 4 pm)* ⊘ *Closed Tues.*

Centro de Arte Contemporáneo (*Contemporary Arts Center*)
ART MUSEUM | This museum includes photographic studies and paintings, some of them immense. The 7,900 square feet of bright exhibition space is used to showcase ultramodern artistic trends—the four exhibitions feature changing exhibits from the permanent collection, two temporary shows, and one show dedicated to up-and-coming Spanish artists. The gallery attracts world-class modern artists like Mark Ryden, KAWS, and Jules de Balincourt. Outside, don't miss the giant murals behind the museum painted by the street artists Shepard Fairey (aka Obey) and Dean Stockton (aka D*Face). ⊠ *Alemania s/n,* ⊠ *952/120055* ⊕ *www. centrodeartecontemporaneo.gob.ec* ⊡ *Free* ⊘ *Closed Mon.*

Gibralfaro (*Fortress*)
VIEWPOINT | Surrounded by magnificent vistas and floodlit at night, these fortifications were built for Yusuf I in the 14th century; the Moors called them Jebelfaro, from the Arab word for "mount" and the Greek word for "lighthouse," after a beacon that stood here to guide ships into the harbor and warn of pirates. The lighthouse has been succeeded by a small parador. ⊠ *Gibralfaro Mountain, Málaga* ✛ *Drive by way of Calle Victoria, or take Bus 35 (10 departures per day, roughly every 45 mins 10–7) from stop in park near Pl. de la Marina* ⊡ *From €4 (free Sun. from 2 pm).*

La Concepción
GARDEN | This botanical garden was created in 1855 by the daughter of the British consul, who married a Spanish shipping magnate—the captains of the Spaniard's fleet had standing orders to bring back seedlings and cuttings from every "exotic" port of call. The wisteria

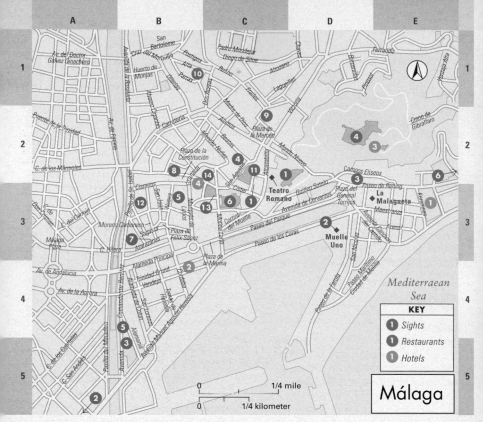

Málaga

KEY
- ① Sights
- ① Restaurants
- ① Hotels

pergola, in bloom in early April, is one of the highlights. The garden is just off the exit road to Granada—too far to walk, but well worth the cab fare or the bus journey (No. 2 from La Alameda, then a 20-minute walk or on the Málaga Tour Bus) from the city center. ⊠ *Ctra. de las Pedrizas, Km 216, Málaga* ☎ *951/926180* 🎟 *€6 (free Sun. afternoon)* ⊘ *Closed Mon.*

Málaga Cathedral

CHURCH | Built between 1528 and 1782, the cathedral is a triumph, although a generally unappreciated one, having been left unfinished when funds ran out. Because it lacks one of its two towers, the building is nicknamed "La Manquita" (the One-Armed Lady). The enclosed choir (restored in 2019), which miraculously survived the burnings of the civil war, is the work of 17th-century artist Pedro de Mena, who carved the wood wafer-thin in some places to express the fold of a robe or shape of a finger. The choir also has a pair of massive 18th-century pipe organs, one of which is still used for the occasional concert. Adjoining the cathedral is a small museum of religious art and artifacts. A walk around the cathedral on Calle Cister will take you to the magnificent Gothic Puerta del Sagrario. A rooftop walkway (guided tours only) gives you stunning views of the ocher domes and the city. ⊠ *Calle Molina Lario, Málaga* ☎ *640/871711* 🎟 *From €6* ⊘ *Closed Sun. morning.*

Mercado de Atarazanas

MARKET | From the Plaza Felix Saenz, at the southern end of Calle Nueva, turn onto Sagasta to reach the Mercado de Atarazanas. The typical 19th-century iron structure incorporates the original **Puerta de Atarazanas,** the exquisitely crafted 14th-century Moorish gate that once connected the city with the port. Don't miss the magnificent stained-glass window depicting highlights of this historic port city as you stroll around the stalls, filled with local produce. The bars at the entrance offer good-value tapas, open at lunchtime only. ⊠ *Calle Atarazanas, Málaga* ⊘ *Closed Sun.*

Museo Carmen Thyssen Málaga

ART MUSEUM | Like Madrid, Málaga has its own branch of this museum, with more than 200 works from Baroness Thyssen's private collection. Shown in a renovated 16th-century palace, the collection features mainly Spanish paintings from the 19th century but also has work from two great 20th-century artists, Joaquín Sorolla y Bastida and Romero de Torres. The museum also hosts regular exhibitions, concerts, talks, and art workshops. ⊠ *Calle Compañía 10, Málaga* ☎ *902/303131* ⊕ *www.carmenthyssen-malaga.org* 🎟 *From €10 (free Sun. from 5 pm)* ⊘ *Closed Mon.*

Museo Casa Natal de Picasso (*Picasso's Birthplace*)

ART MUSEUM | Málaga's most famous native son, Pablo Picasso, was born here in 1881. The building has been painted and furnished in the style of the era and houses a permanent exhibition of the artist's early sketches and sculptures, as well as memorabilia, including his christening robe and family photos. ⊠ *Pl. de la Merced 15, Málaga* ☎ *951/926060* ⊕ *www.fundacionpicasso.malaga.eu* 🎟 *€3.*

Museo del Vidrio y Cristal (*Museum of Glass and Crystal*)

ART MUSEUM | More than 3,000 pieces of glass and crystal, lovingly collected by the owner, are displayed throughout this 18th-century mansion, which is a museum piece in its own right. The pieces, whether ancient Egyptian or from Europe's Lalique and Whitefriars, give a unique insight into man's decorative use of glass. Visits are by guided tour only. ⊠ *Plazuela Santísimo Cristo de la Sangre 2, Málaga* ☎ *952/220271* ⊕ *www.museovidrioycristalmalaga.com* 🎟 *€7* ⊘ *Closed Mon., and Aug.*

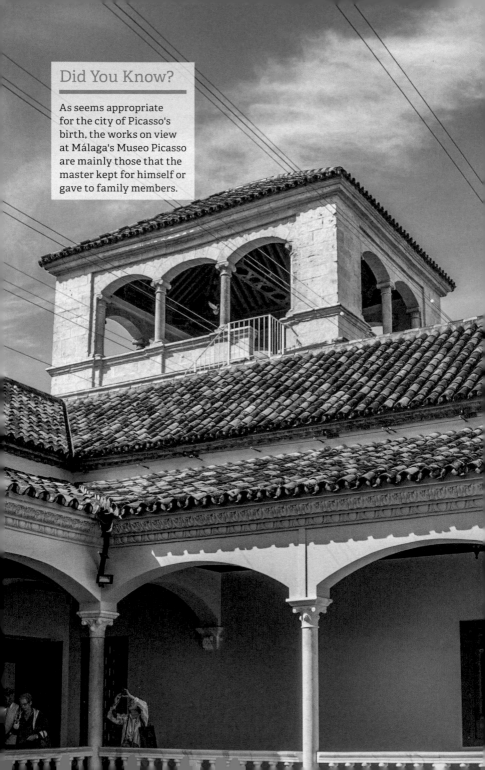

★ Museo Picasso Málaga
ART GALLERY | Part of the charm of this art gallery, one of the city's most prestigious museums, is that its small collection is such a family affair. These are the works that Pablo Picasso kept for himself or gave to his family, including the exquisite *Portrait of Lola*, the artist's sister, which he painted when he was 13, and the stunning *Three Graces*. The holdings were largely donated by two family members—Christine and Bernard Ruiz-Picasso, the artist's daughter-in-law and her son. The works are displayed in chronological order according to the periods that marked Picasso's 73-year development as an artist. The museum is housed in a former palace where, during restoration work, Roman and Moorish remains were discovered. These are now on display, together with the permanent collection of Picassos and temporary exhibitions. Guided tours in English are available; book at least five days ahead. ✉ *Calle San Agustín, Málaga* ☎ *952/127600* 🌐 *www.museopicassomalaga.org* 🎫 *From €9 (free last 2 hrs on Sun.).*

Museo Unicaja de Artes y Costumbres Populares (*Arts and Crafts Museum*)
HISTORY MUSEUM | **FAMILY** | In the old Mesón de la Victoria, a 17th-century inn, this museum displays horse-drawn carriages and carts, old agricultural implements, folk costumes, a forge, a bakery, an ancient grape press, and painted clay figures and ceramics. ✉ *Pasillo de Santa Isabel 10, Málaga* ☎ *952/217137* 🌐 *www.museoartespopulares.com* 🎫 *€4 (free Tues. 1-5pm)* 🕒 *Closed Sun.*

Palacio Episcopal (*Bishop's Palace*)
CASTLE/PALACE | Facing the cathedral's main entrance, this is a fine 18th-century mansion with one of the most stunning facades in the city, as well as interesting interior details. Temporary exhibitions, usually with a religious theme, take place regularly. ✉ *Pl. Obispo 6, Málaga* ☎ *951/294051* 🎫 *€6.*

Something Sweet 🍴

For coffee and cakes, malagueños favor **Lepanto**, the classy shop at Calle Marqués de Larios 7, where uniform-clad staff serve a variety of pastries, cakes, and other sweets. Just next door at **Casa Mira** is delicious homemade ice cream.

Pasaje Chinitas
STREET | The narrow streets and alleys on each side of Calle Marqués de Larios have charms of their own. The most famous is Pasaje Chinitas, off Plaza de la Constitución and named for the notorious Chinitas cabaret here. Peep into the dark, vaulted *bodegas* (wineries) where old men down glasses of *seco añejo* or Málaga Virgen, local wines made from Málaga's muscat grapes. Silversmiths and vendors of religious books and statues ply their trades in shops that have changed little since the early 1900s. Backtrack across Larios, and, in the streets leading to Calle Nueva and Calle San Juan, you can see shoeshine boys, lottery-ticket vendors, street guitarists, and tapas bars serving wine from huge barrels. ✉ *Málaga*

🍴 Restaurants

Araboka
$$ | **SPANISH** | Tucked behind the Picasso Museum, Araboka has a well-deserved reputation as an excellent gastro bar serving Mediterranean dishes made from local produce. Inside, the restaurant is contemporary with low lighting and plant motifs on the walls, and outside there's a pleasant terrace. **Known for:** outdoor terrace; wine list; sharing plates. [$] *Average main: €15* ✉ *Calle Pedro de Toledo 4, Málaga* ☎ *952/124671* 🌐 *www.araboka-restaurante.com.*

Chiringuito Maria

$$ | SPANISH | Fresh seafood and crisp fried fish star on the menu at this busy *chiringuito* (beach restaurant) on the western seafront near the tall chimney. Eat inside in nautically themed decor or outside on the terrace on the sand. **Known for:** efficient service; grilled sardines; fresh fish and seafood. $ *Average main: €12* ⊠ *Calle Pacífico 129, Málaga* ☎ *952/245681* ⊗ *Closed Mon. and Feb. No dinner in the winter.*

El Ambigú de la Coracha

$$ | MEDITERRANEAN | Located beneath the Gibralfaro, this modern restaurant with a lovely terrace offers sweeping views of Málaga below—more than worth the climb to get here—and local cuisine with an international influence. Starters, like king prawn ceviche with local avocado, make ideal sharing plates. **Known for:** olive oil tasting; views of Málaga; local wines and produce. $ *Average main: €15* ⊠ *Calle Campo Eliseos, Málaga* ☎ *951/900046* ⊕ *elambigudelacoracha. com* ⊗ *Closed Mon.*

★ Los Patios de Beatas

$$$ | SPANISH | Sandwiched between the Museo Picasso and Fundación Picasso is one of Málaga's largest wine collections (there are more than 500 on the list). The two historic mansions that make up this restaurant include an original patio and 17th-century stone wine vats; you can sit on barstools in the beamed tapas section, where the walls are lined with dozens of wine bottles, or dine on the airy patio, which is covered with stained glass. **Known for:** wine list; stunning interior; innovative tapas. $ *Average main: €20* ⊠ *Calle Beatas 43, Málaga* ☎ *952/210350* ⊕ *www.lospatiosdebeatas.com.*

Óleo Restaurante

$$$ | INTERNATIONAL | Attached to the Centro de Arte Contemporáneo, this small restaurant offers a range of Mediterranean dishes and sushi best enjoyed on the riverside terrace. Sharing plates include hummus or Vietnamese rolls with Málaga kid goat; highlights on the main menu are *carrillada ibérica* (stewed Iberian pork) with couscous, tuna steak, and a long list of sushi. **Known for:** riverside dining; sushi; stewed Iberian pork. $ *Average main: €18* ⊠ *Calle Alemania, Málaga* ⊕ *Next to CAC* ☎ *952/219062* ⊕ *www. oleorestaurante.es* ⊗ *Closed Mon.*

 Hotels

Gran Hotel Miramar

$$$$ | HOTEL | Málaga's giant "wedding-cake" palace was opened by King Alfonso XIII in 1926 as one of the city's first hotels and fully restored to its former glory in 2017; if you can't splurge on a room, at least treat yourself to a coffee or cocktail here. **Pros:** most luxurious accommodations in town; stunning interior patio; personal butler service. **Cons:** pricey; faces a busy road; short walk from city center. $ *Rooms from: €350* ⊠ *Paseo de Reding 22, Málaga* ☎ *952/603000* ⊕ *www.granhotelmiramarmalaga.com* ⊐ *190 rooms* ⊗| *No Meals.*

Hotel Castilla Guerrero

$$ | HOTEL | This centrally located and gracious hotel has well-priced rooms that are small but functional, with double glazing to block out any late-night street revelry—those facing the side street or the interior patio are the quietest. **Pros:** rooms are clean and modern; great location between the city center and the port; parking. **Cons:** friendly owners don't speak much English; rooms are small; breakfast is not free in adjoining café. $ *Rooms from: €100* ⊠ *Calle Córdoba 7, Málaga* ☎ *952/218635* ⊕ *www.hotelcastillaguerrero.com* ⊐ *51 rooms* ⊗| *No Meals.*

★ Parador de Málaga–Gibralfaro

$$$$ | HOTEL | The attractive rooms at this cozy, gray-stone parador are some of the best in Málaga, with spectacular views of the city and the bay, so reserve well in advance. **Pros:** flawless Málaga-and-Mediterranean vistas from balconies; rooftop pool; popular restaurant. **Cons:** can be very busy; tired communal areas; some distance uphill from town. $ *Rooms from:* €190 ⊠ *Monte de Gibralfaro s/n, Monte,* ☎ 952/221902 ⊕ *www.parador. es* ⇆ *38 rooms* ⦿ *No Meals.*

Room Mate Larios

$$$ | HOTEL | On the central Plaza de la Constitución, in the middle of a sophisticated shopping area, this elegantly restored 19th-century building holds luxuriously furnished rooms. **Pros:** rooftop bar with cathedral views; stylish; king-size beds. **Cons:** interior rooms are dark; daytime noise from shopping street; Cathedral bells ring every 15 mins (from 7 am to midnight). $ *Rooms from:* €150 ⊠ *Marqués de Larios 2, Málaga* ☎ 952/222200 ⊕ *www.room-matehotels. com* ⇆ *45 rooms* ⦿ *No Meals.*

🎭 Performing Arts

Málaga's main nightlife districts are Maestranza, between the bullring and the Paseo Marítimo, and the beachfront in the suburb of Pedregalejo. Central Málaga also has a lively bar scene around the Plaza Uncibay and Plaza de la Merced. Malaga holds a biennial flamenco festival with events throughout the year; the next one is in 2023.

Museo de Flamenco Juan Breva

CULTURAL FESTIVALS | The Juan Breva Flamenco Museum offers flamenco performances featuring local artists on Thursday and Saturday at 8:30 pm. Get there early to admire the museum's extensive collection of flamenco memorabilia. ⊠ *Calle Ramón Franquelo 8, Málaga* ☎ 687/607526 ⇆ €15.

Antequera

64 km (40 miles) north of Málaga, 87 km (54 miles) northeast of Ronda.

The town of Antequera holds a surprising number of magnificent baroque monuments (including some 30 churches)—it provides a unique snapshot of a historic Andalusian town, one a world away from the resorts on the Costa del Sol. It became a stronghold of the Moors after their defeat at Córdoba and Seville in the 13th century. Its fall to the Christians in 1410 paved the way for the Reconquest of Granada; the Moors' retreat left a fortress on the town heights.

Next to the town fortress is the former church of **Santa María la Mayor.** Built of sandstone in the 16th century, it has a ribbed vault and is now used as a concert hall. The church of **San Sebastián** has a brick baroque Mudejar tower topped by a winged figure called the Angelote (Big Angel), the symbol of Antequera. The church of **Nuestra Señora del Carmen** (Our Lady of Carmen) has an extraordinary baroque altarpiece that towers to the ceiling. On Thursday, Friday, and Saturday evening, mid-June–mid-September, many monuments are floodlit and open until late.

GETTING HERE AND AROUND

There are several daily buses from Málaga and Ronda to Antequera. Drivers will arrive via the A367 and A384, and should head for the underground parking lot on Calle Diego Ponce in the center of town, which is well signposted. Antequera is small and compact, and most monuments are within easy walking distance, although the castle is up a fairly steep hill. You need a car to visit the Dolmens.

VISITOR INFORMATION

CONTACTS **Municipal Tourist Office.** ⊠ *Calle Encarnación 4, Antequera* ☎ 952/702505 ⊕ *turismo.antequera.es.*

Sights

Archidona
TOWN | About 8 km (5 miles) from Antequera's Lovers' Rock, the village of Archidona winds its way up a steep mountain slope beneath the ruins of a Moorish castle. This unspoiled village is worth a detour for its **Plaza Ochavada,** a magnificent 17th-century octagon resplendent with contrasting red and ocher stone. ⊠ *A45, Archidona.*

★ Dolmens
RUINS | These mysterious prehistoric megalithic burial chambers, just outside Antequera, were built some 4,000 years ago out of massive slabs of stone weighing more than 100 tons each. The best-preserved dolmen is La Menga. Declared UNESCO World Heritage sites in 2016, the Dolmens offer an interesting insight into the area's first inhabitants and their burial customs, well explained at the visitor center. Note that gates close 30 minutes before closing time. ⊠ *Antequera* ✛ *Signposted off Málaga exit rd.* ☎ *952/712206* 🎫 *Free* ⊙ *Closed Mon.*

Laguna de Fuente de Piedra
NATURE PRESERVE | Europe's major nesting area for the greater flamingo is a shallow saltwater lagoon. In February and March, these birds arrive from Africa by the thousands to breed, returning to Africa in August when the water dries up. The visitor center has information on wildlife. Bring binoculars if you have them. On weekends and public holidays in April–June—flamingo hatching time—the visitor center suspends its usual lunchtime closure. Guided tours are available in English (€8 per person; book ahead online). ⊠ *Antequera* ✛ *10 km (6 miles) northwest of Antequera, off A92 to Seville* ☎ *675/645957* ⊕ *www.visitasfuentepiedra.es* 🎫 *Free* ⊙ *Closed lunchtime.*

Museo de la Ciudad de Antequera
ART MUSEUM | The town's pride and joy is *Efebo,* a beautiful bronze statue of a boy that dates back to Roman times. Standing almost 5 feet high, it's on display along with other ancient, medieval, and Renaissance art and artifacts in this impressive museum. ⊠ *Pl. Coso Viejo, Antequera* ☎ *952/708300* ⊕ *turismo.antequera.es* 🎫 *Free* ⊙ *Closed Mon.*

★ Parque Natural del Torcal de Antequera
(*El Torcal Nature Park*)
NATURE SIGHT | Well-marked walking trails (stay on them) guide you at this park, where you can walk among eerie pillars of pink limestone sculpted by eons of wind and rain. Guided hikes (in Spanish only) can be arranged, as well as stargazing in July and August. The visitor center has a small museum. ⊠ *Centro de Visitantes, Antequera* ✛ *10 km (6 miles) south on Ctra. C3310* ☎ *952/243324* 🎫 *Free.*

🍽 Restaurants

Restaurante Arte de Cozina
$$ | SPANISH | As the name suggests, this cozy restaurant offers art in cooking, and its take on typical local dishes is one of the best in Málaga province. The menu is seasonal with an emphasis on local produce; it might include a selection of *porras* (thick, cold soup) and the *choto malagueño* (kid goat in spicy sauce). **Known for:** bienmesabe dessert; traditional dishes; kid goat. Ⓢ *Average main: €16* ⊠ *Calle Calzada 25, Antequera* ☎ *952/840014* ⊕ *artedecozina.com.*

🛏 Hotels

Parador de Antequera
$$$ | HOTEL | Within a few minutes' walk of the historic center, this parador provides a welcome oasis of calm for relaxing after sightseeing, and panoramic vistas of the Peña de los Enamorados can be seen from the gardens, restaurant, and some rooms. **Pros:** pool with

loungers; views; quiet, romantic setting. **Cons:** not all rooms have views; interior design could be too impersonal for some; slightly out of town. $ *Rooms from: €150* ✉ *Pl. García del Olmo 2, Antequera* ☎ *952/840261* ⊕ *www.parador.es* ⚲ 58 *rooms* ⦿ *No Meals.*

The Guadalhorce Valley

About 34 km (21 miles) from Antequera, 66 km (41 miles) from Málaga.

The awe-inspiring **Garganta del Chorro** (Gorge of the Stream) is a deep lime-stone chasm where the Río Guadalhorce churns and snakes its way some 600 feet below the road. The railroad track that worms in and out of tunnels in the cleft was, amazingly, the main line heading north from Málaga for Bobadilla junction and, eventually, Madrid until the AVE track was built.

North of the gorge, the Guadalhorce has been dammed to form a series of scenic reservoirs surrounded by piney hills, which constitute the **Parque de Ardales** nature area. Informal, open-air restau-rants overlook the lakes and a number of picnic spots. Driving along the southern shore of the lake, you reach Ardales and, turning onto the A357, the old spa town of **Carratraca.** Once a favorite watering hole for both Spanish and foreign aristoc-racy, it has a Moorish-style *ayuntamiento* (town hall) and an unusual polygonal bullring. Today the 1830 guesthouse has been renovated into the luxury Villa Padierna spa hotel. The splendid Roman-style marble-and-tile bathhouse has benefited from extensive restoration.

GETTING HERE AND AROUND

Coming from Antequera, take the "El Torcal" exit, turning right onto the A343, then from the village of Alora, follow the minor road north. From Málaga go west on the A357 through Cártama, Pizarra, Carratraca, and Ardales. There's also a train (one service daily) from Málaga to El Chorro station, which is handy if you're planning to walk the Caminito del Rey.

⊙ Sights

★ Caminito del Rey

TRAIL | Clinging to the cliff side in the valley, the "King's Walk" is a suspended catwalk built for a visit by King Alfonso XIII at the beginning of the 19th century. It reopened in March 2015 after many years and a €9 million restoration and is now one of the province's main tourist attractions—as well as one of the world's dizziest. No more than 400 visitors are admitted daily for the walk, which includes nearly 3 km (2 miles) on the boardwalk itself and nearly 5 km (3 miles) on the access paths. It takes four to five hours to complete, and it's a one-way walk, so you need to make your own way back to the start point at the visitor center at the Ardales end (shuttle buses offer regular service; check when the last bus leaves and time your walk according-ly). A certain level of fitness is required and the walk is not recommended for young children or anyone who suffers from vertigo. This is one of the Costa del Sol's busiest attractions; book ahead. ✉ *Valle del Guadalhorce* ⊕ *reservas.cam-initodelrey.info* ⚲ *From €10* ⚲ *Closed Mon.*

Torremolinos

11 km (7 miles) west of Málaga, 16 km (10 miles) northeast of Fuengirola, 43 km (27 miles) east of Marbella.

Torremolinos is all about fun in the sun. It may be more subdued than it was in the action-packed 1960s and '70s, but it remains the gay capital of the Costa del Sol. Scantily attired Northern Europeans of all ages still jam the streets in season, shopping for bargains on Calle San Miguel, downing sangria in the bars of La Nogalera, and congregating in the bars and English pubs. By day, the sunseekers

Beach umbrellas at the edge of the surf in Torremolinos

flock to El Bajondillo and La Carihuela beaches, where, in high summer, it's hard to find towel space on the sand.

Torremolinos has two sections. The first, Central Torremolinos, is built around the Plaza Costa del Sol, refurbished and fully pedestrianized in 2019; Calle San Miguel, the main shopping street; and the brash Plaza de la Nogalera, which is full of overpriced bars and restaurants. The Pueblo Blanco area, off Calle Casablanca, is more pleasant; and the Cuesta del Tajo, at the far end of Calle San Miguel, winds down a steep slope to El Bajondillo beach. Here, crumbling walls, bougainvillea-clad patios, and old cottages hint at the quiet fishing village of bygone years.

The second, more sedate, section of Torremolinos is La Carihuela. To get here, head west out of town on Avenida Carlota Alessandri and turn left following the signs. This more authentically Spanish area still has a few fishermen's cottages and excellent seafood restaurants. The traffic-free esplanade is pleasant for strolling, especially on a summer evening or Sunday at lunchtime, when it's packed with Spanish families. Just 10 minutes' walk north from the beach is the Parque de la Batería, a very pleasant park with fountains, ornamental gardens, and good views of the sea.

GETTING HERE AND AROUND
Torremolinos is a short train or bus journey from Málaga. The town itself is mostly flat, except for the steep slope to El Bajondillo—if you don't want to walk, take the free elevator.

BUS CONTACT Bus Station. ⊠ *Calle Hoyo, Torremolinos* ☎ *No phone.*

TAXI CONTACT Radio Taxi Torremolinos. ⊠ *Torremolinos* ☎ *952/380600.*

VISITOR INFORMATION
CONTACTS Plaza del Remo. ⊠ *Pl. del Remo, Torremolinos* ⊕ *At the center of La Carihuela beach on the seafront* ☎ *952/372956* ⊕ *www.turismotorremolinos.es.***Torremolinos.** ⊠ *Pl. Comunidades Autónomas, Torremolinos* ☎ *952/371909.*

Beaches

La Carihuela

BEACH | FAMILY | This 2-km (1-mile) stretch of sand running from the Torremolinos headland to Puerto Marina in Benalmádena is a perennial favorite with Málaga residents as well as visitors. Several hotels, including the Tropicana, flank a beach promenade that's perfect for a stroll, and there are plenty of beach bars where you can rent a lounger and parasol—and also enjoy some of the best *pescaíto frito* (fried fish) on the coast. The gray sand is cleaned regularly, and the moderate waves make for safe bathing. Towel space (and street parking) is in short supply during the summer months, but outside high season this is a perfect spot for soaking up some winter sunshine. **Amenities:** food and drink; lifeguards (mid-June–mid-September); showers; toilets; water sports. **Best for:** swimming; walking. ✉ *Torremolinos* ⊕ *West end of town, between center and Puerto Marina.*

Restaurants

Casa Juan Los Mellizos

$$ | SEAFOOD | Thanks to the malagueño families who flock here on weekends for the legendary fresh seafood, this restaurant seats 170 inside and 150 outside in an attractive square, one block back from the seafront. Try for a table overlooking the mermaid fountain. **Known for:** rice dishes; fried fish; zarzuela de marisco (seafood stew). [$] *Average main: €14* ✉ *Pl. San Ginés, La Carihuela, Torremolinos* ☎ *952/373512.*

Yate El Cordobes

$$ | SPANISH | Ask the locals which beachfront chiringuito they prefer and El Yate will probably be the answer. Run and owned by an affable cordobés family, the menu holds few surprises, but the seafood is freshly caught, and meat and vegetables are top quality. **Known for:** beachside dining; grilled dorada (sea bream); fresh seafood. [$] *Average main: €15* ✉ *Paseo Marítimo Playamar s/n, Torremolinos* ☎ *952/384956* ⏲ *Closed Jan.*

Hotels

Hotel Fénix

$$$ | HOTEL | One of the handful of adults-only hotels here, Hotel Fénix offers easy access to both the city center via the main entrance and El Bajondillo beach (one block away) via the first floor. **Pros:** handy location; good breakfast; sea views. **Cons:** some rooms have limited view; no kids allowed; not on the beachfront. [$] *Rooms from: €160* ✉ *Av. de las Mercedes 22, Torremolinos* ☎ *952/051994* 🌐 *www.thepalmexperiencehotels.com* 🛏 *126 rooms* 🍴 *No Meals.*

Hotel La Luna Blanca

$$$ | HOTEL | A touch of Asia comes to Torremolinos at Spain's only Japanese hotel, tucked away at the western end of the resort and a few minutes' walk from La Carihuela. **Pros:** free parking; close to La Carihuela; peaceful. **Cons:** steep walk back from the beach; can be difficult to find. [$] *Rooms from: €140* ✉ *Pasaje del Cerrillo 2, Torremolinos* ☎ *952/053711* 🌐 *hotellalunablanca.es* 🛏 *11 rooms* 🍴 *Free Breakfast.*

Hotel MS Tropicana

$$$ | HOTEL | FAMILY | On the beach at the far end of La Carihuela, in one of the most pleasant parts of Torremolinos, this low-rise resort hotel has a loyal following for its friendly and homey style and comfortable, bright rooms. **Pros:** great for families; has its own beach club; surrounded by bars and restaurants. **Cons:** minimum four-night stay in July and August; a half-hour walk to the center of Torremolinos; can be noisy. [$] *Rooms from: €140* ✉ *Trópico 6, La Carihuela* ☎ *951/615102* 🌐 *www.hotelmstropicana.com* 🍴 *Free Breakfast* 🛏 *84 rooms.*

Nightlife

Most nocturnal action is in the center of Torremolinos, and most of its gay bars are in or around the Plaza de la Nogalera, in the center, just off the Calle San Miguel.

Parthenon
DANCE CLUBS | One of the longest-established gay bars in Torremolinos has live music and drag shows most nights. Check the club's Facebook page for details. ⊠ La Nogalera 716, Torremolinos ☎ 678/479381.

Performing Arts

Taberna Flamenca Pepe López
ARTS CENTERS | Many of the better hotels stage flamenco shows, but you may also want to check out this venue, which has shows throughout the year (call or check the website to confirm times). ⊠ Pl. de la Gamba Alegre, Torremolinos ☎ 952/381284 ⊕ www.tabernaflamenca-pepelopez.com ☑ €30.

Fuengirola

16 km (10 miles) west of Torremolinos, 27 km (17 miles) east of Marbella.

Fuengirola is less frenetic than Torremolinos. Many of its waterfront high-rises are vacation apartments that cater to budget-minded sunseekers from Northern Europe and, in summer, a large contingent from Córdoba and other parts of Spain. The town is also a haven for British retirees (with plenty of English and Irish pubs to serve them) and a shopping and business center for the rest of the Costa del Sol. The Tuesday market here is the largest on the coast and a major tourist attraction.

GETTING HERE AND AROUND
Fuengirola is the last stop on the train line from Málaga. There are also regular buses that leave from Málaga's and Marbella's main bus stations.

BIKE RENTAL CONTACT **Route Electric Bike.** ⊠ Paseo Marítimo Rey de España 10, Fuengirola ☎ 681/691178 ⊕ www.phoenixrentalfuengirola.com.

BUS CONTACT **Bus Station.** ⊠ Av. Alfonso XIII 5, Fuengirola ☎ No phone.

TAXI CONTACT **Radio Taxi Fuengirola.** ⊠ Fuengirola ☎ 952/471000.

VISITOR INFORMATION
CONTACTS **Fuengirola Tourist Office.** ⊠ Av. Jesús Santos Rein 6, Fuengirola ☎ 952/467457 ⊕ turismo.fuengirola.es.

 Sights

Bioparc Fuengirola
ZOO | FAMILY | In this modern zoo, wildlife live in a cageless environment as close as possible to their natural habitats. The Bioparc is involved in almost 50 international breeding programs for species in danger of extinction and also supports conservation projects in Africa and several prominent ecological initiatives. Four different habitats have been created, and chimpanzees, big cats, and crocodiles may be viewed, together with other mammals such as white tigers and pygmy hippos, as well as reptiles and birds. There are also daily shows and exhibitions, and various places to get refreshments. In July and August the zoo stays open until 11 pm to allow visitors to see the nocturnal animals. ⊠ Av. José Cela 6, Fuengirola ☎ 952/666301 ⊕ bioparcfuengirola.es ☑ €22.

Castillo de Sohail
CASTLE/PALACE | On the hill at the far west of town is the impressive Castillo de Sohail, built as a fortress against pirate attacks in the 10th century and named for the Moorish term for Fuengirola. Don't miss the views of the valley, sea,

A horseback rider in Fuengirola's El Real de la Feria

and coast from the battlements. Concerts are held here during the summer months. ✉ *Calle Tartessos, Fuengirola* ✣ *15-min walk west from center* ☎ *663/996727* 🎟 *Free* ⏲ *Closed Mon.*

Beaches

Carvajal

BEACH | FAMILY | Lined with low-rises and plenty of greenery, this typically urban beach is between Benalmádena and Fuengirola. One of the Costa del Sol's Blue Flag holders (awarded to the cleanest beaches with the best facilities), the 1¼-km (¾-mile) beach has yellow sand and safe swimming conditions, which make it very popular with families. Beach bars rent lounge chairs and umbrellas, and there's regular live music in the summer. Like most beaches in the area, Playa Carvajal is packed throughout July and August, and most summer weekends, but at any other time this beach is quite quiet. The Benalmádena end has a seafront promenade and street parking, and the Carvajal train station (on the Fuengirola–Málaga line) is just a few yards from the beach. **Amenities:** food and drink; lifeguards (mid-June–mid-September); parking (no fee); showers; toilets; water sports. **Best for:** sunrise; swimming. ✉ *N340, Km 214–216, Fuengirola.*

Restaurants

Bodega Charolais

$$$ | SPANISH | Andalusian cuisine meets Basque tradition at this authentic restaurant in the heart of the older part of Fuengirola. Dine on fresh local produce either outside on the pleasant corner terrace or inside the rustic dining room. **Known for:** excellent wine list; Basque-Andalusian fusion; duck. [$] *Average main: €18* ✉ *Calle Larga 14, Fuengirola* ☎ *952/475441* 🌐 *www.bodegacharolais.com.*

★ Sollo

$$$$ | SPANISH | Perched high in the hills above Fuengirola, this is one of the best seafood restaurants on the Costa del Sol.

Michelin-starred chef Diego Gallegos champions sustainable and healthy cuisine, and his on-site aquaponics facility raises most of the fish and vegetables used here. **Known for:** coastal views; sustainable and innovative cuisine; Latin American touches in dishes. $ *Average main: €130* ⊠ *Higuerón Hotel, Avda. del Higuerón 48, Reserva del Higuerón, Fuengirola* ☎ *951/385 622* ⊕ *www.sollo. es* ⊙ *Closed Sun. and Mon. No lunch.*

★ Vegetalia

$ | VEGETARIAN | This attractive, long-established vegetarian restaurant has a large, pleasant dining space decorated with vibrant artwork. It's best known for its excellent, vast, and bargain-priced lunchtime buffet, which includes salads and hot dishes like red-lentil croquettes, vegetable paella, and soy "meatballs." Leave room for the house-made desserts, all delicious. **Known for:** soy meatballs; vegetable dishes; lunch buffet. $ *Average main: €10* ⊠ *Calle Santa Isabel 8, Fuengirola* ☎ *952/586031* ⊕ *www. restaurantevegetalia.com* ⊙ *No dinner. Closed July, Aug., and Sun.*

Hotels

Hostal Italia

$ | B&B/INN | Right off the main plaza and near the beach, this deservedly popular family-run hotel has bright and comfortable but small rooms; guests return year after year, particularly during the October *feria* (fair). **Pros:** most rooms have balconies; friendly owners; surrounded by restaurants and bars. **Cons:** some street noise; rooms are small. $ *Rooms from: €75* ⊠ *Calle de la Cruz 1, Fuengirola* ☎ *952/474193* ⊕ *www.hostalitalia.com* ⤳ *40 rooms* ¶○¶ *No Meals.*

Hotel Florida Spa

$$$ | HOTEL | This glossy spa hotel has a sophisticated edge on its high-rise neighbors, with light and airy rooms and private terraces overlooking the port and surrounding beach. **Pros:** views of mountains and coast; in-house spa; great location. **Cons:** three-night minimum stay in July and August; very small pool; can be an overload of tour groups. $ *Rooms from: €150* ⊠ *Calle Dr. Galvez Ginachero, Fuengirola* ☎ *952/922700* ⊕ *www. hotel-florida.es* ⤳ *184 rooms* ¶○¶ *Free Breakfast.*

Mijas

8 km (5 miles) north of Fuengirola, 18 km (11 miles) west of Torremolinos.

Mijas is in the foothills of the sierra just north of the coast. Long ago foreign retirees discovered the pretty, whitewashed town, and though the large, touristy square may look like an extension of the Costa, beyond it are hilly residential streets with timeworn homes. Try to visit late in the afternoon, after the tour buses have left.

Mijas extends down to the coast, and the coastal strip between Fuengirola and Marbella is officially called **Mijas-Costa.** This area has several hotels, restaurants, and golf courses.

GETTING HERE AND AROUND

Buses leave Fuengirola every half hour for the 25-minute drive through hills peppered with large houses. If you have a car and don't mind a mildly hair-raising drive, take the more dramatic approach from Benalmádena-Pueblo, a winding mountain road with splendid views. You can park in the underground parking garage signposted on the approach to the village.

VISITOR INFORMATION

CONTACTS Mijas Tourist Office. ⊠ *Av. Virgen de la Peña, Mijas* ☎ *952/589034* ⊕ *turismo.mijas.es.*

⊙ Sights

Centro de Arte Contemporáneo

ARTS CENTER | This modern art center contains more than 400 works from the Remedios Medina Collection, including the second largest collection of Picasso ceramics in the world. A total of 130 works by Picasso are on display alongside paintings, etchings, and other pieces by artists such as Dalí, Braque, and Foujita. ⊠ *Calle Málaga 28, Mijas* ☎ *952/590442* ⊕ *www.cacmijas.info* ⚐ *€3* ⊙ *Closed Sun.*

Iglesia Parroquial de la Inmaculada Concepción (*Immaculate Conception*)

CHURCH | This delightful village church, up the hill from the bullring, is worth a visit. It's impeccably decorated, especially at Easter, and the terrace and spacious gardens have a splendid panoramic view. ⊠ *Pl. de la Constitución, Mijas* ⚐ *Free.*

Museo Mijas

ART MUSEUM | This charming museum occupies the former *ayuntamiento*. Its themed rooms, including an old-fashioned bakery and *bodega*, surround a patio, and regular art exhibitions are mounted in the upstairs gallery. ⊠ *Pl. de la Libertad, Mijas* ☎ *952/590380* ⚐ *€1.*

🍴 Restaurants

Restaurante El Mirlo Blanco

$$$ | SPANISH | In an old house on the pleasant Plaza de la Constitución, this restaurant is run by a Basque family that's been in the Costa del Sol restaurant business since 1968. The cozy indoor dining room, with log fire for cooler days, is welcoming and intimate, with original and noteworthy artwork interspersed among the arches, hanging plants, and traditional white paintwork. **Known for:** Grand Marnier soufflé; reputation as a local institution; Basque specialties. ⓢ *Average main: €22* ⊠ *Calle Cuesta de la Villa 13, Mijas* ☎ *952/485700* ⊕ *www.mirlo-blanco.es* ⊙ *Closed Tues. and Jan.*

Tomillo Limón

$ | INTERNATIONAL | A bright and airy tapas bar offering traditional Spanish staples—croquettes and patatas bravas—as well more modern takes on quick bites. Try the *pan bao de cochinillo* (suckling pig bao with peanuts and mint) or the *torta de boquerones y anchoas* (anchovy toast). **Known for:** quick bites, delicious desserts; patatas bravas. ⓢ *Average main: €6* ⊠ *Av. Virgen de la Peña 11,* ☎ *951/437298* ⊙ *Closed Mon.*

Marbella

27 km (17 miles) west of Fuengirola, 28 km (17 miles) east of Estepona, 50 km (31 miles) southeast of Ronda.

Thanks to its year-round mild climate and a spectacular natural backdrop, Marbella has been a playground for the rich and famous since the 1950s, when wealthy Europeans first put it on the map as a high-end tourist destination. Grand hotels, luxury restaurants, and multimillion-euro mansions line the waterfront. The town is a mixture of a charming *casco antiguo* (old quarter), where visitors can get a taste of the real Andalusia; an ordinary, tree-lined main thoroughfare (Avenida Ricardo Soriano) flanked by high-rises; and a buzzing Paseo Marítimo (Seafront Promenade), which now stretches some 10 km (6 miles) to San Pedro in the west. The best beaches are to the east of the town between El Rosario and the Don Carlos Hotel. Puerto Banús, the place to see and be seen during the summer, is Spain's most luxurious marina, home to some of the most expensive yachts you will see anywhere. A bevy of restaurants, bars, and designer boutiques is nearby.

GETTING HERE AND AROUND

There are regular buses to and from the surrounding resorts and towns, including Fuengirola, Estepona (both every 30 minutes), and Málaga (hourly).

BUS CONTACT Bus Station. ✉ *Av. Trapiche, Marbella* ☎ *No phone.*

VISITOR INFORMATION CONTACTS Marbella Tourist Office. ✉ *Pl. de los Naranjos 1, Marbella* ☎ *952/768707.*

Sights

Museo del Grabado Español Contemporáneo

ART MUSEUM | In a restored 16th-century palace in the casco antiguo, this museum shows some of the best in contemporary Spanish prints. Some of Spain's most famous 20th-century artists, including Picasso, Miró, and Tàpies, are on show. Temporary exhibitions are also mounted here. ✉ *Calle Hospital Bazán, Marbella* ☎ *952/765741* 🖃 *€3* ☉ *Closed Sun.*

Plaza de los Naranjos

PLAZA/SQUARE | Marbella's appeal lies in the heart of its *casco antiguo*, which remains surprisingly intact. Here, a block or two back from the main highway, narrow alleys of whitewashed houses cluster around the central Plaza de los Naranjos (Orange Tree Square), where colorful, albeit pricey, restaurants vie for space under the orange trees. Climb onto what remains of the old fortifications and stroll along the Calle Virgen de los Dolores to the Plaza de Santo Cristo. ✉ *Marbella.*

Puerto Banús

MARINA/PIER | Marbella's wealth glitters most brightly along the Golden Mile, a tiara of star-studded clubs, restaurants, and hotels west of town and stretching from Marbella to Puerto Banús. A mosque and the former residence of Saudi Arabia's late King Fahd reveal the influence of Middle Eastern oil money in this wealthy enclave. About 7 km (4½ miles) west of central Marbella (between Km 175 and Km 174), a sign indicates the turnoff leading down to Puerto Banús. Though now hemmed in by a belt of high-rises, Marbella's plush marina, with 915 berths, is a gem of ostentatious wealth; a Spanish answer to St. Tropez. Huge yachts and countless expensive stores and restaurants make for a glittering parade of beautiful people that continues long into the night. The backdrop is an Andalusian pueblo—built in the 1960s to resemble the fishing villages that once lined this coast. ✉ *Marbella.*

Beaches

Marbella East Side Beaches

BEACH | FAMILY | Marbella's best beaches are to the east of town, between the Monteros and Don Carlos hotels, and include Costa Bella and El Alicate. The 6-km (4-mile) stretch of yellow sand is lined with residential complexes and sand dunes (some of the last remaining on the Costa del Sol). The sea remains shallow for some distance, so bathing is safe. Beach bars catering to all tastes and budgets dot the sands, as do several exclusive beach clubs (look for Nikki Beach, for instance, where luxury yachts are anchored offshore). Tourists and locals flock to these beaches in the summer, but take a short walk away from the beach bars and parking lots, and you'll find a less crowded spot for your towel. **Amenities:** food and drink; lifeguards (mid-June–mid-September); parking (fee in summer); showers; toilets; water sports. **Best for:** swimming; walking. ✉ *A7, Km 187–193, Marbella.*

Playas de Puerto Banús

BEACH | These small sandy coves are packed almost to bursting in the summer, when they're crowded with young, bronzed, perfect bodies: topless sunbathing is almost de rigueur. The sea is shallow along the entire stretch, which is practically wave-free and seems warmer than other beaches nearby. In the area are excellent Caribbean-style beach bars with good seafood and fish, as well as lots of options for sundown drinks. This is also home to the famous Ocean and Sala Beach clubs with their oversize sun beds, Champagne, and nightlong parties.

Amenities: food and drink; lifeguards (mid-June–mid-September); showers; toilets; water sports. **Best for:** partiers; sunset; swimming. ⊠ *Puerto Banús, Marbella.*

🍴 Restaurants

Altamirano

$$ | SEAFOOD | The modest, old-fashioned exterior of this local favorite is a bit deceiving: inside you'll be greeted not with stodgy decor but rather with three spacious dining rooms with Spanish soccer memorabilia, photos of famous patrons, and tanks of fish. Seafood choices run long and include fried or grilled squid, spider crab, lobster, sole, red snapper, and sea bass. **Known for:** outdoor dining; homemade rice pudding; seafood. $ *Average main: €14* ⊠ *Pl. Altamirano, Marbella* ☎ *952/824932* ⊕ *www.baraltamirano.es.*

★ Cappuccino

$$$ | INTERNATIONAL | Just under the Don Pepe Hotel and right on the promenade, this is the perfect spot for some refreshment before or after you tackle a long stroll along the seafront. Done in navy and white with wicker chairs, this outdoor café-restaurant has a fitting nautical theme, and if the temperature drops, blankets and gas heaters are at the ready. **Known for:** stylish terrace; brunch; ocean views. $ *Average main: €20* ⊠ *Calle de José Meliá, Marbella* ☎ *952/868790.*

Kava Marbella

$$$$ | INTERNATIONAL | This rising star on the Marbella dining scene might be a new arrival, but chef Fernando Alcalá, at just 25, is already a rising star and seems set to pick up the baton from Dani García, whose Michelin-starred restaurant closed in fall 2019. Simplicity is his key to success with dishes consisting solely of a main and secondary ingredient plus sauce. **Known for:** good-value tasting menu; innovative cuisine; famous cheesecake. $ *Average main: €55* ⊠ *Av.*

Antonio Belón 4, ☎ *952/824108* ⊕ *www.kavamarbella.com* ⊗ *Closed Sun. and Mon.*

La Niña del Pisto

$ | SPANISH | Tucked away in the *casco antiguo*, this small venue with upstairs and downstairs dining offers a taste of Córdoba tapas and Montilla wine in Marbella. There is a good choice of tapas and sharing plates, including homemade croquettes, cold cuts, fried fish (the squid is particularly good), and the house *pisto* (ratatouille) served with a fried egg or pork. **Known for:** Montilla wine; tapas; pisto. $ *Average main: €10* ⊠ *Calle Lázaro 2, Marbella* ☎ *633/320022* ⊗ *No lunch. Closed Sun. and Mon.*

Messina

$$$$ | MEDITERRANEAN | Between the *casco antiguo* and the seafront, this innovative restaurant has an unpromising plain exterior, but forge ahead: the interior's chocolate browns and deep reds make for cozy surroundings for a quiet dinner from chef Mauricio Giovanni, who renewed his Michelin star in 2020. The menu has an international slant, with more than a sprinkling of Spanish cuisine in its unusual fusion dishes. **Known for:** cozy atmosphere; innovative dining; good-value tasting menus. $ *Average main: €25* ⊠ *Av. Severo Ochoa 12, Marbella* ☎ *952/864895* ⊕ *www.restaurante-messina.com* ⊗ *Closed Sun. No lunch.*

Paellas y Más

$$$ | SPANISH | Located on the west side of town, about a 10-minute walk from the center, this modern restaurant specializes in rice dishes; there are 14 on the menu, including the signature baked rice with pork and the squid rice with prawns and chickpeas. *Fideuá* (similar to paella but made with noodles instead of rice) also features on the menu. There's a good choice of sharing plates of croquettes, cold cuts, and seafood, as well as innovative salads. **Known for:** baked rice with pork; rice dishes; fideuá (a noodle version of paella). $ *Average main:*

€20 ✉ Calle Hermanos Salom 3, Marbella ☎ 952/822511 🌐 www.restaurantepaellasymas.com.

Hotels

Boho Club

$$$$ | **HOTEL** | At the far western end of the Golden Mile (and a few minutes' walk from the beach and Puerto Banús), Boho Club offers a chilled vibe in Scandinavian-style surroundings. **Pros:** excellent restaurant on-site; stunning interiors; pool and gardens with mountain views. **Cons:** some distance from Marbella center; traffic noise in some rooms; expensive. [$] *Rooms from: €400* ✉ *Urb. Lomas de Río Verde, 144, Ctra. N-340, Km 176, Marbella* ☎ *952/157221* 🌐 *bohoclub.com* 🍴 *No Meals* 🛏 *39 rooms.*

Hotel Lima

$$$ | **HOTEL** | Two blocks from the beach and a short walk from the *casco antiguo* stands one of Marbella's oldest hotels, which had a total overhaul in 2019 to elevate it to a four-star property. **Pros:** open all year; downtown location is good for town and beach; newly refurbished. **Cons:** street noise in some rooms; room size varies considerably; lacks character of other properties. [$] *Rooms from: €160* ✉ *Av. Antonio Belón 2, Marbella* ☎ *952/770500* 🌐 *hotellimamarbella.com* 🛏 *61 rooms* 🍴 *No Meals.*

La Morada Mas Hermosa

$$$ | **HOTEL** | On one of Marbella's prettiest plant-filled pedestrian streets (on the right just up Calle Ancha), this small hotel has a warm, homey feel, and the rooms are lovely. **Pros:** short walk from the beach; real character; quiet street, yet near the action. **Cons:** no parking; some rooms accessed by steep stairs; breakfast is a little basic. [$] *Rooms from: €130* ✉ *Calle Ancha 12, Marbella* ☎ *952/924467* 🌐 *www.lamoradamashermosa.com* 🕒 *Closed Jan.–mid-Feb.* 🛏 *7 rooms* 🍴 *No Meals.*

La Villa Marbella

$$ | **HOTEL** | Just a short walk from the Plaza de los Naranjos, these private rooms and apartments, decorated in Asian style with Thai screens, offer a quiet hideaway. **Pros:** good breakfast (but not always included); central but quiet location; rooftop terrace and pool. **Cons:** no on-site parking; multiple buildings; three-night minimum stay in July and August. [$] *Rooms from: €120* ✉ *Calle Príncipe 10, Marbella* ☎ *952/766220* 🌐 *www.lavillamarbella.com* 🛏 *12 rooms* 🍴 *No Meals.*

★ **Marbella Club**

$$$$ | **HOTEL** | The grande dame of Marbella hotels offers luxurious rooms, tropical grounds, and sky-high rates; the sense of seclusion is emphasized by its lofty palm trees, dazzling flower beds, and a beachside tropical pool area. **Pros:** some bungalow rooms have private pools; superb facilities; luxurious, classic hotel. **Cons:** a drive from Marbella's restaurants and nightlife; three-night minimum stay in July and August; extremely expensive. [$] *Rooms from: €900* ✉ *Blvd. Principe Alfonso von Hohenlohe at Ctra. de Cádiz, Km 178, Marbella* ✥ *3 km (2 miles) west of Marbella* ☎ *952/822211* 🌐 *www.marbellaclub.com* 🛏 *130 rooms* 🍴 *No Meals.*

★ **The Town House**

$$$$ | **HOTEL** | In a choice location on one of old Marbella's prettiest squares, this former family home is now a luxurious boutique hotel. **Pros:** upbeat design; rooftop terrace and bar; great central location. **Cons:** while charming, the attic rooms are not for tall guests; street-facing rooms are noisy on weekends; no parking. [$] *Rooms from: €185* ✉ *Pl. Tetuan, Calle Alderete 7, Marbella* ☎ *952/901791* 🌐 *www.townhousemarbella.com* 🛏 *9 rooms* 🍴 *Free Breakfast.*

Nightlife

Casino Marbella
GATHERING PLACES | This chic gambling spot is in the Hotel Andalucía Plaza, just west of Puerto Banús. Shorts and sports shoes are not allowed, and passports are required. It's open daily 8 pm–4 am (9 pm–5 am in August). ✉ *Hotel Andalucía Pl., N340, Marbella* ☎ *952/814000* 🌐 *www.casinomarbella.com.*

La Sala Banús
DANCE CLUBS | This is one of Marbella's most popular nightspots for "older" clubbers (those out or nearly out of their twenties). Dine in before you dance to the live music. ✉ *Calle Juan Belmonte, near bullring, Puerto Banús* ☎ *952/814145* 🌐 *www.lasalabanus.com.*

Olivia Valére
DANCE CLUBS | Marbella's most famous nightspot, with an impressive celebrity guest list, attracts a sophisticated crowd with its roster of big-name DJs and stylish surroundings that resemble a Moorish palace. To get here, head inland from the town's mosque (it's easy to spot). Doors open at midnight (daily in July and August; Friday and Saturday only, September–June) and close at 7 am. ✉ *Ctra. de Istán, Km 0.8, Marbella* ☎ *952/828861.*

Ojén

10 km (6 miles) north of Marbella.

For a contrast to the glamour of the coast, drive up to Ojén, in the hills above Marbella. Take note of the beautiful pottery and, if you're here the first week in August, don't miss the **Festival de Flamenco,** which attracts some of Spain's most respected flamenco names, including Juan Peńa Fernández (aka El Lebrijano), Miguel Póveda, and Marina Heredia. Four kilometers (2½ miles) from Ojén is the **Refugio del Juanar,** a former hunting lodge in the heart of the Sierra Blanca, at the southern edge of the Serranía de Ronda, a mountainous wilderness. A walking trail takes you a mile from the *refugio* to the *mirador* (lookout), with a sweeping view of the Costa del Sol and the coast of North Africa.

GETTING HERE AND AROUND

Approximately three buses leave from the Marbella main bus station for Ojén on weekdays, two on Saturday, and none on Sunday.

Hotels

La Posada del Angel
$$ | **B&B/INN** | With friendly Dutch owners and rooms with lots of traditional Andalusian features and even a few Moroccan touches, this hotel makes a perfect rural retreat. **Pros:** chance to sample Andalusian village life; some rooms have terraces with a view; heated pool. **Cons:** minimum two-night stay mid-July–mid-September; slightly off the beaten track; could be too quiet for some. [$] *Rooms from: €98* ✉ *Calle Mesones 21, Ojén* ☎ *952/881808* 🌐 *www.laposadadel-angel.net* 🛏 *16 rooms* 🍴 *Free Breakfast.*

Estepona

17 km (11 miles) west of San Pedro de Alcántara, 22 km (14 miles) west of Marbella.

Estepona is a pleasant and relatively tranquil seaside resort, despite being surrounded by lots of urban developments. The beach, more than 1 km (½ mile) long, has better-quality sand than the Costa norm, and the promenade is lined with well-kept, aromatic flower gardens. The gleaming white **Puerto Deportivo** is packed with bars and restaurants, serving everything from fresh fish to Chinese food. Back from the main Avenida de España, the old quarter of cobbled narrow streets and squares is surprisingly unspoiled and decorated with flowerpots. Keep your eyes open for the many modern sculptures in the squares and 60-odd giant murals that cover entire facades throughout the town. The tourist office provides a guide to the artists and a mural map.

GETTING HERE AND AROUND

Buses run every half hour 6:30 am–11 pm from Marbella to Estepona and there are around four buses a day from Málaga Airport. The town is compact enough to make most places accessible via foot.

BUS CONTACT Bus Station. ⊠ *Av. de España, Estepona* ☎ *No phone.*

VISITOR INFORMATION
CONTACTS Estepona Tourist Office.
⊠ *Pl. de las Flores s/n, Estepona*
☎ *952/802002.*

Sights

Museo de Arte de la Diputación
ART MUSEUM | Housed in the historic 18th-century Casa de las Tejerinas palace, this art museum, which opened in 2018 and is known as MAD, showcases contemporary Andalusian and Spanish artists. Focusing on work produced this century, the museum has 50 pieces from artists including Málaga-born Dadi Dreucol and Chema Lumbreras, Santiago Idáñez from Seville, and Judas Arrieta from the Basque Country. Also worthy of note are the central patio and ornate facade. ⊠ *Casa de las Tejerinas, Pl. de las Flores, Estepona* ☎ *952/069695* ⊕ *www. madantequera.com* ☾ *Closed Sun. and Mon.* ⌨ *Free.*

★ Orchidarium
GARDEN | This lush green space in the middle of Estepona houses Europe's largest orchidarium. More than 1,600 species, from South America and Asia, are exhibited under a futuristic 100-foot glass dome containing a giant cascade. Guided tours are available, but the garden is only open for a half-day on Sunday (in the morning). ⊠ *Calle Terraza*

86, Estepona ☎ *951/517074* ⊕ *www. orchidariumestepona.com* ⌨ *€3.*

Beaches

El Saladillo
BEACH | Something of a Costa del Sol secret, this quiet 4-km (2½-mile) beach of gray sand has long, empty stretches with plenty of room for towels, even in high summer, making it a great place to relax, walk, or swim. The water's safe for swimming when waves are low, but watch out for the undertow when it's windy. Between San Pedro and Estepona, and flanked by residential developments, El Saladillo has the occasional beach bar. **Amenities:** food and drink; lifeguards (mid-June–mid-September); showers; toilets; water sports. **Best for:** solitude; sunset; walking. ⊠ *A7, Km 166–172, Estepona.*

Restaurants

La Casa del Rey
$$$ | SPANISH | Just a block from Plaza de las Flores, a 200-year-old building hides this sleek, modern wine bar, serving some of the best tapas in town. Choose from a long list of hot and cold *pinchos* (small snacks)—the *rabo de toro en hojaldre* (oxtail in pastry) and *graten de bacalao* (cod gratin) are perennial favorites—tostas, and miniburgers, or from the à la carte menu, where meat dishes star. **Known for:** rabo de toro; tapas; wine list. Ⓢ *Average main: €18* ⊠ *Calle Raphael 7, Estepona* ☎ *951/965414* ⊕ *lacasadelreyestepona. com.*

La Escollera
$$ | SPANISH | Located at the heart of Estepona port, this is one of the best places on the western Costa del Sol to try simply cooked fresh fish, delivered daily off the restaurant's own boat. The very busy venue (on weekends it's packed to bursting) has excellent service and a quick turnaround so you never

have to wait very long for a table. **Known for:** authentic atmosphere; liveliness on weekends; fresh fish. $ *Average main: €15* ⊠ *Calle Puerto Pesquero s/n,* ⌖ *Near lighthouse at east end of port* ☎ *952/806354* ⊘ *No dinner Sun. Closed Mon.*

 Hotels

Kempinski Hotel Bahía

$$$$ | **RESORT** | Entirely refurbished in 2018, this luxury resort, between the coastal highway and the sea, looks like a cross between a Moroccan casbah and a take on the Hanging Gardens of Babylon, with tropical gardens and a succession of large swimming pools meandering down to the beach. **Pros:** all rooms have balconies with sea views; excellent amenities; great location. **Cons:** so-so beach; expensive; some distance from Estepona. $ *Rooms from: €490* ⊠ *Playa El Padrón, Ctra. A7, Km 159, Estepona* ☎ *952/809500* ⊕ *www.kempinski.com* ⦿ *No Meals* ⇴ *144 rooms.*

Casares

20 km (12 miles) northwest of Estepona.

The mountain village of Casares lies high above Estepona in the Sierra Bermeja, with streets of ancient white houses piled one on top of the other, perched on the slopes beneath a ruined but impressive Moorish castle. The heights afford stunning views over orchards, olive groves, and woods to the Mediterranean sparkling in the distance.

GETTING HERE AND AROUND

Buses are few and far between to Casares and the best way to visit the village is by your own means. Be prepared for some steep slopes when you sightsee.

🍴 Restaurants

Sarmiento

$$$ | **SPANISH** | **FAMILY** | This restaurant has a loyal following among locals and visitors with its stunning location—the terrace has far-reaching views over the village and to the Strait of Gibraltar (don't miss the eagles soaring the thermals above you)—and delicious food. Local produce takes center stage, and you can try Casares cheese, goat, and lamb as well as locally sourced tropical fruits and fresh fish from the coast. **Known for:** meat croquettes; Casares cheese, goat, and lamb; stunning views. $ *Average main: €18* ⊠ *Ctra. de Casares, Km 12.5, Estepona* ☎ *952/895035* ⊕ *restaurante-sarmiento.com* ⊘ *No dinner Sun. and Mon. Closed Tues.*

Tarifa

74 km (46 miles) southwest of San Roque.

Tarifa's strong winds helped keep it off the tourist maps for years, but now it is Europe's biggest center for windsurfing and kiteboarding, and the wide, white-sand beaches stretching north of the town have become a huge attraction. Those winds have proven a source of wealth in more direct ways also, via the electricity created by vast wind farms on the surrounding hills. This town at the southernmost tip of mainland Europe—where the Mediterranean and the Atlantic meet—has continued to prosper. Downtown cafés, which not that long ago were filled with men playing dominoes and drinking *anís* (a Spanish liquor), now serve croissants with their *café con leche* and make fancy tapas for a cosmopolitan crowd. The lovely hilltop village of Vejer de la Frontera, 51 km (32 miles) west of Tarifa, is an easy side trip, and its coastline offers stunning beaches and the historic Cape Trafalgar, where the

Windsurfing at Tarifa

English Armada beat Napoléon in an epic naval battle in 1805.

GETTING HERE AND AROUND
Buses connect Tarifa and Vejer de la Frontera with Algeciras, but this is an area best visited by car, especially if you want to explore the coastline. There's no public transportation to Baelo Claudia or NMAC.

VISITOR INFORMATION
CONTACTS Tarifa Tourist Office. ☒ *Paseo de la Alameda s/n, Tarifa* ☎ *956/680993* ⊕ *turismodetarifa.com.*

Sights

★ Baelo Claudia
RUINS | On the Atlantic coast, 24 km (15 miles) north of Tarifa, stand the impressive Roman ruins of Baelo Claudia, once a thriving production center of garum, a salty, pungent fish paste appreciated in Rome. The visitor center includes a museum. Concerts are regularly held at the restored amphitheater during the summer months. ☒ *Tarifa* ✛ *Take N340*
toward Cádiz 16 km (10 miles), then turn left for Bolonia on CA8202* ☎ *956/106797* ☽ *Closed Mon.* ☒ *€2.*

Castle
CASTLE/PALACE | Tarifa's 10th-century castle is famous for the siege of 1292, when the defender Guzmán el Bueno refused to surrender even though the attacking Moors threatened to kill his captive son. In defiance, he flung his own dagger down to them, shouting, "Here, use this," or something to that effect (they did indeed kill his son). The Spanish military turned the castle over to the town in the mid-1990s, and it now has a **museum** about Guzmán and the sacrifice of his son. There are impressive views of the African coast from the battlements and towers. ☒ *Av. Fuerza Armadas, Tarifa* ☒ *€4* ☽ *Closed Mon.*

★ Fundación NMAC (*Contemporary Art and Nature*)
ART MUSEUM | The rolling hills and forest between Tarifa and Vejer provide the perfect stage for this unique outdoor art

museum. The sculptures and installations are placed along the guided route and in restored army barracks, and include works by international and Spanish artists such as Olafur Eliasson, Marina Abramovic, James Turrell, Pascale Marthine Tayou, and Fernando Sánchez Castillo. Visit first thing to avoid the crowds and get the best of the birdsong. ✉ *Dehesa de Montenmedio, Ctra. N340, Km 42.5, Vejer de la Frontera* ☎ *956/455134* 🌐 *www.fundacionnmac.org* 🎟 *€5 (free 1st Sun. of month)* 🕓 *Closed Mon.*

Beaches

Playa Los Lances
BEACH | This part of the Atlantic coast consists of miles of white and mostly unspoiled beaches, and this, to the north of Tarifa and the town's main beach, is one of the longest. Backed by low-lying scrub and lagoons, the beach is also close to the odd campground, boho-chic hotel, and kitesurfing school. Its windswept sands make for perfect kitesurfing: together with Punta Paloma (just up the coast) it's where you'll see most sails surfing the waves and wind. Amenities are concentrated at the Tarifa end of the beach, where there are a few bars and cafés, usually open mid-June–mid-September, and this is naturally where the crowds congregate in the summer. Otherwise, most of the beach is deserted year-round. Swimming is safe here, except in high winds, when there's a strong undertow. **Amenities:** food and drink (mid-June–mid-September); lifeguards; showers; toilets. **Best for:** solitude; sunset; walking; windsurfing. ✉ *Tarifa.*

Hotels

★ Hotel V... Vejer
$$$$ | **HOTEL** | The spacious rooms at this restored 16th-century mansion in the heart of the spectacular village of Vejer de la Frontera overlook the coast and the countryside with white villages speckling the horizon. **Pros:** rooftop terrace; exquisite decor; stunning views. **Cons:** no on-site parking; no elevator; roads around hotel too narrow to drive. [$] *Rooms from: €225* ✉ *Calle Rosario 11–13, Vejer de la Frontera* ☎ *956/451757* 🌐 *www.hotelv-vejer.com* 🛏 *11 rooms* 🍴 *Free Breakfast.*

Hurricane Hotel
$$$$ | **HOTEL** | Surrounded by lush subtropical gardens and fronting the beach, the Hurricane is one of the best-loved hip hotels on this stretch of coastline, famous for its Club Mistral wind- and kitesurfing school and its horseback-riding center. **Pros:** excellent restaurant; lovely gardens with beach access; fun and sophisticated. **Cons:** some noise from the highway; rooms are plain; 6 km (3½ miles) from Tarifa proper. [$] *Rooms from: €190* ✉ *N340, Km 78, Tarifa* ☎ *956/684919* 🌐 *www.hotelhurricane.com* 🛏 *21 rooms* 🍴 *Free Breakfast.*

Gibraltar

20 km (12 miles) east of Algeciras, 77 km (48 miles) southwest of Marbella.

The Rock of today is a bizarre anomaly of Moorish, Spanish, and—especially—British influences. There are double-decker buses, "bobbies" in helmets, and red mailboxes. Millions of pounds have been spent in developing its tourist potential, and a steady flow of expat Brits comes here from Spain to shop at Morrisons supermarket and other stores. This tiny British colony, whose impressive silhouette dominates the strait between Spain and Morocco, was one of the two Pillars of Hercules in ancient times, marking the western limits of the known world and commanding the narrow pathway between the Mediterranean Sea and the Atlantic Ocean. The Moors, headed by Tariq ibn Ziyad, seized the peninsula in 711, preliminary to the conquest of Spain.

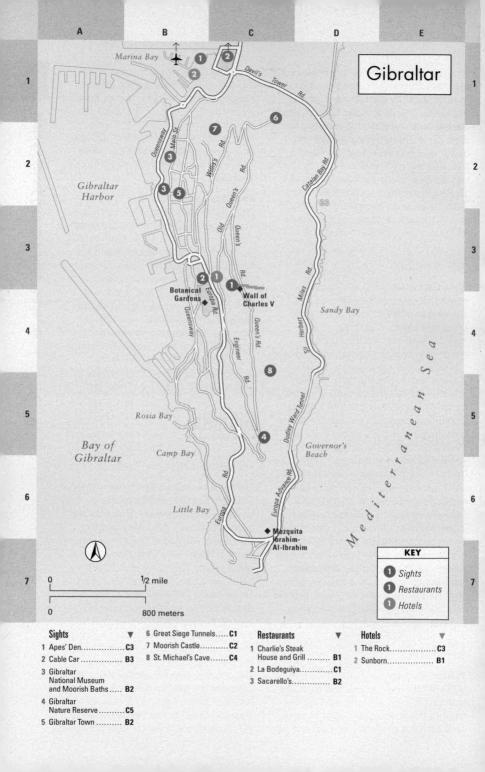

Gibraltar

Marina Bay

Devil's Tower Rd.

Gibraltar Harbor

Queensway

Main St.

Willis's Rd.

Queen's Rd.

Catalan Bay Rd.

33

Old Queen's Rd.

Queen's Rd.

Europa Rd.

Botanical Gardens

Wall of Charles V

Queensway

Sir Herbert Miles Rd.

Sandy Bay

Engineer Rd.

Rosia Bay

Camp Bay

Bay of Gibraltar

Dudley Ward Tunnel

Governor's Beach

Little Bay

Europa Rd.

Europa Advance Rd.

Mezquita Ibrahim-Al-Ibrahim

Mediterranean Sea

0 ___ 1/2 mile

0 ___ 800 meters

KEY

1 *Sights*

1 *Restaurants*

1 *Hotels*

Sights ▼

1 Apes' Den.................**C3**

2 Cable Car **B3**

3 Gibraltar National Museum and Moorish Baths **B2**

4 Gibraltar Nature Reserve **C5**

5 Gibraltar Town **B2**

6 Great Siege Tunnels.....**C1**

7 Moorish Castle...........**C2**

8 St. Michael's Cave.......**C4**

Restaurants ▼

1 Charlie's Steak House and Grill **B1**

2 La Bodeguiya.............**C1**

3 Sacarello's...............**B2**

Hotels ▼

1 The Rock.................**C3**

2 Sunborn.................**B1**

The Spaniards recaptured Tariq's Rock in 1462. The English, heading an Anglo-Dutch fleet in the War of the Spanish Succession, gained control in 1704, and, after several years of local skirmishes, Gibraltar was finally ceded to Great Britain in 1713 by the Treaty of Utrecht. Spain has been trying to get it back ever since. In 1779 a combined French and Spanish force laid siege to the Rock for three years, to no avail. During the Napoleonic Wars, Gibraltar served as Admiral Horatio Nelson's base for the decisive naval Battle of Trafalgar, and during the two world wars, it served the Allies well as a naval and air base. In 1967 Franco closed the land border with Spain to strengthen his claims over the colony, and it remained closed until 1985.

There are likely few places in the world that you enter by walking or driving across an airport runway, but that's what happens in Gibraltar. First you show your passport; then you make your way out onto the narrow strip of land linking Spain's Línea with Britain's Rock. Unless you have a good reason to take your car—such as loading up on cheap gas or duty-free goods—you're best off leaving it in a guarded parking area in La Línea, the Spanish border town.

In 2021, tensions between Gibraltar and Spain lessened due mainly to the entry of Gibraltar into the Schengen Area until 2025. However, there is occasional diplomatic tension between the two sides, which usually result in lines for leaving the colony, both via car and on foot. They can be long—it can take up to three hours to cross the border into Spain. This situation is unlikely to change, as there's little sign of any progress on any sort of joint Anglo-Spanish sovereignty, which the majority of Gibraltarians fiercely oppose.

When you call Gibraltar from Spain or another country, prefix the seven-digit telephone number with 00–350. Gibraltar's currency is the Gibraltar pound (£), whose exchange rate is the same as the British pound. Euros are accepted everywhere, although you will get a better exchange rate if you use pounds.

GETTING HERE AND AROUND
There are frequent day tours organized from the Costa del Sol resorts, either via your hotel or any reputable travel agency.

VISITOR INFORMATION
CONTACTS Gibraltar. ✉ *13 John Mackintosh St., Gibraltar* ☎ *200/45000* ⊕ *www.visitgibraltar.gi.*

Sights

Apes' Den
NATURE SIGHT | The famous Barbary Apes are a breed of cinnamon-color, tailless macaques (not apes, despite their name) native to Morocco's Atlas Mountains. Legend holds that as long as they remain in Gibraltar, the British will keep the Rock; Winston Churchill went so far as to issue an order for their preservation when their numbers began to dwindle during World War II. They are publicly fed twice daily, at 8 and 4, at Apes' Den, a rocky area down Old Queens Road near the Wall of Carlos V. Among the macaques' talents are their grabbing of food, purses, cell phones, and cameras, so be on guard. ✉ *Old Queens Rd., Gibraltar* ☎ *200/71633* 💲 *£5 to enter Upper Rock Nature Reserve.*

★ Cable Car
VIEWPOINT | You can reach St. Michael's Cave—or ride all the way to the top of Gibraltar—on a cable car. The car doesn't go high off the ground, but the views of Spain and Africa from the Rock's pinnacle are superb. It leaves from a station at the southern end of Main Street, which is known as the Grand Parade. ✉ *Grand Parade* 💲 *£17 round-trip.*

Gibraltar National Museum and Moorish Baths
HISTORY MUSEUM | Often overlooked by visitors heading to the Upper Rock Reserve, this museum houses a beautiful

The Rock of Gibraltar

14th-century Moorish bathhouse and an 1865 model of the Rock; the displays evoke the Great Siege and the Battle of Trafalgar. There's also a reproduction of the "Gibraltar Woman," the Neanderthal skull discovered here in 1848 and the remains of some Moorish baths, from the 14th-century Marinid dynasty, which are considered to be among the best-preserved in Europe. The museum also serves as an interpretation hub for the prehistoric remains found in the limestone caves of Gorham's Cave Complex, which received UNESCO World Heritage status in 2016. ⊠ *Bomb House La.* ☎ *200/74289* ⊕ *www.gibmuseum.gi* 🖼 *£5* ⊙ *Closed Sun.*

Gibraltar Nature Reserve

NATURE PRESERVE | The reserve, accessible from Jews' Gate, includes St. Michael's Cave, the Apes' Den, the Great Siege Tunnels, the Moorish Castle, and the Military Heritage Center, which chronicles the British regiments that have served on the Rock. The Skywalk, a glass viewing platform opened (appropriately) by Mark Hamill, aka Luke Skywalker, in 2018, offers 360-degree views of the Rock and ocean from 370 yards up. You can access the reserve via the cable car. ⊕ *From Rosia Bay, drive along Queensway and Europa Rd. as far as Casino, above Alameda Gardens. Make a sharp right here, up Engineer Rd. to Jews' Gate, a lookout over docks and Bay of Gibraltar toward Algeciras* ☎ *200/71633* 🖼 *£13 for all attractions.*

Gibraltar Town

TOWN | The dignified Regency architecture of Great Britain blends well with the shutters, balconies, and patios of southern Spain in colorful, congested Gibraltar town, where shops, restaurants, and pubs beckon on Main Street. At the Governor's Residence, the ceremonial Changing of the Guard takes place six times a year, and the Ceremony of the Keys takes place twice a year. Make sure you see the Anglican Cathedral of the Holy Trinity; the Catholic Cathedral of St. Mary; and the Crowned Law Courts, where the famous case of the sailing ship *Mary Celeste* was heard in 1872.

Great Siege Tunnels

TUNNEL | Formerly known as the Upper Galleries, these tunnels were carved out during the Great Siege of 1779–82. At the northern end of Old Queen's Road, you can plainly see the openings from which the guns were pointed at the Spanish invaders. They form part of what is arguably the most impressive defense system anywhere in the world. The privately managed World War II tunnels nearby (prebooking essential via email) are also open to the public but are less dramatic. ✉ *Old Queen's Rd.* 🌐 *www.visitgibraltar.gi/see-and-do/military-history/the-great-siege-tunnels-50* 🎫 *£13 for Nature Reserve, Upper Rock, and attractions including tunnels.*

Moorish Castle

CASTLE/PALACE | The castle was built by the descendants of the Moorish general Tariq ibn Ziyad (670–720), who conquered the Rock in 711. The present Tower of Homage dates to 1333, and its besieged walls bear the scars of stones from medieval catapults (and later, cannonballs). Admiral George Rooke hoisted the British flag from its summit when he captured the Rock in 1704, and it has flown here ever since. The castle may be viewed from the outside only. ✉ *Willis's Rd.*

St. Michael's Cave

CAVE | This is the largest of Gibraltar's 150 caves; a visit here is part of the tour of the Upper Rock Nature Preserve. This series of underground chambers full of stalactites and stalagmites is sometimes used for very atmospheric (albeit damp) concerts and other events. The skull of a Neanderthal woman (now in the British Museum) was found at the nearby Forbes Quarry eight years before the world-famous discovery in Germany's Neander Valley in 1856; nobody paid much attention to it at the time, which is why the prehistoric species is called Neanderthal rather than *Homo calpensis* (literally, "Gibraltar Man," after the Romans' name for the Rock: Calpe). A Lower St. Michael's Tour with guide has a separate fee and can be arranged in advance by email ✉ *Queen's Rd.* 🌐 *gibraltarinfo.gi/top-10-attractions/#st-michaels-cave* 🎫 *Included in Nature Reserve ticket (£13); £25 for tour of Lower Cave.*

🍴 Restaurants

Charlie's Steak House and Grill

$$ | **STEAKHOUSE** | Don't let the brash neon exterior put you off: inside is one of the best steak houses in the region. Hugely popular among locals for its long list of juicy steaks, this diner-style venue also serves lamb, fried fish, and Indian curries. **Known for:** English desserts; Indian curries; steak. [$] *Average main: £14* ✉ *Marina Bay, 4/5 Britannia House, Gibraltar* ☎ *200/69993* 🌐 *www.charliessteakandgrill.com.*

La Bodeguiya

$ | **SPANISH** | After nearly two decades on the Spanish side of the Rock, the owners of La Bodeguiya decided to open a sister Spanish tapas bar at this location in Gibraltar. Packed to the brim at lunchtime, the restaurant serves tapas of Iberian pork and seafood (shrimp and king prawn are specialties), plus Spanish staples such as croquettes and potato salad. **Known for:** tapas; loyal following; Iberian pork and seafood. [$] *Average main: £10* ✉ *10 Chatham Courterguard, Gibraltar* ☎ *200/64211* 🕓 *Closed Sun. and Mon.*

Sacarello's

$ | **BRITISH** | Right off Main Street, this busy restaurant is as well known for its excellent coffee and cakes as it is for the rest of its food. There's a varied salad and quiche buffet, as well as stuffed baked potatoes and daily specials, which could include beef curry, or baked lamb with honey mustard. **Known for:** coffee and cakes; lunch menu; cozy, old-fashioned English setting. [$] *Average main: £10*

✉ 57 Irish Town ☎ 200/70625 🌐 www.sacarellosgibraltar.com ⏲ Closed Sun. No dinner.

Hotels

The Rock

$$$ | HOTEL | This hotel overlooking the straits first opened in 1932, and although furnishings in the rooms and restaurants are elegant and colorful, they still preserve something of the English colonial style, with bamboo, ceiling fans, and a terrace bar covered with wisteria. **Pros:** good breakfast; old-world atmosphere; magnificent bay views. **Cons:** up a steep hill; inconvenient for shopping; some bathrooms are very small. *[$] Rooms from: £155 ✉ 3 Europa Rd. ☎ 200/73000 🌐 www.rockhotelgibraltar.com 🍴 No Meals 🛏 84 rooms.*

Sunborn

$$$$ | HOTEL | This giant yacht hotel (it's seven floors high and 155 yards long) has a permanent home in Gibraltar's marina and offers luxury accommodations complete with ocean views, a casino, a spa, and a restaurant on the top deck, plus lots of luxury extras. **Pros:** unusual place to stay; central, waterfront location; luxury extras. **Cons:** some may find it claustrophobic; not all cabins have views; noise from airport and nearby bars. *[$] Rooms from: £250 ✉ 35 Ocean Village Promenade, Gibraltar ☎ 200/16000 🌐 www.sunborngibraltar.com 🛏 189 rooms 🍴 No Meals.*

Nightlife

Lord Nelson

BARS | A restaurant during the day and a lively bar at night, the Lord Nelson has karaoke on Saturday night and jam sessions and live music during the week. Many ales are on tap. *✉ Grand Casemates Sq. ☎ 200/50009 🌐 www.lordnelson.gi.*

Chapter 14

THE CANARY ISLANDS

Updated by
Benjamin Kemper

👁 **Sights**
★★★★☆

🍴 **Restaurants**
★★★☆☆

🛏 **Hotels**
★★★★☆

🛍 **Shopping**
★★★☆☆

🍸 **Nightlife**
★★★★☆

WELCOME TO THE CANARY ISLANDS

TOP REASONS TO GO

★ **Carnaval:** Judge for yourself if Carnaval festivities in Santa Cruz de Tenerife and Las Palmas rival those of Rio.

★ **El Teide:** Be blown away by the views of Spain's highest peak, visible from most of the island of Tenerife and from the shores of neighboring islands.

★ **Relaxation:** Seek out solitude and tranquility in national parks, protected biospheres, rolling sand dunes, and secret beaches.

★ **Volcanoes:** Marvel at the stark beauty of Lanzarote's volcanoes and lava flows.

★ **Wine:** Go vineyard-hopping and taste distinctive award-winning wines made from Canarian grapes.

★ **Beaches:** Sunbathe on the pure white sands lapped by pristine turquoise sea on Fuerteventura.

1 Tenerife. Ride a cable car up the slopes of El Teide, swim in a huge artificial lake, wander botanical gardens, or dance at beachside discos.

2 Gran Canaria. Maspalomas is one of the islands' most arresting beach resorts, and the magnificent sand dunes behind it are a must-visit nature reserve. The seaside capital, Las Palmas, is the Canaries' most cosmopolitan city.

3 Lanzarote. Lanzarote has golden beaches, white villages, caves, and a volcanic national park where heat from an eruption in 1730 is still rising through vents in the earth.

4 Fuerteventura. Fuerteventura is remote and beachy, perfect for those who come to windsurf and kitesurf and enjoy the endless white beaches, reminiscent of the Caribbean.

5 La Palma. The terrain is dizzyingly varied—a hiker's dream—with misty laurel forests in the north, rocky trails in the center, and steep vineyards and jet-black volcanic landscapes in the south.

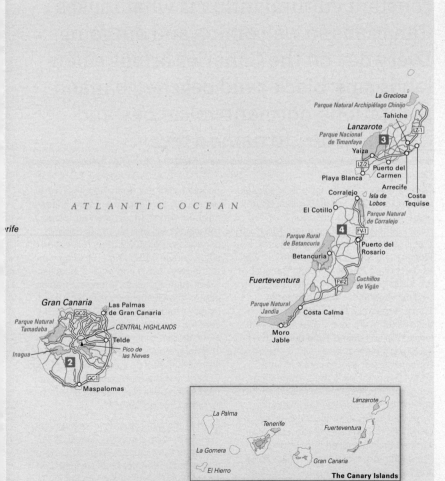

ATLANTIC OCEAN

A historic way station between the Old and New Worlds, the Canary Islands have been influenced over the centuries by African, European, and South American waves of immigration. Perhaps that constant cultural influx is what makes Canarians so welcoming and outgoing. Every day on the Canaries brings a new landscape: black-sand beaches, banana plantations, dormant volcanoes, and colonial cities, to name a few.

There are eight Canary Islands, a volcanic archipelago 1,280 km (800 miles) southwest of mainland Spain and 112 km (70 miles) off the coast of southern Morocco that lie at about the same latitude as Florida. La Gomera and El Hierro, as well as parts of La Palma and Gran Canaria, are fertile and overgrown with exotic tropical vegetation, while Lanzarote, Fuerteventura, La Graciosa, and stretches of Tenerife are as dry as a bone, with lava caves and desert sand dunes. Even so, Spain's highest peak, Mt. Teide, on Tenerife, is sometimes capped with snow. Geographically the Canaries are African, but culturally they're European; spiritually, some say they're Latin American (many islanders have close blood ties to Cuba and Venezuela). After all, the Spanish spoken here sounds more Latin American than Iberian. Salsa and reggaeton, less popular in mainland Spain, are basically all you'll hear at the wild Carnaval fiestas here.

Before the Spanish arrived, the Canaries were populated by a cave-dwelling people called the Guanches who were genetically similar to the Berber tribes of northern Africa. In the late 15th century, the islands fell one by one to Spanish conquistadores. Columbus resupplied his ships here in 1492 before heading west to the New World and helped establish the archipelago as an important trading center. The Guanches were decimated by slave traders by the end of the 16th century, and to this day, their customs and culture remain largely a mystery. The most significant Guanche remains are the Cenobio de Valerón ruins on Gran Canaria and the mummies on display at the Museo de la Naturaleza y el Hombre in Santa Cruz de Tenerife.

Each of the eight islands is a world unto itself with unique charms, landscapes, and patrimony. Our coverage focuses on five islands: Tenerife, Gran Canaria, Lanzarote, Fuerteventura, and La Palma. The smaller islands of El Hierro, La Gomera, and La Graciosa are no less attractive though a bit harder to get to. If you have a few days to spare, visit them from the larger islands via plane or boat.

Planning

When to Go

The Canaries enjoy warmth in the winter and cool breezes in summer. Regardless of the time of year you visit, expect highs of about 75°F and lows of about 60°F. Winter, especially Christmas, and Easter are peak tourism periods for northern Europeans, while Spaniards and Italians tend to come in the summer, particularly August, to escape the sweltering heat. October, when the summer heat and the winds drop, and spring, when a profusion of wildflowers colors the islands, are the most beautiful times to be here. Since the Canaries are a year-round destination, prices tend to be roughly the same no matter when you come, barring the holiday season. You may have some luck negotiating discounts during the slowest months, May and November.

Getting Here and Around

AIR
There are no nonstop flights to the Canary Islands from the United States. Americans usually transfer in Madrid or elsewhere in Europe. Iberia, its budget carrier Vueling, and Air Europa have direct flights to Tenerife, Gran Canaria, Lanzarote, Fuerteventura, and La Palma from mainland Spain (three hours from Madrid). Budget airlines like Ryanair and Easyjet often have unbeatable deals as well.

Inter-island flights are handled by carriers Binter Canarias and Canaryfly using small jets and turboprop planes with stunning low-altitude views of the islands.

FLIGHT INFORMATION Air Europa. ☎ 911/401501 ⊕ www.aireuropa.

com.**Binter Canarias.** ☎ 902/875787 ⊕ www.bintercanarias.com.**Canaryfly.** ☎ 902/808065 ⊕ www.canaryfly.es.**Iberia.** ☎ 901/111500 ⊕ www.iberia.com.**Vueling.** ☎ 902/808005 ⊕ www.vueling.com.

AIRPORTS Fuerteventura. ☎ 913/211000 ⊕ www.aena.es.**Gran Canaria.** ☎ 928/579130 ⊕ www.aena.es.**Lanzarote.** ☎ 902/404704 ⊕ www.aena.es.**Tenerife North.** ☎ 902/404704 ⊕ www.aena.es.**Tenerife South.** ☎ 902/404704 ⊕ www.aena.es.**La Palma.** ☎ 91/321–1000 ⊕ www.aena.es.

TRANSFERS ON TENERIFE
Tenerife has two airports: Tenerife South (TFS), near Playa de las Américas, and Tenerife North (TFN), near the capital city of Santa Cruz. Choose the airport closest to the area of the island that you'll be spending the most time in. The TITSA bus (Route 343, roughly €10) connects the airports directly; travel takes about 50 minutes. Driving time from one airport to the other is also about 50 minutes; you can hire a taxi for about €90 or rent a car for around €35.

BOAT AND FERRY
Fred Olsen, Naviera Armas, Líneas Romero, and Trasmediterránea operate inexpensive ferries between all eight islands, although if you're traveling to or from El Hierro, La Gomera, or La Palma to the eastern islands, you usually need to get a connecting ferry from Tenerife. Most inter-island trips take one to four hours; the few boats departing near midnight are equipped with sleeping cabins. Note that schedules change, particularly in high winds or storms, so it's imperative to call ahead to double-check. Fred Olsen's fleet has several ultra-sleek trimarans, which accommodate vehicles and are the quickest way to go between islands. Trasmediterránea runs a slow, comfortable ferry service weekly between Andalusia and the Canary Islands with trajectories ranging from 34 to 49 hours. Note that this is not a luxury cruise and clearly rather impractical,

both money- and time-wise, for most travelers.

CONTACTS Fred Olsen. ☎ *902/100107 general information* ⊕ *www.fredolsen. es.***Líneas Romero.** ☎ *928/596107* ⊕ *www. lineasromero.com.***Naviera Armas.** ☎ *902/456500 general information* ⊕ *www.navieraarmas.com.***Trasmediter- ránea.** ☎ *902/454645 general information* ⊕ *www.trasmediterranea.es.*

BUS

On the Canaries, buses are known as *guaguas* (pronounced *wa*-was), likely a hispanicization of the English word "wagon." A bus terminal is usually called an *intercambiador* rather than an *estación de autobuses.* Expect to see these terms on signs and brochures.

Bus travel is generally good between the main resorts, airports, and capitals. In Tenerife, TITSA runs a wide-reaching network of routes connecting the airports with Santa Cruz and the south, and Los Rodeos airport with Santa Cruz and Puerto de la Cruz. Global on Gran Canaria connects the capital and the south with the airport. Buses also transport ferry passengers to and from bus terminals and ports.

Each island has its own bus service geared toward residents. Buses generally leave each village early in the morning for the capital, then depart from the main plaza in early afternoon. Tourist offices have details, and Google Maps is gener- ally reliable.

CONTACTS Fuerteventura Buses. ☎ *928/855726* ⊕ *www.tiadhe.com.***Gran Canaria Buses.** ☎ *928/939407* ⊕ *www.glo- balsu.net.***Lanzarote Buses.** ☎ *928/811522* ⊕ *www.intercitybuslanzarote.es.***Tenerife Buses.** ☎ *922/531300* ⊕ *www.titsa.com.*

CAR

Most travelers rent a car for at least part of their stay on the Canaries, as this is by far the best way to explore the coun- tryside. Mountain roads are sometimes

narrow, which can be hair-raising if you meet a bus head on, so be alert. Expect traffic around urban centers. Rental hubs are found in all ferry terminals and airports.

CAR RENTAL

Car-rental companies abound on every island. Reservations are usually neces- sary in high season. Cicar and Europcar, with branches in all the airports and major towns on all seven islands, tend to have the best rates.

CONTACTS Cicar Fuerteventura. ✉ *Aer- opuerto de Fuerteventura, Puerto del Rosario* ☎ *928/822900* ⊕ *www.cicar.com.* **Cicar Gran Canaria.** ✉ *Aeropuerto de Las Palmas, Gando* ☎ *928/822900* ⊕ *www. cicar.com.***Cicar Lanzarote.** ✉ *Aeropuerto de Lanzarote, Arrecife* ☎ *928/822900* ⊕ *www.cicar.com.***Cicar Tenerife South.** ✉ *Tenerife South Airport, Granadilla de Abona* ☎ *928/822900* ⊕ *www.cicar. com.***Europcar Fuerteventura.** ✉ *Aero- puerto de Fuerteventura* ☎ *902/105055* ⊕ *www.europcar.es.***Europcar Gran Canaria.** ✉ *Aeropuerto de Las Pal- mas* ☎ *902/105055* ⊕ *www.europcar. es.***Europcar Lanzarote.** ✉ *Aeropuerto de Lanzarote* ☎ *902/105055* ⊕ *www.europ- car.es.***Europcar Tenerife North.** ✉ *Tenerife North Airport, La Laguna* ☎ *902/105055* www.europcar.es.**Europcar Tenerife South.** ✉ *Tenerife South Airport, Granadilla de Abona* ☎ *902/105055* ⊕ *www.europcar.es.*

CRUISE

Cruises to the Canaries were becoming increasingly popular before the pandemic, but itineraries remained limited as of 2021. Las Palmas de Gran Canaria and Santa Cruz de Tenerife are Spain's most visited cruise ports after Barcelona and Palma de Mallorca. The islands are frequent stops on cruises that also visit Madeira, the Azores, and the west coast of Africa.

TAXI

In major towns, taxis can be hailed on the street. Alternately, ask for the nearest taxi stand (*parada de taxi*). Taxis use meters to calculate the fare, though (*shh*) a cheaper flat rate can sometimes be negotiated in advance and paid in cash; passengers may be charged extra fees for luggage and holiday, weekend, and late-night trips. There are currently no ride-hailing apps such as Uber or Cabify in service.

CONTACTS Lanzarote Taxi. (*Asociación Cooperativa de Taxistas Ajey–Tamia*) ☎ *630/207305* ⊕ *www.lanzarotetaxi.com.***Radio-Taxi San Marcos Tenerife.** ☎ *922/641112, 922/641459, 682/391930 mobile/WhatsApp* ⊕ *www.taxisanmarcos.es.***Taxis Fuerteventura.** ☎ *928/850216* ⊕ *www.taxisfuerteventura.es.***Taxi Radio Gran Canaria.** (*Taragranca Sociedad Cooperativa de Taxistas*) ☎ *928/460000* ⊕ *www.taragranca.org.***Taxi La Palma.** ☎ *686/553868* ⊕ *www.taxilapalma.com.*

Restaurants

Canarian cuisine hinges on local seafood, tropical fruits, potatoes, bread, and goat cheese. Meals often begin with *platos de cuchara,* hearty dishes eaten with a spoon, such as *potaje canario* (containing garden vegetables, pork, potatoes, chickpeas, and sometimes pears), *rancho canario* (with beef, noodles, and legumes), and *potaje de berros* (watercress soup). *Gofio,* a thick, savory porridge made with corn or wheat flour and enriched with milk or stock, adds ballast to otherwise light meals. The main culinary event is often fresh native fish, the best of which are white-fleshed *vieja* (parrotfish), *cherne* (wreckfish), and *sama* (red-banded seabream) and the wonderfully rich *patudo* (bigeye) tuna, most of which is exported to Japan and other luxury markets. The most inescapable Canarian delicacy is *papas arrugadas,* "wrinkled" baby potatoes cooked in an abundance of salt water. The best examples use *papas bonitas* ("pretty") potatoes), the moniker for locally grown heirloom varieties.

Other specialties include *cabrito* (roast baby goat) and *conejo* (rabbit), both often served in *salmorejo,* a slightly spicy paprika sauce. No Canarian meal is complete without a dab of *mojo*: the spicy "rojo" (red) version is made with *pimientas palmeras* (mild local red chilies), garlic, and vinegar, plus any number of secret ingredients, while the "verde" (green) is milder and features parsley and cilantro. Most restaurants serve both sauces virtually by default, and Canarians heap it liberally on dishes as varied as fish and papas arrugadas. Another island specialty is goat cheese, whose most prized specimens are aged in the seaside caves of La Palma.

Canarian wines are good and varied. The most popular red grape is listán negro, which makes a fruity, highly drinkable wine with a faint smokiness—probably that volcanic soil talking. Common whites include Malvasía and Listán Blanco, often blended to create floral, fruity expressions. Confusingly, off-dry wines are frequently labled as *afrutado* ("fruity"), so if you like your whites on the dry side, ask for a *vino seco* ("dry") . Wine production on the Canaries dates back centuries—the Malmsey (fortified sweet) wines from Lanzarote were a favorite with Shakespeare's Falstaff. On the stronger side, the Canaries are also famous for dark rum and liqueurs flavored with everything from coffee to cocoa and hazelnut.

■ TIP→ Although the tap water in the Canary Islands is technically safe to drink according to the Ministry of Health, most of it comes from desalination plants and is of inferior quality (and taste). Bottled water is the norm in both hotels and restaurants, and hotels generally do not charge restocking fees. To cut down on plastic waste, purchase large-format bottles, and ask your hotel to recycle empties. Fuente Alta is the only bottled water brand in the Canaries that uses recycled materials in its production.

Restaurant reviews have been shortened. For full information, visit Fodors. com.

WHAT IT COSTS In Euros			
$	$$	$$$	$$$$
AT DINNER			
Under €12	€12–€17	€18–€22	over €22

Hotels

It's important to read reviews closely and not jump at the first seemingly good deal when selecting accommodations. With a few exceptions, noted in the individual reviews, it's best to stay in newer facilities, ones that weren't built shoddily during the Canaries' tourism boom many decades ago. Many hotels include either a full buffet breakfast or a meal plan of breakfast and lunch or dinner in the price of a room. Hotels with spas and pools generally include the use of these in their rates, but be sure to check the fine print when comparing prices.

Apartment, villa, and cabin rentals at every budget have become wildly popular in recent years. Airbnb is the most common booking resource. Most accommodations are simply furnished with a kitchenette and small living space, though there are certainly diamond-in-the-rough design properties to be discovered for those willing to pony up the extra euros.

Package tours are generally best suited to groups as opposed to independent travelers. Especially in the post-pandemic economy, check for offers on hotel websites, and inquire about discounts for long stays or during low season. Always call properties directly before booking via a third party to see if they'll offer you a lower rate.

High season varies depending on the island and locale. In Tenerife, La Palma, and Gran Canaria, high season is from November to April with a second spike in July and August. Lanzarote and Fuerteventura's high seasons are during December and January plus July and August. Airfare to Tenerife and Gran Canaria increases during those islands' respective Carnaval celebrations in late February, so if you're keen to attend, make reservations a few months out if possible.

Note that many four- and five-star hotels have fusty dress codes that require you to change out of beachwear, shorts, and flip-flops at mealtimes.

Hotel reviews have been shortened. For full information, visit Fodors.com.

WHAT IT COSTS In Euros			
$	$$	$$$	$$$$
FOR TWO PEOPLE			
under €90	€90–€125	€126–€180	over €180

Tenerife

Tenerife is the largest of the Canary Islands. Its standout feature is the volcanic peak of El Teide (also known as Mount Teide or Monte Teide), which, at 12,198 feet, is Spain's highest mountain. The slopes leading up to Teide are blanketed with pines in the north and with barren lava fields in the south. Tenerife's capital, Santa Cruz de Tenerife, is a giant urban center—forget whitewashed villas and sleepy streets, and imagine the traffic, activity, and crowds of an important shipping port. In the wetter north, mixed among the tourist attractions, are banana plantations and vineyards. In the dry south, resorts lining the coast spring up at the edge of a virtual desert.

VILLA AND APARTMENT RENTAL

Villas and apartments abound in the Canary Islands. Self-catering apartments are competitively priced, and you can often find excellent deals, particularly if you stay for a week or more and do price comparisons on Airbnb and similar sites. For detailed listings and photos of apartments, villas and hotels throughout the islands, check out *www.booking.com*, *www.vrbo.com, www.airbnb.com, www. nice2stay.com,* and *www.spain-holiday. com.*

LOCAL AGENTS Atlantic Horizons. ⊠ *Av. Amsterdam 3, Los Cristianos* ☎ *922/790299* ⊕ *www.atlantichorizons. com.***Tenerife Royal Gardens.** ⊠ *Apartamentos Royal Gardens 4, Playa de las Américas* ☎ *922/790211* ⊕ *www.tenerife-holiday-apartments.com.*

VISITOR INFORMATION

CONTACTS Santa Cruz de Tenerife. ⊠ *Pl. de España, Santa Cruz de Tenerife* ☎ *922/892903* ⊕ *www.webtenerife. co.uk.* **Puerto de la Cruz.** ⊠ *Casa de la Aduana, Las Lonjas, Puerto de la Cruz, Canary Islands, 38400, Spain* ☎ *(922) 386000* ⊕ *www.webtenerife.co.uk.*

Santa Cruz de Tenerife

10 km (6 miles) southeast of Los Rodeos Airport, 75 km (45 miles) northeast of Playa de las Américas.

Although Tenerife's busy capital is smaller, quieter, and less attractive than Las Palmas in Gran Canaria, it has worthwhile attractions and monuments. Until 1833, the island's capital was La Laguna, not Santa Cruz, making the latter "new," at least by Spanish standards; the city's oldest buildings (the fishermen's houses on Calle de la Noria) date to the 18th century. At the busy Plaza de España, modernized in 2006 by Swiss architects Herzog & de Meuron, there are several pedestrian streets leading north and to the area west of the port, where you'll find a stunning auditorium and maritime park. Be sure to go for a stroll down the *ramblas,* long, tree-lined boulevards that fall steeply from the north end of the city to the sea.

Santa Cruz is an ideal home base for adventures into the Parque Rural de Anaga (Anaga Nature Park), one of Tenerife's most scenic and untouched corners. Brave the switchbacks, and you'll be rewarded with subtropical forests, volcanic formations, and charming white villages.

GETTING HERE AND AROUND

If you're arriving by sea, it can be a long and fairly uninteresting walk from your cruise ship into town, so take a shuttle bus if one is provided (most cruise companies do) to the Estación Marítima cruise station. From here, you can walk 10 minutes to Plaza de España, where there's a branch of the tourist office, and on to any of the main sights. If you're heading south to Los Cristianos or north to Puerto de la Cruz, go to the bus terminal (about a 15-minute walk from Plaza de España), where there are frequent connections. La Laguna can be reached by tram: There are stops at the

Playa de las Teresitas is one of Tenerife's most popular beaches, thanks to its golden sand, many facilities, and beachfront restaurants.

bus station and near the Puente General Serrador.

From Tenerife you can catch a ferry to any of the other seven islands. From Santa Cruz, sail to Gran Canaria's two main ports: Agaete in the west (Fred Olsen is the quickest, at about an hour) or Las Palmas in the north. Ferries to La Palma (Santa Cruz de la Palma), La Gomera (San Sebastián), and El Hierro (Puerto de la Estaca) leave from Los Cristianos, in southern Tenerife. La Gomera can also be reached by a ferry from Los Cristianos (55 minutes; 35 minutes by Fred Olsen's trimaran).

Sights

Auditorio de Tenerife Adán Martín
PERFORMANCE VENUE | A magnificent avant-garde auditorium designed by Santiago Calatrava dominates the west end of the city. To keep its pearly white *trencadís* (broken tile mosaics) exterior clear of pooping pigeons, a falconer comes twice a day to scare them off with his raptors. The auditorium has a year-round program of concerts and opera, though you can sometimes catch impromptu music acts rehearsing or performing in the adjacent square overlooking the sea. Guided tours are given in English and Spanish; book ahead by phone or email. ⊠ *Av. de la Constitución 1, Santa Cruz de Tenerife* ☎ *922/568625* ⊕ *www.auditoriodetenerife.com* ⊠ *Tours €8* ⊗ *No tours Sun.*

Castillo de San Cristóbal (*St. Christopher's Castle*)
RUINS | FAMILY | The walls of this castle were uncovered when the car park under the Plaza de España was being built. The site is now a small museum that includes the 18th-century "Tigre Cannon" that reputedly cost Britain's Admiral Nelson his right arm in an attack he led in 1797. Entrance to the museum is via a stairway opposite the lake. ⊠ *Pl. de España,* ⊠ *Free* ⊗ *Closed Sun.*

Iglesia do Nuestra Senora de la Concepción

(*Church of Our Lady of the Conception*)
CHURCH | A six-story Moorish bell tower tops this church, which was renovated as part of an urban-renewal project that razed blocks of slums in this area. Church opening times vary, but you can generally visit before and after Mass. ✉ *Pl. de la Iglesia, Santa Cruz de Tenerife* ☎ *922/242387* ⚫ *Free.*

Mercado de Nuestra Señora de África (*La Recova Market*)

MARKET | **FAMILY** | This colorful city market is part bazaar and part food emporium. Stalls outside sell household goods; inside, stands displaying everything from flowers to canaries are arranged around a patio. Downstairs, a stroll through the seafood section will acquaint you with the local fish. A flea market with antiques and secondhand goods is held here on Sunday morning. Check the website for a monthly schedule of nighttime activities. ✉ *Av. de San Sebastián, Santa Cruz de Tenerife* ⊕ *www.la-recova.com.*

Museo de la Naturaleza y Arqueología

(*Museum of Nature and Archaeology*)
SCIENCE MUSEUM | **FAMILY** | Primitive ceramics and mummies are this museum's highlights. The ancient Guanches mummified their dead by rubbing the bodies with pine resin and salt and leaving them in the sun to dry for two weeks. ✉ *Calle Fuente Morales,* ☎ *922/535816* ⊕ *www.museosdetenerife.org* ⚫ *€5 (free Fri. and Sat. 4–8)* ⊘ *Closed Mon.*

Museo Municipal de Bellas Artes (*Museum of Fine Arts*)

ART MUSEUM | This 14-room, two-story gallery is lined with canvases by Breughel, Coecke, and Ribera as well as other famed works created between the 16th and 20th centuries. Many depict local events. The museum is on the Plaza Príncipe de Asturias. ✉ *Calle José Murphy 12, Santa Cruz de Tenerife* ☎ *922/274786* ⊘ *Closed Mon.* ⚫ *Free.*

Palmetum

GARDEN | **FAMILY** | Up on the hill just behind Parque Marítimo is Europe's largest collection of palms with some 600 species. The 29½-acre site, built over the former city dump and opened in 2014, houses palm trees from all over the world set around waterfalls and lagoons, all with panoramic views of the ocean and city. Guided tours in English cost €3 extra and last approximately one hour. ✉ *Av. Constitución 5, Santa Cruz de Tenerife* ☎ *697/651127* ⊕ *palmetumtenerife.es* ⊘ *Closed Mon.* ⚫ *€6.*

Parque Marítimo César Manrique

WATER PARK | **FAMILY** | West of the auditorium, this public water park with its three saltwater pools and tropical gardens is a favorite with locals. Designed by the Lanzarote-born architect César Manrique, it combines volcanic rock with palms and local flora. ✉ *Av. de la Constitución 5, Santa Cruz de Tenerife* ☎ *922/229368* ⊕ *www.parquemaritimosantacruz.es* ⚫ *€3.*

★ Parque Rural de Anaga (*Anaga Nature Park*)

NATURE PRESERVE | **FAMILY** | Thanks to its ornery terrain, Anaga Nature Park has managed to keep the tour-bus crowd (mostly) at bay—their loss. This magical oasis takes in misty laurel forests (aka laurisilva) with numerous endemic species, bizarre rock formations that jut above the trees, and hidden mountain villages like Taganana, founded in 1501. Explore the area by car, stopping to take a dip at Playa de Benijo, where you can catch a hiking trail into the surrounding countryside, and to snap a few postcard-worthy pics at the Pico de Inglés viewpoint. ✉ *Santa Cruz de Tenerife* ☎ *922/633576 for Anaga Visitor Center.*

Plaza de España

PLAZA/SQUARE | The heart of Santa Cruz de Tenerife is the Plaza de España. The cross at the southern end is a memorial to those who died in the Spanish Civil War, which—it bears remembering—was

Tenerife

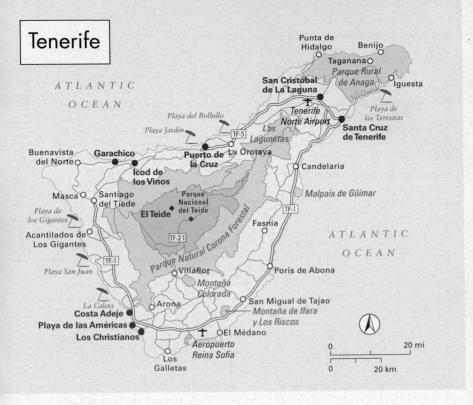

launched from Tenerife by General Franco during his exile here. The controversial monument's architect was Juan de Ávalos, who also designed the Francoist memorial and basilica at Valle de los Caídos. A 2006 refresh of the entire square by Swiss firm Herzog & de Meuron added a shallow oblong pond, new pavilions, and modern lighting The plaza is a vibrant center for Carnaval festivities. Castillo San Cristóbal and the tourist office are both here.

★ Tenerife Espacio de las Artes (*TEA*)

ART MUSEUM | This museum is the leader in contemporary art on the islands due to its sleek low-rise design and avant-garde exhibitions. Designed by the Swiss architects Herzog & de Meuron, it's next to the Museo de la Naturaleza. Expect 20th- and 21st-century art with a political or sociological bent. TEA's crown jewel is the hall dedicated to *Tinerfeño* surrealist artist Óscar Domínguez. ⊠ *Av. San Sebastián 8, Santa Cruz de Tenerife* ☎ *922/849057* ⊕ *www.teatenerife.es* ⊠ *€7* ⊗ *Closed Mon.*

Beaches

Playa de las Teresitas

BEACH | FAMILY | Santa Cruz's beach, Las Teresitas, is about 7 km (4½ miles) northeast of the city, near the town of San Andrés. The 1½ km (1 mile) of beach was created using white sand imported from the Sahara in 1973 and adorned with palms. Beachgoers in the 1970s were purportedly bitten by the occasional scorpion that had hitched a ride from Africa (they've since been eradicated). A man-made barrier runs parallel to the sands and ensures rip-tide-free bathing. Busy in the summer and on weekends, this beach is especially popular with local families. The 910 TITSA bus route connects the beach with Santa Cruz. There's a good choice of bars and restaurants, and plenty of lounge chairs for rent. **Amenities:** food and drink; lifeguards; parking (no fee); showers; toilets. **Good for:** sunrise; swimming; walking. ✉ *San Andrés.*

🍴 Restaurants

Bar Delicatessen La Garriga

$ | **SPANISH** | **FAMILY** | Some of the best sandwiches in town are made here, and the *tortilla* (potato omelet) may be the tastiest on the island. Eat in or take your purchases to the quiet gardens in the Plaza de Príncipe, just down the road, for an impromptu picnic. **Known for:** fine cheeses and charcuterie; terrific tortilla; greasy-spoon sandwiches. [$] *Average main: €5* ✉ *Calle Pérez Galdós 24, Santa Cruz de Tenerife* ☎ *922/285501* 🌐 *www.facebook.com/lagarrigatf* 🕒 *Closed Sun. No dinner Sat.*

El Coto de Antonio

$$ | **SPANISH** | **FAMILY** | The buzz around this down-home Santa Cruz standby is well-deserved, as you'll see when you sample chef Carlos's steak tartare, the best in town, or his rustic snail stew enriched with trotters (don't knock it till you try it). The star dessert is *huevo mole,* egg yolk and sugar whipped into a creamy mousse. **Known for:** homey atmosphere; Canarian comfort food; knockout steak tartare. [$] *Average main: €17* ✉ *Calle de General Goded 13, Santa Cruz de Tenerife* ☎ *922/272105* 🕒 *No dinner Sun.*

El Lateral 27

$$ | **SPANISH** | **FAMILY** | Situated on the main shopping street, this restaurant is a convenient place to stop for a meal after sightseeing, especially since the kitchen is open from 11 am to midnight. Try to snag a table on the terrace that overflows onto the leafy pedestrian street (the interior dining room is comparatively drab). **Known for:** good value for the city center; fresh fish; wide selection of salads. [$] *Average main: €15* ✉ *Calle Bethencourt Alfonso 27, Santa Cruz de Tenerife* ☎ *922/287774* 🕒 *Closed Sun.*

Los Pinchitos

$$ | **SEAFOOD** | **FAMILY** | Los Pinchitos is one of those dying-breed restaurants where you can eat your fill of pristine seafood without maxing out your credit card. Settle in for a leisurely no-frills feast of octopus, scallops, squid, and whatever other sea creatures were hauled up onto the pier that morning, and wash it all down with a carafe of (surprisingly solid) house wine. **Known for:** heaping seafood platters; homey atmosphere; mojo-topped limpets. [$] *Average main: €14* ✉ *Calle Guillén 14, Santa Cruz de Tenerife* ☎ *643/176630.*

★ San Sebastián 57

$$$$ | **FUSION** | To fully grasp the potential of Canarian cuisine, book a table at this white-tablecloth standby that coaxes market ingredients—such as *patudo* (bigeye) tuna, black potatoes, and local heirloom tomatoes—into flawless, modern preparations like *tataki* (lightly seared), *ensaladilla rusa* (salade Olivier), and vinaigrette, respectively. Staff aren't on island time and happily attend to your every need. **Known for:** subdued, minimalist decor; rave-worthy tasting menus; Canarian fusion cuisine. [$] *Average main: €24* ✉ *Av. de San Sebastián 57, Santa Cruz de Tenerife* ☎ *822/104325* 🕒 *Closed Sun.*

Tasca Tagoror

$ | **SPANISH** | **FAMILY** | Opposite the Iberostar Grand Mencey, this tiny no-frills bar serves simple Canarian cuisine—think grilled sardines and tomato-avocado salads—in abundant portions at reasonable prices. The dining room has a beamed ceiling, low wooden stools, and barrels for tables—in other words, it's fine for a quick bite but not ideal for lingering. **Known for:** solid seafood and

Spanish omelet; casual local crowd; budget-friendly tapas. Ⓢ *Average main: €10 ⊠ Calle Dr. José Naveiras 9, Santa Cruz de Tenerife ☎ 922/274163 ⊕ www. facebook.com/TascaTagoror ⊙ Closed Sun.*

Hotels

Hotel Colón Rambla

$ | HOTEL | FAMILY | This cheery budget hotel is situated in a residential area north of the city center, just off the Rambla Santa Cruz. **Pros:** large bathrooms; quiet oasis in the city center; well-maintained pool. **Cons:** some rooms get noise from street traffic; breakfasts don't vary; could use an update. Ⓢ *Rooms from: €65 ⊠ Calle Viera y Clavijo 49, Santa Cruz de Tenerife ☎ 922/272550 ⊕ www. hotelcolonrambla.com* ⇶ *40 rooms* ☉ *No Meals.*

★ Iberostar Heritage Grand Mencey

$$ | HOTEL | The ancient Guanches' name for their kings was "Mencey," and you'll feel like one at this grand, white stucco-and-marble hotel north of the city center. **Pros:** quiet, leafy neighborhood; fairy-tale garden; well-oiled-machine staff. **Cons:** no kid-centric areas or programming; high fees for parking and spa access; far from the action. Ⓢ *Rooms from: €115 ⊠ Calle Dr. José Naveiras 38, Santa Cruz de Tenerife ☎ 922/609900 ⊕ www.iberostar.com* ⇶ *286 rooms* ☉ *No Meals.*

Nightlife

Santa Cruz nightlife revolves around Calle Antonio D. Alfonso, known locally as Calle de la Noria, west of the Iglesia de la Concepción. Here you'll find plenty of good cocktail bars and pubs. If you're looking for tapas, try Callejón del Combate, west of the Plaza del Príncipe. For upscale disco bars and dance clubs, head for **Avenida Anaga,** facing the port.

★ Bambú Lounge

DANCE CLUBS | Shimmy—and twerk, if you want—at this Southeast Asian-inflected rooftop *discoteca* that attracts a young local crowd. Sunday nights are reserved for Latin (salsa, bachata, and more) dance parties. ⊠ *Calle Fernando Arozena Quintero 5, Santa Cruz de Tenerife ☎ 922/202296 ⊕ www.bambulounge.es.*

Café Atlántico

CAFÉS | Opposite the tourist office, this is one of the city's oldest café-bars (est. 1945), famous as a venue for business and cultural gatherings. The original interior includes Moorish tiling, typical Canary wooden beams, and a very large oil painting of Monte Teide. Open morning to night, this is the place for café con leche or a leisurely cocktail. Ownership changed hands in 2020, and it remains to be seen what the new, younger management has in store for Café Atlántico's revamp. ⊠ *Pl. de España 1, Santa Cruz de Tenerife ☎ 922/246909.*

Shopping

Santa Cruz de Tenerife is a major shopping center. Calle Castillo, the main pedestrian street through the center of town, is lined with souvenir shops, trendy boutiques, and big-brand apparel stores (e.g., Massimo Dutti, Bimba y Lola, Foot Locker). Calle del Pilar has higher-end fashions and the department stores Marks & Spencer and El Corte Inglés (another branch is next to the bus terminal).

Artenerife

CRAFTS | Traditional crafts sold at this kiosk near the tourist office are made by local artisans and guaranteed by the island's government as "productos artesanos ." The selection includes *calado*— exquisitely embroidered linen tablecloths and place mats—and clay pottery made using the same methods as those used by the island's aboriginal settlers. (The Guanches didn't use potter's wheels;

rather, they rolled the clay into *churros*, or cylindrical strips, and hand-kneaded these into bowls. Pebbles, branches, and shells were used to buff the results.) ✉ *Pl. de España, Santa Cruz de Tenerife* ☎ *922/291523* 🌐 *www.artenerife.com* 🕒 *Closed Sat. afternoon and Sun.*

San Cristóbal de La Laguna

5 km (3 miles) northwest of Santa Cruz.

Known colloquially as "La Laguna," this university town was the first capital of Tenerife. It was planned and built in a Renaissance style in 1500, a design that was later adopted in New World cities like La Habana (modern-day Havana) and Cartagena de Indias (in Colombia), and many original, UNESCO-protected buildings remain. The old town has kept its colonial feel through the centuries with its tree-lined promenades, pastel-colored facades, and elegant palaces. Pick up a map at the tourist office, on Calle Obispo Rey Redondo, and snake your way through the pedestrianized streets to be transported to Spain's Golden Age.

GETTING HERE AND AROUND

CONTACTS Tram. ✉ *La Laguna* 🌐 *www.metrotenerife.com.*

VISITOR INFORMATION

CONTACTS La Laguna Tourist Office. ✉ *Calle Obispo Rey Redondo 7, La Laguna* ☎ *922/631194* 🌐 *www.turismodelalaguna.com.*

👁 Sights

Museo de Historia y Antropología (*Museum of History and Anthropology of Tenerife*)
HISTORY MUSEUM | FAMILY | Occupying the splendid 17th-century palace of an Italian merchant, this museum chronicles Tenerife's sociocultural history from the 15th to the 20th century with documents, artifacts, and religious relics. Signage is in Spanish only, but you can download a free English audio guide on your smartphone (ask museum personnel for details). The elegant courtyard blends Italian Renaissance architecture, like white marble columns, with local materials such as hardy Canary Island pine. ✉ *Calle San Agustín 22,* ☎ *922/825949* 🌐 *www.museosdetenerife.org* 🎫 *€5 (free Fri. and Sat. 4–8).*

Parroquia Matriz de Nuestra Señora de la Concepción
VIEWPOINT | FAMILY | The arcaded bell tower of this 16th-century church is an architectural icon of La Laguna, visible from almost everywhere in the city. Climb to the top for 360-degree views of the city and surrounding countryside. ✉ *Pl. de la Concepción 10, La Laguna* 🎫 *€1.*

🍴 Restaurants

★ Tasca el Obispado
$$ | SPANISH | FAMILY | Figurines of the Virgin Mary and other religious paraphernalia line the walls of this eclectic tavern with low ceilings and a cozy, countrified feel. Hand-cut *jamón* (ham) and runny-in-the-center tortillas make wonderful appetizers; save room for the *conejo en salmorejo* (roast rabbit in a paprika-garlic sauce) and homemade desserts. **Known for:** one of the best tortillas on the island; cheery service; rustic decor. [$] *Average main: €15* ✉ *Calle Herradores 88,* ☎ *922/251450* 🕒 *Closed Sun.*

Zumería Tamarindo
$ | SPANISH | FAMILY | Students and penny-pinching travelers flock to this no-frills juice bar, as famous for its colorful smoothies (made with local fruit) as it is for its club sandwiches and filling *platos combinados* (lunch and dinner combos), served with fries and salad. **Known for:** collegiate atmosphere; tropical fruit juices and smoothies; full lunches for under €5. [$] *Average main: €4* ✉ *Calle Consistorio 22, La Laguna* ☎ *922/314353* 🌐 *www.facebook.com/ZumeriaTamarindo* 🕒 *Closed Sun.*

La Laguna was the first unwalled colonial city and still preserves its original 15th century layout almost intact.

Hotels

Hotel Aguere

$ | HOTEL | Get a taste of historic life in La Laguna at this 18th-century palace that became a hotel in 1885. **Pros:** historic building; welcoming staff; good value. **Cons:** no elevator and steep stairs; antique doors and walls mean poor soundproofing; small rooms with basic furnishings and space heaters. *$ Rooms from: €80 ⊠ Calle Obispo Rey Redondo 55, La Laguna ☎ 922/314036 ⊕ www. hotelaguere.es ⇨ 23 rooms ❚⊘❚ Free Breakfast.*

★ La Laguna Gran Hotel

$$ | HOTEL | This chic four-star housed in an 18th-century palace opened in 2017. **Pros:** Michelin-starred restaurant on-site; rooftop pool, gym, and bar; varied breakfasts with local items. **Cons:** poor soundproofing; inconsistent service; strong-smelling cleaning products. *$ Rooms from: €97 ⊠ Calle Nava y Grimon 18, La Laguna ☎ 922/108080*

⊕ *www.lalagunagranhotel.com ⇨ 123 rooms ❚⊘❚ No Meals.*

Activities

Centro Hípico La Esperanza

HORSEBACK RIDING | FAMILY | This equestrian center, 8 km (5 miles) west of La Laguna, offers trail rides and equitation lessons. Advanced riders shouldn't miss the "Adrenaline" experience that lets you do what most other riding companies won't: gallop at full tilt. *⊠ Camino Guillén s/n, ☎ 677/479544 ⊕ horszen.com ⊠ From €50.*

Puerto de la Cruz

36 km (22 miles) west of Santa Cruz.

This is the oldest resort in the Canaries, and sadly, cheap mass tourism and urban sprawl have all but drained it of local charm and island character. There are a few diamonds in the rough, though, and several sights on the outskirts of town make the area worth a visit. Don't stay at any of the bland, overpriced resorts by the beach, though, and when exploring, stick to the old sections of town, which have colonial plazas and paseos for evening strolls.

GETTING HERE AND AROUND

An excellent bus service connects Puerto de la Cruz with the airport and Santa Cruz's bus terminal. Buses leave every 30 minutes weekdays and every 45–60 minutes on weekends; the journey takes around 50 minutes. You can also rent a car (from €30 a day) or take a taxi (€42).

The town is very hilly and getting anywhere outside the port involves a steep climb. To visit the Jardín Botánico or Parque Taoro, your best bet is to take a cab or rent a motorcycle or bike.

VISITOR INFORMATION

CONTACTS Más Que Motos Tenerife. ⊠ *Av. Marques Villanueva del Prado 15, Local 8, Puerto de la Cruz* ☎ *922/371131* ⊕ *www. masquemotostenerife.com.*

 Sights

★ **Casa del Vino de Tenerife**

WINERY | FAMILY | Wine and food lovers shouldn't miss this wine museum and tasting room, opened by the Canary Islands' government to promote local vintners. The surprisingly well-appointed museum, which describes local grapes, viticultural methods, and history, has English-language placards; reasonably priced tastings in various formats are held in the abutting bar area, and you can buy your favorite bottle in the shop. The complex also has a tapas bar and a restaurant with creative Canarian fare and a curious little honey museum with exhibits and tastings. Casa del Vino lies about halfway between Puerto de la Cruz and Tenerife North Airport, at the El Sauzal exit on the main highway. ⊠ *Calle San Simon 49, at Autopista General del Norte, Km 21, Sauzal* ☎ *922/572535* ⊕ *www.casadelvinotenerife.com* ☞ *€3* ☺ *Closed Mon.*

Costa Martiánez (*Lago Martiánez*)

POOL | FAMILY | Because Puerto de la Cruz has uninviting black-sand beaches, the town commissioned Lanzarote artist César Manrique in 1965 to build Costa Martiánez, a forerunner of today's water parks. It's an immense, and immensely fun, public pool on the waterfront, with landscaped islands, bridges, and a volcano-like fountain that sprays sky-high. The complex also includes several smaller pools and a restaurant-nightclub. All facilities are cash-only. ⊠ *Av. de Colón, Puerto de la Cruz* ☎ *922/385955* ☞ *From €6.*

Jardín Botánico (*Botanical Garden*)

GARDEN | FAMILY | Filled with more than 4,000 varieties of tropical trees and plants, and sonorous birds, the Jardín Botánico was founded in 1788, on the orders of King Carlos III, to propagate warm-climate species brought back to Spain from the Americas. The gardens are closed during stormy weather or when the wind speed exceeds 40 kph (25 mph). ⊠ *Calle Retama 2, Puerto de la Cruz* ☎ *922/383572* ☞ *€3.*

Loro Parque

ZOO | FAMILY | This huge subtropical garden and zoo holds 1,300 parrots, many of which are trained to ride bicycles and perform other tricks. The garden also has the world's largest penguin zoo. The dapper Antarctic birds receive round-the-clock care from marine biologists and other veterinary specialists in a climate-controlled environment. Also here is one of Europe's largest aquariums, with an underwater tunnel, a dolphin and killer-whale (orca) show, and some gorillas. Free trains leave for the park from the Plaza Reyes Católicos. ⊠ *Av. Loro Parque, Puerto de la Cruz* ☎ *922/373841* ⊕ *www.loroparque.com* ☞ *€38.*

Plaza de la Iglesia

PLAZA/SQUARE | Stroll from Lago Martiánez along the coastal walkway to reach the Plaza de la Iglesia, which is beautifully landscaped with flowering plants. Be sure to visit the Nuestra Señora de la

Jardín Beach in Puerto de la Cruz is a famous beach filled with dark-colored volcanic sand, palm trees, and hotels.

Peña Church (open before and after Mass) with its baroque altarpiece and elaborate pulpit. ✉ *Pl. de la Iglesia, Puerto de la Cruz.*

Plaza del Charco

PLAZA/SQUARE | It's a two-minute walk from the Plaza de la Iglesia to this square, one of the prettiest and liveliest in town, with plenty of cafés and tapas bars. ✉ *Pl. del Charco, Puerto de la Cruz.*

Tourist Office

VISITOR CENTER | Occupying a meticulously preserved royal customhouse from the 17th century, the tourist office is outfitted with balconies, an interior patio, and intricate wood carvings. ✉ *Casa de la Aduana, Calle Las Lonjas, Puerto de la Cruz* ☎ *922/386000* 🌐 *www.webtenerife.com.*

🍴 Restaurants

★ Bodegas Monje

$$ | **SPANISH** | A five-minute drive from the Casa del Vino, in the township of El Sauzal, you'll find this award-winning winery and restaurant perched on a bluff overlooking the ocean. After a lunch of crackly pulled (local heritage-breed *cochino negro*) pork and roasted potatoes, waddle over to the bodega for a tour and tasting, and if you're looking for a gluggable souvenir, snap up a bottle of the Tintilla, a smoky, complex red aged in French oak barrels that's nearly impossible to find in shops. **Known for:** production of some of the finest wines on the island; heritage-breed pulled pork; mojo-making demonstrations (call ahead to book). [$] *Average main: €14* ✉ *Calle Cruz de Leandro 36, Sauzal* ☎ *922/585027* 🌐 *www.bodegasmonje.com* 🕒 *No dinner.*

Casa Pache

$ | **SPANISH** | **FAMILY** | Down a plant-lined alley off the Plaza del Charco, this family-run restaurant is in a typical local house, with a labyrinth of small rooms leading off the main hall; you might find yourself sitting next to a collection of old photos, a pile of hats, or some rustic artifacts. Standouts on the traditional Canarian menu include *puchero canario* (chickpea stew with vegetables, pork, and chicken), *piñas con costillas y papas* (corn on the cob with spareribs and potatoes), and rabbit with *salmorejo*-sauce. **Known for:** staff who treat you like family; Canarian comfort food; romantic ambience. $ *Average main: €10* ✉ *Calle La Verdad 6, Puerto de la Cruz* ☎ *922/372524* ⊕ *www.facebook.com/ casapache.rest* ⊘ *Closed Wed.*

Tropical

$ | SPANISH | Those in the know come here for typical Canarian food, especially the local dayboat fish. The best tables are outside on the pedestrian street, a couple of blocks behind the port, but the interior's cheap and cheerful wooden tables and fishing nets have their charm. **Known for:** local wines; ocean-fresh seafood; unbeatable set lunch deal. $ *Average main: €9* ✉ *Calle El Lomo 7, Puerto de la Cruz* ☎ *922/385312* ⊘ *Closed Sat. and July.*

Hotels

★ Hacienda Cuatro Ventanas

$$$ | HOUSE | Until recently, if you wanted luxury on Tenerife, you had to settle for one of the big-brand resorts in the south—no longer; Cuatro Ventanas, hidden among rolling banana plantations that tumble into the sea, is the kind of place a celebrity might rent to disappear to for a few weeks. **Pros:** highly Insta-grammable infinity pool; high-design interiors; a world away from the tourist hubbub. **Cons:** slow Wi-Fi; no full-time staff or daily cleaning service; a bit remote. $ *Rooms from: €162* ✉ *Calle Playa del Socorro 1–2, Puerto de la Cruz* ☎ *660/866678* ⊕ *www.haciendacuatro-ventanas.com* ⟿ *4 rooms* ⦿ *No Meals.*

Hotel Tigaiga

$$ | HOTEL | Take in sweeping views of the city, ocean, La Palma island, and Monte Teide from the lush tropical gardens at this family-owned hotel above Taoro Park. **Pros:** well-appointed breakfast buffet;

intimate, noncorporate feel; magnificent views. **Cons:** 230-stair climb to the hotel from the city; slightly dated rooms; older clientele means it's quiet. $ *Rooms from: €124* ✉ *Parque Taoro 28, Puerto de la Cruz* ☎ *922/383500* ⊕ *www.tigaiga. com* ⟿ *76 rooms* ⦿ *Free Breakfast.*

Monopol

$ | HOTEL | Monopol has had more than a century to perfect its brand of hospitality: built as a private home in 1742, opened as a hotel in 1888, and run by the same family for several decades, this three-star has neatly furnished rooms with wooden balconies set around a verdant courtyard. **Pros:** serene pool area; historic building; central location. **Cons:** dowdy decor; communal areas could use refurbishment; proximity to loud church bells. $ *Rooms from: €65* ✉ *Calle Quintana 15, Puerto de la Cruz* ☎ *922/384611* ⊕ *www.monopoltf. com* ⟿ *92 rooms* ⦿ *No Meals.*

🍸 Nightlife

Hotels often have live music or other entertainment at night, mostly geared toward a 50s-and-up crowd.

The side streets of Avenida Colón are packed with bars and underground clubs catering to a wider range of ages and musical tastes. For the pop and DJ beats, head to Blanco Bar and the venues on neighboring Calle Blanco.

Azúcar

DANCE CLUBS | You can dance to Cuban rhythms and live Latin jams at this busy nightclub that opens at 11 nightly. ⊠ *Calle Obispo Pérez Cáceres 12, Puerto de la Cruz* ☎ *682/286705.*

Casino Taoro

CABARET | Try your luck in games of chance in the beautiful surroundings of Costa Martiánez. You must be over 18 and flash a photo ID to get into this unfancy casino. No beachwear or shorts are allowed. ⊠ *Av. de Colón 1, Puerto de la Cruz* ☎ *922/368842* ⊕ *www.casinos-tenerife.com.*

 Performing Arts

Sala Timanfaya

ARTS CENTERS | The town's theater (a five-minute walk south of Plaza del Charco) has a year-round calendar of cultural events including a classical music concert every Sunday at noon (€10). Purchase tickets for events at the tourist office. ⊠ *Calle Las Damas 1, Puerto de la Cruz* ☎ *922/376106.*

Icod de los Vinos

26 km (16 miles) west of Puerto de la Cruz.

Attractive plazas rimmed by unspoiled colonial architecture and pine balconies form the heart of Tenerife's most historic wine district. A 1,000-year-old dragon tree, the natural symbol of Tenerife, towers 57 feet above the coastal highway, C820. It's arguably the oldest living specimen of this species on earth, and special measures (like installing an electrical fan inside its trunk to prevent mold) have been undertaken to preserve it. The Guanches worshiped these trees as symbols of fertility and knowledge; the sap, which turns red upon contact with air, was used in healing rituals.

GETTING HERE AND AROUND
Buses run every hour between here and Santa Cruz, and there's also reasonably frequent service from Puerto de la Cruz. Otherwise, drive here so you can also explore farther afield.

Garachico

5 km (3 miles) west of Icod de los Vinos.

Garachico is one of the most idyllic and historic towns on the islands, and it's well worth a stop. It was the main port of Tenerife until May 5, 1706, when El Teide blew its top, sending twin rivers of lava downhill—one filled Garachico's harbor, and the other wiped out about 90% of the town (hence Garachico's nickname: "Pompeii of the Canaries"). Though most of the buildings are faithful reconstructions from the 18th century, a handful of original structures survived including the Castillo de San Miguel, a tiny 16th-century fortress on the waterfront. Save for the odd art exhibition or cultural event, it's closed to the public. The restored Convento de San Francisco (open Monday–Saturday), was also unscathed, as was the 18th-century parish church of Santa Ana with its elaborate baroque altarpiece.

Sights

Piscinas Naturales El Caletón

HOT SPRING | **FAMILY** | Lava flows formed these seaside natural pools, to which stairs, paths, and railings have been added for easy access. There's a pleasant café selling drinks and snacks and a conventional swimming pool that comes in handy when the surf is rough. Far from luxurious or exclusive, the pools are owned by the town and popular with born-and-bred tinerfeños of all ages. ⊠ *Av. Tome Cano 5, Garachico.*

Hotels

★ Boutique Hotel San Roque
$$$$ | HOTEL | Museum-quality art by well-known painters lines the walls of this Bauhaus-inspired design property occupying a colonial palace in the old town. **Pros:** art by renowned artists; 17th-century building with great bones; paradisiacal pool and spa. **Cons:** cold when the weather is uncooperative; rooms and bathrooms a bit gloomy; kids not allowed. [$] *Rooms from: €212* ✉ *Calle Esteban de Ponte 31, Garachico* ☎ *922/133435* 🌐 *www.hotelsanroque.com* 🛏 *20 rooms* 🍴 *No Meals.*

Shopping

Tabacos Arturo
TOBACCO | Snap up local cigars at this tiny mom-and-pop shop that rolls its own smokes on-site. ✉ *Av. Tome Cano 8, Garachico* ☎ *689/359158* ⏲ *Closed Sun.*

El Teide

60 km (36 miles) southwest of Puerto de la Cruz, 63 km (39 miles) north of Playa de las Américas.

The dormant volcano of El Teide, Spain's highest peak, looms on the horizon no matter where you are on the island, and its (often snowcapped) peak is visible from the neighboring islands of Gran Canaria and La Palma on clear days. You need a special permit (approximate processing time: two months; apply at www.reservasparquesnacionales.es) to reach the highest point, but most hikers and tourists will be content with hitching a ride up most of the way on the cable car.

GETTING HERE AND AROUND

Four roads lead to El Teide from different parts of Tenerife, each getting you to the park in about an hour, but the most beautiful approach is the road from Orotava, which is a mile uphill from Puerto de la Cruz. Orotava has a row of stately mansions on Calle San Francisco, north of the baroque church Nuestra Señora de la Concepción. Roads into the park are occasionally closed due to icy conditions; try to visit early on in your trip so you have an opportunity to return if this is the case.

Sights

Cable Car
VIEWPOINT | On its way to the top of El Teide, the cable car soars over sulfur steam vents. You can get a good view of southern Tenerife and Gran Canaria from the top, although you'll be confined to the tiny terrace of a bar. The station also has a basic restaurant. It's strongly recommended to reserve your spot online, though it's important to note that there are no ticket refunds should the cable car be closed due to wind. ✉ ☎ *922/010440* 🌐 *www.volcanoteide.com* 🎫 *€14.*

★ Parque Nacional del Teide (*Teide National Park*)
MOUNTAIN | FAMILY | This park includes the volcano itself and the **Cañadas del Teide,** a violent jumble of volcanic leftovers from El Teide and the neighboring Pico Viejo. The last eruption here was in 1798. Within the park you can find blue-tinged hills (the result of a process called hydrothermal alteration); spiky, knobby rock protrusions; and lava in varied colors and textures. The bizarre, photogenic rock formations known as **Los Roques de García** are especially memorable; a two-hour trail around these rocks—one of 30 well-marked hikes inside the park—is a highlight. Visit in late May or early June to see the crimson, horn-shaped *tajinaste* flowers in bloom, a dramatic sight. You enter the Parque Nacional del Teide at El Portillo. Exhibits at the visitor center explain the region's natural history; a garden outside labels the flora found within the park. The center also offers trail maps, video presentations, guided hikes, and bus tours. A second park

The last eruption of the mountain El Teide was in 1909, on the northwestern flank of the volcano.

information center is located near Los Roques de García beside the Parador Nacional Cañadas del Teide. ✉ *La Orotava* ☎ *922/922371*.

Shopping

Not surprisingly for one of the most visited places in Spain, the area around El Teide provides plenty of places for buying souvenirs. Beware of imitation lace and embroidery.

Casa de los Balcones
CRAFTS | Regional arts and crafts are available here. ✉ *La Orotava* ✛ *Next to cable car* ☎ *922/694060* ⊕ *www.casa-balcones. com*.

Activities

Climbing the Teide Crater
HIKING & WALKING | If you're planning on hiking in the park, plan ahead. Take warm clothing even in summer, suitable footwear, sun protection, snacks, and plenty of drinking water. The trail to the top

(No. 10) of of the volcano is closed when it's snowy, usually three or four months of the year. The difficult final 656 feet to the volcano crater itself take about 40 minutes to climb, and you need a special (free) pass to do so—apply online (at least two months in advance in high season). If you stay at the refuge and access the crater before 9 am, you don't need a pass. ✉ *Teide National Park, La Orotava* ⊕ *www.reservasparquesnacionales.es*.

Los Cristianos, Playa de las Américas, and Costa Adeje

74 km (44 miles) southwest of Santa Cruz, 10 km (6 miles) west of Reina Sofía Airport.

The sunniest—and most touristy—area on Tenerife is the southwestern coast, where high-rise hotels are built chockablock above the beaches without a lick of feng-shui sensibility. Costa Adeje, to the west of Playa de las Américas, is the newest addition with lower-rise apartments and hotels packed into the hillside. Sun, beaches, and nightlife—no cultural or nature activities—constitute the attractions here for millions of northern Europeans desperate for sunshine in the winter months. Playa de las Américas, particularly in the area around Las Verónicas, is a loud and brash resort, while Los Cristianos and Costa Adeje are quieter and more sedate, attracting a more mature crowd of holidaymakers. However, if you're looking for pin-drop-quiet solitude, you'll probably want to give this area a wide berth.

GETTING HERE AND AROUND

Hourly buses connect the south of the island with the capital, stopping at Tenerife South Airport on the way. If you rent a car from Santa Cruz (from €30 a day), expect to get to the southern resorts in just over an hour. Once there, a good bus service connects the different locales, and hotels that are not within easy walking distance of the beach provide a shuttle service to the seafront.

Beaches

El Médano

BEACH | Stretching for more than 2 km (1 mile), this is the longest beach on the island and also one of the most distinctive—the conical top of Montaña Roja (Red Mountain) lies at its southern tip. The golden sands and exemplary facilities earn it the country's "Blue Flag" rating, and the gentle waves make for safe swimming. Strong winds make it a good beach for those who want to try their hand at windsurfing. To get here, drive along the TF1 past the Reina Sofía Airport and take the TF64 south shortly afterward. **Amenities:** food and drink; lifeguards; showers; toilets; water sports. **Best for:** sunset; swimming; walking; windsurfing. ⊠ *Arona.*

Las Vistas

BEACH | Part of the eight beaches making up the sands in Playa de las Américas and Los Cristianos, Las Vistas has clean yellow sand and perfect bathing conditions thanks to a series of breakwalls that protect the beaches from high waves. Lounge chairs and parasols are available for rent. After sunbathing on this Blue Flag beach, take a stroll along the seafront promenade, one of the longest of its kind in Europe. **Amenities:** food and drink; lifeguards; showers; toilets; water sports. **Best for:** sunset; swimming; walking. ⊠ *Los Cristianos.*

Los Cristianos

BEACH | This was the first beach on the island to receive international tourists en masse, from the 1960s on; today its golden sands are flanked by apartment blocks and hotels. The nearby port protects the beach from high winds and waves, so bathing is safe. Lounge chairs and parasols are available for rent. This is a lively beach, with frequent concerts and sporting events, and finding a space for your towel can be a challenge in the summer. **Amenities:** food and drink; lifeguards; showers; toilets; water sports. **Best for:** partiers; sunset; swimming.

★ Playa de los Guíos

BEACH | This small, placid cove situated 12 km (7 miles) from Playa de las Américas is dwarfed by Los Gigantes, the towering cliffs nearby. Its natural black sand, striking in appearance, can be hot on the toes, so be sure to strap on some sandals. A nearby marina provides boat trips along the coast to take in the full beauty of the cliffs. **Amenities:** food and drink; lifeguards; showers; toilets; water sports. **Best for:** sunset; swimming. ⊠ *Los Gigantes, Santiago del Teide.*

Restaurants

Bar Baku

$ | RUSSIAN | Try wrapping your head around the fact that there's an Azerbaijani restaurant in Tenerife, where you can find Georgian specialties served by Russian waiters. Improbably, the food here—lamb kebabs, lemony stuffed grape leaves, plump *pelmeni*, juicy *khinkali* (Georgian soup dumplings), and other Russian and Caucasian delicacies—is fresh, well-spiced, and wildly affordable. **Known for:** Caucasian cuisine like it's made in the Old Country; Russian crowd; grilled kebabs and boiled dumplings. [$] *Average main: €9* ✉ *Centro Comercial Terra Nova, Av. de España 25, Costa Adeje* ✥ *Follow "Bar Baku" signs from shopping center's main entrance* ☎ *662/028096.*

La Vieja

$$$ | **SPANISH** | A few minutes' drive from Costa Adeje lies this oceanfront restaurant overlooking the quaint harbor of La Caleta. Watch the sun set over La Gomera island while you savor fresh local fish and shellfish and Tenerife wines. **Known for:** local wines; fresh fish; ocean views. [$] *Average main: €20* ✉ *Edificio Las Terrazas 1, La Caleta* ☎ *922/711548* 🌐 *www.restaurantelavieja.com.*

Masca

Approximately 16 km (10 miles) north of Guía de Isora, tucked deep in the Macizo de Teno mountains, lies Masca, colloquially known as the Macchu Picchu of the Canaries. If you squint, you can see the resemblance—the huddle of houses is perched on a misty ridge beneath a massive, pyramid-shaped rock. Descend the cobblestone steps into the town center, grab a quick coffee or sandwich, and, if you're feeling adventurous, embark on the three-hour (each way) hike down to the beach.

Hotels

Arona Gran Hotel

$$$ | **HOTEL** | Prime views of the marina at Los Cristianos and La Gomera island are what you get from the balconies at this hotel, which is especially popular among retirees. **Pros:** good choice for those with mobility difficulties; adults-only policy means plenty of peace and quiet; professional, amicable service. **Cons:** poolside real estate fills up fast; younger guests may feel out of place; access to spa and infinity pool costs extra. [$] *Rooms from: €154* ✉ *Av. Juan Carlos I 38, Los Cristianos* ☎ *922/750678* 🌐 *springhoteles.com/en/arona-gran-hotel-tenerife* 🛏 *392 rooms* 🍴 *No Meals.*

★ Bahía del Duque

$$$$ | **RESORT** | **FAMILY** | Built to resemble a 19th-century Canarian village—complete with a bell tower, Italianate villas, and leafy courtyards—this sprawling luxury resort takes in eight restaurants, five swimming pools, a 24-hour gym, and two tennis courts. **Pros:** bountiful poolside real estate; warm, helpful staff; excellent breakfast buffet with made-to-order eggs. **Cons:** leaks in public areas when it rains; most pools aren't climatized; overpriced spa treatments. [$] *Rooms from: €300* ✉ *Av. de Bruselas, Adeje* ☎ *922/746932* 🌐 *www.thetaishotels.com* 🛏 *351 rooms* 🍴 *No Meals.*

Jardines de Nivaria

$$$$ | **HOTEL** | Step inside from views of El Teide to a world of Tiffany glass, palms, and orchids crowned by the largest privately owned stained-glass window in the world. **Pros:** seafront location; fantastic spa; tranquil atmosphere. **Cons:** evening entertainment sometimes a snooze; some may prefer a more modern style; dinner always in the same dated restaurant. [$] *Rooms from: €215* ✉ *Calle Bruselas, Playa de Fanabé* ☎ *922/713333* 🌐 *www.hoteljardinesnivaria.com* 🛏 *271 rooms* 🍴 *Free Breakfast.*

The Ritz-Carlton Abama

$$$$ | **RESORT** | **FAMILY** | Rising like a Moorish citadel from the banana fields, the Ritz-Carlton Abama is an architectural stunner with a coral-red exterior, a semiprivate beach, seven pools, and

a two-Michelin-star restaurant and award-winning golf course. **Pros:** kids club with original activities; top-notch gym, spa, and restaurants; gorgeous ocean views. **Cons:** the main building and pools can be overrun with families; small beach with ugly views; below-average breakfast. [$] *Rooms from: €294* ✉ *TF47, Km 9, Guía de Isora* ☎ *922/126000* 🌐 *www.ritzcarlton.com* 🛏 *461 rooms* 🍴 *No Meals.*

Vincci Selección La Plantación del Sur

$$$$ | HOTEL | Centering around an original banana plantation house, this modern hotel retains its colonial essence with spacious communal areas, teak furniture, and potted palms. **Pros:** tranquil ambience; views of the mountains and Costa Adeje; excellent service. **Cons:** some noise from other rooms; 10- to 15-minute walk to nightlife; some distance from beach. [$] *Rooms from: €210* ✉ *Calle Roque Nublo 1, Costa Adeje* ☎ *902/454585* 🌐 *www.vinccihoteles.com* 🛏 *165 rooms* 🍴 *Free Breakfast.*

Nightlife

Most of the area nightlife is centered in Playa de las Américas, in three main areas: Veronica's (or Veronica's Strip), Starco, and the Patch. Dozens of bars, pubs, and nightclubs compete here for the young, rowdy, mostly foreign crowds drawn to clubs.

Activities

DIVING

Dive Center Aquanautic Club Tenerife

DIVING & SNORKELING | FAMILY | This PADI-licensed diving center in the small resort of Playa Paraíso is one of the most well established on the island. ✉ *Lago Playa Paraíso, Playa Paraíso, Adeje* ☎ *922/741881* 🌐 *www.diving-tenerife.com.*

GOLF

Southern Tenerife has five of the island's eight golf courses, and these five lie within 20 km (12 miles) of each other.

Amarilla Golf Club

GOLF | In San Miguel, not far from Campo Golf, this 18-hole course has greens that front the ocean. ✉ *Urbanizacion Amarilla Golf, San Miguel* ☎ *922/730319* 🌐 *www.amarillagolf.com* 🎫 *€59* ⛳ *18 holes, 6684 yards, par 72.*

Campo Golf del Sur

GOLF | Near Reina Sofía Airport, this course has 27 holes and spectacular greens that are surrounded by cacti and palms. ✉ *Urbanización Golf del Sur, Av. Galván Bello, San Miguel* ☎ *922/738170* 🌐 *www.golfdelsur.es* 🎫 *From €58* ⛳ *27 holes, 6458 yards, par 72.*

Centro de Golf Los Palos

GOLF | In Arona, near Los Cristianos, Centro de Golf Los Palos has 9 holes (par 27) and is a good practice course. ✉ *Ctra. Guaza, Las Galletas, Km 7, Los Cristianos* ☎ *922/169080* 🌐 *www.golflospalos.com* ⛳ *9 holes, 1040 yards, par 27* 🎫 *From €20.*

Golf Abama

GOLF | This exclusive course surrounded by banana plantations boasts more than 22 lakes and 90,000 palms along its 18 holes. It's part of the Ritz-Carlton Abama resort complex. ✉ *Playa de San Juan, Ctra. Gral TF47, Km 9, Guía de Isora* ☎ *922/126000* 🌐 *www.abamagolf.com* 🎫 *€250* ⛳ *18 holes, 6858 yards, par 72.*

Golf Costa Adeje

GOLF | There's a 27-hole course that runs alongside the ocean and has a small number of palm trees dotted throughout, black volcanic sand bunkers, and views of the sea. ✉ *Fince de los Olivos, Adeje* ☎ *922/710000* 🌐 *www.golfcostaadeje.com* 🎫 *€102* ⛳ *27 holes, 6440 yards, par 72.*

Golf Las Américas

GOLF | Adjacent to Playa de las Américas, Golf Las Américas has an 18-hole course with views of the ocean and La Gomera island. ✉ *Playa de las Américas, Arona* ☎ *922/752005* ⊕ *https://www.golflasamericas.com* ✉ *€110* ⚲ *18 holes, 6409 yards, par 72.*

KITESURFING

Azul Kiteboarding

WINDSURFING | **FAMILY** | Kiteboard, surfboard, and windboard rentals and classes are available at this club on the seafront in Playa del Médano, which happens to be one of the best places on the island for beginners. If you're experienced and enjoy big waves, try Playa El Cabezo. ✉ *Edificio El Toscón, Paseo Nuestra Señora de Roja 26, El Médano* ☎ *922/178314* ⊕ *www.azulkiteboarding.com.*

Gran Canaria

Gran Canaria has three distinct identities. Its capital, Las Palmas (pop. 381,000), is a thriving business center and important shipping and cruise port; the white-sand beaches of the south coast are tourist magnets; and the rural interior has a forgotten-in-time allure and spectacular landscapes.

Las Palmas, the largest city in the Canary Islands, is awash with tourists, traffic, and hordes of locals—in other words, it's a *city,* the likes of which most first-time travelers don't readily associate with the archipelago. (Even so, it consistently ranks as number one in air quality among Spanish metropolises.) There are a number of worthwhile cultural attractions including the 7-km (4½-mile) Canteras beach and well-preserved old town.

The south coast, a boxy '60s development along wide avenues, is a family resort, popular with millions of northern Europeans. At the southern tip of the island, the Playa del Inglés (a popular gay-friendly retreat) gives way to the vast, empty dunes of Maspalomas. The isle's interior is a steep highland that reaches 6,435 feet at Pozo de las Nieves. Although it's green in winter, Gran Canaria does not have the luxurious tropical foliage of the archipelago's western islands, and the landscape is often stark the rest of the year.

As of mid-2021, Gran Canaria (and to a lesser extent, Tenerife) is in the midst of a migration crisis. It's estimated that over 10,000 North Africans fleeing violence and poverty have come ashore in the Canaries, but the clunky gears of bureaucracy are not moving fast enough, creating a bottleneck and leaving most migrants stranded, stateless, and in unsafe living conditions. There is tension within the native population: Some Canarians are helping the migrants (several hotels graciously transformed into makeshift shelters to house them), many others simply look on, while a vocal minority is actively antagonizing them—throwing rocks at shelters and organizing vigilante groups—and seeking their extradition. The desperation—of both the migrants and the Canarians, who suffered greatly due to the pandemic—has understandably led to an uptick in petty crime, so it's best to keep your wits about you, particularly at night, in large resort towns and cities like La Palma and Santa Cruz de Tenerife. Traveling in the Canaries? Consider making a donation to the National Commission for Refugee Aid via www.cear.es. Both the migrants and the local population need all the assistance they can get.

Las Palmas

35 km (21 miles) north of Gran Canaria Airport, 60 km (36 miles) north of Maspalomas.

Las Palmas is a long, sprawling city, strung out for 10 km (6 miles) along two waterfronts of a peninsula. Though most

Gran Canaria

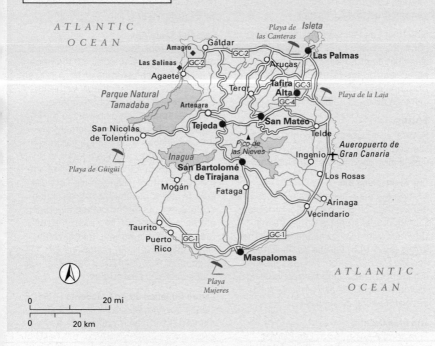

ATLANTIC OCEAN

Playa de las Canteras Isleta

Amagro Gáldar
GC-2
Las Salinas GC-2 **Las Palmas**
Agaete Arucas

Parque Natural Tamadaba Teror **Tafira Alta** GC-3 *Playa de la Laja*
Artenara GC-4

San Nicolás de Tolentino **Tejeda** **San Mateo** Telde

Inagua ▲ *Pico de las Nieves* Ingenio **Aueropuerto de Gran Canaria**

Playa de Güigüi **San Bartolomé de Tirajana** Los Rosas

Mogán Fataga Arinaga
Vecindario

Taurito
Puerto Rico GC-1 GC-1

Maspalomas *ATLANTIC OCEAN*

Playa Mujeres

0 20 mi
0 20 km

---

of the action centers on the peninsula's northern end along the lovely Las Canteras beach, the historical sights are clustered around the city's southern edge. Begin in the old quarter, La Vegueta, at the **Plaza Santa Ana** (don't miss the bronze dog statues), for a tour through attractive colonial architecture. Then make your way to the neighboring quarter of Triana, a treasure trove of small shops and cafés and restaurants. Both neighborhoods are protected by UNESCO. It's quite a walk from one end of town to the other, so at any point you may want to hop on one of the many canary-yellow buses. Buses 1, 2, and 12 run the length of the city.

GETTING HERE AND AROUND

It's a short stroll from the cruise terminal into the northern part of Las Palmas. Here you can explore the beach and

check out the market and the stores in El Muelle shopping mall and Calle Mesa y López, or take a bus (1, 2, or 12) into the older part of the city.

If you're planning to go north to Agaete or Teror, or south to Maspalomas or Puerto Mogán, good bus services run frequently from the Santa Catalina terminal just outside the port. You can also get an airport bus from here. Alternatively, you can rent a car (from €30 a day) or take a taxi.

For those planning to island-hop, Las Palmas and Agaete have good connections with Santa Cruz de Tenerife. Fred Olsen provides the quickest travel between Santa Cruz de Tenerife and Gran Canaria (Agaete)—the trimaran takes an hour. Free bus service is provided between Agaete and Las Palmas in both directions. You can also ferry to Lanzarote (Arrecife) and Fuerteventura (Puerto del

Rosario and Morro Jable). Fred Olsen runs several ferries a week between Las Palmas, Lanzarote (Arrecife), and Fuerteventura (Puerto del Rosario).

Note that Las Palmas and the highway south are always busy with traffic, so allow plenty of time for your journey, particularly on the return. Even a bus trip from one end of Las Palmas to the other can take up to an hour during rush hour.

TOURS

Several companies offer sightseeing and themed tours. The hop-on, hop-off, service is also good for just getting around.

City Sightseeing Bus

Visiting the main sites of Las Palmas, this hop-on, hop-off bus has a Monumental City Tour (nine stops) and the Atlantic City Tour, with two additional stops. The buses leave from Parque Santa Catalina and Parque San Telmo. Tickets (cheaper if bought online) include a free walking tour in Vegueta. ⊠ *Las Palmas* ⊕ *www. city-sightseeing.com* 🖃 *€22.*

Trip Gran Canaria

This company's tours in Las Palmas cover Vegueta and Triana and take 2–3 hours. There are culinary tours available. Book ahead. ⊠ *Calle Colón 2, Vegueta* ☎ *674/128849* ⊕ *www.tripgrancanaria. com* 🖃 *From €8.*

 Sights

★ Casa Museo Colón (*Columbus Museum*)

HISTORY MUSEUM | **FAMILY** | In a palace where Christopher Columbus may have stayed when he stopped to repair the *Pinta*'s rudder, nautical instruments, copies of early navigational maps, and models of Columbus's three ships are on display in addition to interactive exhibits. The palace, which retains many original features, has two rooms holding pre-Columbian artifacts and one floor dedicated to paintings from the 16th to the 19th century. There's a glaring

absence of criticism of Columbus's complicated legacy. ⊠ *Calle Colón 1, Vegueta* ☎ *928/312373* ⊕ *www.casadecolon.com* 🖃 *€4 (free Sun.).*

Catedral Santa Ana

CHURCH | It took four centuries to complete St. Anne's Cathedral, so the neoclassical Roman columns of the 19th-century exterior contrast sharply with the Gothic ceiling vaulting of the interior. Baroque statues are displayed in the cathedral's **Museo de Arte Sacro** (Museum of Religious Art), arranged around a peaceful cloister. Ask the curator to open the *sala capitular* (chapter house) to see the 16th-century Valencian tile floor. Be sure to check out the black-bronze dog sculptures outside the cathedral's main entrance—these are four examples of the Gran Canaria hounds that gave the island its name. ⊠ *Pl. Santa Ana 13, Vegueta* ☎ *928/314430* 🖃 *Cathedral free, museum €3* ⊗ *Closed Sun.*

Centro Atlántico de Arte Moderno (*Atlantic Center for Modern Art*)

ART GALLERY | This art gallery has earned a name for curating some of the best avant-garde shows in Spain, with a year-round calendar of exhibitions. The excellent permanent collection includes Canarian art from the 1930s and 1940s and works by the well-known Lanzarote artist César Manrique. The center also has a fine collection of contemporary African art. ⊠ *Calle los Balcones 11, Vegueta* ☎ *928/311800* ⊕ *www.caam.net* 🖃 *Free* ⊗ *Closed Mon.*

Ermita de San Telmo (*Parroquia de San Bernardo*)

CHURCH | Destroyed by Dutch attackers in 1599, this chapel was rebuilt in the 17th century. Inside is a fine baroque altarpiece with rich gold leaf and wooden details. The chapel is generally open only before and after Mass. ⊠ *Pl. de San Telmo, Triana.*

The irregularity of house shapes in the colorful barrios of San Nicolas and San Juan in Las Palmas are an iconic image of the city.

Fundación de Arte y Pensamiento Martín Chirino

ART MUSEUM | Housed in the Castillo de la Luz—the Canary Islands' oldest defensive fortress that once protected the port from pirates and other invaders—the Fundación de Arte y Pensamiento Martín Chirino opened in 2015 to celebrate the legacy of the Canaries' most famous modern sculptor. Chirino's swooping, abstract designs are more poignant than ever given his death in 2019. ⊠ *Calle Juan Rejón, La Isleta* ☏ *928/463162* ⊕ *www.fundacionmartinchirino.org* ✉ *€4* ⊘ *Closed Mon.*

Parque de Santa Catalina

CITY PARK | **FAMILY** | Ride a guagua (city bus) to this park, where you can visit the **Museo Néstor,** home to neoclassical and modernist works by brothers Miguel (architect) and Néstor (artist) Martín Fernández. There's also a kids' play area and cultural center with temporary exhibitions. On the way there, stop off at the neighboring Parque Doramas (stops are listed on big yellow signs; buses 2,

3, and 12 generally cover the entire city) to peek at the elegant Santa Catalina Hotel. Next to the Parque Doramas is the **Pueblo Canario,** a model village with typical Canarian architecture. ⊠ *Calle León y Castilo, Las Palmas.*

Poema del Mar Aquarium

AQUARIUM | This ultramodern fresh- and saltwater aquarium opened in 2017. It's organized by altitude: you start your visit gazing at the aquatic life of mountain lakes and rivers and finish in a room dedicated to alien-like deep-sea critters. The coral-filled pool is a highlight. ⊠ *Muelle del Sanapú 22, Las Palmas* ☏ *928/010350* ⊕ *www.poema-del-mar.com* ✉ *€25.*

 Beaches

Although it can't quite compete with the endless stretches of golden sand to the south of the island, the northern beach here, frequented by locals of all ages, is one of Las Palmas's major attractions.

★ Las Canteras

BEACH | **FAMILY** | One of the best urban beaches in Spain is found at the northwest end of the city. Its yellow sands are flanked by a pleasant promenade that stretches more than 3 km (nearly 2 miles) from the Alfredo Kraus Auditorium, in the south, where surfers congregate, to the Playa del Confital, in the north. The beach is protected by a natural volcanic reef, La Barra, which runs parallel to the shore and makes for safe swimming. Lounge chairs and sunshades can be rented year-round. **Amenities:** food and drink; lifeguards; showers; toilets; water sports. **Best for:** sunset; surfing; swimming; walking. ✉ *Paseo Las Canteras, Las Palmas.*

🍴 Restaurants

Bikina

$ | **INTERNATIONAL** | **FAMILY** | Skip the middling tourist-packed cafés and sandwich shops on the Las Canteras boardwalk and instead grab a bite at this sunny, casual storefront that serves tropical fare ranging from tacos to Cubano melts to pad Thai. **Known for:** beachside patio; "slow" fast food; craveable tacos and quesadillas. [$] *Average main: €8* ✉ *Paseo las Canteras 63, Las Palmas* ☎ *828/065357* 🌐 *www.facebook.com/labikinacantina* ⏲ *Closed Tues.*

Bistro La Champiñonería

$$ | **SPANISH** | **FAMILY** | Halfway up a pleasant pedestrian street in Vegueta, this French café-restaurant with red walls and old photos of Las Palmas specializes in mushroom dishes. Choose from more than 15 preparations, or forego the fungi and try the meat dishes and giant scrambled-egg *revueltos*. **Known for:** cozy atmosphere; mushroom everything; large portions for the money. [$] *Average main: €14* ✉ *Calle Mendizábal 30, Vegueta* ☎ *928/334516* 🌐 *lachampivegueta.es.tl* ⏲ *Closed Mon.*

Deliciosa Marta

$$ | **SPANISH** | Tables are hard to come by at this busy restaurant in a typical Triana house: there's usually a line outside the door. The concise, contemporary menu includes truffled gnocchi, baked cod with seasonal vegetables, and steak tartare, the house specialty. **Known for:** well-heeled local crowd; consistently fantastic food quality; steak tartare. [$] *Average main: €15* ✉ *Calle Pérez Galdos 23, Triana* ☎ *676/377032* ⏲ *Closed Sun.*

★ El Santo

$$$ | **FUSION** | Freshly dug baby potatoes with mole sauce, tempura octopus with aerated spirulina, Canarian blood sausage soufflé with beer ice cream—these are a few of the palate-bending dishes you'll find on the menu at El Santo, one of Gran Canaria's most exciting fusion spots. Rustic stone walls give the restaurant an intimate, relaxed feel, while the white tablecloths and professional waiters hint that young-gun chef Abraham Ortega means business. **Known for:** foams, reductions, and fine-dining touches; experimental Canarian cuisine; subdued yet stylish dining room. [$] *Average main: €22* ✉ *Calle Escritor Benito Pérez Galdós 23, Las Palmas* ☎ *928/283366* 🌐 *www.elsantorestaurante.com* ⏲ *Closed Sun. and Mon.*

★ Neodimio 60

$$$ | **FUSION** | If you manage to snag one of the four tables at this *nueva cocina* restaurant, you're in for a decadent feast of local seafood, meats, and vegetables prepared with Latin and Asian twists (think chipotle-rubbed octopus, cod ceviche with passion fruit and ginger, and ricotta-stuffed agnolotti with fresh corn sauce). The cocktails, which could be described as "cheffy," don't disappoint either. **Known for:** pocket-size digs; fine-dining fusion cuisine without the smoke and mirrors; concise market-driven menu. [$] *Average main: €21* ✉ *Calle Alfredo L. Jones 28, Las Palmas* ☎ *674/746695* ⏲ *Closed Sun. and Mon.*

Te Lo Dije Pérez
$ | **INTERNATIONAL** | Just below the cathedral square is one of the island's best bars for having a beer—there's a huge selection—along with some tapas. The bar feels a bit like a French café, with high ceilings and black and red furnishings. **Known for:** good tapas; choice of beers; fun ambience. [$] *Average main: €8* ✉ *Calle Obispo Codina 6, Vegueta* ☎ *928/249087* 🌐 *www.telodijeperez.com* 🕓 *Closed Sun.*

Zoe Food
$ | **VEGETARIAN** | A magnet for vegetarians and vegans, this restaurant has retro decor and a pleasant, shady terrace. Specialties include vegetable woks with tofu, vegan meatballs, and healthy organic breakfasts. **Known for:** organic produce; range of vegan, gluten-free, and vegetarian options; fab menú del día (prix fixe). [$] *Average main: €10* ✉ *Calle Domingo J. Navarro 35, Triana* ☎ *928/586507* 🌐 *www.facebook.com/zoefoodlaspalmas* 🕓 *Closed Sun. No dinner.*

Coffee and Quick Bites

Cafetería Casa Suecia (*Swiss Tea House*)
$ | **CAFÉ** | Escape to the tranquil, air-conditioned quiet of the Casa Suecia Salon de Té on Tomás Miller 70—near Playa de las Canteras—for comfortable booths, foreign newspapers, picture windows, pastries, breakfast plates, sandwiches, and perhaps the only free coffee refills on the islands. [$] *Average main: €6* ✉ *Calle Tomás Miller 70, Las Palmas* ☎ *928/271626* 🕓 *Closed Mon.*

Guirlache
$ | **ICE CREAM** | **FAMILY** | For a sweet treat, try Guirlache. There are at least 20 ice-cream flavors, and many of the cakes are made with that trusty island staple, condensed milk. **Known for:** popular with locals; delicious cakes, ice creams, and chocolates; quality ingredients. [$] *Average main: €4* ✉ *Calle Triana 68, Triana* ☎ *928/366723* 🌐 *www.guirlachelaspalmas.com.*

Hotels

Bull Reina Isabel and Spa
$$ | **HOTEL** | **FAMILY** | With a location right on Las Canteras, this is a good midrange option for visiting the city and taking in its beach. **Pros:** rooftop swimming pool; solid breakfasts and dining in general; beachfront location. **Cons:** some areas look a little tired; street-view rooms are dreary; steep competition to get a sunbed by the pool. [$] *Rooms from: €120* ✉ *Calle Alfredo Jones 40, Las Canteras* ☎ *928/260100* 🌐 *www.bullhotels.com* 🛏 *225 rooms* 🍴 *Free Breakfast.*

Hotel Verol
$ | **HOTEL** | **FAMILY** | This no-frills budget hotel has an uninspiring facade, but its location, sandwiched between the Las Canteras seafront promenade and the main shopping street, makes a great base for exploring and beach-going. **Pros:** kid- and pet-friendly; excellent value; beachside location. **Cons:** some street noise; basic, with small bathrooms; poor-quality bath amenities. [$] *Rooms from: €50* ✉ *Calle Sagasta 25, Las Canteras* ☎ *928/262104* 🌐 *www.hotelverol.com* 🛏 *25 rooms* 🍴 *No Meals.*

★ **Veintiuno**
$$$ | **HOTEL** | This boutique adults-only hotel is a social-media darling, thanks to its drool-worthy rooftop pool overlooking the cathedral. **Pros:** local art and quirky library; rooftop splash pool; serene and stylish decor. **Cons:** no tea- and coffee-making facilities in entry-level rooms; cramped breakfast area; noisy ground-floor room. [$] *Rooms from: €145* ✉ *Calle Espíritu Santo 21, Las Palmas* ☎ *683/369723* 🌐 *www.hotelveintiuno.com* 🛏 *11 rooms* 🍴 *No Meals.*

Nightlife

Lively and sometimes a little rough around the edges, the bars and discos in Las Palmas are clustered between Playa de las Canteras and Parque Santa Catalina. The seafront promenade and **Calle Tomás Miller** are lined with restaurants serving dishes from every corner of the globe. Live music and entertainment are common—check out the online La Brújula guide for a lowdown on cultural events (www.labrujulaociocyultura.com).

Ginger
COCKTAIL LOUNGES | Sip a colorful tiki drink while watching the tide come in at this Las Canteras hot spot, whose fishbowl *gin-tónics* and zippy mojitos lure a mixed local and international crowd until 2 am. ⊠ *Paseo de las Canteras 2, Las Palmas* ☎ *696/728992.*

★ Tao Club & Garden
DANCE CLUBS | Open until 5 am on weekends and past 1 am every other night, this swanky tropical nightclub playing a mix of pop and DJ music draws a local crowd of revelers ages 25 and up. The palm-lined outdoor terrace, with music and its own bar, is one of the city's top see-and-be-seen spots in the summer. Be sure to dress to impress (no shorts, sandals, or tanks). ⊠ *Paseo Alonso Quesada, Las Palmas* ☎ *928/243730* ⊕ *www.taolaspalmas.com.*

Performing Arts

Orquesta Filarmónica de Gran Canaria
CONCERTS | One of Spain's oldest orchestras, the Filarmónica has an ample calendar of concerts between September and July that take place at the emblematic Auditorio Alfonso Kraus at the southwestern end of the Las Canteras seafront promenade. ⊠ *Paseo Príncipe de Asturias, Las Palmas* ☎ *928/472570* ⊕ *www.ofgrancanaria.com.*

Teatro Pérez Galdós
THEATER | A varied program of plays, concerts, and opera is performed throughout the year at this 19th-century theater at the end of the Vegueta district. Spanish theater buffs shouldn't miss the guided 40-minute tours, which ran Monday through Saturday at 10:15, 11:15, and 12:15 (€5; no reservation required) prior to the pandemic but remained on pause at the time of writing. ⊠ *Pl. Stagno 1, Vegueta* ☎ *928/433334, 928/491770 box office* ⊕ *www.auditorioteatrolaspalmasgc.es.*

Shopping

Las Palmas easily has the best shopping on the islands. The main commercial areas are around Calle Mesa y López (south of the port) and Triana in the old quarter. You'll find all the major international and Spanish fashion stores, duty-free stores, and shops selling local crafts, hats and clothes, tackle for fishing and catching crabs, surf gear, and lots more.

Artesanía Santa Catalina
CRAFTS | Genuine crafts, souvenirs, and handiwork can be found in this shop two blocks west of Parque Santa Catalina. ⊠ *Calle Ripoche 4, Las Canteras* ☎ *696/335965* ⊗ *Closed Sun.*

Fundación Para El Estudio y Desarrollo de la Artesanía Canaria *(FEDAC)*
CRAFTS | This government-funded shop carries a selection of Gran Canaria crafts and handiwork. ⊠ *Calle Domingo J. Navarro 7, Triana* ☎ *928/369661* ⊕ *www.fedac.org* ⊗ *Closed weekends.*

José Juan Sosa
CRAFTS | Out of his studio in Gáldar, a town west of Las Palmas, this award-winning knife maker sells handmade blades with ornate handles made from ebony, gold, silver, steel, and nickel. Every piece is one of a kind. Visits are by email appointment only: *kneron77@gmail.com.* ⊠ *Lomo San Antón 90B,*

Las Palmas ⊕ *www.cuchilloscanarios. blogspot.com.*

Trastornados Showroom

FURNITURE | Part furniture showroom, part fashion boutique, and part home decorating store, this ultracool shopping spot sells designer wares from Spanish and international brands. If you're looking for a fancy gift for someone special—a beautiful handmade vase, perhaps, or a scented candle—you've come to the right place. ⊠ *Calle Pérez Galdós 13, Las Palmas* ☎ *928/433053* ⊙ *Closed Sun.*

 Activities

GOLF

El Cortijo Club de Campo

GOLF | Just outside Las Palmas on the freeway to the south, this 18-hole, par-72 course is one of the longest in Spain. Set among magnificent palm groves and six lakes, it has several holes with ocean views. ⊠ *Autopista del Sur, Km 6.4, Telde* ☎ *928/711111* ⊕ *www.elcortijo.es* ⚑ *€100* ⚓ *18 holes, 6899 yards, par 72.*

Real Club de Golf de Las Palmas

GOLF | Founded in 1891, the Real Club de Golf de Las Palmas is Spain's oldest course. Redesigned and relocated in 1956, it has 18 holes (par 71), two putting greens, two tennis courts, a restaurant, and a bar. Fifteen minutes outside Las Palmas, the course sits on the rim of the impressive Bandama Crater overlooking the extinct Bandama Volcano. The club also rents horses; it has 48 stables and five riding rings. ⊠ *Ctra. de Bandama, Santa Brígida* ☎ *928/351050* ⊕ *www. realclubdegolfdelaspalmas.com* ⚑ *€70* ⚓ *18 holes, 6288 yards, par 71.*

Maspalomas and the Southern Coast

60 km (36 miles) southwest of Las Palmas, 25 km (15 miles) southwest of Gran Canaria Airport.

One of the first places in Spain to welcome international tourists (starting in 1962), Maspalomas remains a beach resort with all the trappings. It's improbably backed by empty sand dunes that resemble the Sahara—despite beachfront overdevelopment in the town—and retains appealing stretches of isolated beach on the outskirts, as well as a bird sanctuary. Much of the area around the dunes is a protected nature reserve.

GETTING HERE AND AROUND

From Las Palmas, a short bus journey (45 minutes, longer at rush hour) runs to the southern resorts. Note that not all return buses go to the bus terminal near the port (Intercambiador de Parque Santa Catalina); some end at Intercambiador de San Telmo in central Las Palmas. You may therefore need to take a bus from here to the port if you're on a cruise (buses 1 and 12 are the best options). If you rent a car from the port, it's an easy drive to the south coast via the GC1 highway, and there's plenty of parking in and around Maspalomas.

 Sights

Aqualand Maspalomas

WATER PARK | **FAMILY** | The largest water park in the Canary Islands has wave pools, slides, and just about everything else splash-related. ⊠ *Ctra. Palmitos Park, Km 3, Maspalomas* ☎ *928/140525* ⊕ *www.aqualand.es* ⚑ *€30.*

Palmitos Park

ZOO | **FAMILY** | One of the main attractions in this part of the island, inland from Maspalomas, this part botanical garden

The dunes of Maspalomas were formed by sand from the bottom of the ocean, during the last ice age.

and part zoo has 1,500 tropical birds, a butterfly sanctuary, an orchid house, 160 species of tropical fish, many crocodiles, and parrot shows. ✉ *Ctra. Palmitos, Km 6, Maspalomas* ☏ *928/797070* ⊕ *www. palmitospark.es* ✉ *€32.*

Beaches

The below beaches abut one another, and you can walk them in sequence (hindered only by a pair of rocky dividers) along the shore. A boardwalk links Playa de Tarajalillo to the rest of the beaches until the dunes separate the boardwalk from the Maspalomas beach and Playa de la Mujer.

★ Maspalomas

BEACH | The island's most emblematic beach and one of the most beautiful, Maspalomas has golden sand that stretches for 2¾ km (1¾ miles) along the southern tip of Gran Canaria. Behind this beach are the famous Maspalomas dunes as well as palm groves and a saltwater lagoon, which lend an air

of isolation and refuge to the beach. Bathing is safe everywhere except at La Punta de Maspalomas, where currents converge. Topless bathing is acceptable, and there's a nudist area at La Cañada de la Penca. This beach is busy year-round. **Amenities:** food and drink; lifeguards; showers; toilets. **Best for:** nudists; sunrise; sunset; walking. ✉ *Maspalomas.*

Playa de las Burras

BEACH | Sandwiched between Playa del Inglés and Playa de San Agustín, this little sandy beach is protected by a breakwall, making it a favorite with families. Small fishing boats are moored in the bay, and the seafront promenade connects the neighboring resorts. Swimming is safe. There are plenty of lounge chairs and sunshades. **Amenities:** food and drink; lifeguards; showers; toilets. **Best for:** sunrise; swimming. ✉ *San Agustín.*

Playa de las Mujeres

BEACH | The co-ed "Women's Beach" is around the corner from the Maspalomas lighthouse in Meloneras. A natural beach with gray shingles and small rocks, this quiet enclave currently has no amenities, although the expansion of Meloneras, along with the construction of several high-end hotels, may change that in the future. Swimming is generally safe. **Amenities:** none. **Best for:** solitude; sunset; walking. ✉ *Meloneras*

Playa de San Agustín

BEACH | To the east of Maspalomas, this smaller beach consists of brown-black sand and some rocks. The promenade has lush vegetation nearby, making it one of the most picturesque on the island. This is a quieter beach than Maspalomas and Playa del Inglés. Bathing is safe in calm conditions, but watch out for strong currents when the waves get up. Lounge chairs and sunshades line the beach. **Amenities:** food and drink; lifeguards; showers; toilets; water sports. **Best for:** sunrise; walking. ✉ *San Agustín.*

Playa del Inglés

BEACH | Rivaling Maspalomas for popularity, Playa del Inglés has a lot going for it, including partying at the beach bars, sports, competitions, and concerts. There are nearly 3 km (2 miles) of golden sands, flanked by a pleasant seafront promenade that's great for early-morning and evening strolls. Swimming is generally safe, although windy conditions can create waves—it's a favorite spot with surfers. Lounge chairs and sunshades are available along the beach, and there's also a nudist area, which is signposted. **Amenities:** food and drink; lifeguards; showers; toilets; water sports. **Best for:** nudists; partiers; swimming; windsurfing. ✉ *Playa del Inglés.*

Hotels

★ Bohemia Suites & Spa

$$$$ | RESORT | When Swiss architect Pia Smith was tasked with refurbishing the Hotel Apolo, the first hotel on the Playa del Inglés, she reached for the sledgehammer. **Pros:** most avant-garde cocktail bar in the Canaries; characterful modern decor; standout spa and brand-new wellness facilities. **Cons:** certain areas undergoing renovation or repair; garden-view rooms face noisy construction site; poolside waiter service is slow. [$] *Rooms from: €250* ✉ *Av. Estados Unidos 28, Maspalomas* ☎ *928/563400* 🌐 *www.bohemia-grancanaria.com* 🛏 *67 rooms* 🍴 *Free Breakfast.*

Bull Costa Canaria & Spa

$$$$ | RESORT | One of the few hotels in the south of the island with direct access to the beach, Costa Canaria sits just behind the Blue Flag sands on Playa de San Agustín. **Pros:** ultramodern pool facilities; unbeatable oceanfront location; one of the area's few adults-only hotels. **Cons:** young travelers may feel out of place given older clientele; some distance from attractions; unremarkable food. [$] *Rooms from: €200* ✉ *Calle Las Retamas 1, San Agustín* ☎ *928/760200* 🌐 *www.bullhotels.com* 🛏 *229 rooms, 15 bungalows* 🍴 *All-Inclusive.*

Bull Eugenia Victoria & Spa

$$$ | HOTEL | One of the first hotels to pop up in the Playa del Inglés area in 1975, this is a longtime favorite among older northern Europeans in search of sun. **Pros:** huge spa and gym; rooms overlook the pool and garden area; Dead Sea pool. **Cons:** one-night stays not possible; not beachfront; young travelers may feel out of place among older crowd. [$] *Rooms from: €140* ✉ *Av. Gran Canaria 26, Maspalomas* ☎ *928/762500* 🌐 *www.bullhotels.com* 🛏 *400 rooms* 🍴 *Free Breakfast.*

Parque Tropical

$$$ | HOTEL | One of the first hotels to be built in Playa del Inglés, Parque Tropical remains a peaceful oasis of tropical palms, colorful blooms, and cascades. **Pros:** meticulously maintained gardens; direct beach access; made-to-order pancakes at breakfast. **Cons:** antiquated no-shorts policy at dinner; only twin beds available; some rooms are dark because of vegetation. [$] *Rooms from: €150* ✉ *Av.*

Italia 1, Playa del Inglés ☎ *928/774012* ⊕ *www.hotelparquetropical.com* ⇌ *221 rooms* ⦿ *Free Breakfast.*

★ Seaside Palm Beach

$$$$ | HOTEL | Sophisticated and luxurious, this hotel is a stone's throw from the edge of Maspalomas beach. **Pros:** exceptional design and facilities; room cleaning twice a day; above-and-beyond service. **Cons:** almost everyone is German and over 60; small bathrooms; expensive in high season. Ⓢ *Rooms from: €300* ⊠ *Av. del Oasis,* ☎ *928/721032* ⊕ *www.hotel-palm-beach.es* ⇌ *328 rooms* ⦿ *Free Breakfast.*

Nightlife

The days may be long, but the nights are even longer in Maspalomas and Playa del Inglés, party central of the Canary Islands. Freshly tanned vacationers pack the pubs at sundown; later, the clubs fill with writhing masses dancing to disco. Gran Canaria is one of Europe's biggest gay destinations, and gay bars and clubs abound near the four-story Yumbo Centrum shopping center at Playa del Inglés. Las Meloneras is another nightlife center, where Aqua Ocean Club is one of the big attractions.

Eiffel Bar

Slurping down a strawberry daiquiri at the gay-friendly Eiffel Bar is a rite of passage on the Playa del Inglés nightlife circuit; every cocktail comes with a complimentary bowl of peanuts and marshmallows. ⊠ *Yumbo Centrum, Av. Estados Unidos, Planta Baja, Local 121, Playa del Inglés* ☎ *634/310227.*

Pachá Gran Canaria

DANCE CLUBS | The Canarian outpost of this renowned discotheque megachain doesn't disappoint with its DJ beats and sundown-to-sunup dancing. Expect a mix of locals and foreigners; the club isn't gay per se but is gay-friendly. ⊠ *Av. Sargentos Provisionales 10, Maspalomas*

☎ *928/771730* ⊕ *www.facebook.com/pachagrancanaria.*

Activities

BICYCLING

Bike 10Mil

BIKING | FAMILY | The tours offered by this company cater to all ages and fitness levels, or you can rent a bike and go it alone. ⊠ *Centro Comercial Gran Chaparral, Av. de Gran Canaria 30, Playa del Inglés* ☎ *663/535038* ⊕ *www.bike10mil.com.*

BOAT TOURS

CoolPlaySail

SAILING | FAMILY | Hop on a sunset cruise or full-day sailing adventure on this 15.5-meter yacht complete with refreshments, tunes, and paddleboards. ⊠ *Puerto Deportivo Pasito Blanco, Maspalomas* ☎ *629/505606* ⊕ *www.coolplaysail.com.*

Multiacuatic

WILDLIFE-WATCHING | FAMILY | Two-hour whale- and dolphin-watching trips leave from Playa de Puerto Rico, about 13 km (8 miles) west of Maspalomas. Avoid rough-sea days. ⊠ *Muelle Puerto Base, Puerto Rico* ☎ *626/982152* ⊕ *www.dolphinwhales.es* ⇌ *€29.*

CAMEL RIDES

Camello Safari

LOCAL SPORTS | FAMILY | Join a quick camel trek across the Maspalomas dunes. The rides, which take about 30 minutes, leave every 15 minutes. ⊠ *Calle Oceania, Maspalomas* ☎ *928/760781* ⊕ *www.camellosafari.com* ⇌ *€12.*

GOLF

Lopesan Meloneras Golf

GOLF | Half of the 18 holes at this par-71 course face the mountains, and the other half face the sea. Several are practically on the beach. ⊠ *Autopista GC 500,* ☎ *928/145309* ⊕ *www.grancanariagolf.com* ⇌ *€85* ⚹ *18 holes, 6350 yards, par 71.*

Maspalomas Golf

GOLF | Surrounded by the famous Maspalomas dunes, this 18-hole, par-73 course has ocean views from many of its long, wide greens. The course was designed by Mackenzie Ross. ⊠ *Av. T. O. Neckerman, Maspalomas* ☎ *928/762581* ⊕ *www.maspalomasgolf.net* ⊴ *€120* ⚑ *18 holes, 6723 yards, par 73.*

HORSEBACK RIDING
El Salobre

HORSEBACK RIDING | Horseback riding trips near Maspalomas are for one (€30) or two (€45) hours, with longer trips available on request. The company can pick you up from your hotel and take you to the stables. ⊠ *Calle Islas Malvinas 3, El Salobre* ☎ *616/418363* ⊕ *www. elsalobrehr.es.*

WINDSURFING
Pro Surfing

SURFING | FAMILY | Learn from scratch or improve your windsurfing, kitesurfing, and paddleboarding skills here; they also have gear to rent. ⊠ *Centro Comercial Eurocenter Loc. 80, Av. de Moya 6, Playa del Inglés* ☎ *928/769719* ⊕ *www. prsurfing.com.*

San Bartolomé de Tirajana

23 km (14 miles) north of Maspalomas, 20 km (12 miles) east of Cruz de San Antonio.

The administrative center of the south coast, San Bartolomé de Tirajana is an attractive town planted with pink geraniums. At its popular Sunday morning market, held every two weeks in front of the church, you'll find tropical produce and island crafts. To the east, the village of **Santa Lucía** has crafts shops and a small museum devoted to Guanche artifacts.

Side Trip

Drive up to the Cruz Grande summit on GC520. To the left are several of the island's reservoirs, known as the lakes of Gran Canaria; they're stocked with trout and carp, and you can fish in them with a permit (obtained in advance) from the island environmental agency (*928/301591*). Continue along GC520 in the direction of Tejeda, past rural mountain villages. On the right is the Roque Nublo, an eroded volcanic chimney worshiped by the Guanches that juts 80 meters (262 feet) into the air. Explore the Roque and its surrounding trails, pausing for a picnic in the shade.

Tejeda

About 7 km (4½ miles) southwest of Las Palmas.

At the misty mountain village of Tejeda, the road begins to ascend through a pine forest dotted with picnic spots to the Parador Cruz de Tejeda. From the parador, continue uphill about 21 km (13 miles) to the Mirador Pico de las Nieves, the highest lookout on Gran Canaria. Here, too, is the Pozo de la Nieve, a well built by clergymen in 1699 to store snow. Tejeda is locally famous for its fragrant almonds, which bakers incorporate into delectable confections sold in the town center.

◉ Sights

Artenara

TOWN | From the road leading to the Parador Cruz de Tejeda, follow signs west to the village of Artenara (about 13 km [8 miles]) for views of the rocky valley and its chimney-like formations. You can see both Roque Nublo and Roque Ventaiga, sitting like temples on a long ridge in the valley. ✉ *Artenara* 🌐 *www.artenara.es.*

Mirador de la Cilla

RESTAURANT | The entrance to the touristy restaurant Mirador de la Cilla takes you through a 164-foot tunnel. Don't eat here—the food is subpar—but it's worth making a stop to take in the spectacular mountain view with a beer or coffee. ✉ *Camino de la Silla 3, Artenara* ☎ *609/163944.*

Hotels

Parador Cruz de Tejeda

$$ | **HOTEL** | In the geographical center of the island, this is the perfect spot to get away from it all and to take in some of Gran Canaria's best views. **Pros:** incredible sunsets from the rooms; large rooms; fantastic spa (€25 fee). **Cons:** difficult access up a mountain road; limited dining options outside hotel; inconsistent service. [$] *Rooms from: €113* ✉ *Calle Cruz de Tejeda, Tejeda* ☎ *928/012500* 🌐 *www.parador.es* 🛏 *43 rooms* 🍴 *No Meals.*

San Mateo

15 km (9 miles) northeast of Parador Cruz de Tejeda.

From Tejeda, the road winds down to San Mateo, whose goat cheese is famous across Gran Canaria. You can find it at the weekend market and in shops the island over. Pass Santa Brigida and turn right toward the golf club on the rim of the Bandama Crater. Continue to the village of Atalaya, where there are cave houses and pottery workshops carrying on a millennia-old tradition.

Tafira Alta

7 km (4½ miles) west of Las Palmas.

Along the main road leading into Las Palmas from San Mateo is Tafira Alta, an exclusive suburb with a colonial air where many of the city's wealthiest families live.

Sights

Jardín Botánico Canario Viero y Clavijo

GARDEN | In Tafira Alta (just north of Las Palmas) is one of Spain's largest botanical gardens, with plants from all the islands grouped in their natural habitats. ✉ *Ctra. de Centro, Km 7, Tafira Alta* ☎ *928/219580* 🌐 *www.jardincanario.org.*

Lanzarote

With hardened lava fields, black and red dunes, and treeless mountainsides, Lanzarote's interior is right out of a science-fiction movie (literally—*Clash of the Titans, One Million Years B.C.* and a number of other blockbusters were filmed here). The entire island is a UNESCO biosphere reserve. There are no springs or lakes, and it rarely rains, so all freshwater comes from desalination plants. Despite its surreal and sometimes intimidating volcanic landscape, Lanzarote—the fourth-largest Canary—has turned itself into an inviting resort through good planning (although not so good around Playa Blanca, where illegal construction is slightly out of hand), an emphasis on outdoor adventure, and conservation of its natural beauty. No buildings taller than two stories are allowed in most places, and billboards are forbidden, leaving views of the spectacular geology unobstructed.

Lanzarote was named for the Italian explorer Lancelotto Alocello, who arrived in the 14th century, but the name most synonymous with the island today is César Manrique, the internationally acclaimed artist and architect who helped shape modern-day Canarian culture and share it on the world stage. Manrique designed many of the island's tourist attractions and convinced authorities to require that all new buildings be painted white with green or brown trim (white with blue on the coast), to suggest coolness and fertility. He also joined local activists in the fight against overdevelopment, lying down in front of bulldozers and galvanizing islanders. All over this island, and especially in Arrecife, Lanzarote has a North African feel. Like Moroccans, many locals sip their hot drinks, in this case *café bombón* (coffee with condensed milk), from little glasses rather than mugs.

Vying with Fuerteventura for the title of warmest island, Lanzarote often bakes in the summer. It's also very windy, particularly during July and August, when the trade winds (*vientos alisios*) from the northeast batter the island.

Despite the heat and lack of precipitation, the island produces some surprisingly excellent wine. Vines are buried (sometimes up to several feet deep) in a mantle of black lava shingle known as *picón* that attracts and retains moisture from dew, the only source of water for vines on this arid island. There are two designated wine tours that take in the main vineyards on the west side of the island. Ask at a tourist office for a wine-tour map.

VISITOR INFORMATION
CONTACTS Airport Tourist Office.
✉ *César Manrique-Lanzarote Airport,* ☎ *928/820704* ⊕ *www.turismolanzarote. com.* **Arrecife Tourist Office.** ✉ *Parque Municipal, Arrecife* ☎ *928/811762.*

Arrecife

6 km (4 miles) east of the airport.

Although Arrecife houses one-third of Lanzarote's population (146,000), it exudes a leisurely island energy, unlike bustling Santa Cruz or Las Palmas. Real talk: It's not an especially pretty city, and some Canarians will even tell you to skip it altogether, but it does have some of the best shopping and nightlife on the island. It's also a practical place to crash before an early-morning departure or after a late-night landing. The coastline is strung with line after line of rocky reefs (in fact, "reef" is what arrecife means in Spanish). While you're here, don't miss its two castles or its inland saltwater lagoon, Charco de San Ginés, where there's a gorgeous fleet of small fishing craft. A stroll around the backstreets near the lagoon gives you an idea of the old Arrecife. The local Playa del Reducto is a good place to squeeze in some beach time if you're spending the day here.

From Arrecife, you can walk or bike to Puerto del Carmen along the 12-km (7½-mile) seafront promenade, which takes in lovely stretches of golden sand and views of the Ajaches mountains in the south. Stop for a bite to eat in Playa Honda, and take the bus back if you're not up for the return trip.

GETTING HERE AND AROUND
Cruise ships dock at Puerto Mármoles, about 3 km (2 miles) east of the capital. A walkway traces the shore from the port into the town, but it's a long and unattractive walk. Consider hopping on a shuttle bus or hailing a taxi outside the terminal.

Once in Arrecife, there are buses to Costa Teguise, Puerto del Carmen, and Playa Blanca run by the ambitiously named Intercity Bus company. If you want to travel farther afield, it's best to rent a car.

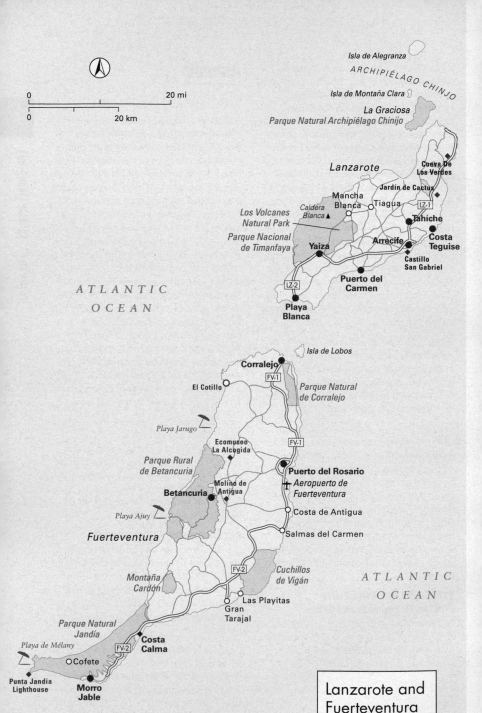

Lanzarote and Fuerteventura

Island-hopping is possible by ferry from Arrecife to Fuerteventura and on to Gran Canaria, although the quickest way to get to Fuerteventura is from Playa Blanca. Southern Lanzarote and northern Fuerteventura are linked by two companies, Fred Olsen and Naviera Armas, both of which make six round trips a day from Lanzarote. Interisland planes link Lanzarote quickly and frequently with the other islands.

VISITOR INFORMATION

Tourist Office Center

Arrecife isn't the most attractive part of Lanzarote, but the old town is interesting, particularly the area around the Charco de San Ginés (lagoon). The **tourist office** , housed in the original bandstand in the municipal park, has detailed maps and information about local points of interest. ⊠ *Parque Municipal, Arrecife* ☎ *928/811762* ⊗ *Closed Sun.*

Tourist Office Cruise Terminal

⊠ *Muelle de los Mármoles, Arrecife* ☎ *928/844690.*

Sights

Castillo San Gabriel

CASTLE/PALACE | This double-wall fortress was once used to keep pirates at bay. You can walk out to the fortress over Puente de las Bolas with lovely views of the port and city and then explore the small (Spanish-only) museum inside. ⊠ *Arrecife* ☎ *€3*

Museo Internacional de Arte Contemporáneo Castillo de San José (*MIAC*)

ART MUSEUM | The old waterfront fortress Castillo San José was turned into this stunning modern art museum by the architect César Manrique. One of his paintings is on display, along with works by Cardenas, Beaudin, Zóbel, Tàpies, and others. ⊠ *Carretera de los Castillos, Arrecife* ☎ *901/200300* ☎ *€4.*

Beaches

Playa del Reducto

BEACH | **FAMILY** | Playa del Reducto is an attractive urban beach, ideal for relaxing after you've looked around Arrecife. It's well-maintained and protected by natural reefs, so swimming is usually like swimming in a warm lake (just watch out for rocky outcrops at low tide). The beach, overlooked at the eastern end by the high-rise Arrecife Gran Hotel, is backed by a pleasant promenade that goes all the way to Puerto del Carmen. **Amenities:** food and drink; showers; toilets. **Best for:** sunrise; walking. ⊠ *Arrecife*

Restaurants

Casa Ginory

$ | **SPANISH** | Decorated in a nautical theme, Casa Ginory has indoor and outdoor seating, with tables overlooking the sea or the Charco de San Ginés lagoon. House specials include *matrimonio* (a "marriage" of squid rings and fish) and clams washed down with local wines. **Known for:** waterfront views; local vibe; fresh fish. $ *Average main: €9* ⊠ *Calle Juan de Quesada 7, Arrecife* ☎ *922/804046* ⊗ *Closed Sun.*

Lilium

$$ | **SPANISH** | Creative cooking with Canarian roots is the philosophy behind the dishes at this modern restaurant east of the San Ginés lagoon. Although there are a few tables outdoors, the dining mainly takes place inside, where copper and chocolate tones accompany floral touches. **Known for:** tasting menu; innovative cuisine; elevated Canarian cuisine. $ *Average main: €15* ⊠ *Centro Comercial Marina Lanzarote, Av. Olof Palme, Arrecife* ☎ *928/524978* ⊕ *restaurantelilium.com* ⊗ *Closed Sun.*

Naia

$$ | **SPANISH** | From your patio table overlooking the harbor, feast on attractively plated modern Spanish fare such

Lanzarote is known for its year-round warm weather, volcanic landscape, and conservation of its natural beauty.

as heirloom tomato *salmorejo* (creamy gazpacho), griddled Iberian pork with sautéed vegetables, and slow-poached cod over black rice. The interior dining area is almost as charming with pendant lights and mismatched vintage chairs. **Known for:** creative Canarian cuisine; artfully plated dishes; pleasant harborside patio. [$] *Average main: €13* ✉ *Av. César Manrique 33, Arrecife* ☎ *928/805797* ⏲ *Closed Sun.*

Hotels

Arrecife Gran Hotel
$$ | HOTEL | This 17-story glass tower is a bit of an eyesore on an island where low-rises are the norm, but once inside, it's hard to hate the bird's-eye views from the rooms and the inviting, comfy communal areas. **Pros:** soothing, well-maintained spa; great views; spacious rooms. **Cons:** average breakfast; cleanliness not quite five-star; slow, forgetful service staff. [$] *Rooms from: €124* ✉ *Av. Fred Olsen 1, Arrecife* ☎ *928/800000* 🌐 *www.aghotelspa.com* 🛏 *160 rooms* 🍴 *No Meals.*

Hotel Lancelot
$ | HOTEL | Facing the attractive Playa del Reducto, this is a good budget option for a quick overnight. **Pros:** rooftop pool; beachside location; good value. **Cons:** mattresses can be a little uncomfortable; dull breakfast that stops at 10 am; drab environs. [$] *Rooms from: €76* ✉ *Av. de la Mancomunidad 9, Arrecife* ☎ *928/805099* 🌐 *www.hotellancelot.com* 🛏 *110 rooms* 🍴 *No Meals.*

Nightlife

The Garden
DANCE CLUBS | This 21-plus nightclub plays mostly chart-topping bangers to a stylish local set. Drinks are reasonably priced. No shorts, sandals, or beachwear allowed. ✉ *Marina Lanzarote, Avenida Olof Palme, Arrecife* ☎ *651/120883* 🌐 *www.facebook.com/thegardenarrecife.*

The Red Lion

BARS | Grab a beer at this quirky locals-only sports bar to watch spirited *fútbol* matches and bet on horse races. An Elvis impersonator frequently provides the musical entertainment. ⊠ *Av. de las Islas Canarias, Local 10, Arrecife* ☎ *651/593485.*

🛍 Shopping

Shopping is low-key in Arrecife. The main shops are on and around the pedestrian-only Calle León y Castilla.

★ Queso Project

FOOD | Some of Lanzarote's top artisan cheeses (and a wide selection of mainland European ones) are sold at this charming city-center shop. ⊠ *Calle José Molina 7, Arrecife* ☎ *636/714348* ⊕ *www.quesoproject.com* ⏱ *Closed Sun. and Mon.*

🏃 Activities

★ Eco Insider

HIKING & WALKING | **FAMILY** | Discover hidden corners of Lanzarote with this company's specialty trips, which include bird-watching, volcano walks, food and wine tours, and visits to the remote islets of La Graciosa and uninhabited La Alegranza. Tours are led by local experts. The company can pick you up by prior arrangement from your hotel or cruise ship; book well in advance. Prices include lunch and transportation. ⊠ *Arrecife* ☎ *650/819069* ⊕ *www.eco-insider.com* ⎘ *From €42.*

Costa Teguise

7 km (4½ miles) northeast of Arrecife.

A green-and-white puzzle of apartments and several large hotels, Costa Teguise is a typical '80s resort that some would say is past its heyday, although it still draws thousands of visitors every year. King Juan Carlos used to own a villa here, near the Meliá Salinas hotel. Teguise proper (aka La Villa de Teguise or, colloquially, just La Villa), on the other hand, is situated 15 km (9 miles) inland from the coastal enclave and is another experience entirely: It is Lanzarote's historic capital and the oldest settlement in the archipelago, dating to 1402. Many of local visionary artist César Manrique's architectural masterpieces are situated within easy driving distance of Teguise.

GETTING HERE AND AROUND

Lanzarote Intercity buses connect the resort and Arrecife. On weekdays, a bus leaves every 20 minutes, and every 30 minutes on weekends. The trip takes about 20 minutes.

VISITOR INFORMATION

CONTACTS Costa Teguise Tourist Office. ⊠ *Av. Islas Canarias s/n, Costa Teguise* ☎ *928/592542* ⊕ *www.turismoteguise. com.*

👁 Sights

Castillo de Santa Bárbara (*Museo de la Piratería*)

CASTLE/PALACE | **FAMILY** | For sweeping aerial views of Lanzarote's craggy coast and parched volcanic landscape, climb to the top of this 16th-century fortress that, since 2011, houses the Canaries' Museo de la Piratería (Piracy Museum). The *castillo* warded off pirates for centuries from its perch on the Guanapay volcano. ⊠ *Calle Herrera y Rojas 5, Teguise* ☎ *686/470376, 928/594802* ⊕ *www. museodelapirateria.com.*

★ César Manrique House Museum

HISTORIC HOME | On a hillock overlooking the sleepy town of Haría you'll find César Manrique's final home, preserved as if in amber. The artist lived in this architecturally stunning estate, which he built for himself, until his untimely death by auto accident in 1992. Plant-filled courtyards lead into Bohemian living areas brimming with sculptures, paintings, and iconic furniture; the bathroom, with a

The incredible Jardín de Cactus was designed by César Manrique, the island's most influential artist and architect.

floor-to-ceiling window into a leafy garden, is a highlight, as is the outdoor pool area and art studio, kept precisely how it was left on the day he died. ⊠ *Calle Elvira Sánchez 30, Haria* ☎ *928/843138* ⊕ *www.fcmanrique.org* ⊠ *€10.*

Cueva de los Verdes (*Verdes's Cave*)
CAVE | FAMILY | Guided walks take you through this 1-km (½-mile) section of an underground lava tube, said to be the longest in the world. It's one of the most stunning natural sights on the island. You'll find the entrance to the north of Costa Teguise, beyond Punta Mujeres. ⊠ *LZ204, Costa Teguise* ☎ *901/200300* ⊠ *€10.*

Jameos del Agua
NATURE SIGHT | These water caverns, turned into an architectural destination by César Manrique, is situated 15 km (9 miles) north of the Costa Teguise. They were created when molten lava streamed through an underground tunnel and hissed into the sea. Look for the tiny albino crabs on the rocks in the underground lake—this species, which is blind, is found nowhere else in the world. There's a pleasant if basic restaurant by the lake, and the Casa de los Volcanes is a good museum of volcanic science. Night visits are possible on Saturday. ⊠ *Punta de Mujeres, Costa Teguise* ☎ *901/200300* ⊠ *€10.*

★ **Jardín de Cactus** (*Cactus Garden*)
CITY PARK | FAMILY | North of Costa Teguise between Guatiza and Mala, this cactus garden with 10,000 specimens of more than 1,500 varieties was César Manrique's last creation for Lanzarote. Look beyond the park and you'll see prickly pear fields: for centuries locals have cultivated these plants for their cochineal, an insect living on the cacti from which scarlet carmine dye is extracted. ⊠ *Ctra. General del Norte, Guatiza* ☎ *901/200300* ⊠ *€6.*

Mirador del Río
NOTABLE BUILDING | Designed by César Manrique, this lookout at the northerly tip of a hairpin bend in the LZ202 road lets you see the islet of La Graciosa from an altitude of 1,550 feet. From the lookout

you can also see smaller protected isles—Montaña Clara, Alegranza (the Canary closest to Europe), and Roque del Este. Arrive early to beat the crowds. ✉ *LZ202,* 🎫 *€5.*

Órzola

TOWN | The little fishing village of Órzola is 9 km (5½ miles) north of Jameos del Agua. Small-boat excursions leave here each day for the neighboring one-town islet of La Graciosa, where there are fewer than 500 residents and plenty of quiet beaches. ✉ *Órzola.*

Beaches

★ Playa de Famara

BEACH | Directly opposite Costa Teguise on the north coast of Lanzarote is perhaps the island's most breathtaking beach. Set in a natural cove, its 6 km (4 miles) of sand are flanked by spectacularly high cliffs. The riptide here makes for excellent surfing and windsurfing, and Playa de Famara is regularly used for world championships for those sports. That said, the strong currents mean swimming can be dangerous. **Amenities:** food and drink; lifeguards; showers; toilets; water sports. **Best for:** sunset; surfing; walking; windsurfing. ✉ *Av. el Marinero, Las Palmas.*

Playa de la Garita

BEACH | FAMILY | Not far from the Jardín de Cactus, Playa de la Garita is a wide bay of crystalline water favored by surfers in winter and snorkelers in summer. Almost a kilometer (½ mile) of golden sands is safe for swimming, making this a popular spot for families. The beach gets busy in the summer but is reasonably quiet the rest of the year. Lounge chairs and umbrellas are available for rent. **Amenities:** food and drink; lifeguards; showers; toilets; water sports. **Best for:** snorkeling; surfing; swimming. ✉ *Arrieta.*

Playa de las Cucharas

BEACH | This is the best of Costa Teguise's several small beaches. The sands are protected from high wind and waves by the natural bay formed in the coastline. A pleasant seafront promenade takes you around the beach and into the southern stretches of the resort. Getting a spot for your towel in the summer can be a challenge, especially on weekends. **Amenities:** food and drink; lifeguards; showers; toilets; water sports. **Best for:** sunrise; swimming. ✉ *Av. Arenas Blancas, Costa Teguise.*

Restaurants

El Navarro

$$ | INTERNATIONAL | Although it's on a busy access road and inside a drab building, this restaurant is well worth a stop. Menu highlights include salad with crispy ham, cheese, and dates, and curry croquettes. **Known for:** killer cheesecake; curry croquettes; pleasant terrace. [$] *Average main: €14* ✉ *Av. del Mar 13, Costa Teguise* ☎ *928/592145* 🕒 *Closed Tues. and July.*

Restaurante Las Caletas Casa Tomás

$$ | SPANISH | Off the tourist track, this no-frills seafood restaurant with stunning sea views is a favorite with locals. The outdoor terrace seems to hover over the sea. **Known for:** affordable seafood dishes; pleasant terrace; ocean views. [$] *Average main: €13* ✉ *Calle Bambilote 2, Costa Teguise* ☎ *928/591046* 🌐 *www.facebook.com/casatomaslascaletas* 🕒 *Closed Mon. and Tues.*

Hotels

Club Santa Rosa Apartamentos

$ | RESORT | Outstanding value in pristine surroundings is the hallmark of the Santa Rosa resort, a collection of one- and two-bedroom apartments and villas centered around a large swimming pool. **Pros:** spotlessly clean; well-appointed gym; indoor pool and bowling (fee). **Cons:** maintenance could be improved; longish walk to the beach; single beds only. [$] *Rooms from: €87* ✉ *Av. del Mar*

19, ☎ *928/346038* 🌐 *www.apartamentossantarosa.com* 🛏 *128 rooms* 🍴 *Free Breakfast.*

H10 Lanzarote Gardens

$$$ | **RESORT** | **FAMILY** | For a good, all-inclusive deal in tropical surroundings, this is one of the best bets in the area for families. **Pros:** entertainment for all ages; excellent service; good value. **Cons:** no elevators; can be crowded in high season; noisy breakfasts. [$] *Rooms from: €160* ✉ *Av. Islas Canarias 13, Costa Teguise* ☎ *900/444666* 🌐 *www.hotelh-10lanzarotegardens.com* 🛏 *242 rooms* 🍴 *Free Breakfast.*

Shopping

For island crafts and produce, go to the open market (one of the largest on the islands) in the village of **Teguise** on Sunday between 9 and 2. Some vendors set up stalls in the plaza; others just lay out a blanket in the street and sell embroidered tablecloths, leather goods, costume jewelry, African masks, and other items.

Aloe Plus Lanzarote

COSMETICS | A wide range of lotions, balms, and serums made from locally grown aloe vera are sold at this shop, which also has a small "museum" detailing the history and uses of the plant. There are other branches in Yaiza, Arrieta, Punta Mujeres, and La Graciosa. ✉ *Pl. de la Constitución 4, Teguise* ☎ *928/594894* 🌐 *www.aloepluslanzarote.com* 🕒 *Closed Sun. afternoon.*

Activities

BIKING

Evolution Bikes

BIKING | **FAMILY** | Both novice and expert cyclists are well-served at this shop that rents mountain bikes, road bikes, quadricycles, and more. Child seats and trailers are also available. Should any technical issues arise while riding, a store associate will drive out and fix it. Rates start at €12 per day. ✉ *Complejo La Galea, Paseo Marítimo 2, Costa Teguise* ☎ *672/330251* 🌐 *www.evolution-bikes.com.*

DIVING

One of the island's official diving centers is located very near to Las Cucharas beach.

Aquatis Diving Center

SCUBA DIVING | Diving Lanzarote rents equipment, leads dives, and offers a certification course. Adrenaline junkies shouldn't miss the "Diving With Sharks" outing. ✉ *Playa de las Cucharas, Local 6, Costa Teguise* ☎ *928/590407* 🌐 *en.divinginlanzarote.com.*

Calipso Diving Lanzarote

DIVING & SNORKELING | This well-established dive school has PADI Resort Center status and offers experiences for kids and adults. Hotel pickup can be arranged. ✉ *Centro Comercial Calipso, Av. Islas Canarias, Local 3, Costa Teguise* ☎ *928/590879* 🌐 *www.calipso-diving.com.*

GOLF

Costa Teguise Golf

GOLF | These 18 holes, which are outside the Costa Teguise development, have unusual sand traps filled with black-lava cinders. ✉ *Av. del Golf, Costa Teguise* ☎ *928/590512* 🌐 *www.lanzarote-golf.com* 🎫 *€90* ⛳ *18 holes, 7082 yards, par 72.*

SURFING

Some of the best surfing in the world is on Lanzarote's west coast, particularly at Famara beach where regular surfing championships take place. The variety of beaches and winds on the island makes it an excellent location for surfers of all abilities.

★ SurfCanarias Surf School Lanzarote

SURFING | Surfers of all experience levels can take classes and rent gear from this company. ✉ *Av. el Marinero 13, Teguise* ☎ *928/528528* 🌐 *www.surfcanarias.com.*

WINDSURFING

Windsurfing Club Las Cucharas

WINDSURFING | The most thrilling place on the island for windsurfing is at Playa de las Cucharas; this club provides lessons and equipment rental. ⊠ *Centro Comercial Las Maretas 2, Calle de Marajo, Costa Teguise* ☎ *928/590731* ⊕ *www.lanzarotewindsurf.com.*

Puerto del Carmen

11 km (7 miles) southwest of Arrecife.

Most beach-bound travelers to Lanzarote wind up in the sands of the Puerto del Carmen area, the island's busiest resort. The small fishing port and historic marina (called El Varadero) are surrounded by cafés and restaurants, with the main commercial center behind them. The charming Puerto Carlero, 6 km (4 miles) west, is the newest addition to the resort and makes a quieter base.

GETTING HERE AND AROUND

Take the bus from Arrecife or the airport. Services run every 20 minutes on weekdays and every 30 on weekends. The trip takes 40 minutes. If you're feeling energetic, walk or bike on the seafront promenade all the way to Puerto del Carmen from the capital.

VISITOR INFORMATION

CONTACTS **Puerto del Carmen Tourist Office.** ⊠ *Av. de las Playas 6, Puerto del Carmen* ☎ *928/513351.*

 Beaches

Playa de los Pocillos

BEACH | Slightly north of Puerto del Carmen, this beach is near most of the area's development; hotels and apartments are restricted, however, to the other side of the highway, leaving the 2-km (1-mile) yellow-sand beach surprisingly pristine. Finding a spot to lay your towel can be difficult in summer. Lounge chairs and umbrellas are available.

Amenities: food and drink; lifeguards; showers; toilets; water sports. **Best for:** sunrise; swimming; walking. ⊠ *Av. de las Playas, Tías.*

Playa Grande

BEACH | Puerto del Carmen's main beach is a busy strip of yellow sand that's as close as you can get to an urban beach on Lanzarote outside Arrecife. Lounge chairs and umbrellas are available for rent. Backing the beach is a seafront promenade with plenty of souvenir shops and restaurants. You can take the promenade all the way to Arrecife. **Amenities:** food and drink; lifeguards; showers; toilets; water sports. **Best for:** swimming. ⊠ *Av. de las Playas.*

Playa Matagorda

BEACH | On this northern extension of Playa de los Pocillos, there are alternating sections of gravel and gray sand. A perpetually windy spot, this busy beach has gentle waves that are perfect for those learning to surf. Lounge chairs and beach umbrellas are available. **Amenities:** food and drink; lifeguards; showers; toilets; water sports. **Best for:** surfing; swimming; walking. ⊠ *Av. de las Playas, Tías.*

🍴 Restaurants

Everest Indian Restaurant

$ | INDIAN | FAMILY | When you can't look at another plate of fish and taters without moaning—*mira*, it happens to the best of us in the Canaries—spring for a palate-jolting curry at Everest, whose heady dishes ranging from vindaloo to korma and *jalfrezi* (curry dish) are probably better than your neighborhood Indian joint's renditions. **Known for:** cheery service; blistered made-to-order naan; unapologetically spicy curries. $ *Average main: €10* ⊠ *Av. de las Playas 41, Puerto del Carmen* ☎ *928/511181.*

La Lonja

$ | TAPAS | Every morning, fishermen haul in their catch steps from this converted fishermen's warehouse whose upstairs

Did You Know?

The grapes used to make wines in Lanzarote are cultivated in a singular manner. Here, rows of volcanic stone semi-circles replace patchwork green fields. Called Zocos, these have been built for each individual vine and provide much needed protection from the sometimes-fierce winds.

dining room has sweeping views of the busy harbor. The Canarian menu includes simply roasted and fried fish and papas arrugadas. **Known for:** great value; heaping seafood and fish platters; harbor and sea views. $ *Average main: €11* ✉ *Calle Varadero 22, Puerto del Carmen* ☎ *928/511377.*

★ Mardeleva

$$ | SEAFOOD | On a hill overlooking the port, this small family-run restaurant is all about the catch of the day (try the barracuda if available), served either fried or grilled and always accompanied by papas arrugadas. *Arroz caldoso con bogavante* (soupy rice with lobster) is another highlight. Try to score a table on the outdoor terrace, where you can watch the boats ply across the harbor; inside, eclectic family artworks are on display. **Known for:** intimate, family-run atmosphere; pleasant marina views; pristine seafood. $ *Average main: €12* ✉ *Calle los Infantes 10, Puerto del Carmen* ☎ *928/510686* ⊕ *www.facebook.com/mardelevarestaurant* ⊙ *Closed Mon. and Tues.*

 ## Hotels

Hotel Costa Calero Talaso & Spa

$$ | HOTEL | Sprawling gardens and serene pools await guests at this modern hotel, just south of Puerto del Carmen in the Puerto Calero marina. **Pros:** spa with Roman baths; free shuttle bus to the beach; quiet location with lovely gardens. **Cons:** slightly off the beaten track; little food variety; dull entertainment. $ *Rooms from: €124* ✉ *Urbanización Puerto Calero, Puerto del Carmen* ☎ *928/849595* ⊕ *www.hotelcostacalero. es* ⇗ *312 rooms, 12 suites* ⭗ *Free Breakfast.*

Seaside Los Jameos Playa

$$$ | HOTEL | FAMILY | César Manrique disciples were behind this giant colonial resort, where the tropical gardens, wooden balconies, and cane furniture all evoke old-school Havana. **Pros:** stunning architecture; complimentary glass of cava at check-in; renowned tennis club. **Cons:** not much variety for vegetarians; kids' activities are sometimes lackluster; communal areas need a refresh. $ *Rooms from: €170* ✉ *Calle Marte 2, Playa de los Pocillos* ☎ *928/763308* ⊕ *www.los-jameos.com* ⇗ *526 rooms, 4 suites* ⭗ *Free Breakfast.*

 ## Nightlife

This is the center of Lanzarote's nightlife. The main party strip is Avenida de las Playas. For a more relaxed night out, head to the old town, where most locals spend their time. There, the crowd is still mostly foreign, but the bars are more intimate and the drinks cheaper.

The Dubliner Live Music Lounge

LIVE MUSIC | These cover musicians are pros at getting everyone into party mode (and they keep it bumping till 3:30)—so grab a pint of Guinness and jump on the dance floor. Nobody takes themselves too seriously at the Dubliner, and that's precisely its allure. ✉ *Centro Comercial Marítimo, Av. de las Playas, Puerto del Carmen* ☎ *636/713861.*

Gran Casino de Lanzarote

GATHERING PLACES | Try your luck at the only casino on Lanzarote—it's as laid-back as the island itself. You must be over 18 and must show your passport to get in. ✉ *Av. de las Playas 12, Puerto del Carmen* ☎ *928/515000* ⊕ *www.grancasinolanzarote.com.*

Ruta 66

BARS | At the American bar Ruta 66, you can sip a frothy mixed drink on a cushioned wicker chair while taking in catchy tunes and ocean views. This is also the town's liveliest spot to catch a sports game and root for your team among fellow fans. ✉ *Av. de las Playas 19, Puerto del Carmen.*

Scotch Corner Bar

BARS | Guitars hang from the ceiling, and old pictures of Scotland adorn the walls in the Scotch Corner Bar. There's live music nightly usually acoustic and sometimes Scottish. Regulars love the mojitos. ✉ *Calle Tenerife 14, Puerto del Carmen.*

Activities

Lanzarote Golf

GOLF | This 18-hole course, which is between Puerto del Carmen and Tías, comes with spectacular ocean views along its wide greens. ✉ *Ctra. del Puerto del Carmen–Tías,* ☎ *928/514050* ⊕ *www.lanzarotegolfresort.com* ✉ *€73* ⚑ *18 holes, 6707 yards, par 72.*

Tahíche

5 km (3 miles) south of Teguise.

Only one thing makes Tahíche a destination rather than a drive-through town between Arrecife and the north of the island: the former estate of César Manrique.

GETTING HERE AND AROUND

By car, head north out of Arrecife on the main avenue, Avenida Campoamor. The Fundación César Manrique is off to the left before you enter the village (follow the signs). From Arrecife, buses 7 and 9 go this way several times a day; Bus 10 runs weekdays only; all stop at the César Manrique Crossing.

Sights

★ Fundación César Manrique

HISTORIC HOME | César Manrique (1919–92) made this high-design bachelor pad called Taro de Tahíche for himself in 1968 upon returning from New York City, where he'd been living and working thanks to a grant from Nelson Rockefeller. The artist managed to turn a barren lava field into an inviting and architecturally stunning abode—the first of its kind in the Canaries—that would play host to international celebrities and become the islands' most emblematic residence. The artist called Taro home for 20 years and created some of his most celebrated works while residing here; his studio now displays original paintings. The real attraction is the house itself with its cave dwellings outfitted with splashy furniture, crystalline pools tucked between boulders, and palms shooting up through holes between floors. ✉ *Calle Jorge Luis Borges 16,* ☎ *928/843138* ⊕ *www.fcmanrique.org* ✉ *€8.*

Yaiza

13 km (8 miles) west of Puerto del Carmen.

Yaiza is a quiet whitewashed village with good restaurants. Largely destroyed by a river of lava in the 1700s, it's best known as the gateway to the volcanic national park. The hamlet of El Golfo, situated within the Yaiza municipality, is a whitewashed coastal town with seafood restaurants and views of the **Charco Verde,** or "Green Lake."

GETTING HERE AND AROUND

Bus service is infrequent, so rent a car to get here. To get to the volcanoes, you have to take a tour bus. There's no access for private vehicles.

Sights

El Charco Verde (*Charco de los Clicos*)

NATURE SIGHT | This bizarre green lagoon, which looks like something out of a sci-fi thriller, is situated at the outer limits of Timanfaya National Park just uphill from El Golfo. It gets its radioactive hue from its sulfuric content and *Ruppia maritima* seagrass. It's forbidden to walk to the lake as it's within the reserve, but there's a viewpoint that's clearly marked at the turn-off to El Golfo where you can snap some excellent photos, especially at sunset. Wear grippy shoes and watch your

The spectacular volcanic landscape of Timanfaya National Park was created over six years of near-continuous volcanic eruptions that took place between 1730 and 1736.

step as there are no guardrails around the viewpoint. ✉ *Yaiza.*

★ Parque Nacional de Timanfaya (*Timanfaya National Park*)

VOLCANO | FAMILY | Popularly known as "the Fire Mountains," this national park takes up much of southern Lanzarote. As you enter the park from Yaiza, you'll see the staging area for the Canaries' best-known camel rides; a bumpy camel trek among the rust-red dunes lasts about 20 minutes. The volcanic landscape inside Timanfaya is a violent jumble of exploded craters, cinder cones, lava formations, and heat fissures. The park is protected, and you can't drive or hike through it yourself (leave your car in the lot beside the volcano-top restaurant, El Diablo); the only way to see the central volcanic area is on a 14-km (9-mile) bus circuit called the Ruta de los Volcanes, designed to have minimal environmental impact. (Photographers will be bummed that the only pics you can take on tour are through smudged windows.) A taped English commentary explains how the parish priest of Yaiza took notes during the 1730 eruption that buried two villages. He had plenty of time—the eruption lasted six years, making it the longest known eruption in volcanic history. By the time it was over, more than 75% of Lanzarote was covered in lava. Throughout the park, on signs and road markers, you'll see a little devil with a pitchfork; this *diablito* was designed by Manrique. During summer, visit in late afternoon to avoid the crowds. ✉ *Centro de Visitantes Mancha Blancha, Ctra. de Yaiza a Tinajo, Km 11.5, Tinajo* ☎ *928/118042* 🌐 *Ruta de los Volcanes €9.*

🍽 Restaurants

El Diablo

$$ | SPANISH | This must be one of the world's most unusual restaurants. Here, in the heart of Timanfaya National Park, chicken, steaks, and spicy sausages are cooked over a volcanic crater using the earth's natural heat. **Known for:** food cooked over crater; unique location; volcano views. 💲 *Average main: €15*

✉ *Timanfaya National Park, Tinajo* ☎ *928/840057.*

★ La Bodega de Santiago

$$ | SPANISH | Shaded by a splendid ficus that keeps the *terraza* cool in the midday heat, La Bodega de Santiago is worth going out of your way to visit. The traditional Canarian menu is exquisite, integrating meats and produce from the surrounding farms and complementing dishes with island wines. **Known for:** locavore cuisine; romantic dining beneath a gorgeous tree; terrific goat and roast meats. [$] *Average main: €17* ✉ *Calle Montañas del Fuego 27, Yaiza* ☎ *928/836204* 🌐 *www.labodegadesantiago.es* 🕓 *Closed Mon.*

Restaurante Mar Azul

$$ | SEAFOOD | Of all the seafood restaurants in the tiny hamlet of El Golfo, this harborside standby stands out for its ultra-fresh fish and homemade Canarian dishes. Order the *parrillada de marisco*, or grilled seafood platter, for a sampling of local fish (the barracuda is consistently exceptional), calamari, and fried shellfish, all of which soar to new heights when dunked in cilantro-packed *mojo verde*. **Known for:** not-your-average mojos; romantic seaside terrace; bountiful seafood platters. [$] *Average main: €15* ✉ *Av. Marítima 42, Yaiza* ☎ *928/173132.*

Shopping

Ahumadería de Uga

FOOD | The hamlet of Uga is the improbable home of what's arguably Spain's finest smoked salmon producer. The Guerrero family won't relinquish its secret recipe, but what we know is that the salmon is imported from Scotland and Norway, cured with salt culled from nearby Janubio beach, and smoked over La Geria grapevines. The smoked fish is so delectable that the tiny shop sells more than 200 pounds of it each day. ✉ *LZ2 3, Yaiza* ☎ *928/830132* 🌐 *www.facebook.com/ahumaderiadeuga.*

Playa Blanca

Hotels

★ Hotel Casa del Embajador

$$$$ | B&B/INN | Tucked behind one of Lanzarote's typically green front doors is an oasis of calm where all you'll want to do is curl up in one of the loungers and take in the views of Fuerteventura and the Isla de Lobos. **Pros:** peace and quiet by the sea; fresh fruit in the rooms; good breakfast. **Cons:** pricey for what it is; rooms need a revamp; no a/c. [$] *Rooms from: €270* ✉ *Calle La Tegala 56, Playa Blanca* ☎ *928/519191* 🌐 *www.hotelcasadelembajador.com* 🛏 *13 rooms* 🍴 *Free Breakfast.*

Iberostar Selection Lanzarote Park

$$$$ | RESORT | FAMILY | Travelers looking for accessible luxury and all-inclusive pampering should look no further than this Iberostar outpost, a chic yet unpretentious oceanfront resort that reopened in 2017 after major renovations. **Pros:** newly renovated public areas; separate family and adults-only areas; spacious rooms. **Cons:** you can hear the evening entertainment from some rooms; underwhelming food across the board; bland interiors convey no sense of place. [$] *Rooms from: €205* ✉ *Av. Archipiélago 7, Playa Blanca* ☎ *928/517048* 🌐 *www.iberostar.com* 🛏 *388 rooms* 🍴 *No Meals.*

Princesa Yaiza Suite Hotel Resort

$$$$ | HOTEL | FAMILY | It might be big, but this sprawling white hotel still manages to feel luxurious. **Pros:** great service; fantastic buffet breakfast with eggs cooked to order; superb spa. **Cons:** communal areas need a refresh; overpriced food at pool bar; long walk to some rooms. [$] *Rooms from: €220* ✉ *Av. de Papagayo, Playa Blanca* ☎ *928/519300* 🌐 *www.princesayaiza.com* 🛏 *385 rooms* 🍴 *Free Breakfast.*

Activities

Papagayo Bike
BIKING | Daily bike rental starts at €12. Guided bike tours are also available. ✉ *Calle La Tegala 13, Playa Blanca* ☎ *928/349861* ⊕ *www.papagayobike. com.*

Fuerteventura

Some of Fuerteventura's towering sand dunes blew in from the Sahara Desert, 96 km (60 miles) away, and indeed it's not hard to imagine Fuerteventura as a detached piece of Africa. Despite being the second-largest Canary Island by area, Fuerteventura's population only reaches 115,000. Tourism arrived relatively late on the island, compared to Gran Canaria and Lanzarote, and it's still a comparatively minor tourist destination. Visitors come mainly to enjoy the stunning white beaches and to windsurf; there's little else to do. The two main resort areas are at the island's far north and south ends: Corralejo, across from Lanzarote, known for its miles of protected dunes, and the Jandía peninsula with dozens of long beaches, respectively. Fuerteventura didn't fully escape the Spanish construction boom of the early 2000s, but it remains a relatively unspoiled island and has been a UNESCO biosphere reserve since 2009.

Prior to being conquered in the early 15th century by French crusaders, the island was inhabited by a tribal people called the Maxos with roots in North Africa; at the time of the colonists' arrival, the Maxos were split between two kingdoms, Jandía, in the south, and Maxorata, in the north. A stone wall, remnants of which have survived to the present, divided the two areas. The Catholic Monarchs claimed sovereignty over Fuerteventura in 1476 but were met with dozens of pirate attacks in the following decades, which led them to decree the construction of several fortifications along the coast, some of which are still visible today. The island was largely dismissed by Spaniards as a desert wasteland until famed novelist Miguel de Unamuno chronicled his exile there in the 1920s under Primo de Rivera's reign—contrary to the dictator's wishes, Unamuno found Fuerteventura rather paradisiacal and would come to appreciate its "eternal springtime" temperatures and "naked hills that look like camels' humps."

Like Lanzarote, Fuerteventura is often windy, especially during the summer, when the northeast trade winds blow hard for days at a time. It's also one of the hottest islands in the summer, and its winters are warm and dry.

VISITOR INFORMATION

CONTACTS Airport Tourist Office. ✉ *Fuerteventura Airport, Puerto del Rosario* ☎ *928/860604* ⊕ *www.visitfuerteventura.es.* **Center Tourist Office.** ✉ *Av. Reyes de España, Puerto del Rosario* ☎ *928/530844.*

Puerto del Rosario

Fuerteventura's capital, Puerto del Rosario, has suffered from an image problem for a long time. It used to be called Puerto de Cabra (Goat Port), but the "rebranding" as Rosary Port has not changed the fact that there's little of interest here to the average traveler. If you arrive by boat, your best bet is to rent a car (from €20 a day; Cicar has an office by the cruise terminal), skip town, and explore the island's natural wonders.

If you find yourself in Puerto del Rosario with an hour or two to spare before your boat leaves, stroll round the Parque Escultórico (Park of Sculptures) in the center of town, where there are more than 50 works on display. The tourist office outside the port can provide a map and guide to the 15 most prominent sculptures.

GETTING HERE AND AROUND

Cruise ships dock at a terminal that's within easy walking distance of the town center. From there you can take a bus to Caleta de Fuste or Corralejo (departures every 30 minutes) or Morro Jable (every hour). If you plan to visit the southern beaches, make sure you rent a vehicle that's suitable for the dirt roads— you may need a 4x4 (inquire at the rental agency).

Ferries leave from Puerto del Rosario for Arrecife in Lanzarote and Las Palmas (via Morro Jable). Southern Lanzarote (Playa Blanca) and northern Fuerteventura (Corralejo) are linked by two companies, Fred Olsen and Naviera Armas. They both make six daily round trips from Lanzarote.

CONTACTS Tiadhe Fuerteventura Bus.
⊠ *Bus Station, Av. de la Constitución, Puerto del Rosario* ☎ *928/855726* ⊕ *www.tiadhe.com.*

 Activities

BIKING AND HIKING
Natouraladventure
BIKING | Bike rentals and guided tours and hikes around the island are all available from this company, which can tailor excursions to different fitness levels. Horseback riding and boat trips can also be arranged. ⊠ *Calle Marisco 7,* ☎ *664/849411* ⊕ *www.natouraladventure.com.*

GOLF
Fuerteventura Golf Club
GOLF | This course with ocean views is near Caleta de Fuste, just south of Puerto del Rosario. ⊠ *Ctra. de Jandía, Km 11, Antigua* ☎ *928/160034* ⊕ *www.fuerteventuragolfclub.com* ☜ *€66* ⚲ *18 holes, 6637 yards, par 70.*

Golf Club Salinas de Antigua
GOLF | Just down the road from Fuerteventura Golf Club, this course is surrounded by sand dunes. ⊠ *Ctra. de*

Jandía, Km 12, Antigua ☎ *928/877272* ⊕ *www.salinasgolf.com* ☜ *€62* ⚲ *18 holes, 6105 yards, par 70.*

Corralejo

38 km (23 miles) north of Puerto del Rosario.

Most people visit this part of Fuerteventura for its magnificent sand dunes. Corralejo, a small port town where ferries from Lanzarote dock, has one street of tourist restaurants and some pedestrian plazas with good seafood.

GETTING HERE AND AROUND

A bus service that leaves every 30 minutes connects Corralejo with Puerto del Rosario. Ferries leave from the marina, next to the original fishing port, for Lanzarote and Isla de Lobos, an uninhabited island that sits off the northwest coast.

 Sights

Casa de los Coroneles (*The Colonels' House*)
HISTORIC HOME | The island's most famous historic building is 19 km (11 miles) south on the inland road. Military governors built the immense house in the 1600s and ruled the island from it until the turn of the 20th century. The interior, which you can see in under 30 minutes, is defined by heavy wooden doors and charming courtyards, though rooms are devoid of furniture. Placards are in Spanish only. ⊠ *Calle los Coroneles 28, La Oliva* ⊕ *www.lacasadeloscoroneles.org* ☜ *€3* ⊙ *Closed Sun. and Mon.*

El Cotillo
TOWN | On Fuerteventura's most northwesterly tip, this fishing village has quaint and colorful houses and a sleepy, lost-in-time feel. Go at sunset, when the surrounding sands take on a red-orange glow, and peek into the 17th-century Castillo de El Toston (Tostón Tower),

which often holds temporary art exhibits. ✉ *Corralejo.*

Beaches

Playa de Corralejo

BEACH | Also known as Grandes Playas, Playa de Corralejo runs about 3½ km (2 miles) south from the Tres Islas hotel to the Playa de la Barreta. Its white sands are fringed by high sand dunes on one side and the ocean and Isla de Lobos on the other, so views are magnificent. Like many Fuerteventura beaches, it's windy, so waves can be rough. Lounge chairs and umbrellas are available on some parts of the beach, and nude sunbathing is common at the more remote spots. **Amenities:** food and drink; lifeguards; showers; toilets; water sports. **Best for:** nudists; sunrise; walking; windsurfing. ✉ *Corralejo.*

Playa del Aljibe de la Cueva

BEACH | On the northwest side of the island, this beach has a castle that once repelled pirates. The small stretch of white sand is rather isolated and is popular with locals. The beach is backed by dramatic ocher cliffs, and the sea tends to be rough. **Amenities:** none. **Best for:** solitude; nudists; sunset; windsurfing. ✉ *Corralejo.*

Restaurants

La Taberna Juan & Ana

$$ | **SPANISH** | Behind the Atlantic Center shopping mall, this well-established favorite is one of the oldest restaurants in town and has been under the same Spanish management since 1989. As you might expect from the name, its interior resembles a typical Spanish tavern, with wooden furniture and beams and cozy lighting. **Known for:** cheery staff; to-die-for paella; traditional Spanish ambience. [$] *Average main: €14* ✉ *Calle Hernán Cortés 10, Corralejo* ☎ *928/535027* 🕒 *Closed Sun. No lunch.*

★ Restaurante El Moral

$$ | **SPANISH** | In the small town of Villaverde, halfway between Puerto del Rosario and Corralejo, is one of the island's best-kept culinary secrets. At this small restaurant, Canarian dishes are served family style in the center of the table. **Known for:** excellent house wines; homemade Canarian tapas; good value. [$] *Average main: €12* ✉ *Ctra. General 94, Villaverde* ☎ *928/868285* 🕒 *Closed Mon.*

Hotels

★ Avanti Lifestyle Hotel

$$$ | **HOTEL** | Fresh, ultramodern (and ultra-Instagrammable) design defines the aesthetic at Avanti, a 15-room adults-only hotel with gleaming blue-and-white rooms and an elegant rooftop bar. **Pros:** exclusive (but not stuffy) feel; destination-worthy restaurant; trendy interiors. **Cons:** small Jacuzzis; first-floor rooms are noisy; rooftop bar open only in high season. [$] *Rooms from: €145* ✉ *Calle Delfín 1, Corralejo* ☎ *928/867523* 🌐 *www.avantihotelboutique.com* 🕒 *Restaurant closed Wed.* 🛏 *15 rooms* 🍴 *Free Breakfast.*

★ Bahiazul Villas & Club

$$$ | **APARTMENT** | Villas sleeping up to six comprise this private, tranquil luxury hotel with a blue-and-white color palette. **Pros:** spotlessly clean; inviting public areas; great for both families and couples. **Cons:** iffy Wi-Fi; no bar service during the day; the occasional cockroach (par for the course on this island but still jarring). [$] *Rooms from: €167* ✉ *Calle Pardelas 7, Corralejo* ☎ *928/854598* 🌐 *www.bahiazul.com* 🍴 *Free Breakfast.*

★ Gran Hotel Bahía Real

$$$ | **RESORT** | Straight out of the *Arabian Nights*, this oceanfront resort renovated in 2021 is a romantic retreat. **Pros:** first-class cuisine; newly renovated; excellent service. **Cons:** beach rocky in places; overpriced restaurant; no bars or shops in the vicinity. [$] *Rooms from: €176* ✉ *Av. Grandes Playas s/n, Corralejo*

☎ *928/537153* 🌐 *www.atlantisbahiareal.com* 🛏 *170 rooms, 72 suites* 🍴 *Free Breakfast.*

Hotel Riu Palace Tres Islas
$$$ | **RESORT** | You can step right onto Grandes Playas, one of the best beaches on the island, from this hotel, which resembles a cruise ship with its six stories and curved white facade. **Pros:** beachfront location; two large, well-maintained pools; excellent service. **Cons:** older clientele may not make it the best fit for families; some distance from Corralejo; dull entertainment. [$] *Rooms from: €170* ✉ *Av. Grandes Playas, Corralejo* ☎ *928/535700* 🌐 *www.riu.es* 🛏 *372 rooms* 🍴 *Free Breakfast.*

Shopping

★ Lapa Studio
CRAFTS | Snap up jewelry, hats, paper goods, and home decor items at this gorgeous little boutique (est. 2018) in El Cotillo run by four women. Many of the wares are made by local artisans. ✉ *Avenida 3 de Abril de 1979 13, Corralejo* ✣ *in El Cotillo* ☎ *669/616144* 🌐 *www.lapastudio.es.*

Activities

BICYCLING

Easy Riders
BIKING | In addition to bike rental, Easy Riders also runs guided tours around the north of the island that cover 20–80 km (12½–50 miles) and can be made to suit most fitness levels. Some include a visit to the Isla de Lobos, off the north coast of the island. ✉ *Suite Atlantis Fuerteventura Resort, Las Dunas, Local 2, Corralejo* ☎ *928/867005* 🌐 *www.easyriders-bikecenter.com.*

BOATING AND OTHER WATER SPORTS

The channel between Corralejo and the tiny Isla de Lobos is rich in undersea life and favored by divers as well as sport fishermen.

Abyss Fuerteventura
DIVING & SNORKELING | This company organizes dives as well as PADI courses. ✉ *Calle Gravina 10, Corralejo* ☎ *928/949004* 🌐 *www.abyssfuerteventura.com.*

Fuertecharter Boat Trips
BOATING | This company, located in the marina, offers boat and fishing trips. ✉ *Marina, Muelle Deportivo, Corralejo* ☎ *928/344734* 🌐 *www.fuertecharter.com.*

Kailua Surf School Fuerteventura
SURFING | Even if you've never surfed before, let the enthusiastic staff at Kailua show you the ropes. Classes for more advanced surfers are also available in addition to 7- and 14-night surf camps. Rates start at approximately €40 per four-hour group lesson. ✉ *Av. Corralejo Grandes Playas 75, Corralejo* ☎ *630/345560* 🌐 *www.kailuasurfschool.com.*

Betancuria

25 km (15 miles) west of Puerto del Rosario.

Betancuria (pop. 839), set in the fertile center of the island, was once Fuerteventura's capital and has several historical monuments. Its quiet streets display typical Fuerteventura architecture.

GETTING HERE AND AROUND

Betancuria and surroundings are best explored by car (hire from €20 a day in Puerto del Rosario).

Sights

Molino de Antigua (*Antigua Windmill*)

WINDMILL | In Antigua, 8 km (5 miles) east of Betancuria, you can visit a restored white Don Quixote–style windmill that was once used for grinding gofio flour and now displays an exhibition about cheese-making on the island. Next to the windmill are a craft shop and cactus garden. Incidentally, the modern metal windmills throughout the island were imported from the United States and are used for pumping water. ✉ *Antigua* ☎ *928/878041* ✉ *€2* ⊘ *Closed Sun. and Mon.*

Museo de Arte Sacro

ART MUSEUM | The town's Church Museum contains a replica of the banner carried by the Norman conqueror Juan de Bethancourt when he seized Fuerteventura in the 15th century. Most of the artwork was salvaged from the nearby convent, now in ruins. The museum is generally open weekday mornings but has no official opening hours. ✉ *Betancuria* ☎ *928/878003* ✉ *€2.*

Santa María de Betancuria

CHURCH | The weatherworn colonial church of Santa María de Betancuria was built in the early 15th century as the island's main church when Betancuria was the capital. The church was almost completely destroyed by Berbers in 1593 and then rebuilt. Outside Mass times, the church has no official opening hours, though weekday mornings are often a safe bet. ✉ *Pl. Santa María de Betancuria 1, Betancuria* ☎ *928/549616* ✉ *€2.*

Costa Calma

7 km (4½ miles) south of Matas Blancas.

As you continue south along the coast from Matas Blancas, the beaches get longer, the sand gets whiter, and the water gets bluer.

GETTING HERE AND AROUND

The bus connecting Puerto del Rosario and Morro Jable stops at Costa Calma. Buses leave roughly every 30 minutes weekdays and every hour on weekends.

Beaches

Playa Costa Calma

BEACH | Like so many of the Fuerteventura beaches, this is yet another stretch of perfect white sands. Playa Costa Calma is actually made up of three beaches, a large one flanked by two smaller ones. You can walk along all three at low tide, but don't be caught by the rising tide: the rocky outcrops between the beaches will prevent your return. Lounge chair and umbrella rental is available near the hotels. Windy conditions draw windsurfers here. **Amenities:** food and drink; lifeguards; showers; toilets; water sports. **Best for:** sunrise; swimming; walking; windsurfing. ✉ *Costa Calma.*

★ Playa de Sotavento

BEACH | This famous stretch of pure white sand rivals Corralejo for the title of best Fuerteventura beach. It extends for 6½ glorious km (4 miles)—at low tide you can walk over to neighboring beaches for 9 km (5½ miles). A sandbank that runs parallel to the beach creates a shallow lagoon that's perfect for swimming and for getting down the basics of windsurfing. Nude sunning is favored here, except directly in front of hotels—these areas are also the only place where amenities are available. **Amenities:** food and drink; water sports. **Best for:** nudists; solitude; sunrise; windsurfing. ✉ *Jandía.*

Hotels

H10 Tindaya

$$$$ | **HOTEL** | Tuscany meets the Canary Islands at this neoclassical hotel with soaring towers and ocher-colored columns. **Pros:** good service; hotel has its own sheltered beach; squeaky-clean.

Surrounded by mountains, Betancuria is a charming colonial village with cobbled streets, whitewashed cottages, and friendly villagers.

Cons: all dining is buffet style; small beach; entertainment can be noisy at times. $ *Rooms from: €200* ⊠ *Punta del Roquito, Costa Calma* ☎ *900/444666* ⊕ *www.h10hotels.com* 🛏 *354 rooms* ¶Ol *All-Inclusive.*

VIK Suite Hotel Risco Del Gato

$$$ | HOTEL | A far cry from the big-box resorts that abound on Fuerteventura, this suites-only sanctuary has spectacular ocean views—it's 2 km (1 mile) to the west of Costa Calma resort and perched about 650 feet above the magnificent Playa de Sotavento. **Pros:** tranquil location and setting; quality service; intriguing architecture. **Cons:** evening meals are bland; some rooms could use a refresh; slightly out of town. $ *Rooms from: €160* ⊠ *Calle Sicasumbre 2,* ☎ *902/160630* ⊕ *www.hotelriscodelgato.com* 🛏 *51 suites* ¶Ol *No Meals.*

 Nightlife

Los Piratas de Costa Calma

COCKTAIL LOUNGES | Pedro, the bartender at this popular tiki joint, will happily get you buzzed on his flamboyantly garnished concoctions. ⊠ *Calle Punta de los Molinillos, Costa Calma* ☎ *663/357689.*

 Activities

GOLF
Playitas Golf

GOLF | This challenging course designed by Scottish golf course architect John Chilver Stainer is between Caleta de Fuste and Costa Calma. ⊠ *Guanchinerfe 2, Las Playitas* ☎ *928/860400* ⊕ *www. playitas.net* 🖾 *€69* 🏌 *18 holes, 5276 yards, par 67.*

Morro Jable

At the southernmost tip of the island.

The old fishing port of Morro Jable has a long stretch of golden sand. Many more miles of virgin coast stretch beyond here, down a dirt road that eventually leads to the lighthouse. Beaches along the entire windward side of the peninsula remain untouched.

GETTING HERE AND AROUND

You can get to Morro Jable by bus from Puerto del Rosario. Buses leave every 30 minutes on weekdays and every hour weekends, but if you want to explore the main attraction in this part of the island (the stunning beaches), a car is a must.

 Beaches

Beyond the town of Morro Jable, a dirt road leads to the isolated hamlet of Puerto de la Cruz, where there's a lighthouse. If you follow the dirt path across the narrow strip of land (make sure ahead of time that your rental is up to it), you can enjoy the equally empty beaches here. For scuba diving and snorkeling, head for the rocky outcrops on the windward side of Jandía.

Playa de Barlovento de Jandía

BEACH | Barlovento is yet another spectacular and unspoiled beach in this part of Fuenteventura. The fact that it can only be reached by 4x4s or other heavy-duty vehicles means it receives few visitors; in low season you could have this 6-km (4-mile) stretch practically to yourself. Take plenty of drinking water, and watch out for strong currents, especially when the wind is strong. **Amenities: none. Best for:** solitude; nudists; sunset; windsurfing. ⊠ *Morro del Jable.*

Playa de Cofete

BEACH | Along with Barlovento next door, Playa de Cofete is one of Spain's most pristine beaches. This 14-km (9-mile) strip

of golden sand faces north, making it the perfect spot for sunbathing, walking, and just getting away from it all. Currents are strong here, particularly when it's gusty. Take plenty of drinking water. **Amenities: none. Best for:** solitude; nudists; sunset; walking; windsurfing. ⊠ *Morro del Jable.*

Playa de Morro Jable

BEACH | The long stretch of powdery white sand and safe swimming conditions make Morro Jable's beach one of the island's most emblematic. It gets busy on weekends and during the summer, and finding a space for your towel can be difficult unless you're prepared to walk a ways. Lounge chairs and umbrellas are both available. **Amenities:** food and drink; lifeguards; showers; toilets; water sports. **Best for:** sunset; swimming; walking; windsurfing.

La Palma

La Palma, the Canaries' most northwestern island, is known as "La Isla Bonita" (The Pretty Island) for a reason: Its landscapes are some of the most breathtaking in the archipelago. This is a hiker's paradise, and it remains virtually unspoiled by tourism. Some 1,000 km (621 miles) of waymarked trails spoke out from the center of the island, where the Caldera de Taburiente National Park, named for the pine-blanketed volcanic caldera, stretches 10 km (6 miles) across. The terrain is so varied on La Palma that you can take a morning hike in a misty subtropical rainforest and unwind in the evening with a glass of local wine overlooking barren lava fields and black-sand beaches.

The capital, Santa Cruz de La Palma, is a quaint colonial city of 16,000 with painted row houses and enough shops and restaurants to keep you busy for a few hours. Outside the urban centers, banana plantations stretch in virtually

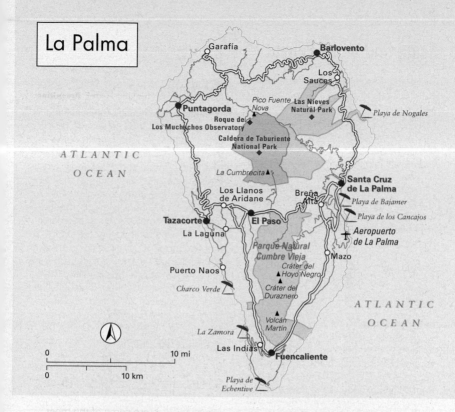

La Palma

Garafía
Barlovento
Los
Sauces
Pico Fuente Nova
Las Nieves Natural Park
Puntagorda
Playa de Nogales
Roque de Los Muchachos Observatory
Caldera de Taburiente National Park
ATLANTIC
OCEAN
La Cumbrecita
Los Llanos de Aridane
Santa Cruz de La Palma
Breña Alta
Playa de Bajamar
Tazacorte
El Paso
Playa de los Cancajos
La Laguna
Aeropuerto de La Palma
Parque Natural Cumbre Vieja
Mazo
Puerto Naos
Cráter del Hoyo Negro
Charco Verde
Cráter del Duraznero
ATLANTIC
OCEAN
Volcán Martín
La Zamora
Las Indias
Fuencaliente
Playa de Echentive

0   10 mi
0   10 km

every direction, tumbling down to the coast, which is rocky and virtually beach-less (relative to, say, Gran Canaria or Fuerteventura). Tropical fruits—most notably, delectable little pineapples—and flowers are the island's other main cultivars; some of the finest goat cheeses and wines in the Canaries are produced here as well.

In September 2021, an earthquake on the Cumbre Vieja ridge shook La Palma, and the ashfall and lava destroyed many homes and buildings. At the time of writing, the situation was ongoing, so confirm openings and closings before planning your trip.

GETTING HERE AND AROUND
AIR TRAVEL La Palma. ☎ 91/321–1000 ⊕ www.aena.es.

CAR TRAVEL Cicar Puerto de La Palma. ✉ Harbor of Santa Cruz, Estación Marítima de Santa Cruz de La Palma, Santa Cruz de la Palma, Canary Islands, 38700, Spain ☎ (92) 242–0159 ⊕ www.cicar.com. **Europcar La Palma Aeropuerto.** ✉ La Palma Airport, Calle La Bajita, LP-5, Canary Islands, 38738, Spain ☎ (92) 242--6192 ⊕ www.europcar.com

TAXI TRAVEL Taxi La Palma. ☎ 686/553868 ⊕ www.taxilapalma.com.

VISITOR INFORMATION
CONTACTS Airport Tourist Office. ✉ La Palma Airport ☎ 922/967044 ⊕ www.visitlapalma.es.

Santa Cruz de La Palma

The island's capital and main port of entry is Santa Cruz de La Palma, situated halfway down the east coast. Ferries depart here for Lanzarote, Tenerife, and Gran Canaria. Santa Cruz is far mellower than other Canarian capitals and has a certain Caribbean air, thanks to the colorful colonial houses dating to the 16th and 17th centuries and cobblestone streets shaded by palms and tropical plants. It's a pleasant enough place to crash after a long day of travel or ahead of an early-morning departure, but you'll want to head for more interesting environs for longer stays.

Hotels

Hotel San Telmo

$$ | B&B/INN | FAMILY | In a centuries-old building with painted wooden balconies and a plant-filled courtyard, this tiny, independently owned hotel offers charm and tranquility at a good value. **Pros:** comfy, homey feel; roof deck with views; on a quiet side street. **Cons:** no pool or gym; no air conditioning; small TVs. [$] *Rooms from: €90* ✉ *Calle San Telmo 5, Santa Cruz de la Palma* ☎ *922/415385* 🌐 *www.hotel-santelmo.com* 🍴 *Free Breakfast* 🛏 *8 rooms.*

El Paso

27 km (17 miles) from Santa Cruz de La Palma.

El Paso is the only landlocked municipality in La Palma, and it's home to the island's premier attraction, Caldera de Taburiente National Park. The area is sparsely populated with fewer than 10,000 inhabitants. Stone carvings show that El Paso has ancient roots; it is believed that the indigenous Benahoarite people, a subset of Guanche culture native to La Palma, tended to livestock here before being colonized from the 15th century onward.

Sights

★ Caldera de Taburiente National Park

NATIONAL PARK | What strikes you first about Caldera de Taburiente National Park its sheer verticality, jutting over 3,000 feet (900 meters) above sea level, which feels dramatic considering that the ocean is only a couple of miles away as the crow flies. Trails here take you through dense Canarian pine forests, meadows of wildflowers, dramatic gorges, and burbling streams. All around you are even higher, jagged cliff-tops whose peaks are often hidden above the cloudline. There are essentially two routes: one uphill and one downhill. The latter is far and away more enjoyable, but you'll have to hire a taxi (approximately €55; try to split the fee with other hikers) at the Barranco de las Angustias (aka Parking de la Villa) to drop you at the trailhead at Mirador Los Brecitos. You then walk the scenic route from Los Brecitos back down to the taxi stand, 4–7 hours depending on how pokey you are. The hike is steep with lots of uneven surfaces and not suited to all travelers. Bring plenty of water and snacks. If you visit in spring or early summer, you'll be treated to jaw-dropping indigo tajinaste flowers in bloom. Islabonitatours (www.islabonitatours.com) is an outstanding English-speaking tour company that can make all transportation arrangements and provide knowledgeable mountain guides. ✉ *Parque Nacional Caldera de Taburiente* ☎ *922/922280* 🌐 *www.reservasparquesnacionales.es.*

Roque de Los Muchachos Observatory

OBSERVATORY | FAMILY | Little do many science buffs know that La Palma boasts the second-best astronomy observatory in the Northern Hemisphere, outdone only by Mauna Kea in Hawaii. Situated within the Caldera de Taburiente National Park, it has three extremely powerful telescopes and sits above the clouds at an altitude of 7,861 feet (2,396 meters). Though the site is operated by an astrophysics institute, small-group visits, lasting 70–90 minutes and always held at dawn, are subcontracted to a company called Ad Astra. The tour with a certified guide includes entry into one of the telescopes. ✉ *Parque Nacional Caldera de Taburiente* ☎ *696/186633* 🌐 *www.adastralapalma.com/tours-en/observatory-tour* 🎟 *€9* ✍ *Reservations essential.*

🍴 Restaurants

El Duende del Fuego

$$ | SPANISH | FAMILY | This eccentric indoor-outdoor restaurant one municipality over from El Paso specializes in flavorful allergen-free food prepared for guests with any range of dietary requirements. All ingredients are organic; nearly every dish is gluten-, dairy-, and nut-free; and the best part is, you don't miss these common ingredients, thanks to the chef's creativity. **Known for:** characterful local wines; allergen-free food; zero-kilometer menu. [$] *Average main: €15* ✉ *Plaza Elías Santos Abreu, Plaza Chica 2* ☎ *92/2401002* 🌐 *www.elduendedelfuego.com* 🕓 *Closed Mon. lunch and Sun.*

Fuencaliente

22 km (14 miles) from El Paso.

This municipality occupies the southernmost tip of La Palma. It stands out for its dramatic black-and-red volcanic landscape dotted with cacti and succulents. It's also a center of wine production.

👁 Sights

Matías i Torres

WINERY | La Palma native Victoria Torres Pecis has been quietly making some of the finest Canarian wine on the market since taking the reins at her late father's hilltop winery in 2010. A fifth-generation winemaker, she has a deep understanding of the island's soils and microclimates, and she adheres to a minimal-intervention philosophy both in the vineyard and at the cellar. Snap up as many bottles as you can—her wines (ranging from floral Malvasía to earthy Negramoll) sell out quickly and are hard to come by anywhere else. Visits are private and by email appointment only. ✉ *in Los Canarios village* ☎ *617/967499* 📧 *victoriatorrespecis@gmail.com* 🌐 *www.facebook.com/matiasitorres* ✍ *Reservations essential.*

Salinas de Fuencaliente

NATURE SIGHT | FAMILY | Beside two picturesque lighthouses (one built in 1903 and the other in 1985) are salt flats set amid a starkly black lava landscape. Placards along a footpath explain how salt is extracted from ocean water according to an ancient method. There's a souvenir shop selling various types and textures of salt as well as local wines, T-shirts, postcards, and more, and a good oceanfront restaurant specializing in salt-baked fish that's filleted tableside. ✉ *Ctra. la Costa el Faro 5* ☎ *922/696002* 🌐 *www.salinasdefuencaliente.es* 🎟 *Free.*

Barlovento and the Northeast

36 km (22 miles) from Santa Cruz de La Palma.

The banana-tree-blanketed northeastern municipalities of Barlovento, San Andrés y Sauces, and Puntallana contain some of the most pristine nature on the island, with a highlight being the misty laurel forests of Las Nieves Natural Park.

👁 Sights

Las Nieves Natural Park

NATURE PRESERVE | FAMILY | Also known as Bosque de Los Tilos, this protected biosphere is home to one of the best-preserved laurisilva forests in the archipelago. Take a leisurely walk beneath mossy lianas and towering laurel trees up to the Espigón Atravesado viewpoint, about one hour each way, or take a 3–5-hour hike along the Marcos y Cordero route, skirting beneath waterfalls. There's also a quick out-and-back trail (30 minutes total, give or take) to the Los Tilos Waterfall; follow signs for "Sendero a la Cascada." There's a well-appointed visitor center at the end of the LP-105 road (follow signs for "Los Tilos") with maps and English placards on local history, flora, and fauna. Mudslides and inclement weather cause occasional closures; check with your hotel or the tourist office for updates. ✉ *Parque Natural de Las Nieves, Calle Los Tilos* ☎ *922/451246.*

Hotels

Faro de Punta Cumplida
$$$$ | **B&B/INN** | The Punta Cumplida lighthouse has been guiding ships to safety for 154 years, but since 2019, it has doubled as an end-of-the-earth luxury retreat for travelers looking for solitude amid the rolling banana plantations and crashing waves. **Pros:** breakfast basket dropped at your door each morning; bucket-list experience; steps from La Fajana natural pools. **Cons:** unheated pool; sparse seating in living areas; uncomfortably windy at times. [$] *Rooms from: €210* ✉ *Faro de Punta Cumplida* ☎ *91/4879017* 🌐 *www.floatel.de/en/hideaways/faro-cumplida* 🛏 *4 suites* 🍴 *Free Breakfast.*

Tazacorte

37 km (23 miles) from Santa Cruz de la Palma.

The municipality of Tazacorte, midway down the western coast, is named for a small inland town and port (Puerto de Tazacorte). The former is home to the island's most iconic hotel, while the latter is a popular beach destination. This is a good home base for hikes in the Caldera de Taburiente National Park, a 20-minute drive away.

Beaches

Playa de Tazacorte
BEACH | **FAMILY** | Powdery black sand is the main draw at this urban beach with a boardwalk. When the ocean is calm and the weather is slightly overcast (which makes the sand less likely lest you singe your toes!), it's an idyllic spot to relax and swim. There's a playground for kids. **Amenities:** food and drink; lifeguards; parking (free). **Best for:** sunset; swimming; walking. ✉ *Av. El Emigrante 15.*

Restaurants

★ Playa Mont
$ | **SEAFOOD** | **FAMILY** | Expertly grilled fish and fried seafood lure crowds night after night to this open-air restaurant steps from the beach. Let the chatty waitstaff talk you through the extensive, well-priced menu, which runs the gamut from *morena frita* (crisp-fried eel) to *alfonsino* (a delectable red-skinned fish) to *escaldón,* a hearty gofio porridge made with fish stock and topped with mojo. **Known for:** heavenly tres leches cake; beachy vibe; perfectly cooked fish. [$] *Average main: €11* ✉ *Av. Taburiente 2* ☎ *922/480443* 🌐 *www.playamont.com* 🕒 *Closed Wed.*

Hotels

★ Hacienda de Abajo
$$$$ | **HOTEL** | This sumptuous retreat tucked amid sloping banana plantations and set against the open Atlantic is a tropical oasis with colonial architecture and a distinctly Old World feel. **Pros:** tranquil garden and pool; a living museum dripping with priceless works of art; lovingly made breakfasts. **Cons:** underwhelming restaurant; riches procured

through multigenerational colonialism; bad lighting throughout the hotel doesn't do justice to the art. $ *Rooms from: €400* ✉ *Calle Miguel de Unamuno 11* ☎ *922/406000* ⊕ *www.hotelhaciendadea-bajo.com* ¶◎¶ *Free Breakfast* ⇌ *32 rooms.*

Puntagorda and the Northwest

28 km (17 miles) from Tazacorte.

The dry northwest of the island is covered in cacti and low shrubs and succulents as well as Canarian pine forests in some areas. Many affluent Northern Europeans have vacation homes here that they rent as luxury villas for much of the year. Though rural tourism is on the upswing, the economy still relies heavily on agriculture: You'll spot orange, lemon, avocado, and almond trees. The sleepy town of Puntagorda is a pleasant place to stroll (and stock up on groceries, should you be staying in a vacation rental). There's a quaint farmers' market held on Saturday afternoon and Sunday morning a mile north of the town center (Mercadillo del Agricultor de Puntagorda, Camino el Pinar 56A, Puntagorda).

🍴 Restaurants

Jardín de los Naranjos
$$ | SPANISH | FAMILY | In a dining room oozing rustic charm (think green tablecloths, beamed ceilings, and squat wine glasses), feast on rich fall-off-the-bone goat stew made with local meat, or opt for the catch of the day, served with salad and *papas arrugadas* (boiled potatoes with a spicy sauce). **Known for:** local wines; warm service; slow-simmered goat stew. $ *Average main: €14* ✉ *Camino el Pinar 33* ☎ *619/571125* ⊗ *Closed Mon.*

Hotels

Villa Gran Atlántico
$$$$ | HOUSE | There's a smattering of villa rentals available in this tranquil corner of La Palma, but the most intriguing of the bunch—for both its magazine-cover-worthy Bauhaus-esque design and jaw-dropping views—is Villa Gran Atlántico, whose two ample suites comfortably sleep four guests each. **Pros:** heated outdoor lap pool; architectural home with 180-degree ocean views; high-end perks like Vitamix blender. **Cons:** spotty Wi-Fi; far from main sights; booking through application. $ *Rooms from: €320* ✉ *Villa Gran Atlántico* ☎ *687/791163* ⊕ *www.villagranatlantico.com* ¶◎¶ *No Meals* ⇌ *2 suites* ▭ *No credit cards.*

Index

Photo Credits

Solodovnikova Elena/Shutterstock (473). Catarina Belova/shutterstock (478). **Chapter 9: Catalonia, Valencia, and the Costa Blanca:** Robwilson39/Dreamstime (483). Patty Orly/Shutterstock (486). Mauricio Pellegrinetti/Flickr, [CC BY-ND 2.0] (487). Kauka Jarvi/iStockphoto (487). zebra0209/Shutterstock (495). Alexey Fedorenko/Shutterstock (498). Sevka3/Dreamstime (500). 4H4 Photography/Shutterstock (503). Amoklv/Dreamstime (504). Helio San Miguel (511). Adam Zoltan/Shutterstock (513). Elenaphotos/Dreamstime (525). LisyMoreno/Shutterstock (527). Alex Tihonovs/Shutterstock (529). BAHDANOVICH ALENA/Shutterstock (532). Zigres/Shutterstock (535). **Chapter 10: Ibiza and the Balearic Islands:** Alex/iStockphoto (537). Travelling-light/Dreamstime (540). Rafael Campillo / age fotostock (541). Laurie Geffert Phelps / Fodor's member (541). tagstiles (542). Anibal Trejo/Shutterstock (543). ArtesiaWells/iStock Editorial (543). lara-sh/Shutterstock (552). Skowron/Shutterstock (562). kovop58/Shutterstock (571). Bkrzyzanek/Shutterstock (576). Philippe Fritsch/iStockphoto (578). LUNAMARINA/iStockphoto (586). **Chapter 11: Seville and Around:** LucVi/Shutterstock (591). VicPhotoria/Shutterstock (594). Pyroshot/Dreamstime (595). KikoStock/Shutterstock (595). Sina Ettmer Photography/Shutterstock (600). Cezary Wojtkowski/Shutterstock (607). sorincolac/iStock Editorial (623). RudiErnst/Shutterstock (624). riverside / fodors.com member (628). mamadela/iStock Editorial (630). miquelito/Shutterstock (635). Fulcanelli/Shutterstock (636). **Chapter 12: Granada and Around:** Balate Dorin/Shutterstock (639). Pat_Hastings/Shutterstock (642). ampFotoStudio/Shutterstock (643). Carmen Martínez Banús/iStockphoto (643). Botond Horvath/Shutterstock (651). Vladimir Korostyshevskiy/Shutterstock (651). joserpizarro/Shutterstock (652). Cezary Wojtkowski/Shutterstock (653). Ivan Soto Cobos/Shutterstock (654). Arenaphotouk/Dreamstime (654). joserpizarro/Shutterstock (654). Reimar/Shutterstock (654). guss.95/Shutterstock (654). Leon Rafael/Shutterstock (655). Kiev.Victor/Shutterstock (656). Fotografiecor.nl/Shutterstock (657). Julian Maldonado/Shutterstock (657). **Chapter 13: Costa del Sol and Costa de Almería:** Shutterstock / Artur Bogacki (673). Baghitsha/Dreamstime (676). gildemax/wikipedia.org (677). Lia Sanz/Shutterstock (677). Valery Bareta/Shutterstock (678). sunshinecity (679). Claus Mikosch/iStockphoto (679). Daniela Sachsenheimer/Shutterstock (686). Westend61 GmbH / Alamy Stock Photo (691). Anastasia Galkina/Shutterstock (700). Arsty/Dreamstime (706). Jupitersounds/Shutterstock (709). trabantos/Shutterstock (714). Sabine Klein/Shutterstock (718). two_meerkats/Shutterstock (720). Freefly/iStockphoto (724). **Chapter 14: The Canary Islands:** Turismo Lanzarote (727). leoks/shutterstock (736). RossHelen/shutterstock (742). Elena19/shutterstock (744). Mikadun/shutterstock (748). bellena/shutterstock (755). Valery Bareta/shutterstock (760). alexilena/shutterstock (768). MisterStock/shutterstock (770). Turismo Lanzarote (774-775). Sergey Kelin/shutterstock (778). RossHelen/shutterstock (785). **About Our Writers:** All photos are courtesy of the writers except for the following: Isabelle Kliger, courtesy of Ilia Robert Kliger.

*Every effort has been made to trace the copyright holders, and we apologize in advance for any accidental errors. We would be happy to apply the corrections in the following edition of this publication.

Notes

Notes

Notes

Notes

Notes

Notes

Notes

Notes

Notes

Notes

Notes

Fodor's ESSENTIAL SPAIN 2022

Publisher: Stephen Horowitz, *General Manager*

Editorial: Douglas Stallings, *Editorial Director*; Jill Fergus, Amanda Sadlowski, Caroline Trefler, *Senior Editors*; Kayla Becker, Alexis Kelly, *Editors;* Angelique Kennedy-Chavannes, *Assistant Editor*

Design: Tina Malaney, *Director of Design and Production*; Jessica Gonzalez, *Graphic Designer*

Production: Jennifer DePrima, *Editorial Production Manager*; Elyse Rozelle, *Senior Production Editor;* Monica White, *Production Editor*

Maps: Rebecca Baer, *Senior Map Editor*; Mark Stroud (Moon Street Cartography), David Lindroth, *Cartographers*

Photography: Viviane Teles, *Senior Photo Editor;* Namrata Aggarwal, Payal Gupta, Ashok Kumar, *Photo Editors;* Rebecca Rimmer, *Photo Production Associate;* Eddie Aldrete, *Photo Production Intern*

Business and Operations: Chuck Hoover, *Chief Marketing Officer*; Robert Ames, *Group General Manager*; Devin Duckworth, *Director of Print Publishing*

Public Relations and Marketing: Joe Ewaskiw, *Senior Director of Communications and Public Relations*

Fodors.com: Jeremy Tarr, *Editorial Director;* Rachael Levitt, *Managing Editor*

Technology: Jon Atkinson, *Director of Technology;* Rudresh Teotia, *Lead Developer*; Jacob Ashpis, *Content Operations Manager*

Writers: Benjamin Kemper, Isabelle Kliger, Elizabeth Prosser, Joanna Styles

Editor: Caroline Trefler

Production Editor: Elyse Rozelle

4th Edition

ISBN 978-1-64097-416-6

ISSN 2471-920X

All details in this book are based on information supplied to us at press time. Always confirm information when it matters, especially if you're making a detour to visit a specific place. Fodor's expressly disclaims any liability, loss, or risk, personal or otherwise, that is incurred as a consequence of the use of any of the contents of this book.

SPECIAL SALES
This book is available at special discounts for bulk purchases for sales promotions or premiums. For more information, e-mail SpecialMarkets@fodors.com.

PRINTED IN THE UNITED STATES OF AMERICA

10 9 8 7 6 5 4 3 2 1

About Our Writers

 Raised in Sweden, educated in the UK, and currently based in Barcelona, **Isabelle Kliger** is a freelance writer specializing in travel, food, and pop culture. Her work has appeared in *Condé Nast Traveler, Forbes, The Guardian, The Times*, and other publications. Isabelle can usually be found in a local restaurant, eating all the food and drinking all the wine—preferably somewhere in Spain, Italy, Tel Aviv, or Southeast Asia. Follow her on Instagram at @ikliger.

 Benjamin Kemper is a native New Englander based in Madrid, Spain, where he writes about the places that make him hungriest. The Caucasus and—*por supuesto*—Spain are his main beats. Beyond Benjamin's frequent contributions to Fodor's, his work appears regularly in *The Wall Street Journal, Bon Appétit, Condé Nast Traveler, AFAR,* and *Travel + Leisure*, among other publications. He is also a travel planner and culinary tour guide. Eavesdrop on his adventures on Instagram: @benjaminkemper.

 Originally from the north of England, **Elizabeth Prosser** has lived in Barcelona since 2007. When she is not indulging in her passion for travel, she works as a freelance writer and editor covering a range of topics including travel, lifestyle, property and technology for a range of print and online publications.

 Joanna Styles is a freelance writer based in Malaga, Andalusia, just about the perfect place to live. Since she first spotted orange trees in the sunshine and the snow-capped Sierra Nevada, she's been passionate about Andalusia, its people, places, and culture. Thirty years later she's still discovering hidden corners. Joanna is the author of www.guidetomalaga.com. Follow her and Malaga on social media @ GuidetoMalaga.